Basic Marketing

Basic Marketing

Fourth Canadian Edition

E. JEROME McCARTHY
Professor of Marketing
Michigan State University

STANLEY J. SHAPIRO
Professor of Marketing
Faculty of Business Administration
Simon Fraser University

WILLIAM D. PERREAULT, JR.
School of Business Administration
University of North Carolina

1986

Homewood, Illinois   60430

ISBN 0-256-03725-6

Library of Congress Catalog Card No. 85-82558

Printed in the United States of America

3 4 5 6 7 8 9 0 V 3 2 1 0 9 8 7

■ Preface

The more things change, the more they are the same. This is the fourth time a special edition of McCarthy has been prepared for the Canadian market. In each case the American edition on which a Canadianization was to be based differed in many significant respects from its predecessor. However, each subsequent American edition has been revised in a manner consistent with the tried-and-true McCarthy format that has proven so successful in the classroom. Subsequent Canadian editions also built upon their predecessors. But while each such effort contained increasing amounts of Canadian content, this material was always provided within a McCarthy context. All the above being so, readers are correct in assuming that radical changes in this text, as compared to earlier editions, are not to be found.

Important modifications have been made, however, both in the American source publication and in this Canadianization. As the title page reveals, perhaps the most significant development affecting the Eighth American Edition was the participation of Bill Perreault as co-author. Professor Perreault brings to that edition the perspective of one thoroughly versed in all aspects of the behavioral sciences. An outstanding record of academic achievement resulted in his selection, at a very early age, as editor of the *Journal of Marketing Research*. *Basic Marketing* can not help but benefit greatly from Professor Perreault's involvement in the Eighth and all subsequent American editions.

But what changes in content are to be found in the Eighth American Edition as compared to its predecessors? The discussion of strategic planning is now presented in a manner that more clearly highlights how marketing relates to this activity. There are major revisions in the treatment of such important topics as marketing research, consumer behavior, and sales management. Careful readers will note a myriad of other changes, individually less significant but collectively most impressive. Improvements in format and layout give the text an attractive new appearance. This new format, coupled with Professor McCarthy's long-standing commitment to language that communicates rather than confuses, means that an already easy-to-read publication has become even more so.

What changes have been made as far as Canadian content is concerned? All relevant economic and demographic data has been updated, and this type of material is again used far more extensively than in any competing textbook. For example, a special appendix appearing for the first time discusses what census data reveals about Canada's ethnic population. Some new inserts from the business press are also included. However, previously used material of this type again appears when such repeat use, all things considered, seemed more likely than any substitute insert to achieve the intended pedagogical objective.

The most significant changes in Canadian content, however, are the result of the views expressed by adopters of the preceding edition. Those surveyed for their opinions indicated that far more coverage of service marketing was required, that the treatment of market segmentation should be modified to reflect the development of new techniques, and that somewhat longer Canadian cases should be included. Marketing professors who practice what they preach must take their marching orders from the market. *Basic Marketing,* Fourth Canadian Edition contains a lengthy appendix covering various aspects of service marketing. The text's treatment of how one actually goes about segmenting markets, both industrial and consumer, has been entirely rewritten. The longer Canadian cases that were desired are also to be found.

Basic Marketing is more than a textbook. It is also part of a pedagogical package. As is only appropriate, the other components of that package have also been updated. The accompanying Learning Aid includes a number of new exercises. In addition, many of the other "how-to" exercises have been modified in that new data or illustrations have been substituted for what previously appeared in those exercises. The Instructor's Manual has a large number of newspaper and magazine discussions of contemporary developments in marketing. Instructors are free to use such material as classroom handouts in order to demonstrate the "real-world" relevance of what is covered in the text. Finally, the Manual of Objective Tests will now be available to instructors both in its conventional hard-copy format and, for the first time, on computer disk.

The ultimate test of any textbook is its degree of acceptance. Previous Canadian editions of *Basic Marketing* have been well received by both students and colleagues. We have tried to justify this past confidence by preparing an even better Fourth Canadian Edition that emphasizes both what is universal about marketing and what is uniquely Canadian. Once more, we submit our joint effort to the judgment of the marketplace. The authors welcome comments, suggestions, and corrections on any subject. Canadian concerns might best be discussed with me as I alone am responsible for any errors, either of omission or of commission, in the Canadianized sections of this text.

Stanley J. Shapiro

■ Acknowledgments

The acknowledgments section of a text cannot be prepared until after the entire manuscript has been completed. Only then can the author be certain that no additional requests for information will be made either of outside experts or well-informed colleagues. Since that stage has finally been reached, I can now acknowledge my very substantial debts of gratitude to those who have assisted me in this Canadianization of McCarthy and Perreault.

How this Canadian edition differs from its predecessors is discussed in the accompanying Preface. However, each succeeding edition of any text builds upon and refines what has preceded it. Consequently, all those who assisted in the preparation of previous Canadian editions are again deserving of thanks for they have contributed as well to this latest effort. A complete listing of those individuals is found in the three preceding acknowledgment sections.

Two thirds of the cases found in this volume have been prepared by other Canadian marketing professors. Because they have held up so well in classroom use, I have again included eight cases originally written for a previous edition by, respectively, D. Aronchik, Ryerson Polytechnical Institute; W. Balderson, University of Lethbridge; G. Byers, Humber College; J. Graham, University of Calgary; R. Rotenberg, Brock University; J. Liefeld, University of Guelph; R. Tamilia, University of Quebec at Montreal; and R. Wyckham, Simon Fraser University. I have also included two new cases by Professor L. Meredith of Simon Fraser University, one by Mr. G. Jacob of the British Columbia Institute of Technology, and two prepared under the joint direction of Professors C. Lawrence and K. Wong of Queen's University.

Professors P. Banting of McMaster University, K. Hardy of the University of Western Ontario, and R. Wyckham of Simon Fraser University kindly granted permission to use previously published cases either authored by them or prepared under their direction. Thanks are also due to the respective publishers of this material—McGraw-Hill Ryerson of Professor Banting's casebook, Allyn & Bacon of Professor Hardy's casebook, and John Wiley of the Small Business volume co-authored by Professor Wyckham—for agreeing to make this material available.

Adopters of the third edition of this text were asked in the spring of 1985 how the forthcoming fourth edition should be modified to better meet their needs. Thanks are due to Morris Chandross, The George Brown College of Applied Arts and Technology; B. B. Everest, McMaster University; Elko Kleinschmidt, McMaster University; I. L. McLean, Cariboo College; H. L. Mills, University of Toronto; and J. C. Selby, East Kootenay Community College for responding in such detail to that letter of inquiry. Useful suggestions regarding possible areas of revision were also received from two long-time friends and McGill colleagues, Dr. Ralph Marcus, now also associated with Dawson College, and Mr. Maurice Bortz. A final, very important source of guidance was my periodic contacts, culminating in a lengthy meeting devoted solely to an assessment of the Third Canadian Edition, with members of the Marketing Management Department of the British Columbia Institute of Technology.

A number of colleagues also assisted in the preparation either of the text or the appendices. First of all, I am again greatly indebted to Professor Carl Lawrence of Queens University, a friend and colleague for close to 30 years. As he did for the Third Canadian Edition, Professor Lawrence again researched and wrote all of the material in Chapter 6 dealing with the demographic and economic dimensions of the Canadian consumer market. He also prepared all of the Canadian content found in the chapters on retailing and wholesaling. Finally, Professor Lawrence and Ms. Shaheen Lalji co-authored with me the material on Canada's ethnic market that appears in Appendix C.

Professor Ron Fullerton prepared, especially for this Canadian edition of *Basic Marketing*, the new discussion of the evolution of marketing thought and practice found in Chapter 2. Mrs. Mary Roberts of the Simon Fraser University Library System again updated the sources of Marketing Information discussion that appears as Appendix B. Professor Bob Tamilia of the University of Quebec at Montreal provided a first draft of the discussion of the French Canadian market now to be found in Appendix D following Chapter 7. Thanks are due to all of these individuals for the assistance so graciously rendered.

Finally, I am indebted to a number of SFU Faculty of Business Administration support staff members who became involved in preparing the manuscript that was to become *Basic Marketing*, Fourth Canadian Edition. A long and demanding word processing task was carried out willingly, ably, and with great professionalism by Ms. Janet Dunford. Overload typing services were cheerfully provided by Mrs. Betty Chung and Ms. Felicity Warburton. The sisters Dieter, Anita and Doris, successfully completed the very difficult task of revising the accompanying Learning Aid. Mrs. Carol Murrell, keeper of both our financial records and our computer supplies, conclusively demonstrated that in this world one gets what one pays for. The patience and understanding shown by Robbie and Roberta also deserve acknowledgment.

Each Canadianization of McCarthy has benefited from the invaluable contribution of a research associate who "made it all happen." That indispensible role was played for the Fourth Canadian Edition by Mr. Karim Lalji. Karim is the third member of the Lalji family who has worked with me since I arrived at Simon Fraser University some five years ago. Personally, professionally, and politically, I am not sure how I would have gotten along without "the family." Karim repeatedly demonstrated the commitment to completion, the attention to detail, the sense of professionalism, and the recognition of deadlines that his task required. That this volume was eventually ready for publication is more his doing than my own.

S.J.S.

■ Contents

Basic Marketing

Part I ■ Introduction to Marketing and Its Environment

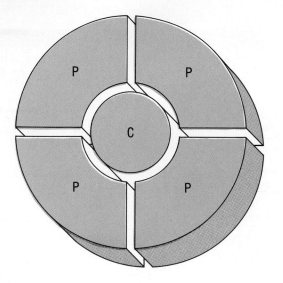

Product	
Place	
Promotion	
Price	
Customer	

The first four chapters (and Appendix A, which follows Chapter 2) present a "big picture" of what marketing is all about. First, we will see how marketing fits into our whole economic system—and then discuss where marketing fits within a business firm or a non-profit organization. You will learn what marketing strategy planning is all about—and get an overview of the rest of the book. You will also learn about finding attractive opportunities—and even "breakthrough opportunities"—which will help you plan and implement "hard-to-copy" strategies.

Marketing strategy planning doesn't happen in a vacuum, however, so in Chapters 3 and 4 (and Appendix A), we will discuss the uncontrollable environments which the marketing manager must understand and work with when planning marketing strategies. These uncontrollable variables are becoming more and more important as the role of government expands—and changes in the economic environment have a greater impact on individual companies.

A marketing manager must know how to plan strategies—but this must be done with full understanding of the uncontrollable environments. It is almost suicide to try to plan in a vacuum. This emphasizes the importance of a marketer having a broad view of the world—being an "educated person" in the best sense of the word. In fact, marketing can be thought of as an integrating discipline. An effective marketer must be able to tie together the various parts of a business—and help it adjust to the uncontrollable environments in which it must operate.

Chapter 1 ■ Marketing's role in society

When you finish this chapter, you should:

1. Know what marketing is and why you should learn about it.
2. Know why and how macro-marketing systems develop.
3. Know why marketing specialists—including middlemen and facilitators—develop.
4. Know the marketing functions and who performs them.
5. Recognize the important new terms (shown in red).

"Marketing affects almost every aspect of your daily life."

Some students take an introductory marketing course because friends tell them it's really interesting. Some students study marketing because they've heard many good job opportunities are available to marketing graduates. Others take it just to be able to list some business courses on their resumés—or simply because it's a required subject.

Regardless of why they decide to study marketing, most beginning marketing students have one thing in common: at the start they have little idea of what marketing is all about. If you are one of these students, don't worry—you're not alone! Also be assured that you have something to look forward to! As you read this book—and learn more about the many areas of marketing—you will see that it affects every aspect of your daily life. You will also find it *is* interesting. We can say this with confidence—since that is the experience of the thousands of students who read this book before you.

Before defining marketing, we will give you a general idea of what marketing is all about—and how you can benefit from studying marketing.

Marketing—What's It All About?

Marketing is more than selling or advertising

If forced to define marketing, many beginning students would probably say that marketing means "selling" or "advertising." Advertising and selling are, in fact, important parts of marketing. But, it is crucial that you recognize that *marketing is much more than just selling and advertising.*

5

How did all those tennis rackets get here?

To illustrate some of the *other* important things that are included in marketing, consider all the tennis rackets being swung with varying degrees of accuracy by millions of tennis players all around the world. Most of us weren't born with a tennis racket in our hand. Nor do most of us make our own tennis rackets. Instead, the tennis rackets we use were manufactured by firms such as Wilson, Spalding, Slazenger, Davis, Head, and Prince.

Most tennis rackets look pretty much alike. All are intended to do the same thing—hit the ball over the net. Nevertheless, a tennis player can choose from a wide assortment of rackets. Not only do tennis rackets come in different shapes, weights, and handle sizes, but one can also choose from rackets made of different materials—wood, steel, aluminum, fiberglass, or graphite. In addition, a racket can be strung with various types of nylon or gut. These different materials involve various trade-offs, not the least of which is price. You can purchase a prestrung racket for less than $15. Or you can spend more than $200 just for a frame!

This variety—of sizes and materials—complicates the production and sale of tennis rackets. To illustrate how involved the whole process can be, let's consider some of the many things a firm should do *before* and *after* it decides to manufacture tennis rackets. In addition to simply manufacturing rackets, the firm should:

1. Estimate how many people will be playing tennis over the next several years and how many tennis rackets they will buy—to make certain that there are enough customers to even justify manufacturing.
2. Determine which types of rackets—handle sizes, shapes, weights, and materials—people will want and in what proportion—so that the *right* products are produced.
3. Estimate what price the different tennis players will be willing to pay for their rackets—to see if producing and selling rackets can be profitable.
4. Determine where these tennis players will be located and when they'll want to buy tennis rackets so that a method of distribution—including selecting the best wholesalers and retailers—can be set up to reach them.
5. Decide which kinds of promotion should be used to tell potential customers about the firm's tennis rackets.
6. Estimate how many other firms will be manufacturing tennis rackets, how many rackets they will produce, what kind, at what prices, and so forth.

The above activities are *not* part of what is called **manufacturing**—actually *producing* goods and services. Rather, they are part of the larger marketing process. If the process is carried out effectively, it can provide needed direction for manufacturing—and ensure that the right products find their way into the hands of final consumers.

As our tennis racket example shows, marketing involves far more than selling or advertising. In fact, marketing involves many other activities not mentioned in our example. We will describe these activities in the next chapter, and you'll learn much more about them before you finish this book. For now, it is enough to see that marketing plays an essential role in providing consumers with need-satisfying goods and services.

All tennis racquets can hit the ball over the net—but there are many variations to meet the needs of different people.

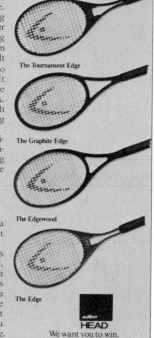

How Marketing Relates to Manufacturing

Manufacturing is a very important economic activity. Whether for lack of skill, resources, or just plain time, most people don't make most of the products they consume. Picture yourself, for example, building a 10-speed bicycle, a component stereo system, or a digital watch—starting from scratch! Clearly, the high standard of living that most Canadians enjoy is not possible without modern manufacturing.

Tennis rackets, like mousetraps, don't sell themselves

Although manufacturing is an essential economic activity, some people over-rate its importance in relation to marketing. Their attitude is reflected in Emerson's old saying: "If a man . . . makes a better mousetrap . . . the world will beat a path to his door." In other words, they think that all you need to succeed in business is a good product—that customers will search you out if you make that product.

The mousetrap theory probably wasn't true in Emerson's time. And it certainly isn't true today. In modern economies, the grass grows high on the path to the Better Mousetrap Factory—if the new mousetrap is *not* properly marketed. We have already seen, for example, that there's a lot more to selling tennis rackets than simply manufacturing them. The same holds true for most other products.

The point is that manufacturing and marketing are both important parts of a total business system—whose purpose is providing consumers with need-satis-fying goods and services. Together, manufacturing and marketing are able to combine to provide economic **utility**—value that comes from satisfying human needs. We will be concerned with four basic types of utility—form, time, place, and possession utility.

Tennis rackets do not automatically provide utility

Form utility is provided when a manufacturer makes something—for in-stance, a tennis racket—out of something else. But contrary to those who believe in the mousetrap theory, just producing tennis rackets doesn't result in consumer satisfaction. The product must be something that consumers want—or there is no need to be satisfied and no utility. This is how marketing thinking guides the manufacturing side of the business. Marketing decisions focus on the cus-tomer—and that includes decisions about what products to produce, what fea-tures to include, and what materials to use. It doesn't make sense to waste money producing a product consumers don't want—and may not value—when there are so many things that they do want or need. This is an important idea that we will develop more completely later.

Even if marketing and manufacturing do combine to provide form utility, con-sumers will not be satisfied until time, place, and possession utility are also pro-vided. **Time utility** means having the product available *when* the customer wants it. And **place utility** means having the product available *where* the customer wants it. For example, how much satisfaction does a tennis player in British Columbia get from a tennis racket in a manufacturer's warehouse in Winnipeg? Obviously, that tennis racket won't win many games unless it is available *when* (time utility) and *where* (place utility) the tennis player wants it. Further, to have the legal right to use the racket, the tennis player has to pay for it before enjoying possession utility. **Possession utility** means completing a transaction and gain-ing possession so that one has the right to use a product.

It should be clear that successful manufacturing depends on successful mar-keting—getting the right goods to the right place at the right time at a price that will allow the buyer to take possession. How marketing creates time, place, and possession utility will be explored later in this chapter. First, we want to tell you why you should study marketing—and then we'll define marketing.

Marketing and You

Why you should study marketing

One reason for studying marketing is that a large share of your buying dollar goes for marketing. It is widely thought that about 50 cents of each consumer's dollar pays for the *cost of marketing activities*.[1] This also means that more effective marketing decisions—those that create the same amount of utility for less money—can do a lot to cut costs.

Another important reason for learning about marketing is that marketing is all around you. It *affects your daily life*. The products you buy, the stores where you shop, the salespeople that approach you, all that advertising you see and hear—they are all part of marketing. Further, the newspapers and magazines you read, the radio programs you listen to, and the television shows you watch are largely paid for by advertisers—again, part of marketing. Even your job resumé is part of a marketing campaign to sell yourself to some employer. Some courses are interesting when you take them—but never relevant again once they are over. Not so with marketing—you will be a consumer dealing with marketing for the rest of your life.

Still another reason for studying marketing is that there are many exciting and rewarding *career opportunities in marketing*. Marketing is often the route to the top executive's job. At several places in this book, you will find descriptions of career opportunities in marketing—in sales, advertising, product management, marketing research, physical distribution, and other areas.

Marketing is important to the success of every organization. So if you take a non-marketing job in business, you will better understand how marketing activities relate to your job. In the final analysis, a company that cannot successfully market its products will have no need for accountants, computer programmers, financial managers, personnel managers, production managers, traffic managers, credit managers, and so on. As is often said: "Nothing happens unless the cash register rings."

Even if you are not planning a business career, marketing concepts and techniques have broad *application for nonprofit organizations,* too. The same basic approaches used to sell soap can also be used to "sell" ideas, politicians, mass transportation, health care services, energy conservation, and museums. Some hospitals even have "marketing directors."[2]

A final and even more basic reason for studying marketing is that *marketing is vital for economic growth and development*. Marketing stimulates research and innovation—resulting in new products—which—if found attractive by customers—can lead to fuller employment, higher incomes, and a higher standard of living. An effective marketing system is vital, therefore, to the future of our nation—as well as all other nations.

How Should We Define Marketing?

As we said earlier, some people define marketing in terms of just some of its parts—selling and advertising. This is too narrow. On the other hand, one professor defined marketing as "the creation and delivery of a standard of living."[3] That definition is probably too broad.

An important difference between the two definitions may be less obvious. The first definition focuses on activities performed by an individual business firm. The second focuses on the economic welfare of a whole society. In other words, the first is a *micro*-level definition while the second is a *macro*-level definition.

This is a very important difference. Traditionally, marketing has been seen at the micro level—as a set of activities performed by individual business firms or nonprofit organizations. Some students of marketing feel that a micro-level view of marketing is too limiting. They prefer to view marketing from a macro level—as a "fundamental societal process which . . . evolves within a society to facilitate the effective and efficient resolution of the society's needs for exchange of consumption values."[4]

Micro- or macro-marketing?

Which view is correct? Is marketing a set of activities done by individual firms or organizations? Or is it a social process?

To answer this question, let's go back to our tennis racket example. We saw that to be successful, a manufacturer of tennis rackets has to perform several customer-related activities in addition to simply producing rackets. The same is true for an art museum or a family service agency. This seems to support the idea of viewing marketing as a set of activities done by individual organizations.

On the other hand, people cannot live on tennis rackets and art museums alone! In an advanced economy—like that of Canada—it takes thousands of goods and services to satisfy the many needs of society. A large supermarket may handle as many as 20,000 products. And a typical K mart stocks 15,000 different items.[5] Clearly, a society needs some sort of marketing system to or-

A society needs some sort of marketing system to organize the efforts of producers to satisfy the needs of different customers.

ganize the efforts of all the producers and middlemen necessary to satisfy the needs of all citizens. Thus, it appears that marketing is a vital social process.

The answer to our question is that *marketing is both a set of activities performed by organizations* **and** *a social process.* In other words, marketing exists at both the micro and macro levels. Therefore, it must be defined at both levels. We will present two definitions of marketing—one for *micro*-marketing and another for *macro*-marketing. The first focuses on customers and the organizations that serve them. The second one takes a broad view of our whole production-distribution system.

Micro-Marketing Defined

Micro-marketing is the performance of activities which seek to accomplish an organization's objectives by anticipating customer or client needs and directing a flow of need-satisfying goods and services from producer to customer or client.

Let's examine this definition.

Applies to profit and non-profit organizations

To begin with, this definition applies to both profit and non-profit organizations. Their customers or clients may be individual consumers, business firms, non-profit organizations, government agencies, or even foreign nations. While most customers and clients pay for the goods and services they receive, others may receive them free of charge or at a reduced cost—through private or government subsidies.

Marketing is concerned with supplying need-satisfying goods and services.

More than just persuading customers

You already know that micro-marketing is not just personal selling and advertising. Unfortunately, many executives still think this is true. They feel that the job of marketing is to "get rid of" whatever the company happens to produce. They think of marketing as "persuading"—even if the unsuspecting customers don't want or need what is to be "pushed."

This view of marketing should be rejected. As noted management consultant Peter Drucker has stated:

> There will always, one can assume, be a need for some selling. But the aim of marketing is to make selling superfluous. The aim of marketing is to know and understand the customer so well that the product or service sells itself. Ideally, marketing should result in a customer who is *ready* to buy.[6]

Thus, when we defined micro-marketing as those activities which anticipate customer or client needs and direct a flow of need-satisfying goods and services, we meant just that—*anticipate* and *direct*.

Begins with customer needs

Marketing should begin with potential customer needs—not with the production process. Marketing should try to anticipate needs. And then marketing, rather than production, should determine what products are to be made—including decisions about product development, product design, and packaging; what prices or fees are to be charged; credit and collection policies; transporting and storing policies; when and how the products are to be advertised and sold; and after the sale—warranty, service, and perhaps even disposal policies.

Marketing does not do it alone

This does *not* mean that marketing should try to take over production, accounting, and financial activities. Rather, it means that marketing—by interpreting customers' needs—should provide direction for these activities and seek to coordinate them. After all, the purpose of a business or non-profit organization is to satisfy customer or client needs. It is *not* to supply goods or service which are *convenient* to produce and which *might* sell or be accepted free.

The Focus of This Text—Management-Oriented Micro-Marketing

Assuming that most of you are preparing for a career in management, the main focus of this text will be on micro-marketing—as seen from the viewpoint of the marketing manager. But the concepts we will discuss are also directly relevant if you plan to be a manager for a non-profit organization.

It is very important, however, that marketing managers never forget that their organizations are just small interacting components of an enormously complex macro-marketing system. Changes in the system can affect any marketing manager. And good decisions by many individual marketing managers can in turn affect the system. Therefore, the rest of this chapter will examine the macro—or "big picture"—view of marketing. Let's begin by defining macro-marketing and review some basic concepts. Then—in Chapter 2—we will explain the key marketing management decision areas we will be discussing in the rest of the book.

Macro-Marketing Defined

Macro-marketing is a social process which directs an economy's flow of goods and services from producers to consumers in a way which effectively matches supply and demand and accomplishes the objectives of society.

Emphasis is on whole system

Like micro-marketing, macro-marketing is concerned with the flow of need-satisfying goods and services from producer to consumer. However, the emphasis is not on the activities that *individual* organizations perform. Rather, the emphasis is on *how the whole system works*—and how it affects society, and vice versa.

Every society needs a macro-marketing system—but not all systems are equally "good." They can vary both in how *effectively* the society uses its scarce resources and how *fairly* it allocates its output of goods and services.

Supply and demand must be matched

Achieving effectiveness and fairness isn't easy. Not all producers share the same objectives, resources, and skills. Likewise, not all consumers share the same objectives, resources, and needs. In other words, within any society there are both heterogeneous supply capabilities and heterogeneous demands for goods and services. The role of a macro-marketing system is to effectively match this heterogeneous supply and demand—*and* at the same time accomplish society's objectives.

Is it effective and fair?

Given that not all nations share the same objectives, the effectiveness and fairness of a particular macro-marketing system must be evaluated in terms of that society's objectives. For example, the citizens of Sweden receive many "human services"—like health care and retirement benefits—and the goods and services produced seem to be quite evenly distributed among the total population. Russia, by contrast, places much less emphasis on goods and services for individual consumers—and more on military spending. In Venezuela, the distribution of goods and services is very uneven—with a big gap between the "have-nots" and the elite "haves." Which of these systems is called "fair" or "effective" depends on the objectives of the society—and who sets the objectives for that society. Even in our democratic society, the objectives of different elected leaders may vary dramatically.

Let's look more closely at macro-marketing.[7] And to make this more meaningful to you, consider (1) what kind of a macro-marketing system we have and (2) how effective and fair it is.

Every Society Needs an Economic System

All societies must provide for the needs of their members. Therefore, every society needs some sort of **economic system**—the way an economy is organized (with or without the use of money) to use *scarce* productive resources (which could have alternative uses) to produce goods and services and distribute them for consumption—now and in the future—among various people and groups in the society.

How an economic system operates will depend on a society's objectives and the nature of its political institutions.[8] But, regardless of what form these take, all economic systems must develop some method—along with appropriate economic institutions—to decide *what and how much* is to be produced and distributed *by whom, when, and to whom. How* these decisions are made may vary from nation to nation—but the macro-level objectives are basically similar: to create goods and services and make them available when and where they are needed—to maintain or improve each nation's standard of living.

We are producers and consumers

It is very useful (although greatly oversimplified) to think of an economic system as consisting of *producers* and *consumers.* In a pure subsistence economy, individual family units produce all the goods that they themselves consume. In more advanced economies, most people are also both producers and consumers—but the goods and services that they produce are usually not the same ones they consume.

As *producers,* we are mainly concerned with our income. This represents our reward for contributing to the output of the economy. As *consumers,* on the other hand, we are concerned with what our income will buy. While these two roles are inherent in any economy, they can lead to conflicts and difficulties. This is called the **micro-macro dilemma**—*what is "good" for some producers and consumers may not be "good" for society as a whole.* This problem complicates economic decision making considerably. It means that there may not always be

There is a dilemma if what is "good" for some producers and consumers creates problems for society as a whole.

obvious right answers that everyone will agree on. Many compromises may have to be reached.

Let's consider a simple—but emotionally charged—example. Each year automobile accidents kill thousands of people who would have lived if they were wearing seat belts. In spite of this, the vast majority of motorists don't wear seat belts. Is it "good" to force producers (by law) to offer impact-cushioning safety airbags to protect these people from themselves—and cut the kill ratio? This may increase car costs and prices—and reduce producers' car sales and profits. Further, is it "good" to make people who wear seat belts anyway pay extra for a car with airbags—because someone else is not safety conscious?

Sometimes such decisions don't involve a matter of life and death but are still important. For example, many consumers want the convenience of soft drinks in cheap, non-returnable aluminum cans. But often these same cans end up sprinkled along the highways—and need to be picked up at taxpayer expense. Should just can buyers (through special charges)—or everyone—have to pay for this littering?

How Economic Decisions Are Made

There are two basic kinds of economic systems: planned systems and market-directed systems. Actually, no economy is *entirely* planned or market-directed. Most fall somewhere between the two extremes.

In **planned economic systems**, government planners decide what and how much is to be produced and distributed by whom, when, and to whom. Producers generally have very little choice about product design. Their main task is to meet their assigned production quotas. Prices are set by the planners and tend to be very rigid—not fluctuating according to supply and demand. Consumers usually have *some* freedom of choice—because it is impossible to control every single detail. But the assortment of goods and services offered to them is often quite limited. Activities such as market research, branding, and advertising typically receive little emphasis. Sometimes they aren't done at all.

Government planning may work fairly well as long as an economy is simple—and the variety of goods and services is small. It may even be necessary under certain conditions—during wartime, for example. However, as economies become more complex, government planning becomes more difficult. It may even break down. Planners may find themselves overwhelmed by many complex decisions. And consumers may lose patience if the planning bureaucracy does not respond satisfactorily to their needs. In an effort to reduce consumer dissatisfaction, planners in the Soviet Union and other socialist countries have placed more emphasis on marketing (branding, advertising, and market research) in recent years.[9]

A market-directed economy adjusts itself

In **market-directed economic systems**, the individual decisions of the many producers and consumers result in the macro-level decisions for the whole economy. For the most part, such an economy is free from the bureaucratic controls that go along with government planning.

In a pure market-directed economy, consumers determine a society's production decisions when they make their choices in the marketplace. In a sense, they decide what is to be produced and by whom—through their dollar "votes." If some producer puts out a product that no one wants—it goes unpurchased, and in time the producer goes out of business. At the same time, whenever a new consumer need arises, an opportunity is created for some profit-minded business. All consumer needs that can be served profitably—not just the needs of the majority—will generate producers to meet those needs. Thus, ideally, the control of the economy is completely democratic—with power spread throughout the economy.

Consumers in a market-directed economy enjoy maximum freedom of choice. They are not forced to buy any goods or services, except those that must be provided for the good of society—things such as national defense, schools, police and fire protection, mass transportation, and public health services. These are provided by the community—and citizens are taxed to pay for them. Even some of these "purchases" can be influenced—by whoever consumers vote into political office.

Similarly, producers are free to do whatever they wish—provided that they stay within the rules of the game established by government *and* that they receive sufficient dollar "votes" from consumers. If they do their job well—if, through sound decision making, they satisfy enough consumers—they will earn a profit and stay in business. But profit, survival, and growth are not guaranteed.

Price is a measure of value

Since the bulk of the Canadian economy (and most Western economies) is market-directed, it is important that you understand how such an economy works—in particular, the role of market price. The prices of consumer goods and services serve roughly as a measure of their social importance. If consumers are willing to pay the market prices, they apparently feel they are getting at least their money's worth. Similarly, the cost of labor and materials is a rough measure of the value of the resources used in the production of these goods and services. In a market-directed economy, the prices in both the production sector (for resources) and the consumption sector (for goods and services) fluctuate to allocate resources and distribute income in the light of consumers' preferences. The result is a balance of demand and supply—and the coordination of the economic activity of many people and institutions.

Consumers and producers must continually interact

The interaction among various people and institutions in a market-directed economy is shown in a very simplified manner in Figure 1–1. The figure helps to show that there are really *several* markets operating. On the right side of Figure 1–1, consumers "vote" for goods and services in a product-market by spending their money—which the producers receive as income.

At the same time, there is a market for resources to be used in production—see the left side of Figure 1–1. In this market, consumers offer their production

■   FIGURE 1–1   Model of a market-directed economy

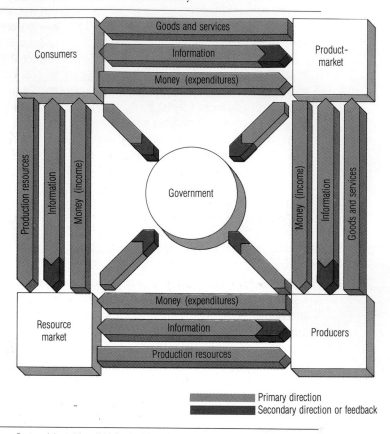

Source: Adapted from Y. H. Furuhashi and E. J. McCarthy, *Social Issues in the American Economy* (Columbus, Ohio: Grid, 1971), p. 5.

resources—such as their labor or use of their investment capital—to the producers in exchange for income. The process continues as consumers again exchange their incomes for goods and services.

Continual flows are required to keep this system working. Ideally, the participants have enough information to make wise decisions about where they offer their resources for sale and what they buy. This way, all the buyers and sellers influence the direction of the economy.

The role of government

Government is included in Figure 1–1 to show that a market-directed society may assign the supervision of the system to the government. Since proper functioning of a market-directed system depends on continual, smooth flows throughout the system, the government is expected to make sure that the market system continues to work properly. In an effort to protect the rights and freedoms of both

consumers and producers, the government usually sets rules for the system. The aim of the rules is to ensure that property is protected, contracts are enforced, individuals are not exploited, no group monopolizes the resource market or the product-market, and that producers do, in fact, deliver the kinds and quality of goods they claim to be offering.

The Canadian economy is mainly—but not entirely—market-directed. For example, in addition to the tasks we have mentioned, the Bank of Canada influences the supply of money and influences interest rates. The federal government sets import and export restrictions, regulates radio and TV broadcasting, alternately restricts and stimulates agricultural production, controls prices and wages on occasion, and so on. Some observers see increasing government interference as a growing threat to the survival of our market-directed system—and the economic and political freedom that goes with it.[10]

All Economies Need Macro-Marketing Systems

At this point, you may be saying to yourself: All this sounds like economics—where does *marketing* fit in? Studying a *macro-marketing system* is a lot like studying an economic system—except more detailed attention is given to the "marketing" components of the system—including consumers and other customers, middlemen, and marketing specialists. The focus is on the activities they perform—and how the interaction of the components affects the effectiveness and fairness of a particular system.

In general, we can say that no economic system—whether centrally planned or market-directed—is likely to achieve its macro-level objectives without an effective macro-marketing system. In explaining why this is so, we will first look at the role of marketing in primitive economies. Then, we will see how macro-marketing tends to become increasingly complex in advanced economic systems.

Marketing involves exchange

Our earlier statement that all economies need macro-marketing systems was not entirely true. One big exception is a **pure subsistence economy**—where each family unit produces all the goods that it consumes. In such a primitive economy, there is no need for producers and consumers to exchange goods and services. Each producer-consumer unit is totally self-sufficient. Therefore, no marketing takes place. *Marketing does not occur unless there are two or more parties who each have something of value they want to exchange for something else.*

This doesn't mean that marketing begins and ends with the exchange process. As our tennis racket example showed, much comes before and after exchange. So there is more to marketing than simply producing and selling something in exchange for cash or something else of value. However, the need to facilitate exchange—which is found in almost all societies—is at the core of marketing.

What is a market?

The term "marketing" comes from the word **market**—which means a group of sellers and buyers (usually producers and consumers) bargaining over the terms of exchange for goods and/or services. This can be done face-to-face at some physical location (for example, a farmers' market). Or it can be done indirectly—through a complex network of middlemen who link buyers and sellers who are separated geographically (for example, when producers of auto batteries sell to wholesalers who sell to retailers who sell to widely spread consumers).

In primitive economies, exchanges tend to occur in central markets. **Central markets** are convenient places where buyers and sellers can meet face-to-face to exchange goods and services. You will understand macro-marketing better by analyzing how and why central markets develop.

Central markets facilitate exchange

Imagine a small village consisting of five families—each with some special skill for producing some need-satisfying product. After meeting basic subsistence needs, each family decides to specialize. This decision is very practical. It's easier for one family to make two pots and another to make two baskets than it is for either to make one pot and one basket. Specialization makes labor more efficient and more productive. It may also increase the total amount of form utility created.

If these five families specialize in one product each, they will have to trade with each other. As Figure 1–2 shows, it will take the five families 10 separate exchanges to obtain some of each of the products. If the families live near each other, the exchange process is relatively simple. But if they are far apart, travel back and forth will be time-consuming. And who will do the traveling—and when? Obviously, this type of marketing system is not very effective for creating time, place, and possession utilities.[11]

Faced with this problem, the families may agree to come to a central market and trade on a certain day. Then, each family needs to make only one trip to the market to trade with all the others—reducing the total number of trips. This facilitates exchange, leaves more time for production and consumption, and also provides for social gatherings. In total, much more time, place, possession, and even form utility is enjoyed by the five families.

Money system speeds trading

While a central meeting place simplifies exchange, the individual bartering transactions may still take much time. Bartering only works when someone else wants what you have—and vice versa. Each trader must find others who have products of approximately equal value. After trading with one group, a family may find itself with a collection of baskets, knives, and pots. Then it has to find others willing to trade for these products.

A money system changes all of this. A seller merely has to find a buyer who wants his product, negotiate the price, and be free to spend his money to buy whatever he wants.

Middlemen facilitate exchange even more

Even though the development of a central market and a money system simplifies the exchange process among the five families in our imaginary village, a total of 10 separate transactions are still required. Thus, it still takes much time and

■ FIGURE 1–2   Ten exchanges required when a central market is not used

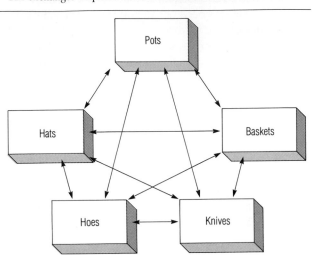

Source: Wroe Alderson, "Factors Governing the Development of Marketing
Channels," in *Marketing Channels for Manufactured Products,*
ed. Richard M. Clewett (Homewood, Ill.: Richard D. Irwin, 1954), p. 7.

effort to carry out exchange among the five families. Each family head may have
to operate (and pay for) a stall at the market—while other family members shop
at other parts of the market.

This clumsy exchange process can be made much simpler by the appearance
of a **middleman**—someone who specializes in trade rather than production—
who is willing to buy each family's goods and then sell each family whatever it
needs. He charges for the service, of course. But this charge may be more than
offset by savings in time and effort.

In our simple example, using the services of a middleman at a central market
reduces the necessary number of transactions for all five families from 10 to 5.
See Figure 1–3. Each family has more time for production, consumption, and
visits with other families. Moreover, each family can specialize in production—
thereby creating greater form utility. Meanwhile, by specializing in trade, the middleman provides additional time, place, and possession utility. In total, all the
villagers may enjoy greater economic utility—and thus greater consumer satisfaction—as a result of using a middleman in the central market.

Note that the reduction in transactions that results from using a middleman in
a central market becomes more significant as the number of families increases.
For example, if the population of our imaginary village increases from 5 to 10
families, 45 transactions will be required without a middleman. Using a middleman reduces the necessary number of transactions to 10—1 for each family.

Such middlemen—offering permanent trading facilities—are known today as
wholesalers and *retailers*. The advantages of working with middlemen increase
rapidly as the number of producers and consumers, their distance from each

■ FIGURE 1–3   Only five exchanges are required when a middleman in a central market is used

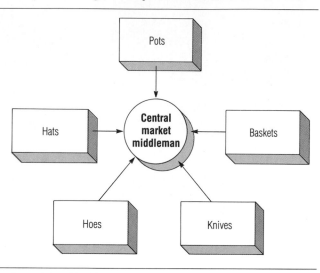

Source: Adapted from Wroe Alderson, "Factors Governing the Development of
Marketing Channels," in *Marketing Channels for Manufactured Products*,
ed. Richard M. Clewett (Homewood, Ill.: Richard D. Irwin, 1954), p. 7.

other, and the number and variety of competing products increase. That is why
there are so many wholesalers and retailers in more complex economic systems.

The Role of Marketing in Economic Development

Modern economies have advanced well beyond the five-family village—but
the same principles still apply. The main purpose of markets and middlemen is to
facilitate exchange and allow greater time for production, consumption, and other
activities—including recreation.

**Effective marketing
system is necessary**

Although it is tempting to conclude that more effective macro-marketing systems are the result of greater economic development, just the opposite is true.
*An effective macro-marketing system is a necessary ingredient for economic
development.* Some experts think that improved marketing is the *key* to economic development in these situations. Marketing is usually the *most* backward
part in poorly developed economic systems—but the part which can be improved
most rapidly. And improving it also leads to better use of the economy's resources—so they meet consumer needs better. As management expert Peter
Drucker has put it, marketing "mobilizes latent economic energy. It contributes to
the greatest needs: that for the rapid development of entrepreneurs and managers, and at the same time it may be the easiest area of managerial work to get
going."[12]

Without an effective ma-cro-marketing system, people will not leave their subsistence way of life to produce for the market.

Breaking the vicious circle of poverty

Without an effective macro-marketing system, the less-developed nations may be doomed to a "vicious circle of poverty"—that is, people will not leave their subsistence way of life to produce for the market because there are no buyers for any goods they may produce. And there are no buyers because everyone else is producing for their own needs.[13]

How can this vicious circle of poverty be broken? Evidence suggests that what may be needed most is a major overhaul of the antiquated micro- and macro-marketing systems that are typical in the less-developed nations.

The inefficiency of these marketing systems results in very high food prices in the rapidly growing urban areas of these nations. The majority of the population in these urban areas often spends two thirds or more of their disposable income on food—as compared to only about 20 percent on food for the average Canadian household. The high food prices leave the urban consumers with little discretionary income to spend on non-food products. This discourages the manufacture of non-food items. High prices also reduce the demand for food—so farmers are reluctant to increase their production. As a result, real income doesn't increase.

A "marketing revolution" may help developing countries break out of this cycle. Effort probably should focus on development of marketing middlemen who are willing to adopt newer methods, assume greater risks, increase their operating efficiency, and create multi-product retail outlets with high turnover–low margin operations.[14]

Can Mass Production Satisfy a Society's Consumption Needs?

Urbanization brings together large masses of people who must rely on others to produce the bulk of the goods and services that are necessary to satisfy their basic needs. Further, in advanced economies, consumers often enjoy considerable discretionary income. This allows them to seek goods and services that satisfy higher-level needs as well. Such economies face a stiff challenge to create sufficient economic utility to satisfy these consumption needs.

Fortunately, advanced economies can take advantage of mass production with its **economies of scale**—i.e., as a company produces larger numbers of a particular product, the cost for each of these products goes down. Further, aided by specialization and the division of labor, modern economies can apply modern manufacturing methods to convert raw materials into a massive output of goods and services with need-satisfying potential.

Is mass production the solution to the problem of satisfying a society's consumption needs? Some will answer *yes* to this question. But the truth is that mass production is a necessary *but not the only* condition for satisfying consumers' needs. Effective marketing is also needed.

Barriers to effective marketing

Effective marketing involves getting all the goods and services that consumers need and want to them at the right time, in the right place, and at prices that will allow them to take possession. This is a complicated task, given the heterogeneous nature of supply in an advanced economy's production sector and the heterogeneous nature of demand in its consumption sector.

Achieving effective marketing in an advanced economy is complicated further by the fact that producers are separated from consumers in several ways.[15] As Figure 1–4 illustrates, exchange between producers and consumers is generally hampered by spatial separation, separation in time, separation in information, separation in values, and separation of ownership. Exchange is complicated further by "discrepancies of quantity" and "discrepancies of assortment" between producers and consumers. That is, individual producers specialize in producing and selling large quantities of a narrow assortment of goods and services, while individual consumers need small quantities of a wide assortment of goods and services.

Marketing helps adjust the discrepancies between the quantity and assortment of goods produced and what is desired by customers.

■ FIGURE 1–4   Marketing facilitates production and consumption

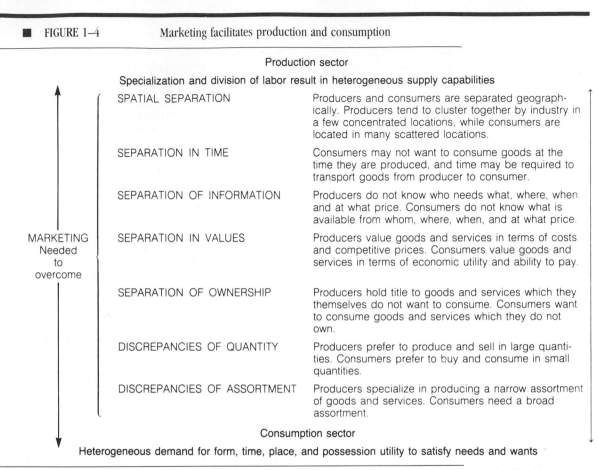

Source: Adapted from William McInnes, "A Conceptual Approach to Marketing," in *Theory in Marketing*, 2d ser., ed. Reavis Cox, Wroe Alderson, and Stanley J. Shapiro (Homewood, Ill.: Richard D. Irwin, 1964), pp 51–67.

Universal marketing functions must be performed

The role of a macro-marketing system is to provide the marketing capability that is necessary to overcome these separations and discrepancies—and thereby provide for an effective matching of heterogeneous supply and demand between producers and consumers. This is achieved through the performance of the **universal functions of marketing**: buying, selling, transporting, storing, standardization and grading, financing, risk taking, and market information.

These marketing functions are *universal* in the sense that they must be performed in *all* macro-marketing systems—regardless of whether an economy is planned or market-directed. It is largely through these marketing functions that economic utility is created. *How* these functions are performed and *by whom* may differ among nations and systems, but their performance is essential in the marketing of all goods and services.

Because these functions are the foundation for any macro-marketing system, some explanation is necessary to help you understand what they involve.

The exchange functions

Buying and selling lead to exchange. The **buying function** involves looking for and evaluating goods and services. For middlemen, this means a search for products that will appeal to their customers. The **selling function** involves promoting the product. It includes the use of personal selling and advertising and other mass selling methods. This is the most "visible" function of marketing.

The physical distribution functions

The **transporting function** means the movement of goods from one place to another. This provides place utility. The **storing function** involves holding goods until customers need them. These are the major activities of many marketing institutions—especially warehouses, transportation agencies, wholesalers, and some retailers.

The facilitating functions

Standardization and grading, financing, risk taking, and market information are the facilitating functions that aid the performance of the exchange and physical distribution functions. **Standardization** and **grading** involve sorting products according to size and quality. This simplifies the exchange process by reducing the need for inspection and sampling. For example, you buy a dozen "extra large" eggs without weighing each one because someone has already done that job. **Financing** provides the necessary money to manufacture, transport, store, sell, and buy products. **Risk taking** involves bearing the uncertainties that are a part of the marketing process. A firm can never be sure that customers will want to buy its products, and the products can also become damaged, stolen, or obsolete. The **market information function** involves the collection, analysis, and distribution of information needed to plan, carry out, and control marketing activities.

Who Performs Marketing Functions?

Producers, consumers, and marketing specialists

From a macro-level viewpoint, these marketing functions are all part of the marketing process and must be performed by someone. *None* of them can be eliminated. In a planned economy, some of the functions may be performed by government agencies, while others may be left to individual producers and consumers. In a market-directed economy, marketing functions are performed by producers, consumers, and a variety of marketing institutions which serve as producers of time, place, and possession utilities. See Figure 1–5.

It is possible for individual producers and consumers to perform all the marketing functions themselves. In a very simple economy, this may actually happen. Usually, however, while producers and consumers must perform *some* marketing functions themselves, it generally is not very efficient if they try to perform *all* the functions.

■ **FIGURE 1–5**   Model of Canadian macro-marketing system*

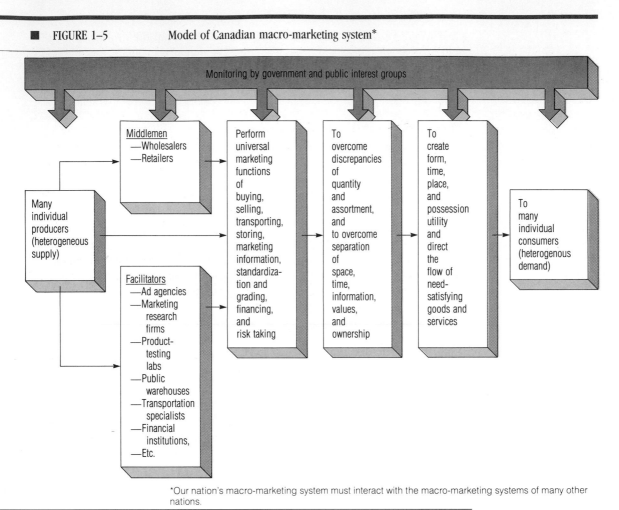

Monitoring by government and public interest groups

Many individual producers (heterogeneous supply)

Middlemen
—Wholesalers
—Retailers

Facilitators
—Ad agencies
—Marketing research firms
—Product-testing labs
—Public warehouses
—Transportation specialists
—Financial institutions,
—Etc.

Perform universal marketing functions of buying, selling, transporting, storing, marketing information, standardization and grading, financing, and risk taking

To overcome discrepancies of quantity and assortment, and to overcome separation of space, time, information, values, and ownership

To create form, time, place, and possession utility and direct the flow of need-satisfying goods and services

To many individual consumers (heterogenous demand)

*Our nation's macro-marketing system must interact with the macro-marketing systems of many other nations.

Source: This model was suggested by Professor A. A. Brogowicz of Western Michigan University.

Earlier in this chapter, we saw that the addition of a middleman in a simple five-family village of producers and consumers both simplified exchange and increased the total amount of economic utility. This effect is multiplied many times over in a large, complex economy. This helps explain why the bulk of the products sold in Canada are distributed through wholesalers and retailers—rather than directly from producers to consumers.

Just as producers and consumers benefit when marketing specialists take over the exchange functions of buying and selling, they also benefit when marketing specialists perform the other marketing functions. Thus, we find marketing functions being performed not only by marketing middlemen—but also by a variety of other **facilitators**—firms which provide one or more of the marketing functions *other than buying or selling.* These include advertising agencies, marketing research firms, independent product-testing laboratories, public warehouses, transportation firms, and financial institutions (including banks). Through specialization and economies of scale, marketing middlemen and facilitators are often able to perform the marketing functions more effectively—and at a lower cost—than producers or consumers can. At the same time, they allow producers and consumers to spend more of their time on production and consumption.

Functions can be shifted and shared

From a macro viewpoint, all of the marketing functions must be performed by someone. But, *from a micro viewpoint, not every firm must perform all of the functions.* While some marketing specialists perform all the functions, others specialize in only one or two. Marketing research firms, for example, specialize in the market information function.

Determining the most efficient path to the consumer's door is one of the most important jobs of marketing management. Because of the benefits of specialization, distributing goods through a series of marketing specialists is often more efficient than distributing directly from producer to consumer. When several specialists are used, some of the marketing functions may be performed several times. But the key point to remember is this: *responsibility for performing the marketing functions can be shifted and shared in a variety of ways, but no function can be completely eliminated!*

How Well Does Our Macro-Marketing System Work?

It connects remote producers and consumers

A macro-marketing system does more than link an economy's production and consumption sectors. It also provides an organizational, transportation, and communications network linking small, geographically isolated markets to larger, inter-regional markets which have enough demand to make mass production possible. This also helps distribute goods from surplus areas to deficit areas under changing supply and demand conditions.[16]

It encourages growth and new ideas

In addition to making possible the mass production of goods, our market-directed macro-marketing system encourages **innovation**—the development and spread of new ideas and products. Research effort and investment capital are attracted when customers are willing to pay for a new good or service. And competitive pressures and changing consumer needs force firms to develop further innovations and improvements. In recent years, industries that have followed this pattern include communications and electronics.

It has its critics

In explaining marketing's role in society, we described some of the benefits of our macro-marketing system. This is reasonable when we see that our macro-marketing system has provided us—at least in material terms—with one of the highest standards of living in the world. It seems to be "effective" and "fair" in many ways.

This is not to suggest that the marketing system in Canada is above criticism. And it does have its critics! Marketing activity is especially open to criticism—

because it is the part of business most visible to the public. There is nothing like a pocketbook issue for getting consumers aroused!

Typical complaints about marketing include:

Advertising is too often annoying, deceptive, and wasteful.

Products are not safe or the quality is poor.

Marketing makes people too materialistic—it motivates them toward the "almighty dollar" instead of social needs.

Easy consumer credit makes people—especially the poor—buy things they don't need and really can't afford.

Style changes and planned product obsolescence waste our precious resources.

Packaging and labeling are often confusing and deceptive.

Middlemen add to the cost of distribution and raise prices without providing anything in return.

Marketing creates interest in products that pollute the environment.

Advertising manipulates consumers—especially children—to buy things they don't really want.

Marketing helps create monopolies which restrict output and raise prices.

Marketing serves the rich and exploits the poor.

Note that some of these complaints deal with the whole macro-marketing system. Others apply to practices of specific firms—and are micro-marketing oriented.

Such complaints cannot and should not be taken lightly.[17] They show that many Canadians are less than enchanted with some parts of our marketing system. Certainly, the strong public support that consumer protection laws have received proves that not all consumers feel they are being treated like kings and queens. There are some legitimate problems which need attention. But there is also some confusion—and some of the complaints are because people don't

Some critics argue that marketing serves the rich and exploits the poor.

understand marketing. Throughout the rest of this book, we will raise some of these criticisms again—and deal with them in more detail. Then we will return to a more complete appraisal of marketing in our final chapter.

■ CONCLUSION

In this chapter, we defined two levels of marketing: micro-marketing and macro-marketing. Macro-marketing is concerned with marketing's overall role in the economy and in society. Micro-marketing, on the other hand, is concerned with the activities of individual firms. We discussed the role of marketing in economic development—and talked about the functions of marketing and who performs them. We concluded by raising some of the criticisms of marketing—both criticisms of the whole macro system and criticisms aimed at individual firms.

The major thrust of this book is on *micro*-marketing. Most students of marketing are preparing for careers in management, so it is important to understand marketing decision making—to be more efficient and socially responsible decision makers. This will not only improve the performance of individual firms and organizations, but it should also make our macro-marketing system perform more effectively.

In the chapters that follow, we will see how organizations can better satisfy their customers' and clients' needs. We will not focus just on how present organizations operate. Instead, we will focus on *why* they do what they do and *how* they might do it better. Ultimately, you should be able to understand the *why* of present marketing efforts, *how* they might be improved, and *how* you can contribute to the marketing process in the future.

The impact of micro-level marketing decisions on society will be discussed throughout the text. Then—in Chapter 24—after you have had time to develop a deeper understanding of how and why producers and consumers think and behave the way they do—we will look at macro-marketing again. There we will evaluate how well both micro-marketing and macro-marketing perform in our market-directed economic system.

■ QUESTIONS AND PROBLEMS

1. It is fairly easy to see why people do not beat a path to the mousetrap manufacturer's door, but would they be similarly indifferent if some food processor developed a revolutionary new food product which would provide all necessary nutrients in small pills for about $100 per year per person?

2. Distinguish between macro- and micro-marketing. Then explain how they are interrelated, if they are.

3. Explain in your own words what the macro-micro dilemma is, using an example.

4. Identify the two roles that most individuals play in our economic system. Are these roles incompatible? Why?

5. Distinguish between how economic decisions are made in a centrally planned economy and in a market-directed economy.

6. Explain (*a*) how a central market facilitates exchange and (*b*) how the addition of a middleman facilitates exchange even more.

7. Identify a "central market" in your city and explain how it facilitates exchange.

8. Discuss the nature of marketing in a socialist economy. Would the functions which must be provided and the development of wholesaling and retailing systems be any different?

9. Describe a recent purchase you have made and indicate why that particular product was available at a store and, in particular, at that store.

10. Define the functions of marketing in your own words. Using an example, explain how they can be shifted and shared.

11. Explain, in your own words, why the emphasis in this text is on micro-marketing.

12. Why is satisfying customers or clients considered equally as important as satisfying an organization's objectives—in the text's definition of micro-marketing?

■ SUGGESTED CASES

2. Kaskaid Communications

4. Tot-Switch

■ NOTES

1. To see the basis for such estimates, see Reavis Cox, *Distribution in a High-Level Economy* (Englewood Cliffs, N.J.: Prentice-Hall, 1965), p. 149; and Paul W. Stewart and J. Frederick Dewhurst, *Does Distribution Cost Too Much?* (New York: Twentieth Century Fund, 1963), pp. 117–18.

2. Christopher H. Lovelock and Charles B. Weinberg, "Public and Nonprofit Marketing Comes of Age," in *Review of Marketing,* ed. Gerald Zaltman and Thomas V. Bononia (Chicago: American Marketing Association, 1978), pp. 413–52; Phillip Kotler, "Strategies for Introducing Marketing into Nonprofit Organizations," *Journal of Marketing,* January 1979, pp. 37–44; Shelby D. Hunt, "The Nature and Scope of Marketing," *Journal of Marketing,* July 1976, pp. 17–28; and Paul N. Bloom and William D. Novelli, *Journal of Marketing* 45, no. 2 (Spring 1981), pp. 79–88.

3. Malcolm P. McNair, "Marketing and the Social Challenge of Our Times," in *A New Measure of Responsibility for Marketing,* ed. Keith Cox and Ben M. Enis (Chicago: American Marketing Association, 1968).

4. Daniel J. Sweeney, "Marketing: Management Technology or Social Process," *Journal of Marketing,* October 1972, p. 7.

5. "The Hot Discounter," *Newsweek,* April 25, 1977, p. 70.

6. Peter F. Drucker, *Management: Tasks, Responsibilities, Practices* (New York: Harper & Row, 1973), pp. 64–65.

7. George Fisk, "Editor's Working Definition of Macromarketing," *Journal of Macromarketing* 2, no.1 (Spring 1982), pp. 3–4; and Shelby D. Hunt and John J. Burnett, "The Macromarketing/Micromarketing Dichotomy: A Taxonomical Model," *Journal of Marketing* 46, no. 3 (Summer 1982), pp. 11–26.

8. Much of the material on this topic has been adapted from Y. H. Furuhashi and E. J. McCarthy, *Social Issues of Marketing in the American Economy* (Columbus, Ohio: Grid, 1971), pp. 4–6. See also J. F. Grashof and A. Kelman, *Introduction to Macro-Marketing* (Columbus, Ohio: Grid, 1973).

9. For more on this topic, see Thomas V. Greer, *Marketing in the Soviet Union* (New York: Praeger Publishers, 1973); "Free Enterprise Helps to Keep Russians Fed but Creates Problems," *The Wall Street Journal,* May 2, 1983, pp. 1 and 22; Reed Moyer, "Marketing in the Iron Curtain Countries," *Journal of Marketing,* October 1966, pp. 3–9; G. Peter Lauter, "The Changing Role of Marketing in the Eastern European Socialist Economies, *Journal of Marketing,* October 1971, pp. 16–20; Coskun Samli, *Marketing and Distribution Systems in Eastern Europe* (New York: Praeger Publishers, 1978); and John F. Gaski, "Current Russian Marketing Practice: A Report of the 1982 AMA Study Tour of the Soviet Union," in *1983 American Marketing Association Educators' Proceedings,* ed. P. Murphy et al. (Chicago: American Marketing Association, 1983), pp. 74–77.

10. See, for example, Milton Friedman, *Capitalism and Freedom* (Chicago: University of Chicago Press, 1962); and Murray L. Weidenbaum, *Business Government, and the Public* (Englewood Cliffs, N.J.: Prentice-Hall, 1977). For a contrasting point of view, see John Kenneth Galbraith, *Economics and the Public Purpose* (Boston: Houghton-Mifflin, 1973).

11. Wroe Alderson, "Factors Governing the Development of Marketing Channels," in *Marketing Channels for Manufactured Products,* ed. Richard M. Clewett (Homewood, Ill.: Richard D. Irwin, 1954).

12. Peter F. Drucker, "Marketing and Economic Development," *Journal of Marketing,* January 1958, p. 253.

13. Ragnar Nurkse, *Problems of Capital Formation in Underdeveloped Countries* (Oxford: Basil Blackwell, 1953), p.4.

14. Robert W. Nason and Phillip D. White, "The Visions of Charles C. Slater: Social Consequences of Marketing," *Journal of Macromarketing* 1, no. 2 (Fall 1981), pp. 4–18; and D. F. Dixon, "The Role of Marketing in Early Theories of Economic Development," *Journal of Macromarketing* 1, no. 2 (Fall 1981), pp. 19–27.

15. This discussion is based largely on William McInnes, "A Conceptual Approach to Marketing," in *Theory in Marketing,* second series, ed. Reavis Cox, Wroe Alerson, and Stanley J. Shapiro (Homewood, Ill.: Richard D. Irwin, 1964), pp. 51–67. See also Grashof and Kelman, *Introduction to Macro-Marketing,* pp. 69–78.

16. Reed Moyer, *Macro Marketing: A Social Perspective* (New York: John Wiley & Sons, 1972), pp. 3–5.

17. *Forging America's Future: Strategies for National Growth and Development,* Report of the Advisory Committee on National Growth Policy Processes, reprinted in *Challenge,* January/February 1977.

Chapter 2 ■ Marketing's role within the firm

When you finish this chapter, you should:

1. Know what the marketing concept is—and how it should affect a firm's strategy planning.

2. Understand what a marketing manager does.

3. Know what marketing strategy planning is—and why it will be the focus of this book.

4. Understand target marketing.

5. Be familiar with the four Ps in a marketing mix.

6. Know the difference between a marketing strategy, a marketing plan, and a marketing program.

7. Recognize the important new terms (shown in red).

*"A master plan to hit the target" is not a Star Wars story line—
but the goal of a good marketing manager.*

Marketing and marketing management are important in our society—and in business firms. As you saw in Chapter 1, marketing is concerned with anticipating needs and directing the flow of goods and services from producers to consumers. This is done to satisfy the needs of consumers—and achieve the objectives of the firm (the micro view) and of society as a whole (the macro view).

To get a better understanding of marketing, we are going to look at things from the point of view of the marketing manager—the one who makes a company's important marketing decisions. Let's consider the kinds of decisions that have to be made by marketing managers—to get you thinking about the ideas we will be developing in this chapter and in the rest of the book.

Procter & Gamble is one of the most successful marketing organizations in North America. Most of the products marketed in the United States are also sold in Canada, but up to now Folger's coffee has not been distributed in this country. Let's assume Procter & Gamble wants to launch Folger's in Canada. To bring this product to market many decisions would be required.

First of all the company would have to study the market to see how large it is and to find out who their main competitors would be. The Folger blend used in the United States would also have to be tested—to make sure Canadians liked the taste. Marketing management would have to decide whether to use the same kind of packaging and how labels could be redesigned so that both English and

French would appear. Marketing managers would also have to decide how to tell consumers about the product—i.e., choose which people were to be the main target, pick a theme for the advertising campaign and determine how much to spend on advertising and where to spend it. Decisions would also have to be made as to how the new brand would be promoted to the grocery trade—the "middlemen" who actually offer products at places where customers can buy them. Folger's marketing managers would have to decide how they would price their new brand as compared to its competitors and whether to set a special low price during the introductory period. They would either have to pick regions of the country in which to introduce the product first—to see how it sold—or decide to distribute it in as many places as possible all at once.

These are only a few of many important decisions Folger's marketing mangers need to make—and you can see that each of the decisions affects the others. Making effective marketing decisions is never easy—but knowing ahead of time what basic decision areas need to be considered is an important part of arriving at a sensible whole. This chapter will get you started in this direction by giving you a framework to think about all the marketing management decision areas—which is what the rest of this book is all about.

Marketing's Role Has Changed a Lot over the Years*

In our Folger's example, it is clear that marketing management plays a very important role. Marketing today is a highly sophisticated process—but it did not become this way overnight. Some of the practices used today are based on practices introduced many years ago. During its long historical development marketing has been a significant force in human history.

Early Marketing: Prehistory to 1700 A.D.

Early marketing took the form of trading activities—activities involved in people exchanging items of value with one another. Trading activities were carried on by prehistoric people more than 10,000 years ago. Trade enabled them to obtain items which they could not find in their own areas. This has been the basic motivation for trade ever since.

When civilization developed in China, India, and the Middle East, trade became common. Civilizations provided military protection for traders, and cities developed whose inhabitants required both basic supplies and luxuries. The Romans purchased luxuries from as far away as China, wheat from North America, and oysters from Britain. Some Roman merchants advertised on walls. When Roman authority collapsed, trade deceased in Europe. But it never died out entirely—some trade was essential to life. Trade increased again when strong governments developed in Europe.

---

*This brief review of marketing's historical development was written for Basic Marketing, Fourth Canadian Edition, by Professor Ronald Fullerton of Providence College, Providence, R.I.

Early trade activities did vary in intensity from time to time and place to place. But even at their most active, they were very limited compared to today.[1] Thus exchange activities played a much smaller role in the lives of most people than they do now. Merchants had lower status than in our culture. Most people lived in rural areas and were largely self-sufficient—they made or grew most of what they consumed.

Aside from luxury goods intended for tiny elites, there were few manufactured products for sale. Styles changed slowly, and business practices were conservative. This state of affairs lasted until the 19th century in much of Europe, the Americas, and Asia. Some places even today are still in the Early Trade Stage.

Early trade did have some important consequences. Many of today's major population centers grew up along ancient trade routes. Trade contacts among different cultures stimulated change and progress in art, science, technology, and business.[2] British trade contacts with the non-European world helped to stimulate the birth of modern marketing.

The birth of modern marketing: Britain and the Industrial Revolution, 1700–1860

The Industrial Revolution made Britain the first modern economy. It brought about the greatest changes in the way people lived since the development of agriculture 10,000 years before. Historians now know that many of these changes were due to the development of modern, energetic, marketing activities.[3]

The Industrial Revolution was caused by the work of energetic and creative entrepreneurs. These entrepreneurs were capitalists—they used resources (capital) to build up their businesses. They believed that their businesses should grow indefinitely, a very different attitude from previous business people. The British entrepreneurs strove continually to create new markets and to enlarge older ones. They had to overcome old technological constraints in order to produce more. Equally important, they had to overcome the age-old limits on demand—the deeply rooted custom of buying few material possessions.

The entrepreneurs overcame both constraints. They introduced factories and steam power in order to produce a great array of inexpensive products. They developed marketing techniques to determine what products to produce, which styles to produce them in, and how to promote and distribute them. The techniques developed by British entrepreneurs in the 1700s are the bases of several of the present-day practices which will be described in this book. These include: close attention to customer needs, vigorous advertising, attractive retail stores, creative incentives to buy, and targeting of promising groups for special attention.

By increasing supply and demand at the same time, British business people made their economy the most dynamic the world had ever seen. Rich earlier economies like those of Rome and China had reached a point of development and stopped growing—the British economy kept expanding, and expanding.

The entire way of life changed. Britons increasingly abandoned self-sufficient living and specialized in their work. The Industrial Revolution created countless new jobs of all types for them to fill. Britons purchased their needs on a regular basis—they became consumers in the modern sense. Market transactions became a pervasive part of life for most people. There were still poor people—and people who suffered more than they gained from the Industrial Revolution. But the living standards of even average Britons astounded foreign observers. During the 1800s the British innovations in marketing and manufacturing began to spread. They had great influence in Western Europe and North America.

The development of marketing in North America

Most of the early settlers to North America lived largely self-sufficient lives. Marketing activity was limited. But in the second half of the 19th century the economy and styles of life modernized rapidly. Marketing activities played an ever-larger role in everyday life. By 1900, marketing practices were as highly developed in North America as they were in Britain itself.

The period between 1870 and 1930 was the *Age of Marketing Development* in North America. During these years the lessons of British marketers were absorbed—and improved upon in some cases. Most of today's marketing institutions and practices originated in this period. These include: national brands, mail-order selling, market research, advertising agencies, sophisticated large-scale advertising, consumer credit, well-trained sales forces, and attractive retail stores. Many stores were organized into chains by the end of the period. Wholesalers developed into their modern form.

North America pioneered the development of marketing education during this period. Marketing courses made it possible for students to learn quickly what it had previously taken the most capable business people years to figure out by trial and error.

Energetic and astute marketing practices helped raise the material standard of living enormously in North America just as they had earlier in Britain. In fact, by 1929 North America's standard of living was the highest in the world. A majority of families owned automobiles—something Britain did not achieve until 25 years later.

1930–1979: The age of marketing refinement

During this period the basic institutions and practices of marketing were further developed and refined.

Noteworthy advances were made in the development of market research techniques and in the understanding of consumer behavior. Marketing planning and evaluation techniques were improved and became widely used. New technologies like television and the computer were quickly adopted by marketers—today marketing executives are among the largest users of personal computers. Marketing education spread widely, and most colleges and universities offered marketing courses. The courses themselves were increasingly designed to teach students to think like marketing managers. Within most medium- and large-sized firms, marketing managers worked within the formal marketing departments which were established during this period. Sometimes these marketing departments set the tone of the entire company—orienting the company toward discovering and satisfying buyers' needs.

But not all firms showed a marketing orientation. The top management of some companies was preoccupied with finance or production. There were complaints that some firms took their customers for granted and did not respond to their needs. A few areas of marketing practice did decline in quality during the period—retail selling and magazine advertising. So there were problems along with the solid advances in marketing. During the past few years serious efforts have been made to correct the most serious of the problems—lack of attention to customer needs.

Marketing today: The top priority of enterprise

Intense international competition during the past several years has convinced most companies that effective marketing "will provide the cutting edge in the 1980s."[4] Experienced marketing people are now the favored candidates for top management positions. In addition, there is an intense interest in marketing on the part of government agencies, non-profit institutions, and some professions. The prestige of marketing has never been higher than it is now—this is a good time to be learning marketing.

What Does the Marketing Concept Mean?

The **marketing concept** means that an organization aims *all* its efforts at satisfying its *customers*—at a *profit.* The marketing concept is a simple but very important idea.

It is not really a new idea in business—it has been around for most of your life. But, some managers act as if they are stuck at the beginning of the production era—when there were shortages of most products—and show little motivation to worry about customers' needs. These managers still have a **production orientation**—making products which are easy to produce and *then* trying to sell them. They think of customers as existing to buy the firm's output—rather than the firm existing to serve customers.

In well-managed firms, this production orientation has been replaced with a marketing orientation. A **marketing orientation** means trying to carry out the marketing concept. Instead of just trying to get customers to buy what the firm has produced, a marketing-oriented firm tries to produce what customers need.

Three basic ideas are included in the definition of the marketing concept:

1. A customer orientation.
2. A total company effort.
3. Profit—not just sales—as an objective.

These three ideas deserve more discussion.

A customer orientation guides the whole system

"Give the customers what they need"—this may seem so obvious that it may be hard for you to understand why the marketing concept requires special attention. However, people don't always do the logical and obvious—especially when it means changing what they have done in the past. Twenty years ago—in a typical company—production managers thought mainly about getting out the product. Accountants were interested only in balancing the books. Financial people looked after the company's cash position. And salespeople were mainly concerned with getting orders. Each department thought of its own activity as the center of the business—with others working around "the edges." No one was concerned with the whole system. As long as the company made a profit, each department went merrily on—"doing its own thing." Unfortunately, this is still true in many companies today.

Work together . . . do a better job

Ideally, all managers should work together—because the output from one department may be the input to another. But managers tend to build "fences" around their own departments—as seen in Figure 2–1A. Each department runs its own affairs for its own benefit. There may be meetings to try to get them to work together—but usually each department head comes to such meetings with the idea of protecting his own department's interests.

We use the term "production orientation" as a shorthand way to refer to this kind of narrow thinking—and lack of a central focus—in a business firm. But keep in mind that this problem may be seen in sales-oriented sales representatives, advertising-oriented agency people, finance-oriented finance people, and so on. It is not a criticism of people who manage production—because they aren't necessarily any more guilty of narrow thinking than anyone else in the firm.

In a firm that has accepted the marketing concept, however, the fences come down. There are still departments, of course, because there are efficiencies in specialization. But the total system's effort is guided by what customers want—instead of what each department would like to do.

In such a firm, it is more realistic to view the business as a box with both internal and external activities—as shown in Figure 2–1B. Some internal departments—production, accounting, and research and development (R&D)—are mainly concerned with affairs inside the firm. And the external departments are concerned with outsiders—sales, advertising, and sales promotion. Finally, some

---

■ FIGURE 2–1

A. A business as a box
(most departments have high fences)

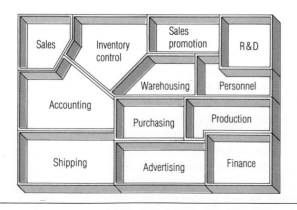

B. Total system view of a business (implementing marketing concept; still have departments but all guided by what customers want)

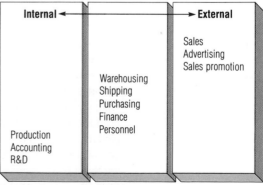

departments work with both insiders and outsiders—warehousing, shipping, purchasing, finance, and personnel.

The important point is having a guiding focus that all departments adopt. It helps the organization work as a total "system"—not a lot of separate parts. The marketing concept, however, is more complete than many "systems-oriented" ideas. It actually specifies a "high-level" objective—customer satisfaction—that is logical for each and every part of the system. It also specifies a profit objective—which is necessary for the system's survival.

It's easy to slip into a production orientation

The marketing concept may be obvious, but it is very easy to slip into a production-oriented way of thinking. For example, a retailer might prefer only weekday hours—avoiding nights, Saturdays, and Sundays—when many customers would prefer to shop. Or a company might rush to produce a clever new product idea developed in its laboratory—rather than first finding out if it fills a need.

■ FIGURE 2–2   Some differences in outlook between adopters of the marketing concept and the typical production-oriented managers

Marketing orientation	Attitudes and procedures	Production orientation
Customer needs determine company plans ←	Attitudes toward customers →	They should be glad we exist, trying to cut costs and bring out better products
Company makes what it can sell ←	Product offering →	Company sells what it can make
To determine customer needs and how well company is satisfying them ←	Role of marketing research →	To determine customer reaction, if used at all
Focus on locating new opportunities ←	Interest in innovation →	Focus is on technology and cost cutting
A critical objective ←	Importance of profit →	A residual, what's left after all costs are covered
Seen as a customer service ←	Role of customer credit →	Seen as a necessary evil
Designed for customer convenience and as a selling tool ←	Role of packaging →	Seen merely as protection for the product
Set with customer requirements and costs in mind ←	Inventory levels →	Set with production requirements in mind
Seen as a customer service ←	Transportation arrangements →	Seen as an extension of production and storage activities, with emphasis on cost minimization
Need-satisfying benefits of products and services ←	Focus of advertising →	Product features and quality, maybe how products are made
Help the customer to buy if the product fits his needs, while coordinating with rest of firm—including production, inventory control, advertising, etc. ←	Role of sales force →	Sell the customer, don't worry about coordination with other promotion efforts or rest of firm

Source: Adapted from R. F. Vizza, T. E. Chambers, and E. J. Cook, *Adoption of the Marketing Concept—Fact or Fiction* (New York: Sales Executive Club, Inc., 1967), pp. 13–15.

Take a look at Figure 2–2 on page 39. It shows some differences in outlook between adopters of the marketing concept and typical production-oriented managers. As this suggests, the marketing concept is really very powerful—if taken seriously. It forces the company to think through what it is doing—and why. And it motivates the company to develop plans for accomplishing its objectives.

Adoption of the Marketing Concept Has Not Been Easy or Universal

The marketing concept seems so logical that you would think that it would have been quickly adopted by most firms. In fact, it was not. Many firms are still production-oriented. In fact, the majority are either production-oriented—or regularly slip back that way—and must consciously bring the customers' interests to bear in their planning.

The marketing concept was first accepted by consumer goods companies—such as General Electric and Procter & Gamble. Competition was intense in some of their markets—and trying to satisfy customers' needs more fully was a way to win in this competition. Widespread publicity about the success of the marketing concept at companies like General Electric and Procter & Gamble helped spread the "message" to other consumer goods and industrial goods companies.[5]

Producers of industrial commodities—steel, coal, paper, glass, chemicals—have accepted the marketing concept more slowly—if at all. Similarly, many retailers have been slow to accept the marketing concept—in part because they are so close to final consumers that they "feel" that they really know their customers.

Service industries are catching on fast

In the last 10 years or so, many "service" industries—including airlines, lawyers, physicians, accountants, and insurance companies—have begun to apply the marketing concept. Banking illustrates the trend. Banks used to be open for limited hours that were convenient to the bankers—not customers. Now, banks stay open longer—and many are open evenings and Saturdays. They also offer more services for their customers—automatic banking machines that take credit cards—or a "personal banker" to give financial advice. And interest rates are not all the same. Some banks advertise their interest rates—so customers can see that they vary. The marketing of services is discussed as some length in the Appendix that follows Chapter 21.

Marketing concept applies directly to non-profit organization

The same ideas apply directly to non-profit organizations. All that must be changed are the objectives against which possible plans are measured. The Red Cross, art museums, and government agencies, for example, are all seeking to satisfy some consumer groups.[6]

A simple example shows how marketing concept thinking helped one non-profit service organization do a better job of achieving its objectives. First, it had to overcome a production orientation.

The police chief in a small town had too few officers to cope with the increasing number of residential break-ins. He asked the town manager for a larger budget—to pay for additional police officers and to buy extra cars so that he could patrol in neighborhoods more often. The town manager realized that this was really a narrow view—one that "increased production" but did not necessarily meet the needs of the residents they were trying to serve. Instead of raising the budget, the town manager suggested another approach. She took one police officer "off the beat"—and put him in charge of a "community watch" program. The officer set up meetings and helped neighbors organize to look after each others' property—and to notify the police of anything unusual. She also set up a program to engrave identification numbers on belongings—and put up signs in neighborhoods that warned thieves that a "community watch" was in effect. Break-ins all but stopped—and it didn't require higher taxes. What the town *really needed* was more effective crime prevention—not just more police officers.

Through this text, we will be discussing the marketing concept and related ideas as they apply in many different settings. Often we will simply say "in a firm" or "in a business"—but you should keep in mind that most of the ideas discussed in the book can be applied in *any* type of organization.

How far should the marketing concept go?

The marketing concept is so logical that it's hard to argue with it. Yet, it does raise some important questions—for which there are not always "easy" answers.

Should all consumer needs be satisfied?

When a firm focuses its efforts on satisfying some consumers—to gain its objectives—the effect of this on society may be completely ignored. Remember that we discussed this micro-macro dilemma in Chapter 1.

Further, the long-run welfare of consumers may be neglected in favor of satisfying their short-term wants. For example, some critics argue that businesses should not offer cigarettes, high-heeled shoes, alcoholic beverages, sugar-coated cereals, soft drinks, and many processed foods—because they are either "empty calories" or may be detrimental to health in the long run. Should manufacturers continue to produce these products because consumers want them? The critics look at these issues and raise the basic question: "Is the marketing concept really desirable?"[7]

Some marketing managers and socially conscious marketing companies are beginning to face this problem. Their definition of customer satisfaction is changing to include long-range effects—as well as immediate customer satisfaction. They are trying to bring social cost/benefit analysis into their decision making—with a view to balancing consumer, company, and social interests.

What if it cuts into profits?

Being more "socially conscious" often seems to lead to positive customer response. For example, one baby food company had great success when it improved the nutritional quality of its products.

But what about the not-so-easy changes that will cut into profits? A toy maker recently took a profitable new game off the market when a child accidentally swallowed one of the parts and choked to death. Other companies might have to go out of business altogether. Motorcycles, lawnmowers, bicycles, small cars, skis, and many other products are extremely hazardous to users. Should these be offered to consumers just because they want them? Who should decide? Is this a micro-marketing issue or a macro-marketing issue?

Being "socially conscious" and trying to carry out the marketing concept can be difficult. It may mean reducing short-term profitability. But socially responsible business managers have to face this issue. We will discuss some of the social issues in marketing management throughout the book, and we will focus on them again in Chapter 24—after you have a better understanding of marketing.

The Management Job in Marketing

Now that you know about the marketing concept—as a philosophy to guide the whole firm—we can look more closely at how marketing managers help the firm to achieve its objectives. The marketing manager is a *manager,* so let's look at the *marketing management process.*

The **marketing management process** is the process of (1) *planning* marketing activities, (2) directing the *implementation* of the plans, and (3) *controlling* these plans. Planning, implementation, and control are basic tasks of *all* managers—but here we will emphasize what they mean to marketing managers.

Figure 2–3 shows the relationships among the key steps in the marketing management process. The steps are all connected to show that the marketing management process is continuous. The planning job sets guidelines for the implementing job and specifies expected results. These expected results are used in the control job—to determine if everything has worked out as planned. The link from the control job to the planning job is especially important. This feedback often leads to changes in the plans—or even to totally new plans.

Marketing managers should seek new opportunities

Figure 2–3 shows that marketing managers must seek attractive new opportunities—as customer needs change or as the organization's ability to meet customer needs changes. In the next two chapters, we will discuss how marketing managers seek and evaluate opportunities.

For now, however, it is important to see that—in dynamic marketplaces—marketing managers cannot be satisfied just planning present activities. Competitors continually search for ways of improving their offerings—and consumers are usually willing to try something newer and better.

A marketing manager for a company that installs electric water heaters, for example, might see an opportunity to meet the need for lower-cost hot water with a solar energy system. This might be a "good" opportunity for the company. But, not every opportunity will be "good." Really attractive opportunities are those that fit with what the whole company wants to—and is able to do.

Strategic management planning concerns the whole firm

The job of planning strategies to guide a *whole company* is called **strategic (management) planning**—the managerial process of developing and maintaining a match between the resources of an organization and its market opportuni-

■   FIGURE 2–3   The marketing management process

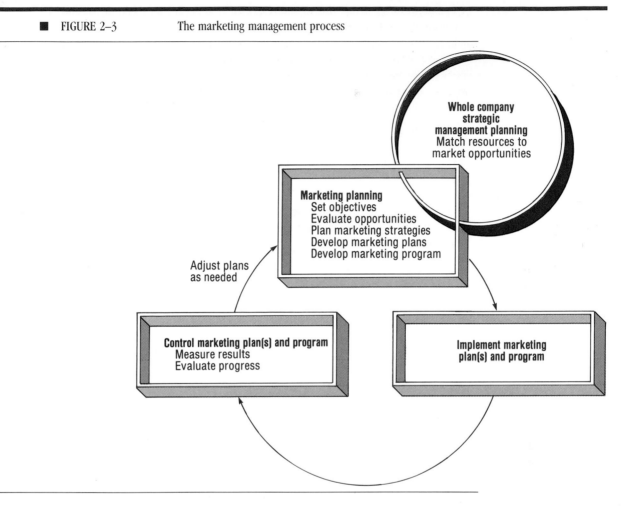

Whole company
strategic
management planning
Match resources to
market opportunities

Marketing planning
Set objectives
Evaluate opportunities
Plan marketing strategies
Develop marketing plans
Develop marketing program

Adjust plans
as needed

Control marketing plan(s) and program
Measure results
Evaluate progress

**Implement marketing
plan(s) and program**

ties. This is a big job that includes not only marketing activities but also major financial decisions, planning for production, research and development, and other functional areas. Ultimately, the top executive in a firm is responsible for such whole-company strategic planning. But, because the strategic (management) planning job is so important—and has such far-reaching effects—other top managers in the firm are almost always involved.

We will not get into such detail in this text—and it is important to see that the marketing department's plans are not the overall strategic management plan. On the other hand, the overall plan should be market-oriented. And in most organizations, there is at least some form of **bottom-up planning**—in which plans developed at lower levels in the organization are compiled into an overall plan. To the extent that the overall plan is the sum of the various department plans, the marketing department's plans may help set the tone and direction for the whole company. If the marketing department applies the marketing concept, then this can lead the whole company to follow. So we will use "strategy planning" and "marketing strategy planning" interchangeably.[8]

What Is Marketing Strategy Planning?

Marketing strategy planning means finding attractive opportunities and developing profitable marketing strategies. But what is a "marketing strategy?" We have used these words rather casually so far. Now let's see what they really mean.

What is a marketing strategy?

A **marketing strategy** specifies a target market and a related marketing mix. It is a "big picture" of what a firm will do in some market. Two interrelated parts are needed:

1. A **target market**—a fairly homogeneous (similar) group of customers to whom a company wishes to appeal.
2. A **marketing mix**—the controllable variables which the company puts together to satisfy this target group.

The importance of target customers in this process can be seen in Figure 2–4, where the customer—the "C"—is at the center of the diagram. The customer is surrounded by the controllable variables which we call the "marketing mix." A typical marketing mix would include some product, offered at a price, with some promotion to tell potential customers about the product, and the place where it is available.

Hanes Corporation's strategy for L'eggs hosiery is to aim at convenience-oriented young women in urban areas with a consistently high quality product that comes in a distinctive package. The strategy calls for the product to be available at as many grocery and drug stores as possible. While its pricing is more or less competitive, the company supports the whole effort with much promotion—including advertising to final consumers, personal selling to retailers, and sales promotion to both consumers and retailers.

■ FIGURE 2–4   A marketing strategy

L'eggs made its distinctive package conveniently available.

Selecting a Market-Oriented Strategy Is Target Marketing

Target marketing is not mass marketing

It is important to see that a marketing strategy specifies some *particular* target customers. This approach is called "target marketing" to distinguish it from "mass marketing." **Target marketing** says that a marketing mix must be tailored to fit some specific target customers. In contrast, **mass marketing**—the typical production-oriented approach—vaguely aims at "everyone" with the same marketing mix. Mass marketing assumes that everyone is the same—and everyone is considered a potential customer. See Figure 2–5.

"Mass marketers" may do target marketing

Commonly used terms can be confusing here. The terms "mass market*ing*" and "mass market*ers*" do not mean the same thing. Far from it! "Mass marketing" means trying to sell to "everyone," as we explained above—while "mass marketers" like General Foods and Sears, are not aiming at "everyone." They do aim at clearly defined target markets. The confusion with "mass marketing" occurs because their target markets usually are large and spread out.

Target marketing— can mean big markets and profits

Remember that target marketing is not limited to small market segments— only to fairly homogeneous ones. A very large market—even what is sometimes called the "mass market"—may be fairly homogeneous in some cases—and a target marketer will deliberately aim at it.

The basic reason for this focus on some specific target customers is to gain a competitive advantage by developing a more satisfying marketing mix—which should also be more profitable for the firm.

■ FIGURE 2–5   Production-oriented and marketing-oriented managers have different views of the market

Production-oriented manager sees everyone as basically similar and practices "mass marketing"

Marketing-oriented manager sees everyone as different and practices "target marketing"

Developing Marketing Mixes for Target Markets

There are many marketing mix variables

There are many possible ways to satisfy the needs of target customers. A product can have many different features, colors, and appearances. The package can be of various sizes, colors, or materials. The brand names and trademarks can be changed. Services—like delivery or installation—can be adjusted. Various advertising media—newspapers, magazines, radio, television, billboards—may be used. A company's own sales force or other sales specialists can be used. Different prices can be charged, and so on. With so many variables available, the question is: Is there any way of simplifying the selection of marketing mixes? And the answer is: Yes.

The four "Ps" make up a marketing mix

It is useful to reduce the number of variables in the marketing mix to four basic ones:

Product.
Place.
Promotion.
Price.

It helps to think of the four major parts of a marketing mix as the "four Ps." Figure 2–6 emphasizes their relationship and their focus on the customer—"C."

■ FIGURE 2–6   A marketing strategy—showing the 4 Ps of a marketing mix

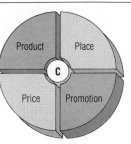

Customer is not part of the marketing mix

The customer is shown surrounded by the four Ps in Figure 2–6. Some students assume that the customer is part of the marketing mix—but this is not so. The customer should be the *target* of all marketing efforts. The customer is placed in the center of the diagram to show this—the C stands for some specific customers, the target market.

Table 2–1 shows some of the variables in the four Ps—which will be discussed in later chapters. For now, let's just describe each P briefly.

Product—the right one for the target

The Product area is concerned with developing the right "product" for the target market. This offering may involve a physical good and/or service. For example, the product of a taxi company is a ride to your destination. The important thing to remember in the Product area is that your good—and/or service—should satisfy some customers' needs.

■ TABLE 2–1   Strategic decision areas

Product	Place	Promotion	Price
Features	Objectives	Objectives	Objectives
Accessories	Channel type	Promotion blend	Flexibility
Installation	Market exposure	Sales people	Level over product
Instructions	Kinds of middlemen	Kind	life cycle
Service	Kinds and locations	Number	Geographic terms
Warranty	of stores	Selection	Discounts
Product lines	Who handles	Training	Allowances
Packaging	transporting	Motivation	
Branding	and storing	Advertising	
	Service levels	Targets	
	Recruiting	Kind of ads	
	middlemen	Media type	
	Managing	Copy thrust	
	channels	Prepared by whom	
		Sales promotion	
		Publicity	

Along with other Product decisions, we will talk about developing and managing new products and whole product lines. We will also discuss the characteristics of various kinds of products—so that you will be able to make generalizations about product classes. This will help you to develop whole marketing mixes more quickly.

Keep in mind that Product is not limited to "physical goods." It refers to the whole offering of the firm—which may involve some service with a physical good or a service by itself. This is important—because the service side of our economy is large and growing.

Place—reaching the target

Place is concerned with getting the right product to the target market. A product isn't much good to a customer if it isn't available when and where it's wanted. In the Place chapters, we will see where, when, and by whom the goods and services can be offered for sale.

Goods and services often move to customers through channels of distribution. A **channel of distribution** is any series of firms (or individuals) from producer to final user or consumer. A channel can include several kinds of middlemen and specialists. Marketing managers work with these channels. So our study of Place is very important to marketing strategy planning.

Sometimes a channel system is quite short. It may run directly from a producer to a final user or consumer. Usually, it is more complex—involving many different kinds of middlemen and specialists. And if a marketing manager has several different target markets, several channels of distribution might be needed. See Figure 2–7. We will also see how transporting and storing relates to the other Place decisions—and the rest of the marketing mix.

■   FIGURE 2–7   Four possible (basic) channels of distribution for consumer goods

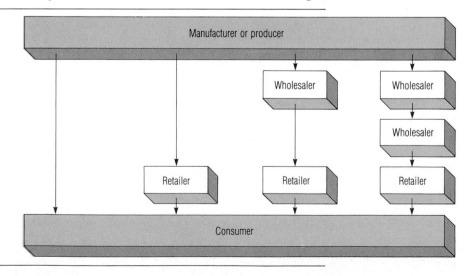

Promotion—telling and selling the customer

The third P—Promotion—is concerned with telling the target market about the "right" product. Promotion includes personal selling, mass selling, and sales promotion. It is the marketing manager's job to blend these methods.

Personal selling involves direct face-to-face communication between sellers and potential customers. Personal selling lets the salesperson adapt the firm's marketing mix to each potential customer. But this individual attention comes at a price. Personal selling can be very expensive. Often this personal effort has to be blended with mass selling and sales promotion. Sales and marketing managers make decisions about how to select, train, supervise, compensate, and control the sales force.

Mass selling is communicating with large numbers of customers at the same time. **Advertising** is any paid form of non-personal presentation of ideas, goods, or services by an identified sponsor. It is the main form of mass selling. **Publicity** is any *unpaid* form of non-personal presentation of ideas, goods, or services.

Sales promotion refers to those promotion activities—other than advertising, publicity, and personal selling—which stimulate interest, trial, or purchase by final customers or others in the channel. This can involve designing and arranging for the distribution of coupons, point-of-purchase materials, store signs, catalogs, novelties, and circulars. Sales promotion people try to help the personal selling and mass selling specialists.

Price—making it right

In addition to developing the right Product, Place, and Promotion, marketing managers must also decide the right Price. In setting a price, they must consider the kind of competition in the target market. They must also try to estimate customer reaction to possible prices. Besides this, they also must know current practices as to markups, discounts, and other terms of sale. Further, they must be aware of legal restrictions on pricing.

If customers won't accept the Price, all of the planning effort will be wasted. So you can see that Price is an important area for the marketing manager.

Each of the four Ps contributes to the whole

All four Ps are needed in a marketing mix. In fact, they should all be tied together. But is any one more important than the others? Generally speaking, the answer is *no*—all contribute to one whole. When a marketing mix is being developed, all (final) decisions about the Ps should be made at the same time. That's why the four Ps are arranged around the customer (C) in a circle—to show that they all are equally important.

Strategy guides implementing

Let's sum up our discussion of marketing mix planning this far. We develop a *Product* that we feel will satisfy the target customers. We find a way—*Place*—to reach our target customers. *Promotion* tells the target customers about the availability of the product that has been designed for them. Then the *Price* is set after estimating expected customer reaction to the total offering and the costs of getting it to them.

Both jobs must be done together

It is important to stress—*it cannot be overemphasized*—that selecting a target market and developing a marketing mix are interrelated. A marketing manager cannot do one step and then another. Both steps must be done together. It is *strategies* which must be evaluated against the company's objectives—not alternative target markets or alternative marketing mixes.

Strategy sets details of implementation

The needs of a target market virtually determine the nature of an appropriate marketing mix. So it is necessary for marketers to analyze their potential target markets with great care. This book will explore ways of identifying attractive market opportunities and developing appropriate strategies. Ideally, we will try to understand not only the needs and attitudes of potential target markets, but also enough of their other dimensions so that logical marketing mixes will follow quickly. Such target market descriptions may require imaginative combining of several dimensions to completely describe potential target markets. Further, it will help in estimating the size of potential markets if we can tie each to demographic characteristics such as age, sex, income, geographic area, and so on.

Ideally, our target market dimensions should be complete enough to guide marketing mix planning. Table 2–2 shows some of the kinds of dimensions we will be considering in later chapters and their probable effect on marketing decisions. Ideally, we would like to describe any potential market in terms of all three types of dimensions because these dimensions will help us develop more appealing—and profitable—marketing mixes.

These ideas can be seen more clearly with an example in the home decorating market.

A British paint manufacturer looks at the home decorating market

The experience of a paint manufacturer in England illustrates the strategy planning process—and how strategic decisions help decide how the plan is carried out.

■ TABLE 2–2   Relation of potential target market dimensions to marketing mix decision areas

Potential target market dimensions	Effects on decision areas
1. Geographic location and other demographic characteristics of potential customers	Affects size of *Target Markets* (economic potential) and *Place* (where products should be made available) and *Promotion* (where and to whom to advertise)
2. Behavioral needs, attitudes, and how present and potential goods or services fit into customers' consumption patterns	Affects *Product* (design, packaging, length or width of product line) and *Promotion* (what potential customers need and what to know about the product offering, and what appeals should be used)
3. Urgency to get need satisfied and desire and willingness to compare and shop	Affects *Place* (how directly products are distributed from producer to consumer, how extensively they are made available, and the level of service needed) and *Price* (how much potential customers are willing to pay)

First, this paint manufacturer's marketing manager interviewed many potential customers and studied the various needs for the products he could offer. By combining several kinds of customer needs and some available demographic data, he came up with the view of the market shown in Figure 2–8. In the following description of these markets, note that useful marketing mixes come to mind immediately.

There turned out to be a large (but hard to describe) market for "general-purpose paint"—about 60 percent of the potential for all kinds of paint products. The manufacturer did not consider this market—because he did not want to compete "head-on" with the many companies already in this market. The other four markets—which were placed in the four corners of a market diagram simply to show that they were different markets—he called Helpless Homemaker, Handy Helper, Crafty Craftsman, and Cost-Conscious Couple.

The *Helpless Homemaker*—the manufacturer found out—really didn't know much about home painting or specific products. This customer needed a helpful paint retailer who could supply not only paint and other supplies—but also much advice. And the retailer who sold the paint would want it to be of fairly good quality so that the homemaker would be satisfied with the results.

The *Handy Helper* was a jack-of-all-trades who knew a great deal about paint and painting. He wanted a good-quality product and was satisfied to buy from an old-fashioned hardware store or lumber yard—which usually sells mainly to men. Similarly, the *Crafty Craftsman* was willing to buy from a retailer who would not attract female customers. In fact, these older men didn't want to buy paint at all. They wanted pigments, oils, and other things to mix their own paint.

Finally, the *Cost-Conscious Couple* was young, had low income, and lived in an apartment. In England, an apartment dweller must paint the apartment during the course of the lease. This is an important factor for some tenants as they choose their paint. If you were a young apartment dweller with limited income,

■ FIGURE 2–8   The home decorating market (paint area) in England

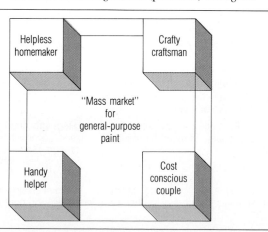

what sort of paint would you want? Some couples in England—the manufacturer discovered—did not want very good paint! In fact, something not much better than whitewash would do fine.

The paint manufacturer decided to cater to "Cost-Conscious Couples" with a marketing mix flowing from the description of that market. That is, knowing what he did about them, he offered a low-quality paint (Product), made it available in lower-income apartment neighborhoods (Place), aimed his price-oriented ads at these areas (Promotion), and, of course, offered an attractive low price (Price). The manufacturer has been extremely successful with this strategy—giving his customers what they really want—even though the product is of low quality.

Differentiating between Strategic Decisions and Operational Decisions

Strategies work out as planned only when they are effectively carried out. Many **operational decisions**—short-run decisions to help implement strategies—may be needed.

Operational decisions can enhance the basic strategy

Operational decisions should be made within the guidelines set down during strategy planning. Product policies, place policies, and so on are developed as part of strategy planning. Then, operational decisions within these policies probably will be necessary—while carrying out the basic strategy. It is important to realize, however, that as long as these operational decisions stay within the guidelines, no change is being made in the basic strategy. If operational decisions do not produce the desired results, however, it may be necessary to re-

■ TABLE 2–3   Relation of strategic policies to operational decisions for paint manufacturer

Strategic policies	Likely operational decisions
Product—Carry as limited a line of colors and sizes as will satisfy the target market.	Add, change, or drop colors and/or can sizes as customer tastes and preferences dictate.
Place—Try to obtain distribution in every conceivable retail outlet which will handle this type of paint in the areas where the target customers live or buy.	If a new retailer opens for business in these market areas, immediately solicit his order.
Promotion—Promote the "low price" and "satisfactory quality" to meet the needs of the market.	Regularly change the point-of-purchase and advertising copy to produce a "fresh" image. Media changes may be necessary also. Salespeople have to be trained, motivated, etc.
Price—Maintain a low "one-price" policy without "specials" or other promotional deals.	If paint companies in other markets cut prices, do not follow.

evaluate the whole strategy—rather than just "redoubling the effort" in an operational decision area.

It's easier to see the difference between strategic policies and operational decisions if we illustrate these ideas using our paint manufacturer example. Possible four-P or basic strategic policies are shown in the left-hand column in Table 2–3—and likely operational decisions are shown in the right-hand column.

It should be clear that some operational decisions are made regularly—even daily—and such decisions should not be confused with strategic ones. Certainly, a great deal of effort can be involved in these operational decisions. They might take up a good part of the time of a sales manager, advertising manager, and others. But they are not the strategic decisions that will be our primary concern.

The Marketing Plan Is a Guide to Implementation and Control

Now that the key ideas of marketing strategy planning have been introduced, we can return to our overview of the marketing management process. You will see how a marketing strategy leads to a marketing plan and ultimately to implementation and control (see Figure 2–3).

Marketing plan fills out marketing strategy

A marketing strategy is a "big picture" of what a firm will do in some market. A marketing plan goes farther. A **marketing plan** is a written statement of a marketing strategy *and* the time-related details for carrying out the strategy. It should spell out the following in detail: (1) what marketing mix is to be offered to whom (that is, the target market) and for how long; (2) what company resources (shown as costs) will be needed—at what rate (month by month perhaps); and (3) what results are expected (sales and profits perhaps monthly or quarterly). It should also include some control procedures—so that whoever is to carry out the plan will know when things are going wrong. This might be something as simple as comparing actual sales against expected sales—with a "warning flag" to be raised whenever total sales fall below a certain level.

Our focus has been—and will continue to be—on developing marketing strategies. But it is also important to see that eventually marketing managers must develop marketing plans. We discuss them more fully in Chapter 21—after you have studied more about what is involved.

Implementation puts strategies and marketing plans to work

After a basic marketing strategy is developed, a marketing manager is concerned with implementation—that is, with putting the marketing plans into operation. For the marketing manager, this may involve personnel selection, salary administration, middlemen selection, setting commission rates, selection of promotion materials, organizing storage and transportation, and so on. The details of implementation may be simple—or quite complicated. Often this depends on whether the marketing mix is really new. A "start from scratch" effort may be really involved.

Often implementation will take up a greater part of the manager's time than does marketing strategy planning. But implementation is not the major concern of this text. The details of implementation must be left for advanced texts and courses in marketing—after you have learned about planning marketing strategies. Of course, as you learn more about each of the Ps—Product, Place, Promotion, and Price—you will also be learning what managers need to know to implement a strategy.[9]

Several plans make a whole marketing program

Most companies implement more than one marketing strategy—and associated marketing plan—at the same time. They may have a whole line of products—some of them quite different—that were designed to appeal to different target markets. The other elements of the marketing mix might vary, too. A Bic pen, a Bic windsurfer, and a Bic razor all involve different target markets and different marketing mixes, and yet the strategies for each must be implemented at the same time.

A **marketing program** blends all of the firm's marketing plans into one "big" plan. See Figure 2–9. This program, then, is the responsibility of the whole company. Typically, the whole *marketing program* will be an integrated part of the whole-company strategic plans we discussed earlier.

Ultimately, marketing managers plan and manage a whole marketing program. In this text, however, we will put more emphasis on planning one marketing strategy at a time, rather than on planning—or implementing—a whole marketing program. The same basic ideas apply, but our focus on planning individual strategies—as the key building block in the marketing management process—emphasizes how important it is for you to plan each and every one carefully. Too many marketing managers fall into the trap of "sloppy thinking" because they try to worry about too many strategies all at once—and none is developed very carefully.

Control is analyzing and correcting what you've done

The control job provides the feedback that leads to modifying marketing strategies. To maintain control, the marketing manager uses a number of tools—like computer sales analysis, marketing research surveys, and accounting analysis of expenses and profits. We will be devoting all of Chapter 22 to the important topic of controlling marketing plans and programs.

In addition, as we talk about each of the marketing decision areas, we will discuss some of the control issues. This will help you see the specifics of how control keeps the firm on course—or shows the need to plan a new course.

■ FIGURE 2–9   Elements of a firm's marketing program

All marketing jobs require planning and control

At first, it might appear that planning and control are of concern only to high-level management—or in really large companies. This is not true. Every organization needs planning—and without control you never know where things stand.

Similarly, all salespeople—however limited their territory or department—also must have a plan of attack. They may not have complete freedom—because of the master strategy already outlined—but they usually have some choice. They should develop their own strategies—in the light of their abilities and the problems of their particular areas.

The Importance of Marketing Strategy Planning

Most of our emphasis in this book will be on the planning part of the marketing manager's job—for a good reason. The "one-time" strategy decisions—the decisions that decide what business the company is in and the strategies it will follow—are usually basic to success or failure. An extremely good plan might be carried out badly and still be profitable, while a poor but well-implemented plan can lose money. The case histories that follow show the importance of planning—and why we are going to emphasize marketing strategy planning throughout this text.

Henry Ford's strategy worked—until General Motors caught up

Henry Ford is remembered for developing the mass production techniques that produced a car for the masses. His own view of his approach, however, was that mass production developed *because* of his basic decision to build a car for the masses. Cars then were almost custom-built for wealthy buyers. Ford decided on a different strategy. He wanted to produce a car that could appeal to most potential buyers.

Certainly, new production ideas were needed to carry out Ford's strategy. But the really important decision was the initial market-oriented decision that there was a market for millions of cars in the $500 price range. Much of what followed was just carrying out his decision. Ford's strategy to offer a low-priced car was an outstanding success—and millions of Model Ts were sold during the 1910s and 1920s. But there was a defect in his strategy. To keep the price down, a very basic car was offered in "any color you want as long as it's black."

In the 1920s, General Motors felt there was room for a new strategy. They hit on the idea of looking at the market as having several segments (based on price and quality)—and offered a full line of cars with different styles and colors in each price range. The GM strategy was not an immediate success. But they stuck with it and slowly caught up with Ford. In 1927, Ford finally closed down his assembly line for 18 months, switched his strategy, and introduced the more market-oriented Model A. By then GM was already well on its way to the strong market position it still holds.[10]

General Motors didn't see all the opportunities

While GM was successfully capturing a giant share of the automobile market, it was neglecting another very important market—the automobile replacement parts market. Supplying parts was seen more as a "necessary evil" than an important business in itself. As a result, this profitable market was left to many smaller suppliers. Even today, GM does not have the dominance in the repair parts and service market that it has in the car market. In other words, the successful strategy of General Motors was concerned with making and selling *automobiles*—not with the broader business of meeting the customers' needs for personal transportation and keeping the cars moving.

GM also failed to learn the lesson that it had, years earlier, hammered home to Ford. GM concentrated on producing and trying to sell what it wanted—high-priced big cars—even after rising gas prices changed some consumers' preferences to smaller, more economical cars. Foreign manufacturers had geared to that target market in their own countries much earlier—and they successfully seized the opportunity when the North American firms were slow to respond. It has been a long, hard battle for the Detroit auto makers to recapture some of their lost customers.

The watch industry sees new strategies

The conventional watch makers—both domestic and foreign—had always aimed at customers who thought of watches as high-priced, high-quality symbols to mark special events—like graduations or retirement. Advertising was concentrated around Christmas and graduation time and stressed a watch's symbolic appeal. Expensive jewelry stores were the main retail outlets.

This commonly accepted strategy of the major watch companies ignored people in the target market that just wanted to tell the time—and were interested in a reliable, low-priced watch. So the U.S. Time Company developed a successful strategy around its "Timex" watches—and became the world's largest watch company. Timex completely upset the watch industry—both foreign and domestic—by not only offering a good product (with a one-year repair or replace guarantee) at a lower price, but also by using new, lower-cost channels of distribution. Its watches were widely available in drug stores, discount houses, and nearly any other retail stores that would carry them.

Recently, Timex was surprised by new competitors who were ready for the electronic revolution in watch making. Texas Instruments took the industry by storm with its low-cost but very accurate digital readout watches—using the same channels Timex had originally developed. But others soon developed a more stylish watch that used liquid crystal display. Texas Instruments could not change quickly enough to keep up—so others came into the low-priced market.

Now, Seiko has captured a commanding share of the high priced "gift" market by focusing on accurate quartz watches with a good sense for consumer styling preferences. All of this has forced some of the traditional watch makers—like the once famous Swiss—to close their factories.[11] Texas Instruments stopped marketing watches altogether. Timex introduced new technology and styling to compete in the higher-priced market—and broadened its offering to defend its position in the low- to mid-priced segment.

Creative strategy planning needed for survival

Such dramatic shifts in strategy may surprise conventional, production-oriented managers. But such changes are becoming much more common—and should be expected. Industries or firms that have accepted the marketing

Timex pioneered new ways to market watches, but now faces tough competition from other makers of watches.

Timex:
The Beautiful Quartz

Timex believes these are the most beautiful quartz watches available to you, at any price. The design is handsome. Rich. Gleaming in the look of silver or gold. With accuracy to within 30 seconds a month. From $29.95 to $79.95 (suggested retail prices). Great design and great beauty are not expensive. Just rare.

TIMEX®

We make technology beautiful

concept realize that they cannot simply define their line of business in terms of the products they currently produce or sell. Rather, they need to think about the basic consumer needs they serve—and how those needs may change in the future. If they are too nearsighted, they may fail to see what's coming until too late.

Creative strategy planning is becoming even more important—because profits no longer can be won just by spending more money on plant and equipment. Moreover, domestic and foreign competition threatens those who can't create more satisfying goods and services. New markets, new customers, and new ways of doing things must be found if companies are to operate profitably in the future—and contribute to our macro-marketing system.

Strategy Planning Doesn't Take Place in a Vacuum

Strategy planning takes place within a framework

The examples above show that a marketing manager's strategy planning cannot take place in a vacuum. Instead, the manager works with controllable variables within a framework involving many uncontrollable variables—which must be considered even though the manager can't control them. Figure 2–10 illustrates this framework and shows that the typical marketing manager must be concerned about the competitive environment, economic and technological environment, political and legal environment, cultural and social environment, and the resources and objectives of the firm. These uncontrollable variables are discussed in more detail in the next two chapters. But clearly, the framework within which the marketing manager operates affects his strategy planning.

■   FIGURE 2–10   Marketing manager's framework

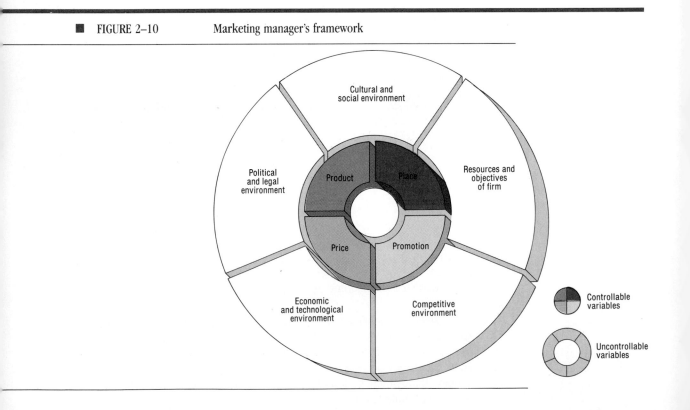

Market-Oriented Strategy Planning Helps Non-Marketing People, Too

While market-oriented strategy planning is helpful to marketers, it is also important to recognize that it is needed by accountants, production and personnel people, and all other specialists. A market-oriented plan lets everybody in the firm know what "ballpark" they are playing in—and what they are trying to accomplish. In other words, it gives direction to the whole business effort. It helps them to proceed with their various jobs. For example, an accountant cannot set budgets if there is no plan, except perhaps by mechanically projecting last year's budget. Similarly, a financial manager cannot project cash needs without some notion of expected sales to some customers—and the costs of satisfying them.

We will use the term "marketing manager" for editorial convenience, but really, when we are talking about marketing strategy planning, we are talking about the planning that a market-oriented manager should do when developing a firm's strategic plans. This kind of thinking should be done—or at least understood—by everyone in an organization who is responsible for planning—and this means even the lowest-level salesperson, production supervisor, retail buyer, or personnel counselor.

■ CONCLUSION

Marketing's role within a marketing-oriented firm is to tie the company together. The marketing concept provides direction. It stresses that the firm's efforts should be focused on satisfying some target customers—at a profit. Production-oriented firms tend to forget this. Often the various departments within such a firm let their natural conflicts of interest lead them to building "fences."

The job of marketing management is one of continuous planning, implementing, and control. The marketing manager must constantly study the environment—seeking attractive opportunities. And new strategies must be planned continually. Potential target markets must be matched with marketing mixes that the firm can offer. Then, attractive strategies—really, whole marketing plans—are chosen for implementation. Controls are needed to be sure that the plans are carried out successfully, If anything goes wrong along the way, this continual feedback should cause the process to be started over again—with the marketing manager planning more attractive marketing strategies.

A marketing mix has four variables—the four Ps—Product, Place, Promotion, and Price. Most of this text is concerned with developing profitable marketing mixes for clearly defined target markets. So, after several chapters on analyzing target markets, we will discuss each of the four Ps in greater detail.

■ QUESTIONS AND PROBLEMS

1. Define the marketing concept in your own words and then explain why the notion of profit is usually included in this definition.

2. Define the marketing concept in your own words and then suggest how acceptance of this concept might affect the organization and operation of your college.

3. Distinguish between "production orientation" and "marketing orientation" illustrating with local examples.

4. Explain why a firm should view its internal activities as part of a "total system." Illustrate your answer for (*a*) a large grocery products manufacturer, (*b*) a plumbing wholesaler, and (*c*) a department store chain.

5. Does the acceptance of the marketing concept always require that a firm view itself as a "total system?"

6. Distinguish clearly between a marketing strategy and a marketing mix. Use an example.

7. Distinguish clearly between mass marketing and target marketing. Use an example.

8. Why is the customer placed in the center of the four Ps in the text diagram of a marketing strategy? Explain, using a specific example from your own experience.

9. Explain, in your own words, what each of the four Ps involves.

10. Evaluate the text's statement, "A marketing strategy sets the details of implementation."

11. Distinguish between strategic and operational decisions, illustrating for a local retailer.

12. Distinguish between a strategy, a marketing plan, and a marketing program—illustrating for a local retailer.

13. Outline a marketing strategy for each of the following new products: (*a*) a radically new design for a hair comb, (*b*) a new fishing reel, (*c*) a new "wonder drug," (*d*) a new industrial stapling machine.

14. Provide a specific illustration of why marketing strategy planning is important for all business people, not just for those in the marketing department.

■ SUGGESTED CASES

1. Foodco, Inc.

3. Apex Chemical Company

■ NOTES

1. Peter Gamsey, K Hopkins, and C. R. Whittaker, eds., "Trade in the Ancient Economy," Berkeley: University of California Press, 1983.

2. Philip D. Curtin, "Cross-Cultural Trade in World History," Cambridge, England: Cambridge University Press, 1984.

3. Neil McKendrick, John Brewer, and J. J. Plumb, "The Birth of a Consumer Society," Bloomington: Indiana University Press, 1982.

4. *Business Week,* November 21, 1983.

5. For an overview of some of Procter & Gamble's current marketing effort, see "Procter & Gamble Co. Starts to Reformulate Tried and True Ways," *The Wall Street Journal,* March 30, 1983, p.1.

6. Alan R. Andreasen, "Nonprofits: Check Your Attention to Customers," *Harvard Business Review* 60, no. 3 (May-June 1982), pp. 105–10; Edward G. Michales, "Marketing Muscle," *Business Horizons* 25, no. 3 (May/June 1982), pp. 63–79; Gene R. Laczniak and Jon G. Udell, "Dimensions of Future Marketing," *MSU Business Topics,* Autumn 1979, pp. 33–44; J. N. Green, "Strategy, Structure, and Survival: The Application of Marketing Principles in Higher Education During the 1980s," *Journal of Business* 10 (1982), pp. 24–28; and Philip Kotler, "Strategies for Introducing Marketing into Nonprofit Organizations," *Journal of Marketing* 43 (January 1979), pp. 37–44.

7. Roger C. Bennett and Robert G. Cooper, "The Misuses of Marketing: An American Tragedy," *Business Horizons* 24, no. 6 (November/December 1981), pp. 51–61; Alan R. Andreasen, "Judging Marketing in the 1980s," *Journal of Macromarketing* 2, no. 1 (Spring 1982), pp. 7–13; Leslie M. Dawson, "Marketing for Human Needs in a Humane Future," *Business Horizons,* June 1980, pp. 72–82; Hiran C. Barksdale and William D. Perreault, Jr., "Can Consumers Be Satisfied?" *MSU Business Topics,* Spring 1980, pp. 20–30; Peter C. Riesz, "Revenge of the Marketing Concept," *Business Horizons,* June 1980, pp. 49–53; Alan M. Kantrow, "The Strategy-Technology Connection," *Harvard Business Review,* July-August 1980, pp. 6–21; and G. R. Laczniak, R. F. Lusch, and P. E. Murphy, "Social Marketing: Its Ethical Dimensions," *Journal of Marketing* 43 (Spring 1979), pp. 29–36.

8. Ravi Singh Achrol and David L. Apple, "New Developments in Corporate Strategy Planning," in *1983 American Marketing Association Educators' Proceedings,* ed. P. Murphy et al. (Chicago: American Marketing Association, 1983), pp. 305–10; Derek F. Abell and John S. Hammond, *Strategic Market Planning: Problems and Analytical Approaches* (Englewood Cliffs, N.J.: Prentice Hall, 1979); and Subhash C. Jain, *Marketing Planning and Strategy* (Cincinnati, Ohio: South-Western Publishing, 1980).

9. Robert E. Spekman and Kjell Gronhaug, "Insights on Implementation: A Conceptual Framework for Better Understanding the Strategic Marketing Planning Process," in *1983 American Marketing Association Educators' Proceedings,* ed. P. Murphy et al. (Chicago: American Marketing Association, 1983), pp. 311–14.

10. Alfred P. Sloan, Jr., *My Years with General Motors* (New York: MacFadden Books, 1965), Introduction, chaps. 4 and 9; Jack Givens, "Automobile Industry, Heal Thyself," *Advertising Age,* September 29, 1980, pp. 5–32,33; "U.S. Autos Losing a Big Segment of the Market—Forever?" *Business Week,* March 24, 1980, pp. 78; Jack Honomichl, "Consumer Signals: Why U.S. Auto Makers Ignored Them," *Advertising Age,* August 4, 1980, pp. 43–48; "U.S. Auto Makers Reshape the World Competition," *Business Week,* June 21, 1982; and Jean Ross-Skinner, "Global Auto Battle," *Dun's Review,* June 1980.

11. "Japanese Heat on the Watch Industry," *Business Week,* May 5, 1980, pp. 92–106; "A Reclusive Tycoon Takes Over at Timex," *Business Week,* April 14, 1980, p. 32; Texas Instruments Wrestles with the Consumer Market," *Fortune,* December 3, 1979, pp. 50–57; "The Great Digital Watch Shake-Out," *Business Week,* May 2, 1977, pp. 70–80; "The Digital Watch Becomes the World's Cheapest Timepiece," *The Wall Street Journal,* April 18, 1977, p.11; "Gruen Industries Asks Chapter 11 Status," *The Wall Street Journal,* April 15, 1977, p. 9; "Why Gillette Stopped Its Digital Watches," *Business Week,* January 31, 1977, pp. 37–38; "Digital Wristwatch Business is Glowing, but Rivalry Winds Down Prices, Profits," *The Wall Street Journal,* August 24, 1976, p. 6; and "The Long-term Damage From TI's Bombshell," *Business Week,* June 15, 1981, p. 36.

Appendix A ■ Economics fundamentals

When you finish this appendix, you should:

1. Understand the "law of diminishing demand."
2. Know what a market is.
3. Understand demand and supply curves—and how they set the size of a market and its price level.
4. Know about elasticity of demand and supply.
5. Recognize the important new terms (shown in red).

A good marketing manager should be an expert on markets—and the nature of competition in markets. The economist's traditional demand and supply analysis are useful tools for analyzing the nature of demand. In particular, you should master the concepts of a demand curve and demand elasticity. A firm's demand curve shows how the target customers view the firm's Product—really its whole marketing mix. And the interaction of demand and supply curves helps set the size of the market—and the market price. These ideas are discussed more fully in the following sections.

Products and Markets as Seen by Customers and Potential Customers

Economists provide useful insights

How potential customers (not the firm) see a firm's product (marketing mix) affects how much they are willing to pay for it, where it should be made available, and how eager they are to obtain it—if at all. In other words, it has a very direct bearing on marketing strategy planning.

Economists have been concerned with these basic problems for years—and their analytical tools can be quite helpful in summarizing how customers view products and how markets behave.

Economists see individual customers choosing among alternatives

Economics is sometimes called the "dismal" science—because It says that customers simply cannot buy everything they want. Since most customers have a limited income over any period of time, they must balance their needs and the prices of various products.

Economists usually assume that customers have a fairly definite set of preferences—and that they evaluate alternatives in terms of whether they will make them feel better (or worse)—or in some way improve (or change) their situation.

But what exactly is the nature of a customer's desire for a particular product?

Usually the argument is given in terms of the extra utility the customer can obtain by buying more of a particular product—or how much utility would be lost were the customer to have less of the product. (Students who wish further discussion of this approach should refer to indifference curve analysis in any standard economics text.)

Utility is a conceptual framework. It may be easier to grasp this idea if we look at what happens when the price of one of the customer's usual purchases changes.

The law of diminishing demand

Suppose that a consumer buys potatoes in 10-pound bags at the same time he buys other foods—such as meat and vegetables. If the consumer is mainly interested in buying a certain amount of foodstuffs—and the price of the potatoes drops—it seems reasonable to expect that he will switch some of his food money to potatoes—and away from some other foods. But if the price of potatoes rises, you expect our consumer to buy fewer potatoes—and more of other foods.

The general interaction of price and quantity illustrated by this example is called the **law of diminishing demand**—which says that if the price of a product is raised, a smaller quantity will be demanded—and if the price of a product is lowered, a greater quantity will be demanded.

A group of customers makes a market

When our hypothetical consumers are considered as a group, we have a "market." It seems reasonable that many consumers in a market will behave in a similar way—that is, if price declines, the total quantity demanded will increase—and if price rises, the quantity demanded will decrease. Experience supports this reasoning—especially for broad product categories, or commodities such as potatoes.

The relationship between price and quantity demanded in a market is shown in Table A–1. It is an example of what economists call a "demand schedule." Note that as the price drops, the quantity demanded rises. In the third column, total dollar sales—total revenue of the potato market—is shown. Notice, however, that as prices go lower, the total *unit* quantity increases, yet the total *revenue* decreases. It is suggested that you fill in the missing blanks and observe the behavior of total revenue—an important number for the marketing manager. We will explain what you should have noticed—and why—a little later.

The demand curve— usually down-sloping

If your only interest is seeing at which price customers will be willing to pay the greatest total revenue, the demand schedule may be adequate. But a demand curve may be more helpful. A **demand curve** is a "picture" of the relationship between price and quantity demanded in a market—assuming that all other things stay the same. It is a graph of the demand schedule. Figure A–1 shows the demand curve for potatoes—really just a plotting of the demand schedule. It shows how many potatoes would be demanded by potential customers at various possible prices. This is known as a "down-sloping demand curve."

Most demand curves are down-sloping. This just means that if prices are decreased, the quantity that customers will demand will increase.

Note that the demand curve only shows how customers will react to various prices. In a market, we see only one price at a time—not all of these prices. The curve, however, shows what quantities will be demanded—depending on what

---

■   TABLE A–1   Demand schedule for potatoes

Point	(1) Price of potatoes per bag (P)	(2) Quantity demanded (bags per month) (Q)	(3) Total revenue per month (P × Q = TR)
A	$0.80	8,000,000	$6,400,000
B	0.65	9,000,000	
C	0.50	11,000,000	5,500,000
D	0.35	14,000,000	
E	0.20	19,000,000	

FIGURE A–1 Demand curve for potatoes (10-pound bags)

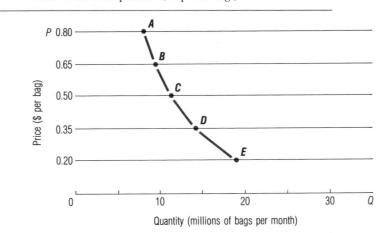

price is set. It would seem that most business people would like to see the price set at the point where the resulting revenue would be large.

Before discussing this, however, we should consider the demand schedule and curve for another product—to get a more complete picture of what is involved in demand-curve analysis.

A refrigerator demand curve looks different

A different demand schedule is the one for refrigerators shown in Table A–2. Column (3) shows the total revenue that will be obtained at various possible prices and quantities. Again, as the price of refrigerators goes down, the quantity demanded goes up. But here, unlike the potato example, total revenue increases—at least until the price drops to $150.

Every market has a demand curve—for some time period

These general demand relationships are typical for all products—but each product has its own demand schedule and curve in each potential market—no matter how small the market. In other words, a particular demand curve has

■ TABLE A–2 Demand schedule for refrigerators

Point	(1) Price per refrigerator (P)	(2) Quantity de- manded per year (Q)	(3) Total revenue per year (P × Q = TR)
A	$300	20,000	$ 6,000,000
B	250	70,000	17,500,000
C	200	130,000	26,000,000
D	150	210,000	31,500,000
E	100	310,000	31,000,000

■ FIGURE A–2   Demand curve for refrigerators

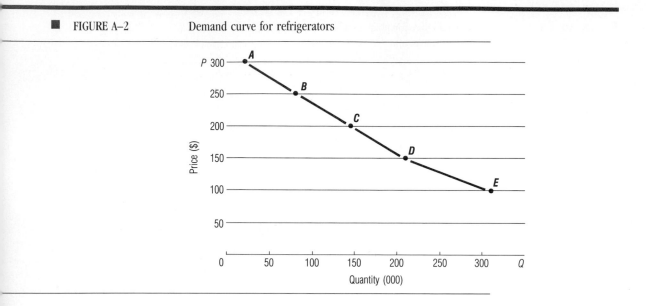

meaning only with reference to a particular market. We can think of demand curves for individuals, regions, and even countries. And the time period covered really should be specified—although this is often neglected, as we usually think of monthly or yearly periods.

The difference between elastic and inelastic

The demand curve for refrigerators (see Figure A–2) is down-sloping—but note that it is flatter than the curve for potatoes. It is quite important that we understand what this flatness means.

We will consider the flatness in terms of total revenue—since this is what interests business managers.*

When you filled in the total revenue column for potatoes, you should have noticed that total revenue drops continually if the price is reduced. This looks undesirable from a manager's point of view—and illustrates inelastic demand. **Inelastic demand** means that although the quantity demanded increases if the price is decreased, the quantity demanded will not "stretch" enough—that is, it is not elastic enough—to avoid a decrease in total revenue.

In contrast, **elastic demand** means that if prices are dropped, the quantity demanded will stretch enough to increase total revenue. The upper part of the refrigerator demand curve is an example of elastic demand.

But note that if the refrigerator price is dropped from $150 to $100, total revenue will decrease. We can say, therefore, that between $150 and $100, demand is inelastic—that is, total revenue will decrease if price is lowered to $100.

---

* Strictly speaking, two curves should not be compared for flatness if the graph scales are different, but for our purposes now, we will do so to illustrate the idea of "elasticity of demand." Actually, it would be more correct to compare two curves for one product—on the same graph. Then both the shape of the demand curve and its position on the graph would be important.

Thus, elasticity can be defined in terms of changes in total revenue. *If total revenue will increase if price is lowered, then demand is elastic. If total revenue will decrease if price is lowered, then demand is inelastic.*

Total revenue may decrease if price is raised

A point that is often missed in discussions of demand is what happens when prices are raised instead of lowered. With elastic demand, total revenue will *decrease* if the price is *raised.* If total revenue remains the same when prices change, then we have a special case known as "unitary elasticity of demand."

The possibility of raising price and increasing revenue at the same time is of special interest to managers. This only occurs if the demand curve is inelastic. If this is the case, it is obviously an attractive situation. Total revenue will increase if price is raised, but costs probably will not increase—and may actually go down. So profits will increase as price is increased.

The ways total revenue changes as prices are raised are shown in Figure A–3. Here, total revenue is the rectangular area formed by a price and its related quantity.

P_1 is the original price here—and the total potential revenue with this original price is shown by the area with the diagonal lines slanted down from the left. The total revenue area with the new price, P_2, is shaded with lines running diagonally upward from the left. In both cases, there is some overlap—so the important

■ FIGURE A–3   Changes in total revenue as prices increase

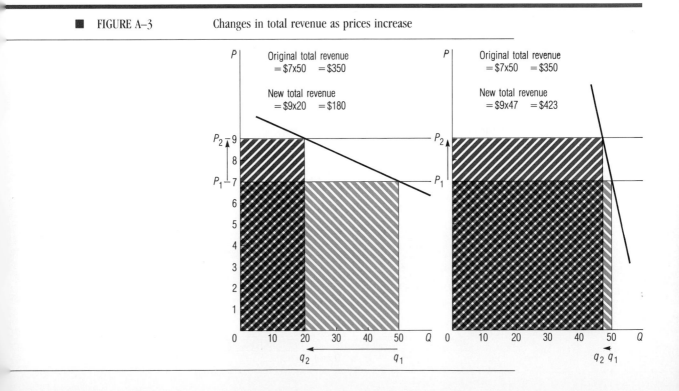

areas are those with only a single shading. Note that in the left-hand figure—where demand is elastic—the revenue added when the price is increased is less than the revenue lost (compare only the single-shaded areas). When demand is inelastic, however, only a small single-shaded revenue area is given up for a much larger one when price is raised.

An entire curve is not elastic or inelastic

It is important to see that it is *wrong to refer to a whole demand curve as elastic or inelastic.* Rather, elasticity for a particular curve refers to the change in total revenue between two points on a curve—and not along the whole curve. The change from elasticity to inelasticity can be seen in the refrigerator example. Generally, however, nearby points are either elastic or inelastic—so it is common to refer to a whole curve by the degree of elasticity of the curve in the price range that normally is of interest—the *relevant range.*

Demand elasticities affected by availability of substitutes and urgency of need

At first, it may be difficult to see why one product has an elastic demand and another an inelastic demand. Many factors affect elasticity—such as the availability of substitutes, the importance of the item in the customer's budget, and the urgency of the customer's need and its relation to other needs. By looking at one of these factors—the availability of substitutes—we should better understand why demand elasticities vary.

Substitutes are goods or services that offer a choice to the buyer. The greater the number of "good" substitutes available, the greater will be the elasticity of demand—"good" here referring to the degree of similarity—or homogeneity—that customers see. If they see a product as extremely different—or heterogeneous—then a particular need cannot easily be satisfied by substitution—and the demand for the most satisfactory product may be quite inelastic.

As an example, if the price of hamburger is lowered (and other prices stay the same), the quantity demanded will increase a lot—as will total revenue. The reason is that not only will regular hamburger users buy more hamburger, but those consumers who formerly bought hot dogs, steaks, or bacon probably will buy

■ FIGURE A–4   Demand curve for hamburger (a product with many substitutes)

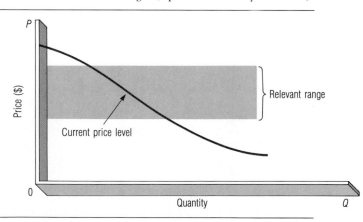

■ FIGURE A–5   Demand curve for salt (a product with few substitutes)

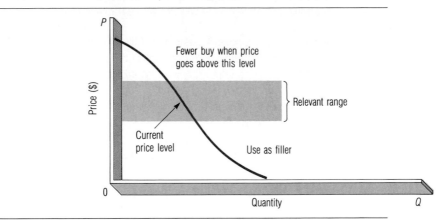

hamburger, too. But if the price of hamburger rises, the quantity demanded will decrease—perhaps sharply. Consumers will still purchase some hamburger—depending on how much the price has risen, their individual tastes, and what their guests expect (see Figure A–4).

In contrast to a product which has many "substitutes"—such as hamburger—consider a product with few or no substitutes. Its demand curve will tend to be inelastic. Salt is a good example. Salt is needed to flavor food. Yet no one person or family uses great quantities of salt. And even with price changes *within a reasonable range,* it is not likely that the quantity of salt purchased will change much. Of course, if the price is dropped to an extremely low level, manufacturers may buy more—say, for low-cost filler, instead of clay or sand (Figure A–5). Or, if the price is raised to a staggering figure, many people will have to do without. But these extremes are outside the relevant range.

Markets as Seen by Suppliers

Demand curves are introduced here because the degree of elasticity of demand shows how potential customers feel about a product—and especially whether there are substitutes for the product. But to get a better understanding of markets, we must extend this economic analysis.

Customers may want some product—but if suppliers are not willing to supply it, then there is no market. So we will study the economist's analysis of supply—and then bring supply and demand together for a more complete understanding of markets.

Economists often use the kind of analysis we are discussing here to explain pricing in the marketplace. This is *not* our intention. Here we are interested in how and why markets work—and the interaction of customers and potential suppliers. The discussion in this appendix does *not* explain how individual firms set prices—or should set prices. That will come in Chapters 19–20.

Supply curves reflect supplier thinking

Generally speaking, suppliers' costs affect the quantity of products they are willing to offer in a market during any period. In other words, their costs affect their supply schedules and supply curves. While a demand curve shows the quantity of goods customers will be willing to buy at various prices, a **supply curve** shows the quantity of goods that will be supplied at various possible prices. Eventually, only one quantity of goods will be offered and purchased—so a supply curve is really a hypothetical description of what will be offered at various prices. It is, however, a very important curve. Together with a demand curve, it summarizes the attitudes and probable behavior of buyers and sellers about a particular product in a particular market—i.e., in a product-market.

Some supply curves are vertical

We usually assume that supply curves tend to slope upward—that is, suppliers will be willing to offer greater quantities at higher prices. If a product's market price is very high, it seems only reasonable that producers will be anxious to produce more of the product—and even put workers on overtime or perhaps hire additional workers to increase the quantity they can offer. Going further, it seems likely that producers of other products will switch their resources (farms, factories, labor, or retail facilities) to the product that is in great demand.

On the other hand, if a very low price is being offered for a particular product, it's reasonable to expect that producers will switch to other products—reducing supply. A supply schedule (Table A–3) and a supply curve (Figure A–6) for potatoes illustrate these ideas. This supply curve shows how many potatoes would be produced and offered for sale at each possible market price in a given month.

In the very short run (say, over a few hours, a day, or a week), a supplier may not be able to increase the supply at all. In this situation, we would see a vertical supply curve. This situation is often relevant in the market for fresh produce. Fresh strawberries, for example, continue to ripen, and a supplier wants to sell them quickly—preferably at a higher price—but in any case, he wants to sell them. For less perishable products, he may set a minimum price and, if necessary, store them until market conditions are better.

■ TABLE A–3   Supply schedule for potatoes

Point	Possible market price per 10-lb. bag	Number of bags sellers will supply per month at each possible market place
A.	$0.80	17,000,000
B.	0.65	14,000,000
C.	0.50	11,000,000
D.	0.35	8,000,000
E.	0.20	3,000,000

Note: This supply curve is for a month to emphasize that farmers might have some control over when they deliver their potatoes. There would be a different curve for each month.

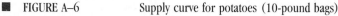

■ FIGURE A–6   Supply curve for potatoes (10-pound bags)

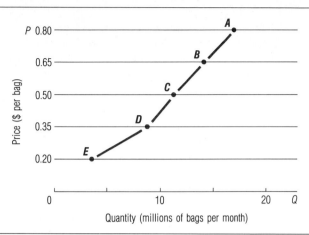

If the product is a service, it may not be easy to expand the supply in the short run—and there is no way to store it either. Additional barbers or medical doctors are not quickly trained and licensed—and they only have so much time to give each day. When the day is done, the unused "supply" is lost. Further, the prospect of much higher prices in the near future cannot easily expand the supply of many services. For example, a good play or an "in" restaurant or nightclub is limited in the amount of "product" it can offer at a particular time.

Elasticity of supply

The term *elasticity* also is used to describe supply curves. An extremely steep or almost vertical supply curve—often found in the short run—is called **inelastic supply** because the quantity supplied does not stretch much (if at all) if the price is raised. A flatter curve is called **elastic supply** because the quantity supplied does stretch more if the price is raised. A slightly up-sloping supply curve is typical in longer-run market situations. Given more time, suppliers have a chance to adjust their offerings—and competitors may enter or leave the market.

Demand and Supply Interact to Determine the Size of the Market and Price Level

We have treated market demand and supply forces separately. Now we must bring them together to show their interaction. The *intersection* of these two forces determines the size of the market and the market price—at which point (price and quantity) the market is said to be in *equilibrium*.

The intersection of demand and supply is shown for the potato data discussed above. The demand curve for potatoes is now graphed against the supply curve in Figure A–6—see Figure A–7.

■   FIGURE A–7   Equilibrium of supply and demand for potatoes

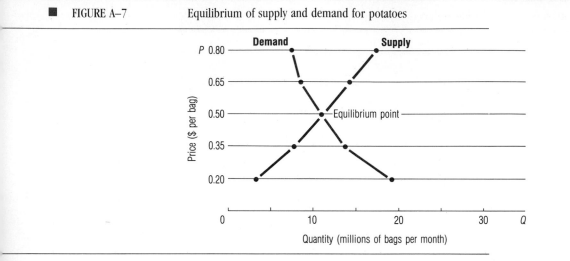

In this potato market, demand is inelastic—the total revenue of all the potato producers would be greater at higher prices. But the market price is at the **equilibrium point**—where the quantity and the price sellers are willing to offer are equal to the quantity and price that buyers are willing to accept. The $0.50 equilibrium price for potatoes yields a smaller *total revenue* to potato producers than a higher price would. This lower equilibrium price comes about because the many producers are willing to supply enough potatoes at the lower price. *Demand is not the only determiner of price level. Cost also must be considered—via the supply curve.*

Some consumers get a surplus

It is important to note that not everyone gets *only* his money's worth in a sales transaction. Presumably, a sale takes place *only* if both buyer and seller feel they will be better off after the sale. But sometimes the price is better than "right."

The price we are talking about is the market price set by demand and supply forces. Typically, demand curves are down-sloping, and some of the demand curve is above the equilibrium price. This is simply a graphic way of showing that some customers are willing to pay more than the equilibrium price if they have to. In effect, some of them are getting a "bargain" by being able to buy at the equilibrium price. Economists have traditionally called these bargains the **consumer surplus**—that is, the difference to consumers between the value of a purchase and the price they pay.

It is important to see that there is such a surplus—because some business critics assume that consumers do badly in any business transaction. In fact, a sale takes place only if the consumer feels he is at least "getting his money's worth." As we can see here, some are willing to pay much more than the market price.

Demand and Supply Help Understand the Nature of Competition

The elasticity of demand and supply curves—and their interaction—help predict the nature of competition a marketing manager is likely to face. For example, extremely inelastic demand curves together with the usual up-sloping supply curves mean that the firm will have much latitude in its strategy planning. Apparently customers like the product and see few substitutes—they are willing to pay higher prices before cutting back much on their consumption.

Clearly, the elasticity of a firm's demand curves has great relevance for strategy planning—but there are other factors which affect the nature of competition. Among these are the number and size of competitors—and the uniqueness of each firm's marketing mix. These ideas are discussed more fully in Chapters 3 and 4. Those discussions presume a real understanding of the contents of this appendix—so now you should be ready to handle that—and later material involving demand and supply analysis (especially Chapters 19 and 20).

■ CONCLUSION

The economist's traditional demand and supply analysis provides useful tools for analyzing the nature of demand and competition. It is especially important that you master the concepts of a demand curve and demand elasticity. How demand and supply interact helps determine the size of a market—and its price level. It also helps explain the nature of competition in different market situations. These ideas are discussed in Chapters 3 and 4—and then built upon throughout the text. So careful study of this appendix will build a good foundation for later work.

■ QUESTIONS AND PROBLEMS

1. Explain in your own words how economists look at markets—and arrive at the "law of diminishing demand."

2. Explain what a demand curve is—and why it is usually down-sloping.

3. What is the length of life of the typical demand curve? Illustrate your answer.

4. If the general market demand for men's shoes is fairly elastic, how does the demand for men's dress shoes compare to it? How does the demand curve for women's shoes compare to the demand curve for men's shoes?

5. If the demand for fountain pens is inelastic above and below the present price, should the price be raised? Why or why not?

6. If the demand for steak is highly elastic below the present price, should the price be lowered?

7. Discuss what factors lead to inelastic demand and supply curves. Are they likely to be found together in the same situation?

Chapter 3 ■ Finding attractive marketing opportunities

When you finish this chapter, you should:

1. Understand how to find marketing opportunities.

2. Understand how to define relevant markets, generic markets, and product-markets.

3. Know about the different kinds of marketing opportunities.

4. Understand how to screen and evaluate opportunities.

5. Understand how the resources and objectives of a firm can help in the search for opportunities.

6. Understand why a firm should match its opportunities to its resources and objectives.

7. Recognize the important new terms (shown in red).

"Finding attractive opportunities is part of marketing strategy planning."

The main focus of this book is on marketing strategy planning—an important part of which is finding attractive opportunities. But what are "attractive opportunities?"

Should North American auto manufacturers seriously consider producing computers? The auto market is flat and very competitive, while the computer market seems to be growing rapidly.

Should a small gift shop owner look into converting to a computer store—to sell both hardware and software? There is a lot of competition in the "stagnant" gift market, while the demand for computers is likely to continue to grow for years.

This chapter will define what we mean by "attractive opportunities"—and then see how the company's objectives and resources can affect the search for these opportunities. Remember, strategy planning is concerned with matching a firm's resources to its market opportunities. Thus, we will discuss not only finding opportunities but also how to evaluate them. This chapter is important—because attractive opportunities make the rest of marketing strategy planning easier.

What Are Attractive Opportunities?

Optimists see opportunities everywhere. Should a marketing manager go after all of the possibilities? Is every one really an attractive opportunity for his firm? The answer, in general, is *no!* Attractive opportunities for a particular firm are those which the firm has some chance of doing something about—given its resources and objectives. Marketing strategy planning tries to match opportunities to the firm's resources—what it can do—and its objectives—what it wants to do.

Usually, attractive opportunities are fairly close to markets the firm already knows. It makes sense to build on a firm's strengths—and avoid its weaknesses. This may allow it to capitalize on changes in its present markets—or more basic changes in the uncontrollable environments.

How many opportunities a firm "sees" depends on the thinking of top management—and the objectives of the firm. Some want to be innovators—and eagerly search out new opportunities. Others are willing to be creative imitators of the leaders. And others are risk-avoiding "me-too" marketers.

Figure 3–1 shows the process we will be discussing in this chapter—finding possible opportunities and screening them to choose the ones to be turned into strategies and strategic plans. As Figure 3–1 shows, we will look first at possible opportunities—and then evaluate them against screening criteria. These criteria grow out of analysis of the company's resources, the long-run trends facing the firm, and the objectives of top management.

■ FIGURE 3–1   Finding and evaluating opportunities

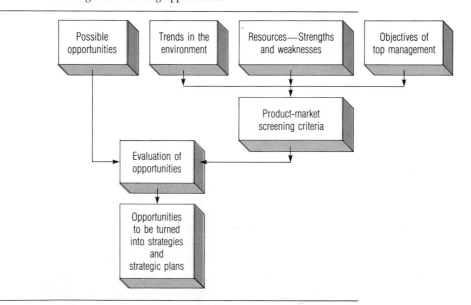

**Breakthrough oppor-
tunities are wanted**

Throughout this book, we will emphasize finding **breakthrough opportunities**—opportunities which help innovators develop hard-to-copy marketing mixes
that will be very profitable for a long time. Such an opportunity can give the firm
a "competitive advantage" over other firms—and at least a temporary monopoly
"in its own little market." Such a breakthrough opportunity may help the firm
capture a large market share—which may delay "imitators." This can prolong its
monopoly—and the attractive profits which come with real breakthrough
opportunities.

Our emphasis on finding breakthrough opportunities is important because
such opportunities are becoming more necessary—just for survival—in our increasingly competitive markets. The "me-too" products which production-oriented people like to turn out are not very profitable anymore. They must face
head-on competition with similar products from all over the world—and much of
this competition emphasizes lower prices.

*Kodak tries to identify
breakthrough opportuni-
ties—ones which com-
petitors can't copy
quickly.*

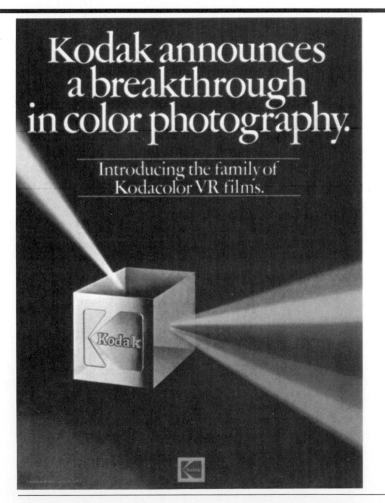

Competitive advantage is needed—at least

Even if a breakthrough opportunity is not possible, the firm should try to obtain some "competitive advantage"—to increase its chances for profit and survival. This may only involve "fine tuning" a firm's marketing mix(es). But it is vital to have some "competitive advantage"—so the promotion people have "something different" to sell—and success does not hinge on offering lower and lower prices. Too many competitors are "competitive"—rather than "innovative." They try to get by with yesterday's strategies—rather than creating more effective new ones. This accounts, in part, for the declining profit rates we see in some industries and firms.

Search for Opportunities Can Begin by Naming Present Markets

Accurately describing a marketer's present or possible markets may suggest attractive opportunities—even breakthrough opportunities—which production-oriented competitors won't see. The following Eastman Kodak example shows the possibilities. Eastman Kodak—well known for cameras and photographic supplies—also produces an industrial good, X-ray film. Until a few years ago, Kodak felt this market wanted faster X-ray pictures at cheaper prices. Their marketing mix was aimed to satisfy those needs. But closer study of this market showed that the real need in hospitals and health-care units was saving the radiologist's time. Time was precious—and just giving the radiologist a faster picture wasn't enough. Something more was needed to help do the job faster. Kodak came to see that its business was not just supplying X-ray pictures, but really helping to improve the health care supplied to patients. As a result, Kodak came up with new time-savers for radiologists: a handy cassette film pack—and a special identification camera that records all vital patient data directly on X-ray at the time the X-ray is made. Before, this tagging had to be done in the back room during developing—which took more time and created the risk of error. This was a different marketing mix aimed at satisfying a different need. And it worked very well.

What is a company's market?

What is a company's market is a very important—but sticky—question. A **market** is a group of potential customers with similar needs—and sellers offering various products—that is, ways of satisfying those needs. Obviously, the description of a market should focus on customers—and the needs they want satisfied. But how specific should we get? We all have a need for food—but should a food producer call its market the hunger market? The food market? The flour market? The flour producer will have to compete with other flour producers—but all of them must also compete with producers of other kinds of food in a "bigger" market. You can see this more clearly if you think of a market as including sellers who offer substitute ways of satisfying needs. So wheat flour has to compete with other kinds of flour, as well as rice, potatoes, and beans—and perhaps even less direct substitutes like meat, vegetables, and dairy products.

Companies sometimes avoid the difficulties of naming markets by describing them in terms of products the firm sells. This production-oriented approach is easy—but it may also make the firm miss opportunities. Producers and retailers of Christmas cards, for example, may define their market very narrowly as the "Christmas-card" market. Or, if they think a little broader, they may call their market the "greeting-card" market—including birthday cards, Easter cards, all-occasion cards, and humorous cards. But by taking a more customer-oriented view, the firm may define its market as the "personal-expression" market. This may lead the firm to offer all kinds of products which can be sent as gifts—to express one person's feelings towards another. The possibilities—besides greeting cards—include jewelry, plaques, candles, puzzles, etc. Companies like Hallmark have this bigger view—and they have expanded far beyond just selling standard greeting cards for the major greeting-card occasions—birthdays and Christmas.

From generic markets to product-markets

It is useful to think of two basic types of market—a generic market and a product-market. A **generic market** is a market with *broadly* similar needs and sellers offering various *often diverse* ways of satisfying those needs. In contrast, a **product-market** is a market with *very* similar needs and sellers offering various *close substitute* ways of satisfying those needs.[1]

A generic market description looks at markets broadly—and from a customer's viewpoint. Status-seekers, for example, have several very different ways to satisfy their status needs. A status-seeker may buy an expensive car, take a luxury cruise to Hawaii, or buy designer clothes at an exclusive shop. See Figure 3–2. Any one of these very different products may satisfy their status need. Sellers In this generic status-seeker market have to focus on the *needs* the customers want satisfied—not on how one seller's product (car, vacation, or designer label) is better than that of another producer. By really understanding the people's needs and attitudes, it may be possible for producers of "status symbols" to encourage shifts to their particular product.

■ FIGURE 3–2   The position of some products in a "status-seeker" market

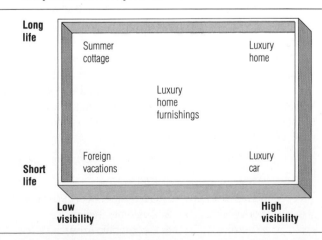

The fact that quite different products may compete with each other in the same generic market makes it harder to understand and define the market. But if customers see all these products as substitutes—as competitors in the same generic market—then marketers will have to live with this complication.

Suppose, however, that one of our status seekers decides to satisfy this status need with a new, expensive car. Then—in this *product*-market— Mercedes, Cadillac, and Ferrari may compete with each other for the status- seeker's dollars.

To summarize—in the broad *generic* market for status—cars, designer clothes, and expensive vacations may all be competing with each other. In a narrower *product*-market concerned with cars *and* status (not just personal transportation!)—consumers
compare similar products to satisfy their status need (e.g., a Ferrari with a Mercedes or a Cadillac).

Most companies quickly narrow their focus to product-markets—because of the firm's past experience, resource commitments, or management preferences. And we will usually be thinking of product-markets when we refer to markets. But this should be done carefully when looking for opportunities—because it is so easy to miss opportunities—as the Christmas card example showed.

Broaden market definitions for finding opportunities

Broader market definitions—including broader product-market definitions and generic market definitions—are useful for finding opportunities. But deciding how broad to go is not easy. Too narrow a definition will limit a firm's opportunities— but too broad a definition will make the company's efforts and resources look insignificant.

Our strategy planning process can help to define a firm's **relevant market**— the market which is suitable for the firm's purpose. Here we are trying to match opportunities to a firm's resources and objectives—so the *relevant market for finding opportunities* should be bigger than the firm's present product-market— but not so big that the firm couldn't expand and be an important competitor in the relevant market. A small manufacturer of screwdrivers, for example, shouldn't define its market as broadly as "the world-wide tool users market" or as narrowly or "our present screwdriver customers." But it may have the production and/or marketing capabilities to consider "the Canadian handyman's hand tool market." Or it may be able to consider expanding its market coverage from the west coast of Canada to the whole country. Or it may be able to offer other tools—such as hammers, pliers, or wrenches—to its present customers or to the whole country. You can see that knowing what market you are in will help you see possible opportunities. So, let's see what you have to think about to do a good job naming a market.

Naming a product- market

A product-market definition should include a four-part description:[2]

What:	1. Product Type
To Meet What:	2. Customer (User) Functional Needs
For Whom:	3. Customer Types
Where:	4. Geographic Area

In other words, a product-market description must include some customer-related terms—*not* just product-related terms. Product-related terms are *not*—by themselves—an adequate description of a market.

Note: a generic market description *doesn't include any product-related terms.* It consists of the last three parts of a product-market definition—omitting the product type. This emphasizes the functional needs—for example, the needs for personal expression, or status, or personal transportation. Figure 3–3 emphasizes the relationship between generic market and product-market definitions.

It helps to think of the naming process as "hypothesizing" the names of likely product-markets. "Hypothesize" is used to emphasize that all suggested product-market names should be thought of as tentative. This is a "commonsense" step—to make full use of current experience. For example, a North American car manufacturer might proceed in the following way. One tentative product-market definition might be: cars for transporting done by final consumers in Canada. But

Lanier knows that its office machines compete with other alternatives in the same generic market.

■ FIGURE 3–3   Relationship between generic and product-market definitions

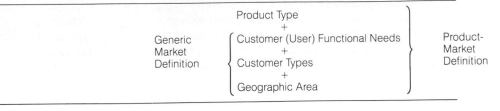

on further thought, it probably would be obvious that different product types were being offered to satisfy different functional needs of different customer types. And this would lead to more specific product-market definitions. It might become clearer, for example, that cars sold to Canadian final consumers must satisfy at least two different transporting needs: (1) the need for economical transportation by consumers who usually carry only one or two people and (2) the need for transporting families or other groups of three to six people and/or bulky parcels. These different needs suggest different products—and different strategies might be needed for these product-markets. So, at the least, a tentative product-market—cars for transporting done by final consumers in Canada—could be split and expanded into two more specific product-markets:

1. Small personal cars for economical "personal" transportation by final consumers in Canada.
2. Station wagons for "family" transportation by final consumers in Canada.

Getting started on naming product-markets

It usually is useful to start with a broad description of "product type" and "functional need(s)" that this product type is satisfying. The "product type" can be a general description of the product area of interest to the company—or the actual product type it is now selling. Both "product type" and "functional need(s)" should be defined together, because a single physical product may satisfy different functional needs—and provide an obvious basis for identifying two different product-markets.

Somewhere in the description of either product type and/or functional need, you must define what the product type does for someone. Sometimes naming the product type gets at the functional need at the same time—for example, caulking products are for caulking. In other cases, naming the functional need requires much thought—because the same product type may solve several functional needs—or even sets of functional needs. Cars, for example, can be for transporting and socializing and status and fun.

Once some combination(s) of product type and functional need(s) has been described—to get the process going—then the next step is to hypothesize (describe) major differences in functional needs of different customer types in different geographic areas. Possible major differences may be based on whether they now require/permit different marketing strategies.

Defining customer types

Here, we want to choose a general name which describes *all* present (possible) *types* of customers. The emphasis should be on identifying the final consumer or user of the product type, rather than the buyer—if they are different. If the product type flows through middlemen on the way to final customers, avoid treating middlemen as a customer type—*unless* these middlemen actually use the product in their own business. For example, retailers regularly use all kinds of office supplies which are also sold to manufacturers, government agencies, and so on. Here, the middlemen should be treated just as any other user of office supplies. In this case, customer type might be defined as all business and nonprofit organizations. This customer type name would cover manufacturers, wholesalers, retailers, government agencies, hospitals, churches, etc.—that is, all present users of the firm's products (e.g., paper clips and other fasteners).

Understanding customers' functional needs helps develop better products.

(Portion of Child Guidance ® ad reproduced here)

Such a broad name implies that all of these customer types may be the basis for many different product-markets.

Defining functional needs

The functional needs satisfied by a product type refers to what the product type does for the customer type. Product types supply functions, such as nourishing, protecting, warming, cooling, transporting, reassuring, holding, drilling, assembling, etc. It is such "basic" functions which we should seek first—to be sure that the right functional needs are identified.

Functional needs in a generic market can be understood by considering the substitutes which are now meeting some people's needs in this area. If we were interested in the "world-wide transporting market," for example, we would look at how this basic need is being satisfied—and we would see that various competitors are offering mass and personal solutions to this need. In varying degrees, the following products are substitutes—airplanes, pickup trucks, cars, motorcycles, mopeds, bicycles, skateboards, skates, and even shoes. By thinking about why some of these substitutes are better than others, we can convert these product types to more specific needs or benefits sought. For example, some of these substitutes are better than others with respect to speed, fun, amount of cargo, and economy. See Figure 3–4 for other characteristics and a graphical aid to understanding the basic needs in a generic or broad product-market area.

Often it's necessary to go beyond "basic" needs, like transporting, to emotive needs, such as for status, fun, excitement, pleasing appearance, etc. Correctly defining the functional need(s) is quite important and requires a good understanding of peoples' needs and wants. These topics are discussed more fully in Chapters 7 and 8.

Defining product type for a product-market

Defining product type is straightforward—simply use commonly understood product-related terms that will adequately describe all of the product elements which are being offered to a product-market. The major problem here is being sure that the whole product offering is described—or at least understood by all. Typically, the product offering is much more than just a physical product. Installation, warranties, service, etc. may be included.

In some markets, these "extras" may be far more important than the basic physical product—which may be considered as a "commodity" by customers. Generally, within a company, the ingredients of the "complete product" may be understood by some people—so a "nickname" may be adequate. But it is generally desirable to have a legend which fully explains what the product type means.

Defining geographic area

The geographic area definition is simply the geographic area in which the firm is now competing—or thinking of competing. If the firm is only interested in the Canadian market—or parts of the Canadian market—then it should specify this in the market name. Some managers may think they are selling in Canada—or world-wide—but further study may show that they are competing in only a part of

■ FIGURE 3–4   Using a tree diagram to help understand the basic needs in the generic
transporting market

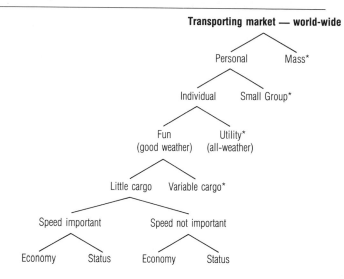

Transporting market — world-wide

Personal   Mass*

Individual   Small Group*

Fun   Utility*
(good weather)   (all-weather)

Little cargo   Variable cargo*

Speed important   Speed not important

Economy   Status   Economy   Status

By considering the benefits offered by "substitutes," a tree diagram can show the complex sets of needs satisfied by different transporting possibilities. All the "needs" along any branch are the "needs" of that sub-market of the generic transporting market—e.g., expensive 10-speed bicycles, mopeds, and motorcycles might compete in the personal-individual-fun-little cargo-speed important-status" world-wide transporting market.

*The rest of the "needs" of this branch are ignored to simplify this figure. But a complete analysis would fill out all of the relevant branches.

Source: F. R. Bacon, Jr., T. W. Butler, Jr., E. J. McCarthy, *Planned Innovation Procedures*, 1983.

these broader geographic areas. So, while naming the geographic area may seem trivial, it should be taken seriously. Just identifying the current geographic boundaries can suggest new opportunities. A supermarket in Vancouver is not catering to all consumers in the Vancouver area—and so there may be opportunities for expansion to unsatisfied customers in that market.[3]

Creativity is needed   Creative analysis of the needs and attitudes of present and potential target markets—in relation to the benefits being offered by the firm and competitors—will help you see new opportunities. In the next several chapters, we will be studying the many possible dimensions of markets. But, for now, you should see that markets can be defined in various ways—and defining them only in terms of current *products* is *not* the best way of finding new opportunities—and planning marketing strategies. Instead, you should try to define generic markets and product-markets—with emphasis on the customer-related characteristics, including geographic dimensions—and needs and attitudes.

Market Segmentation Leads to Three Approaches to Target Marketing

What is market segmentation?

We just discussed how to get started on naming product-markets—and finding new opportunities. Marketing managers can use these broad product-market names to describe their general area of interest—and then segment these broad areas into more "relevant" product-markets which they might pursue. So let's take a closer look at what segmenting involves.

Market segmentation is the process of *naming* product-markets and then *segmenting* these broad product-markets into more homogeneous sub-markets—also called product-markets—for the purpose of selecting target markets and developing suitable marketing mixes. You can see that market segmentation—and "segmenting"—are *not* planning marketing strategies. Segmenting is concerned only with identifying more homogeneous product-markets or sub-markets which may become parts of marketing strategies.

The basic idea underlying market segmentation is that any broad product-market usually consists of sub-markets—which may need separate marketing mixes. So target marketers segment broad product-markets into smaller, more homogeneous product-markets—which they may be able to satisfy better than if they treated everybody alike.

Market grid is a visual aid to segmenting

Assuming that any market may consist of sub-markets, it helps our understanding to picture a market as a rectangle with boxes representing smaller, more homogeneous product-markets. See Figure 3–5.

Think of the whole rectangle as representing a broad product-market—or even a generic market—and then label each of the boxes as sub-markets. Product-markets require several dimensions to adequately describe them—and within a broad product-market, the sub-markets may require very different dimensions. We saw this in Chapter 2 with respect to the British home decorating market.

■ FIGURE 3–5   Market grid diagram with sub-markets (numbered)

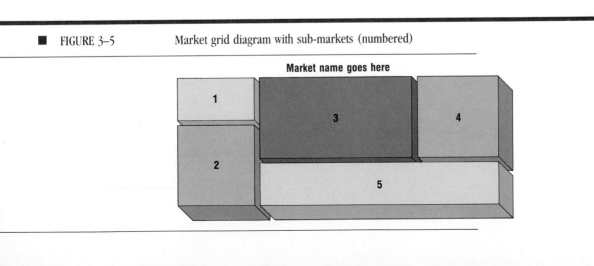

Market name goes here

Target marketers aim at specific targets

Once we accept the idea that broad product-markets may have sub-markets, then it is clear that target marketers may have a problem choosing among the many possible target markets.

There are three basic ways of developing market-oriented strategies for a broad product-market:

1. The **single target market approach**—segmenting the market and picking one of the homogeneous sub-markets as the target market.
2. The **multiple target market approach**—segmenting the market and choosing two or more homogeneous sub-markets—each of which will be treated as a separate target market needing a different marketing mix (as Procter & Gamble does with Crest, Gleem, and so on).
3. The **combined target market approach**—combining two or more homogeneous sub-markets into one larger target market as a basis for one strategy.

Note that all three approaches involve target marketing—they are all aiming at specific—and clearly defined—target markets. See Figure 3–6. For convenience, we will call people who follow the first two approaches the "segmenters" and the people who use the third approach "combiners."

Combiners try to satisfy pretty well

Combiners try to increase the size of their target markets by combining two or more sub-markets—perhaps to gain some economies of scale, to minimize

■ FIGURE 3–6   Target marketers have specific aims

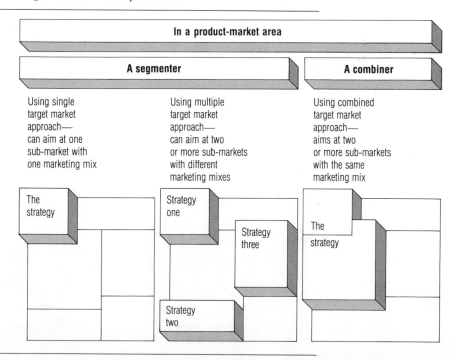

their risk, or just because they don't have enough resources to develop more than one marketing mix. Combiners look at various sub-markets for similarities—rather than differences. Then they try to extend or modify their basic offering to appeal to these "combined" customers—with just one marketing mix. See Figure 3–7. For example, combiners may try a new package, a new brand, or new flavors. But even if physical changes are made, their aim is not at smaller sub-markets. Instead, combiners try to improve the general appeal of their marketing mix—to appeal to a bigger "combined" target market.

Combiners often rely heavily on promotion to convince the different sub-markets that a single product or marketing mix satisfies each market's needs. Relying more on promotion is often practical when there are few product differences between competitors—and the differences may be quite small. But these little differences—in color, texture, or ease of use—may be very important to some customers. Also, the many different customers combined into one target market may be interested in different features of the same product. In the "cosmetics" market, the same product may have different meanings—and fill different needs—for each customer. For example, some women may be concerned with cleanliness, others with beauty, and others with glamour. One ad for one cosmetic product may appeal to all of them—but for different reasons. A combiner may see that the firm can serve *all* these needs at the same time. If the needs aren't too different, this may not only be possible—but may make economic sense for the firm.

Segmenters try to satisfy "very well"

Segmenters, on the other hand, aim at one or more homogeneous sub-markets and try to develop a different marketing mix for each sub-market—one that will satisfy each sub-market very well.

■ FIGURE 3–7   There may be different demand curves in different market segments

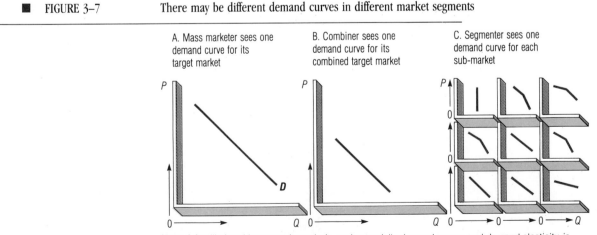

Note: A familiarity with economic analysis, and especially demand curves and demand elasticity, is assumed in this text. Those desiring a review of these materials should see Appendix A at the end of Chapter 2.

Segmenters may make more basic changes in marketing mixes—perhaps in the physical product itself—because they are aiming at smaller, more homogeneous target markets—each needing a separate marketing mix. A segmenter worries that trying to appeal to *several* sub-markets at the same time—with the same mix—may confuse the customers. For example, some of the early entries in the "instant breakfast" market failed with combination appeals to dieters (as a low-calorie lunch), harried commuters (as a fast breakfast), working mothers (for a convenient, wholesome breakfast for kids), and homemakers (as a nutritious snack between meals). Now, some segmenters have aimed at the "nutritious-snack" market—and succeeded with "crunchy granola" bars. It is interesting to note that while they aim at the "nutritious-snack" market, they are also getting some of the "quick-lunch" and "fast-breakfast" customers.

Segmenters see each sub-market's demand curve

Segmenters see different demand curves in different parts of a market area. Instead of assuming that the whole market consists of a fairly homogeneous set of customers—as the mass marketer does—or merging various sub-markets together—as the combiner does—the segmenter sees sub-markets with their own demand curves—as shown in Figure 3–7. Segmenters believe that aiming at one—or some—of these smaller markets will provide greater satisfaction to the target customers—and greater profit potential and security for the segmenter.

Segmenting may produce bigger sales

It is very important to understand that a segmenter is not settling for a smaller sales potential. Instead, by aiming the firm's efforts at only a part of a larger product-market, the segmenter expects to get a much larger share of his target market(s). In the process, total sales may be larger. The segmenter may even get almost a monopoly in "his" market(s).

A segmenter may be able to avoid extremely competitive market conditions. For example, Apple came out with a "home computer" that moved the firm into the very competitive "computer" market with spectacular success—while conventional computer manufacturers were still offering only bigger, more expensive machines and facing growing competition.

Should you segment or combine

Which approach should be used? This depends on many things, including the firm's resources, the nature of competition, and—most important—the similarity of customer needs, attitudes, and buying behavior.

It is tempting to aim at larger combined markets—instead of smaller segmented markets. If successful, such a strategy can result in economies of scale. Also, offering one marketing mix to two or more sub-markets usually requires less investment—and may appear to involve less risk—than offering different marketing mixes to different sub-markets.

However, a combiner faces the continual risk of segmenters "chipping away" at the various sub-markets of the combined target market—especially if the combined market is quite heterogeneous. In the extreme, a combiner may create a fairly attractive marketing mix, but then watch segmenters capture one after another of its sub-markets with more targeted marketing mixes—until finally the combiner is left with no market at all!

The single or multiple target market approaches may be better

In general, it's safer to be a segmenter—that is, to try to satisfy customers very well—instead of just fairly well. That's why many firms use the single or multiple target market approach—instead of the combined target market approach. Procter & Gamble, for example, markets many products which—on the surface—appear to be directly competitive with each other (e.g., Tide versus Cheer or Crest versus Gleem). However, P&G offers "tailor-made" marketing mixes (including products) to each sub-market that is large enough and profitable enough to deserve a separate marketing mix. This approach can be extremely effective—but it may not be possible for a smaller firm with more limited resources. It may have to use the single target market approach—aiming at the one sub-market which looks "best" for it.

Types of Opportunities to Pursue

Most people have unsatisfied needs—and alert marketers can find opportunities all around them. Starting with the firm's present product-markets is useful. By carefully defining its product-markets, it may see new opportunities. Or it may see opportunities beyond its present activities.

It helps to see the kinds of opportunities which may be found. Figure 3–8 shows the four broad possibilities: market penetration, market development, product development, and diversification.

Market penetration

Market penetration is trying to increase sales of a firm's present products in its present markets—probably through a more aggressive marketing mix. The firm may try to increase the customers' rate of use—or attract either the competitors' customers or current nonusers. New promotion appeals may be effective. McDonald's may have Ronald McDonald invite the kids in for a special offer. More stores may be added in present areas—for greater convenience. Short-term price cuts or coupon offers may help. Obviously, effective planning is aided

■ FIGURE 3–8   Four basic types of opportunities

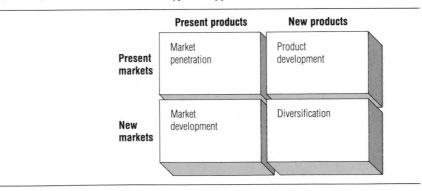

by a real understanding of why some people are buying now—and what will motivate them to buy more—or motivate others to shift brands or begin or resume buying.

Market development

Market development is trying to increase sales by selling present products in new markets. This may involve, for example, McDonald's adding new stores in new areas—perhaps in downtown locations, in schools or hospital lobbies, or even in foreign countries. Or it may only involve advertising in different media to reach new target customers.

Product development

Product development is offering new or improved products for present markets. Here, the firm should know the market's needs—and may see ways of adding or modifying product features, or creating several quality levels, or add-

Burger King developed new products for its old market—because it wants to be "King" of fast food, not just burgers.

At our new salad bar!

Come stuff, tuck, fill, and top our tasty pita bread with any of 23 tempting fixings from the new Burger King® salad bar. Or, if you prefer, build a salad platter. Salad in a pita! Or on a platter! New! From Burger King!

BURGER KING

ing more types or sizes—to better satisfy the present market. For example, McDonald's now offers breakfast for adults—and cookies for kids.

Diversification

Diversification is moving into totally different lines of business—which may include entirely unfamiliar products, markets, or even levels in the production-marketing system. For example, manufacturers may go into wholesaling or retailing—or buy their suppliers.[4]

Which opportunities come first?

Most firms tend to be production oriented—and think first of greater market penetration. If they already have as big a share as they can get in their present markets, they may think of market development—finding new markets for their present products—including expanding regionally, nationally, or even internationally.

Marketers who have a good understanding of their present markets may see opportunities in product development—especially because they already have a way of reaching their present customers.

The most challenging opportunities involve diversification. Here, both new products and new markets are involved. The further the opportunity is from what the firm is already doing, the more attractive it may look to the optimists—and the harder it will be to evaluate. The firm may have a good understanding of all the problems close to its current operations—that's why it's considering other opportunities! But opportunities which are far from a firm's current operations may involve much higher risks. This is why it is very important to have ways of avoiding wasteful searches for opportunities—as well as for efficiently evaluating those which are finally considered. How this can be done is discussed in the following pages.

Company Resources May Limit Search for Opportunities

Every firm has some resources—hopefully some unique resources—which set it apart from other firms. Attractive opportunities should make use of these strong points—while avoiding direct competition with firms having similar strengths.

To find its strengths, the firm must evaluate functional areas (production, research and engineering, marketing, general management, and finance) as well as present products and markets. By analyzing outstanding successes and failures—in relation to the firm's capabilities, talents, and skills—it should be possible to find patterns which explain why it was successful—or why it failed—in the past.

Resources which should be considered—as part of an evaluation of strengths and weaknesses—are discussed in the following sections.

Financial strength

Some industries—such as steel and public utilities—need large amounts of capital to obtain economies of scale. For them, the cost of production per unit

decreases as the quantities produced increase. Therefore, smaller producers would be at a great disadvantage if they tried to compete in these lines. Some industries, however, do not have economies of scale—and smaller, more flexible firms may be quite effective. In fact, large companies often have difficulties when they enter low-investment businesses. A large chemical processor tried to make and sell decorated shower curtains—because it was producing the basic plastic sheets. It lost heavily on the experiment, however. The smaller shower curtain manufacturers and middlemen were much more flexible—changing their styles and price policies more rapidly. Here, financial strength was a strength in the basic plastic sheet business—but it was a weakness where style and flexibility in adapting to customer needs were important.

Raw material reserves

Firms that own or have assured sources for basic raw materials have a head start in businesses that need these resources. But companies—large or small— that are not in this position may find—especially in times of short supply—that they have difficulty even staying in business. Chemical and paper manufacturers, for example, usually try to control timber resources. Metals and petroleum companies control their own resources. Now that we see a growing scarcity of raw materials, it probably will be wise for a firm to control or have assurances of supply before building a marketing strategy which depends on raw materials.

Physical plant

Some lines of business—railroads, utilities, oil refineries, tennis clubs, ice-skating rinks—require large, special-purpose physical plants. If these are well located, they are a strength. On the other hand, badly located or obsolete plants—or wholesale or retail facilities—can be real weaknesses. The existing physical plant can have a big impact on marketing strategy planning—because one of the firm's objectives probably will be to use the existing plant as fully as possible. Any logical strategy will, therefore, try to use the existing facilities—or provide for their disposal so that the capital can be used more effectively elsewhere.

Patents

Patents are of primary concern to manufacturers. A patent owner has a 17-year "monopoly" to develop and use its new product, process, or material as it sees fit. If a firm has a patent on a basic process, potential competitors will be forced to use second-rate processes—and their efforts may be doomed to failure. If a firm has such a patent, it is a resource—while if its competitors have it, it may be a weakness which cannot be overcome with other aspects of a marketing mix.

Brands

If a firm has developed a loyal following of customers which prefer—or insist on—its product, others may have difficulty invading this market. A strong brand is a valuable resource that a marketing manager can use in developing marketing strategies.

Skilled people

Some firms deliberately pay high wages to attract and retain skilled workers— so they can offer high-quality products. A skilled sales force is also a strength— lack of good salespeople can limit strategy planning. Even if skilled employees can produce a new product, the sales force may not have the contacts or know-how to sell it. This is a common weakness when a firm moves from consumer products to industrial products—or vice versa.

Management attitudes   The attitude of top management toward growth is important in strategy planning—especially as it affects the development and introduction of new products.

The president of a Nova Scotia manufacturing company was enthusiastic about the prospects for a new product. But after evaluating the attitudes of his company's personnel—and especially his management people—he dropped his plans for the product. Why? He found that his employees had no ambition or interest in growth.[5]

Objectives May Limit the Search for Opportunities

A company's objectives should shape the direction and operation of the whole business. If it has already been decided that the firm is to stay small—so the owner has plenty of time for golf—then this objective will obviously limit the firm's opportunities. (Actually, of course, it probably won't even be looking for opportunities!) On the other hand, if a large, aggressive firm seeks sales growth—then the range of opportunities expands quickly. If this firm has almost unlimited capital, then the strategy planners have even more freedom to search for good opportunities.

You can see that company objectives are important regarding marketing strategy planning. So we will treat this matter in some depth—referring to its effect both on finding attractive opportunities and developing marketing strategies.

Objectives Should Set Firm's Course

A company should know where it is going—or it is likely to fall into the trap expressed so well by the quotation: "Having lost sight of our objective, we redoubled our efforts." In spite of their importance, objectives are seldom stated explicitly. In small businesses, they often are stated *after the fact!* And in some large businesses, there may be *several* unspoken and conflicting objectives held by different managers. The relative importance of these objectives may depend on the point of view of the person being interviewed.

It would be convenient if a company could set one objective—such as making a profit—and let that serve as the guide. Actually, however, setting objectives is much more complicated—which explains why it is done so poorly, if it's done at all.

Setting objectives that really guide the present and future development of the company is difficult. It forces top management to look at the whole business, relate its present objectives and resources to the external environment, and then decide what it wants to accomplish in the future.

Three basic objectives provide guidelines

Taken together, the following three objectives provide a useful starting point for objective setting for a particular firm. They should be sought *together* because—in the long run—a failure in even one of the three areas could lead to total failure of the business.

1. Engage in some specific business activity that will perform a socially and economically useful function.
2. Develop an organization to carry on the business and implement its strategies.
3. Earn enough profit to survive.[6]

Should be socially useful

The first objective suggests that the company should do something society considers useful. This isn't just a "do good" objective. Businesses exist on the approval of consumers. If the activities of a business appear to be against the consumer "good," that firm can be wiped out almost overnight by political or legal action—or the consumer's own negative response.

The first objective also implies that a firm should see its purpose as satisfying customer needs—rather than focusing only on internal concerns—such as using the company's resources, exploiting a patent, and so on.

A firm should define its efforts broadly setting need-satisfying objectives rather than production-oriented objectives. Too narrow a view may lead the company into a product-market in which the product itself—because of changing customer needs—will soon be obsolete.[7]

Should organize to innovate

In a macro-marketing sense, consumers have granted businesses the right to operate—and to make a profit if they can. They also expect businesses to be dynamic—agents of change—adjusting their offerings to consumers' needs. Competition is supposed to encourage innovation and efficiency. Assuming that our society will continue this approach, a business firm should develop an organization that will ensure that these consumer-assigned tasks are effectively carried out—and that the firm itself continues to prosper.

Should earn some profit

It is sometimes assumed that profit is the only objective of business—and it certainly is true that in the long run a firm must make a profit to survive. But just saying that a firm should try to make a profit isn't enough. The time period involved must also be specified—since long-run profit maximization may require losing money during the first few years of a plan.

Further, trying to maximize profit won't necessarily lead to large profits. Competition may be so fierce that failure may be almost guaranteed in a particular industry. It might be better to set some target rate of profit return that will lead the firm into areas having some possibility of such a return.

Setting objectives is complicated further by the need for specifying the degree of risk that management is willing to assume for larger returns. Very large profits are possible in the oil exploration business, for example, but the probability of success in that field is quite low. If the business is to take a long-run view—if it intends to survive and be a useful member of the business community—it probably should include the costs of risk and potential losses in its estimates of long-run returns.

Both hands must work toward the same objective

Whatever objectives are chosen by top management, they should be compatible with each other—or frustrations and even failure may result. The three broad objectives suggested above help a firm avoid this mistake. But as these three guidelines are made more specific, care is necessary. For example, top management may set a 20 percent return on investment each year as one objective, while at the same time specifying that the current plant and equipment be used as fully as possible. Competition may make it impossible to use the resources fully and achieve the 20 percent return—but the managers may try to follow the resource-use objective through the course of the year and only discover at the end of the year that the two objectives are impossible to achieve together!

Top-management myopia may straitjacket marketing

We are assuming that it is the marketing manager's job to work within the framework of objectives provided by top management. But some of these objectives may limit marketing strategies—perhaps damaging the whole business. This is why it is desirable for the marketing manager to help shape the company's objectives.

A few examples will help show how the marketing manager may be forced to choose undesirable strategies.

A quick return on investment is sometimes sought by top management. This may lead the marketing manager to choose marketing strategies that yield quick returns in the short run—but kill brand loyalty in the long run.

Top management may decide on diversification. This may force the marketing manager to choose strategies that are badly matched to the company's resources.

Some top managements want a large sales volume or a large market share—because they feel this assures greater profitability. Recent studies seem to support the idea that larger market share leads to greater profitability. But a better explanation may be found in the quality of the marketing strategies—rather than the quantity of sales or market share. Recently, there have been many bankruptcies of large firms with big market shares—some railroads, for example, which seemed to dominate their markets. And A&P has been a leader in some food store markets, and yet profits have been very disappointing. Increasingly, companies are shifting their objectives toward *profitable* sales growth rather than just larger market share—as they realize that the two do not necessarily go together.[8]

Objectives should guide the whole management process

Ideally, the marketing manager should be involved in setting objectives, but regardless, these objectives should guide the search for and evaluation of opportunities—as well as later planning of marketing strategies. Particular marketing objectives should be set within the framework of these overall objectives. As shown in Figure 3–9, there should be a hierarchy of objectives—moving from company objectives, to marketing department objectives. For each marketing strategy, there should also be objectives for each of the four Ps—as well as subobjectives. For example, in the Promotion area, we may need advertising objectives, sales promotion objectives, and personal selling objectives.

The company objectives are also used as input to the development of product-market screening criteria—for screening opportunities—as explained below.

■   FIGURE 3–9   A hierarchy of objectives

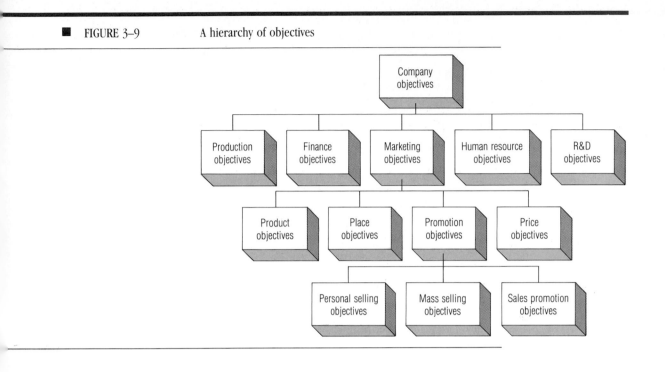

How to Evaluate Opportunities

Once some opportunities have been identified, then they must be screened and evaluated. Usually, it isn't possible for a firm to pursue all of its opportunities. Instead, it should try to match its opportunities to its resources and objectives. So, the first step is to quickly screen out the obvious mismatches. Then, it can analyze the others more carefully. Let's look at some approaches for screening and evaluating opportunities.

Developing and applying screening criteria

After we have analyzed the firm's resources (for strengths and weaknesses), the environmental trends facing the firm (Chapter 4), and the objectives of top management, they all should be merged into a set of product-market screening criteria. These criteria should include both quantitative and qualitative components. The quantitative components summarize the objectives of the firm—sales, profit, and return on investment (ROI) targets for each strategy.* The qualitative components summarize what kinds of businesses the firm wants to be in, what businesses it wants to exclude, what weaknesses it should avoid, and what strengths and trends it should build on.[9]

_____

*See Appendix E (following Chapter 19) for definitions of these terms.

■ FIGURE 3–10

An example of product-market screening criteria for a sales company
(retail and wholesale—$1 million annual sales)

1. Quantitative criteria
   a. Increase sales by $200,000 per year for the next five years.
   b. Earn ROI of *at least* 25 percent before taxes on new ventures.
   c. Break even within one year on new ventures.
   d. Opportunity must be large enough to justify interest (to help meet objectives) but small enough so company can handle with the resources available.
   e. Several opportunities should be needed to reach the objectives—to spread the risks.
2. Qualitative criteria
   a. Nature of business preferred.
      (1) Goods and services sold to present customers.
      (2) "Quality" products which can be sold at "high prices" with full margins.
      (3) Competition should be weak and opportunity should be hard to copy for several years.
      (4) Should build on our strong sales skills.
      (5) There should be strongly felt (even unsatisfied) needs—to reduce promotion costs and permit "high" prices.
   b. Constraints
      (1) Nature of businesses to exclude.
         (a) Manufacturing.
         (b) Any requiring large fixed capital investments.
         (c) Any requiring many people who must be "good" all the time and would require much supervision (e.g., "quality" restaurant).
      (2) Geographic
         (a) United States and Canada only.
      (3) General
         (a) Make use of current strengths.
         (b) Attractiveness of market should be reinforced by *more than one* of the following basic trends: technological, demographic, social, economic, political.
         (c) Market should not be bucking *any* of above trends.

Developing screening criteria is difficult—because they summarize in one place what the firm wants to accomplish—in quantitative terms—as well as roughly how and where it wants to accomplish it. The criteria should be realistic—that is, they should be achievable. Opportunities that pass the screen ought to be able to be turned into strategies which the firm can implement with its resources.

Figure 3–10 illustrates the product-market screening criteria for a small sales company (retailer and wholesaler). This whole set would help the firm's managers eliminate unsuitable opportunities—and find attractive ones to turn into strategies and plans.

Whole plans should be evaluated

Forecasts of the probable results of implementing whole product-market strategic plans are needed to apply the quantitative part of the screening criteria—because it is "implemented plans" which generate sales, profits, and return on investment (ROI). For a rough screening, we only need an estimate of the likely results of implementing each opportunity over a logical planning period. If a product's life is likely to be three years, for example, then a good strategy may not produce profitable results during the first six months to a year. But evaluate the plan over the projected three-year life, and it might look like a winner. When evaluating the potential of possible opportunities—product-market strategic plans—it is important to evaluate similar things—that is, *whole* plans.

Opportunities that pass the screen—or any opportunities, if screening criteria are not used—may be evaluated in more detail before being accepted as *the* strategic plans for implementation. Usually, there are more opportunities than resources, and the marketing manager must choose among them—to match the firm's opportunities to its resources and objectives. The following approaches can be useful in selecting among possible strategic plans.

Total profit approach can help evaluate possible plans

The total profit approach to evaluating plans requires forecasts of potential sales and costs during the life of the plan—to estimate likely profitability.

The prospects for each plan may be evaluated over a five-year planning period—with monthly and/or annual estimates of sales and costs. This is shown graphically in Figure 3–11.

Note that—as shown in Figure 3–11—quite different strategic plans can be evaluated at the same time. In this case, a much improved product and product concept (Product A) is being compared with a "me-too" product for the same target market. In the short run, the "me-too" product would break even sooner and might look like the better choice—if only one year's results were considered. The new product, on the other hand, will take a good deal of pioneering but—over its five-year life—will be much more profitable.

Return-on-investment (ROI) approach can help evaluate possible plans, too

Besides evaluating the profit potential of possible plans, it may also be desirable to calculate the return on investment of resources needed to implement plans. One plan may require a heavy investment in advertising and channel development, for example, while another relies primarlly on lower price. (Note: ROI analysis is discussed briefly in Appendix E, which follows Chapter 19.)

■ FIGURE 3–11   Expected sales and cost curves of two strategies over five-year planning periods

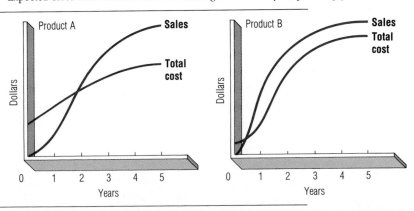

ROI analyses can be useful for selecting among possible plans—because equally profitable plans may require vastly different resources—and offer different rates of return on investment. Some firms are very much concerned with ROI—because they must borrow money for working capital and there is little point in borrowing to implement strategies that won't even return enough to meet the cost of borrowing.[10]

Expected-value approach can handle uncertainty

The total profit approach and the ROI approach require estimates of sales, costs, and profits. If fairly definite estimates can be made for possible product-market plans, these can be compared and the "best" one selected.

Where there is uncertainty about the likely outcome of individual plans, however, which profit figures do you use? If you can estimate the probability of the possibilities happening, however, then it is possible to use the *expected-value approach*—that is, to compute the expected profit (or sales) and compare these expected profits for possible plans.

Table 3–1 shows how *expected profit* can be calculated for four alternatives. Assuming that the marketing manager is willing to use expected profit as the objective, then the strategy that is likely to produce the highest expected profit can be chosen. For example, in Table 3–1, Strategy 3 will be chosen. A more conservative decision maker, however, may select Strategy 2 because of the certainty of *some* profit. In other words, even though profit is one of the objectives of management, the risk associated with alternative plans may lead different managers to select different plans.

Decision trees may show alternatives more clearly

When many possible plans must be evaluated, a visual aid—called a *decision tree*—may be helpful. The tree diagram in Figure 3–12 shows several alternatives clearly. At the end of each branch, a measure of effectiveness—such as total profit and/or return on investment—can be shown for comparison. And, if the success of any of the plans is uncertain, the expected values can be calcu-

■ TABLE 3–1   Evaluation of various alternatives with expected-value approach

Alternative strategies	Payoff (in dollars of profit)	Probability of occurrence	Expected profit
1	100,000 or 0	.50 .50	$ 50,000
2	25,000 or 10,000	.90 .10	23,500
3	1,000,000 or – 10,000	.20 .80	192,000
4	500,000 or – 100,000	.30 .70	80,000

■ FIGURE 3–12   Decision tree for evaluation of possible one-year marketing plans—given that the target market and Product have already been selected and one-year plans are realistic

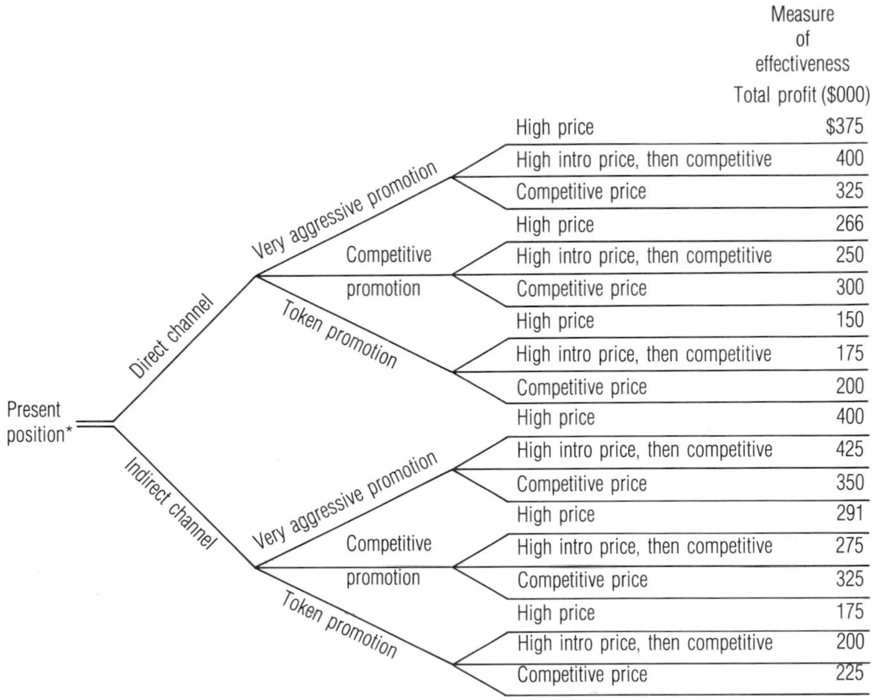

Measure
of
effectiveness
Total profit ($000)

			Measure of effectiveness Total profit ($000)
		High price	$375
	Very aggressive promotion	High intro price, then competitive	400
		Competitive price	325
Direct channel	Competitive promotion	High price	266
		High intro price, then competitive	250
		Competitive price	300
	Token promotion	High price	150
		High intro price, then competitive	175
Present position*		Competitive price	200
		High price	400
	Very aggressive promotion	High intro price, then competitive	425
		Competitive price	350
Indirect channel	Competitive promotion	High price	291
		High intro price, then competitive	275
		Competitive price	325
	Token promotion	High price	175
		High intro price, then competitive	200
		Competitive price	225

*Target market and Product have been selected.

lated and compared. As a further aid, it might be useful to show the resources required for each alternative—beside the total profit and return on investment. Most firms try to make a profit—while using their resources effectively—but sometimes these are conflicting objectives. So, it helps to have all the relevant information conveniently displayed when management attempts to apply its judgment in choosing the best opportunities.

Planning Grids Help Evaluate Different Kinds of Opportunities

When a firm has many possibilities to evaluate, it usually has to compare quite different ones. This can present a real problem—but the problem has been reduced by the development of graphical approaches—such as the nine-box strategic planning grid developed by General Electric.

General Electric looks for green positions

General Electric's strategic planning grid—see Figure 3–13—forces company managers to make three-part judgments (high, medium, and low) about the business strengths and industry attractiveness of all proposed or existing products or businesses.

GE feels that opportunities that fall into the dark gray boxes in the upper left-hand corner of the grid are its growth opportunities—the ones that will lead the company to invest and grow with these businesses. The red boxes in the lower right-hand corner of the grid, on the other hand, suggest a no-growth policy. Existing red businesses may continue to generate earnings—but GE figures they no longer deserve much investment. The light gray businesses are the borderline cases—which can go either way. An existing light gray business may be continued and supported—but a proposal for a new one has a greater chance of being rejected by top management.

GE's "stop light" evaluation method is a very subjective, multiple-factor approach—because GE has concluded that there are too many traps and possible errors if it tries to use over-simplified, single-number criteria—like ROI and market share—for judging "attractiveness" or "strength." Instead, top managers review written summaries of about a dozen factors (see Figure 3–12) which help them make summary judgments. Then they make a collective judgment based on the importance they attach to each of the factors. GE reports that the approach generally leads to agreement and, further, a good understanding about why some businesses or new opportunities are supported—while others are not. Further, it appears that high-high dark gray businesses are uniformly good on almost any quantitative or qualitative measure used. This interaction among the relevant variables makes it practical to boil them all down into a "stop light" framework.[11]

■ FIGURE 3–13   General Electric's strategic planning grid

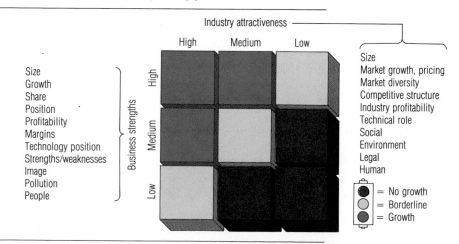

Source: Adapted from M. G. Allen, "Strategic Problems Facing Today's Corporate Planner, speech given at the Academy of Management, 36th Annual Meeting, Kansas City, Missouri, 1976.

Factors reflect GE's objectives

The various factors which General Electric considers in its subjective evaluation do, of course, reflect the corporation's objectives. The various "business strength" factors are related to the size of business it wants to be in—and the business's growth potential and profitability. The "industry attractiveness" variables also reflect GE's objectives in that ideally it wants to be involved in industries where the firm has a good chance of growth and profitability—while still contributing to the economy. In summary, the use of many factors simply helps ensure that all the concerns of the corporation are properly considered when it is evaluating alternative opportunities. Figure 3–14 elaborates on the specific factors contributing to each individual market's attractiveness and the relative position of the firms in that product market.

Multi-Product Firms Have a Difficult Strategy Planning Job

Multi-product firms—like General Electric—obviously have a more difficult strategic planning job than a firm with only a few products or product lines aimed at the same or similar target markets. They have to develop strategic plans for very different businesses. And the corporate level must try to balance the plans and needed resources for the various businesses in such a way that the whole corporation reaches its objectives. This requires analyses of the various alternatives—using approaches similar to the General Electric strategic planning grid—and approving strategic plans which make sense for the whole corporation—even if it means "harvesting" some divisions and eliminating others.

Details on how to manage such a complicated firm are beyond our scope. But it is important to recognize (1) that there are such firms and (2) that the principles we will discuss in this text are applicable—they just may have to be extended. For example, some firms have developed strategic business units (SBUs) and others are applying a portfolio management approach. These topics are discussed next.

Strategic business units may help

Some multi-product firms have tried to improve their operations by forming strategic business units. A **strategic business unit (SBU)** is an organizational unit within a larger company which focuses its efforts on some product-markets and is treated as a separate profit center. Forming SBUs formally recognizes that a company is composed of quite different activities. Some may be growing rapidly and require a great deal of attention and resources—while others may be only in the middle in terms of profitability and should be "harvested"—that is, they should be allowed to generate cash for the businesses with more potential. There also may be product lines with poor market position, low profits, and poor growth prospects. These should be dropped or sold.

Companies which set up strategic business units usually do change their attitudes and methods of operation. Managers are rated in terms of achieving their strategic plans—rather than short-term profits. Without SBUs, it is all too easy

■ FIGURE 3–14   Factors contributing to market attractiveness and business position

Attractiveness of your market	Status/position of your business
Market factors	
Size (dollars, units, or both)	Your share (in equivalent terms)
Size of key segments	Your share of key segments
Growth rate per year	Your annual growth rate
Total	Total
Segments	Segments
Diversity of market	Diversity of your participation
Sensitivity to price, service features, and external factors	Your influence on the market
Cyclicality	Lags or leads in your sales
Seasonality	
Bargaining power of upstream suppliers	Bargaining power of your suppliers
Bargaining power of downstream suppliers	Bargaining power of your customers
Competition	
Types of competitors	Where you fit, how you compare in terms
Degree of concentration	of products, marketing capability,
Changes in type and mix	service, production strength, financial
	strength, management
Entries and exits	Segments you have entered or left
Changes in share	Your relative share change
Substitution by new technology	Your vulnerability to new technology
Degrees and types of integration	Your own level of integration
Financial and economic factors	
Contribution margins	Your margins
Leveraging factors, such as economies of scale and experience	Your scale and experience
Barriers to entry or exit (both financial and nonfinancial)	Barriers to your entry or exit (both financial and nonfinancial)
Capacity utilization	Your capacity utilization
Technological factors	
Maturity and volatility	Your ability to cope with change
Complexity	Depths of your skills
Differentiation	Types of your technological skills
Patents and copyrights	Your patent protection
Manufacturing process technology required	Your manufacturing technology
Sociopolitical factors in your environment	
Social attitudes and trends	Your company's responsiveness and flexibility
Laws and government agency regulations	Your company's ability to cope
Influence with pressure groups and government representatives	Your company's aggressiveness
Human factors, such as unionization and community acceptance	Your company's relationships

Source: Derek F. Abell and John S. Hammond, *Strategic Market Planning: Problems and Analytical Approaches,*
© 1979, p. 214. Reprinted by permission of Prentice-Hall, Inc., Englewood Cliffs, New Jersey.

to emphasize only profits—especially short-run profits. It is a temptation for an eager manager to go for the short-term results—while sacrificing long-term gains. With SBUs, the emphasis is on developing plans which, when accepted, are to be implemented aggressively. Under this concept, some managers would be rewarded for successfully phasing out product lines, while other managers are moving ahead aggressively—expanding sales in other markets.

The point here is that each manager is carrying out a market-oriented strategic plan approved by top management. The manager's job is to help develop effective plans and then implement them to ensure that the company's resources are used effectively—and that the firm accomplishes its corporate objectives.

Some firms use portfolio management

Some top managements handle strategic planning for a multi-product firm with an approach called **portfolio management**—which treats alternative products, divisions, or strategic business units (SBUs) as though they were stock investments—to be bought and sold using financial criteria. These managers see themselves making trade-offs among very different opportunities. They simply treat the various alternatives as investments—which should be supported, "milked," or sold off—depending on profitability and return on investment (ROI). In effect, each alternative is evaluated as a stock market trader evaluates a stock.[12]

This approach makes some sense if the alternatives are really quite different. It is unlikely that top managers can become very familiar with the prospects for all of their alternatives. So they fall back on the easy-to-compare quantitative criteria. And because the short run is much clearer than the long run, heavy emphasis is usually placed on *current* profitability and return on investment. This puts great pressure on the operating managers to "deliver" *in the short run*—perhaps even neglecting the long run. (There have even been cases of managers manipulating their accounting records—to make the short-run results look better!)

Portfolio management is greatly improved by encouraging the development of market-oriented strategic plans—which make it possible to more accurately evaluate the short-run and long-run prospects of the many alternatives. If market-oriented strategies are spelled out in detail, it is easier for experienced managers to evaluate the quality of the plans. They not only have a better basis for deciding how to allocate resources among the various plans, but they also are able to make specific suggestions about modifying plans. In other words, they actually become involved—again—in the management process—instead of relying on a few financial criteria which may fail to capture the long-run value of their alternatives.

■ CONCLUSION

Innovative strategy planning is needed for survival in our increasingly competitive marketplaces. In this chapter, we discussed ways of finding attractive opportunities—and breakthrough opportunities. And we saw that the firm's own resources and objectives may help limit the search for opportunities. We learned that carefully defining generic markets and product-markets can help find new opportunities. And segmenting broad product-markets may force target marketers to choose among three approaches to target marketing: (1) the single target market approach, (2) the multiple target market approach, and (3) the combined target market approach. In general, we encouraged marketers to be segmenters (single or multiple) rather than combiners.

Eventually, some procedures are needed for screening and evaluating opportunities. We explained an approach for developing screening criteria—from the output of an analysis of the strengths and weaknesses of the company's re-sources, the environmental trends it faces, and top management's objectives. We also considered some quantitative techniques for evaluating opportunities. And we discussed a way for evaluating quite different opportunities—using the GE strategic planning grid. We also recognized that a multi-product firm may use SBUs or a portfolio management approach to developing its whole program.

We looked at the resources and objectives of the firm—uncontrollable variables to the marketing manager—to help in finding attractive opportunities. Now—before going on to discuss how to turn opportunities into profitable marketing strategies in the rest of the book—we will look at the rest of the uncontrollable variables (in Chapter 4). They are important because changes in these environments present new opportunities—as well as problems— a marketing manager must deal with in marketing strategy planning.

■ QUESTIONS AND PROBLEMS

1. Distinguish between an attractive opportunity and a breakthrough opportunity.

2. Explain how new opportunities may be seen by defining a firm's markets more precisely. Illustrate for a situation where you feel there is an opportunity—i.e., an unsatisfied market segment— even if it is not very large.

3. Distinguish between a generic market and a product-market. Illustrate your answer.

4. Explain the major differences among the four basic types of opportunities discussed in the text and cite examples for two of these types of opportunities.

5. Explain why a firm may want to pursue a market penetration opportunity before pursuing one involving product development or diversification.

6. Explain how a firm's resources may limit its search for opportunities. Cite a specific example for a specific resource.

7. Discuss how a company's financial strength may have a bearing on the kinds of products it produces. Will it have an impact on the other three Ps as well? If so, how? Use an example in your answer.

8. Explain how a firm's objectives may affect its search for opportunities.

9. Specifically, how would various company objectives affect the development of a marketing mix for a new type of baby shoe? If this company were just being formed by a former shoe maker with limited financial resources, list the objectives he might have. Then discuss how they would affect the development of his marketing strategy.

10. Explain the components of product-market screening criteria—which can be used to evaluate opportunities.

11. Explain the differences among the following approaches to evaluating alternative plans: total profit approach, return-on-investment approach, and expected-value approach.

12. Explain General Electric's strategic planning grid approach to evaluating opportunities.

13. Distinguish between the operation of a strategic business unit and a firm which only pays "lip service" to adopting the marketing concept.

■ SUGGESTED CASES

---

9. West Coast International Resources

17. Black & Decker Company

■ NOTES

---

1. F. R. Bacon, Jr., T. W.Butler, Jr., and E. J. McCarthy, *Planned Innovation Procedures* (printed by authors, 1983). See also George S. Day, A. D. Shocker, and R. K. Srivastava, "Customer-Oriented Approaches to Identifying Product-Markets, *Journal of Marketing* 43 (Fall 1979), pp. 8–19.

2. Ibid.

3. Ibid.

4. Igor Ansoff, *Corporate Strategy* (New York: McGraw-Hill, 1965).

5. Based on a classic article by Charles H. Kline, "The Strategy of Product Policy," *Harvard Business Review,* July-August 1955, pp. 91–100.

6. Adapted from Peter F. Drucker, "Business Objectives and Survival Needs: Notes on a Discipline of Business Enterprise," *Journal of Business,* April 1958, pp. 181–90.

7. This point of view is discussed at much greater length in a classic article by T. Levitt, "Marketing Myopia," *Harvard Business Review,* September-October 1975, 1 f.

8. Carolyn Y. Woo and Arnold C. Cooper, "The Surprising Case for Low Market Share," *Harvard Business Review* 60, no. 6 (November-December 1982), pp. 106–13; and "Reichhold Chemicals: Now the Emphasis is on Profits Rather than Volume," *Business Week,* June 20, 1983, pp. 178–79.

9. Frank R. Bacon, Jr., and Thomas W. Butler, Jr., *Planned In-*novation, rev. ed. (Ann Arbor: Institute of Science and Technology, University of Michigan, 1980).

10. Paul F. Anderson, "Marketing, Strategic Planning and the Theory of the Firm," *Journal of Marketing* 46, no. 2 (Spring 1982), pp. 15–26; George S. Day, "Analytical Approaches to Strategic Market Planning," in *Review of Marketing 1981,* ed. Ben M. Enis and Kenneth J. Roering (Chicago: American Marketing Association, 1981), pp. 89–105; and Michael E. Porter, "How Competitive Forces Shape Strategy," *Harvard Business Review,* March/April 1979, pp. 137–45.

11. M. G. Allen, "Strategic Problems Facing Today's Corporate Planner," speech given to the Academy of Management, 36th Annual Meeting, Kansas City, Missouri, 1976.

12. Richard N. Cardozo and David K. Smith, Jr., "Applying Financial Portfolio Theory to Product Portfolio Decisions: An Empirical Study," *Journal of Marketing* 47, no. 2 (Spring 1983), pp. 110–19; Yoram Wind, Vijay Mahajan, and Donald J. Swire, "An Empirical Comparison of Standardized Portfolio Models," *Journal of Marketing* 47, no. 2 (Spring 1983), pp. 89–99; Philippe Haspeslagh, "Portfolio Planning: Uses and Limits," *Harvard Business Review* 60, no. 1 (January-February 1982), pp. 58–73; and H. Kurt Christensen, Arnold C. Cooper, and Cornelius A. DeKluyver, "The Dog Business: A Re-examination," *Business Horizons* 25, no. 6 (November/December 1982), pp. 12–18.

Chapter 4 ■ Uncontrollable environments affecting marketing management

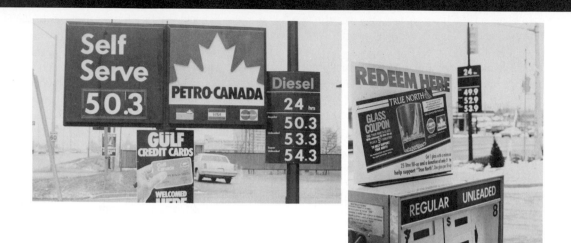

When you finish this chapter, you should:

1. Know the uncontrollable variables the marketing manager must work with.

2. Know how—and how quickly—the cultural and social environment can change.

3. Understand how the economic and technological environment can affect strategy planning.

4. Know the effect of the different kinds of market situations on strategy planning.

5. Know why you can go to prison by ignoring the political and legal environment.

6. Recognize the important new terms (shown in red).

"Marketing managers do not plan strategies in a vacuum."

Marketing managers do not plan strategies in a vacuum. They have to work with several uncontrollable variables when choosing target markets and developing the four Ps.

North American manufacturers, for example, have been hurt by fluctuating gasoline prices. When prices were rising rapidly in the 1970s—due to the oil cartel—sales of big cars dropped drastically as buyers switched to smaller, fuel-efficient foreign cars. Then, in the late 70s and again in the early 80s, when gas prices leveled off and even dropped in some places, buyers again wanted the big cars. But, then the auto producers were geared up to produce the small cars required by government regulations. In 1983, the industry even had to drop prices and subsidize interest rates—on the small cars—to sell them.

In the early 1980s, IBM's competitors were shocked to find that IBM was no longer going to play the role of "gentle leader"—enabling quick followers to match its offerings at lower prices or supply peripheral equipment. Instead, it began aggressive pricing—sometimes dropping prices 20 to 30 percent on a new model within a year—and introducing products more rapidly, with adequate quantities to meet market demand fairly quickly. Further, IBM's product-price "bundling" made it harder for manufacturers of "add on" accessories to pick the accessory areas where they wanted to compete—and then use lower price to "steal" business away from IBM.

109

■ FIGURE 4–1 Marketing manager's framework

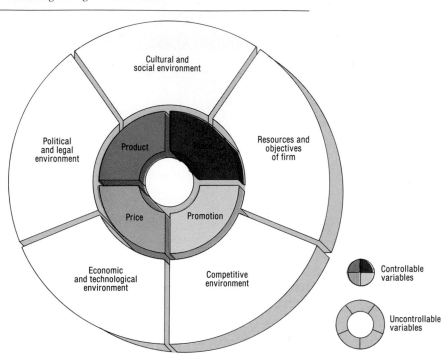

As we saw in Chapter 2—and as shown again in Figure 4–1—such uncontrollable variables fall into the following areas:

1. Cultural and social environment.
2. Economic and technological environment.
3. Competitive environment.
4. Political and legal environment.
5. Resources and objectives of the firm.

We have already seen—in Chapter 3—how the resources and objectives of a firm may affect marketing strategy planning. Now we will consider how the first four uncontrollable variables add to the complexity and challenge of marketing management.

Cultural and Social Environment

The **cultural and social environment** affects how and why people live and behave as they do. This variable is very important—because it has a direct effect on customer buying behavior.

Markets consist of real people with money to spend. But the number and location of these people is pretty much set. And many of their attitudes and behavior patterns are fixed—or changing only slowly. In other words, we already know a great deal about our cultural and social environment.

Since the demographic and behavioral dimensions of buyer behavior are treated in detail in Chapters 6 through 8, we will present only a few examples here—to emphasize the possible impact of this variable on marketing strategy planning.

Cultural similarities and differences

Is there a distinct Canadian culture? If so, how do cultural differences and so-called national characteristics effect the way Canadians live, work, and consume? It is easy to ask such questions but difficult to answer them in a manner helpful to marketers. All we can do now is indicate some of the cultural similarities and differences that must be taken into consideration.

Some observers maintain that four key concepts help shape the Canadian cultural environment. *Negative nationalism* is the tendency of Canadians to characterize themselves by what they are not and how they differ from Americans rather than by what they are or what they do. *Ultraconservatism,* viewed as a legacy from England, has encouraged stable political institutions, public dignity, and social orderliness. The third distinguishing feature is *mosaic diversity.* This follows from Canadian immigrants maintaining more of their original cultural heritage than would have been possible within the American melting pot. Finally, Canada is characterized by the *biculturalism* associated with the coexistence of the founding English and French cultures.[1]

The Canadian personality is often presented as somewhat subdued, less as-

Sometimes we take our own culture for granted.

■ FIGURE 4-2   Summary of significant English Canadian characteristics

A. As a function of being a part of the North American reality:
    Modern orientation.
    Openness to new ideas.
    Egalitarianism.
    A rich developing society with many needs and high materialistic expectations.
    Growing, more diffuse "middle class."
B. In relation to the United States:
    Conservative tendencies.
    Traditional bias.
    Greater confidence in bureaucratic institutions.
    Collectivity orientation—reliance on institutions such as state, big business, and the
        church versus personal risk taking.
    Less achievement oriented.
    Lower optimism—less willing to take risks.
    Greater acceptance of hierarchical order and stratification.
    Tolerance for diversity—acceptance of cultural mosaic.
    Family stability.

Source: Adapted from M. Dale Beckman, "Canadian Life Style: Values and Attributes of the Canadian Consumer," in *Problems in Canadian Marketing*, ed. Donald N. Thompson (Chicago: American Marketing Association, 1977), p. 44.

sertive, and more tolerant of dissenting viewpoints than its American counterpart. Internationally, Canadians are perceived as reserved, conservative, and a trifle self-conscious. Americans, in contrast, are usually described as gregarious, outspoken, ethnocentric, self-confident, and proud. Other significant English Canadian characteristics are presented in Figure 4–2. Nevertheless, the similarities that exist in values, living patterns, work roles, familial relationships, and consumer behavior far outweigh and are much more obvious than any differences that might exist between American and Anglo-Canadian families.[2]

Canada is indeed a "mosaic"

The Canadian population is far from homogeneous. To the contrary, one of the important characteristics of the Canadian market is its distinctive regional disparities. The United States is often considered a "melting pot." It is best to think of Canada in terms of a mosaic, where the pieces at times converge and other times remain far apart. Incomes, consumption patterns, life styles, dialects, and attitudes vary from province to province. For example, mean personal disposable income per household, family size, and number of persons per dwelling are substantially higher in Ontario than in Prince Edward Island. Unemployment is generally higher in the Atlantic Provinces than in the rest of Canada.[3] Life in the Prairie Provinces is usually more relaxed than in other regions—people expect and often experience "Western hospitality." Consumption patterns also reflect regional differences. The further west you go in Canada, the more milk people drink. West Coast dwellers prefer foreign cars; Maritimers opt for compacts. Consumers in the Atlantic region consume more tea per capita than other Canadians.[4]

Cultural differences similar to those found between regional areas are also common within large urban areas. Montreal and Toronto, for example, have large Italian, Greek, Jewish, and Chinese communities. Over 200,000 residents of

Metropolitan Toronto report Italian as their mother tongue—an important factor marketers cannot overlook. Food stores, newsstands, travel agencies, credit unions, and restaurants cater specifically to this and other culturally defined markets. The ethnic market is discussed in greater detail in Appendix C.

The women's movement

The appropriate role of women in North American society has been an important topic for two decades. Some of the resulting discussion has generated more heat than understanding. However, a shift in thinking is clearly taking place. Women are now freer to seek any kind of job they want. This greater degree of financial freedom, in turn, is making many women less dependent on marriage as a career and a source of financial security. More women are either not marrying at all or marrying later. And the number of children such women plan to have is declining. We shall see in Chapter 6 that a falling birth rate has a marked impact on manufacturers of housing, baby foods, convenience foods, clothing, and cosmetics, among other things.

Women and advertising

Women have become especially sensitive to the way they are represented in television commercials and advertisements in magazines and newspapers. Studies conducted both in the United States and Canada show that there is legitimate cause for this concern. Women are typically portrayed as fulfilling only "female" roles or are otherwise unfavorably sex stereotyped. A Task Force on Women and Advertising, established by the Canadian Advertising Advisory Board, concluded that the situation in Canada had improved. However, the Task Force maintained that women still had to be more realistically represented and that alert marketers might well benefit from advertisements more in tune with today's social realities and life styles.[5] As is indicated by Figure 4–3 some women's groups believe that there is still far too much sex-role stereotyping in Canadian advertising.

Work and growth are important to some

We also must take into account cultural attitudes toward life and work. These are a reflection of religious, ethical, and moral values. It is evident that national attitudes have an effect on a country's rate of growth and the direction of its development.[6]

North American culture tends to encourage the belief that hard work leads to achievement and material rewards. This has led to a preoccupation with economic growth, production, and the distribution of goods and services. Much of our analysis of the Canadian market will take place within this cultural framework.

Other societies seem far less concerned about what they feel are materialistic values. Far greater stress is placed on leisure and enjoyment of life. More holidays are built into the working year. The output of such economies may not be quite as high as it could be. However, people may not feel that they are suffering in any way because of this lower physical output.

Are North American values changing?

Interestingly enough, the North American values just mentioned are not as widely accepted as they once were. The traditional emphasis on growth, mass production, and consumption is being questioned by advocates of ecological

■ FIGURE 4–3   The sterotyping controversy continues

Study discovers advertisers failing to eliminate sexism

By DOROTHY LIPOVENKO

Self-policing by the Canadian advertising industry is not working because sex-role stereotyping of women persists, a national watchdog group warns in a report to the federal Government.

"Woman continues to be cumulatively portrayed in ways that suggest her place is in the home, her interests do not include issues of the world or public affairs but are limited to interests in other people and her own appearance. Her primary roles are those of caretaker of men and children and sexual object of men," says MediaWatch, a women's group that monitors images of women in the media.

"Even in terms of the (advertising and broadcasting) industries' own guidelines, these findings suggest a poor job in eliminating sexist content from broadcast material," the group concludes in a report to the Canadian Radio-Television and Telecommunications Commission to be released today.

MediaWatch did the study to determine the extent of sex-role stereotyping since the advertising industry embarked on a two-year period of self-regulation which ended in September, 1984.

The industry had set up voluntary guidelines to encourage the elimination of sex-role stereotyping and a CRTC task force had recommended they be given an opportunity to police themselves rather than be required to conform to a regulatory code.

Among the findings of Media-Watch:

● Female characters are more passive and use seductive non-verbal behavior;
● Men outnumbered women more than two to one in voice-overs for commercials;
● Men exclusively pitch products such as cars and financial services while women are more likely to present cosmetics and health care products;
● Women were more likely to be partly or provocatively clothed;
● Men are shown to be more interested in their careers or business, while women are shown to be more interested in clothes and their appearance.

"Women continue to be psychologically and physically abused in the guise of entertainment. . . . She is usually submissive and has no power," the report said.

An official with the Canadian Advertising Advisory Board, the organization that produced the voluntary sex-role stereotyping guidelines, said improvements have been made in the portrayal of women.

"The complaints we receive have to do with ads directed to women themselves — underwear, clothing — where five years ago, the complaints were about the dumb housewife," Suzanne Keeler, staff coordinator at the board, said in an interview yesterday.

She refused to comment on MediaWatch's criticisms because said she had not seen the report.

Ms Keeler said most of the complaints about ads come from MediaWatch and not individual consumers. Asked whether the industry finds their complaints tiresome, she replied: "No . . . they are strong feminists with deeper concerns than the average Canadian."

The average Canadian would not be offended by the images that offend MediaWatch, she added. Some of their complaints "overwork the word pornographic. . . . Pornography is what you find in Hustler magazine."

Source: *The Globe and Mail*, Thursday, June 6, 1985.

awareness, more job satisfaction, and less wasteful forms of consumption. A small but still significant number of North Americans have "voluntarily simplified" their life styles. A much larger percentage are beginning to question our society's long-time acceptance of materialism.[7] If a major shift in values occurs, this change will have a profound impact on North American marketing.

Bribes or standard operating procedure

Differences between countries in the way that business is done is both a fact of life and a cause of widespread concern. What some North Americans call a "bribe" may be accepted as a necessary business expense in other countries. Some cultures even have a special word for financial "favors" and treat them much like Canadians and Americans treat tips. It's "just the way things are done." Recently, however, an increasing reluctance at home to sanction "bribes" and related practices to obtain overseas sales has gotten some firms and even crown corporations into legal "hot water." The methods used to sell American aircraft overseas were widely criticized in the United States. In this country, many observers bitterly attacked Atomic Energy of Canada for paying "special commissions" to well-placed foreign sales representatives who helped AEC sell its CANDU reactors. Some felt that such practices violated the spirit, if not the letter, of Canadian law.[8]

In reply, many North American firms say that they are merely following the prevailing practices of customer countries. It has also been argued that Canadian firms cannot refuse to offer "kickbacks" or other special inducements as long as companies headquartered elsewhere continue to do business "as usual." Unfortunately for the firms concerned, such arguments are no longer accepted by many Canadians as good enough reasons for making illegal or morally questionable payments.

Changes come slowly

Regarding the possibility of changing the cultural environment, it is important to recognize that changes in basic attitudes come slowly. An individual firm can't

Attitudes toward materialism vary among different groups in the society.

hope to encourage big changes in the short run. Instead, it should identify these attitudes and work within these constraints in the short run, while making long-run plans.

Sometimes, however, strong outside forces, such as the energy crisis, riots, or boycotts, may force more rapid changes in the cultural and social environment, or cause clashes with the political and economic environments.

Economic Environment

The **economic and technological environment** affects the way firms—and the whole economy—use resources. We will treat the economic and technological environments separately—to emphasize that the technological environment provides a base for the economic environment. Technical skills and equipment affect the way resources of an economy are converted into output. The economic environment, on the other hand, is affected by the way all of the parts of our macro-economic system interact. This, then, affects such things as national income, economic growth, and inflation.

Obviously, the marketing manager also has a big stake in the economic environment. In contrast to the legal and cultural environments, economic conditions change continuously. And they can move rapidly up or down, requiring tactical and even strategic responses.

National income changes make a difference

Changes in the overall level of economic activity are obviously important. Even the best possible marketing strategy may prove unsuccessful when Canada is in the midst of a depression or suffering from a rapid business decline. As consumers' incomes go down, people have less money to spend and they spend it in different ways. In a mild recession, for example, firms offering luxury goods can be badly hurt while those offering lower-priced goods may continue to prosper. More serious or more prolonged crises, however, can also hurt those who produce or retail lower-priced goods. For example, spending of all kinds tends to decline during periods when Quebec's consumers and investors are uncertain about that province's place in Confederation.

Resource scarcities may depress economic conditions

The growing shortage of some natural resources—in particular, energy resources—may cause severe upsets. In the petrochemical industry, for example, some plastic manufacturers' costs are so high that they are priced out of some markets. High gasoline prices have caused some consumers to be less interested in the larger, more profitable (to the auto industry) cars. Further, shifts in auto-buying patterns have a ripple effect throughout the economy—because the automobile industry is a major buyer of metals, plastics, fabrics, and tires.[9]

High fuel prices may cut economic growth

The continued economic growth which we have come to accept may be slowed or stopped by high fuel costs. High fuel prices for imported oil have shifted income to fuel producing nations outside North America. Furthermore, lower real incomes are possible in the future because of technological factors. Much of our existing plant and equipment is energy intensive. Some industrial processes that were profitable when energy was cheap are now less profitable or may actually be obsolete. So it is likely that the average job in the future will use less machinery and be less productive. In effect, high energy costs will increase real incomes in the few countries with large energy reserves, but the balance of the world may see lower real incomes. Canada will definitely be hurt both because we are big energy users and, contrary to what people believe, because we are large net importers of crude oil.[10]

Continued inflation changes government policies and business strategies

Inflation is a major factor in many economies. When people assume that prices will keep going up, they buy and sell accordingly. This behavior adds fuel to the inflationary fires. Some Latin American countries have had from 25 to 100 percent inflation per year for many years. In contrast, the 8, 10, or even 12 percent levels reached in recent years in Canada were "low." Nevertheless, these Canadian rates caused—properly—great concern about whether our inflation was out of control. This led to restrictive monetary and fiscal policies which did reduce income and employment *and* consumer spending. The federal government also considered it necessary in 1975 to introduce legislation which controlled wages, prices, profits, and dividends for a three-year period.[11]

You can see that the marketing manager must watch the economic environment carefully. In contrast to the cultural and social environment, economic conditions change continuously. And they move rapidly—up or down—requiring tactical and even strategic responses.

Technological Environment

The technological base affects opportunities

Underlying any economic environment is the **technological base**—the technical skills and equipment which affect the way the resources of an economy are converted to output. In tradition-bound societies, relatively little technology may be used—and output may be small. Modern economies, on the other hand, make greater use of the technological base—so labor can be more productive.

Spectacular advances in technology were made in the last 40 years. This was due in part to our new-found interest in and support of research and development. Almost all of the technological developments since the beginning of man have occurred in that time period. It is estimated that about 90 percent of the scientists that ever lived are alive and working today. This has caused an explosion of scientific literature, which makes it difficult—and in some fields, impossible—to keep up. New engineers who are not working on the frontiers of their field become obsolete in about 10 years!

More technological developments probably can be expected—although not as many from the United States. Support in the United States for R&D has been cut back in recent years as fighting recessions, inflation, and energy shortages have taken center stage. Canadian R&D expenditures, as a percentage of gross domestic product (GDP), have always been low compared to those of other industrialized nations. One explanation for the difference is the large number of foreign-owned firms that do no R&D in Canada. But whatever the cause, the problems became serious enough for the federal government to offer tax incentives to firms increasing R&D outlays. Some foreign producers—especially Japan—have pioneered recent breakthroughs, for example, in applying basic research findings to electronic products.

Some of these developments certainly will affect marketing—just as previous ones have had their impact. The modern automobile, for example, has enabled farmers to come to town—and urban people to go wherever they want—thereby destroying the local "monopolies" of some retailers and wholesalers. Modern trucks and airplanes have opened up many new markets and permitted production for national or international markets—with resulting competition and benefits for consumers. Electronic developments have permitted mass promotion via radio, TV, and telephone—reducing the relative importance of other media. And, in time, we may be able to shop in the home with a combination TV-computer system—eliminating the need for some retailers and wholesalers.

Computers have also permitted more sophisticated planning and control of business. Electronic equipment may allow us to return to custom production methods—but this time in automated factories which will let customers decide more exactly what they want and then get almost immediate delivery. This will cause drastic changes in internal company affairs—including sales forecasting, production scheduling, warehousing, and so on.

As we move through the text, you should see that some of the major advances in business have come from creative and early recognition of new ways to do things. Additional breakthrough opportunities probably will arise as our technological base changes.

Marketers should help their firms see such opportunities by trying to understand the "why" of present methods—and what is keeping their firms from meeting needs more effectively. Then, as new developments come along, they will be sensitive to possible applications—and be able to see how opportunities can be turned into profitable realities.

Further, they can make a contribution by developing a sense of what technical developments will be acceptable to society. With the growing concern about environmental pollution, the quality of life, working conditions, and so on, it is possible that some potentially attractive technological developments should be rejected—because of their long-run impact. Perhaps what is good for the firm and the economy's *economic* growth will not fit with the cultural and social environment—and thus the political and legal environment. The marketer's closeness to the market should give him a better feel for what people are thinking—and allow him to help his firm avoid blunders.[12]

The Competitive Environment

(Note: The following materials assume some familiarity with economic analysis—and especially the nature of demand curves and demand elasticity. For those wishing a review of these materials, see Appendix A, which follows Chapter 2.)

The **competitive environment** refers to the number and types of competitors the marketing manager must face—and how they may behave. Although these factors can't be controlled by the marketing manager, he can choose strategies which will avoid head-on competition.

Manager may be able to avoid head-on competition

By correctly understanding the nature of the competitive environment, the manager's chances may be improved. He should expect many competitors—and probably price competition—in an industry composed of many small producers and retailers. This is the case, for example, in the boating industry—where hundreds of boat builders and thousands of engine and accessory manufacturers try to sell their products through more than 20,000 retailers. Competitive strategies in this industry are very different from those in the aluminum or steel industries—where there are relatively few competitors.

You can get a better understanding of the nature of competition by identifying four kinds of market situations. We will emphasize three kinds: pure competition, oligopoly, and monopolistic competition—since the fourth kind, monopoly, is simply an extreme case of monopolistic competition.

Understanding these market situations is important—because the freedom of a marketing manager is greatly reduced in some situations. The important dimensions in these situations are summarized in Figure 4–4.

■ FIGURE 4–4   Some important dimensions regarding market competitors

Important dimensions \ Types of situations	Pure competition	Oligopoly	Monopolistic competition	Monopoly
Uniqueness of each firm's product	None	None	Some	Unique
Number of competitors	Many	Few	Few to many	None
Size of competitors (compared to size of market)	Small	Large	Large to small	None
Elasticity of demand facing firm	Completely elastic	Kinked demand curve (elastic and inelastic)	Either	Either
Elasticity of industry demand	Either	Inelastic	Either	Either
Control of price by firm	None	Some (with care)	Some	Complete

| When competition is pure | **Many competitors offer about the same thing** |

Pure competition is a market situation which develops when a market has:

1. Homogeneous (similar) products.
2. Many buyers and sellers, who have full knowledge of the market.
3. Ease of entry for buyers and sellers; that is, new firms have little difficulty starting in business—and new customers can easily come into the market.

More or less pure competition is found in many agricultural markets. In the potato industry, for example, there are tens of thousands of producers—and they are in pure competition. Let's look more closely at these producers.

In pure competition, the many (usually small) producers each face an almost perfectly flat demand curve. The relation between the industry demand curve and the demand curve facing the individual farmer in pure competition is shown in Figure 4–5. Although the potato industry as a whole has a down-sloping demand curve, each individual potato producer has a demand curve that is perfectly flat at the **equilibrium price**—the going market price.

To explain this more clearly, let's look at the demand curve for the individual potato producer. Assume that the equilibrium price for the industry is 50 cents. This means the producer can sell as many potatoes as he chooses at 50 cents. The quantity that all producers choose to sell makes up the supply curve. But acting alone, a small producer can do almost anything he wants to do.

If this individual farmer raises 1/10,000th of the quantity offered in the market, for example, you can see that there will be little effect on the market if he goes out of business—or doubles his production.

The reason an individual's demand curve is flat in this example is that the farmer probably could not sell any potatoes above the market price. And there is no point in selling below 50 cents.

■ FIGURE 4–5   Interaction of demand and supply in the potato industry and the resulting demand curve facing individual potato producers

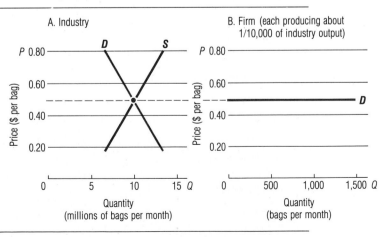

Not many markets are *purely* competitive. But many are close enough to allow us to talk about "almost" pure competition situations—ones in which the marketing manager has to accept the going price.

Squeeze on the orange growers

Florida orange growers, for example, have basically homogeneous products. They have no control over price. When there is a very large supply, prices drop rapidly and are beyond the producers' control. When supplies are short, the reverse happens. During one year, the crop was 50 percent larger than the previous crop—and most growers sold their oranges below their costs. Oranges "on the tree" which cost 75 cents a box to grow were selling for 35 cents a box. Supply turned around the next year, however, and oranges were selling for $2.40 to $2.60 a box.

Similar situations are found with many agricultural commodities. Farmers often seek government help to "save" them from pure competition. Agricultural parity programs are designed in part for this purpose—usually working to increase price by reducing supply.

Profit squeeze is on in many markets

Such highly competitive situations are not limited to agriculture. In any field where many competitors sell homogeneous products—such as chemicals, plastics, lumber, coal, printing, and laundry services—the demand curve seen by *each producer* tends to be flat. Assuming no collusion among the firms, there is a tendency for each firm to expand production—and the action of all producers forces down the market price.

Industries tend to become more competitive—that is, move toward pure competition (except in oligopolies—see below). More competitors enter the market, the supply is increased, and the current equilibrium price is pushed downward. This tends to force profits down—until some competitors are eliminated. Economists describe the final equilibrium position as that point at which there is only enough return to keep the survivors in business.

On the way to this final equilibrium position, competition becomes so tough that companies actually lose money—as the price goes below the long-run equilibrium level—and some firms are driven out of the market. It also may take some time before the industry price moves up to the equilibrium level—so that the remaining companies can survive. At the economist's final equilibrium point, however, none of the firms makes a profit! Each just covers all its costs.

When competition is oligopolistic

Few competitors offering similar things

Not all industries or markets move toward pure competition. Some become oligopolies.

Oligopoly situations are special market situations which develop when a market has:

1. Essentially homogeneous products—such as basic industrial chemicals or gasoline.

2. Relatively few sellers—or a few large firms and many smaller ones who follow the lead of the larger ones.
3. Fairly inelastic industry demand curves.

The demand curve facing each firm is unusual in an oligopoly situation. Although the industry demand curve can be inelastic throughout the relevant
range, the demand curve facing each competitor looks "kinked." See Figure 4–6.
Each marketing manager must expect that raising his own price above the market for such a homogeneous product would cause a big loss of sales. Few, if any,
competitors would follow his price increase. So, his demand curve is relatively
flat above the market price. But if he lowers his price, he must expect competitors to follow. Therefore, given inelastic industry demand, his own demand curve
is inelastic at lower prices. Since lowering prices along such a curve would reduce total revenue, he probably should not do it. That is, he should leave his
price at the kink—the market price.

Actually, however, there are price fluctuations in oligopolistic markets. Sometimes this is due to firms that don't understand the market situation—and cut
their prices to get business. In other cases, big increases in demand or supply
change the basic nature of the situation—and lead to price cutting. Sometimes
the price cuts are drastic—such as Du Pont's Dacron price cut of 25 percent.
This happened when Du Pont decided that industry production capacity already
exceeded demand—and more plants were due to start into production.

Price wars are sometimes started

A common example of price fluctuations can be seen in retail gasoline marketing—at a major intersection where there are several obvious competitors. Apparently enough final consumers think of gasoline as homogeneous to create
oligopoly conditions. And oligopoly-type "price wars" are common. These usually
start when some gasoline discounter successfully attracts "too much" busi-

■ FIGURE 4–6   Oligopoly—kinked demand curve—situation

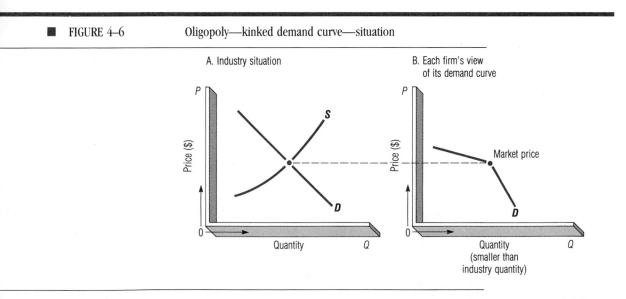

ness—perhaps by cutting his prices one cent a gallon below his usual price. The war proceeds for a time—with everyone losing money—until one of the retailers calls a meeting and suggests that they all "get a little sense." Sometimes these price wars will end immediately after such a meeting—with prices returning to a "reasonable and proper" level.

As in pure competition, oligopolists face a long-run trend toward an equilibrium level—with profits driven toward zero. Along the way, a marketing manager may try to avoid price competition—relying more on other elements in the marketing mix. This is extremely difficult, however. If all of the potential customers view the products as essentially similar, how can a firm obtain some competitive advantage?

When competition is monopolistic

A price must be set

You can see why marketing managers want to avoid pure competition or oligopoly situations. They prefer a market in which they have more control. Aggressive marketing managers do seek to develop a differentiated product and/or marketing mix (in the eyes of some consumers, not just the firm)—in order to gain more control. But if they still have to face some fairly direct competitors, we have a market situation called monopolistic competition.

Monopolistic competition is a market situation which develops when a market has:

1. Different (heterogeneous) products—in the eyes of some customers.
2. Sellers who feel they do have some competition in this market.

The word *monopolistic* means that each firm is trying to get its own little monopoly. But the word *competition* means that there are still substitutes. The vigorous competition of the purely competitive market is reduced. Each firm has its own down-sloping demand curve. But the shape of the curve depends on the similarity of competitors' products and marketing mixes. Each monopolistic competitor has freedom—but not complete freedom—in its own little "industry."

Judging elasticity will help set the price

Since a firm in monopolistic competition has its own down-sloping demand curve, it must make a price decision as part of its marketing strategy planning. Here, estimating the elasticity of the firm's own demand curve is helpful. If it is highly inelastic, the firm may decide to raise prices to increase total revenue. But if demand is highly elastic, this may mean many competitors with acceptable substitutes. Then the price may have to be set near "competition." And the marketing manager probably should try to develop a better marketing mix.

Why some products are offered in pure competition

Why would anyone compete in profitless pure competition? The usual explanation is that the firm was either already in the industry—or enters without knowing what is happening or is going to happen—and must stick it out until its resources are gone.

Production-oriented people seem more likely to make such a mistake than market-oriented managers. Avoiding pure competition seems advisable—and certainly fits with our emphasis on target marketing.

Pure competition cannot always be avoided

Despite their desire to avoid pure competition, some firms find that (at least for part of their operation) they can't. In some cases, production processes make this inevitable. For instance, in the chemical industry, caustic soda is produced as a by-product in the production of more profitable chlorine. At one time, the supply of caustic soda was so great that it was dumped as waste into the Gulf of Mexico. Obviously, this large supply had a depressing influence on the price (to say nothing about the water)!

Some industries appear to be almost purely competitive, yet new firms keep entering—replacing the casualties—possibly because they don't have more attractive alternatives and can at least earn a living in the industry. Examples include small retailers and wholesalers—especially in less-developed economies. Also, farmers continually try to shift their production to more profitable crops, but since there are many thousands of other farmers making similar choices, almost pure competition is typical.

Political Environment

The attitudes and reactions of people, social critics, and governments are becoming increasingly important to the marketing manager, because they all affect the political environment. In our discussion, we will separate political and legal questions, although in practice the separation is hard to maintain. A change in the political environment often leads to changes in the legal environment or the administration of existing laws.

Consumerism is here and basic

Perhaps the consumerism movement should have been treated under the cultural environment, because it reflects the values of many people in our society. But it is discussed here because these values may be changing rapidly. As a well-known business consultant, Peter Drucker, wrote: "We have been a very patient people, by and large. Now people are fed up, and I do not blame them."[13]

Consumerism is a social movement seeking to increase the rights and powers of consumers and buyers in relation to sellers and the government. Its continued growth may flow out of a change in thinking which began in the 1950s with books like Rachel Carson's *Silent Spring* and was reinforced by U.S. President John F. Kennedy's "Consumer Bill of Rights." He stated these in March 1962 and, although they did not become law, they have affected people's thinking, including government regulatory agencies and some courts.

President Kennedy's "Consumer Bill of Rights" included the following:

> *The right to safety*—to be protected against the marketing of goods which are hazardous to health or life."
>
> "*The right to be informed*—to be protected against fraudulent, deceitful, or grossly misleading information, advertising, labeling, or practices, and to be given the facts he needs to make an informed choice.

Public interest groups influence legislation—and marketing strategies.

"*The right to choose*—to be assured, whenever possible, of access to a variety of products and services at competitive prices, and in those industries in which competition is not workable and government regulation is substituted, to be assured satisfactory quality and service at fair prices.

"*The right to be heard*—to be assured that consumer interest will receive full and sympathetic consideration in the formulation of governmental policy, and fair and expeditious treatment in its administrative tribunals."

Kennedy did not include "the right to a clean and safe environment," probably because the environment had not yet become a public concern. But most people are now concerned with such a right. Increasingly, government pressure is being applied on everyone, including businesses and government units, to improve our waste handling and clean our chimneys and motor exhaust systems. This is probably the outstanding recent example of a rapid change in cultural values which was converted into action by the political authorities. This change was speeded by the rapid and visible deterioration of the physical environment coupled with our democratic political process which capitalizes on "dramatic" problems. And we may see more changes if the notions of "safety" and "quality of life" are applied to personal and property safety (from criminals) and moral safety (from pornographers, and movie and mass media producers).

These "rights" are generally not as susceptible to dramatic changes as the antipollution moves. Instead, individual firms and government agencies must change their behavior on a day-to-day basis. This is not nearly as easy to legislate. Basic changes in attitudes about what is "right" and "wrong" are needed, and this doesn't happen quickly. So there may be an ongoing need for consumerists to help assure that the "little guy" is not ignored or "wronged" by business or government authorities. And this need is being filled by institutions at the federal, provincial, and local levels. So the consumerism movement is not likely to die overnight.

The Canadian consumer scene

Canadian consumerism has been an important movement since the mid 1960s. One reason for this increased consumer consciousness was the establishment in 1968 of Consumer and Corporate Affairs Canada. This action gave one department the responsibility for administering a number of existing consumer protection laws. It also provided support for a wide variety of new programs designed to further the interests of the Canadian consumer.

Consumer and Corporate Affairs Canada (CCAC) has moved aggressively in the area of consumer protection. Additional laws have been passed and existing legislation has been enforced far more vigorously than in the past. (The laws which CCAC now administers in whole or in part are discussed in the next section covering the legal environment.)

Great emphasis has also been placed on educating and informing consumers. The kind of complaints received by CCAC have been studied to determine the serious problem areas that remain and the corrective action that seems best. At the provincial level, consumer protection bureaus and agencies have also been greatly strengthened in recent years. Some of these units are becoming at least as active as their federal counterpart.

Consumerists—often but not always working through the Consumers' Association of Canada (CAC)—also try to safeguard the legitimate interest of all consumers. The CAC is an especially influential group at both the provincial and federal level. Since most consumers are unorganized, the CAC is now widely recognized as "the voice of the Canadian consumer." And the organization speaks out whenever it believes that new consumer protection legislation is needed, defective products must be removed from the market, or some other interest group—business, government, or agriculture—is taking unfair advantage of consumers.[14]

Government efforts at consumer education as well as the *Canadian Consumer* and other CAC publications also increase consumer awareness. Specialized groups with a more limited focus, such as the Automobile Protection Association, are also busy educating and informing consumers. A number of consumer self-help and "rip off" protection books are now sold across Canada. Many Canadian newspapers publish articles on more intelligent purchasing—and run columns designed to help complaining consumers obtain a "fair deal" from local merchants. Also, consumer-oriented programs on network television and radio "talk shows" frequently deal with marketplace problems.

Not meeting consumers' expectations could be drastic

Generally, the public seems to like what the consumerists are trying to do. Marketers shouldn't forget that the role of businesses is to satisfy consumers. No firm has a God-given right to operate any way it sees fit. This means that the marketing manager, as well as top management, should give more serious consideration to consumer attitudes in marketing planning. The alternative could be pretty drastic from a macro point of view—the rules governing business could change. From a micro point of view, specific businesses might be banned—or they might be forced out of business by heavy fines.

Nationalism can be limiting in international markets

Strong sentiments of **nationalism**—the country's national interest before everything else—may also affect the work of some marketing managers. These feelings can reduce sales or even block marketing activity in some international markets. Oil producers and copper mining firms have felt such pressures in recent years, for example, in Latin America, Africa, and the Middle East. To whom the firms could sell, and how much, have been dictated by national interest. The Arab boycott of firms doing business with Israel is probably the outstanding example in recent years.

"Buy Canadian" policy is another form of nationalism. There also seems to be support for protecting Canadian producers from foreign competition, especially in footwear and textiles. Similarly, Philippine business executives have tried to drive "excessively aggressive" Chinese merchants out of the Philippines. And Africans have driven out Indian merchants. Countries may issue guidelines to foreign firms—as Canada has done recently to encourage "good corporate behavior." These guidelines are sometimes supplemented with new laws or the threat of legislation.

Nationalistic feelings can be extremely important in international business. In some countries, obtaining permission to operate is only a routine formality; in others, a lot of red tape is involved and personal influence and/or "bribes" are sometimes expected.

Multinational firms may be affected

Corporations that routinely operate in several countries have grown in size and importance in the last few decades. But growing nationalistic sentiments must be even more seriously considered by such firms in the future. Many countries require firms to employ nationals, use locally produced parts, and so on. Multinational corporations are discussed at some length in Chapter 23; here it need only be noted that their occasional disregard for feelings in individual countries has now given way to serious efforts to understand the people and the politicians within each particular country.

Political environment may offer new opportunities

The political environment can be a plus as well as a minus. Governments may decide that encouraging business and opening markets are constructive steps for their people. China and Japan recently opened their markets more to foreign investors and competitors. The United States and other highly developed countries may give industrial development a boost in Latin America, Africa, and Asia by allowing manufactured goods from those areas to be imported at lower duty rates.

Within Canada, the Department of Regional Economic Expansion (DREE), created in the late 1960s, uses developmental incentives such as accelerated depreciation, commercial loan guarantees, and start-up grants to encourage growth in depressed areas. In January 1982, DREE merged with the Department of Industry, Trade and Commerce. However, that reorganization had no real effect on federal efforts at regional development. Although the new Conservative government may go about it in different ways, it also seems committed to helping depressed areas. Provincial and local governments also try to attract and hold businesses, sometimes with tax incentives.[15]

Some business executives have become very successful by studying the political environment and developing strategies which use these political opportunities.

Legal Environment

American law has been a far more important factor in the shaping of prevailing business practices than has corresponding Canadian legislation. Why is this so? First of all, Canada traditionally has not been as committed as the United States to protecting either competition or the existence of a large number of competing small firms. Monopoly has not always been automatically condemned by Canadian economists and legislators.

Note also that Combines Act offenses had to be treated as violations of criminal law. The government, to win a case, had to prove guilt "beyond any reasonable doubt." Difficulties in establishing this degree of proof discouraged prosecution. They also reduced the likelihood that any firm brought to court would be found guilty.

How effective, then, was the Combines Investigation Act as amended through 1960? The legislation prevented two kinds of marketing activity—price fixing by competitors and misleading price advertising. Even though resale price maintenance was specifically prohibited in 1951, considerable difference of opinion exists as to how often and how effectively manufacturers still controlled retail prices.

Aside from these two or three areas, the Combines Investigation Act had little effect on either prevailing marketing practices or the structure of the Canadian economy. No firm was ever found guilty of price discrimination. In two key cases brought to court under the merger provisions, the government lost and did not appeal.[16]

Bill C-2: The "new" Competition Act— Stage 1

Dissatisfaction with the Combines Investigation Act led to the passage by Parliament, in December of 1975, of Bill C-2—the first part of a proposed two-stage major revision of the existing legislation. The minister who introduced this legislation said the following were its most important features.[17]

1. The bill clarifies and strengthens provisions concerning misleading advertising. It adds new protection in the area of warranties and guarantees. It deals with certain undesirable selling practices, such as pyramid selling, referral selling, bait-and-switch selling, selling at a price higher than advertised, the use of promotional contests, and "double-ticketing."
2. The bill covers some trade practices which could be acceptable in some circumstances but not in others. The Restrictive Trade Practices Commission is authorized to review these practices (refusal to deal, consignment selling, exclusive dealing, tied sales, and market restriction) and to issue orders prohibiting or modifying them.
3. The commission also has the power to issue orders forbidding the implementation within Canada of foreign judgments, laws, or directives where it finds them contrary to the Canadian public interest.
4. The bill makes bid-rigging an indictable offense. It also strengthens the existing provisions regarding resale price maintenance.
5. Services are to be covered by the provisions of the Combines Investigation

Act. Service activities have become a very important part of the Canadian economy, and there is no logical case for their continued exclusion from our competition legislation.

6. All economic activity in the private sector is covered by federal competition policy. However, activities regulated or authorized by valid federal or provincial legislation will continue to be exempted from the provisions of the Combines Investigation Act.

7. The bill proposes that, in order to prove that an agreement prevents or lessens competition "unduly," it is not necessary to establish complete or virtual elimination of competition in the relevant market.

8. The courts, for the first time, are able to issue interim injunctions to prevent the commission or continuation of suspected offenses against the Act until the main issue is settled.

9. Also for the first time the bill provides for bringing civil actions by any one adversely affected by violation of the Act to enable such a person to recover his damages and full costs.

Other federal legislation exists

Other laws and regulations are designed primarily to strengthen and maintain two of the previously mentioned consumer rights—to be protected against the marketing of hazardous goods (the right to safety) and to be safeguarded against deceptive promotion (the right to be informed). Here we will mention only a few of the many federal laws and regulations designed to protect public well-being.

The Food and Drug Act regulates the sale of foods, drugs, cosmetics, and medical devices. This legislation deals with quality standards, packaging, labeling, and advertising, as well as the manufacturing practices and selling policies of food and drug manufacturers. Certain forms of misrepresentation in food labeling, packaging, selling, and advertising are specifically outlawed by the Food and Drug Act.

The Canadian Radio-Television Commission regulates broadcast advertising. The Standards Branch of Consumer and Corporate Affairs Canada is one of many federal agencies that establish product standards and grades. There are also laws concerning the labeling of wool, furs, precious metals, and flammable fabrics. One form of promotional self-regulation is the voluntary ban on cigarette advertising on Canadian radio and television, which became effective January 1, 1972.

Provincial and local regulations

Marketers must also be aware of provincial and local laws which affect the four Ps. There are provincial and city laws regulating minimum prices and the setting of prices (to be discussed in Chapter 19); regulations for starting up a business (licenses, examinations, and even tax payments); and, in some communities, regulations prohibiting certain activities, such as door-to-door selling or selling on Sundays or during evenings. The sale and advertising of alcoholic beverages also is provincially controlled.

The provinces have become far more active in the protection of consumer rights. All of them have passed laws which regulate the granting of credit and otherwise call for "truth in lending." Purchasers are often provided with a "cooling-off period" within which they may cancel the contract, return any merchandise actually received, and obtain a full refund. The provinces are also more actively exercising their regulatory authority over car dealers, travel agents, and many other types of business that deal with large numbers of consumers spending considerable amounts of money.

Perhaps the most significant development on the provincial scene has been the passage by a number of governments of "trade practices" legislation. Such legislation protects the consumer from unconscionable and deceptive practices. Though the laws passed by different provinces are not identical, they all attempt to deal with the same set of problems.

The legislative environment in Quebec

Like every other major governmental jurisdiction in Canada, Quebec has passed a number of laws to protect its consumers. The most recent Quebec legislation, the Consumer Protection Act of 1978, is modeled after, but goes considerably beyond, trade practices legislation previously passed in British Columbia, Ontario, and Alberta. One unique feature of the Quebec Statute is its virtual ban on all advertising directed toward children.

Some laws reflect a growing concern with assuring the preeminence of the French language in every aspect of Quebec life. Long before the Parti Quebecois came to power, laws required that French be featured either exclusively or as prominently as any other language on the labels of all food products sold in that province. Similar legislation governing billboards, direct mail, and point-of-sale displays was passed in 1974. Bill 101, enacted in August 1977, provides even greater legal support for the primary and sometimes exclusive use of French in all aspects of advertising and promotion.

Although Quebec is too large a part of the total Canadian market to be neglected by most major North American manufacturers, such firms are certain to incur additional costs in complying with language legislation. Smaller Canadian and foreign corporations, on the other hand, may well cease marketing in Quebec. They could decide that the size of this market—as compared with the rest of North America—does not justify modifying the firm's promotional efforts to the extent compliance would require.

Consumerists and the law say "let the seller beware"

Traditional thinking about buyer-seller relations has been *let the buyer beware*—but now it seems to be shifting to *let the seller beware.* The number of consumer protection laws has been increasing. These laws and court interpretations suggest that the emphasis now is on protecting consumers *directly*—rather than *indirectly* by protecting competition. Production-oriented businesses may find this frustrating—but they will just have to adapt to this new political and legal environment.

Much of the impact of consumer protection legislation tends to fall on manufacturers. They are the producers of the product, and under common law, they are supposed to stand behind what they make. Generally, common law warranties have been fairly weak—what was "reasonable" or what the courts would consider "reasonable." But increasingly, the courts are putting greater responsibility on the manufacturers and even holding them liable for any injury that their product causes, even injury caused by users' carelessness. In such an environment, it is clear that businesses must "lean over backward." Times have changed—let the seller beware.

Know the laws—follow the courts

Because the real meaning of a law depends in large part on how it is interpreted, marketers must also be aware of how legislation is being implemented and enforced. Often good legal assistance is needed to keep up with new rules, regulations, and interpretations.

If marketing managers had a better understanding of the intent of the makers and interpreters of the laws, there would be less conflict between business and government and fewer embarrassing mistakes. With such an understanding, managers might come to accept the political-legal environment as simply another framework within which business must function and develop its marketing strategies. After all, it is the consumers, through their government representatives, who determine the kind of economic system they want.

■ CONCLUSION

This chapter was concerned with the forces which—while beyond the marketing manager's control—greatly affect marketing strategy planning. Some uncontrollable variables may change faster than others. But all can change—requiring adjustments in plans. Ideally, likely changes are considered in the strategy planning.

As we have seen, a marketer must develop marketing mixes appropriate to the customs of the people in his target markets. He must be aware, for example, that promotion which is suitable in Toronto may be offensive to citizens of Red Deer, Alberta, or Yokohama, Japan.

The marketing manager must also be aware of legal restrictions—and sensitive to changing political climates. The growing acceptance of consumerism may force many changes.

The economic environment—the chances of business recessions or spiraling inflation—also will affect the choice of strategies. And the marketer must try to anticipate, understand, and deal with such changes—as well as changes in the technological base underlying the economic environment.

A manager must also examine the competitive environment. How well established are competitors? What action might they take? What is the nature of competition?

Developing good strategies is obviously a very complicated job. The marketing manager must be well informed. He can benefit by increased knowledge of the social and natural sciences. Most important, he must know his own field thoroughly—for he will have to use the information from all these sources when developing his own strategies. Marketing management—as you can see—is an integrating and challenging discipline.

■ QUESTIONS AND PROBLEMS

1. For a new design of hair comb, or one of the items mentioned in Question 13 of Chapter 2, discuss the uncontrollable factors that the marketing manager will have to consider.

2. Discuss the relative importance of the uncontrollable variables, given the speed with which these variables move. If some must be neglected because of a shortage of executive time, which do you recommend for neglect?

3. Discuss the probable impact on your hometown of a major technological breakthrough in air transportation which would permit foreign producers to ship into any Canadian market for about the same transportation cost that domestic producers incur.

4. If a manufacturer's well-known product is sold at the same price by many retailers in the same community, is this an example of pure competition? When a community has many small grocery stores, are they in pure competition? What characteristics are needed to have a purely competitive market?

5. List three products that are sold in purely competitive markets and three sold in monopolistically competitive markets. Do any of these products have anything in common? Can any generalizations be made about competitive situations and marketing mix planning?

6. Cite a local example of an oligopoly—explaining why it is an oligopoly.

7. Which way does the Canadian political and legal environment seem to be moving (with respect to business-related affairs)?

8. Why is it necessary to have so many laws regulating business? Why hasn't Parliament just passed one set of laws to take care of business problems?

9. What and who is the government attempting to protect in its effort to preserve and regulate competition?

10. Are consumer protection laws really new? Discuss the evolution of consumer protection. Is more such legislation likely?

■ SUGGESTED CASES

1. Foodco, Inc.

5. Indian Steel Company

■ NOTES

1. Bruce Mallen, V. Kirpalani, and G. Lane, *Marketing in the Canadian Environment* (Scarborough, Ont.: Prentice-Hall of Canada, 1973), pp. 51–52.

2. Gerald B. McCready, *Profile Canada: Social and Economic Projections* (Georgetown, Ont.: Irwin-Dorsey, 1977), p. 58.

3. Peter M. Banting and Randolph E. Ross, "Canada: Obstacles and Opportunities," *Journal of the Academy of Marketing Science,* Winter 1975, pp. 11–13.

4. Gerald B. McCready, *Canadian Marketing Trends* (Georgetown, Ont.: Irwin-Dorsey, 1972), p. 52.

5. Report of the Task Force on *Women and Advertising* (Ottawa: The Canadian Advertising Advisory Board, November 1977). For a more definitive treatment of the controversy preceding formulation of these guidelines, see Louise A Heslop and Alice E. Courteney, "Advertising and Women," in *Marketplace Canada: Some Controversial Dimensions,* ed. Stanley J. Shapiro and Louise A. Heslop (Toronto: McGraw-Hill Ryerson, 1982), pp. 68–77.

6. David C. McClelland, "Business Drive and National Achievement," *Harvard Business Review,* July-August 1962, pp. 99–112.

7. Duane S. Elgin and Arnold Mitchell, "Voluntary Simplicity: Lifestyle of the Future," *The Futurist,* August 1977, p. 209.

8. "Candu Report Gets Steam up in House," *Financial Post,* May 28, 1977, p. 9; "Politics and Nuclear Power," *Financial Post,* December 10, 1977, p. 8; "CANDU'S, Stuggle—Safeguards Competition, Payoffs Take Toll," *Financial Times of Canada,* March 7, 1978, p. 3.

9. "The Petro-Crash of the 80's," *Business Week,* November 19, 1979, pp. 176–90; "The Shrinking Standard of Living," *Business Week,* January 28, 1980, pp. 72–78; "Howard Johnson Says Inflation Fuel Woes Could Hurt Business," *The Wall Street Journal,* April 3, 1980, p. 29; "Tire Industry Drops into Deep Recession; Gasoline Shortage, Rising Costs Take Toll," *The Wall Street Journal,* October 17, 1979, p. 40; "For Some U.S. Concerns, Energy Crisis Fuels Greater Profits and Employment," *The Wall Street Journal,* December 7, 1979, p. 18; "How OPEC's High Prices Stran-

gle World Growth," *Business Week,* December 20, 1976, pp. 44–50; "Will Energy Conservation Throttle Economic Growth?" *Business Week,* April 25, 1977, pp. 66–80; and "Economic Shock Wave from Oil Price Rises in '73 Still Hurts West," *The Wall Street Journal,* March 10, 1977, pp. 1f.

10. McCready, *Profile Canada: Social And Economic Projections,* p. 282.

11. J. Allison Barnhill, "Marketing in the Increasingly Controlled Economy of Canada," *1976 Educators Proceedings,* ed. K. L. Bernhardt (Chicago: American Marketing Association, 1976), pp. 456–60.

12. Maxwell R. Morton, "Technology and Strategy: Creating a Successful Partnership," *Business Horizons* 26, no. 1 (January/February 1983), pp. 44–48; Henry R. Norman and Patricia Blair, "The Coming Growth in 'Appropriate' Technology," *Harvard Business Review* 60, no. 6 (November-December 1982), pp. 62–67; and Alan L. Frohman, "Technology as a Competitive Weapon," *Harvard Business Review* 60, no. 1 (January-February 1982), pp. 97–104.

13. "The U.S.'s Toughest Customer," *Time,* December 12, 1969, pp. 89–98. "Supreme Court, 1975–1981," *Journal of Marketing* 46, no. 2 (Spring 1982), pp. 141–46.

14. Marion Brechin, "The Consumer Movement in Canada," in *Cases and Readings in Marketing,* ed. V. H. Kirpalani and R. H. Rotenberg (Toronto: Holt, Rinehart, & Winston of Canada, 1974), pp. 141–46.

15. Muriel Armstrong, *The Canadian Economy and Its Problems* (Scarborough, Ont.: Prentice-Hall of Canada, 1970), pp. 148–49.

16. D. N. Thompson, "Competition Policy and Marketing Regulation" in *Canadian Marketing: Problems and Prospects,* ed. D. N. Thompson and David S. R. Leighton (Toronto: Wiley Publishers of Canada, 1973), pp. 14–15.

17. Herb Gray, "Notes for Remarks to a York University Seminar on a Competition Policy," mimeographed, Toronto, January 25, 1974, pp. 5–7.

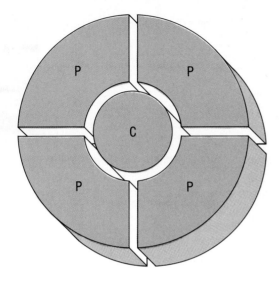

Product

Place

Promotion

Price

Customer

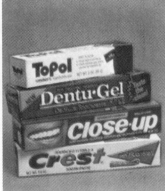

In this part, we will talk about finding potentially attractive target markets. First (in Chapter 5), we will discuss how to gather information to aid in marketing strategy planning. This "marketing research" chapter is really concerned with much more than just analyzing target markets—so it could be studied here or near the end of the book, when you have questions about marketing mix planning.

The next three chapters (Chapters 6–8) are concerned with possible dimensions of target markets. In Chapters 6 and 7, we will look at the dimensions of the consumer market—both demographic and behavioral. And in Chapter 8, the possible dimensions of many different kinds of intermediate customers will be considered.

Finally, in Chapter 9, we will wind up this part with a discussion of segmenting markets and estimating their potential. This is a very important chapter because it is necessary to correctly define markets and their relevant dimensions—to be able to plan effective marketing mixes.

Part II leads logically into the next part—on developing marketing mixes. In fact, it is not possible to select target markets without tying them to marketing mixes. You implement whole strategies and marketing plans, not target markets, so you should see Part II as the first step in learning how to develop more effective marketing mixes—and eventually effective marketing plans.

Chapter 5 ◼ Getting information for marketing decisions

When you finish this chapter, you should:

1. Understand a scientific approach to marketing research.
2. Know how to go about defining and solving marketing problems.
3. Know about getting secondary and primary data.
4. Understand the use of observation, direct questioning, and experimental methods in marketing research.
5. Know about marketing information systems.
6. Recognize the important new terms (shown in red).

> *"Marketing research doesn't prove that you're right. It gives you a way to find out."*

Successful planning of marketing strategies requires information—information about potential target markets and their likely responses to various marketing mixes—and about competition and other uncontrollable factors. Without good marketing information, managers have to operate on intuition or guesses—and in our dynamic and highly competitive economy, this invites failure.

On the other hand, a manager seldom has *all* the information needed to make the best decision. After all, both customers and competitors are unpredictable. Getting more information to improve a decision may cost too much—or take too long. So a manager often must decide if it is sensible to seek more information and—if so—how to get it. In this chapter, we'll talk about how a marketing manager gets the information he needs to plan successful strategies.

The marketing manager for a coffee company, for example, may wonder how effective its discount coupons really are. Do they draw new customers—or do current customers simply use the coupons to stock up? If consumers switch from another brand, do they go back to their old brand the next time they buy? The answers to these questions are important to planning marketing strategies—and now a marketing manager can get those answers more easily. Groups of consumers in some cities are participating in a project started by an independent marketing research firm. The consumers give an identification number when they do their weekly grocery shopping. The check-out clerk keys in the number, and then uses a computer scanner that records all of the purchases—including prices and any coupons used. Every food purchase made by the consumer—for over a year—is recorded on the computer. For a fee, a company can use the data and tabulate the actual purchase patterns—and find answers to questions like those worrying our coffee company manager. Other information—like demographic characteristics—already has been collected using standard questionnaires and is also available for each consumer. This data can be used to analyze the purchase behavior of different target markets—or even identify possible segmenting dimensions. The same consumers are also hooked up to a special TV cable system. It is possible for a company to direct advertisements to some houses—and not others. Then, the effect of the ads on the purchases can be evaluated by comparing the different groups of consumers. The information possibilities are more limited by imagination—and money—than technology.[1]

Not all marketing research requires computers. A museum director wanted to know which of the many exhibits was most popular. A survey didn't help. Visitors seemed to want to please the interviewer—and generally responded that *all* of the exhibits were interesting. Then observers were put nearby to record how long visitors spent at each exhibit. That didn't help either. The curious visitors stood around to find out what was being recorded—and that messed up the measures. Finally, a simpler approach was used. The museum floors were waxed to a glossy shine. Several weeks later, the floors around the exhibits were inspected. It was easy to tell the popularity of an exhibit—based on how much wax had worn off the floor!

What Is Marketing Research?

Research provides a bridge to customers

The marketing concept says that marketing managers should meet the needs of customers. Yet today, many marketing managers are isolated in company offices—far from their potential customers. Their products are sold all over the country—and even all around the world. Producers typically don't even deal with consumers directly—products are sold through middlemen. The growth of big, centrally managed retail chains means that even those directing the retailing end of the channel of distribution may be out of touch with local customers. Similarly, industrial marketers may sell to companies in many different industries—so it's impossible for a manager to keep up with changes in all of them on a first-hand basis.

This forces marketing managers to rely on help from **marketing research**—procedures to gather and analyze information to help marketing managers make decisions. One of the important jobs of a marketing researcher is to get the "facts." This can be done with special projects—or on a continuing basis—depending on the purpose.

Continued improvements—in sampling procedures and the use of computers to quickly analyze data, for example—have increased the dependability of marketing research information. This has encouraged firms to put more money—and trust—in research. In some consumer goods companies, no major decisions are made without the support—and sometimes even the official approval—of the marketing research department. As a result, some marketing research directors rise to high levels in the organization.

Who does the work?

Most larger companies have a separate marketing research department to plan and conduct research projects. These departments often use outside specialists—such as interviewing or tabulating services—to handle technical assignments. Further, specialized marketing consultants and marketing research organizations may be called in to take charge of the research for special problems. The kinds of marketing research studies conducted by and for large Canadian firms are revealed by Table 5–1.

Small companies—those with less than $3 or $4 million in sales—usually do not have separate marketing research departments—they rely instead on salespeople or top managers for what research they do.

Effective research usually requires cooperation

Often marketing research involves technical details—but good marketing research is much more than just statistical techniques—or specialists who do computer work. Good marketing researchers must be oriented toward both research *and* management—to be sure their research focuses on real problems on which action can be taken. Marketing researchers must understand the marketing manager's information needs.

Marketing managers must be involved in marketing research, too. Many marketing research details may be handled by staff or outside specialists—but marketing managers must know how to plan and evaluate research projects. They should be able to communicate with specialists in *their* language. They may only be "consumers" of research. But they should be informed consumers—and be able to specify exactly what they need from the research. They should also know about some of the basic decisions made during the research process—so they know the limitations of the findings.

Marketing research often must try to provide answers to urgent questions. Sometimes answers are needed so soon that quick research work must be done—even if speed means that it isn't possible to consider every question. A little information may be better than total ignorance. Even if time is short—and a really complete research effort is not possible—it's important that both managers and researchers approach marketing research in a logical way.

As all this suggests, our discussion of marketing research will not focus on mechanics—but rather on how to plan and evaluate research. You will learn about the steps in the marketing research process—and how those steps are guided by the philosophy of the scientific method.[2]

The Scientific Method and Marketing Research

The **scientific method** is a decision-making approach that focuses on being objective and orderly in testing ideas before accepting them. With the scientific method, managers don't simply *assume* that their intuition is correct. Rather,

■ TABLE 5–1

Activities of marketing research groups in Canada, 1977
(percentage analysis by industry)

| | All companies (152 = 100%) | | |
| | | Research done by* | |
Type of research	Frequency of use	Marketing research depart-ment	Another depart-ment	Outside firm
Business economic, and corporate research:				
Short-range forecasting	97%	67%	56%	7%
Long-range forecasting	98	66	53	8
Studies of business trends	93	69	43	9
Pricing studies	92	48	62	4
Product mix studies	85	50	49	3
Acquisition studies	81	31	60	7
Internal company employee studies	79	25	58	8
Plant and warehouse location	77	21	66	4
Export and international studies	62	34	35	5
Sales and market research:				
Measurement of market potentials	99	92	29	9
Market share analysis	99	88	31	11
Determination of market characteristics	99	88	28	13
Sales analysis	97	70	52	1
Establish sales quotas, territories	90	26	75	—
Distribution channel studies	77	38	53	6
Sales compensation studies	68	14	55	4
Test markets, store audits	60	42	23	16
Promotional studies	56	32	29	10
Consumer panel operations	45	30	15	19
Advertising research:				
Studies of ad effectiveness	73	44	31	21
Copy research	73	32	30	23
Media research	73	26	32	29
Product research:				
Competitive product studies	89	64	41	7
New product acceptance and potential	86	66	36	8
Testing existing products	79	47	41	8
Packaging research: physical design	62	32	36	8
Others	23%	22%	5%	1%
Number of companies reporting	152	152	152	152

*Totals may exceed 100 percent due to multiple response.

Source: *Marketing Research in Canada: A Status Report,* The Conference Board of Canada, July 1978.

they use their intuition and observations to develop **hypotheses**—educated guesses about the relationships between things or what will happen in the future—such as "There is no significant difference between brands A and B in the minds of consumers." Then they test each hypothesis.

The scientific method helps managers *and* researchers reduce the possibili-

Pepsi and other soft drink companies use consumer taste-tests to find out about consumer preferences.

ties of sloppy work. It focuses attention on the *best* ideas and takes a common-sense but objective approach—developing hypotheses, testing the hypotheses, perhaps modifying them, and testing again. The feedback principle is applied throughout the process. Decisions are based on evidence—not just hunches.

A manager who does not rely on the scientific method might say, "I know that consumers will like the taste of our new product—so let's go ahead and introduce it nationwide." A manager who uses the scientific method might say, "I think (hypothesize) that consumers who currently buy the most popular brand will prefer the taste of our new product. Let's run some consumer taste-tests. If the test results show that at least 60 percent of the consumers prefer our product, let's introduce it in a regional test market. If the taste is *not* preferred, we may need to change the flavors and try again—or even drop the idea."

The scientific method is objective. Some foolish managers are only interested in research if they think it will "prove" that their intuition is correct. They aren't interested in any information that might be contrary to what they have already decided to do. They miss the point of the scientific method. They place intuition over facts. If they really asked for research that *tested* their ideas, then the real problems might be isolated—and the final decisions might be better.

The scientific method forces an orderly process. Some managers don't think carefully about what information they need to make a decision. They blindly forge ahead hoping that research will give them "the answer"—even if they don't know what the question is. Other managers may have a clearly defined problem or question, but don't know how to proceed in a logical fashion. These "hit-or-miss" approaches waste both time and money. This waste can be avoided with a scientific approach to solving marketing problems. We'll talk about this approach next.

Five-Step Approach to Marketing Research

The **marketing research process** is a five-step application of the scientific method that includes:

1. Definition of the problem.
2. Situation analysis.
3. Obtaining problem-specific data.
4. Interpretation of data.
5. Problem solution.

Figure 5–1 shows the five steps in the process. Note that the process may lead to a logical conclusion before all of the steps are completed. Or, as the feedback arrows suggest, the process may cycle back to an earlier step if needed. For example, the interpretation step may point to a new question—or reveal the need for additional information—before a final decision can be made. As you will see in the sections which follow, this scientific approach helps clarify what is involved in marketing research.

Definition of the Problem—Step One

Defining the problem is the most important—and often the most difficult—step in the marketing research process. In this step, the objective(s) of the research must be clearly defined. The manager must think about what decisions need to be made—and clearly specify what information is really needed to make them.

■ FIGURE 5–1   Five-step scientific approach to marketing research process

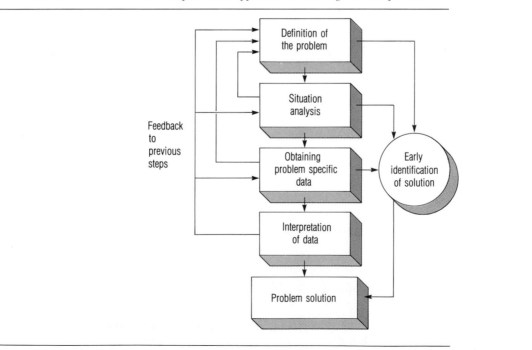

The manager and the researcher should both be involved—so that both agree on the major objectives of the research. The best research job on the wrong problem is wasted effort.

Finding the right problem level almost solves the problem

The strategy planning framework introduced in Chapter 2 can be especially useful here. It can help the researcher see where the real problem lies—and what information is needed. Do we really know enough about target markets to work out all of the four Ps? Do we know enough to specify what background music to use in an advertisement—or how to handle a price war in Montreal or Tokyo? Where our information is inadequate, we may want to do research— rather than rely on intuition.

The importance of understanding the nature of the problem—and then trying to solve *that* problem—can be seen more clearly in the following example of a manufacturer of a new easy-to-bake cake mix. Top management chose apartment dwellers, younger couples, and the too-busy-to-cook crowd as the target market—a logical market at first glance. Managers asked the research department for some research on the *size* of this market—and information about their life styles. The results indicated that if these consumers responded as expected, there were enough of them to be a profitable target market. The company decided to aim at this market—and developed a logical marketing mix.

But why didn't this baking mix sell?

During the first few months, sales were disappointing. The manufacturer "guessed" that the product itself might be unacceptable—since the promotion seemed to be adequate. At this point, a consumer survey was run—with surprising results. The taste of the cake was apparently satisfactory—but the target consumers were just *not interested* in the product concept. Easy baking didn't particularly grab them—it was easier yet to buy a cake at the store. Instead, the best market turned out to be families who did their own cooking. They appreciated the convenience of the mix—especially when they needed something in a hurry.

In this case, the original strategy planning was done sloppily. The choice of target market was based on executive guesswork. This led to an unsuitable strategy—and wasted promotion money. Some research with consumers—about their needs and attitudes—might have avoided this costly error. Both marketing research and management fumbled the ball—by not studying the attitudes of the target market. Then, when sales were poor, the company compounded the error by assuming that the problem was the product—overlooking consumers' real attitudes about the product. Fortunately, the real problem was finally uncovered— and the strategy was changed quickly.

The moral of this story is that our strategy planning framework can be useful for guiding the problem definition step of the marketing research process. If marketing managers have the facts on the potential target markets, then they can focus their research on marketing mix ingredients—and the markets' sensitivity to change. Without such a framework, marketing researchers can get sidetracked into working on the wrong problems.

Don't confuse problems with symptoms

The problem definition step sounds simple—and that's the danger. A manager may assume that all of the questionable areas are obvious—or that the researcher really understands what information is needed. That may not be the case. Too frequently, research objectives are not stated clearly—if at all. It's also easy to fall into the trap of mistaking symptoms for the definition of the problem. The key questions may be ignored—while less important questions may be analyzed in depth.

Setting priorities may require more understanding

Sometimes the research priorities are very clear—as when a manager only wants to know if the targeted households have tried a new product—and what percent of them bought it a second time. But usually it's harder than this. The manager might also want to know why some didn't buy—or if they had even heard of the product. There is rarely enough time and money to study everything. The manager will have to narrow things down. Developing a priority list that includes all the possible problem areas is sensible. The various items on the list may need to be considered more completely in the situation analysis step before final priorities can be set.

Situation Analysis—Step Two

What information do we already have?

When the marketing manager feels the real problem(s) has begun to surface, a situation analysis is useful. A **situation analysis** is an informal study of what information is already available in the problem area. The situation analysis may help refine the problem definition and specify what additional information—if any—is needed.

Pick the brains around you

The situation analysis usually involves informal talks with informed people. By informed people, we mean others in the firm, perhaps a few good middlemen who have close contact with customers, or others knowledgeable about the industry. In industrial marketing—where relationships with customers are close—the customers themselves may be called. Perhaps one of these people has already worked on the same problem—or knows about a useful source of relevant information. Their inputs may help to sharpen the problem definition, too.

Situation analysis helps educate a researcher

The situation analysis is especially important if the researcher is a research specialist who doesn't know much about the management decisions to be made—or if the marketing manager is dealing with unfamiliar areas. They must be sure they understand the problem area—including the nature of the target market, the marketing mix, competition, and other external factors. Otherwise, the researcher may rush ahead and make foolish mistakes—or simply "discover" what is already well known by management. A simple example illustrates this hazard.

A marketing manager at the home office for a large retail chain hired a research firm to do "in-store" interviews to learn what customers liked most—and least—about some of their stores in other cities. Interviewers diligently filled in their questionnaires. When the results came back, it was apparent that neither the marketing manager nor the researcher had done their homework. No one had even talked with the local store managers! Several of the stores were in the middle of some messy remodeling—so all the customers' responses concerned the inconvenience of the noise and dust from the remodeling. The "research" was a waste of money.

Secondary data may provide the answers—or some background

The situation analysis should also find relevant **secondary data**—information that has been collected or published already. **Primary data**—information specifically collected to solve a current problem—will be discussed later. See Figure 5–2. For now, keep in mind that researchers too often rush out to gather primary data when a plentiful supply of relevant secondary information is already available. And this data may be available immediately—at little or no cost!

One source of good secondary data may be the company's own computer system, files, or reports. Secondary data also is available from libraries, trade associations, or government agencies.

Much secondary data is available

One of the first places a researcher should look for secondary data, after looking at internal data, is a good library. Familiarity with the references in the library's card catalog and bibliographies helps the researcher pursue secondary sources more knowledgeably. Appendix B, following this chapter, gives an excellent list of secondary sources available to the Canadian marketer, from both government and private sources.

Situation analysis yields a lot—for very little

The virtue of a good situation analysis is that it can be very informative—but takes little time. It is inexpensive compared with more formal research efforts—like a large-scale survey. The fact that further research *may* be improved—or even eliminated—is important. The situation analyst is really trying to determine

Much marketing research information is available in libraries—and a good librarian can help you find it.

■ FIGURE 5–2   Sources of secondary and primary data

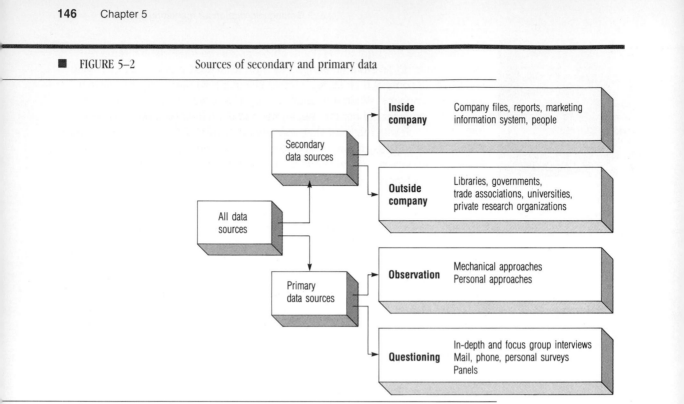

the exact nature of the situation—and the problem. Too-hasty researchers may try to skip this step—perhaps rushing to get out questionnaires. Often these researchers find the real problem only when the questionnaires are returned—and they must start over. One marketing expert puts it this way: "Some people don't have time to do research right the first time, but they seem to have time to do it over again."

Determine what else is needed

At the end of the situation analysis, you can see which research questions—from the priority list developed during the problem definition step—remain unanswered. Then, you have to decide exactly what information is needed to answer those questions—and what is involved to get it.

This often requires discussion between the technical experts and the marketing manager. Often a written **research proposal**—a plan that specifies what information will be obtained and how—is used to be sure that no one is surprised later by some misunderstanding. The research plan may include information about costs, what data will be collected, how it will be collected, who will analyze it and how, and how long it will all take. Then the marketing manager must decide if it makes sense to go ahead—if the time and costs involved seem worthwhile. It's foolish to pay $100,000 for information to solve a $50,000 problem! Often the decision is not so clear-cut—so marketing managers need to know more about the next steps in the marketing research process.

Getting Problem-Specific Data—Step Three

Gathering primary data

The next step is to plan a formal research project to gather data—usually primary data. There are different methods for collecting primary data—and which approach is best depends on how precisely the research problem has been defined, the nature of the problem, and how much time and money is available. The approach may also vary depending on how important it is for management to draw firm conclusions about whole target markets—perhaps based on only a small group of people.

The vast majority of primary data collection focuses on finding what customers think about some topic—or how they behave under some conditions. There are two basic methods for obtaining information about people: *questioning* and *observing*. Questioning can range from qualitative to quantitative research. And many kinds of observing are possible. Either basic method can be used in the experimental method. In the following sections, we will review some of the advantages and limitations of these different methods for gathering information—since the marketing manager may have to choose which one to use for a research project.

Qualitative questioning—open-ended with a hidden purpose

Qualitative research seeks in-depth, open-ended responses. The researcher tries to get people to share their thoughts on a topic—but without giving them many directions or guidelines about what to say. The people may be asked to write out some of their thoughts—but usually they just talk through their ideas.

For example, a researcher may ask different consumers "What do you think about when you decide where to shop for food?" One person may talk about convenience of the location, another about service in the store, and others about the quality of the fresh produce. The real advantage of this approach is *depth*. Each person can be asked follow-up questions so that the researcher really understands what *that* respondent is thinking. For example, if the consumer says "I want good service at a store," the researcher can say "What kind of service do you have in mind?" The customer might be thinking about fast check-out, knowledgeable salespeople available on the floor, courteous check cashing, or something else. The depth of the qualitative approach gets at the details—even if a lot of judgment is involved in summarizing it all.

There is not even a specific question in some types of qualitative research. For example, cartoons with unfilled word-balloons may be used. The cartoon may show a situation—such as a woman and a man buying coffee in a supermarket. The respondent may be asked to fill in the balloon—explaining what the woman is saying to the man. Or the balloon might be removed and the respondent asked to comment on the picture itself. Or the consumer might simply be shown a product—or an ad—and asked to comment.

At one time, marketers tried to use the qualitative questioning approaches of psychoanalysis and personality interviews to better understand consumer motivations. Most companies dropped these approaches because they weren't very successful. Theories that helped explain unusual psychological behavior were just not very appropriate for explaining normal consumer behavior.

Focus groups focus the discussion

Now the most widely used form of qualitative questioning in marketing research is the **focus group interview**—which involves interviewing 6 to 10 people in an informal group setting. It uses the general types of interviewing techniques described above—but the purpose is to get group interaction—to stimulate thinking and get immediate reaction—perhaps expanding an idea and then moving to another. Focus groups are used more with final consumers—but sometimes industrial buyers or middlemen will participate.

A trained focus group leader can get a lot of valuable information from this approach. A typical session may last an hour—so a lot of ground can be covered. This approach can be useful for finding out how consumers think about a product or a market—what interests them, or what they don't like. An example shows a simple application.

A large discount store was losing business. A marketing research firm was hired to find what was wrong. After developing some tentative hypotheses about what might be wrong, the researchers organized a focus group interview with consumers recruited from the store. No matter what topics were raised by the interview leader, the consumers often turned the discussion back to the clutter in the store—and how difficult it was to find anything. The researchers suggested to the store manager that he was ordering too much merchandise for the amount of space. The offended manager argued that the store was not so crowded that it could hurt business. He changed his mind when the researchers showed him a videotape of the focus group. The tape showed one woman humorously acting out the difficulty of getting down an aisle in the store—with much laughter and encouragement from the other consumers.

In this case, everyone reached the same conclusion. But the conclusions reached from watching a focus group session often vary depending on who watches it! This is typical of qualitative research. There is little or no possibility of quantifying the answers—or developing an objective measure of the results. This is an important criticism, because the results seem to depend so heavily on the point of view of the research worker. Even if different viewers arrive at the same conclusion for one group—the results may not apply to a different group.[3]

Some researchers make effective use of qualitative research in preparation for quantitative research. The qualitative research may suggest what questions to ask, how to ask them, and even what possible answers to provide. In other words, strictly qualitative research can provide ideas. But, the ideas may need to be tested in some other way. Other approaches—perhaps based on more representative samples and structured questionnaires—provide more objective measurements which give marketing managers more confidence in taking action. Let's turn our attention to some of these approaches.

Structured questioning gives more objective results

With formal questionnaires, you can ask many people questions in the same way. Because identical questions and response alternatives are used, you can summarize the information quantitatively. Samples can be larger and more representative. Various statistics can be used in drawing conclusions. For these reasons, most survey research is **quantitative research**—which seeks structured responses that can be summarized in numbers—like percentages, averages, or other statistics. For example, a marketing researcher might calculate what percentage of respondents had tried a new product—and even figure an average "score" for how satisfied they were with the experience.

Alternative answers speed answering and analysis

Designers of survey questionnaires usually try to provide fixed responses to questions—to simplify analysis of the replies. This "multiple-choice" approach also makes it easier and faster for respondents to reply to the questions. Simple fill-in-a-number questions are also widely used in quantitative research. For example, a questionnaire might ask an industrial buyer "From approximately how many suppliers do you currently purchase electronic parts?"

Some questionnaires have open-ended questions—and ask respondents to write out their thoughts. But this is less common since open-ended responses on a big survey can be very difficult to summarize. Fixed responses are also more convenient for computer analysis—which is the way most surveys are analyzed now.

Quantitative summaries keep tabs on the market

Some companies routinely survey consumers to keep "tabs" on the market. Quantitative summaries of the results help tell what, when, and where consumers are buying.[4] By keeping up-to-date on what the consumer is doing and thinking, management may be able to spot a trend—or see relationships between responses to different questions.

Keeping up with current activity is especially important for consumer goods—because of the time lag between purchases at the retail level and the restocking of the product by the retailer through the wholesaler and then restocking by the wholesaler from the manufacturer. The time lag may be three to six months. If consumer demand falls off drastically, the manufacturer may be stuck with a large stock of goods produced in anticipation of continued consumer purchases.

Quantitative surveys of attitudes and feelings, too

One common quantitative approach to summarize consumers' opinions and preferences is to have respondents indicate their level of agreement or disagreement with a statement given in a questionnaire. For example, a researcher interested in what different consumers think about frozen pizzas may include a few statements like those at the top of Figure 5–3. The five levels of response—ranging from "strongly agree" to "strongly disagree"—can be tabulated and then the researcher may compute the percent of responses in each category.

Another approach is to have respondents *rate* a product, feature, or store. Figure 5–3 shows that it is common to use rating "scales" to see how important respondents consider some feature—or how satisfied they are. Sometimes rating scales are labeled with adjectives—like excellent, good, fair, poor.

Surveys by mail, phone, or in person

Decisions about what specific questions to ask and how to ask them are usually related to how you will contact respondents—by mail, on the phone, or in person.

■ FIGURE 5–3   Sample questioning methods to measure attitudes and opinions

A. Please check your level of agreement with each of the following statements.

	Strongly agree	Agree	Uncertain	Dis- agree	Strongly disagree
1. In general I prefer frozen pizza to a frozen chicken pot pie	____	____	____	____	____
2. A frozen pizza dinner is more expensive than eating at a fast food restaurant	____	____	____	____	____

B. Please rate how important each of the following is to you in selecting a brand of frozen pizza:

	Not at all important					Very important
1. Price per serving	____	____	____	____	____	____
2. Toppings available	____	____	____	____	____	____
3. Amount of cheese	____	____	____	____	____	____
4. Cooking time	____	____	____	____	____	____

C. Please check the rating which best describes your feelings about the last frozen pizza which you prepared.

	Poor	Fair	Good	Excellent
1. Price per serving	____	____	____	____
2. Toppings available	____	____	____	____
3. Amount of cheese	____	____	____	____
4. Cooking time	____	____	____	____

Mail surveys are the most common and very convenient

The mail questionnaire is useful when extensive questioning is necessary. This is especially true if potential respondents are far apart geographically. With a mail questionnaire, respondents can complete the questions at their convenience. They may be more willing to fill in personal or family characteristics—since a mail questionnaire can be returned anonymously. But the questions must be simple and easy to follow—since there is no interviewer to help.

A big problem with mail questionnaires is that many people don't complete or return them. The **response rate**—the percent of people contacted who complete the questionnaire—is usually around 25 percent in consumer surveys—and it can be even lower. Also, those who respond may not be representative. For example, people who are most interested in the questionnaire topic may respond—but answers from the most interested group may be very different than the typical "don't care" group. Results based on the very interested responders can be very misleading.

Mail surveys are economical per questionnaire—if a large number of people respond. But they may be quite expensive if the response rate is poor. With mail questionnaires, moreover, it is difficult to probe for additional answers—or to encourage respondents to expand on particular points. In spite of these limits, the convenience and economy of mail surveys makes them a popular approach to collecting primary data.

Telephone surveys—if the information is not too personal

Telephone interviews are growing in popularity. They are effective for getting quick answers to simple questions. People will stay on the phone with a good interviewer longer than you might expect—10 to 20 minutes is not unusual. Telephone interviews allow the interviewer to probe—and really understand what the respondent is thinking. On the other hand, the telephone is usually not a very good contact method if you are trying to get confidential personal information—such as details of family income. Respondents are not certain who is calling—or how this personal information might be used.

Research firms—with up to 50 interviewers calling on low-cost, long distance lines at the same time—can complete 1,000 or more interviews in one evening. The popularity of telephone surveys is in part due to this speed—and the high response rates that can be obtained. The high response rates may mean that the results are more representative—but only if the researcher is primarily interested in people who own telephones. In some areas, 10 to 20 percent of the families don't have telephones—and excluding these families may distort the results.[5]

Personal interview surveys—can be in-depth

It is usually possible to keep the respondent's attention longer when the interviewer is right there. The interviewer can also help explain complicated directions—and perhaps get better responses. A personal interview survey is usually much more expensive per interview than a mail or telephone survey—but it offers a chance to investigate certain questions in depth.

Being there also allows the interviewer to follow a different line of questioning—depending on earlier answers. New problems may be uncovered in a personal interview. There is a chance for the interviewer to judge some characteristics—like socio-economic status. The interviewer can follow up people who weren't available earlier—or who don't ordinarily answer mail questionnaires. For these reasons, personal interviews are commonly used for interviewing industrial customers.

Researchers need to be careful that having an interviewer involved doesn't affect answers. Sometimes people won't give an answer they consider embarrassing—or they may try to impress or please the interviewer. For example, when asked what magazines they read, respondents may report a "respectable" magazine like *National Geographic*—even if they don't read it—but fail to report magazines like *Playboy* or *Playgirl*.

Obviously, direct questions can be used in varied situations, but—as you have seen—there are times when questioning has limitations. In these cases—the observation method may be more accurate or economical.

Observing—what you see is what you get

Observing—as a method of collecting data—focuses on a well-defined problem. Here we are not talking about the "casual" observations that may stimulate ideas in the early steps of a research project.

With the observation method, the researcher avoids talking to the subjects. He tries to see what they do naturally—not to influence them at all. For example, a bread manufacturer interested in bread-buying behavior in supermarkets could station an observer near the bread counter. The observer could gather information about the length of deliberation, the choice of a brand, the amount of label reading that takes place, or the extent of multiple purchases.

In some situations, consumers are recorded on videotape. Later, the tape can be analyzed carefully by running the films at very slow speeds—or actually analyzing each frame. This might be useful, for example, in studying product selection in a department store—or studying the routes consumers follow through a grocery store.

Observation data may be analyzed in a number of ways. For example, Taubman Company—a shopping center developer—wondered if one of its shopping centers was attracting customers from all the surrounding areas. Taubman hired a firm to observe and record the license plate numbers of cars in the parking lot. The addresses of all license holders were then obtained—using registration information—and plotted on a map. Very few customers were coming from one large area. The developers aimed direct mail advertising at that area and generated a lot of new business.

Traffic counts provide a simple measure that can tell a shopping center developer how many people go past a location each day.

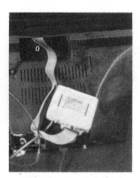

Various observation methods are common in advertising research. For example, a device called an "audimeter" permits adaptation of the observation method to television audience research. This machine is attached to the TV set in the homes of selected families, and records when the set is on and what station is tuned in. This method is used by the A. C. Nielsen Company—and the results are widely used for popularity ratings. It is claimed that once families get used to the meter, their behavior is no longer influenced by its presence. Note, however, that the meter only records if the TV is on and what channel—not whether anyone is viewing it.

Other types of special equipment are used to "observe" a consumer's response to an advertisement. Special cameras can record the flow of a consumer's eyes over a printed ad to be certain that key points—like the brand name—attract attention. And some broadcast ads are tested in movie-theater settings. The audience is "wired" to special meters so that it is possible to tell how much they are stimulated by an ad.[6]

Experimental method controls conditions

A different kind of information can be obtained—with questioning or observing—using the *experimental method*. With the **experimental method**, the responses of groups which are similar—except on the characteristic being tested—are compared. The researcher wants to determine if the investigated characteristic—which varies among groups—*causes* differences in some *response* among the groups. The "response" might be an observed behavior—like the purchase of a product—or the answer to some question—like "How much do you like the taste of our new product?"

The marketing manager of Amboy, Inc., has to decide whether to use the company president, Mr. Amboy, as spokesman in a TV ad. The manager has decided to use the president—rather than a professional actor—*if* consumers who see the ad featuring Mr. Amboy feel more favorable toward the company's product. An experiment is set up in which otherwise similar consumers are shown different commercials. One group will see an ad with Mr. Amboy, and the other group will see an actor. Then the consumers will be asked to indicate their feelings about the company's product. If the group that is shown the ad with the president is—on the average—more favorable toward Amboy's products than the other group, the researcher will conclude that it is *because of* the spokesman in the ad—since other variables were the same.

The experimental method is not used in marketing research as frequently as are surveys and focus groups. Part of the reason for this is that in the "real world" it's difficult to set up controlled situations in which one marketing variable is different—but everything else is the same. But there is probably another reason, too. Many managers don't understand the valuable information that can be gained by controlled comparisons—and they don't like the idea of some researcher "experimenting" with their business.[7]

Research by subscription—shares data collection costs

Some private research firms specialize in supplying data that is regularly collected to aid marketing managers with specific problems. This data may be collected by surveys, observation, or some combination of the two. Often the marketing manager subscribes to the research service—and gets regular updates.

Many different marketing managers have to make the same kinds of decisions—and have the same type of data needs. So, the most economical approach is to have one specialist firm collect the data and distribute it to the different users—who share the cost.

Research by subscription

Two of the better-known organizations in Canada specializing in subscription research are International Surveys Limited (ISL) and A. C. Nielsen Co. ISL studies product movements using data from a consumer panel of over 3,500 households located throughout the country. These households record in diaries their total purchases from all sources and for each item list the day and date of purchase, the type and size of package, the retail price, and the source of purchase. This data is used by many large food and drug manufacturers to measure the rate of consumption of their products at the consumer level.

Subscription reports are also provided by A. C. Nielsen, which audits 750 retail food stores and drug stores to measure movement at the retail level. Nielsen provides additional information about competitors' use of retail displays, two-for-one sales, and other activities. In contrast, ISL furnishes more detailed information on buyer characteristics. For this reason, some large companies subscribe to both services.

Computers help subscribers to ISL, Nielsen, and other syndicated services analyze the substantial amounts of data generated. Nielsen now supplies audit data on computer tape along with the software required for easy retrieval and analysis on both mainframe and microcomputers.[8]

A subscription or participation is also sold in syndicated services that provide reliable data on the audience characteristics of both print and broadcast media. Nielsen and The Bureau of Broadcast Measurement (BBM) both provide station-by-station television audience estimates and program ratings. BBM also reports on the Canadian audience of all its member radio stations throughout the day.

The Print Measurement Bureau provides equally detailed information to its subscribers on both the readers and the readership of over 50 major Canadian magazines. Very specific demographic data is gathered along with information on life style and exposure to other media. Also valuable to marketing managers is PMB's information bank on actual purchase and usage, by type of customer, of 862 different products or services, and 55 other measures of life style including media consumption and psychographics. Having comparable information available on both purchases and readership greatly facilitates print media planning.[9]

Electronic scanning and the more advanced methods of measuring at-home television viewing will almost certainly lead to the development of a new generation of Canadian subscription services. These new services will provide information on both the viewing and the purchasing habits of a sample or panel of consumers with known economic, demographic, and behavioral characteristics. In other words, the service will indicate what kinds of people (and how many) bought different types of products in a given period after having been exposed to TV advertising for those products. It will also reveal what kinds of people bought those small products without seeing any advertising for them and what kinds saw the advertising but didn't buy the advertised brands. The A. C. Nielsen press release shown in Figure 5–4 describes one of the most promising new approaches now being developed in Canada.

Interpretation of Data—Step Four

What does it really mean?

When data has been collected—or purchased—it must be interpreted to decide "what it all means." With quantitative research, this step usually includes the use of statistics to analyze the data. **Statistical packages**—easy-to-use computer programs that analyze data—have opened up many new possibilities. Technical specialists often are involved at this step—and the details are beyond the scope of this book. But a good manager should know at least enough to understand some of the limitations of a research project. It's possible to understand these problems without worrying about *how* the technical people compute the statistics.[10]

Is your sample really representative?

For most marketing research, it is economically and physically impossible to collect all the information you might want about *everyone* in a *population.* Here, **population** means the total group in which you are interested. In a marketing

■ FIGURE 5–4   Nielsen tests single source data collection

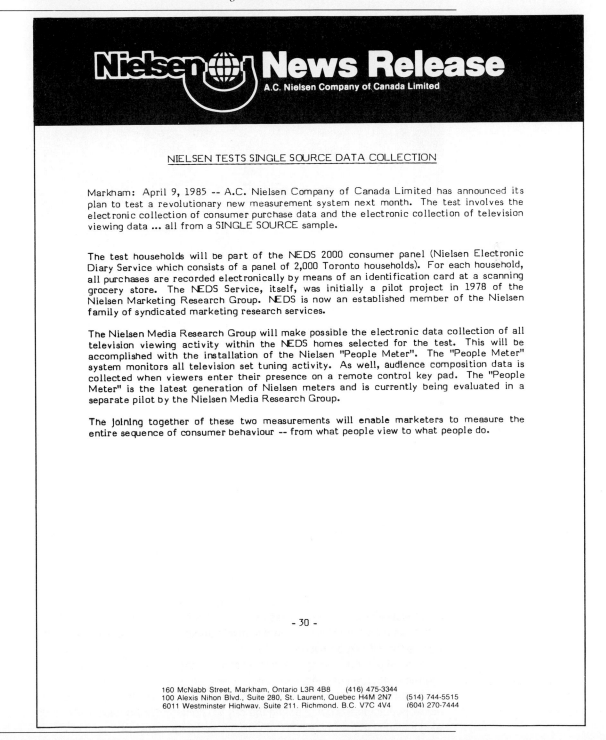

Nielsen ⊕ News Release
A.C. Nielsen Company of Canada Limited

NIELSEN TESTS SINGLE SOURCE DATA COLLECTION

Markham: April 9, 1985 -- A.C. Nielsen Company of Canada Limited has announced its plan to test a revolutionary new measurement system next month. The test involves the electronic collection of consumer purchase data and the electronic collection of television viewing data ... all from a SINGLE SOURCE sample.

The test households will be part of the NEDS 2000 consumer panel (Nielsen Electronic Diary Service which consists of a panel of 2,000 Toronto households). For each household, all purchases are recorded electronically by means of an identification card at a scanning grocery store. The NEDS Service, itself, was initially a pilot project in 1978 of the Nielsen Marketing Research Group. NEDS is now an established member of the Nielsen family of syndicated marketing research services.

The Nielsen Media Research Group will make possible the electronic data collection of all television viewing activity within the NEDS homes selected for the test. This will be accomplished with the installation of the Nielsen "People Meter". The "People Meter" system monitors all television set tuning activity. As well, audience composition data is collected when viewers enter their presence on a remote control key pad. The "People Meter" is the latest generation of Nielsen meters and is currently being evaluated in a separate pilot by the Nielsen Media Research Group.

The joining together of these two measurements will enable marketers to measure the entire sequence of consumer behaviour -- from what people view to what people do.

- 30 -

160 McNabb Street, Markham, Ontario L3R 4B8   (416) 475-3344
100 Alexis Nihon Blvd., Suite 280, St. Laurent, Quebec H4M 2N7   (514) 744-5515
6011 Westminster Highway, Suite 211, Richmond, B.C. V7C 4V4   (604) 270-7444

SPSS/Pro is a microcomputer statistical software program that makes it easy to summarize market research data.

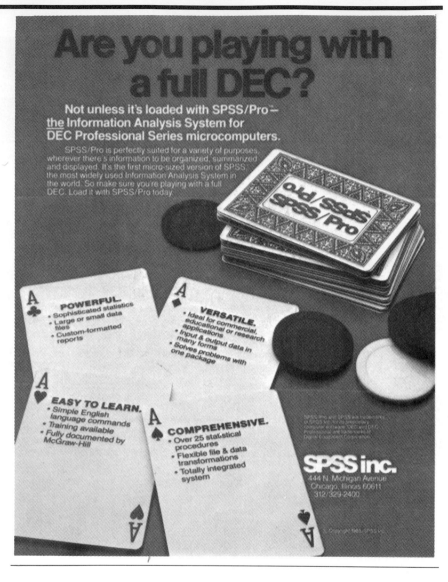

research study, only a **sample**—a part of the relevant population—may be surveyed. How well a sample *represents* the total population affects the results. Results obtained from an unrepresentative sample may be "biased"—and not apply to the whole population.

For example, the manager of a retail store might want a phone survey to determine attitudes of consumers about the store hours. If interviewers made all of the calls during the day, the sample might not be representative. Consumers who work outside the home during the day would not have an equal chance of being included in the survey. People interviewed might say the limited store hours were "satisfactory." Yet to assume from this that *all* consumers are satisfied would be misleading.

Random samples are intentional

You can see that getting a representative sample is very important. The most common method for getting a representative sample is **random sampling**—where each member of the population has the *same* chance of being included in the sample. Great care must be used to ensure that sampling is really random—and not just haphazard.

If a random sample is chosen from a population, it will *tend to* have the same characteristics and be representative of the population. "Tend to" is important because it is *only* a tendency. Random selection alone does not *ensure* a representative sample. A simple example will help you see this.

A marketing manager for a manufacturer wants to find out about the attitudes of his 1,000 customers—the "population." One hundred customers—the sample—are randomly selected for a survey. The survey may include a simple yes or no question: "Were you satisfied with the delivery service you received on your last order?" Of the 100 firms sampled, 20 firms may respond no. The manager can interpret this to mean—based on the 20 out of 100 (20 percent) sample response—that 200 of the 1,000 customers in the population are dissatisfied with delivery service. Because each member of the population had an equal chance of being included in the sample, it is *possible* that all of the dissatisfied customers ended up in the sample. So the random sample may not be representative—and the true percentage of dissatisfied customers may be different than the sample estimate.

Research results are not exact

The point is that the estimate from a sample—even a randomly selected one—usually varies somewhat from the "true value" for the total population. Many managers forget this. They assume that survey results are exact. Instead, when interpreting sample estimates, it is better to think of them as *suggesting* an approximate result.

If random selection is used in developing the sample, then methods are available for stating the likely accuracy of the sample. This is done in terms of **confidence intervals**—the range on either side of an estimate which is likely to contain the "true" value for the whole population. For instance, in our example we might say—based on the 20 percent estimate and a sample of 100—that we are 95 percent "confident" that the percentage of dissatisfied customers is in the confidence interval between 12 and 28 percent.[11]

The accuracy of estimates from a random sample usually increases with a larger sample size. With a larger sample, a few "unusual" responses are less likely to make a big difference. Much marketing research is based on non-random sampling—because of the higher cost and difficulty of obtaining a truly random sample. Sometimes non-random samples give very good results—especially in the industrial area where the total number of customers may be relatively small—and the customers may be fairly similar. But results from non-random samples must be interpreted—and used—with care.

Clearly, the nature of the sample—and how it is selected—makes a big difference in how the results of a study can be interpreted. This should be considered as part of planning data collection—to make sure that the final results can be interpreted with enough confidence so the marketing manager can use them in his planning.

Even if the sampling is carefully planned, it is also important to evaluate the quality of the research data itself.

Validity problems can destroy research

Marketers often take research data at "face value"—assuming that it really measures what it is supposed to measure. Managers and researchers should be cautious about this—because many of the variables that are of interest to marketing managers are hard to measure accurately. We can create a questionnaire that will allow us to assign numbers to consumer responses, but that doesn't assure that the result is precise. For example, a questionnaire might ask "How much did you spend on soft drinks last week?" You might be perfectly willing to cooperate—and be part of a representative sample—but still not be able to remember the correct amount. This problem may be increased when trying to assign numbers to consumer attitudes or opinions.

Validity concerns the extent to which data measures what it is intended to measure. You will understand this idea better by thinking about validity in the context of a score you might get on a test in one of your courses. The instructor might interpret that test score as a measure of what you have learned in the course. If you lost points because the answer to one question was not really covered in the course—or because you made careless errors—or because the question was poorly worded—the grade might not be a *valid* measure of what you learned.

Validity problems are important in marketing research because most respondents are obliging and will give a response—even when they don't think very carefully about their answer or even know what they're talking about. Sometimes a poorly worded question means different things to different people. Although respondents may not care—a manager should see that he only pays for research results which are representative and valid.

Interpretation of data can destroy research

Besides sampling and validity problems, a marketing manager should consider whether the analysis of the data supports the conclusions drawn in the interpretation step. Sometimes the technical people pick the right statistical procedure—their calculations are exact—but they offer a wrong interpretation because they don't understand the management problem. In one survey automobile buyers were asked to rank five cars in order—from most preferred to least preferred. One car was ranked first by slightly more respondents than any other car—so the researcher reported it as the "most liked car." That interpretation, however, ignored the fact that most of the other respondents ranked the car last.

Interpretation problems like this can be subtle, but crucial. Some people draw misleading interpretations intentionally—to suit their own purposes. There is even a book called *How to Lie With Statistics.* A marketing manager must decide whether all of the results support the interpretation—and are relevant to his problem.

Results of a marketing research computer analysis may not be very helpful—unless they are correctly interpreted and carefully communicated.

Marketing manager and researcher should work together

Conducting and interpreting a research project involves some technical details. But it should be obvious that the marketing researcher and the marketing manager must have a close working relationship—to be sure that they really do solve the problems facing the firm. If the whole research process has been a joint effort, then the interpretation step can move quickly into decision making—problem solution.

Problem Solution—Step Five

The last step is solving the problem

In the problem solution step, the results of the research are used in making marketing decisions.

Some researchers—and inexperienced managers—are fascinated by the interesting tidbits of information that may come from the research process. They are satisfied if the research reveals something they didn't know before—or if the pattern of results can be clearly summarized. But if research doesn't have action applications, it may have little value to management—and it suggests poor planning by the researcher.

At the conclusion of the research process, the marketing manager should be able to apply the research findings to marketing strategy planning—the choice of a target market or the mix of the four Ps. If the research doesn't provide relevant information to help guide these decisions, the research money probably was wasted.

We are emphasizing this step because it is the logical conclusion to the whole research process. This final step must be anticipated in every one of the preceding steps. It is the *reason* for these earlier steps.

How Much Research Should Be Done?

**Research is costly—
but reduces risk**

Dependable research can be expensive. A large-scale survey can cost from $20,000 to $100,000—and the continuing research available from companies such as A. C. Nielsen can cost a company from $25,000 to well over $100,000 a year. And a market test for 6 to 12 months may cost $100,000 to $300,000 per test market. But companies willing and able to pay the cost of marketing research may more than recover the cost in benefits. They are more likely to select the right target market and marketing mix—or know about a potential problem before it becomes a costly crisis.

**What is the value of
information?**

The high cost of good research must be balanced against its probable value to management. You never get all the information you would like to have. Very sophisticated surveys or experiments may be "too good" or "too expensive" or "too late"—if all that is needed is a rough sampling of retailer attitudes toward a new pricing plan—*by tomorrow.* Further, no matter how good the research may be, the findings are always out of date—because "past" behavior was studied. It's the decision maker's job to evaluate—beforehand—whether research findings will still be relevant.

Complicating things for Canadian firms is the fact that, relatively speaking, it is far more costly to do marketing research in Canada than in the United States. Canada's population and the Canadian market for almost every product are many times smaller than those of the United States. However, the same number of consumers often have to be surveyed, questionnaires must be as skillfully prepared, and the results just as carefully analyzed. Consequently, it is not surprising to find Canadian research studies costing about as much as American ones. The same dollar figure, however, becomes a much more significant proportion of total Canadian sales. This helps explain why Canadian marketing managers are more reluctant than their American counterparts to carry out a full-scale marketing research program.[12]

Must marketing research be "done over" in Canada when the parent organization has already researched a product or advertising message elsewhere? Many marketers who work for Canadian subsidiaries of multinational firms must routinely answer that question. There are differences of opinion as to how often test market results or other research findings can be "imported"—and when separate studies are necessary. Some foreign-owned firms are active researchers. Other organizations, including some very large ones, do far less research. They assume that U.S. findings will apply to Canada except in unusual cases. This is not always the wisest course of action, but it is a tempting one—since the market is so much smaller but research is just as costly.[13]

Marketing managers must take risks because of incomplete information. That's part of their job—and always will be. They might like more data—but they must weigh the cost of getting it against its likely value. If the risk is not too great, the cost of getting more information may be greater than the potential loss from a poor decision. A decision to expand into a new territory with the present marketing mix, for example, might be made with greater confidence after a $25,000 survey. But just sending a sales rep into the territory for a few weeks to try to sell the potential customers would be a lot cheaper—and, if successful, the answer is in *and* so are some sales.

Faced with many risky decisions, the marketing manager should only seek help from research for problems where the risk can be reduced at a reasonable cost—or where the value of information is likely to be greater than the cost.

Some Firms Are Building Marketing Information Systems

Marketing research is an important source of decision-making information. But some firms don't understand the difference between "one-shot" research to answer specific questions and developing a *continual flow of information* to help marketing managers make better decisions. Marketing managers for some companies make decisions based almost totally on their own judgment—with very little hard data—even though much information is or can be made readily available on an ongoing basis.

It is worthwhile to think about the difference between data that is *available* and data that is *accessible*. In some companies, all kinds of information are available—but no one uses it for a decision. It's not organized in a useful fashion. Therefore, it's not really accessible. Some companies are now facing this problem and organizing for current and future information needs with a marketing information system.

MIS makes available data accessible

Some companies are setting up marketing information systems to improve the quality and quantity of information available—and accessible—to their man-

Once marketing managers learn how a functioning MIS can help their decision making, they are eager for more information.

agers. A **marketing information system (MIS)** is an organized way of continually gathering and analyzing data to get information to help marketing managers make decisions. Sometimes this is handled by the marketing research department. In other companies, this information function is separated into a new department that provides *all* departments in the firm with information.

The need for a marketing information system (MIS) grows out of the recognition that most firms can generate more market-related data than they can possibly digest—and turn into useful information. Computers can now print much faster than anyone can read. Some way must be found to convert raw data into information. Fortunately, you can build up to an MIS in stages. The sales and cost analysis techniques discussed in Chapter 22 illustrate relatively easy kinds of analysis that are possible.

Computer-aided analysis can make the accessible data easier to understand, too. For example, many marketing managers have desktop computer terminals to display requested data—and plot trends or draw simple graphs that summarize complicated and otherwise hard to "see" relationships.

■ FIGURE 5–5   A diagram of a marketing information system showing various inputs and outputs to managers

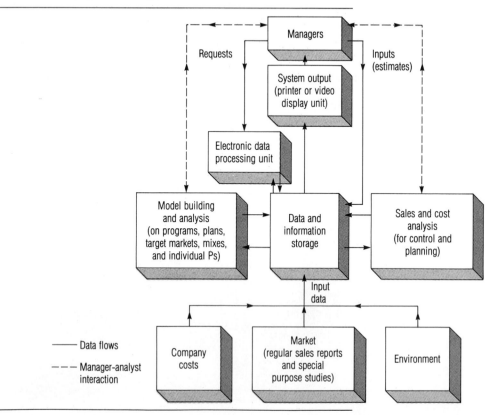

Information may make managers greedy

Once marketing managers see how a functioning MIS can help their decision making, they are eager for more information. They see that they can improve all aspects of their planning—blending individual Ps, combining the four Ps into mixes, and developing and selecting plans. Further, they can monitor the implementation of current plans—comparing results against plans and making necessary changes more quickly. Figure 5–5 shows all the interacting parts in an MIS. As you can see, it really is an information *system* intended to help managers make better decisions—not just to collect and manipulate data.

We are now seeing many more marketing information systems—as managers are becoming more sensitive to the possibilities and computer costs continue to drop. The major obstacle may be the inexperience of marketing managers in asking for information in the most useful form. They are used to doing it the "old way." For example, one sales manager thought he was progressive when he asked the MIS director for a monthly report listing each sales rep's sales—for the previous month and the current month. The MIS director provided the report—but later was surprised to see the sales manager working on the list with a calculator. He was figuring the change in sales and percentage change during the month—and then ranking the names from largest increase in sales to smallest. The computer could easily have done all of that—but the sales manager didn't know how to ask for what he really needed. Marketing managers must be sure that data processing people understand the problems to be solved—and the real information needs.

Many MIS changes are underway—even in small firms. There is still room in marketing for able students willing to apply advanced techniques to solving real marketing problems.[14]

■ CONCLUSION

In this chapter, we have seen that marketing research is not magic worked by statisticians. It is a management tool that helps the marketing manager make better decisions—based not just on feel and intuition, but on objective information. The manager should understand research procedures—and the researcher should understand management's problems of planning, implementing, and controlling marketing strategies. Without this close cooperation, the output of a marketing research department may be useless.

Marketing researchers should apply the scientific method to solve marketing problems. Some objective and organized approach is needed—because very often a researcher does not have the time or money to complete a whole research project. If the early steps of the research effort have

been done effectively, he may be able to "jump" to a solution early in the process. A scientific approach to solving marketing problems involves five steps: definition of the problem, a situation analysis, obtaining data, interpreting data, and solving the problem.

Definition of the problem is obviously the most crucial step—because good research on the wrong problem is useless. Then, a good situation analysis—perhaps using inexpensive secondary data—may help the researcher solve the problem without going on to further steps in the process.

Primary data is then collected—if it is still needed after the situation analysis. Both qualitative and quantitative research may be needed. This step often involves surveys. Surveys can provide helpful information, but often other methods provide better information—at the same or lower cost. Focus groups and observation, for example, may be better when researchers need more ideas about what to study.

Great care must be taken in the interpretation step—to be certain that the research results are properly understood. Marketing managers should not assume results to be more precise than they really are. The interpretation step must be considered when the data collection steps are designed—so there can be enough confidence in the results to take action.

Proper interpretation should lead directly to the problem solution step. Research results should suggest specific action which management might take to solve its problem.

Our strategy planning framework can be helpful in finding the real problem. By focusing on the real problem, the researcher may be able to move quickly to a useful solution—without the cost and risks of a formal research project. If the firm has more time—and an adequate budget—it may be able to enjoy the luxury of more detailed and more sophisticated analysis. And if there is a need for ongoing information, the "answers" may be routinely accessible in a marketing information system.

■ QUESTIONS AND PROBLEMS

1. Marketing research involves expense—sometimes a considerable expense. Why does the text recommend the use of marketing research even though a highly experienced marketing executive is available?

2. Explain the key characteristics of the scientific method and then show why these are important to managers concerned with research.

3. How is the situation analysis different from the data collection step. Can both these steps be done at the same time to obtain answers sooner? Is this wise?

4. Explain how you might use different types of research (focus groups, observation, survey, and experiment) to forecast market reaction to a new kind of margarine which is to receive no promotion other than what the retailer will give it. Further, assume that the new margarine's name will not be associated with other known products. The product will be offered at competitive prices.

5. Distinguish between primary data and secondary data and illustrate your answer.

6. If a firm were interested in estimating the distribution of income in the province of Ontario, how could it proceed? Be specific.

7. If a firm were interested in estimating sand and clay production in Alberta, how could it proceed? Be specific.

8. Go to the library and find (in some government publication) three marketing-oriented "facts" which you did not know existed or were available. Record on one page and show sources.

9. Distinguish between reliability and validity of marketing research measures—and illustrate your answer.

10. Distinguish between qualitative and quantitative approaches to research—and give some of the key advantages and limitations of each approach.

11. Discuss the concept that some information may be too expensive to obtain in relation to its value. Illustrate.

12. Discuss the concept of a marketing information system and how its output might differ from the output of a typical marketing research department.

13. Discuss some of the likely problems facing the marketer in a small firm which has just purchased an inexpensive "personal computer" to help develop a marketing information system.

■ SUGGESTED CASES

6. West City Fitness
8. Last Mountain Ski Resort, Ltd.

20. The Niagara Peninsula Rehabilitation Centre

■ NOTES

1. A. Parasuraman, "Research's Place in the Marketing Budget," *Business Horizons* 26, no. 2 (March/April 1983), pp. 25–29; J. G. Keane, "Some Observations on Marketing Research in Top Management Decision Making," *Journal of Marketing,* October 1969, pp. 10–15; R. J. Small and L. J. Rosenberg, "The Marketing Researcher as a Decision Maker: Myth of Reality?" *Journal of Marketing,* January 1975, pp. 2–7; Danny N. Bellenger, "The Marketing Manager's View of Marketing Research," *Business Horizons,* June 1979, pp. 59–65; and *The Role and Organization of Marketing Research,* Experiences in Marketing Management, No. 20 (New York: National Industrial Conference Board, 1969), 65 pp.

2. For more details on doing marketing research, see *A Basic Bibliography on Marketing Research,* ed. Robert Ferber et al. (Chicago: American Marketing Association, 1972). Good readable discussion is found in Harper W. Boyd, Jr., Ralph Westfall, and Stanley F. Stasch, *Marketing Research: Text and Cases* (Homewood, Ill.: Richard D. Irwin, 1977).

3. For more on focus groups see William Wells, "Group Interviewing," in *Handbook of Marketing Research,* ed. R. Ferber (New York: McGraw-Hill, 1975); and Bobby J. Calder, "Focus Groups and the Nature of Qualitative Marketing Research," *Journal of Marketing Research,* August 1977, pp. 353–64.

4. "Good Listener: At Procter & Gamble Success is Largely Due to Heeding Consumer," *The Wall Street Journal,* April 29, 1980, pp. 1–2.

5. Tyzoon T. Tyebjee, "Telephone Survey Methods: The State of the Art," *Journal of Marketing* 43, no. 3 (Summer 1979), pp. 68–77.

6. For more detail on some of these observational approaches, see "Market Research by Scanner," *Business Week,* May 5, 1980, pp. 113–16; "License Plates Locate Customers," *The Wall Street Journal,* February 5, 1981, p. 23; and Eugene Webb, Donald Campbell, Richard Swartz, and Lee Secrest, *Unobtrusive Measures: Nonreactive Research in the Social Sciences* (Chicago: Rand McNally, 1966).

7. Alan G. Sawyer, Parker M. Worthing, and Paul E. Fendak, "The Role of Laboratory Experiments to Test Marketing Strategies," *Journal of Marketing,* Summer 1979, pp. 60–67.

8. "The A.C. Nielsen Company—Master of the Numbers Game," *Senescan,* January 1984, a magazine published by Seneca College of Applied Arts and Technology.

9. *The Canadian Media Directors Council Media Digest, 1984/1985* (published by Marketing).

10. A number of surveys have been done that reveal which marketing research areas and techniques are most common. See, for example, Dik Warren Twedt, *1978 Survey of Marketing Research* (Chicago: American Marketing Association, 1978); Rohit Deshpande and Gerald Zaltman, "Factors Affecting the Use of Market Research Information: A Path Analysis," *Journal of Marketing Research* 19 (February 1982), pp. 14–31; and Barnett A. Greenberg, Jac L. Goldstucker, and Danny N. Bellenger, "What Techniques Are Used by Marketing Researchers in Business," *Journal of Marketing* 41 (April 1977), pp. 62–68.

11. Detailed treatment of confidence intervals is beyond the scope of this text, but it is covered in most marketing research texts, such as Donald R. Lehmann, *Marketing Research and Analysis* (Homewood, Ill.: Richard D. Irwin, 1979); also see Alan G. Sawyer and J. Paul Peter, "The Significance of Statistical Significance Tests in Marketing Research," *Journal of Marketing Research* 20 (May 1983), pp. 122–33.

12. Winston H. Mahatoo, *Marketing Research in Canada* (Toronto: Thomas Nelson & Sons, 1968), p. 2.

13. W. J. Stanton, M. S. Sommers and J. G. Barnes, *Fundamentals of Marketing,* 2d Canadian ed. (Toronto: McGraw-Ryerson, 1977), pp. 639–41.

14. Richard H. Brien and James E. Stafford, "Marketing Information Systems: A New Dimension for Marketing Research," *Journal of Marketing,* July 1968, p. 21; David B. Montgomery and Charles B. Weinberg, "Toward Strategic Intelligence Systems," *Journal of Marketing,* Fall 1979, pp. 41–52; Donald F. Cox and Robert E. Good, "How to Build a Marketing Information System," *Harvard Business Review* 45, no. 3 (May-June 1967), pp. 145–56; Allen S. King, "Computer Decision Support Systems Must be Credible, Consistent, and Provide Timely Data," *Marketing News,* December 12, 1980, p. 11; Robert Hershey, "Commercial Intelligence on a Shoestring," *Harvard Business Review* 43, no. 3 (Summer 1979), pp. 22–48; and Martin D. J. Buss, "Managing International Information Systems," *Harvard Business Review* 60, no. 5 (September-October 1982), pp. 153–62.

Appendix B ■ Key sources of marketing information in Canada*

*This appendix was originally an abridged version of the article by the same name written by Ronald Rotenberg and Beth Hutton and published in the Spring 1974 issue of *The Canadian Marketer.* However, it was revised and completely updated for *Basic Marketing,* 4th Canadian edition, after a detailed review by Mary Roberts, librarian for business administration and economics, Simon Fraser University Library, Burnaby, British Columbia. The authors wish to express their gratitude to Mrs. Roberts for the professional assistance she so graciously provided.

1. General Sources of Information

A. Newspapers and periodicals

The leading financial newspapers in Canada are the *Globe and Mail Report on Business,* the *Financial Post,* and the *Financial Times of Canada.* The Globe and Mail is now accessible through its own system called InfoGlobe. Information about this may be obtained from a library or by calling InfoGlobe in Toronto. Other important general business journals include the *Business Quarterly, Canada Commerce, Canadian Business, Canadian Business Review,* and *Executive.* Periodicals which focus on marketing include *Marketing* (a weekly newspaper), *Modern Purchasing, Sales and Marketing Management in Canada,* and *Volume Retail Merchandising.* Consumer issues are dealt with in the *Canadian Consumer,* the monthly magazine of the Consumers Association of Canada.

B. Indexing services

A number of useful indexes report on what has been published in Canadian newspapers and magazines. These include the *Canadian News Index,* which covers seven daily newspapers; the *Canadian Periodical Index,* which covers 123 English-language and 13 French-language periodicals; and the *Canadian Business Index,* which covers 163 business periodicals and newspapers; as well as the *Financial Post,* the *Financial Times,* and the *Globe and Mail. Canadian News Index* and *Canadian Business Index* are available online through either the QL or DIALOG systems. Ask at a library for information about accessing these systems, or contact QL in Ottawa or Micromedia/DIALOG in Toronto. The leading French language index is *Point de repere: index analytique d'articles de periodiques quebecois et etrangers.* Montreal, Centrale des bibliotheques, Bibliotheque nationale du Quebec. Bimonthly.

Business Periodicals Index covers about 310 journals, primarily American, in accounting, advertising, banking and finance, insurance, labor and management, marketing and purchasing, taxation, and general business.

Predicasts in Cleveland, Ohio, publishes *Predicasts F&S Index United States* (covering approximately 1,000 newspapers, periodicals, financial and special reports, *Predicasts F&S Index International* (reporting on more than 400 sources in Canada, Latin America, Africa, the Mideast, and Oceania), and *Predicasts F&S Index Europe* (extensive coverage of European newspapers, trade and business magazines, and financial reports. The predicasts indexes are also accessible online, as the PTS databases, through DIALOG and other systems.

Summaries of useful marketing literature are found through spring 1985 in the Marketing Abstracts section of each *Journal of Marketing.* The *Journal of Marketing,* beginning with the Summer 1985 issue, introduced a new section entitled "Marketing literature review." This section reports on a larger number of articles than the former Marketing Abstracts section did; they will be grouped into categories with title, author(s), source, and key descriptors given, but no abstracts. *Market Research Abstracts,* published twice a year by the Market Research Society in Britain, covers 35 journals in the fields of sociology, psychology, and statistics as well as marketing.

C. Trade sources

Numerous trade periodicals serve to keep their readers up-to-date on technical innovations and new product developments. Some devote one issue per year to a listing of products and suppliers as a guide to buyers. *Canadian Advertising Rates and Data* provides a complete listing of such publications. Some specialized trade journals are: *Automotive Marketer, Canadian Vending, Drug Merchandising, Hardware and Housewares Merchandising,* and *Home Goods Retailing.*

The bulletins and newsletters issued by major Canadian banks and investment houses provide information on current financial and economic developments and are often available free of charge.

Business, trade, and professional associations issue bulletins, journals, and other regular publications. They are authoritative sources of information in their particular fields. The *Directory of Associations in Canada,* 5th edition, 1984, published by Micromedia, Toronto, groups associations by subjects as well as listing them by name.

D. Government

For detailed information on the structure of the federal government, see *Organization of the Government of Canada,* 1980, 13th edition, published by the Ministry of Supply and Services. The 13th edition unfortunately is the last published and is now quite out-of-date. A continually updated non-government source of the same information is the loose-leaf *Canadian Government Programs and Services,* published by CCH Canadian, Toronto. The scope of this publication includes addresses, principal officers, historical background, overall responsibilities, statutes administered, programs, and departmental structure. *Assistance to Business in Canada,* ABC 1984, 3d edition, issued by the Federal Business Development Bank, gives information on Federal and Provincial Programs, explains who qualifies, and indicates how to apply.

The official publishing and distributing agency for Parliament and federal government departments is the Department of Supply and Services. Through its "full depository" service, large libraries in major cities in each province provide access to most government publications, including those generated by Statistics Canada. Publication lists may be consulted at these libraries.

Canada's national statistical agency is Statistics Canada (formerly the Dominion Bureau of Statistics); to assist users it maintains regional service offices at which all current publications are available. Consult the latest *Statistics Canada Catalogue* for information about their publications. Statistics Canada has an ever-increasing databank of machine-readable information which may be accessed through universities and colleges or by contacting Statistics Canada offices in larger cities.

The reports of councils and of federal and provincial boards and commissions established to deal with special problems can also be useful. Such undertakings usually involve the collection of a great deal of background data. See, for example, the submissions to the Royal Commission on the Economic Union and Development Prospects, or Macdonald Commission. The commission's preliminary report, "Challenges and Choices," was released in 1984. The *Canada Year Book* lists under "Commissions of Inquiry" all recent commissions, federal and provincial. However, the *Canada Year Book* is no longer a "year" book: it covers two years at a time. The 1982–1983 edition appearing in July 1985 is the most recent edition to date. To find out about current commissions of inquiry, check the following non-government loose-leaf services: *Canadian News Facts* under the heading "Governmental Investigations," *Ottawa Letter* under "Royal Commissions," and *Provincial Pulse* under "Commissions."

2. Guides to Reference Sources and Bibliographies

A. General

Canadian Reference Sources: A Selective Guide, 2d edition, by Dorthy E. Rider, Canadian Library Association, 1981, includes material up to the end of 1980, arranged by subject. *Canadian Books in Print: Subject Index,* 1985 edition, by Marian Butler and published by University of Toronto Press, lists books that are available now and is frequently updated.

The most useful reference is *Canadian Business & Economics: A Guide to Sources of Information,* 2nd edition, edited by Barbara E. Brown, Canadian Library Association, 1984. This contains a general demographic, statistical, and directory section, as well as coverage of specific subject areas such as "Consumers" or "Service Industries," which include marketing. Be aware when using this source that coverage is only up to early 1981.

B. Government publications

Federal

Supply and Services issues a *Weekly Checklist* and a *Quarterly Catalogue of Canadian Government Publications.* A *Monthly Catalogue of Government Publications* and an *Annual Catalogue of Government Publications* were previously published.

Statistics Canada, responsible for the bulk of the federal government's statistical output, reports on its own current publications in *The Daily* and in *Informat Weekly Bulletin.* Its annual *Statistics Canada Catalogue* and *Historical Catalogue of Statistics Canada Publications, 1918–1980* cover the rest of its published output. Statistics Canada has also published a useful *Bibliography of Federal Data Sources Excluding Statistics Canada 1981,* Catalogue number 11-513, to complement its own material.

Additional information

Canadiana, published monthly by the National Library in Ottawa, includes a listing of federal, provincial, and municipal documents. *Microlog* is a monthly paper and microfiche index and document delivery service emanating from Micromedia, Toronto. The monthly indexes cumulate annually—note the broad subject categories on microfiche, e.g., "Business and Economics." Many libraries have the indexed documents on microfiche.

Provincial and municipal

All provinces and the Northwest Territories issue periodic checklists or catalogues of their own publications. *Canadiana* and *Microlog* are other sources to check.

Statistics Canada's *Index to Municipal Data 1982,* Catalogue number 11-515, is the key to statistics for cities and towns.

Canadian Urban Trends (Ottawa: Minister of Supply and Services, 1976–77) and *Urban Indicator: Statistical Profiles on Quality of Life for Canadian Cities,* revised edition (Ottawa: Ministry of State for Urban Affairs, 1978), are two other exceedingly useful source books on Canada's cities.

Urban and Regional References 1945–1972, published by the Canadian Council on Urban and Regional Research in Ottawa, contains references to periodical articles, books, and government publications on urban and regional research in Canada. Many municipal government publications are included. Subsequent annual editions of this material appear as *Canadian Urban Sources (1973–1975), Urban Canada (1976–1978),* and *Microlog Index* (1979 to date).

3. Directories

A. Trade directories

Trade directories supply information on the companies covered, including addresses, names of executives, product range, and brand names of the products. Information on parent companies and/or subsidiaries and agents is often included. There is usually a product listing as well, providing the names of companies involved in a particular field. The major trade directories in Canada include the *Canadian Trade Index, Fraser's Canadian Directory, Scott's Industrial Directories,* and *Canadian Key Business Directory,* a Dun & Bradstreet publication which classifies Canadian firms by U.S. SIC numbers.

Some provincial departments of industry publish directories of products manufactured by local industries. For more information contact the proper department of each province, a listing of which can be found in *Canadian Almanac and Directory or Corpus Directory and Canadian Sourcebook.* There are also a number of specialized product directories such as *Pulp & Paper Canada: Annual and Directory* and the *Canadian Textile Directory.*

B. Financial directories

A number of services provide detailed financial information about companies. This information usually includes names of executives, a summary of the company's history and activities, details on stock issued, and comparative balance sheet figures covering several years.

The Financial Post Corporation Service issues basic and up-dated cards on companies whose securities are listed on Canadian stock exchanges. This data is also accessible by computer. Maclean-Hunter publishes the *Financial Post Survey of Industrials* and the *Financial Post Survey of Mines and Energy Resources,* both of which give concise financial information for a large number of companies.

C. Biographical directories

The *Financial Post Directory of Directors* lists key executives residing in Canada. It also provides a listing of major Canadian companies, giving the names and positions of their executive officers and directors. Other useful biographical information is provided in *Canadian Who's Who,* the *Blue Book of Canadian Business, Who's Who in Canadian Finance,* and *Who's Who in Canadian Business.*

Specialized directories listing members of particular professions are also published. Organizations such as the American Marketing Association provide lists of members' names, titles, and business addresses.

D. Associations and service organizations

The *Directory of Associations in Canada,* 5th edition, 1984, is the best source for this information as it lists associations by subject, e.g., "Marketing," as well as alphabetically by their names. The *Canadian Almanac* and *Corpus Directory* both have large sections of associations arranged by subject and giving address, phone number, and officers' names.

Scientific and Technical Societies of Canada, compiled biennially by the Canadian Institute for Scientific and Technical Information, lists more than 200 societies and provides information on officers, history, membership, and publications.

E. Media

Canadian Advertising Rates and Data contains a geographical listing of daily newspapers and radio and television stations, as well as special subjects listings of periodicals such as "Farm," "Consumer," "Labor," "Foreign Language," and "Business." Detailed information on rates and how advertisements should be submitted is provided. Other advertising media, such as aerial, bench, transit, theater screen, and outdoor advertising, are also listed.

The National List of Advertisers includes all firms which have advertised in Canadian media. It includes details on size of the company, product range, agency employed, approximate budget appropriated to advertising, and media used. There is a cross-index covering brand names and product advertised. A list of advertising agencies with the names of accounts handled is also provided.

Canadian Industry Shows and Exhibitions, published annually in September, provides details on major industrial and trade shows and exhibitions scheduled to take place in the coming year.

F. Government

Canadian Almanac & Directory and *Corpus Directory and Canadian Sourcebook* contain the names and addresses of provincial and municipal, as well as federal, government departments and officials.

Government Directory: National Capital Region gives addresses and telephone numbers of federal government departments and personnel. Regional telephone directories have also been issued by the Government of Canada.

Several provincial governments also issue telephone and organizational directories for their own departments. Some provide lists of municipal officials in that province.

4. Geographical Market and Population Data

A. Governmental

The primary source of demographic data is the census conducted by Statistics Canada for the years ending in 1 and 6. It tabulates information on Canada's population by numbers, geographical distribution, age, sex, mother tongue, marital status, educational attainment, occupation, income level, and housing. Religion was tabulated through the 1981 census but will no longer be included as of the 1986 census.

Some of the data generated by the 1981 census is not in published form; instead it is stored in a databank and available on demand at a modest cost. The amount of printed output will decrease further in future censuses, and custom tabulation will grow. Users with specialized needs should contact the nearest Statistics Canada office.

The following studies on topics of special interest were issued after the 1981 census. Statistics Canada catalogue numbers are given. *Canada's Changing Population Distribution,* 99-931; *The Elderly in Canada,* 99-932; *Canada's Lone-parent Families,* 99-933; *Living Alone,* 99-934; *Language in Canada,* 99-935; *Canada's Immigrants,* 99-936; *Canada's Native People,* 99-937; *Schooling in Canada,* 99-938; *Canada's Young Family Home-owners,* 99-939; *Women in the Work World,* 99-940; *Changes in Income in Canada: 1970–1980,* 99-941; *Urban Growth in Canada,* 99-942.

B. Other Statistics Canada publications

Finding and Using Statistics, 1980, is a general guide to Stats Can publications. *How a Manufacturer Can Profit from Facts,* 1976; *How a Retailer Can Profit from Facts,* 1978; *How Contractors and Builders Can Profit from Facts,* 1979; and *How Communities Can Use Statistics,* 1981 are all booklets which give information both on what statistics are available and on how to track down and use them.

Small area data program

Detailed publications on small area data began in 1984 for each of the 282 Federal Electoral Districts in Canada. A gold mine of information is presented in narrative form and tables. Data are drawn from a variety of sources including the Censuses of Population and Agriculture, and household and business establishment surveys. Sources are indicated at the end of each section.

Women in Canada: A Statistical Report, 89-503, March 1985; *Historical Statistics of New Brunswick,* 11-X-526, December 1984; and *Toronto 150: Portrait of a Changing City,* 11-X0523, April 1984 are just a few examples of special-interest material being produced by Stats Can.

The *Market Research Handbook* contains selected economic indicators and statistics on such topics as merchandising, advertising and media, population characteristics, and personal income expenditures. Data is presented for Canada as a whole and often for regions, provinces, counties, and metropolitan areas. Other occasionally issued Statistics Canada publications dealing with such topics as buying power, leisure activities, and consumption include *Current Demographic Analysis, 1983,* 91-203; *Family Food Expenditures Canada, 1982,* 62-554; *Family Expenditures in Canada, 1982,* 62-555; and *Household Facilities by Income and other Characteristics, 1982,* 13-567.

Perspectives Canada III, a compendium of social statistics, is one of a series which group Statistics Canada figures under headings dealing with such topics as the family, leisure, and consumption. Maps and diagrams are included as well as a useful bibliography.

C. Nongovernmental

The *Financial Post's Canadian Markets,* formerly the *Survey of Markets,* contains marketing facts drawn from Statistics Canada sources and projections based on census figures. Market data is provided annually by province, county, city, town, and census division. Statistics and trends for each major Canadian industry are also presented. *Handbook of Canadian Consumer Markets,* 3d edition, 1984, published biennially by the Conference Board of Canada, is another useful source of data on population, employment, income, expenditures, and prices. (A companion publication is the quarterly *Survey of Consumer Buying Intentions,* which surveys the coming six months.) The *Sales & Marketing Management* July "Survey of Buying Power" issue gives population, effective buying income, and retail sales by provinces and metro areas. All three publications can be used to calculate each area's market potential.

Marketstat 1982, published by Sorecom, Inc., contains information from the 1981 census on over 5,700 Canadian municipalities. Data on such topics as provincial and urban activity in the retail sector, GNP, inflation, and price indexes are also provided. The annual *Woods Gordon Report on Canada's Markets* very effectively employs graphics in its presentations of actual and projected data.

The BBM (Bureau of Broadcast Measurement) is a nonprofit organization which conducts impartial audience measurements of Canadian radio and television. (The A. C. Nielsen organization also provides this type of data.) The Audit Bureau of Circulations and the Canadian Circulations Audit Board provides similar service for the general and business press. The Print Measurement Bureau published *PMB '84: Magazine Readership,* a four-volume survey covering total Canada and English language, Montreal, Toronto, Vancouver, and exposure to other media. Volume 4 is of particular interest as it contains a questionnaire on product use and a set of microfiche giving detailed tabulations by educational levels, sex, age, regions, etc.

A number of newspapers and magazines, including the *Financial Post,* the *Financial Times,* and *Marketing,* publish annual reports on both regional Canadian markets and key Canadian industries. Prevailing conditions and problems of interest at the time are usually stressed.

5. Economic and Business Statistics

A. Summary publications and special studies

The *Canada Year Book* provides summary data on resources, demography, political institutions, social issues, and economic conditions. There is an index to special material published in former editions. Such material can be updated by consulting the latest Statistics Canada Bulletins given as sources at the bottom of each table. As was indicated earlier, that Year Book is now issued every other year, and the data of publication maybe as long as 18 months after the close of the period being covered.

Canadian Statistical Review is issued monthly, with an annual supplement, by Statistics Canada. Its summary of current statistics on population, national accounts, labor, industry, trade, and finance shows the monthly or quarterly figures as well as the annual totals for a period of at least two years. Each issue also contains a special section of seasonally adjusted major economic indicators and one or more feature articles. *Current Economic Indicators,* 13-005, is a monthly report on trends.

The information in *Canadian Statistical Review* is also available from a computerized data bank called CANSIM *(Canadian Socio-Economic Information Management System),* accessible through universities or Statistics Canada. A directory of all series contained in the database and a user's manual for data retrieval are available from Statistics Canada.

Economic reports and projections are published by such organizations as: The Conference Board of Canada, *Quarterly Canadian Forecast, Quarterly Provincial Forecast* and *Survey of Business Attitudes,* The C. D. Howe Research Institute, *Policy Review and Outlook,* Maclean Hunter Research Bureau, *Report on Canada,* Wood Gundy Limited, *Forecast,* The Royal Bank, *Econoscope,* The Economic Council of Canada *Annual Review,* and The Organization for Economic Cooperation and Development, *Economic Surveys: Canada.* The *Financial Times* forecasts every six months, with the first issues of January and June. The *Financial Post* forecasts quarterly. *Canadian Business Service* opens each year with a forecast. Some regional organizations conduct local forecasts; e.g., the Business Council of British Columbia produces the *B.C. Industrial Employment Index,* compiled by Dr. R. A. Holmes of Simon Fraser University.

Newsletters, Bulletins, and annual reports issued by the various Canadian chartered banks contain useful data compiled by their research departments. There are also regional compendiums of statistics such as *Annuaire du Quebec* or *British Columbia Facts and Statistics.*

B. Industry statistics

Governmental

Statistics Canada conducts annual surveys of all Canadian industries asking for data on number and types of employees, wages and salaries, volume of goods produced and value of shipments, imports and exports, inventories, capacity utilization, etc. All these statistics are used to compile the reports listed in the *Statistics Canada* and are accessible through the index at the back of that catalogue by subject (e.g. "Steel industry" or "Drug stores") or by product name (e.g., "Beer").

Nongovernmental

Various trade associations publish statistics on aspects of their particular industry; one example is the Canadian Petroleum Association's *Statistical Handbook.*

In the field of retailing, the Retail Council of Canada Publishes *Financial and Operating Results of Canadian Department Stores* on an annual basis. The data is arranged by store departments, and total store results are tabulated by geographical regions.

Maclean Hunter Research Bureau produces reports on specific industries such as electronics, packaging, or materials handling, and on particular markets, such as Quebec. The PTS online databases produced by Predicasts in Cleveland also give industry or product forecasts from periodicals and other sources.

Chapter 6 ■ Demographic dimensions of the Canadian consumer market*

When you finish this chapter, you should:

1. Know about population and income trends—and how they affect marketers.
2. Understand how population is growing—but at different rates for different age groups.
3. Know about the distribution of income.
4. Know how final consumer spending is related to population, income, family life cycle, and other variables.
5. Know how to estimate likely consumer purchases for broad classes of products.
6. Recognize the important new terms (shown in red).

---

*The Canadian content of this chapter was written for *Basic Marketing, Fourth Canadian Edition,* by Professor Carl Lawrence of Queen's University.

"Markets are people with money to spend to satisfy needs."

Target marketers believe that the *Customer* should be the focus of all business and marketing activity. These marketers hope to develop unique marketing strategies—by finding unsatisfied customers and offering them more attractive marketing mixes. They want to work in less competitive markets with more inelastic demand curves. Finding these attractive opportunities takes real knowledge of what makes potential customers tick. This means finding those market dimensions that make a difference—in terms of population, income, needs, attitudes, and buying behavior.

Three important questions should be answered about any potential market:

1. What are its relevant segmenting dimensions?
2. How big is it?
3. Where is it?

The first question—about relevant dimensions—is basic. Management judgment—perhaps aided by analysis of existing data and new findings from marketing research—is needed to pick the right dimensions.

To help build your judgment regarding buying behavior, this and the following two chapters will discuss what we know about various kinds of customers and their buying behavior. Keep in mind that we aren't trying to make generalizations about "average customers" or how the "mass market" behaves—but rather how *some* people in *some* markets behave. You should expect to find differences.

We will begin with final consumer demographics—because markets consist of *people* with *money* to spend to satisfy needs. The importance of these ideas to marketing managers can be seen in many different types of strategy decisions. For example, firms change their product offerings—by introducing new products or repositioning old ones—as the demographic characteristics of the population change.

Consider the breakfast food manufacturers of Canada. Children under 13 were their prime target and had been for years. But the presweetened cereals aimed at children are now fighting for shelf space with new products targeted at adults. When Total was introduced it was aimed at adults—featuring not sugar, but low calories, and high fiber content. Some of the sugar cereals are now attempting to reposition themselves as also appropriate for adults. Numerous examples from all kinds of businesses illustrate how firms adjust to changes in the population mix. Consider, for example, Johnson & Johnson's baby shampoo—originally designed for babies with the promise of "no tears" but now being sold to adults with a unisex theme—or McDonald's introduction of breakfast for working adults with commercials stressing nutrition.

When a trust company wants to expand to a new city or county there are thousands of possible locations. Which markets would be best to study in detail? With a simple visit to the library you can get information about each county, city, or even a section of a city—information on such things as total population, income, retail sales, number and kinds of manufacturers, retailers, and banks. No doubt you would decide to focus in areas where there appeared to be a real opportunity—a good many people with money—and less competition. So for each county or city, you would divide the total income, the total population, and other statistics by the number of bank outlets and trust company offices. This would help to identify the most promising counties or cities. For example, a location which had a much higher than average total income per branch would seem to deserve more careful study—especially if it were growing in population and income. Retail organizations of all kinds (McDonald's, A&P, Sears, etc.) carry out the same kind of studies when making decisions on where to locate each new outlet.

Get the facts straight—for good marketing decisions

Everybody "knows" that there are lots of retired people in Victoria, that Calgary has many "oil millionaires," that many residents of Quebec speak French, and that the population is growing rapidly in major metropolitan areas. Generalities and stereotypes like these may be partly true—but "partly true" usually is not good enough when it comes to making important marketing strategy decisions. Major investments may be involved. Marketing managers should know the "facts" about the size, location, and characteristics of their target markets.

Fortunately, much useful information is available on the demographic dimensions of the Canadian consumer market. Most of it is free—because it has been collected by government agencies like Statistics Canada. When valid data is available, there is no excuse for decisions based on guesses—or rumors. Try to see the data in the next few chapters in terms of selecting relevant market dimensions—and estimating the potential in different market segments. Also, check your own assumptions against this data. Now is a good time to get your facts straight!

Population—People with Money Make Markets

Present population and its distribution

Table 6–1 shows the population of Canada by province for the years 1971, 1976, 1981, and 1983. The percentage change in each area between 1971 and 1983 is also indicated. The consumer market in 1983 consisted of about 25 million people, with the bulk of that group (61.6 percent) living in Quebec and Ontario. Note also that the provinces of British Columbia and Alberta, with 11.6 and 9.4 percent of the total population respectively, are each larger in population than the four Atlantic provinces combined (9.1 percent).

The relative size of Quebec and Ontario has important marketing implications. These two provinces contain slightly more than three fifths of the country's population. They also account for the majority of consumer income and expenditures, and the lion's share of the industrial market. Consequently, a strong presence in these markets is a must for any national marketing strategy. On the other hand, competition is tough since such markets tend to be attractive to everyone. The marketer also has an added challenge in that these two provinces reflect different linguistic and cultural heritages.

■ TABLE 6–1 Population of Canada by Province 1971, 1976, 1981, 1983 (000)

	1971		1976		1981		1983		Percent change, 1971–1983
	Total	Percent	Total	Percent	Total	Percent	Total	Percent	
Canada	21,568	100.0	22,993	100.0	24,343	100.0	24,890	100.0	15.4
Atlantic Provinces	2,057	9.5	2,182	9.5	2,234	9.2	2,268	9.1	10.3
Newfoundland	522	2.4	558	2.4	568	2.3	578	2.3	10.7
Prince Edward Island	112	0.5	118	0.5	123	0.5	124	0.5	10.7
Nova Scotia.	789	3.7	829	3.6	847	3.5	859	3.5	8.9
New Brunswick.	635	2.9	677	2.9	696	2.9	707	2.8	11.3
Quebec	6,028	28.0	6,234	27.1	6,438	26.5	6,522	26.2	8.2
Ontario.	7,703	35.7	8,265	36.0	8,625	35.4	8,816	35.4	14.5
Manitoba/ Saskatchewan. . . .	1,915	8.9	1,943	8.5	1,994	8.2	2,040	8.2	6.5
Manitoba	988	4.6	1,022	4.4	1,026	4.2	1,047	4.2	6.0
Saskatchewan.	926	4.3	921	4.0	968	4.0	993	4.0	7.2
Alberta.	1,628	7.5	1,838	8.0	2,238	9.2	2,350	9.4	44.4
British Columbia/ Territories.	2,238	10.4	2,532	11.0	2,814	11.6	2,894	11.6	29.3
British Columbia. . . .	2,185	10.1	2,467	10.7	2,745	11.3	2,824	11.4	29.2
Yukon	18	0.1	22	0.1	23	0.1	22	0.1	22.2
Northwest Territories	35	0.2	43	0.2	46	0.2	48	0.2	37.1

Note: Totals may exceed 100 due to rounding.

Sources: Statistics Canada: *Current Demographic Analysis, Report on the Demographic Situation in Canada, 1983*, Cat. 91-209E, October 1984, and *Population Projections for Canada, Provinces and Territories, 1984–2006*, Cat. 91–520, May 1985 (Ottawa: Minister of Supply and Services).

However, the importance of the Atlantic provinces, the Prairies, or the West as regional markets should not be overlooked. Some mass marketers pay little attention to these regions because of their relatively small size. Yet they can provide an opportunity for an alert marketer who is looking for areas with fewer competitors or for the company interested in selling a product of particular interest to a sizable market segment in one of these regions.

Where are the people today and tomorrow?

Population figures for a single year don't show the dynamic aspects of markets. The population of Canada has been growing continuously since the founding of the country, more than doubling in the years between 1945 and 1983. But—and this is important to marketers—the population did *not* double everywhere. Marketers are always looking for markets that are growing fast. They want to know where the more recent growth has been—and where it is likely to be in the future.

Glance again at the changes between 1971 and 1983 as revealed by Table 6–1. The national growth rate of 15.4 percent was exceeded in only two provinces, Alberta (44.4 percent) and British Columbia (29.3 percent). All of the other provinces grew at rates below the national average. Notice too that some of the most populated areas are not the ones that have been growing the fastest. For example, Quebec with its 6.5 million people increased by only 8.2 percent in this 12-year period. Ontario, Canada's most populous province, had the largest absolute increase—some 1.1 million—but a percentage gain very near the national average.

These different rates of growth are especially important to marketers. For example, sudden growth in one area may create a demand for many new shopping centers—while existing centers may be more than adequate in other areas. In fact, the introduction of new marketing facilities in slow-growing areas can create severe competitive problems for existing retailers. In growing areas, however, demand may increase so rapidly that the profits in even poorly planned facilities may be very good.

Table 6–1 presents summary data at the national and provincial level. It gives you the big picture. Keep in mind, however, that much more detailed population data are available. Indeed, detailed census data and updated estimates are available from Statistics Canada for very small geographic areas. Just as we have considered population changes at the provincial level, a local marketer must divide a city or a big metropolitan area into smaller areas to figure out "where the population action is."

Immigration can also affect growth

The level of immigration is also a factor to take into account. Immigration levels fluctuate sharply from year to year, depending on economic and political circumstances both within and outside Canada. Net international immigration had a strong influence on Canada's population growth in the early and mid 1950s. However, in recent years that influence has been declining. Statistics Canada is now predicting a net increase from immigration of between 50,000 and 100,000 people each year.

Immigrants can bring growth and diversification to a community. It is important for marketers to keep track of where the immigrants settle, so that their unique marketing needs can be satisfied.

A Look at the Future

Population will keep growing, but . . .

The world's population is growing rapidly—it is expected to double in the next 30 years—but this is in contrast to the situation in Canada. Our own population growth has slowed dramatically—Canada ranks among the slow-growth population countries in a world where most developing countries are growing quite rapidly. Many Canadian marketers who previously enjoyed rapid and profitable growth in this country are beginning to turn to international markets—to the United States, Europe, and Asia—where in the future population growth will be much larger than in our own country.

This doesn't mean, however, that our population has stopped increasing. Canada's population will continue to grow—at least for another 45 years or even longer. This leaves us with two big questions: how much and how fast? Statistics Canada has released an in-depth study of population growth in Canada which tries to answer these questions.[1] Based on the 1981 census, this report updates earlier projections to account for changes in fertility rates, mortality rates, and migration trends. Let's look at some of these trends—and what they mean to marketing managers.

Total population projections

Starting with the present population and looking at data on regional growth, birth rates, and immigration makes it possible to get an idea of how many people will live where in Canada. Table 6–2 shows expected population increases for Canada to the year 2031, using different projection assumptions. By the turn of the century Canada's population will be between 27.8 million and 30.3 million, a modest growth of some 3 to 5 million from today's 25 million.

Which projection will turn out to be most accurate? What changes in these projections might the next few years bring? This will depend upon the attitudes of Canadians toward marriage, family size, and family planning. These trends should be watched carefully by marketers because of their impact on future mar-

■ **TABLE 6–2**   Population of Canada, selected years 1981 to 2031 (millions)

	1981	1983	1986	1991	1996	2001	2006	2011	2016	2021	2026	2031
Low growth	24.3	24.9	25.6	26.6	27.3	27.8	28.1	28.2	28.2	27.9	27.5	26.8
Medium growth:												
Projection A	24.3	24.9	25.6	26.8	27.8	28.5	29.1	29.5	29.9	30.0	30.0	29.8
Projection B	24.3	24.9	25.6	26.9	28.1	29.2	30.1	30.9	31.6	32.1	32.5	32.7
High growth	24.3	24.9	25.6	27.1	28.7	30.3	31.6	33.0	34.3	35.6	36.9	38.1

Sources: 1971–1983: Statistics Canada, *Postcensal Annual Estimates of Population by Marital Status, Age, Sex and Components of Growth for Canada and the Provinces, June 1, 1982 and 1983,* Vol. 1, Cat. 91-210, annual, 1984; 1984–2031: Detailed tables, Part II.

kets. For the present, however, it is clear that the population will continue to grow although at a much slower rate than was true in the past. When you consider the dip in the birth rate—and think about the declining market for baby products—you can understand why Johnson & Johnson started to promote its well-known "baby" shampoo to *adults* who wanted a gentle product for frequent shampoos.

Fertility rate is declining

Canada's rapid increase in population following World War II ended in the late 1950s. The slowdown in the rate of population growth since that time is due mainly to a drop in fertility levels. The fertility level declined to a low of 1.757 in 1978 from a high of 3.95 in 1959. That level is now down to 1.4 in the major metropolitan areas of Montreal, Ottawa, Toronto, Vancouver, and Quebec—and it seems that the rest of the country will soon follow suit. The greater availability of birth control devices made a lower birth rate possible, rising economic expectation made it necessary, and changing social attitudes toward deferring or forgoing child rearing made it acceptable. The relevant data suggest that more women have opted to remain in the educational system for longer periods of time, and that both young men and young women are delaying first marriages. Also, there are more women in the labor force than ever before. In 1965 only 25 percent of all women over 20 years old were in the labor force—but by 1983 that figure had risen to 53 percent!

Even though the fertility rate has been dropping, both 1982 and 1983 saw a slight increase in the number of live births. This occurred because the baby boom generation is entering the child-bearing years. There are now more women of child-bearing age. However, the number of children per family may still stay low. If so, there may be less need for big "family" homes and large "family size" packages of food—and more demand for small apartments, out-of-home entertainment, travel, and smaller food packages.

A smaller number of children in the family means that parents can spend more money per child. For example, high-priced 10-speed bikes, home video games, and designer clothes for children have all done well in recent years—because parents can indulge one or two children more easily than they could a whole house full.

Average age will rise

An increase in the average age of the population will have a major impact on our society. That increase follows from the fact that the percentage of the population in different age groups is changing. The percentage change—growth or decline—in some key age groups for the period 1983–2001 is given in Figure 6–1.

The major reason for the changing age distribution is the post-World War II baby boom. This large group crowded into the schools in the 1950s and 60s—and then into the job market in the 1970s. In the 1980s, they are swelling the middle-aged group. And early in the 21st century, they will reach retirement—still a dominant group in the total population. According to one population expert, "It's like a goat passing through a boa constrictor."

Some of the effects of this big target market are apparent. For example, recording industry sales exploded—to the beat of rock and roll music and the

■ FIGURE 6–1 Projected changes in size of age groups, 1983–2006 (low-growth scenario)

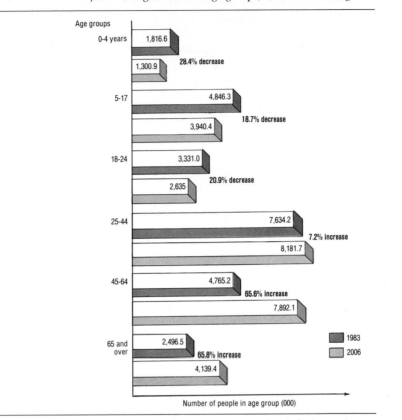

Source: Statistics Canada, *Population Projections for Canada, Provinces and Territories, 1984–2006*, Cat. 91-520 (Ottawa: Minister of Supply and Services, March 1985).

Beatles—as the baby boom group moved into its record-buying teens. Soon after, colleges added facilities and faculty to handle the surge—then had to cope with excess capacity—and loss of revenue—when the student-age population dwindled. Many colleges are adding special courses and programs for adults—in an attempt to attract the now-aging baby boom students and to relieve financial strain. On the other hand, the "fitness" industry is reaping the benefit of a middle-aged bulge in the population.

Medical advances that help people live longer are also adding to the proportion of the population in the senior citizen group. The median age will continue to rise—from 30 years of age in 1983 to 41 years in 2031. The most dramatic change is in the size of the age group over 65. In 1983 this group made up about 10 percent of the total population. As can be seen from Figure 6–1 those over 65 will continue to increase both in numbers and as a percentage of the total population. It is expected that this age group will make up 14.7 percent of the total population in 2006 and about 27 percent in 2031! This trend will have obvious effects on many industries—like tourism and health care.

Older people will want a larger share of the resources

Eventually, Canada's "youth culture" will give way to a new kind of society. In fact, the aging of the population is seriously concerning some planners—because it is possible that younger people will not be able—or willing—to support all of the older people in the style they now expect. Certainly, the costs will continue to rise—as there are relatively more retired people being supported by fewer young people. The cost of Canada's old age pension plan is already attracting the attention of our federal Parliament. However, we saw in 1985 how those over 65 could exercise their political power to prevent the de-indexing of pensions.

Household composition is changing

We often think of the "typical" Canadian household as a married couple with two children living in the suburbs. This never was true—and it is even less true now. Although almost all Canadians marry, they are marrying later, delaying child bearing, and having fewer children. Couples with no children now account for almost 32 percent of all families.

And couples don't stay together as long as they used to. Overall, the divorce rate has risen by 82 percent in the past 10 years, reaching 365 divorces for every 100,000 people by 1982. However, many of those divorced eventually remarry. In 1982 about 20 percent of all marriages were "remarriages"—resulting in a growing number of "his and her" families. So even with all the delayed marriages and the increase in the divorce rate, the majority of adults are married at any one time.

Non-family households are increasing

Once we get rid of the "couple-with-two-children" image of family life, we should also recognize that many households are not families in the usual sense. *Single-adult households* account for about 20 percent of all households—more than 1.6 million people! These households include young adults who leave home when they finish school—as well as divorced and widowed people who live alone.

In Canada's urban areas the percentage of single-person households is even higher—reaching 22 percent of all urban households. There are also several million unmarried people living together—some in groups but most as couples. Some of these arrangements are temporary—as in college towns or in large cities when recent graduates go to the "big city" for their first "real" job. These people need smaller apartments, smaller cars, smaller food packages—and in some cases, less expensive household furnishings because they don't have very much money. Other singles have ample discretionary income—and are attractive markets for "top-of-the-line" stereos, clothing, "status" cars, travel, and nice restaurants and bars.

The number of these non-traditional households is still relatively small. But marketers should probably pay special attention to them—because they are growing at a much higher rate than are traditional family households. This trend will no doubt continue—particularly if the age projections indicated earlier prove true. And such households have different needs and attitudes than does the stereotyped Canadian family. To reach this market, some banks have changed their policies about loans to unmarried couples for homes, cars, and other major purchases—and some insurance companies are now designing coverage oriented toward unmarried couples.

The shift to urban and suburban areas

Migration from rural to urban areas has been the pattern in Canada for the last 100 years. The urban population rose from 19.6 percent in 1871 to 76.1 percent in 1971. It then declined slightly to 75.7 percent in 1981. The past 10 years have been marked by a new trend: a decline in the percentage of the population classed as urban residents. More people are moving to the country from the city than the reverse. But this increase in the rural population does not mean a return to farms—as a matter of fact the number of farms decreased between 1976 and 1981. Rather, what seems to be happening is that more Canadians are settling outside the large Census Metropolitan Areas—preferring instead to live in smaller, average-sized cities. And more people within metropolitan areas are choosing to live in the urban and rural fringe areas of those cities rather than in the urban core. But this trend to exurbia is not being experienced all across the country—the urbanization rate is still rising in the Prairie provinces while declining in all other provinces.[2]

From city to suburbs—and then a trickle back

Not only people—but also industries—have been fleeing the cities. This continuing decentralization of industry has moved many jobs closer to the suburbs. We may be developing an urban economic system which is not as dependent on central cities. A growing population must go somewhere—and the suburbs can combine pleasant neighborhoods with easy transportation to higher-paying jobs nearby or in the city.

Purchase patterns are different in the suburbs. For example, a big city resident may not need—or own—a car. But with no mass transportation, living carless in the suburbs is difficult—and in some areas, it almost seems that a station wagon—to carpool kids, and haul lawn supplies or pets—is a necessity.

Some families, however, have become disenchanted with the suburban dream. They found it to be a nightmare of commuting, yard and house work, rising local taxes, and gossiping neighbors. These people are reversing the trend to suburbia. The movement back to the city is most evident among older—and sometimes wealthier—families. They feel crowded by the expansion of suburbia—and especially by the large number of lower-income families moving in. Their children have left home—or are ready to leave. These older families are creating a market for luxury condominiums and high-rise apartments close to downtown and its shopping, recreation, and office facilities. Some young people are also moving into downtown areas—fixing up old homes that still offer convenience and charm at a reasonable price. They are big buyers in the market for "do-it-yourself" home repair products—like paint, insulation, and flooring. They also spend much of their extra money on the city's cultural events and interesting restaurants.

There is also early evidence of a movement back to the peace and quiet of the truly rural areas—at least by some people who are fed up with the hustle and bustle of the modern life style. This increase in the non-metropolitan growth rate may be the beginning of a national trend to "deconcentration" that would make some target markets harder to reach.

Local political boundaries don't define market areas

These continuing shifts to and from urban and suburban areas mean that recording population by arbitrary city and county boundaries may result in misleading descriptions of markets. Marketers are more interested in the size of homogeneous marketing areas than in the number of people within political boundaries. To meet this need, Statistics Canada has developed a separate population classification, the **Census Metropolitan Area (CMA)**. The CMA is the "main labor market area" of a continuous built-up area having 100,000 or more population. It is a zone in which a significant number of people are able to commute on a daily basis to their work places in the main built-up area.[3]

■ TABLE 6–3   Canada's major metropolitan areas (000)

Atlantic provinces:	1976	1981	1983	Percent change, 1976–1983
Halifax	268.0	277.7	280.7	4.7
St. John's, Newfoundland	145.4	154.8	155.5	7.0
St. John, New Brunswick	113.0	114.0	114.4	1.2
Quebec:				
Chicoutimi-Jonquiere	128.6	135.2	138.	7.3
Montreal	2,802.5	2,828.3	2,862.3	2.1
Ottawa-Hull	693.3	718.0	737.6	6.4
Quebec	542.2	576.0	580.4	7.0
Trois-Rivières	106.0	111.4	113.4	7.0
Ontario:				
Hamilton	529.4	542.1	548.1	3.5
Kitchener	272.2	287.8	294.4	8.2
London	270.4	283.7	287.2	6.2
Oshawa	135.2	154.2	160.0	18.3
St. Catharines–Niagara	301.9	304.4	304.4	0.8
Sudbury	157.0	149.9	148.4	− 5.5
Thunder Bay	119.8	121.4	122.2	2.0
Toronto	2,803.1	2,998.7	3,067.1	9.4
Windsor	247.6	246.1	244.8	− 1.1
Manitoba/Saskatchewan:				
Regina	151.2	164.3	172.7	14.2
Saskatoon	133.8	154.2	162.5	21.4
Winnipeg	578.2	584.8	600.7	3.9
Alberta:				
Calgary	471.4	592.6	620.5	31.6
Edmonton	556.3	656.9	698.6	25.6
British Columbia:				
Vancouver	1,166.3	1,268.1	1,310.6	12.4
Victoria	218.3	233.5	240.4	10.1
Total CMAs	12,911.0	13,658.1	13,965.1	8.2
Total Canada	22,992.6	24,341.7	24,889.8	8.3
Percent CMAs	56.2	56.1	56.1	

Source: Statistics Canada, *Postcensal Annual Estimates of Population Census Division and Census Metropolitan Areas, June 1, 1982 and 1983.* Cat. 91-211, Vol. I (Ottawa: Minister of Supply and Services, February 1985).

In other words, CMAs represent integrated economic and social units with a large population. They are usually known by the name of their largest city. In 1983 there were 24 CMAs in Canada, with a total population of nearly 14 million. This figure amounts to 56 percent of the 1981 Canadian total. Table 6–3 shows the location of Canada's largest urban areas.

As can be seen from Table 6–3, certain of these CMAs make formidable target markets. Montreal and Toronto together account for 5.9 million persons, or 24 percent of Canada's total population. While the CMAs in general grew only slightly less than the Canadian population as a whole, the growth pattern was uneven across the country. In the east, only Oshawa exceeded the national average—with Sudbury and Windsor actually suffering a decline in population. Note especially the high rates of growth experienced by all the major centers in the west except Winnipeg.

Big targets are attractive—but very competitive

Some marketers sell only in these metro areas—because of the large, concentrated population. They know that having so many customers packed into a small area can simplify the marketing effort. Fewer middlemen can be used—while still offering products conveniently. One or two local advertising media—city newspaper or TV station—can reach most residents. If a sales force is needed, it will have less wasted travel time and expense—because people are closer together.

Metro areas are also attractive markets because they offer greater sales potential than large population alone would indicate. Metro consumers have more money to spend because wages tend to be higher in these areas. In addition, professional occupations—with higher salaries—are concentrated in these areas. Densely populated areas offer great opportunities—if the competition is not too strong.

Megalopolis—the continuous city

In 1983, 11 of Canada's 24 CMAs fell within Canada's megalopolis. This is a strip of land running approximately 750 miles from Quebec in the east to Windsor in the west, passing through such cities as Trois Rivieres, Montreal, Ottawa, Oshawa, Kitchener, Toronto, Hamilton, London, and St. Catharines. This strip represents less than 2 percent of the country's total land mass. But in contains about 37 percent of the country's population.

Another concentration of population is developing in British Columbia in the vicinity of Vancouver and Victoria. Also, population corridors are building up between Calgary and Edmonton and between Regina and Saskatoon.

The mobile ones are an attractive market

People move, stay awhile, and then move again. In fact, the 1981 census classed nearly half (47.8 percent) of the Canadian population as movers over the last five years—and about half of that group moved to a new community. Both the long-distance and local mobiles are important market segments.

Often when people move in the same city, it is to "trade-up" to a bigger or better house or neighborhood. Those who move tend to be younger, better educated people who are "on the way up" in their careers. Their income is rising—and they have money to spend. Buying a new house may spark many other purchases, too. The old draperies may look shabby in the new house—and the bigger yard may require a new lawnmower or even a yard service.

Lately we have been seeing a new development—the moving of older or retired persons. Some are moving from suburbia to "downtown" areas in their own city. Others are leaving the larger population centers for smaller towns and cities such as Victoria, British Columbia, and Kingston, Ontario.

Many market-oriented decisions have to be made fairly quickly after moves. People must locate new sources of food, clothing, medical and dental care, and household goods. Once these basic buying decisions are made, they may not change for a long time.

Alert marketers should try to locate these mobile people—and inform them of their marketing mixes.[4] The mobile market gives special opportunities to retail chains, "national" brands, and franchised services that are available in different areas. The customer who moves to a new town may find the familiar A&P grocery store sign down the street—and never even try the local competitor.

Not only are Canadians mobile with respect to their home base, they also like to travel and try new things. Better highways have encouraged more distant vacationing—and ownership of second homes, vacation cabins, travel trailers, and boats. This, in turn, has led to more retail stores, marinas, and recreation areas. Even the growth of suburban areas was encouraged by a willingness to travel farther to work. And growing suburban areas encouraged the growth of outlying shopping centers. With rising energy costs, we may see less growth of this kind—or even a reversal. Such a change could offer new opportunities for alert marketers closer to population centers.

Income—People with Money Make Markets

So far, we have been concerned mainly with the *number* of different types of people—and *where* they are located. It is obvious, however, that people without money are not potential customers. The amount of money they can spend also will affect the type of goods people are likely to buy. For this reason, most marketers study income levels, too.

Changing growth rates

Income comes from producing and selling goods or services in the marketplace. A widely available measure of the output of the whole economy is the **gross national product (GNP)**—the total market value of goods and services produced in a year.

In 1971 Canada's GNP was $94.5 billion. By 1983 it had risen to $390.3 billion. In absolute terms GNP has grown at an annual rate of about 13 percent. Much of the change, however, does not represent "real" growth but rather the effects of inflation. In "constant" 1971 dollars the relevant GNP figures were $94.5 billion for 1971 and $134.4 billion for 1983. This is an increase of about 42 percent over a 12-year period, or an annual rate of growth of about 3 percent. But recently, Canada's growth rate has slowed. GNP actually fell 1.3 percent in real terms between 1981 and 1982 before picking up again in 1983.

Family and household incomes in Canada also increased between 1971 and 1983 but not as much as you might have expected. And the distribution of income hardly changed at all. Let's look more closely at these two developments.

Family income continues to rise

The data in Table 6–4 reveals that in current dollars the average family income in 1971 was $10,368. This figure grew steadily till it reached $34,748 in 1983, representing a growth of some 235 percent over the period or an annual growth rate of slightly over 10 percent. However, note the stark contrast when the same data is presented in real terms (constant 1983 dollars). Over the 12-year period real average family income has increased—but only at a rate of slightly over 1 percent per year. Of particular interest is the fact that real average family income has declined each year since 1980 and was lower in 1983 than it had been in 1979.

On a regional basis, average family incomes in 1983 ranged from a low of $28,511 in the Atlantic provinces to a high of $37,465 in Ontario. Family incomes in Quebec, the Prairie provinces, and British Columbia averaged $31,987, $35,642, and $36,034, respectively. As would be expected, variations in the level of family incomes follow from differences in family characteristics (such as age, sex, occupation, the educational levels of family members) and in the number of wage earners or income recipients in the family.[5]

Distribution of families by income level

Table 6–5 reveals that the percentage distribution of families by income level has also changed. Since this data is in constant 1983 dollars, the effects of inflation have been taken into account. Table 6–5 shows that between 1971 and 1977 the number of families whose real income was below $15,000 declined significantly (from 22.8 percent to 16.6 of all families). Also, the percentage earning over $25,000 increased from 52.5 percent to 65.8 percent of all families. The largest gains took place in the percentage of families earning over $35,000. Note, however, that by 1983 this distribution had altered somewhat. By 1983 a greater percentage of families were earning less than $15,000 than had been the case in 1977, while fewer were earning over $25,000 (62.7 percent versus 65.8

■ TABLE 6–4   Family incomes in Canada, 1971–1983

Year	Unadjusted average	Constant 1983 dollars average
1971	10,368	28,798
1973	12,716	31,312
1975	16,613	33,275
1977	20,101	34,701
1979	24,245	35,206
1980	27,579	36,363
1981	30,440	35,676
1982	32,981	34,886
1983	34,748	34,748

Source: Statistics Canada. *Income Distribution by Size in Canada, 1983.* Cat. 13-207 (Ottawa: Minister of Supply and Services. March 1985).

■ TABLE 6–5   Percentage distribution of families by income levels (selected years in 1983 dollars)

Income class	1971	1977	1983
45,000 and over	13.1	25.6	25.1
35,000–44,999.	14.4	17.9	16.9
30,000–34,999.	11.5	11.3	9.9
25,000–29,999.	13.5	11.0	10.8
20,000–24,999.	13.6	9.6	10.3
15,000–19,999.	11.0	8.1	9.7
10,000–14,999.	9.8	8.4	10.4
Under 10,000.	13.0	8.2	7.0

Source: Statistics Canada, *Income Distribution by Size in Canada, 1983*, Cat. 13-207
(Ottawa: Minister of Supply and Services, March 1985).

percent). As can be seen from the chart, this decline held true for all upper
income classes.

The rising income level of the 1970s was significant in that it broadened markets and drastically changed our marketing system. More families became important customers—with money to spend. Many products which might previously
have been thought of as "luxuries" could now be sold to "mass" markets. In this
way the standard of living improved even more—because large markets can lead
to economies of scale. Are we going to slide backward all through the 80s, or will
family incomes in Canada again rise during the last half of this decade? That is
the question on everyone's lips—politicians in Ottawa and the provinces, business leaders, and concerned citizens.

**The higher-income
groups still receive a
big share**

Although the distribution of families by income level has changed, the higher-
income groups still receive a very large share of total income. This can be seen
in Figure 6–2, which divides all households into five equal size groups—from
lowest income to highest. Note that although the median income of Canadian

■ FIGURE 6–2   Percent of total family income going to different income groups in 1983
(in current dollars)

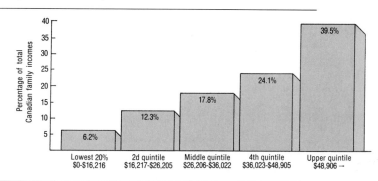

Source: Statistics Canada, *Income Distribution by Size in Canada, 1983*, Cat. 13-207 (Ottawa:
Minister of Supply and Services, March 1985).

families in 1983 was $30,896, the top 20 percent of the households—those with incomes over $48,905 (current dollars) received about 40 percent of all total income. This gave them extra buying power—especially for "luxury" items.

At the lower end of the scale, about 1.5 million families had less than $16,216 income. They also account for 20 percent of the total number of families, but they only receive about 6 percent of total income. Even this low-income group—many of whose members are below the poverty level—is an attractive market for some basic commodities—especially food and clothing. Some marketers target this group—usually with a lower-price marketing mix.

Historically, the distribution of income in Canada has varied very little over the years since 1965. The lowest 20 percent have never received more 6.4 percent of total family income, and the top 20 percent have always received more than 38 percent. Obviously the top two quintiles are attractive markets for high-ticket luxury items.

How much income is enough?

The importance of income distribution cannot be stressed too much. Bad marketing strategy errors have been made by overestimating the amount of income in various target markets. It is all too easy for marketers to fall into such errors because of our natural tendency to associate with others in similar circumstances—and to assume that almost everyone lives the same way.

The 1983 median family income of about $30,000 is a useful reference point. A young working couple together can easily go way over this figure. What's being earned may seem like more than enough in the initial flush of making money—but it is surprising how soon needs and expenses rise and adjust to available income. Before long, it's difficult to see how anyone can live on less.

In fact many Canadian families must make do on much less. Statistics Canada has for many years used "low-income cutoffs" as a measure of well-being and a basis for welfare and other transfer payments. Families required to spend more than 62 percent of their income on basic necessities such as food, shelter, and clothing are said to be in "strained circumstances." The size of the family unit as well as the size of the community in which it lives are also taken into account. For example, a family of four living in a rural area had a low-income or poverty-line cutoff of $12,277 in 1983. For a similar family in a metropolitan area of 500,000, the low-income cutoff figure was $16,885. So, the fact that there *is* an income distribution—and that many households must make do on much less than the median—should not be forgotten in marketing strategy planning.

But who are the poor?

In 1983 17.1 percent of the population was living below the low income cut-off level—up from 16 percent in 1982 and 14.7 percent in 1981. While poverty is widespread, it seems to be particularly prevalent among young families, the elderly, singles, and women. For example, 34.7 percent of all families whose household head was under 24 years of age and one out of every four elderly over 65 have incomes below the low-income cutoff level. This helps explain why the elderly were so vocal in the recent controversy over old age pensions.

Many women also live in poverty. They represent by sex 55.6 percent of all those living below the poverty cut-off line. As for singles classified as poor, 63 percent of them were female, both young and old. Some 43.4 percent of all

■ TABLE 6–6   Personal income, geographical distribution, 1983

Province	Personal income ($ millions)	Percent of total	Personal income per capita ($)
Newfoundland	5,287	1.6	9,179
Prince Edward Island	1,247	0.4	10,056
Nova Scotia	9,354	2.8	10,889
New Brunswick	7,098	2.1	10,040
Quebec.	81,641	24.2	12,531
Ontario	130,333	38.7	14,784
Manitoba.	13,183	3.9	12,603
Saskatchewan	12,585	3.7	12,686
Alberta	34,490	10.2	14,652
British Columbia	40,523	12.0	14,339
Yukon and Northwest Territories	1,014	0.3	14,282
Foreign countries.	229	0.07	
Canada.	336,984		13,541

Source: Statistics Canada, *National Income and Expenditure Accounts, 1969–1983,* Cat. 13-201 (Ottawa: Minister of Supply and Services, November 1984).

families headed by a female was deemed to be poor—as opposed to but 10 percent of those headed by a male.

Income is not equally distributed geographically

Earlier, we stressed that population is concentrated in some areas of the country—and pointed out that consumers in urban areas tend to have higher incomes than their country cousins. Table 6–6 shows how total personal income is distributed in Canada and highlights provincial differences in per capita personal income. Companies often map the income of different areas when picking markets. A market area—a city, county, CMA, or province—that has more income will often be more attractive. For example, a chain of retail dress shops might decide to locate in the suburbs around Toronto or Edmonton because there are a lot of people in these areas with high incomes.

Consumer Spending Patterns Are Related to Population and Income

We have been using the term *family income* because consumer budget studies show that most consumers spend their incomes as part of family or household units. If both adults work—or children work—they usually pool their incomes when planning expenditures. Thus, most of our discussion will be on how households or families spend their income.

Disposable income is what you get to spend

It should be remembered, however, that families do not get to spend all of their income. **Disposable income** is what is left after taxes. Out of this disposable income—together with gifts, pensions, cash savings, or other assets—the family makes its expenditures. Some families don't spend all their disposable income—they save part of it. Therefore, we should distinguish between disposable income and actual expenditures when trying to estimate potential expenditures in target markets.

Discretionary income is elusive

Most households spend a good portion of their income on "necessities"—food, rent or house payments, car and home furnishings payments, insurance, and so on—which are defined in various ways by different researchers and consumers. A family's purchase of "luxuries" comes from **discretionary income**—what is left of disposable income after paying for necessities.

Discretionary income is an elusive concept—because the definition of "necessities" varies from family to family—and over time. A color television set might be purchased out of discretionary income by a lower-income family—while being considered a necessity by a higher-income family. But if many people in a lower-income neighborhood start buying color television sets, then this might become a necessity for the others—and severely reduce the discretionary income available for other purchases.

Measuring discretionary income in a specific situation requires marketing research—but it is clear that the majority of Canadian families *do not* have enough discretionary income to afford the leisure-class life styles seen on TV and in other mass media. On the other hand, some young adults and older people without family responsibilities may have a large share of the discretionary income in a market. They may be especially attractive markets for sellers of stereos, cameras, new cars, foreign travel, and various kinds of recreation—tennis, skiing, plays, concerts, and fine restaurants.

Expenditure data tells how target markets spend

It is common sense that a wealthy family will spend more money than a poor one—and that the money will be spent on different things. But how it is spent—and how that varies for different target markets—is important to marketers.

This question is not a new one. Over a hundred years ago in Germany, a statistician named Engel studied how people spent their income. He looked at basic questions—like what percent of a family's income was spent on clothing, food, or housing as income increased. Followers have rephrased these laws, until now they are stated in three parts:

1. As a family's income increases, the percentage spent on food will decrease.
2. As a family's income increases, the percentage spent on housing and household operations will be roughly constant (with the exception of fuel, light, and refrigeration, which will decrease).
3. As a family's income increases, the percentage spent on all other categories and the amount saved will increase (with the exception of medical care and personal care items, which are fairly constant).

Engel studied working-class families who spent *all* their income. This fits in with our emphasis on analyzing consumer *expenditures*. Note that as a family's income increases, *more money will be spent in total in all categories*. The decreases or increases are in percentage terms.

Summary of family expenditure, by family income, Canada, 10 Provinces, 1982

	All classes		Family income							
	All classes	Under $10,000	$10,000–14,999	$15,000–19,999	$20,000–24,999	$25,000–29,999	$30,000–34,999	$35,000–39,999	$40,000–49,999	$50,000 and over
Percentage distribution										
Food	15.3	24.3	21.0	18.5	17.2	16.3	15.5	14.6	13.9	11.5
Shelter	17.5	29.8	23.8	20.5	18.7	18.3	17.3	16.5	16.0	14.0
Principal accommodation	16.5	29.5	23.2	19.8	18.0	17.4	16.4	15.4	15.0	12.5
Rented	4.8	17.1	10.7	9.5	7.2	5.4	4.5	3.3	2.3	1.4
Owned	8.2	5.6	6.6	6.1	7.1	8.5	8.7	8.9	9.6	8.6
Water, fuel and electricity	3.5	6.8	6.0	4.1	3.8	3.6	3.3	3.2	3.1	2.5
Other accommodation	1.0	.3	.6	.7	.7	.9	.9	1.0	1.0	1.5
Household operation	4.3	6.4	5.7	5.1	4.5	4.4	4.3	4.2	3.9	3.7
Household furnishings and equipment	3.6	3.2	3.8	3.6	3.3	3.6	3.6	3.7	4.0	3.4
Household furnishings	1.8	1.6	1.7	1.8	1.6	1.8	1.7	1.9	2.0	1.8
Household equipment	1.6	1.4	1.8	1.7	1.5	1.7	1.7	1.7	1.7	1.4
Services	.2	.2	.3	.2	.2	.2	.2	.2	.2	.2
Clothing	6.1	5.6	6.1	6.4	5.8	5.9	6.2	6.3	6.4	5.9
Transportation	12.1	9.6	12.4	13.8	14.2	12.8	11.6	13.0	11.7	11.0
Private transportation	10.9	7.6	10.6	12.4	13.1	11.5	10.5	12.0	10.6	9.8
Public transportation	1.2	2.0	1.7	1.3	1.1	1.3	1.1	1.0	1.0	1.2
Health care	1.9	2.4	2.4	2.4	2.2	2.1	1.9	1.8	1.8	1.6
Personal care	1.8	2.5	2.2	2.2	2.0	1.9	1.8	1.8	1.7	1.5
Recreation	4.7	3.1	4.0	4.2	4.3	4.5	4.8	4.4	4.7	5.4
Reading materials and other printed matter	.6	.8	.8	.7	.6	.6	.6	.5	.5	.5
Education	.7	.7	.6	.5	.6	.5	.6	.6	.8	.9
Tobacco products and alcoholic beverages	3.3	4.4	4.3	4.2	3.9	3.8	3.5	3.0	3.1	2.4
Miscellaneous	2.9	2.8	2.7	2.9	3.1	2.9	3.4	3.2	2.9	2.7
Total current consumption	74.8	95.6	89.9	84.9	80.4	77.6	75.3	73.7	71.3	64.5
Personal taxes	17.9	.3	4.5	8.8	12.8	15.5	17.3	19.0	20.6	27.2
Security	4.3	.9	1.9	3.3	4.0	4.4	4.5	4.8	5.0	5.0
Gifts and contributions	3.0	3.3	3.8	3.0	2.8	2.5	2.8	2.5	3.0	3.3
Total expenditure	100.0	100.0	100.0	100.0	100.0	100.0	100.0	100.0	100.0	100.0

Source: Statistics Canada, Family Expenditures in Canada, 1982, Cat. 62-55 (Ottawa: Minister of Supply and Services, October 1984).

Estimating how potential customers spend their money

More detailed family spending data than Engel ever dreamed of having is now available from Statistics Canada. Table 6–7 shows the annual spending by families—for several family income levels—for major categories of expenditures. This data can serve as a reference point—and should keep you from making wild estimates based only on your own experience. The amount spent on major categories—such as food, housing, clothing, transportation, and so on—does vary by income level. And the relationships are logical when you realize that many of the purchases in these categories are "necessities."

Data such as that in Table 6–7 can help you understand how potential target customers spend their money. Let's make this more concrete—with a simple example. You are a marketing manager for a swimming pool manufacturer. You are considering a mail advertisement to consumers in a neighborhood where most families fall in the $35,000 to $40,000 income category. Looking at the appropriate column of Table 6–7, you can see how families in this category spend their money. For example, the table suggests that such families spend about $1,520 a year on recreation of all kinds. If you know that it would cost a family at least $1,200 a year for depreciation and maintenance of a pool, it follows that the average family in this income category would have to make a big shift in its life style in order to purchase a pool.

Data like this will not tell you whether a specific family will buy the pool. But it does supply useful input to help make a sound decision. If more information is needed, perhaps about the strength of the target market's attitudes toward recreation products, then some marketing research may be needed. Perhaps you might want to see a budget study on consumers who already have swimming pools to see how they adjusted their spending patterns—and how they felt before and after the purchase.

Expenditure Patterns Vary with Other Measurable Factors

Income has a direct bearing on spending patterns—but there are other factors that should not be ignored in any careful analysis of potential markets.

Expenditure patterns in Canada vary with the size and type of family. Differences are also noted between renters and home owners. And even among home owners spending patterns are not the same between those with a mortgage and those without a mortgage.

Spending affected by urban-rural location

Consumer spending data shows that the location of a consumer's household does affect the household's spending habits. We will not present detailed tables here—but will summarize a few important differences. Detailed Statistics Canada data should be analyzed to answer specific questions.

Expenditures on transportation, housing, and food do seem to vary by geographic location. Consumers in urban areas spend a lower percentage of their income on transportation and more on housing than those in rural areas—probably because of higher land and construction costs, and greater population density. A rural family spends a larger percentage on food—but lower rural incomes mean that the absolute amount is not very different.

Also, by region of the country

Geographic boundaries are also related to spending. Total expenditures in the Atlantic Provinces are lower than in other regions—but this isn't surprising. You can't spend what you don't have—and incomes in this region are lower than elsewhere in Canada. But the important differences are in the relative shares going for food and housing. Consumers in Newfoundland spend about 21 percent of their incomes on food, as opposed to 13.4 percent for those in Alberta. Shelter accounts for an average of 17.5 percent of total consumer expenditures in all regions. But more is spent on shelter in Prince Edward Island (20 percent), Ontario (17.8 percent), the Prairies (18.1 percent), Alberta (18.8 percent), and British Columbia (19.1 percent).

Stage of family life cycle affects spending

Two other demographic dimensions affect spending patterns—age of the adults and age of any children. For example, families of adults spent more money for both food and clothing than families of the same size that also include children. Put together, these dimensions tell us about the life-cycle stage of a family. See Figure 6–3 for a summary of life cycle and buying behavior.

Young people and families accept new ideas

Singles and young couples seem to be more receptive to new products and brands—but they are careful, price-conscious shoppers. Although the income of these younger people is often lower than that of older groups, they spend a greater proportion of their income on "discretionary" items—because they don't have major financial responsibilities for housing, education, and family rearing.[6] Although many are waiting longer to marry—most young people do "tie the knot" eventually. These younger families—especially those with no children—are still accumulating durable goods, such as automobiles and home furnishings. They need less food. It is only as children begin to arrive and grow that family spending shifts to soft goods and services—such as education, medical, and personal care. This usually happens when the household head reaches the 35–44 age group.

Reallocation for teenagers

Once the children become teenagers, further shifts in expenditures occur. Teenagers eat more, want to wear expensive clothes, and develop recreation and education needs that are hard on the family budget. The parents may be forced to reallocate their expenditures to cover these expenses—by spending less on durable goods, such as appliances, automobiles, household goods, and houses. A family can easily spend $7,000 a year to send a son or daughter away to college.

Many teenagers do earn much or all of their own spending money—and this has made them an attractive market. But marketers who have catered to teenagers are beginning to feel the decline in the birth rate—and probably will face harder times in the near future. Motorcycle manufacturers, for example, have already been hurt—because teenagers are their heaviest buyers.[7]

■ FIGURE 6–3   Stages in the family life cycle and buying behavior

Stage	Characteristics and buying behavior
1. Singles: unmarried people living away from parents	Feel "affluent" and "free." Buy basic household goods. More interested in recreation, cars, vacations, clothes, cosmetics, and personal care items.
2. Divorced or separated	May be financially squeezed to pay for alimony or maintaining two households. Buying may be limited to "necessities"—especially for women who have no job skills.
3. Newly married couples: no children	Both may work and so they feel financially well-off. Buy durables: cars, refrigerators, stoves, basic furniture—and recreation equipment and vacations.
4. Full nest I: youngest child under six	Feel squeezed financially because they are buying homes and household durables—furniture, washers, dryers, and TV. Also buying child-related products—food, medicines, clothes, and toys. Really interested in new products.
5. Full nest II: youngest child over five	Financially are better off as husband earns more and/or wife goes to work as last child goes to school. More spent on food, clothing, education, and recreation for growing children.
6. Full nest III: older couples with dependent children	Financially even better off as husband earns more and more wives work. May replace durables and furniture, and buy cars, boats, dental services, and more expensive recreation and travel. May buy bigger houses.
7. Empty nest: older couples, no children living with them, head still working	Feel financially "well-off." Home ownership at peak, and house may be paid for. May make home improvements or move into apartments. And may travel, entertain, go to school, and make gifts and contributions. Not interested in new products.
8. Sole survivor, still working	Income still good. Likely to sell home and continue with previous life style.
9. Senior citizen I: older married couple, no children living with them, head retired	Big drop in income. May keep home but cut back on most buying as purchases of medical care, drugs, and other health-related items go up.
10. Senior citizen II: sole survivor, not working	Same as senior citizen I, except likely to sell home, and has special need for attention, affection, and security.

Source: Adapted from William D. Wells and George Gubar, "Life Cycle Concept in Marketing Research," *Journal of Marketing Research*, August 1968, p. 267.

Selling to the empty nesters

An important category is the **empty nesters**—people whose children are grown—and who are now able to spend their money in other ways. Usually these people are in the 50–64 age group—but it is an elusive group because some people marry later and are still raising a family at this age. It is the empty nesters who move back into the smaller, more luxurious apartments in the city. They may also be more interested in travel, small sports cars, and other things that they couldn't afford before. Much depends on their income, of course, but this is a high-income period for many workers—especially white-collar workers.

Senior citizens are a big new market

Finally, the **senior citizens**—people over 65—should not be neglected. The number of people over 65 is increasing rapidly—because of modern medicine,

The senior citizen segment is a growing market for vacation travel, health care, and retirement housing.

improved sanitary conditions, and better nutrition. This group is now about 10 percent of the population and growing.

Although older people generally have reduced incomes, many have adequate resources and very different needs. Many firms, in fact, are already catering to the senior citizen market—and more will be entering this market. Gerber (in baby foods)—faced with a declining baby market—started producing products for older people.[8] Some firms have gone into special diet supplements and drug products. Others have designed housing developments to appeal to older people. Senior citizen discounts at drug stores are more than just a courtesy—the elderly are the biggest spenders for medicine.

Ethnic diversity

Language and culture also greatly influence the Canadian marketplace. More than one quarter of Canada's total population comes from a French ethnic background, with its own distinct and separate culture and life style. Those marketing nationally must give full weight and attention to this unique feature of the Canadian marketplace. The French Canadian market will be dealt with more fully in Appendix D following Chapter 7.

But Canada is rich, too, in other cultures. The country has often been called a "mosaic." In contrast to the United States, where it has been the practice for cultural minorities to assimilate as quickly as possible, the Canadian environment has encouraged cultural diversity. Thus there are still many relatively distinct ethnic groups that require special consideration. Canada's ethnic characteristics are discussed in detail in Appendix C, which follows this chapter.

The wide range of ethnic backgrounds has created a whole host of demands for new products and services. Also, the market for such items as Greek food and bagels is not confined to the ethnic group with which the demand originated. Since Canadians of all backgrounds are being exposed to a wide range of cultural influences, their consumption patterns are constantly changing. This factor

This ad is from a magazine sold widely in the United States and illustrates the targeting of Spanish-speaking readers—a fast-growing market.

«Cuando vuelo con Lufthansa no me puedo permitir llegar tarde.»

Comentario auténtico de un pasajero.

Lufthansa

Lufthansa
Lineas Aéreas Alemanas

contributes to the growth of specialized market segments for a wide variety of goods and services. Conversely, other markets also expand as ethnic groups become more fully assimilated within the Canadian scene.

When the wife earns, the family spends

A final factor that deserves attention is the growing number of married women with paying jobs. In 1965 only 25 percent of all wives worked outside the home. Some 59.4 percent of all families in Canada now have more than one wage earner. Also, the percentage of families with more than one earner increases as incomes go up. In the lowest quintile 79 percent of all families had at most one wage earner. In the highest quintile 87.1 percent had more than one wage earner. For the second, third, and fourth quintiles the percentage of families with more than one wage earner was 47.4, 64.9, and 76.5 percent, respectively.

In families where the wife works family spending power is increased. This is why the median family income is as high as it is. But many families feel they need this income to make ends meet.

The data shows that working wives do *spend more* for food—and probably choose more expensive types of food. Families with working wives also spend more on clothing, alcohol and tobacco, home furnishings and equipment, and automobiles. In short, when a wife works, it affects the spending habits of the family. This fact must be considered when analyzing markets and planning marketing strategies.

■ CONCLUSION

We studied population data—getting rid of various misconceptions about how our more than 25 million people are spread over Canada. We learned that the potential of a given market cannot be determined by population figures alone. Income, stage in life cycle, geographic location of people, and other factors are important, too. We talked about some of the ways that these dimensions—and changes in them—affect marketing strategy planning.

We also noted the growth of sprawling metropolitan areas. These urban-suburban systems suggest the shape of future growth in this country. The very high concentration of population—and spending power—in these markets has already made them attractive and easily reached target markets. Competition in these markets, however is often tough.

One of the outstanding characteristics of Canadians is their mobility. This emphasizes the need for paying attention to changes in markets. The high mobility also reminds us that even relatively new data is not foolproof. Available data can only aid judgment—not replace it.

Canadian consumers are among the most affluent in the world. And this affluence affects purchasing behavior. Beyond buying the "necessities" of life, they have "discretionary income"—and are able to buy a wide variety of "luxuries." Even when buying "necessities"—like food and clothing—they have many choices. And they use them.

The kind of data discussed in this chapter can be very useful for estimating the market potential within possible target markets. But, unfortunately, it is not very helpful in explaining specific customer behavior—why people buy *specific* products and *specific* brands. And such detailed forecasts are obviously important to marketing managers. Fortunately, better estimates can come from a fuller understanding of consumer behavior—which is the subject of the next chapter.

■ QUESTIONS AND PROBLEMS

1. Discuss how slower population growth—and especially the smaller number of young people, will affect the businesses in your local community.

2. Discuss the impact of our "aging culture" on marketing strategy planning.

3. Some demographic characteristics are likely to be more important than others in determining market potential. For each of the following characteristics, identify two products for which this characteristic is *most* important: (*a*) size of geographic area, (*b*) population, (*c*) income, (*d*) stage of life cycle.

4. Name three specific examples (specific products or brands—not just product categories) illustrating how demand will differ by geographic location *and* urban-rural location.

5. Explain how the continuing mobility of consumers—as well as the development of big metropolitan areas—should affect marketing strategy planning in the future. Be sure to consider the impact on the four Ps.

6. Explain how the redistribution of income has affected marketing planning thus far—and its likely impact in the future.

7. Explain why the concept of the Census Metropolitan Area was developed. Is it the most useful breakdown for retailers?

8. Does the growing homogeneity of the consumer market mean there will be fewer opportunities to segment markets? Do you feel that all consumers of about equal income will probably spend their incomes similarly—and demand similar products?

■ **SUGGESTED CASES**

28. Multi Foods Limited

16. New Start Furniture

■ **NOTES**

1. Statistics Canada, *Population Projections for Canada, Provinces and Territories, 1984-2006,* Cat. 91-520 (Ottawa: Minister of Supply and Services, May 1985).

2. Statistics Canada, *Urban Growth in Canada,* Cat. 99-942 (Ottawa: Minister of Supply and Services Canada, May 1984).

3. Statistics Canada, *Dictionary of the 1971 Census Terms,* Cat. 12-540 (Ottawa: Information Canada, December 1972).

4. James E. Bell, Jr., "Mobiles—A Possible Segment for Retailer Cultivation," *Journal of Retailing,* Fall 1970, pp. 3–15; and "Mobile Americans: A Moving Target with Sales Potential," *Sales & Marketing Management,* April 7, 1980, p. 40.

5. Statistics Canada, *Income Distribution by Size in Canada 1983,* Cat. 13-207 (Ottawa: Minister of Supply and Services, March 1985).

6. "Young Market Becoming More Conventional," *Advertising Age,* May 16, 1977, p. 84; "On a Fast Track to the Good Life," *Fortune,* April 7, 1980, pp. 74–84; "Demography's Good News for the 80s," *Fortune,* November 5, 1979, pp. 92–106; and "The Upbeat Outlook for Family Incomes," *Fortune,* February 25, 1980, pp. 122–30.

7. "Motorcycles: The Dip Continues," *Business Week,* May 3, 1976, pp. 80–81.

8. "Why Gerber Makes an Inviting Target," *Business Week,* June 27, 1977, pp. 26–27.

Appendix C* ■ Canada's ethnic markets—fact and fancy

*This appendix draws heavily on "Ethnic Markets—A Canadian Perspective," a Simon Fraser University Working Paper by Carl Lawrence, Stanley J. Shapiro, and Shaheen Lalji.

Many religious, social, and cultural institutions have been established to meet the needs of Canada's different ethnic communities. More relevant for marketing purposes are the large number of ethnic publications and a significant amount of ethnic-oriented broadcasting. Now there are advertising agencies and marketing research firms with a distinct ethnic focus. Despite the size of Canada's ethnic communities and the existence of specialized marketing agencies, 1981 Census of Canada data has not previously been analyzed in a way that provides a statistical overview of Canada's ethnic mix. Until recently, any such analysis would have been impossible. Many of the most relevant census reports were not published until the spring of 1984. But now that the necessary raw data is available, we will attempt to fill the existing "ethnic analysis" gap.

Talking about Canada's "ethnic market" makes little or no sense. Rather, Canada is a nation with many different ethnic markets. The demographic importance of each such market depends on whether we choose as the key determinant declared ethnic origin, each individual's reported mother tongue, the language spoken most at home, or place of birth. A careful analysis of the 1981 Census of Canada is only a necessary first step in effective ethnic target marketing. Individual ethnic markets are not, for marketing planning purposes, as large or as important as readily available data suggests. Unless a large number of individuals from the same ethnic background cluster together geographically and share a real sense of ethnic identity, a significant ethnic market does not exist. In this regard, ethnic target segments are no different than any other. To be worth cultivating, the ethnic target market must be clearly distinguishable, large enough to be profitable, and capable of being reached.

We will investigate four major aspects of Canada's ethnic markets in the following analysis. First, we will cover the size of each ethnic community, expressed both in absolute terms and as a percentage of Canada's total population. Next, we will explore the relationship, again on a national basis, between reported ethnic origin, mother tongue, language spoken most often at home, and place of birth. We will also discuss the size of the major ethnic groupings in each of Canada's 24 Census Metropolitan Areas. Finally, in a concluding section we will summarize both what census data reveals and what can only be learned from studies of ethnic consumption patterns.

Ethnic Aggregates—What's Revealed and What's Concealed

Table C–1 shows the size and relative importance of the "British," "French," the "other single origins," and the "multiple ethnic origin" categories as revealed by the 1981 Census of Canada. The fact that the aggregate, non-British–non-French percentage was considerable larger (33.1 percent to 26.7 percent) than the French ethnic origin figure apparently triggered much of the recent interest in "the ethnic market." However, lets take a closer look at the data.

Table C–2 shows that over three quarters of the multiple ethnic origin respondents referred to a British and/or French component in their ethnic background.

■ TABLE C–1   Ethnic aggregates, 1981

	Number	Percent
British	9,674,250	40.2%
French	6,439,100	26.7
Other single origins	6,054,685	25.1
Multiple ethnic origin	1,915,460	8.0
Total population	24,083,495	100

■ TABLE C–2   A closer look at ethnic multiples, 1981

	Number	Percent of total population
British and French	430,260	1.8%
British and other	859,805	3.6
French and other	124,940	0.5
British, French, and other	107,080	0.4
European and other	238,450	1.0
Native People and other	78,080	0.3
Other (reported as single and/or multiple origin)	76,845	0.32

The census does not tell us anything about the relative marketing impact of each ethnic component of those from mixed ethnic ancestry. However, a large proportion of this group may have abandoned ethnic consumption traits in favor of more traditional English or French patterns. For purposes of target marketing, all individuals of multiple ethnic origin cannot be considered as inherently different from those of either English or French ethnic origin and/or as more closely akin to those from "other single origins."

The marketing homogeneity of "the British" can also be questioned. Table C–3 reveals that Canada has over 1.4 million residents of Scotch descent and 1.15 million of Irish origin. If treated separately, the Scotch and the Irish would be

■ TABLE C–3   A closer look at "the British"

Ethnic group	Number	Percent of British total	Percent of total population
English	6,109,235	63.2%	25.4
Scottish	1,415,200	14.6	4.8
Irish	1,151,955	11.9	5.9
Welsh	46,620	0.5	0.2
British not otherwise specified	951,235	9.8	4.0
Total	9,674,245	100%	40.3

Canada's third and fourth largest ethnic groups, exceeded in size by only the English and the French! Should these components of the "British" aggregate be treated as separate and distinct ethnic markets? For example, would their consumption patterns differ from "English" consumption patterns to a greater extent than do those of Canadians of German ethnic origin? Would it be appropriate, for marketing purposes, to combine recent immigrants from England with the descendants of the United Empire Loyalists who, some 200 years ago, moved to Canada from what was to become the United States? Such questions cannot be answered on the basis of available census data.

Table C–4 rank orders Canada's population by ethnic origin. It provides information on all ethnic groupings of more than 40,000 people. Due to the degree of aggregation involved, however, this listing should be used with great caution. Many of the ethnic groups listed in Table C–4 are not nationally or linguistically homogeneous. For example, the Scandinavian aggregate of 282,795 includes 102,735 Canadian residents of Norwegian ethnic origin, 78,360 of Swedish origin, 57,940 of Danish origin, and 22,755 of Icelandic origin. Another 21,005 classified themselves as Scandinavian but gave no further details. A substantial Native Peoples figure (413,380) breaks down into 266,420 status or registered Indians from many different tribes, 47,235 non-status Indians, 76,520 Metis, and 23,200 Inuit. What is collectively presented in Table C–4 as the Indo-Pakistani,

■ TABLE C–4   Population by major ethnic group in rank order

Ethnic group	Number	Percent of total
British	9,674,250	40.2
French	6,439,105	26.7
German	1,142,365	4.7
Italian	747,970	3.1
Ukrainian	529,615	2.2
Native Peoples	413,380	1.7
Dutch	408,240	1.7
Chinese	289,245	1.2
Scandinavian	282,795	1.2
Jewish	264,020	1.1
Polish	254,480	1.1
Indo-Pakistani	196,390	0.8
Portuguese	188,105	0.8
Greek	154,365	0.6
Balkans	129,075	0.5
Hungarians	116,395	0.5
Pacific Islands	80,340	0.3
Czech/Slovak	67,695	0.3
Asian Arab	60,135	0.3
Spanish	53,545	0.2
Finnish	52,320	0.2
Russian	49,430	0.2
African	45,220	0.2
Indo-Chinese	43,725	0.2
Belgian & Luxembourg	43,000	0.2
Japanese	40,995	0.2
Austrian	40,630	0.2

Balkans, Pacific Islands, Asian-Arab, and African ethnic groupings also requires more detailed analysis. Data on the component elements of these aggregations is available from Statistics Canada. However, closer study often reveals that many of the ethnic groupings lumped together are too small or too widely scattered to be appropriate target markets.

Ethnic Analysis—By Mother Tongue, Language Spoken Most at Home, and Place of Birth

Table C–5 provides an aggregate overview of ethnic language relationships. The movement of ethnics linguistically from their mother tongue primarily to English is the most important development highlighted by this table. Just under 40 percent of those either of multiple ethnic origin or of single ethnic origin (other than French or English) indicated that some third language was their mother tongue. Just under 50 percent of that group reported that this "other" mother tongue is also the language most often spoken at home. Finally, of the 1,567,400 individuals who report that a language other than English or French is the one most often spoken at home, approximately half were born outside Canada.

Table C–6 shows the percentage of those belonging to each ethnic group with more than 40,000 members who reported a mother tongue and home language other than French or English and/or a place of birth outside Canada. Canada's various ethnic groups differ greatly along both linguistic and place-of-birth dimensions. A significant proportion of the members of most ethnic groups have a good working knowledge of a language other than English or French. (The relevant "mother tongue" question read "What is the language you first learned in childhood and still understand?") Presumably such individuals understand both

---

■ TABLE C–5   Ethnic language patterns

Of those of single or multiple ethnic origin (8,044,330):

58.6% or 4,672,960 identify *English* as their mother tongue
 2.7% or   214,585 identify *French* as their mother tongue
39.6% or 3,156,785 identify some *other* language as their mother tongue

Of the 3,156,785 who have mother tongues other than English or French:

47.4% or 1,496,145 report *English* as the language spoken most at home
 1.7% or   52,000 report *French* as the language spoken most at home
49.7% or 1,567,400 report the mother tongue to be the language spoken most at home
 1.3% or   41,240 report some other non-official language as the one spoken most at
                    home

Of the 1,567,400 who report the mother tongue to be the language spoken most at home:
49.9% or 782,133 were born outside Canada

■ TABLE C–6   Ethnics by three key measures—percent of ethnic origin

Ethnic group	Number	Percent of total	Ethnic mother tongue	Ethnic home language	Born outside Canada
German	1,142,365	4.7	36.9	11.6	24.6
Italian	747,970	3.1	69.0	47.8	52.5
Ukrainian	529,615	2.2	49.0	16.7	14.5
Native Peoples	413,380	1.7	38.3	28.6	0.29
Dutch	408,240	1.7	40.4	7.8	37.3
Chinese	289,245	1.2	77.8	65.2	74.7
Scandinavian	282,795	1.2	22.0	22.6	21.5
Jewish	264,020	1.1	25.1	9.7	35.5
Polish	254,480	1.1	50.7	22.6	37.5
Indo-Pakistani	196,390	0.8	55.7	44.7	77.1
Portuguese	188,105	0.8	83.2	67.3	75.5
Greek	154,365	0.6	79.4	61.7	60.5
Balkans	129,075	0.5	74.0	45.0	63.0
Hungarians	116,395	0.5	63.3	26.1	51.5
Pacific Islands	80,340	0.3	58.5	39.7	80.9
Czech/Slovak	67,695	0.3	60.2	27.1	51.3
Asian Arab	60,135	0.3	56.5	37.6	63.0
Spanish	53,545	0.2	78.9	59.3	78.5
Finnish	52,320	0.2	61.2	24.3	40.0
Russian	49,430	0.2	55.3	22.9	22.5
African	45,220	0.2	10.9	7.3	62.6
Indo-Chinese	43,725	0.2	83.2	82.9	94.0
Belgian & Luxembourg	43,000	0.2	23.1	5.2	33.6
Japanese	40,995	0.2	46.5	25.8	27.0
Austrian	40,630	0.2	51.3	15.1	41.9

print and broadcast advertising in that same language. This would be true even of the significant percentage of those who indicated that their mother tongue is no longer the language spoken most often at home.

It is not yet clear whether foreign birth or most often speaking a language other than English or French at home is the more important influence on ethnic product and brand choice. In any case, language spoken at home and place of birth are not the only important determinants of ethnic purchasing patterns. The absolute size of an ethnic community, its geographic concentration, the proportion of second- and third-generation Canadians it contains, and the strength of its ethnic institutions will also have an impact on consumption patterns. The extent and nature of each factor's influence remain unresolved mysteries of ethnic marketing.

Ethnic Groupings by CMA

All things considered, data on ethnic population by province is not especially useful to marketers. Urban-based ethnic communities are more likely to satisfy the requirements of effective segmentation. They are clearly distinguishable, accessible or capable of being effectively reached, and, finally, substantial or profitable enough to be worth cultivating. Consequently, the major geographic focus of ethnic marketing attention should be the various Canadian Census Metropolitan Areas (CMAs).

■ **TABLE G–7**   Census and Metropolitan Areas, ethnic groups (number and percent)

CMAs*	Total population	%	British	%	French	%	Dutch	%	German	%	Italian	%
St. John's	152,475	100	142,105	93.2	1,960	1.3	200	0.1	650	0.4	155	0.1
Halifax	275,745	100	194,970	70.7	19,650	7.1	4,345	1.6	9,200	3.3	1,335	0.5
St. John	112,395	100	84,800	75.5	11,960	10.6	825	0.7	1,155	1.0	270	0.2
Chicoutimi-Jonquiere	134,390	100	3,015	2.2	129,010	96.0	10	0.007	260	0.2	75	0.06
Montreal	2,798,040	100	318,920	11.4	1,837,905	65.9	5,265	0.2	22,290	0.8	156,535	5.6
Ottawa-Hull	711,920	100	275,190	38.7	257,315	36.1	6,835	1.0	15,565	2.2	16,210	2.3
Quebec	569,005	100	16,365	2.9	535,680	94.1	270	0.05	1,430	0.3	1,250	0.2
Trois Rivieres	110,500	100	2,575	2.3	105,265	95.3	40	0.04	185	0.2	165	0.2
Hamilton	537,645	100	298,785	55.6	18,185	3.4	16,960	3.2	20,420	3.8	41,335	7.7
Kitchener	285,140	100	132,165	46.4	9,055	3.2	5,470	1.9	55,865	19.6	3,170	1.1
London	280,060	100	180,965	64.6	7,935	2.8	9,780	3.5	11,665	4.2	7,320	2.6
Oshawa	152,690	100	98,645	64.6	6,565	4.3	4,325	2.8	4,225	2.8	4,435	2.9
St. Catharines-Niagara	301,565	100	149,925	49.7	21,960	7.3	9,600	3.2	18,405	6.1	27,620	9.2
Sudbury	148,690	100	47,690	32.1	51,415	34.6	930	0.6	3,290	2.2	8,110	5.5
Thunder Bay	119,720	100	47,425	39.6	6,880	5.8	1,800	1.5	3,290	2.8	9,710	8.1
Toronto	2,975,495	100	1,390,000	46.7	74,795	2.5	34,220	1.2	82,930	2.8	297,205	10.0
Windsor	243,645	100	100,070	41.1	39,385	16.2	2,060	0.9	8,695	3.6	18,960	7.8
Winnipeg	578,625	100	210,070	36.3	44,180	7.6	12,605	2.2	54,170	9.4	8,760	1.5
Regina	162,390	100	64,065	39.5	5,830	3.6	2,125	1.3	29,350	18.1	1,195	0.7
Saskatoon	152,270	100	58,855	38.7	6,520	4.3	3,520	2.3	22,745	14.9	690	4.5
Calgary	587,025	100	287,840	49.0	24,550	4.2	14,150	2.4	48,765	8.3	11,240	1.9
Edmonton	650,895	100	254,055	39.0	38,730	6.0	17,475	2.7	56,520	8.7	10,135	1.6
Vancouver	1,250,610	100	612,140	49.0	36,820	2.9	28,220	2.3	73,960	5.9	30,685	2.5
Victoria	229,495	100	153,475	66.9	6,010	2.6	4,815	2.1	8,580	3.7	1,920	0.8
Total	13,520,430		5,124,110		3,297,560		185,845		553,610		658,485	
CMA population as percent of national	56.1%*		53.0%		51.2%		45.5%		48.5%		88.0%	

CMAs*	Total population	%	Polish	%	Ukrainian	%	Chinese	%	Jewish	%	Portuguese	%	Greek	%
St. John's	152,475	100	80	0.05	40	0.03	360	0.24	180	0.1	—	—	—	—
Halifax	275,745	100	670	0.2	625	0.2	1,000	0.36	1,220	0.4	345	0.13	1,410	0.51
St. John	112,395	100	70	0.06	175	0.2	290	0.26	180	0.2	—	—	250	0.22
Chicoutimi-Jonquiere	134,390	100	45	0.03	25	0.02	—	—	10	0.007	—	—	—	—
Montreal	2,798,040	100	17,095	0.6	13,005	0.5	17,200	0.61	101,365	3.6	23,250	0.83	48,255	1.7
Ottawa-Hull	711,920	100	5,035	0.7	4,700	0.7	8,080	1.13	8,470	1.2	4,990	0.10	2,615	0.31
Quebec	569,005	100	250	0.04	80	0.01	715	0.12	135	0.02	380		255	0.07
Trois Rivieres	110,500	100	35	0.03	15	0.01	—	—	25	0.02	—	—	—	—
Hamilton	537,645	100	12,225	2.3	11,620	2.2	3,405	0.63	4,300	0.8	6,500	1.2	3,435	0.64
Kitchener	285,140	100	5,360	1.9	3,030	1.1	1,710	0.60	1,300	0.5	10,620	8.0	1,855	0.65
London	280,060	100	3,520	1.3	3,105	1.1	1,960	0.70	2,095	0.8	4,160	1.5	2,875	1.0
Oshawa	152,690	100	3,460	2.3	4,270	2.8	650	0.43	490	0.3	3,115	2.0	420	0.28
St. Catharines-Niagara	301,565	100	7,115	2.4	9,395	3.1	980	0.32	1,100	0.4	—	—	980	0.32
Sudbury	148,690	100	1,835	1.2	3,395	2.3	545	0.37	115	0.08	—	—	3,285	2.2
Thunder Bay	119,720	100	3,270	2.7	9,440	7.9	440	0.37	105	0.09	650	0.54	410	0.34
Toronto	2,975,495	100	47,690	1.6	50,705	1.7	89,590	3.0	123,725	4.2	88,885	3.0	65,025	2.2
Windsor	243,645	100	4,255	1.8	5,200	2.1	2,325	0.8	2,025	0.8	405	0.16	1,945	0.8
Winnipeg	578,625	100	18,900	3.3	58,970	10.2	6,195	1.1	15,355	2.7	7,330	3.5	2,190	0.38
Regina	162,390	100	2,985	1.8	9,820	6.0	1,835	1.1	710	0.4	—	—	520	0.32
Saskatoon	152,270	100	2,915	1.9	14,590	9.6	2,410	1.6	540	0.4	385	0.25	310	0.20
Calgary	587,025	100	7,345	1.3	18,045	3.1	15,545	2.6	5,580	1.0	1,610	0.27	2,060	0.35
Edmonton	650,895	100	14,040	2.2	63,125	10.0	16,300	2.5	4,250	0.7	3,955	0.61	1,875	0.29
Vancouver	1,250,610	100	11,495	0.9	29,280	2.3	83,845	6.7	12,865	1.0	7,965	0.64	6,125	0.50
Victoria	229,495	100	1,590	0.7	3,070	1.3	5,285	2.5	655	0.3	1,300	0.57	530	0.23
Total	13,520,430		315,725		315,725		261,205		296,925		163,865		146,715	
CMA population as percent of national	56.1%		67.3%		59.6%		90.3%		%		88.2%		95.0%	

*56.1 percent of the Canadian population lives in these 24 CMAs.

Table C–7 gives the number of those belonging to the 11 largest ethnic groupings (including English and French) who reside in each of Canada's 24 CMAs. The relative importance of each ethnic group in the various metropolitan areas is also indicated along with the percentage of each group's total population who are CMA residents. Note the substantial proportion of the Italian (88.0 percent), Portuguese (88.2 percent), Chinese (90.3 percent), and Greek (95 percent) ethnic groups who reside in CMAs (compared to 56 percent for all Canadians). The Jewish community is also highly urbanized, but the information in Table C–7 is for Jews as a religious rather than an ethnic group. The table also shows a substantial clustering of certain ethnic groups not only in the larger Canadian CMAs but in some smaller ones as well. For example, 27,620 people of Italian ethnic origin resided in St. Catharines–Niagara, where the total population was 301,565. The corresponding Italian population of Vancouver was just a little larger (30,685) even though the Vancouver CMA had a total population four times that of St. Catharines–Niagara.

What if two ethnic communities are approximately the same size but the CMAs in which they are located are not? Will the ethnic market in the smaller CMA be the more economical one to reach? This depends on the geographic clustering (or, alternately, the degree of dispersal) of that particular community in the two CMAs in question. Despite Vancouver's large physical size and substantial population, the Italian community in that city still lives in a fairly restricted geographic areas. Those of Italian ethnic origin residing in St. Catharines–Niagara, on the other hand, might be more evenly dispersed throughout that entire CMA. Data on ethnic origin by smaller geographic reporting unit (enumeration district, census tract, or electoral riding) is not always published by Statistics Canada. However, such information is available to those willing to pay the modest cost of a special statistical run.

Information on the percentage of ethnics with a mother tongue other than French or English who still most often spoke some other language at home and/or who were foreign born is available for every metropolitan ethnic cluster of 10,000 or more people. For example, of the 156,535 residents of Montreal who are of Italian ethnic origin, 130,285 first spoke Italian and still understand that language, 92,495 indicated that Italian is the language they speak most often at home, and 85,905 were born outside of Canada.

There are interesting linguistic and place-of-birth variations between different ethnic groups in the same metropolitan area and, somewhat more surprisingly, between groups with the same ethnic background living in different cities. In the German and Ukrainian communities in Toronto and Montreal, for example, a much higher proportion of residents were born outside Canada and still most often speak their native languages at home than is true of the German and Ukrainian communities in Prairie province CMAs. The marketing significance of such differences, however, cannot be deduced from census data.

■   CONCLUSION: Blending Census Data and Ethnic Consumption Studies

Any sizable ethnic group resident in a given metropolitan area can be considered a market segment potentially worth cultivating. But census data must be supplemented by ethnic-specific studies of consumption habits and practices before we can decide whether any ethnic community is large enough, different enough, and potentially profitable enough to be treated as a target market for a given product or service. The necessary consumption studies should reveal the percentage of each ethnic group's disposable income that is spent on shelter and related expenditures, transportation, clothing, vacations, education, and appliances. Brand loyalty and frequency of purchases data is also necessary. Ethnic consumption studies should provide, in addition, as much information as possible on media exposure (with particular reference to ethnic media) and on the characteristics of the retail outlets currently being frequented by members of that ethnic community.

Careful examination of the 1981 Census of Canada is a necessary first step, but only a first step, for ethnic marketers. Only when the findings of ethnic consumption studies are combined with prior painstaking analysis of census data can marketers develop effective marketing programs targeted at specific ethnic communities.

Chapter 7 ■ Behavioral dimensions of the consumer market

When you finish this chapter, you should:

1. Know about the various "black box" models of buyer behavior.

2. Understand how the intra-personal variables affect an individual's buying behavior.

3. Understand how the inter-personal variables affect an individual's and household's buying behavior.

4. Know how consumers use problem-solving processes.

5. Have some "feel" for how all the behavioral variables and incoming stimuli are handled by a consumer.

6. Recognize the important new terms (shown in red).

"Which car will the customer buy—the Ford Mustang or the Audi Fox?"

How can marketing managers predict which specific products consumers will buy—and in what quantities? Why does a consumer choose a particular product?

Basic data on population, income, and consumer spending patterns in Canadian markets were presented in the last chapter. With this information, it is possible to predict basic *trends* in consumer spending patterns.

Unfortunately, when many firms sell similar products, this demographic analysis isn't much help in predicting which *products* and *brands* will be purchased. Yet whether its products and brands will be chosen—and to what extent—is extremely important to a firm.

To find better answers, we need to understand more about people. For this reason, many marketers have turned to the behavorial sciences for help. In this chapter, we will explore some of the approaches and thinking in psychology, sociology, and the other behavorial disciplines. The following example introduces some of the concepts we'll be discussing.

Pam Bowers was very satisfied with the car she had been driving for six years. But a careless driver ran a stop sign—and Pam's dependable old used car was "totaled." She had to buy another one—but what kind? Pam hadn't paid any attention to car ads—she was amazed by all the styles and features offered.

Pam needed reliable transportation—but she also liked some of the advertised features like air conditioning and electric door locks. She had enjoyed the roominess of her old car—and didn't like the cramped seating in the new compacts. Her husband asked her not to buy a small car. He thought a bigger car would be safer in case there was another accident. On the other hand, Pam didn't want a *really* big car that would be more expensive and harder to drive and park.

Pam went to several car dealers. The salespeople weren't much help—and often couldn't answer even basic questions. So, Pam and her husband studied *Canadian Consumer* and asked opinions of friends—and even relatives in another city. Pam's busy suburban life style was really complicated without a car— so she finally stopped searching and bought one. Even after driving it for awhile, she continued to read the car ads—to be sure she had made the right decision.

Note that Pam's car purchase was *motivated by a need.* Her satisfaction with her old car was a *learning* experience—that shaped her *attitudes* in choosing a new car. *Beliefs* about safety were relevant, too. Both husband and wife influenced the purchase decision. In fact, a *reference group*—people who weren't directly involved—had some effect. Pam used *extended* problem solving. She considered different inputs—including test drives, sales presentations, friends' opinions, and magazine articles. Information that she had *selectively* ignored suddenly was relevant. Even after Pam bought the car, her evaluation continued. She kept looking for new information to reinforce her decision.

In the next few pages, you will see how all these concepts fit together—and why they are important. Our discussion will focus on *final consumers,* but keep in mind that many of these behavioral influences can apply to industrial and other intermediate buyers, too. (We will be talking about them in more detail in the next chapter.)

The Behavioral Sciences Help Understand Buying Process

Buying in a black box

A simplified view of how behavioral scientists think about customer buying behavior is shown in Figure 7–1. Potential customers are exposed to various stimuli—including the marketing mixes of competitors. Somehow, an individual takes in some or all of these stimuli and then, for some reason, responds to the stimuli. We can't see into the mysterious black box—so we can't observe the consumer's decision-making processes. We can only see resulting behavior— such as whether a purchase is made.

This is a simple version of the classical model of buyer behavior. This **stimulus-response model** says that people respond in some predictable way to a stimulus. The model doesn't explain *why* they behave the way they do—only that there is a predictable response to a stimulus.

There are many black box theories

There are many different opinions about how the black box works. These varying theories lead to different predictions about how consumers will react. So

■ FIGURE 7–1 Simplified buyer behavior model

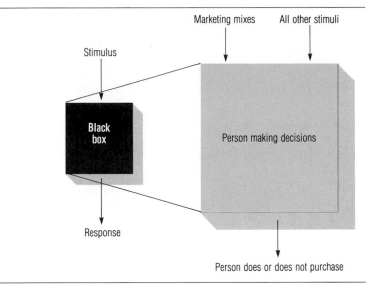

it helps to have some feel for the differences. Let's start with a view that doesn't pay much attention to behavioral dimensions.

Most economists feel that consumers are **economic men**—people who logically compare choices in terms of cost and value received—in order to maximize their satisfaction from spending their time, energy, and money. The economists assume that each consumer knows everything about all possible products—and can see in advance which particular one will be best. The economists' view of the black box for the most part ignores individual and social differences among consumers—and their effect on behavior.

How we will view the black box

The economists' view of consumers is a narrow one—which seems to focus only on cost and value received. But we know that consumers are multi-dimensional—so we will try to combine some of these dimensions into a more complete model of how consumers make decisions.

Figure 7–2 shows how other people influence the black box. Here, we see the individual consumer—shown by a dot in the center of the diagram—surrounded by many social forces. Each individual is influenced by family, social class, other reference groups—and the whole culture. These inter-personal variables, however, are not the whole story.

A more detailed view of the black box is shown in Figure 7–3. Here we see both intra-personal and inter-personal variables affecting the person making decisions. Both sets of variables affect how a person sees and processes incoming stimuli. Let's look at these topics next.

■ FIGURE 7–2 The individual decision maker (shown as a dot) nestled in an environment

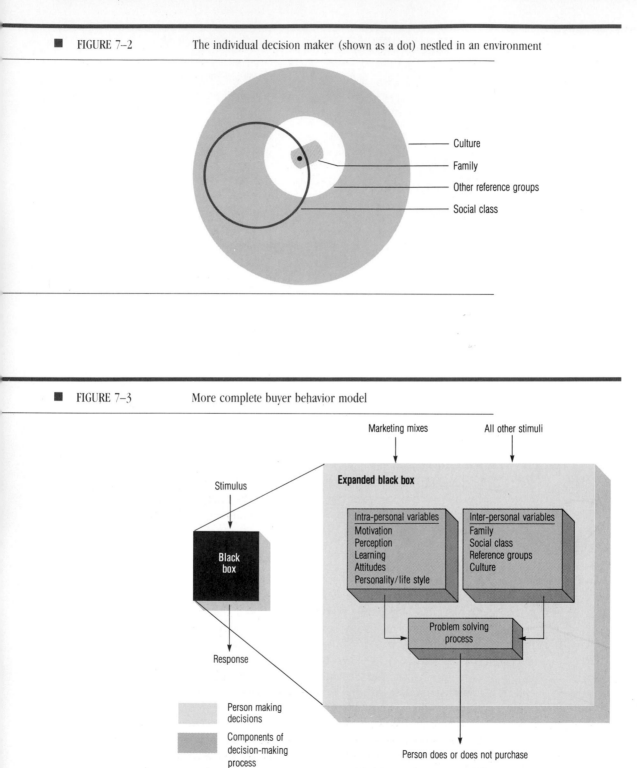

- Culture
- Family
- Other reference groups
- Social class

■ FIGURE 7–3 More complete buyer behavior model

Marketing mixes   All other stimuli

Expanded black box

Stimulus

Black box

Response

Intra-personal variables
Motivation
Perception
Learning
Attitudes
Personality/life style

Inter-personal variables
Family
Social class
Reference groups
Culture

Problem solving process

Person making decisions

Components of decision-making process

Person does or does not purchase

Intra-Personal Variables Focus on the Individual

Here we will discuss some variables of special interest to marketers—including motivation, perception, learning, attitudes, and life style. Much of what we know about these intra-personal variables draws from ideas originally developed in the field of psychology.

Motivation determines what consumers want

Everybody is motivated by needs and wants. Needs are the basic forces which motivate an individual to do something. Some needs are concerned with a person's physical well-being—the need for food or shelter. Other needs are psychological—concerned with the individual's self-view and relationship with others. Needs are more basic than *wants*. Wants are "needs" which are learned during an individual's life. For example, everyone needs food, but some people also have learned to want a "Big Mac."

When a need has not been satisfied, it may lead to a drive. The food need, for example, leads to a hunger drive. A drive is a strong stimulus that encourages action—to reduce a need. Drives are internal—they are the reasons behind certain behavior patterns. In marketing, a product purchase is the result of a drive to satisfy some need.   *also + desires*

A marketing mix can't create a drive—but it can satisfy a need

Marketing managers can't create internal drives in consumers. Some critics imply that they do—that marketers can somehow manipulate consumers to buy products against their will. Most marketing managers realize that trying to get consumers to act against their will isn't a very fruitful activity. Instead, a good marketing manager studies what consumer drives and needs already exist—and how they can be satisfied better.

We all are a bundle of needs and wants. Figure 7–4 presents a list of some important consumer needs. These are people-related needs. They can also be thought of as *benefits* which consumers might seek from a marketing mix. This list should *not* be thought of as complete. Some marketers work with long lists like this to help locate what specific needs relate to a marketing mix. But working with such lists can be frustrating. It's easy to ignore a need (or benefit sought) which may turn out to be key to understanding some consumer's behavior.

When a marketing manager has defined a product-market, then the benefits sought may become quite specific. For example, the food need might be as specific as wanting a pizza. You can see that consumers' needs must be studied when developing a marketing strategy. Then the marketer can try to match what consumers want and what the firm can offer in its marketing mix.

Are there hierarchies of needs?

Some psychologists feel that a person may have several reasons for buying—at the same time. They think that people try to develop a balance among the forces driving them. Some even see a hierarchy of needs. Maslow is well known for his five-level hierarchy. But we will discuss a similar four-level hierarchy which is easier to apply—and is supported by more recent research on human motivation.[1] The four levels are illustrated in Figure 7–5. The lowest-level needs are

■ FIGURE 7–4   Possible needs motivating a person to some action

Physiological needs

Food	Warmth	Activity
Drink	Coolness	Rest
Sex—tension release	Body elimination	Self-preservation
Sleep		

Psychological needs

Abasement	Deference	Order
Acquisition	Distinctive	Personal fulfillment
Affiliation	Discriminating	Playing—competitive
Aggression	Discriminatory	Playing—relaxing
Beauty	Dominance	Power
Belonging	Emulation	Pride
Being constructive	Exhibition	Security
Being part of a group	Family preservation	Self-expression
Being responsible	Imitation	Self-identification
Being well thought of	Independence	Symmetry
Companionship	Individualism	Tenderness
Conserving	Love	Striving
Curiosity	Nurturing	Understanding (knowledge)
Discovery		

Desire for:

Acceptance	Prestige
Achievement	Recognition
Affection	Respect
Affiliation	Retaliation
Appreciation	Satisfaction with self
Comfort	Security
Contrariness	Self-confidence
Dependence	Sensuous experiences
Distance—"space"	Sexual satisfaction
Distinctiveness	Sociability
Fame	Status
Happiness	Sympathy
Identification	

Freedom from:

Anxiety	Imitation
Depression	Loss of prestige
Discomfort	Pain
Fear	Pressure
Harm—Psychological	Ridicule
Harm—Physical	Sadness

Source: Adapted from C. Glenn Walters, *Consumer Behavior*, 3d ed. (Homewood, Ill.: Richard D. Irwin, 1979); R. M. Liebert and M. D. Spiegler, *Personality*, 3d ed., (Homewood, Ill.: Dorsey Press, 1978); and others. © 1979 by Richard D. Irwin, Inc. and © 1978 by The Dorsey Press.

physiological. Then come safety, social, and personal needs. As a study aid, think of the "PSSP needs."

The physiological needs are concerned with biological needs—food, drink, rest, and sex. The safety needs are concerned with protection and physical well-being (perhaps involving health, food, medicine, and exercise). The

■ FIGURE 7–5   The PSSP hierarchy of needs

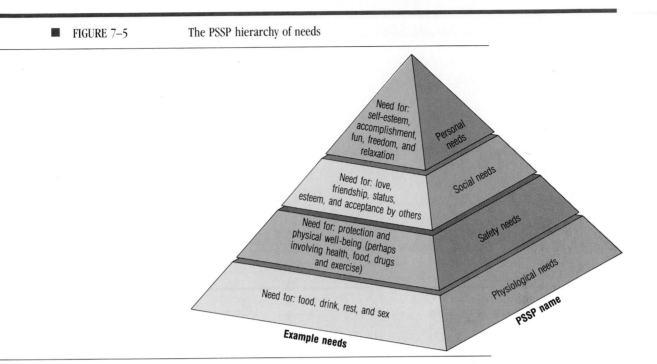

social needs are concerned with love, friendship, status, and esteem—all things that involve a person's interaction with others. The personal needs, on the other hand, are concerned with the need of an individual to achieve personal satisfaction—unrelated to what others think or do. Examples here include self-esteem, accomplishment, fun, freedom, and relaxation.

Motivation theory suggests that we never reach a state of complete satisfaction. As soon as lower-level needs are reasonably satisfied, those at higher levels become more dominant. It is important to see, however, that a particular good or service may satisfy more than one need at the same time. A hamburger in a friendly environment, for example, might satisfy not only the physiological need to satisfy hunger—but also some social need. In fact, it seems necessary to think of individuals as need-satisfying mechanisms who try to fill a *set* of needs—rather than just one need or another in sequence. You should also be aware that: (1) a higher-level need may develop before lower needs are satisfied, and (2) the order in which needs are satisfied can vary from one group to another.

Higher-level needs may be important for "commodities"

While the four basic needs can help us understand some buying behavior, other market situations may involve such basic "commodities" that neither producers nor consumers give much thought to what needs are being satisfied—resulting in undifferentiated marketing mixes. But a creative marketer may see that *several* basic needs are involved—and be able to segment the market. Or if this isn't possible, he may be able to appeal to the higher-level needs to differen-

These jewelry-like pens satisfy a functional need for writing—but also higher-level needs.

From Sheaffer in 23-karat gold electroplate: fountain pen, ballpoint, pencil, and our Dual Writing System with interchangeable micro tip marker and rolling ball—engraved in straight lines, barleycorn, geometric, or diamond square. Golden gift ideas, all.

SHEAFFER.
JEWELRY FOR WRITING

tiate his marketing mix. Gasoline illustrates this idea. Gasoline might help one consumer get food to satisfy a hunger (physiological) need—by driving safely to a store and therefore avoiding a walk through a dangerous neighborhood (safety need). But gasoline could be used to pick up a friend and satisfy social needs—or simply for a drive to satisfy a personal need for "freedom." Here, since motorists must buy gas to get around, there is no point in selling the "gas is a good commodity" story. But a particular brand might offer more safety and dependability because of quality control. Or racing or beach scenes might try to associate the brand with fun, speed, and excitement.

While these "commodity-type" markets are often identified with product-related names—like the gasoline market—relying on such product-related "needs" is risky—because it's easy to miss seeing what is really motivating (or could motivate) some consumers. Just a simple knife, for example, might be treated as a commodity for satisfying the "knife" or "food cutting" need. But the same knife might help a cook satisfy several levels of need. A market-oriented firm might see that some cooks are interested in high-quality cutlery for their own personal satisfaction—or name brands to impress their guests. In these cases, different markets are involved, and the appropriate marketing mixes should be different. An imaginative marketer might be able to develop a unique strategy—while competitors wouldn't even understand what's going on.

Economic needs affect how we satisfy basic needs

The need hierarchy idea can help explain *what* consumers will buy—but the economic needs help explain *why* they want specific product features.

Economic needs are concerned with making the best use of a consumer's limited resources—as the consumer sees it. Some people look for the best price. Others want the best quality—almost regardless of price. And others settle for the best value. Some economic needs are:

1. Economy of purchase or use.
2. Convenience.
3. Efficiency in operation or use.
4. Dependability in use.
5. Improvement of earnings.

Economic needs often can be explained in terms of measurable factors—including specific dollar savings, the length of the guarantee, and the time or money saved in using the product.

Unfortunately, it may not be easy for a marketer to identify the relevant needs—either informally or through marketing research. Consumers really may not know what drives them. Or if they do, they may not be willing to admit, for instance, that they have a need for "status." One clothes-conscious woman argued that her expensive designer shoes were a good buy because "they last forever!" Actually, she bought the newest style each season—long before less expensive shoes would wear out—and discarded her "old" ones.

Perception determines what is seen and felt

We are constantly bombarded by stimuli—ads, products, stores—yet we may not hear or see anything. This is because we apply the following selective processes:

1. **Selective exposure**—our eyes and minds seek out and notice only information that interests us.
2. **Selective perception**—we screen out or modify ideas, messages, and information that conflict with previously learned attitudes and beliefs.
3. **Selective retention**—we remember only what we want to remember.

These selective processes help explain why some people are not at all affected by some advertising—even offensive advertising. They just don't see or remember it!

Our needs affect these selective processes. Decisions that we are currently concerned about will receive more attention. In our car purchase example, Pam Bowers became interested in available cars, people's attitudes toward them, and car advertising *only* when she had to replace her old car.

Marketers are interested in these selective processes mainly because they limit what new information a consumer gets and retains. This in turn is likely to affect how they act—and what products they select and buy. This is also why marketers are interested in how consumers *learn.*

Learning determines what response is likely

Learning is a change in a person's thought processes caused by prior experience. A little girl tastes her first ice cream cone, and learning occurs! In fact, almost all consumer behavior is learned—so understanding more about how consumers learn should help you develop more effective marketing mixes.[2]

Experts describe a number of steps in the learning process. We have already discussed the idea of a *drive* as a strong stimulus that encourages action. Depending on the **cues**—products, signs, ads, and other stimuli in the environment—an individual chooses some specific response. A **response** is an effort to satisfy a drive. The specific response chosen depends on the cues and the person's past experience.

Reinforcement—of the learning process—occurs when the response is followed by satisfaction—that is, reducing the drive. Reinforcement strengthens the relationship between the cue and the response. And it may lead to a similar response the next time the drive occurs. Repeated reinforcement leads to the development of a habit—making the decision process routine for the individual. The relationships of the important variables in the learning process are shown in Figure 7–6.

The learning process can be illustrated by a thirsty person. The thirst *drive* could be satisfied in a variety of ways. But if the person happened to walk past a vending machine and saw a 7up sign—a *cue*—then he might satisfy the drive with a *response*—buying a 7up. If the experience is satisfactory, positive *reinforcement* will occur—and our friend may be quicker to satisfy this drive in the same way in the future. This emphasizes the importance of developing good products which live up to the promises of the firm's advertising. People can learn to like or dislike 7up—that is, learning works both ways.

Good experiences can lead to positive attitudes about a firm's product. Bad experiences can lead to negative attitudes—which even good promotion won't

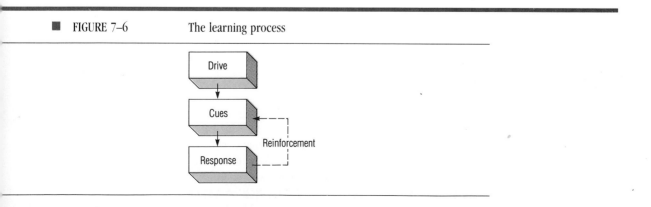

■ FIGURE 7–6   The learning process

be able to change. In fact, the subject of attitudes is extremely important to marketers—and is discussed more fully in a following section.

Positive cues may help a marketing mix

Sometimes marketers try to identify cues that have positive associations from some other situation and relate them to their marketing mix. Many people associate the smell of lemons with a fresh, natural cleanliness. Lemon scent is added to many household cleaning products—because it has these associations.

Using positive cues is especially common when new products are introduced—because consumers have no past experience with the product itself. Some "competitive advantage" is required if consumers are already satisfied with a competing product. Their likely response is to just buy the same thing again.

Some firms copy favorable cues associated with a competitor's popular product—hoping that the same consumer response will carry over to their product. They may use a similar package or brand name. Campbell's soup—long a consumer favorite—has a label with distinctive colors and lettering. Some lesser-known brands of soup use look-alike colors and type styles on their labels. They hope that consumers' positive feelings toward Campbell will encourage purchase of *their* soup. Ideally, they hope the buyer will simply respond to the cue with the same learned response—and not even discriminate between Campbell's and their brand.

Some needs may be learned

Some needs may be culturally (or socially) learned. When babies are born, their needs are simple. But as they grow, they learn more sophisticated and specific ways to meet a need. The need for food, for instance, may lead to many specific food wants—depending on the person's experience. The people of Western nations like beef—and their children learn to like it. In India, however, Hindus regard the cow as sacred and will not eat beef. Hindu children learn to eat and like other foods. Many foods, in other words, can satisfy hunger—but in a particular culture, an individual may have learned a strong preference for a specific food.

Some critics argue that marketing efforts encourage people to spend money on learned wants that relate to no "basic need" at all. For example, Europeans are less concerned about body odor, and few buy or use a deodorant. Millions of dollars are spent on such products in North America. Advertising implies that the use of deodorants "takes the worry out of being close." It is harder to argue, however, that marketing activity is the cause of the difference in the two cultures. Most of the research evidence says that advertising is not very convincing if it is not consistent with consumer needs—or if it tries to convince buyers of something which is contrary to their basic *attitudes.*

Attitudes relate to buying

An **attitude** is a person's point of view toward something. The "something" may be a product, an advertisement, a salesperson, a firm, or an idea. A good marketing mix will encourage positive attitudes among target customers. Attitudes are an important topic for marketers—because attitudes affect the selective processes, learning, and eventually the buying decisions people make.

Attitudes are usually thought of as involving liking or disliking—and therefore have some action implications. *Beliefs* are not so action-oriented. A **belief** is a person's conviction about something. Beliefs may help shape a consumer's attitudes—but don't necessarily involve any liking or disliking. It is possible to have a belief—say that Listerine has a medicinal taste—without really caring what it tastes like. On the other hand, beliefs about a product may have a positive or negative effect in shaping consumers' attitudes. Marketing managers for M&M candies realized this. "Red dye number 2"—used in some food products—was shown to be dangerous. M&M's candies were made with another, harmless, red dye—but managers didn't want consumers' fears to hurt the company—so they stopped including red candies in the M&M package.

Some marketers have stretched the attitude concept to include consumer "preferences" or "intention to buy"—in an attempt to relate attitude more closely to purchase behavior.

It is the "intention to buy" which is of most interest to practical managers who must forecast how much of their brand customers will buy. This would be easier if attitudes were good predictors of intentions to buy. Unfortunately, the relationships usually are not that simple. A person might have positive attitudes toward a Cadillac without having any intention of buying one. Even so, measuring consumer attitudes can sometimes *help* a marketing manager get a better picture of present and potential markets. For example, some customers may already have very positive attitudes toward competitors' offerings. Or consumers may not have very strong attitudes toward a proposed product. They may be perfectly satisfied with their present ways of doing things—or just "don't care." Or they may have beliefs that would discourage them from liking the product category—or wanting to buy it.

We have noted that attitudes may sometimes cause a person to act one way or another. A customer's experience with a purchased product is likely to shape attitudes. For example, from 1979 to 1982, Oldsmobile sold many cars with diesel engines to consumers who had favorable attitudes about getting good gas mileage from a low-maintenance North American car. But after buying the cars,

M&M's managers did away with red M&Ms—because of some consumers' beliefs that the red dye would be a health hazard.

the consumers' attitudes changed. They found that the early diesel engine was poorly designed and that fuel was often hard to find and rising in price.

Marketers generally try to understand the attitudes of their potential customers—and work with them. We'll discuss this idea more later when we review the way consumers evaluate product alternatives. For now, we want to emphasize that it is more economical to work with consumer attitudes than to try to *change* them. Changing present attitudes—especially negative ones—is probably the most difficult job that marketers face. Attitudes tend to be enduring. If really negative attitudes are held by a target market, it may be more practical to try another strategy.[3]

Personality affects how people see things

Much research has been done on how personality affects people's behavior—but the results have generally been disappointing to marketers. Certainly, personality traits, such as dominance, aggressiveness, dependence, sociability, responsibility, and friendliness, are relevant to how people behave. And traits like neatness have been associated with users of certain types of products—like cleaning materials. But personality traits haven't been much help in predicting which specific products or brands are chosen. Further, trying to develop marketing strategy based on personality traits is impractical. Moodiness, for example, might be found among buyers of a product class—but of what use would this information be? Copywriters couldn't make a direct appeal to this trait. And salespeople wouldn't be able to persuade customers to take a personality test before a sales call.[4]

People's individual personalities probably do affect their buying behavior, but we haven't found a way to use personality to help in strategy planning. Part of the problem is that most personality measures were originally developed to identify people whose behavior was abnormal and who needed medical care. Most consumer behavior—on the other hand—is quite normal. When marketers realized this distinction, they quit focusing on personality measures borrowed from psychologists—and instead developed *life-style analysis*.

Psychographic and life-style analysis focuses on activities, interests, and opinions

Psychographics or **life-style analysis** is the analysis of a person's day-to-day pattern of living—as expressed in his *Activities*, *Interests*, and *Opinions*—sometimes referred to as "AIOs." A number of variables for each of the AIO dimensions are shown in Table 7–1—along with some demographics which are sometimes used to add detail to the life-style profile of a target market.

Life-style analysis assumes that you can plan more effective strategies to reach your target market if you know more about them. Understanding the life style of target customers has been especially helpful in providing ideas for advertising themes. Let's see how it adds to a typical demographic description. It may not help a marketer much to know that an average member of the target market for a small station wagon is 30.8 years old, married, lives in a three-bedroom home, and has 2.3 children. Life styles help marketers to paint a more human portrait of the target market. For example, life-style analysis might show that the 30.8-year-old is also a community-oriented consumer with a traditional life style who especially enjoys spectator sports and spends much time in other activities

TABLE 7–1   Life-style dimensions

Activities	Interests	Opinions	Demographics
Work	Family	Themselves	Age
Hobbies	Home	Social issues	Education
Social events	Job	Politics	Income
Vacation	Community	Business	Occupation
Entertainment	Recreation	Economics	Family size
Club membership	Fashion	Education	Dwelling
Community	Food	Products	Geography
Shopping	Media	Future	City size
Sports	Achievements	Culture	Stage in life cycle

Source: Joseph T. Plummer, "The Concept and Application of Life-Style Segmentation," *Journal of Marketing*, January 1974, pp. 33–37.

with the whole family. An ad might show the product being used by a happy family at a ball game—so the target market could really identify with the ad.

Life-style analysis is usually developed from consumer responses to a long questionnaire—sometimes up to 25 pages. Each life-style variable is scored based on consumer reactions to several statements. For example, if a marketer wanted to learn if the target market included "sports spectators," the following types of statements would be included:

"I like to watch or listen to baseball or football games."

"I usually read the sports pages in the daily paper."

"I thoroughly enjoy conversations about sports."

"I would rather go to a sporting event than a dance."[5]

Potential customers are asked how strongly they agree with the statements—from "definitely agree" to "definitely disagree." Hundreds of such statements are used—tapping relevant life-style variables—and then a computer analysis is used to "profile" the target market. Life-style research often provides interesting insights about specific target markets—but usually a new analysis is needed for each target market.[6]

Inter-Personal Variables Affect the Individual's Buying Behavior

We have been discussing some of the ways that needs, attitudes, and other intra-personal variables influence the buying process. Now, you will see that these variables—and the buying process—are usually affected by relations with other people, too. We will look at how the individual interacts with family, social class, and other groups who may have influence. Many ideas about inter-personal influences on consumer behavior are based on theories originally developed in sociology, anthropology, and social psychology.

Who is the real decision maker in family purchases?

Not long ago, marketers assumed that the wife was the family purchasing agent. She was usually the one who shopped for household items. As a result, most promotion for those products was aimed at women. But times are changing. As more women work—and as night and weekend shopping become more popular—men are playing a more visible role as family "buyer" and decision maker.

Although one member of the family may go to the store and make a specific purchase, it is important in planning marketing strategy to know who else may be involved. Other family members may have influenced the decision—or really decided what to buy. Still others may use the product.

You don't need to watch much Saturday morning TV to see that the cereal companies know this. Cartoon characters tell kids about the goodies found in certain cereal packages—and urge them to remind Dad or Mom to pick up that brand next time at the store. Studies show that older sons and daughters may even influence big purchases—like cars and television sets.

Family considerations may overwhelm personal ones

A husband or wife may do a lot of thinking about personal preferences for various products and services. Such individual preferences may be modified if the husband and wife have different priorities. A wife might want to spend more on the family vacation—and the husband might want a power boat. The actual outcome in such a situation is unpredictable. The final decision might be determined by social processes—such as power, domination, and affection.

Buying responsibility and influence vary greatly—depending on the product and the family. A marketer trying to plan a strategy will find specific research—aimed at a definite target market—helpful. Remember—many buying decisions are made jointly—and thinking only about who actually buys the product can misdirect the marketing strategy.[7]

Social class affects attitudes, values, and buying

Up to now, we have been concerned with the individual and his relation to his family. Now let's consider how society looks at an individual and perhaps the family—in terms of social class. A **social class** is a group of people who have approximately equal social position—as viewed by others in the society.

Almost every society has some social class structure. The Canadian class system is far less pronounced than those in European and Asian nations—where the system is tied to religion, blood kinship, or landed wealth. Social class in this country is less rigid. Children may start out in the same social class as their parents—but can move to a different social class depending on their educational levels or the jobs they hold.

Marketers want to know what people are like in various social classes. They can get help from sociologists who have developed simple approaches for measuring social class groupings—based on a person's *occupation, education,* and *type and location of housing.* These can be studied in marketing research surveys—or in available Census data—to get a feel for the social class of a target market.

Notice that the person's income level is not included in this list. There is *some* general relationship between income level and social class. But the income level

People from the same so-
cial class often have sim-
ilar values—and even
similar preferences for
products.

of people within the same social class can vary greatly—and people with the same income level may be in different social classes.

People with the same level of income—but belonging to different social classes—tend to spend their money in different ways. This doesn't mean that income is unimportant. Rather it emphasizes that social class is important, too—it adds another dimension.

The marketing manager should understand differences among social classes—to be able to develop better marketing strategies. We will briefly describe a five-level social class structure developed for the United States. First, look at the relative sizes of the groupings in Figure 7–7—which also names the groups using the traditional technical terms like "upper," "middle," and "lower." These terms are used here because they are in general use—but a word of warning is in order. The terms may seem to imply "superior" and "inferior." In sociological and marketing usage, however, no value judgment is intended. In fact, it is not possible to state that any one class is "better" or "happier" than another.

Characteristics of so-
cial classes in the
United States

The **upper class** (2 percent of the population) consists of people from old, wealthy families (upper-upper)—as well as the socially prominent new rich (lower-upper). They often live in large homes with luxury features. They are a good market for antiques, art, rare jewelry, luxury travel, and unique designer products. They are likely to shop at exclusive shops where they receive special services—and may avoid mass-merchandisers.

The **upper-middle class** (11 percent of the population) consists of successful professionals, owners of small businesses, or managers for large corporations. These people are concerned about their quality of life—their homes and furnishings are selected for entertaining and gracious living. Their purchases are viewed as symbols of success—so they want quality products. They want to be seen as socially acceptable and fashionable. They support the arts and are civic-minded. They are ambitious for their children—and in general are more "future-oriented" than the lower-class groups.

The **lower-middle class** (36 percent of the population) consists of small business people, office workers, teachers, and technicians—the "white-collar workers." The American moral code and the emphasis on hard work have come from this class. This has been the most conforming, church-going, morally serious segment of society. They are home- and family-oriented. We speak of America as a middle-class society, but the middle-class value system stops here. More than half of our society is *not* middle class.

The **upper-lower class** (38 percent of the population) consists of factory production line workers, skilled workers, and service people—the "blue-collar workers." Most earn good incomes but are still very concerned about security. People in these families adopt traditional male-female roles. They are less confident in their own judgments about products—and may rely more on salespeople and advertising.

The **lower-lower class** (13 percent of the population) consists of unskilled laborers and people in non-respectable occupations. They usually don't have much income. But they are good markets for "necessities" and products which help them enjoy the present.[8]

■ FIGURE 7–7   Sizes of five social class groups

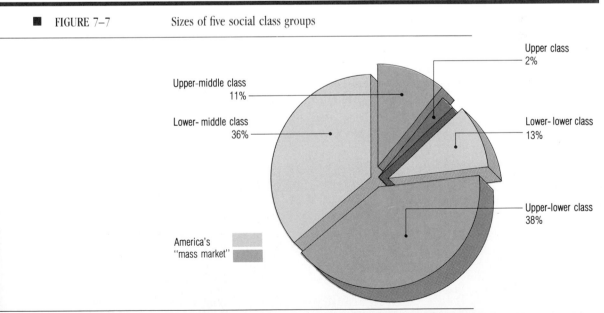

Source: Adapted from Steven L. Diamond, Thomas S. Robertson, and F. Kent Mitchel, "Consumer Motivation and Behavior," in *Marketing Manager's Handbook*, ed. S. H. Britt and N. F. Guess (Chicago: Dartnell, 1983), p. 239.

Class system in Canada

Canadian sociologists generally agree that Canada has a clearly definable class structure which can be classified according to the above five categories. However, the type of micro-level field study carried out in the United States has few Canadian counterparts. Instead, Canadian studies of social class have focused more on national or ethnic class profiles, on the factors hindering movement between classes, and on the social background of Canada's economic elite. The method used to assign individuals to a social class has usually involved a measure reflecting some combination of income, education, and occupation.[9]

What do these classes mean?

Social class studies suggest that an old saying—"A rich man is simply a poor man with more money"—is not true. It appears that a person belonging to the lower classes—given the same income as a middle-class person—handles himself and his money very differently. The various classes shop at different stores. They prefer different treatment from salespeople. They buy different brands of products—even though their prices are about the same—and they have different spending-saving attitudes. Some of these differences are shown in Figure 7–8.

The impact on strategy planning is most interesting. Selection of advertising media should be related to social class, for example. Customers in the lower classes have little interest in *Fortune, Holiday, Vogue,* or *Ladies' Home Journal.* The middle and upper classes probably have little desire to read *True Story, Modern Romances,* or *True Confessions.*

Class should also affect product design—and the kinds of goods carried by retailers. Lower-class people seem to prefer "flashy" home furnishings. Those in the middle and upper classes prefer functional or "classic" styles. Further, those in the lower classes seem to be confused by variety—and have difficulty making choices. As a result, such buyers look on furniture salespeople as friends and advisors. The middle-class buyers, on the other hand, are more self-confident. They know what they want. They prefer the sales clerk to be an impersonal guide.

Reference groups have relevance, too

A **reference group** is the people to whom an individual looks when forming attitudes about a particular topic. People normally have several reference groups—for different topics. Some they meet face-to-face. Others they may just wish to imitate. In either case, they may take values from these reference groups—and make buying decisions based on what the group might accept.

■   FIGURE 7–8   Characteristics and attitudes of middle and lower classes

Middle classes	Lower classes
Plan and save for the future ←———————→	Live for the present
Analyze alternatives ←———————→	"Feel" what is "best"
Understand how the world works ←———————→	Have simplistic ideas about how things work
Feel they have opportunities ←———————→	Feel controlled by the world
Willing to take risks ←———————→	"Play it safe"
Confident about decision making ←———————→	Want help with decision making
Want long-run quality or value ←———————→	Want short-run satisfaction

■ FIGURE 7–9   Examples of different levels of group influence for different types
                           and brands of products

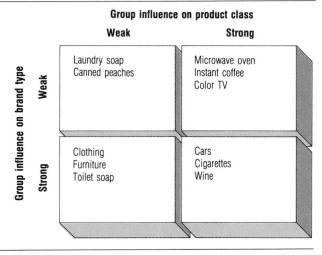

Source: Adapted and updated by authors from H. Kassarijan and Thomas S. Robertson, eds., *Perspectives on Consumer Behavior*, 3rd ed. (Glenview, Ill.: Scott, Foresman, 1981). p. 318; and the work of the Bureau of Applied Social Research,
Columbia University, New York.

Young college graduates—for example—who aspire to be accepted quickly by
co-workers—may buy clothes In the same style and from the same stores.

The importance of reference groups depends somewhat on the nature of the
product—and on whether anyone else will be able to "see" which product and
which brand is being used. Figure 7–9 shows products with different amounts of
reference group influence.[10]

**Reaching the opinion
leaders who are
buyers**

Opinion leaders are people who influence others. Opinion leaders aren't necessarily wealthier or better educated. And opinion leaders on one subject are not
necessarily opinion leaders on another subject. Capable homemakers with large
families may be consulted for advice on family budgeting. Young women may be
opinion leaders for new clothing styles and cosmetics. Each social class tends to
have its own opinion leaders. Some marketing mixes are aimed especially at
these people—since their opinions affect others and research shows that they
are involved in many product-related discussions with "followers."[11]

**Culture surrounds
the whole decision-
making process**

Culture is the whole set of beliefs, attitudes, and ways of doing things of a
reasonably homogeneous set of people. We can think of the Canadian culture,
the French culture, or the Latin American culture. People within these cultural
groupings are more similar in outlook and behavior. And sometimes it is useful to
think of sub-cultures within such groupings. For example, within the Canadian
culture, there are various religious and ethnic sub-cultures.

From a target marketing point of view, a marketing manager will probably want
to aim at people within one culture. If a firm were developing strategies for two
cultures, two different marketing plans might be needed.[12]

The attitudes and beliefs that we usually associate with culture tend to change slowly. So once you develop a good understanding of the culture for which you are planning, it probably will be practical to concentrate on the more dynamic variables discussed above.

Consumers Use Problem-Solving Processes

It is clear that the individual and social variables we have been discussing affect *what* products a consumer finally decides to purchase. It is also important for marketing managers to understand *how* buyers use a problem-solving process to select particular products.

A common problem-solving process that seems to be used by most consumers consists of five steps:

1. Becoming aware of—or interested in—the problem.
2. Gathering information about possible solutions.
3. Evaluating alternative solutions—perhaps trying some out.
4. Deciding on the appropriate solution.
5. Evaluating the decision.[13]

An expanded version of this basic process is presented in Figure 7–10. Note that this figure integrates the problem-solving process with the whole set of intra-personal and inter-personal forces we have been reviewing.

A consumer's evaluation of information about purchase alternatives includes not only a product type in relation to other types of products, but also differences in brand within a product type *and* the stores where they may be available. This can be a very complicated evaluation procedure—and depending on their choice criteria, consumers may make seemingly "irrational" decisions. If convenient service is crucial, for example, a person might pay list price for an "unexciting" car from a *very convenient* dealer. Marketers need a way to think about these decisions.

Grid of evaluative criteria helps

Based on studies of how consumers seek out and evaluate information about products, researchers have suggested that marketing managers use an evaluative grid which shows features common to different products (or marketing mixes). For example, Figure 7–11 shows some of the features common to three different cars which a consumer might consider.

The grid encourages marketing managers to view each product as a "bundle" of features or "attributes." The pluses and minuses in Figure 7–11 indicate one consumer's attitude toward each feature of each different car.

This information is collected with market research. If members of the target market don't rate a feature of the marketing manager's brand with "pluses," it may indicate a problem. The manager might want to change the product to improve that feature—or perhaps use more promotion to emphasize an already acceptable feature. For example, in Figure 7–11, the Nissan has a minus under

■   FIGURE 7–10   Consumer's problem-solving process

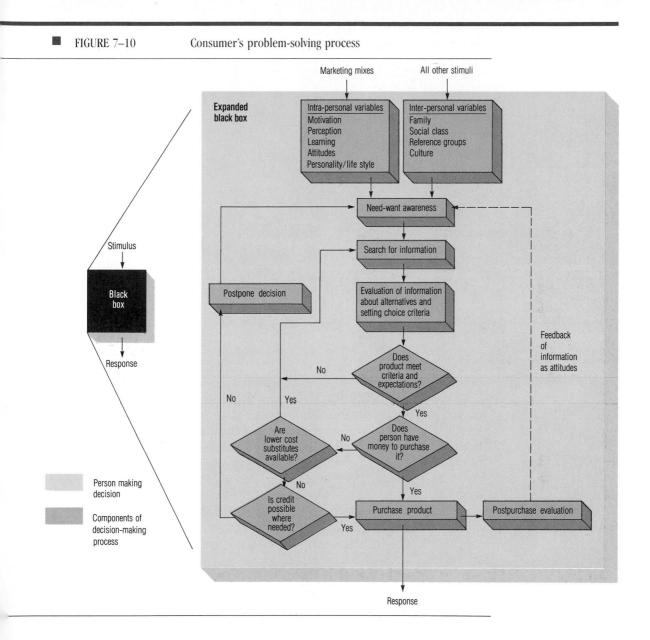

gas mileage for this consumer. If the Nissan really gets better gas mileage than the other cars, promotion might focus on this feature, trying to improve consumer attitudes toward it, and toward the whole product.

Some consumers will reject a product if *one* feature is below standard—regardless of how favorable they might be about other features of the product. The consumer represented in Figure 7–11 might avoid the DeLorean—which was perceived to be less than satisfactory on ease of service—even if it were supe-

■ FIGURE 7–11   Grid of evaluative criteria for three car brands

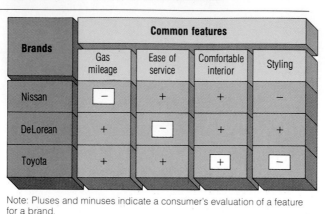

Note: Pluses and minuses indicate a consumer's evaluation of a feature
for a brand.

rior in all other aspects. In other instances, a consumer's overall attitude toward
the product might be such that a few good features could make up for some
shortcomings. The comfortable interior of the Toyota (Figure 7–11) might make
up for less exciting styling—especially if comfort were viewed as really important.

Of course, consumers don't use a grid like this. However, constructing such a
grid will help managers think about what evaluative criteria are really important to
their target consumers, what consumers' attitudes are toward their product (or
marketing mix) on each criteria, and how consumers combine the criteria to
reach a final decision. Having a better understanding of the process may help
the manager develop a marketing mix that will "rate" higher.[14]

**Three levels of prob-
lem solving are useful**

The basic problem-solving process shows the steps a consumer may go
through while trying to find a way to satisfy his needs—but it does not show how
long this will take—or how much thought will be given to each step. Some individuals have had much experience solving certain problems—and can move
quickly through some of the steps or almost directly to a decision.

It is helpful, therefore, to recognize three levels of problem solving: extensive
problem solving, limited problem solving, and routinized response behavior. See
Figure 7–12. These problem-solving approaches might be used for any kind of
good or service.

Extensive problem solving is involved when a need is completely new to a
person—and much effort is taken to understand the need and how to satisfy it. A
new college student, for example, may have feelings of loneliness, a need for
companionship, a need for achievement, and so on. It may take him some time
to figure out what he wants to do—and how to do it.

Limited problem solving involves *some* effort to understand a person's need
and how best to satisfy it. Our college student, for example, might have tried
various ways of satisfying his needs and come up with several fairly good

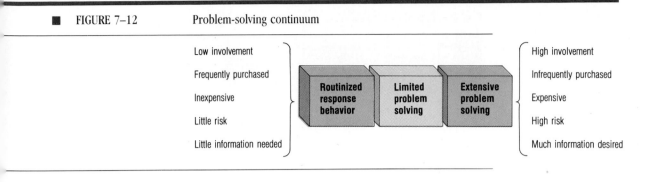

■ FIGURE 7–12   Problem-solving continuum

Low involvement   High involvement

Frequently purchased   Infrequently purchased

Inexpensive | Routinized | Limited | Extensive | Expensive
                     | response | problem | problem |
                     | behavior | solving | solving |

Little risk   High risk

Little information needed   Much information desired

choices. So, limited problem solving means deciding which choice is best at a particular time.

Routinized response behavior involves mechanically selecting a particular way of satisfying a need whenever it occurs. When our college student feels the need for companionship, for example, it might be quickly solved by meeting with friends in familiar surroundings. A daily trip to the local "hangout" might become the answer to this problem.

Routinized response behavior is typical for **low involvement products**—products which do not have high personal importance or relevance for the customer. Let's face it—buying a box of salt is probably not one of the burning issues in your life. Most marketing managers would like their target consumers to always buy their products—in a routinized way.[15]

Problem solving is a learning process

The reason problem solving becomes simpler with time is that people learn from experience—both positive and negative things. As a person approaches the problem-solving process, he brings with him attitudes formed by previous experiences and social training. Each new problem-solving process may then contribute to or modify this attitude set.

New concepts require an adoption process

Really new concepts present a problem solver with a harder job—handling the adoption process. The **adoption process** means the steps which individuals go through on the way to accepting or rejecting a new idea. It is similar to the problem-solving process, but the adoption process makes clearer the role of learning—and the potential contribution of promotion in a marketing mix.

The adoption process for an individual moves through some fairly definite steps, as follows:

1. Awareness—the potential customer comes to know about the product but lacks details. He may not even know how it works or what it will do.
2. Interest—*if* he becomes interested, he gathers general information and facts about the product.
3. Evaluation—he begins to make a mental trial, applying the product to his personal situation.

Marketing managers sometimes offer trial sizes of products free—to speed the adoption process.

4. Trial—the customer may buy the product so that he can experiment with it in use. A product that is either too expensive to try or isn't available for trial may never be adopted.
5. Decision—he decides on either adoption or rejection. A satisfactory evaluation and trial may lead to adoption of the product and regular use. According to psychological learning theory, reinforcement will lead to adoption.
6. Confirmation—the adopter continues to rethink the decision and searches for support for the decision—that is, further reinforcement.[16]

Dissonance may set in after the decision

After a decision has been made, a buyer may have second thoughts. He may have had to choose from among several attractive alternatives—weighing the pros and cons and finally making a decision. Later doubts, however, may lead to

dissonance—tension caused by uncertainty about the rightness of a decision. Dissonance may lead a buyer to search for additional information—to confirm the wisdom of the decision and so reduce tension. Without this confirmation, the adopter might buy something else next time—or not give positive comments to others.[17]

Several Processes Are Related and Relevant to Strategy Planning

The interrelation of the problem-solving process, the adoption process, and learning can be seen in Figure 7–13. It is important to see this interrelation—and to understand that it can be modified or accelerated by promotion. Also note that the problem-solving behavior of potential buyers should affect the design of physical distribution systems. If customers aren't willing to travel far to shop, then more outlets may be needed to get their business. Similarly, their attitudes help determine what price to charge. Clearly, knowing how a target market handles these processes will aid marketing strategy planning.

■ FIGURE 7–13   Relation of problem-solving process, adoption process, and learning (given a problem)

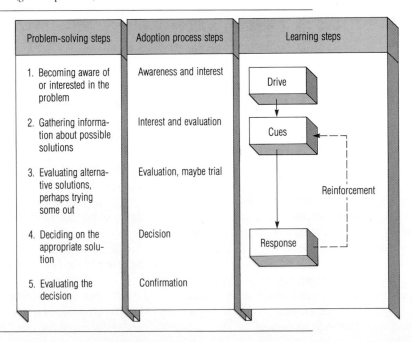

■ CONCLUSION

In this chapter, we have analyzed the individual consumer as a problem solver who is influenced by intra- and inter-personal variables. Our "black box" model of buyer behavior helps integrate a large number of variables into one process. A good grasp of this material is needed in marketing strategy planning—because an assumption that everyone behaves the way you do—or even like your family or friends do—can lead to expensive marketing errors.

Consumer buying behavior results from the consumer's efforts to satisfy needs and wants. We discussed some reasons why consumers buy—and saw that consumer behavior can't be fully explained by only a list of needs.

We also saw that our society is divided into social classes—which helps explain some consumer behavior. The impact of reference groups and opinion leaders was discussed, too.

A buyer behavior model was presented to help you interpret and integrate the present findings—and any new data you might obtain from marketing research. As of now, the behavorial sciences can only offer insights and theories which the marketing manager must blend with intuition and judgment in developing marketing strategies.

Marketing research may have to be used to answer specific questions. But if neither the money nor the time is available for research, then marketing managers will have to rely on the available description of present behavior and "guesstimates" about future behavior. You should study the popular magazines and the leading newspapers carefully—they often reflect the public's shifting attitudes. You also should be familiar with the many studies concerning the changing consumer that are published regularly in the business and trade press. This material—added and related to the information in these last two chapters—will help your marketing strategy planning.

Remember that consumers—with all their needs and attitudes—may be elusive—but not invisible. We have more data and understanding of consumer behavior than is generally used by business managers. Applying this information may help you find your breakthrough opportunity.

■ QUESTIONS AND PROBLEMS

1. What is the behavioral science concept which underlies the "black box" model of consumer behavior? Does this concept have operational relevance to marketing managers; i.e., if it is a valid concept, can they make use of it?

2. Explain what is meant by a hierarchy of needs and provide examples of one or more products which enable you to satisfy each of the four levels of need.

3. Cut out two recent advertisements: one full-page color ad from a magazine and one large display from a newspaper. Indicate which needs are being appealed to in each case.

4. Explain how an understanding of consumers' learning processes might affect marketing strategy planning.

5. Explain psychographics and life-style analysis. Explain how it might be useful for planning marketing strategies to reach college students as compared to the "average" consumer.

6. How do cultural values affect purchasing behavior? Give two specific examples.

7. How should the social class structure affect the planning of a new restaurant in a large city? How might the four Ps be adjusted?

8. What social class would you associate with each of the following phrases or items?

a. Sport cars.
b. *True Story, True Romances,* etc.
c. *New Yorker.*
d. *Playboy.*
e. People watching "soap operas."
f. TV bowling shows.
g. Families that serve martinis, especially before dinner.
h. Families who dress formally for dinner regularly.
i. Families who are distrustful of banks (keep money in socks or mattresses).
j. Owners of French poodles.

In each case, choose one class, if you can. If you are not able to choose one class, but rather feel that several classes are equally likely, then so indicate. In those cases where you feel that all classes are equally interested or characterized by a particular item, choose all five classes.

9. Illustrate how the reference group concept may apply in practice by explaining how you personally are influenced by some reference group for some product. What are the implications of such behavior for marketing managers?

10. What new status symbols are replacing the piano and automobile? Do these products have any characteristics in common? If they do, what are some possible status symbols of the future?

11. Illustrate the three levels of problem solving with an example from your own personal experience.

12. On the basis of the data and analysis presented in Chapters 6 and 7, what kind of buying behavior would you expect to find for the following products: (*a*) canned peas, (*b*) toothpaste, (*c*) ballpoint pens, (*d*) baseball gloves, (*e*) sport coats, (*f*) dishwashers, (*g*) encyclopedias, (*h*) automobiles, and (*i*) motorboats? Set up a chart for your answer with products along the left-hand margin as the row headings and the following factors as headings for the columns: (*a*) how consumers would shop for these products, (*b*) how far they would go, (*c*) whether they would buy by brand, (*d*) whether they would wish to compare with other products, and (*e*) any other factors they should consider. Insert short answers—words or phrases are satisfactory—in the various boxes. Be prepared to discuss how the answers you put in the chart would affect each product's marketing mix.

■ SUGGESTED CASES

22. Canadian Hydrogardens, Ltd.

28. Multi Foods, Ltd.

■ NOTES

1. K. H. Chung, *Motivational Theories and Practices* (Columbus, Ohio: Grid, 1977), pp. 40–43; and A. H. Maslow, *Motivation and Personality* (New York: Harper & Brothers, 1954).

2. Walter R. Nord and J. Paul Peter, "A Behavior Modification Perspective on Marketing," *Journal of Marketing,* Spring 1980, pp. 36–47; and James R. Bettman, "Memory Factors in Consumer Choice: A Review," *Journal of Marketing* 43 (Spring 1979), pp. 37–53.

3. For just a few references, see Alvin A. Achenbaum, "Advertising Doesn't Manipulate Consumers," *Journal of Advertis-*

ing Research 12 (April 1972), pp. 3–14; and Steven J. Gross and C. Michael Niman, "Attitude-Behavior Consistency: A Review," *Public Opinion Quarterly* 39 (Fall 1975), pp. 358–68; Paul W. Miniard and Joel B. Cohen, "Isolating Attitudinal and Normative Influences in Behavioral Intentions Models," *Journal of Marketing Research,* February 1979, pp. 102–10; Paul R. Warshaw, "A New Model for Predicting Behavioral Intentions: An Alternative to Fishbein," *Journal of Marketing Research,* Spring 1980, pp. 82–95; J. Pavasars and W. D. Wells, "Measures of Brand Attitudes Can Be Used to Predict Buying Behavior," *Marketing News,* April 11, 1975, p. 6; Joel Huber and John McCann, "The

Impact of Inferential Beliefs on Product Evaluations," *Journal of Marketing Research* 19 (August 1982), pp. 324–33; and Calvin P. Duncan and Richard W. Olshavsky, "External Search: The Role of Consumer Beliefs," *Journal of Marketing Research* 19 (February 1982), pp. 32–43.

4. H. H. Kassarjian, "Personality and Consumer Behavior: A Review," *Journal of Marketing Research,* November 1971, pp. 409–18; and W. D. Wells and A. D. Beard, "Personality and Consumer Behavior," in *Consumer Behavior: Theoretical Sources,* ed. Scott Ward and T. S. Robinson (Englewood Cliffs, N.J.: Prentice-Hall, 1973).

5. William D. Wells and Douglas J. Tigert, "Activities, Interests, and Opinions," in *Market Segmentation,* ed. James F. Engel et al. (New York: Holt, Rinehart & Winston, 1972), p. 258.

6. W. D. Wells, "Psychographics: A Critical Review," *Journal of Marketing Research,* May 1975, pp. 196–213; Alvin C. Burns and Mary C. Harrison, "A Test of the Reliability of Psychographics," *Journal of Marketing Research,* February 1979, pp. 32–38; "Information on Values and Lifestyles Needed to Identify Buying Patterns," *Marketing News,* October 5, 1979, p. 1 f; and *Marketing News,* December 31, 1976, p. 8. See also "Life Style Research Inappropriate for Some Categories of Products," *Marketing News,* June 17, 1977, p. 9; and M. E. Goldberg, "Identifying Relevant Psychographic Segments: How Specifying Product Functions Can Help," *Journal of Consumer Research,* December 1976, pp. 163–69.

7. W. H. Reynolds and James H. Myers, "Marketing and the American Family," *Business Topics,* Spring 1966, pp. 58–59. See also G. M. Munsinger, J. E. Weber, and R. W. Hansen, "Joint Home Purchasing Decisions by Husbands and Wives," *Journal of Consumer Research,* March 1975, pp. 60–66; E. P. Cox III, "Family Purchase Decision Making and the Process of Adjustment," *Journal of Marketing Research,* May 1975, pp. 189-95; I. C. M. Cunningham and R. R. Green, "Purchasing Roles in the U.S. Family, 1955 & 1973," *Journal of Marketing,* October 1974, pp. 61–64; Harry L. Davis, "Decision Making within the Household," *Journal of Consumer Research,* March 1976, pp. 241–60; Patrick E. Murphy and William A. Staples; "A Modernized Family Life Cycle," *Consumer Research,* June 1979, pp. 12–22; and George J. Szybillo et al., "Family Member Influence in Household Decision Making," *Journal of Consumer Research,* December 1979, pp. 312–16.

8. P. Martineau, "The Pattern of Social Classes," in *Marketing's Role in Scientific Management,* ed. R. L. Clewett (Chicago: American Marketing Association, 1957), pp. 246–47. See also James A. Carman, *The Application of Social Class in Market Segmentation* (Berkeley: Institute of Business and Economic Research, University of California, 1965); William H. Peters, "Relative Occupational Class Income: A Significant Variable in the Marketing of Automobiles," *Journal of Marketing,* April 1970, pp. 74–78; and Arun K. Jain; "A Method for Investigating and Representing an Implicit Theory of Social Class," *Journal of Consumer Research,* June 1975, pp. 53–59.

9. For an especially useful collection of relatively recent articles on Canadian class structure, see J. E. Curtis and W. G. Scott, *Social Stratification: Canada* (Scarborough, Ont.: Prentice-Hall of Canada, 1973).

10. David F. Midgley, "Patterns of Interpersonal Information Seeking for the Purchase of a Symbolic Product," *Journal of Marketing Research* 20 (February 1983), pp. 74–83; James H. Donnelly, Jr., "Social Character and Acceptance of New Products," *Journal of Marketing Research,* February 1970, pp. 111–16; Jeffrey D. Ford and Elwood A. Ellis, "A Reexamination of Group Influence on Member Brand Preference," *Journal of Marketing Research,* February 1980, pp. 125–32; William O. Bearden and Jesse E. Teel, "An Investigation of Personal Influences on Consumer Complaining," *Journal of Retailing* 56, no. 3 (Fall 1980), pp. 3–20; and George P. Moschis, "Social Comparison and Informal Group Influence," *Journal of Marketing Research,* August 1976, pp. 237–44.

11. Harold H. Kassarjian, "Social Character and Differential Preference for Mass Communication," *Journal of Marketing Research,* May 1965, pp. 146–53; James H. Myers and Thomas S. Robertson, "Dimensions of Opinion Leadership," *Journal of Marketing Research,* February 1972, pp. 41–46; and Charles W. King and John O. Summers, "Overlap of Opinion Leadership Across Consumer Product Categories," *Journal of Marketing Research,* February 1970, pp. 43–50.

12. Walter A. Henry, "Cultural Values Do Correlate with Consumer Behavior," *Journal of Marketing Research,* May 1976, pp. 121–27.

13. Adapted from James H. Myers and William H. Reynolds, *Consumer Behavior and Marketing Management* (Boston: Houghton Mifflin, 1967), p. 49.

14. James R. Bettman, *An Information Processing Theory of Consumer Choice,* (Reading, Mass.: Addison-Wesley Publishing, 1979); Richard W. Olshavsky and Donald H. Granbois, "Consumer Decision Making—Fact or Fiction?" *Journal of Consumer Research,* September 1979, pp. 93–100; David A. Sheluga, James Jaccard, and Jacob Jacoby, "Preference, Search, and Choice: An Integrative Approach," *Journal of Consumer Research,* September 1979, pp. 166–176; Lawrence X. Tarpey, Sr., and J. Paul Peter, "A Comparative Analysis of Three Consumer Decision Strategies," *Journal of Consumer Research,* June 1975, pp. 29–37; and J. H. Myers and M. I. Alpert, "Determinant Buying Attributes: Meaning and Measurement," *Journal of Marketing* 32 (October 1968), pp. 13–20.

15. John A. Howard and Jagdish N. Sheth, *The Theory of Buyer Behavior* (New York: John Wiley & Sons, 1969), pp. 46–48.

16. Adapted from E. M. Rogers, *The Diffusion of Innovations* (New York: Free Press, 1962); and E. M. Rogers with F. Shoemaker, *Communication of Innovation: A Cross Cultural Approach* (New York: Free Press, 1968).

17. For further discussion on this topic, see James H. Myers and William H. Reynolds, *Consumer Behavior and Marketing Management* (Boston: Houghton Mifflin, 1967); and J. F. Engel and R. D. Blackwell, *Consumer Behavior* (New York: Holt, Rinehart & Winston, 1981).

Appendix D ■ French Canada—adding behavioral insights to economic and demographic data

Can behavioral science provide a better understanding of the differences between French Canadian consumers and their English counterparts? Does a behavioral approach generate additional insights—ones not available from economic and demographic data? The answer to both these questions is a qualified "yes." Behavioral science may be able to provide new and useful perspectives on French-English differences. However, it has not revealed all we need to know about the French Canadian market. This is true even though Canadian marketers have spent a great deal of time and money studying *specific differences* in marketplace behavior.

Unfortunately, not enough *basic research* has been conducted on the factors that might underlie and help to explain differences in consumption patterns. This is due, in part, to the fact that corporate marketing researchers are not that interested in fundamental and basic research. Their job is to help sell a certain brand or product. In any case, much of what commercial marketing researchers learned about French and English differences is kept confidential by those who paid for the research.

Conducting cross-cultural research in two languages is no easy task. We must be sure, for example, that the two questionnaires used mean exactly the same thing and that the samples used are equivalent in all important respects. Even when the results of such research are known, we still cannot be sure that cultural factors are the cause of any French-English differences discovered. As we shall see, a number of factors, alone or in combination, have been advanced as the reason why French Canadian consumers behave differently than their English-speaking counterparts. So executives studying the French Canadian market should be prepared to borrow from the behavioral sciences whenever appropriate. What they will learn will always be interesting and sometimes useful. However, "the real reason" why French Canadian and English Canadian consumers have different purchasing habits and consumption practices is unlikely to be discovered in the foreseeable future. In the paragraphs that follow, we will discuss relevant economic, geographic, and demographic material and explore behavioral dimensions of the French Canadian market.

Before we proceed, keep one additional point in mind. The fact that English Canadians speak the same language does not make them a homogeneous market! There are very real differences in brand preferences, purchasing habits, and consumption practices between and even within the Atlantic provinces, Ontario, the Prairie provinces, and British Columbia. Similarly, many regional and linguistic differences (i.e., Acadian versus French Canadian background) are overlooked whenever people generalize about the French-speaking market.

Size and Scope of That Market

There are some important questions we should ask about the French Canadian market.

1. What is a French Canadian consumer?

French Canadians can be defined in many ways. Let's accept the position that a French Canadian consumer is any one whose mother tongue is French or who tends to speak French rather than English at home.[1] However, marketers must realize that a large number of French Canadians are truly bilingual. They watch English-language television and read English-language publications. For example, most of the people in Montreal who watch English-language television programs such as "The Price Is Right" are French-speaking.[2] A significant number of French Canadians who are not truly bilingual on occasion still prefer to listen to English radio, watch English TV, or read English-language publications. Marketers must carefully study the media preferences of French Canadians. They cannot rely exclusively on census discussions of mother tongue or language most often spoken at home.

2. Where is the French Canadian market?

Is that market essentially Quebec, or should it be defined more broadly? For marketing purposes, Quebec and the French Canadian market are not identical. However, a French Canadian market does not exist in every location where French is the mother tongue of a few consumers. Marketers cannot afford to develop special programs for very small market segments.

One approach defines the French Canadian market to include Quebec, eight adjacent counties in Ontario, and seven counties in the northern part of New Brunswick. At least 25 percent of the residents in each of these 15 additional counties claim French as their mother tongue. For the 15 taken together, the mother tongue of 49 percent of the population is French, and 16 percent speak only French. In addition, flourishing French Canadian institutions are found in these counties. French Canadian assimilation into the English culture is somewhat limited. Also, the same areas receive a significant amount of overflow advertising from Quebec, and they are frequently served by Quebec-based distributors.[3]

Joel Garreau, the author of the recent best-seller *The Nine Nations of North America,* selected Quebec as one of North America's nine nations. Material provided by Garreau is now being used by advertising agencies and research firms in their efforts to delineate life-style segments.[4]

Of all Canadians reporting *French* as their mother tongue, 91 percent, or over 5.6 million people, live in Quebec or in the 15 adjacent counties. The figure includes immigrants from France, North Africa, Vietnam, Haiti, and other French-speaking nations. A substantial Acadian population in New Brunswick is also unique in some ways. Nevertheless, for marketing planning purposes, Acadians are usually considered to be part of the larger "French" market. Table D–1 gives more detailed mother tongue information for Metropolitan Montreal, the rest of Quebec, and the adjacent counties in Ontario and New Brunswick.

3. How important is the English market in the same area?

Some 694,915 English "mother tongue" individuals, 9.4 percent of the total Quebec population, live in that province. The English-speaking community of Quebec is also believed to account for an even larger share of the area's total purchasing power. In addition, Quebec has 425,715 residents who report some third language as their mother tongue. In the adjacent 15 counties, another

■   TABLE D–1   Mother tongue—The French Canadian market, 1981*

	Population	Percentage
Quebec		
Montreal CMA		
French	1,912,865	68.36
English	512,170	18.30
Other†	373,005	13.33
	2,798,040	
Rest of province		
French	3,335,575	93.41
English	182,745	5.12
Other	52,710	1.48
	3,571,030	
New Brunswick‡		
French	217,260	58.31
English	151,735	40.74
Other	3,570	0.95
	372,565	
Ontario§		
French	140,725	39.15
English	198,470	55.22
Other	20,215	5.62
	359,410	
Totals		
French	5,606,425	78.95
English	1,045,120	14.72
Other	449,500	6.33
	7,101,045	

*Counties in which French is the mother tongue of at least one fourth of the population—accounts in total for 92 percent of all Canadians having French as their mother tongue.
†Includes "did not declare."
‡Includes the counties of Gloucester, Kent, Madawaska, Northumberland, Restigouche, Victoria, and Westmorland.
§Includes the counties of Cochrane, Glengarry, Nipissing, Prescott, Russell, Stormont, Sudbury, and Timiskaming.

Source: Statistics Canada, Cat. 93-929, Volume 2, 1984, 93-940, 1984, 93-942, 1984.

350,205 claim English as their mother tongue and 23,785 a language other than English or French. Such segments are obviously too large to be neglected.

Although some English-speaking consumers have left Quebec, the number of Quebec residents whose mother tongue is not French is still larger than the total population of Manitoba or Saskatchewan. This "other Quebec" market is also less expensive to reach—because almost 80 percent of these consumers live in or around Montreal. Obviously, a significant "other" market well worth cultivating still exists in Quebec. In fact, statistics show that "other than French-speaking" Montreal is Canada's fourth largest city after Toronto, French-speaking Montreal, and Vancouver.

Differences in Consumption

4. Are there French-English differences in product usage?

Yes, and in some cases, these differences are great. One report suggests that, in comparison with their English counterparts, French Canadians buy relatively more packaged soups, instant coffee, olives, wine, cosmetics, ale-type beer, linoleum tile, baby food, Geneva Gin, and soft drinks. They buy relatively less frozen goods, canned fish and meats, chocolate chips, pickles, vinyl tile, tea, and dietetic foods.[5]

French Canadians may also have a sweet tooth. Quebec leads all other provinces in per capita sales of soft drinks, corn and maple syrup, molasses, and several other sweets and delicacies.[6]

The above are but a few of the many differences in product usage and preference that have been reported. However, alert marketers must regularly reexamine the market to find whether such differences or preferences still exist. One of

■ FIGURE D–1

Marketing scholar deplores death of French market data

There is a disturbing lack of information available about the whole Quebec market, not just the French market in Quebec, in the opinion of Robert Tamilia, professor of marketing at the Université du Québec à Montreal.

Comparisons of the level of consumption between Quebec and the rest of Canada are not a particularly good means of identifying the cultural uniqueness of the Quebec market, according to Tamilia.

"To begin with," he says, "the data regarding consumption from the Quebec "francophone" market isn't available from Statistics Canada, which doesn't break down statistics by language groups. "Further, Stats Can figures often correspond to the level of manufacturing, not the level of consumption. And the data used to compare the level of consumption between Quebec and the rest of Canada that is available likely comes from private sources, so it is difficult to judge the validity of the figures."

Tamilia also says that available data can be outdated and not correspond to the actual consumption level. "Perhaps 25 years ago certain consumption differences existed between Quebec and Canada. But I wonder if they are still true today? For example, Quebec was known 10 years ago to be the biggest consumer of beer. Now both the Northwest Territories and British Columbia are higher on a per capita basis."

"Sugar consumption is said to be higher in Quebec, but is it really true on a consumption basis? There's a large production of sugar in Quebec, but no figures readily available about consumption." "Historically, Quebec women were said to spend more on cosmetics than other women, but that may not be true today."

Quebec/Canada or Quebec/Ontario comparisons do not consider the heterogeneous mix in Quebec. There are people from all over the world in Quebec. The English-language market of the province is about 1 million persons. Perhaps they are what cause differences.

"If you want to know about the francophone, you'll have difficulty because, in marketing, the exact definition of the francophone does not yet exist," says Tamilia. "About 40 percent of the people in the Montreal area alone are bilingual." (A conservative estimate.)

Much research classifies francophones by the language spoken at home or the maternal language, but often the person who speaks French in his home tends to use English media to obtain information.

Tamilia finds that there is greater similarity between the buying behavior of a Quebecois and Ontarian than there is between an Albertan and a Newfoundlander. "Too much energy is dispensed in perceiving the Quebec market as culturally different."

Source: Robert Tamilia, "Marketing Scholar Deplores Dearth of French Market Data." *Marketing*, June 1. 1981. p. 12.

Canada's most knowledgeable observers stresses in Figure D–1 the importance of up-to-date information on French Canadian consumption patterns.

It is not clear what marketers should do when they discover differences in consumption. Should manufacturers of the underconsumed frozen vegetables pay more attention to the Quebec market? Perhaps there are insurmountable barriers involved in increasing sales to French Canadians. If so, marketing time and effort could be more profitably spent elsewhere.

On the other hand, differences in consumption habits and practices exist not only between French and English consumers but between French consumers living in Montreal, Quebec City, Sherbrooke, or elsewhere in Quebec. Just about every major market in the United States has its own major consumption profile. There is no reason to believe that Canadian markets are any different in this respect.[7]

Unique Purchasing Habits and Practices

5. What do we know about the purchasing habits and practices of French Canadians?

French Canadian housewives seem to like the friendly atmosphere of the boutique and the personal contact with store employees.

In the past, such personal contact could only be obtained at small neighborhood food stores offering credit and delivery. In time, these stores expanded, and other, more "specialized" food stores appeared on the scene. This may account for Quebec's omnipresent epicierie (grocery store), charcuterie (butcher shop), depanneur (convenience store), and patisserie (bakery). It may also help explain the greater importance of small retail outlets in Quebec as compared to Ontario.

Is there another reason for the apparent Quebec preference both for national brands and for purchasing at relatively small food stores rather than supermarket chains? In Quebec, until 1984, beer and wine were available for home consumption only from corner groceries, depanneurs, and independent supermarkets having three employees or less. This legal restriction generated additional customers for such outlets. It also increased the relative popularity of the national brands these stores carry. Independent outlets are still allowed to have longer operating hours than supermarket chains. Peculiarities of the distributive market may explain, at least in part, French-English differences in purchasing habits and practices.

Many neighborhood food stores have recently become members either of retailer cooperatives such as Metro or wholesaler-sponsored voluntary chains such as Provigo. Even the ever-present depanneur is now often part of a franchised chain such as Le Maisonnee owned by Steinberg and Provi-Soir owned by Provigo. This trend toward vertical integration and franchising, found not only in the food business but in other sectors of the economy as well (hardware stores, drugs, books, etc.), has an impact on French Canadian purchasing habits and practices.

Household Decision Making

6. What about household decision making in the marketplace?

BCP Publicite, one of Montreal's largest advertising agencies, found the following when it studied middle-aged, middle-class French Canadian couples:

a. Automobiles, insurance, and lodging are viewed primarily as male responsibilities.
b. Food, clothing, and allowances are recognized as female responsibilities.
c. Decisions regarding the education of children are jointly made.
d. Furniture was considered by females as a female responsibility, while men perceived such purchases as a joint decision.
e. Clothing for males was regarded by men as a joint decision, but women claimed it as their area of responsibility.[8]

Another source concluded that when it comes to major purchases such as an automobile:

a. The higher the degree of influence of the husband, the less joint decisions are likely to be made.
b. Newlyweds or recently married women had more to say in such purchases.
c. Women lost competence and influence in decision making the longer they stayed at home and the larger the family.
d. Husbands judged their wives more competent if they held jobs outside the home.[9]

These findings may have applied to French Canadian consumers in the past. Are they still valid? How have they been affected by the feminist movement and other recent developments? To what extent do such dimensions differentiate French-speaking from English-speaking consumers? Unfortunately, it is impossible to answer these questions.

The Search for the "Reason Why"

Now we will explore the issue of greatest importance to Canadian marketers. If French-speaking and English-speaking Canadians differ in product usage, brand preference, and shopping habits, what factors account for such differences? With an answer to that question, firms could develop far more effective strategies for these two important segments of the Canadian market. Unfortunately, general agreement is yet to be reached as to the "reasons why" marked variations often exist. What are some of the different explanations that have been advanced?

Is language the reason?

The difference in language is an obvious one with far-reaching marketing consequences. Fifty-five percent of the French Canadians living in Quebec plus the 16 county regions speak only French. Another significant proportion is somewhat bilingual but exposed primarily to French-language advertising media. Such customers should obviously be addressed in their mother tongue. Does this mean, however, that English-language advertising intelligently adapted into French will not be effective? Most marketers now believe that the extra costs involved in developing a separate campaign are more than offset by the increased effectiveness of advertising created in an entirely French environment.[10]

Language-related differences in response to advertising do exist. For example, French Canadians are believed to react far more positively when products or services are endorsed by prominent French Canadian athletes or entertainers.[11] French Canadians, a recent study concluded, pay more attention to the source of advertisements (i.e., spokespersons), while English Canadians are more affected by the content of the message.[12] But despite such differences, language is not generally considered a major cause of existing French-English differences in brand preferences and consumption patterns. We must look beyond language for an explanation.

Is the explanation socioeconomic?

Does the answer lie in the social and economic differences between French Canadian consumers and their English-speaking counterparts? It has been argued that a much larger proportion of French Canadian families belong to the lower socioeconomic classes and that they consume accordingly. As evidence of this fact, some cite the many parallels between the values of French Canadian women and those of American working-class wives. The more commonly mentioned marketing differences between French Canadian and English Canadian consumers, one observer maintained, are similar to those that American researchers have found between the middle and lower classes.[13]

What logically follows from such a socioeconomic explanation? Differences between consumption practices should decline as the relative income and education of French Canadians approaches that of English Canadians. The marketplace behavior of French and English families of equivalent socioeconomic class should be pretty much the same.

Socioeconomic factors, however, are not universally accepted as either explanations for French-English differences in consumption or predictions of what is likely to happen. There are those who believe comparable incomes and educations do not necessarily mean similar consumption patterns. They maintain that a different heritage affecting ideas, attitudes, values, and habits could lead to very different French Canadian purchasing patterns.[14] And there is evidence to support this position. Two studies have shown that consumption patterns differed markedly between Quebec (French language) and Ontario (English language) households of similar size, income level, and educational background.[15]

What about law and regulation

Provincial laws and regulations unique to Quebec contribute, at least to some extent, to existing French-English differences in consumption habits and practices. We have already seen that until recently Quebec's laws aided small stores at the expense of supermarkets. Quebec's best-known piece of marketing legislation is Bill 101, which restricts the use of English in all commercial communications. Consequently, French is the primary language used in advertising, sales slips, catalogs, posters, point-of-purchase displays, direct mail, and even packaging. This legislation makes marketing in Quebec very different from marketing in other parts of Canada. However, it is not clear exactly how Bill 101 affects French-English differences in consumption habits and practices. Two other bills also affect marketing in Quebec. Bill 67 restricts the use of coupons, contests, and lotteries in Quebec, and Bill 34 prohibits advertising directed toward children 13 years of age or under.

Does culture make the difference?

Many believe that culture, broadly defined, underlies many French-English differences in consumption patterns. In addition to language, some important French Canadian culture traits are said to be:

A more homogeneous society with rigid barriers against assimilation forces.

A philosophical and psychological outlook which tends to be more humanistic, more historically oriented, more emotional, and less pragmatic with lower achievement motivation.

A relatively stronger sense of religious authority.

A greater role for the family unit and the kinship system.

However, the changes associated with Quebec's Quiet Revolution have influenced the prevailing philosophical outlook. In particular, it reduced the importance of both church and family.[16]

A leading French Canadian advertising executive believes that the history of the French Canadian community helps to explain some of the behavioral differences between French and English Canadian consumers. He identifies six determining influences on the French Canadian: moral origin, minority group status within Canada, a North American environment, and Catholic, Latin, and French origins.[17]

Unfortunately, a generalized statement that culture and heritage make the difference does not help in developing more appropriate strategies. We need to know how and why social, psychological, cultural, or other market-related factors are reflected in the French Canadian consumer's search for information, in his exposure to advertising media, and in the selection of the products and brands actually purchased.

And what about social change?

Rapid social and cultural evolution is affecting this market. French Canadian society has transformed itself over the last few years. Today, that society is determined to exercise economic and social authority within its province. There has also been an increasing level of education, a weakening of family ties, and a distinct rejection of religious constraints. Such changes have far-reaching marketing implications. For example, consider how products and markets have been affected by a sharp decline in the Quebec birth rate and a marked increase in the number of working French Canadian women!

The sense of belonging to a unique and original French Canadian society is very strong in Quebec. Many advertisers now believe that a positive brand image can be built by appealing to this sense of identity. Such marketers have modified their French-language advertising appeals accordingly.

What psychographics teaches us

A life-style study of activities, interests, opinions, and behavior revealed, among other things, that compared to her English counterpart, the French Canadian female is:

1. More oriented toward the home, the family, the children, and the kitchen.
2. More interested in baking and cooking and more negative toward convenience foods.
3. More concerned about personal and home cleanliness, and more fashion and personal appearance conscious.
4. More price conscious.
5. Much more concerned about a number of social, political, and consumer issues.
6. More religious, especially in feelings about the life hereafter.
7. More security conscious and less prone to take risks.
8. More positive toward television and less positive toward newspapers.
9. More negative toward bank borrowing and the use of credit cards.
10. Characterized by a set of values described as steady and consistent.[18]

Although the data for this study was collected in 1970, a subsequent life-style investigation some years later produced similar results. In addition, researchers learned that the French Canadian housewife, as compared with her English-speaking counterpart, was more liberal and perhaps less prudish in her views, more concerned about education, and less confident about her decision-making abilities. The only significant difference in the two studies concerned the apparent degree of price consciousness. The more recent investigation concluded that French-speaking housewives were less rather than more price conscious than English-speaking ones.[19]

■ CONCLUSION

What have we covered in this appendix? First, we tried to define a French Canadian consumer. We discussed geographic boundaries of the French Canadian markets and French-English differences in product usage. However efforts to explain such differences were not very successful. Neither language nor socioeconomic factors appeared to be "the reason why." Cultural factors and a rapid period of social change are obviously important. They are not, however, easily related to specific brand preferences and overall consumption patterns. As Figure D–1 indicated, we are a long way from knowing what we should about the French Canadian market.

■ NOTES

1. P. C. Lefrancois and Giles Chatel, "The French-Canadian Consumer: Fact and Fancy," in *New Ideas for Successful Marketing Proceedings of the 1966 World Congress,* ed. J. S. Wright and J. L. Goldstucker (Chicago: American Marketing Association, 1966), p. 706.

2. See Ron Boychuk, "The Impact of English Media on Francophones," *Marketing,* June 13, 1983, pp. 23–25.

3. The approach used in answering this question and the following one draws heavily on Lefrancois and Chatel, but 1981 census figures have been utilized instead of the 1961 census data they employed.

4. "Data Base Offers Consumer Profiles from 'Nine Nations,'" *Marketing News* 18 (May 25, 1984), p. 13.

5. Frederick Elkin, *Rebels and Colleagues: Advertising and Social Change in French Canada* (Montreal: McGill-Queen's Press, 1973), p. 73.

6. The preceding are but a few of many drawn from numerous sources and cited by Bruce Mallen, "The Present State of Knowledge and Research in Marketing to the French-Canadian Market," in *Canadian Marketing: Problems and Prospects,* ed. D. N. Thompson and D. S. R. Leighton (Toronto: Wiley of Canada, 1973), pp. 100–101.

7. Robert Tamilia, "Advanced Research Skills Needed to Probe Consumption Patterns of French Canadians," *Marketing News,* 13 (April 18, 1980), p. 3.

8. Jean M. Lefevre, "A Compilation of Empirical Studies of Family Roles in French-Canadian Families," mimeographed and undated.

9. Ibid.

10. Robert D. Tamilia, "International Advertising Revisited," in *Perspectives in International Business: Readings and Essays,* ed. Harold W. Berkman and Ivan R. Vernon (New York: Rand McNally, 1979).

11. Michael Patterson, "French Agencies Have No Golden Touch—Just a Better Feel for the Quebecois Taste," *Marketing,* October 27, 1975.

12. Robert D. Tamilia, "A Cross-Cultural Study of Source Effects in a Canadian Advertising Situation," in *Marketing 1978: New Trends in Canadian Marketing,* ed. J. M. Boisvert and R. Savitt (Edmonton: Administrative Sciences Association of Canada, 1978), pp. 250–56.

13. Lefrancois and Chatel, "French Canadian Consumer," pp. 710–15.

14. C. R. McGoldrick, "The French Canadian Consumer: The Past Is Prologue," speech before the 4th Annual Conference Association of Canadian Advertisers, in *Marketing: A Canadian Perspective,* ed. M. D. Beckman and R. H. Evans (Scarborough, Ontario: Prentice-Hall of Canada, 1972), p. 92.

15. K. S. Palda, "A Comparison of Consumer Expenditures in Quebec and Ontario," *Canadian Journal of Economics and Political Science* 33, (February 1967), p. 26. See also Dwight R. Thomas, "Culture and Consumption Behavior in English and French Canada," in *Marketing in the 1970's and Beyond,* ed. Bent Stidsen (Canadian Association of Administrative Sciences, Marketing Division, 1975), pp. 255–61.

16. Mallen, "The Present State of Knowledge and Research in Marketing to the French-Canadian Market," p. 105.

17. Jaques Bouchard, "Les 36 cordes sensibles du consommateur quebecois," unpublished paper, 1973, quoted in *Communication de Masse, Consommation de Masse,* ed. Claude Cossette (Sillery: Le Borial Express, 1975), pp. 257–58.

18. D. J. Tigert, "Can A Separate Marketing Strategy for French Canada Be Justified: Profiling English-French Markets through Life-Style Analysis," in *Canadian Marketing,* ed. Thompson and Leighton, p. 128.

19. Marion Plunkett, "The Difference between French and English Speaking Canadians," paper presented to the Academy of Marketing Science, Ohio, May 1977.

Chapter 8 ■ Industrial and organizational customers and their buying behavior

When you finish this chapter, you should:

1. Know who the organizational customers are.
2. Know about the number and distribution of manufacturers.
3. Understand the problem-solving behavior of manufacturers' purchasing agents.
4. Know the basic methods used in industrial buying.
5. Know how buying by retailers, wholesalers, and governments is similar to—and different from—industrial buying.
6. Recognize the important new terms (shown in red).

"Organizational customers buy more than final consumers!"

Most of us think of the term *customer* as meaning only the individual final consumer. Actually, more purchases are made by organizational customers. This chapter will discuss these organizational consumers: who they are; where they are; how they buy.

Organizational customers are any buyers from producers of basic raw materials to final consumers. Some examples include:

Manufacturers, farmers, and other producers of goods or services;

Wholesalers and retailers;

Hospitals, universities, and other non-profit organizations;

Government units—including federal agencies in Canada or other countries, as well as all the provincial and local-level governments.

Many of the behavioral influences we discussed in the last chapter apply to organizational customers, too. After all, *people* do the buying. But there are also some important differences—as the following example shows.

General Motors needed to cut the weight of its cars—to improve gas mileage and be able to compete with the imports. Reynolds Aluminum assigned a sales rep to the account—because its lightweight metals were a possible solution. Meetings were arranged with those involved in the decision. GM engineers, production managers, quality-control and safety experts all had different concerns. The sales rep listened to each one and offered advice about which parts could be made of lighter metals—and what technical problems had to be considered.

After more than a year, GM wrote detailed specifications of the lightweight parts it wanted—and invited a few suppliers to submit bids. In preparing a bid, the sales rep from Reynolds was pleased to see that many of his suggestions—favorable to his products—appeared in the GM specifications. He was finally called by a GM buyer—who told him that top GM executives had selected several suppliers—to ensure supply and keep suppliers on their toes—but Reynolds would get a nice share of the new business.

The main focus in this chapter will be on the buying behavior of manufacturers—because we know most about them. Other organizational customers seem to buy in much the same way. In fact, often buyers for all kinds of organizations are loosely referred to as "industrial buyers."

Organizational Customers Are Different

There are about 500,000 organizational customers in Canada—spread across different buying categories. These customers do many different jobs—and many different market dimensions are needed to describe all these different markets.

Organizational customers buy for a purpose

Organizational buyers purchase goods and services to meet needs—just as final consumers do. But here the needs are usually easier to define. Organizational customers buy for specific purposes. A business firm wants to make a profit—usually by making or reselling products. A town government wants to meet its legal and social obligations to citizens. A country club wants to help its members enjoy their leisure times. Such organizations buy goods and services which will *help them meet the demand* for the goods and services which they in turn supply to their markets.

Even small differences are important

Understanding how and why organizational customers buy is important because competition is often rugged in organizational markets. Even "trivial" differences may affect the success of a marketing mix.

Since sellers usually approach each organizational customer directly—through a sales representative—there is more chance to adjust the marketing mix for each individual customer. It is even possible that there will be a special marketing strategy for each individual customer. This is carrying target marketing to its extreme. But when the customer's size and sales volume make this possible, it may be not only desirable but necessary in order to compete.

In such situations, the individual sales rep will have to carry more responsibility for strategy planning. This is relevant to your career planning—since these jobs are very challenging and pay well.

Manufacturers Are Important Customers

There are not many big ones

One of the most striking facts about manufacturers is how few there are compared to final consumers. In the industrial market, Table 8–1 shows there were under 36,000 factories in 1982, and the majority of these are quite small. The

■ TABLE 8–1 Canadian manufacturing establishments, 1982

					Number employed					
	Under 5	5–9	10–19	20–49	50–99	100–199	200–499	500–999	1,000 +	Total
Number of establishments	10,710	6,521	6,072	6,246	2,897	1,847	1,129	274	138	35,834
Percent of total establishments	29.89	18.20	16.95	17.43	8.08	5.15	3.15	.76	.39	100%
Number of employees	19,885	38,415	68,403	150,020	152,962	194,412	247,973	133,748	206,606	1,212,424
Percent of total employees	1.64	3.17	5.64	12.37	12.62	16.04	20.45	11.03	17.04	100%
Percent of manufacturing shipments	.93	1.58	3.48	8.98	10.71	15.00	25.04	13.03	21.25	100%

Source: Statistics Canada, Cat. 31-203, Table 57, 1984.

owners may also be the buyers in small plants. And they buy less formally than in the relatively few large manufacturing plants which employ the majority of workers and do most of the manufacturing. In 1982, plants with 200 or more employees numbered only 1,541—about 4 percent of the total—yet they employed 48.5 percent of all production employees and produced 59.3 percent of all manufacturing shipments. These large plants are important, and it may be desirable to segment industrial markets on the basis of size.

Customers cluster in geographic areas

In addition to concentration by size, industrial markets are concentrated in particular geographic areas—both regions and cities. Quebec and Ontario are important industrial markets, as are the big metropolitan areas in the other provinces. Tables 8–2 and 8–3 tell us more about the distribution of Canadian manufacturing by province and by industry group.

The buyers for some of these larger manufacturers are even further concentrated in home offices, often in large metropolitan areas. One of the large building material manufacturers, for example, does the bulk of its buying for more than 50 North American plants from its Chicago office. In such a case, a sales representative may be able to sell all over the country without leaving the home city. This makes selling easier for competitors also, and the market may be extremely competitive. The importance of these big buyers has led some companies to set up "national account" sales forces specially trained to cater to their needs. A geographically bound salesperson can be at a real disadvantage against such competitors.

Concentration by industry

Not only do we see concentrations by size of firm and geographic location, but also by industry. Iron and steel mills center in Ontario, while flour mills are in Saskatchewan. Paper and allied industries tend to group in Quebec and British Columbia. Other industries have similar concentration based on the availability of natural or human resources.

■ TABLE 8–2   Number of manufacturing establishments and volume of shipments by province, 1982

Province	Number of establishments	Percent of establishments	Value of shipments ($000)	Percent of shipment value
Newfoundland	295	.82%	$ 1,288,536	.69%
Prince Edward Island	127	.35	255,173	.13
Nova Scotia	781	2.18	3,610,726	1.92
New Brunswick	591	1.65	3,323,697	1.77
Quebec	10,753	30.01	49,179,416	26.17
Ontario	14,822	41.36	93,939,308	49.99
Manitoba	1,279	3.57	4,839,481	2.57
Saskatchewan	749	2.09	2,488,065	1.32
Alberta	2,490	6.95	13,278,317	7.07
British Columbia	3,919	10.94	15,689,780	8.35
Yukon and Northwest Territories	28		40,384	.02
Total	35,834		$187,932,882	100.00%

Source: Statistics Canada, Cat. 31-203, Table 57, 1984.

■ TABLE 8–3   Value of manufactured shipments (by industry group, 1982)

Industry group	1982 value ($000)	Percent of all manufactured shipments
Foods and beverages industries	$ 32,930,113	17.52%
Tobacco products industries.	1,493,756	.79
Rubber and plastics products industries	4,433,639	2.36
Leather industries	1,105,960	.59
Textile industries	4,507,573	2.40
Knitting mills	947,795	.50
Clothing industries	3,962,352	2.12
Wood industries.	7,173,003	3.81
Furniture and fixture industries	2,494,082	1.33
Paper and allied industries	14,783,955	7.87
Printing, publishing, and allied industries	6,779,341	3.61
Primary metal industries	12,402,450	6.60
Metal fabricating industries (except machinery and transportation equipment industries).	11,765,669	6.26
Machinery industries (except electrical machinery)	7,662,220	4.08
Transportation equipment industries	22,656,564	12.05
Electrical products industries	8,714,421	4.64
Nonmetallic mineral products industries. . .	4,385,269	2.33
Petroleum and coal products industries . . .	21,709,154	11.55
Chemical and chemical products industries	4,095,400	7.50
Miscellaneous manufacturing industries . .	3,930,165	2.09
Total	$187,932,882	100.00%

Source: Statistics Canada, Cat. 31-203, 1984, Table 3.

Much data is available on industrial markets by SIC code

In industrial markets, marketing managers can focus their attention on a relatively few clearly defined markets and reach the majority of the business. Their efforts can be aided by the availability of very detailed information. The federal government regularly collects data on the number of establishments, their sales volumes, and the number of employees of a large number of industry groups, broken down by Census Metropolitan Areas. The data is reported for Standard Industrial Classification code industries (**SIC codes**). These codes greatly facilitate research by firms which can relate their own sales to their *customers'* type of activity. Figure 8–1 provides more detailed information on how the SIC code goes from the general to the very specific.

Four-digit detail is not available for all industries in every geographic area. To preserve confidentiality, the census will not reveal data when only one or two plants are located in an area. But the point is that a lot of good basic information is available. If companies aiming at industrial target markets can specify who they are aiming at, readily available data organized by SIC codes may be extremely valuable. Besides the federal government, most trade associations and private organizations which gather data in the industrial area do so according to SIC code.[1]

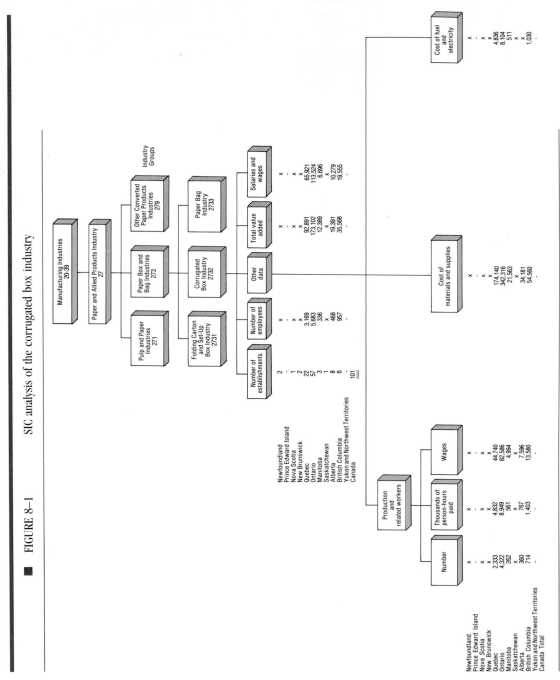

■ FIGURE 8–1   SIC analysis of the corrugated box industry

Source: From an unpublished research paper by Shaheen Lalji, Simon Fraser University. Statistical source: Statistics Canada. Cat. 36-216. 1982.

Industrial Buyers Are Problem Solvers

Some people think of industrial buying as entirely different from consumer buying—but a closer look at buying processes suggests that there are many similarities. In fact, the problem-solving framework introduced in Chapter 7 can be applied here.

Three kinds of buying processes are useful

In Chapter 7, we discussed problem solving by consumers and how it might vary from extended problem solving to routine buying. In industrial markets, it is useful to adapt these concepts slightly—and work with three similar buying processes, a *new-task buying* process, a *modified rebuy* process, or a *straight rebuy.*[2]

New-task buying occurs when a firm has a new need and the buyer wants a great deal of information. New-task buying can involve setting product specifications, sources of supply, and an order routine which can be followed in the future—if satisfactory results are obtained.

The **modified rebuy** is the in-between process where some review of the buying situation is done—though not as much as in new-task buying. Sometimes a competitor will get lazy enjoying a straight rebuy situation. An alert marketer can turn these situations into opportunities—by providing more information.

A **straight rebuy** is a routine repurchase which may have been made many times before. Buyers probably would not bother looking for new information—or new sources of supply. Most of a company's small or recurring purchases might be this type—but they take only a small part of an organized buyer's time.

A particular product may be considered in any of the three ways. Careful market analysis is needed to determine how the firm's products are accepted—and by whom. A new-task buy will take much longer than a straight rebuy—and provide much more chance for a promotion impact by the seller. This can be seen in Figure 8–2—which shows the time and many influences involved in the purchase of a special drill.

Industrial buyers are becoming specialists

The large size of some manufacturers has created a need for buying specialists. **Purchasing agents** are buying specialists for manufacturers. Some of these have banded together—forming the Purchasing Management Association of Canada—in an effort to improve the effectiveness and status of professional buyers. This is the well-informed, modern buyer who will face *you* if you want to sell to the industrial market.

The industrial buyer—or purchasing agent—usually must be seen first—before any other employee is contacted. These buyers hold important positions and take a dim view of sales reps who try to go around them. In large companies, purchasing agents usually specialize by product area—and are real experts.

Rather than being "sold," these buyers expect accurate information that will help them buy wisely. They like information on new goods and services—and tips on potential price changes, strikes, and other changes in business conditions.

■ FIGURE 8–2　　　　　Decision network diagram of the buying situations: Special drill

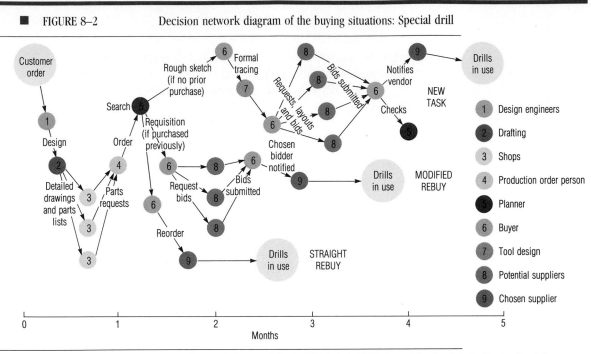

Source: Patrick J. Robinson and Charles W. Faris, *Industrial Buying and Creative Marketing* (Boston: Allyn & Bacon, 1967), p. 33. Reprinted by permission of the publisher.

Most industrial buyers are serious and well educated—and sales representatives should treat them accordingly.

Basic purchasing needs are economic

Industrial buyers are usually less emotional in their buying than final consumers. Buyers look for certain product characteristics—including economy both in original cost and in use, productivity, uniformity, purity, and ability to make the buyer's final product better.

In addition to product characteristics, buyers consider the reliability of the seller, general cooperativeness, ability to provide speedy maintenance and repair, past and present relationships (including previous favors), continuous supply under all conditions, and reliable and fast delivery.

Many buyers use **vendor analysis**—formal rating of suppliers on all relevant areas of performance. Evaluating suppliers and how they are working out can result in better buying decisions.

Emotional needs are relevant, too

Vendor analysis tries to focus on economic factors—but industrial purchasing does have some emotional overtones. Modern buyers are human—and want friendly relationships with suppliers. Some buyers seem eager to imitate progressive competitors—or even to be the first to try new products. Such "innovators" might deserve special attention—when new products are being introduced.

Buyers are also human with respect to protecting their own interests—and their own position in the company. Most buyers—like people everywhere—want to survive and improve their chances for promotion—without taking too many risks. "Looking good" is a serious matter for some purchasing agents—because they have to buy a wide variety of things from many sources and make decisions involving many factors beyond their control. Spending a few dollars more on a well-known supplier may not be noticed or criticized. But if a new source delivers low-quality materials, you can guess who will be blamed. Poor service or late delivery also will reflect on the buyer's ability. Therefore, anyone or anything that helps the buyer look good to higher-ups has a definite appeal. In fact, this one factor may make the difference between a successful and an unsuccessful marketing mix.

Supply sources must be dependable

This matter of dependability deserves further emphasis. There is nothing worse to a purchasing agent and a production manager than shutting down a production line because sellers haven't delivered the goods. Product quality is important, too. The cost of a small item may have little to do with its importance. If it causes the breakdown of a larger unit into which it goes, it may result in a large loss completely out of proportion to its own cost.

To try to assure dependable quality, some buyers inspect all incoming lots with statistical quality control procedures. Such buyers give preference to producers whose products are slightly better than required specifications—thereby giving greater assurance of reliability and quality. This is *the* important selling

■ FIGURE 8–3   Overlapping needs of an individual industrial buyer and of the firm (shaded area)

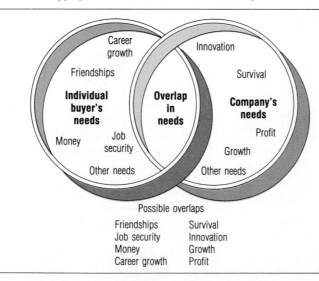

point for some firms. In effect, this "makes" their marketing mix—because it gives the buyer an extra margin of safety.

A seller's marketing mix should satisfy both the needs of the buyer's company as well as the buyer's individual needs. Therefore, it helps to find an overlapping area where both can be satisfied. See Figure 8–3 (page 263) for a graphic model of this concept.

Multiple buying influences in a buying center

Much of the work of the typical purchasing agent consists of straight rebuys—routine placing of orders to fill requisitions flowing from various production, warehouse, and office departments. For such requisitions, the order can be placed without consultation with anyone.

In other cases—especially new-task buying—a multiple buying influence may be important. **Multiple buying influence** means the buyer shares the purchas-

Borden Chemical knows that industrial buyers want dependable sources of supply.

ZERO DEFECTS. In service, in delivery. That's our goal.

At Borden Graphics, our service, delivery and production systems interact with each other. This chain of systems improves performance and enables us to achieve the same standard for each one. The very highest.

Our staff of quality control, R&D and sales professionals are dedicated to delivering the best inks, pigments and flushes. Their expertise, aided by the most sophisticated testing equipment in the business, enables them to respond to any problem, however complex.

If there's a pressroom problem, they can rectify it immediately. And if, for any reason, you have an unexpected customer request, they can help you respond to it without delay.

Zero defects is our goal. Our chain of systems and our people make sure we reach it.

ZERO DEFECTS. That's our goal.

For more information on these or any ink subject call toll-free*: K. Fritz, 1-800-543-1670. *In Ohio call 1-800-582-1621. Or write Borden Chemical, Graphics Division, 630 Glendale-Milford Road, Cincinnati, Ohio 45215.

ing decision with several people—perhaps even top management. Possible buying influences include:

1. *Users*—perhaps production line workers or their supervisors.
2. *Influencers*—perhaps engineering or R&D people who help write specifications or supply information for evaluating alternatives.
3. *Buyers*—the purchasing agents who have the responsibility for selecting suppliers and arranging the terms of the sale.
4. *Deciders*—the persons in the organization who have the power to select or approve the supplier—usually the purchasing agent for small items, but perhaps top management for larger purchases.
5. *Gatekeepers*—people who control the flow of information within the organization—perhaps purchasing agents who shield users or other deciders. Gatekeepers can also include receptionists, secretaries, research assistants, and others who influence the flow of information about potential purchases.[3] An example will help to show how the different buying influences work in a business situation.

Multiple-buying influence is often involved in industrial purchase decisions.

■ FIGURE 8–4   Major elements of organizational buying behavior

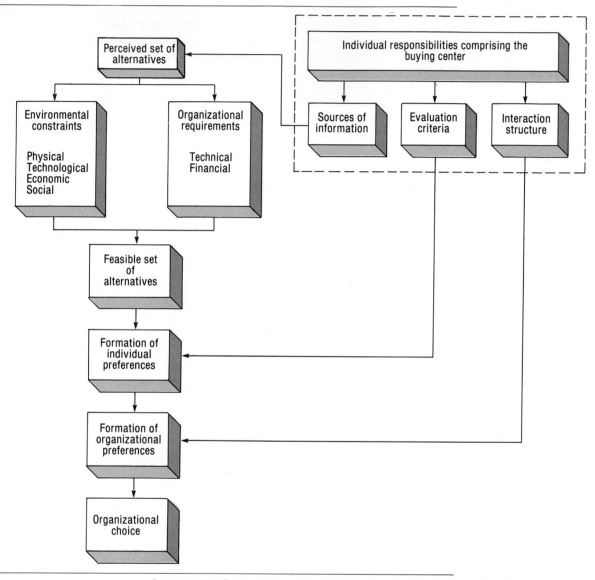

Source: Jean-Marie Choffray and Gary L. Lilien, *Market Planning for New Industrial Products*, Ronald Series on Marketing Management (New York: John Wiley & Sons, 1980), p.35.

A manufacturer of running shoes wants to buy a machine that will attach shoe soles to the tops. Different vendors are eager for the business. Several people (*influencers*) help to evaluate the choices. A finance manager is worried about the high cost, and just wants to lease the machine. The quality control people want a machine that will do a more accurate job—although it's more expensive.

The production manager is interested in speed of operation. The production line workers and their supervisors want the machine that is easiest to use—so workers can continue to rotate jobs.

The company president has notified the purchasing department to assemble all the information—but says he will reserve the power to select and approve the supplier (to be the *decider.*) The administrative assistant for the purchasing manager has been deciding what information to pass on to higher-ups and scheduling visits for salespeople (a gatekeeper. After all these buying influences are considered, one of the purchasing agents for the firm will be the *buyer*—with responsibility for making recommendations and arranging the details of the terms of the sale.

It is helpful to think of a **buying center** that consists of all the people who participate in or influence a purchase. The people who make up a buying center probably will be different from one decision to the next. Who is involved will also vary a lot from firm to firm—depending on how they operate. This makes the marketing job difficult.

The salesperson must study each case carefully. Just finding out who to talk with may be hard—but thinking about the various roles in the buying center can help.

The salesperson might have to talk to every member of the buying center—stressing different topics for each. This not only complicates the promotion job—but also lengthens it. Approval of a routine order may take anywhere from a week to several months. On very important purchases—a new computer system, a new plant, or major equipment—the selling period may stretch out to a year or more.[4] Figure 8–4 shows an organizational buying behavior model similar to what was shown for individuals in Figure 7–3.

Basic Methods and Practices in Industrial Buying

Not only the nature of the buyer—but also the nature of the buying situation—may be the basis for segmenting markets. Some buyers use different methods of evaluating products and sellers. And because of the way they buy, there may be times when the market potential dries up completely—and there is no way for a new supplier to break into a market.

Should you inspect, sample, describe, or negotiate?

Industrial buyers (really, buyers of all types, including final consumers) can use four basic approaches to evaluating and buying products: (1) *inspection,* (2) *sampling,* (3) *description,* and (4) *negotiated contracts.* Understanding the differences in these buying methods is important in strategy planning—so let's briefly look at each approach.

Inspection looks at everything

Inspection buying means looking at every item. It is used for products that are not standardized—and require examination. Here each product is different—as in the case of livestock or used equipment. These products are often sold in open markets—or at auction if there are several potential buyers. Buyers inspect the goods and either "haggle" with the seller—or bid against competitors.

Sampling looks at some

Sampling buying means looking at only part of a potential purchase. Sampling is logical when a buyer is evaluating a large quantity that is standardized—perhaps because of careful grading or quality control. Sampling is necessary when it is too expensive or impractical to inspect every item. For example, a power company might buy miles of heavy electric cable. A sample section might be heated to the melting point—to be certain it is safe.

Prices may be based on a sample. The general price level may be set by demand and supply factors—but the actual price level may vary from this level, depending on the quality of a specific sample. This kind of buying is used in grain markets, for example—where the actual price is based on a sample which has been withdrawn from a carload of grain and analyzed.

Description just describes accurately

Description (specification) buying means buying from a written (or verbal) description of the product. Most manufactured items and many agricultural commodities are bought this way—because quality control or grading procedures can be used. When quality can almost be guaranteed, buying by description—grade, brand, or specification—may be satisfactory—especially when there is mutual trust between buyers and sellers. Many fruits and vegetables are sorted according to government grading standards when picked—and then bought without further inspection. This, of course, reduces the cost of buying and is used by buyers whenever practical.

Negotiated contracts explain how to handle relationships

Negotiated contract buying means agreeing to a contract that allows for changing the purchase arrangements.

Sometimes, the buyer knows roughly what is needed—but can't fix all the details in advance. The specifications or total requirements may change as the job progresses. This is found, for example, in research and development work—and in the building of special-purpose machinery or buildings. In such cases, the general project is described, and a basic price may be agreed on—with provision for changes and price adjustments up or down. Or a supplier may be willing to accept a contract that provides some type of incentive—such as full coverage of costs plus a fixed fee or full costs plus a percentage profit based on costs. The whole contract may even be subject to renegotiation as the work proceeds.

In modern economies, most products are purchased by some combination of description or negotiated contracts. Laws make it easy to enforce the contracts. By contrast, most buying in less-developed economies is done by inspection or sampling—regardless of the products. The reason is skepticism and uncertainty about quality—or lack of faith in the seller.

**Buyers may favor
loyal, helpful
suppliers**

To be sure of dependable quality, a buyer may develop loyalty to certain suppliers. This is especially important when buying non-standardized products. When a friendly relationship is developed over the years, the supplier practically becomes a part of the buyer's organization. (Sometimes the buyer will design a product—and then simply ask the supplier to build and deliver it—at a fair price.)

When a seller proposes a new idea that saves the buyer's company money, the seller is usually rewarded with orders. Most buyers have a sense of fair play—and this also encourages future suggestions. In contrast, buyers who use a bid system exclusively—either by choice or necessity, as in some government and institutional purchasing—may not be offered much beyond the basic goods or services. They are interested primarily in price. Marketing managers who have developed better products may not seek such business—at least with their better marketing mixes.

**But buyers must
spread their risk—by
seeking several
sources**

Even if a firm has developed the most ideal marketing mix possible, it probably will not get all the business of its industrial customers. Purchasing agents usually look for several dependable sources of supply—to protect themselves from unpredictable events, such as strikes, fires, or floods in one of their suppliers' plants. Still, a good marketing mix is likely to win a larger share of the total business.

**Most buyers try to
routinize buying**

Most firms use a buying procedure that tries to routinize the process. When some person or unit wants to buy something, a **requisition**—a request to buy something—is filled out. After approval by some operating supervisor, the requisition is forwarded to the buyer for placement with the "best" seller. These requisitions have already been approved—and now the buyer is responsible for placing a purchase order and getting delivery by the date requested.

**Ordering may be rou-
tine after
requisitioning**

The requisitions are converted to purchase orders as quickly as possible. Straight rebuys are usually made the day the requisition is received—while new-task and modified rebuys take longer. If time is important, the buyer may place the order by telephone—and then a confirming purchase order is typed and sent out. Routine straight rebuys consist of the buyer (1) deciding which of several sellers will get the order, (2) filling in the seller's name and other details on the requisition, and (3) forwarding it to the clerical pool for typing into a purchase order and mailing.

**It pays to know the
buyer**

Notice the importance of being one of the regular sources of supply. The buyers don't even call potential sources for straight rebuys. Sellers' sales reps regularly call on these buyers—*not* to sell a particular item but to maintain relations—or to become a source—and/or to point out new developments which might cause the buyer to reevaluate the present "straight rebuy" procedure and give some business to the sales rep's company.

Obviously, having a favorable image is an advantage for a seller. Unless a definite share of the business must be allocated to each of several sources, it is likely that a favored source will get a slightly larger share. Moving from a 20 percent to a 30 percent share may not seem like much from a buyer's point of view, but for the seller it is a 50 percent increase in sales!

Some buy by computer

Some buyers delegate a large part of their routine order-placing to computers. They program decision rules that tell the computer how to order—and leave the details of following through to the machine. When economic conditions change, the buyers modify the computer instructions. When nothing unusual happens, however, the computer system continues to routinely rebuy as needs develop—printing out new purchase orders to the regular suppliers.

Obviously, it is a big "sale" to be selected as a major supplier and routinely called up in the computer program. It is also obvious that such a buyer will be more impressed by an attractive marketing mix for a whole *line* of products than just a lower price for a particular order. It may be too expensive and too much trouble to change the whole buying system just because somebody is offering a low price on a particular day.

Paying taxes affects spending decisions

How the cost of a particular purchase is handled on a firm's profit and loss statement has a big effect on the buyer. If—in computing profits—the cost of a large machine could be charged to the current year's expenses, the company might be more willing to buy it. Even though the cost of the equipment reduced current profits, it also would reduce taxes and increase the company's assets. Typically, however, such purchases *cannot* be charged off in one year, due to government regulations.

There are two general methods of charging costs: as capital and as expense items. Both are determined primarily by Revenue Canada Taxation regulations.

Capital items are depreciated

Capital items are durable goods—such as large machinery or factories—which are charged off over many years, that is, depreciated. As a general rule, depreciable assets fall into one of over 30 classes, each with a separate depreciation rate. Revenue Canada regulations and accepted accounting procedure require that that rate be applied to determine what portion of the original cost should be charged off each year.[5]

The federal government has relaxed depreciation rules to stimulate the economy and then tightened them—to cool inflationary booms. These efforts have been effective—and you can see why managers do look at capital investments differently from expense items. Capital items are likely to lead to "new task" purchasing—because of their importance to a company.

Expense items are expensed

In contrast to capital items, **expense items** are short-lived goods and services which are charged off as they are used—usually in the year of purchase. The potential value is more easily forecast—and can be compared with the cost. Since the company is not mortgaging its future when it buys expense items, it tends to be less concerned about these costs—especially if business is good. the multiple buying influence is less here—and straight rebuys become more common. If a firm's sales decline, however, some expense purchases may be cut back sharply—or eliminated temporarily. There may also be a return to the modified rebuy process—as buyers reevaluate their sources of supply and the prices being offered to them.

Inventory policy may determine purchases

Industrial firms generally try to maintain an adequate inventory—certainly enough to keep production lines moving. There is no greater disaster in a factory than to have a production line close down.

Adequate inventory is often expressed in terms of number of days' supply—for example, 60- or 90-days' supply. But what is a 60- or 90-days' supply depends on the level of demand for the company's own products. If the demand rises sharply—say by 10 percent—then total purchases will expand by more than 10 percent to maintain customary inventory levels *and* meet the new needs. On the other hand, if sales decrease by 10 percent, actual needs and inventory requirements decrease—and total purchases may decrease drâstically while inventory is being "worked off." During such a cutback, a seller probably couldn't stimulate sales—even by reducing price—or offering more favorable credit terms. The buyer is just not in the market at that time.

Anticipating the future may lead to buying fluctuations

Demand at the manufacturer level may fluctuate much more than at the final consumer level—because manufacturers earlier in the channel try to predict the behavior of middlemen and other producers. If manufacturers believe prices are going to drop further, they may postpone all purchases. If they feel that prices are at their lowest point, they may buy in large quantities—anticipating future needs.

Buyers' needs may be hard to forecast when other organizational customers try to anticipate growing demand. Home air-conditioners, for example, are sold to

A printing press is a capital purchase, but the paper is an expense item.

final consumers mostly in hot weather. Orders for air-conditioner compressors, however, may be heavy *before* the summer selling season because retailers and wholesalers are building their stocks. Compressor producers may have to accelerate production—perhaps even going on overtime. If really hot weather never comes, however, then everyone may be overstocked—and the orders for compressors may stop completely. Yet, a prolonged heat wave may run down retailers' stocks—and start a chain reaction backward to the component manufacturers—and all their suppliers.

Reciprocity helps sales, but . . .

Reciprocity means trading sales for sales—that is, "if you buy from me, I'll buy from you." If a company's customers also can supply products which the firm buys, then the sales departments of both buyer and seller may try to "trade" sales for sales. Purchasing agents generally resist reciprocity—but often there is pressure from the sales departments.

When prices and quality are otherwise competitive, an outside supplier seldom can break such a reciprocal relationship. The supplier can only hope to become an alternate source of supply—and wait for the competitors to let their quality slip or prices rise.

Although the U.S. Justice Department has attacked reciprocity as a monopolistic practice which restricts the normal operation of the free market,[6] the legality of reciprocal agreements has not as yet been seriously challenged under Canadian law. Any such move in this direction would force those firms that place heavy reliance upon reciprocal dealing to reevaluate their marketing strategies.

Buying practices vary by product

These general buying methods and practices apply in the purchase of many industrial products. Specific habits and practices, however, vary according to the type of product—a subject covered in Chapter 10.

Retailers and Wholesalers Are Problem Solvers, Too

They must buy for their customers

Most retail and wholesale buyers see themselves as purchasing agents for their target customers—remembering the old saying that "Goods well bought are half sold." Typically, retailers do *not* see themselves as sales agents for particular manufacturers. They buy what they think they can sell. And wholesalers buy what they think their retailers can sell. They don't try to make value judgments about the desirability or "worth" of what they are selling. Rather, they focus on the needs and attitudes of *their* target customers. Recognizing the close relationship of buying and selling, the buyers in some smaller firms are also responsible for sales and the sales force. This allows immediate feedback from the salespeople to affect buying.

They must buy too many items

Most retailers carry a large number of items—drug stores up to 12,000 items, hardware stores from 3,000 to 25,000, and grocery stores up to 20,000 items—and they just don't have the time to pay close attention to every individual item.

This wholesaler uses a computer-to-telephone hookup to place orders and control inventory.

Often retail buyers are annoyed by the number of wholesalers' and manufacturers' representatives who call on them. The retailers feel that their sales of each item are so small that they can't afford to spend much time on each product.

Wholesalers, too, handle so many items that they can't give continuous attention to each one of them. A drug wholesaler—for example—may stock up to 125,000 items—and a dry-goods (textiles and sewing supplies) wholesaler up to 250,000 items. Understandably, most retailers and wholesalers buy most of their products on a routine, automatic reorder basis—straight rebuys—once the initial decision to stock products has been made. Sellers to these markets must understand the size of the buyer's job—and have something useful to say and do when they call. For example, they might try to save the middleman time by taking inventory, setting up displays, or arranging shelves—while trying to get a chance to talk about specific products and maintain the relationship.

In larger firms, on the other hand, we see buyers spending more time on individual items. Buyers may specialize in certain lines. Some large chains buy such large lots that they assign buyers to find additional and lower-cost sources of supply.[7]

They must watch inventories and computer output

The large number of items bought and stocked by wholesalers and retailers means that inventories must be watched carefully. Smart retailers and wholesalers try to carry adequate but *not* excessive inventories. Instead, they want to maintain a selling stock and some reserve stock—and then depend on a continual flow through the channel.

Most larger firms now use sophisticated computer-controlled inventory control systems. Even small firms are using automated control systems now that electronic cash registers and countertop microcomputers can keep a count of items sold at relatively low cost. Such systems can print daily unit control reports—which show sales of every product on the manager's shelves. This is important to marketing managers selling to them—because buyers with this kind of information know their needs and become more demanding about dependability of delivery. They also know more about how goods move—and where promotion assistance might be desirable.

Automatic computer ordering is a natural outgrowth of such systems. For example, some wholesale drug companies give retail pharmacists a microcomputer to maintain all inventory records. At the end of the day, the druggist types in a command—and the computer automatically dials the computer at the wholesaler and places an order which arrives the next morning.

Some are not always "open to buy"

Just as manufacturers may sometimes be trying to reduce their inventory—and are "not in the market"—retailers and wholesalers may stop buying for similar reasons. No amount of special promotion or price cutting will cause them to buy in these situations.

In retailing, another dimension may become important—buyers may be controlled by a miniature profit and loss statement for each department or merchandise line. In an effort to make a profit, the buyer tries to forecast sales, merchandise costs, and expenses. The figure for "cost of merchandise" is the amount the buyer has to spend over the budget period. If the money has not yet been spent, the buyer is **open to buy**—that is, the buyer has budgeted funds which he can spend during the current time period.

Owners or professional buyers may buy

The buyers in small stores and for many wholesalers are the owners or managers—since there is a very close relationship between buying and selling. In larger operations, buyers may specialize in certain lines—but they may also supervise the salespeople who sell what they buy. These buyers are in close contact with their customers—*and* with their salespeople, who are sensitive to the effectiveness of the buyer's efforts—especially when they are on commission. A buyer may even buy some items to satisfy the preferences of salespeople. Therefore, the salespeople should not be neglected in the promotion effort. The multiple buying influence may be important.

As sales volumes rise, a buyer may specialize in buying only—and have no responsibility for sales. Sears is an extreme case, but it has a buying department of more than 3,000—supported by a staff department exceeding 1,400. These are professional buyers—who frequently know more about prices and quality and trends in the market than their suppliers. Obviously, they are big potential customers—and should be approached differently than the typical small retailer.

Resident buyers may help a firm's buyers

Resident buyers are independent buying agents who work in central markets for several retailer or wholesaler customers from outlying areas. They work in cities like New York, Montreal, Toronto, and Los Angeles. They buy new styles and fashions—and fill-in items—as their customers run out of stock during the year. Some resident buyers have hundreds of employees—and buy more than $1 billion worth of goods a year.

Resident buying organizations fill a need—helping small channel members (producers and middlemen)—reach each other inexpensively. Resident buyers usually are paid an annual fee—based on their purchases.

Committee buying happens, too

In some large companies—especially chains selling foods and drugs—the major decisions to add or drop lines or change buying policies may be handled by a *buying committee.* The seller still calls on and gives a "pitch" to a buyer—but the buyer does not have final responsibility. In such companies, the buyer prepares forms summarizing proposals for new products. The forms are passed on to the committee for evaluation. The seller may not get to present his story to the buying committee in person.

This rational, almost cold-blooded approach reduces the impact of the persuasive salesperson. It has become necessary because of the flood of new products. Consider the problem facing grocery chains. In an average week, 150 to 250 new items are offered to the buying offices of the larger food chains. If all were accepted, 10,000 new items would be added during a single year! Obviously, buyers must be hard-headed and impersonal. About 90 percent of the new items presented to food stores are rejected.

Wholesalers' and manufacturers' marketing managers must develop good marketing mixes when buying becomes this sophisticated and competitive. This approach is likely to become more common—as computers improve sales analysis and inventory control. Obviously, how possible target markets buy should affect marketing strategy planning.

The Farm Market

Agriculture plays a large and important role in the Canadian economy, accounting for almost one quarter of all economic activity. Agricultural production continues to climb from year to year, and agricultural exports account for about one fifth of the foreign exchange earned from tourism and all forms of exporting.[8] However, farm incomes are greatly influenced by the prices received for crops, the cost of supplies that are purchased, and interest rates.

The number of farms has slowly and steadily declined for many years. Average farm size, on the other hand, continues to increase. Although there are still many small units, large firms produce most of the output. The modern commercial farm is highly mechanized, highly specialized, and marked by a large capital investment in the business.[9] Consequently, the owners of large farms tend to run them as a business rather than a way of life. They respond to sales presentations stressing savings and increases in productivity. Further, they are more knowledgeable and receptive to change—and, they may have the money to buy what they need.

Some studies of farmer purchasing behavior, however, indicate that for some products, buying motivations are not much different from those for consumer goods. This is understandable when you consider that a farmer's home and place of business are the same. Some manufacturers take pride in office facilities and factories, and the same sort of motive may affect farmer purchasing behavior. And among owners of smaller farms, a new tractor may offer just as much status as a new car would to an urban resident. Moreover, the farmer's roles in business and as a final consumer sometimes overlap. For example, a station wagon might be used for carrying feed and also the family's groceries. Thus the motives of final consumers and business managers may coincide.

Farmers tend to specialize in one or a few products—such as wheat and other grains, dairy, poultry, and so forth. These specializations seem to have developed in response to geographic and climatic regions. A farmer in the Prairies growing wheat will undoubtedly have different needs from a farmer in the Central Region engaged in the dairy business. Or a fruit farmer in the Niagara Peninsula would have different needs from a fruit farmer in British Columbia, where fruit is grown on irrigated terraces.

Marketing mixes may have to be developed for each type of farm and, occasionally, even for individual farmers. Fertilizer producers, for example, have moved far beyond selling an all-purpose bag of fertilizer. Now they are able to blend the exact type needed for each farm and load it directly onto fertilizer spreaders which do the job more economically than manual methods. Some producers, in fact, are working directly with farmers, providing a complete service—including fertilizing, weeding, and debugging—all tailored to each individual farmer's needs.[10]

Agriculture is becoming agribusiness

Another increasing important factor is the tendency for farmers to engage in **contract farming**. Here, the farmer obtains his supplies and perhaps working capital from local dealers or manufacturers who agree to purchase his output, sometimes at guaranteed prices. This limits the farmer's buying freedom, since he becomes, in effect, an employee. Such arrangements are becoming more frequent, especially in raising chickens and turkeys and in growing fresh vegetables for commercial canning. A farmer, for example, may contract with Canada Packers, who will supply him with chicks and feed. The company, in turn, will receive all output through a predetermined arrangement. These arrangements offer security, but they also limit the markets for sellers. It is all part of the move toward bigger and more businesslike agricultural enterprises—what has been called **agribusiness.**

Where such contractual arrangements (or actual ownership) are common, marketing managers will have to adjust their marketing mixes. They may have to sell directly to large manufacturers or dealers who are handling the arrangements—rather than to the farmer himself.

Farmers constitute a market, of course, because farm products are themselves marketed. This is done through a blend of private trading, public sales and auctions, sales under contract, sales through cooperatives, and sales by marketing boards. Methods vary with the type of product, the region, and the preference of producers. Most products, except western grains and a few special crops, are marketed in more than one way.

For many years, large central markets served as price-making centers for agricultural products, as places where supply and demand forces came together. It is no longer economically feasible, however, for all commodities to be physically present when buying and selling occurs and, with the introduction of standardized grading procedures, it is no longer necessary.

Canada's principal livestock markets are at Montreal, Toronto, Winnipeg, Calgary, and Edmonton, but there are many other outlets ranging from large stockyards to country collection points. Egg sales are regulated by the Canadian Egg Marketing Agency, and the Canadian Turkey Marketing Agency performs similar services for turkey producers. The marketing of fluid milk is a provincial responsibility with quality, prices, and deliveries regulated by provincial marketing agencies. Fruit and vegetables are distributed through fresh and frozen food markets, canneries, and other processors. Most products are grown under a contract or a prearranged marketing scheme.[11]

Marketing boards

Marketing boards are an important type of marketing institution for agricultural products. For example, the Canadian Wheat Board is responsible for various aspects of marketing the wheat, oats, barley, rye, flax, and rapeseed grown in western Canada. In Ontario, all wheat is sold through the Ontario Wheat Producers' Marketing Board.

Other products sold under marketing boards include hogs, milk, fruit, potatoes and other vegetables, tobacco, poultry, eggs, wood, soybeans, honey, maple products, and pulpwood. There are 2 federally authorized marketing boards operating in Canada and over 100 provincial ones. Although these boards differ in the powers they exercise, their mandate generally includes pricing, quotas for production and/or marketing, licensing promotion, and the control of interprovincial and export trade.[12]

The Government Market

Size and diversity

Governments in Canada represent a sizable market, a market concentrated in relatively few hands. On the federal level, for example, much of the buying is done through Supply and Services Canada, a department which purchases billions of dollars' worth of goods and services a year for other federal departments and agencies. The Department of National Defence is generally Canada's largest single customer. Other major purchasers include the Canadian Commercial Corporation (a Crown corporation that helps foreign governments purchase goods made in Canada), Transport Canada, and Public Works Canada. Collectively, provincial and local governments are even more important markets than the federal government.

The range of goods and services purchased by the government is vast, including everything from advertising services to appliances. Governments not only run schools, police departments, and military organizations, but also supermarkets, public utilities, research laboratories, offices hospitals, and liquor stores. And it is expected that government expenditures for these operations will continue to grow. Such opportunities cannot be ignored by an aggressive marketing manager.

Government buying methods

Most goods and services are purchased through contracts awarded after a requisition is received from the ultimate user. Any Canadian business supplying the necessary goods and services is eligible to bid. The only requirements are a desire to sell and evidence of the ability to supply the goods or services under the terms and conditions of the contract. Any size firm can bid—the overall size of government expenditures is no indication of the size of individual contracts. Despite the overall amount spent by government, firms of all sizes can and do bid for such business since many thousands of contracts are for less than $10,000.

Bidding is common

Although bidding procedures may vary slightly between departments and levels of government, the general procedures are common. A firm merely requests to be placed on the supplier list for a particular commodity group or service. (At the present time, there are about 20,000 commodities and some 60,000 interested suppliers listed by Supply and Services Canada.)

Interested suppliers are invited to tender on a particular contract. The government department in question has drawn up its list of specifications carefully in order to clarify what the supplier must bid on and to simplify the selection procedure. The contract is then awarded to the firm submitting the lowest bid which also answers the specifications of the tender call most closely.

Writing specifications is not easy, and buyers usually appreciate the help of knowledgeable salespeople. Legally, the buyer cannot draw the specifications so that only one supplier will be able to meet them (although this has been done!). However, you may get the business, even with a bid that is not the lowest, because the lower bids do not meet the minimum specifications.

Not all government purchases, however, are made this way. Many branded or standardized items are routinely purchased through standing offer arrangements. These offers are issued to suppliers for specific time periods. They, in turn, agree to supply the goods or services at prearranged prices and delivery conditions. Pharmaceutical supplies, tires and tubes, and petroleum and oil would fall into this category.

Negotiated contracts also used

Contracts may also be negotiated rather than put up for tender. This procedure is followed when only one acceptable tender has been received, when there is only one known source of supply, or when the contract is for a proprietary item (an item made and sold by a firm having exclusive rights of manufacture and sale. Negotiated contracts represent one area where favoritism and "influence" can slip in. However, negotiation remains an important and legitimate buying method in government sales.

Learning what government wants

Since most government contracts are advertised, a prospective supplier can focus on particular government agencies or departments. Marketers can learn about potential government target markets, using the assistance available from government publications. For example, Supply and Services Canada offers a purchasing and sales directory that explains its procedures.[13] Information on successful bidders for contracts of $10,000 and over is found in a *Weekly Bulletin of*

■   FIGURE 8–5   A DSS advertisement directed at potential suppliers

Supply and Services   Approvisionnements et Services
Canada   Canada

B.C. BUSINESS — ARE YOU LOOKING FOR NEW CUSTOMERS?

If the Federal Government is not already listed as one of your clients, you could be missing sales opportunities. Supply and Services Canada is the Federal Government department responsible for buying goods and services on behalf of other Federal Government departments and agencies. SSC also acquires goods and services from Canadian suppliers at the request of foreign governments.

Why not learn how you can do business with us, by attending a free **"Selling to Supply and Services Canada"** seminar on **April 25, 1985** at the **Holiday Inn Harbourside, Commonwealth Ballroom.** Choose the seminar or seminars that best describe your sales orientation.

Commercial Acquisitions (General off-the-shelf goods and
                                       services oriented industry)
Science Procurement (Research and Development)
Marine and Industrial Machinery Procurement
Printing Procurement
Disposal Operations (Sale of government surplus)

Call 438-6337 for reservations and to confirm seminar time (space is limited, so reserve early).

For B.C. Business already selling to the Federal Government, you are invited to the Holiday Inn to discuss tendering procedures or any other purchasing concerns with SSC procurement specialists. These specialists, representing all areas of SSC, will be located at the **Holiday Inn, Commonwealth Room Centre** from **9 a.m.-4 p.m. on April 25.** No reservations are necessary for drop-in consultations.

Canadä

Business Opportunities. Research and development contract awards information appears in a monthly *Research and Development Bulletin.* As Figure 8–5 shows, Supply and Services Canada even conducts briefing sessions at which interested firms can learn more about the federal market.

Various provincial and local governments also offer assistance. There are trade magazines and trade associations providing information on how to reach schools, hospitals, highway departments, park departments, and so on. These are unique target markets and must be treated as such when developing marketing strategies.

Of course, marketers interested in selling to provincial and local governments must be aware of any "province-first" procurement policies. Most of the provinces tend to favor local suppliers at the expense of firms manufacturing elsewhere. Although provincial preference in purchasing may make political sense, it poses real problems for firms trying to sell nationally in what is already a very small "internal common market."[14]

■ CONCLUSION

In this chapter, we have considered the number, size, location, and buying habits of various organizational customers—to try to identify logical dimensions for segmenting markets. We saw that the nature of the buyer and the buying situation are relevant—and that the problem-solving models of buyer behavior introduced in Chapter 7 apply here—with modifications.

The chapter focused mainly on buying in the industrial market—because more is known about manufacturers' buying behavior, and buying in other organizational markets is similar. Some differences in buying by retailers and wholesalers were discussed. Characteristics of the farm and government markets were also considered. The government market was described as an extremely large, complex set of markets that require much market analysis—but also offer opportunities for the target marketer.

A clear understanding of organizational customer buying habits, needs, and attitudes can aid marketing strategy planning. And since there are fewer organizational customers than final consumers, it may even be possible for some marketing managers (and their salespeople) to develop a unique strategy for each potential customer.

This chapter suggested some general principles which would be useful in strategy planning—but the nature of the products being offered may require some adjustments in the plans. The nature of specific industrial products is discussed in Chapter 10. These variations by product may provide additional segmenting dimensions—to help the marketing manager fine tune his marketing strategies.

■ QUESTIONS AND PROBLEMS

1. Discuss the importance of thinking "target marketing" when analyzing organizational customer markets. How easy is it to isolate homogeneous market segments in these markets?

2. Explain how SIC codes might be helpful in evaluating and understanding industrial markets.

3. Compare and contrast the problem-solving approaches used by final consumers and by industrial buyers.

4. Describe the situations which would lead to the use of the three different buying processes for a particular product—such as computer tapes.

5. Compare and contrast the buying processes of final consumers and industrial buyers.

6. Distinguish among the four methods of evaluating and buying (inspection, sampling, etc.) and indicate which would probably be most suitable for furniture, baseball gloves, coal, and pencils—assuming that some organizational customer is the buyer.

7. Discuss the advantages and disadvantages of reciprocity from the industrial buyer's point of view. Are the advantages and disadvantages merely reversed from the seller's point of view?

8. Is it always advisable to buy the highest-quality product?

9. Discuss how much latitude an industrial buyer has in selecting the specific brand and the specific source of supply for that product, once a product has been requisitioned by some production department. Consider this question with specific reference to pencils, paint for the offices, plastic materials for the production line, a new factory, and a large printing press. How should the buyer's attitudes affect the seller's marketing mix?

10. How does the kind of industrial good affect manufacturers' buying habits and practices? Consider lumber for furniture, a lathe, nails for a box factory, and a floor cleaner.

11. Considering the nature of retail buying, outline the basic ingredients of promotion to retail buyers. Does it make any difference what kinds of products are involved? Are any other factors relevant?

12. Discuss the impact of the decline in the number of commercial farmers on the marketing mixes of manufacturers and middlemen supplying this market. Also consider the impact on rural trading communities which have been meeting the needs of farmers.

13. The government market is obviously an extremely large one, yet it is often slighted or even ignored by many firms. "Red tape" is certainly one reason, but there are others. Discuss the situation and be sure to include the possibility of segmenting in your analysis.

14. Based on your understanding of buying by manufacturers and governments, outline the basic ingredients of promotion to each type of customer. Use two products as examples for each type. Is the promotion job the same for each pair?

■ SUGGESTED CASES

3. Apex Chemical Company
5. Indian Steel Company

9. West Coast International Resources

■ NOTES

1. For more detail, see *Facts for Marketers,* U.S. Department of Commerce.

2. Patrick J. Robinson and Charles W. Faris, *Industrial Buying and Creative Marketing* (Boston: Allyn & Bacon, 1967), chap. 2. See also Frederick E. Webster, Jr., and Yoram Wind, "A General Model for Understanding Organizational Buying Behavior," *Journal of Marketing,* April 1972, pp. 12–19; Urban B. Ozanne and Gilbert A. Churchill, Jr., "Five Dimensions of the Industrial Adoption Process," *Journal of Marketing Research,* August 1971, pp. 322–28; J. Patrick Kelly and James W. Coaker, "The Importance of Price as a Choice Criterion for Industrial Purchasing Decisions," *Industrial Marketing Management* 5 (1976), pp. 281–93; Lowell E. Crow, Richard W. Olshavsky, and John O. Summers, "Industrial Buyers' Choice Strategies: A Protocol Analysis," *Journal of Marketing Research,* February 1980, pp. 34–44; Robert E. Spekman and Louis W. Stern; "Environmental Uncertainties and Buying Group Structure: An Empirical Investigation," *Journal of Marketing,* Spring 1979, pp. 54–64; and Arch G. Woodside and David M. Samuel, "Decision Systems Analysis of Corporate Purchase Agreements," *Industrial Marketing Management* 10 (1981), pp. 191–205.

3. Frederick E. Webster, Jr., and Yoram Wind, *Organizational Buying Behavior* (Englewood Cliffs, N.J.: Prentice-Hall, 1972).

4. Thomas V. Bonoma, "Major Sales: Who Really Does the Buying?" *Harvard Business Review* 60, no. 3 (May-June 1982), pp. 120–27; Wesley J. Johnston and Thomas V. Bonoma, "The Buying Center: Structure and Interaction Patterns," *Journal of Marketing* 45, no. 3 (Summer 1981), pp. 143–56; and Rowland T. Moriarty and John E. G. Bateson, "Exploring Complex Decision Making Units: A New Approach," *Journal of Marketing Research* 19 (May 1982), pp. 182–91.

5. Peter Lusztig and Bernhard Schwab, *Managerial Finance in a Canadian Setting,* 2d ed. (Toronto: Butterworth & Co., 1977) p. 49.

6. "Federal Suit Charges GE with Reciprocity on Purchasing; Vigorous Defense Is Vowed," *The Wall Street Journal,* May 19, 1972, p. 2. See also Robert E. Weigand, "The Problems of Managing Reciprocity," *California Management Review,* Fall 1973, pp. 40–48; and Reed Moyer, "Reciprocity: Retrospect and Prospect," *Journal of Marketing,* October 1970, pp. 37–54.

7. For a detailed discussion of supermarket chain buying, see J. F. Grashof, *Information Management for Supermarket Chain Product Mix Decisions,* Ph.D. thesis, Michigan State University, 1968.

8. The following information is from Statistics Canada, *1971 Census of Canada,* Cat. 96-701, July 1973; Statistics Canada, Canada Year Book 1972 (Ottawa: Information Canada, 1972).

9. Total investment in farm capital in Canada for 1976 amounted to $48.8 billion. *Quarterly Bulletin of Agricultural Statistics,* April-June 77, Table 1.

10. "Monsanto Moves into Farmers' Backyard," *Business Week,* February 6, 1965, pp. 60–62; see also "Agricorporations Run into Growing Criticism as Their Role Expands," *The Wall Street Journal,* May 2, 1972, p. 1 f.

11. *Canada Year Book 1976–77,* p. 516.

12. H. Pellicer, P. Moncrieff, and O. Weaver, *Canadian Agricultural Systems,* 2d ed., Department of Agricultural Economics, McDonald College, 1977.

13. *Policy and Guidelines on Contracting in the Government of Canada,* Treasury Board, Administrative Policy Branch, June 1975; *The Federal Government Your Client,* Supply and Services Canada, Ministers of Supply and Services, 1978.

14. Larry Grossman, "Constitutional Renewal Requires a Canadian Common Market," *Policy Options,* September-October 1980, p. 10.

Chapter 9 ■ Segmenting markets and forecasting their potential

When you finish this chapter, you should:

1. Know what market segmentation is.
2. Know dimensions which may be useful for segmenting markets.
3. Understand how to segment markets into sub-markets.
4. Understand several forecasting approaches which extend past behavior.
5. Understand several forecasting approaches which do not rely on extending past behavior.
6. Recognize the important new terms (shown in red).

"You have to aim at somebody—not just everybody—to make a profit."

Aiming at specific "somebodies" is the big difference between production-oriented managers and target marketers.

Production-oriented managers think of their markets in terms of *products* and aim at everybody. They think of the "women's clothing" market or the "car" market.

Target marketers think of satisfying people in product-markets. They think first of markets in terms of *customers' needs*—and then products to satisfy these needs. They may segment these product-markets into sub-markets—as they look for attractive opportunities. A computer manufacturer, for example, might aim only at the government market or the large Fortune 500 companies. And a restaurant owner might choose to aim only at people seeking gourmet dining—rather than everyone who "eats out."

The great importance of segmenting product-markets as part of marketing strategy planning helps explain why we have been talking about possible market dimensions for several chapters.

In Chapter 3, we started talking about market segmentation—including *naming* generic markets and broad product-markets. Now we will go into more depth—seeing if it is practical to segment broad product-markets into sub-markets. Then we'll go on to talk about forecasting sales in these product-markets. Segmenting markets isn't just a classroom exercise—if a product isn't aimed at a specific target market big enough to support the effort, all the effort may be wasted.

Market Segmentation Requires Judgment

Effective market segmentation requires a two-step process: (1) *naming* broad product-markets and then (2) *segmenting* these broad product-markets into more homogeneous sub-markets—also called product-markets—for the purpose of selecting target markets and developing suitable marketing mixes.

This two-step process is not well understood. Market segmentation efforts have often been unsuccessful because of a common tendency to start with the whole "mass market" and then try to "break it down" into sub-markets—often using one or two demographic characteristics. This approach usually fails—because customer behavior is too complex to be explained in terms of just one or two demographic characteristics. For example, not all old men or all young

One of E. F. Hutton's target markets is the growing segment of professional women.

Are a woman's financial requirements different from a man's?

Some are astonishingly similar, others vastly different.

Financial requirements are as diverse as individuals. But the need for wise investing is common to all.

That is why for over 78 years, people have been listening to E.F. Hutton.

When EF Hutton talks, people listen.

women buy the same products or brands. Other dimensions usually must be considered—starting with customer needs.

Sometimes, many different dimensions are needed to describe the sub-markets within a broad product-market. This was the case in the home-decorating market example we studied in Chapter 2. Recall that the British paint manufacturer finally settled on the "cost-conscious-couple" as its target market. In that case, four possible target markets with very different dimensions were placed in the four corners of a market diagram. This is the kind of market segmentation we want to do.

Naming markets is dis-aggregating

The first step in effective market segmentation is to name the broad product-market of interest to the firm. This was discussed in Chapter 3. And as you recall, we suggested that a product-market name should consist of four parts: product type, customer (user) functional needs, customer type, and geographic area. Such a four-part definition can be clumsy, so it's practical to reduce it to a "nick-name"—as long as everyone understands what the nickname stands for.

The important point here, however, is that the product-market naming approach discussed in Chapter 3 helps get us in the "right ballpark," but it usually does *not* yield the detailed product-market names which segmenters are seeking. The naming step is simply a narrowing down process—a dis-aggregating process—rather than the end of the market segmentation process. It places primary emphasis on functional needs, while not ignoring customer types in geographic areas. Now we will go on to *segmenting*—which focuses more on the different needs and wants of different customer types within the geographic area named in a broad product-market.

Segmenting is an aggregating process

Marketing-oriented managers think of **segmenting** as an aggregating process. They start with the idea that each person is "one of a kind"—and can be described by a special set of dimensions. However, while it might be ideal to treat each person as a unique target market, this usually isn't practical in terms of manufacturing and distribution costs—the marketing mix might cost more than the customer is willing and able to pay.

Therefore, segmenters look for similarities—customers who are quite similar in terms of their special set of dimensions—and then aggregate these customers into relatively homogeneous sub-markets that can be served effectively—and profitably. This is shown in Figure 9–1—where the many dots show each person's position in a broad product-market with respect to two possible segmenting dimensions—need for status and need for dependability. While each person's position is unique, it can also be seen that many of the people are similar in terms of how much status and dependability they want. Thus, a segmenter can aggregate these people into three (an arbitrary number) relatively homogeneous sub-markets—A, B, and C. Group A might be called "Status Oriented" and group C "Dependability Oriented." Members of group B want both—and might be called the "Demanders."

One of the difficult things about segmenting is that some potential customers just don't "fit" neatly into market segments. For example, not everyone in Figure 9–1 was put into one of the three groups. Forcing them into one of the three

■ FIGURE 9–1   Every individual has his or her own unique position in the market—those with
                      similar positions can be aggregated into potential target markets

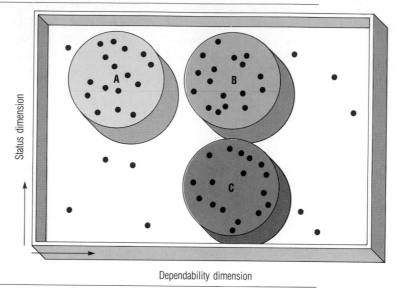

groups would have made these sub-markets more heterogeneous—and harder
to please. Further, forming additional segments for them probably wouldn't be
profitable—because they are too few in number and not very similar in terms of
the two dimensions. These people are simply too "unique" to be catered to and
may have to be ignored—unless they are willing to pay a high price for special
treatment.

**How far should the
aggregating go?**

Segmenters have basically three choices: they can treat everybody alike; they
can treat everybody differently; or they can try to aggregate people into some
workable number of relatively homogeneous sub-markets—and treat each sub-
market differently. The first choice is seldom (if ever) effective—it is "mass marketing." The second choice is seldom practical because of costs (of production
and/or distribution). Thus, the only real choice is to look for homogeneous sub-
markets that can be served profitably. The major problems with this choice are
deciding: (1) *how many* sub-markets should be formed and (2) what the *boundaries* of these sub-markets should be.

Looking back at Figure 9–1, we assumed that there were three sub-markets.
This was an arbitrary number, however. As Figure 9–2 shows, it may be that
there are really *six* sub-markets. What do you think—does this product-market
consist of three segments or six segments?

**It's a matter of
judgment**

Actually, the number of sub-markets that should be formed is based more on
judgment than on some scientific rule. This decision is influenced by two factors:

how heterogeneous the market is with respect to the segmenting dimensions and how well the firm wants to—and can afford to—satisfy the needs of each potential customer.

There would be no point in trying to segment a market if customer needs were all basically the same. Typically, however, there are some important differences—and segmenting is desirable. In fact, in very competitive markets, even seemingly minor differences may make a big difference in how well a firm does against tough competitors. But it is necessary to have decision rules about how far to go.

Basically, a profit-oriented firm will probably want to continue aggregating potential customers into a larger market as long as its marketing mix is reasonably satisfying to all those within the segment—*and* the firm is able to offer this marketing mix at a profit. The interaction of customer needs with what the firm can offer profitably should be noted. And present or potential competition must be considered when calculating profitability.

Criteria for segmenting product-markets into sub-product-markets

Ideally, "good" product-market segments meet the following criteria:

1. *Homogeneous within*—the people within a market segment should be as homogeneous as possible with respect to the segmenting dimensions *and* their likely responses to marketing mix variables.
2. *Heterogeneous between*—the people in different market segments should be as heterogeneous as possible with respect to the segmenting dimensions *and* their likely responses to marketing mix variables.
3. *Substantial*—the product-market segments should be big enough to be profitable.
4. *Operational*—the segmenting dimensions should be useful for identifying customers and deciding on marketing mix variables.

■ FIGURE 9–2   How many segments are there?

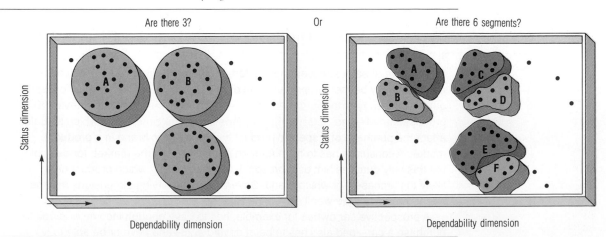

There is no point in having a dimension that isn't usable.

Criterion 4 is especially critical—because it is possible to find dimensions which are useless. A personality trait such as moodiness, for example, might be found among the traits of particularly heavy buyers of a product—but what could anyone do with this knowledge? Personal salespeople would have to take a personality inventory of each prospective buyer—clearly an impossible task. Similarly, advertising media buyers or copywriters could not make much use of this information. So although moodiness might be related in some way to previous purchases, it would not be a useful dimension for segmenting purposes.

Criterion 4 may lead to including readily available dimensions—such as demographics—to aid marketing mix planning. Dimensions such as age, income, location, and family size may be very useful—at least for Place and Promotion planning. In fact, it is difficult to make some Place and Promotion decisions without such information.

Profit is the balancing point

Target marketers develop whole strategies—they don't just segment markets. As a practical matter, this means that cost considerations probably encourage *more aggregating*—to achieve economies of scale—while demand considerations suggest less aggregating—to satisfy needs more exactly.

Profit is the balancing point—it determines how unique a marketing mix the firm can afford to offer to a particular group.

Too much aggregation leaves you vulnerable

Segmenters must be careful not to aggregate too far in search of profit. As sub-markets are made larger, they become less homogeneous—and individual differences within each sub-market may begin to outweigh the similarities. This makes it harder to develop marketing mixes which can do an effective job of satisfying potential customers within each of the sub-markets. And this in turn leaves the firm more vulnerable to competitive efforts—especially from innovative segmenters who are willing to offer more attractive marketing mixes to more homogeneous sub-markets.[1]

There May Be Both Qualifying and Determining Dimensions

We have already stressed that customers are multi-dimensional. Some dimensions may be more important than others, however, and it is useful to distinguish between **qualifying dimensions**—the dimensions which are relevant to a product-market—and **determining dimensions**—the dimensions which actually affect the purchase of a specific product type or specific brand in a product-market. A consumer has to have enough money to be in the market, for example, but this only qualifies him as a prospect. It doesn't tell us which product he is likely to purchase—or which brand. Several such qualifying dimensions may be needed—and still we won't determine what he will do.

A prospective car owner, for example, has to have enough income or credit to purchase a car—and also has to be of driving age—and have or be able to

The 4-wheel drive benefits of this car meet the needs of some consumers— who have been aggregated into a target market.

obtain a driver's license. This still doesn't determine that he will buy a car. He may simply rent one—or continue borrowing his parents' or friends' cars—or hitchhike. He may not get around to actually buying a car until not having one is annoying—until, for example, his status with his buddies is falling because he doesn't have "wheels." This need may lead him to buy *some* car—but it is not determining with respect to a specific brand or a specific model within a particular brand.

Determining dimensions may have to be very specialized

How specific the determining dimensions have to get depends on whether we are concerned with a general product type or a specific brand. This is shown in Figure 9–3. The more specific we want to be, the more particular the determining dimensions may have to be. In a particular case, the determining dimensions may seem minor—but they are important because they *are* the determining di-

■   FIGURE 9–3   Finding the relevant segmenting dimensions

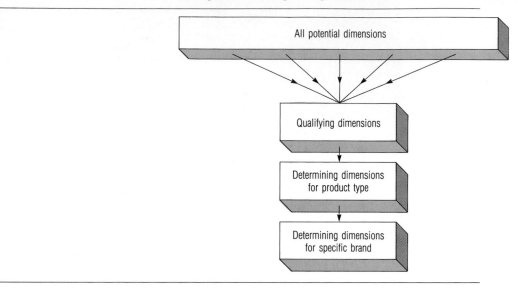

mensions. In the car–status-seekers market, for example, paint colors or the brand name may determine which cars people buy.

Qualifying dimensions are important, too

The qualifying dimensions are necessary to narrow down to the determining dimensions. But, once the determining dimensions have been identified, we can go back to the qualifying dimensions—for insights which can aid marketing mix planning and implementation. The qualifying dimensions may help identify the "core features" which will have to be offered to everyone in the broad product-market. In other words, qualifying and determining dimensions work together to affect marketing strategy planning.

Different dimensions may be needed for different segments in a market

It is important to see that each different product-market *within* the same broad product-market may be motivated by a different set of dimensions. In the "snack food" market, for example, health food enthusiasts might be interested in nutrition, while dieters might care only about calories—and economical shoppers with lots of kids might be interested in volume to "fill them up." The related product-markets might be called: "health-conscious snack food market," "dieters snack food market," and "kids snack food market."

What Dimensions Are Used to Segment Markets?

Segmenting forces the marketing manager to decide which product-market dimensions might be useful for planning marketing mixes. Ideally, of course, the dimensions should help guide marketing mix planning. Table 9–1 shows some of

■ TABLE 9–1   Relation of potential target market dimensions to marketing mix decision areas

Potential target market dimensions	Effects on decision areas
1. Geographic location and other demographic characteristics of potential customers	Affects size of *Target Markets* (economic potential) and *Place* (where products should be made available) and *Promotion* (where and to whom to advertise)
2. Behavioral needs, attitudes, and how present and potential goods or services fit into customers' consumption patterns	Affects *Product* (design, packaging, length or width of product line) and *Promotion* (what potential customers need and want to know about the product offering, and what appeals should be used)
3. Urgency to get need satisfied and desire and willingness to compare and shop	Affects *Place* (how directly products are distributed from producer to consumer, how extensively they are made available, and the level of service needed) and *Price* (how much potential customers are willing to pay)

the kinds of dimensions we have been talking about in the last several chapters—and their probable effect on the four Ps. Ideally, we would like to describe any potential product-market in terms of all three types of customer-related dimensions—plus a product type description—because these four types of dimensions will help us develop better marketing mixes. Further, some situation-related dimensions may be determining in some cases.

Consumers have many dimensions—and several may be useful for segmenting a broad product-market. Table 9–2 shows some possible consumer market segmenting dimensions—and their typical breakdowns. As Table 9–2 shows, there are customer-related dimensions and situation-related dimensions—which may be more important in some situations. When all the competitors in a market are imitating each other, for example, then some product feature may be *the most important dimension.* Or, the degree of brand loyalty or even whether the brand is in a store where it is wanted (that is, the buying situation) may decide which product is purchased.[2]

With so many possible dimensions—and knowing that several dimensions may be needed to capture what is determining in specific product-markets, how should we proceed? This is obviously a difficult—multi-dimensional—task. And it does require creativity and intuition. But it is not impossible! All it takes is some understanding of the product-market area of interest and determination to try to understand why people think and behave as they do.

Basically, we start with the assumption that potential customers are reasonably sensible problem solvers who have needs they want to satisfy. This doesn't mean they always solve their problems in a strictly economic way—or the way the marketer might solve them. But we assume that they do follow a somewhat logical process. Further, research seems to support the hypothesis that most customers only have a few really important determining dimensions—so the task is to try to understand the "few" determining dimensions of groups of customers.

■ **TABLE 9–2**   Possible segmenting dimensions and typical breakdowns for consumer markets

Dimensions	Typical breakdowns
Customer related	
Geographic	
Region..................	Atlantic provinces, Quebec, Ontario, Prairie provinces, and British Columbia
City, county, CMA size	Under 5,000; 5,000–19,999; 20,000–49,999; 50,000–99,999; 100,000–249,999; 250,000–499,999; 500,000–999,999; 1,000,000–3,999,999; 4,000,000 or over
Demographic	
Age	Infant, under 6; 6–11; 12–17; 18–24; 25–34; 35–49; 50–64; 65 and over
Sex......................	Male, female
Family size	1–2, 3–4, 5+
Family life cycle...........	Young, single; young, married, no children; young, married, youngest child under 6; young, married, youngest child 6 or over; older, married, with children; older, married, no children under 18; older, single; other
Income	Under $5,000; $5,000–$7,999; $8,000–$9,999; $10,000–$14,999; $15,000–$24,999; $25,000 or over
Occupation	Professional and technical; managers, officials, and proprietors; clerical, sales; craftsmen, foremen; operatives; farmers; retired; students; housewives; unemployed
Education................	Grade school or less, some high school, graduated high school, some college, college graduate
Religion..................	Catholic, Protestant, Jewish, other
Race	White, Black, Oriental, other
Nationality	Canadian, British, French, German, etc.
Social class	Lower-lower, upper-lower, lower-middle, upper-middle, lower-upper, upper-upper
Situation related	
Benefits offered	
Need satisfiers............	PSSP, economic, and more detailed needs
Product features	Situation specific, but to satisfy specific or general needs
Consumption or use patterns	
Rate of use...............	Heavy, medium, light, non-users
Use with other products	Situation specific, e.g., gas with a traveling vacation
Brand familiarity	Insistence, preference, recognition, non-recognition, rejection
Buying situation	
Kind of store..............	Convenience, shopping, specialty
Kind of shopping...........	Serious versus browsing, rushed versus leisurely
Depth of assortment.......	Out of stock, shallow, deep
Type of good	Convenience, shopping, specialty, unsought

Segmenting the Market—Prospective American Visitors to Canada*

We have reviewed the various ways in which markets for different consumer products and services *could* be segmented. However, the marketing manager must decide on each occasion how the market *should* be segmented. Given all the possible segmentation attributes, this is no easy task. Both sound judgment and research "know-how" are required. The following illustrates both the kind of problems encountered in segmentation studies and how those problems were solved in a particular study.

The Canadian Government Office of Tourism decided to conduct a market segmentation study of the U.S. travel market to obtain a better understanding of Americans as potential vacation travelers to Canada. A segmentation study was done to identify different groups of potential vacation travelers and to determine what each such group was looking for in a vacation. Once the various segments were identified and described, they could be evaluated in terms of vacation business potential. Advertising and promotion campaigns showing the advantages of a Canadian vacation of the specific type each group preferred could then be directed toward those segments deemed attractive enough to cultivate. However, three critical issues had to be resolved before this study could be carried out.

Who should be interviewed

Because the purpose of the travel study was to expand the number of Canadian vacations taken by U.S. travelers, interviewing obviously could not be limited to the 5 percent of the U.S. population who had already taken Canadian vacations. Researchers had to interview prospective new visitors to Canada—but how could they define prospective visitor status? After careful consideration, it was decided that (*a*) only those who had taken at least a week-long vacation in the past three years would be interviewed; (*b*) the distance traveled on that vacation had to be at least three quarters of the distance from each respondent's current home to Canada; and (*c*) the 1,750 individuals interviewed had to be the family's vacation decision maker.

The frame of reference or context for questioning

Most respondents would be prospects for more than one type of vacation. To question those individuals about "vacations in general" would not prove all that helpful. Consumer needs and desires would vary by the type of vacation being considered. Also, asking about an "ideal vacation" would generate a lot of fantasies. To make answers relevant and realistic, researchers asked interviewees to respond in terms of the last vacation they had taken. So behavioral and attitudinal information would then be based on a specific and recent vacation experience.

---

*This section is a somewhat modified version of the tourism study first discussed in "Some Practical Considerations in Market Segmentation," an article by S Young, L. Ott, and B. Feigin that appeared in the August 1978 issue of the *Journal of Marketing Research*. See the original source for more information on this study and two other interesting discussions of how markets are actually segmented.

The basis of segmentation

Because the best way to segment or group potential U.S. travelers to Canada was not clear, three alternate bases of segmentation were investigated in a pilot study of 200 interviews.

1. *By segmenting consumers on favorability toward Canada as a vacation area,* U.S. travelers could be grouped on the basis of their attitudes toward Canada. This approach could have been the most appropriate if Canada offered only one type of vacation and if attitudes toward vacationing in Canada were polarized. This was not the case.
2. *By segmenting on geographic area or proximity to selected areas of Canada,* respondents would be assigned by their place of residence in the United States. This would have been a reasonable segmentation alternative if traveler vacation behavior and desires varied dramatically by region within the United States. However, such regional differences do not exist.
3. *By segmenting consumers on desires (or benefits) sought on their last vacation,* respondents could be grouped in terms of what they were seeking in a vacation of the last type taken. This approach yielded the most helpful marketing insights. Consequently, it was the approach employed in the major study.

Results of the study

That major study of 1,750 eligible respondents revealed six distinct vacation market segments.

1. *Friends and relatives—nonactive visitor (29 percent).* These vacationers seek familiar surroundings where they can visit friends and relatives. They are not inclined to participate in any activity.
2. *Friends and relatives—active city visitor (12 percent).* These vacationers also seek familiar surroundings where they can visit friends and relatives, but they are more inclined to participate in activities—especially sightseeing, shopping, and cultural and other entertainment.
3. *Family sightseers (6 percent).* These vacationers are looking for a new vacation place which would be a treat for the children and an enriching experience.
4. *Outdoor vacationer (19 percent).* These vacationers seek clean air, rest and quiet, and beautiful scenery. Many are campers so availability of recreation facilities is important. Children's needs are also an important factor.
5. *Resort vacationer (19 percent).* These vacationers are most interested in water sports (e.g., swimming) and good weather. They prefer a popular place with a big-city atmosphere.
6. *Foreign vacationer (26 percent).* These vacationers look for vacations in a place they have never been before with a foreign atmosphere and beautiful scenery. Money is not their major concern but good accommodations and service are. They want an exciting, enriching experience.[3]

Results also suggested that segments I and II were far less attractive target markets than were the other four segments. This was true for two reasons. People who visited friends and relatives tended to spend less on their vacations than did the other categories of visitors. Also, there was no way that a marketing campaign could generate more friends or relatives for prospective U.S. visitors. In contrast, the vacation needs and desires of the other segments could be satisfied by different types of Canadian vacations. For each of the remaining four segments data from the questionnaire was used to generate a prospective customer profile that focused on behavior, psychographics, travel incentives, and image of a Canadian vacation.

Use made of the study

The results of this study led to a number of changes in the way Canada was promoted in the United States as a tourist destination.

1. Advertising content

Advertising was designed to be more compatible with the personality traits and life styles of the four target groups Creatively, the advertising message stressed the specific benefits sought by each segment, reinforced the positive interests in Canada that each group already had, and corrected undesirable impressions they may have held. Television commercials were changed in mood, tempo, and emphasis.

2. Advertising media

The study facilitated the selection of media outlets with the life style, demographic features, and personality traits of the target group. In particular, selecting magazines in which to advertise was made much easier. Both the readership characteristics and the editorial content of each magazine under consideration could be compared with the profile and vacation desires of the four target segments.

3. Merchandising and promotional efforts

Specific types of vacation "tours" or packages were developed along the lines suggested by the study's finding. These special offerings were then promoted to the appropriate target markets.

4. Provincial and private sector involvement

The results of the segmentation study were passed on to the provinces so that they could adopt a segmented promotional effort—and to tourist-related businesses that could deliver the benefits sought by one or more of the target groups. In addition to providing this type of marketing guidance, the study's results were useful in planning new hotels, other types of accommodations, and tourist attractions.

Segmenting Industrial Markets

Up to now we have only talked about segmenting consumer markets. But industrial markets can and should also be segmented. Once again, the marketing manager must choose the dimensions along which the industrial market of interest should be segmented. Some of those possible segmenting dimensions

■ TABLE 9–3   Possible segmenting dimensions for industrial markets

Type of organization—Manufacturing, institutional, government, public utility, military, farm, etc.

Demographics—Size
         Employees
         Sales volume
     SIC code
     Number of plants
     Geographic location:
         Atlantic provinces, Quebec, Ontario, Prairie provinces, British Columbia
         Large city $\longrightarrow$ rural

Type of good—Installations, accessories, components, raw materials, supplies, services

Type of buying situation—Decentralized $\longrightarrow$ centralized
                                Buyer $\longrightarrow$ multiple buying influence
                                Straight rebuy $\longrightarrow$ modified rebuy $\longrightarrow$ new buy

Source loyalty—Weak $\longrightarrow$ strong loyalty
                  Last resort $\longrightarrow$ second source $\longrightarrow$ first source

Kinds of commitments—Contracts, agreements, financial aids

Reciprocity—None $\longrightarrow$ complete

are identified in Table 9–3. However, when segmenting industrial markets you need not always reject some bases of segmentation in favor of others. Rather, you may be far better off moving systematically from more general and easily available segmenting dimensions to more difficult to learn about but potentially more useful dimensions. A new method of industrial market segmentation that follows this approach is described in Figure 9–4. This method, based on a great deal of careful research, deserves your close attention. Just about every industrial market can be segmented using what the authors call their "nested" approach.

■ FIGURE 9–4   The "nested" approach to segmenting industrial markets

We have identified five general segmentation criteria, which we have arranged as a *nested* hierarchy—like a set of boxes that fit one into the other or a set of wooden Russian dolls. Moving from the outer nest toward the inner, these criteria are: demographics, operating variables, customer purchasing approaches, situational factors, and personal characteristics of the buyers.

Exhibit 1 shows how the criteria relate to one another as nests. The segmentation criteria of the largest, outermost nest are demographics—general, easily observable characteristics about industries and companies; those of the smallest, inmost nest are personal characteristics—specific, subtle, hard-to-assess traits. The marketer moves from the more general, easily observable segmentation characteristics to the more specific, subtle ones. This approach will become clearer as we explain each criterion.

We should note at this point that it may not be necessary or even desirable for every industrial marketer to use every stage of the nested approach for every product. Although it is possible to skip irrelevant criteria, it is important that the marketer completely understand the approach before deciding on omissions and shortcuts.

■   FIGURE 9–4   (*continued*)

Demographics

We begin with the outermost nest, which contains the most general segmentation criteria: demographics. These variables give a broad description of the company and relate to general customer needs and usage patterns. They can be determined without visiting the customer and include industry and company size, and customer location.

Operating Variables

The second segmentation nest contains a variety of segmentation criteria called "operating variables." Most of these enable more precise identification of existing and potential customers within demographic categories. Operating variables are generally stable and include technology, user-nonuser status (by product and brand), and customer capabilities (operating, technical, and financial).

Purchasing Approaches

One of the most neglected but valuable methods of segmenting an industrial market involves consumers' purchasing approaches and company philosophy. The factors in this middle segmentation nest include the formal organization of the purchasing function, the power structure, the nature of buyer-seller relationships, the general purchasing policies, and the purchasing criteria.

■   EXHIBIT 1   Nested approach

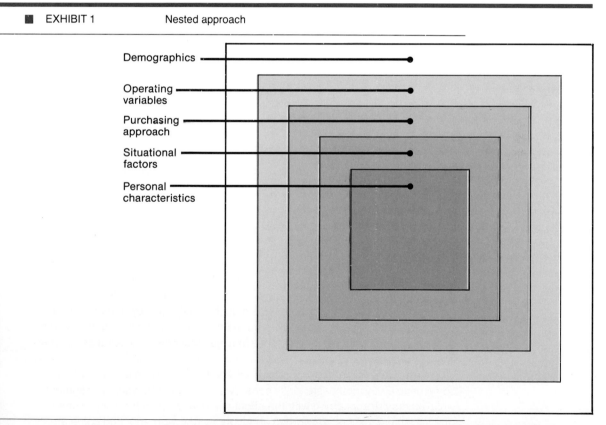

Source: Benson P. Shapiro and Thomas V. Bonoma, "How to Segment Industrial Markets," *Harvard Business Review* 63 (May-June 1984), pp. 104–10.

■ FIGURE 9-4 *(concluded)*

Situational Factors

Up to this point we have focused on the grouping of customer companies. Now we consider the role of the purchase situation, even single-line entries on the order form.

Situational factors resemble operating variables but are temporary and require a more detailed knowledge of the customer. They include the urgency of order fulfillment, product application, and the size of order.

Buyers' Personal Characteristics

People, not companies, make purchase decisions, although the organizational framework in which they work and company policies and needs may constrain their choices. Marketers for industrial goods, like those for consumer products, can segment markets according to the individuals involved in a purchase in terms of buyer-seller similarity, buyer motivation, individual perceptions, and risk-management strategies.

Reassembling the Nest

As we move from the outer to the inner nests, the segmentation criteria change in terms of visibility, permanence, and intimacy. The data in the outer nests are generally highly visible, even to outsiders, are more or less permanent, and require little intimate knowledge of customers. But situational factors and personal characteristics are less visible, are more transient, and require extensive vendor research.

A fine line exists between minimizing the cost and difficulty of segmentation by staying in the outer nests on the one hand and gaining the useful data of the inner nests at appreciable direct and indirect cost on the other. The outer-nest criteria are generally inadequate when used by themselves in all but the most simple or homogeneous markets because they ignore buying differences among customers. Overemphasis on the inner-nest factors, however, can be too expensive and time-consuming for small markets. We suggest achieving a sense of balance between the simplicity and low cost of the outer nests and the richness and expense of the inner ones by making the choices explicit and the process clear and disciplined.

More Sophisticated Techniques May Help in Segmenting

Clustering usually requires a computer

Clustering techniques usually require market research to gather primary data and then computer analysis try to find similar patterns within sets of data. This data could include anything which might possibly turn out to be relevant—including demographic characteristics, attitudes toward the product or life in general, and previous purchasing behavior. The computer searches among all the data for homogeneous groups of people. When such groups are found, then the dimensions of the people in the groups must be analyzed—by humans—for insights as to why the computer clustered them together. If the results make some sense—if they have face validity—they may suggest new, or at least better, marketing strategies.

A cluster analysis of the toothpaste market, for example, might show that some people buy toothpaste for its sensory satisfaction (the sensory segment), while others are concerned with the effect of clean teeth on their social image (the sociables). Others are worried about decay (the worriers), and some are strictly interested in the best value for their money (the economic men). See

■ FIGURE 9–5   Toothpaste market segment description

Segment name	The sensory segment	The sociables	The worriers	The independent segment
Principal benefit sought	Flavor, product appearance	Brightness of teeth	Decay prevention	Price
Demographic strengths	Children	Teens, young people	Large families	Men
Special behavioral characteristics	Users of spearmint flavored toothpaste	Smokers	Heavy users	Heavy users
Brands disproportionately favored:	Colgate, Stripe	Macleans, Plus White, Ultra Brite	Crest	Brands on sale
Personality characteristics	High self-involvement	High sociability	High hypochon-driasis	High autonomy
Life style characteristics	Hedonistic	Active	Conservative	Value-oriented

Source: Russell I. Haley, "Benefit Segmentation: A Decision-Oriented Research Tool," *Journal of Marketing,*
July 1968, p. 33.

Figure 9–5. Each of these market segments calls for a different marketing mix—although some of the four Ps may be similar. Finally, a marketing manager has to decide which one (or more) of these segments will be the firm's target market(s).

Much experimental work is being done with these techniques—and the results are encouraging.[4] For example, consumer-based clustering techniques were used in the study of prospective American visitors to Canada discussed earlier in this chapter. It should be clear, however, that these techniques only aid the manager. Judgment is still required in the design and conduct of a segmentation study.[5]

Clustering works for services and also industrial goods

These clustering techniques are generally useful for both goods and services—and for industrial goods as well as consumer goods.

In a study of the commercial banking market, for example, six different groups were isolated—each having relevance for marketing strategy planning. These groups were called the non-borrowers, value seekers, non-saving convenience seekers, loan seekers, one-stop bankers, and an "other" group (which was not particularly different on any dimensions). Subsequently, changes were made in the bank's strategy—focusing on each of the markets and treating them as the basis for separate product-market strategies. Instead of the previous "we are friendly people" advertising campaign, the bank decided to appeal to the different markets. The non-borrowers segment was appealed to with messages about the bank's checking account, bank charge card, insurance, and investment counseling. For the convenience seekers, on the other hand, stress was placed on faster teller service, express drive-in windows, overnight drop boxes, and deposit-by-mail accounts. In an effort to reach the loan seekers, promotion stressed auto-loan checking accounts, mail-loan request forms, and loan programs through automobile dealers.[6]

Forecasting Target Market Potential and Sales

Target markets do not have potential all by themselves. Their attractiveness depends on the likely response of the potential customers to a marketing mix—which is the subject of the rest of the book. So as you are learning to plan marketing mixes, keep in mind that eventually you will have to evaluate alternative product-market marketing plans—not just target markets—and then pick those plans which will be carried out by the company.

Estimates of target market potential and likely sales volumes are necessary for effective strategy planning. But a manager can't forecast *sales* without some possible plans. Sales are *not* just "out there for the taking." Market opportunities may be there—but whether a firm can change these opportunities into sales depends on the strategy it selects.

Much of our discussion in the rest of the chapter will be concerned with estimating **market potential**—what a whole market segment might buy—rather than a sales forecast. A **sales forecast** is an estimate of how much an industry or firm hopes to sell to a market segment. We must first try to judge the market potential before we can estimate what share a particular firm might be able to win—because of its marketing strategy and how well it implements it.

Our primary focus will be on forecasting for a reasonable planning period—such as a year—rather than on long-run estimates, or weekly or monthly forecasts to guide current operations. Such forecasts require different techniques and are beyond our scope.

Two Approaches to Forecasting

Many methods are used in forecasting market potential and sales—but they can be grouped under two basic approaches: (1) extending past behavior and (2) predicting future behavior. The large number of methods may seem confusing at first—but this variety is an advantage. Forecasts are so important that management often prefers to develop forecasts in two or three different ways—and then compare the differences before preparing a final forecast.

Extending past behavior

Trend extension can miss important turning points

When we forecast for existing products, we usually have some past data to go on. The basic approach—called **trend extension**—extends past experience into the future. See Figure 9–6.

Ideally—when extending past sales behavior—we should decide why sales vary. This is the difficult and time-consuming part of sales forecasting. Usually we can gather a lot of data about the product or market—or about the economic environment. But unless the *reason* for past sales variations is known, it's hard to predict in what direction—and by how much—sales will move. Graphing the data

■ FIGURE 9–6 Straight-line trend projection—extends past sales into the future

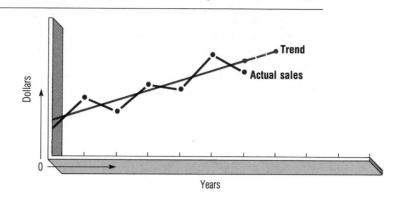

and statistical techniques—including correlation and regression analysis—can be useful here. These techniques are beyond our scope. They are discussed in beginning statistics courses.

Once we know why sales vary, we usually can develop a specific forecast. Sales may be moving directly up as population grows, for example. So we can just get an estimate of how population is expected to grow and project the impact on sales.

The weakness of the trend extension method is that it assumes past conditions will continue unchanged into the future. In fact, the future is not always like the past. And, unfortunately, trend extension will be wrong whenever there are important variations. For this reason—although they may extend past behavior for one estimate—most managers look for another way to help them forecast sharp economic changes.

Predicting future behavior takes judgment

When we try to predict what will happen in the future—instead of just extending the past—we have to use other methods and add a bit more judgment. Some of these methods—to be discussed later—include juries of executive opinion, salespeople's estimates, surveys, panels, and market tests.

Three Levels of Forecast Are Useful

We are interested in forecasting the potential in specific market segments. To do this, it helps to make several kinds of forecasts.

Some economic conditions affect the entire economy. Others may influence only one industry. And some may affect only one company or one product's sales potential. For this reason, a common approach to forecasting is to:

1. Develop a *national income forecast* and use this to:
2. Develop an *industry sales forecast,* which then is used to:
3. Develop *specific company* and *product forecasts.*

Generally, a marketing manager doesn't have to make forecasts for the national economy. This kind of forecasting—basically, trend projecting—is a specialty in itself. These forecasts are available in business and government publications, so managers can simply use one source's forecast or combine several together.

Developing industry sales forecasts	Once the future of the whole economy has been estimated, the next step is to make a forecast for industry sales, that is, sales in the firm's broad product-market area. Since the two are often closely related, simply extending this past relationship may be effective. Automobile sales, for example, reflect the level of national income—since auto sales normally go up as national income rises. But it would be most unusual for such a relationship to be direct; that is, a 1 percent increase in some national figure seldom leads to a 1 percent increase in industry sales. Therefore, some statistical analysis is needed—to determine the relationship between the two (or more) variables. This relationship can then be used to adjust the forecast of national income to estimate future industry sales.

Someone else may do the forecasting

Just as marketing managers do not have to develop their own national economy estimates, they may not have to do industry estimates either. Some industry estimates are published regularly by government agencies, banks, trade associations, and business publications—for such broad categories as steel, cement, plywood, and housing.

Unfortunately, most readily available industry forecasts are for general commodity groups—and reflect what appears to be production-oriented thinking. Such estimates may show market potential for broad *product* classes, but too narrow a view of a market can miss many opportunities. The relevant "industry" should be defined carefully—before the available data is assembled to make an industry forecast.

The more imaginative the previous product-market naming and segmenting effort has been, the less likely that available industry data will fit the firm's chosen product-markets. In fact, aggressive segmenters may create their own little "industries"—and thus have to move directly to estimating potential for their own company and specific products.

Developing company and product forecasts	Next, the marketing manager must try to forecast the size of product-market segments of interest only to his firm and direct competitors. This is the subject of the rest of this chapter.

Forecasting sales for new products is a tougher assignment than forecasting for established products—and calls for slightly different techniques. Therefore, we will discuss these two forecasting jobs separately. |

Forecasting Company and Product Sales by Extending Past Behavior

Past sales can be extended

At the very least, a marketing manager ought to know what the firm's present markets look like—and what it has sold to them in the past. A detailed sales analysis—for products and geographic areas—gives such facts for projecting future results.

Just extending past sales into the future may not seem like much of a forecasting method. But it is better than just assuming that next year's *total* sales will be the same as this year's.

Factor method includes more than time

Simple extension of past sales gives one forecast. But it usually is desirable to tie future sales to something more than the passage of time. The factor method tries to do this.

The **factor method** tries to forecast sales by finding a relation between the company's sales and some other factor (or factors). The basic formula is: something (past sales, industry sales, etc.) *times* some factor *equals* sales forecast. A **factor** is a variable which shows the relation of some variable to the item being forecasted.

A bread manufacturer example

The following example for a bread manufacturer shows how forecasts can be made for many geographic market segments—using the factor method and available data. This general approach can be useful for any firm—manufacturer, wholesaler, or retailer.

Analysis of past sales relationships showed that a particular bread manufacturer regularly sold one half of 1 percent (0.005) of the total retail food sales in its various target markets. This is a single factor. By using this single factor, estimates of the manufacturer's sales for the coming period could be obtained by multiplying a forecast of expected retail food sales by 0.005.

Retail food sales estimates are made each year by *Sales & Marketing Management* magazine. Figure 9–7 shows the kind of geographically detailed data which is updated.

Let's carry this bread example further, using the data in Figure 9–7 for Victoria, British Columbia. Victoria's food sales were $302,122,000 for the previous year. Start by simply accepting last year's food sales as an estimate of current year's sales. Then multiply the food sales estimate for Victoria by the 0.005 factor (the firm's usual share in such markets). The manager would now have an estimate of his current year's bread sales in Victoria. That is, last year's food sales estimate ($302,122,000) times 0.005 equals this year's bread sales estimate of $1,510,610.

Going further, let's assume the marketing manager expected that an especially aggressive promotion campaign would increase the firm's share by 10 percent. The single factor could be increased from 0.005 to 0.0055—and then

■ FIGURE 9–7   Sample of pages from *Sales & Marketing Management's* "Survey of Buying Power"

CENSUS METROPOLITAN AREA SUMMARIES
OF 1984 POPULATION & RETAIL SALES

PROVINCE Census Metropolitan Area	POPULATION 12/31/84 Total Pop (thousands)	% Of Canada	House-holds (thousands)	% Of Canada	RETAIL SALES BY STORE GROUP—1984 Total Retail Sales ($000)	% Of Canada	Food ($000)	Eating & Drinking Places ($000)	General Mdse ($000)	Apparel & Accessories ($000)	Furniture/ Furnish./ Appliance ($000)	Auto-motive ($000)	Gas Stations ($000)	Hard-ware ($000)	Drug ($000)	SALES/ ADVERTISING INDEXES Sales Activity	Buying Power	Quality
ALBERTA																		
Calgary	613.7	2.4292	230.6	2.5128	4,129,272	3.3379	951,644	384,373	634,050	286,092	202,632	945,612	256,560	14,308	147,981	137	2.9604	122
Edmonton	680.2	2.6925	255.9	2.7881	3,831,889	3.0976	736,038	361,939	806,040	221,984	148,958	498,740	182,950	17,363	214,706	115	2.9803	111
BRITISH COLUMBIA																		
Vancouver	1,336.1	5.2889	530.1	5.7766	6,454,123	5.2172	1,470,804	761,104	1,209,241	295,541	274,754	1,080,237	401,661	23,397	326,478	99	5.6162	106
Victoria	243.9	.9653	106.1	1.1560	1,372,371	1.1094	302,122	139,242	281,939	55,563	65,969	173,399	83,952	4,437	51,249	115	1.0539	109
MANITOBA																		
Winnipeg	607.8	2.4062	241.1	2.6286	3,058,065	2.4720	757,499	251,212	532,517	124,373	107,517	516,482	218,399	5,420	90,612	103	2.5467	106
TOTAL ABOVE AREAS	14,165.4	56.0734	5,364.0	58.4504	74,331,461	60.0874	18,144,594	7,182,105	10,459,633	4,107,488	2,875,753	14,176,663	5,091,182	520,474	2,962,075	107	60.2983	108

S&MM METROPOLITAN AREA SUMMARIES OF 1984 EFFECTIVE BUYING INCOME

PROVINCE S&MM Metropolitan Area	EFFECTIVE BUYING INCOME—1984 Total EBI ($000)	% Of Canada	Per Capita EBI	Average Hsld EBI	% of Households by EBI Group (A) $0–$4,999 (B) $5,000–$7,999 (C) $8,000–$9,999 (D) $10,000–$14,999 (E) $15,000 & Over A	B	C	D	E
ALBERTA									
Calgary	9,440,806	3.2754	13,639	36,821	2.1	3.7	3.2	19.6	71.4
Edmonton	9,991,428	3.4664	12,611	34,358	1.5	2.9	2.6	15.7	77.3
BRITISH COLUMBIA									
Kamloops	1,039,147	.3605	10,079	28,085	3.9	3.2	3.4	18.3	71.2
Kelowna	946,018	.3282	10,535	27,107	4.2	5.4	4.3	16.7	69.4
Prince George	985,739	.3420	10,832	31,798	1.6	2.8	2.9	14.8	77.9
Vancouver	16,129,795	5.5960	13,149	32,758	3.1	2.8	2.4	16.2	75.5
Victoria	3,253,056	1.1287	12,478	28,865	3.7	3.8	3.3	15.9	73.3
MANITOBA									
Winnipeg	7,406,569	2.5696	12,626	31,611	3.6	4.0	3.8	26.1	62.5
NEW BRUNSWICK									
Moncton	1,301,063	.4514	9,553	27,860	3.2	4.2	6.2	18.7	67.7
St. John	1,387,089	.4813	9,950	29,019	2.9	4.2	5.7	22.0	65.2
NEWFOUNDLAND									
St. John's	2,247,246	.7797	9,047	30,954	4.0	6.0	6.2	24.6	59.2
NOVA SCOTIA									
Halifax-Dartmouth	3,467,914	1.2032	11,583	31,584	3.2	4.9	6.8	29.9	55.2
Sydney-Glace Bay	1,084,285	.3762	8,354	26,772	5.2	5.7	5.7	36.4	47.0
ONTARIO									
Brantford	1,178,616	.4089	10,954	30,377	3.0	3.8	3.0	19.3	70.9
Guelph	1,606,812	.5575	11,720	32,725	3.5	5.3	3.1	22.9	65.2

PROVINCE S&MM Metropolitan Area	EFFECTIVE BUYING INCOME—1984 Total EBI ($000)	% Of Canada	Per Capita EBI	Average Hsld EBI	% of Households by EBI Group (A) $0–$4,999 (B) $5,000–$7,999 (C) $8,000–$9,999 (D) $10,000–$14,999 (E) $15,000 & Over A	B	C	D	E
Hamilton	5,020,650	1.7418	11,900	31,537	3.7	2.4	1.8	14.4	77.7
Kingston	1,366,258	.4740	11,953	31,264	3.6	4.8	4.4	16.0	71.2
Kitchener-Cambridge	3,789,010	1.3145	11,863	32,608	2.3	3.5	3.4	21.8	69.0
London	4,043,357	1.4028	12,282	31,271	3.5	3.5	3.2	23.7	66.1
North Bay	850,261	2950	10,433	29,523	4.7	4.0	3.2	17.1	71.0
Oshawa	3,842,748	1.3332	12,297	36,632	1.5	1.5	1.3	11.1	84.6
Ottawa	11,470,579	3.9796	14,195	37,002	2.2	2.9	2.7	17.0	75.2
Peterborough	1,189,846	.4128	11,225	29,452	5.3	4.8	3.4	20.9	65.6
St. Catharines-Niagara	4,325,602	1.5007	11,569	31,277	3.4	2.9	2.2	14.7	76.8
Sarnia	1,615,411	.5605	12,474	34,009	2.7	2.3	1.7	6.8	86.5
Sault Ste. Marie	1,583,311	.5494	11,229	32,512	1.9	1.1	.8	4.3	91.9
Sudbury	1,661,353	.5763	10,515	30,372	1.5	1.4	1.2	6.4	89.5
Thunder Bay	1,930,990	.6699	12,442	34,359	2.5	1.6	1.5	8.2	86.2
Toronto	46,525,005	16.1414	14,094	38,607	2.1	2.2	2.3	16.6	76.8
Windsor	3,626,548	1.2582	11,451	31,399	3.2	2.9	2.1	7.4	84.4
QUEBEC									
Chicoutimi-Jonquiere	1,597,131	.5541	8,873	27,776	1.2	1.7	2.1	16.5	78.5
Montreal	34,119,196	11.8371	11,515	29,594	2.9	3.8	3.7	24.2	65.4
Quebec	6,682,483	2.3184	11,222	30,654	1.9	2.7	3.3	20.2	71.9
Sherbrooke	1,178,513	.4089	10,013	26,424	3.6	3.4	3.4	28.3	61.3
Trois Rivieres-Shawinigan	2,198,859	.7629	9,433	25,598	3.9	4.2	3.6	17.3	71.0
SASKATCHEWAN									
Regina	2,692,663	.9342	12,565	33,533	2.2	2.8	3.0	19.3	72.7
Saskatoon	2,532,462	.8786	12,088	30,884	2.4	3.7	3.2	19.3	71.4
TOTAL ABOVE AREAS	205,307,819	71.2293	12,352	33,037	2.7	3.2	3.0	18.9	72.2

Source: *Sales & Marketing Management*, July 22, 1985, D-5 and D-6.

multiplied by the food sales estimate for Victoria—to obtain an estimate for his Victoria bread sales.

Factor method can use several factors

The factor method is not limited to using just one factor. Several factors can be used together. For example, *Sales & Marketing Management* regularly gives a "buying power index" (BPI) as a measure of the potential in different geographic areas. See Figure 9–7. This index takes into consideration (1) the population in a market, (2) the market's income, and (3) retail sales in that market. The BPI for Calgary, Alberta, for example, is 2.9604—meaning that Calgary accounts for 2.9604 percent of the total Canadian buying power. This means that Calgary is a fairly attractive market, because its BPI is much greater than would be expected based on population alone. That is, although Calgary accounts for 2.4292 percent of the Canadian population, it has a much larger share of the buying power—because its income and retail sales are above average.

Using several factors rather than only one factor enables us to work with more information. And in the case of the BPI, it gives a measure of a market's potential, which may be quite important if, for example, a company's sales are not limited to one type of retail store. Then, rather than falling back to using population only, or income only, or trying to develop one's own special index, the BPI can be used in the same way that we used the 0.005 factor in the bread example.

When several factors are used, they may be put together—as with the BPI—or used separately. But the basic factor method is the same. This is shown for a retailer who might be interested in estimating the potential for sets of novelty beer mugs in the Winnipeg area. If about 10 percent of its target market could be expected to buy a $5 set within a one-year period, and this target market consisted of average- or middle-income households, the appropriate numbers could be multiplied to get a forecast as shown below. The example shows that 15,070 buying households spend $5 each, for a total sales potential of $75,350.

Households in Winnipeg	241,100
× Number earning $15,000 + (62.5%)	.625
	150,700
× Share of market (10%)	.10
	15,070
× Price of product ($5.)	5
Total sales potential	$ 75,350

Manufacturers of industrial goods can use several factors, too

Table 9–4 shows how one manufacturer estimated the market for fiber boxes for a particular CMA. This approach could be used in each CMA—to estimate the potential in many geographic target markets.

In this case, SIC code data is used. This is common in the industrial area—because SIC code data is readily available and often very relevant. In this case, the value of box shipments by SIC code were collected by a trade association—but the rest of the data was available from government sources.

Basically, the approach is to calculate the typical consumption per employee—for each SIC industry group in the particular CMA—to get a market potential estimate for each group. Then, the sum of these estimates becomes the total market potential in that CMA. A firm thinking of going into that market would need to estimate the share it could get with its own marketing mix.

Note that this approach can also aid management's control job. If the firm were already in this industry, it could compare its actual sales (by SIC code) with the potential and see how it is doing. If its typical market share is 10 percent of

■   TABLE 9-4   Estimated market for corrugated boxes and cartons (by industry groups,
                      Toronto CMA, 1981)

Industry	(1) Value of box shipments (by end use) ($000)	(2) Production workers (by industry group)	(3) Consumption per worker (1) ÷ (2) (dollars)	(4) Toronto Production workers (by industry group)	(5) Estimated size of the market (3) × (4) ($000)
Food and beverage	$316,752	159,703	$1,983	24,343	$48,272
Tobacco products.	6,100	5,606	1,088	—	—
Rubber and plastics products . .	35,375	45,681	774	12,546	9,711
Leather.	6,450	22,577	286	3,986	1,140
Textile	19,504	53,073	367	7,195	2,641
Knitting mills	3,140	17,851	179	3,288	589
Clothing	10,670	83,418	128	13,467	1,724
Wood.	4,694	94,328	48	3,499	168
Furniture and fixtures.	30,968	44,328	699	13,780	9,632
Paper	51,785	99,491	520	12,824	6,668
Printing and publishing	9,492	63,964	148	19,020	2,815
Primary metal	2,916	92,337	32	—	—
Metal fabricating.	38,895	120,450	323	30,024	9,698
Machinery	9,883	70,784	140	14,238	1,993
Transportation equipment.	11,905	136,102	87	25,899	2,253
Electrical products	40,856	84,282	485	26,834	13,014
Nonmetallic mineral products. . .	40,294	40,145	1,004	5,919	5,943
Petroleum and coal products . . .	3,800	8,457	449	—	—
Chemical and chemical products.	50,176	46,398	1,081	11,600	12,540
Miscellaneous manufacturing . .	25,292	48,354	523	19,263	10,075
Total.	$718,947				138,876

Source: Statistics Canada, Cat. 31-209, 31-203 and 31-212, 1981.

the market—and it is obtaining only 2–5 percent of the market in various SIC sub-markets—then some marketing mix changes may be in order.

Time series and leading series may help estimate a fluctuating future

Not all past economic or sales behavior can be neatly extended with a straight line or some manipulation. Much economic activity has ups and downs. To cope with such variation, statisticians have developed *time series* analysis techniques. **Time series** are historical records of the fluctuations in economic variables. We cannot go into a detailed discussion of these techniques here—but note that there are techniques to handle daily, weekly, monthly, seasonal, and annual variations.[7]

The dream of all forecasters is to find an accurate **leading series**—a time series which changes in the same direction *but ahead of* the series to be forecasted. For example, if an index of electrical power consumption always went up three months before a company's own sales of products which have some logical relation to electric power consumption (it is important that there be some logical relation!), then the managers might watch this "leading" series very carefully when forecasting monthly sales of its products.

No single series has yet been found that leads GNP—or other important quantities. Lacking such a series, forecasters develop **indices**—statistical combinations of several time series—in an effort to find some time series that will lead the series they are attempting to forecast. The Bank of Canada, The Conference Board in Canada, and the chartered banks offer statistical information in their monthly reviews. The Conference Board also provides detailed information on many generally accepted measures of economic activity. And business magazines, such as *Canadian Business,* publish their own series and predictions.

Predicting Future Behavior Calls for More Judgment and Some Opinions

The past-extending methods discussed above make use of "hard" data—projecting past experience into the future on the assumption that the future will be like the past. But this is a dangerous assumption in dynamic markets. Usually, it is desirable to add judgment to hard data to get better—or at least other—forecasts to be compared on the way to making the final forecast.

The following methods—which tend to be more qualitative—may be especially useful when: (1) conditions are changing in the marketplace, (2) the company's marketing mix has changed a lot, (3) the company is in unstable, fluctuating markets (such as fashion goods or seasonal businesses), and (4) the company is introducing new products which have no past history.

Jury of executive opinion adds judgment

One of the oldest and simplest methods of forecasting—the **jury of executive opinion**—combines the opinions of experienced executives—perhaps from marketing, production, finance, purchasing, and top management. Basically, each executive is asked to estimate market potential and sales for the *coming years.* Then, they try to work out a consensus. The idea is to use as much seasoned judgment as possible—in combination with past data.

The main advantage of the jury approach is that it can be done quickly—and easily. On the other hand, the results may not be very good. There may be excessive reliance on extending the past—because some of the executives may have little contact with outside market forces. At the worst, it could be an averaging of naive extensions of the past. At the best, however, it could alert the forecasters to major shifts in customer demand or competition.

Estimates from salespeople can help, too

Using salespeople's estimates to forecast is like the jury approach. But salespeople are more likely than home office managers to be familiar with customer reactions—and what competitors are doing. Their estimates are especially useful in industrial markets—where the limited number of customers may be well known to the salespeople. But this approach is useful in any type of market. Good retail clerks have a "feel" for the market—their opinions should not be ignored.

Two limitations concerning the use of salespeople's estimates should be kept in mind. First, salespeople usually don't know about possible changes in

Salespeople know their market and can be helpful in sales forecasting.

the national economic climate—or even about changes in the company's marketing mix.

Second, salespeople may have little to offer if they change jobs often.

Surveys, panels, and market tests

Instead of relying heavily on salespeople to estimate customers' intentions, it may be desirable to do some marketing research. Special surveys of final buyers, retailers, and/or wholesalers can show what is happening in different market segments. Some firms use panels of stores—or final consumers—to keep track of buying behavior—and to determine when simply extending past behavior has become inadequate.

Surveys are sometimes combined with market tests—when the company wants to estimate the reaction of customers to possible changes in its marketing mix. A market test might show that a product increased its share of the market by 10 percent when its price was dropped one cent below competition. Yet this extra business might be quickly lost if the price were increased one cent above competition. Such market experiments help the marketing manager make realistic estimates of future sales when one or more of the four Ps are changed.

Sometimes the only way to estimate the market potential of a new product is to actually try it in the market. Several test markets can be used—and assuming they are fairly representative (a big assumption!)—the results can be projected to a larger area.

Forecasting from market test results can be misleading, however—since the very novelty of the product seems to attract some customers. This means that sales may shoot up just after a new product is introduced, then decline quickly, level off, and then *perhaps* rise as a market of repeat customers develops.

Another problem with market test results is that competitors may run special pricing offers or extra promotion—to meet or beat the introductory effort. And there's also the danger of wanting to rush the market test—which probably should take from 6 to 12 months—because of an initial sales boom *and* an eagerness to offer the product ahead of competition. This is a serious matter. Extensive market testing may be a luxury in our highly competitive markets—especially if more aggressive competitors are monitoring the tests to try to beat the innovator to national distribution. This has happened often enough to discourage some firms from testing new products.

**Substitute method—
nothing is completely
new**

The **substitute method** involves careful analysis of the sales of products which a new one may displace. Since few products are entirely new, this method can provide an upper limit on potential sales. With imagination and research, a company can list most possible uses and estimate the potential in the present markets. Once the potential of the markets has been estimated, these figures can be scaled down by market realities—including likely customer preferences at various price levels, and the availability of good or better substitutes. Research and judgment are obviously needed with this approach—and several of the methods discussed above would be helpful. In the industrial goods area, SIC data would be especially useful—in estimating the potential in quite different kinds of markets.

Application of the substitute method can be illustrated by the forecasting done by Du Pont for a plastic resin product.[8]

■ FIGURE 9–8   Estimating the size of the market possibilities

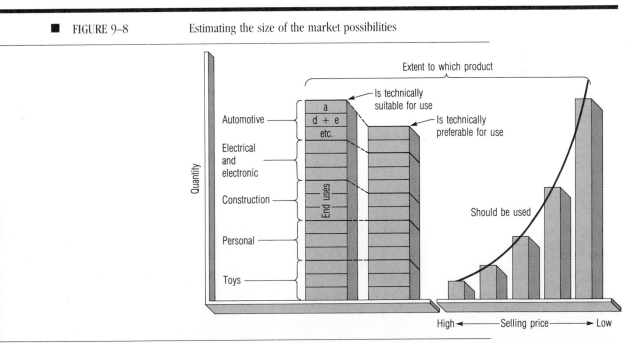

Source: G. T. Borchert, "Design of the Marketing Program for a New Product," in *Marketing's Role in Scientific Management*, ed. Robert L. Clewett (Chicago: American Marketing, 1957), p. 64.

The chemical company began by estimating the size of the various end-use markets—shown as the left series of boxes in Figure 9–8 (page 311). These were markets where the resin product was technically suitable for use—including automotive, electrical, electronic, construction, personal, and toy products. The sum of the potential in all these boxes indicated the upper limit on demand. Then a harder look at the suitability of the product in comparison with those currently being used indicated that one of the planned automotive and construction applications should be dropped.

The markets where the new product was technically preferable for use are shown in Figure 9–8 in the second bar from the left. These first two market possibility bars, however, ignore potential selling prices—which are realities in any market. So the potential demand at various selling prices was considered. The five right-hand bars in Figure 9–8 show the various quantities of the product that, technically, should be used at various price levels. The extreme right-hand bar indicates that if prices were low enough, all of the potential users would use the product.

■ FIGURE 9–9   Another way of seeing Figure 9–8

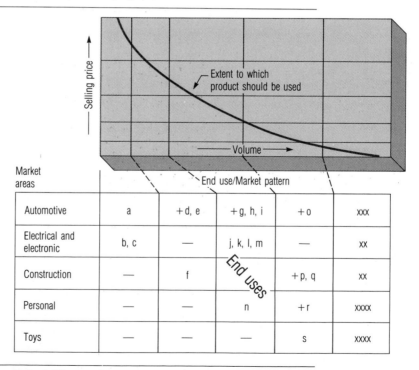

Market areas			End use/Market pattern		
Automotive	a	+d, e	+g, h, i	+o	xxx
Electrical and electronic	b, c	—	j, k, l, m	—	xx
Construction	—	f		+p, q	xx
Personal	—	—	n	+r	xxxx
Toys	—	—	—	s	xxxx

Source: G. T. Borchert, "Design of the Marketing Program for a New Product," in *Marketing's Role in Scientific Management*, ed. Robert L. Clewett (Chicago: American Marketing Association, 1957), p. 66.

Many potentials but one forecast

The data in Figure 9–8 is shown in a different way and with more detail in Figure 9–9.

Here the impact of demand curves in different markets on marketing strategy planning becomes clearer. At a high selling price, interest would be shown by one of the potential automotive markets and by electrical and electronic users (markets a, b, and c). If the price were dropped slightly, additional automotive users (d and e) and a construction industry user (f) would add to the potential market. In other words, potential target markets are being specified as part of the sales forecasting procedure.

Need analysis in possible market segments

If a product is so new that no present market can be used as a guide, then the marketing manager may have to use **need analysis**—market research to determine who might be interested in the new product and how strongly felt are the needs it will satisfy. This—combined with demographic data—can lead to a forecast.

This kind of forecasting may seem crude in comparison with the techniques described earlier—but it is still important. Careful analysis may produce clear alternatives. It may show that either the highest potential sales volume for a product is too small to justify further effort—or the outlook may prove to be so attractive that, despite the crude estimate, enthusiasm seems justified.

Calculations killed this slide rule

The following simple example illustrates this approach.

A firm developed a five-inch plastic slide rule that would help a shopper determine the "best buy" among several products and packages at a supermarket. After discussion with a few friends, the company's managers were sure that some shoppers would be interested. But how many? And which ones? Men probably should have been considered, too, because they do some shopping—but the managers limited their initial survey to women.

A small-scale survey was discouraging. Only 5 percent showed any interest. The survey was not large enough to enable the managers to understand all the relevant dimensions, but it appeared that only more highly educated, younger women might be interested—and only if the retail price of the slide rule were under 70 cents.

The company then talked to retailers to see how they reacted to the product. Some retailers indicated a lack of enthusiasm—though some were willing to give it a try.

It looked as if the achievable potential would be quite low. Specific figures confirmed this. The 5 percent of the women who *might* be interested—multiplied by approximately 70 million American households—suggested an upper limit of 3.5 million units. When potential retail availability was considered, this potential upper limit was reduced to 100,000 units *or less.* In view of the fact that a premium price could not be obtained (the rule itself would cost about 25 cents to make) and that repeat sales were highly unlikely, the project was dropped. Not enough people had strongly felt needs to make the product worthwhile to the firm.

Accuracy of Forecasts

The accuracy of forecasts varies a lot—depending on the number of components in the number being forecast. The more general the number being forecast, the more accurate the forecast is likely to be. This is because small errors in various components of the estimate tend to offset each other—and make the whole estimate more accurate.

Annual forecasts of national totals—such as GNP—may be accurate within 5 percent. Industry sales forecasts—which tend to be more specific—are usually accurate within 10 percent—depending on the variability of the industry.

When estimates are made for individual products, there is even less chance of offsetting errors—except where errors from one salesperson or territory offset those in another. Where style and innovation are important factors in an industry, forecast errors of 10 to 20 percent for *established products* are not uncommon. The accuracy of specific *new-product* forecasts is even lower. Many new products fail completely—while others are extremely successful.

One forecaster of new consumer and industrial products claimed he had an excellent overall forecasting average for a particular year. He was off by only 2 percent on the average. His inaccuracy on specific product forecasts, however, was frightening. Many products did not sell at all—he missed by 100 percent—and others exceeded his expectations by 200 to 300 percent.[9]

■ CONCLUSION

This chapter discussed market segmentation—the process of naming and segmenting broad product-markets—to find potentially attractive target markets. Some people try to segment markets by breaking them down into smaller sub-markets. But this can lead to poor results. Instead, segmenting should be seen as an aggregating process. The more similar the potential customers are, the larger the sub-markets can be. Four criteria for evaluating possible market segments were presented.

Even "rough and ready" segmenting can add perspective about the nature of possible product-markets—and may lead to breakthrough opportunities. Seemingly trivial determining dimensions may make a "winner" out of what appears to be a "me-too" strategy.

We also talked about two basic approaches to forecasting market potential and sales: (1) extend-ing past behavior and (2) predicting future behavior. The most common approach is to extend past behavior into the future. This gives reasonably good results if market conditions are fairly stable. Methods here include extension of past sales data and the factor method. We saw that projecting the past into the future is risky when big market changes are likely. To make up for this possible weakness, marketers must predict future behavior using their own experience and judgment. They also may be able to bring in the judgment of others—using the jury of executive opinion method and salespeople's estimates. They may also use surveys, panels, market tests, the substitute method, and need analysis.

We saw that the accuracy of forecasts depends on how general a forecast is being made. The most error occurs with specific forecasts for products—and especially new products.

Even though forecasts are subject to error, they are still necessary to help the firm choose among possible product-market marketing plans. Sloppy forecasting can lead to poor strategies. No forecasting at all is stupid!

In summary, good marketers should be experts on markets and likely relevant dimensions. By creatively segmenting markets, they may spot opportunities—even breakthrough opportunities—and help their firms to succeed against aggressive competitors offering similar products. Segmenting is basic to target marketing. And the more you practice segmenting, the more meaningful market segments you will see.

■ QUESTIONS AND PROBLEMS

1. Explain what market segmentation is.

2. List the types of potential segmenting dimensions and explain which you would try to apply first, second, and third in a particular situation. If the nature of the situation would affect your answer, explain how.

3. Explain why "first-time" segmentation efforts may be very disappointing.

4. Illustrate the concept that segmenting is an aggregating process by referring to the apparent admissions policies of your own college and a nearby college or university.

5. Review the types of segmenting dimensions listed in Tables 9–2 and 9–3, and select the ones which you feel should be combined to fully explain the market segment you, personally, would be in if you were planning to buy a new automobile today. Do not hesitate to list several dimensions, but when you have done so, try to develop a shorthand name, like "swinger," to describe your own personal market segment. Then try to estimate what proportion of the total automobile market would be accounted for by your market segment. Next, explain if there are any offerings which come close to meeting the needs of your market. If not, what sort of a marketing mix is needed? Do you feel it would be economically attractive for anyone to try to satisfy your market segment? Why or why not?

6. Identify the determining dimension or dimensions which explain why you bought the specific brand you did in your most recent purchase of a (*a*) soft drink, (*b*) pen, (*c*) shirt or blouse, and (*d*) larger, more expensive item, such as a bicycle, camera, boat, and so on. Try to express the determining dimension(s) in terms of your own personal characteristics rather than the product's characteristics. Estimate what share of the market would probably be motivated by the same determining dimension(s).

7. Explain the difference between a forecast of market potential and a sales forecast.

8. Suggest a plausible explanation for sales fluctuations for (*a*) bicycles, (*b*) baby food, (*c*) motor boats, (*d*) baseball gloves, (*e*) wheat, (*f*) woodworking tools, and (*g*) latex for rubber-based paint.

9. Explain the factor method. Illustrate your answer.

10. Discuss the relative accuracy of the various forecasting methods. Explain why some are more accurate than others.

11. Given the following annual sales data for a company which is not planning any spectacular marketing strategy changes, forecast sales for the coming year (7) and explain your method and reasoning.

	(a)		(b)
Year	Sales ($000)	Year	Sales ($000)
1	$200	1	$160
2	230	2	155
3	210	3	165
4	220	4	160
5	200	5	170
6	220	6	165

12. Discuss the relative market potential of Oshawa and Sudbury, Ontario, for: (*a*) prepared cereals, (*b*) automobiles, and (*c*) furniture.

13. Discuss how a General Motors market analyst might use the substitute method if the company were considering the potential for an electric car suitable for salespeople, commuters, homemakers, farmers, and perhaps other groups. The analyst is trying to consider the potential in terms of possible price levels—$2,000, $4,000, $6,000, $8,000, and $10,000—and driving ranges—10 miles, 20 miles, 50 miles, 100 miles, and 200 miles—which would typically be desired or needed before recharging. He is assuming that gasoline-powered vehicles will become illegal for use within the major urban cities. Further, it is expected that while personal gasoline-driven cars still will be used in rural and suburban areas, they will not be permitted within some suburban areas, especially around the major metropolitan areas.

■ **SUGGESTED CASES**

12. Miller Shoes Limited

16. New Start Furniture

■ NOTES

1. Terry Elrod and Russell S. Winer, "An Empirical Evaluation of Aggregation Approaches for Developing Market Segments," *Journal of Marketing* 46, no. 4 (Fall 1982), pp. 32–34.

2. Peter R. Dickerson, "Person-Situation: Segmentation's Missing Link," *Journal of Marketing* 46, no. 4, (Fall 1982), pp. 56–64. For a classic article on the subject, see Russell I. Haley, "Benefit Segmentation: A Decision-Oriented Research Tool," *Journal of Marketing,* July 1968, pp. 30–35. See also Richard M. Johnson, "Marketing Segmentation: A Strategic Management Tool," *Journal of Marketing Research,* February 1971, pp. 13–18; James H. Myers, "Benefit Structure Analysis: A New Tool for Product Planning," *Journal of Marketing,* October 1976, pp. 23–32; and Roger J. Calantone and Alan G. Sawyer, "The Stability of Benefit Segments," *Journal of Marketing Research,* August 1978, pp. 395–404.

3. Shirley Young, Leland Ott, and Barbara Feigin, "Some Practical Considerations in Market Segmentation," *Journal of Marketing Research,* August 1978, p. 408, as reproduced in Joseph P. Guiltinan and Gordan W. Paul, *Marketing Management-Strategies and Programs* (New York: McGraw-Hill, 1982), p. 78.

4. Danny N. Bellenger and Pradeep K. Korgaonkartation, "Profiling the Recreational Shopper," *Journal of Retailing* 56, no. 3 (Fall 1980), pp. 77–92; Miriam Tatzel, "Skill and Motivation in Clothes Shopping: Fashion-Conscious, Independent, and Apathetic Consumers," *Journal of Retailing* 58, no. 4 (Winter 1982), pp. 90–96; and "The Sky's the Limit in Luring the Frequent Flier," *Business Week,* October 18, 1982, pp. 152–53.

5. Girish Punj and David W. Stewart, "Cluster Analysis in Marketing Research: Review and Suggestions for Application," *Journal of Marketing Research* 20 (May 1983), pp. 134–48; T. D. Klastorin, "Assessing Cluster Analysis Results," *Journal of Marketing Research* 20 (February 1983), pp. 92–98; Rajendra K. Srivastava, Robert P. Leone, and Allen D.

Shocker, "Market Structure Analysis: Hierarchical Clustering of Products Based on Substitution-in-Use," *Journal of Marketing* 45, no. 3 (Summer 1981), pp. 38–48; Frederick W. Winter, "A Cost-Benefit Approach to Market Segmentation," *Journal of Marketing,* Fall 1979, pp. 103–11; Phillip E. Downs, "Multidimensional Scaling versus the Hand-Drawn Technique," *Journal of Business Research,* December 1979, pp. 349–58; and Henry Assael, "Segmenting Markets by Response Elasticity," *Journal of Advertising Research,* April 1976, pp. 27–35.

6. S. Arbeit and A. G. Sawyer, "Benefit Segmentation in a Retail Banking Environment," paper presented at the American Marketing Association Fall Conference, Washington D.C., 1973.

7. See most basic statistics textbooks under time series analysis.

8. G. T. Borchert, "Design of the Marketing Program for a New Product," in *Marketing's Role in Scientific Management,* ed. Robert L. Clewett (Chicago: American Marketing Association, 1957), pp. 64–66.

9. Checking the accuracy of forecasts is a difficult subject. See R. Ferber, W. J. Hawkes, Jr., and M. D. Plotkin, "How Reliable Are National Retail Sales Estimates?" *Journal of Marketing,* October 1976, pp. 13–22; D. J. Dalrymple, "Sales Forecasting Methods and Accuracy," *Business Horizons,* December 1975, pp. 69–73; P. R. Wotruba and M. L. Thurlow, "Sales Force Participation in Quota Setting and Sales Forecasting, *Journal of Marketing,* April 1976, pp. 11–16; R. Shoemaker and R. Staelin, "The Effects of Sampling Variation on Sales Forecasts for New Consumer Products," *Journal of Marketing Research,* May 1976, pp. 138–43; and R. Staelin and R. E. Turner, "Error in Judgmental Sales Forecasts: Theory and Results," *Journal of Marketing Research,* February 1973, pp. 10–16.

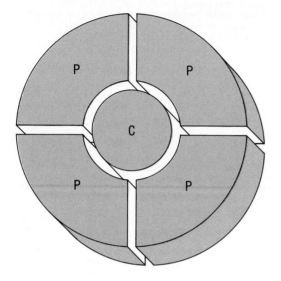

Product

Place

Promotion

Price

Customer

Here (Chapters 10–20) we are concerned with developing effective marketing mixes for the possible target markets we discussed in Part II. We discuss the "four Ps"—the ingredients of a marketing mix. The four Ps are interrelated and must be blended into one integrated whole—to satisfy some target market's needs and preferences.

First, we will discuss Product—in Chapters 10 and 11. We will explore what a "product" is, and introduce some goods classes to speed the development of your marketing sense—because they suggest the outlines of a marketing mix. Combined with a knowledge of the target market, you can "rough out" a marketing mix fairly quickly.

Place is covered in Chapters 12–15. Chapter 12 is concerned with the development and management of channel systems. Chapters 13–15 introduce some of the components of channel systems—retailers, wholesalers, warehousers, and transporters. The Place chapters are very important—because this is where most of the "action" in marketing takes place.

Promotion is discussed in three chapters (Chapters 16–18). Chapter 16 explains the various promotion methods—personal selling, advertising, and sales promotion—and shows that a blend of these methods is usually needed. Chapters 17 and 18 go into more detail about personal selling and advertising.

The final two chapters in this part (as well as Appendix E on Marketing Arithmetic) are concerned with Price. Chapter 19 discusses price objectives—and how they affect the strategic decisions in the pricing area. Then, Chapter 20 talks about price setting in the real world.

In summary, by the time you have studied this part, you should have a good understanding of how to develop a *profitable* strategy—i.e., selecting the "right" Product (including packaging and branding) which will be made available in the "right" Place, supported with the "right" Promotion, at the "right" Price—to satisfy some target market. So the next job—Part IV—will be to evaluate potentially attractive strategies to decide which one or ones you will select for implementation.

Chapter 10 ■ Elements of product planning

When you finish this chapter, you should:

1. Understand what "Product" really means.

2. Know the differences among the various consumer and industrial goods classes.

3. Understand how the goods classes can help a marketing manager plan marketing strategies.

4. Understand what branding is and how it can be used in strategy planning.

5. Understand the strategic importance of packaging.

6. Recognize the important new terms (shown in red).

"The product must satisfy customers—what they want is what they'll get."

Developing the "right" product isn't easy—because customer needs and attitudes keep changing. Further, *most customers want some combination of goods and services in their product.*

A young couple with a new baby has a new need—getting diapers clean. They decide to buy a washing machine. Since it's a big purchase, they shop at several stores for a machine with just the right features. They want a well-known brand—like Whirlpool—that will assure them of quality. They also want the washer delivered—so this service is part of the product they're considering. And they want to be sure that the machine will last—so they're concerned about the warranty included with the product.

This simple situation includes many of the important topics we'll discuss in this chapter. First, we'll look at how customers view a firm's product—based on the needs it meets. Then, we'll talk about goods classes. These consumer and industrial goods classes help us understand how Product relates to other aspects of marketing strategy planning—and can speed your development as a strategy planner.

We will also talk about branding and packaging. Both goods and services should be branded. A successful marketer wants to be sure that satisfied customers will know what to ask for the next time. Packaging helps to protect goods, but it's also important in promoting the product—or making it easier to use.

■ FIGURE 10–1   Strategy planning for Product

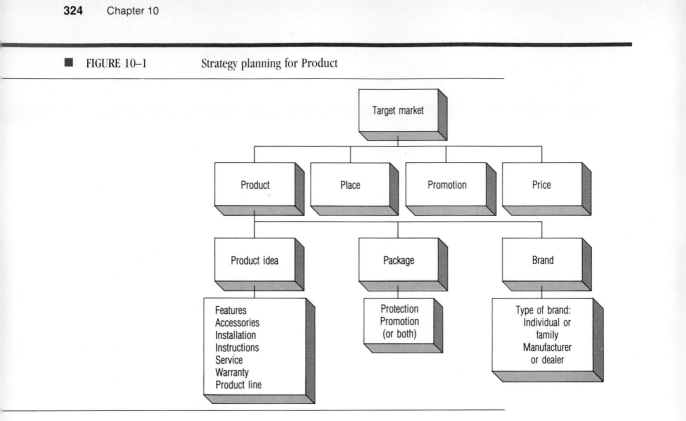

In summary, we will talk about the strategic decisions of manufacturers or middlemen who make these Product decisions. These strategic decisions are shown in Figure 10–1.

What Is a Product?

Need-satisfying offer-ing of a firm

First, we have to define what we mean by a "product." **Product** means the need-satisfying offering of a firm.

If we sell an automobile, are we selling a certain number of nuts and bolts, some sheet metal, an engine, and four wheels?

If we sell a detergent to be used in a washing machine, are we selling just a box of chemicals?

If we sell a delivery service, are we selling so much wear and tear on a delivery truck and so much operator fatigue?

The answer to all these questions is *no*. Instead, what we are really selling is the satisfaction, use, or profit the customer wants.

The idea of Product as potential customer satisfactions or benefits is very important. It means that what matters is how *customers* see what is being of-fered—not how the seller sees it. It also means that the Product is not just limited to the physical features of a good. It can include accessories, installation, instructions on use, the package, a warranty, and confidence that service will be available after the purchase if it is needed. In fact, Product may simply be a service that satisfies a need—it may have no physical features at all. These ideas are important, so we will talk about each of them in more detail.[1]

Customers buy satisfaction—not parts

The product must satisfy the customers' needs—or they won't buy it. So what is important is how customers see what is offered—not how the seller sees it. And these two views may be far apart.

A customer buying a radio thinks about the benefits it will provide—what needs it will satisfy. Will it tune in the desired stations? Is the sound good? Is it convenient to use? Does it look attractive? Answers to these questions might vary for different customers. They listen to different stations. They have different ideas about sound quality and appearance.

Many business managers—trained in the production side of business—get wrapped up in technical details. They think of Product as a collection of physical parts—like transistors and resistors. But most customers just want a good-looking product that works. They don't want to know how it's made.

These ideas apply to industrial customers, too. When producers and middlemen buy products, they are interested in the profit they will make from their purchase—through its use and resale—not how the products were made.

Managers who think of products only as collections of parts often have problems. They think the product is the same to all customers—because the parts are the same. They may even forget to provide things needed to meet the customers' needs.

A Japanese company had trouble selling its camera in Canada. The camera had many good features, but the instructions were so confusing that buyers couldn't operate it. With improved instructions, sales of this camera took off.

Product may only be a service

"Product" may not include a physical good at all! The product of a hair stylist is the trimming or styling of your hair. A doctor may just look at you—neither taking anything away nor giving you anything other than an opinion. An accounting firm may only review the correctness of a firm's tax records. Nevertheless, each satisfies needs—and provides a product in the sense we will use "product" in this book.

Goods and/or services are our product

Most products are a blend of physical goods *and* services. Figure 10–2 emphasizes this by showing that a "product" can range from 100 percent physical good—such as commodities like common nails or dried beans—to 100 percent service, like a taxi ride.

This bigger view of a product must be understood completely—it's too easy to slip into a *physical product* point of view. We want to think of a product in terms of the *needs it satisfies*. Customer needs are satisfied not only by physical goods, but also by services. If the objective of a firm is to satisfy customer needs, it must see that service is part of the product—or service may be *the* product—and has to be provided as part of the marketing mix.

Given the logic discussed above, we will not make a distinction between

■ FIGURE 10–2   Possible blends of goods and services in a product

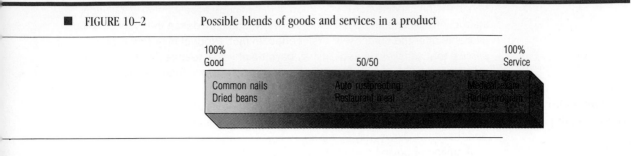

goods and services—but will call them all *Products.* Within this broader concept of a Product, we can also consider the assortment of goods and services offered by a firm.

Product Assortments and Product Lines Must Be Developed, Too

We will usually talk about one product at a time—to simplify the discussion. But most businesses sell many products—each of which may require a separate strategy. So, it is useful to define **product assortment**—the set of all product lines and items that a firm sells—and **product line**—a set of products that are closely related. They may be seen as related by the seller because they are produced and/or operate in a similar way, or are sold to the same target market, or are sold through the same types of outlets, or are priced at about the same level. Procter & Gamble, for example, has many product lines in its product assortment—including coffee, detergents, toothpastes, shampoo, toilet tissue, and disposable diapers. **Product item**—a particular product within a product line—usually is differentiated by brand, size, price, or some other characteristic—and identified with its own stockkeeping number. For example, each size of a brand of soap would be a separate item—and may require a separate strategy.

Most companies have to offer product assortments to satisfy their customers. This makes the job of product planning harder. But it is important to fully understand the needs and attitudes of target customers—and then develop a *complete* offering to satisfy their needs.

Goods Classes Help Plan Marketing Strategies

A firm's Product decisions are important in planning the rest of the strategy. But it isn't necessary to treat *every* product as unique when planning strategies. There are classes of products that require similar strategies. Understanding these classes is important. It helps you to see *general* patterns that guide marketing strategy planning. This also means that you don't have to memorize long lists of products—and how each is marketed.

We will call these classes "goods classes"—because this is traditional in marketing. But remember, goods classes refer to *products*—which can be goods and/or services.

Goods classes start with type of customer

All products fit into one of two broad groups—based on what type of customer will use them. **Consumer goods** are those products meant for the final consumer. **Industrial goods** are products meant for use in producing other products. Note, however, that the same product might be in both groups. Paper clips are sold to both final consumers and industrial customers—and require (at least) two different strategies for these different goods class groups.

There are goods classes within each of these two groups. The basis for the classes is different in each. This is because final consumers and industrial customers usually view purchases differently. Consumer goods classes are based on *how consumers think about and shop for products.* Industrial customers typically do little shopping—especially compared to final consumers. Usually the seller comes to the industrial buyer. So industrial goods classes are based on *how the product will be used.*

We will talk about consumer goods classes first.

Consumer Goods Classes

Consumer goods are divided into four groups: (1) convenience goods, (2) shopping goods, (3) specialty goods, and (4) unsought goods. See Figure 10–3 for a summary of how goods classes are related to marketing mixes.[2]

■   FIGURE 10–3   Consumer goods classes and marketing mix planning

1. *Convenience goods.*
    a. Staples—need maximum exposure—need widespread distribution at low cost.
    b. Impulse goods—need maximum exposure—need widespread distribution but with assurance of preferred display or counter position.
2. *Shopping goods.*
    a. Homogeneous—need enough exposure to facilitate price comparison.
    b. Heterogeneous—need adequate representation in major shopping districts or large shopping centers near other, similar shopping goods.
3. *Specialty goods*—can have limited availability, but in general should be treated as a convenience or shopping good (in whichever category product would normally be included), to reach persons not yet sold on its specialty-goods status.
4. *Unsought goods*—need attention directed to product and aggressive promotion in outlets, or must be available in places where similar products would be sought.

Convenience Goods—Purchased Quickly with Little Effort

Convenience goods are products a consumer needs but isn't willing to spend much time or effort shopping for. These products are bought often, require little service or selling, don't cost much, and may even be bought by habit. Examples are toothpaste, chewing gum, candy, soap, newspapers, magazines, and most grocery products.

Convenience goods are of three types—staples, impulse goods, and emergency goods—again based on how customers think about products—not the features of the products themselves.

Staples—purchased and used regularly

Staples are goods which are bought often and routinely—without much thought. Examples include most packaged foods, health and beauty aids like toothpaste and shampoo, and cleaning products like soap and paper towels—all items which are used frequently in every household.

Because staples are purchased often, they are sold in convenient places like food stores or drug stores, or even delivered to the home (bread, milk, eggs). Branding can also be important to help customers cut shopping effort.

Impulse goods— bought immediately on sight

Impulse goods are goods which are bought quickly—as unplanned purchases—because of a strongly felt need. True impulse goods are items that the customer had not planned to buy, decides to buy on sight, may have bought the same way many times before, and wants "right now." If the customer doesn't buy an impulse good immediately, the need may disappear, and no purchase will be made.

This is important because it affects Place and the whole marketing mix for impulse goods. If the buyer doesn't see an item at the "right" time, the sale may be lost. As a result, impulse goods are put where they will be seen and bought—near the check-out counters or in other heavy traffic areas of a store. Gum, candy bars, and magazines are often sold this way in grocery stores. An ice cream seller at the beach sells impulse goods. If sunbathers don't buy then, the need goes away, and the impulse purchase won't be made later.[3]

Emergency goods— purchased only when urgently needed

Emergency goods are goods which are purchased immediately when the need is great. The customer does not have the time to shop around—so price isn't important. Examples are ambulance services, umbrellas or raincoats during a rainstorm, and tire chains during a snowstorm.

An item which is usually a staple good may be purchased as an emergency good when time is short. A customer may think of a purchase of milk, soft drinks, or ice as "an emergency" if he's in a hurry. Meeting customers' needs for immediate service may require a different marketing mix—especially regarding Place. Some small neighborhood stores provide "emergency" service—staying open "7 till 11" and stocking items that are needed fast. Usually, these stores charge higher prices. But customers pay them because they think of these goods as "emergencies."

Shopping Goods—Are Compared

Shopping goods are those products that a customer feels are worth the time and effort to compare with competing products. Shopping goods can be divided into two types—depending on what customers are comparing: (1) homogeneous and (2) heterogeneous shopping goods.

Homogeneous shopping goods—the price must be right

Homogeneous shopping goods are shopping goods that the customer sees as basically the same—and wants at the lowest price. Some consumers feel that certain sizes and types of refrigerators, television sets, washing machines, and even automobiles are very similar. They are mainly concerned about shopping for the best price.

Manufacturers may try to emphasize their product differences—and retailers may try to promote their "better service." But if the customers don't believe these differences are real, they will just look at price.

Some sellers realize that a slight price cut on such products can greatly increase sales volume—because they are facing almost perfectly elastic demand curves. So, price competition is often vigorous. In fact, this helps to explain the rise of certain types of discount houses—and why some retailers emphasize "low prices" and "price cuts."

Low-price items are seen this way, too

Even some relatively inexpensive items like butter, coffee, and other food items may be thought of as homogeneous shopping goods. Some customers carefully read food store advertising for the lowest prices—and then go from store to store getting the items. They wouldn't do this for staples.

For this woman, these shirts are a heterogeneous shopping good—but other people might see them differently.

Heterogeneous shopping goods—the product must be right

Heterogeneous shopping goods are shopping goods that the customer sees as different—and wants to inspect for quality and suitability. Examples are furniture, clothing, dishes, and some cameras. Quality and style are important—price is less important.

For non-standardized products, it's harder to compare prices. Once the customer has found the right product, price may not be determining—provided it is reasonable. That is, the demand for the product may be quite inelastic. The more close substitutes there are, the more elastic the demand becomes. But it does not approach the extreme elasticity found with homogeneous shopping goods.

Branding may be less important for heterogeneous shopping goods. The more consumers want to make their own comparisons of price and quality, the less they rely on brand names and labels. Some retailers carry competing brands so consumers don't need to go to a competitor to compare items.

The buyer of heterogeneous shopping goods not only wants—but expects—some kind of help in buying. Knowledgeable sales clerks can be important. Promotion often highlights "special" features for customers. And if the product is expensive, the buyer may want extra service—such as alteration of clothing or installation of appliances.

Specialty Goods—No Substitutes Please!

Specialty goods are consumer goods that the customer really wants—and is willing to make a special effort to find. Shopping for a specialty good doesn't mean comparing—the buyer wants that special product and is willing to search for it. It is not the extent of searching, but the customer's *willingness* to search—that makes it a specialty good.

Any item that consumers insist on by brand name is a specialty good. So, specialty goods usually are specific branded products—not broad product categories. A college student who wants a Ralph Lauren shirt with the polo symbol sees it as a specialty good—if he won't accept an otherwise identical shirt.

Don't want substitutes!

Contrary to a common view, specialty goods need not be expensive, durable items that are purchased infrequently. Consumers have been observed asking for a drug product by its brand name and, when offered a substitute (even though chemically identical), actually leaving the store in anger.

As might be expected, the demand for specialty goods is relatively inelastic—at least within reasonable price ranges—since target customers are willing to insist on the product. All marketing managers would like buyers to see their products as specialty goods—but competition may make this impossible.

Unsought Goods—Need Promotion

Unsought goods are goods that potential customers do not yet want or know they can buy. Therefore, they don't search for them at all. In fact, consumers probably won't buy these goods if they see them—unless Promotion can show their value.

There are two types of unsought goods. **New unsought goods** are products offering really new ideas that potential customers don't know about yet. Informative promotion can help convince customers to accept or even seek out the product—ending their unsought status. When microwave ovens were first introduced, consumers didn't know what the oven could do. It was an unsought good. But promotion showed the benefits provided by the new product, and now many consumers buy them.

Regularly unsought goods are products—like gravestones, life insurance, and encyclopedias—that stay unsought but not unbought forever. There may be a need—but the potential customers are not motivated to satisfy it. And there probably is little hope that they will move out of the unsought class for most consumers. For this kind of product, personal selling is very important.

One Product May Be Seen as Several Consumer Goods

We have been looking at product classes *one at a time.* But, a marketing manager might find that a product-market consists of several groups of people which have different attitudes toward the product. And some customers may see the same product as different types of good, depending on the situation. Each of these groups might need a different marketing mix.

A tale of four motels

Motels are a good example of a service that can be seen as *four different* kinds of goods. Some tired motorists are satisfied with the first motel they come to—a convenience good. Others shop for acceptable facilities at the lowest price—a homogeneous shopping good. Other travelers shop for the kind of place they want at a fair price—a heterogeneous shopping good. And others study tourist guides, talk with traveling friends, and phone ahead to reserve a place in a recommended motel—a specialty good.

How an individual views a motel may vary, too. During a cross-country move, one type of motel may be needed. Another may be needed for a family vacation.

Perhaps one motel could satisfy all potential customers—all of the time. But it would be hard to produce a marketing mix attractive to everyone—easy access for convenience, good facilities at the right price for shopping goods buyers, and qualities special enough to attract the specialty goods travelers. As a result, we see very different kinds of motels seemingly—but not really—competing with each other.

Industrial Goods Are Different

Industrial goods classes are useful for developing marketing mixes, too—since industrial firms use a logical system of buying related to these goods classes.

Before looking at industrial good *differences,* however, we will note some important *similarities* that have a direct impact on marketing strategy planning.

One demand derived from another

The outstanding characteristic of the industrial goods market is **derived demand**—the demand for industrial goods is derived from the demand for final consumer goods. For example, about one fifth of all steel products are typically sold to auto manufacturers. But, if demand for automobiles is down, the auto makers won't buy as much steel. The auto makers' demand for steel is derived from consumer demand for automobiles.

As long as business is good and markets are growing, the derived nature of industrial demand is often ignored. But it becomes very important when final consumer demands are shifting rapidly—or in times of recession when even the most efficient and aggressive industrial goods companies lose sales because their customers can't get business.

Price increases might not reduce quantity purchased

The fact that demand for most industrial goods is derived means that *industry* demand for such goods will be fairly inelastic. To satisfy final consumer needs, producers need a certain quantity of each of the components of their products—almost regardless of price. Since each of the components costs only a fraction of the total cost of their product, the price of any one item may have relatively little to do with the quantity of that item purchased. The cost of a spice in a box of cake mix, for example, might be only one half of 1 percent of the cake manufacturer's total cost. Even if the price of this spice were doubled and passed directly along to consumers, it would have relatively little impact on the cake producer's price—or the quantity demanded by final consumers. Therefore, the price increase might not reduce the quantity of spice purchased.

Suppliers may face almost pure competition

Although the total industry demand for industrial goods may be inelastic, the demand facing individual sellers may be extremely elastic. This is true if competitive products are similar and there are many sellers—that is, if the market approaches pure competition.

In the case of the spice ingredient, if the spices available from all suppliers are basically the same and one spice supplier increases its price while competitors do not, buyers probably will shift to another supplier. Thus, *there may be nearly pure competition among the suppliers of a product even though there is inelastic industry demand.*

Buyers will help make the market as competitive as they can. Most industrial buyers seek several sources of supply to ensure production in their own plants. Their job is to buy as economically as possible—and they will be quick to spread the word that competitors are offering lower prices.

Industrial Goods Classes

Industrial goods classes are based on how buyers see products—and how the products are to be used. Expensive and/or long-lasting products are treated

■ FIGURE 10—4   Industrial goods and marketing mix planning

1. *Installations.*
   a. Buildings (used) and land rights—need widespread and/or knowledgeable contacts. depending upon specialized nature of product.
   b. Buildings (new)—need technical and experienced personal contact. probably at top management level (multiple buying influence).
   c. Major equipment.
      i. Custom-made—need technical (design) contacts by person able to visualize and design applications. and present to high-level and technical management.
      ii. Standard—need experienced (not necessarily highly technical) contacts by person able to visualize applications and present to high-level and technical management.
2. *Accessory equipment*—need fairly widespread and numerous contacts by experienced and sometimes technically trained personnel.
3. *Raw materials.*
   a. Farm products—need contacts with many small farmer producers and fairly widespread contact with users.
   b. Natural products—need fairly widespread contacts with users.
4. *Component parts and materials*—need technical contacts to determine specifications required—widespread contacts usually not necessary.
5. *Supplies.*
   a. Maintenance—need very widespread distribution for prompt delivery.
   b. Repairs—need widespread distribution for some. and prompt service from factory for others (depends on customers' preferences).
   c. Operating supplies—need fair to widespread distribution for prompt delivery.
6. *Services*—most need very widespread availability.

differently than inexpensive items. Products that become a part of a firm's own product are seen differently from those which only aid production. Finally, the relative size of a particular purchase can make a difference. An air compressor might be a very important purchase for a small garage owner, but not for General Motors.

The industrial goods classes are related to the way industrial purchasing departments and accounting control systems operate. Buyers, for example, often specialize by product categories. And categories similar to our industrial goods classes are used for buying, maintenance, costing of orders, and control purposes.

The classes of industrial goods are: (1) installations, (2) accessory equipment, (3) raw materials, (4) component parts and materials, (5) supplies, and (6) services. See Figure 10–4 for a summary of how these goods classes are related to what is needed in a marketing mix.

Installations—Major Capital Items

Installations are important long-lived capital items—durable goods which are depreciated over many years. They include buildings, land rights, and major equipment. One-of-a-kind installations—like buildings and custom-made equipment—generally require special negotiations for each sale. Standard major equipment is more homogeneous—and is treated more routinely. Even so, negotiations for installations can stretch over months or even years.

Multiple buying influence important

The importance of installations leads to much multiple buying influence. Top managers of the company are likely to be involved. This may complicate Promotion since these managers may be concerned with quite different problems than purchasing agents—and may evaluate the items differently. The top managers may be less concerned, for example, with the product's suitability for current needs than with its flexibility and possible usefulness in a new venture being considered. The seller may need different sales approaches for each of the possible influences.

Small number of customers at any one time

Installations are long-lasting goods—so they aren't bought very often. The number of potential buyers *at any particular time* usually is small. For custom-made machines, there may be only a half-dozen potential customers—compared to a thousand or more potential buyers for similar standard machines.

Potential customers are generally in the same industry. Their plants are likely to be near each other—which makes personal selling easier. The automobile industry, for example, is heavily concentrated in Central Canada. The oil industry is in Alberta. And the aircraft industry—from a world view—is in the United States.

Buying needs basically economic

Buying needs are basically economic—and concerned with the performance of the installation over its expected life. After comparing expected performance to present costs and figuring interest, the expected return on capital can be determined. Yet emotional needs—such as a desire for industry leadership and status—also may be involved.

To meet customers' needs, installations may have to be leased or rented.

Industry demand may be very inelastic, but sellers see elastic curves

The demand for a particular installation may be completely inelastic up to a certain price—especially if the firm badly needs more capacity. The potential return on the new investment may be so attractive that any reasonable price may be accepted.

While the buyers' demand can be very inelastic, however, the situation for sellers may be different. There may be many suppliers—such as building contractors. So, buyers of installations may be able to request bids and buy in a very competitive market.

Installation industry, a "boom-or-bust" business

The installation industry has been described as a "boom-or-bust" business. During the upswing of a business cycle, businesses want to expand capacity rapidly—and are willing to pay almost any reasonable price to do it. Competition is less vigorous—and profits are higher for the installation sellers. But during a downswing, buyers have little or no need for new installations—and sales fall off sharply.

Installations may have to be leased or rented

Since installations are relatively expensive, the producer will often lease or rent the product rather than sell it outright. Such lease or rental arrangements are attractive to some target markets. Capital can be invested in other opportunities—since the payment is not made all at once. Leasing may make it easier for a firm to make changes if its future needs are different. For example, many firms lease computers so they can expand to bigger systems as the firm grows.

There is another possible advantage of leasing or renting. The expenditure is shifted from being a capital item to an expense item. For accounting and tax purposes, an expense item is usually written off in the year the payment Is made. Capital expenditures usually are written off (depreciated) slowly—over a longer time period.

Specialized services are needed as part of the product

The expected return on an installation is based on efficient operation. The supplier may have to provide special services to assure this efficiency. The more homogeneous the physical good, the more likely that the seller will try to differentiate the product by offering special services—such as aid in installing the machine in the buyer's plant, training employees in its use, supplying repair service, and taking trade-ins. Service people may even be permanently assigned to a company.

Firms selling equipment to dentists setting up a new office offer such services. They may assign a service rep to stay with the dentist until he can use the equipment easily. They will even provide plans for a building to hold the dental equipment. The cost is included in the price.

Accessory Equipment—Important but Short-Lived Capital Items

Accessory equipment includes short-lived capital items. They are the tools and equipment used in production or office activities. Examples include portable drills, sanding machines, electric lift trucks, typewriters, and filing cabinets.

Since these products cost less and last a shorter time than installations, multiple buying influence is less important. Operating people and purchasing agents—rather than top managers—may do the buying. As with installations, however, some customers may wish to lease or rent—to expense the cost.

More target markets requiring different marketing mixes

Accessories are more standardized than installations. And they are usually needed by more customers! A large, special-purpose belt sanding machine, for example, may be produced as a custom-made installation for wood-working firms. But small portable sanding machines are needed accessory equipment for many types of businesses. And different types of customers are likely to be spread out geographically.

Because the market for less expensive and more standardized accessories is larger, more competitors are likely. So, although individual buyers may have inelastic demands, they still may be able to compare substitute products in fairly competitive markets.

The larger number of different kinds of customers and increased competition mean that different marketing mixes are needed for accessory equipment than for installations.

Special services may be attractive

Ordinarily, engineering services or special advice is less important for accessory equipment—because of its simpler operation. Yet some companies have managed to add attractive services to their accessories. Office equipment firms, for example, offer advice on office layout and office systems.

Raw Materials—Farm Products and Natural Products Are Expense Items

They become part of a physical good

Raw materials are unprocessed goods—such as logs, iron ore, wheat, and cotton—that are handled as little as is needed to move them to the next production process. Unlike installations and accessories, *raw materials become part of a physical good*—and are expense items.

We can break raw materials into two types: (1) farm products and (2) natural products. **Farm products** are grown by farmers—examples are oranges, wheat, strawberries, sugar cane, cattle, hogs, poultry, eggs, and milk. **Natural products** are products which occur in nature—such as fish and game, lumber and maple syrup, and copper, zinc, iron ore, oil, and coal.

Farm Products Vary in Quality and Quantity

Involve grading, storage, and transportation

The need for grading is one of the important differences between farm products and other industrial goods. Nature produces what it will—and someone must sort and grade farm products to satisfy various market segments. Some of

Natural products and farm products vary in quality and usually need to be graded.

the top grades of fruits and vegetables find their way into the consumer goods market. The lower grades are treated as industrial goods—and used in juices, sauces, and soup.

Most farm products are produced seasonally—yet the demand for them is fairly constant all year. As a result, storage and transportation are important.

Buyers of industrial goods usually don't seek suppliers. This complicates the marketing of farm products. The many small farms usually are widely scattered—sometimes far from potential buyers. Selling direct to final users would be difficult. So Place and Promotion are important in marketing mixes for these products.

Large buyers may encourage contract farming

Most buyers of farm products have specific uses in mind—and generally prefer that these products be sorted and graded. But since large buyers may have difficulty getting the quantities of the grades and types they want, they may encourage contract farming. **Contract farming** means the farmer gets supplies and perhaps working capital from local middlemen or manufacturers who agree to buy the farmer's output—sometimes at guaranteed prices. This makes the supplier a part of the buyer's operation—and removes one more producer from the competitive market. This may be desirable from the suppliers' point of view—because it isolates them from a purely competitive market.

Each seller's demand curve is elastic

Most farm products have an inelastic *industry* (market) demand—even though the many small producers are in nearly pure competition. The industry demand becomes more elastic when there are many substitutes (such as beef for pork or corn for wheat). But within the usual price ranges, the industry demand for agricultural products is generally inelastic. So these producers often try to control output and prices—through various farm marketing boards.

Natural Products—Quantities Are Adjustable

In contrast to the farm products market with its many producers, natural products are usually produced by fewer and larger companies. There are some exceptions—such as in the coal and lumber industries which have almost pure competition—but oligopoly conditions are common for natural products. The producers know that industry demand for natural products is derived and basically inelastic. As in other oligopoly situations, they are inclined to adjust supply to maintain stable prices. The supply of natural products harvested or mined in any one year can be adjusted up or down—at least within limits. And storage is less of a problem—since few are perishable.

As with farm products, buyers of natural products usually need specific grades and dependable supply sources—to be sure of continued production in their own plants. Large buyers, therefore, often try to control—or even buy—their sources of supply. Some control can be gained through contracts—perhaps negotiated by top-level managers—using standard grades and specifications.

Other large buyers want even more assurance of supply. One way is with **vertical integration**—ownership of the natural product source by the user. Examples are paper manufacturers who own timber resources, oil refiners who control crude oil sources, and tire manufacturers who own rubber plantations.

Component Parts and Materials—Important Expense Items

The whole is no better than . . .

Component parts and materials are expense items which have had more processing than raw materials. They require different marketing mixes than raw materials—even though they both become part of a finished product.

Component *parts* include those items that are (1) finished and ready for assembly or (2) nearly finished—requiring only minor processing (such as grinding or polishing) before being assembled into the final product. Examples are automobile batteries, small motors, and tires—all of which go directly into a finished product. Some simpler component parts, like rivets and electronic transistors and resistors, may be inexpensive as individual items but are used in very large quantities.

Component *materials* are items such as wire, paper, textiles, or cement. They have already been processed—but must be processed further before becoming part of the final product.

Multiple buying influences

Some component parts are custom-made. Much negotiation may be necessary between the engineering staffs of both buyer and seller to arrive at the right specifications. If the price of the item is high—or if it is extremely important in the final product—top managers may be involved. New-task buying is found here—to help set the specifications and sources.

Other component parts and materials are produced to commonly accepted standards or specifications—and produced in quantity. Production people in the buying firm may specify quality—but the purchasing agent will do the buying. And he will want several dependable sources of supply. Modified rebuys and straight rebuys are seen here.

Buying needs are economic

The needs involved in buying components are basically economic—price, availability, quality, and suitability. Since components become part of the firm's own product, quality is extremely important. The buyer's own name and whole marketing mix are at stake.

Assurances of availability and prompt delivery are also relevant. A purchasing agent must do everything possible to avoid a plant shutdown caused by lack of materials. Moreover, a prompt source of supply means that the buyer can carry smaller inventory. This reduces the cost of inventory investment—as well as the risk that goods in stock will become obsolete or be damaged.

Market may be very competitive

Although the demand for component parts and materials may be fairly inelastic, there are usually many willing suppliers and an extremely competitive market. There are several reasons for this:

1. There usually are many small producers—small fabricators, machine shops, and foundries—with general-purpose machinery that can produce a great variety of component parts.
2. There usually are many component materials suppliers willing to produce to widely accepted specifications or standards.
3. Most component buyers want to have several sources of supply—and encourage new suppliers.

Profitable replacement markets may develop

Since component parts go into finished products, a replacement market often develops. This market can be both large and very profitable—as in the case of automobile tires and batteries.

This replacement market (*after market*) may involve new target markets. The part originally may have been considered a component part when it was sold in the *OEM* (*original equipment market*), but as a replacement, the same product might become a consumer good. The target markets are different—and probably different marketing mixes will be necessary.

Some component parts suppliers are eager to have their parts used in the OEM market—because the "after market" is so attractive.

The Mallory Battery Company worked hard to get its small batteries installed as original components in cameras, watches, hearing aids, and dictating equipment—because marketing research told them that half of all final consumer battery buyers don't know what kind of battery powers their equipment. They simply walk into a store and say, "I want one just like this."

Mallory coordinated its efforts in both markets—the components and final consumer markets—and achieved a 50 percent increase in profits.[4]

Supplies—Everybody Wants These Expense Items, but How Much?

Supplies are expense items that do not become a part of a final product. They may be treated less seriously by buyers. Although they are necessary, most supplies are not as vital to continued operations as the products in the first four classes. When a firm cuts its budget, orders for supplies may be the first to go.

They are called MRO items

Supplies can be divided into three types: (1) maintenance, (2) repair, and (3) operating supplies—giving them their common name: "MRO items."

Maintenance items include such things as paint, nails, light bulbs, sweeping compounds, brooms, and cleaning equipment. *Repair items* are parts—like filters, bearings, and gears—needed to fix worn or broken equipment. *Operating supplies* include lubricating oils and greases, grinding compounds, typing paper, ink, pencils, and paper clips.

Important operating supplies

Operating supplies needed regularly and in large amounts receive special treatment from buyers. Some companies buy coal and fuel oil in carload or tank-car quantities. Usually there are several sources for such homogeneous products—and large volumes may be purchased in highly competitive markets. Or contracts may be negotiated—perhaps by high-level executives. Such contracts have several advantages. Later purchase orders can be drawn routinely against them—as straight rebuys. They sometimes assure lower prices. And they eliminate the buyer's concern about a dependable source for these important operating supplies.

Maintenance and small operating supplies

These items are similar to consumer's convenience goods—and are so numerous that a purchasing agent cannot possibly be an expert in buying all of them. There usually is little multiple buying influence. They are often purchased on a straight rebuy basis.

Each requisition for maintenance and small operating supplies may be for relatively few items. A purchase order may amount to only $1 or $2. Although the cost of handling a purchase order may be from $5 to $10, the item will be ordered—because it is needed—but not much time will be spent on it.

Branding may become important for such products. It makes product identification and buying easier for such "nuisance" purchases.

Industry demand for supplies is fairly inelastic—and sellers may see quite inelastic demand curves, too. Since only small amounts of money are involved—and shopping around for bargains is hardly worth the time—a purchasing agent may find several dependable sources of supply and buy from them for the bulk of such items.

A new company offering only one supply item may have trouble entering such a market. The job of buying these small items is difficult enough—and buyers usually don't have time to review the small advantages of some new product or supplier.

The purchasing agent is usually less concerned about price for such items—the breadth of assortment and dependability of the source are more important in buying supply items. But price is not unimportant—and a skilled purchasing agent continually shops for good value. The threat of losing a large amount of business from one buyer tends to keep the various suppliers' prices in line for their whole assortment.

Repair items

The original supplier of installations or accessory equipment may be the only source of supply for repairs or parts. The cost of repairs relative to the cost of disrupted production may be so small that buyers are willing to pay the price charged—whatever it is.

Demand for repair items is quite inelastic. But if the demand for such items is large and steady—say, for truck mufflers or power transmission belts—there may be many suppliers. The market then may become quite competitive—even though each buyer's demand is inelastic.

Services—You Expense Them

Services are expense items which support the operations of a firm. Engineering or management consulting services can improve the plant layout or the operation of a company. Design services can supply designs for a physical plant, products, and promotion materials. Maintenance services can handle window-cleaning, painting, or general housekeeping. Other companies can supply in-plant lunches—and piped-in music—to improve employee morale and production.

The cost of buying services outside the firm is compared with the cost of having company people do them. For special skills needed only occasionally, an outsider can be the best source. And service specialists are growing in number in our complex economy.

The demand for special services is often inelastic—if the supplier has a unique product. And the supply may be fairly inelastic, too. The suppliers may consider themselves professionals and charge accordingly. For example, engineers, architects, and lawyers have commonly accepted fee schedules. The competition among them is not based on price—but on quality of service.

Goods Classes and Marketing Mixes Are Related

This focus on goods classes may not seem exciting—but it is vital because how customers view products affects how they buy them. This obviously has a direct effect on planning marketing mixes.

We will be referring to goods classes as we talk about other elements of the marketing mix. In the rest of this chapter, however, we will focus on other strategic decisions related to Product—including branding, packaging, and warranty policies.

Branding Is a Strategy Decision, Too

There are so many brands—and we're so used to seeing them—that we take them for granted. In the grocery products area alone, there are more than 40,000 brands. But brands are of great importance to their owners—because

■ FIGURE 10–5   Recognized trademarks and symbols help in promotion

they help identify the company's marketing mix—and help consumers recognize the firm's products and advertising. Branding is an important Product decision area which is ignored by many business people. So we will treat it in some detail.

What is branding, brand name, and trademark?

Branding means the use of a name, term, symbol, or design—or a combination of these—to identify a product. It includes the use of brand names, trademarks, and practically all other means of product identification.

Brand name has a narrower meaning. A **brand name** is a word, letter, or a group of words or letters.

Trademark is a legal term. A **trademark** includes only those words, symbols, or marks that are legally registered for use by a single company.

The word Buick can be used to explain these differences. The Buick car is *branded* under the *brand name* "Buick" (whether it is spoken or printed in any manner). When "Buick" is printed in a certain kind of script, however, it becomes a *trademark*. A trademark need not be attached to the product. It need not even be a word. A symbol can be used. Figure 10–5 shows some common trademarks.

These differences may seem technical. But they are very important to business firms that spend much money on brands—to make consumers familiar with their brands and to protect them.

Branding—Why It Developed

Brands emerged long ago—to meet needs

Branding started during the Middle Ages—when craft guilds (similar to labor unions) and merchant guilds formed to control the quantity and quality of production. Each producer had to mark his goods, so output could be cut back when necessary. This also meant that poor quality—which might reflect unfavorably on other guild products and discourage future trade—could be traced back to the guilty producer. Early trademarks were also a protection to the buyer—who could now know the source of the product.

The earliest and most aggressive brand promoters in North America were the patent medicine companies. They were joined by the food manufacturers—who grew in size after the American Civil War. Some of the brands started in the 1860s and 1870s (and still going strong) are Borden's Condensed Milk, Quaker Oats, Pillsbury's Best Flour, and Ivory Soap.

These brands—and the thousands developed since—have mainly been for identification. Product identification is important to both sellers and consumers. Branding provides this identification.

Soviets adopted brands

The need for branding is illustrated by the experience in the Soviet Union, where central planners originally thought that branding was not necessary.

Several Russian factories were manufacturing supposedly identical 17-inch TV sets—but actually one of the plants was shipping "lemons." When customers became aware of this, many stopped buying any 17-inch set—because they couldn't identify the bad ones. This obviously caused inventory problems for the central planners. It also caused public discontent with the Soviet system.

Shortly thereafter, factory numbers on products were required—to help the planners identify the production source. Subsequently, consumers discovered the factory numbers—and plants that were producing poorer-quality products began to have difficulties meeting their economic plans. Soviet consumers—rather than planners—forced the plants to pay more attention to quality. Before long, there were more than 25 state-sponsored advertising agencies—to tell people about the "quality" of various factories. Now, advertising courses are even offered in Russian universities.[5]

The important thing to note here is that the "brands" were created by the customers—rather than the planners. The factory identification numbers had been added to help the planners—but the consumers quickly adapted them to their own use.

How Branding Helps Customers

Makes shopping more efficient

Well-recognized brands make shopping possible in a modern economy. Think of the problem of buying groceries, for example, if you had to consider seriously the advantages and disadvantages of each of 10,000 items every time you went to a supermarket.

Assures regular satisfaction

Many customers are willing to buy new things—but having gambled and won, they like to buy a "sure thing" the next time. Customers are willing to pay a premium for brands that they like.

Sunkist brand means quality to its loyal customers.

May be dependable guides to quality

There is evidence that consumers use well-known brands as an indication of good quality. Customers are willing to buy by brand—without inspection—when they are sure of quality. In many countries, however, the consumer doesn't feel so sure. In India, for example, inspecting the product is common—because there is little faith in packaged goods and brands. There is good reason for this. Foods are often mixed with sawdust, husks, and colored earth—which may be 10 to 50 percent of the weight of packaged or prepared foods. And an Indian car battery manufacturer has had great success with its brand by *correctly* advertising "the battery you don't have to test."

May satisfy status need

Some customers buy well-recognized brands for assurance of quality. Other customers, however, seem to be less concerned with the physical characteristics of the product and more concerned with the symbolic value. They seem to get psychic satisfaction from the use of well-known brands—perhaps because they feel some of the status or prestige of the product may rub off on them. The success of designer jeans—like those with the Calvin Klein brand—illustrate this.

How Branding Helps Branders

Encourages repeat buying and lowers costs

Brands obviously would not be used so aggressively by companies if target customers didn't respond to them. Many advantages of brand promotion to the branders are related to the advantages to customers. A good brand speeds up shopping for the customer—and so reduces the marketer's selling time and effort. When a customer repeats purchases by brand, promotion costs are reduced, and sales volume is increased.

May develop loyal customers

Another important advantage of successful branding is that the brander may be able to carve out a market of loyal customers. Whether the brander is a manufacturer, wholesaler, or retailer, this brand loyalty protects against competition.

May build corporate image

Good brands can improve the company's image—speeding acceptance of new products marketed under the same name. The idea of improving the company's image—as well as its brands—has been growing. When customers think a company is big and successful, they often have a better impression of it and its products. The U.S. Steel Corporation, with its many large subsidiaries, found that industrial customers who were aware of the relationship of U.S. Steel to its subsidiaries viewed the subsidiaries more favorably. This was important in their choice of supplier—especially when competing products were basically similar. For this reason, U.S. Steel redesigned its trademark and used it to identify all its subsidiaries.

Growing acceptance of the idea that a good customer image is important has led some companies to change their corporate name—so that the name is more descriptive of the firm's activities. U.S. Rubber, with many foreign subsidiaries, adopted the Uniroyal name and trademark—because it felt that the new name was more accurate. And the Bankamericard companies changed their name to VISA to have a common name with an international image.

Conditions Favorable to Branding

Most marketing managers accept branding—and are concerned with seeing that their brands succeed.

The following conditions are favorable to successful branding:

1. The demand for the general product class should be large.
2. The demand should be strong enough so that the market price can be high enough to make the effort profitable.
3. There should be economies of scale. If the branding is really successful, the cost of production should drop, and profits should increase.
4. The product quality should be the best for the price—that is, the best "value" for the price. And the quality should be easily maintained.
5. The product should be easy to identify by brand or trademark.
6. Dependable and widespread availability should be possible. When customers start using a brand, they want to be able to continue finding it in their stores.
7. Favorable shelf locations or display space in stores will help. This is something retailers can control when they brand their own products. Manufacturers must use aggressive sales forces to get favorable positions.

Achieving Brand Familiarity Is Not Easy

Brand acceptance must be earned with a good product and regular promotion. **Brand familiarity** means how well customers recognize and accept a company's brand. The level of brand familiarity may affect development of the whole marketing mix. But sometimes it's hard to know what consumers think about a brand—or if they think about it at all! Marketing research is sometimes needed to learn how well the brand is known—and in which target markets.

There are many brands which—for practical purposes—have no value because they have no meaning to customers. And there are others which have actually been rejected by potential customers.

Five levels of brand familiarity

Five levels of brand familiarity are useful for strategy planning: (1) rejection, (2) non-recognition, (3) recognition, (4) preference, and (5) insistence.

Some brands have been tried and found wanting. **Rejection** means the potential customers won't buy a brand—unless its current image is changed. Rejection may suggest a change in the product—or perhaps only a shift to target

customers who have a better image of the brand. Overcoming negative images is difficult—and can be very expensive. Many customers rejected "extra-strength" Tylenol capsules when there was much bad publicity about some poisoned bottles. The company wasn't responsible for the problem, but it had to work hard to rebuild consumer faith in the brand.

Some products are seen as basically the same. **Non-recognition** means a brand is not recognized by final customers at all—even though middlemen may use the brand name for identification and inventory control. Examples here are school supplies, novelties, inexpensive dinnerware, and similar goods found in discount stores.

Brand recognition means that customers have heard of and remember the brand. This can be a big advantage if there are many "nothing" brands on the market. Even if consumers can't recall the brand without help, they may be reminded when they see it in a store among other less familiar products.

Most branders would like to win **brand preference**—which means target customers will generally choose the brand over other brands—perhaps because of habit or past experience. They might use another brand at times, however. For example, a consumer who generally prefers Maxwell House coffee might buy another brand on a special sale, or if Maxwell House is out of stock. Occasionally, a consumer may even switch from a preferred brand for variety. Even so, brand preference can help a firm achieve a favorable position in a monopolistic competition situation.

Brand insistence means customers insist on a firm's branded product and are willing to search for it. This is an objective of many target marketers. Here, the firm may enjoy a very inelastic demand curve.

The right brand name can help

A good brand name can help build brand familiarity. It can help tell something important about the company or its product. Figure 10–6 lists some characteristics of a good brand name. Some successful brand names seem to break all these rules. Many of these names, however, got started when there was less competition.

■ FIGURE 10–6   Characteristics of a good brand name

Short and simple.
Easy to spell and read.
Easy to recognize and remember.
Pleasing when read or heard—and easy to pronounce.
Pronounceable in only one way.
Pronounceable in all languages (for goods to be exported).
Always timely (does not get out of date).
Adaptable to packaging or labeling needs.
Legally available for use (not in use by another firm).
Not offensive, obscene, or negative.
Suggestive of product benefits.
Adaptable to any advertising medium (especially billboards and television).

Protecting Canadian Trademarks

Benefits of trademark registration

Common law protects the owners of trademarks and brand names. Ownership of brand names and trademarks is established by continued usage without abandonment.

Since the basic right is found in "use," a Canadian firm need not register its trademark under the **Trade Marks Act**. But when a trademark is so registered, the registering firm is legally protected against any other company using a trademark that might be confused with its own. In contrast the holder of an unregistered trademark could not sue a firm merely for using a similar trademark. The owner of the unregistered trademark would have to prove that the defendant was deliberately trying to create confusion in the minds of consumers.

Canadian and U.S. legislation differ in the types of trademark protection they provide. In Canada, a firm producing a substantially different product may use the same trade name as another product used for some other purpose. This is not so in the United States. On the other hand, there is less likelihood of a Canadian trade name being ruled "generic" or a common descriptive term—and therefore no longer protectable by its original owner. For example, Bayer's Aspirin is still a protected trademark in Canada, even though "aspirin" has become a generic term in the United States.[6]

You must protect your own

A brand or trademark can be a real asset to a company. So each firm should try to see that it doesn't become a common descriptive term for its kind of product. When this happens, the brand name or the trademark becomes public property—the owner loses all rights to it. This happened in the United States with cellophane, aspirin, shredded wheat, and kerosene. There was concern that Teflon and Scotch Tape might become public property—and Miller Brewing Company tried unsuccessfully to protect its Lite beer by suing brewers who wanted to use the word *light*.[7]

What Kind of Brand to Use?

Keep it in the family

Branders who manufacture or handle more than one item must decide whether they are going to use a **family brand**—the same brand name for several products—or individual brands for each product. Examples of family brands are the Kraft food products, the three A&P brands (Ann Page, Sultana, and Iona), and Sears' "Craftsman" tools and "Kenmore" appliances.

The use of the same brand for many products makes sense if all are similar in type and quality. The goodwill attached to one or two products may help the others—which cuts promotion costs. It also tends to build loyalty to the family brand—and makes it easier to introduce new products.

Kraft sells many different products under its family name.

A **licensed brand** is a well-known brand which different sellers pay a fee to use. For example, the creators of "Sesame Street" allow different sellers to brand their products with the Sesame Street name and trademark—for a fee. In this case, many different companies may be in the "family."

Individual brands for outside and inside competition

Individual brands—separate brand names for each product—are used by a brander when its products are of varying quality or type. If the products are really different—such as motor oil and cooking oil—individual brands are better. Or an individual brand may be better if the high-quality image of one of the company's well-known brands is to be protected while another brand (perhaps identifying a lower-priced line) is used as a **fighting brand**—an individual brand which is used to meet competition. Individual brands are also preferred if there is any risk of failure of one product—thereby damaging the reputation of others in the product line.

Sometimes firms use individual brands to encourage competition within the organization. Each brand is the responsibility of a different group. Management feels that internal competition keeps everyone alert. The theory is that if anyone is going to take business away from them, it ought to be their own brand. This kind of competition is found among General Motors' brands. Chevrolet, Pontiac, Oldsmobile, Buick, and even Cadillac compete with each other in some markets.

Who Should Do the Branding?

Manufacturer brands versus dealer brands

Manufacturer brands are brands which are created by manufacturers. These are sometimes called "national brands"—because manufacturers often promote these brands all across the country or in large regions. Such brands include Kellogg's, Stokely, Whirlpool, Ford, and IBM.

Dealer brands are brands created by middlemen. These are sometimes called "private brands." Examples of dealer brands include the brands of Eaton's, The Bay, Sears, and Radio Shack. Some of these are advertised and distributed more widely than many "national brands."

Generic brands for "commodities"

Products which are seen by consumers as "commodities" may be difficult to brand meaningfully. Recently, some manufacturers and middlemen have faced up to this problem and come up with **generic products**—products which have no brand at all other than identification of their contents and the manufacturer or middleman. Generic products are most common for staple goods—especially food products and drug items. For example, many supermarkets offer generic paper towels, macaroni, beans, noodles, and dog food. Typically, these are offered in plain packages at lower prices. Product quality may be lower for generic products, but some consumers do not think that the differences are important. For example, generic peanuts may be smaller in size, or the nuts may be broken. But the nutritional value and taste may be the same.

Some generic products have been well accepted by some target markets. These consumers don't see big differences among these products—except in price. When generic products were first introduced, many critics predicted that they wouldn't last. It now appears that some products—"commodities"—will continue to be offered in this way.[8]

So far, we have been focusing on the value of branding in general, but branding has some special advantages and disadvantages for middlemen. These affect whether they should use manufacturers' brands or develop their own dealer brands.

Advantages of manufacturers' brands— more prestige, less inventory

The major advantage of selling a popular manufacturer's brand is that the product already is presold to some target customers. It may bring in new customers. It can encourage higher turnover with reduced selling cost—and some of the prestige of the manufacturer's brand may rub off on the middleman. And in

Many "commodity" products are now sold as generic "brands."

Generics, manufacturer brands, and dealer brands often battle for the consumer's dollar.

case quality slips, the manufacturer receives the blame, not the middleman. The customer can be shifted to another manufacturer's brand or a dealer brand. The middleman doesn't lose *his* customer.

Since manufacturers' brands usually are readily available at wholesalers' or manufacturers' warehouses, the middleman can carry less inventory. Another advantage for some retailers is that the retailer can advertise special prices on items which are carried in other stores—calling attention to his store as a source of bargains.

Disadvantages of manufacturers' brands—lost products, lost customers

The major disadvantage of manufacturers' brands is that manufacturers normally offer a lower gross margin than the middleman might be able to earn with his own brands. This, however, may be offset by high turnover.

Another disadvantage is that the manufacturer maintains control of his brand—and may withdraw it from the middleman at any time. Wholesalers are especially vulnerable. If customers become loyal to a manufacturer's brand and the wholesaler does not or cannot carry the product, then the customers may go elsewhere. Here, loyalty may be tied to the brand—rather than to the retailer or wholesaler.

Advantages of dealer brands—loyal sales reps, the best shelves

The advantages of dealer brands are—roughly—the reverse of the disadvantages of manufacturers' brands. The middleman may be able to buy products at lower prices—and so be able to obtain higher gross margins, even with lower retail prices. He can have greater price flexibility with his own brands because (1) price comparisons are not as easy as with manufacturers' brands and (2) there is no manufacturer setting pricing policy. The middleman can also control the point of sale—and give the dealer brand special shelf position or display.

Another advantage of dealer brands is that middlemen can easily change from one supplier to another. For example, if the company that manufactures Lady Kenmore sewing machines for Sears doesn't supply the quality or price Sears wants, that supplier can be dropped. Customers may not even be aware that the manufacturer is different.

Dealer brands protect wholesalers from the defection of their sales reps—and their customer following—to other wholesalers. Why? Dealer brands give the wholesaler—rather than the sales force—a claim to customer loyalty.

Disadvantages of dealer brands—taking the blame, buying big quantities

Dealer branders must stimulate their own demand. This may be costly, especially if turnover is slow in the lines being considered. Also, they must take the blame for inferior quality. They may have difficulty getting consistently good quality at low prices—especially during times of short supply. And they probably will have to buy in fairly large quantities from suppliers—thus assuming the risk and cost of carrying inventory.

Dealer brands have a chance if . . .

Branding by middlemen begins to move them into the traditional role of a manufacturer. They must assume all of the marketing responsibilities of a manufacturer—and plan their marketing strategies accordingly. Therefore, the decision to go into dealer branding should not be made lightly. The chances of a middleman being successful are increased if a number of conditions exist:

1. If several manufacturer's brands are in the market, none should be strongly established.
2. A dependable quality and quantity of ingredients or raw materials for the dealer brand should be available at a reasonable price—to ensure a good margin if the brand is accepted.
3. It helps if manufacturers' brands are overpriced—so the dealer brand can be priced under them, yet with a larger-than-normal gross margin—to cover higher promotion costs.
4. Although dealer brands must be promoted, the promotion should not be so expensive as to use up the extra gross margin.
5. There should be an adequate, well-established market—middlemen may find it expensive to pioneer the introduction of new products.
6. Product quality should be easily and economically determined by inspection or use—customers will be more willing to experiment if a dealer brand is not much of a risk.
7. If the dealer brand is lower-priced, depressed business conditions may help its sale—customers are more price conscious then.

Dealer brands in the food and drug lines usually are offered at slightly lower prices than manufacturers' brands. Middleman-sponsored generic products are really "low-price" dealer brands.

Dealer brands, however, are not always priced lower. Sometimes middlemen—having analyzed their target markets—offer a prestige-laden, higher-quality product and price it even higher than major manufacturers' brands.

Manufacturer Brands Compete with Dealer Brands

Whether a manufacturer should produce dealer brands is an important decision. Sales of a dealer brand may take customers away from the manufacturer's own brand. Yet a manufacturer who decides not to produce dealer brands for a middleman may lose the customers anyway—if the middleman finds other willing manufacturers.

The battle of the brands—who's winning?

The **battle of the brands** is the competition between dealer brands and manufacturer brands. The "battle" is just a question of whose brands will be more popular—and who will be in the control.

At one time, manufacturer brands were much more popular than dealer brands. But sales of dealer brands have continued to grow—so now sales are about equal. Middlemen have some advantages in this battle. They can control scarce shelf space. They often price their own brands lower, which can make a difference in inflationary times—especially when many consumers know that well-known manufacturers make the dealer brands anyway. Customers can benefit from the "battle." Price differences between manufacturer brands and well-known dealer brands have already narrowed due to the competition.[9]

The Strategic Importance of Packaging

Packaging involves protecting and promoting the product. Packaging can be important to both sellers and customers. Packaging can make a product more convenient to use or store. It can prevent spoiling or damage. Good packaging makes products easier to identify—and promotes the brand at the store, and even in use.

Packaging can make the difference

A new package can make *the* important difference in a new marketing strategy—by meeting customers' needs better. A better box, wrapper, can, or bottle may help create a "new" product—or a new market. A small, relatively unknown producer—Minnetonka, Inc.—was able to enter in the tough soap market with a liquid hand soap in a push-top container. Consumers preferred this "Soft Soap" because it was neater and less wasteful than bar soap.

Sometimes a new package improves a product by making it easier to use. Some oil companies—trying to appeal to "self-service" gas customers—now sell oil in reusable plastic containers with a built-in pouring spout. A producer of light-sensitive X-ray films increased sales by packing each sheet in a separate foil pack—making it easier for doctors to handle. Many frozen convenience foods are now packaged in containers that can be used in microwave ovens.

Packaging can improve product safety. Shampoo comes in plastic bottles—that won't break if dropped in the shower. Many drugs are sold in child-proof bottles and tamper-resistant packages.

Packaging can tie the product to the rest of the marketing strategy. Expensive perfume may come in a crystal glass bottle—adding to the prestige image. The design may reinforce advertising messages customers have seen or heard before. L'eggs pantyhose—in their distinctive plastic eggs—set the product apart in stores and remind customers of the name.

The amount spent is large and rising

The importance of packaging is partly shown by its cost. Packaging is itself a major Canadian industry—it is estimated the Canadian manufacturers spent $5.6 billion dollars on packaging materials in 1981.[10] For perspective, this is roughly equal to the total amount spent on advertising. And the actual cost of packaging might be twice as high, if all costs of handling, storing, and moving containers were included. These rising outlays for packaging are due in part to a shift from an earlier emphasis on protection to the current interest in protection and the promotional potential of the package.

May lower total distribution costs

While packaging can be expensive, it can help reduce total distribution costs. Better protective packaging is especially important to manufacturers and wholesalers. They often have to pay the cost of goods damaged in shipment. There are also costs for settling such claims. Goods damaged in shipment also may delay production—or cause lost sales.

Retailers need good packaging, too. Packaging which provides better protection can reduce store costs by cutting breakage, preventing discoloration, and stopping theft. Packages that are easier to handle can cut costs by speeding price marking, improving handling and display, and saving space.

Promotion-oriented packaging may be "better" than advertising

A good package sometimes gives a firm more promotion effect than it could possibly afford with advertising. Packaged products are regularly seen in retail stores—when customers are actually buying products. The package may actually be seen by many more potential customers than the company's advertising. An attractive package may speed turnover so much that total costs will decline as a percentage of sales.

Or . . . may raise total costs

In other cases, total distribution costs may rise because of packaging. But customers may be more satisfied because the packaging improves the product—perhaps by offering much greater convenience or reducing waste.

Packaging costs as a percentage of a manufacturer's selling price vary widely—ranging from 1 to 70 percent. Let's look at sugar as an example. In 100-pound bags, the cost of packaging sugar is only 1 percent of the selling price. In two- and five-pound cartons, it is 25 to 30 percent. And for individual serving packages, it is 50 percent. Most customers don't want to haul a 100-pound bag home—and are quite willing to pay for more convenient packages. Restaurants use one-serving envelopes of sugar—finding that they reduce the cost of filling and washing sugar bowls—and that customers prefer the more sanitary little packages. In both cases, packaging adds value to the product. Actually, it creates new products and new marketing strategies.

What Makes a Good Packaging Design?

The right packaging is just enough packaging

A specific package must be designed for each product. The package must safely transport its contents, serve in a specific climate (especially if the product is to be exported), and last for a specific time. Underpackaging costs money—for damage claims or poor sales. But overpackaging also costs money—because dollars are spent for no benefit.

Glassware, for example, needs to be protected from even relatively light blows that might smash it. Heavy-duty machinery doesn't need protection from blows—

■ FIGURE 10–7   Award-winning design firm creates "definable difference" for each client's products

Robert Burns is preparing for a New York City meeting with a client. He asks his secretary to book a reservation at a good restaurant, but "somewhere I can go without a bloody tie." Ties are definitely not the right packaging for creative graphics designers moving in on their quarry.

And as Burns, a partner in the design firm of Burns, Cooper, Hynes Ltd., Toronto, says, "Visual appearance will give you definable differences in the product. Labeling can significantly infuence people's perceptions."

Influencing perceptions is Burns' business. And, judging from the many awards his firm has won since it started 11 years ago, it's a skill at which he's more than adept. Burns, Cooper, Hynes has designed everything from shoes, to cosmetics, matches, suntan lotion, and sanitary napkins, activities which boosted revenues to $1 million last year.

Creating an effective package—one that increases product sales—is part practical, part artistic, explains Burns. "But I don't make any distinction between the time I'm sitting down with a client and the time I'm designing. I regard the analytical aspect as just as creative as the actual design.

No matter what the product, the design package follows a set procedure: research, creative development, and execution. "We lay great emphasis on the basic research and investigative procedure," says Burns. This means looking at every side of three important aspects—the sender of the message, the receiver (consumer), and the context in which the product is sold.

All these things must be investigated before the actual design is started, says Burns. And once all the information is assembled, the designer may be able to redefine the problem. "You look at the store environment itself. What's the lighting, for instance. We look at how the color reacts in the light it's being presented in."

That done, the designer considers all the different ways to tackle the packaging problem. What does the product have that its competitors don't? How can it be reinforced? The designer has to look at what the product is telling the customer visually.

Design assignments range from a single new package for $5,000–$10,000 to a corporate image involving perhaps two dozen products and a total price tag of $200,000.

In fact, that was the cost of Burns, Cooper, Hynes' redesign of the Yardley cosmetic line in 1978. Working with the company on the three-month project resulted in a trimmed product line (to 22 from 40), streamlined packaging, even new merchandising displays, redesigned products, and new (higher) prices. The results? Within a year, sales tripled.

Burns, Cooper, Hynes' designs are marked by simplicity—in the approach, process, and end product itself. For example, in the Yardley redesign a package with 27 separate components was replaced by one with only two parts. "We live in an age where consumers consider it too vulgar to overpackage," says Burns, "and quite rightly, too."

New packaging can't perform miracles though. "All a well-designed package can do is to induce the customer to buy it once, but you can't put a good package around a bad product and expect it to do well."

Source: Gary Weiss, "Award-winning design firm creates 'definable difference' for each client's products," *Financial Post,* May 10, 1980, p. S1.

but may need protection from moisture. To provide such packaging, the manufacturer must know about the product, the target customers, and how the product will be delivered. Packaging suppliers typically have highly trained sales people who can help the marketing manager blend the package into the whole marketing mix. Figure 10–7 (page 355) shows how one of Canada's top packaging designers has helped a number of firms increase their sales.

What Is Socially Responsible Packaging?

Some consumers say that some package designs are misleading—perhaps on purpose. They feel that the great variety of package designs makes it hard to compare values.

Packaging can make a new product.

**Federal law tries
to help**

The **Hazardous Products Act** gives Consumer and Corporate Affairs Canada the authority either to ban or to regulate the sale, distribution, and labelling of hazardous products.

Since 1971, all products considered potentially hazardous—such as cleaning substances, chemicals, and aerosol products—have had to carry on their labels an appropriate symbol which reveals both the possible danger and the necessary precautions. Figure 10–8 shows the symbols used to indicate whether the product is poisonous, flammable, explosive, or corrosive.

The **Consumer Packaging and Labelling Act** calls for bilingual labels as well as the standardization of package sizes and shapes. It also required that all food products be labelled in metric terms as well as in traditional Canadian measures by March 1976. When reference is made on a label or package to the number of servings being provided, the average size of these servings must also be indicated. The term *best before* must appear in both official languages along with a date reflecting the durability of the product.

Labelling requirements for certain specified products are also set forth in the National Trademark and True Labelling Act, the Textile Labelling Act, and the Precious Metals Marking Act. Other federal initiatives include the Textile Care Labelling Program that provides for all garments and other textiles being labelled with washing or dry cleaning instructions. Similarly, the CANTAG program now

■   FIGURE 10–8

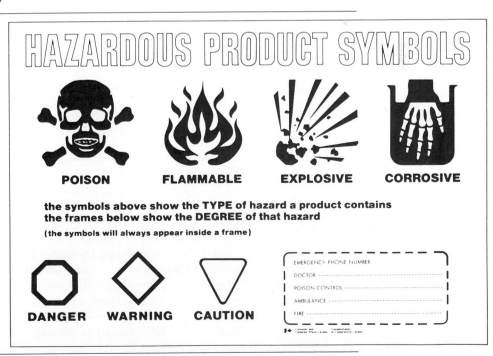

■ FIGURE 10–9 An illustration of a universal product code for a ballpoint pen

0

70330 00105

being widely used provides customers with performance, capacity, and energy consumption data on major appliances.

Unit-pricing—a possible help

There is a growing interest in unit-pricing, which aids comparison shopping—using weight and volume. **Unit-pricing** involves placing the price per ounce (or some other standard measure) on or near the product. Some supermarket chains offer unit-pricing. And many consumers do appreciate this service.[11]

Universal product codes allow more information

To "automate" the handling of fast-selling products, government and industry representatives have developed a **universal product code (UPC)**—which identifies each product with marks that can be "read" by electronic scanners. Through a computer, each code is related to the type of product—and its price. Supermarkets and other high-volume retailers have been eager to use these codes. They speed the check-out process—and get rid of the need for marking the price on every item. They also reduce errors by cashiers—and make it easy to control inventory and track sales of specific products. Figure 10–9 shows a universal product code mark.

Some consumers don't like the codes because they can't compare prices—either in the store or at home. To reduce these concerns, most new systems now print a receipt showing the prices of products bought. In the future, the codes probably will become even more widely used—because they can lower operating costs—and perhaps prices.

Warranties Are Important, Too

Warranty should mean something

Common law says that producers should stand behind—i.e., provide a **warranty** for—their products. And both present and proposed warranty legislation tries to see that such warranties or guarantees are neither deceptive nor unfair. Warranties are a major source of consumer complaint and dissatisfaction.

Both provincial and federal legislation attempts to see that any warranty offered is fair to the consumer, easy to understand, and precise as to what is and what is not covered. Prior to this increased government concern, some firms simply said their products were "fully warranted" or "absolutely guaranteed" without either specifying a time period or spelling out the meaning of the guarantee.

A warranty explains what the seller guarantees about its product.

> ## LIMITED WARRANTY
> ## SHEPARD'S SHOES, INC. GUARANTEE
>
> Except as specifically otherwise provided below, we will repair or replace for no charge any part of any leather shoe that wears out during the guarantee period according to the following schedule:
>
> **Children:** (age 15 or under) — 3 months from date of purchase.
> **Women:** (age 16 and over) — 4 months from date of purchase.
> **Men:** (age 16 and over) — 6 months from date of purchase.
>
> SPECIFICALLY EXCLUDED FROM THIS GUARANTEE OF REPAIR OR REPLACEMENT ARE THE FOLLOWING:
>
> 1. This guarantee does not cover any part of a patent leather shoe.
> 2. This guarantee does not cover any damage caused by water.
> 3. This guarantee does not cover more than a single repair or replacement to each part of a leather shoe.
>
> This guarantee will be honored in all cases where the condition of the shoe is such that repair or replacement of any part is required in order to render it fit for the normal use required of it.
>
> To receive the free repair or replacement, this guarantee must be presented at any Shepard's Shoes location before expiration of the guarantee period. Shepard's Shoe Stores are located at Downtown Lansing, East Lansing, Frandor and Lansing Mall.
>
> Category _Women's Bass_   Authorization _Laurie Froh_
>
> Stock No. _2501_   Size _8 M_   _Marie Johnson_
>   Name
> Date _12 - 27 - 86_   _6948 Uhinta_
>   Address
> _Marie Johnson_   _Houston_
>   Signature   City

On the federal level, protection against misleading warranties is provided by one of the Stage 1 amendments to the Combines Investigation Act. Specifically prohibited are warranties that seem unlikely to be carried out, warranties where excessive labor or handling charges are used to cover the manufacturer's cost of allegedly replacing defective parts "free of charge," and warranties that reduce a purchaser's usual rights under common law.[12]

Provincial legislation designed to make warranties more meaningful was greatly influenced by the recommendations of a 1972 study of warranties and guarantees made by the Ontario Law Reform Commission.[13] However, changes have not occurred all that quickly! Ten years after the Law Reform study, only Saskatchewan had its new legislation in force.

Customers might like a strong warranty—but it can be very expensive. It might even be economically impossible for small producers. Some customers abuse products and demand a lot of service on warranties. Backing up warranties can be a problem, too. Although manufacturers may be responsible, they may have to depend upon reluctant middlemen to do the job—or set up their own service companies. This can make it hard for a small firm to compete with larger firms that have many service centers. Foreign auto producers and small domestic auto producers, for example, can't match the number of Chevrolet or Ford service locations.

Deciding on the warranty is a strategic matter. Specific decisions should be made about what the warranty will cover—and then it must be communicated clearly to the target customers. In some cases, the warranty may make the difference between success and failure for a whole strategy.

■ CONCLUSION

In this chapter, we looked at Product very broadly. A Product may not be a physical good at all. It may be a service. Or it may be some combination—like a meal at a restaurant.

A firm's Product is what satisfies the needs of its target market. This *may* be a physical good—but also could include a package, brand, installation, repair service, a warranty, and so on—whatever is needed to satisfy target customers.

Consumer goods and industrial goods classes were introduced to simplify your study of marketing—and help in planning marketing mixes. The consumer goods classes are based on consumers' buying behavior. Industrial goods classes are based on how buyers see the products—and how they are used. Knowing these goods classes—and learning how marketers handle specific products within these classes—will speed the development of your "marketing sense."

The fact that different people may view the same product in different goods classes helps explain why "competitors" may use very different marketing mixes—quite successfully.

Packaging and branding can create new and more satisfying products. Variations in packaging can make a product salable in various target markets. A specific package must be developed for each strategy. Both under-packaging and over-packaging can be expensive.

To customers, the main value of brands is as a guarantee of quality. This leads to repeat purchasing. For marketers, such "routine" buying means lower promotion costs and higher sales.

Should brands be stressed? The decision depends on whether the costs of brand promotion and honoring the brand guarantee can be more than covered by a higher price or more rapid turnover—or both. The cost of branding may reduce other costs—by reducing pressure on the other three Ps.

Branding gives marketing managers choice. They can add brands—and use individual or family brands. In the end, however, customers express their approval or disapproval of the whole Product (including the brand). The degree of brand familiarity is a measure of the marketing manager's ability to carve out a separate market—and affects Place, Price, and Promotion decisions.

Warranties are also important in strategy planning. A warranty need not be strong—it just has to be clearly stated. But some customers find strong warranties attractive.

So it should be clear that Product is concerned with much more than a physical good or service. The marketing manager must also be concerned about packaging, branding, and warranties—if he is to help his firm succeed in our increasingly competitive marketplaces.

■ QUESTIONS AND PROBLEMS

1. Define, in your own words, what a Product is.

2. Explain how the addition of warranties, service, and credit can improve a "product." Cite a specific case where this has been done and explain how customers viewed this new "product."

3. What "products" are being offered by an exclusive men's shop? By a nightclub? By a soda fountain? By a supermarket?

4. What kinds of consumer goods are the following: (*a*) fountain pens, (*b*) men's shirts, (*c*) cosmetics? Explain your reasoning and draw a picture of the market in each case to help illustrate your thinking.

5. Some goods seem to be treated perpetually as unsought goods by their producers. Give an example and explain why.

6. How would the marketing mix for a staple convenience good differ from the one for a homogeneous shopping good? How would the mix for a specialty good differ from the mix for a heterogeneous shopping good? Use examples.

7. Which of the Ps would receive the greatest emphasis in the marketing mix for a new unsought good? Explain why, using an example.

8. In what types of stores would you expect to find: (a) convenience goods, (b) shopping goods, (c) specialty goods, and (d) unsought goods?

9. Cite two examples of industrial goods which require a substantial amount of service in order to make them useful "products."

10. Would you expect to find any wholesalers selling the various types of industrial goods? Are retail stores required (or something like retail stores)?

11. What kinds of industrial goods are the following: (a) nails and screws, (b) paint, (c) dust-collecting and ventilating systems, (d) an electric lift truck? Explain your reasoning?

12. What impact does the fact that demand for industrial goods is derived and fairly inelastic have on the development of industrial goods marketing mixes? Use examples.

13. How do farm product raw materials differ from other raw materials or other industrial goods? Do the differences have any impact on their marketing mixes? If so, what specifically?

14. For the kinds of industrial goods described in this chapter, complete the following table (use one or a few well-chosen words).

Goods	1	2	3
Installations			
Buildings and			
land rights			
Major equipment			
Standard			
Custom made			
Accessory equipment			
Raw materials			
Farm products			
Natural products			
Components			
Parts			
Materials			
Supplies			
Operating supplies			
Maintenance and			
small operating			
supplies			
Services			

1—Kind of distribution facility(ies) needed and functions they will provide.
2—Caliber of salespeople required.
3—Kind of advertising required.

15. Is there any difference between a brand name and a trademark? If so, why is this difference important?

16. Is a well-known brand valuable only to the owner of the brand?

17. Would it be profitable for a firm to spend large sums of money to establish a brand for any type product in any competitive situation? Why or why not? If the answer is no, suggest examples.

18. Evaluate the suitability of the following brand names: (a) Star (sausage), (b) Pleasing (books), (c) Rugged (shoes), (d) Shiny (shoe polish), (e) Lord Jim (ties).

19. Explain family brands. Sears and A&P use family brands, but they have several different family brands. If the idea is a good one, why don't they have just one brand?

20. What is the "battle of the brands?" Who do you think will win and why?

21. What does the degree of brand familiarity imply about previous promotion efforts and the future promotion task? Also, how does the degree of brand familiarity affect the Place and Price variables?

22. If you have been operating a small supermarket with emphasis on manufacturers' brands and have barely been breaking even, how should

you evaluate the proposal of a large wholesaler who offers a full line of dealer-branded groceries at substantially lower prices? Specify any assumptions necessary to obtain a definite answer.

23. Explain the increasing interest in packaging not only for consumer goods but also for industrial goods. Is this likely to continue?

24. Suggest an example where packaging costs probably: (*a*) lower total distribution costs and (*b*) raise total distribution costs.

■ **SUGGESTED CASES**

13. McIntosh Filing System

17. Black & Decker Company

■ **NOTES**

1. Stanley C. Hollander, "Is There a Generic Demand for Services?" *MSU Business Topics,* Spring 1979, pp. 41–46; John M. Rathmell, "What Is Meant by Services?" *Journal of Marketing,* October 1966, pp. 32–36; T. Levitt, "The Industrialization of Service," *Harvard Business Review,* September-October 1976, pp. 63–74; R. W. Obenberger and S. W. Brown, "A Marketing Alternative: Consumer Leasing and Renting," *Business Horizons,* October 1976, pp. 82–86; Richard B. Chase, "Where Does the Customer Fit in a Service Operation?" *Harvard Business Review,* November-December 1978, pp. 137–42; Dan R. E. Thomas, "Strategy Is Different in Service Industries," *Harvard Business Review,* July-August 1978, pp. 158–65; Paul F. Anderson and William Lazer, "Industrial Lease Marketing," *Journal of Marketing,* January 1978, pp. 71–79; Robert E. Sabath, "How Much Service Do Customers Really Want?" *Business Horizons,* April 1978, pp. 26–32; "Sony's U.S. Operation Goes in for Repairs," *Business Week,* March 13, 1978, pp. 31–32; Bernard Wysocki, Jr., "Branching Out: Major Retailers Offer Varied Services to Lure Customers, Lift Profits," *The Wall Street Journal,* June 12, 1978, pp. 1, 21; and Phillip D. White and Edward W. Cundiff, "Assessing the Quality of Industrial Products," *Journal of Marketing* 42 (January 1978), pp. 80–86.

2. J. B. Mason and M. L. Mayer, "Empirical Observations of Consumer Behavior as Related to Goods Classification and Retail Strategy," *Journal of Retailing,* Fall 1972, pp. 17–31; Arno K. Kleinenhagen, "Shopping, Specialty, or Convenience Goods?" *Journal of Retailing,* Winter 1966–67, pp. 32–39 ff; Louis P. Bucklin, "Testing Propensities to Shop," *Journal of Marketing,* January 1966, pp. 22–27; William P. Dommermuth, "The Shopping Matrix and Marketing

Strategy," *Journal of Marketing Research,* May 1965, pp. 128–132; Richard H. Holton, "The Distinction Between Convenience Goods, Shopping Goods, and Specialty Goods," *Journal of Marketing,* July 1958, pp. 53–56; Perry Bliss, "Supply Considerations and Shopper Convenience," *Journal of Marketing,* July 1966, pp. 43–45; and S. Kaish, "Cognitive Dissonance and the Classification of Consumer Goods," and W. P. Dommermuth and E. W. Cundiff, "Shopping Goods, Shopping Centers, and Selling Strategies," *Journal of Marketing,* October 1967, pp. 28–36; Edward M. Tauber, "Why Do People Shop?" *Journal of Marketing,* October 1972, pp. 46–49.

3. David T. Kollat and Ronald P. Willett, "Customer Impulse Purchasing Behavior," *Journal of Marketing Research,* February 1967, pp. 21–31. See also David T. Kollat and Ronald P. Willett, "Is Impulse Purchasing Really a Useful Concept for Marketing Decisions?" *Journal of Marketing,* January 1969, pp. 79–83; and Danny N. Bellenger, Dan H. Robertson, and Elizabeth C. Hirschman, "Impulse Buying Varies by Product," *Journal of Advertising Research* 18 (December 1978), pp. 15–18.

4. "Will Tiny Cells Power Big Sales," *Business Week,* January 14, 1967, pp. 60–64.

5. T. Levitt, "Branding on Trial," *Harvard Business Review,* March-April 1966, pp. 28–32.

6. The source of this discussion of Canadian trademark policy is B. E. Mallen, V. Kirpalani, and G. Lane, *Marketing and the Canadian Environment* (Toronto: Prentice-Hall of Canada, 1973), p. 137.

7. "DuPont's Teflon Trademark Survives Attack," *Advertising Age,* July 14, 1975, p. 93; George Miaoulis and Nancy

D'Amato, "Consumer Confusion and Trademark Infringement," *Journal of Marketing,* April 1978, pp. 48–55; but see also "Miller Beer Wins Round over Use of Lite Name," *The Wall Street Journal,* October 10, 1980, p. 9.

8. K. L. Granzin, "An Investigation of the Market for Generic Products," *Journal of Retailing* 57 (1981), pp. 39–55; "Checklist Tells If Generic Products 'Threaten' Your Brand," *Marketing News,* October 31, 1980; Patrick E. Murphy and Gene R. Laczniak, "Generic Supermarket Items: A Product and Consumer Analysis," *Journal of Retailing* 55 (Summer 1979), pp. 3–14; "Co-opting Generics," *Advertising Age,* March 31, 1981; "Generic Products Are Winning Noticeable Shares of Market from National Brands, Private Labels," *The Wall Street Journal,* August 10, 1979, p. 6; and Betsy D. Gelb, "'No-Name' Products: A Step Toward 'No Name' Retailing," *Business Horizons,* June 1980, pp. 9–13.

9. J. A. Bellizzi, H. F. Kruekeberg, J. R. Hamilton, and W. S. Martin, "Consumer Perceptions of National, Private, and Generic Brands," *Journal of Retailing* 57 (1981), pp. 56–70; J. C. M. Cunningham, A. P. Hardy, and G. Imperia, "Generic Brands versus National Brands and Store Brands," *Journal of Advertising Research* 22, no. 5 (October/November 1982), pp. 25–32; "Is the Private Label Battle Heating Up?" *Grey Matter* 44, no. 7 (July 1973); Zarrel V. Lambert, Paul L. Doering, Eric Goldstein, and William C. McCormick, "Predisposition toward Generic Drug Acceptance," *Consumer*

Research, June 1980, pp. 14–23; "Private-Label Firms Aided by Inflation, Expected to Post Healthy Growth in 1980," *The Wall Street Journal,* March 31, 1980, p. 20; Victor J. Cook and T. F. Schutte, *Brand Policy Determination* (Boston: Allyn & Bacon, 1967); Arthur I. Cohen and Ana Loud Jones, "Brand Marketing in the New Retail Environment," *Harvard Business Review,* September-October 1978, pp. 141–48; "The Drugmaker's Rx for Living with Generics," *Business Week,* November 6, 1978, pp. 205–8; "No-Name Goods Catching on with Grocers," *Detroit Free Press,* April 9, 1978, p. 16D; and "The Marketing of Licensed Characters for Kids, Or How the Lovable Care Bears Were Conceived," *The Wall Street Journal,* September 24, 1982, p. 44.

10. "Packagers Take Steps to Avoid Being Boxed in by Unpredictable Economy," *The Financial Post,* May 1, 1982, p. 18.

11. J. E. Russo, "The Value of Unit Price Information," *Journal of Marketing Research,* May 1977, pp. 193–201; and K. B. Monroe and P. J. LaPlaca, "What are the Benefits of Unit Pricing?" *Journal of Marketing,* July 1972, pp. 16–22.

12. *Stage 1 Competition Policy,* Background Papers, Section 36(1)(c)—Misleading Warranties, Etc." (Ottawa: Consumer and Corporate Affairs), p. 42.

13. Arleen N. Hynd, speech delivered to the Association of Canadian Advertisers, Toronto, 1975, p. 9.

Chapter 11 ■ Product management and new-product development

When you finish this chapter, you should:

1. Understand how product life cycles affect strategy planning.
2. Know what is involved in designing new products and what "new products" really are.
3. Understand a new-product development process.
4. Understand product positioning.
5. Understand the need for product or brand managers.
6. Recognize the important new terms (shown in red).

> *"Product management is a dynamic, full-time job for product managers."*

As recently as 15 years ago, almost every engineer in the country owned a slide rule. Now slide rules have all been replaced with pocket calculators. Once-popular fountain pens have lost out to disposable ballpoint and felt-tip pens. Wood stoves all but disappeared for 40 years, but the recent energy crunch brought them back again. Electric cars and solar-powered water heaters haven't caught on yet—but may be common in another 20 years.

The point of these examples is simple. Products, markets, and competition change over time. This makes marketing management difficult—but also exciting. Developing new products and managing existing products in changing conditions is important to the success of every firm. In this chapter, we focus on some key ideas in these areas.

Products—like consumers—go through life cycles. Understanding these cycles is vital in product management and marketing strategy planning. We will talk about these product life cycles in detail.

We will also discuss different ways a product can be "new." Then, we'll review an organized process for new-product development. It helps to ensure that a company continues to produce successful products. Then we will discuss some analytical aids for managing both old and new products. Finally, we'll see why some companies have "product managers" who are responsible for all of these important Product decisions.

Management of Products over Their Life Cycles

If we could see the future, marketing decisions would be easier. But, we never have a perfect view of the future. However, we can sometimes identify patterns of events that have occurred over and over again—and come to understand and expect them. This can help us plan marketing strategies for the future—and better manage marketing mixes in the present. Fortunately, almost every product idea—during its "life"—follows such a logical pattern.

Product life cycle has four major stages

We call this pattern the **product life cycle**—the stages a new product idea goes through from beginning to end. The product life cycle is divided into four major stages: market introduction, market growth, market maturity, and sales decline.

A particular firm's marketing mix for a product usually must change during the life cycle—for several reasons. Customers' attitudes and needs may change through the course of the product's life cycle. Entirely different target markets may be appealed to at different stages. And the nature of competition moves toward pure competition or oligopoly.

Further, total sales of the product—by all competitors in the industry—vary in each of its four stages. They move from very low in the introductory stage—to high at maturity—and then back to low in the decline stage. More importantly, the profit picture changes, too. These general relationships can be seen in Figure 11–1. It is important to see that the level of sales and the level of profit do not move together over time. *Industry profits decline—while industry sales are still rising.* The reasons for this pattern will become clear when you understand more about the stages in the product life cycle.[1]

Market introduction— investing in the future

In the **market introduction** stage, sales are low as a new idea is first introduced to a market. Customers aren't looking for the product. They don't even know about it. Informative promotion is needed to tell potential customers about the advantages and uses of the new product.

■ FIGURE 11–1   Life cycle of a typical product

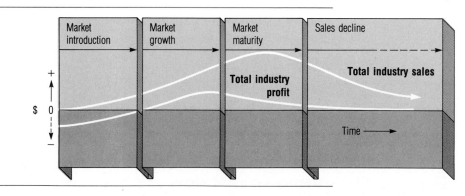

Microwave ovens have been selling well—and probably haven't reached the market maturity stage.

Even though a firm promotes its new product, it takes time for customers to learn that the product is available. The introductory stage usually is marked by losses—with much money spent for Promotion, Product, and Place development. Money is being invested in the hope of future profits.

Market growth—profits and then competition grow, too

In the **market growth** stage, industry sales are growing fast—but industry profits rise and then start falling. The innovator begins to make big profits—as more and more customers buy. But competitors see the opportunity and enter the market. Some improve the product design—to compete better. This results in much product variety. Others just copy the most successful products. Monopolistic competition—with down-sloping demand curves—is typical of the market growth stage.

This is the time of biggest profits—*for the industry. But it is also when industry profits begin to decline*—as competition increases. See Figure 11–1.

Some firms make big strategy planning mistakes at this stage—by not understanding the product life cycle. They see the big sales and profit opportunities of the early market growth stage—but ignore the competition that will soon follow. When they realize their mistake, it may be too late.

Market maturity—sales level off, profits go down

The **market maturity** stage is when industry sales level off—and competition gets tougher. Many aggressive competitors have entered the race for profits—except in oligopoly. Industry profits go down throughout the market maturity stage—because promotion costs rise and some competitors cut prices to attract business. Less efficient firms can't compete with this pressure—and they drop out of the market. Even in oligopoly situations, there is a long-run downward pressure on prices.

New firms may still enter the market at this stage—increasing competition even more. Note that late entries skip the early life-cycle stages—including the profitable market growth stage. And they must try to take a share of the market from established firms—which is difficult and expensive.

Persuasive promotion becomes more important during the market maturity stage. Products may differ only slightly—if at all. Most competitors have discovered the most effective appeals—or copied the leaders. Although each firm may still have its own demand curve, the curves become increasingly elastic—as the various products become almost the same in the minds of potential consumers.

In Canada as well as in the United States, the markets for most automobiles, boats, many household appliances, most groceries, and television sets are in market maturity.[2] This stage may continue for many years—until a basically new product idea comes along. This is true even though individual brands or models may come and go.

Sales decline—a time of replacement

During the **sales decline** stage new products replace the old. Price competition from dying products becomes more vigorous—but firms with strong brands may make profits almost until the end. These firms have down-sloping demand curves—because they have successfully differentiated their products.

As the new products go through their introductory stage, the old ones may keep some sales—by appealing to the most loyal target customers or those who are slow to try new ideas. These conservative buyers might switch later—smoothing the sales decline.

Product Life Cycles Vary in Length

How long a whole product life cycle will take—and the length of each stage—varies a lot across products. The cycle may vary from 90 days—in the case of a toy like Rubic's Cube—to possibly 90 years for gas-powered automobiles.

The product life cycle concept does not tell a manager precisely *how long* the cycle will last. But, often a good "guess" is possible—based on the life cycle for similar products. Sometimes marketing research can help, too. However, it may be more important to expect and plan for the different stages than to know the precise length of each cycle.

Product life cycles are getting shorter

Although the life of different products varies, in general, product life cycles are getting shorter. This is partly due to rapidly changing technology. One new invention may make possible many new products which replace old ones. Plastics changed many products—and created new ones. Tiny electronic "microchips" led to hundreds of new products—from pocket calculators and digital watches to video games.

Some markets move quickly to market maturity—if there are fast "copiers." In the highly competitive grocery products industry, cycles are down to 12 to 18 months for really new ideas. Simple variations of a new idea may have even shorter life cycles. Competitors sometimes copy flavor or packaging changes in a matter of weeks or months.

Fast copying is also common in industrial goods markets—where buyers buy by specification and want to have several sources of supply. And several companies may be working on the same new product idea at the same time. A top Du Pont manager said: "Lead time is gone . . . there's no company so outstanding technically today that it can expect a long lead time in a new discovery." Du Pont had nylon to itself for 15 years. But in just two years, a major competitor—Celanese Corporation—came out with something very competitive to Delrin—another synthetic fiber discovery that Du Pont hoped would be as important as nylon. Similarly, six months after U.S. Steel came out with a new "thin tin" plate, competitors were out with even better products.

Patents may not be much protection for a new product. The product's life may be over before a patent case can get through the courts. The copy-cat competitor may be out of business by then. Or competitors may find other ways to produce the product—without violating a specific patent.

The short happy life of fashions and fads

The sales of some products are influenced by **fashion**—the currently accepted or popular style. Fashion-related products tend to have short life cycles. What is "currently" popular can shift rapidly. A certain color or style of clothing—such as mini-skirts—may be in fashion one season, and outdated the next.

Fashion cycles have stages, too

Consumer acceptance of fashion products usually goes through a **fashion cycle** consisting of three stages: the *distinctiveness, emulation,* and *economic emulation* stages—which roughly parallel the product life cycle stages.

During the **distinctiveness stage**, some consumers seek—and are willing to pay for—products different from those that satisfy the majority. They have products custom-made—or patronize manufacturers or middlemen who offer products in small quantities and/or in "distinctive" places.

If a particular style catches on with a number of fashion leaders, then other consumers—because of their desire to emulate—may copy them. This is the **emulation stage**—when many more consumers want to buy what is satisfying the original users. Emulation is easier because manufacturers begin to make large quantities of the products that seem to be catching on. This stage is similar to the early market growth stage of the product life cycle.

In the **economic emulation stage**, many consumers want the currently popular fashion—but at a lower price. When this happens, manufacturers mass produce large quantities of the product at low cost—and the product moves quickly through the market growth stage and maybe through the market maturity stage into sales decline.

Perhaps in the second stage—and certainly in the third stage—the style that began as the private fling of the few is no longer attractive to these original fashion leaders. They already are trying other styles—which eventually may become fashions and run through another cycle.

It's not really clear how a particular fashion gets started. Most present fashions are adaptations or revivals of previously popular styles. Designers and business firms are always looking for styles that will satisfy consumers who crave distinctiveness. The speed of fashion changes increases the cost of producing and marketing products. There are losses due to trial and error in finding acceptable styles, then producing them on a limited basis because of uncertainty about the length of the cycle. These increased costs are not always charged directly to

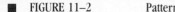

■   FIGURE 11–2   Patterns of fashion, fad, and style cycles for fashion products

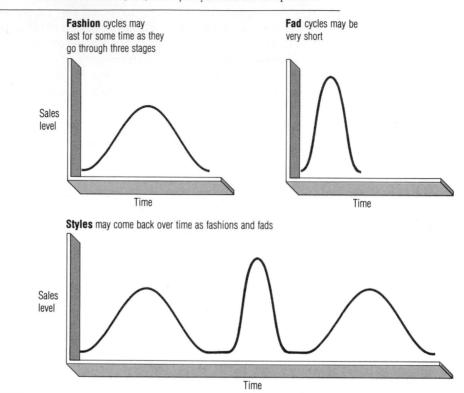

Fashion cycles may last for some time as they go through three stages

Sales level

Time

Fad cycles may be very short

Time

Styles may come back over time as fashions and fads

Sales level

Time

the consumer—since some firms lose their investment and go out of business. But in total, fashion changes cost consumers money.

A **fad** is an idea that is fashionable only to certain groups who are enthusiastic about it—but so fickle that it is even more short-lived than a regular fashion. A few years ago, it was a fad to own a "Pet Rock." Some teenagers' music tastes are fads. Figure 11–2 summarizes the shape of typical life cycles for fashions, fads, and styles. Note that the pattern for a style may go up and down—as it comes back into fashion over time.[3]

The early bird makes the profits

The increasing speed of the product life cycle means that firms must be developing new products all the time. Further, they must try to have marketing mixes that will make the most of the market growth stage—when profits are highest. But the profits do not necessarily go to the innovator. Sometimes fast copiers of the basic idea will share in the market growth stage. They may even be faster in adapting more exactly to the market's needs. This emphasizes the importance of being flexible *but also* correctly understanding the needs and attitudes of target markets.

Product Life Cycles Should Be Related to Specific Markets

Each market should be carefully defined

To fully understand the *why* of a particular product life cycle, we should carefully define the market area we are considering. The way we define a market makes a difference in the way we see product life cycles—and who the competitors are. If a market is defined too generally, there may be many competitors—and the market may appear to be in market maturity. On the other hand, if we focus on a narrow area—and a particular way of satisfying specific needs—then we may see much shorter product life cycles, as improved product ideas come along to replace the old. For example, the general market demand for power lawn mowers appears to be in the market maturity stage—where only minor product changes are expected. If we think of lawn mowers using different technical principles, however, we see a different view. "Air-cushion" mowers for very uneven lawns were introduced recently and may take some of the "wheeled" mower business. Power lawn mower producers who defined their market too generally may miss this opportunity.

Each market segment has its own product life cycle

Too narrow a view of a market segment can also result in misreading the nature of competition—and the speed of the relevant product life cycle. A firm producing exercise machines, for example, may focus on only the "exercise machine" market. But this narrow view may lead it to compete only with other exercise machine producers, when it might be more sensible to compete in the "fitness" market. Certainly, it should not ignore competitors' machines, but even tougher competition may come from health clubs—and suppliers of jogging suits, athletic shoes, and other fitness-related goods. In other words, there may be two markets and life cycles to work with—the exercise machine market and the fitness market. Each may require a different strategy.

Individual products don't have product life cycles

Remember that product life cycles describe *industry* sales and profits for a product idea within a particular product-market—*not* the sales and profits of an *individual* product or brand. Individual products or brands may be introduced or withdrawn during any stage of the product life cycle. Further, their sales and profits may vary up and down throughout the life cycle—sometimes moving in the opposite direction of industry sales and profits.

A "me-too" product introduced during the market growth stage, for example, may reach its peak and start to decline even before the market maturity stage begins—or it may never get any sales at all and suffer a quick death. Market leaders may enjoy high profits during the market maturity stage—even though industry profits are declining. Weaker products, on the other hand, may not earn a profit during any stage of the product life cycle.

What this discussion means, therefore, is that sales of *individual* products often do not follow the general product life cycle pattern—and expecting such patterns can be misleading for strategy planning purposes. It's the life cycle for the product idea in the whole product-market—including all current or potential competitors—that marketing managers must consider when planning their strategies. In fact, it might be more sensible to think in terms of "market life cycles" or "product-market life cycles" rather than product life cycles—but we will use the term *product life cycle* because it is commonly accepted and widely used.

Planning for Different Stages of the Product Life Cycle

Length of cycle affects strategy planning

The probable length of the cycle affects strategy planning—realistic plans must be made for the later stages. In fact, where a product is in its life cycle—and how fast it's moving to the next stage—should affect strategy planning. Figure 11–3 shows the relation of the product life cycle to the marketing mix variables. The technical terms in this figure are discussed later in the book.

■ FIGURE 11–3   Typical changes in marketing variables over the course of the product life cycle

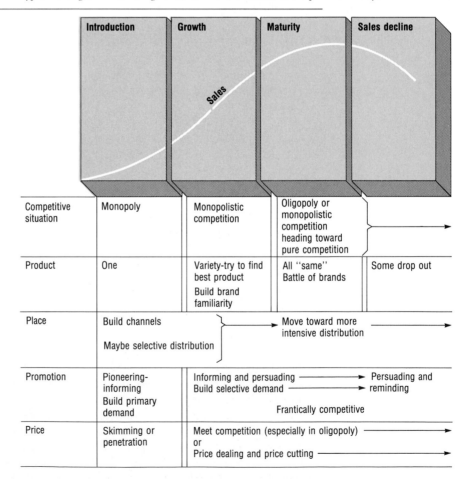

	Introduction	Growth	Maturity	Sales decline
Competitive situation	Monopoly	Monopolistic competition	Oligopoly or monopolistic competition heading toward pure competition	
Product	One	Variety-try to find best product — Build brand familiarity	All "same" Battle of brands	Some drop out
Place	Build channels — Maybe selective distribution		Move toward more intensive distribution	
Promotion	Pioneering-informing — Build primary demand	Informing and persuading ——— Persuading and — Build selective demand ——— reminding — Frantically competitive		
Price	Skimming or penetration	Meet competition (especially in oligopoly) ——— or — Price dealing and price cutting ———		

Introducing new products

Figure 11–3 shows that a marketing manager has to do a lot of work to introduce a really new product—and this should be reflected in the strategy planning. Money must be spent designing and developing the new product. Even if the product is unique—this doesn't mean that everyone will immediately come running to the producer's door. The firm will have to build channels of distribution—perhaps offering special incentives to win cooperation. Promotion is needed to build demand *for the whole idea*—not just to sell a specific brand. Because all of this is expensive, it may lead the marketing manager to try to "skim" the market—charging a relatively high price to help pay for the introductory costs.

The correct strategy, however, depends on how fast the product life cycle is likely to move—that is, how quickly the new idea will be accepted by customers—and how quickly competitors will follow with their own versions of the product. When the early stages of the cycle will be fast, a low initial price may make sense—helping to develop loyal customers early and keep competitors out.

Also relevant is how quickly the firm can change its strategy as the life cycle moves on. Some firms are very flexible—and are able to compete effectively with larger, less adaptable competitors by adjusting their strategies more frequently.

Managing maturing products

Whether you have developed some competitive advantage is important as you move into market maturity. Even a small advantage can make a big difference—and some firms do very well by careful management of maturing products. They are able to capitalize on a slightly better product—or perhaps lower production and/or marketing costs. Or they are simply more successful at promotion—allowing them to differentiate their more-or-less homogeneous product from competitors.

An important point to remember here, however, is that industry profits are declining in market maturity. Financially oriented top management must see this—or they will continue to expect the attractive profits of the market growth stage—profits that are no longer possible. If top managers don't understand the situation, they may place impossible burdens on the marketing department—causing marketing managers to think about collusion with competitors, deceptive advertising, or some other desperate way of reaching impossible objectives.

Improved products can push existing products into the sales decline stage.

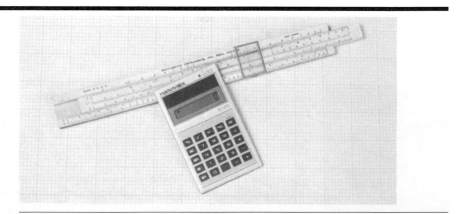

■ FIGURE 11–4   Significantly improved product starts a new cycle, but maybe with short introductory stage

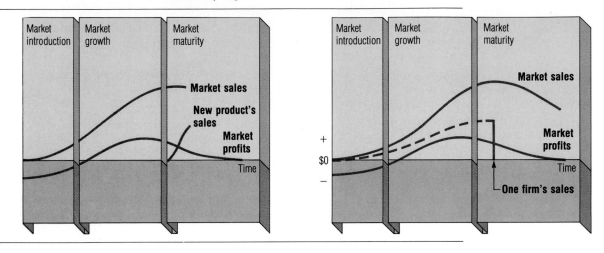

Top management must see that there is an upper limit in any product-market. The product life cycle concept has been very useful in communicating this unhappy message. It is one of the powerful tools of marketing which is turning up in finance and top management literature—because it is useful for overall corporate planning and objective setting.

Product life cycles keep moving. But if a company doesn't have any competitive advantage, it doesn't have to sit by and watch its products go through a complete product life cycle. It has choices. It can improve the product—for the same or a different market—and let it start on a different cycle. Or it can withdraw the product before it completes the cycle. These two choices are shown in Figure 11–4.

Product life cycles can be extended

When a firm's product wins the position of "the product that meets my needs," its life will last as long as it continues to meet these needs. If the needs change, the product may have to change—but the target consumers will continue to buy it if it still meets their needs. An outstanding example is Procter & Gamble's Tide. Introduced in 1947, this synthetic detergent gave consumers a significantly cleaner wash than they were able to get before—because it did away with soap film. Tide led to a whole new generation of laundry products—because it produced better cleaning with fewer suds. Since 1947, consumers' needs have changed, washing machines have changed, and fabrics have changed—so the Tide sold today is much different than the one sold in 1947. In fact, there were 55 modifications during its first 29 years of life. But the product continues to sell well—because it continues to meet consumers' needs.[4]

Do product modifications—like those made with Tide—create a wholly new product which should have its own product life cycle—or are they simply technical adjustments of the original product idea? We will take the latter position—focusing on the product idea rather than changes in features. This means that some of these Tide changes were made in the current market maturity stage. It also means that for strategy planning purposes—"new" brands which are similar to present competitors must immediately enter the product life cycle stage of the already competing brands.

Phasing out dying products

Not all strategies have to be "exciting" growth strategies. If prospects are poor in some product-market, then a "phase-out" strategy may be needed. The need for phasing out becomes more obvious as the sales decline stage arrives. But even in market maturity, it may be clear that a particular product is not going to be profitable enough to reach the company's objectives. Then, the wisest move may be to develop a strategy which helps the firm get out of the product-market as quickly as possible—even before the sales decline stage sets in—while minimizing possible losses.

Marketing plans are implemented as "ongoing" strategies—with salespeople making calls, inventory moving in the channel, advertising scheduled for several months into the future, and so on. So usually it is not possible to avoid losses if a plan is ended abruptly. Sometimes it is better to phase out the product gradually. This involves selective materials ordering—so that production can end with a minimum of unused inventory. Salespeople are shifted to other jobs. The advertising and other promotion efforts are canceled or phased out quickly—since there is no point in promoting for the long run anymore. These various actions obviously affect morale within the company—and may cause channel members to pull back also. So the company may have to offer price inducements in the channels. And the company's people should be told that a phase-out strategy is being implemented—and reassured that they will be shifted to other jobs as the plan is completed.

Obviously, there are some difficult implementation problems here, but phase-out is also a *strategy*—and it must be market-oriented to cut losses. In fact, it is even possible to "milk out" a dying product for some time if competitors move out more quickly. This situation occurs when there is still ongoing demand—although it is declining—and some customers are willing to pay attractive prices to get their "old favorite." Further, there may be an ongoing need for repair parts and service—which helps maintain the overall profitability of the phase-out strategy. Alternately, a new strategy could handle just the repairs and service—even as the basic product is being phased out.

So you can see that whole product life cycles should be planned—for each strategy. A company with many strategies needs to plan for many life cycles. And the product life cycle concept adds depth to the portfolio management analysis which we discussed in Chapter 3. There we were concerned with planning and evaluating the prospects for various kinds of opportunities. Now you can see that these opportunities will have different product life cycles—and that product life cycles should be considered when estimating the attractiveness of alternative opportunities.

New-Product Planning

Competition is so strong and dynamic in most markets, that it is essential for a firm to keep developing new products—as well as modifying its current products—to meet changing customer needs and competitors' actions. Not having an active new product development process means that consciously—or subconsciously—the firm has decided to "milk" its current products and go out of business. New-product planning is not an optional matter—it has to be done—just to survive in our dynamic marketplaces.

Eggs are not new—but this frozen egg roll is a new product with many possibilities.

What is a new product?

A **new product** is one that is new *in any way* for the company concerned. A product can become "new" in many ways. A fresh idea can be turned into a new item or service. Small changes in an existing product also can make it "new."

Some marketers focus on relatively small changes to make products "new"—but such minor changes may not lead to long-lived strategies. To develop really good strategies, marketers must find better ways to satisfy needs. Perhaps the needs were there all along—just not seen in the way that the firm now sees them—and a "good" marketing mix can satisfy these needs "very well." This may require a "really new" product which will need much "pioneering" effort. This is obviously harder than emphasizing small changes—but it may lead to the break-through opportunities we've been talking about.

CCAC says product is "new" only 12 months

A product can be called "new" for only a limited time. Twelve months is the longest time that a product should be called new—according to Consumer and Corporate Affairs Canada. To be called new, a product must be entirely new or changed in a "functionally significant or substantial respect."[5] While 12 months may seem a short time for production-oriented managers, it may be reasonable, given the short life cycles of many products.

New markets can lead to "new" products

Sometimes existing products can become "new" products in a new market. Lemons are a good example.

In the marketing of Sunkist lemons, no physical changes were made—but promotion created many "new" products. The same old lemons were promoted successfully for lemonade, mixed drinks, diet supplements, cold remedies, lemon cream pies, a salad dressing, sauce for fish, and many other uses.[6] Note that several product life cycles are involved here—not just one. For each of these markets, each product idea had to go through the early stages of its own product life cycle.

This broad approach to what a new product is deserves more emphasis—because one or more of the other Ps may have to be modified when no physical changes are made in the product. The experience of a dictating machine manufacturer illustrates this. Its normal target markets were office managers and efficiency experts. But the dictating machines had less appeal to the much larger potential market of general business executives—although the products were technically good.

Motivation research revealed several facts. One was that the promotion appeals being used—speed, economy, and efficiency—were not psychologically appealing to the executives. They felt they might lose prestige by using the machines—because it might reduce or eliminate the need for their secretaries. The research also showed that secretaries believed that machines might set up a wall between them and their bosses—and that they might become nothing but "slaves to machines." As a result, management was afraid to order the machines for fear that employees would quit.

The solution here—which in effect created a new product—was to explain that the machines were office management tools which speeded up work and made the secretary, manager, and machines a happy team. Advertisements stressed "no more staying at the office after hours . . . time to relax . . . secretary free to be a real assistant . . . I can get ahead and still get home while the kids are still awake." Note the close interrelation of two Ps—Product and Promotion.

An Organized New-Product Development Process Is Critical

Identifying and developing new product ideas—and effective strategies to go with them—is often the key to a firm's success and survival. But this is not easy. New-product development demands effort, time, and talent—and still the risks and costs of failure are high. The failure rate on new products actually placed in the market may be as high as 50 percent.[7]

To improve this effort, it is useful to follow an organized new-product development process. The following pages describe such a process—moving logically through five steps: (1) idea generation, (2) screening, (3) idea evaluation, (4) development (of product and marketing mix), and (5) commercialization.[8] See Figure 11–5.

■ FIGURE 11–5   New-product development process

Industrial markets	Consumer markets
1. Idea generation	1. Idea generation
2. Screening	2. Screening
Rough ROI estimate	*Rough ROI estimate*
3. Idea evaluation	3. Idea evaluation
Exploratory	Concept testing
Rough ROI verification	*Rough ROI verification*
Qualitative	
Quantitative	
ROI estimate	
4. Development	4. Development
R&D	R&D
Build model	Engineering
Engineering test	Build model(s)
Test in market	Test in market
ROI estimate	*ROI estimate*
	Revise product specifications
	Pilot production
	Production and quality
	control test
	Market testing
	Product variations
	Variations of marketing mix
	ROI estimates
5. Commercialization	5. Commercialization
Finalize production model	Finalize product
Finalize marketing mix (plan)	Finalize market mix (plan)
Final ROI estimate	*Final ROI estimate*
Start full-scale production	Start full-scale production
and marketing plan	and marketing plan

Source: Adapted from Frank R. Bacon, Jr. and Thomas W. Butler, Jr., *Planned Innovation,* rev. ed. (Ann Arbor: The University of Michigan, Institute of Science and Technology, 1980).

The general process is similar for both consumer and industrial markets. There are some significant differences, but we will emphasize the similarities in the following discussion.

Process tries to kill new ideas— economically

An important element in the new-product development process for both markets is continued evaluation of the likely profitability and return on investment of new ideas. In fact, it is desirable to apply the hypothesis-testing approach discussed in Chapter 5 to new-product development. The hypothesis which is tested is that the new idea will *not* be profitable. This puts the burden on the new idea to prove itself—or be rejected. This may seem harsh, but experience shows that most new ideas have some flaw which can lead to problems—and even substantial losses. Marketers try to discover those flaws early—and either find a remedy or reject the idea completely. Applying this process requires much analysis of the idea—both within and outside the firm—*before* any money is spent by research and development (R&D) or engineering to develop a physical item. This is a major departure from the usual production-oriented approach—which develops a product first and then asks sales to "get rid of it."

The value of an organized new-product development process can be seen in Figure 11–6. It shows how few ideas survive when they are carefully evaluated— from the screening stage to commercialization. It is estimated that out of 40 new ideas, only one is left after the ideas have passed through an organized development process of the type described below. The rate of rejection varies among industries and companies—but the general shape of the decay curve seems to be typical. An especially conservative company may have even more rejects, of course. In summary, it is important to see that if a firm doesn't use this sort of

■ FIGURE 11–6   Decay of new-product ideas during an organized new-product development process

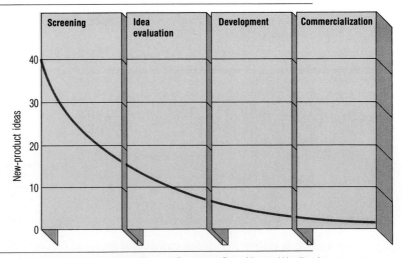

Source: Adapted from Management Research Department, Booz, Allen, and Hamilton, Inc.

organized process, it probably will bring many bad or weak ideas to market—at a big loss.

Step 1: Idea generation

New ideas can come from a company's own sales or production staff, middlemen, competitors, consumer surveys, or other sources—such as trade associations, advertising agencies, or government agencies. Analyzing new and different views of the company's markets helps spot opportunities which have not yet occurred to competitors—or even to potential customers. Basic studies of present consumer behavior point up opportunities, too.

When looking for ideas, the consumer's viewpoint is all-important. It may be helpful to consider the image that potential customers have of the firm. The makers of Cracker Jack had a familiar brand of caramel-coated popcorn—so they introduced a line of plain popping corn because consumers saw them as makers of "good" popcorn.

If potential customers think of a firm as a food manufacturer—rather than just a snack producer—then many food products become logical additions to the line. This kind of thinking led the Maryland Cup Corporation—the world's largest

Consumers saw Cracker Jack as makers of good caramel-covered corn—so Cracker Jack introduced a plain popping corn, too.

manufacturer of paper drinking straws and a leading manufacturer of paper drinking cups—to produce plastic food containers of all types. Customers identified them with the "disposable container" business—rather than just the straw and cup business. Similarly, S. C. Johnson & Son, Inc., expanded from a line of paste waxes to many other household products.

Research shows that many new ideas for industrial markets come from customers who identify a need they have. Then they approach a manufacturer with the idea—and perhaps even with the particular design or specification.

But finding new-product ideas should not be left to chance. Companies need a formal procedure for seeking new ideas. The lists of considerations and checkpoints discussed below—as well as the hierarchy of needs and other behavioral elements discussed earlier—should be reviewed regularly to assure a continual flow of new—but sound—ideas. The importance of a continual flow is obvious. Though later steps will eliminate many ideas, a company must have some which succeed in the market—if it is to survive.

Step 2: Screening step

Screening involves evaluating the new ideas with the product-market screening criteria described in Chapter 3. Recall that these criteria include the combined output of a resource (strengths and weaknesses) analysis, a long-run trends analysis, and the objectives of the company. See Figure 3–10. The criteria include the nature of the product-markets the company would like to be in—as well as those it wants to avoid. Further, the qualitative part of the criteria includes statements that help select ideas which will allow the company to lead from its strengths and avoid its weaknesses. Ideally, a company matches its resources to the size of its opportunities. A "good" new idea should eventually lead to a product (and marketing mix) which will give the firm a competitive advantage—hopefully one that will last.

Some companies screen based on consumer welfare

The firm's final choice in product design should fit with the company's overall objectives—and make good use of the firm's resources. But it is also desirable to create a need-satisfying product which will appeal to consumers—in the long run as well as the short run. Ideally, the product will increase consumer welfare, too—not just satisfy a whim. Different kinds of new-product opportunities are shown in Figure 11–7. Obviously, a socially responsible firm tries to find "desirable" opportunities—rather than "deficient" ones. This may not be as easy as it sounds, however. Some consumers want "pleasing products"—instead of "desirable products." They emphasize immediate satisfaction and give little thought to their own long-term welfare. And some competitors are quite willing to offer what consumers want in the short run. Generating "socially responsible," new-product ideas is a challenge for new-product planners. Consumer groups are helping to force this awareness on more firms.

Safety should be considered in screening ideas

Real acceptance of the marketing concept certainly leads to the design of safe products. But some inherently risky products are purchased because they do provide thrills and excitement—for example, bicycles, skis, and hang gliders.

■ FIGURE 11–7   Types of new-product opportunities

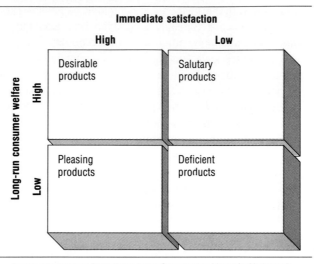

Immediate satisfaction

Source: Adapted from Philip Kotler, "What Consumerism Means for Marketers," *Harvard Business Review*, May-June 1972, pp. 55–56.

Even so, safety features usually can be added—and are desired by some potential customers.

The **Hazardous Products Act**, passed by the Canadian Parliament in June 1969, gives Consumer and Corporate Affairs Canada the authority either to ban outright or to regulate the sale, distribution, labeling, and advertising of potentially dangerous products. This act reemphasizes the need for business persons to become more safety oriented.

The consumers' new-found interest in safety is also worth noting. Early efforts (in the early 1950s) to "sell" seat belts to Canadian motorists were not successful. The Ford Motor Company backed off from its attempt to sell safety when it found that consumers were not too concerned about needs which they personally did not feel. However, a change in the social environment has made consumers far more safety conscious and caused much more interest in the matter by both politicians and businessmen.[9] The use of seat belts in now compulsory in many provinces.

Product safety complicates strategy planning because not all customers—including some who want better safety features—are willing to pay more for safer products. And some features cost a lot to add—increasing prices considerably. These safety concerns must be considered at the screening step—because a firm can later be held liable for unsafe products.

Product liability must be taken seriously

Product liability means the legal obligation of sellers to pay damages to individuals who are injured by defective products or unsafely designed products. Some firms find their product liability insurance costs rising to the point where they have to "self-insure"—take the risk themselves—or go out of business. For example, Nissen Corporation, a maker of gym equipment, recently was offered a product liability insurance policy costing about $400,000 to cover $300,000 worth of protection (because of uncertainty about the size of court settlements). This is an extreme example—but machine tool makers have seen their insurance premiums increase drastically in recent years. The major reason for these rising premiums is a growing number of claims, lawsuits, *and* settlements. And the potential for more suits is great. Recently, users of two paper-making presses sued the manufacturer for damages arising out of industrial accidents. One of the presses was built in 1895 and the other in 1897!

Obviously, the uncontrollable environment has changed—and it's more important than ever to take new-product planning—and in particular the safety of products—seriously. It is hard to consider all aspects of product safety and liability at the screening stage—but managers must start analyzing these issues earlier in the new-product development process.[10]

ROI is a crucial screening criterion

Getting by the initial screening criteria does not guarantee success for the new idea—but it does show that at least the new idea is "in the right ballpark"— *for this firm.* If many ideas pass the screening criteria, then it is necessary to set priorities for which ones go on to the next step in the process. This can be done by comparing the ROI (return on investment) for each idea—assuming the firm is ROI-oriented. The most attractive alternatives are to be pursued first.

Step 3: Idea evaluation step

Once an idea moves past the screening step, the basic concept is evaluated more carefully. Note that no tangible product has yet been developed—and this handicaps concept testing from the start. Final consumers, especially, have difficulty visualizing "ideas" or "concepts." Nevertheless, this kind of research can help guide the next step—where actual models are developed.

Concept testing involves market research—anywhere from informal focus groups to formal surveys of potential customers' attitudes toward the idea. It is

A new product idea can be killed by negative consumer reaction during marketing research.

possible to make a rough ROI estimate after a survey. Even informal focus groups are useful—especially if they show that potential users aren't excited about the new idea. And if the results are discouraging, it may be best to kill the idea at this stage. Remember, in this hypothesis-testing process, we are looking for any evidence that an idea is *not* a good opportunity for this firm—and should be rejected.

Product planners must not only think about final customers—but intermediate customers, too. For example, middlemen may have special concerns about handling a proposed product—or recognize problems that a final consumer wouldn't think about. For example, a manufacturer was considering adding hot-tubs to its line of plumbing items. But it found that its current wholesalers did not want to handle hot-tubs because of problems with storage and handling. Consumer reactions were good, but the company dropped the idea because it didn't want to develop new channels of distribution.

Idea evaluation is more precise in industrial markets. Here, potential customers are more informed about their needs—and their buying is more economical and less emotional. Further, given the derived nature of demand in industrial markets, most needs are already being satisfied in some way. So new products are "substitutes" for existing ways of doing things. This means that a relatively small number of interviews with well-informed people can help determine the range of variation in product requirements—and whether there is an opportunity.

In one case—where this process was not used—a large manufacturer of food machinery and equipment completed the design of a large citrus juicer without making an adequate study of the juice industry. Management went ahead with engineering development—confident that the machine would find a market. After spending nearly $1 million on design and engineering work, the company learned that the machine was built for the top of the market rather than for the bulk of potential users—the smaller processors. The machine was too big and expensive—only a few firms could afford it. If the company had spent a few thousand dollars to determine how many citrus processors there were by size, types of machines used and wanted, and related facts, it might have avoided a costly mistake.

A form similar to Figure 11–8 can be helpful in gathering the kind of information which will be useful in deciding whether there is an opportunity—and whether it fits with the firm's resources—*and* whether there is a basis for developing a competitive advantage. With such information, it is possible to estimate likely ROI in the various market segments—and decide whether to continue the new product development process.

Step 4: Development step

Product ideas which have survived the screening and idea evaluation steps must now be analyzed further. Usually, this involves some research and development (R&D) and engineering—to design and develop the physical part of the product. Input from the earlier efforts helps guide this technical work.

But it is still desirable to test models and early versions of the product in the market. This process may have several cycles—building a model, testing it, revising product specifications based on the tests—and so on—*before* pilot plant production.

■ FIGURE 11–8   Information requirements to develop new products

Information requirements

	1 How is basic function performed now?	2 What do present methods cost?	3 What's wrong with present methods?	4 What value do improvements have?
A. Physical need	―――――	―――――	―――――	―――――
B. Technical product design (R&D)	―――――	―――――	―――――	―――――
C. Production methods	―――――	―――――	―――――	―――――
D. Marketing and distribution methods	―――――	―――――	―――――	―――――
E. Economic cost and value consideration				

Source: Adapted from Frank R. Bacon, Jr., and Thomas W. Butler, Jr., *Planned Innovation*, rev. ed. (Ann Arbor: The University of Michigan, Institute of Science and Technology, 1980).

With actual models, it is possible to show potential customers how the idea has been converted into a tangible product. Using small focus groups, panels, and larger surveys, marketers can get reactions to specific features and the whole product idea. This can lead to revision of product specifications—for different markets. Sometimes months or even years of research are necessary to focus on precisely what different market segments will find acceptable. It took Procter & Gamble over 10 years and $800 million to develop Pringles Potato Chips!

An example shows how important customer analysis is to successful product design—especially if there are different demands in different segments of a market. When the Powers Regulator Company wanted to enter the home-building market with a shower control, it found it had to redesign the product it was already selling to schools, hotels, and hospitals. Research found this product "too severe and institutional" to win the acceptance of the new target market—builders and homeowners. Then, Powers developed a more attractive—and successful—product for home use.

After testing the tangible product, pilot production begins—to be sure that the product can be produced economically. This product then goes into the market for testing—perhaps testing product variations if there are still questions—as well as variations in the marketing mix. For example, alternative brands, prices, or advertising copy may be tested. Test marketing is risky. It not only tests ideas for the company—but also gives information to the competition. But not testing is dangerous, too. Fortunately, if this new-product development process was used carefully, the market test will provide a lot more information to the firm than to its competitors. Presumably, the company will be testing specific variables—rather than just vaguely testing whether a new idea will "sell." After the market test, an estimate of likely ROI for various strategies will determine whether the idea moves on to commercialization.

Sometimes a market test is not run because it isn't practical. In fashion goods, for example, speed is extremely important, and products are usually just tried in the market. And durable goods—which have high fixed production costs and long production lead times—may have to go directly to the market. In these cases, it is especially important that the early steps are done carefully—to reduce the chances for failure in the marketplace.

Step 5:
Commercialization

A product idea which has survived this far can finally be placed on the market. First, the new-product people decide exactly which product form or line will be sold. Then, they complete the marketing mix—really a whole strategic plan. And an ROI estimate for this plan has to get top management approval before it is implemented. Finally, the product idea emerges from the new-product development process—and success will require the cooperation of the whole company.

Putting a product on the market is expensive—because manufacturing facilities have to be set up and enough product has to be produced to fill the channels of distribution. Further, introductory promotion is costly. This is especially true if the company has to develop new channels of distribution.

Because of the size of the job, some firms introduce their products city by city or region by region—in a gradual "roll out"—until they have complete market coverage. This also permits more market testing—but that is not the purpose of the roll out. All implementation efforts should be controlled—to be sure the strategic plan is still on target.

Eventually, the "new" product is no longer "new"—and it becomes just another product. About this time, the "new-product people" turn the product over to the regular operating people—and go on to developing other new ideas. Of course, product management doesn't stop here. In the next section, we will discuss several analytical tools which help managers keep score on how their products are doing.

Keeping Score on Products

Ongoing analysis of present and/or potential customers' needs and attitudes—as well as the needs of channel members—is obviously important in product management. Ignoring those influences—as is typical with production-oriented managers—helps contribute to the relatively high failure rate on new as well as existing products.

Most of these "failures" are due to inadequate analysis of market demands to begin with—or changing market demands *and* competitive moves. Therefore, it is extremely important for a marketing manager to continually evaluate present products—as well as carefully study possible new ones.

■ FIGURE 11–9   Good design: Does your product have it?

	Yes	No
1. Does the product's present design reflect quality?	———	———
2. Is the present design economical to manufacture?	———	———
3. Is the design well accepted by wholesalers, retailers, sales people and customers?	———	———
4. Is the design in tune with current design trends?	———	———
5. Does the design have a comparatively long life?	———	———
6. Are the details of the product well designed?	———	———
7. Does the design contribute to the product's usefulness, safety, and convenience?	———	———
8. Are the materials used practical for product's end use?	———	———
9. Is the color right for use and environment?	———	———
10. Is the size right for best use?	———	———
11. Is the weight right for best use?	———	———
12. Does the design stand up well with competition?	———	———
13. Does the design meet environmental requirements?	———	———

As a starting point, it is important to keep track of how well a product design competes. The checklist in Figure 11–9 can help in this ongoing monitoring. This checklist is useful because it usually is safer to make 13 separate small judgments—than one large "yes" or "no" judgment.

On this checklist, a yes on 11 to 13 questions indicates a good design; 9 or 10 points, a fair design (with "no" answers indicating weak spots to be corrected); and below 9 points, a poor design—suggesting that profits may be reduced through lost sales and/or high manufacturing costs. This list is suitable for most manufactured products—except high-fashion items which are in a world of their own. Adaptations must be made for services.

This checklist helps to keep track of product design. But a purely *physical product* point of view is too narrow. Managers must also keep track of how a product is viewed by customers. One important tool is discussed next.

Product positioning aids product management

A new aid to marketing management—**product positioning**—shows where proposed and/or present brands are located in a market—as seen by customers. It requires some formal marketing research. The results are usually plotted on graphs to help show where the products are "positioned" in relation to competitors. Usually, the products' positions are related to two product features which are important to the target customers.

Assuming the picture is reasonably accurate, managers then decide whether they want to leave their product (and marketing mix) alone—or reposition the product. This may mean *physical changes* in the product—or simply *image changes based on promotion.* For example, most beer drinkers can't pick out their "favorite" brand in a blind test—so physical changes might not be necessary (and might not even work) to reposition a beer brand.

The graphs for product positioning decisions are obtained by asking product users to make judgments about different brands—and then computer programs summarize the ratings and plot the results. In addition to current brands, consumers are sometimes asked to rate their "ideal" brand—and it is included in the analysis. The details of product positioning techniques—sometimes called "perceptual mapping"—are beyond the scope of this text.[11] But, Figure 11–10 shows the possibilities.

Figure 11–10 shows the "product space" for different brands of bar soap using two dimensions—the extent to which consumers think the soaps moisturize and deodorize their skin. For example, consumers see Dial as quite low on moisturizing—but high on deodorizing. Lifebuoy and Dial are close together—implying that consumers think of them as similar on these characteristics. Dove is viewed as different—and is further away on the graph. Remember that positioning maps are based on customers' perceptions—the actual characteristics of the products (as determined by a chemical test) might be different!

The circles on Figure 11–10 show sets of consumers clustered near their "ideal" soap preferences. Groups of respondents with a similar "ideal" product are circled to show apparent customer concentrations. In this graph, the size of the circles suggests the size of the segments for the different ideals.

Ideal clusters 1 and 2 are the largest and are close to two popular brands—Dial and Safeguard. It appears that customers in cluster 1 want more moisturizing than they see in Dial and Lifebuoy. However, exactly what these brands

■ FIGURE 11–10   "Product space" representing consumers' perceptions for different brands of soap

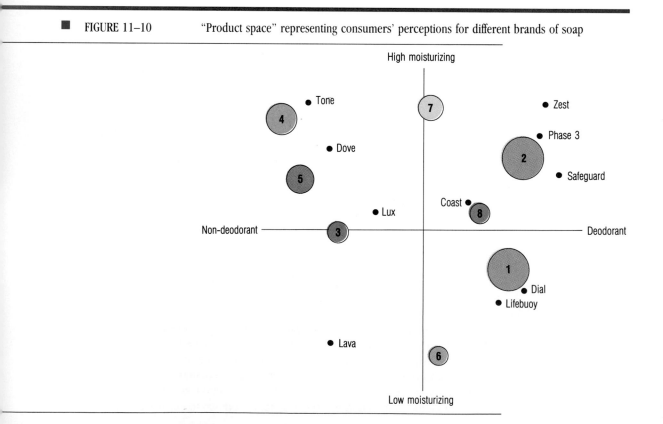

should do about this requires some thought. Perhaps both of these brands should leave their physical products alone—but emphasize moisturizing more in their promotion, to make a stronger appeal to those who want moisturizers.

Lava does not appear to satisfy any of the "ideal clusters" very well. Therefore, some attempt probably should be made to reposition Lava—either through physical or image changes. However, management must make important strategy decisions here. Should Lava aim for cluster 1, for example, and compete head-on with Dial and Lifebuoy? Or should it compete with Lux for cluster 3? Or should it try to capture the smaller cluster 6 all by itself—and minimize direct competition?

Note that ideal cluster 7 is not near any of the present brands. This may suggest an opportunity for introducing a new product—a strong moisturizer with some deodorizers. If some firm chose to follow this approach, we would think of it as a segmenting effort.

Combining versus segmenting

Product positioning analysis may lead a firm to combining—rather than segmenting—if managers think they can make several general appeals to different parts of a "combined" market. For example, by varying its promotion, Coast might try to appeal to clusters 8, 1, and 2 with one product. On the other hand, there may be clearly defined sub-markets—and some parts of the market may be "owned" by one product or brand. In this case, segmenting efforts may be practical—moving the firm's own product into another segment of the general market area, where competition is weaker. This might require modifying the product—or simply changing the promotion appeal to make the product's image fit more closely with the desires of those customers.

Positioning as part of broader analysis

The major value of product positioning is to help managers see how customers see their market—it is a visual aid to understanding a product-market area. But product positioning usually focuses on specific product features—that is, it is product-oriented. There is the risk that important customer-related dimensions—including needs and attitudes—may be overlooked. But as part of a broader analysis of target markets, product positioning can be very useful. The first time such an analysis is done, managers may be shocked to see how much customers' perceptions of a market differ from their own. For this reason alone, product positioning is useful.

Premature emphasis on product features is dangerous, however. And it is easy to do if you start with a product-oriented definition of a market—as in the bar soap example. This leads to positioning bar soaps against bar soaps. But this can make a firm miss more basic shifts in markets. For example, bars might be losing popularity to liquid soaps. Or other products—like bath oils or bubble baths—may be part of the relevant competition. Such shifts would not be seen by only looking at alternative bar soap brands. The focus is just too narrow. Similarly, studying only alternative luxury cars is too narrow—if potential customers are considering spending their money not only on luxury cars but also on foreign travel or vacation homes. Recall our discussion of the status-symbol market in Chapter 3. See Figure 3–2. Focusing on the physical characteristics of different luxury cars might completely miss the relevant competition—and what should be emphasized in the promotion effort.

As we have emphasized throughout the text, it *is* necessary to understand potential needs and attitudes when planning products and marketing strategies. If customers are treating quite different products as substitutes, then a firm has to position itself against those products, too. Great care must be used to avoid focusing on physical product characteristics which are not the determining dimensions of the target market.

New-Product Development: A Total Company Effort

Top-level support is vital

New-product development must have the enthusiastic support of top management. New products tend to upset old routines that managers of established products often try in subtle but effective ways to maintain. So someone with top-level support needs to be responsible for new product development.[12]

Some organization helps

What specific product development organization is used may not be too important—as long as there is top management support. But rather than just leaving new-product development to anyone who is interested—perhaps in engineering, R&D, or sales—it is better to put someone in charge. This can be a person, a department, or a committee.

A new-product development department or committee helps make sure that new ideas are carefully evaluated and good ones profitably marketed. Who is involved in this evaluation is important. Conservative managers may kill too many—or even all—new ideas. Or they may create delays. Delays lead to late introduction—and give competitors a head start. A delay of even six months can make the difference between a product's success or failure.

A well-organized development process even makes it possible for a firm to copy others' successful ideas—quickly and profitably. This possibility should not be overlooked. No one company can always be first with the best new ideas.[13]

A complicated, integrated effort is needed

Developing new products should be a total company effort. The whole process—involving people in management, research, production, promotion, packaging, and branding—must move in steps from early exploration of ideas to development of the product. Even with a careful development process, many new products do fail. This usually happens, however, when the process has been hurried—or some steps have been skipped. It is always tempting to do this when some part of the process seems to indicate that the company has a "really good idea." But the process moves in steps—gathering different kinds of information along the way. Skipping some of the steps may lead to missing an important aspect that will make a whole strategy less profitable—or actually cause it to fail.

Learning from the mistakes of others

The importance of following a systematic market-oriented approach to new product introduction is not hard to prove. The efforts of Canada's industrial marketers to launch new products have been extensively studied.[14] Particular attention has been paid to why some of these products succeeded and others failed.

One important study concluded that the main general reason for product failure was that sales failed to materialize. "Underestimating competitive strength, overestimating the number of potential uses, and overestimating the price customers would pay for the new product were the three major causes of low sales. The majority of the dimensions or factors which appeared to explain many of the causes of low sales were also market related—a lack of understanding of the marketplace, the customer, and the competition."[15]

Another major factor distinguishing between success and failure appears to be the amount of time, effort, and money devoted to researching the market at various stages of development and commercialization. New-product failures were characterized by an almost complete neglect of marketing research and a corresponding overemphasis on technical considerations and on spending for R&D.[16] In contrast, marketing considerations had received far more attention in successful new-product launches.[17]

Need for Product Managers

Product variety leads to product managers

When a firm has only one or a few related products, everyone is interested in them. But when many new products are being developed, someone should be put in charge of new-product planning—to be sure it is not neglected. Similarly, when a firm has several different kinds of products, management may decide to put someone in charge of each kind—or even each brand—to be sure they are not lost in the rush of everyday business. **Product managers** or **brand managers** manage specific products—often taking over the jobs formerly handled by an advertising manager. That gives a clue to what is often their major responsibility—Promotion—since the products have already been developed by the "new-product" people.

Product managers are especially common in large companies which produce many kinds of products. Several product managers may serve under a marketing manager. Sometimes these product managers are responsible for the profitable operation of the whole marketing effort for a particular product. Then, they have to coordinate their efforts with others—including the sales manager, advertising agencies, and production and research people.

In some companies, the product manager has a lot of power—and profit responsibility. He has difficulties, however, because although he has responsibility for profit, he usually has no authority over other functional areas whose efforts he is expected to direct and coordinate!

In other companies, the product manager may serve mainly as a "product champion"—concerned with planning and getting the promotion effort implemented. The activities of product managers vary a lot—depending on their experience and aggressiveness—and the company's organizational philosophy. Today, companies are emphasizing marketing *experience*—as it becomes clearer that this important job takes more than academic training and enthusiasm. But it is clear that someone must be responsible for developing and implementing product-related plans—especially when a company has many products.[18]

Can as strong a case for the product management system be made in Canada? Differences of opinion exist on this issue. One detailed study of American-owned producers of frequently purchased, relatively low-priced packaged goods concluded that these Canadian-based firms were applying the product management concept in a manner similar to their U.S. parents and encountering the same kinds of successes and problems.[19]

Another study of Canada's leading advertisers revealed, however, that a substantial proportion of American-owned firms and a majority of the larger Canadian-owned advertisers do not use the product manager system.[20] In such firms, responsibility for the advertising of all products is assigned to the advertising manager, responsibility for sales promotion to the manager of that activity, and so forth.

The popularity of this alternate, so-called functional, approach is consistent with the view that the Canadian market for a given product or brand often is not large enough to justify a product management system. American-owned packaged goods manufacturers have also been criticized for importing into Canada, without paying enough attention to local conditions, a form of marketing organization that may be too costly or otherwise inappropriate.

■ CONCLUSION

Product planning is an increasingly important activity in a modern economy—because it is no longer very profitable to sell just "commodities." Product positioning was described as an aid to product planning—helping to see where products and brands are positioned in a market.

The product life cycle concept is especially important to marketing strategy planning because it shows that different marketing mixes—and even strategies—are needed as a product moves through its cycle. This is an important point, because profits change during the life cycle—with most of the profits going to the innovators or fast copiers.

We pointed out that a new product is not limited to physical newness. We will call a product "new" if

it is new in any way—to any target market. But Consumer and Corporate Affairs Canada takes a narrower view of what you can call "new."

New products are so important to the survival of firms that some organized process for developing them is needed. Such a process was discussed—and it is obvious that it must be a total company effort to be successful.

The failure rate of new products is high—but it is lower for larger and better-managed firms that recognize product development and management as vital processes. Some firms appoint product managers to manage individual products—and new-product committees to assure that the process is carried out successfully.

■ QUESTIONS AND PROBLEMS

1. Explain how industry sales and industry profits behave over the product life cycle.

2. Cite two examples of products which you feel are currently in each of the product life cycle stages.

3. Explain how different conclusions might be reached with respect to the correct product life cycle stage(s) in the automobile market—especially if different views of the market are held.

4. Can product life cycles be extended? Illustrate your answer for a specific product.

5. Discuss the life cycle of a product in terms of its probable impact on a manufacturer's marketing mix. Illustrate using battery-operated toothbrushes.

6. Distinguish between fad and fashion. How should a retailer adapt to them? Some people maintain that fads or fashions can be created by businesses. Can you give an example of any companies that have *consistently* created successful fads or fashions? *Consistently* is important because anyone can be lucky a few times; the successes are publicized, but the failures are not.

7. Explain how product positioning differs from segmenting markets. Is target marketing involved in product positioning?

8. What is a new product? Illustrate your answer.

9. Discuss how the checklist "Good design: Does your product have it?" (Figure 11–9) can be used to evaluate (*a*) a can opener, (*b*) a baby stroller, (*c*) men's hats (fedoras), (*d*) a coffeemaker.

10. Explain the importance of an organized new-product development process and illustrate how it might be used for (*a*) an improved phonograph, (*b*) new frozen-food items, (*c*) a new children's toy.

11. Explain the role of product or brand managers. Are they usually put in charge of new-product development?

12. Discuss the social value of new-product development activities which seem to encourage people to discard products that are not "all worn out." Is this an economic waste? How worn out is "all worn out"? Must a shirt have holes in it? How big?

■ SUGGESTED CASES

8. Last Mountain Ski Resort, Ltd.

33. Diamond Jim's Pizza Company

■ NOTES

1. George Day, "The Product Life Cycle: Analysis and Applications Issues," *Journal of Marketing* 45, no. 4 (Fall 1981), pp. 60–67; John E. Swan and David R. Rink, "Fitting Marketing Strategy to Varying Product Life Cycles," *Business Horizons* 25, no. 1 (January/February 1982), pp. 72–76; Igal Ayal, "International Product Life Cycle: A Reassessment and Prod-

uct Policy Implications," *Journal of Marketing* 45, no. 4 (Fall 1981), pp. 91–96; Stephen G. Harrell and Elmer D. Taylor, "Modeling the Product Life Cycle for Consumer Durables," *Journal of Marketing* 45, no. 4 (Fall 1981), pp. 68–75; William Qualls, Richard W. Olshavsky, and Ronald E. Michaels, "Shortening of the PLC—An Empirical Test," *Journal of Mar-

keting 45, no. 4 (Fall 1981), pp. 76–80; Gerard J. Tellis and C. Merle Crawford, "An Evolutionary Approach to Product Growth Theory," *Journal of Marketing* 45, no. 4 (Fall 1981), pp. 125–32; Hans B. Thorelli and Stephen C. Burnett, "The Nature of Product Life Cycles for Industrial Goods Businesses," *Journal of Marketing* 45, no. 4 (Fall 1981), pp. 97–108; David F. Midgley, "Toward a Theory of the Product Life Cycle: Explaining Diversity," *Journal of Marketing* 45, no. 4 (Fall 1981), pp. 109–15; and Bernard Catry and Michel Chevalier, "Market Share Strategy and the Product Life Cycle," *Journal of Marketing*, October 1974, pp. 29–34.

2. "RCA to Cut Prices on Eight Color TVs in Promotion Effort," *The Wall Street Journal*, December 31, 1976, p. 16; "Sales of Major Appliances, TV Sets Gain; But Profits Fail to Keep Up: Gap May Widen," *The Wall Street Journal*, August 21, 1972, p. 22; "What Do You Do When Snowmobiles Go on a Steep Slide?" *The Wall Street Journal*, March 8, 1978, pp. 1,33; "After Their Slow Year, Fast-Food Chains Use Ploys to Speed Up Sales," *The Wall Street Journal*, April 4, 1980, p. 1 f; "Home Smoke Detectors Fall On Hard Times as Sales Apparently Peaked," *The Wall Street Journal*, April 3, 1980, p. 1; and "As Once Bright Market for CAT Scanners Dims, Smaller Makers of the X-Ray Devices Fade Out," *The Wall Street Journal*, May 6, 1980, p. 40.

3. George B. Sproles, "Analyzing Fashion Life Cycles—Principles and Perspectives," *Journal of Marketing* 45, no. 4 (Fall 1981), pp. 116–24; "Fad, Fashion, or Style?" *Saturday Review*, February 5, 1977, pp. 52–53; Claude R. Martin, Jr., "What Consumers of Fashion Want to Know," *Journal of Retailing*, Winter 1971–72, pp. 65–71; Alfred H. Daniels, "Fashion Merchandising," *Harvard Business Review*, May 1951, pp. 51–60. See also Chester R. Wasson, "How Predictable Are Fashion and Other Product Life Cycles?" *Journal of Marketing*, July 1968, pp. 36–43; "Troubled Industry (Apparel)" and "Durable Denims," *The Wall Street Journal*, January 11, 1977, p. 1, and February 7, 1977, p. 1.; Dwight E. Robinson, "Style Changes: Cyclical, Inexorable, and Foreseeable," *Harvard Business Review*, November-December 1975, pp. 121–31; "Playtex: Buying Its Way from Function to Fashion," *Business Week*, July 7, 1980, pp. 40–41; and Jonathon Gutman and Michael K. Mills, "Fashion Life-Style, Self-Concept, Shopping Orientation, and Store Patronage," *Journal of Retailing* 58, no. 2, (Summer 1982), pp. 64–86.

4. "'Good Products Don't Die,' P&G Chairman Declares," *Advertising Age*, November 1, 1976, p. 8; "Detroit Brings Back the Fast, Flashy Auto to Aid Sluggish Sales," *The Wall Street Journal*, December 9, 1976, p. 1 f; and "Ten Ways to Restore Vitality to Old, Worn-Out Products," *The Wall Street Journal*, February 18, 1982, p. 25.

5. *Business Week*, April 22, 1967, p.120.

6. Chester R. Wasson, "What is 'New' About New Products?" *Journal of Marketing*, July 1960, pp. 52–56; Patrick M. Dunne, "What Really Are New Products?" *Journal of Business*, December 1974, pp. 20–25; and S. H. Britt and V. M. Nelson, "The Marketing Importance of the 'Just Noticeable Difference,'" *Business Horizons*, August 1976, pp. 38–40.

7. *Marketing News*, February 8, 1980; C. Merle Crawford, "Marketing Research and the New-Product Failure Rate," *Journal of Marketing*, April 1977, pp. 51–61.

8. Adapted from Frank R. Bacon, Jr., and Thomas W. Butler, Jr., *Planned Innovation*, rev. ed. (Ann Arbor: Institute of Science and Technology, University of Michigan, 1980). See also John R. Rockwell and Marc C. Particelli, "New Product Strategy: How the Pros Do It," *Industrial Marketing*, May 1982, 49 ff; G. Urban and J. Hauser, *Design and Marketing of New Products* (Englewood Cliffs, N.J.: Prentice Hall, 1980); David S. Hopkins, "New Emphasis in Product Plan-

ning and Strategy Development," *Industrial Marketing Management Journal* 6 (1977), pp. 410–19; Richard P. Greenthal and John A. Larson, "Venturing Into Venture Capital," *Business Horizons* 25, no. 5 (September/October 1982), pp. 18–23; Eric von Hippel, "Get New Products from Customers," *Harvard Business Review* 60, no. 2, (March-April 1982), pp. 117–22; Shelby H. McIntyre and Meir Statman, "Managing the Risk of New Product Development," *Business Horizons* 25, no. 3 (May/June 1982), pp. 51–55; and "Listening to the Voice of the Marketplace," *Business Week*, February 21, 1983, p. 90 f.

9. "Dictating Product Safety," *Business Week*, May 18, 1974, pp 56–62; L. A. Bennigson and A. I. Bennigson, "Product Liability: Manufacturers Beware!" *Harvard Business Review*, May-June 1974, pp. 122–32; and L. J. Loudenback and J. W. Goebel, "Marketing in the Age of Strict Liability," *Journal of Marketing*, January 1974, pp. 62–66.

10. "Inflation in Product Liability," *Business Week*, May 31, 1976, p. 60; Jane Mallor, "In Brief: Recent Products Liability Cases," *Business Horizons*, October 1979, pp. 47–49; and William L. Trombetta, "Products Liability: What New Court Ruling Means for Management," *Business Horizons*, August 1979, pp. 67–72.

11. David A. Aaker and J. Gary Shansby, "Positioning Your Product," *Business Horizons* 25, no. 3 (May/June 1982), pp. 56–62; Al Ries and Jack Trout, *Positioning: The Battle for Your Mind* (New York: McGraw-Hill, 1981), p. 53; and D. W. Cravens, "Marketing Strategy Positioning," *Business Horizons*, December 1975, pp. 47–54.

12. Phillip R. McDonald and Joseph O. Eastlack, Jr., "Top Management Involvement with New Products," *Business Horizons*, December 1971, pp. 23–31; John H. Murphy, "New Products Need Special Management," *Journal of Marketing*, October 1962, pp. 46–49; and E. J. McCarthy, "Organization for New-Product Development?" *Journal of Business of the University of Chicago*, April 1959, pp. 128–32.

13. See T. Levitt, "Innovation Imitation," *Harvard Business Review*, September-October 1966, pp. 63–70; and Shelby H. McIntyre, "Obstacles to Corporate Innovation," *Business Horizons* 25, no. 1 (January/February 1982), pp. 23–28.

14. Blair Little, "Characterizing the New Product for Better Evaluation and Planning," *Working Paper Series*, no. 21 (London: University of Western Ontario, July 1970); and Robert G. Cooper and Blair Little, "Reducing the Risk of Industrial New-Product Development," *The Canadian Marketer* 7, no. 2 (Fall 1974), pp. 7–12.

15. Robert G. Cooper, "Why New Industrial Products Fail," *Industrial Marketing Management* 4 (1975), pp. 315–26.

16. Ibid.

17. Robert G. Cooper, *Winning the New Product Game* (Montreal: McGill Faculty of Management, 1976).

18. Richard T. Hise and J. Patrick Kelly, "Product Management on Trial," *Journal of Marketing*, October 1978, pp. 28–33; and Victor P. Buell, "The Changing Role of the Product Manager in Consumer Goods Companies," *Journal of Marketing*, July 1975, pp. 3–11.

19. A. M. Ragab and A. W. Babcock, "An Investigation into the Practice of the Product Manager Concept by Selected Canadian Companies," in *Marketing in the 1970s and Beyond*, ed. Bent Stidsen, proceedings of the 1975 meetings of the Marketing Association of the Canadian Association of Administrative Sciences, Edmonton, Alberta, 1975.

20. Charles LeRoyer and Edward Clements, *How Companies in Canada Plan, Manage, and Control Their Advertising Programs* (Montreal: Faculty of Management, McGill University, 1975). Funding for the study was provided by the Advertising and Sales Executives Club of Montreal.

Chapter 12 ■ Place and development of channel systems

When you finish this chapter, you should:

1. Understand how and why marketing specialists adjust discrepancies of quantity and assortment.
2. Understand what goods classes suggest about place objectives.
3. Know about the different kinds of channel systems.
4. Understand how much market exposure is "ideal."
5. Understand how to obtain cooperation and avoid conflict in channel systems.
6. Know how channel systems can shift and share functions.
7. Recognize the important new terms (shown in red).

You may build a "better mousetrap," but if it's not in the right place at the right time, it won't do anyone any good.

Offering customers a good product at a reasonable price is important to a successful marketing strategy—but it isn't enough. Managers must also think about **Place**—which involves making products available in the right quantities and locations when customers want them. Place often requires the selection and use of marketing specialists—middlemen and facilitators—to provide target customers with time, place, and possession utilities.

There are many ways to provide Place—so, many decisions are involved. Magnavox televisions are sold by a selected group of stores—while Zenith televisions are sold by many more retailers. Many industrial goods are sold by the producer direct to the customer. But most consumer goods are sold to middlemen—who later sell to the final consumer. Some middlemen carry only one brand in a product category. Others carry competing brands from different producers.

The many Place variations raise important questions. Why are some products sold by the producer direct to customers, while others are sold with the help of middlemen? Why are some products carried by many retailers—and others by only a few? In the next four chapters we will deal with these important questions. See Figure 12–1 for a "picture" of the Place decision areas we are going to discuss.

■ FIGURE 12–1   Strategic decision areas in Place

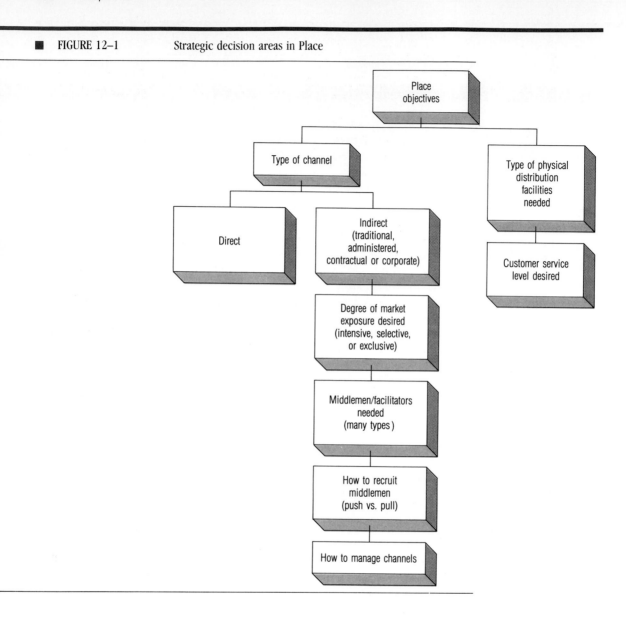

In this chapter, we will first consider Place objectives—and how they relate to goods classes. Then we'll take a look at some of the activities needed to provide Place. We will show why specialists are often involved and how they come together to form a **channel of distribution**—any series of firms or individuals who participate in the flow of goods and services from producer to final user or consumer. We will also consider how much market exposure is "ideal." Finally, we will discuss how relations among channel members can be managed—to reduce conflict and improve cooperation.

"Ideal" Place Objectives Suggested by Goods Classes

Obviously, the needs and attitudes of potential target markets should be considered when developing Place. We expect that people in a particular target market have similar attitudes and, therefore, can be satisfied with the same Place system. Their attitudes about urgency to have needs satisfied and willingness to shop are already included in the goods classes. Now you should be able to use the goods classes to suggest how Place should be handled.

The relationship between goods classes and *ideal Place objectives* was shown in Figure 10–3 for consumer goods and Figure 10–4 for industrial goods. Study these figures carefully—they set the framework for solving the whole Place problem. In particular, the goods classes help us to think about how much market exposure will be needed in each geographic area.

The marketing manager must also consider Place objectives in relation to the product life cycle when making Place decisions. Place decisions have long-run effects. They are harder to change than Product, Price, and Promotion decisions. Effective working arrangements with others in the channel may take several years—and a good deal of money—to develop. Legal contracts with channel partners may also limit changes. And it's hard to move retail stores and wholesale facilities once leases have been signed—and customer movement patterns are settled.

Place system is not automatic

Just as there are no automatic classifications of products, we cannot automatically determine the one "best" Place arrangement. If two or three market segments hold different views of the product, then different Place arrangements may be required.

Discrepancies Require Channel Specialists

In addition, Place depends on both (1) what customers prefer and (2) what channel members can provide profitably. And planning Place is complicated by the fact that the assortment and quantity of goods wanted by customers may be different than the assortment and quantity of goods normally produced.[1] Remember that we discussed this briefly in Chapter 1. Now we need to go into more detail—so you will be able to plan all kinds of channels of distribution.

Discrepancy of quantity—only a few golf balls are wanted

It is economically sensible for a producer to specialize and offer those products that it can produce most efficiently—given its resources and objectives. This specialization usually causes a producer to create a discrepancy of quantity. **Discrepancy of quantity** means the difference between the quantity of goods it is economical for a producer to make and the quantity normally wanted by final users or consumers. For example, most manufacturers of golf balls produce large quantities—200,000 to 500,000—in a given time period. See Figure 12–2.

■   FIGURE 12–2   Movement of golf from a manufacturer to consumers—showing discrepancy of
                               quantity produced, handled, handled by wholesalers and retailers, and desired
                               by consumers*

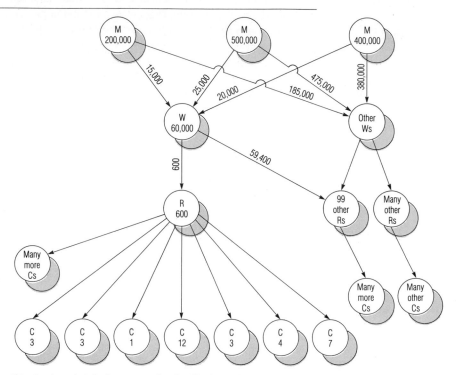

*Number in a circle indicates quantity of golf balls produced, handled, or desired: *M* = Manufacturer;
W = Wholesaler; *R* = Retailer; *C* = Consumer

The average golfer, however, is interested only in a few balls at a time. For a golf
ball manufacturer to deal directly with thousands of golfers would be a big job.
Each individual order would have to be mailed to the customer's home (unless he
lived right down the street). And then there would be a question of credit.

The solution to this problem is a local specialist—a retailer—who can fill the
various needs of individual consumers for a product—and ease the manufacturer's headaches. We now have one link in a channel of distribution.

But there still may be a great discrepancy between the quantity the manufacturer produces and the quantity each retailer wants. The solution to this problem
is wholesalers. They can serve perhaps 100 retailers each—another link in our
channel of distribution.

If we limit our discussion to the golf ball example alone, however, we only
partially explain the development of specialists. Why doesn't the producer simply
open wholesale branches and retail outlets—to adjust these discrepancies in
quantity?

Discrepancies of assortment and quantity explain why golf balls are sold in shops with other golfing products.

Discrepancy of assortment—clubs, bags, and shoes are wanted, too

The typical consumer usually doesn't want a large quantity of each item—but rather an assortment of products. The typical golfer, for example, needs more than golf balls. Golfers want golf shoes, gloves, clubs, a bag, and other golf needs. They probably don't want to shop around for each item.

While the typical consumer wants an assortment, the typical producer specializes by product—and so another discrepancy develops. **Discrepancy of assortment** means the difference between the lines the typical producer makes and the assortment wanted by final consumers or users. It is the job of specialists—wholesalers and retailers—to adjust the discrepancy of assortment by assembling assortments for their target customers. If retailers offer a wide assortment, they may sell enough to be an economical transaction for wholesalers. Along with orders for golf balls, for example, they might also place orders for other golf supplies—for delivery at the same time. The wholesalers, in turn, while assembling attractive size orders for their manufacturers, are also able to run profitable businesses—because of the large total sales volumes they get by selling for many manufacturers. See Figure 12–3.

In actual practice, bringing goods to customers isn't as simple as in the golf example. Specializing only in golfing products may not achieve all the economies possible in a channel of distribution. Sporting goods retailers usually carry even wider assortments of goods. And they buy from a variety of wholesalers who specialize by product line. Some of these wholesalers are supplied by other wholesalers. These complications will be discussed later. The important thing to remember is that discrepancies in quantity and assortment cause distribution problems for manufacturers—and explain why specialists develop.

Channel specialists adjust discrepancies with regrouping activities

It is not always necessary to overcome discrepancies of quantity and assortment, but if it is, regrouping activities are needed. **Regrouping activities** adjust the quantities and/or assortments of goods handled at each level in a channel of distribution.

■ FIGURE 12–3   Movement of golf supplies from manufacturers to consumers—showing adjustment of discrepancies of quantity and assortment

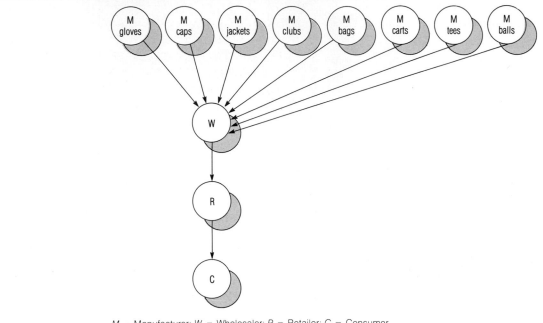

M = Manufacturer; W = Wholesaler; R = Retailer; C = Consumer

There are four regrouping activities: accumulating, bulk-breaking, sorting, and assorting. When one or more of these activities is required, a marketing specialist might develop to fill this need.

Adjusting quantity discrepancies by accumulating and bulk-breaking

Accumulating involves collecting products from many small producers. This is common for agricultural products—because they are often produced in relatively small quantities. Small apple farmers, for example, bring their apples in their own trucks to collecting points. Collecting larger quantities of such products is necessary so that the products can be handled economically further along the channel. It is especially important for obtaining the lowest transportation rate—by accumulating and shipping goods in truckload or carload quantities.

Bulk-breaking involves dividing larger quantities into smaller quantities as goods get closer to the final market. Sometimes this even starts at the manufacturer's level. A golf ball manufacturer may need 25 wholesalers to help sell the output of its ball-making machines. And the bulk-breaking may involve several levels of middlemen. Wholesalers may sell smaller quantities to other wholesalers—or directly to retailers. Retailers continue the bulk-breaking as they sell individual items to their customers.

Adjusting assortment discrepancies by sorting and assorting

Different types of specialists are needed to adjust assortment discrepancies. Two types of regrouping activities may be needed: sorting and assorting.

Sorting means separating products into grades and qualities desired by different target markets. This is a common process for agricultural products. Nature produces what it will, and these products must be sorted into grades and qualities desired by different target markets. For example, at an accumulating point for fresh apples, the fruit is sorted by grades and quality. Some is packed in boxes for food stores and restaurants. The rest is shipped to canneries for juice or applesauce.

Sorting may create assortments the producers or middlemen won't want. Some products may be of lower quality—or may not fit into the company's product line at all—and must be distributed to entirely different target markets. Minor defects in clothing, tires, and sporting goods, for example, may force the marketing manager to offer them—perhaps at little profit—as "seconds" in special "outlet stores."

Assorting means putting together a variety of products to give a target market what it wants. This usually is done by those close to the final consumer or user—retailers or wholesalers who try to supply a wide assortment of products for the convenience of their customers. A grocery store is a good example. But some assortments involve very different products—a wholesaler that wants to sell tractors and mowers to golf courses might also carry grass seed, fertilizer, and even irrigation systems—for the customers' convenience.

Watch for changes

Sometimes these discrepancies are adjusted badly—especially when rapid shifts in wants and attitudes occur. When jogging became popular, an opportunity developed for a new specialist. Consumers were interested in an assortment of running shoes, jogging clothes, and running information—all in one place.

Channel specialists sort products—in this case, eggs—according to grades and sizes desired by different target markets.

Rapid shifts in buying habits or preferences can result in discrepancies of assortment—and new marketing opportunities.

Most sporting goods stores placed more emphasis on other sports—and on equipment rather than on shoes and clothes. "Runners" stores developed to meet the need.

Specialists should develop to adjust discrepancies—*if they must be adjusted.* But there is no point in having middlemen just because "that's the way it has always been done." Sometimes a breakthrough opportunity can come from finding a better way to reduce discrepancies—and eliminate some middlemen specialists. For example, the Columbia Record Company found that it could sell records—profitably—by direct mail, thereby bypassing retail stores and the wholesalers who served them.

Marketing manager must choose type of channel

Middlemen specialists can help make a channel more efficient. But there may be problems getting different firms in a channel to work together well. How well the channel members work together depends on the type of relationship they have. This should be carefully considered—since marketing managers usually have choices about what type of channel system to join—or develop.

Marketing managers must choose among direct and indirect channel systems—see Figure 12–1. We'll talk about direct channels first and then the various indirect channels. (Figure 12–4 summarizes some characteristics of indirect channel systems.)

Direct Channel Systems May Be Best, Sometimes

Some producers would prefer to handle the whole distribution job themselves. They do not want to rely on independent middlemen—who have different objectives. Or they think they can adjust the discrepancies as well as available middle-

■   FIGURE 12–4   Types of indirect channel systems

	Traditional	Vertical marketing systems		
		Administered	Contractual	Corporate
Amount of cooperation	Little or none	Some to good	Fairly good to good	Complete
Control maintained by	None	Economic power and leadership	Contracts	Ownership by one company
Examples	Typical channel of "independents"	General Electric, Miller's Beer, O.M. Scott & Sons (lawn products)	McDonald's, Holiday Inn, IGA, Super Valu, Coca-Cola, Chevrolet	Florsheim Shoes, Firestone Tire

men. And some just want to control a large organization. In any case, there often *are* great advantages in selling direct to the final user or consumer.

If a firm is in direct contact with its customers, it is more aware of changes in customer attitudes. It is in a better position to adjust its marketing mix quickly—there is no need to convince other channel members to help. If aggressive selling effort or special technical service is needed, management can be sure that the sales force receives the necessary training and motivation. In contrast, middlemen often carry products of several competing manufacturers—and aren't willing to give any one item the special emphasis its manufacturer wants.

Direct-to-user channels are not uncommon. Many industrial products are sold direct. This is understandable—since there are fewer transactions and orders are larger. In some cases, leasing—rather than selling—may be sensible. Or producers and customers may need to talk directly about product specifications. Of course, some consumer goods are sold direct too. Avon cosmetics, Electrolux vacuum cleaners, Amway cleaning products, and Fuller Brush products are examples.

Some consumer goods companies—like Avon and Fuller Brush—have been very successful with direct-to-user channels.

Indirect Channels May Be Best, Sometimes

Although a producer might prefer to handle the whole distribution job, this is just not economically possible for many kinds of goods—unless the firm integrates and forms its own "vertical marketing system." Typically, producers have to use middlemen—like it or not. They join or develop one of the indirect channel systems described below—and summarized in Figure 12–4.

Traditional channel systems are common

In **traditional channel systems**—the various channel members make little or no effort to cooperate with each other. They buy and sell from each other—and that's all. Each channel member does only what it considers to be in its own best interest. It does not worry much about the effect of its policies on other members of the channel. This is shortsighted—but it is clear how it can happen. The objectives of different firms may be different. For example, an electrical building supplies producer wants a wholesaler to sell *his* products. But if the wholesaler carries an assortment of products from different manufacturers, he may not care whose products are sold—as long as his customers are happy and a fair profit margin is achieved.

Specialization has the potential to make a channel more efficient—but not if the specialists are so independent that the channel does not work smoothly. For example, in some very "independent" traditional channels, buyers may even prefer to wait until sellers desperately need to sell—hoping to force the price down. This leads to erratic production, inventory, and employment patterns that can only increase total costs.

Traditional channel members have their independence—but they may pay for it, too. As we will see, such channels are declining in importance—with good reason. But they are still typical in some industries.

Vertical marketing systems focus on final customers

In contrast to traditional channel systems are **vertical marketing systems**—channel systems in which the whole channel shares a common focus on the same target market at the end of the channel. Such systems make sense and are growing in importance—because if the final customer doesn't buy the product, the whole channel suffers. The three types of vertical marketing systems—corporate, administered, and contractual—are discussed below.

Corporate channel systems—shorten channels

Some corporations develop their own vertical marketing systems by internal expansion and/or buying other firms. With **corporate channel systems**—corporate ownership all along the channel—we might say the firm is going "direct"—but actually it may be handling manufacturing, wholesaling, *and* retailing—and it is more accurate to think of it as running a vertical marketing system.

Vertical integration is at different levels

Corporate channel systems are often developed by **vertical integration**—acquiring firms at different levels of channel activity—for example, two or more successive stages of production or distribution. Firestone, for example, has rub-

ber plantations in Liberia, tire plants in Quebec, Ontario, and Alberta, and Firestone wholesale and retail outlets all across the country.

Corporate channel systems are not always started by manufacturers. A retailer might integrate into wholesaling—and perhaps even manufacturing. A&P has fish canning plants. Bata and Florsheim make their own shoes. Steinberg has its own bakeries.

There are many possible advantages to vertical integration—stability of operations, assurance of materials and supplies, better control of distribution, better quality control, larger research facilities, greater buying power, and lower executive overhead. The economies of vertical integration benefit the consumer, too, through lower prices and better products.

Provided that the discrepancies of quantity and assortment are not too great at each level in a channel—that is, the firms fit together well—vertical integration can be extremely efficient and profitable.

Horizontal integration may be needed, too

At first, it may seem that **horizontal integration**—acquiring of firms at the same level of activity—has little to do with channels of distribution—which are usually shown as vertical. But discrepancies of quantity and assortment are relevant here, too.

To have enough sales volume to integrate vertically, a firm might have to integrate horizontally—or expand its horizontal operations by internal expansion. Woolworth's, K mart, A&P, Safeway Stores, and Florsheim Shoes have expanded or integrated horizontally at the retail level. General Motors of Canada integrated horizontally at the producer level—with plants and divisions around the country and the world.

Administered and contractual systems may work well

Although a company may prefer to handle the whole distribution job, this just isn't economically feasible for many kinds of goods. Often the advantages of a vertical marketing system can be had without building a corporate channel. A firm can develop administered or contractual channel systems instead. In **administered channel systems**, the various channel members informally agree to cooperate with each other. This can include agreements to routinize ordering, standardize accounting, and coordinate promotion efforts. In **contractual channel systems**, the various channel members agree by contract to cooperate with each other. With both of these systems, the members achieve some of the advantages of corporate integration—while retaining some of the flexibility of a traditional channel system.

A U.S. appliance manufacturer, for example, developed an informal arrangement with the independent wholesalers in its administered channel system—agreeing to keep production and inventory levels in the system balanced—using sales data from the wholesalers. Every week, its managers make a thorough item-by-item analysis of up to 130,000 major appliance units located in the many warehouses operated by its 87 wholesalers throughout the country. This helps the manufacturer plan production and shipments to maintain adequate inventory levels and helps the wholesalers manage their inventories. The wholesalers can be sure that they have enough inventory—but not the expense of too much—or the need to worry about it. And the manufacturer has better information to plan its manufacturing and marketing efforts.

Similar systems have been developed and coordinated by middlemen in the grocery, hardware, and drug industries. Electronic cash registers keep track of what has been sold. The information is sent to the wholesaler's computer, and an order is automatically entered. This reduces buying and selling costs, inventory investment, and customer frustration with "out-of-stock" items.

The Best Channel System Should Achieve Ideal Market Exposure

Although it might seem that all marketing managers would want their products to have maximum exposure to potential customers, this isn't true. Some goods classes require much less market exposure that others.

Ideal market exposure makes a product widely enough available to satisfy target customers' needs—but not exceed them. Too much exposure only increases the total marketing cost.

Market exposure can be intensive, selective, or exclusive

We will discuss three degrees of market exposure.

Intensive distribution is selling a product through all responsible and suitable wholesalers or retailers who will stock and/or sell the product. **Selective distribution** is selling through only those middlemen who will give the product special attention. **Exclusive distribution** is selling through only one middleman in a particular geographic area. As we move from intensive to exclusive distribution, we give up exposure in return for some other advantage—including, but not limited to, lower cost.

In practice, this means that cigarettes are handled—through intensive distribution—by at least 90,000 Canadian outlets, while Rolls Royces or expensive chinaware are handled—through exclusive distribution—by only a limited number of middlemen across the country.

Intensive distribution—sell it where they buy it

Intensive distribution is commonly needed for convenience goods and for industrial supplies—such as pencils, paper clips, and typing paper—used by all plants and offices. Customers want such goods nearby.

Manufacturers of new unsought goods that must compete with convenience goods usually want to achieve intensive distribution. They may not be able to get this degree of exposure—because customers aren't demanding their products and so the channel isn't willing to carry them. Nevertheless, these manufacturers may choose an intensive distribution policy.

The seller's *intent* is important here. Intensive distribution refers to the *desire* to sell through *all* responsible and suitable outlets. What this means depends on customer habits and preferences. If target customers normally buy a certain product at a certain type of outlet, ideally, you would specify this type of outlet in your Place policies. If customers prefer to buy hardware items only at hardware

Many designer fashions are distributed selectively.

stores, you would try to sell all hardware stores to achieve intensive distribution. Today, however, many customers buy some hardware items at any convenient outlet—including drug stores and food stores. Logically, this means that an intensive distribution policy requires use of these outlets—and more than one channel—to reach one target market.

Intensive distribution usually requires help from more middlemen. More channels may be involved—and discrepancies of assortment may be solved through additional levels of specialists who do bulk-breaking and assorting.

Selective distribution—sell it where it sells best

Selective distribution covers the broad band of market exposure between intensive and exclusive distribution. It may be suitable for all categories of products. Only the better middlemen are used here. The usual reason for going to selective distribution is to gain some of the advantages of exclusive distribution—while still achieving fairly widespread market coverage.

A selective policy might be used to avoid selling to wholesalers or retailers who (1) have a poor credit rating, (2) have a reputation for making too many returns or requesting too much service, (3) place orders that are too small to justify making calls or providing service, or (4) are not in a position to do a satisfactory job.

Selective distribution is growing in popularity—over intensive distribution—as firms see that it is not necessary to have 100 percent coverage of a market to justify or support national advertising. Often, the majority of sales come from relatively few customers—and the others buy too little compared to the cost of working with them. That is, they are unprofitable to serve. This is called the "80/20 rule"—because 80 percent of a company's sales often come from only 20 percent of its customers—*until it becomes more selective in choosing customers.*

Selective distribution can produce greater profits for all channel members—because of the closer cooperation among them. Transactions become more routine—requiring less negotiation in the buying and selling process. Wholesalers and retailers are more willing to give aggressive promotion to products—if they know they are going to obtain the majority of sales produced through their own efforts. They may carry more stock and wider lines, do more promotion, and provide more service—all of which contribute to increased sales.

Selective distribution makes sense for shopping and specialty goods—and for those industrial goods that need special efforts from channel members. It reduces interchannel competition and gives each of the members a greater opportunity for profit.

When selective distribution is used by manufacturers, fewer sales contacts have to be made—and fewer wholesalers are needed. In fact—as in the garment industry—a manufacturer may be able to contact retailers directly if selective distribution is suitable at the retail level.

In the early part of the life cycle of a new unsought good, a manufacturer's marketing manager may have to use selective distribution to encourage enough middlemen to handle the product. The manager wants to get the product out of the unsought category as soon as possible—but he can't as long as it lacks distribution. Well-known middlemen may have the power to get such a product introduced—but sometimes on their own terms, which often include limiting the number of competing wholesalers and retailers. The manufacturer may be happy with such an arrangement at the time but dislike it later when other retailers want to carry the product.

Exclusive distribution sometimes makes sense

Exclusive distribution is just an extreme case of selective distribution—only one middleman is selected in each geographic area. Besides the various advantages of selective distribution, manufacturers might want to use exclusive distribution—to help control prices and the service offered in a channel.

Unlike selective distribution, exclusive distribution arrangements usually involve a verbal or written agreement stating that channel members will buy all or most of a given kind of product line from the seller. In return, these middlemen are granted the exclusive rights to that product in their territories. Many middlemen are so anxious to get a manufacturer's exclusive franchise that they will do practically anything to satisfy the manufacturer's demands. Retailers of shopping goods and specialty goods often try to get exclusive distribution rights in their territories. And owners of fast-food franchises—like McDonald's—willingly pay a share of sales and follow company strategy to have the exclusive right to a market.

But is limiting market exposure legal?

Marketing managers must operate within the law, and any consideration of Place must raise the question of the legality of limiting market exposure.

Exclusive distribution, as such, is not illegal in Canada. Indeed, "vertical" exclusive distribution contracts between a manufacturer and middleman have yet to be successfully challenged in the courts. "Horizontal" arrangements among competing retailers, wholesalers, and/or manufacturers would almost certainly be judged a violation of Section 32 of the Combines Act which deals with monopolies. However, it would have to be proven that such agreements had "unduly lessened competition."

Stage 1 Amendments to the Combines Act gave the Restrictive Trade Practices Commission the authority to review "vertical" agreements and to act against those judged as having an adverse effect upon competition. This legislation (Bill C-2) also specified that "unduly lessening competition" meant lessening it to any extent judged detrimental to the public interest. (Previously it had to be shown that competition would be completely or virtually eliminated). The Stage 1 amendments also allow temporary exclusive dealing arrangements in order to permit the introduction of a new product or where there is some technological justification for such a policy.

Caution is suggested

Obviously, considerable caution must be exercised before firms enter into any exclusive dealing arrangement. The same probably holds true for selective distribution. Here, however, less formal and binding arrangements are typical—and the chance of an adverse impact on competition being proven is more remote.

Channel Systems Can Be Complex

Trying to achieve the desired degree of market exposure can lead to complex channels of distribution. Different channels may be required to reach different segments of a broad product-market—or to be sure that each segment is reached. Sometimes this results in competition between different channels. Figure 12–5 shows the many channels used by manufacturers of paperback books. These books are both consumer goods and industrial goods—so this helps explain why some channels develop. But note that the books go through wholesalers and retailers—independent and chain bookstores, drug stores, supermarkets, and convenience stores. This can cause problems—because these wholesalers supply retailers who take different markups. This increases competition—including price competition. And the different markups may lead to open price wars—especially on branded products.

■ FIGURE 12–5   Sales of paperback books are made through many kinds of wholesalers and retailers

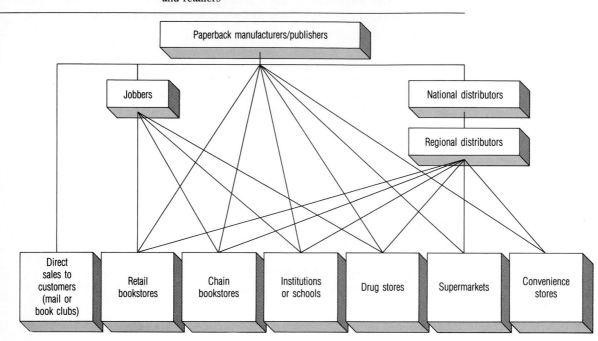

Source: Neil Suits, Suits News Company, Lansing, Michigan.

Dual distribution systems may be needed

Dual distribution occurs when a manufacturer uses several competing channels to reach the same target market—perhaps using several middlemen in addition to selling directly itself. This is becoming more common. Big retail chains want to deal directly with producers. They want large quantities—and low prices. The producer will sell direct to retail chains—and rely on wholesalers to sell to smaller accounts. Some established middlemen resent this because they do not appreciate *any* competition—but especially price competition set up by their own suppliers. Other times, manufacturers are forced to use dual distribution because their present channels are doing a poor job—or aren't reaching some potential customers.

Sometimes there's not much choice of middlemen

The paperback example seems to suggest that there are plenty of middlemen around to form almost any kind of channel system. But this isn't true. Sometimes there is only one key middleman serving a market. To reach this market, producers may have no choice but to use this one middleman—if he is willing.

In other cases, there are no middleman at all! Then a producer may try to go directly to target customers. If this isn't economically possible, the product may die! Some products aren't wanted in big enough volume and/or at high enough prices to justify any middlemen providing the regrouping activities needed to reach potential customers.

How to Recruit Middlemen

A producer has a special challenge ensuring that the product reaches the end of the channel. Middlemen—especially retailers—don't have this problem since they already control that end of the channel. To reach the target market, a producer may have to recruit middlemen.

The two basic methods of recruiting middlemen are pushing and pulling.

Pushing policy—get a hand from the firms in the channel

Pushing (a product through a channel) means using normal promotion effort—personal selling and advertising—to help sell the whole marketing mix to possible channel members. This method is common—since these sales transactions are usually between rational, presumably profit-oriented buyers and sellers. The approach emphasizes the importance of building a channel—and securing the wholehearted cooperation of channel members. The producer—in effect—

When the channel system for this product changed, the package and other elements of the marketing mix changed, too.

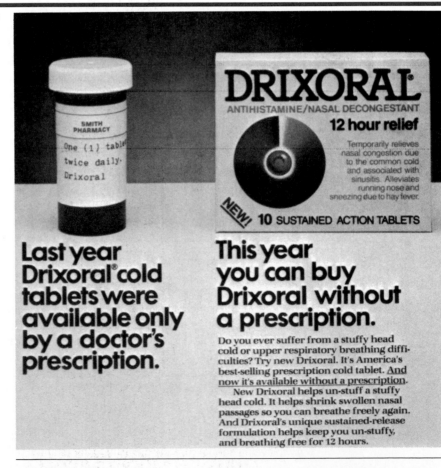

Last year Drixoral® cold tablets were available only by a doctor's prescription.

This year you can buy Drixoral without a prescription.

Do you ever suffer from a stuffy head cold or upper respiratory breathing difficulties? Try new Drixoral. It's America's best-selling prescription cold tablet. And now it's available without a prescription.

New Drixoral helps un-stuff a stuffy head cold. It helps shrink swollen nasal passages so you can breathe freely again. And Drixoral's unique sustained-release formulation helps keep you un-stuffy, and breathing free for 12 hours.

tries to develop a team that will work well—to "push" the product down the channel to the final user.

**Pulling policy—
makes them reach for
it out there**

By contrast, **pulling** means getting consumers to ask middlemen for the product. This usually involves highly aggressive and expensive promotion to final consumers or users—perhaps using coupons or samples—and temporary bypassing of middlemen. If the promotion works, the middlemen are forced to carry the product—to satisfy customer requests.

This method may be used if many products are already competing in all desired outlets—and channel members are reluctant to handle a new product. But channel members should be told about the planned pulling effort—so they can be ready if the promotion is successful.

Channels Need to Be Managed

**Some conflict is
natural**

Our discussion of vertical marketing systems makes it clear there are many good reasons for cooperation within a channel system. But there are also reasons why conflicts arise—and these should be anticipated and managed, if possible. For example, horizontal conflicts occur when middlemen's territories overlap and they argue over taking each other's business or "predatory pricing." In these cases, careful administration of selective or even exclusive distribution policies is helpful. But problems should be expected—and middlemen are now forming their own "dealer councils" to discuss problems—as well as potential vertical conflicts with their suppliers.

Vertical conflicts can occur also. Policies which may be "good" for the producer—perhaps expanding *its* sales by lowering suggested retail prices (by reducing the middlemen's margins)—may not be quite as "good" for the middlemen. And dual distribution conflicts can easily happen unless channel systems are very carefully planned. This leads us to the channel captain concept.

**Channel captain can
guide channel
planning**

We can now see that it is logical that each channel system should act as a unit—perhaps directed by a **channel captain**—a manager who helps direct the activities of a whole channel and tries to avoid—or solve—channel conflicts.

The concept of a single channel captain is logical. But some channels—including most traditional channels—do not have a recognized captain. The various firms do not act as a system. The reason may be lack of leadership—or members of the system may not understand their interrelationship. Many managers—more concerned with those firms immediately above and below them—seem unaware that they are part of a channel.[2]

But, like it or not, firms are interrelated—even if poorly—by their policies. And there is potential for conflict in the buyer-seller relationship. So it makes sense to try to avoid channel conflicts by planning for channel relations.

Manufacturer or middleman?	In North America, manufacturers frequently take the lead in channel relations. Middlemen wait to see what the manufacturer intends to do—and what he wants done. After the manufacturer sets Price, Promotion, and Place policies, middlemen decide whether their roles will be profitable—and whether they want to join in the manufacturer's plans. Middlemen may not play an active role in building the channel—but they must be considered by manufacturers in their planning, if only because middlemen have the power to say *no*.
Some middlemen dominate their channels	There are large or well-located middlemen who do take the lead—especially in foreign markets where there are fewer large manufacturers. Such middlemen analyze the types of products their customers want and then seek out manufacturers—perhaps small ones—who can provide these products at reasonable prices.

Sometimes these middlemen develop their own dealer brands. Or they handle manufacturers' brands—but on their own terms. In effect, strong middlemen like this act like manufacturers. They specify the whole marketing mix for a product—and merely delegate production to a factory.

Middlemen are closer to the final user or consumer—and are in an ideal position to assume the channel captain role. It is even possible that middlemen—especially retailers—may dominate the marketing system of the future.

Middlemen are especially likely to serve as channel captains when a limited number of companies account for a substantial proportion of retail sales. This is often the case in Canada and especially true in the grocery trade. Five Canadian chains account for about 40 percent of all grocery outlet sales.[3] Few manufacturers can afford to argue with these chains on pricing or merchandising matters for fear that their products will no longer be carried.[4]

The whole channel competes with other channels	It is extremely important for a whole channel system to view itself in competition with other systems. Without this view, one firm might adopt policies clearly unfavorable to another member of the same system. In the short run, a stronger firm might succeed in forcing its policies by sheer weight of market power. Yet, in the long run, this might lead to failure—not only of a weaker channel member but of the whole team.

The person or firm that helps direct a vertical marketing system is the leader. We will consider that person the channel captain. The captain's identity may change from time to time—depending on the success of product development or promotion efforts, financial reserves, or management personalities—but this does not change the concept or its impact on marketing.[5]

Product-market commitment can guide strategy	It helps to think of all the members of a vertical marketing system having a *product-market commitment*—with all members focusing on the same target market at the end of the channel—and sharing the various marketing functions in appropriate ways.

The job of the channel captain is to arrange for the performance of the necessary functions in the most effective way. This might be done as shown in Figure 12–6 in a manufacturer-dominated channel system. Here, the manufacturer has selected the target market and developed the Product, set the Price structure,

■ FIGURE 12–6   How channel strategy might be handled in a manufacturer-dominated system

Manufacturer's part of the job   Middleman's part of the job

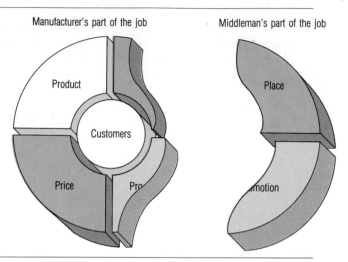

Source: Adapted from D. J. Bowersox and E. J. McCarthy, "Strategic Development of
Planned Vertical Marketing Systems," in *Vertical Marketing Systems*, ed. Louis Bucklin
(Glenview, Ill.: Scott, Foresman, 1970).

done some consumer Promotion and Promotion in the channels, and developed
the Place setup. Middlemen are then expected to finish the Promotion job in their
respective places.

In a middleman-dominated channel system, we would see quite different diagrams. In the extreme, in a channel similar to that dominated by Eaton's, the
middleman circle would show the dominance of Eaton's. Producers would be
almost solely concerned with manufacturing the product to meet Eaton's
specifications.

New and better ways of organizing channel systems may evolve out of this
way of thinking. By rearranging who does what functions, unnecessary and
costly duplication is avoided—and the flow of information and physical goods is
smoothed and speeded. Franchising organizations—like McDonald's—have
grown rapidly in recent years by developing systems in which the members have
the same product-market commitment. In the fast-food franchise industry, for
example, successful franchisers run training programs to teach prospective franchise holders how to carry out company strategies effectively. These programs
stress the importance of sticking to the basic strategies—in fact, it may even be
required by contract. If the franchiser earns a share of the franchise holder's
sales, it will feel even more strongly about franchisees implementing the basic
strategies.[6]

**A coordinated chan-
nel system can help
everyone**

A channel system in which the members have accepted a common product-
market commitment can work very well—even though not everyone in the channel system is strongly market-oriented. As long as someone—say, the channel

captain—is market-oriented, it may be possible to win the confidence and support of production-oriented firms—and make the whole channel work effectively.

Small production-oriented producers in Japan or Hong Kong, for example, may become part of an effective channel reaching the Canadian market—if a middleman correctly analyzes market needs and relays them clearly to the producers. The producers may not even know where their products are going—but the system can still be competitive with other systems and profitable for the members.

The channel system may shift and share functions

Ultimately, a successful *channel system* must deliver the goods and services desired by target customers—at reasonable prices. Regardless of whether the marketing manager uses long or short channels, the channels must provide all the functions of marketing. Some buying and selling are required. Transporting, grading, or sorting, financing, risk taking, and market information functions are necessary in all channels. These functions can be *shifted and shared—but not eliminated.* Note that the customer can participate in this shifting and sharing. How costly the whole process is depends on how well the functions are combined *and* how much work has to be done.

If a manufacturer is successful in differentiating his marketing mix in the minds of customers, other channel members may have little to contribute—and the manufacturer may not have to offer channel members very attractive returns for their efforts. Auto and appliance manufacturers, for instance, offer retailers lower margins on fast-selling, lower-priced models than on less popular, top-of-the-line models.

Even if a producer takes goods directly to the user, the channel functions are not eliminated. The direct-to-user route reduces the number of times the functions are performed—but it does not eliminate them. It *may* or *may not* reduce the cost—depending on the situation and the Place objectives. As explained

Channels can be short, but marketing functions can't be eliminated.

earlier in the chapter, middlemen may be more efficient at performing the regrouping activities—as well as the marketing functions. Middlemen may have economies of scale which allow them to operate at lower costs. This might be as simple as having regular and friendly contacts with the target customers—which speeds the promotion job—while "going direct" might be very expensive for the producer.

In summary, the choice of who should do which marketing functions in a channel is an important strategy decision—it must be decided not only on the basis of costs but also on how Place fits in with the rest of the marketing strategy.

■ CONCLUSION

This chapter has discussed the role of Place—and noted that Place decisions are especially important because they may be difficult and expensive to change.

Marketing specialists—and channel systems—develop to adjust discrepancies of quantity and assortment. Their regrouping activities are basic in any economic system—and adjusting discrepancies provides opportunities for creative marketers.

The importance of planning channel systems was discussed—along with the role of a channel captain. It was stressed that channel systems compete with each other.

Channel planning requires deciding on the degree of market exposure desired. The legality of limiting market exposure should also be considered—to avoid having to undo an expensively developed channel system—or even going to jail!

Channel systems compete with each other. In this broader context, the "battle of the brands" is only a skirmish in the battle between various channel systems. And, it should be emphasized that producers are not necessarily channel captains. Often, middlemen control or even dominate channels of distribution. The degree of this control must be considered by producers when they decide whether to push or pull their product though a channel system—or simply join some channel captain's system.

■ QUESTIONS AND PROBLEMS

1. Explain "discrepancies of quantity and assortment" using the clothing business as an example. How does the application of these concepts change when selling coal to the steel industry? What impact does this have on the number and kinds of marketing specialists required?

2. Explain the four regrouping activities with an example from the building supply industry (nails, paint, flooring, plumbing fixtures, etc.). Do you think that many specialists develop in this industry, or do manufacturers handle the job themselves? What kinds of marketing channels would you expect to find in this industry and what functions would various channel members provide?

3. In view of the Place objectives suggested for convenience goods, what kinds of marketing specialists would a manufacturer hope to find in this market? What kinds for shopping goods? For unsought goods? For industrial goods? (Don't be concerned with whether there *are* any such specialists—just indicate what you would *like* to find.)

4. Discuss the Place objectives and distribution arrangements that are appropriate for the following products (indicate any special assumptions you have to make to obtain an answer):

a. A postal scale for products weighing up to two pounds.
b. Children's toys: (1) electric train sets costing $20 or more, (2) balloons.
c. Pneumatic nut tighteners for factory production lines.
d. Caustic soda used in making paper.

5. If a manufacturer has five different markets to reach, how many channels is he likely to use? If only one, why? If more than one, what problems may this cause?

6. Find an example of horizontal integration within your city. Are there any particular advantages to this horizontal integration? If so, what are they? If there are no such advantages, how do you explain the integration?'

7. Explain how a "channel captain" could help traditional independent firms compete with a corporate (integrated) channel system.

8. What would happen if retailer-organized integrated channels (either formally integrated or administered) dominated consumer goods marketing.

9. Relate the nature of the product to the degree of market exposure desired.

10. Why would middlemen want to be exclusive distributors for a product? Why would producers want exclusive distribution? Would middlemen be equally anxious to get exclusive distribution for any type of product? Why or why not? Explain with reference to the following products: cornflakes, razor blades, golf clubs, golf balls, steak knives, hi-fi equipment, and industrial wood-working machinery.

11. Explain the present legal status of exclusive distribution. Describe a situation where exclusive distribution is almost sure to be legal. Describe the nature and size of competitors and the industry, as well as the nature of the exclusive arrangement. Would this exclusive arrangement be of any value to the producer or middleman?

12. Discuss the promotion a grocery products manufacturer would need in order to develop appropriate channels and move goods through those channels. Would the nature of this job change at all for a dress manufacturer? How about for a small producer of installations?

13. Discuss the advantages and disadvantages of either a pushing or pulling policy for a very small manufacturer just entering into the candy business with a line of inexpensive candy bars. Which policy would probably be most appropriate? State any assumptions you need to obtain a definite answer.

■ SUGGESTED CASES

14. Cooper Lumber Company

25. Lafontaine Potteries Limited

■ **NOTES**

1. For a classic discussion of the discrepancy concepts, see Wroe Alderson, "Factors Governing the Development of Marketing Channels," in *Marketing Channels for Manufactured Goods,* ed. Richard M. Clewett (Homewood, Ill.: Richard D. Irwin, 1954), pp. 7–9. See also Lee Dahringer, "Colloquium on the Role of Marketing in Developing Nations: Public Policy Implications of Reverse Channel Mapping for Lesotho," *Journal of Macromarketing* 3, no. 1 (Spring 1983), pp. 69–75; Louis W. Stern and Adel I. El-Ansary, *Marketing Channels* (Englewood Cliffs, N.J.: Prentice-Hall, 1977); Bruce Mallen, *Principles of Marketing Channel Management* (Lexington, Mass.: D. C. Heath, 1977); and R. D. Michman and S. D. Sibley, *Marketing Channels and Strategies* (Columbus, Ohio: Grid, 1980).

2. Robert W. Little, "The Marketing Channel: Who Should Lead this Extra Corporate Organization?" *Journal of Marketing,* January 1970, pp. 31–39; Phillip McVey, "Are Channels of Distribution What the Textbooks Say?" *Journal of Marketing,* January 1960, pp. 61–65; Bruce Mallen, "Functional Spin-Off: A Key to Anticipating Change in Distribution Structure," *Journal of Marketing,* July 1973, pp. 18–25; and Gary L. Frazier, "On the Measurement of Interfirm Power in Channels of Distribution," *Journal of Marketing Research* 20, (May 1983), pp. 158–66.

3. Claude Raymond, "A Seminar with A. C. Nielsen," special presentation to Junior Advertising Sales Club of Montreal, April 18, 1978.

4. Tony Thompson, "Are the Food Chains Really Putting the Squeeze on Their Suppliers?" *Marketing,* July 3, 1978, p. 9.

5. Michael Etgar, "Selection of an Effective Channel Control Mix," *Journal of Marketing,* July 1978, pp. 53–58; Michael Etgar, "Intrachannel Conflict and Use of Power," *Journal of Marketing Research,* May 1978, pp. 273–74; Robert F. Lusch, "Sources of Power: Their Impact on Intrachannel Conflict," *Journal of Marketing Research,* November 1976, pp. 382–90; William P. Dommermuth, "Profiting from Distribution Conflicts," *Business Horizons,* December 1976, pp. 4–13; Shelby D. Hunt and John R. Nevin, "Power in a Channel of Distribution: Sources and Consequences," *Journal of Marketing Research,* May 1974, pp. 186–93; Louis P. Bucklin, "A Theory of Channel Control," *Journal of Marketing,* January 1973, pp. 39–47; Joseph B. Mason, "Power and Channel Conflicts in Shopping Center Development," *Journal of Marketing,* April 1975, pp. 28–35; Stanley D. Sibley and Donald A. Michie, "An Exploratory Investigation of Cooperation in a Franchise Channel," *Journal of Retailing* 58, no. 4 (Winter 1982), pp. 23–45; James R. Brown, "A Cross-Channel Comparison of Supplier-Retailer Relations," *Journal of Retailing* 57, no. 4 (Winter 1981), pp. 3–18; and John E. Robbins, Thomas W. Speh, and Morris L. Mayer, "Retailers' Perceptions of Channel Conflict Issues," *Journal of Retailing* 58, no. 4 (Winter 1982), pp. 46–67.

6. Shelby D. Hunt and John R. Nevin, "Full Disclosure Laws in Franchising: An Empirical Investigation," *Journal of Marketing,* April 1976, pp. 53–62; S. D. Hunt and J. R. Nevin, "Tying Agreements and Franchising," *Journal of Marketing,* July 1975, pp. 20–26; Shelby D. Hunt, "The Socioeconomic Consequences of the Franchise System of Distribution," *Journal of Marketing,* July 1972, pp. 32–38; P. Ronald Stephenson and Robert G. House, "A Perspective on Franchising," *Business Horizons,* August 1971, pp. 35–42; Bruce J. Walker and Michael J. Etzel, "The Internationalization of U.S. Franchise Systems: Progress and Procedures," *Journal of Marketing,* April 1973, pp. 38–46; "Supreme Court Declines Review of Franchise Suit," *The Wall Street Journal,* October 30, 1979, p. 4; and James M. Carman, "Private Property and the Regulation of Vertical Channel Systems," *Journal of Macromarketing* 2, no. 1 (Spring 1982), pp. 20–26.

Chapter 13 ■ Retailing*

When you finish this chapter, you should:

1. Understand about retailers planning their own marketing strategies.

2. Know about the many kinds of retailers which might become members of producers' or wholesalers' channel systems.

3. Understand the differences among the conventional and non-conventional retailers—including those who accept the mass-merchandising concept.

4. Understand scrambled merchandising and the "wheel of retailing."

5. Recognize the important new terms (shown in red).

*The Canadian context of this chapter was researched and written for *Basic Marketing*, Fourth Canadian Edition, by Professor Carl Lawrence of Queen's University.

"If the goods aren't sold, nobody makes any money."

Retailing covers all of the activities involved in the sale of goods and/or services to final consumers. Retailing is important to all of us. As consumers, Canadians spend about $109 billion a year buying goods and services from retailers. If the retailing effort isn't effective, everyone in the channel suffers—and some products aren't sold at all. So retailing is important to marketing managers of consumer goods at *all* channel levels.

Retailers must select their own target markets and marketing mixes very carefully. Retailing is very competitive—and constantly changing. An example shows some of the problems retailers face.

Almost every household has a telephone. But until recently, most people didn't *own* a phone. Few stores bothered to sell them—because phone companies required that customers rent their phones. Then, the government ruled that consumers must be allowed to buy their own phones if they choose. Now many phone producers compete in a very big market for phones. They have had to find ways to sell their products—and the phone companies have not been interested in helping them! Some firms' phones are sold at big general merchandise stores—like Sears. Some sell phones at electronics stores—which also handle phone answering devices, automatic dialers, and related items. Some phones—including expensive cordless ones—are sold in specialty mail-order catalogs. Even the phone companies are setting up "phone stores." Each of these retailers offers different marketing mixes to consumers—perhaps aimed at quite different target markets.

Telephones are now available in many different types of retail stores—which probably reach different target markets.

What are the different kinds of retailers—and why did they develop? How do their strategies vary? What trends are likely in the future? In this chapter, we'll try to answer these important questions. We will talk about the major decision areas summarized in Figure 13–1. We will not discuss the promotion and pricing decisions of retailers in detail here. These problems are similar for all firms—and are discussed in later chapters.

Planning a Retailer's Strategy

Remember that retailing is *not* concerned with industrial goods—or with the sale of consumer goods in the channels. Retailing is concerned with *final consumers.* In fact, retailers are so directly involved with final consumers that their strategy planning is critical to their survival. If a retail customer is lost to a competitor, the retailer loses the sale—even though manufacturers and wholesalers in this channel make *their* sale—regardless of which retailer sells their product. Further, retailers don't have an opportunity to "load" middlemen with products that won't sell. They must be guided by the old maxim: Goods well bought are half sold.

A retailer is usually selling more than just individual items. It is useful to think of the retailer's whole offering—assortment of goods and services, advice from sales clerks, convenience in parking, and the like—as a "Product." And in the case of service retailing—dry cleaning, lawn care, or dental work, for example—the retailer is also the producer. So, most of what we said in the Product area applies here—and we can extend our thinking beyond why people buy specific products to why they select particular retailers.

■ FIGURE 13–1   Strategic decision areas for a retailer

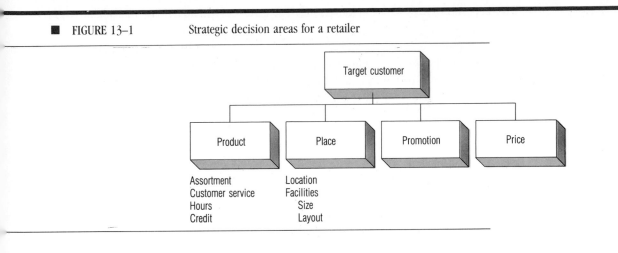

Assortment   Location
Customer service Facilities
Hours   Size
Credit   Layout

Consumers have reasons for buying from particular retailers

It may seem obvious that different consumers prefer particular kinds of retailers—but why they do is often ignored by retailers. Just renting a store and assuming that customers will come running is all too common among beginning small retailers—and the failure rate is quite high. More than three fourths of new retailing ventures die a slow and costly death during the first year.[1] To avoid this fate, a new retailer—or one trying to adjust to changing conditions—should carefully identify possible target markets and try to understand why people buy where they do.

Economic needs—which store has the best value?

Consumers consider many factors in choosing a particular retailer. Some of the most important ones are:

1. Convenience.
2. Variety of selection.
3. Quality of products—freshness, purity, craftsmanship, and so on.
4. Courtesy of salespeople.
5. Integrity—reputation for fairness in dealings.
6. Services offered—delivery, credit, returned-goods privileges.
7. Value offered.

Just as different customers may want different features in a product, consumers shop in stores that offer the assortment and conveniences they want—at the lowest prices consistent with all the service they want. Some consumers want a great deal of service—and are willing to pay for it. The conventional thinking in retailing, however, tends to emphasize economic needs—especially the value offered or, more narrowly, low prices.

Emotional needs—the importance of social class

There may also be important emotional reasons for preferring particular retailers. Many people equate a store with a certain level of social status. They might be embarrassed to carry home packages bearing the brand of an obviously "inferior" store. In contrast, some people get an ego boost from shopping in a "prestigious" store. They patronize these stores—and wear their labels with pride—to emulate the social leaders.

Different stores do seem to attract customers from different social classes. People like to shop where salespeople and other customers are similar to themselves. No one wants to feel "out of place." Some people even go to particular stores hoping they will meet friends there. For them, a trip to the store is also a social event.

The emotional needs that a store fills are related to its target market(s). Zellers—a chain of variety stores—has been very successful with a "budget" image that appeals to lower-class people. Holt Renfrew works at its upper-class image—and appeals to more "upscale" customers. But not all stores have—or want—a particular class image. Some try to avoid creating one—because they want to appeal to a wide audience. Eaton's, for example, tries to create a fairly universal appeal. It has departments that carry some very expensive merchandise—and others that handle goods for the masses.

There is no one "right" answer as to whom a store should appeal. But, ignorance about emotional dimensions—including social class appeal—could lead to serious errors in marketing strategy planning.

Goods classes help understand store types

Retail strategy planning can be simplified by recalling our earlier discussion of consumer behavior and the consumer goods classes—convenience goods, shopping goods, and specialty goods. We can also use these classes to define three types of stores.

A **convenience store** is a convenient place to shop—either centrally located "downtown" or "in the neighborhood." Such stores attract many customers because they are so handy. Easy parking, fast check-out, and easy-to-find merchandise add to the convenience. **Shopping stores** attract customers from greater distances because of the width and depth of their assortments. They may also keep shoppers with displays, demonstrations, information, and knowledgeable sales clerks. **Specialty stores** are those for which customers have developed a strong attraction. For whatever reasons—service, selection, or reputation—some customers will consistently buy at these stores. We may think of them as insisting on the store—just as some customers have brand insistence for certain products.

Store types based on how customers see store

It is important to see that these store types refer to *customers' images of the store*—not just the kind of products they carry. Moreover, different market segments might see or use a particular store differently. Remember that this was true with the goods classes, too. So a retailer's strategy planning must consider potential customers' attitudes toward *both* the product and the store. Classifying market segments by how they see both the store type and the product class—as shown in Figure 13–2—helps to understand this complete view.

When planning strategy, a retailer will obtain a deeper understanding of a market by estimating the relative size of each of the boxes shown in Figure 13–2. By identifying which competitors are satisfying which market segments, the retailer may see that some boxes are already "filled." In fact, a manager may

■ FIGURE 13–2   How customers view store-product combinations

Store type Product class	Convenience	Shopping	Specialty
Convenience	Will buy any brand at most accessible store	Shop around to find better service and/or lower prices	Prefer store. Brand may be important
Shopping	Want some selection but will settle for assortment at most accessible store	Want to compare both products and store mixes	Prefer store but insist on adequate assortment
Specialty	Prefer particular product but like place convenience too	Prefer particular product but still seeking best total product and mix	Prefer both store and product

Source: Adapted from Louis Bucklin, "Retail Strategy and the Classification of Consumer Goods," *Journal of Marketing*, January 1963, pp. 50–55.

find that he and his competitors are all charging head-on after the same customers and completely ignoring others.

For example, until recently household plants were sold only by florists and greenhouses. This served some market segments well. They wanted a "shopping store" variety from which to select their plants. But, for many people, this was too much trouble for plants—and they went without. Then, some retailers went after the "convenience store" segment—with small house plant departments and stores at neighborhood shopping centers. They quickly found a big market segment that wanted to buy plants at convenience stores.

Figure 13–2 suggests another approach to retail strategy planning, too. A specific store might try to satisfy the people in two or more segments—by adding something to its "Product." A "shopping store" which normally emphasizes shopping goods might also try to become a shopping store for convenience goods for the many staple clothing, and health and beauty aids wanted by nearby office workers. And lower prices could be offered to attract "price-conscious shoppers" to the "staple" convenience goods.

Whole channel system is involved

The store-goods classes are also important to manufacturers and wholesalers. If, for example, the majority of a manufacturer's target customers patronize convenience stores, then intensive distribution may be necessary. Similarly, if a large group of customers treat particular stores—or a chain—as specialty stores, manufacturers will have to be in those stores if they want to reach those customers. Unfortunately, if those stores use dealer brands, the manufacturers may be blocked from those customers. Some customers see Sears as a specialty store, for example, and regularly buy their paint, hardware, and major appliances at Sears—without shopping at other stores. Competing manufacturers simply have to accept Sears' position—and cater to other markets.

While store types based on how consumers see stores can help guide strategy planning, other dimensions of retailers are useful, too. So let's go on to see what kinds of retailers are already competing in the marketplace—and how they have developed.

Types of Retailers and the Nature of Their Offerings

There are about 160,000 retailers in Canada—and they are constantly evolving. To speed your understanding, therefore, it is useful to describe basic types of retailers—and key aspects of their strategies.

Retailers vary in many ways. They differ in terms of the product assortments they sell. A paint store and a fabric store, for example, focus on different lines. But both have depth in their line. By contrast, a department store might have less depth—but more different lines and more width within lines. Some retailers expect customers to serve themselves—to select products without assistance—or to pump their own gas. Other retailers give "full service." They provide helpful sales clerks as well as credit, delivery, trade-ins, giftwrap, special orders, and returns. Some retailers have fancy locations—downtown or at a mall with other stores. But some sell from vending machines or in a customer's home—without any store at all. Some retailers try to make a profit by selling large quantities at low prices. Others have higher than conventional prices, but also offer something extra—like an especially convenient location or sales clerks who remember customers' names.

Each retailer's offering represents some *mix* of all of these different characteristics. So, any classification of retailers based on a single characteristic is incomplete.

Over time, new types of retailers have evolved who emphasize different characteristics. We can see this by first looking at some of the conventional retailers, and then describing how others have modified the conventional offering and survived—because they met the needs of *some* consumers.

Conventional Retailers—Avoid Price Competition

Single-line, limited-line retailers specialize by Product

Historically, trading posts or general stores—that carried anything they could sell in reasonable volume—were the main type of retailers. Today, such stores are usually found only in rural communities. Because of the growing variety of consumer goods it is hard for general stores to offer depth and width in all of their traditional lines. So some stores chose to specialize in dry goods, apparel, furniture, or groceries.

Most conventional retailers are single-line or limited-line stores—like this one which specializes in men's casual wear.

Now, most conventional retailers are **single-line** or **limited-line stores** that specialize in certain lines of related products rather than a wide assortment. Many stores specialize not only in a single line—such as clothing—but also in a *limited-line* within the broader line. For example, within the clothing line a store might carry *only* shoes, formal wear, men's casual wear, or even neckties—but offer depth in that limited line. This specialization will probably continue as long as customer demands are varied—and large enough to support such stores.

■ FIGURE 13–3   Types of retailers and the nature of their offerings

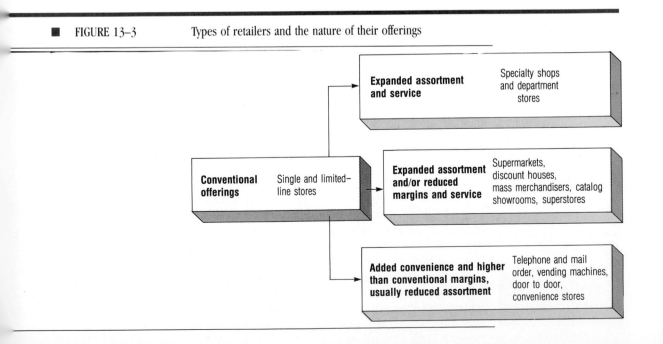

Single-line, limited-line stores are being squeezed

The main advantage of these stores is that they can satisfy some target markets better. Some even achieve specialty-store status by adjusting the marketing mix—including store hours, credit, and product assortment—to suit certain customers. But these stores face the costly problem of having to stock some slow-moving items in order to satisfy the store's target market. Further, many of these stores have the disadvantage of being small—with high expenses relative to sales. Stores of this type have traditionally applied the retailing philosophy of "buy low and sell high." If they face much competition, they may expand assortment—specialize further—trying to keep costs down and prices up by avoiding competition on identical products.

Conventional retailers of this sort have been around for a long time—and are still found in every community. They are a durable lot—and clearly satisfy some people's needs. But, they will continue to be squeezed by retailers who have modified their mixes in the various ways suggested in Figure 13–3 (page 429). Let's have a closer look at some of these other types of retailers.

Expand Assortment and Service—To Compete at a High Price

Specialty shops usually sell shopping goods

A **specialty shop**—a type of conventional limited-line store—usually is small, with a distinct "personality." Specialty shops often deal in special types of shopping goods—such as high-quality sporting goods, exclusive clothing, or leather goods.[2] They aim at a carefully defined market segment by offering a unique product assortment, knowledgeable sales clerks, and better service. For example, small specialty shops have developed to satisfy the growing market of "joggers." The clerks are runners themselves. They know the sport—and are eager to explain the advantages of different types of running shoes to their customers. These stores also carry a selection of books on running—as well as clothes for the jogger. They even offer discounts to customers who are members of local track teams.

Using the term "specialty" should not cause us to confuse specialty *shops*, specialty *stores*, and specialty *goods*. A successful specialty shop might achieve a specialty-store status among a small group of target customers—but the owner probably would rather be well known among a larger group as a "good" shopping store—because of the distinctiveness of its line and the special services offered. Similarly, a specialty shop might carry specialty goods—but only if those goods fit into its narrow line and would benefit by the additional service and display the specialty shop offers. For example, "The Kitchen Korner"—a specialty *shop*—might become a specialty *store* for some gourmet-cook customers. And the owner of "The Kitchen Korner" might be willing—because it fits into "The Kitchen Korner's" line—to carry a well-respected brand of pots and pans which are considered specialty *goods* by the gourmet-cook customers.

The specialty shop's major advantage is that it caters to certain types of customers whom the management and salespeople come to know well. This familiarity simplifies buying, speeds turnover, and cuts the costs due to obsolescence and style changes. Specialty shops probably will continue to be a part of the retailing scene as long as customers have varied tastes—and the money to satisfy them.

Department stores combine many limited-line stores and specialty shops

Department stores are larger stores—organized into many separate departments. For purposes of buying, promotion, service, and control, each department is like a separate limited-line store or specialty shop. They usually handle a wide variety of products—such as women's ready-to-wear and accessories, men's and boys' wear, textiles, housewares, and home furnishings.

Some specialty shops—grown large and departmentalized—appear to be department stores—and we will treat them as such. As a rule, however, specialty shops do not carry complete lines. They frequently omit housewares, home furnishings, and furniture—and prefer instead to emphasize depth and distinctiveness in the lines they do choose to carry.

Department stores are often looked to as the retailing leaders in a community. They usually do lead in customer services—including credit, merchandise return, delivery, fashion shows, and Christmas displays. They also are leaders because of their size. In 1982 there were 810 department store locations (346 major and 464 junior) with sales of $10.3 billion, accounting for 10.5 percent of total retail trade. Of this total volume the 346 major department stores accounted for $6.7 billion or an average of $19.4 million per store. In comparison, the junior department stores had average sales per outlet of $9.9 million. Chain stores had average sales of $1.3 million, while the independent store average was only $412,000.[3]

Certain department stores have a strong grip on their market. Some market segments can be reached *only* through particular department stores. These stores have achieved a strong specialty-store status—and their buyers can make it tough on suppliers. In other words, because of their strength, they may either choose to play the role of channel captain or simply demand all the concessions they can get.[4] Across Canada the department store sector is dominated by three giant chains—Hudson's Bay, Eaton's, and Sears. In 1983, Eaton's, the Hudson's Bay Company, and Sears together accounted for slightly over 54 percent of all the sales made by department and general merchandise stores in Canada. This is in marked contrast to the situation in the United States, where there are many large department store operations with branches across the country, as well as several regional department store groups. No one group has achieved the share of market enjoyed by their Canadian counterparts.

Department stores generally try to cater to customers seeking shopping goods. But some special departments—like a beauty salon or candy department—may help attract and satisfy customers. If these special departments require unusual management skills, the store may lease out space for the department. Decisions about the operation of the department are then left to the proprietor—who usually pays some share of sales as rent.

Originally, most department stores were downtown—close to other, similar stores. This was convenient for many potential customers. Many downtown stores suffered after World War II, however, as middle- and upper-income groups moved to the suburbs. Some are making efforts to renew the appeal of their traditional downtown locations by (1) carrying wide lines in the major shopping goods items for which they have long been famous; (2) attracting conventioneers and tourists; and (3) appealing to low-income groups remaining in the residential neighborhoods near the downtown area. New urban trends—including downtown apartment units, urban redevelopment, and improved mass transit—may save some of the big downtown stores.[5]

Simpsons is a prime example of a department store trying to upgrade its image in downtown Toronto. For decades that cavernous somewhat musty store seemed to be the favorite outlet of elderly ladies who paused for tea and scones between polite purchases of white gloves. Today the store is undergoing extensive renovation. It is also bidding to attract the admirers of Madonna, Prince, and Corey Hart. The changing merchandise mix will emphasize more soft goods and fewer high-ticket items such as appliances and furniture. It is expected that the flagship store (along with others in the chain) will carry up to 11 different designer lines of clothing—that's more than the average carried by most major U.S. department stores![6]

The department stores responded to the growth of suburbia by opening suburban branches—usually in shopping centers—to be more convenient for their customers. This has helped offset some of the problems of downtown stores. But traditional department stores still face many challenges—especially price competition from mass-merchandising retailers who operate with lower costs and sell larger volumes. We'll discuss them next.

Evolution of New, Mass-Merchandising Retailers

Mass-merchandising is different than conventional retailing

So far we have been describing retailers primarily in terms of the *assortment carried*. This reflects traditional thinking about retailing. But there are many important kinds of retailers that can't be adequately described this way. Supermarkets and discount houses, for example, can be shoved into the single-line or limited-line category. But, by so doing, we would miss their essence—just as some conventional retailers did when these stores first appeared.

Conventional retailers believe in a fixed demand for a territory and have a "buy low and sell high" philosophy. Some modern retailers reject these notions. They have accepted the **mass-merchandising concept**—which says that retailers should offer low prices to get faster turnover and greater sales volumes—by appealing to larger markets. Some mass-merchandising stores were started by people outside of retailing who were willing to depart from the conventional wisdom of existing retailers. To better understand mass-merchandising, let's look at its evolution from the development of supermarkets and discounters to the modern mass-merchandisers—like K mart.

Supermarkets started the move to mass-merchandising

A **supermarket** is a large store specializing in groceries—with self-service and wide assortments. As late as 1930, most food stores were relatively small single- or limited-line operations. In the early Depression years, some innovators

Supermarkets were the first retailers to adopt the mass-merchandising concept.

felt that price appeals could move goods in volume. They introduced self-service, provided a very broad product assortment in large stores, and emphasized low price by reducing high-cost services. Their early experiments in vacant warehouses were an immediate success. Profits came from large volume sales—not from "high" traditional markups. Many conventional retailers—both independents and chains—quickly copied the innovators—emphasizing lower prices and self-service.[7]

Supermarkets sell convenience goods—but in quantity. Their target customers don't want to shop for groceries every day—like grandma did. To make volume shopping easier, supermarkets typically carry more than 7,000 product items. Stores are large—around 20,000 square feet. And free parking is provided. According to the Food Marketing Institute, $1 million is considered the minimum annual sales volume for a store to be called a supermarket. According to Statistics Canada each of the 1,900 supermarkets in Canada had an average sales volume in 1982 of about $7 million. And the same high degree of concentration that existed among department stores also holds true for supermarkets. The five grocery and supermarket chains which reported annual sales of over $700 million in 1982 controlled only 25.8 percent of the total sales of all chain outlets. However, these five chains accounted for 63 percent of the total sales of all supermarket and grocery chains.[8] Today, supermarkets are beginning to reach the saturation level—yet new ones still do well when they are wisely located.[9]

Present-day supermarkets are planned for maximum efficiency. Some carefully analyze the sales and profit of each item—and allocate space accordingly. This approach helps sell more goods in less time, reduces the investment in inventory, makes stocking easier, and reduces the cost of handling goods. Such efficiency is essential. Grocery competition is keen—and net profits after taxes in grocery supermarkets usually run a thin 1 percent of sales—*or less*!

Supermarkets have continued to change and evolve. But, remember that they were the first retailers to adopt the mass-merchandising concept.

Catalog showroom retailers preceded discount houses

Catalog showroom retailers sell several lines out of a catalog and display showroom—with backup inventories. Before 1940, catalog sellers were usually wholesalers who also sold at retail to friends and members of groups—such as labor unions or church groups. In the 1970s, however, these operations expanded rapidly. Catalogs intended for consumer use were developed. The average catalog retailer can offer lower prices and deliver almost all the items in its catalog from its backroom warehouse. Price is the important variable here—and big price savings can be had in jewelry, gifts, luggage, and small appliances—the areas where these retailers specialize.[10] Catalog showrooms tend to focus on well-known manufacturers' brands. They offer few services.

A fine example is Consumers Distributing. A typical Consumers unit has 9,000 square feet of space. Its aim is to concentrate on variety in a few well-chosen product lines. It offers those products at the lowest possible price by blanketing the market with showrooms which use warehouse techniques and relatively little labor.[11]

The early catalog operations did not bother the conventional retailers—because they were not well publicized and accounted for only a small portion of total retail sales. If they had moved ahead aggressively—as the current catalog retailers are doing—the retailing scene might be different. But instead, discount houses developed.

Discount houses upset some conventional retailers

Right after World War II, some retailers moved aggressively beyond offering discounts to selected customers—or those who happened to hear about their catalog operations. These **discount houses** offered "hard goods" (cameras, TVs, appliances) at substantial price cuts—to customers who would go to the discounter's low-rent store, pay cash, and take care of any service or repair problems. They were much more open about their operations. Some even advertised widely in newspapers—and on radio and television. These retailers sold at perhaps 20 to 30 percent off the list price being charged by conventional retailers—for similar or the same nationally advertised brands. The emphasis in these discount houses was on cutting prices to get fast turnover.

In the early 1950s—with war shortages finally over—manufacturers' brands became more available, and a buyers' market developed. The discount houses were able to get any brands they wanted—and to offer fuller assortments. The early Canadian discount operations were aided tremendously when the practice of Resale Price Maintenance was declared illegal in 1951. At this stage, many discounters "turned respectable"—moving to better locations and offering more services and guarantees. They began to act more like regular retailers—but kept their prices lower than conventional outlets to keep turnover high.

Conventional retailers fight back by cutting prices

The discount-house strategy was a new approach to "hard goods" retailing. Faced with discount house competition, some conventional hard goods retailers resorted to price cutting on highly competitive items. But these purely defensive moves were just that—price cutting—while discounters make a standard practice of selling everything with lower than usual markups.

More than simple price cutting is involved in a successful discount house, however. Careful buying with the firm's target markets in mind is essential—to assure high turnover. A major discounter's first venture into apparel sales flopped, for instance, because its buyers were appliance experts—who knew nothing about fashions. The discount house approach worked only after they hired experienced fashion buyers.

Mass-merchandisers are more than discounters

Mass-merchandisers are large, self-service stores with many departments—which emphasize "soft goods" (housewares, clothing, and fabrics) but still follow the discount house's emphasis on lower margins to get faster turnover. Mass-merchandisers—like K mart and Zellers—have check-out counters in the front of the store and little or no sales help on the floor. This is in contrast to more conventional retailers—such as Sears and Hudson's Bay—who still offer some service and have sales stations and cash registers in most departments. The more conventional retailer may try to reorder sizes and stocks in lines it carries, whereas mass-merchandisers do less of this. They want to move merchandise—fast—and are less concerned with continuity of lines and assortment.

Mass-merchandisers—as contrasted with department stores—have less expensive locations which attract fewer "walk by" customers. Although many are now renovating their stores, they are still plain compared to the fancy fixtures and displays in most department stores.

The average mass-merchandiser has nearly 60,000 square feet of floor space. This is three to four times the size of the average supermarket.[12]

Mass-merchandisers have grown rapidly. In fact, they expanded so rapidly in some areas that they were no longer taking customers from conventional retailers—but from each other.[13] Because of this saturation, profits have been declining—and many stores have gone bankrupt. Seeing the declining potential in major metropolitan areas, K mart and others have started moving into smaller towns. This has really upset some small-town merchants—who felt they were safe from this competitive "rat-race."

Consumers appreciate mass-merchandisers

The mass-merchandisers grew rapidly between 1970 and 1980. Their emphasis on "value" (quality products at reasonable prices) met an important consumer need. Perhaps this was because inflation rates forced consumers to be more careful with their shopping dollars. At any rate, the success of mass-merchandisers shows that at least some customers weren't fully satisfied with the conventional retailers' strategies. Clearly, there is a demand for this type of store. Mass-merchandisers probably will continue to use their present methods—because they see these methods as "conventional" for their type of operation.

Super-stores meet all routine needs

Some supermarkets and mass-merchandisers have moved toward becoming **super-stores**—very large stores that try to carry not only foods, but all goods and services which the consumer purchases *routinely*. Such a store may *look* like a mass-merchandiser, but it is different in concept. A super-store is trying to meet *all* the customer's routine needs—at a low price.

The super-store concept is bigger than the supermarket or mass-merchandiser concept. The super-store carries not only foods—but also personal care products, some apparel products, some lawn and garden products, gasoline—and services such as laundry, dry cleaning, shoe repair, check cashing, and bill paying.[14] Some mass-merchandisers have moved in this direction—and if they spread, the food-oriented supermarkets may suffer. Their present buildings and parking lots are not large enough to convert to super-stores.

Some Retailers Focus on Added Convenience

The supermarkets, discounters, and mass merchandisers provide many different products "under one roof." Yet, they are inconvenient in other ways. There may be few customer services, or check-out lines may be longer. It may be hard to find the right product in the store, or they may be in less convenient, "low-rent" locations. The savings may justify these inconveniences when a consumer has a lot to buy. But, there are times when convenience is much more important—even if it means that the consumer must pay a bit extra. Let's take a look at some retailers who have met a need by focusing on convenience.

Convenience (food) stores must have the right assortment

Convenience (food) stores are a convenience-oriented variation of the conventional limited-line food stores. Instead of expanding their assortment, however, convenience stores severely limit their assortment to those "pick-up" or "fill-in" items like bread, milk, ice cream, and beer. Stores such as Becker's, Mac's Milk, and 7-Eleven fill needs between major shopping trips to a supermarket. They are offering convenience—not assortment—and often charge prices 10 to 20 percent higher than those charged at nearby supermarkets. Apparently this price difference is more than offset by the convenience offered—because these stores continue to spread all over the country. Further, the higher margins—coupled with faster turnover of a narrow assortment—makes them much more profitable than supermarkets. They net approximately 4 percent on sales—rather than the 1 percent earned by supermarkets. This helps explain why the number of such stores has increased steadily in the past few years.[15]

Vending machines are convenient

Automatic vending is selling and delivering products through vending machines. Although vending machine growth has been spectacular, automatic vending sales generate only about 0.3 percent of Canadian retail sales. Many small operators (434 or 64 percent of all operators) with annual sales of less than $250,000 account for about 11.9 percent of total sales of vending machines. On the other hand, in 1983, seven operators (1 percent of all owners) owned 22 percent of all machines and accounted for 36 percent of the total sales. Cigarette machines generated the largest proportion of sales (34 percent); followed by soft drink machines (20 percent) and coffee machines (18 percent).[16] For some target markets, this retailing method cannot be ignored.

The major stumbling block in automatic vending is the high cost of operation. The machines are expensive to buy, stock, and repair—relative to the volume they sell. Marketers of similar non-vended products can operate profitably on a margin of about 20 percent—while the vending industry requires about 41 percent to break even. So they must charge higher prices.[17] If costs come down—and consumers' desire for convenience rises—we may see more growth in this method of retailing. Automatic bank teller machines—which give a customer cash, using a "money card"—provide a hint of how technology may change automatic vending.

Shop at home—with telephone and mail-order retailing

Telephone and mail-order retailing allows consumers to shop at home—usually placing orders by mail or telephone—and charging the purchase to a credit card. Typically, catalogs let customers "see" the offerings—and purchases are delivered by mail. This can be a real convenience to consumers, especially if desired products are not available at local stores. For some products, the target market is widely scattered. Retail stores don't want to carry an item for which there are few local customers. Telephone and mail-order retailing works well in these situations.

The early mail-order houses in Canada were offshoots of department store operations. They were brought about by the extension of the railroads and the improvement in postal facilities in the late 19th century. They targeted their efforts to rural areas—where consumers had fewer shopping alternatives. They were not only convenient, but also low-priced. They were so successful with their low prices and wide variety of shopping and convenience goods that some conventional retailers sought laws to restrict them.

The mail-order houses have continued to grow. According to Statistics Canada mail-order sales reached some $504 million in 1983—up slightly more than 8 percent from the previous year—but still representing less than one half of 1 percent of total retail sales.[18] Today, however, "mail-order" isn't what it used to be. Many companies provide toll-free long distance telephone numbers for ordering and information—and there is an increasing emphasis on expensive fashion, gift,

Mail and telephone order catalogs are the classic consumer "wish books."

and luxury items. Computer mailing lists help these retailers target their catalogs and promotions more effectively. Catalogs for narrow lines—like car stereos, exotic fruits, and classical records—are common.

The big mail-order houses started all this—but now oil companies and limited-line stores are seeing the profit possibilities and selling this way, too. Not only can they get additional business this way—but costs may be lower because they can use warehouse-type buildings and limited sales help. Shoplifting—a big expense for most retailers—isn't a problem. After-tax profits for mail-order retailers average 7 percent of sales—more than twice the profit margins for most other types of retailers.

Rapid growth is expected to continue for "at home" retailers. And more changes are expected, too. Experiments are now under way with two-way cable television systems—so consumers may see a product advertised on TV and order it with the push of a button. Videotapes and disks—or signals from satellites to televisions or home computers—may be the "catalogs" of the future.

Door-to-door retailers—give more personal attention

Door-to-door selling means going directly to the consumer's home. It is an old—but still effective—method. It accounts for slightly over 1 percent of retail sales—but it is an important form of retailing for some products. For example, Avon—the largest cosmetics firm in the world—has nearly a million door-to-door representatives. Door-to-door selling meets some consumers' needs for convenience and personal attention. It is also useful when unsought goods—like encyclopedias—need a special push.

This is an expensive method of selling. Markups range from 30 to 50 percent—often higher. Overhead costs are lower—because there is no store—but travel is costly, and the number of personal contacts possible in a day is limited. And reaching people at home—especially during the day—is becoming more difficult because there are more single-person households and households with all the adults working outside the home.

Retailing Types Are Explained by Consumer Needs Filled

We have talked about many different types of retailers—and how they have evolved. Earlier, we noted that no single characteristic provided a good basis for classifying all retailers. Now, it helps to see the three-dimensional view of retailing presented in Figure 13–4. It positions different types of retailers in terms of three consumer-oriented dimensions: (1) width of assortment desired, (2) depth of assortment desired, and (3) a price/service combination. Price and service are combined because they are often indirectly related. Services are costly to provide. So, a retailer that wants to emphasize low prices will usually need to cut some services—and stores with a lot of service must charge prices that cover the added costs.

Within this three-dimensional market diagram, it is possible to position most existing retailers. Figure 13–4, for example, suggests the *why* of vending machines. Some people—in the front upper left-hand corner—have a strong need

■ FIGURE 13–4   A three-dimensional view of the market for retail facilities and the probable
                      position of some present offerings

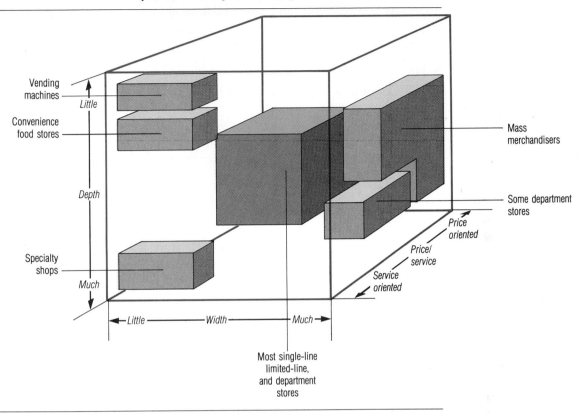

for a specific item—and are *not* interested in the width of assortment, the depth
of assortment, *or* the price.

On the other hand, some people have very specific needs and would like to
be able to select from a very deep assortment—and a range of price alternatives
as well. Various kinds of specialty shops fill these needs. This market can be
seen in the lower left front corner of Figure 13–4.

At another extreme, customers wanting to shop for a broad assortment of
items with reasonable depth might choose a large department store or a mass-
merchandiser—depending on their price/service preferences.

It's no surprise to find that some modern success stories in retailing are retailers which aim at needs along the edges of the market shown in Figure 13–4.
Convenience food stores, for example, don't just sell food—but deliberately sell a
particular assortment-service combination to meet special needs. The same can
be said for specialty shops as well as some of the mass-merchandisers and
department store chains.[19]

Drawing a three-dimensional picture is easy—but it doesn't guarantee that all
parts of the market have the same number of people to be satisfied. In fact, it's

quite possible that some parts would be almost empty. This points out the importance of retailers studying market needs *before* developing their strategies. Retailers should also evaluate the competition in each part of the market—the potential customers may already be loyal to some competing stores.

Why Retailers Evolve and Change

Figure 13–4 helps to summarize relationships among different types of existing stores. Now, we will look at some of the important evolutionary changes in retailing.

Scrambled merchandising—mixing product lines for higher profits

Conventional retailers tend to specialize by product line. But most modern retailers have moved toward **scrambled merchandising**—carrying *any* product lines which they feel they can sell profitably. Traditional grocery stores sold food items. Drug stores sold health and beauty aids. Now, supermarkets and "drug stores" are selling anything they can move in volume—pantyhose, magazines, antifreeze, and potted plants. Mass-merchandisers aren't just selling everyday items, but also cameras, jewelry, and even home computers. Why has scrambled merchandising become so common?

To survive, a retailer must consistently show at least some profit. But typical retailers' net profit margins on sales are very slim—from 0 to 5 percent. And new types of retailers are continually evolving—and putting even more pressure on profits.

Although competition changes, many conventional retailers have rigid pricing policies. Pricing is discussed more in later chapters, but it should be noted here that many conventional retailers have traditionally used fixed percentage markups for *all* items—regardless of the rate of turnover. The fast-moving items contribute nicely to profit—while the slow-moving items tend to reduce profits. So, a firm looking for better profits wants to sell more fast-moving, high-profit items. And it is exactly these items that are scrambling across traditional lines and appearing in unexpected places.

Will retailers keep scrambling for profits?

Figure 13–5 shows the ranges of gross margins conventional retailers have found necessary—to assure staying in business and making *some* profit. *Some* is emphasized because usually the net profit—the difference between a seemingly big gross margin and apparently necessary expenses—is only 1 or a few percent.

Mass-merchandisers and discounters like to operate on gross margins and markups of 15 to 30 percent but—as shown in Figure 13–5—conventional retailers usually need much higher percentages. This figure should give you a better idea of the *why* of scrambled merchandising—and suggest possible directions it will take. Figure 13–5 shows, for example, why scramblers want to sell bakery goods, jewelry, appliances, refreshments, and gifts. Try to analyze why some of

■ FIGURE 13–5   Gross margins in selected retail trades for recent years

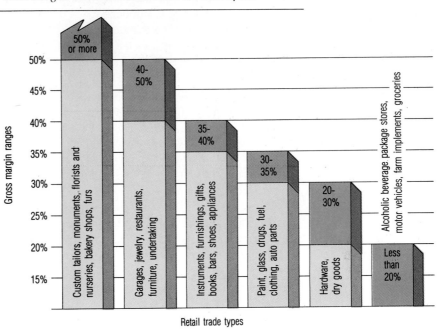

the conventional retailers have such high gross margins—and why other types of retailers can operate more economically.

The wheel of retailing keeps rolling

The **wheel of retailing theory** says that new types of retailers enter the market as low-status, low-margin, low-price operators and then—if they are successful—evolve into more conventional retailers offering more services—with resulting higher operating costs and higher prices. Then they are threatened by new low-status, low-margin, low-price retailers—and the wheel turns again.

Early department stores began this way. Then they became higher priced—and added basement departments to serve the more price-conscious customers. The 5-and-10 cent store and the mail-order house were developed on a price basis—as were the food chains, economy apparel chains, drug chains, and the automotive accessory chains which developed during the 1920s. The supermarket, in turn, was started with low prices and little service.

Some innovators start with high margins

The wheel idea describes a pattern of evolution that holds for many major retailing developments. But there are major exceptions. Vending machines entered retailing as high-cost, high-margin operations. Convenience food stores are high-priced. The branch trend of the department stores—and shopping centers—have not been low-price-oriented. On the contrary, they are sometimes high-price operations.

Product life-cycle concept applies to retailer types, too

Earlier, we talked about the life cycles which products go through. The same ideas help us better understand the evolutionary changes we see when a new development in retailing is introduced. At a given time, many different retailers are trying out new retailing strategies. Many of these don't really fill a need—or they cost too much—and they fail quickly. But, when a good idea catches on—a number of different retailers imitate the strategy and try to attract the same target market. Competition makes it harder to achieve the growth they become used to. So they try to be more attractive to customers. That usually means giving the consumer more—of something. It may be more service, variety, convenience, or value. The battle for customers goes on—until a new type of retailer develops and the process starts over again. This applies to scrambled merchandising, too. The "high-profit" products attract competitors. Over time, some competitors lower the margins on those products as they add them to their traditional lines.

Some types of retailers are far along in their cycles and may be declining. And recent innovators are already in the market maturity stage. See Figure 13–6. Note that the cycles—from introduction to maturity—keep getting shorter.

The retailers who are confused by the scrambling going on around them don't see this evolutionary process—and don't understand that some of their more successful competitors are aiming at different market segments—rather than just

■ FIGURE 13–6   Retailer life-cycle positions

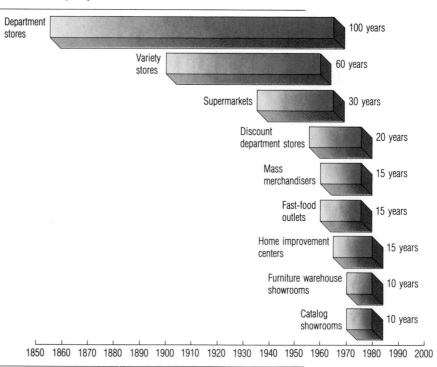

selling products. These product-oriented retailers can get away with focusing on their internal problems during the early stages of the life cycle of a retailer type. But eventually, market maturity sets in, and profits are squeezed. Then they, too, may blindly scramble for more profitable opportunities—or go out of business.

Economies of Scale in Retailing

We have talked about different characteristics of retailers—and how they have evolved. Now let's look at the size of stores—and how they are owned—because this too is related to retailer strategy planning. It is also another area where there has been much change.

The number of retailers is very large

There are lots of retailers—in part because it is easy to enter retailing. Kids can open and close a lemonade stand in one day. A more serious retailer can rent an empty store and be in business with relatively little capital in a few weeks. The large number of retailers might suggest that retailing is a field of small businesses. To an extent, this is true. But as we shall see, small retailers are not that important in any line of business.

Still, the many small retailers can't be ignored. They do reach many consumers—and often are valuable channel members. But they frequently cause difficult problems for producers and wholesalers. Their large number—and relatively small sales volume—make working with them expensive. They often require separate marketing mixes.

Small size may be hard to overcome

A small retailer may satisfy some personal needs—by remaining independent. And a small retailer can be very helpful to some target customers—because of more flexibility. But a small store may only *seem* profitable because some of the costs of doing business are ignored. There may be no allowance for depreciation—or for family members working without pay. Many small retailers gross less than $50,000 in sales annually—which, after expenses, leaves hardly enough to support one person.

Even the average retail store is too small to gain economies of scale. Annual sales for the average store of only $412,000 is not very impressive—especially considering that net profits as a percentage of sales range from 1 to 5 percent.

Larger stores may get some economies of scale—if they can buy in quantity at lower prices, take advantage of mass advertising, and hire specialists. But, larger size alone doesn't guarantee more efficient operation. For example, the departments in a department store might not be any larger than independent limited-line stores—and so there may be little possibility for volume buying.

Being in a chain may help

One way for a retailer to achieve economies of scale is with a corporate chain. Statistics Canada defines a **corporate chain** as "an organization operating four or more retail outlets in the same kind of business, under the same legal ownership." All department stores are considered to be chains, even if they have fewer

Chain stores—like Sears—win a very large share of all retail business.

than four outlets. However, department store statistics are usually not included when figures on corporate chains are quoted. The definition also excludes voluntary chains and franchise operations unless they can meet all the conditions of the chain definition. [20] Most chains have at least some central buying for different stores—which allows them to take advantage of quantity discounts or opportunities for vertical integration. They may also have advantages over independent stores in promotion and management—spreading the costs to many stores. Often, it is the retail chains that have their own dealer brands, too.

Chains grew slowly until after World War I—then spurted ahead during the 1920s. In Canada, there were approximately 8,000 corporate chain outlets by 1930 with sales of $487 million, which then equaled about 18 percent of total retail trade.

From 1930 until the early 1950s, chain stores enjoyed mixed success in Canada, due to the Depression, the war, and the legal restraints placed on chain store operations in the United States, which had a spillover effect into Canada. Chain store share of retail sales hopped around in the 16 to 19 percent range for much of this time.[21] But chains have continued to grow. In 1982 they accounted for slightly more than 33 percent of retail sales—and about 17 percent of all retail outlets.

Chains have done even better in certain lines. They have 100percent of the department store business. Sears, Eaton's, The Bay, and Woodwards are in this category. The mass-merchandisers—like K mart—are usually operated as chains. That gives them more buying power—and makes it easier to fight the price competition.

Independents form chains, too

The growth of corporate chains has encouraged the development of both cooperative chains and voluntary chains.

Cooperative chains are retailer-sponsored groups—formed by independent retailers—to run their own buying organization and conduct joint promotion efforts. Sales of cooperative chains have been rising as they have learned how to meet the corporate chain competition. Examples include Associated Grocers, Certified Grocers, and True Value (in hardware).

Voluntary chains are wholesaler-sponsored groups which work with "independent" retailers. Some are linked by contracts stating common operating procedures—and the use of common store front designs, store name, and joint promotion efforts. The wholesaler-sponsor often provides training programs, computer and accounting assistance, and dealer brands. Examples include IGA in groceries, Home in hardware, and Canadian Tire in auto supplies.

Franchising is similar

In **franchise operations** the franchiser develops a good marketing strategy, and the retail franchise holders carry out the strategy in their own units. They are like voluntary chains. The idea is that the franchise holder benefits from the experience, buying power, and image of a large "chain." In return, the franchise holder usually signs a contract to pay fees and commissions—and to strictly follow franchise rules. Examples include McDonald's (fast food), Midas Mufflers (auto repair), Century 21 (real estate), and Baskin-Robbins (ice cream).

The voluntary chains have tended to work with existing retailers, while some franchisers like to work with newcomers—whom they train and get started. Sometimes they will locate the site—as well as supervise building and the initial promotion and opening.[22]

Consumer co-ops try—but usually in vain

Cooperative and voluntary chains should not be confused with **consumer cooperatives**—which are groups of *consumers* who buy together. These groups usually operate on a non-profit basis—with voluntary or poorly paid management. Consumer cooperatives have never made much of an impact in Canada. Consumer cooperatives have been more successful in Europe—where most retailers have been high-priced and inefficient.

The fate of consumer cooperatives is further evidence that size or goodwill alone does not make an efficient channel system. Economies of scale may be possible, but it takes some hard-headed business decisions to link the members of a channel system efficiently.

Location of Retail Facilities

Consumers will travel only so far to shop at a store—even a special one. Location determines how convenient the store is for customers—and what competition is nearby. But, what is a "good location" can change—as target markets, competitors, costs, and other nearby stores change. Let's review some of the ideas a retailer should consider in selecting a location.

Downtown and shopping strips—evolve without a plan

Most cities have a downtown "central business district"—where many retail stores are found. At first, it may appear that such a district was developed according to some plan. Actually, the location of individual stores is more an accident of time—and what spaces were available. As time goes on, however, the cost of rent downtown forces less profitable stores away from the busiest streets. Further, some streets may begin to specialize by product line—because new retailers want to be close to others who are already attracting customers.

As cities grow, "shopping strips" of convenience stores develop along major roads. Generally, they emphasize convenience goods. But a variety of single-line and limited-line stores may enter too, adding shopping goods to the mix. Often these have difficulty, however, if there is not enough demand nearby. There may be a lot of turnover—as one goes out of business and another takes its place. All of these retail areas are more or less unplanned—except that city planners sometimes restrict commercial development. They certainly are not the planned shopping centers which have developed in the last 30 years.

Planned shopping centers—not just a group of stores

A **planned shopping center** is a set of stores planned as a unit—to satisfy some market needs. The number and type of stores are balanced to the needs of the surrounding market. The idea is that each store will attract more customers because it is with the others. The stores sometimes act together for Promotion purposes too. Many centers are enclosed to make shopping more pleasant. Free parking is usually provided. These centers vary in their mix of stores, size, and location.

Neighborhood shopping centers consist of 5 to 15 retail establishments. These centers usually include a supermarket, drug store, hardware store, beauty shop, laundry, dry cleaner, gas station, and perhaps others—such as a bakery or appliance shop. They normally must serve 7,500 to 40,000 people living within 6 to 10 minutes driving distance.

Community shopping centers are larger with 16 to 30 retail outlets and offer some shopping stores as well as the convenience stores found in neighborhood shopping centers. They usually include a small department store which carries shopping goods (clothing and home furnishings). But most sales in these centers are convenience goods. These centers must serve 40,000 to 150,000 people within a radius of five to six miles.

Many cities are trying to renovate and revitalize downtown shopping areas.

Regional shopping centers are the largest centers. They have over 30 outlets and emphasize shopping stores and shopping goods. They include one or more large department stores—and as many as 200 smaller stores. Stores that feature convenience goods are often placed at the edge of the center—so they won't get in the way of customers primarily interested in shopping.

Regional centers usually serve 150,000 or more persons. They are like downtown shopping districts of larger cities. Regional centers usually are found near populated suburban areas. They draw customers from a radius of 7 to 10 miles—or even further from rural areas where shopping facilities are poor. Regional shopping centers being built now are often in the 2 million square foot range—as large as 40 football fields!

Canadian retailing statistics

In 1983 there were about 160,000 retail outlets in Canada, as compared to almost 60,000 wholesale locations and about 36,000 manufacturers. That same year total trade in Canada amounted to $109.1 billion. The greater portion of this (97.3 percent or $106.2 billion) was accounted for by retail stores. Non-store retailers were responsible for just under $2.9 billion in sales, some 2.7 percent of total retailing. About 80 percent of this $2.9 billion was accounted for by direct sellers—primarily those who sell door-to-door or through mail order. Vending machines and campus book stores made the remainder of the sales in this category.

Although the dollar volume of non-store retailing in Canada has grown about 13 percent since 1980—its share of total retail trade has declined from 3.2 percent to 2.9 percent. All things considered, non-store retailing has not been that effective a way to reach Canada's consumers.

Retailing—the trend toward bigness

Retail store sales in 1983 totaled some $106.2 billion, making retailing a key element in the Canadian economy. The dollar volume of retail trade done by independently owned retail organizations has continued to increase. However, the percentage share of business done by independents has declined steadily from a high of 72.5 percent in the early 1950s to a low of 56.6 percent in 1983. Over the same period the department stores' share of total retail sales has grown from slightly over 8 percent to its present level of 10.3 percent—a slight decrease from the 11 percent level achieved through the 70s and early 80s. Meanwhile, the share of sales accounted for by chain stores has increased from 18.2 percent of all retail sales in 1950 to 33.1 percent in 1983.

Clearly there appears to be an increasing trend to bigness. A review of the nation's largest companies reveals that the Hudson's Bay Company and Provigo, Inc., are 15th and 16th, respectively, in sales ahead of such corporate giants as Trans Canada Pipelines, Ontario Hydro, and the Canada Development Corporation. Also, Canada Safeway, Ltd. (24th), Steinberg (25th), and Sears Canada (26th) are larger than such corporations as the Seagram Co., Air Canada, Stelco, and John Labatt Ltd.[23]

As already noted chain stores dominate the grocery field. In the last 10 years, they have also enjoyed tremendous growth in the apparel trade—where they now account for 53 percent, 62 percent, and 60 percent of the sales of men's clothing stores, women's clothing stores, and family clothing stores, respectively.[24]

Concentration—even among chains

Much of the growth in chain stores' sales has been concentrated in the hands of the big chains. Of the total 1,001 chain store organizations that existed in Canada in 1982—the 22 largest (each with over 200 stores) controlled 30 percent of all chain outlets and made 44.5 percent of all chain store sales. Put another way, the 50 chain organizations with annual sales volumes over $100 million controlled 9,571 stores (35 percent of the total number of outlets) but did 70 percent of all chain store business. While the exact numbers vary somewhat, these general trends appear to hold true for all classes of business in which chains are prominent—supermarkets, men's wear, women's clothing, shoes, and the like.

Concentration among department stores is even greater. Of the 25 department stores organizations operating in 1982 the top 9 chains (over 20 stores each) controlled 93 percent of all department store outlets and 87.8 percent of total department store sales volume. However, the top three organizations—The Bay, Sears, and Eaton's—each had annual sales volumes of over $1.3 billion. Together they accounted for 54.4 percent of all department store sales! And some individual stores are very big. In 1982 there were 27 department stores (out of the 810 in Canada) with annual sales volumes in excess of $50 million. These stores accounted for slightly over 20 percent of all sales made by department store outlets.[25]

Retailing is also geographically concentrated

Since retailers sell to final consumers, they are usually located nearer to people than to production facilities. It is not surprising, then, to find that in 1983, 83.5 percent of Canada's total retail trade was concentrated in the four provinces of Ontario (37.1 percent), Quebec (24.3 percent), British Columbia (11.5 percent), and Alberta (10.6 percent). These figures are close to the share of total disposable personal income for these same four provinces. Indeed, the percentage of retail trade and of disposable personal income is roughly proportional across the country.

Retail trade is also concentrated by city size. In 1983 the four metropolitan centers of Toronto, Montreal, Vancouver, and Winnipeg accounted for slightly more than one third of Canada's total retail trade.[26] Toronto led the way with 13.8 percent followed by Montreal (11.4 percent), Vancouver (5.8 percent), and Winnipeg (2.6 percent).

What Does the Future Look Like?

The changes in retailing in the last 30 years have been rapid—and seem to be continuing. Scrambled merchandising may become more scrambled. Some people are forecasting larger stores—while others are predicting smaller ones.

**More customer-
oriented retailing
may be coming**

Any effort to forecast trends in such a situation is risky—but our three-dimensional picture of the retailing market (Figure 13–4) can be helpful. Those who suggest bigger and bigger stores may be primarily concerned with the center of the market. Those who look for more small stores and specialty shops may be anticipating more small—but increasingly wealthy—target markets able to afford higher prices for special products.

To serve small but wealthy markets, convenience food stores continue to spread. And sales by vending machines—even with their higher operating costs and prices—may grow. Certainly, some customers are getting tired of the large supermarkets that take so much of their time. Logically, convenience goods should be offered at the customer's—rather than the retailer's—convenience. For example, some retailers still fight night and weekend hours—hours when it is most convenient for many families to shop.

**In-home shopping
will become more
popular**

Telephone shopping will become more popular also. The mail-order houses and department stores already find phone business attractive. Telephone supermarkets—now a reality—sell only by phone and deliver all orders. Linking the phone to closed-circuit TV would let the customer see the products at home—while hearing well-prepared sales presentations. The customer could place an order through a home computer system—which would also handle the billing and delivery.

We now have far greater electronic capabilities than we are using. There seems to be no reason why the customer couldn't shop in the home—saving time and gasoline. Such automated retailing could take over a large share of the convenience goods and homogeneous shopping goods business.[27]

**Retailers becoming
manufacturers, and
vice versa**

We may also see more horizontal and vertical arrangements in channel systems. This would certainly affect present manufacturers—who already see retailers developing their own brands, using manufacturers mainly as production arms.

Laura Secord (candy), Glidden and Sherwin Williams (paint), Firestone (rubber), and Bata and Florsheim (shoes) are but some of the firms that already control or own retail outlets. Other manufacturers lease departments in major or junior department stores.

The function of retailing will continue to be needed. But the role of individual retailers—and even the concept of a retail store—may have to change. Customers will always have needs—and they will probably want to satisfy these needs with combinations of goods and services. But retail *stores* aren't necessarily the only way to do this.

**Renting may elimi-
nate buying**

Just as builders of tract homes shifted some home appliance sales from retailers, the builders of new cities may sell completely furnished homes—and eliminate the need for retail home furnishing stores. And apartment builders catering to the mobile young may rent furnished apartments—or offer assortments of furniture for rent from a selection owned by the management. This may fit the needs of a mobile population better than *owning* goods. But it will also have a direct impact on present retailers. Some won't be needed at all!

**Retailers must face
the challenge**

One thing is certain—change in retailing is inevitable. For years, conventional retailers' profits have declined. Even some of the discounters—like the warehouse furniture retailers—and shopping centers have had disappointing results. Department stores, and food and drug chains have seen profit declines. The old variety stores have done even worse. Some shifted into mass merchandising operations—yet that area is less attractive now as limited-line stores try to "meet competition" with lower margins.

A few firms—especially K mart—have avoided this general profit squeeze. But the future doesn't look too bright for retailers who stick with the status quo. New technical developments—like automatic check-out counters—require capital to save labor costs. But the developments are available to all competitors. In our competitive markets, the benefits are passed on to the consumers—but the firms are stuck with higher fixed costs. Further, unionization is increasing labor costs in the traditionally non-union retailing sector.

**No easy way for more
profit**

In fact, it appears that the "fat" has been squeezed out of the retailing sector—and there is no easy route to greater profitability. Instead, careful strategy planning—and great care in implementation—will be needed for success in the future. This means more careful market segmenting to find unsatisfied needs which (1) have a long life expectancy and (2) can be satisfied with low levels of investment. This is a big order. But it is safe to say that the imaginative marketer will find more profitable opportunities than the conventional retailer who doesn't know that the product life cycle is moving along—and is just "hoping for the best."[28]

■ CONCLUSION

Modern retailing is scrambled—and we will probably see more changes in the future. In such a dynamic environment, a producer's marketing manager must choose very carefully among the available kinds of retailers. And retailers must plan their marketing mixes with their target customers' needs in mind—while at the same time trying to be part of an effective channel system.

We described many types of retailers—and saw that each has its advantages and disadvantages. We also saw that modern retailers have discarded conventional practices. The old "buy low and sell high" philosophy is no longer a safe guide. Lower margins for faster turnover seems to be the modern philosophy—as retailers move into mass-merchandising. But even this is no guarantee of success—as retailers' product life cycles move on.

Scrambled merchandising will probably continue as retailing evolves to meet changing consumer demands. But important breakthroughs are still possible—because it seems unlikely that consumers will continue to want all the conventional retail services. Convenience goods, for example, may be made more easily available by some combination of electronic ordering and home delivery or vending. The big, all-purpose department store may not be able to satisfy anyone's needs exactly. Some combination of mail-order and electronic ordering might make a larger assortment of goods available to more people—to better meet their particular needs.

In the face of declining profit margins, new approaches will be tried. Our society needs a retailing function—but it is not certain that all the present retailers are needed. It is safe to say that the future retail scene will offer the marketing manager new challenges and opportunities.

■ QUESTIONS AND PROBLEMS

1. Identify a specialty store selling convenience goods in your city. Explain why you feel it is that kind of a store and why an awareness of this status would be important to a manufacturer. Does it give the retailer any particular advantage? If so, with whom?

2. What sort of a "product" are specialty shops offering? What are the prospects for organizing a chain of specialty shops?

3. A department store consists of many departments. Is this horizontal integration? Are all of the advantages of horizontal integration achieved in a department store operation?

4. Many department stores have a bargain basement. Does the basement represent just another department, like the hat department or the luggage department, for example, or is some whole new concept involved?

5. Distinguish among discount houses, discount selling, and mass-merchandising. Forecast the future of low-price selling in food, clothing, and appliances.

6. In view of the wide range of gross margins (and expenses) in various lines of trade, suggest what the supermarket or scrambled merchandising outlet of the future may be like. Use care here. Are products with high gross margins necessarily highly profitable?

7. List five products which seem suitable for automatic vending and yet are not normally sold in this manner. Generally, what characteristics are required?

8. Apply the "wheel of retailing" theory to your local community. What changes seem likely? Does it seem likely that established retailers will see the need for change, or will entirely new firms have to develop?

9. Discuss the kinds of markets served by the three types of shopping centers. Are they directly competitive? Do they contain the same kinds of stores? Is the long-run outlook for all of them similar?

10. Explain the growth and decline of various retailers and shopping centers in your own community. Use the text's three-dimensional drawing (Figure 13–4) and the product life cycle concept. Also, treat each retailers' whole offering as a "product."

■ SUGGESTED CASES

■ NOTES

1. *Client's Monthly Alert*, June 1977, p. 3.
2. "Bonwit's Turns Up the Heat," *Business Week*, October 11, 1976, pp. 120–22.
3. Statistics Canada, *Retail Chain and Department Stores, 1982*, Cat. 63-210 (Ottawa: Minister of Supply and Services, Canada, April 1984).
4. *Financial Times of Canada*, December 15, 1980, p. 12; and *Globe and Mail*, December 19, 1980, p. B5.
5. "Why Profits Shrink at a Grand Old Name (Marshall Field)," *Business Week*, April 11, 1977, pp. 66–78; Louis H. Grossman, "Merchandising Strategies of a Department Store Facing Change," *MSU Business Topics*, Winter 1970, pp. 31–42; "Suburban Malls Go Downtown," *Business Week*, November 10, 1973, pp. 90–94; and "Smaller Cities, With No End to Suburbanization," *Business Week*, September 3, 1979, pp. 204–6.
6. *Financial Post*, July 6, 1985, p. 1.
7. David Appel, "The Supermarket: Early Development of an Institutional Innovation," *Journal of Retailing*, Spring 1972, pp. 39–53.
8. Statistics Canada, *Retail Chain and Department Stores, 1982*, Cat. 63-210 (Ottawa: Minister of Supply and Services Canada, April 1984).
9. "Supermarkets Eye the Sunbelt," *Business Week*, September 27, 1976, pp. 61–62; "Safeway: Selling Nongrocery Items to Cure the Supermarket Blahs," *Business Week*, March 7, 1977, pp. 52–58; "How a Long Price War Dragged on and Hurt Chicago Food Chains," *The Wall Street Journal*, July 19, 1976, p. 1 f.; and Gilbert D. Harrell and Michael D. Hutt, "Crowding in Retail Stores," *MSU Business Topics*, Winter 1976, pp. 33–39.
10. "Discount Catalogs: A New Way to Sell," *Business Week*, April 29, 1972, pp. 72–74; "Catalog Discounting Is a Small Man's Game," *Business Week*, October 13, 1973, pp. 70–76; and Pradeep K. Korgaonkar, "Consumer Preferences for Catalog Showrooms and Discount Stores," *Journal of Retailing* 58, no. 3 (Fall 1982), pp. 76–88.
11. Douglas J. Tigert and George H. Haines Jr., "The Death of a Discount Store: Analysis of the Changing Structure of Retailing in Canada," in *Problems in Canadian Marketing*, ed. Donald N. Thompson (Chicago: American Marketing Association, 1977), p. 171.
12. Claudia Ricci, "Discount Business Burns, Pleasing Buyers, Irking Department Stores," *The Wall Street Journal*, May 3, 1983, p. 31; and "Mass Merchandisers Move toward Stability," *The Nielsen Researcher*, no. 3 (1976), pp. 19–25.
13. "Those 1,215 K's Stand for Kresge, K mart's, and the Key to Success," *The Wall Street Journal*, March 8, 1977, p. 1 f.; and "Where K mart Goes Next Now That It's No. 2," *Business Week*, June 2, 1980, p. 109.
14. Walter J. Salmon, Robert D. Buzzell, and Stanton G. Cort, "Today the Shopping Center, Tomorrow the Superstore," *Harvard Business Review*, January-February 1974, pp. 89–98; "Super-Stores May Suit Customers to a T—a T-Shirt or a T-Bone," *The Wall Street Journal*, March 13, 1973, p. 1 f.; and *The Super-Store—Strategic Implications For the Seventies* (Cambridge, Mass.: The Marketing Science Institute, 1972).
15. "Convenience Stores: A $7.4 Billion Mushroom," *Business Week*, March 21, 1977, pp. 61–64; "Convenience Stores Battle Lagging Sales by Adding Items and Cleaning Up Image," *The Wall Street Journal*, March 28, 1980, p. 16; and "Arco Takes on Convenience Stores," *Advertising Age*, December 17, 1979, p. 1 f.
16. Statistics Canada, *Vending Machine Operators, 1983*, Cat. 63-213 (Ottawa: Minister of Supply and Services Canada, May 1984).
17. Douglas J. Dalrymple, "Will Automatic Vending Topple Retail Precedence?" *Journal of Retailing*, Spring 1963, pp. 27–31.
18. Statistics Canada, *Direct Selling in Canada, 1983*, Cat. 63-218 (Ottawa: Minister of Supply and Services Canada, May 1984).
19. For more discussion on segmenting of retail markets, see "Fast-Food Franchisers Invade the City," *Business Week*, April 22, 1974, pp. 92–93; "Korvettes Tries for a Little Chic," *Business Week*, May 12, 1973, pp. 124–26; Phillip D. Cooper, "Will Success Produce Problems for the Convenience Store?" *MSU Business Topics*, Winter 1972, pp. 39–43; "Levitz: The Hot Name in 'Instant' Furniture," *Business Week*, December 4, 1971, pp. 90–93; David L. Appel, "Market Segmentation—A Response to Retail Innovation," *Journal of Marketing*, April 1970, pp. 64–67; Steven R. Flaster, "A Consumer Approach to the Specialty Store," *Journal of Retailing*, Spring 1969, pp. 21–31; and A. Coskun Samli, "Segmentation and Carving a Niche in the Market Place," *Journal of Retailing*, Summer 1968, pp. 35–49.
20. Statistics Canada, *Retail Chain and Department Stores, 1982*, Cat. 63-210 (Ottawa: Minister of Supply and Services Canada, April 1984).
21. M. S. Moyer and G. Snyder, "Trends in Canadian Marketing" (Ottawa: Dominion Bureau of Statistics, 1967), pp. 125–48.
22. E. H. Lewis and R. Hancock, *The Franchise System of Distribution* (Minneapolis: University of Minnesota Press, 1963). See also the special issue on franchising in the *Journal of Retailing*, Winter 1968–69.
23. *The Financial Post 500*, Summer 1985, May 25 1985, p. 68.
24. Statistics Canada, *Retail Trade, March 1984*, Cat. 63-005 (Ottawa: Minister of Supply and Services Canada, June 1984).
25. Statistics Canada, *Retail Chain and Department Stores 1982*, Cat. 63-210 (Ottawa: Minister of Supply and Services Canada, April 1984).
26. Statistics Canada, *Retail Trade March 1984*, Cat. 63-005 (Ottawa: Minister of Supply and Services Canada, June 1984).
27. Larry J. Rosenberg and Elizabeth C. Hirschman, "Retailing Without Stores," *Harvard Business Review*, July-August 1980, pp. 103–12.
28. Albert D. Bates, "The Troubled Future of Retailing," *Business Horizons*, August 1976, pp. 22–28; William R. Davidson, Albert D. Bates, and Stephen J. Bass, "Retail Life Cycle," *Harvard Business Review*, November-December 1976, pp. 89–96; "Investigating the Collapse of W. T. Grant," *Business Week*, July 19, 1976, pp. 60–62; "Shopping Center Boom Appears to Be Fading Due to Overbuilding," *The Wall Street Journal*, September 7, 1976, p. 1 f; "Jewel Co. Discloses Operations Review in Search of a More Successful Strategy," *The Wall Street Journal*, March 23, 1977, p. 12; Ronald D. Michman, "Changing Patterns in Retailing," *Business Horizons*, October 1979, pp. 33–38; "The Discount Twist in Suburban Shopping Malls," *Business Week*, July 7, 1980, pp. 95–96; "Sears Mulls Test of Catalog Sales via Warner Cable," *Advertising Age*, February 18, 1980, p. 1 f; and Patrick J. Kelly and William R. George, "Strategic Management Issues for the Retailing of Services," *Journal of Retailing* 58, no. 2 (Summer 1982), pp. 26–43.

Chapter 14 ■ Wholesaling

When you finish this chapter, you should:

1. Understand what wholesalers are and the wholesaling functions they *may* provide for others in channel systems.

2. Know the various kinds of merchant wholesalers and agent middlemen.

3. Understand when and where the various kinds of merchant wholesalers and agent middlemen would be most useful to channel planners.

4. Understand why wholesalers have lasted.

5. Recognize the important new terms (shown in red).

"I can get it for you wholesale," the man said. But could he? Would it be a good deal?

George Mims is a heating contractor. His company sells heating systems—and his crew installs them in new buildings. Mr. Mims gets a lot of help from Air Control Company, the wholesaler who supplies this equipment. When Mims isn't certain what type of furnace to install, the experts at the wholesale company give him good technical advice. They also keep an inventory of products from a number of different manufacturers. This means that Mr. Mims can order a piece of equipment when he is ready to install it. He doesn't need to tie up his money in a big inventory—or wait for a part to be shipped cross country from the producer. Air Control Company even helps him to finance his business. Mims doesn't have to pay for his purchases until 30 days after he takes delivery. By then, he has finished his work and been paid by his customers. Mr. Mim's whole way of doing business would be different without this wholesaler—who provides channel functions.

Alice Hansen took a job right out of college as a sales rep for a big toy producer. She called on toy and hobby stores, and department stores in British Columbia. After a while, she developed a good relationship with her customers—and a "feel" for what would sell well in their stores. She also realized that there were many small toy producers who couldn't afford to hire their own sales force. So she quit her job—and formed her own sales company. She contracted with many small producers to sell their toys and games to the stores she had called on. At a given store, she might sell toys from several producers. She didn't have a warehouse—or even buy any inventory of her own. She sent in orders to the producers—who shipped directly to the stores. She was paid a percentage of the total dollar sales. The toy makers were pleased to have a way to reach some new markets—and the retailers were glad to have some new toy lines that consumers liked. Before long, Hansen had to hire additional salespeople to work for her—so more retailers could be served.

These examples show that wholesalers can perform very different functions. They also show that a wholesaler is often a vital link in a channel system—and in the whole marketing process—helping both their suppliers and customers. Of course, wholesalers—like other businesses—must select their target markets and marketing mixes carefully. But you can understand wholesalers better if you look at them as members of channels—rather than as separate business firms.

In this chapter, you will learn more about wholesalers. You will see how they have evolved, how they fit into various channels, why they are used, and what functions they perform.

What Is a Wholesaler?

This question is hard to answer exactly, but one way to get at a definition is to find out why a firm might want to be considered a wholesaler rather than a retailer. There are several reasons.

How to tell a wholesaler from a retailer

First—in some channels—manufacturers sell only to wholesalers. The wholesalers, in turn, are expected to sell only to other middlemen or producers—but *not* to final consumers. Exactly which firms will be allowed to buy from a manufacturer depends on how the manufacturer defines a wholesaler.

Second, is the amount of discount granted. If retailers in a certain line normally expect a 30 percent discount off the suggested retail list price, then the

There is wide variation in the way wholesalers operate, but they do not sell in large amounts to final consumers.

wholesalers supplying them may be given a 45 percent discount off retail list. They, in turn, are expected to pass on a 30 percent discount to their retailers. In practice, this can be much more complicated.

Some manufacturers set up a scale of wholesale discounts—depending on sales size and services offered. These "trade discounts" are discussed further in the pricing chapters. Correctly determining which firms are entitled to what trade discounts is a serious matter—because of the possibility of violating the price discrimination laws.

Third, some cities and provinces have retail sales taxes—or taxes on inventories or gross receipts—that apply only to retailers. These taxes require record keeping—and out-of-pocket costs when the tax is not collected from the consumer. You can understand why some firms try to avoid being classified as retailers.

Any of these three points explains why a firm might wish to be labeled a wholesaler rather than a retailer.

A wholesaler—by any other name—is still a middleman

It is hard to write a definition of wholesaling that is both short and complete. The *main* source of this difficulty is the *wide variation* in the way wholesale firms operate, the functions performed, the cost of operations, and the operating policies followed.

Many wholesalers perform more functions than we usually associate with the term. Some wholesalers engage in all four regrouping activities—and some of their sorting and accumulating activities may even seem like manufacturing. As a result, we find some firms calling themselves "manufacturer and jobber" or "manufacturer and dealer." In addition, some use general terms such as merchant, dealer, distributor, or jobber because their actual operations are flexible—and they don't wish to be narrowly classified.

We will use the Statistics Canada definition of wholesalers:

> **wholesalers** are primarily engaged in buying merchandise for resale to retailers; to industrial, commercial, institutional, and professional users; to other wholesalers; for export; to farmers for use in farm production; or acting as agents in such transactions.
>
> Mixed activity business (such as firms engaged in both wholesaling and retailing, contracting, service trades, manufacturing, etc.) are considered to be in wholesale trade whenever they derive the largest portion of their gross margin from their wholesaling activity.[1]

It should be noted that producers who take over wholesaling activities are not considered wholesalers. However, if separate establishments—such as branch warehouses—are set up, some of these facilities are counted as wholesalers by Statistics Canada. Wholesaling is a middleman activity. When a manufacturer goes direct, it still must assume the marketing functions that an independent wholesaler might provide. This is important from a channel standpoint. Wholesaling functions usually must be performed by some channel member—whether a wholesaler, the manufacturer, or a retailer.

Possible Wholesaling Functions

Wholesalers may perform certain functions for both their own customers and their suppliers—in short, for those above and below them in a channel. These *wholesaling functions* really are variations of the basic marketing functions—buying, selling, grading, storing, transporting, financing, risk taking, and gathering market information. These wholesaling functions are basic to the following discussion and should be studied carefully now. But *keep in mind that these functions are provided by some, but not all, wholesalers.*

What a wholesaler might do for customers

1. *Regroup goods*—provide at least one and sometimes all four regrouping activities—to provide the quantity and assortment wanted by customers at the lowest possible cost.
2. *Anticipate needs*—forecast customers' demands and buy accordingly.
3. *Carry stocks*—carry inventory so customers don't have to store a large inventory.
4. *Deliver goods*—provide prompt delivery at low cost.
5. *Grant credit*—give credit to customers, perhaps supplying their working capital. Note: This financing function may be *very* important to small customers—and is sometimes the main reason why they use wholesalers—rather than buying directly from manufacturers.
6. *Provide information and advisory service*—supply price and technical information as well as suggestions on how to install and sell products. Note: The wholesaler's sales reps may be experts in the products they sell.
7. *Provide part of buying function*—offer products to potential customers so they don't have to hunt for supply sources.
8. *Own and transfer title to goods*—permits completing a sale without the need for other middlemen—speeding the whole buying and selling process.

What a wholesaler might do for producer-suppliers

1. *Provide part of producer's selling function*—by going to producer-suppliers instead of waiting for their sales reps to call.
2. *Store inventory*—reducing a producer's need to carry large stocks—and cutting his warehousing expenses.
3. *Supply capital*—reducing a producer's need for working capital by buying his output and carrying it in inventory until it is sold.
4. *Reduce credit risk*—by selling to customers the wholesaler knows—and taking the loss if these customers don't pay. Note: A producer's target customers may be numerous. And some may be poor credit risks. It is expensive for a small producer—especially one far away—to evaluate all these potential credit risks when selling only one or a few products. The wholesaler who sells these customers many products is in a better position to evaluate their credit status. Also, if the wholesaler is a source of supply for many products, the customers may be more likely to pay a helpful wholesaler than a producer from whom they may not reorder.
5. *Provide market information*—as an informed buyer and seller closer to the market, the wholesaler reduces the producer's need for market research.[2]

Kinds and Costs of Available Wholesalers

Why do manufacturers use merchant wholesalers costing about 19 percent of sales as opposed to using their own sales branches?

Why use either when brokers cost only about 3.0 percent?

Is the use of wholesalers with higher operating expenses the reason why marketing costs are high—if, in fact, they are?

To answer these questions, we must understand what these wholesalers do—and don't do. Figure 14–1 gives a big-picture view of the wholesalers described in more detail below. Note that a major difference is whether they *own* the goods they sell.

Each wholesaler found a niche

In this text, we are emphasizing the evolution of our marketing system—and this certainly applies to wholesaling. Canada has transformed itself from a colonial territory—dependent on England for its finished goods in exchange for raw materials—into an industrial nation. As output grew, so did the need for middlemen to handle it.

■ FIGURE 14–1   Type of wholesalers

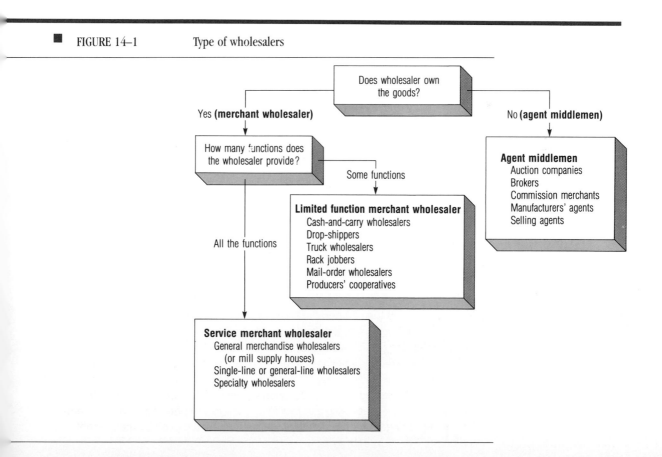

To serve the retail general stores of earlier times, wholesalers carried a wide line of merchandise. They were called "general merchandise" wholesalers—because their merchandise was so varied. We already have seen that the general store developed into a single- or limited-line store—as towns grew and more goods became available. To serve these stores, "single-line" wholesalers developed. Those specializing in very narrow lines were called "specialty" wholesalers.

As wholesaling changed to distribute the greater production of the factories to a growing population, wholesalers served not only retailers and final consumers—but also manufacturers. Many manufacturers were so small that it was hard for them to contact the growing number of wholesalers or other manufacturer customers, so special wholesalers—called agent middlemen—developed to make these contacts. In general, specialized needs arose—and specialized wholesalers developed to meet them. The wholesalers changed as the needs changed.[3]

Wholesaler provides access to a target market

One of the principal assets of a wholesaler is its customers. The wholesaler tries to offer a unique service to certain customers—and may be the only one who does this particular job. The manufacturer who wants to reach the market segment served by the wholesaler *may have no choice but to use that wholesaler.* What customers does this wholesaler serve should be one of the first questions you ask when planning a channel of distribution.[4]

Learn the pure to understand the real

The next important question would be, What functions does this particular wholesaler provide? Wholesalers typically specialize by product line—a fact which should please product-oriented manufacturers! But they do provide different functions—and probably will keep doing what they are doing—no matter what others might like them to do.

To get a clear understanding of wholesaling, we will identify and analyze different "pure types" of wholesalers—as if only certain pure types performed a specific set of functions. In practice, it may be difficult to find examples of these pure types—because many wholesalers are mixtures. Further, the names commonly used in a particular industry may be misleading. Some so-called "brokers" actually behave as limited-function merchant wholesalers—and some "manufacturers' agents" operate as full-service wholesalers. This casual use of terms makes it all the more important for you to thoroughly understand the pure types before trying to understand the blends—and the names given to them in the business world. Similarly, a manufacturer's or retailer's marketing manager should understand these differences *and* clearly specify *desired* Place objectives—before trying to select suitable wholesalers.

In the following pages, we will discuss the major types of wholesalers which have been identified by Statistics Canada—to guide its data collection. Remember, detailed data is available by kind of business, by product line, and by geographic territory. Among other things, such detailed data can be valuable in strategy planning—especially in determining if there are potential channel members serving a target market—and the sales volumes achieved by the present middlemen.

In international markets, we find the same kinds of wholesalers as in Canada—although good data may be lacking. In addition, different names may be used. And this again emphasizes the importance of understanding the pure types.

Merchant Wholesalers Are the Most Numerous

Merchant wholesalers own (take title to) the goods they sell. For example, a wholesale lumber yard that buys plywood from the producer is a merchant wholesaler. It actually owns—"takes title to"—the lumber for some period of time before selling to its customers.

In addition to taking title, merchant wholesalers also provide some—or all—of the wholesaling functions. There are two basic kinds of merchant wholesalers: (1) service—sometimes called full-service wholesalers and (2) limited-function or limited-service wholesalers. Their names explain their difference.

Service wholesalers provide all the functions

Service wholesalers provide all the wholesaling functions. Within this basic group are three types: (1) *general merchandise,* (2) *single line,* and (3) *specialty.*

General merchandise wholesalers carry a wide variety of non-perishable items such as hardware, electrical supplies, plumbing supplies, furniture, drugs, cosmetics, and automobile equipment. With this broad line of convenience and shopping goods, they serve general stores, hardware stores, drug stores, electric appliance shops, and small department stores. In the industrial goods field, the *mill supply house* operates in a similar way. Somewhat like a hardware store, the mill supply house carries a broad variety of accessories and supplies for industrial customers.

General merchandise wholesalers carry a wide variety of non-perishable staple items.

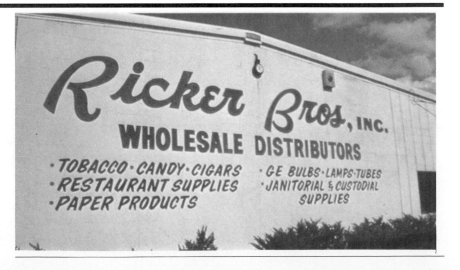

Single-line (or general-line) wholesalers carry a narrower line of merchandise than general merchandise wholesalers. For example, they might carry only groceries, or wearing apparel, or certain types of industrial tools or supplies. In consumer goods, they service the single- and limited-line stores. In industrial goods, they cover a wider geographic area and offer more specialized service.

Specialty wholesalers carry a very narrow range of products. A consumer goods specialty wholesaler might carry only health foods or oriental foods—instead of a full line of groceries. Or a specialty house might carry only automotive items—selling exclusively to mass-merchandisers.

Specialty wholesalers often know a great deal about the final target markets in their channel. One wholesaler, for example, is willing to arrange and stock mass-merchandisers' shelves—an important service to these retailers because their customers' behavior seems to vary according to geography. Final consumers in Quebec, for instance, respond to different shelf arrangements and products than do those in western Canada. The specialty wholesalers' job is to learn these differences—and adjust stocks and displays accordingly. In this effort, they go further than most merchant wholesalers—providing some of the customers' selling function—since displays do most of the selling in mass-merchandising outlets. Figure 14–2 tells how one Saskatchewan firm has become a major distributor of jeans by being ready to sell in small quantities.

An industrial goods specialty wholesaler might limit himself to fields requiring technical knowledge or service—perhaps electronics or plastics. The Cadillac Plastic and Chemical Company in Detroit became a specialty wholesaler serving the needs of both plastics makers and users. Neither the large plastics manufacturers nor the merchant wholesalers with wide lines were able to give technical advice to each of the many customers (who often have little knowledge of which product would be best for them). Cadillac carries 10,000 items and sells to 25,000 customers—ranging in size from very small firms to General Motors.

Limited-function wholesalers provide some functions

Limited-function wholesalers provide only *some* wholesaling functions. Figure 14–3 shows the functions typically provided—and not provided. In the following paragraphs, the main features of these wholesalers will be discussed. Some are not very numerous. In fact, they are not counted separately by Statistics Canada. Nevertheless, these wholesalers are very important for some products.

Cash-and-carry wholesalers want cash

Cash-and-carry wholesalers operate like service wholesalers—except that the customer must pay cash.

Many small retailers—especially small grocers and garages—are too small to be served profitably by a service wholesaler. So service wholesalers set a minimum charge, or just refuse to handle certain customers' business. Or they may set up a *cash-and-carry department* to give the small retailer the products needed in exchange for cash on the counter. This works like a retail store—but for small retailers. It can operate at lower cost—because the retailers take over many wholesaling functions. And using cash-and-carry outlets may allow the small retailer to stay in business.

■   FIGURE 14–2   Joyner finds big market serving small retailers

Sixty-five Ontario retailers are buying jeans manufactured in Toronto from a jean distributorship in Moose Jaw, which is one illustration of the success of Ted Joyner in finding a profitable market niche.

Joyner's business venture started as a favor to a fellow retailer, and grew into a jean distributorship with gross sales of more than $2 million a year.

Joyner's, Ltd., Associated Services Buying Office sells jeans to 1,000 small retailers located in small towns from Ontario to British Columbia. The majority of Joyner's customers buy in volumes which are often too small to interest large manufacturers and traditional wholesalers. Joyner pools his customers' orders.

The distributorship started in mid-1974, when a retailer from a southern Saskatchewan town walked into Joyner's Department Store in Moose Jaw, and told Joyner of the trouble he was having getting service from jean manufacturers. Joyner has heard much the same story, he says, from other retailers many times since.

Jean manufacturers are geared to serve the large-volume purchaser. The bulk of the selling is done for the spring and fall seasons, and supplement or "fill-in" orders are placed throughout the year to bolster supplies of a popular style, or to replenish sold-out sizes.

For a large chain, fill-in orders are usually sizable, and the purchaser can expect preferred shipping. A small retailer usually is faced with about three months' lead time to get an order in the store—and that poses some problems. The retailer has to anticipate what market trends will be three months down the road, to tie up money in inventories and face the possibility of selling out of a particular size or style.

For the past six years, Joe Orban of Joe's Men's Wear in Assiniboia, Saskatchewan, 125 kilometers south of Moose Jaw, has solved the problem by buying his jeans from Joyner's. He says the minimum order he can place with a manufacturer is two or three dozen pairs, with a lead time of three months. If he buys from Joyner's, he says he can buy what he needs and usually gets delivery the same day by bus.

Wayne Buck, owner of Fay's Fashions in Gull Lake, Saskatchewan, says it is virtually impossible for him to buy jeans from the manufacturers. "By the time I can get an order in, the styles have changed," he says.

Joyner says he can compete successfully with the traditional wholesalers or "jobbers" because his prices and selection are better.

After six years in the business, he says he is able to anticipate what market demands for the major styles will be, and in practice, actually buys some of his stock in advance. During peak periods, Joyner says, he holds about $200,000-worth of jeans in inventory, which he uses to fill orders from his regular supply list. An order from a customer can usually be shipped out the same day by bus, rail, or mail.

Joyner also sells less widely known lines from what he calls a "fringe list." Orders for these jeans are pooled until the collective order is large enough to place with a manufacturer.

Despite the "intestinal fortitude" it sometimes takes retailers to admit they buy their jeans in Moose Jaw, Joyner says the service has caught on well with small-town retailers. While he has salesmen in all the provinces he operates in except Saskatchewan, he says the majority of his new customers have been referred by other customers.

Phil Slade, owner of Clothes Encounter in Moose Jaw, says the ability to buy in small volumes to try out new styles has proved invaluable to his operation: "Instead of gambling with $1,000 you can gamble with $100."

Despite gross sales for the distributorship of $2 million in 1979 which, Joyner says, from all indications will be surpassed this year, he says the profit margin on the distributorship is slim, and retail business continues to be his main source of income.

Source: "Joyner Finds Big Market Serving Small Retailers," Western Business Section, *Financial Post,* June 7, 1980.

■   FIGURE 14–3   Functions provided by limited-function merchant wholesalers

Functions	Cash-and-carry	Drop-shipper	Truck	Mail-order	Cooperatives	Rack jobbers
For customers:						
Anticipates needs	X		X	X	X	X
"Regroups" goods (one or more of four steps)	X		X	X	X	X
Carries stocks	X		X	X	X	X
Delivers goods			X		X	X
Grants credit		X	Maybe	Maybe	Maybe	Consignment (in some cases)
Provides information and advisory services		X	Some	Some	X	
Provides buying function		X	X	X	Some	X
Owns and transfers title to goods	X	X	X	X	X	X
For producers:						
Provides producers' selling function	X	X	X	X	X	X
Stores inventory	X		X	X	X	X
Helps finance by owning stocks	X		X	X	X	X
Reduces credit risk	X	X	X	X	X	X
Provides market information	X	X	Some	X	X	Some

Drop-shipper does not handle the goods

Drop-shippers own the goods they sell—but do not actually handle, stock, or deliver them. These wholesalers are mainly involved in selling. They get orders—from wholesalers, retailers, or industrial users—and pass these orders on to producers. Then the orders are shipped directly to the customers. Because drop-shippers do not have to handle the goods, their operating costs are lower.

Drop-shippers commonly sell products which are so bulky that additional handling would be expensive—and possibly damaging. Also, the quantities they usually sell are so large that there is little need for regrouping—for example, rail carload shipments of coal, lumber, oil, or chemical products.

Truck wholesalers deliver—at a cost

Truck wholesalers specialize in delivering goods which they stock in their own trucks. Handling perishable products in general demand—tobacco, candy, potato chips, and salad dressings—truck wholesalers may provide almost the same functions as full-service wholesalers. Their big advantage is that they deliver perishable products that regular wholesalers prefer not to carry. Also, they may call on many small service stations and "back-alley" garages—providing local delivery of the many small items these customers often forget to pick up from a service wholesaler. Truck wholesalers' operating costs are relatively high—because they provide a lot of service for the little they sell.

Mail-order whole-salers reach outlying stores

Mail-order wholesalers sell out of catalogs which may be distributed widely to smaller industrial customers or retailers. These wholesalers operate in the hardware, jewelry, sporting goods, and general merchandise lines. Their markets are often small industrial or retailer customers who might not be called on by other middlemen.

Producers' coopera-tives do sorting

Producers' cooperatives operate almost as full-service wholesalers—with the "profits" going to the cooperative's customer-members—in the form of "pa-tronage dividends." They develop in agricultural markets—where there are many small producers.

The successful producers' cooperatives have emphasized sorting—to im-prove the quality of farm products offered to the market. Some have also branded these improved products—and then promoted the brands. Farmers' co-operatives and marketing boards have also been successful in restricting output and increasing price—by taking advantage of the normally inelastic demand for agricultural commodities.

Rack jobbers sell hard-to-handle assortments

Rack jobbers specialize in non-food items which are sold through grocery stores and supermarkets—and they often display them on their own wire racks. Most grocers don't want to bother with reordering and maintaining displays of non-food items (housewares, hardware items, and health and beauty aids) be-cause they sell small quantities of so many different kinds of goods. And regular wholesalers handling such items may not be too interested in this business either—because opening up this new channel might strain relations with their present retailer customers. Rack jobbers are almost service wholesalers—except that they usually are paid cash for the amount of stock sold or delivered.

This is a relatively expensive operation—with operating costs of about 18 per-cent of sales. The large volume of sales from these racks has encouraged some large chains to experiment with handling such items themselves. But they often find that rack jobbers can provide this service as well as—or better than—they can themselves. For example, a rack jobber that wholesales paperback books studies which titles are selling in the local area—and applies that knowledge in many stores. The chain has many stores, perhaps, but in different areas where preferences vary. It may not be worth the extra effort to try to study the market in each area.

Agent Middlemen Are Strong on Selling

They don't own the goods

Agent middlemen are wholesalers who do not own the goods they sell. Their main purpose is to help in buying and selling. They usually provide even fewer functions than the limited-function wholesalers. In certain trades, however, they are extremely valuable. They may operate at relatively low cost, too—sometimes 2 to 6 percent of their selling price.

■ **FIGURE 14–4**   Functions provided by agent middlemen

Functions	Manufacturers' agents	Brokers	Commission merchants	Selling agents	Auction companies
For customers:					
Anticipates needs	Sometimes	Some			
"Regroups" goods (one or more of four steps)	Some		X		X
Carries stocks	Sometimes		X		Sometimes
Delivers goods	Sometimes		X		
Grants credit			Sometimes	X	Some
Provides information and advisory services	X	X	X	X	
Provides buying function	X	Some	X	X	X
Owns and transfers title to goods			Transfers only		Transfers only
For producer:					
Provides producers' selling function	X	Some	X	X	X
Stores inventory	Sometimes		X		X
Helps finance by owning stocks					
Reduces credit risk				X	Some
Provides market information	X	X	X	X	

Agent middlemen—like merchant wholesalers—normally specialize by customer type—and by product or product line—and so it is important to determine exactly what each one does.

In the following paragraphs, only the most important points about each type will be mentioned. See Figure 14–4 for details on the functions provided by each. It is obvious from the number of empty spaces in Figure 14–4 that agent middlemen provide fewer functions than merchant wholesalers.

Manufacturers' agents—free-wheeling sales reps

A **manufacturers' agent** sells similar products for several noncompeting manufacturers—for a commission on what is actually sold. Such agents work almost as members of each company's sales force—but they are really independent middlemen. Manufacturers' agents account for more than half of all agent middlemen.

Their big "plus" is that they already call on a group of customers and can add another product line at relatively low cost and no cost to the producer until they sell something! If the sales potential in an area is low, a manufacturers' agent may be used instead of a company's own sales rep because the agent can do the job at lower cost. A small producer often has to use agents everywhere—because its sales volume is too small or too spread out to justify its own sales force.

Manufacturers' agents are very useful in fields where there are many small manufacturers who need to contact customers. These agents are often used in the sale of machinery and equipment, electrical goods, automobile products, clothing and apparel accessories, and some food products. They may cover one city or several provinces.

The agent's main job is selling. The agent—or the agent's customer—sends the orders to the producer. The agent, of course, gets credit for the sale. Agents seldom have any part in setting prices—or deciding on the producer's policies. Basically, they are independent, aggressive salespeople.

Agents can be especially useful in introducing new products. For this service, they may earn 10 to 15 percent commission. (In contrast, their commission on large-volume established goods may be quite low—perhaps only 2 percent.) The higher rates for new products often become the agent's major disadvantage for the manufacturer. The 10 to 15 percent commission rate may have seemed small when the product was new—and sales volume was low. Once the product is selling well, the rate seems high. At about this time, the producer often begins using its own sales reps—and the manufacturers' agents must look for other new products to develop. Agents are well aware of this possibility. Most try to work for many manufacturers—so they are not dependent on only one or a few lines.

Brokers provide information

Brokers bring buyers and sellers together. Brokers usually have a temporary relationship with the buyer and seller—while a particular deal is negotiated. Their "product" is information about what buyers need—and what supplies are available. They aid in buyer-seller negotiation. If the transaction is completed, they earn a commission from whichever party hired them.

Usually, some kind of broker will develop whenever and wherever market information is inadequate. Brokers are especially useful for selling seasonal products. For example, they could represent a small food canner during the canning season—then go on to other activities.

Brokers are also active in used machinery, real estate, and even ships. These products are not similar, but the needed marketing functions are. In each case, buyers don't come into the market often. Someone with knowledge of available

Some kind of broker will develop whenever and wherever market information is inadequate.

products is needed to help both buyers and sellers complete the transaction quickly and inexpensively.

Commission merchants handle and sell goods in distant markets

Commission merchants handle goods shipped to them by sellers, complete the sale, and send the money—minus their commission—to each seller.

Commission merchants are common in agricultural markets where farmers must ship to big-city central markets. They need someone to handle the goods there—as well as to sell them—since the farmer can't go with each shipment. Although commission merchants do not own the goods, they generally are allowed to sell them at the market price—or the best price above some stated minimum. Prices in these markets usually are published in newspapers, so the producer-seller has a check on the commission merchant. Costs are usually low because commission merchants handle large volumes of goods—and buyers usually come to them.

Commission merchants are sometimes used in other trades—such as textiles. Here, many small producers wish to reach buyers in a central market—without having to maintain their own sales force.

Selling agents— almost marketing managers

Selling agents take over the whole marketing job of manufacturers—not just the selling function. A selling agent may handle the entire output of one or more producers—even competing producers—with almost complete control of pricing, selling, and advertising. In effect, the agent becomes each producer's marketing manager.

Financial trouble is one of the main reasons a producer calls in a selling agent. The selling agent may provide working capital—but also may take over the affairs of the business.

Selling agents have been especially common in highly competitive fields— like textiles and coal. They also have been used for marketing lumber, certain food products, clothing items, and some metal products. In all these industries, marketing is much more important than production for the survival of firms. The selling agent provides the necessary financial assistance and marketing know-how.

Auction companies— display the goods

Auction companies provide a place where buyers and sellers can come together and complete a transaction. Auction companies are not numerous, but they are important in certain lines—such as livestock, fur, tobacco, and used cars. For these products, demand and supply conditions change rapidly—and the product must be seen to be evaluated. Buyers and sellers, therefore, are brought together by the auction company—and demand and supply interact to determine the price while the goods are being inspected.

Facilities can be plain—keeping overhead costs low. Frequently, auction sheds are close to transportation so that the commodities can be reshipped quickly. The auction company charges a set fee or commission for the use of its facilities and services.

International marketing is not so different

We find agent middlemen in international trade, too. Most operate much like those just described. **Export or import agents** are basically manufacturers' agents. **Export or import commission houses** and **export or import brokers** are really brokers. A **combination export manager** is a blend of manufacturers' agent and selling agent—handling the entire export function for several manufacturers of similar but non-competing lines. As with domestic agent middlemen, it is necessary to determine exactly what functions each one provides before deciding to use it in a channel system.

Agent middlemen are more common in international trade because of the critical problem of financing. Many markets have only a few well-financed merchant wholesalers. The best many manufacturers can do is get local representation through agents—and then arrange financing through banks which specialize in international trade.

Manufacturers' Sales Branches Provide Wholesaling Functions, Too

The drive toward horizontal and vertical integration that began in the late 1880s had its effect in wholesaling, too. Many manufacturers set up their own sales branches whenever the sales volume—or the nature of their products—justified it. These branches also sell products produced by others.

Manufacturers' sales branches are separate businesses which manufacturers set up away from their factories. For example, computer manufacturers such as IBM set up local branches to provide service, display equipment, and handle sales. As these branches are usually placed in the best market areas, many of them do a considerable amount of business. This also helps explain why their operating costs are often lower. But cost comparisons between various channels can be misleading, since sometimes the cost of selling is not charged to the

Sales finance companies provide financing of expensive display stocks.

branch. If all the expenses of the manufacturers' sales branches were charged to them, they probably would be more costly than they seem now.

In Canada, if goods are transferred to the sales branches at final market value, they are considered an arm of the plant and therefore not wholesalers. However, when goods are provided at manufacturers' final selling price (manufacturer's cost plus markup), then the sales branches are considered to be separate entities. They are, therefore, defined as wholesalers. These definitions hold true only for branches owned by Canadian manufacturing plants. If a sales branch is owned by a foreign plant, it is considered to be a wholesale merchant.

Other Specialized Middlemen—Facilitators—Fill Unique Roles

Factors—like a credit department

In some competitive markets, sellers must provide customers long-term financing to make a sale. For example, a textile company might buy some specialized fabric dying equipment only if the producer will finance the sale for five years. To close the deal, the seller might agree to the terms. But then the textile company might wish to sell its account receivable to a factor—for less than the amount due—to get cash quicker and be sure it can make the equipment payments on time.

Factors are wholesalers of credit—who buy their clients' accounts receivable. In buying accounts receivable, factors provide their clients with working capital—the financing function. A factor may provide advice on customer selection and collection, too. In effect, the factor may assume the function of a credit department—relieving clients of this expense. Sometimes, factors also provide management assistance—and almost become selling agents.

Usually factors specialize in certain lines of trade—such as textiles—and are willing to extend credit for longer periods than commercial banks. By specializing in a certain line, they get to know most of the buyers in that trade—and are better able to evaluate the credit risks.

Field warehousing— cash for goods on hand

Another specialist in financing is the **field warehouser**—a firm which segregates some of a company's finished goods on its own property and issues warehouse receipts which can be used to borrow money. If a firm has accounts receivable, it can use a factor or even borrow at a bank. But if it has financial problems and its goods are not yet sold, then borrowing may be more difficult. One solution is to move the goods to a public warehouse and obtain a warehouse receipt—which can then be used as collateral for borrowing at a bank. But moving goods can be expensive.

In field warehousing, the producer's own warehouse is used, but an area is formally segregated by the field warehouser. The producer retains title to the goods, but control of them passes to the field warehouser. A receipt is issued which can be used as collateral in borrowing. These field warehousing organizations usually know capital sources—and may be able to arrange loans at lower cost than is possible locally.

Using this method, large stocks can be maintained at various distribution points—in anticipation of future needs. Or economical production runs can be made—and then stored at the factory against future needs.

Sales finance companies—do floor planning

Some **sales finance companies** finance inventories. **Floor planning** is the financing of display stocks for auto and appliance retailers. Many auto dealers, for example, do not own any of the cars on their display floors. They may have only a 10 percent interest in each of them—the other 90 percent belonging to a sales finance company. The auto dealer has physical possession. But the finance company owns the cars—and the proceeds from sales may go directly to it to pay off the loan. Any "surplus" is returned to the auto dealer, of course.

In effect, these companies are providing part of the retailer's financing function. But because the goods are usually well branded—and therefore easily resold—there is relatively little risk. The charge to the retailer for these services may be as low as 12 percent a year—just a little above the finance company's cost of borrowing money.

Wholesalers Tend to Concentrate Together

Different wholesalers are found in different places

Some wholesalers—such as grain elevator operators—are located close to producers. But most wholesaling is done in or near large cities.

This heavy concentration of wholesale sales in large cities is caused, in part, by the concentration of manufacturers' sales offices and branches in these attractive markets. It also is caused by the tendency of agent middlemen to locate in these large cities—near the many large wholesalers and industrial buyers.

Some progressive wholesalers are using automated warehouses to provide better service.

Some large manufacturers buy for many plants through one purchasing department located in the general offices in these cities. And large general merchandise wholesalers often are located in these transportation and commerce centers. This is true not only in Canada—but also in world markets. Wholesalers tend to concentrate together—near transporting, storing, and financing facilities—as well as near a large population.

Comeback and Future of Wholesalers

In the 1800s, wholesalers held a dominant position in marketing. The many small producers and small retailers needed their services. As producers became larger, some bypassed the wholesalers—by setting up their own sales organizations or by selling directly to industrial customers. When retailers also began to grow larger—especially during the 1920s when chain stores began to spread rapidly—many predicted a gloomy future for wholesalers. Chain stores normally assume the wholesaling functions—and it was thought that the days of independent wholesalers were numbered.

Not fat and lazy, but enduring

Some analysts and critics felt that the decline of wholesalers might be desirable from the social point of view—because many wholesalers had apparently grown "fat and lazy"—contributing little more than bulk-breaking. Their salespeople were often only order takers. The selling function was neglected. High-caliber management was not attracted to the wholesaling industry. It became a domain of vested interests—which many persons felt should be eliminated.

Our review here, however, has shown that wholesaling functions *are* necessary, and wholesalers have not been eliminated. The traditional, merchant wholesaler did go through a critical period in the late 1940s and early 1950s but seems to have recovered from his problems and has adapted to new market conditions.[5] The manufacturer's agent has also experienced the need to adapt to changing market conditions, particularly those brought about by the increasing size of the Canadian market, making better communications and direct buying more feasible.[6]

Producing profits, not chasing orders

Wholesalers have held their own, in part, because of new management and new techniques. To be sure, there are still many operating in the old ways—and wholesaling has had nothing comparable to the rapid changes in retailing. Yet progressive wholesalers have become more concerned with their customers—and with channel systems. Some are offering more services to their independent customers—and others are developing voluntary chains that bind them more closely to their customers. Their customers' ordering can now be done routinely by mail or telephone—or directly by telephone to computer.

Today's *progressive* wholesaler is no longer a passive order taker. As part of the new look in wholesaling, many sales representatives have been eliminated. In place of the old order takers, wholesalers are now using order slips similar to those used between a chain's warehouse and retail stores.

Some modern wholesalers no longer require all customers to pay for all the services offered—simply because certain customers use them. This traditional practice had the effect of encouraging limited-function wholesalers and direct channels. Now some wholesalers are making a basic service available at a minimum cost—then charging additional fees for any special services required. In the grocery field, for instance, the basic servicing of a store might cost the store 3 to 4 percent of wholesale sales. Then promotion assistance and other aids are offered at extra cost.

Modern wholesalers also are becoming more selective in picking customers—i.e., choosing a selective distribution policy—as cost analysis shows that many of their smaller customers are clearly unprofitable. With these less desirable customers gone, wholesalers can give even more attention to more profitable customers. In this way, they are helping to promote healthy retailers—who are able to compete in any market.

Some wholesalers have renamed their salespeople "store advisers" or "supervisors" to reflect their new roles. These representatives provide many management advisory services—including location analysis, store design and modernization, legal assistance on new leases or adjustments in old leases, store-opening services, sales training and merchandising assistance, and advertising help. Such salespeople—really acting as management consultants—must be more competent than the mere order takers of other days.

Progress—or fail

Training a modern wholesaler's sales force isn't easy—and it's sometimes beyond the management skills in small wholesale firms. In some fields—such as the plumbing industry—wholesaler trade associations have taken over the job. They organize training schools designed to show the wholesaler's salespeople how they, in turn, can help their customers manage their businesses and promote sales. These schools give instruction in bookkeeping, figuring a markup, collecting accounts receivable, advertising, and selling—all in an effort to train the wholesalers' salespeople to improve the effectiveness of other channel members.[7]

Many wholesalers are now using electronic data processing systems to control inventory. And some are modernizing their warehouses and physical handling facilities.

Some wholesalers are offering central bookkeeping facilities for their retailers—realizing that their own survival is linked to their customers' survival. In this sense, some wholesalers are becoming more channel system minded—no longer trying to overload retailers' shelves. Now they are trying to clear the merchandise *off* retailers' shelves. They follow the old adage, "Nothing is really sold until it is sold at retail."

Perhaps good-bye to some

Despite these changes, however, not all wholesalers today are progressive. Many still follow outmoded practices. Some of the smaller, less efficient ones may have difficulty in the future. While the average operating expense ratio is 19 percent for merchant wholesalers, some small wholesalers have expense ratios in excess of 30 percent.

Low cost, however, is not the only criterion for success. The higher operating expenses for some smaller wholesalers may be a reflection of the special services they offer to some market segments. Truck distributors are usually small—and have high operating costs—yet some customers are willing to pay the higher cost of this service. Some of the apparently expensive, older, full-service wholesalers probably will continue operating—because they offer the services and contacts needed by some small manufacturers. And, of course, some goods and some markets traditionally have slow turnover. Wholesalers may be the best choice—even though they have high operating expenses.

Even making these allowances, though, it is clear that the smaller wholesalers—and the larger, less progressive ones—face future difficulty unless each has carved out a specific market for itself. Profit margins are not large in wholesaling—typically ranging from less than 1 percent to 2 percent of sales. And they have been declining in recent years—as the competitive squeeze has tightened. In short, the institution of wholesaling certainly will survive—but weaker, less progressive wholesalers may not.

A Statistical Overview of Canadian Wholesaling*

An introductory note of caution

Wholesaling is a difficult area in which to collect meaningful data. This is due in part to the difficulty of classifying wholesalers by type of operation. Also, the reporting procedures used by Statistics Canada have changed over time. This makes comparability of data a problem. Marketers must carefully examine the particular definitions used in *each* study of the wholesaling sector.

Statistics Canada recognizes five different types of wholesale operations. These include wholesale merchants (buying and selling goods on own account), agents and brokers (buying and selling goods for others on a commission basis), manufacturers' sales branches (wholesale businesses owned by manufacturing firms for marketing their own products), primary product dealers (including cooperative marketing associations), and petroleum bulk tank plants and truck distributors (wholesale distributors of petroleum products).

Wholesale merchants

Key 1982 statistics on wholesaling indicate that 44,513 wholesale merchant organizations (operating at 54,742 different locations) had a total volume of trade of $143 billion.

Wholesale merchant activity is concentrated in Quebec and Ontario. These two provinces accounted for 62.6 percent of all establishments and 57.8 percent of all wholesale trade. This is not surprising, given the relative importance of these provinces as measured by population, manufacturing activity, retail trade, and so forth.

Table 14–1 reports on wholesale merchants by kind of business. Are you surprised to find food accounting for only 15.4 percent of the total volume of whole-

*The Canadian context of this section was researched and written for *Basic Marketing*, Fourth Canadian edition, by Professor Carl Lawrence of Queen's University.

■ TABLE 14–1   Wholesale merchants principal statistics by kind of business, Canada 1982

Kind of business (three-digit SIC)	Number of establish-ments	Percent-age dis-tribution	Percentage distribution volume of trade	Gross margins (percent)
Total, all trades.	44,513	100.0%	100.0%	19%
Farm products	964	2.1	13.2	11
Coal, coke, and petroleum products	1,875	4.2	17.5	19
Paper and paper products.	483	1.1	1.9	18
General merchandise	497	1.1	0.4	17
Food.	3,926	8.8	15.4	10
Tobacco, drugs, and toilet preparations	624	1.4	2.7	13
Apparel and dry goods	1,266	2.8	1.5	27
Household furniture and house furnishings	716	1.6	1.1	28
Motor vehicles and accessories	2,389	5.3	6.6	25
Electrical machinery, equipment, and supplies . . .	2,343	5.2	5.0	25
Farm machinery and equipment.	2,380	5.4	3.2	22
Machinery and equipment (n.e.s.*)	7,382	16.8	9.1	31
Hardware plumbing and heating equipment	1,803	4.1	2.7	24
Metals and metal products	522	1.2	3.7	13
Lumber and building supplies	4,445	10.0	6.2	19
Scrap and waste materials.	1,680	3.8	0.6	29
Wholesalers (n.e.s.*)	11,198	25.1	9.2	22

*n.e.s. = Not elsewhere specified.

Source: Statistics Canada, *Wholesale Trade Statistics—Wholesale Merchants Agents and Brokers, 1982*, Cat. 63-226 (Ottawa: Minister of Supply and Services Canada, March 1984).

sale merchant trade? This is due to the way that the data is collected. These figures do not include the sales made at wholesale merchant locations operated by large supermarkets such as Safeway, Steinberg's, A&P, and Loblaw's.

Costs and profits vary with product sold

Is the cost of doing business the same for all classes of wholesale merchants? Table 14–1 indicates otherwise. Gross margins, as a percentage of net sales, average 19 percent for all wholesale merchants. However, specific margins range from 8 percent in the food business to 31 percent for hardware, plumbing, and heating wholesalers. Why do such differences exist? Again, it depends upon the type of product. It obviously costs more to assemble some products than it does others. The services demanded by the customers for one product category also may be much more expensive than those demanded by those purchasing other items. Also, one wholesale business may be much more labor intensive than another. In short, wholesale merchants with high gross margins are not necessarily the most profitable. Many of these firms also have high operating expenses.

Statistics Canada reports that in 1982 5,009 agents and brokers operating at 5,183 locations had a total trade volume of $27.1 billion. As was the case for wholesale merchants, the two provinces of Quebec and Ontario dominate agent and broker trade. They account for 48.1 percent of the establishments and 52.7 percent of total dollar volume. The relative importance of Manitoba should also be noted. That province has 8.7 percent of all agents and brokers, accounting for

18 percent of the total volume of trade. (For comparison purposes, Manitoba's 3.8 percent of all wholesale merchant establishments accounted for 11.6 percent of all wholesale merchant trade).

Agents and brokers engaged in the petroleum products business account for just under half of all establishments, but they do only 16 percent of all agent and broker trade. In contrast, the 3.4 percent of all establishments engaged in the distribution of farm products together accounted for a very significant 40.5 percent of all the business done by agents and brokers.

■ CONCLUSION

Wholesalers can provide functions for those both above and below them in a channel of distribution. These services are closely related to the basic marketing functions. There are many types of wholesalers. Some provide all the wholesaling functions—while others specialize in only a few. Eliminating wholesalers would not eliminate the need for the functions they provide. And we cannot assume that direct channels will be more efficient.

Merchant wholesalers are the most numerous and account for most of the establishment's locations and volume of wholesale trade. Their distinguishing characteristic is that they take title—and often physical possession—of goods. Agent mid-

dlemen, on the other hand, act more like sales representatives for sellers or buyers—and do not take title.

Despite various predictions of the end of wholesalers, they continue to exist. And the more progressive ones have adapted to a changing environment. No such revolutions as we saw in retailing have yet taken place in the wholesaling area—and none seem likely. But it is probable that some smaller—and less progressive—wholesalers will fail, while larger and more marketoriented wholesalers will continue to provide these necessary functions.

■ QUESTIONS AND PROBLEMS

1. Discuss the evolution of wholesaling in relation to the evolution of retailing.

2. What risks do merchant wholesalers assume by taking title to goods? Is the size of this risk about constant for all merchant wholesalers?

3. Why would a manufacturer set up its own sales branches if established wholesalers were already available?

4. What is an agent middleman's marketing mix? Why don't manufacturers use their own salespeople instead of agent middlemen?

5. Discuss the future growth and nature of wholesaling if low margin retailing and scrambled merchandising become more important. How will wholesalers have to adjust their mixes if retail establishments become larger and the retail managers more professional? Might the wholesalers be eliminated? If not, what wholesaling functions would be most important? Are there any particular lines of trade where wholesalers may have increasing difficulty?

6. Which types of wholesalers would be most appropriate for the following products? If more than one type of wholesaler could be used, provide the specifications for the situation in each case. For example, if size or financial strength of a company has a bearing, then so indicate. If several wholesalers could be used in this same channel, explain this also.

a. Fresh tomatoes.

b. Paper-stapling machines.

c. Auto mechanics' tools.

d. Men's shoes.

e. An industrial accessory machine.

f. Ballpoint pens.

g. Shoelaces.

7. Would a drop-shipper be desirable for the following products: coal, lumber, iron ore, sand and gravel, steel, furniture, or tractors? Why or why not? What channels might be used for each of these products if drop-shippers were not used?

8. Explain why factors developed.

9. Explain how field warehousing could help a marketing manager.

10. Which types of wholesalers are likely to become more important in the next 25 years? Why?

■ SUGGESTED CASES

4. Tot-Switch

14. Cooper Lumber Company

25. Lafontaine Potteries Limited

■ NOTES

1. For a detailed discussion of wholesaling and the operation and management of a wholesale business, see T. N. Beckman, N. H. Engle, and R. D. Buzzell, *Wholesaling,* 3d ed. (New York: Ronald Press, 1959).

2. For interesting case studies of the activities of different types of wholesalers, see M. P. Brown, William Applebaum, and W. J. Salmon, *Strategy Problems of Mass Retailers and Wholesalers* (Homewood, Ill.: Richard D. Irwin, 1970).

3. P. Ronald Stephenson, "Wholesale Distribution: An Analysis of Structure, Strategy, and Profit Performance," in *Foundations of Marketing Channels,* ed. Arch G. Woodside et al. (Austin, Texas: Lone Star Publishers, 1978), pp. 103–7.

4. James D. Hlavacek and Tommy J. McCuistion, "Industrial Distributors—When, Who, and How?" *Harvard Business Review* 61, no. 2 (January-February 1983), pp. 96–101; and Steven Flax, "Wholesalers," *Forbes,* January 4, 1982.

5. Isiah A. Litvak and Peter M. Banting, "Manufacturers' Agent—Adoption or Atrophy," *Industrial Canada,* January 1967, p. 25. This and five other articles by these authors appearing in *Industrial Canada* between October 1966 and March 1967 offer a good detailed view of wholesaling in Canada, its problems and prospects.

6. *Dealer Development Institute* (Chicago: Central Supply Association).

7. James R. Moore and Kendall A. Adams, "Functional Wholesaler Sales: Trends and Analysis," in *Combined Proceedings of the American Marketing Association,* ed. E. M. Mazze (Chicago: American Marketing Association, 1976), pp. 403–5; Richard S. Lopata, "Faster Pace in Wholesaling," *Harvard Business Review,* July-August 1969, pp. 130–43; and "Napco: Seeking a National Network as a Nonfood Supermarket Supplier," *Business Week,* November 8, 1982, p. 70.

Chapter 15 ■ Physical distribution

When you finish this chapter, you should:

1. Understand why physical distribution is such an important part of Place *and* marketing.

2. Know about the advantages and disadvantages of the various transporting methods.

3. Know what storing possibilities a marketing manager can use.

4. Understand the distribution center concept.

5. Understand the total cost approach to physical distribution.

6. Understand customer service level as a strategic variable.

7. Recognize the important new terms (shown in red).

"If it got to you, it probably came at least part way by truck."

Physical distribution (PD) is the transporting and storing of physical goods within individual firms and along channel systems. Nearly half the cost of marketing is spent on physical distribution!

PD is very important to the firm—and the macro-marketing system—since goods that remain in the factory or on the farm really have no "use" at all. *Possession* utility is not possible until *time* and *place* utility has been provided. This usually requires the transporting and storing functions that are part of physical distribution.

PD decisions can influence the cost of the whole *Place* system—and good PD decisions can help a firm attract and keep customers. A few examples help to show some of the different ways that PD can affect other aspects of the marketing mix.

Each week, a grocery chain advertised special items at low sale prices—to attract customers. But it often ran out of inventory early the first day—and some weeks it had no supply at all. This may have just been bad planning—but it made many customers angry—and it was a violation of a Combines Act Requirement that advertised items must be in stock.

A manufacturer of exhaust pipes and mufflers contracted with trucking firms to deliver orders to car parts wholesalers around the country. Then a new marketing manager suggested a change. The company rented space in public warehouses near its key markets. It shipped large quantities to the warehouses by train—at lower carload rates. Economical small trucks were leased for local deliveries. Savings in transport costs more than offset the increased inventory and warehousing expenses. And sales increased because some of the savings were passed on in lower prices—and because the wholesalers liked being able to get needed parts quickly from the local warehouse.

These examples show that managers at all channel levels need to think about physical distribution functions. They are important in Place decisions—and can affect a whole marketing strategy. Wise PD decisions may help attract new customers by providing better service—or by cutting costs and lowering prices. And effective management of PD will help assure that the "right" *Product* actually is in the "right" *Place* when the customer wants to buy. Providing *time, place,* and *possession utilities* is important—sales are often lost just because the product is not available!

Products can be moved and stored in many ways. The benefits and limitations of the different ways vary—as do costs. And the lowest cost approaches may not be best—if customers aren't satisfied. In this chapter, we talk about these ideas in more detail. It is useful to start by emphasizing that the physical distribution functions can be shared by different members of a channel—and competitors may share these functions in different ways with different costs.

Deciding who will haul and store is strategic

As a marketing manager develops the Place part of a strategy, it is important to decide how transporting and storing functions can and should be divided within the channel. Who will store and transport the goods—and who will pay for these services? Just deciding to use certain types of wholesalers or retailers doesn't automatically—or completely—answer these questions. A wholesaler may use its own trucks to haul goods from a producer to its warehouse—and from there to retailers—but only because the manufacturer gives a transportation allowance. Another wholesaler may want the goods delivered.

When developing a marketing strategy, the marketing manager must decide how these functions are to be shared—since this will affect the other three Ps—and especially Price. The truth is, however, that there is no "ideal" sharing arrangement. Physical distribution can be varied endlessly in a marketing mix—and in a channel system.

These are important strategic decisions—because they can make or break a strategy. The case of a small firm that had been making inexpensive "rabbit ear" TV antennas illustrates these ideas. The growth of cable TV was hurting sales. So the firm developed a new product—a large dish-like antenna used by motels to receive TV signals from satellites. The product looked like it could be a real success—but the small company didn't have the money to invest in a large inventory. So it decided to work only with wholesalers who were willing to buy several units—to be used for demonstrations and to ensure that buyers got immediate delivery. In the first few months, the firm had $2 million in sales—and recovered its development cost—just providing inventory for the channel. And the wholesalers paid the interest cost of their inventory investment—which was over $300,000 the first year. Here, the wholesalers helped share the risk of the new venture—but it was a good decision for them, too. They won many sales from a competing channel that expected customers to wait several months for delivery.

So, as we discuss the transporting and storing functions in the next sections, keep in mind that different members of the channel may share these responsibilities.

The Transporting Function

Transporting aids economic development and exchange

Transporting is the marketing function of moving goods. It provides time and place utilities. Before the coming of powered vehicles, transporting was slow, and the movement of goods was limited to what a person could carry or haul in a wagon. People lived where the goods were—on self-sufficient farms—and traded their surplus in nearby markets.

The basic idea in transporting is that the value added to products by moving them must be greater than the cost of the transporting—or there is little reason to ship in the first place. Without transporting, there could be no mass distribution with its regrouping activities—or any urban life as we know it today. We understand this most clearly during a major rail or truck strike.

Early Canadian society settled on or near the water's edge, particularly the drainage area of the St. Lawrence.[1] Although roads existed, transport by water was more feasible, except for two drawbacks. These were the winter ice, which was unavoidable, and the many falls and rapids along the waterways. Thus canoes provided the best means of transport. However, with the introduction of the steamship in the early 1800s, and the construction of canals and locks as ways around the natural obstacles, Canada quickly adopted vessels as part of its transportation system in order to increase the amounts and types of cargo carried.

Compared with the United States, Canada was slow to build railroads. For example, in 1850 Canada had only 66 miles of railway, whereas the United States had 10,000. It was not until 1885 that all of Canada was connected by rail, Once the hinterlands were linked with the commercial centers both at home and abroad, the economic development of the west was made possible. Water and rail transport dominated for generations. However, the increased use of the automobile after 1920 prompted the building of better highways between large cities, and roads connecting outlying areas with major markets.

Transporting can be costly

How transport costs affect the final price varies a lot by product. As a general rule, transport costs add less significantly to the price of products which are already valuable relative to their size and weight. Transporting costs can be an important part of the total, however, for large, heavy products of low value—like many minerals and raw materials. This is illustrated in Figure 15–1, which shows transporting costs as a percent of total sales dollars for a number of different products.[2]

Can you afford to get to the target?

Transporting costs may limit the target markets that a marketing manager can consider. Shipping costs increase delivered cost—and this is what really interests the customer. High costs for goods in outlying areas—caused by higher trans-

■   FIGURE 15–1   Transporting cost as a percent of sales dollars for different products

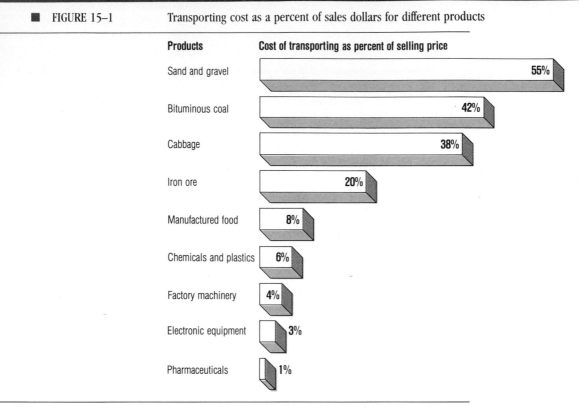

Source: Adapted from B. J. LaLonde and P. H. Zinszer, *Customer Service: Meaning and Measurement* (Chicago: National Council of Physical Distribution Management, 1976); and D. Phillip Locklin, *Transportation for Management* (Homewood, Ill.: Richard D. Irwin, 1972).

porting costs—encourage local production. For example, gravel is expensive to ship—relative to its value. This means that it is usually sold only near the pits where it is extracted.

The Five Modes of Transportation

There are five basic modes of freight movement: railroads, trucks, waterways, pipelines, and airplanes. Today, a marketing manager generally has several carriers in one or more modes competing for the firm's transportation business. So it is important to know about the different modes.

A common measure of the importance of various methods of transportation is ton-miles carried. A **ton-mile** means the movement of 2,000 pounds (one ton) of goods one mile. If, for example, 10 tons of sand were carried 10 miles, the total movement would be 100 ton-miles.

Using this measure makes it obvious that railways are the backbone of the

Canadian transportation system. Rail accounts for more than five times as many ton-miles as highway does. Unfortunately, reliable information on changes over time in the number of ton-miles carried by each of the five basic modes of transport—railroads, trucks, waterways, pipelines, and airways—is not available.[3] Discussions of ton-miles, however, do not tell the whole story. By 1968, trucks were carrying as many tons of freight as the railroads but not for as many miles.[4] And the products trucks carry are usually those with higher freight rates.

Which Transporting Alternative Is Best

Transporting function must fit the whole strategy

The transporting function should fit into the whole marketing strategy. But picking the best transporting alternative can be difficult. What is "best" depends on the product, other distribution decisions, and what the company wants to achieve. The best transporting alternative should not only be as low in cost as possible—but also provide the level of service (for example, speed and dependability) required. See Figure 15–2. The figure makes it clear that different modes have different strengths and weaknesses.[5] It is important to see from the beginning that lowest transporting cost is *not* the only criterion for selecting the best method.

Railroads—workhorse of the nation

The railroad—the workhorse of Canadian transportation—has been important mainly for carrying heavy and bulky freight, such as coal, steel, lumber, chemicals, cars, and canned goods, over long distances.

Government regulatory commissions encouraged low rates on such "basic commodities"—to encourage wider distribution. At the same time, higher rates

■ FIGURE 15–2   Relative benefits of different transport modes

were permitted on higher-valued, less bulky goods like electrical and electronic goods—to give the railroads a chance for profits.

Many of the goods shipped by rail are not particularly perishable or in urgent demand—and as a result, much railroad freight moves more slowly than truck shipments. By handling large quantities, the railroads are able to transport at relatively low cost. Railroads are most efficient at handling full carloads of goods. Less-than-carload (LCL) shipments take a lot of handling and rehandling—which means they usually move slowly—and at a higher price per 100 pounds than carload shipments.

Competition has forced railroads to innovate

Railroads have had low profits in recent years—in part because trucking firms have taken a large share of the most profitable business. The railroads have fought back—cutting costs—and often services—to bring their profits up. Catering more specifically to the needs of some target customers has helped, too.

Rails now offer more special services

The rails won back a large share of new car transporting from trucks—by introducing specially designed railcars that carry 30 small automobiles. So many cars can be carried because they are loaded vertically rather than horizontally. Similarly, the design of special refrigerator cars, tank cars, hopper cars, and cars especially suited for loading and unloading livestock also has helped attract and hold business.[6]

To offset the shortcomings of low speed and high cost—and still encourage the business of small shippers—some railroads encourage **pool car service**—which allows groups of shippers to pool their shipments of like goods into a full car. Sometimes local retailers buying from a single area—such as Montreal—combine their shipments in single cars. Local truckers then deliver the goods when they arrive. When different commodities are shipped in the same car, it is called a *mixed car* rather than a pool car—and the highest rate for any of the commodities applies to the whole shipment.

Another example of a special railroad service is **diversion in transit**—which allows redirection of carloads already in transit. This lets a marketing manager get the goods rolling—but still stay flexible about target market selection. A carload of British Columbia lumber could be shipped toward a specific destination in Manitoba. But as market demand and supply conditions changed, the shipper could specify another destination in Canada or the United States. The railroad would then reroute the car for a small fee.

Trucks are flexible, fast, dependable, and essential

The flexibility of trucks makes them better at moving small quantities of goods for short distances. They can travel on almost any road. They are not limited to where the rails go—and can give extremely fast service. Truckers compete with railroads for the high-charge items in somewhat the same way retailers compete in "scrambled merchandising." Going after such business makes sense for the truckers—because it is these smaller, high-charge items that trucks are able to handle best. Trucking has opened many new markets—and permitted decentralization—by bringing fast, dependable transport to outlying urban areas, smaller towns, and rural areas. Although critics complain that trucks congest traffic and

Railroads and their suppliers have introduced many specialized new services to better serve transporting needs.

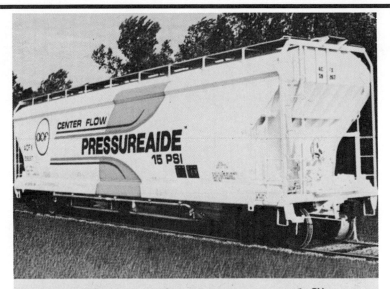

damage highways, it is a fact that trucks are essential to our present macro-marketing system.[7]

Waterways are slow and seasonal, but inexpensive

Waterways play an important role in Canada's transportation network, particularly in two areas of the country. These are the eastern Great Lakes–St. Lawrence coastal system and the British Columbia coastal system.

The availability of ocean transport to the vast industrial and agricultural hinterlands of Canada and the United States, as well as easier movement of traffic in the Great Lakes–St. Lawrence River areas, was made possible in 1959 by the completion of the St. Lawrence Waterway System. This 2,342-mile-long waterway opened the Great Lakes to 80 percent of all ocean vessels. Only the very largest ships are excluded.

Lakers on these internal waterways are used chiefly for bulky, non-perishable

Barges are an inexpensive way to transport bulky, non-perishable products.

products such as iron ore, grain, steel, petroleum products, cement, gravel, sand, coal, and coke. Water transportation is the lowest-cost method, but it is also the slowest and most seasonal. When winter ice closes fresh-water harbors, alternate transportation must be used. Some shippers, such as those dealing in iron ore, ship their total annual supply during the summer months and store it near their production facilities for winter use. Here, low-cost transportation combined with storage reduces total cost.

Bulk movement of a few commodities (particularly forest products) also dominates the British Columbia coastal system. But in contrast to communities along the eastern waterways, British Columbia communities depend almost entirely on ships for receipt of supplies from the Lower Mainland. No other form of transport is available for shipment of freight. The barge and tug are the predominant type of shipping used.

Pipelines are used primarily by the petroleum industry

In Canada, pipelines are used to transport all of the natural gas, most of the crude oil, and the majority of natural gas liquids moving between processing plants and markets. As of 1983 there were just over 32,000 kilometers of oil pipeline in Canada and close to 133,000 kilometers of gas-gathering and transmission distribution pipelines.[8] The majority of this pipeline distance runs from Alberta and Saskatchewan to eastern Canada and the United States. Oil pipeline companies are common carriers, which carry oil for a fixed charge, whereas in most cases gas pipeline companies own the gas being transported.

Airplanes are fast— and expensive

The most expensive cargo transportation mode is airplane—but it is also fast! Airfreight rates normally are at least twice as high as trucking rates—but the

Federal Express provides overnight transporting—and is especially good for high-value, low-weight products.

greater speed may offset the added cost. Trucks took the cream of the railroads' traffic. Now airplanes are taking the cream of the cream.

High-value, low-weight goods—like high-fashion clothing and industrial parts for the electronics and metal-working industries—are often shipped by air. Airfreight is also creating a new transporting business by carrying—across continents and oceans—perishable commodities that simply could not be moved before. Tropical flowers from Hawaii, for example, now are jet-flown to points all over Canada. And airfreight is also becoming very important for small emergency deliveries—like repair parts or special orders.

But airplanes may cut the total cost of distribution

An important advantage of using airplanes is that the cost of packing, unpacking, and preparing the goods for sale may be reduced or eliminated. One manufacturer of electronic products—who makes all deliveries beyond 150 miles by air—merely wraps the complex 600-pound machines in heavy wrapping paper. The increased transporting costs are more than offset by the lower packaging costs—and the firm is now competing for business nationally. The speedy service at lower costs has improved the company's marketing mix—and market position.

Planes may help a firm reduce its inventory costs—by eliminating outlying warehouses. Valuable by-products of airfreight's speed are less spoilage, theft, and damage. Although the *transporting cost* of air shipments may be higher, the *total cost of distribution* may be lower. As more firms have come to realize this, airfreight has enjoyed rapid growth.[9]

Put it in a container—and move it between modes easily

It is easiest to talk about the modes separately. But products are often moved by different modes and carriers during their journey. This is especially common for international shipments. For example, Japanese manufacturers might ship stereos to Canada and the United States by boat. When they arrive on the West Coast, they are loaded on trains and sent across the country. Then, a truck might deliver the units to the wholesaler—if it is not located on a railroad track. The loading and unloading of the goods several times used to be a real problem. Parts of a shipment would become separated, damaged, or even stolen.

Containerization reduces handling and speeds intermodal transfers.

And handling the goods—perhaps many times—raised costs and slowed things down.

Many of the these problems are reduced with **containerization**—grouping individual items into an economical shipping quantity and sealing them in protective containers for transit to the final destination. This protects the products and simplifies handling during shipping. Some containers are as large as truck bodies.

This idea is also carried further. **Piggy-back service** loads truck trailers—or flat-bed trailers carrying containers—on railcars to provide both speed and flexibility. Operating with the apparent philosophy, If you can't beat 'em, haul 'em," railroads now pick up truck trailers at the producer's location, load them onto specially designed rail flatcars, and haul them as close to the customer as rail lines run. The trailers are then picked up by a truck tractor and delivered to the buyer's door. Such service provides all the flexibility of trucking—and on some routes, it costs much less. A loaded truck trailer can be shipped piggy-back from Central Canada to the West Coast for approximately half the cost of sending it over the highways.

Ocean-going ships have also been redesigned to handle large standard-size containers and truck trailers. **Fishy-back service**—similar to rail piggy-back service—but using ships and trucks—allows door-to-door service between Canada and European cities.

Different kinds of carriers fill different roles

Common carriers—such as the railroads and major truck lines—are transporters which maintain regular schedules and accept goods from any shipper. They charge rates which are fixed for all users by government regulators. **Contract carriers** are transporters who are willing to work for anyone for an agreed sum—and for any length of time. They are less strictly regulated. Common carriers provide a dependable transportation service for the many producers and middlemen who make small shipments in various directions. Contract carriers, on the other hand, are a more free-wheeling group—going wherever goods have to be moved.

Private carriers are company-owned transportation facilities. "Do-it-yourself" transporting is always a possibility—but it often isn't economical because the contract or common carriers can make fuller use of their facilities and, therefore, charge less.

Should You Do It Yourself?

To cut transporting costs, some marketing managers do their own transporting—rather than buy from specialists. Trucking has made it easier to "do-it-yourself." Some large manufacturers own thousands of cars and trucks. And some iron ore, gypsum rock, and petroleum producers have their own ships.

What to do depends on discrepancies of quantity and shipment consistency

The concept of discrepancy of quantity is important here. If there is a great difference between the quantity a firm normally ships and the quantity that common carriers find economical, the firm may have to ship via common carrier. But if a company normally ships in the same quantities that common carriers find economical, it may save money by using its own vehicles. This avoids the cost that common carriers must charge for maintaining a regular schedule—or that contract carriers must charge against future uncertainties.

If a marketing manager is fairly certain of the firm's future plans, do-it-yourself transporting may be good business. A wine wholesaler in Central Canada found that it cost much more to ship wine by rail from the West Coast than if a tank truck and driver were hired for the West Coast run. Because this was a regular and frequent shipment, the firm bought a truck—and operated it at a large saving.

The Transporting Rate Structure

The rates—prices—charged by transportation firms are based on many factors. Each transporter, product, and route may have its own rate. When you consider how many products and route combinations there are, it is obvious that the whole rate structure can get very complicated. We won't review the details of the current rate structure here. Rather, we will focus on a few important ideas that will help you see how transportation rates influence marketing functions—and what the marketing manager can do to influence those rates.

Most rates are based on the idea that large quantities of a good can be shipped at a lower transport cost per item than can small quantities. For example, if a furniture producer sends a truck to deliver a single chair, the company still needs to pay for the driver, the truck, the gas, and other expenses like insurance. It is foolish to send a nearly empty truck when many other goods can be sent without any increase in costs. Transporters often give much more favorable rates for quantities that make efficient use of their transport facilities. For example, railroad rates are usually quoted for carloads (CL, 60,000–100,000 pounds), truckloads (TL, 15,000 pounds or more), less than carloads (LCL), and less than truckloads (LTL). Rates for less than full carloads and truckloads vary but are often twice as high as those for full loads.

These quantity rate differences are another reason for the development of wholesalers. They buy in larger quantities than most customers need—to get the advantage of full-load rates—and then sell in the smaller quantities the customers *do* need.

Correct rate not easy to determine

The large number of possible rates make traffic management a difficult job. Carriers frequently charge a higher rate when a lower rate should apply. It is not that they are deliberately overcharging—but rather that the freight agents who determine the appropriate rates must choose from a large number of possible routes and rate combinations. Some companies find it profitable to audit all freight bills before payment. There are even private firms specializing in this kind of work—earning a share of the savings.

Planning the best routing for the lowest rate gets more complex each year—since thousands of rate changes are made annually. Because of this complexity—and the possibility of error—some channel members prefer to have prices quoted on a delivered basis. Some of the problems in this area are being reduced by more use of computers.[10] The computer identifies all the alternatives, and selects the one with the lowest rate.

Marketing Manager May Affect Rates

Present rate structure not permanently fixed

There is nothing final about the present rate structure. Since it is man-made, it could be changed. If it were changed, it might lead to a vastly different—perhaps more efficient or fairer—transportation system. In some other countries, for instance, the rate differences for carload quantities are much smaller—or non-existent. As a result, goods are shipped in much smaller quantities, freight cars are smaller, and wholesalers and retailers handle smaller quantities.

Capitalize on carrier competition

Most rates are based originally on the carrier's cost of providing necessary services—such as loading, product liability, regularly scheduled service, special equipment such as refrigerated cars, and so on. But these supply factors alone do not determine the final rates. Rather, they determine the rate the carrier *would like to charge*. The rates actually charged are determined by competition among the various carriers—*and* alternate methods of transportation. By taking advantage of these factors, an aggressive marketing manager can reduce the cost of transporting.

Carriers are usually interested in stimulating business in their areas. If the marketing manager can show that business could expand if lower rates were granted into certain territories, the carriers may be willing to grant these lower rates. In fact, much adjustment has taken place—so that now distance traveled and total transporting costs are often only weakly related.

Creative marketing managers—by bargaining for rate changes—can help their channel system members with the transporting function. In fact, some manufacturers and middlemen have *traffic departments* to deal with carriers. These departments can be a big help—not only to their own firms but also to their suppliers and customers—finding the best routes and lowest rates.

Freight Forwarders Are Transporting Wholesalers

They accumulate economical shipping quantities

Freight forwarders combine the small shipments of many shippers into more economical shipping quantities. Many marketing managers regularly use freight forwarders to make the best use of available transporting facilities. They are especially good for the many small shipments that may have to move by varied transportation modes.

Freight forwarders do not own their own transporting facilities—except perhaps for delivery trucks. Rather, they wholesale air, ship, railroad, and truck space. Accumulating small shipments from many shippers, they reship in larger quantities to obtain lower transportation rates. Their profits mainly come out of the difference in freight rates between small- and large-quantity shipments—though they sometimes make special service charges.

They help exporters

Freight forwarders can be especially helpful to the marketing manager who ships many small shipments to foreign markets. They handle a large percentage of the general cargo shipped from Canadian ports to foreign countries. Most exporters—including companies with large shipping departments—use their services. An important reason is that the forwarders are located right at the exporting point—and can more easily process all the complicated paper work necessary in overseas shipments.

The Storing Function

Store it and smooth out sales, increase profits and consumer satisfaction

Storing is the marketing function of holding goods. It provides time utility. **Inventory** means the amount of goods which are being stored.

Storing is needed when production doesn't match consumption. This is common with mass production. A steel mill, for example, might produce thousands of bars of one size before changing the machinery to produce another size. Changing the production line can be costly and time-consuming. It is cheaper to produce extra quantities of one size—and then store the surplus for a while—than to change production too often.

*Storing perishables keeps
prices more stable
throughout the year.*

Some products—such as agricultural commodities—can only be produced seasonally although they are in demand year-round. If crops could not be stored when they mature or ripen, all of the crop would be thrown onto the market—and prices might drop sharply. Consumers might benefit temporarily from this "surplus," but later in the year—when supplies were scarce and prices high—they would suffer. Storing, therefore, helps stabilize prices during the consumption period—although prices usually do rise slightly over time to cover storing costs.

The practice of storing and therefore withholding products from the market to get better prices is the basic principle behind the Canadian Wheat Board's operations. It also explains the policies of some farm marketing boards as well as the occasional stockpiling of commodities such as rubber, coffee, and cocoa beans in other countries. Storing, we can see, may be intimately related to Price as well as to Place.

Some buyers purchase in large quantities to get quantity discounts—from the producer or transporter. The extra goods must be stored until there is demand. Other goods are sometimes stored as a hedge against future price rises, strikes, shipping interruptions, and other disruptions.

Storing allows manufacturers and middlemen to keep stocks at convenient locations—ready to meet customers' needs. In fact, storing is one of the major activities of some middlemen.

Storing varies the channel system

Most channel members provide the storing function for varying lengths of time. Even final consumers store some things for their future needs. Since storing can be provided anywhere along the channel, the storing function offers several ways to vary a firm's marketing mix—and its channel system—by: (1) adjusting the time goods are held, (2) sharing the storing costs, and (3) delegating the job to a specialized storing facility. This latter variation would mean adding another member to the distribution channel.

Which channel members store the product—and for how long—affects the behavior of all channel members. If a manufacturer of cake mixes, for example, had a large local stock, wholesalers probably would carry smaller inventories—since they would be sure of dependable local supplies. If final customers "store" the product, more of it may be used or consumed. Soft drink manufacturers know this—and offer 6-, 12-, and 24-packs. They want the consumer to have an "inventory" in the refrigerator when the thirst hits.

Goods are stored at a cost

Storing can increase the value of goods—and make them more available when customers want them. No one wants to lose a sale because goods aren't available. But it is important to remember that the storing function costs money, too. Many businesses forget this—and their profits suffer.

Most new car dealers store cars on their lots—waiting for the right customer. Let's consider their storing costs. First, the dealer has to invest money in the cars. If the money weren't tied up in this inventory, it could be in a bank—or invested some other way—earning interest. Some managers don't think about these costs until times when interest rates are very high.

If a new car on the lot is dented or scratched, there is a repair cost. If a car isn't sold before the new models come out, its value declines. There is also a risk of fire or theft—so the dealer needs insurance. There is also a cost of leasing or owning the display lot where the cars are stored.

Managing storing costs is more difficult if demand is irregular

Storing costs vary for different types of firms. But you should remember that storing always involves *some* costs. The wise manager tries to control these costs—to make certain that the benefits of storing are greater than the costs. This isn't always easy. It's especially difficult to have the right amount of inventory when the manager doesn't know what quantity of a good will be demanded—or when it will be needed. Consider the problem of a record store manager. A new album may be a hit—in which case many could be sold. But if the record is not popular—having extra copies increases his costs.

It's also harder to manage the storing function when the firm doesn't know how long it will take its suppliers to deliver goods. This is another way in which each member of a channel may affect the other members. For example, a printing company may not be able to store every variety of paper which customers might want. But customers may take their business elsewhere if the printer can't tell them how long it will take to get the desired paper from the paper company.

Specialized Storing Facilities Can Be Very Helpful

New cars may be stored outside—on a display lot. An inventory of fuel oil may be stored in a specially designed tank. Coal and other raw materials may be stored in open pits. But most products must be stored inside protective buildings. Often, there are choices among different types of specialized storing facilities. The right choice may reduce costs—or serve customers better.

Private warehouses are common

Private warehouses are storing facilities owned by companies for their own use. Most manufacturers, wholesalers, and retailers have some storing facilities—either in their main buildings or in a warehouse district. Management of a

■ FIGURE 15–3   A comparison of private warehouses and public warehouses

		Type of warehouse	
		Private	Public
1.	Fixed investment	Very high	No fixed investment
2.	Unit cost	High, if volume is low Very low, if volume is very high	Low; charges are made only for space needed
3.	Control.	High	Low managerial control
4.	Adequacy for product line	Highly adequate	May not be convenient
5.	Flexibility.	Low; fixed costs have already been committed	High; easy to end arrangement

Source: Adapted from Louis W. Stern and Adel I. El-Ansary, *Marketing Channels* (Englewood Cliffs, N.J.: Prentice-Hall, 1977), p. 150.

manufacturer's finished-goods warehouse is often the responsibility of a sales manager—especially at sales branches located away from the factory. In retailing, storing is so closely tied to selling that the buyers may control this function.

Private warehouses are used when a large volume of goods must be stored regularly. Owning warehouse space can be expensive, however. If the need changes, the extra space may be hard—or impossible—to rent to others. See Figure 15–3 for a comparison of private and public warehouses.

Public warehouses fill special needs

Public warehouses are independent storing facilities. A company that does not need permanent warehouse space may find public warehouses useful. The customer pays only for the space used—and may purchase a variety of additional services. Public warehouses are useful for manufacturers who must maintain stocks in many locations—including foreign countries.

Some public warehouses provide all the services that could be obtained in the company's own branch warehouse—or from most wholesalers. These warehouses will receive goods in carload quantities, unload and store them, and later reship them in any size lots ordered by the company or its customers. They will inspect goods, package them, and even invoice customers. They will facilitate the financing function—by issuing warehouse receipts that can be used as collateral when borrowing from banks. Some public warehouses will provide desk space and telephone service for a company's salespeople. The public warehouse is responsible for the risk of damage or the loss of the product in the warehouse. Of course, the customer pays for these special services.[11]

Public warehouses are located in all major metropolitan areas—and many smaller cities. Many rural areas also have public warehouses for locally produced agricultural commodities.

Warehousing facilities have modernized

The cost of physical handling is a major storing cost. The goods must be handled once when put into storage—and again when removed to be sold. In older, multi-storied warehouses—located in congested areas—these operations take many hours of high-cost labor. Difficult parking, crowded storage areas, and slow freight elevators delay the process—increasing the cost of distribution.

*Modern warehousing fa-
cilities speed the flow of
goods with computerized
systems.*

Today, modern, one-story buildings are replacing the old multi-story buildings. These new designs eliminate the need for elevators—and permit the use of power-operated lift trucks, battery-operated motor scooters, roller-skating order pickers, electric hoists for heavy items, and hydraulic ramps to speed loading and unloading. Most of these new warehouses use lift trucks and pallets (wooden "trays" which carry many cases) for vertical storage—and better use of space. Some warehouses even have computer-controlled order picking systems that speed the process of locating and assembling the assortment required to fill a particular order.[12]

The Distribution Center—A Different Kind of Warehouse

**Is storing really
needed?**

Discrepancies of assortment or quantity between one channel level and an-other are often adjusted at the place where goods have been stored. It reduces handling costs to regroup and store at the same place—*if both functions are required.* But sometimes regrouping is required when storing is *not* needed. For example, a British Columbia produce canner might want to ship its products across the country the cheapest way—perhaps in carload quantities by rail-road—and then quickly divide the shipment into smaller orders to deliver to local middlemen by truck. In this case, storing is not needed—and it is best to avoid storing expenses. This leads us to the distribution center concept.

Don't store it, distribute it

A **distribution center** is a special kind of warehouse designed to speed the flow of goods and avoid unnecessary storing costs. It makes bulk-breaking operations easier and speeds the rate of inventory turnover—reducing the cost of carrying inventory. This is important—because these costs may run as high as 35 percent a year of the value of the average inventory—and lower costs and faster turnover lead to bigger profits.

Today, the distribution center concept is widely used by firms at all channel levels. But the basic benefits of this approach are still the same as they were 20 years ago—when the idea was pioneered. In fact, a good way to see how the distribution center works is to consider one of the early applications.

Pillsbury's distribution system was overwhelmed by expanding product lines and sales

Pillsbury—the manufacturer of baking products—used to ship directly from the factory to large middlemen in carload quantities. Initially, plants were as near to customers as possible, and each plant produced the whole Pillsbury line. As lines expanded, however, no single plant could produce all the various products. When customers began to ask for mixed carload shipments and faster delivery, Pillsbury added warehouse space—and started hauling goods from plant to plant. In time, Pillsbury had set up 100 branch warehouses—controlled by 33 sales offices. Accounting, credit, and other processing operations were duplicated in each sales office. But it still took the company a week just to process an order. Moreover, turnover was slow, warehousing costs were high, and there was no effective control over inventories. A change to distribution centers was needed.

The distribution center brings it all together

Manufacturing at each plant was specialized to a few product lines—with carload shipments made directly to the distribution centers—almost eliminating storing at the factories. The distribution centers were controlled by four regional data processing centers—which quickly determined where and when goods were to be shipped. Centralized accounting got invoices to customers faster—resulting in quicker payment. And because each distribution center always had adequate inventory, it was possible to ship orders the most economical way.

Because the field sales organization no longer handled physical distribution or inventory, it could focus on sales. And they had something extra to sell—more reliable and faster service. They could guarantee customers delivery within three days.

There are many variations of the distribution center. The Pillsbury example shows it within an integrated operation. But public warehouses offer similar services. A small manufacturer might service markets all over the United States efficiently—using only 10 or 15 such public distribution centers.

Physical Distribution Concept Focuses on the Whole Distribution System

We have talked about the transporting and storing functions as if they were separate activities—partly to simplify discussion. In our examples, however, it's obvious that they are related. In fact, the transporting and storing functions often affect other areas of the firm, too—as we saw in the Pillsbury case. Recognizing how these areas relate leads us to think about the *whole* physical distribution function.

Physical distribution concept—an idea whose time has come

The **physical distribution (PD) concept** says that all transporting and storing activities of a business and a channel system should be thought of as part of one system—which should seek to minimize the cost of distribution for a given level of customer service. Figure 15–4 shows all the elements of such a system and defines physical distribution in more detail.It may be hard to see this as a startling development. But until just a few years ago, even the most progressive companies treated PD functions as separate—and quite unrelated—activities. Responsibility for different distribution activities was spread among various departments. Often the distribution-related costs were not even calculated separately. So the *total* cost of physical distribution was not obvious in most firms—and no one individual was responsible. And planning for a customer service level was almost unheard of—the idea was to "get the goods out the door." Unfortunately this is still the case in most firms.

In some firms, the production department is responsible for storing and shipping—and it builds inventories related to its production activities—rather than market needs. In other companies, storing may be a separate activity. If those in charge of inventory put little faith in sales forecasts, they may simply carry large stocks.

This naive focusing on individual functional activities may actually increase total distribution costs for the firm and even the whole channel. Therefore, those who accept the PD concept usually evaluate the total cost of alternative physical distribution systems—applying the *total cost approach.*

Evaluate Alternative PD Systems with Total Cost Approach

Searching for the lowest total cost

In selecting a PD system, the **total cost approach** involves evaluating each possible PD system—and identifying *all* of the costs of each alternative. This means that all costs—including those which are sometimes ignored—should be considered. Inventory carrying costs, for example, are often ignored—because these costs may be buried in "overhead costs." Yet they may be 10 to 35 percent of the value of average inventory.

The tools of cost accounting and economics are used with this approach. Sometimes, total cost analyses reveal that unconventional physical distribution methods will provide service as good as—or better than—conventional means—and at lower cost, as the following example shows.

Evaluating rail/warehouse versus airfreight

The Good Earth Vegetable Company had been shipping produce to distant markets by train. The cost of shipping a ton of vegetables by train averaged less than half the cost of airfreight. So the company was sure rail was the best

■ FIGURE 15–4   The scope of physical distribution

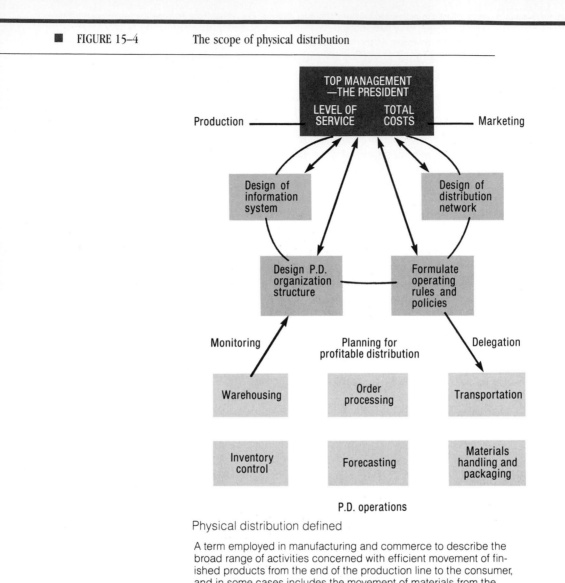

Physical distribution defined

A term employed in manufacturing and commerce to describe the broad range of activities concerned with efficient movement of finished products from the end of the production line to the consumer, and in some cases includes the movement of materials from the source of supply to the beginning of the production line. These activities include freight transportation, warehousing material handling, protective packaging, inventory control, plant and warehouse site selection, order processing, market forecasting, and customer service.

Source: Don Firth et al., *Distribution Management Handbook* (Toronto: McGraw-Hill Ryerson, 1980), p. 21.

method. But when a competitor started to use airfreight, the Good Earth managers were forced to do a more complete analysis. To their surprise, they found the airfreight system was faster and cheaper. See Figure 15–5.

Figure 15–5 compares the costs for the two distribution systems—airplane and railroad. Because shipping by train was slow, Good Earth had to keep a

■   FIGURE 15–5   Comparative costs of airplane versus rail and warehouse

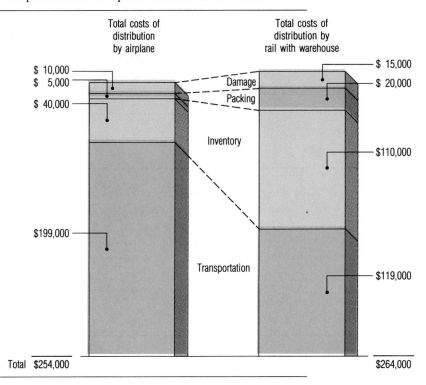

large inventory in a warehouse—to fill orders on time. And the company was also surprised at the extra cost of carrying the inventory "in transit." Good Earth's managers also found that the cost of spoiled vegetables during shipping and in the warehouse—was much higher when rail shipment was used.

Identifying all the alternatives is sometimes difficult

In a total cost analysis of this kind, all practical alternatives should be evaluated. Sometimes, however, there are so many possible combinations that it is difficult to study each one completely. For example, there may be hundreds of possible locations for a warehouse—and each location might require different combinations of transporting and storing costs. Some companies use computer simulation to generate and compare the many possible alternatives.[13] Typically, however, the straightforward total cost analysis discussed above is practical—and will show whether there is need for a more sophisticated analytical approach.

Physical Distribution Planning as Part of a Company's Strategy Planning

Physical distribution not just cost-oriented

Early physical distribution efforts emphasized lowering costs—to increase profits. Now more attention is given to the physical distribution service level in strategy planning. Sometimes, by increasing physical distribution costs somewhat, the customer service level can be increased so much that, in effect, a new and better marketing mix is created.

Decide what level of service to offer

Customer service level is a measure of how rapidly and dependably a firm can deliver what customers want. A company should decide what aspects of service are most important to its customers—and then what level of service to provide. For example, a supplier of repair parts might focus on how long it takes to deliver the product once an order has been received. When a machine breaks down, the customers want the repair parts "yesterday." The service objective might be stated as "we will deliver emergency repair parts within 48 hours." Such a service level might require that almost all such parts be kept in inventory, that order processing be very fast, and that the parts be sent by airfreight. Obviously, supplying this service level will affect costs.

Another company may be more concerned with delivery consistency. For example, a tire manufacturer might send a truckload of tires to a tire retailer. If the delivery arrives too early, there may be no space to put the tires. If it arrives late, ads might have already been run and customers disappointed. Either way, the retailer would be unhappy.

Distribution decisions require trade-offs

Figure 15–6 shows the typical relation between physical distribution costs and customer service level. You can see that there are many "trade-offs" in the physical distribution area. A lower cost in one PD area may offset a higher cost in another area. We have already talked about the possible trade-off between transporting costs and warehouse and inventory costs. The figure also shows the trade-off between customer service levels and costs.

When a firm decides to minimize total cost, it may also be settling for a lower customer service level. By increasing the number of distribution points, the firm might be able to serve more customers—better—within a specified time period. Transporting costs would be reduced—but warehousing and inventory costs would be increased. The higher service level, however, might greatly improve the company's strategy. Clearly, the marketing manager has a strategic decision about what service level to offer. Minimizing cost is not always the right answer.

Higher service level may cost more and sell more

Increasing service levels may be very profitable in highly competitive situations where the firm has relatively little to differentiate its marketing mix—for example, in close to pure competition or oligopoly. Here, simply increasing the service level—perhaps through faster delivery or wider stocks—may allow the firm to make headway in a market without changing Product, Price, or Promo-

FIGURE 15–6   Higher customer service levels are obtained at a cost

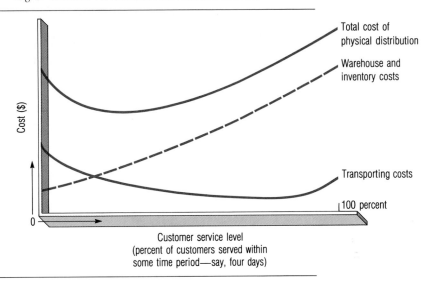

tion. In fact, improved service levels can put a marketing mix across—and competitors may not fully realize what has happened.[14]

The PD concept may not be implemented to the same degree in Canada as in the United States. This could be true for a number of reasons. First, Canada's total population is much smaller, that population is highly concentrated, and the number of alternatives available to distribution managers is limited. After all, there are only two railways (CN and CP), two major airlines (CPA and Air Canada), and one cross-country highway. Also, our waterways are only open for part of the year. In addition, Canada's large retailers—and remember, retailing is more concentrated in Canada than in the United States—often "lay down the law" to manufacturers as to service levels, the size of shipments, and time, place, and mode of delivery. Customer power of this sort discourages manufacturer acceptance of the complete physical distribution concept. Adequately trained physical distribution specialists are also less plentiful in this country than in the United States.[15] Nevertheless, the very real cost savings of a PD system approach should encourage acceptance of the concept and appointment of more Canadian physical distribution managers.[16]

Future Physical Distribution Problems and Opportunities

Getting ready for an age of planning—and costly fuel

New approaches must be found to mass transportation and urban living as more expensive fuel makes present transporting methods based on "cheap" oil look less attractive. Already, the federal government is subsidizing urban mass transportation systems. We see some attempts at developing new residential and commercial building arrangements. England, France, and Sweden have experimented with communities combining residential, working, and recreation facilities in the same center.

Deregulation or adjustments in transporting rate structures may lead to drastic changes in movement patterns—and where and what goods are produced and sold. The railroads have lost more and more of their most profitable business to competitors. But if major changes in the transporting rate structure were to occur, we might see major changes in our whole economy.

Suppose, for example, that the low rail rates charged on bulk commodities such as lumber were raised sharply. A lumber company in British Columbia could not afford to compete nationally. Contractors might shift to other types of building materials. Such a rate increase might even force the whole construction industry to change its methods and materials.

Similarly, high fuel costs and pollution controls increase the cost of truck and air movements—and may make the rails more appealing. Lower speed limits on trucks may make the railroads look even better. Another energy "crisis" might force even more radical changes—such as limiting the use of private cars or even banning them from city streets.

What will such regulations do to our car- and truck-oriented society? How will you and your community change? Such shifts will affect where people live and work—and what they produce and consume—and where and how they buy. In other words, these changes will have an impact on our whole macro-marketing system—and an alert marketing manager should try to anticipate and plan for this future.[17]

■ CONCLUSION

This chapter has dealt with transporting and storing—providing *time* and *place utility*. We discussed various modes of transporting—and their advantages and disadvantages. We also discussed the types of warehousing now available. Examples were given of modern techniques which can cut storing and handling costs.

Although we discussed transporting and storing separately, it was emphasized that both are related. The distribution center approach is an attempt to integrate these two functions to speed inventory turnover and lower costs. The physical distribution concept is concerned with integrating all the storing and transporting activities into a

smoothly working system—to deliver some service level.

While cost is important in evaluating physical distribution alternatives, service level must be considered, too—along with its strategic implications. A marketing manager often wants to improve service—and may select a higher-cost alternative to improve his marketing mix. Or the total cost approach might reveal that it is possible *both* to reduce costs and to improve service—perhaps by eliminating warehouses and using airplanes to speed delivery.

Effective marketing managers make important strategic decisions about physical distribution arrangements. But acceptance of the physical distribution concept probably will continue to be slow. Many "marketing managers" do not see physical distribution as part of their job—even though it accounts for half the cost of marketing.

But high energy costs—and rising transporting costs—may encourage more marketing managers to coordinate storing and transporting in their planning. Creative marketing managers may be able to cut costs—while maintaining or improving service levels—and production-oriented competitors may not even understand what is happening.

■ QUESTIONS AND PROBLEMS

1. Discuss the relative advantages and disadvantages of railroads, trucks, and airlines as transporting methods.

2. Describe how your college town would be changed if there were no incoming or outgoing transportation except by foot, horseback, or horse-drawn covered wagon.

3. Distinguish between common carriers and contract carriers. What role do the contract carriers play in our economic system? How would our economy be different if there were no common carriers?

4. Discuss some of the ways that air transportation can change other aspects of a Place system.

5. Explain which transportation mode would probably be most suitable for shipping the following goods to a large Toronto department store:

a. A 10,000-pound shipment of dishes from Japan.
b. 15 pounds of screwdrivers from Quebec.
c. Three couches from High Point, North Carolina.
d. 500 high-fashion dresses from the garment district in New York City.
e. 300 pounds of Atlantic coast lobsters.
f. 600,000 pounds of various appliances from

Montreal. How would your answers change if this department store were the only one in a large factory town in Ontario?

6. Indicate the nearest location where you would expect to find substantial storage facilities. What kinds of products would be stored there, and why are they stored there instead of some other place?

7. Indicate when a producer or middleman would find it desirable to use a public warehouse rather than a private warehouse. Illustrate, using a specific product or situation.

8. Discuss the distribution center concept. Is this likely to eliminate the storing function of conventional wholesalers? Is it applicable to all products? If not, cite several examples.

9. Clearly differentiate between a warehouse and a distribution center. Explain how a specific product would be handled differently by these marketing institutions.

10. Explain the total cost approach and why it may be controversial in some firms. Give examples of where conflicts might occur.

11. Explain how adjusting the customer service level could improve a marketing mix. Illustrate.

■ SUGGESTED CASES

14. Cooper Lumber Company

15. Partitions Canada

■ NOTES

1. This discussion is taken from A. W. Currie, *Canadian Economic Development* (Toronto: Thomas Nelson & Sons, 1942).

2. Bernard J. LaLonde and P. H. Zinszer, *Customer Service: Meaning and Measurement* (Chicago: National Council of Distribution Management, 1976).

3. H. L. Purdy, *Transport Competition and Public Policy in Canada,* Section 7-3 (Vancouver: University of British Columbia Press, 1972), pp. 48–56.

4. Ibid., p. 59.

5. For a more detailed comparison of mode characteristics, see D. J. Bowersox, *Logistical Management* (New York: Macmillan, 1978), p. 120.

6. "Railcars Haul Vegas Vertically," *Detroit Free Press,* August 6, 1970, p. 8-D; and "High-Mountain Railroad with Profits to Match," *Business Week,* June 10, 1967, pp. 174–80.

7. George L. Stern, "Surface Transportation: Middle-of-the-Road Solution, *Harvard Business Review* 53 (December 1975), pp. 82.

8. Statistics Canada, Cat. 52-201, 57-205 (Ottawa: Minister of Supply and Services Canada, December 31, 1983).

9. "Federal Express Rides the Small-Package Boom," *Business Week,* March 31, 1980, p. 108.

10. "Saving Money When Freight Rates Are Computerized," *Business Week,* February 25, 1980, p. 111.

11. Warren Blanding, "Warehousing: Should You Go Public?" *Sales & Marketing Management,* June 14, 1976, p. 52.; G. O. Pattino, "Public Warehousing: Supermarket For Distribution Services, *Handling and Shipping,* March 1977, p. 59; and "Public Warehouses Perform Many Marketing Functions," *Marketing News,* February 8, 1980, p. 12.

12. Kenneth B. Ackerman and Bernard J. LaLonde, "Making Warehousing More Efficient," *Harvard Business Review* 58, no. 2 (April 1980), p. 94–102.

13. Arthur M. Geoffrion, "Better Distribution Planning with Computer Models," *Harvard Business Review,* July-August 1976, pp. 92–99. See also Donald J. Bowersox, *Logistical Management* (New York: Macmillan, 1974); Kenneth B. Ackerman and Bernard J. LaLonde, "Making Warehousing More Efficient," *Harvard Business Review,* March-April 1980,

pp. 94–102; David P. Herron, "Managing Physical Distributor for Profit," *Harvard Business Review,* May-June 1979, pp. 121–32; and "'What If' Help for Management," *Business Week,* January 21, 1980, p. 73.

14. For more discussion on this point, see William D. Perreault, Jr., and Frederick A. Russ, "Physical Distribution Service in Industrial Purchase Decisions," *Journal of Marketing,* April 1976, pp. 3–10. See also William D. Perreault, Jr., and Frederick A. Russ, "Physical Distribution Service: A Neglected Aspect of Marketing Management," *MSU Business Topics,* Summer 1974, pp. 37–46; Douglas M. Lambert and James R. Stock, "Physical Distribution and Consumer Demands," *MSU Business Topics,* Spring 1978, pp. 49–56; Harvey N. Shycon and Christopher R. Sprague, "Put a Price Tag on Your Customer Servicing Levels," *Harvard Business Review,* July-August 1979, pp. 71–78; Richard A. Matteis, "The New Back Office Focuses on Customer Service," *Harvard Business Review,* March-April 1979, pp. 146–59; M. Murphy Bird, "Small Industrial Buyers Call Late Delivery Worst Problem," *Marketing News,* April 4, 1980, p. 24; and "Apparel Makers Face Consolidation as Stores Stiffen Delivery Terms," *The Wall Street Journal,* February 6, 1978, p. 1.

15. Gerald Byers and Charles S. Mayer, "Physical Distribution in Canada," in *Problems in Canadian Marketing,* ed. Donald N. Thompson (Chicago: American Marketing Association, 1977), pp. 105–109.

16. For a statistical and interest profile on Canadian Physical Distribution executives see Douglas Lambert and Mark Bennear, Jr., "The Changes Predicted as PD Managers Enter the Future," *Canadian Transportation and Distribution Management,* November 1977, pp. 55–60.

17. R. F. Lusch, J. G. Udell, and G. R. Laczniak, "The Future of Marketing Strategy," *Business Horizons,* December 1976, pp. 65–74. See also "A Dark Tunnel Ahead for Mass Transit," *Business Week,* April 18, 1977, pp. 121–23; Walter F. Friedman, "Physical Distribution: The Concept of Shared Services," *Harvard Business Review,* March-April 1975, pp. 24–26; "Back to Railroading for a New Era," *Business Week,* July 14, 1980, pp. 64–69 (Union Pacific Railroad); and "A Sickly Conrail Heads for Radical Surgery," *Business Week,* July 28, 1980, p. 78.

Chapter 16 ■ Promotion—introduction

When you finish this chapter, you should:

1. Know the advantages and disadvantages of the promotion methods which a marketing manager can use in strategy planning.
2. Understand the importance of promotion objectives.
3. Know how the communication process should affect promotion planning.
4. Know how the adoption processes can guide promotion planning.
5. Understand how promotion blends may have to change along the adoption curve.
6. Know how promotion blends may have to change because of the size of the budget, the product life cycle, the nature of competition, the target of the promotion, and the nature of the product.
7. Know how typical promotion budgets are blended.
8. Know who plans and manages promotion blends.
9. Recognize the important new terms (shown in red).

"M*A*S*H" was one of the most popular TV series ever. In fact, the last program attracted the largest audience in TV history. To tell that enormous audience about their products, companies like General Motors paid almost $15,000 *per second* for advertising time—or nearly a half million dollars for each 30-second ad.

Rent-a-car firms—like Avis, Hertz, and Budget—compete vigorously for the attention—and business—of traveling executives. Lower prices alone don't appeal to many executives—since their companies usually pay their travel expenses. To influence the purchase decision, some car rental firms have special sales promotions and give luggage or other "gifts" with a car rental. The executives keep the gifts—even though their companies pay the rental bills.

Many companies have tried to develop additives that would improve the gas mileage of diesel trucks. One small company discovered such an additive—and hired a sales force to promote it. But it didn't sell. The customers had never heard of the company—and they didn't believe its claims. Finally, the company *gave* a large quantity of the product to a big trucking firm for a free trial. When the product reduced fuel costs, a trucking industry newsletter printed a favorable story about the product. Word quickly spread around the industry—and telephone orders poured in.

Promotion—one of the four major marketing mix variables—is communicating information between seller and buyer—to influence attitudes and behavior. The marketing manager's promotion job is to tell target customers that the right

Product is available at the right Place at the right Price. As the examples above suggest, there are many different promotion possibilities.

What the marketing manager communicates is basically determined when the target customers' needs and attitudes are known. *How* the appropriate messages are communicated depends on what blend of the various promotion methods—personal selling, mass selling, and sales promotion—is chosen.

Promotion planning is only part of marketing strategy planning—but it is an important part because it links the seller with potential buyers—hoping to convince them that the seller has the product they need.

In this chapter, we will discuss basic promotion methods, promotion objectives and methods of implementing them, and how these methods can be blended for effective promotion. The next two chapters will cover personal selling and advertising—two important promotion methods.

Several Promotion Methods Are Available

The marketing manager can choose from several promotion methods. These include personal selling, mass selling, and sales promotion (see Figure 16–1).

Personal selling— flexibility is the biggest asset

Personal selling involves direct face-to-face communication between sellers and potential customers. Salespeople can be very important parts of a marketing mix—because they are able to adapt the company's marketing mix to the needs

■ FIGURE 16–1   Basic promotion methods and strategy planning

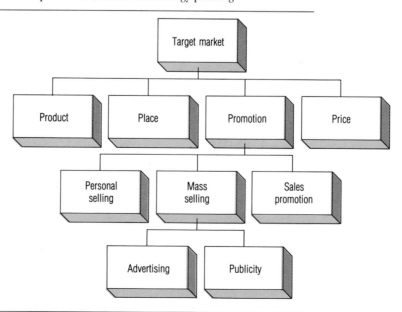

Sales promotions can attract consumer attention—and often spark sales.

of each target market—and, in the extreme, to each potential customer. Face-to-face selling also provides immediate feedback—which helps salespeople to adapt effectively. Salespeople are included in most marketing mixes—especially when target customers are industrial buyers. But their services come at a price. Sometimes personal selling is very expensive—and it is desirable to supplement this effort with mass selling and sales promotion.

Mass selling—reaching millions at a price or even free

Mass selling is communicating with large numbers of customers at the same time. It is less flexible than personal selling. But when the target market is large and scattered—mass selling can be less expensive.

Advertising is the main form of mass selling. **Advertising** is any *paid* form of non-personal presentation of ideas, goods, or services by an identified sponsor. It includes the use of such media as magazines, newspapers, radio and TV, signs, and direct mail. While advertising must be paid for, another form of mass selling—publicity—is "free."

Publicity is "free"

Publicity is any *unpaid* form of non-personal presentation of ideas, goods, or services. Although, of course, publicity people get paid, they try to attract attention to the firm and its offerings *without having to pay media costs.* For example, book publishers try to get authors on TV "talk shows" because this generates a lot of interest—and book sales—at no cost to the publisher.

If a firm has a really new message, publicity may be more effective than advertising. Trade magazines, for example, may carry articles featuring the newsworthy products of regular advertisers—in part because they *are* regular advertisers. Often a firm's publicity people write the basic "copy"—and then try to convince magazine editors to print it. Each year, the auto manufacturers send magazine publishers photos, news releases, and even draft stories about new car models and features. Magazines print many pages based on these materials. This publicity may even raise more interest than the company's paid advertising. A potential customer might not pay any attention to an ad—but might carefully read a trade magazine story with the same information.

Large firms have specialists to handle this job. Usually though, it is treated as just another kind of advertising—and often it isn't used as effectively as it could be. Much more attention needs to be paid to publicity in the future.[1]

Sales promotion tries to spark immediate interest

Sales promotion refers to those promotion activities—other than advertising, publicity, and personal selling—which stimulate interest, trial, or purchase by final customers or others in the channel. Sales promotion may be aimed at consumers, at middlemen, or even at a firm's own sales force. Examples include displays at trade shows, samples of consumer products, and special sweepstakes and contests. Many more examples are listed in Table 16–1.

It's hard to generalize about sales promotion—because it includes such a wide variety of activities. But usually its objective is to complement mass selling and personal selling—which are often seen as the basic methods, while sales promotion is seen as more short-run oriented. And since the sales manager may be responsible for short-run price adjustments, "price dealing" may come to be thought of as sales promotion. It may be necessary to decide whether the money which might be "lost" on a price deal should be used instead for special advertising allowances, contests, or other activities which are usually called "sales promotion." Figure 16–2 spells out a way of seeing that both publicity and sales promotion dollars are well spent.

We will talk more about sales promotion at the end of this chapter. First, however, you need to understand the role of the whole promotion blend—personal selling, mass selling, and sales promotion combined—so you can see how promotion fits into the rest of the marketing mix.

Which Methods to Use Depends on Promotion Objectives

Overall objective is to affect behavior

The different promotion methods can all be viewed as different forms of communication. But good marketers are not interested in just "communicating." They

■ TABLE 16–1   Examples of sales promotion activities

Aimed at final consumers or users	Aimed at middlemen	Aimed at company's own sales force
Banners	Price deals	Contests
Streamers	Promotion allowances	Bonuses
Samples	Sales contests	Meetings
Calendars	Calendars	Portfolios
Point-of-purchase materials	Gifts	Displays
Aisle displays	Trade shows	Sales aids
Contests	Meetings	Training materials
Coupons	Catalogs	
Trade shows	Merchandising aids	
Trading stamps		

■ FIGURE 16–2   The management of sales promotion and publicity

The effective use of sales promotion requires careful planning, consisting of six steps. The first step is to develop clear objectives for sales promotion that derive from the larger marketing communication objectives and still broader marketing objectives set for the product. The second step calls for choosing the sales promotion tools that can accomplish these objectives in the most cost-effective way. The third step calls for rounding out the sales promotion program by making decisions on the specific size of the promotion incentive, conditions for participation, distribution vehicles, duration and timing of promotion, and the overall budget for promotion. The fourth step calls for pretesting the proposed promotion in a limited geographical area or market group to assess its effectiveness. The fifth step calls for the careful implementation and control of the sales promotion program. Finally, the sixth step calls for evaluating the sales promotion results to improve the future use of this tool.

There are four steps in the effective use of publicity. The first step is to establish the objectives for publicity in support of the broader marketing objectives. The second step is to select the publicity messages and vehicles that would be most cost effective. The third step calls for implementing the publicity plan through seeking the cooperation of media people and arranging planned events. The final step is to evaluate the publicity results in terms of the number of exposures achieved, changes in awareness/comprehension/attitude in the target audience and, ultimately, increases in sales and profits.

Source: Philip Kotler, *Marketing Management—Analysis, Planning, and Control*, 4th ed., 1980, p. 541. Reprinted by permission of Prentice-Hall, Inc., Englewood Cliffs, New Jersey.

want to communicate information which will lead to decisions favorable to the firm. They know that if they have a better offering for some target market, informed customers are more likely to buy. Therefore, they are interested in (1) reinforcing present attitudes that might lead to favorable behavior or (2) actually changing the attitudes and behavior of the firm's target market. In terms of demand curves, promotion may help the firm make its present demand curve more inelastic—or shift the demand curve to the right—or both. These possibilities are shown in Figure 16–3.

■ FIGURE 16–3   Promotion seeks to shift the demand curve

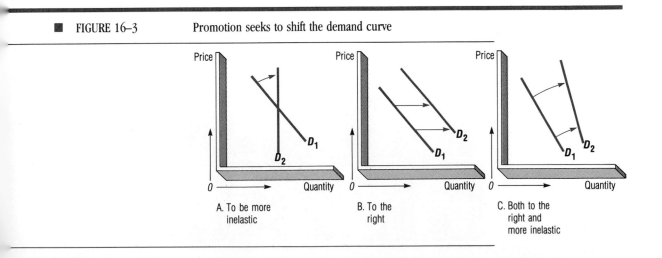

A. To be more
inelastic

B. To the
right

C. Both to the
right and
more inelastic

The buyer behavior model introduced in Chapter 7 showed the many influences on buying behavior. You saw there that affecting behavior is a tough job—and now you should see that it is the overall objective of Promotion.

Informing, persuading, and reminding are basic promotion objectives

If a firm's promotion is to be effective, agreeing on and defining promotion objectives is critical—because the right promotion blend depends on what the firm wants to accomplish. It's helpful to think of three basic *promotion objectives:* to *inform, persuade,* and *remind* target customers about the company and its marketing mix. All are concerned with affecting behavior—by providing more information.

A more specific set of promotion objectives that states *exactly who* you want to inform, persuade, or remind, and *why,* is even more useful—but this is unique to each company's strategy—and too detailed to discuss here. Instead, we will limit ourselves to the three basic promotion objectives—and how you might reach them.

Informing is educating

We know that potential customers must know something about a product if they are to buy at all. Therefore, *informing* may be the most important objective. For example, a cable TV company found that whenever it offered service to a new neighborhood, most of the families subscribed. The main job for the cable company was to inform prospects that cable was available.

A firm with a distinctly new product may not have to do anything but *inform* consumers about it—and show that it works better than other products. Newness and uniqueness in a product can simplify the promotion job. They may even get free publicity for the seller.

Persuading usually becomes necessary

When competitors are offering similar products, however, the firm must not only inform the customers that its product is available—but also persuade them

Trade show promotions inform and persuade intermediate buyers.

to buy it. A *persuading* objective means the firm will try to develop or reinforce a favorable set of attitudes—in the hope of affecting buying behavior. Here, comparative information can be supplied.

Reminding may be enough, sometimes

If target customers already have positive attitudes about the firm's product, then a *reminding* objective might be suitable. The company would try to reinforce previously satisfactory behavior—by keeping cues in front of the customer. This objective can be extremely important in some cases. Even though customers have been attracted and sold once, they are still open to competitive influences. Reminding them of their past satisfaction may keep them from shifting their purchases to a competitor. Coca-Cola realizes that people know about Coke—so much of its advertising is intended to remind.

Promotion Requires Effective Communication

Promotion obviously must get the attention of the target audience—and communicate effectively—or it is wasted effort. What is obvious, however, is not always easy to do. Much promotion doesn't really communicate. For example, you might listen to the radio for several hours—but never really be aware of any of the ads. There are many ways in which promotional communication can break down.

The same message may be interpreted differently

Different audiences may see the same message in different ways—or interpret the same words differently. Such differences are often found in international marketing—when translation is a problem. General Motors, for example, had trouble in Puerto Rico with its Nova automobile until it discovered that—while Nova means "star" in Spanish—when it is spoken it sounds like "no va," which means "it doesn't go." The company quickly changed the car's name to "Caribe"—and it sold well.[2]

Semantic problems in the same language may not be so obvious—and yet the negative effects can still be serious. For example, a new children's cough syrup was advertised as "extra strength." The advertising people thought that would assure parents that the product worked well. But worried mothers avoided the product because they feared that it might be too strong for their children. Marketing research can help avoid such problems—often caused by the *selective processes* discussed in Chapter 7.

Feedback can lead to better communication

There are many reasons why a message can be misunderstood—or not heard at all. To better understand this, it is useful to think about a whole **communication process** which means a source trying to reach a receiver with a message. Figure 16–4 illustrates the elements of this communication process. Here we see that a **source**—the sender of a message—is trying to deliver a message to a **receiver**—a potential customer. Research shows that customers evaluate not only the message—but also the source of the message—in terms of trustworthi-

■   FIGURE 16–4   The communication process

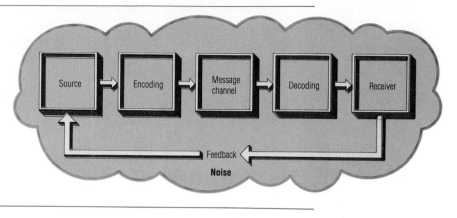

ness and credibility. Information from the president of a company might be viewed as more impressive than from a junior sales representative. A source can deliver a message by many message channels, too. The personal salesperson does it with voice and action. Advertising must do it with mass media—magazines, newspapers, radio, and TV.

A major advantage of personal selling is that the source—the seller—can get immediate feedback from the receiver. It's easier to judge how the message is being received—and change it if necessary. Mass sellers must depend on marketing research or total sales figures for feedback—and that can take too long.

The **noise**—shown in Figure 16–4—is any factor which reduces the effectiveness of the communication process. Any distraction is viewed as "noise"—not just something that makes hearing the message difficult. For example, a motorist on the highway may not see a message on a billboard—because the traffic is

Personal selling allows immediate feedback in the communications process.

■ FIGURE 16–5   Encoding and decoding depend on common frame of reference

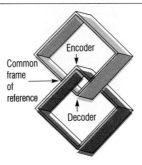

heavy and requires the driver's attention. This is "noise." Advertisers planning messages must recognize that many possible distractions—noise—can interfere with communications.[3]

Encoding and decoding depend on common frame of reference

The basic difficulty in the communication process occurs during encoding and decoding. **Encoding** is the source deciding what it wants to say and translating it into words or symbols that will have the same meaning to the receiver. **Decoding** is the receiver translating the message. This process can be very tricky—because the meanings of various words and symbols may differ, depending on the attitudes and experiences of the two groups. See Figure 16–5.

Average car drivers, for example, might think of the Ford Mustang as a sports car. If they are the target market, they want to hear about ease of handling, acceleration, and racing symbols—such as wide tires. Auto engineers and sports car fanatics, however, don't consider the Mustang a real sports car. So, if they are writing—or approving—copy, they might encode the message in regular "small-car" terms. Errors could be minimized by knowing the relevant market dimensions—in terms of the needs and attitudes of potential customers. This data should be available for strategy planning anyway—and it would be especially useful here.

Whether the message should emphasize only the positive features (one-sided arguments) or both positive and negative features (two-sided arguments) depends on the attitudes of the target market. Sometimes accenting the positive is desirable—it's less confusing. But if the potential customers already know something of the pros and cons, a two-sided approach may be more effective. The marketing manager must realize that such details may affect the effectiveness of communication—and be sure that they are considered during the implementation process.

Message channel is important, too

The communication process is complicated even more because the receiver is aware that the message is not only coming from a source but also coming through some **message channel**—the carrier of the message. The receiver may attach more value to a product if the message comes in a well-respected newspaper or magazine, rather than the over the radio.

Adoption Processes Can Guide Promotion Planning

The adoption process discussed in Chapter 7 is related to effective communication and promotion planning. You learned that there were six steps in that adoption process: awareness, interest, evaluation, trial, decision, and confirmation. Further, in Chapter 7 we saw consumer buying as a problem-solving process in which buyers go through these several steps on the way to adopting (or rejecting) an idea or product. Now we will see that the three basic promotion objectives can be related to these various steps—to show what is needed to achieve the objectives. See Figure 16–6.

Informing and *persuading* may be needed to affect the potential customer's knowledge and attitudes about a product—and then bring about its adoption. Later, promotion can simply remind the customer about that favorable experience—aiming to confirm the adoption decision.

The AIDA model is a practical approach

The basic adoption process fits very neatly with another action-oriented model—called AIDA—which we will use in this and the next two chapters to guide some of our discussion.

The **AIDA model** consists of four promotion jobs—(1) to get *Attention,* (2) to hold *Interest,* (3) to arouse *Desire,* and (4) to obtain *Action.* (As a memory aid, note that the first letters of the four key words spell AIDA—the well-known opera.)

The relationship of the adoption process to the AIDA tasks can be seen in Figure 16–6. *Getting attention* is necessary if the potential customer is to become aware of the company's offering. *Holding interest* gives the communication a chance to really build the prospect's interest in the product. *Arousing desire* affects the evaluation process—perhaps building preference. And *obtaining action* includes obtaining trial—which then may lead to a purchase decision. Continuing promotion is needed to confirm the decision—and encourage continuing action.

■ FIGURE 16–6   Relation of promotion objectives, adoption process, and AIDA model

Promotion objectives	Adoption process (Chapter 7)	AIDA model
Informing	⎰ Awareness	Attention
	⎱ Interest	Interest
Persuading	⎰ Evaluation / Trial	Desire
Reminding	⎱ Decision / Confirmation	Action

Are consumers help-less victims of the mass media?

The AIDA sequence helps us think about the stages that a consumer might go through as promotional communications are received. But it is very important to realize that this sequence can stop at any point—or never even get started. For example, a message may get a consumer's attention. But that certainly does not mean that the consumer will develop a positive attitude toward a product—or buy it.

Some critics of marketing communications seem to imply that promotion is always successful. Consumers are seen as helpless victims of mass media messages which have direct, immediate, and powerful effects—and which make consumers do things against their will.

A good marketing manager knows that this simplistic view is inaccurate—and misleading. Consumers are likely to go through the whole AIDA sequence only if the attitudes and behaviors involved meet their needs. After all, when was the last time that a promotional communication made you do something you didn't want to do? You can see why it is so important for marketing managers to develop promotions—and whole marketing mixes—which fit with consumers' needs and preferences.

Good Communication Varies Promotion Blends along Adoption Curve

The AIDA and adoption processes discussed above look at individuals. This emphasis on individuals helps us understand how people behave. But it's also useful to look at markets as a whole. Different customers within a market may behave differently—with some taking the lead in trying new products and, in turn, influencing others.

Getting attention does not always lead to interest, desire, or action.

**Adoption curve fo-
cuses on market seg-
ments, not
individuals**

Research on how markets accept new ideas has led to the adoption curve idea. The **adoption curve** shows when different groups accept ideas. It shows the need to change the promotion effort as time passes. It also emphasizes the relations among groups. It shows that some groups act as leaders in accepting a new idea.

**Promotion must vary
for different adopter
groups**

The adoption curve for a typical successful product is shown in Figure 16–7. Some of the important characteristics of each of these customer groups are discussed below. Which one are you?

Innovators don't mind taking some risk

The **innovators** are the first to adopt. They are eager to try a new idea—and willing to take risks. Innovators tend to be young and well educated. They are likely to be mobile and sophisticated—with many contacts outside their local social group and community. They are also able to understand and apply complex technical information. Business firms in the innovator group usually are large and rather specialized—and within such firms are people who fight the *status quo*—and encourage innovations.

For promotion purposes, an important characteristic of innovators is that they rely on impersonal and scientific information sources—or other innovators—rather than personal salespeople. They often read articles in technical publications—or informative advertisements in special interest magazines or newspapers. Perhaps you know someone who is among the first to buy a new type of stereo equipment—who reads all the electronics magazines and is interested in all the technical details.

■   FIGURE 16–7   The adoption curve

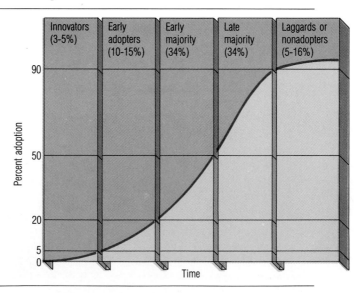

Early adopters are often opinion leaders

Early adopters are well respected by their peers and usually high in opinion leadership. They tend to be younger, more mobile, and more creative than later adopters. But unlike innovators, they have fewer contacts outside their own social group or community. Business firms in this category also tend to be specialized.

This group tends to have the greatest contact—of all the groups—with salespeople. Mass media are important information sources, too. Marketers should be very concerned with attracting and selling the early adopter group. Their acceptance is really important in reaching the next group—because the early majority look to the early adopters. They can help the promotion process—spreading *word-of-mouth* information and advice among other consumers.

Early majority group is deliberate

The **early majority** avoids risk and waits to consider a new idea after many early adopters have tried it—and liked it. They watch the experiences of the early adopters—and ask for their advice. By the time members of this group start to buy, a product is probably in the growth stage of the product life cycle and headed for success—if this group buys.

Average-sized business firms with less specialization often fit in this category. If successful companies in their industry adopt the new idea, they will too.

The early majority seek a lot of purchase information. They have a great deal of contact with mass media, salespeople, *and* early adopter opinion leaders. They interact with their peers, but usually are not opinion leaders.

Late majority is skeptical—but may react to social pressure

The **late majority** are skeptical and cautious about new ideas. Often they are older than the early majority group—and more set in their ways. So they are less likely to follow opinion leaders and early adopters. They may not worry much about "keeping up with the Joneses." In fact, strong social pressure from their own peer group may be needed before they adopt a new product.

Business firms in this group tend to be conservative, smaller-sized firms with little specialization.

The late majority make little use of marketing sources of information—mass media and salespeople. They tend to be oriented more to other late adopters—rather than to outside sources they don't trust.

Laggards or nonadopters hang on to tradition

The **laggards** or **non-adopters** prefer to do things the way they have been done in the past—and are very suspicious of new ideas. They tend to be older and less well educated. They may also be low in social status and income.

The smallest businesses with the least specialization are often in this category. They cling to the status quo—and think it's the safe way. They often don't realize that other companies will search for improved ways of doing things. The laggards stay the same—while those all around them are adopting new ideas.

Laggards tend to be "loners" and have almost no opinion leadership. The main source of information for laggards is other laggards. This certainly is bad news for marketers who are trying to reach a whole market quickly—or who want to use only one promotion method. In fact, it may not pay to bother with this group. By the time they finally adopt a new product, the firm has probably started marketing even newer products to innovators and early adopters.[4]

Promotion Is More Effective if It Reaches Opinion Leaders

The adoption curve concept reinforces our earlier discussion in Chapter 7 of the importance of *opinion leaders*—people who influence other people's attitudes and behavior. To develop the opinion leader idea further—and see how it relates to promotion decisions—we will think about opinion leaders in terms of flows of communication.

Multi-step flow model is useful

Mass communication can be seen as a **multi-step flow model**—which says that messages can flow from the mass media (or other sources) to people in the mass audience in a variety of ways. Figure 16–8 shows some of the important flows. In some cases, the mass media affect people directly. In other cases, mass media messages may flow to opinion leaders and then from opinion leaders to the people with whom they interact. And in some cases, messages may flow through a whole series of opinion leaders and interacting people—that is, there may be more than two steps in the communication process.

The multi-step flow model also recognizes that opinion leaders do not rely only on the mass media as a source of information. Early adopters, for example,

■ FIGURE 16–8   The multi-step model

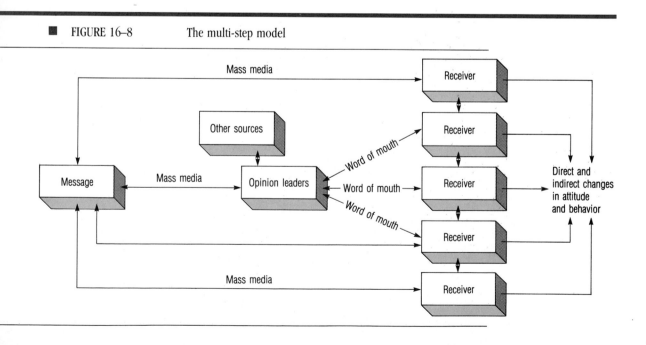

have a lot of contact with salespeople. Further, we aren't passive receivers of information forced on us by the mass media or opinion leaders. Instead, we often seek out information from the mass media or opinion leaders, using the selective processes discussed in Chapter 7—selective exposure, selective perception, and selective retention.

Marketers should try to reach opinion leaders

Opinion leaders and word-of-mouth communication can be important parts of the communication process. They should not be overlooked by strategy planners in their Promotion decisions.

Some companies target special promotions to the opinion leaders. For example, radio announcers are often opinion leaders for new records—so the record companies target promotions to them. Some companies try to encourage more word-of-mouth publicity. When Canon—the camera producer—introduced a high- quality new "automatic" 35 mm camera, they prepared special ads designed to help the opinion leader's explain to others how the camera worked. Other advertisers take a simpler approach. They simply say "tell your friends." Of course, this can backfire if the word-of-mouth is unfavorable.[5]

Opinion leaders may accept or reject new ideas

It's important for marketers to keep in mind that opinion leaders don't always accept new ideas—they can reject them, too. For example, some movie goers are usually among the first to see new movies. If they think a movie is dull, they are quick to tell their friends not to waste their time and money.

If the early adopter group rejects a new product, it may never get off the ground. But if some people in the first two or three groups accept the new product, then opinion leaders in those groups will help spread the message—and may create enough social pressure so the later adopter groups accept the new product. Thus, the "web-of-word-of-mouth"—rather than the firm's mass selling and personal selling efforts—may do the real selling job in the marketplace.

Who are the opinion leaders?

All this shows the importance of trying to reach the opinion leaders in the various adopter groups. But as you may recall from Chapter 7—opinion leaders are often hard to identify. A person can be an opinion leader for some products but not for others. For example, you might ask a friend who is a serious photographer for some advice about buying a camera—but she might come to you for advice about buying a component stereo system. In this case, you would both be opinion leaders—but not all of the time and not for all products.

We know less about the adoption process in industrial goods markets. It seems likely that the same general process is at work—but one study suggests that there is little word-of-mouth communication in these markets. This makes both personal selling and mass selling more important in communicating with industrial buyers *and* the multiple buying influences.[6]

May Need a Different Blend for Each Market Segment

Each unique market segment may need a separate marketing mix—and a different promotion blend. Some mass selling specialists have missed this point.

They think mainly in "mass marketing"—rather than "target marketing"—terms. Aiming at large markets may be desirable in some situations, but unfortunately, promotion aimed at everyone can end up hitting no one. In the Promotion area, we should be especially careful about slipping into a "shotgun" approach when what is really needed is a "rifle" approach—with more careful aiming.

Successful Promotion May Be an Economical Blend

Once promotion objectives for a product-market have been set, a marketing manager may decide to use a blend of promotion methods—since some jobs can be done more economically one way than another. This can be seen most clearly in the industrial goods market. While personal selling dominates most industrial goods promotion budgets, mass selling is necessary, too. Personal

A promotion blend may include advertising, contests, and coupons.

sales representatives nearly always have to complete the sale, but it is seldom practical for them to carry the whole promotion load. The cost of an industrial sales call is estimated to be over $150. This relatively high cost is because sales-people have only limited time and much of it is spent on non-selling activities—traveling, paper work, sales meetings, and strictly service calls. Less than half of their time is available for actual selling.

The job of reaching all the buying influences is made more costly and difficult by the constant turnover of buyers and influencers. An industrial salesperson may be responsible for several hundred customers and prospects—with many buying influences per company. There isn't enough time to get the company's whole message across to every potential customer. The problem is pictured in the classic McGraw-Hill advertisement shown in Figure 16–9. As the ad suggests, too much has been invested in a salesperson to use his time and skill to answer questions that could be better handled through mass selling. It may cost an industrial advertiser much less than a dollar per reader to advertise in a trade magazine—to a targeted group of possible buyers or influencers. After the mass selling has done the ground work, the salesperson can concentrate on answering specific questions—and closing the sale.

Factors Affecting the Selection of a Promotion Blend

Most business firms develop a *promotion blend* of some kind—because the various methods complement each other. But what blend is right in a particular situation?

Wholesalers rely on personal selling. Some retailers do, too—while other retailers advertise aggressively.

At the same time, a food products manufacturer may develop a promotion blend with 10 parts advertising to 1 part personal selling. A lawn seed producer might emphasize advertising 4 to 1—while a paint manufacturer might reverse the ratio. Is there some logical pattern to these differences?

Each promotion blend should be designed to achieve the firm's promotion objectives. But the particular blend selected depends on a number of factors—including (1) the promotion budget available, (2) stage of product in its life cycle, (3) nature of competition, (4) target of the promotion, and (5) nature of the product.

Size of promotion budget affects promotion efficiency

There are some economies of scale in Promotion. In terms of the cost per person reached with an ad, network radio or television may be more economical than local media. City-wide radio, TV, and newspapers may be cheaper than neighborhood newspapers or direct personal contact. But the minimum charge for some "mass media" may force small firms—or those with small promotion budgets—to use the less economical alternatives, in terms of cost per contact. For example, a small retailer might like to use local television but find that there is only enough money for an occasional newspaper ad and perhaps an ad in school bulletins. Similarly, a small manufacturer might see personal selling as the only choice—because a salesperson could be hired for $10,000 to $15,000 a year plus expenses. In contrast, it would cost well over $200,000 to purchase 30 seconds of television time a week for just 13 weeks on the CBC's French and English networks. The TV show might bring the firm's message to more people for less per person, but its total lump sum cost might be too high for a small firm.

When the promotion budget is limited, sales promotion and direct mail may be attractive possibilities. Direct mail selling can be carefully targeted to the desired target market—so there is little wasted expense. Computerized mailing lists—and special firms that supply them—have made a big difference in this area. Mailing lists can be purchased very inexpensively. For example, a company selling medical supplies could buy a list of doctors for less than 3 cents per name—with the names printed on mailing labels. And thousands of very specific lists are available. Most special interest magazines sell their subscription lists. If you were opening a new car service center, you could buy a list of people living in your ZIP Code area who own selected types of cars. Some companies, like Radio Shack, try to get the name and address of every customer—to build their own mailing lists. This is easy to do when most customers pay with check or credit card.

Stage of product in its life cycle

A new product seldom becomes a spectacular success overnight. The adoption curve helps explain why. Further, the product must go through the product life cycle stages described in Chapter 11—market introduction, market growth, market maturity, and sales decline. During these stages, promotion blends may have to change—to achieve different promotion objectives.

Market introduction stage—"this new idea is good"

During market introduction, the basic promotion objective is to inform. If the product is a really new idea, the promotion must build **primary demand**—demand for the general product idea—for example, cordless telephones or video-disk players—not just the company's own brand. There may be few potential innovators during the introduction stage, and personal selling can help find them. Salespeople also are needed to find good channel members—and then persuade them to carry the new product. Special promotions may be targeted at salespeople or channel members to get them interested in the new product.

Since there are few competitors at this stage, mass selling can concentrate on the basic informing job. Initial advertisements may try to get inquiries. Sales promotion may seek to get people to try the product.

Market growth stage—"our brand is best"

In the market growth stage, more competitors begin entering the market—and promotion emphasis must shift from building primary demand to stimulating **selective demand**—that is, demand for a company's own brand. The main job is to persuade customers to buy—and keep buying—the company's product.

Now that more potential customers are trying and adopting the product—mass selling may become more economical. But personal salespeople must still work in the channels—expanding the number of outlets.

Market maturity stage—"our brand is better, really"

In the market maturity stage, more competitors have entered the market. Promotion must become more persuasive. At this stage, mass selling may dominate the promotion blends of consumer products manufacturers. Industrial products might require more aggressive personal selling—perhaps supplemented by more advertising. The total dollars allocated to promotion may rise—as the competitive pressure increases.

If a firm already has high sales—relative to competitors—it may have a real advantage in promotion at this stage. If, for example, General Motors has twice the sales for a certain model of car as Chrysler, its smaller competitor, and they both spend the same *percentage* of total sales on promotion—GM will be spending twice as much, and will probably communicate to more people. GM may get even more than twice as much promotion—because of economies of scale.

Firms that have strong brands at this stage are able to use reminder-type advertising—to remind customers of the product name. This may be much less expensive than persuasive efforts. You can see why it's important for a firm to look for breakthrough opportunities early—and not just try to be a copy-cat later in the life cycle.

Sales decline stage—let's tell those who still want our product

During the sales decline stage, the total amount spent on promotion usually decreases—as firms try to cut costs to remain profitable. Since the product may still be acceptable to some people, more targeted promotion is needed to reach these customers.

On the other hand, some firms may increase promotion to try to slow the cycle—at least temporarily. Crayola had almost all of the market for children's crayons, but sales had been slowly declining as new kinds of marketers came along. Crayola broke the cycle with more promotion spending—and a message to parents to buy their kids a "fresh box."

Nature of competition requires different promotion

Firms in monopolistic competition may favor mass selling—because they have differentiated their marketing mixes—and have something to talk about. As a market tends toward pure competition—or oligopoly—it is difficult to predict what will happen. Competitors in some markets try to "out-promote" each other. The only way for a competitor to stay in this kind of market is to match rivals' promotion efforts—unless the whole marketing mix can be improved in some other way. We see such competitive advertising in our daily newspapers.

In markets that are drifting toward pure competition, some companies resort to price cutting. This *may* increase the number of units sold—temporarily—but it may also reduce total revenue and the amount available for promotion *per unit.* And competitive retaliation may reduce the temporary sales gains—and drag price levels down faster. The cash flowing into the business may decline—and all promotion may have to be cut back.

Once a firm is really in pure competition, there seems to be little reason to promote the product. But someone has to get the business—and using persuasive personal salespeople can be the way to get it. Customers must buy needed products someplace—and often prefer to buy from friendly salespeople who call regularly. This is also true in oligopoly situations. But here, there may be enough profit to support more promotion—including entertaining and business gift-giving.

Target of promotion helps set the blend

Promotion can be directed to five different groups: final consumers, industrial customers, retailers, wholesalers, and even a company's own employees. The right promotion blend for each group can be different.[7]

Promotion to final consumers

The large number of potential customers almost forces consumer goods manufacturers and retailers to emphasize mass selling. Effective mass selling may even win enough brand familiarity so that little personal selling is needed—as in self-service and discount operations.

Promotion planning must consider the whole channel. This ad encourages local McDonald's owners to participate in a promotion.

Mass selling is often the least expensive way to supply information—especially to "hard-to-reach" consumers. The innovators and early adopters—and opinion leaders within social groups—are widely scattered—and it isn't possible to identify and approach each one individually.

Personal selling can be effective too. Some retailers— specialty shops in particular—rely heavily on well-informed salespeople. Some door-to-door retailers have been very successful. But aggressive personal selling to final consumers usually is found only in relatively expensive channel systems.

Promotion to industrial customers

Industrial customers are much less numerous than final consumers—and there is more reason to emphasize personal selling. Industrial customers may have technical questions—or need adjustments in the marketing mix. Manufacturers' or wholesalers' sales reps can be more flexible in adjusting their companies' appeals to suit each customer. They also are able to call back later—and provide confirmation and additional information. Personal selling becomes more practical as the size of each purchase increases—and larger unit purchases are more typical in industrial goods markets.

When it is hard to identify all of the companies—or even industries—that might use a product, ads in trade publications inform potential customers that the product is available and stimulate inquiries. Then a salesperson can follow up.

Promotion to retailers

As with industrial buyers, the relatively small number of retailers makes it practical for manufacturers and wholesalers to emphasize personal selling. Sales promotion and some mass selling in trade magazines and newspapers can be valuable. But most of the promotion is by salespeople—who can answer retailers' questions about what promotion will be directed toward the final consumer, the retailers' own part in selling the product, and important details concerning price, markups, and promotion assistance and allowances.

In other words, promotion to retailers is mainly informative. But since the manufacturer's or wholesaler's sales reps cannot *guarantee* the retailer a profit, the promotion must also be persuasive. The sales rep must convince the retailer that demand for the product exists—and that making a profit will be easy. Further, the rep must establish and maintain good channel relationships. Retailers must be convinced that the manufacturer or wholesaler has their interests at heart. A channel is a human system and depends on the mutual trust and understanding of channel members. This can be built only by personal relations.

Another reason personal selling is so important in dealing with retailers is that marketing mixes may have to be adjusted from one geographic territory to another—to meet competitive situations. The mixes in highly competitive urban areas, for example, may emphasize price more than those in outlying areas.

Promotion to wholesalers

Promotion to wholesalers is very similar to promotion to retailers—except that wholesalers are less numerous—and perhaps even more aware of demand and cost. They respond to economic arguments. They may want to know about the promotion which the producer intends to direct at final customers and retailers. And personal sales reps are needed to cement the relationship between producer and wholesaler.

Promotion to employees

Some companies put a lot of emphasis on promotion to employees—especially salespeople. Sales promotions—like contests that give free trips to big sellers—are common in many businesses. Now, more large companies are trying to design promotions targeted at customers so that they also communicate to employees—and boost their image. This is especially important in service industries—where the quality of the employees' efforts is a big part of the product. General Motors, for example, promotes "Mr. Goodwrench"—the well-qualified mechanic who provides friendly, expert service. The ad communicates primarily to customers—but it also reminds service people that what they do is important and appreciated.

Nature of the product makes a big difference	The target customers' view of the product is the common thread tying together all the variables that must be combined into a marketing mix. The customers' view of the product affects the promotion blend, too. The goods classes introduced in Chapter 10 have a direct bearing on the Place objectives. These goods classes influence the development of promotion blends, too. The way all these factors interact will be discussed in Chapter 21. Here, however, we will consider the impact of some general product characteristics on promotion blends.

Technical nature of product

An extremely technical industrial product may require a heavy emphasis on personal selling by technically trained salespeople. This is the only sure way to make the product understood—and get feedback on how customers use it. The technical sales rep meets with engineers, plant people, purchasing agents, and top managers—and can adjust the sales message to the needs of these various influences.

Mass selling, on the other hand, is practical for many consumer goods—because there is no technical story to be told. If there are some technical details—for example, with cars or appliances—they can be offered to interested customers—perhaps in sales promotion materials at the retailer's showroom.

Degree of brand familiarity

If a product has already won brand preference or insistence—perhaps after years of satisfactory service—aggressive personal selling may not be needed. Reminder-type advertising may be all that's necessary. Hershey Chocolate long prided itself on not having to do any advertising! Recently, however, increasing competition in the United States has forced Hershey to begin some advertising and sales promotion. But in Canada—where it is not well established—Hershey always has advertised aggressively.[8]

If a manufacturer has not differentiated its product and brand, and does not plan to invest in building a brand name—perhaps because of a small budget—then much heavier emphasis on personal selling makes sense. The objective would be to build good channel relations—and encourage channel members to recommend the product.

How Typical Promotion Budgets Are Blended

There is no one right blend

There is no one *right* promotion blend for all situations. Each one must be developed as part of a marketing mix. But to round out our discussion of promotion blends, let's look at ways different manufacturers have allocated their promotion budgets. They do vary considerably—depending on the various factors discussed above. Retailers' blends vary widely also. Wholesalers—on the other hand—use personal selling almost exclusively.

Figure 16–10 shows how manufacturers have allocated their promotion budgets. It shows the ratios of advertising expenditures to personal selling which might be expected in various situations. It's common to find the ratios of advertising to personal selling varying from 10 to 1 to 1 to 10. Note that here we are referring to ratios—not actual expenditures. A 1-to-1 ratio means that the expenditures for advertising and personal selling are roughly equal.

Figure 16–10 shows that manufacturers of well-branded consumer goods (such as cars, breakfast cereals, and non-prescription drugs)—and especially those which are seeking to build brand familiarity—have higher ratios in favor of advertising. The ratio might be even higher if the firm has already built its channel of distribution.

At the other extreme, small companies—even those with new consumer products—use more personal selling—especially if the products are relatively undifferentiated. Middlemen and industrial buyers want several sources of supply—so personal selling is quite important to assure that the seller continues to satisfy—and remain on the supplier list.

Personal selling usually is dominant

The heavier emphasis on personal selling which you might have assumed from the figure is correct. As we will see in the next two chapters—for the econ-

■ FIGURE 16–10   Typical promotion blends of manufacturers (ratio of advertising to personal selling)

10:1	5:1	1:1	1:5	1:10
←———Advertising emphasis ———→		←———Personal selling emphasis ———→		
	Firms with well-branded consumer goods (with established channels)	Blend of consumer and industrial goods	Smaller companies and any firms offering relatively undifferentiated consumer goods or industrial goods	

omy as a whole—far more is spent on personal selling than on advertising. The many ads you see in magazines and newspapers—and on television—are impressive and costly. But you should be aware that most retail sales are completed by sales clerks—and that behind the scenes, much personal selling goes on in the channels. In total, personal selling is several times more expensive than advertising.

Someone Must Plan and Manage the Promotion Blend

Selecting a promotion blend is a strategic decision which should fit with the rest of the marketing strategy. Once the outlines of the promotion blend are set, more detailed plans for the parts of the blend must be developed and implemented. This is the job of specialists—such as the sales and advertising managers.

Sales managers manage salespeople

Sales managers are concerned with managing personal selling. Often the sales manager is responsible for building good distribution channels and implementing Place policies. In smaller companies, the sales manager may act as the marketing manager—and be responsible for advertising and sales promotion, too. Since most sales managers have come up through sales, they usually know more about the power of personal contact. This can be both a strength and a weakness. They may believe in—and be able to develop and motivate—an effective sales force. But they may have less interest in—and respect for—developing a whole promotion blend.

Advertising managers work with ads and agencies

Advertising managers manage their company's mass selling effort—in television, newspapers, magazines, and other media. Their job is choosing the right media for each purpose—and developing the ads. Advertising departments within their own firms may help in these efforts—or they may use outside advertising agencies. They—or their agencies—may handle publicity also. Or it may be handled by whoever handles **public relations**—communication with non-customers—including labor, consumerists, stockholders, and the government.

Advertising managers usually come up through advertising—and have an exaggerated view of its potential power. They may feel that advertising can do the whole promotion job—or that advertising *is* promotion.

Sales promotion managers need many talents

Sales promotion managers manage their company's sales promotion effort. They fill the gaps between the sales and advertising managers—increasing their effectiveness. Nearly everything the sales promotion department does *could* be done by the sales or advertising departments. But sales promotion activities are so varied that specialists tend to develop. In some companies, the sales promotion managers work for the sales managers. In others, they are moving toward independent status—with responsibility to the marketing manager. Where sales promotion expenses exceed those for advertising, it would seem logical to have a separate sales promotion manager.

Marketing manager talks to all, blends all

Because of differences in outlook and experience—the advertising, sales, and sales promotion managers may have difficulty working with each other as partners or equals—especially when each feels that his own approach is the most important. The marketing manager must weigh the pros and cons of the various approaches. Then he must come up with an effective promotion blend—fitting the various departments and personalities into it—and coordinating their efforts.

To be able to evaluate a company's promotion blend, you must first know more about the individual areas of promotion decisions. We start in that direction in the next section—with more discussion of sales promotion. Then, in the following chapters, we will take up personal selling and advertising.

Sales Promotion: Do Something Different to Stimulate Change

Sales promotion refers to those promotion activities—other than advertising, publicity, and personal selling—which stimulate interest, trial, or purchase by final customers or others in the channel. Sales promotion generally tries to complement the other promotion methods—and if properly done, it can be very effective. But there are problems in the sales promotion area.

Sales promotion is a weak spot in marketing

Sales promotion—like publicity—is currently a weak spot in marketing. Table 16–1 shows that sales promotion includes such a wide variety of activities—each of which may be custom-designed and used only once—that little skill can be developed in the typical company. Further, the personal or mass selling managers may be responsible for specific sales promotion activities—but they often treat them as "stepchildren" to whom money is allocated if there is any "left over" or a crisis develops. Many companies—even large ones—don't have a separate budget for sales promotion—or even know what it costs in total.

This neglected method is bigger than advertising

This neglect of sales promotion is most unfortunate, however. Sales promotion expenditures are estimated to be much larger than the total amount spent on advertising. This means that sales promotion deserves more attention—and perhaps separate status within the marketing organization.[9]

The spending on sales promotion is large and growing—sometimes at the expense of other promotion methods—for several reasons. Sales promotion has proved successful in increasingly competitive markets. Sales promotion can usually be implemented quickly—and get results sooner than advertising. Sales promotion activities may help the product manager win support from an already overworked sales force. The sales force may be especially receptive to sales promotion—including promotion in the channels—because competition has been growing and middlemen respond to sales promotion.[10] The sales reps can see that their company is willing to help them win more business.

Creative sales promotion can be very effective, but making sales promotion work is a learned skill—not a sideline for amateurs. In fact, specialists in sales

Coupons have become a big part of promotion—because they stimulate action.

promotion have developed—both inside larger firms and as outside consultants. Some are extremely creative—and might be willing to take over the whole promotion job. But it's the marketing manager's responsibility to set promotion objectives and policies which will fit in with the rest of the marketing strategy.[11]

Earlier, we noted that sales promotion may be aimed at final consumers or users, channel members, and salespeople. Let's take a look at some of the sales promotion tools used for these different target receivers—and what they are expected to accomplish.

Sales promotion for final consumers or users

Sales promotion aimed at final consumers or users usually is trying to increase demand or speed up the time of purchase. Such promotion might involve developing materials to be displayed in retailers' stores—including banners and streamers, sample packages, calendars, and various point-of-purchase materials. The sales promotion people also might develop the aisle displays for supermarkets. They might be responsible for "jackpot" and sweepstakes" contests—as well as coupons designed to get customers to buy a product by a certain date.

All of these efforts are aimed at specific promotion objectives. For example, if customers already have a favorite brand, it may be hard to get them to try anything new. Or it may take a while to become accustomed to a different product. A free sample tube of toothpaste might be just what it takes to get cautious consumers to try—and like—a new product. Such samples might be distributed house to house, by mail, at stores, or attached to other products sold by the firm.

Sales promotion directed at industrial goods customers might use the same kinds of ideas. In addition, the sales promotion people might set up and staff trade show exhibits. Here, attractive models are often used to try to encourage economically oriented buyers to look over a particular firm's product—especially when it is displayed near other similar products in a circus-like atmosphere.

Some industrial sellers give promotional items—pen sets, cigarette lighters, watches, or more expensive items (perhaps with the firm's brand name on them)—to "remind" industrial customers of their products. This is common practice in many industries. But, it can be a sensitive area, too. Some companies frown on buyers taking any gift—of any kind—from a supplier, fearing the buyer's judgment may be influenced by the supplier who gives the best promotional items!

Sales promotion for middlemen

Sales promotion aimed at middlemen—sometimes called *trade promotion*—stresses price-related matters—because the objective assigned to sales promotion may be to encourage stocking new items, or buying in larger quantity, or buying early. The tools used here are price and/or merchandise allowances, promotion allowances, and perhaps sales contests to encourage retailers or wholesalers to sell specific items—or the company's whole line. Offering to send contest winners to Hawaii, for example, may increase sales greatly.

Sales promotion for own sales force

Sales promotion aimed at the company's own sales force might try to encourage getting new customers, selling a new product, or generally stimulating sales of the company's whole line. Depending on the objectives, the tools might be contests, bonuses on sales or number of new accounts, and holding sales meetings at fancy resorts to raise everyone's spirits.

Ongoing sales promotion work might also be aimed at the sales force—to help sales management. Sales promotion might be responsible for preparing sales portfolios, displays, and other sales aids. Sales promotion people might develop the sales training material which the sales force uses in working with customers—and other channel members. They might develop special racks for product displays—which the sales rep sells or gives to retailers. In other words, rather than expecting each individual salesperson—or the sales manager—to develop these sales aids, sales promotion might be given this responsibility.

■ CONCLUSION

Promotion is an important part of any marketing mix. Most consumers and intermediate customers can choose from among many products. To be successful, a manufacturer must not only offer a good product at a reasonable price, but also inform potential customers about the product—and where they can buy it. Further, producers must tell wholesalers and retailers in the channel about their product—and their marketing mix. These middlemen, in turn, must use promotion to reach their customers.

The promotion blend should fit logically into the strategy which is being developed to satisfy a particular target market. *What* should be communicated to them—and *how*—should be stated as part of the strategy planning.

The overall promotion objective is affecting

buying behavior—but basic promotion objectives include informing, persuading, and reminding.

Various promotion methods can be used to reach these objectives. How the promotion methods are combined to achieve effective communication can be guided by behavioral science findings. In particular, we know something about the communications process and how individuals and groups adopt new products.

An action-oriented framework called AIDA can help guide planning of promotion blends—but the marketing manager has the final responsibility for blending the promotion methods into one promotion effort for each marketing mix. Special considerations which may affect the promotion blend are the size of the promotion budget, stage of product in its life cycle, the particular target customers who must be reached, the nature of competition, and the nature of the product.

In this chapter, we have considered some basic ideas. In the next two chapters, we will treat personal and mass selling in more detail. Sales promotion will not be treated anymore—because it is difficult to generalize about all the possibilities.

Further, the fact that most sales promotion activities are short-run efforts—which must be specially tailored—means that sales promotion will probably continue to be a "stepchild"—even though sales promotion costs more than advertising. Marketers must find a better way of handling this important decision area.

■ QUESTIONS AND PROBLEMS

1. Briefly explain the nature of the three basic promotion methods which are available to a marketing manager. Explain why sales promotion is currently a "weak spot" in marketing and suggest what might be done.

2. Relate the three basic promotion objectives to the four tasks (AIDA) of the promotion job, using a specific example.

3. Discuss the communication process in relation to a manufacturer's promotion of an accessory good, say, a portable air hammer used for breaking up concrete pavement.

4. Explain how an understanding of the way individuals adopt new ideas or products (the adoption process) would be helpful in developing a promotion blend. In particular, explain how it might be desirable to change a promotion blend during the course of the adoption process. To make this more concrete, discuss it in relation to the acceptance of a new men's sportcoat style.

5. Explain how opinion leaders should affect a firm's promotion planning. Be sure to refer to the multi-step flow model.

6. Discuss how our understanding of the adoption curve should be applied to planning the promotion blend(s) for a new, small (personal) electric car.

7. Discuss the nature of the promotion job in relation to the life cycle of a product. Illustrate, using household dishwashing machines.

8. Promotion has been the target of considerable criticism. What specific types of promotion are probably the object of this criticism?

9. Might promotion be successful in expanding the general demand for: (*a*) oranges, (*b*) automobiles, (*c*) tennis rackets, (*d*) cashmere sweaters, (*e*) iron ore, (*f*) steel, (*g*) cement? Explain why or why not in each case.

10. Indicate the promotion blend which might be most appropriate for manufacturers of the following established products (assume average- to large-sized firms in each case) and support your answer:
a. Candy bars.
b. Men's T-shirts
c. Castings for automobile engines.
d. Car batteries.
e. Industrial fire insurance.
f. Inexpensive plastic raincoats.
g. A camera which has achieved a specialty-goods status.

11. Discuss the potential conflict among the various promotion managers. How might this be reduced?

■ SUGGESTED CASES

8. Last Mountain Ski Resort, Ltd.

31. Mayfair Detergent Company

■ NOTES

1. "Attention to Public Opinion Helps Firms Avoid Blunders," *The Wall Street Journal,* June 15, 1981, p. 21; Robert S. Mason, "What's a PR Director For, Anyway?" *Harvard Business Review,* September-October 1974, pp. 120–26; "Top Flacks Want Nobodies, Where the Power, Prestige and Big Bucks Are at More Firms," *The Wall Street Journal,* March 4, 1980, p. 1; and Raymond Simon, *Public Relations: Concepts and Practices,* 2d ed. (Columbus Ohio: Grid, 1980).

2. "More Firms Turn to Translation Experts to Avoid Costly Embarrassing Mistakes," *The Wall Street Journal,* January 13, 1977, p. 32.

3. For interesting perspectives on this issue, see Jacob Jacoby and Wayne D. Hoyer, "Viewer Miscomprehension of Televised Communication: Selected Findings," *Journal of Marketing* 46, no. 4 (Fall 1982), pp. 12–26; Gary T. Ford and Richard Yalch, "Viewer Miscomprehension of Televised Communication—A Comment," *Journal of Marketing* 46, no. 4 (Fall 1982), pp. 27–31; and Richard W. Mizerski, "Viewer Miscomprehension Findings Are Measurement Bound," *Journal of Marketing* 46, no. 4 (Fall 1982), pp. 32–34. Also see Reed Sanderlin, "Information Is Not Communication," *Business Horizons* 25, no. 2 (March/April 1982), pp. 40–42; and Robert E. Smith and William R. Swinyard, "Information Response Models: An Integrated Approach," *Journal of Marketing* 46, no. 1 (Winter 1982), pp. 81–93.

4. For further discussion, see Gerald Zaltman, *Marketing: Contributions from the Behavioral Sciences* (New York: Harcourt Brace Jovanovich, 1965), pp. 45–56 and 23–37; Everett M. Rogers, *The Diffusion of Innovations* (New York: Free Press, 1962); Kenneth Uhl, Roman Andrus, and Lance Poulsen, "How Are Laggards Different? An Empirical Inquiry," *Journal of Marketing Research,* February 1970, pp. 43–50; Joseph R. Mancuso, "Why Not Create Opinion Leaders for New Product Introductions?" *Journal of Marketing,* July 1969, pp. 20–25; Thomas S. Robertson, "The Process of Innovation and the Diffusion of Innovation," *Journal of Marketing,* January 1967, pp. 14–19; Robert A. Westbrook and Claes Fornell, "Patterns of Information Source Usage among Durable Goods Buyers," *Journal of Marketing Research,* August 1979, pp. 303–12; V. Mahajan and E. Muller, "Innovation Diffusion and New Products," *Journal of Marketing,* Fall 1979, pp. 55–68; L. E. Ostlund, "Perceived Innovation Attributes as Predictors of Innovativeness," *Consumer Research,* September 1974, pp. 23–29; Richard W. Olshavsky, "Time and the Rate of Adoption of Innovations,"

Consumer Research, March 1980, pp. 425–28; and Thomas S. Robertson and Yoram Wind, "Organizational Psychographics and Innovativeness," *Consumer Research,* June 1980, pp. 24–31.

5. Marsha L. Richins, "Negative Word-of-Mouth by Dissatisfied Consumers: A Pilot Study," *Journal of Marketing* 47, no. 1 (Winter 1983), pp. 68–78.

6. Everett M. Rogers and F. Floyd Shoemaker, *Communication of Innovations: A Cross-Cultural Approach* (New York: Free Press, 1971), pp. 203–9; Frederick E. Webster, Jr., "Informal Communication in Industrial Markets," *Journal of Marketing Research,* May 1970, pp. 186–90; Leon G. Schiffman and Vincent Gaccione, "Opinion Leaders in Institutional Markets," *Journal of Marketing,* April 1974, pp. 49–53; John A. Czepiel, "Word-of-Mouth Processes in the Diffusion of a Major Technological Innovation," *Journal of Marketing Research,* May 1974, pp. 172–80; and John A. Martilla, "Word-of-Mouth Communication in the Industrial Adoption Process," *Journal of Marketing Research,* May 1971, pp. 173–78.

7. Christopher H. Lovelock and John A. Quelch, "Consumer Promotions in Service Marketing," *Business Horizons* 26, no. 3 (May/June 1983), pp. 66–75; John A. Quelch, "It's Time to Make Trade Promotion More Productive," *Harvard Business Review* 61, no. 3 (May-June 1983), pp. 130–36; and Thomas V. Bonoma, "Get More out of Your Trade Shows," *Harvard Business Review* 61, no. 1 (January-February 1983), pp. 75–83.

8. "Hershey's Sweet Tooth Starts Aching," *Business Week,* February 7, 1970, pp. 98–104; and "Big Chocolate Maker, Beset by Profit Slide, Gets More Aggressive," *The Wall Street Journal,* February 18, 1970, p. 1 f.

9. Roger A. Strang, "Sales Promotion—Fast Growth, Faulty Management," *Harvard Business Review,* July-August 1976, pp. 115–24; "Now the Battling Airlines Try Mass Marketing," *Business Week,* April 18, 1980, p. 104; Michel Chevalier, "Increase in Sales Due to In-Store Display," *Journal of Marketing Research,* November 1975, pp. 426–31; "Retailing May Have Overdosed on Coupons," *Business Week,* June 13, 1983, p. 147.

10. Ibid., pp. 116–19.

11. J. F. Engel, M. R. Warshaw, and T. C. Kinnear, *Promotional Strategy,* 5th ed. (Homewood, Ill.: Richard D. Irwin, 1983); and "A New Toothpaste Takes Off, Promoted By Single Employee," *The Wall Street Journal,* May 26, 1983, p. 31.

Chapter 17 ■ Personal selling

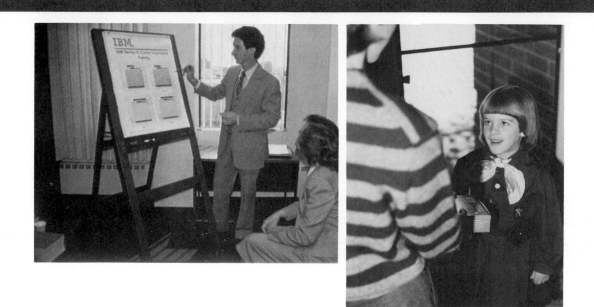

When you finish this chapter, you should:

1. Understand the importance and nature of personal selling.

2. Know the three basic sales tasks and what the various kinds of salespeople can be expected to do.

3. Know what a sales manager must do to carry out the job assigned to personal selling.

4. Understand when and where the three types of sales presentations should be used.

5. Recognize the important new terms (shown in red).

"Today, many salespeople are problem-solving professionals."

Promotion is communicating with potential customers—and personal selling is often the best way to do it. While face-to-face with prospects, salespeople can get more attention than an advertisement or a display. Further, they can adjust the presentation as they move along—and stay in tune with the prospect's feedback. If—and when—the prospect says that "this might be a good idea," the salesperson is there to close the sale—and take the order. A few examples show the importance of personal selling.

A manufacturer of allergy tablets wanted to switch to tamper-proof packages for its products. Some of its managers had been impressed by a sales rep for a supplier of specialty packaging who had called on them before. They arranged another meeting so the sales rep could meet with different departments in the company to learn about their needs and concerns. Then the sales rep made a presentation—which included descriptions of the types of packaging that could be used as well as the probable cost. The company liked the ideas and wanted the packages in a hurry—faster than the supplier could usually fill an order. To win the sale, the sales rep had to coordinate schedules with his company's design, production, and distribution departments to get the packages to the customer on time. Then, he even held a training session for the customer's sales force—to explain the details of the new package. Now, working with this customer is easy. The sales rep simply visits occasionally—to write the routine order and be certain that the customer is still happy. Successful selling isn't just "pushing the goods out the door." Often it means finding creative ways to solve a customer's problems.

Bigelow makes quality carpet for office buildings. Some Bigelow salespeople call only on architects—to help them plan what type of carpet would be best in a new building. They know all of the technical details—such as how well a certain carpet fiber will wear or its effect in reducing noise from office equipment. Often no "selling" is involved—because the architect only suggests specifications and does not actually buy the carpet. But later, the building owner will buy the specified carpet—and think about how many thousands of yards of carpet are used in a 50-story office building!

Marketing managers must decide how much—and what kind of—personal selling effort is needed in each marketing mix. Specifically, as part of their strategy planning, they must decide: (1) how many salespeople will be needed, (2) what kind of salespeople are needed, (3) what kind of sales presentation should be used, (4) how salespeople should be selected and trained, and (5) how they should be supervised and motivated. The sales manager provides inputs into these strategic decisions. And once they are made, it's the sales manager's job to implement the personal selling part of a marketing strategy.

In this chapter, we will discuss the importance and nature of personal selling—so you will understand the strategic decisions which face sales managers and marketing managers. These strategic decisions are shown in Figure 17–1.

■ FIGURE 17–1   Strategy planning for personal selling

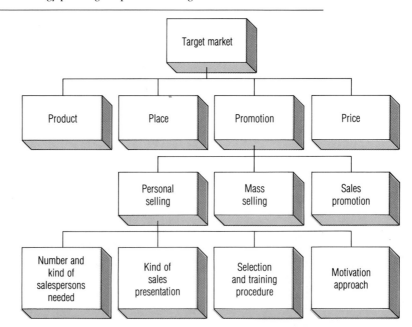

The Importance and Role of Personal Selling

We have already seen that personal selling is important in some promotion blends—and absolutely essential in others. Some of its supporters feel that personal selling is the dynamic element which keeps our economy going. You could better appreciate the importance of personal selling if you regularly had to meet payrolls, and somehow—almost miraculously—your salespeople kept coming in with orders just in time to keep the business from closing.

Personal selling is often a company's largest single operating expense. This is another reason why it is important to understand the decisions in this area. Bad sales management decisions can be costly not only in terms of lost dollar sales, but also in actual out-of-pocket expenses.

Obviously, our economy does need and use many salespeople. Government statistics show that about 1 person out of every 10 in the total labor force is in sales work. By comparison, that's about 15 times more people than in advertising. Any activity that employs so many people—and is so important to the economy—deserves study.

Helping to buy is good selling

Salespeople are important sources of useful information to customers—especially to industrial buyers. The salesperson may even help customers solve their problems. Increasingly, good salespeople don't just try to *sell* the customer. Rather, they try to *help the customer buy*—by presenting both the advantages and disadvantages of their products—and showing how they will satisfy needs. Such helpfulness results in satisfied customers—and long-term relationships. This new approach recognizes the growing sophistication of buyers—especially industrial buyers. You may still think of personal selling in terms of an old-time stereotype: a "bag of wind" with no more to offer than a funny story, a big expense account, and an engaging grin. But that isn't true any more. "Old-time" salespeople are being replaced by real professionals who have something definite to contribute to their customers and employers.

Salespeople represent the whole company— and customers, too

Increasingly, the salesperson is seen as a representative of the whole company—responsible for explaining its total effort to target customers—rather than just "pushing" products. The sales rep is often the only link between the firm and its customers—especially if customers are far away. The salesperson may provide information about products, explain and interpret company policies, and even negotiate price levels. In industrial markets, he may have to diagnose technical problems when a product doesn't work well.

In some cases, the salesperson represents his *customers* back inside his own firm, too. Recall that feedback is an essential part of both the communications process *and* the basic management process of planning, implementing, and control. For example, the sales rep is the likely one to explain to the production manager why a customer is unhappy with product performance or quality—or to the physical distribution manager why slow shipments are causing problems.

As evidence of these changing responsibilities, some companies now give

A salesperson represents the company to the customer—and the customer to the company.

their salespeople such titles as field manager, market specialist, account representative, or sales engineer.

Sales force provides marketing research information as well

In many companies, the sales force plays an important role in the marketing research process. The sales rep may be the first in the company to hear about a new competitor—or a competitor's new product or strategy. It is important that such information get back to the firm—as the following example shows.

A sales rep for Scripto (ballpoint pens) wondered why sales were dropping off in his Ontario stores and asked why. He learned that a new Japanese product—a felt-tip writer—was taking sales from ballpoint pens. But the sales rep failed to report this to management—until months later. By then, it was too late. The new felt-tip pens were sweeping the country—and Scripto did not have one in its product line.

Salespeople can be strategy planners, too

Some salespeople are expected to be marketing managers in their own geographic territories. Or some may become marketing managers by default—because top management hasn't provided detailed strategic guidelines. Either way, salespeople may take the initiative to fill the gap—to develop their own marketing mixes or even their own strategies. The sales rep may be given a geographic territory—but exactly who the target customers should be may be vague. The salesperson may have to start from scratch with strategy planning—the only restrictions being the general product line to sell and probably the price structure. The salesperson may have choices about (1) what target customers to aim at, (2) which particular products in the whole line to push most aggressively, (3) which middlemen to call on or to work with the hardest, (4) how to use any promotion money that may be available, and (5) how to adjust prices.

A salesperson who can put together profitable strategies—and implement them well—can rise very rapidly. A successful sales rep is usually very visible to top management. And it is very likely that such people will be given responsibility for larger and larger territories. The opportunity is there—for those who are prepared and willing to work.

Even the starting job may offer great opportunities. Some beginning sales-

Some salespeople are only given a territory and a product and have to develop their own strategy.

people—especially those working for manufacturers or wholesalers—are responsible for larger sales volumes than are achieved by many retail stores. This is a responsibility which must be taken seriously—and should be prepared for.

Further, the sales job is often used as an entry-level position—to evaluate a person. Success in this job can lead to rapid promotion to higher-level sales and marketing jobs—and more money and security.

Three Basic Sales Tasks Are Needed

If a firm has too few salespeople—or the wrong kind—some important personal selling tasks may not be completed. But having too many salespeople—or the wrong kind—wastes money. A sales manager needs to find a good balance—and have the right number of the right kind of salespeople.

One of the difficulties of determining the right number and kind of salespeople is that every sales job is different. While the engineer or accountant can look forward to fairly specific duties, the salesperson's job is constantly changing. However, there are three basic types of sales tasks. This gives us a starting point for understanding what selling jobs need to be done—and how many people will be needed to do them.

Personal selling is divided into three tasks

The three **basic sales tasks** are *order getting, order taking,* and *supporting.* For convenience, we will describe salespeople by these terms—referring to their primary task—although one person might have to do all three tasks in some situations.

As the names imply, order getters and order takers are interested in obtaining orders for their company. In contrast, supporting salespeople are not directly interested in orders. Their function is to help the order-oriented salespeople. With this variety, you can see that there is a place in personal selling for nearly everyone.[1]

Order Getters Develop New Business

Order getters are concerned with getting new business. **Order getting** means aggressively seeking out possible buyers with a well-organized sales presentation designed to sell a product, service, or idea. Order getters may be interested in selling the advantages of buying from one company rather than from another—or shifting a larger share of purchases to their own company—or finding completely new customers and even entirely new markets.

Order getters must have complete confidence in their abilities, company, and product—since their attitudes show through to customers. They must also know what they are talking about—not be just a personal contact. Order-getting salespeople work for manufacturers, wholesalers, and retailers. They normally are well paid—many earn more than $60,000 per year.

Manufacturers' order getters—find new opportunities

Manufacturers of all kinds of goods—but especially industrial goods—have a great need for order getters. They are needed to locate new prospects, open new accounts, visualize new opportunities, and help establish and build channel relationships.

High-caliber order getters are essential in sales of installations and accessory equipment—where large sums are involved and where top-level management participates in the buying decision.

Top-level customers are more interested in ways to save or make more money than in technical details—and good order getters cater to this interest. They sell concepts and ideas—rather than physical products. The products are merely the means of achieving the ends desired by the customer.

In selling other industrial goods—such as raw materials, components, supplies, and services—skilled order getters also are necessary but mainly for initial contacts. Since many competitors offer nearly the same product, the order getter's crucial selling job here is getting the company's name on the "approved suppliers" list. Persuasion of the highest order—and sometimes deliberate social cultivation of prospects—may be needed.

Industrial goods order getters need the "know-how" to help solve their customers' problems. Often they need to understand both customers' general business concerns—as well as technical details about the product and its applications. To have technically competent order getters, firms often give special technical training to business-trained college graduates. Such salespeople then can deal intelligently with their specialist customers. In fact, they may be more technically competent in their narrow specialty than anyone they are likely to encounter—and so may be able to provide a unique service. For example, a salesperson for sophisticated computerized accounting systems must under-

Firms often give special technical training to marketing graduates to make them competent order getters.

stand how a prospect's records are currently kept, as well as the technical details of converting to computer processing.

Wholesalers' order getters—hand it to the customer, almost

Progressive wholesalers are developing into counselors and store advisors—rather than just order takers. Such order getters are almost "partners" of retailers in the job of moving goods from the wholesale warehouse through the retail store to consumers. These order getters almost become a part of the retailer's staff—helping to check stock, write orders, conduct demonstrations—and plan advertising, special promotions, and other retailing activities.

Agent middlemen often are order getters—particularly the more aggressive manufacturers' agents and brokers. They face the same tasks as manufacturers' order getters. Unfortunately for them, however, once the "order getting" is done and the customers become established and loyal, manufacturers may try to eliminate the agents—and save money with their own order takers.

Retail order getters— visionaries at the refrigerator

Order getters are needed for unsought goods—and desirable for some shopping goods.

Unsought goods need order getters

Convincing customers of the merits of products they haven't seriously considered takes a high degree of personal selling ability. Order getters have to help customers visualize how a particular product will satisfy needs now being filled by something else—or needs they don't even realize they have. Most people reject new ideas or wait for others to accept them first. Without order getters, many of the products we now accept as part of our standard of living—such as refrigerators and window air-conditioners—might have died in the introduction stage. It is the visionary order getter who helps bring products out of the introduction stage—into the market growth and market maturity stages. And some products need order getters throughout their life cycle—because they remain unsought goods. Encyclopedia sales reps, for example, must convince prospects that $400 to $800 is a small price for a lifetime of literacy and enjoyment.

They help sell shopping goods

Order getters are helpful for selling *heterogeneous* shopping goods. Consumers shop for many of these items on the basis of price *and* quality. They welcome useful information. Automobiles, furniture and furnishings, cameras, jewelry, and fashion items can be sold effectively by an aggressive, helpful order getter. Friendly advice—based on thorough knowledge of the product and its alternatives, may really help consumers—and bring profits to the salesperson and retailers.

Many specialty shops and limited-line stores have developed a following because of the help offered by the stores' sales clerks. The sales clerks at Forever Young—a specialty store that sells fashions for working women—know the style preferences of their regular customers and notify them when they get new shipments that might be of interest. They will even advise a customer *not* to buy a particular item—because the color isn't flattering, for example—even though they do not have a suitable substitute. The store may lose an immediate sale—but this kind of service is profitable to retailers seeking loyal customers and repeat business.

Order Takers—Keep the Business Coming

Order takers sell the regular or typical customers. Order takers complete most sales transactions. After a customer becomes interested in the products of a specific firm—from an order getter or a supporting salesperson or through advertising or sales promotion—an order taker usually is needed to answer any final questions and complete the sale. **Order taking** is the routine completion of sales made regularly to the target customers.

Sometimes sales managers or customers will use the term "order taker" as a "put down" when referring to unaggressive salespeople. While a particular salesperson may perform so poorly that criticism is justified, it is a mistake to downgrade the function of order taking. Order taking is extremely important—whether handled by human hands or machines. Many sales are lost just because no one ever asked for the order—and closed the sale.

Manufacturers' order takers—responsible for training and explaining

After order getters open up industrial, wholesale, or retail accounts, regular follow-up is necessary. Someone has to explain details, make adjustments, handle complaints, explain or negotiate new prices and terms, place sales promotion materials, and keep customers informed on new developments. It may also be necessary to train the customers' employees to use machines or products. In sales to middlemen, it may be necessary to train wholesalers' or retailers' salespeople. All these activities are part of the order taker's job.

Usually these salespeople have a regular route with many calls—which they may make at set times. To handle these calls well, they must have energy, persistence, enthusiasm, and a friendly personality that wears well over time. They sometimes have to "take the heat" when something goes wrong with some other element of the marketing mix.

Sometimes jobs that are basically order taking are used to train potential order getters and managers. Such jobs give them an opportunity to meet key customers—and to better understand their needs. Frequently, there may also be some order-getting possibilities.

George Turpin went to work for a manufacturer of supplies for automotive body shops. Usually, this was an order-taking job. George discovered, however, that one of the biggest body shops in his territory was splitting its orders between a number of suppliers. George spent more time at this shop, studying the business. He found ways to speed up their repairs by suggesting products they didn't know about. This increased the shop's profits. The owners were impressed—and it helped George convince them that they could save even more if they let him coordinate *all* of their purchases. They agreed to give it a try. Since the body shop scheduled all repairs a week ahead, George could study the work list in advance, figure out what supplies and paints were needed, and write up the order. The shop found that this approach meant fewer delays due to supplies that had not been ordered or did not arrive—and it saved them the time of working up orders. George used the same approach with other customers—and increased sales in his territory by 50 percent.

Wholesalers' order takers—not getting orders but keeping them

While manufacturers' order takers handle relatively few items—and sometimes even a single item—wholesalers' order takers may sell 125,000 items or more. Most wholesale order takers just sell out of their catalog. They have so many items that they can't possibly give aggressive sales effort to many—except perhaps newer or more profitable items. Once a new product has been featured, the order taker probably won't give it much attention for some time. He has too many items to single any out for special attention. The order taker's strength is a wide assortment—rather than detailed knowledge of individual products.

The wholesale order taker's main job is to maintain close contact with customers—perhaps once a week—and fill any needs that develop. Sometimes such an order taker gets very close to industrial customers or retailers. Some retailers let the salesperson take inventory—and then write up the order. Obviously, this position of trust cannot be abused. After writing up the order, this order taker normally checks to be sure the company fills the order promptly—and accurately. He also handles any adjustments or complaints—and generally acts as a liaison between the company and customers.

Such salespeople are usually the low-pressure type—friendly and easygoing. Usually these jobs aren't as high paying as the order-getting variety—but are attractive to many because they aren't as physically taxing. Relatively little traveling is required—and there is little or no pressure to get new accounts. There can be a social aspect, too. The salesperson sometimes becomes good friends with customers. Some salespeople even schedule their calls so that they will arrive "in time for coffee" with a friendly customer.

Retail order takers—often they are poor sales clerks

Order taking may be almost mechanical at the retail level—for example, at the supermarket check-out counter. For many products, not much is needed—except to fill the customer's order, wrap it, and make change. As a result, retail clerks often are expected to concentrate on setting up and arranging stock—and sometimes they seem to be annoyed by having to complete sales. Many are downright rude. This is most unfortunate because order taking is a vital function. They may be poor orders takers, however, because they aren't paid much—often only the minimum wage. But—they may be paid little because they do little. In any case, order taking at the retail level appears to be declining in quality. And it is likely that there will be far fewer such jobs in the future—as more marketers make adjustments in their mixes and turn to self-service selling. Even check-out counters are being automated—with electronic scanning equipment that reads price codes directly from packages.

Supporting Sales Force—Informs and Promotes in the Channel

Supporting salespeople help the order-oriented salespeople—but don't try to get orders themselves. Their activities are aimed at getting sales in the long run. For the short run, however, they are ambassadors of goodwill—who may provide specialized services. Almost all supporting salespeople work for manufacturers—or middlemen who do this supporting work for manufacturers. There are two types of supporting salespeople: *missionary salespeople* and *technical specialists.*

Missionary salespeople can increase sales

Missionary salespeople work for manufacturers—calling on their middlemen and their customers. They try to develop goodwill and stimulate demand, help the middlemen train their salespeople to do so, and often take orders for delivery by the middlemen. Missionary salespeople are sometimes called *merchandisers* or *detailers.*

They may be needed if a manufacturer uses the typical merchant wholesaler to obtain widespread distribution—and yet knows that the retailers will need promotion help. These salespeople may be able to give an occasional "shot in the arm" to the company's regular wholesalers and retailers. Or they may work regularly with these middlemen—setting up displays, arranging special promotions, and, in general, implementing the sales promotion plans.

A missionary sales rep can focus on a product which otherwise wouldn't get much attention from the middlemen—because it's just one of many they sell. For example, a missionary salesperson for Vicks' cold remedy products might visit druggists during the "cold season" and encourage them to use a special end-of-aisle display for Vicks' cough syrup—and even help set it up. The wholesaler that supplies the drug store would benefit from any increased sales, but might not have taken the time to urge use of the special display.

An imaginative missionary salesperson may double or triple sales. Naturally, this doesn't go unnoticed—and missionary sales jobs are often a route to order-oriented jobs. In fact, this position is often used as a training ground for new salespeople.

Technical specialists are experts who know product applications

Technical specialists provide technical assistance to order-oriented sales people. Technical specialists usually are scientists or engineers with the know-how to explain the advantages of the company's product. Before the specialist's visit, an order getter probably has stimulated interest. The technical specialist provides the details. The order getter probably will complete the sale—but only after the customer's technical people give at least tentative approval. Some technical specialists are more interested in showing the technical details of their product than in helping to persuade customers to buy it. But many of the decision makers who influence industrial purchases are more technical than in the past. As a result, more technical specialist work is needed, and many companies are training their technical specialists in presentations skills—to help them be not only technically correct—but also persuasive salespeople. Technical specialists who are good communicators often become high paid order getters.

Most Selling Requires a Blend of All Three Tasks

We have described three sales tasks—order getting, order taking, and supporting. You should understand, however, that a particular salesperson might be given two—or all three—of these tasks. Ten percent of a particular job may be order getting, 80 percent order taking, and the additional 10 percent supporting. Another company might have three different people handling the different sales tasks.

Strategy planners should consider all the different types of selling tasks to be handled by a sales force. Once the tasks are identified, the sales manager needs to assign responsibility for individual sales jobs—so that the tasks are completed and the personal selling objectives achieved.

Personal Selling Techniques—Prospecting and Presenting

Now, let's discuss selling techniques—so you understand the basic steps which each salesperson should follow—including prospecting, planning sales presentations, making sales presentations, and following up after the sale. Figure 17–2 shows the steps we will consider. From the figure, you can see that the personal salesperson is just carrying out a planned communications process—as discussed in the last chapter.[2]

Finding prospects— the big buyer who wasn't there

Finding "live" prospects isn't as easy as it sounds. Although the marketing strategy should specify the target market, we have already seen that some people within a target market may be innovators, while others are late adopters.

FIGURE 17–2   Personal selling is a communication process

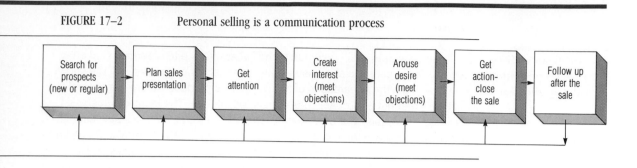

| Search for prospects (new or regular) | → | Plan sales presentation | → | Get attention | → | Create interest (meet objections) | → | Arouse desire (meet objections) | → | Get action—close the sale | → | Follow up after the sale |

Basically, **prospecting** involves following down all the "leads" in the target market. But this only identifies which kinds of people or companies *may* be prospects—not which ones are currently "live" and will help make the buying decision. In the industrial goods area, for example, about two thirds of industrial calls are made on the wrong person—because of multiple buying influences and the fact that companies regularly rearrange their organization structures and buying responsibilities. This means that constant, detailed customer analysis is needed—requiring many personal calls and telephone calls.

Telephone selling—using the telephone to find out about a prospect's interest in the company's marketing mix and even to make a sales presentation or take an order—is becoming especially common as an aid in prospecting. A telephone call has many of the benefits of a personal visit—including the ability to modify the message as feedback is received. It is more efficient in many cases. It can eliminate wasted expense of personal visits—or even sell "hot" prospects on the spot. Usually, it provides information which can be used in a follow-up sales visit. Telephone companies offer training in using the telephone for prospecting—or making sales presentations.

Priority system guides prospecting

Another part of prospecting is deciding how much time to spend on which prospects. The problem is to "qualify" prospects—to see if they deserve more effort. The potential sales volume—as well as the likelihood of a sale—must be

Telephone selling is often used to find out about a prospect's interest in the company's marketing mix.

weighed. If many competitors are concentrating on a few accounts, the probability of any one of them making the sale may be low. It may be more sensible for the salesperson to shift to other prospects. this obviously requires judgment—but well-organized salespeople usually develop some priority system. Attractive accounts may be labeled "A"—and the salesperson may plan to call on them weekly until the sale is made or they are placed in a lower category. "B" customers might offer somewhat lower potential—and be called on monthly. "C" accounts might be called on only once a year—unless they happen to contact the salesperson. And "D" accounts might be ignored—unless the customer takes the initiative.

Some such system is needed to guide prospecting—because most salespeople have too many prospects. They can't afford to "wine and dine" all of them. Some may deserve only a phone call. Taking them to lunch would be a waste of precious time. There are only a few hours each business day for personal sales calls—this time must be used carefully if the salesperson is to succeed. You can see that effective prospecting is important to success—in fact, it may be more important than making a good sales presentation, especially if the company's marketing mix is basically strong.[3]

Three kinds of sales presentations may be useful

Once a promising prospect has been located, it is necessary to make a sale. But someone has to plane the kind of **sales presentation** to be made. This is a strategic matter. The kind of presentation should be set before the sales rep is sent prospecting. And in situations where the customer comes to the salesperson—for example, in a retail store—the planners have to make sure that prospects are brought together with salespeople. Eventually, then, the sales presentation must be made.

The marketing manager can choose two basically different approaches to making sales presentations: the *prepared* approach or the *need-satisfaction* approach. Another approach—the *selling formula approach*—is a combination of the two. Each of these has its place.

The prepared sales presentation

The **prepared sales presentation** approach uses a memorized presentation which is not adapted to each individual customer. A prepared ("canned") presentation builds on the black box (stimulus-response) model discussed in Chapter 7. This model says that a customer faced with a particular stimulus will give the desired response—in this case, a yes answer to the salesperson's prepared statement—which includes a request for an order. In applying the "canned" approach, the salesperson usually doesn't have a very good idea what the customer is thinking. So the prepared presentation includes various appeals—one after the other—hoping to get the desired response.

With a prepared presentation, the salesperson does most of the talking—occasionally letting the customer talk when the salesperson attempts to close. You may be surprised to learn that one of the most frequent reasons for losing a sale is that the salesperson fails to ask for the order! That important point is never left out of prepared presentations. Further, "trial closes" help ensure that the salesperson doesn't have to actually ask for the order and be told no.

A trial close may assume a positive response

There are ways to avoid this awful word. Without asking for a direct yes or no, the experienced salesperson may just assume that "of course" the customer will buy. The salesperson may begin to write up the order—or ask which of various delivery dates would be preferable—or what quantity the customer would like to try in a new display. This may lead the customer into taking action without consciously having to make a direct decision—a difficult psychological step for some people.

If one "trial close" doesn't work, another prepared presentation is tried with another attempt at closing. This can go on for some time—until the salesperson runs out of material—or the customer either buys or decides to leave. The relative participation of the salesperson and customer in the prepared approach is shown in Figure 17–3. Note that salesperson participation dominates.

In modern selling, the "canned" approach is commonly used when the prospective sale is low in value—and only a short presentation is practical. It's also sensible when salespeople are not very skilled. The company can control what is said—and in what order. But this approach has the obvious weakness of treating all potential customers alike. It may work for some and not for others—and the salespeople probably won't know why. Moreover, salespeople don't improve with more experience—because they are just mechanically trying standard presentations. This approach may be suitable for simple order taking—but it is no longer considered good selling for complicated situations.

Need-satisfaction approach—builds on the marketing concept

The **need-satisfaction approach**—in sharp contrast to the prepared approach—involves developing a good understanding of the individual customer's needs before trying to close the sale. Here, after making some general "benefit" statements—to get the customer's attention and interest—the salesperson leads the customer to do most of the talking—to help the salesperson understand the customer's needs. Then, the salesperson begins to enter into the conversation more—trying to get agreement from the customer about what needs or problems are most important. Once they agree on needs, the seller tries to show the customer how the product fills those needs—and closes the sale. This is a problem-solving approach—in which the customer and salesperson work together to

■ FIGURE 17–3   Prepared approach to sales presentations

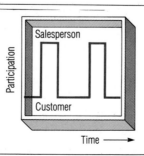

■ FIGURE 17–4   Need-satisfaction approach to sales presentations

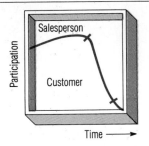

solve the problem. Figure 17–4 shows the participation of the customer and the salesperson during such a sales presentation.

The need-satisfaction approach is most useful if there are many subtle differences among the various customers in one target market. In the extreme, each customer may be thought of as a separate target market—with the salesperson trying to adapt to each one's needs and attitudes.

With this approach, the salesperson is much more on his own—and should have not only a good grounding in the company's product and policies, but also much empathy for people and situations. This kind of selling obviously takes more skill. The salesperson must be able to analyze what motivates a particular customer and show how the company's offering would help the customer satisfy those needs.

Selling formula approach—some of both

The **selling formula approach** starts with a prepared presentation outline—much like the prepared approach—gets the customer to discuss needs, and then leads the customer through some logical steps to a final close. The prepared steps are logical because here we assume that we know something about the target customer's needs and attitudes.

The selling formula approach is shown in Figure 17–5. The salesperson does most of the talking at the beginning of the presentation—to be certain that key

■ FIGURE 17–5   Selling-formula approach to sales presentations

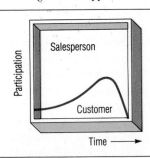

Which sales presentation is best depends on the situation.

points are communicated early. This part of the presentation may even have been prepared as part of the marketing strategy. As the sales presentation moves along, however, the salesperson brings the customer into the discussion—to help clarify just what needs this customer has. In other words, the strategy planners know that the target customers may have several needs. The salesperson's job is to discover the needs of a particular customer—to know how to proceed. Once it is clear what kind of customer this is, the salesperson comes back to show how the product satisfies this specific customer's needs—and to close the sale. In summary, the salesperson learns a number of "canned" arguments to present, and selects from those the ones most relevant to the particular customer. It is like a formula: if the customer raises a certain objection or concern, then the salesperson has a prepared response ready.

This approach can be useful for both order-getting and order-taking situations—where potential customers are similar, and relatively untrained salespeople must be used. Some of the office equipment and computer manufacturers, for example, have used this approach—because they know the kinds of situations their salespeople meet—and roughly what they want them to say. Using this approach speeds training and makes the sales force productive sooner.

AIDA helps plan sales presentations

AIDA—Attention, Interest, Desire, Action. Each sales presentation—except for some very simple canned types—follows this AIDA sequence. The "how-to-do-it" might even be set as part of the marketing strategy. The time spent with each of the steps might vary, depending on the situation—and the selling approach being used—but it is still necessary to begin a presentation by getting the prospect's *attention,* and hopefully moving him to *action* through a close.[4]

Each sales manager—and salesperson—needs to think about this sequence in deciding what sales approach to use—and in evaluating a possible presentation. Does the presentation do a good job of quickly getting the prospect's attention? Will the presentation be interesting? Will the benefits be clear—so that the prospect is moved to buy the product? Are likely objections considered—and problems anticipated—so the sales rep can act to close the sale when the time is right? These may seem like simple things but too frequently they are not done—and a sale is lost.

Sales management must be planned, too

Marketing plans should indicate how personal selling efforts are to fit in with the other elements of the firm's marketing mix. Thus, sales management must plan and execute its sales program within the guidelines set by the overall marketing strategy. Such matters as selecting, training, and motivating salespeople and deciding how the personal selling job will be carried out are obviously important. The sales manager must also allocate territories, set quotes, and control the whole process.[5] Let's see how sales management deals with such problems as organization, selection, training, motivation and control.

The Right Structure Helps Assign Responsibility

A sales manager must organize the sales force so that all the necessary tasks are done well. A large organization might have different salespeople who specialize by different selling tasks *and* by the target markets they serve.

Different target markets need different selling tasks

Sales force responsibilities often are divided based on the type of customer involved. For example, a company that sells upholstery fabrics might have one sales group that calls on furniture manufacturers and another that calls on wholesalers who sell to small upholstery shops. They may buy the same products, but the marketing mixes are very different.

Very large customers often require special selling tasks—and are treated differently. For example, a company that makes plumbing fixtures might have a "regular" sales force to call on building material wholesalers and an "elite" **national accounts sales force** that sells direct to large accounts—like Sears or other major retail chain stores that carry plumbing fixtures.

Sales tasks are done in sales territories

Often companies organize selling tasks on the basis of **sales territory**—a geographic area which is the responsibility of one salesperson or several working in a coordinated effort. A territory might be a region of the country, a province, or part of a city—depending on the market potential. Companies like Lockheed Aircraft Corporation often consider a whole country as *part* of a sales territory for one salesperson.

Carefully set territories can reduce travel time and the cost of sales calls. Assigning territories can also help reduce confusion about who has responsibility for a set of selling tasks. But, sometimes simple geographic division of selling jobs isn't easy. A company may have different products that require very different knowledge or selling skills—even if products are being sold in the same territory—or to the same customer.[5] For example, Du Pont makes special films used in hospital X-ray departments as well as chemicals used in laboratory blood tests. But a salesperson who can talk to a radiologist about what film is best for a complex X-ray probably can't be expected to also know everything about blood chemistry!

Size of sales force depends on workload

Once all the important selling tasks have been identified—and the responsibilities have been divided—the sales manager must decide how many salespeople are needed. The first step is estimating how much work can be done by one person in some time period. Then he can make an "educated guess" about how many people are required in total, as the following example shows.

The Parker Jewelry Company had long been successful in selling its silver jewelry to department and jewelry stores in Western Canada. But management decided to expand into the big urban markets of Quebec and Ontario. They realized that most of the work for the first few years would require order getters. They felt that a salesperson would need to call on each account at least once a month to get a share of this competitive business. They estimated that a salesperson could make only four calls a day on prospective buyers—and still allow time for travel, waiting, and follow-up on orders that came in. This meant that a sales rep who made calls 20 days a month could handle about 80 stores (4 a day × 20 days).

The managers looked at telephone Yellow Pages for their target cities—and estimated the total number of jewelry departments and stores. Then they simply divided the total number of stores by 80 to estimate the number of salespeople needed. This helped them set up territories, too—defining areas that included about 80 stores for each salesperson. Obviously, managers might want to "fine tune" this estimate for differences in territories—such as travel time. But the basic approach can be applied to many different situations.

When a company is starting a new sales force, managers are concerned about its size. But, in many established businesses, this problems is often ignored. Some managers forget that over time the "right" number of salespeople may change—as selling tasks change. Then, when a problem becomes obvious, they try to change everything in a hurry—a big mistake. Finding and training effective salespeople takes time.

Sound Selection and Training to Build a Sales Force

Selecting good salespeople takes judgment, plus

It is important to hire *good, well-qualified* salespeople. But the selection in many companies is a hit-or-miss affair—done without serious thought about exactly what kind of person is needed. Friends and relations—or whoever is available—may be hired because many feel that the only qualifications for sales jobs are a friendly personality and nice appearance. This approach has led to poor sales—and costly sales force turnover—for many companies.

Progressive companies try to be more careful. They constantly update a list of possible job candidates—so they have a pool of applicants when they're needed. They also use more scientific procedures in hiring—including multiple interviews with various executives, and psychological tests. Unfortunately, these techniques can't guarantee success—but using some kind of systematic approach to selection results in a better sales force than using no selection aids at all.

One problem in selecting salespeople is that two different sales jobs with identical titles may involve very different selling tasks—and require different skills. This can lead to a lot of confusion among job applicants—and even result in candidates not very well suited for the job. There can also be confusion among those involved in the selection process about what the job involves—and what kind of person could do it well. One way to avoid this problem is with a carefully prepared *job description.*[6]

Job descriptions should be in writing and specific

A **job description** is a written statement of what a salesperson is expected to do. It might list 10 to 20 specific tasks—as well as routine prospecting and sales report writing. Each company must write its own job specifications—but when they are written, they should provide clear guidelines about what selling tasks are involved in the job. This is critical in determining the kind of salespeople who should be selected—and later it provides a basis for seeing how they need to be trained, how well they are performing, and how they should be paid.

Good salespeople are trained, not born

The idea that good salespeople are born may have some truth in it—but it isn't the whole story. A *born* salesperson—if that term refers to a gregarious, aggressive kind of individual—may not do nearly as well—when the going gets rough—as a less extroverted co-worker who has had solid, specialized training.

What a salesperson needs to be taught—about the company and its products, and about giving effective sales presentations—may seem logical and even obvious. But what is obvious in theory isn't always done. Many salespeople fail—or do a poor job—because they haven't had good training. Many orders are lost simply because the salesperson doesn't have enough information about the product—or doesn't ask for the order. New salespeople often are hired and immediately sent out on the road—or retail selling floor—with no grounding in the basic selling steps and no information about the product or the customer—just a price list and a pat on the back. This isn't enough!

Many sales are lost because the salesperson fails to ask for the order.

All salespeople need some training

It's up to sales and marketing management to be sure that the salespeople know what they're supposed to do—and how to do it. A job description is helpful in telling the salespeople what they are expected to do. But showing them how to get the job done is harder—because people may be hired with different backgrounds, skills, and levels of intelligence. Some trainees are hired with no knowledge of the company or its products—and little knowledge of selling. Others may come in with a lot of industry knowledge and much selling experience—but some bad habits developed at another company. Still others may have some relevant selling experience, but need to know more about the firm's customers and their needs. Even a firm's own sales veterans may get set in their ways and profit greatly by—and often welcome the chance for—additional training.

The kind of initial sales training should be modified based on the experience and skills of the group involved. This might mean skipping certain parts of a complete training program for trainees with better qualifications or backgrounds. But the company's sales training program should cover at least the following areas: (1) company policies and practices, (2) product information, and (3) selling techniques.

Company policies and practices

The salesperson may be the only company representative that a customer ever sees—so the sales reps ought to be thoroughly familiar with the company's policies with respect to credit, size of orders, dating of invoices, delivery, transportation costs, returned goods privileges, and pricing. They must be familiar with the procedures concerning expected reports, expenses and their control, attendance at sales meetings, and other requirements. As far as company practices are concerned, the sales force should understand internal procedures—to better help customers by speeding up orders, securing adjustments, and generally making it easier for them to deal with the company.

Product information

The amount of product information a salesperson needs depends on the type of selling job—and the variety, extent, and technical complexity of the product line. The important thing is that the salesperson have enough information to be able to satisfy customers. Ideally, the sales rep should know a lot about competitors' products, too.

Selling techniques

In most companies, unfortunately, training in selling techniques has been neglected because of the feeling that selling is something "anyone can do." The bulk of the training time is spent on product information. More progressive companies are finding that salesmanship can be taught very effectively by observing senior salespeople, by making trial demonstrations and sales presentations, and by analyzing why present customers buy from the company, why former customers now buy from competitors, and why some prospects remain only prospects. This training is started in the classroom and often supplemented by on-the-job coaching from sales supervisors. Later in this chapter, we will talk about some key ideas in this area—especially related to different kinds of sales presentations.

Training is ongoing

How long the initial training period should be depends on how hard the job is—as shown in the job description. Some training programs go on for two or three years. But training really should never stop. Some form of sales training should go on indefinitely. Many companies use weekly sales meetings or work sessions, annual or semiannual conventions or conferences, and regular weekly or biweekly newsletters—as well as normal sales supervision—to keep salespeople up-to-date.

Compensating and Motivating Salespeople

To recruit—and keep—good salespeople, a firm has to develop an attractive compensation plan. The plan must be designed to motivate salespeople. Ideally, they will be paid so that what they want to do—for personal interest and gain—is in the company's interest, too. Most companies focus on financial motivation—but public recognition, sales contests, and simple personal recognition for a job well done can be highly effective in encouraging greater sales effort.[7] Our main emphasis here, however, will be on financial stimulation.[8]

Two basic decisions must be made in developing a compensation plan: (1) determine the level of compensation and (2) set the method of payment.

Level of compensation depends on needed skills—and job

A written job description is helpful in setting the compensation level. It forces a careful evaluation of the salesperson's role in the total marketing mix. This description shows whether any special skills or responsibilities are required that will command higher pay levels. The next step is to determine how valuable such a salesperson will be to the company. An order getter may be worth $50,000 to $100,000 to a large organization but only $5,000 to $10,000 to a smaller company—simply because it doesn't have enough to sell to justify the higher pay. In some cases, though, smaller companies pay order getters more than they might get in a larger company—because these people carry almost the whole promotion burden—and because their efforts are so necessary to the firm's success.

Most companies must at least meet the going market wage for salespeople of a particular skill level. Conditions in the market usually set the minimum pay for each kind of job. Order getters earn the highest levels—and then the pay scale works down to some of the supporting salespeople and eventually to the lowest-level order takers. Some retail store clerks—basically low-level order takers—may only be paid the minimum wage.

If there are particularly difficult aspects to a job—such as extensive traveling, aggressive pioneering, or contacts with more difficult customers—the level of compensation may have to be increased. It must be kept in mind, however, that the salesperson's compensation level should correspond—at least roughly—with the pay scale of the rest of the firm. Normally, salespeople will be paid more than the office or production force, but seldom more than top management.

Once the general level of compensation has been decided, the method of payment must be set. There are three basic methods of payment: (1) *straight salary,* (2) *straight commission,* or (3) a *combination plan.* Straight salary normally supplies the most security for the salesperson—and straight commission the most incentive. Because these two represent extremes—and most companies want to offer their salespeople some balance between incentive and security—the most popular method of payment is a combination plan which includes some salary and some commission. Bonuses, profit sharing, pensions, insurance, and other fringe benefits may be included, too. Still, some blend of salary and commission provides the basis for most combination plans.

Over 300 Canadian companies with, in total, some 5,000 sales representatives were surveyed as to their sales compensation practices. The results indicated that 22 percent of these representatives were paid a straight salary, while 6 percent live on commission or bonus alone. The remaining 72 percent were compensated through some combination of salary and commission.[9]

What determines the choice of the pay plan? Four standards should be applied: control, incentive, flexibility, and simplicity.

Salary gives control—if there is close supervision

A sales manager's *control* over a salesperson varies directly with what proportion of his compensation is in the form of salary. The straight salary plan permits the maximum amount of supervision—while the person on commission tends to be his own boss. The salesperson on straight salary earns the same amount regardless of how he spends his time—or which product he pushes. If the sales manager wants the salesperson to spend much time on order taking, supporting sales activities, repair work or delivery service, then the salaried salesperson can be expected to do these activities without complaining. The company is paying for the use of his services for a set period of time—and he should expect to work as needed.

It should be noted that straight salary or a large salary element in the compensation plan increases the amount of sales supervision needed. Control is maintained *only* if the sales manager supervises the salesperson. If such personal supervision would be difficult, better control might be obtained by a compensation plan which includes some commission—or even a straight commission with built-in direction. For example, if the company wants its salespeople to devote more time to developing new accounts, the commission could be higher for "first orders" from a new customer.

A poorly designed commission plan can lead to lack of control, however. A manufacturer of industrial fabrics which paid its salespeople a straight commission found its plant was swamped with a large quantity of small yardage orders. Further, the plant was receiving many requests for bids on highly competitive low-margin items. This was disappointing—since the company's personal selling objective was developing new markets, not getting immediate business. In this case, the sales compensation plan was directing the salespeople toward the wrong objective.

Incentives can be direct or indirect

An *incentive* plan can range anywhere from an indirect incentive (a modest sharing of company profits) to very direct incentive—where a salesperson's income is strictly a commission on sales generated by that salesperson. The incentive should be large only if there is a direct relationship between the salesperson's effort and results. If the relationship is less direct, as when a number of people are involved in the sale—engineers, top management, or supporting salespeople—then each one's contribution is less obvious, and greater emphasis on salary may make more sense.

Strong incentives are normally offered order-getting salespeople when a company wants to expand sales rapidly. Strong incentives may be used, too, when the company's objectives are shifting or varied. In this way, the salesperson's activities and efforts can be directed and shifted as needed. One trucking company, for example, has a sales incentive plan that pays commissions on business needed to balance the freight movement—depending on how heavily traffic has been moving in one direction or another.

Flexibility is desirable—but difficult to achieve

Flexibility is probably the most difficult aspect to achieve. One major reason that combination plans have become more popular is that they offer a way to meet varying situations. Four major kinds of flexibility will be considered:

1. *Flexibility in selling costs.* This is important for most small companies. With limited working capital and uncertain markets, small companies like straight commission—or combination plans with a large commission element. When sales drop off, costs do, too. This is similar to using manufacturers' agents who are paid only if they deliver sales. This advantage often dominates in selecting a method of sales compensation.
2. *Flexibility among territories.* Different sales territories have different potentials. Unless the pay plan allows for this fact, the salesperson in a growing territory might have rapidly increasing earnings for the same amount of work—while the sales rep in a poor area will have little to show for his effort. Such a situation isn't fair—and can lead to high turnover and much dissatisfaction. Many companies set different sales objectives—or quotas—depending on the potential in each territory.
3. *Flexibility among people.* Most companies use salespeople at varying stages of their development. Trainees and new salespeople usually require a special pay plan with emphasis on salary. This provides at least some stability of earnings.
4. *Flexibility among products.* Most companies make several different products with different profit potentials. Unless this fact is recognized, the salespeople may push the products which sell best—ignoring overall company profit. A flexible commission system can more easily adjust to changing profit potentials.

Simplicity

A final consideration is the need for *simplicity*. Complicated plans are hard for salespeople to understand—and costly for the accounting department to administer. Dissatisfaction will result if salespeople can't see a direct relationship between their effort and their income.

Simplicity is best achieved with straight salary. In practice, however, it is usually better to sacrifice some simplicity to gain some incentive, flexibility, and control. The actual combination of these factors depends on the job description and the company's objectives. Figure 17–6 shows the general relation between personal selling expenses—for the basic alternatives—and sales volume. It also shows why firms switch from agents to their own sales forces as sales increase.

Sales management must plan, implement, and control

There are, unfortunately, no easy answers to the compensation problem. It is up to the sales manager—together with the marketing manager—to develop a good compensation plan. The sales manager's efforts must be coordinated with the whole marketing mix—because the personal selling objectives can be accomplished only if enough money is allocated for this job. Further, the manager needs to regularly evaluate each salesperson's performance—and be certain that all the needed tasks are being done well. The compensation plan may need to be changed if the pay and work are out of line. And evaluating performance can also identify areas where more attention—by the salesperson or management—is needed.[10] In Chapter 22, we'll talk more about controlling marketing activities.

■ FIGURE 17–6   Relation between personal selling expenses and sales volume—for basic personal selling compensation alternatives

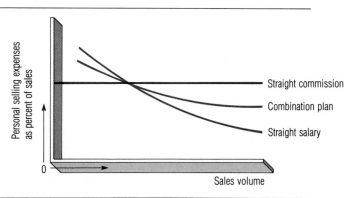

Source: This figure suggested by Professor A. A. Brogowicz, Western Michigan University.

■ CONCLUSION

In this chapter, we have discussed the importance and nature of personal selling. Selling is much more than just "getting rid of the product." In fact, a salesperson who is not provided with strategy guidelines may have to become his own strategy planner. Ideally, however, the sales manager and marketing manger should work together to set some strategic guidelines: the kind and number of salespersons needed, the kind of sales presentation, and selection, training, and motivation approaches.

Three *basic* sales tasks were discussed: (1) order getting, (2) order taking, and (3) supporting. Most sales jobs are a combination of at least two of these three tasks. Once the important tasks have been identified, the structure of the sales organization and the number of salespeople needed to accomplish the tasks can be decided. The nature of the job—and the level and method of compensation—also depend on the blend of these tasks. A job description should be developed for each sales job. This, in turn, provides guidelines for selecting, training, and compensating salespeople.

Once the sales manager's basic plan and budget have been set, the job is to implement the plan—including directing and controlling the sales force. This includes assigning sales territories and controlling performance. More is said on controlling in Chapter 22—but you can see now that the sales manager has more to do than jet around the country sipping martinis and entertaining customers. A sales manager is deeply involved with the basic management tasks of planning and control—as well as ongoing implementing of the personal selling effort.

We also reviewed some fundamentals of salesmanship. Three kinds of sales presentations were identified. Each has its place—but the need-satisfaction approach seems most applicable for higher-level sales jobs. It is in these kinds of jobs that personal selling is achieving a new, professional status—because of the competence and degree of personal responsibility required of the salesperson. The day of the old-time "glad-hander" is passing in favor of the specialist who is creative, industrious, persuasive, knowledgeable, highly trained—and, therefore, able to help the buyer. This type of salesperson always has been—-and probably always will be—in short supply. And the demand for high-level salespeople is growing.

■ QUESTIONS AND PROBLEMS

1. Identify the strategic decisions which are needed in the personal selling area and explain why they should be treated as strategic decisions to be made by the marketing manager.

2. What kind of salesperson (or what blend of the basic sales tasks) is required to sell the following products? If there are several selling jobs in the channel for each product, then indicate the kinds of salespeople required. (Specify any assumptions necessary to give definite answers.)

a. Soy bean oil.
b. Costume jewelry.
c. Nuts and bolts.
d. Handkerchiefs.
e. Mattresses.
f. Corn.
g. Cigarettes.

3. Distinguish among the jobs of manufacturers', wholesalers', and retailers' order-getting salespeople. If one order getter is needed, must all the salespeople in a channel be order getters? Illustrate.

4. Discuss the role of the manufacturers' agent in the marketing manager's promotion plans. What kind of salesperson is a manufacturers' agent?

5. Discuss the future of the specialty shop if manufacturers place greater emphasis on mass selling because of the inadequacy of retail order taking.

6. Compare and contrast missionary salespeople and technical specialists.

7. Explain how a straight commission system might provide flexibility in the sale of a line of women's clothing products which continually vary in profitability.

8. Explain how a compensation system could be developed to provide incentives for older salespeople and yet make some provision for trainees who have not yet learned their job.

9. Cite an actual local example of each of the three kinds of sales presentations discussed in the chapter. Explain for each situation whether a different type of presentation would have been better.

10. Describe a need-satisfaction sales presentation which you have experienced recently and explain how it might have been improved by fuller use of the AIDA framework.

11. Describe the operation of our economy if personal salespeople were outlawed. Could the economy work? If so, how; if not, what is the minimum personal selling effort necessary? Could this minimum personal selling effort be controlled effectively by law?

■ SUGGESTED CASES

1. Foodco, Inc.
18. York Furniture Company

24. Perry Manufacturing Company

■ NOTES

1. "Making Sure the Goods Get on the Shelves," *Business Week,* July 22, 1972, pp. 46–47; P. Ronald Stephenson, William L. Cron, and Gary L. Frazier, "Delegating Pricing Authority to the Sales Force: The Effects on Sales and Profit Performance," *Journal of Marketing,* Spring 1979, pp. 21–24; James H. Fouss and Elaine Solomon, "Salespeople as Researchers: Help or Hazard?" *Journal of Marketing* 44, no. 3 (Summer 1980), pp. 36–39; and Gilbert A. Churchill, Jr., Neil M. Ford, and Orville C. Walker, Jr., *Sales Force Management: Planning, Implementation, and Control* (Homewood, Ill.: Richard D. Irwin, 1981), pp. 60–85.

2. James Holbert and Noel Capon, "Interpersonal Communication in Marketing," *Journal of Marketing Research,* February 1972, pp. 27–32; Paul Busch and David T. Wilson, "An Experimental Analysis of a Salesman's Expert and Referent Bases of Social Power in the Buyer-Seller Dyad," *Journal of Marketing Research,* February 1976, pp. 3–11; Rosann L. Spiro, William D. Perreault, Jr., and Fred D. Reynolds, "The Personal Selling Process: A Critical Review and Model," *Industrial Marketing Management* 5 (December 1977), pp. 351–64; and Rosann L. Spiro and William D. Perreault, Jr., "Influence Used by Industrial Salesmen: Influence Strategy Mixes and Situational Determinants," *Journal of Business* 52 (July 1979), pp. 435–55.

3. Leonard M. Lodish, "Vaguely Right Approach to Sales Force Allocations," *Harvard Business Review,* January-February 1974, pp. 119–24; Gary M. Armstrong, "The SCHEDULE Model and the Salesman's Effort Allocation Problem," *California Management Review,* Summer 1976, pp. 43–51; and "To Computer Salesmen, the 'Big-Ticket' Deal is the One to Look For," *The Wall Street Journal,* January 22, 1974, p. 1.

4. Adapted from Harold C. Cash and W. J. E. Crissy, "Ways of Looking at Selling," *Psychology of Selling,* 1957. See also Barton A. Weitz, "Effectiveness in Sales Interactions: A Contingency Framework," *Journal of Marketing* 45, no. 1 (Winter 1981), pp. 85–103; Marvin A. Jolson, "The Underestimated Potential of the Canned Sales Presentation," *Journal of Marketing,* January 1975, pp. 75–78; and Don Meisel, "Add Sales Power! Ask Questions," *Industrial Distribution,* December 1976, p. 64. For more on sales presentation approaches, see C. A. Pederson, M. D. Wright, and B. A. Weitz, *Selling: Principles and Methods,* 7th ed. (Homewood, Ill.: Richard D. Irwin, 1981), pp. 224–356.

5. A. F. Doody and W. G. Nickels, "Structuring Organizations for Strategic Selling," *MSU Business Topics,* Autumn 1972, pp. 27–34; Davis Fogg and Josef W. Rokus, "A Quantitative Method for Structuring a Profitable Sales Force," *Journal of Marketing,* July 1973, p. 8–17; Porter Henry, "Manage Your Sales Force as a System," *Harvard Business Review,* March-April 1975, pp. 85–94; Charles A. Beswick and David W. Cravens, "A Multistage Decision Model for Salesforce Management," *Journal of Marketing,* May 1977, pp. 135–44; Michael S. Herschel, "Effective Sales Territory Development," *Journal of Marketing,* April, 1977, pp. 39–43; Henry C. Lucas, Jr., Charles B. Weinberg, and Kenneth W. Clowes, "Sales Response as a Function of Territorial Potential and Sales Representative Workload," *Journal of Marketing Research,* August 1975, pp. 298–305; and B. Shapiro and R. Moriarty, "National Account Management," *MSI Report,* Marketing Science Institute, 1980.

6. Kenneth Lawyer, *Training Salesmen to Serve Industrial Markets* (Washington, D.C.: Small Business Management Series No. 36, Small Business Administration, 1975);

"Retailers Discover an Old Tool: Sales Training," *Business Week,* December 22, 1980; Derek A. Newton, "Get the Most out of Your Salesforce," *Harvard Business Review,* September-October, 1967, pp. 130–43; Wesley J. Johnston and Martha Cooper, "Analyzing the Industrial Salesforce Selection Process," *Industrial Marketing Management* 10 (April 1981), pp. 139–47; J. Michael Munson and W. Austin Spivey, "Salesforce Selection that Meets Federal Regulations and Management Needs," *Industrial Marketing Management* 9 (February 1980), pp. 11–21; and A. J. Dubinsky, "Recruiting College Students for the Salesforce," *Industrial Marketing Management* 9 (February 1980), pp. 37–46.

7. Stephen X. Doyle and Benson P. Shapiro, "What Counts Most in Motivating Your Sales Force," *Harvard Business Review,* May-June, 1980, pp. 133–40; The Conference Board, *Incentives for Salesmen,* Experiences in Marketing Management, no. 14 (New York: National Industrial Conference Board, 1967); Richard C. Smyth, "Financial Incentives for Salesmen," *Harvard Business Review,* January-February 1968, pp. 109–17; H. O. Pruden, W. H. Cunningham, and W. D. English, "Nonfinancial Incentives for Salesmen," *Journal of Marketing,* October 1972, pp. 55–59; O. C. Walker, Jr., G. A. Churchill, and N. M. Ford, "Motivation and Performance in Industrial Selling: Present Knowledge and Needed Research," *Journal of Marketing Research,* May 1977, pp. 156–68; R. Y. Darmon, "Salesmen's Responses to Financial Incentives: An Empirical Study," *Journal of Marketing Research,* November 1974, pp. 418–26; and Thomas N. Ingram and Danny N. Bellenger, "Motivational Segments in the Sales Force," *California Management Review* 24 (Spring 1982), pp. 81–88.

8. For more discussion, see F. E. Webster, Jr., "Rationalizing Salesmen's Compensation Plans," *Journal of Marketing,* January 1966, pp. 55–58; R. L. Day and P. D. Bennett, "Should Salesmen's Compensation Be Geared to Profits?" *Journal of Marketing,* October 1962, pp. 6–9; John P. Steinbrink, "How to Pay Your Sales Force," *Harvard Business Review,* July-August 1978, pp. 111–22; D. Wilson, "Common Characteristics of Compensation Plans for Industrial Salesmen," in *Marketing's Role in Scientific Management,* ed. R. L. Clewitt (Chicago: American Marketing Association, 1957), p. 168; "Managers on Compensation Plans: There Has to Be a Better Way," *Sales & Marketing Management,* November 12, 1979, pp. 41–43; and Leon Winer, "A Sales Compensation Plan for Maximum Motivation," *Industrial Marketing Management* 5 (1976), pp. 29–36.

9. James Bagnall, "When Small Is Not Necessarily Beautiful," *Financial Post,* February 4, 1978, pp. 20–21.

10. G. David Hughes, "Computerized Sales Management," *Harvard Business Review* 61, no. 2 (March-April 1983), pp. 102–12; Douglas N. Behrman and William D. Perreault, Jr., "Measuring the Performance of Industrial Salespersons," *Journal of Business Research,* September 1982, pp. 350–70; *Measuring Salesmen's Performance,* Business Policy Study, no. 114 (New York: National Industrial Conference Board, 1965); "'BARS' Performance Rating for Sales Force Personnel," *Journal of Marketing,* July 1978, pp. 87–95; William D. Perreault, Jr., and Frederick A. Russ, "Comparing Multiattribute Evaluation Process Models," *Behavioral Science* 22 (November, 1977), pp. 423–31; and Nicholas C. Williamson, *A Model for Predicting Sales Performance* (Ann Arbor, Mich: U.M.I. International, 1982).

Chapter 18 ■ Advertising

When you finish this chapter, you should:

1. Understand when the various kinds of advertising are needed.
2. Understand how to go about choosing the "best" medium.
3. Understand how to plan the "best" message—that is, the copy thrust.
4. Understand what advertising agencies do—and how they are paid.
5. Understand how to advertise legally.
6. Recognize the important new terms (shown in red).

"To reach a lot of people quickly and cheaply—use advertising."

Advertising facilitates widespread distribution. Although a marketing manager might prefer to use personal selling exclusively, it can be expensive on a per-contact per-sale basis. Advertising is a way around this roadblock. It is not as pinpointed as personal selling, but it does permit communication to large numbers of potential customers at the same time. Today, most promotion blends contain both personal selling and advertising.

Marketing managers have strategic decisions to make about advertising. Working with advertising managers, they must decide: (1) who is to be aimed at, (2) what kind of advertising is to be used, (3) how customers are to be reached (via which types of media), (4) what is to be said to them (the copy thrust), and (5) by whom (i.e., the firm's own advertising department or advertising agencies). (See Figure 18–1). These matters will be discussed in this chapter. We will also consider measuring advertising effectiveness and how to advertise legally.

The Importance of Canadian Advertising

Canadian versus U. S. expenditure

Expenditures in Canada for advertising have been growing continuously, and no end is in sight. Table 18–1 shows the amount spent on advertising between 1962 and 1984 in Canada and the United States both in total and as a percent-

■ FIGURE 18–1 Strategy planning for advertising

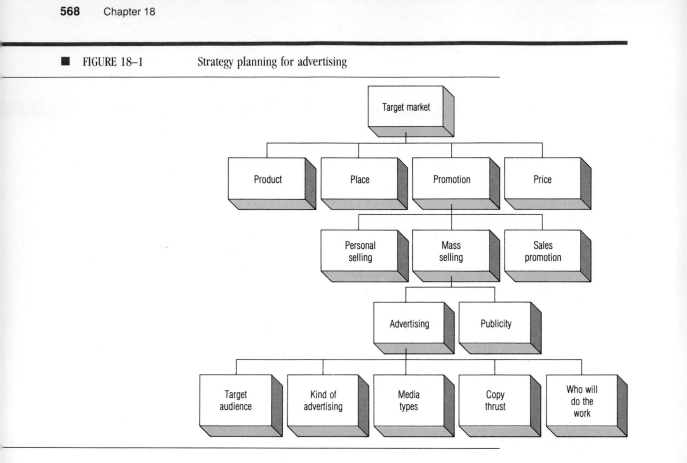

age of each country's GNP. That table also shows annual per capita advertising expenditures in both nations.

Canadian advertising expenditures are substantial. They reached almost $6 billion dollars in 1984, more than tripling in the brief period since 1974. However, both per capita advertising and aggregate U.S. expenditures on advertising, expressed as a percentage of GNP, are consistently about 50 percent greater than the corresponding Canadian figures.

Why does this difference exist? Population obviously isn't the answer since we are making "per capita" and "percent of GNP" comparisons. However, the two estimates of "total advertising expenditures" are not directly comparable. The American figures also include what advertisers spend on their own advertising departments, and the costs of producing their advertisements. The Canadian figures, in contrast, include only what is spent on media, the providers of space and time. Thus a large part of the difference in per capita spending reflects the more inclusive nature of the U.S. figures.

In addition, per capita income is lower in Canada than in the United States. Since Americans have a greater amount of real income, U.S. advertisers may be justified in spending proportionately more on advertising to cultivate this richer market. Also, Canadians see or read a certain amount of "spillover" U.S. adver-

■ TABLE 18–1   Advertising expenditures, United States and Canada, 1962–1984

	Total advertising expenditures ($ millions)		Per capita expenditures		Advertising expenditures, percent of GNP	
	U.S.A.	Canada	U.S.A.	Canada	U.S.A.	Canada
1962	$12,430	$ 643	$ 66	$ 35	2.21%	1.52%
1964	14,150	724	74	38	2.23	1.45
1966	16,630	873	85	44	2.22	1.42
1968	18,090	982	90	47	2.09	1.38
1970	19,550	1,138	95	53	2.00	1.33
1972	23,300	1,391	110	64	1.99	1.32
1974	26,820	1,830	127	82	1.90	1.24
1976	33,690	2,387	157	104	1.97	1.25
1978	43,840	2,973	201	127	2.06	1.29
1980	54,500	4,011	241	168	2.08	1.384
1982	66,580	4,932	286	200	2.17	1.38
1984p	85,000	5,985	356	238	2.26	1.42

p = preliminary.
Expenditures are quoted in national currencies.

Sources: U.S. data from *Advertising Age*; Canadian data from Maclean Hunter Research Bureau.

tising for products available in Canada. If we could estimate the dollar value of such advertising, the U.S. figure could be reduced and the Canadian one increased by that amount. Unfortunately, it is impossible to put a dollar value on spillover advertising.

Table 18–2 shows the changes over time in how Canadian net advertising revenues have been divided among different media. Not surprisingly, television's share of the media dollar has kept on climbing as the percentage of Canadian homes with television sets has steadily increased. But our figures do not always

■ TABLE 18–2   Net advertising revenues percent share by media, 1956–1983

Media	Percent share							
	1956	1960	1964	1968	1972	1976	1980	1983
Radio	9.0%	9.2%	9.7%	10.4%	11.1%	10.8%	11.2%	10.9%
TV	6.3	9.1	12.0	12.6	12.7	14.4	17.6	18.5
Daily newspapers............	32.9	30.9	29.0	28.4	28.7	29.5	20.9	21.1
Weekend newspaper supplements	3.4	3.1	2.7	1.9	2.0	1.1	.9	
Weekly semi-tri..............	4.5	4.3	4.0	5.5	4.9	4.9	5.8	5.5
General magazines	4.1	3.8	2.6	2.6	2.4	3.0	4.8	5.2
Business papers.............	4.8	4.7	3.9	3.1	2.5	3.2	3.7	3.0
Farm papers	1.5	1.2	0.8	0.6	0.6	0.4	.5	.5
Directories—phone, city	3.7	5.2	5.1	4.7	5.5	6.1	6.3	7.1
Religious, school, and other publications	0.6	0.4	0.3	0.4	0.4	0.4	.5	.5
Catalogs, direct mail	23.4	21.4	22.2	20.4	20.8	19.4	21.6	21.1
Billboards, car cards, signs	5.8	6.7	7.7	9.4	8.4	6.8	6.9	6.6

Source: Statistics Canada and *The Canadian Media Directors' Council Media Digest, 1984/85*.

reveal the obvious. Would you have expected in 1956 that radio would more than hold its own over the next few decades? Would you have predicted the continuing importance of catalog selling and direct mail? Aren't you surprised even now to find advertiser expenditures in this category somewhat greater than those in TV?

Canadian and U.S. advertisers also differ in the way they allocate their advertising dollars. Television and general circulation magazines obtain a much larger percentage of the U.S. media dollar than newspapers. Direct mail and radio receive less than their Canadian counterparts. Why such differences exist has never been thoroughly investigated.

U.S. spillover advertising may be one of the reasons television and magazines are relatively less important in Canada. Over 85 percent of all Canadian homes can receive at least one U.S. television station. By 1980 approximately 68 percent of all homes were wired for cable.[1]

Over 9 million issues of U.S. consumer publications are believed to enter Canada every four weeks. (This figure does not include *Time,* which still offers advertisers a separate Canadian edition published in Canada). Such a massive influx of U.S. publications obviously affects the Canadian magazine industry. On the other hand, the circulation of Canadian consumer magazines is now about four times as great as the total spill-in to Canada of U.S. consumer magazines.[2]

Some spend more than others

Canadian firms and industries differ in the percentage of their sales spent on advertising. This reflects the relative importance of advertising to the firm's or the industry's marketing mix. The most recent (1965) Canadian study of advertising as a percentage of industry sales showed that soap and related products manufacturers spent 10.9 percent of industry sales on advertising. Drug manufacturers spent 8.65 percent, and toilet article manufacturers 15.2 percent. At the other extreme, artificial ice manufacturers, pulp and paper mills, and sugar refineries all spent less than one quarter of 1 percent of their sales on advertising.[3]

Table 18–3 lists Canada's top 50 advertisers in print, radio, and TV during 1984. This list also shows that advertising expenditures are concentrated in a limited number of consumer product categories—food products, drugs and cosmetics, automotives, brewers and distillers, financial and insurance, and household supplies).[4] Table 18–3 also shows that the federal, Quebec, and Ontario governments are among Canada's largest advertisers. These totals tell us how much was spent in Canada by different governments. They do not include what was spent for tourist advertising in other countries.

Less costly than personal selling

Clearly, advertising is an important factor in certain markets, especially consumer goods markets. Nevertheless, in total, much less is spent on advertising than on personal selling. And although total advertising expenditures are large, the advertising industry itself employs relatively few people. Probably less than 30,000 people work directly in Canadian advertising. This figure includes everyone who helps create or sell advertising for the different advertising media as well as those in advertising agencies. It also includes those working for retailers, wholesalers, and manufacturers who either create their own advertising or at least manage that activity.[5]

Top 50 National Advertisers 1984

Company	Total $
1. Government of Canada	95,767,946
2. Procter and Gamble	46,339,143
3. John Labatt	37,581,241
4. The Molson Companies	35,297,759
5. Dart and Kraft	32,489,845
6. Government of Ontario	32,086,361
7. Rothmans of Canada	31,045,579
8. General Motors of Canada	30,011,258
9. Nabisco Brands	24,471,874
10. General Foods	22,945,590
11. Unilever	21,830,065
12. Ford Motor of Canada	20,364,261
13. American Home Products	18,327,314
14. Kellogg Salada Canada	17,787,386
15. Government of Quebec	17,781,235
16. Chrysler Canada	17,640,849
17. Canadian Pacific	17,341,827
18. Imperial Oil	15,580,595
19. Warner Lambert Canada	15,500,551
20. Coca-Cola	14,335,015
21. Imasco Holdings Canada	14,216,971
22. McDonald's Restaurants Canada	13,608,806
23. Gillette Canada	12,097,653
24. The Thomson Group	11,939,927
25. Bristol-Myers Canada	11,880,576
26. Rowntree Mackintosh Canada	11,297,038
27. Dairy Bureau of Canada	11,045,297
28. Pepsico	10,905,944
29. Canada Packers	10,733,553
30. Kodak Canada	10,627,891
31. Sears Canada	10,600,922
32. Ralston Purina Canada	10,481,771
33. CKR	10,419,209
34. IBM Canada	9,859,007
35. Bell Enterprises Canada Inc.	9,360,472
36. Eatons of Canada	9,300,706
37. Quaker Oats Co. of Canada	9,274,361
38. Canadian Tire Corporation	9,243,044
39. Johnson and Johnson	9,002,141
40. Union Carbide Canada	8,959,164
41. Kimberly-Clark of Canada	8,944,850
42. Gulf Canada	8,678,255
43. Nissan Automobile Co. of Canada	8,666,836
44. Canadian Imperial Bank of Commerce	8,533,066
45. Nestlé Enterprises	8,527,154
46. Telecom Canada	8,180,212
47. General Mills Canada	7,950,696
48. Bank of Montreal	7,724,703
49. Honda Canada	7,575,819
50. George Weston	6,904,644

Source: Elliot Research Corporation, as reprinted in *Marketing*, May 13, 1984.

Advertising Objectives Are Set by Marketing Strategy

Every advertisement and every advertising campaign should have clearly defined objectives. These should grow out of the overall marketing strategy—and the jobs assigned to advertising. It is not enough for the marketing manager just to say—"Promote the product." The marketing manager should decide exactly what advertising should do—although specifying what should be accomplished in each individual advertisement isn't necessary. Such detailed objectives should be set by the advertising manager—to guide his own efforts.

Advertising may be assigned specific objectives

An advertising manager might be given one or more of the following specific objectives—along with the budget to accomplish them:

1. Aid in the introduction of new products to specific target markets.
2. Help obtain desirable outlets.
3. Prepare the way for salespeople—by presenting the company's name and the merits of its products.
4. Provide ongoing contact with target customers—even when the salesperson isn't available.
5. Get immediate buying action.
6. Help buyers confirm their purchasing decisions.

If you want half the market, say so!

The objectives listed above are not as specific as they could be. The advertising manager might want to sharpen them for his own purposes—or encourage the marketing manager to set more specific objectives. If a marketing manager really wants specific results, then he should state what he wants. A general objective: "To help in the expansion of market share," could be rephrased more specifically: "To increase traffic in our cooperating retail outlets by 25 percent during the next three months."

Such specific objectives obviously affect implementation. Advertising that might be right for building a good image among opinion leaders might be all wrong for getting customers into the retailers' stores. Instead, a combination of advertising and sales promotion—perhaps contests or tie-in sales—might be used. Media would be selected to help particular retailers—perhaps using local newspapers and billboards, rather than national consumer magazines.

Even more specific objectives might be needed in some cases. For new products, for example, most of the target market may have to be brought through the early stages of the adoption process. This might mean that the advertising manager would want to use "teaser" campaigns or free samples—along with informative ads. General Foods recently developed a sugar-free Kool Aid—sweetened with a new, natural sweetener instead of saccharin. The company included samples of the new drink mix in a free coupon offer mailed to consumers' homes. For more established products, advertising's job might be to build brand preference—as well as help purchasers confirm their decisions. This, too, leads to different kinds of advertising—as shown in Figure 18–2.

■ FIGURE 18–2   Advertising should vary for adoption process stages

Adoption process (basically the Lavidge- Steiner model)	Advertising that might be relevant to various stages
Awareness	Teaser campaigns Skywriting Jingles and slogans Classified ads Announcements
Interest	Informative or descriptive ads Status or glamour appeals Image ads
Evaluation and trial	Competitive ads Persuasive copy
Decision	Testimonials Price deal offers "Last-change" offers "Direct-action" retail ads Point-of-purchase ads
Confirmation	Informative "why" ads Reminder ads

Source: Adapted from R. J. Lavidge and G. A. Steiner, "A Model for Predictive Measurements of Advertising Effectiveness," *Journal of Marketing*, October 1961, p. 61.

Advertising objectives should be more specific than personal selling objectives. One of the advantages of personal selling is that the salespeople can shift their presentations to meet customers' needs. Each advertisement, however, is a specific communication that must be effective, not just for one customer, but for thousands—or millions—of target customers. This means that specific objectives should be set for each advertisement—as well as a whole advertising campaign. If specific objectives are not set, a creative advertising staff may pursue its own objectives. The group may set some reasonable objective—like "selling the product"—and then create ads that may win artistic awards within the advertising industry—but fail to do the advertising job expected.

Objectives Determine the Kinds of Advertising Needed

The advertising objectives largely determine which of two basic types of advertising to use—*product or institutional.*

Product advertising tries to sell a product. It may be aimed at final users or channel members.

Institutional advertising tries to develop goodwill for a company or even an industry—instead of a specific product. Its objective is to improve sales—and relations with the various groups with whom the company deals. This includes not only consumers—but also current and prospective channel members, suppliers, shareholders, employees, and the general public.

Product advertising— meet us, like us, remember us

Product advertising falls into three categories: pioneering, competitive, and reminder advertising.

Pioneering advertising—builds primary demand

Pioneering advertising tries to develop **primary demand**—demand for a product category rather than a specific brand. It's needed in the early stages of the adoption process—to inform potential customers about a new product.

Pioneering advertising is used in the introductory stage of the product life cycle—and can be used with several specific advertising objectives (objectives 1, 2, and 3 given above, for example). Its basic job is to inform—not persuade.

Competitive advertising tries to develop selective demand for a specific brand rather than demand for a product category.

The beauty of Crisco Oil

Turns onions into rings of gold with no greasy taste.

Pioneering advertising doesn't have to mention the brand or specific company at all. The California olive industry promoted olives as olives—not certain brands. This was so successful that after only five years of promotion, the industry's surpluses had become shortages. Then it switched promotion funds to horticultural research—to increase production.

Competitive advertising—emphasizes selective demand

Competitive advertising tries to develop **selective demand**—demand for a specific brand rather than a product category. A firm can be forced into competitive advertising as the product life cycle moves along—to hold its own against competitors' products and promotion. The United Fruit Company gave up a 20-year pioneering effort to promote bananas—in favor of advertising its own "Chiquita" brand. The reason was simple. While United Fruit was single-handedly promoting bananas, it slowly lost market share to competitors. The competitive advertising campaign was launched to avoid further losses.

Competitive advertising may be either direct or indirect. The **direct type** aims for immediate buying action. The **indirect type** points out product advantages—to affect future buying decisions.

Much airline advertising is of the competitive variety. Each airline is trying for sales, either immediately—in which case the ads are the *direct type* with price, timetables, and phone numbers to call for reservations—or eventually—in which case the ads are of the *indirect type,* suggesting that you mention the airline's name when talking to your travel agent.

Comparative advertising is even rougher. **Comparative advertising** means making specific brand comparisons—using actual product names. Ban Roll-On deodorant ran ads claiming to be more effective than Right Guard, Secret, Sure, Arrid Extra Dry, Soft & Dri, Body All, and Dial products.

The competitive frenzy caused by comparative advertising has been rising since the U.S. Federal Trade Commission encouraged these kinds of ads several years ago. But this approach has led to legal as well as ethical problems—and some advertisers and their agencies have backed away from it. Supposedly, research evidence should support superiority claims, but the guidelines aren't clear here. Some firms just keep running tests until they get the results they want. Others talk about minor differences that don't reflect the overall benefits of a product. This may make consumers less—rather than more—informed. Some comparative ads leave consumers confused—or even angry if the product they are using has been criticized. Hopefully, the Canadian Advertising Standards Council's guidelines covering comparative advertising in this country will solve many of these problems.

Comparative advertising may be "a can of worms" which some advertisers wish had not been opened. But since it has been, it is likely that the approach will be continued by some advertisers long as the ad copy is not obviously false.[6]

Reminder advertising—reinforces early promotion

Reminder advertising tries to keep the product's name before the public. It may be useful when the product has achieved brand preference or insistence— perhaps in the market maturity or sales decline stages. Here, the advertiser may

■ FIGURE 18–3   Example of a reminder ad

use "soft-sell" ads that just mention or show the name—as a reminder. Much Chanel advertising has been of this variety. See Figure 18–3.

Institutional advertising—remember our name in Vancouver, Toronto, Montreal

Institutional advertising focuses on the name and prestige of a company or industry. It may seek to inform, persuade, or remind.

A persuading kind of promotion is sometimes used by large companies with several divisions. GM, for example, does institutional advertising of the GM name—emphasizing the quality and research behind *all* GM products.

Some large companies—such as General Motors and Imperial Oil—use institutional ads to emphasize the value of large corporations. Their long-run objective is developing a favorable political and legal environment in which to work.

Cooperative Advertising May Buy More

Vertical cooperation—advertising allowances, cooperative advertising

So far, our discussion might suggest that only producers do product or institutional advertising. This is not true, of course, but producers can affect the advertising done by others. Sometimes a manufacturer knows what promotion job or advertising job should be done—but finds that it can be done more effectively or more economically by someone further along in the channel. In this case, the manufacturer may offer **advertising allowances**—price reductions to firms further along in the channel to encourage them to advertise or otherwise promote the firm's products locally. For example, 1 percent off the list price might be allowed to retailers who support their allowance claims with ads which have promoted the manufacturer's products.

Cooperative advertising may get more cooperation

Cooperative advertising involves middlemen and producers sharing in the cost of ads. It helps the manufacturer get more promotion for the advertising dollar—because media rate structures usually give local advertisers lower rates than national firms. In addition, a retailer is more likely to follow through when he is paying a share of the cost.

Cooperative advertising and advertising allowances can be abused, however, because allowances can be given to retailers with little expectation that they will be used for ads. This may become a disguised price concession—and result in price discrimination. To avoid charges of discrimination and to be certain they have received advertising support in return for their allowances, intelligent producers insist on advertising tearsheets and other proof of use.

Horizontal cooperation may be good, too

Some retailers—particularly those in shopping centers—may get together for joint promotion efforts—sponsoring "sale days" and running full-page ads promoting the individual retailers. Similarly, the manufacturers of complementary products—such as home furnishings—may find it desirable to join forces. They might run an ad showing their different products—furniture, lamps, and drapes—used together in a room. Generally, the objective is the same as in vertical cooperation—to get more for the promotion dollar.

Choosing the "Best" Medium—How to Deliver the Message

For effective promotion, specific target customers must be reached. Figure 18–4 shows the vast number of media in which Canadian firms can advertise. As you can see, the possibilities are almost endless. To make things worse, all potential customers do not read all newspapers, magazines, or other printed media or listen to all radio and television programs. So not all media are equally effective for any one advertising campaign.

There is no simple answer to the question—"What is the best medium?" Effectiveness depends on how well it fits with the rest of a marketing strategy—that is , it depends on (1) your promotion objectives, (2) what target markets you want to reach, (3) the funds available for advertising, and (4) the nature of the media—including who they *reach,* with what *frequency,* with what *impact,* at what *cost.* Table 18–4 shows some of the pros and cons of major kinds of media—and some illustrative costs.

■ FIGURE 18–4   A capsule view of major Canadian media

Television—49 television markets covered by 96 commercial television stations, most of which belong to one of five networks.

Radio—614 radio stations (399 AM and 215 FM).

Daily newspapers—113 daily newspapers with a total daily circulation of 5.4 million. Gross circulation as a percentage of households is approximately 70 percent.

Consumer magazines—approximately 419 consumer magazines ranging in content from general editorial to special interest categories (such as photography and music).

Business publications—listed in *Canadian Advertising Rates & Data* (CARD) under 118 classifications.

Ethnic press—160 publications covering 37 ethnic groups other than English and French.

Farm publications—89 farm publications whose circulation ranges from 1,000 copies to large mass-appeal publications with over 200,000 circulation.

Community newspapers—Approximately 870 (697 English and 173 French).

Weekend newspapers—This type of newspaper is essentially a Quebec phenomenon; 11 such papers are published in French.

Religious publications—23 publications listed under the religious category in CARD, which range in circulation from 3,200 to over 310,000 for the largest.

University and school publications—162 university, community college, alumni, and scholarly publications.

Outdoor advertising—Poster space is available in more than 400 Canadian municipalities covering over 70 percent of the Canadian population.

Source: *The Canadian Media Directors' Council Media Digest, 1984/85.*

Specify promotion objectives

Before you can choose the best medium, you must decide on promotion objectives. For example, if the objective is to inform—telling a long story with precise detail—and if pictures are desired, then the print media—including magazines and newspapers—may be better. Jockey switched its annual budget of more than $1 million to magazines from television when it decided to show the variety of colors, patterns, and styles that Jockey briefs offer. They felt that it was too hard to show this in a 30-second TV spot. Further, it is not the kind of product that can be worn on television—the same problem that manufacturers of women's undergarments face! Jockey ads were run in men's magazines—such as *Sports Illustrated, Outdoor Life, Field and Stream, Esquire,* and *Playboy.* But, aware that women buy over 80 percent of men's ordinary underwear—and 50 percent of fashion styles—they also placed the ads in *TV Guide, New Yorker, People, Money, Time,* and *Newsweek.* And a page of scantily clad males was run in *Cosmopolitan.*[7]

When timeliness is not too important, then weekly or monthly magazines may be practical. But if demonstrations are needed, the TV may become desirable— or necessary.

If your objective is to provide technical information to a particular group, you might have to choose specialized journals. Remember, you pay for the audience the media delivers—which may (or may not) be your target audience. The use of men's magazines such as *Esquire* and *True* to reach doctors would be inefficient. Medical journals and direct mail are the most effective advertising media for telling doctors about new drugs.

■ TABLE 18–4   Relative size and costs, and advantages and disadvantages of major kinds of media

Kinds of media	Typical costs, 1985	Advantages	Disadvantages
Newspaper.............	$1,393 for one page in the television tabloid, Winnipeg Free Press	Flexible Timely Local market	May be expensive Short life No "pass-along"
Television	$525 for 30 seconds of prime evening time on CKTV, the CTV station in Regina	Offers sight, sound, and motion Good attention Wide reach	Expensive in total "Clutter" Short exposure Less selective audience
Direct mail and other print	$150 to $200 for 1,500 screened names in selected categories	Selected audience Flexible Can personalize	Relatively expensive per contact "Junk mail"—hard to retain attention
Radio..................	$329 in total for one 60-second commercial on all Regina radio stations combined	Wide reach Segmented audiences Inexpensive	Offers audio only Weak attention Many different rates Short exposure
Periodicals	$29,860 for one page, 4-color, in *Chatelaine*, French and English	Very segmented audiences Credible source Good reproduction Long life Good "pass-along"	Inflexible Long lead times
Outdoor...............	$1,556 for one prime bill-board showing 4 weeks, Regina/Moose Jaw	Flexible Repeat exposure Inexpensive	"Mass market" Very short exposure

Source: *Canadian Advertising Rates & Data*, July 1985.

Match your market with the media

To guarantee good media selection, the advertiser first must *clearly* specify its target market—a step necessary for all marketing strategy planning. Then, media can be chosen that are heard, read, or seen by *those* target customers.

Matching target customers and media is the major problem in effective media selection—because it is not always certain who sees or hears what. Most of the major media use marketing research to develop profiles of the people who buy their publications—or live in their broadcasting area. But they cannot be as definite about who actually reads each page or sees or hears each show. And, they seldom tailor their marketing research to gather information on the market dimensions which *each* advertiser may think important. Generally, media research focuses on demographic characteristics. But what if the really important dimensions are concerned with behavioral needs or attitudes which are difficult to measure—or unique to a particular product-market?

The difficulty of evaluating alternative media has led some media analysts to focus excessively on objective measures—such as cost in relation to audience size or circulation. But preoccupation with keeping these costs down may lead to ignoring the relevant dimensions—and slipping into "mass marketing." The media buyer may become hypnotized by the relatively low cost of "mass media" when, in fact, a more specialized medium might be a much better buy. Its audi-

Billboards are especially good for simple messages and reminder advertising.

ence might have more interest in the product—or more money to spend—or more willingness to buy.

Specialized media help zero in on target markets

Media are now directing more attention to reaching smaller more defined target markets. Large metropolitan newspapers usually have several editions, to cater to city and suburban areas. Where these outlying areas are not adequately covered, however, suburban newspapers are prospering—catering to the desire for a "small town" newspaper.[8]

The major magazines of Canada such as *Chatelaine, Maclean's,* or *Reader's Digest* all offer regional or even metropolitan editions. In addition, there are magazines like *Toronto Life* which serve only a specific city. Another way in which magazines are serving advertisers better is by focusing their editorial content on the interests of special groups. There have long been magazines just for fishermen and hunters, etc., but now there are magazines for motion-picture fans (*Showbill*), for those interested in records, tapes, and related equipment (*Sound Canada*), geography (*Canadian Geographic*), and so on.

In addition to trade magazines bought at newsstands or through subscription, there is an important class of magazine in Canada called controlled circulation.[9] These magazines are distributed free to special-interest groups—the publisher gets all his revenue from advertising. The largest of these is *Homemaker's*. With its French counterpart, *Madame au Foyer,* it offers a combined circulation of over 1.6 million delivered to preselected homes in middle- and upper-income areas. In addition, magazines such as *City Woman* are sent without charge to narrow, well-defined segments.

In comparing print with broadcast media, it is important to remember that circulation is not directly comparable to, say, television or radio audience figures. Readership figures should be used for such comparisons. A magazine or newspaper is usually read by more than one person (just as a television program is often viewed by a family group). Thus, advertising in print media can have a much broader exposure than the circulation figures alone suggest.

Radio suffered at first from the inroads of television. But now, like some magazines and newspapers, it has become a more specialized medium. Some stations cater to particular ethnic, racial, and religious groups, such as Jews,

---

■ FIGURE 18–5   More firms turn to direct mail—low cost, selectivity the keys

Rather than simply informing the public about a product, direct marketing encourages a selected group of potential buyers to act. Television advertisements which give a toll-free number to call, promotional material in newspapers or magazines along with ordering instructions, catalogs, coupons, and flyers are all methods of direct marketing gaining popularity.

The main advantages are selectivity and measurability. Material aimed at a specific target market, unlike traditional advertising, enables a company to calculate exactly how much response is generated and relate it to promotion costs. Customer lists can be compiled from telephone books, voter registration lists, city directories, Yellow Pages, company customer lists, subscriber lists, club lists, and industry directories. "Cost is measured as cost per order, and it's an exact science, not an art," says Ferguson, president of the Canadian Direct Mail Marketing Association (CDMMA).

But now more retailers see another advantage. They look to direct marketing as a means of expanding their sales and geographical base without opening new stores or sales offices in costly locations and hiring new staff. "Direct marketing can be used not only to sell products but to make a salesman's time much more effective, and this results in tremendous cost savings," says Ferguson. "It allows salesmen to know customer's requirements before making a personal sales call."

Adds George Farr, managing director of direct response at Ogilvy and Mather (Canada) Ltd.: "The cost of sales calls is astronomical. Including wages, car allowances, and other expenses a call can cost $100."

"You can mail a lot more information than you can put into a magazine or radio advertisement, and it's going to people who are interested in the product," he says. "If a company fired its two worst salesmen and put their salaries into direct marketing, the rest of the sales force would be far more effective."

On the consumer side, industry executives point to a number of factors working in direct marketing's favor over the past few years. The major catalyst has been the widespread use of credit cards, enabling customers to easily charge for services bought by mail or telephone. Also contributing have been the number of working women who have less time to browse in stores, the rising costs of fuel, traffic congestion in cities, crowds in department stores, and the lack of knowledgeable sales staffs.

CDMMA figures show at least 75 percent of the public opens and at least glances at all direct marketing material received. Eighty-one percent read or at least glance at fund-raising appeals, 76 percent open and read catalogs, and 75 percent read advertising and selling mail. Three out of four persons use samples received, and more than half use coupons received.

Source: "More Firms Turn to Direct Mail—Low Cost, Selectivity the Keys," *Financial Times of Canada,* March 2, 1981, p. 10.

Italians, and French Canadians, while others emphasize country, rock, or classical music.

Perhaps the most specific medium is **direct mail advertising**. The purpose of this medium is to go directly to the customer via his mailbox. This method is to send a specific message to a carefully selected list of names.

Delivery problems of Canada Post notwithstanding, direct mail remains an exceedingly important advertising medium. Figure 18–5 indicates the many advantages of direct mail.

"Must buys" may use up available funds

Selecting which media to use is still pretty much an art. The media buyer may start with a budgeted sum and attempt to buy the best blend to reach the target audience. There may be some media that are obvious **must buys**, such as *the* local newspaper for a retailer in a small or medium-sized town. Such "must" buys may even exhaust the available funds. If not, then the media buyer must begin to think in terms of the relative advantages and disadvantages of the possible alternatives and recognize that trade-offs must be made. Typically, media that have several advantages—for example, television, which permits visual and audio presentations along with movement—are more expensive. So the buyer might want to select a media blend which may permit him to reach additional customers or reinforce the presentation from a different angle.

Ideally, the first media choice would reach a substantial part of the target audience. Then, each successive choice (if any more can be afforded) would reach fewer who had not already been covered. Figure 18–6 illustrates the concept for four equally costly magazines. Here, the first choice reaches 60 percent

■ FIGURE 18–6   Increase in audience coverage as additional magazine ads are purchased

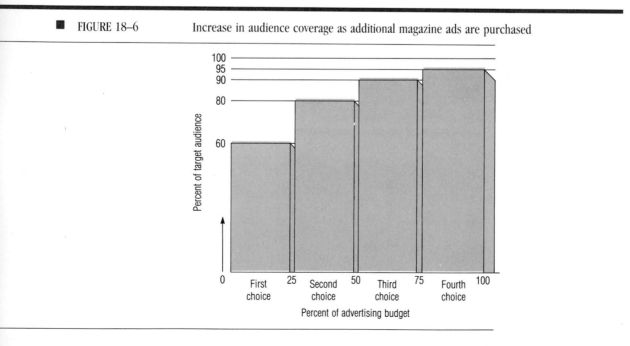

of the target audience. The second choice adds only 20 percent who were not reached before. The third choice adds 10 percent, and the fourth 5 percent. Five percent cannot be reached with only these four magazines.

Planning the "Best" Message—What Is to Be Communicated

Specifying the copy thrust

Once it has been decided *how* the messages are to reach the target audience, then it is necessary to decide on the **copy thrust**—*what* is to be communicated by the written copy and illustrations. This should flow from the promotion objectives—and the specific jobs assigned to advertising. Although the overall *promotion* objective is to affect the target customer's attitudes *and* behavior, a particular advertisement may have the specific objective of informing target customers that the firm's prices have dropped 10 percent. Or it might have the more difficult job of persuading customers that a product with a 10 percent price premium is really a "good buy."

Carrying out the copy thrust is the job of advertising specialists. But the advertising manager and the marketing manager should have an understanding of the process—to be sure that the job is done well.

Communication process is relevant to message planning

Message planning should be guided by a sound understanding of the communication process. As we saw in Chapter 16, common frames of reference and experience are needed for good communication. This is not a small matter in advertising—because advertising professionals are often far removed from their target audiences.

Some advertisers realize the complexity of the communication process—and use marketing research to help them as much as possible. At the very least, research can give clues about perceived needs—and the words or ideas that communicate with potential customers in the company's product-market.

Other advertisers depend almost entirely on their own "creative genius." This is at the root of many poor campaigns. Some are brilliant—and others are miserable failures—and they don't know why.

Few tried-and-true rules exist in message construction. Everything we see—and every new way we see it—changes us in some way. An idea that may have worked a year ago can fail today. A highly successful advertising campaign for beer in Eastern Canada flopped on the West Coast—and one industrial advertiser received more inquiries when it *reduced* the size of its ads.

Behavioral science research does provide some help, however. The concepts of needs, learning, and perception discussed in Chapter 7 are certainly relevant here. We know, for example, that consumers have a fantastic ability for selectively "tuning out" messages or ideas which aren't of current interest. Just think of how much of the daily newspaper you actually "see" as you page through it. We don't see everything the advertisers want us to see—or learn all they would like us to learn. How can an advertiser be more effective?

Let AIDA help guide message planning

Basically, the overall marketing strategy should determine *what* should be said in the message. Then management judgment—perhaps aided by marketing research—can help decide how this content can be encoded so it will be decoded as intended.

As a guide to message planning, we can make use of the AIDA concept: getting *Attention,* holding *Interest,* arousing *Desire,* and obtaining *Action.*

Getting attention

Getting attention is the first job of an advertisement. If this isn't done, it doesn't matter how many people see it. Many readers leaf through magazines and newspapers without paying attention to any of the advertisements. Many listeners or viewers do chores—or get snacks—during commercials on radio and television.

Many attention-getting devices are available. A large headline, newsy or shocking statements, pictures of pretty girls, babies, cartoon characters—or anything that is "different" or eye-catching—may do the trick. But . . . the attention-getting device must not distract from the next step—holding interest.

Holding interest

Holding interest is another matter. A pretty girl may get attention—but once you've seen her, then what? A man may pause to appreciate her. Women may evaluate her. But if there is no relation between the girl and the product, observers of both sexes will move on.

More is known about holding interest than getting attention. The tone and language of the ad must fit with the field of experience and the attitudes of target customers—and their reference groups. An advertisement featuring fox hunters in riding coats, for example, might be noted but passed over by many potential customers who don't "ride to the hounds."

In addition to speaking the target customer's language, the advertising layouts should look "right" to the customer. Print illustrations and copy should be arranged so that the eye is encouraged to move smoothly through the ad—perhaps from the upper left-hand corner to the company or brand name at the lower right-hand corner. Advertisements having this natural flowing characteristic are said to encourage *gaze motion.*

Arousing desire

Arousing desire to own or use a particular product is one of the most difficult jobs for an ad. The advertiser must be successful in communicating with the customer. To communicate effectively, the advertiser should understand how target customers think, behave, and make decisions. Then the ad must convince the customers that the product can meet their needs. An ad may also have the objective—especially during the market growth and market maturity stages—of supplying words that the customer can use for rationalizing a desire to buy. Although products may satisfy certain emotional needs, many consumers find it necessary to justify their purchases on an economic or even moral basis. Desire may develop around emotional needs, but economic reasons must also be reinforced.

An attention-getting picture with good gaze motion "leads" readers through the ad.

Obtaining action

Getting action is the final requirement—and not an easy one. We now know—from communications research—that prospective customers must be led beyond considering how the product *might* fit into their lives—to actually trying it or letting the company's sales rep come in and demonstrate it.

Strongly felt customer needs might be emphasized in the ads to communicate more effectively. Careful research on the attitudes in the target market may help uncover such strongly felt unsatisfied needs.

Appealing to these needs can get more action—and also provide the kind of information the buyers need to confirm their decisions. Post-purchase dissonance may set in—and obtaining confirmation may be one of the important advertising objectives. Some customers seem to read more advertising *after* the purchase than before. What is communicated to them may be very important if satisfied customers are to start—or keep—the web-of-word-of-mouth going. The ad may reassure them about the correctness of their decision—and also supply the words they use to tell others about the product.

Advertising Manager Directs Mass Selling

An advertising manager manages a company's mass selling effort. Many advertising managers—especially those working for retailers—have their own advertising departments that plan the specific advertising campaigns—and carry out the details. Others turn over much of the advertising work to specialists—the advertising agencies.

Advertising Agencies Often Do the Work

Ad agencies are specialists

Advertising agencies are specialists in planning and handling mass selling details for advertisers. Agencies play a useful role—because they are independent of the advertiser and have an outside viewpoint. They bring experience to an individual client's problems, because they work for many other clients. Further, as specialists they often can do the job more economically than a company's own department.

Agencies sometimes handle overall marketing strategy planning—as well as marketing research, product and package development, and sales promotion.

Advertising agencies work with marketing managers to plan ad campaigns.

Some agencies make good marketing partners—and almost assume the role of the firm's marketing department.

One of the ad agency's advantages is that the advertiser is free to cancel the arrangement at any time. This provides extreme flexibility for the advertiser. Some companies even use their advertising agency as a scapegoat. Whenever anything goes wrong—it's the agency's fault—and the advertiser shops around for a new one.

Are they paid too much?

The major users of advertising agencies are manufacturers or national middlemen—because of the media rate structure. Normally, media have two prices: one for national advertisers—and a lower rate for local advertisers, such as retailers. The advertising agency gets a 15 percent commission on national rates (only). This makes it worthwhile for national advertisers to use agencies. The national firm would have to pay the full media rate, anyway. So it makes sense to let the agency experts do the work—and earn their commission. Local retailers—allowed the lower media rate—seldom use agencies.

There is a growing resistance to the traditional method of paying agencies. The chief complaints are (1) that the agencies receive the flat 15 percent commission—regardless of work performed—and (2) that this makes it hard for the agencies to be completely objective about inexpensive media—or promotion campaigns that use little space or time.

Not all agencies are satisfied with the present arrangement either. Some would like to charge additional fees—as they see costs rising and advertisers demanding more services.

The fixed commission system is most favored by accounts—such as producers of industrial goods—that need a lot of service but buy relatively little advertising. These are the firms the agencies would like to—and sometimes do—charge additional fees.

The fixed commission system is generally opposed by very large consumer goods advertisers who do much of their own advertising research and planning. They need only basic services from their agencies. Some of these accounts can be very profitable for agencies. Naturally, these agencies prefer the fixed commission system.

Fee for service commonly used

Canadian advertising budgets are, on the average, much smaller than American ones. And the rates charged by Canadian media serving a more limited audience are, on a "per page" or "per minute" basis, far less than U.S. rates. On the other hand, the tasks that must be performed by Canadian agencies in planning campaigns and preparing effective advertisements are not much different or less demanding, and the salaries they must pay are not much lower. Because of these factors the fee-for-service basis of agency compensation is well established and widely used in Canada.

Agency arrangements are changing

The advertising agency business has seen much change—and profit squeezes—in recent years. Some agencies have given up the full-service approach (for 15 percent) and become more specialized—for example, in media buying or creative functions. Other agencies have gone out of business—some have been purchased by advertisers. Many of the changes are partly due to the work of the less efficient agencies who—under the umbrella of the 15 percent system—were able to get business primarily through social contacts rather than real ability.

Internal conflict causes changes

Some of the changes in the advertising business are due to internal struggles between the creative and the business types—with the latter winning many of the battles because the very survival of the agency is involved. Some of the creative types can properly be called "production-oriented."

At the root of this tension is the fact that the advertiser's product managers or brand managers may be personally responsible for the success of particular products—and feel that they have some right to direct and even veto the work of the creative people. This has resulted in confrontations in which the agency often loses—because the advertiser is paying the bills. A former agency woman—and now an advertiser—said she had lost patience with the "ego-dominated creative type who is blindly in love with his own efforts." She feels the yardstick of successful advertising is whether advertising communicates what it's supposed to communicate to its target audience.[10] Advertisers like this woman have been partly responsible for the changes occurring in the agency business.

Measuring Advertising Effectiveness Is Not Easy

Success depends on the total marketing mix

It would be convenient if we could measure the results of advertising by looking at sales. Unfortunately, we can't—although the advertising literature is filled with success stories that "prove" advertising has increased sales. The total marketing mix—not just promotion generally or advertising specifically—is responsible for the sales result. The one exception to this rule is direct mail advertising. If it doesn't produce immediate results, it's considered a failure.

Research and testing can improve the odds

Ideally, advertisers should pretest advertising before it's run—rather than relying solely on the judgment of creative people or advertising "experts." They too often judge only on the basis of originality—or cleverness—of the copy and illustrations. And advertisers may be no better at deciding how "good" an ad will be.

Some progressive advertisers now demand laboratory or market tests to evaluate the effectiveness of ads. In addition, before ads are run generally, attitude research is sometimes used. Researchers try to evaluate consumers' reaction to particular advertisements—or parts of advertisements—sometimes using laboratory-type devices which measure skin moisture or eye reaction. Split runs on cable TV also are being used to experiment with possible ads.

Hindsight may lead to foresight

After the advertisements have been run, researchers may try to measure how much is recalled about specific products or advertisements. Inquiries from customers may be used as a measure of the effectiveness of particular ads. The recall of, or response to, radio or television commercials can be obtained using various survey techniques such as telephone day-after-recall (D.A.R.) studies or special copy-testing techniques. Starch Readership Service is a regular ongoing service for measuring readership of advertising in print media. It is based on the recognition technique. You can also assume that larger audiences lead directly to greater purchases. Various media audiences are measured by three major services in Canada. These are the Bureau of Broadcast Measurement (BBM) for radio and TV, Nielsen for TV, and the Print Measurement Bureau (PMB) for major consumer magazines and newspaper weekend supplements. In addition, the Canadian Outdoor Measurement Bureau (COMB) measures the total traffic passing by all outdoor advertising.

While advertising research techniques aren't foolproof, they are probably far better than relying on pure judgment by advertising "experts." Until more effective advertising research tools are developed, the present methods—carefully defining specific advertising objectives, choosing media and messages to accomplish these objectives, testing plans, and then evaluating the results of actual advertisements—seem to be most productive.

Government Regulation of Canadian Advertising

Advertising abuses have been a favorite target of Canadian consumerists and of Consumer and Corporate Affairs Canada. A number of Canadian firms and their agencies have been brought to court for alleged violations of the provisions of the Combines Act governing misleading advertising. For up-to-date information on enforcement efforts, take a look at the Misleading Advertising Bulletin, published quarterly by Consumer and Corporate Affairs Canada.

The most recent amendments to the Combines Act strengthened that law by extending its coverage to services as well as to products. All forms of misrepresentation (including the package), not merely published advertisements, are also covered. In addition, not only the literal meaning of an advertisement but also the general impression it conveys and now considered in assessing misrepresentation. Untrue or misleading warranties, "bait and switch" advertising, and contests which mislead the public as to its chances of success are also specifically prohibited.[11]

The Canadian Radio-Television and Telecommunications Commission (CRTC) has "control" (defined to include limiting, rewriting, and banning) over the content of all radio and television commercials. The CRTC has given the Health Protection Branch of the Department of National Health and Welfare authority to regulate the advertising of drugs, cosmetics, and birth control devices. Similarly, the CRTC has delegated its authority to control other types of advertising to Consumer and Corporate Affairs Canada. Firms using broadcast media must obtain approval in advance for every food and drug commercial.

Although these government agencies do not have the same kind of advance "veto power" over print advertising, they can and do insist that print advertisements which violate existing regulations be corrected.

The provinces are also active

Almost all the provinces are also regulating advertising far more aggressively than was previously the case. Such regulation is an especially prominent feature of the "trade practices" acts now in force in many Canadian provinces.

Conflicting or contradictory provincial legislation can make it impossible for national advertisers to use a single advertising theme or the same campaign across Canada. The most extreme case of provincial diversity may be in the advertising of liquor, beer, and wine. Some provinces ban it outright, others restrict what can be said, and still others limit the advertiser to specific media. Complying with all this legislation and frequent changes in regulations is no easy task.

Self-regulation also a factor

Additional forms of regulation are imposed by the media themselves and by industry associations. The CBC and CTV networks also have their own codes of advertising acceptability. The Canadian Advertising Advisory Board is a long established and well accepted industry grouping of advertisers, agencies, and media active in promoting self-regulation. The Advertising Standards Council, which includes public representatives, administers both a Code of Advertising Standards (reprinted as Figure 18–7) and more specific codes governing advertising directed toward children and the advertising of nonprescription drug items. Figure 18–8 tells how many complaints about advertising were made to the Advertising Standards Council and what happened to these complaints.

■ FIGURE 18–7   The Canadian Code of Advertising Standards

As advertising volume increases, so does the responsibility of the industry to the Canadian consumer and the community. The average citizen is now daily exposed to an estimated several hundred advertising messages. It is therefore important that advertising be prepared in ways that respect the taste and values of the public at large. In a society that recognizes the equality of the sexes, advertising should also reflect an awareness of and a sensitivity to this reality and to other human rights issues.

Through the adoption of this Code of Advertising Standards, the participating organizations undertake to apply high ethical standards to the preparation and execution of Canadian advertising. It is their desire and intention to make advertising more effective by continuing to raise the standard of advertising excellence and by ensuring integrity in advertising content.

1. Accuracy, Clarity
Advertisements may not contain inaccurate or deceptive claims or statements, either direct or implied, with regard to price, availability, or performance of a product or service. Advertisers and advertising agencies must be prepared to substantiate their claims promptly to the Council. Note that in assessing the truthfulness of a message, the Council's concern is not with the intent of the sender or the precise legality of the phrasing. Rather the focus is on the message as received or perceived, that is, the general impression conveyed by the advertisement.

2. Disguised Advertising Techniques
No advertisement shall be presented in a format which conceals its commercial intent. Advertising content, for example, should be clearly distinguished from editorial or program content. Similarly, advertisements are not acceptable if they attempt to use images or

■ FIGURE 18–7   *(continued)*

sounds of very brief duration or physically weak visual or oral techniques to convey messages below the threshold of normal human awareness. (Such messages are sometimes referred to as subliminal.)

3. Price Claims

No advertisement shall include deceptive price claims, unrealistic price comparisons, or exaggerated claims as to worth or value. "List price," "suggested retail price," "manufacturer's list price," and "fair market value" are misleading terms when used to imply a savings unless they represent prices at which a reasonable number of the items were actually sold within the preceding six months in the market area where the advertisement appears.

4. Testimonials

Testimonials must reflect the genuine, reasonably current opinion of the endorser and should be based upon adequate information about or experience with the product or service advertised. This is not meant to preclude, however, an actor or actress presenting the true experience of an actual number of users or presenting technical information about the manufacture or testing of the product.

5. Bait and Switch

The consumer must be given a fair opportunity to purchase the goods or services offered at the terms presented. If supply of the sale item is limited, this should be mentioned in the advertisement. Refusal to show or demonstrate the product, disparagement of the advertised product by sales personnel, or demonstration of a product of superior quality are all illustrations of the "bait and switch" technique which is a contravention of the Code.

6. Comparative Advertising

Advertisements must not discredit or attack unfairly other products, services, or advertisements, or exaggerate the nature or importance of competitive differences. When comparisons are made with competing products or services, the advertiser must make substantiation available promptly upon the request from the Council.

7. Professional or Scientific Claims

Advertisements must not distort the true meaning of statements made by professionals or scientific authorities. Advertising claims must not imply they have a scientific basis they do not truly possess. Scientific terms, technical terms, etc., should be used in general advertising only with a full sense of responsibility to the lay public.

8. Slimming, Weight Loss

Advertisements shall not state or imply that foods, food substitutes, appetite depressants, or special devices will enable a person to lose weight or girth except in conjunction with a balanced, calorie-controlled diet; and the part played by such a diet shall be given due prominence in the advertisement.

9. Guarantees

No advertisement shall offer a guarantee or warranty, unless the guarantee or warranty is fully explained as to conditions and limits and the name of the guarantor or warrantor, or it is indicated where such information may be obtained.

10. Imitation

No advertiser shall deliberately imitate the copy, slogans, or illustrations of another advertiser in such a manner as to mislead the consumer. The accidental or unintentional use of similar or like general slogans or themes shall not be considered a contravention of this Code, but advertisers, media, and advertising agencies should be alert to the confusion that can result from such coincidences and should seek to eliminate them when discovered.

11. Safety

Advertisements shall not display a disregard for public safety or depict situations which might encourage inappropriate, unsafe, or dangerous practices.

12. Exploitation of Human Misery

Advertisements may not hold out false hope in the form of a cure or relief for the mental or physically handicapped, either on a temporary or permanent basis.

■ FIGURE 18–7 *(concluded)*

13. Superstition and Fears

Advertisements must not exploit the superstitious, or play upon fears to mislead the consumer into purchasing the advertised product or service.

14. Advertising to Children

Advertisements to children impose a special responsibility upon the advertiser and the media. Such advertisements should not exploit their credulity, lack of experience, or their sense of loyalty, and should not present information or illustrations which might result in their physical, mental, or moral harm. (See also Broadcast Code for Advertising to Children and the Quebec Consumer Protection Act, Bill 72.)

15. Taste, Opinion, Public Decency

a. As a public communication process, advertising should not present demeaning or derogatory portrayals of individuals or groups and should not contain anything likely, in the light of generally prevailing standards, to cause deep or widespread offence. It is recognized, of course, that standards of taste are subjective and vary widely from person to person and community to community, and are, indeed, subject to constant change.

b. The authority of the Code and the jurisdiction of the Council are over the content of advertisements. The Code is not meant to impede in any way the sale of products which some people, for one reason or another, may find offensive—provided, of course, that the advertisements for such products do not contravene section *(a)* of this Clause.

Source: The Canadian Code of Advertising Standards, May, 1982, The Advertising Standards Council.

■ FIGURE 18–8 1984 report of the Advertising Standards Council

Advertising
Standards Council

FOR IMMEDIATE RELEASE

March, 1985

The 411 complaints closed by Toronto Council staff during 1984 represents a slight increase over 1983. Approximately the same percentage of complaints were upheld - 24 percent or a total of 100. There was a significant increase in the number of trade disputes handled by the Council - 26 in 1984 and 15 in 1983. Among the 1984 complaints, which invariably involve comparative advertising, 15 of the initiators of complaints were successful in having their objections upheld.

There was also an increase in the number of complaints upheld under Clause 15, "Taste, Opinion, Public Decency"; however, the 23 complaints involved only 10 different advertisers, since there were multiple complaints against some of the companies.

Le Conseil des Normes de la Publicité closed an additional total of 127 complaints and the regional Councils added another 466 to make a complete total of 998 complaints dealt with by Councils across the country.

The Advertising Standards Councils' complaint handling represents only part of the role it plays in the self-regulatory process. For example, the Toronto staff receives an average of 25 - 30 enquiry calls per week, most of them from the Toronto region; however enquiries do originate regularly from

...2

-2-

centers right across the country, and occasionally from U.S. cities such as New York, Chicago, Los Angeles, and as we were writing this release a call came in from Chattanooga.

Who calls? Advertising agency personnel seeking to clarify some specific regulation, or to ask about issues such as the use of illustration of currency in advertising. Frequently the subject of comparative advertising raises questions such as - "is it ok in a car commercial featuring the roominess of the sponsor's car, to show a big man in a cramped position in a competitor's car which in fact has equal seating space?" Occasionally lawyers in the U.S. and in Canada who are very familiar with misleading advertising law, request information about self-regulation. Students seek general information about the regulation of advertising, and of course members of the public call to question, or to complain about, specific advertising messages.

Station copywriters sometimes call on the Council when they are having difficulty persuading a local client that, for example, he may not describe his product as "the best" unless he can prove that it is. It may be human nature to presume that our product or service is best, but that's not adequate support for an advertising claim. Another overly enthusiastic merchant wished to advertise an unqualified "50% off sale" even though many of the items in the store were not included in the half price sale. And of course advertiser and agency personnel also consult ASC staff with regard to regulations in the Code of Advertising Standards, or in the comparative Advertising Guidelines. The ASC welcomes these opportunities to make Code regulations better known.

■ CONCLUSION

Theoretically, it may seem simple to develop an advertising campaign. Just pick the media and develop a message. But it's not that easy. Effectiveness depends on using the "best" medium and the "best" message, considering: (1) promotion objectives, (2) the target markets, and (3) the funds available for advertising.

Specific advertising objectives will determine what kind of advertising to use—product or institutional. If product advertising is needed, then the particular type must be decided—pioneering, competitive (direct or indirect), or reminder. And advertising allowances and cooperative advertising may be helpful.

Many technical details are involved in advertising, and specialists—advertising agencies—handle some of these jobs. But specific objectives must be set for them—or their advertising may have little direction and be almost impossible to evaluate.

Ultimately, effective advertising should affect sales. But the whole marketing mix affects sales—and the results of advertising can't be measured by sales changes alone. Advertising is only a part of promotion—and promotion is only a part of the total marketing mix that the marketing manager must develop to satisfy target customers.

■ QUESTIONS AND PROBLEMS

1. Identify the strategic decisions a marketing manager must make in the advertising area.

2. Discuss the relation of advertising objectives to marketing strategy planning and the kinds of advertising actually needed. Illustrate.

3. Present three examples where advertising to middlemen might be necessary. What are the objective(s) of such advertising?

4. What does it mean to say that "money is invested in advertising?" Is all advertising an investment? Illustrate.

5. Find advertisements to final consumers which illustrate the following types of advertising: (a) institutional, (b) pioneering, (c) competitive, (d) reminder. What objective(s) does each of these ads have? List the needs appealed to in each of these advertisements.

6. Describe the type of media which might be most suitable for promoting: (a) tomato soup, (b) greeting cards, (c) an industrial component material, (d) playground equipment. Specify any assumptions necessary to obtain a definite answer.

7. Discuss the use of testimonials in advertising. Which of the four AIDA steps might testimonials accomplish? Are they suitable for all types of products? If not, for which types are they most suitable?

8. Find an advertisement which seeks to accomplish all four AIDA steps—and explain how you feel this advertisement is accomplishing each of these steps.

9. Discuss the future of independent advertising agencies now that the 15 percent commission system is not required.

10. Does advertising cost too much? How can this be measured?

11. How would retailing promotion be affected if all local advertising via mass media such as radio, television, and newspapers were prohibited? Would there be any impact on total sales? If so, would it probably affect all goods and stores equally?

12. Is it "unfair" to advertise to children? Is it "unfair" to advertise to less educated or less experienced people of any age? Is it "unfair" to advertise for "unnecessary" products?

■ SUGGESTED CASES

22. Canadian Hydrogardens Limited

31. Mayfair Detergent Company

■ NOTES

1. *The Canadian Media Directors' Council Media Digest, 1981/1982* (Toronto: Marketing, 1981).

2. Jo Marney, "We've Become a Nation of Magazine Addicts," *Marketing,* June 19, 1978, p. 38.

3. Statistics Canada, *Advertising Expenditures in Canada, 1965,* Cat. 63-216, table 19.

4. *Handbook of Canadian Consumer Markets, 1982,* 2d ed. (Ottawa: The Conference Board of Canada, February 1982), p. 220. For more detailed information an aggregate expenditures by industry, see Zarry, "Advertising and Marketing Communications in Canada," in *Canadian Marketing; Problems and Prospects,* ed. Donald N. Thompson and David S. R. Leighton (Toronto: Wiley Publishers of Canada, 1973), pp. 230–34. Though the figures given are dated, the relative importance of the industries Zarry mentions has not changed appreciably.

5. Estimate provided by the Canadian Advertising Advisory Board.

6. William L. Wilkie and Paul W. Farris, "Comparison Advertising: Problems and Potential," *Journal of Marketing,* October 1975, pp. 7–15; V. K. Prasad, "Communications Effectiveness of Comparative Advertising: A Laboratory Analysis," *Journal of Marketing Research,* May 1976, pp. 128–37; Murphy A. Seawall and Michael H. Goldstein, "The Comparative Advertising Controversy: Consumer Perceptions of Catalog Showroom Reference Prices," *Journal of Marketing,* Summer 1979, pp. 85–92; Linda L. Golden, "Consumer Reactions to Explicit Brand Comparisons in Advertisements," *Journal of Marketing Research,* November 1979, pp. 517–32; Stephen Goodwin and Michael Edgar, "An Experimental Investigation of Comparative Advertising: Impact of Message Appeal, Information Load and Utility of Product Class," *Journal of Marketing Research,* May 1980, pp. 187–202; and "Should an Ad Identify Brand X?" *Business Week,* September 24, 1979, pp. 156–61.

7. "Why Jockey Switched Its Ads from TV to Print," *Business Week,* July 26, 1976, pp. 140–42.

8. J. M. Kramer, "Benefits and Use of Suburban Press for Large Metropolitan Buys," *Journal of Marketing,* January 1977, pp. 68–70.

9. "Keep Both Advertiser and the Reader Happy," *Marketing,* July 22, 1974, p. 22.

10. Helen Van Slyke, Vice President, Advertising, Helena Rubenstein, Inc., New York, in a speech to the meeting of the American Association of Advertising Agencies, April 25, 1970; and "The Days of Fun and Games Are Over," *Business Week,* November 10, 1973, p. 84.

11. *Bill C-227: Proposals for a New Competition Policy for Canada* (Ottawa: Department of Consumer and Corporate Affairs, November 1973), p. 5. See also the complete listing of cases as of that date under the misleading advertising provisions of the Combines Act found in Appendix C of that publication.

Chapter 19 ■ Pricing objectives and policies

When you finish this chapter, you should:

1. Understand how pricing objectives should guide pricing decisions.

2. Understand choices the marketing manager must make about price flexibility, and price levels over the product life cycle.

3. Understand the legality of price level and price flexibility policies.

4. Understand the many possible variations of a price structure, including discounts, allowances, and who pays transportation costs.

5. Recognize the important new terms (shown in red).

"Deciding what price to charge can be agonizing."

Price is one of the four major variables a marketing manager controls. Price level decisions are especially important—because they affect both the number of sales a firm will make and how much money is earned.

Pricing is complicated by different perceptions about cost, benefits (value), and price. For instance, a Hollywood starlet rushed into a famous hat designer demanding a new hat—at once—for a party. The designer took a few yards of ribbon, twisted it cleverly, arranged it on her head, and said "There is your hat, madam." The starlet looked in the mirror and exclaimed: "Marvelous!" The designer bowed and said, "That will be $50." "But," complained the starlet, "that's a lot of money for a couple yards of ribbon." Indignant, the designer unwound the ribbon and handed it to her saying, "Madam, the ribbon is _free._"

Guided by the company's objectives, marketing managers must develop a set of pricing objectives and policies. They must spell out what price situations the firm will face and how it will handle them. These policies should explain: (1) how flexible prices will be, (2) at what level they will be set—over the product life cycle, (3) how transportation costs will be handled, and (4) to whom and when discounts and allowances will be given. These strategic pricing decision areas are shown in Figure 19–1.

Price Has Many Dimensions

It is not easy to define price in real-life situations. This is because prices reflect many dimensions—and not realizing this can lead to big mistakes. For example, a catalog might offer—at $175—a pair of stereo speakers which are sold by local retailers for $300.

■ FIGURE 19–1   Strategy planning for Price

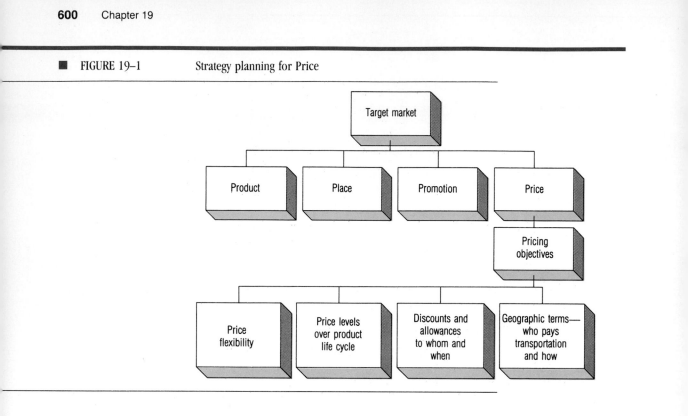

At first, this might seem like a real bargain. However, your view of this "deal" might change if you found that the speakers came in a kit for you to assemble— and that there was no warranty because you were assembling the parts. The price might look even less attractive if you discovered that you had to pay $35 for insurance and shipping from the factory. Further, how would you feel if you ordered the speakers anyway and then learned that delivery takes two months!

■ FIGURE 19–2   Price as seen by consumers or users

Price	equals	Something

List price
Less: *Discounts:*
    Quantity
    Seasonal
    Cash
Less: *Allowances:*
    Trade-ins
    Damaged goods
	equals	*Product:*
		    Physical product
		    Service
		    Assurance of quality
		    Repair facilities
		    Packaging
		    Credit
		    Trading stamps or coupons
		Place of delivery or availability

■ FIGURE 19–3   Price as seen by channel members

Price	equals	Something

List price
Less: *Discounts*:
    Quantity
    Seasonal
    Cash
    Trade or functional
Less: *Allowances*:
    Damaged goods
    Advertising
    Push money
	equals	*Product:*
		    Branded—well known
		    Guaranteed
		    Warranted
		    Service—repair facilities
		    Convenient packaging for handling
		Place:
		    Availability—when and where
		Price:
		    Price-level guarantee
		    Sufficient margin to allow chance for profit
		Promotion:
		    Promotion aimed at customers

The price equation: Price equals something

The speaker example emphasizes that when a price is quoted, it is related to *some* assortment of goods and/or services. So **Price** is what is charged for "something." *Any business transaction in our modern economy can be thought of as an exchange of money—the money being the Price—for Something.*

This description of Price is similar to our broad definition of Product. The *Something* can be a physical product in various stages of completion, with or without supporting services, with or without quality guarantees, and so on. Or it could be a service—dry cleaning, a lawyer's advice, or a taxi ride.

The nature and extent of this *Something* will determine the amount of money to be exchanged. Some customers may pay list price. Others may obtain large discounts or allowances—because something is *not* provided. Some possible variations are summarized in Figure 19–2 for consumers or users and in Figure 19–3 for channel members. Some of these variations will be discussed more fully below. But here it should be clear that Price has many dimensions.

Pricing Objectives Should Guide Pricing

Pricing objectives should flow from—and fit in with—company-level and marketing objectives. Because pricing is so important, price-related topics are sometimes included in the marketing or even the company-level objectives. But pricing objectives should be *explicitly stated*—because they have a direct effect on pricing policies as well as the methods used to set prices.

■ FIGURE 19–4   Possible pricing objectives

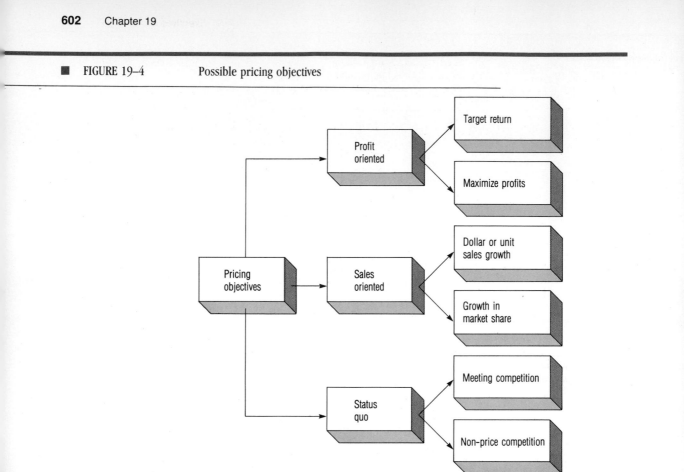

The various types of pricing objectives we will discuss are shown in Figure 19–4. A company may have different pricing objectives for different products aimed at the same target market. Similarly, different objectives may be set for different target markets. In other words, every marketing strategy may have its own pricing objective.

Profit-Oriented Objectives

Target returns provide specific guidelines

A **target return objective** sets a specific level of profit as an objective. Often this amount is stated as a percentage of sales or of capital investment. For example, a large manufacturer might aim for a 25 percent return on investment, while the target for a grocery chain might be a 1 percent return on sales.

Common long-run targets are somewhere between 10 and 30 percent return on investment, after taxes. The actual size depends partly on present or likely competition. Some companies set a relatively low objective—to discourage potential competitors. Others—expecting relatively little competition—set extremely high targets for the short run.

A target return objective has administrative advantages in a large company. The performance of the many divisions and departments—all of which are using capital—can be compared against the target. Some companies will eliminate divisions—or drop products—that aren't yielding the target rate of return on investment.

Some just want satisfactory profits

Some managers aim for only "satisfactory" returns. They just want returns which ensure the firm's survival and convince stockholders that they are "doing a good job." Similarly, some small family run businesses aim for a profit that will provide a "comfortable life style."[1]

Companies which are leaders in their industries—like Alcan, Du Pont of Canada, General Motors of Canada, and Stelco—sometimes pursue only "satisfactory" long-run targets. They are well aware that their activities are in public view.[2] The public—and government officials—expect them to follow policies that are "in the public interest" when they play the role of price leader or wage setter. Too large a return might invite government action.

But this kind of situation can lead to decisions which are not in the public interest. A large company which is afraid of making "too much" profit may not be motivated to keep costs and prices low. Lower costs—reflected in lower prices to consumers—might result in even larger market shares and antitrust actions by the government!

Profit maximization can be socially responsible

A **profit maximization objective** seeks to get as much profit as possible. It might be stated as a desire to earn a rapid return on investment. Or—more bluntly—to charge "all the traffic will bear."

Some people believe that anyone seeking a profit maximization objective will charge *high* prices—prices that are not in the public interest.

Economic theory does not support this idea. *Pricing to achieve profit maximization doesn't always lead to high prices.* Demand and supply *may* bring extremely high prices if competition can't offer good substitutes. But this happens *if and only if* demand is highly inelastic. The oil producers were able to raise prices because of this. But if demand is very elastic, profit maximizers may charge relatively low prices. Low prices may expand the size of the overall market—and result in greater revenues and profits. For example, when prices for electronic calculators were very high, only specialists bought them. When some firms lowered prices, nearly everyone bought calculators. In other words, when demand is elastic, profit maximization may occur at a *lower* price.

Profit maximization objectives can also produce desirable results indirectly. Consumers "vote" with their purchase dollars—for firms which do "the right things." The profits from this "voting" guide other firms in deciding what they should do. If a firm is earning a very large profit, other firms will try to copy or improve on what the company offers. Frequently, this leads to a lower price. We saw this process at work in Chapter 11—in the rise and fall of profits during the life cycle of a product. Contrary to popular belief, a profit maximization objective is often socially desirable.

Sales-Oriented Objectives

A **sales-oriented objective** seeks some level of unit sales, dollar sales, or share of market—without referring to profit.

Sales growth doesn't mean big profits

Some managers are more concerned about sales growth than profits.[3] They think sales growth leads to big profits. This kind of thinking causes problems when a firm's costs are growing faster than sales—or when managers don't keep track of their costs. Recently, many major corporations have had declining profits, in spite of growth in sales.[4] More attention is now being paid to profits—not just sales.

Market share objectives are popular

Many firms seek to gain a specified share (percent) of a market. A benefit of a market share objective is that it forces a manager to pay attention to what competitors are doing in the market. In addition, it's usually easier to measure a firm's market share than it is to determine if profits are being maximized. Large consumer package goods firms—such as Procter & Gamble, Coca-Cola, and General Foods—often use market share objectives.

Aggressive companies often aim to increase market share—or even to control a market. Sometimes this makes sense. If a company has a large market share, it may have better economies of scale than its competitors. Therefore, if it sells at about the same price as its competitors, it gets more profit from each sale. Or, lower costs may allow it to sell at a lower price—and still make a profit.

A company with a longer-run view may decide that increasing market share is a sensible objective when the *overall market is growing*. The logic is that the larger future volume will justify sacrifice of some profit in the short run.

Of course, objectives aimed at increasing market share have the same limitations as straight sales growth objectives. A larger market share—if gained at too low a price—may lead to profitless "success."

Pricing to increase sales units may reduce profits.

The key point regarding sales-oriented objectives is: larger sales volume, by itself, doesn't necessarily lead to higher profits. The wise manager will consider the profit implications of an objective stated only in terms of sales.

Status Quo Pricing Objectives

Don't-rock-the-boat objectives

Managers who are satisfied with their current market share and profits sometime adopt **status quo objectives**—"don't-rock-the-*pricing*-boat" objectives. They may be stated as "stabilizing prices," or "meeting competition," or even "avoiding competition." This "don't-rock-the-boat" thinking is most common when the total market is not growing. Maintaining stable prices may discourage price competition and avoid the need for hard decisions. The managers may have more time for golf!

Or stress non-price competition instead

On the other hand, a status quo *pricing objective* may be part of an aggressive overall marketing strategy focusing on **non-price competition**—aggressive action on one or more of the Ps other than Price. Fast-food chains like McDonald's prefer non-price competition.

Most Firms Set Specific Pricing Policies—To Reach Objectives

Specific pricing policies are vital for any firm. Otherwise, a marketing manager has to rethink the strategy every time a customer asks for a price. This is not only a drain on the manager's time, but customer goodwill can be lost if quoted prices do not appear to follow a logical pattern.

Administered prices help achieve objectives

Price policies usually lead to **administered prices**—consciously set prices—aimed at reaching the firm's objectives. In other words, instead of letting daily market forces decide their prices, most firms (including *all* of those in monopolistic competition) set their own prices. They may even hold them steady for long periods of time.

It is sometimes difficult to administer "final customer" prices if a producer does not sell directly to final customers. Other channel members may also wish to administer prices to achieve their own objectives. For example, a manufacturer of color televisions might prefer to sell sets to TV specialty stores with knowledgeable salespeople and repair service. The manufacturer may have price policies which will allow TV stores sufficient margins to cover the costs of these services. But, some of its wholesalers may decide that they can improve profits by selling in larger quantities to discount stores. The discount stores, in turn, may sell at prices lower than the manufacturer intended—but without the desired service!

Some channel members don't charge the suggested list price.

Some firms don't even try to administer prices. They just "meet competition"—or worse, mark up their costs with little thought to demand. They act like they have no choice in selecting a price policy.

Remember that Price has many dimensions. Managers *do* have many choices. They *should* administer their prices. And they should do it carefully—because, finally, it is these prices which customers must be willing to pay before a whole marketing mix is a success. In the rest of this chapter, we will talk about policies a marketing manager must set to do an effective job of administering Price.

Price Flexibility Policies

One of the first decisions a marketing manager has to make is about price flexibility. Should he have a one-price or a flexible-price policy?

One-price policy—the same price for everyone

A **one-price policy** means offering the *same price to all customers* who purchase goods under essentially the same conditions and in the same quantities. The majority of Canadian firms use a one-price policy—mainly for administrative convenience and to maintain goodwill among customers. Most food stores, department stores, and even the modern discount houses and mass-merchandisers use a one-price policy.

A one-price policy makes pricing easier. But a marketing manager must be careful to avoid a rigid one-price policy. This can amount to broadcasting a price which competitors can undercut—especially if the price is somewhat high. One reason for the growth of discount houses is that conventional retailers rigidly applied traditional margins—and stuck to them.

Flexible-price policy—different prices for different customers

A flexible-price policy means offering the same product and quantities to different customers at different prices. Flexible-price policies often specify a *range* in which the actual price charged must fall.

Flexible pricing is most common in the channels, in direct sales of industrial goods, and at retail for expensive items and homogeneous shopping goods. These situations usually call for personal selling, not mass selling. The advantage of flexible pricing is that the sales rep can make price adjustments—considering prices charged by local competitors, the relationship with the customer, or the customer's bargaining ability.[5]

Flexible pricing was more common when businesses were small—and products weren't standardized. Most customers expected to bargain for a price. These conditions still exist in many countries.

Flexible pricing has disadvantages. A customer who finds that others have paid lower prices for the same marketing mix will be unhappy. If buyers learn that negotiating can be in their interest, the time needed for bargaining will increase. This can affect selling costs. In addition, some sales reps let price cutting become a habit. This reduces the role of price as a competitive tool—and leads to a lower price level. To reduce this problem, some firms require a rep to obtain approval to lower a price.

Flexible prices can also lead to legal difficulties. These will be discussed later in this chapter.

Price Level Policies—Over the Product Life Cycle

When marketing managers administer prices—as most do—they must consciously set a price level policy. As they enter the market, they have to set "introductory" prices which may have long-run effects. They must consider where the product life cycle is—and how fast it is moving. And they must decide if their prices should be above, below, or somewhere in between relative to the "market."

Let's look for a moment at a new product in the introduction stage of its product life cycle. The price level decision should focus first on the nature of market demand. There are few (or no) direct substitute marketing mixes. And considering the demand curve for this product, a high price may lead to higher profit from each sale but also to fewer units sold. A lower price might appeal to more potential customers. With this in mind, should the firm set a "high" or "low" price?

Skimming pricing—feeling out demand at a high price

A skimming price policy tries to sell the top ("skim the cream") of a market—the top of the demand curve—at a high price before aiming at more price-sensitive customers. Skimming is used to maximize profits in the market introduction stage, especially if there is little competition and there are few substitutes. A skimming policy is more attractive if demand is fairly inelastic—at least at the upper price ranges.

A skimming policy usually involves a slow reduction in price over time. It is important to realize that as price is reduced, new target markets are probably being sought. So, as the price level "steps-down" the demand curve, new *Place* and *Promotion* policies may be needed, too.

When Polaroid introduced its camera to make "instant pictures," it initially set a high price. It had patents which excluded competitors. The high-priced camera was sold mainly to professional photographers and serious amateurs—at camera stores. Soon, Polaroid introduced other models which had fewer features. These were sold at lower prices and appealed to different market segments. Finally, before its patents ran out, Polaroid introduced a low-cost camera—sold through department, drug, and discount stores. This is very typical of skimming. It involves changing prices through a series of marketing strategies over the course of the product life cycle.

Skimming is also useful when you don't know very much about the shape of the demand curve. It's easier to start with a high price that customers can refuse—and then to reduce it if needed.

Penetration pricing— get volume at a low price

A **penetration pricing policy** tries to sell the whole market at one low price. The intention is to expand the quantity of the product sold by picking a lower point on the demand curve. This approach might be wise when the "elite" market—willing to pay a high price—is small. This is the case when the whole demand curve is fairly elastic.

A penetration policy is even more attractive if selling larger quantities results in lower costs—because of economies of scale. This is especially important if the firm expects strong competition *very* soon after introduction.

A *low* penetration price may be called a "stay out" price. It discourages competitors from entering the market. Their profits will not be as attractive because the price is low.

The first personal computer companies knew that it would be easy for competitors to copy—and even improve on—what they were doing. Moreover, the potential market for low-priced computers was so large that profits still looked attractive, even at "lower" prices. So the early "penetrators"—like Apple, Radio Shack, and Atari—avoided skimming prices which would be easy to undercut.

Introductory price dealing—temporary price cuts

Price cuts do attract customers. Therefore, marketers often use **introductory price dealing**—temporary price cuts—to speed new products into the market. The low price encourages customers to try the new product and hopefully to buy again later at the regular price. These *temporary* price cuts should not be confused with low penetration prices, however. The plan here is to raise prices as soon as the introductory offer is over.

Established competitors often choose not to meet introductory price dealing—as long as the introductory period is not too long or too successful. But knowing that customers may shift their loyalties if they try competitors' products, some aggressive competitors do meet such introductory price cuts.

Once price dealing gets started in a market, it may continue for some time. So an introductory price dealing policy must be chosen with care.[6]

"Meeting competition" may be wise sometimes

Regardless of their introductory pricing policy, most firms face competition sooner or later in the product life cycle. When that happens, how high or low a price is may be relative not only to the market demand curve, but also to the prices charged by competitors.

The nature of competition will usually affect whether prices are set below, at, or above competition. The clearest case is in pure competition. The decision is really made by the market. To offer goods above or below the market price is foolish.

Similarly, there is little choice in oligopoly situations. Pricing "at the market"—that is, meeting competition—may be the only sensible policy. To raise prices might lead to a large loss in sales—unless competitors adopt the higher price, too. And cutting prices would probably lead to similar reductions by competitors—downward along an inelastic industry demand curve. This can only lead to a decrease in total revenue for the industry and probably for each of the firms. Therefore, each oligopolist may set an objective of status quo pricing—at the competitive level. (Note: some critics call this pricing behavior "conscious parallel action"—and imply that it is the same as intentional conspiracy among firms.)

Price-off promotions are a way of lowering prices—temporarily.

"Low prices" may really be different prices for different market segments.

There are alternatives in monopolistic competition

In monopolistic competition situations, there are more pricing options. Some firms emphasize "below-the-market" prices in their marketing mixes. Prices offered by discounters and mass-merchandisers such as K mart illustrate this approach. At the other extreme, some firms are clearly "above-the-market"—and they may even brag about it. Tiffany's is well known as one of the most expensive jewelry stores in the world. Curtis Mathes advertises that it makes "the most expensive TV you can buy."

But, above or below what market?

These examples raise an important question: Do these various strategies contain prices which are "above" or "below" the market—or are they really different prices *for different market segments*? It is important in thinking about price level policies to clearly define the *relevant target market* and *competitors* when making comparisons of prices.

Perhaps *some* target customers *do* see important differences in the physical product, or in the convenience of location, or in the whole marketing mix. Then what we are talking about are different marketing strategies—not just different price levels.

Consider K mart prices again from this view. It may have lower TV prices than conventional television retailers offering fast, in-house repair service. But it offers less help in the store and depends on outside repair services. K mart may be appealing to budget-oriented shoppers who are comparing prices among different mass-merchandisers. A specialty TV store—appealing to different customers—may not be a direct competitor! Thus, it may be better to think of K mart's price as part of a different marketing mix for a different target market—not as a "below-the-market" price.[7]

Different price level policies through the channel

When a product is sold to channel members instead of final consumers, the price should be set so that the channel members can cover costs and make a profit. To achieve its objectives, a manufacturer may set different price level policies for different levels in the channel. For example, he may set a price level that is low relative to competitors when selling to middlemen, while suggesting an "above-the-market" price at retail. This would encourage middlemen to carry the product—and to emphasize it in their marketing mix—because it yields higher profits.

Most Price Structures Are Built around List Prices

Prices start with a list price

Most price structures are built around a base price schedule or price "list." **Basic list prices** are the prices that final customers or users are normally asked to pay for products or services. Unless noted otherwise, "list price" refers to "basic list price" in this book.

How these list prices are set is discussed in the next chapter. Now, however, we will consider variations of list price—and when adjustments are made to that price.

Unchanging list prices—an administrative convenience

Some companies face a problem in publishing catalogs which must show prices. They don't want to print a new catalog every time a price changes. In this situation, it is convenient to use **unchanging list prices**—published prices that remain the same for a long time—perhaps years—but the actual price is adjusted upward or downward by a list of add-ons or discounts. Such change lists can be issued quickly and inexpensively.

Discount Policies—Reductions from List Prices

Discounts are reductions from list price that are given by a seller to a buyer who either gives up some marketing function or provides the function himself. Discounts can be useful in marketing strategy planning. In the following discussion, think about what function the buyers are giving up—or providing—when they get each of these discounts.

Quantity discounts encourage volume buying

Quantity discounts are discounts offered to encourage customers to buy in larger amounts. This lets a seller get more of a buyer's business, or shifts some of the storing function to the buyer, or reduces shipping and selling costs—or all of these. Such discounts are of two kinds: cumulative and non-cumulative.

Cumulative quantity discounts apply to purchases over a given period—such as a year—and the discount usually increases as the amount purchased increases. Cumulative discounts are intended to encourage *repeat* buying by a single customer—by reducing its cost for additional purchases. For example, a lumber wholesaler might offer its customers—building contractors—a cumulative discount. The contractor is not able to buy all of the materials needed at once, but the wholesaler wants to reward the contractor's patronage—and discourage shopping around.

Non-cumulative quantity discounts apply only to *individual orders.* Such discounts encourage larger orders but do not tie a buyer to the seller after that one purchase. These discounts are often used to discourage small orders—which are expensive to handle. But the main use is to encourage bigger orders. For example, a wholesale lumber yard may purchase and resell the products of several competing producers. One producer might try to encourage the wholesaler to stock larger quantities of its products by offering a non-cumulative quantity discount. The objective would be to encourage the wholesaler to "push" those products to its customers.

Quantity discounts may be based on the dollar value of the entire order, or on the number of units purchased, or on the size of the package purchased. While quantity discounts are usually given as price cuts, sometimes they are given as "free" or "bonus" goods.

Quantity discounts can be a very useful tool for the marketing manager. Some customers are eager to get them. But marketing managers must use quantity discounts carefully—offering them to all customers on equal terms—to avoid price discrimination.

Seasonal discounts— buy sooner and store

Seasonal discounts are discounts offered to encourage buyers to stock earlier than present demand requires. If used by producers, this discount tends to shift the storing function further along in the channel. It also tends to even out sales over the year and, therefore, permit year-round operation. This approach also gives a firm a better idea of what its sales will be—rather than waiting and selling everything all at once. If seasonal discounts are large, they may be passed along to other customers down the channel of distribution. For example, a manufacturer of lawnmowers is likely to offer its wholesalers a lower price if they buy in the fall—when the lawnmower market is slow. The wholesalers can then offer a discount to retailers—who may then sell the mowers during a special "fall sale."

Payment terms and cash discounts set payment dates

Most sales to channel members and final users are made on credit. The seller sends a bill (invoice)—and the buyer's accounting department processes it for payment. Some firms depend on their suppliers for temporary working capital (credit). Therefore, it is very important for both sides to clearly state the terms of payment—including the availability of cash discounts—and to understand the commonly used payment terms.

Net means that payment for the face value of the invoice is due immediately. These terms are sometimes changed to "net 10" or "net 30"—which means payment is due within 10 or 30 days of the date on the invoice.

Cash discounts are reductions in the price to encourage buyers to pay their bills quickly. The terms for a cash discount usually modify the "net" terms.

2/10, net 30 means that a 2 percent discount off the face value of the invoice is allowed if the invoice is paid within 10 days. Otherwise, the full face value is due within 30 days. And it usually is stated or understood that an interest charge will be made after the 30-day free credit period.

An invoice shows the terms of the sale.

Servco, Ltd.

1475 Lake Lansing Road
Port Moody, B.C. V5A 1E6
(604)291-3708

Nº   1522

DATE
10-20-86

CUSTOMER'S ORDER
#179642

SALESMAN
Miller

TERMS
Net 30

F.O.B.
Port Moody

SHIPPED VIA
Truck

Sold To: JONES SUPPLY COMPANY

220 COMMERCIAL DRIVE

BURNABY, B.C. V5G 3H2

Shipped To: JONES SUPPLY CO., 623 KENSINGTON.

VANCOUVER, B.C. V5K 2P9

200	Smoke Alarms, #263 - A	12.	00	2400.	00
		Thank you.			

Why cash discounts are given and should be taken

Smart buyers take advantage of cash discounts. A discount of 2/10, net 30 may not look like much at first. But the 2 percent discount is earned for paying the invoice just 20 days sooner than it would have to be paid anyway. And if it is not taken, the company—in effect—is borrowing at an annual rate of 36 percent. That is, assuming a 360-day year and dividing by 20 days, there are 18 periods during which the company could earn 2 percent—and 18 times 2 equals 36 percent a year.

While the marketing manager can often use the cash discount as a marketing variable, this is not always true. Purchasing agents who value cash discounts may *insist* that the marketing manager offer the same discount offered by competitors. In fact, some buyers automatically deduct the traditional cash discount from their invoices—regardless of the seller's invoice terms!

Some sellers find themselves in trouble when they do not state exactly when payment is due—or what the penalty will be for late payment. Customers may wait as long as possible to pay the invoice, especially if they are short of cash—or if interest rates are high.

Consumers say "charge it," too

Credit sales are also becoming much more common—and important—to retailers. The majority of department store purchases may be made with credit cards. Some stores have their own credit accounts. But most stores use credit card services—such as VISA or MasterCard. The retailers pay a percent of the revenue from each credit sale for this service—from 1 to 7 percent depending on the card company and the store's sales volume. For this reason, some retailers offer discounts to consumers who purchase with cash.

Trade discounts often are set by tradition

A **trade (functional) discount** is a list price reduction given to channel members for the job they are going to do.

A manufacturer, for example, might allow retailers a 30 percent trade discount from the suggested retail list price—to cover the cost of the retailing function and their profit. Similarly, the manufacturer might allow wholesalers a chain discount of 30 percent and 10 percent off the suggested retail price. In this case, the wholesalers would be expected to pass the 30 percent discount on to retailers. But, while such discounts are legal and widely offered in the United states, they violate the price discrimination provisions of the Combines Act. A Canadian wholesaler cannot legally be offered a larger discount than a retailer purchasing the same quantity of merchandise.

Trade discounts might seem to offer manufacturers or wholesalers great flexibility in varying a marketing mix. In fact, however, the customary trade discounts can be so well established in the channel that the manager has to accept them as fixed when setting prices.

Allowance Policies—Off List Prices

Allowances—like discounts—are given to final consumers, customers, or channel members for doing "something" or accepting less of "something."

Bring in the old, ring up the new—with trade-ins

A **trade-in allowance** is a price reduction given for used goods when similar new goods are bought.

Trade-ins give the marketing manager an easy way to lower the price without reducing list price. Proper handling of trade-ins is important when selling durable goods. Customers buying machinery or buildings, for example, buy long-term satisfaction in terms of more manufacturing capacity. If the list price less the trade-in allowance does not offer greater satisfaction—as the customer sees it—then no sales will be made.

Many firms replace machinery slowly—perhaps too slowly—because they value their old equipment above market value. This also applies to new cars. Customers want higher trade-ins for their old cars than the current market value. This encourages the use of high, perhaps "phony," list prices so that high trade-in allowances can be given.

Advertising allowances—something for something

Advertising allowances are price reductions given to firms in the channel to encourage them to advertise or otherwise promote the supplier's products locally. For example, General Electric has given an allowance (1.5 percent of sales) to its wholesalers of housewares and radios. They, in turn, were expected to spend the allowance on local advertising.

PMs—push for cash

Push money (or prize money) allowances—sometimes called "PMs" or "spiffs"—are given to retailers by manufacturers or wholesalers to pass on to the retailers' sales clerks—for aggressively selling certain items. PM allowances are used for new merchandise, slower-moving items, or higher-margin items. They are especially common in the furniture and clothing industries. A sales clerk, for example, might earn an additional $5 for each mattress of a new type sold.

Some Customers Get Extra Somethings

Trading stamps—something for nothing?

Trading stamps are free stamps (such as "Green Stamps") given by some retailers with each purchase.

Retailers can buy trading stamps from trading-stamp companies—or set up their own plans. In either case, customers can trade the stamps for merchandise premiums or cash.

Some retailers offer trading stamps to their customers to try to get a "competitive advantage." Some customers think they are getting something for nothing. And sometimes they are—if the retailer doesn't pass the cost of the stamps (2 to 3 percent of sales) along to customers. This can occur when lower promotion costs or a large increase in sales make up for the cost of the stamps.

There was much interest in trading stamps in the 1950s and 60s. The early users of stamps in a community seemed to gain a competitive advantage. But this soon disappeared as competitors started offering stamps. Now, their use has declined—especially in grocery retailing.

Clipping coupons brings other extras

Many manufacturers and retailers offer discounts (or free items) through the use of coupons distributed in packages, mailings, print advertisements, or at the store. By presenting a coupon to a retailer, the consumer is given a discount off list price ("10 cents off"). This is especially common in the grocery business. "Couponing" has become so common that special firms have been set up to help repay retailers for redeeming manufacturers' coupons. Moreover, the total dollar amounts involved are so large that crime has become a problem. Some dishonest retailers collect for coupons which they have "redeemed" without requiring their customers to buy the products.[8]

Some 3.6 billion marketer-issued coupons were distributed in Canada in 1984, a 500 percent increase over the 1974 figure. During this 10-year period coupon redemption rates (the percentage of coupons actually returned to the store) has ranged between 5 and 9 percent.[9]

List Price May Depend on Geographic Pricing Policies

Retail list prices often include free delivery. Or free delivery may be offered to some customers as an aid to closing the sale. What is included (or not included) in the retail list price may not be formally stated. That way, the retailer can adjust its marketing mix—depending on the needs—or bargaining ability—of a customer.

Deciding who is going to pay the freight is more important on sales to intermediate customers than to final consumers—because more money may be involved. Usually purchase orders specify place, time, method of delivery, freight costs, insurance, handling, and other charges. There are many possible variations for an imaginative marketing manager. Some specialized terms have developed. A few are discussed in the following paragraphs.

F.O.B. pricing is easy

A commonly used transportation term is **F.O.B.**—which means "free on board" some vehicle at some place. Typically, it is used with the place named—often the location of the seller's factory or warehouse—as in "F.O.B. Halifax" or "F.O.B. mill." This means that the seller pays the cost of loading the goods onto some vehicle—usually a truck, railroad car, or ship. At the point of loading, title to the goods passes to the buyer. Then the buyer pays the freight and takes responsibility for damage in transit—except as covered by the transportation company.

Variations are made easily—by changing the place part of the term. If the marketing manager wants to pay the freight for the convenience of customers, he can use: "F.O.B. delivered" or "F.O.B. buyer's factory." In this case, title does not pass until the goods are delivered. If the seller wants title to pass immediately—but is willing to prepay freight (and then include it in the invoice)—"F.O.B. seller's factory–freight prepaid" can be used.

Different geographic pricing policies may be needed to expand into new territories.

F.O.B. "shipping point" pricing simplifies the seller's pricing—but it may narrow the market. Since the delivered cost of goods varies depending on the buyer's location, a customer located farther from the seller must pay more and might buy from closer suppliers.

Zone pricing smooths delivered prices

Zone pricing means making an average freight charge to all buyers within specific geographic areas. The seller pays the actual freight charges and bills each customer for an average charge. Canada might be divided into five zones, and all buyers within each zone would pay the same freight charge.

Zone pricing reduces the wide variation in delivered prices which result from an F.O.B. shipping point pricing policy. It also simplifies charging for transportation.

This approach often is used by manufacturers of hardware and food items—both to lower the chance of price competition in the channels and to simplify figuring transportation charges for the thousands of wholesalers and retailers they serve.

Uniform delivered pricing—one price to all

Uniform delivered pricing means making an average freight charge to all buyers. It is a kind of zone pricing. An entire country may be considered as one zone—and the average cost of delivery is included in the price. It is most often used when (1) transportation costs are relatively low and (2) the seller wishes to sell in all geographic areas at one price—perhaps a nationally advertised price.

Freight-absorption pricing—competing on equal grounds in another territory

When all firms in an industry use F.O.B. shipping point pricing, a firm usually competes well near its shipping point but not farther away. As sales reps look for business farther away, delivered prices rise and the firm finds itself priced out of the market.

This problem can be reduced with **freight absorption pricing**—which means absorbing freight cost so that a firm's delivered price meets the nearest competitor's. This amounts to cutting list price to appeal to new market segments.

With freight absorption pricing, the only limit on the size of a firm's territory is the amount of freight cost it is willing to absorb. These absorbed costs cut net return on each sale, but the new business may raise total profit.

Legality of Pricing Policies

Even very high prices may be OK—if they are not fixed

From our general discussion of legislation in Chapter 4, you might think that companies have little freedom in pricing—or may even need government approval for their prices. Generally speaking, this is *not* true. They can charge what they want—even "outrageously high" prices— if these prices are not fixed with competitors.

But they should be legal—to avoid fines or jail

There are some restrictions on pricing, however. Difficulties with pricing—and perhaps violation of price legislation—usually occur only when competing marketing mixes are quite similar. When the success of an entire marketing strategy depends upon price, there is pressure (and temptation) to make agreements (conspire) with competitors. And **price fixing**—competitors getting together to raise, lower, or stabilize prices—is common and relatively easy. But it is also completely illegal. It is a "conspiracy" under the antimonopoly laws. And fixing prices can be dangerous. Some business managers have already gone to jail! And governments are getting tougher on price fixing—especially by smaller companies.

The first step to understanding pricing legislation is to know the thinking of legislators and the courts. Ideally, they try to help the economy perform more effectively in the consumers' interest. In practice, this doesn't always work out as neatly as planned. But generally their intentions are good. And if we take this view, We get a better idea of the "why" of legislation. This helps us to anticipate future rulings. We will look at Canadian legislation here, but other countries have similar laws on pricing.[10] More specifically we will discuss the kinds of pricing action the Combines Act made illegal, past difficulties in enforcing that law, and recent efforts to make enforcement easier.

Price discrimination as a violation of the Combines Act

Prior to its amendment by Bill C-2, section 34a of the Combines Act made it illegal for a supplier to discriminate in price between competitors purchasing like quantities of goods or for a buyer knowingly to benefit from such discrimination. However, it was not easy to prove that price discrimination had actually occurred.

1. There must have been two or more sales that could be compared.
2. There must have been a discount, rebate, allowance, price concession, or other advantage granted to one purchaser that was not available to another.
3. The persons between whom there was discrimination must have been purchasers in competition with each other.
4. The discriminatory prices must have applied to articles of like quality and like quantity.
5. The discriminatory transaction must have been part of a practice of discrimination.

One-shot deals or arrangements such as store-opening specials, anniversary specials, and stock clearance sales were not ruled out since they failed to constitute "a practice." Quantity and volume discounts also were not prohibited as long as they were available to all competing purchasers of like quantities. However, functional discounts—offering a larger discount to wholesalers than to retailers—were illegal. Such discounts were based on a test other than quality and quantity of the goods purchased.

Section 34a was intended to make price discrimination illegal. But because of difficulties in enforcement, no Canadian manufacturer was ever convicted of price discrimination.[11]

Amendments contained in Bill C-2 dealt with some but not all of these barriers to enforcement. Discrimination in the pricing of services as well as articles is now banned. The provision that requires "a practice" of discrimination has been deleted from the legislation. But defining what constitutes "competing customers" and "like quality" still poses enforcement problems. Also, differences in the amount purchased—even small differences—still justify whatever quantity discount structure a manufacturer chooses to use.[12]

Legal barriers to predatory pricing

Section 34b of the Combines Act outlaws regional price differentials that limit competition. This provision forbids a company making profits in one area from pricing at an unreasonably low level in another area in order to eliminate local competition. But the government must prove (1) that the company had a policy of selling the articles in one area of Canada at prices lower than those charged elsewhere in Canada and (2) that this policy had the effect, tendency, or intent of substantially lessening competition or eliminating a competitor. Section 34c of the same act contained a more general bar to predatory pricing. Very few Canadian firms have been brought to court under either of these two predatory price-cutting provisions. Bill C-2, which less strictly defines a substantial lessening of competition, may lead to more aggressive enforcement.

Discriminatory promotional allowances and the law

Section 35 of the Combines Act makes it an offense, either for a seller to offer or for a customer to seek any form of promotional allowance (including discounts, rebates, and price concessions) not offered on proportionate terms to all other competing customers. A small customer purchasing half as much as a larger competitor must receive a promotional allowance equal to half of what was offered to this competitor. In fact, this means that promotional allowances must be granted on a "per case" or "per dozen" basis. The cost of promotional allowances must also be approximately proportionate to their purchases.

This section of the Combines Act resembles the Robinson-Patman Act, which requires American manufacturers to offer competing customers "proportionately equal" promotional allowances. However, remember that in Canada, unlike in the United States, functional discounts are illegal. Wholesalers and retailers are considered to be directly competing customers who must receive proportionately equal promotional allowances.

A retail chain may get a special functional discount.

No Canadian manufacturer has as yet been convicted under this provision. This is true even though discrimination in the offering of promotional allowances is a *per se* offense. (It need not be part of a practice of discrimination or be proven substantially to have lessened competition). A manufacturer intent on discriminating would use a quantity discount structure favoring large customers, rather than a promotional allowance. For the moment at least, such discount structures are safe from legal challenge.

Legislation against misleading price advertising

The section designed to prevent deceptive price advertising has been actively policed in the courts. More aggressive prosecution may be due to the fact that misleading price advertising is a lesser offense under the Criminal Code and one easier to establish. Although the publicity surrounding a conviction may greatly harm the offender's public image, violations are usually punished by modest fines.

Bill C-2 introduced additional restrictions on misleading price advertising. One such section was directed against "bait and switch" advertising, which lures customers to a store by stressing the low price of an article that the retailer either does not stock at all or stocks only in token amounts. Under the new provision, an advertiser must stock reasonable quantities of any advertised product. However, a merchant is exempt from prosecution if he offers "rain checks" in place of an advertised but unavailable item. These rain checks must be redeemable within a reasonable period of time.

Legislation against resale price maintenance

Resale price maintenance is the marketing practice whereby a producer or brander of an article requires subsequent resellers to offer it at a stipulated (or not below a stated minimum) price. But although such a practice has been illegal in Canada since 1951, has that law been enforced? Some argue that efforts at resale price maintenance are few and far between. Others maintain that this restriction has been relatively ignored.[13]

Section 38 of Bill C-2 was intended to correct one apparent weakness in the existing legislation—its inability to deal with suppliers' exhortations to "get your price up." Any effort to bring about an increase in price or to discourage a reduction is now illegal. A number of other changes were also designed to tighten up the price discrimination rules.

New provisions—consignment selling and refusal to supply

Bill C-2 lets the Restrictive Trade Practices Commission bar **consignment selling** when such a policy is being used (*a*) to fix the price at which a dealer sells the products so supplied or (*b*) to discriminate between those receiving the product for resale.[14] Before this amendment was adopted, a supplier could control the selling price by dealing only on consignment and by specifying the commission level built into the ultimate price. Alternately, a supplier could place a favored customer on consignment and allow him a larger commission than other customers were able to take. The new consignment-selling provision of Bill C-2 made both such practices illegal.

Another Stage 1 provision allows the commission to help someone injured by a **refusal to supply**. It applies to the situation where a firm or individual is unable to obtain, on usual trade terms, adequate supplies of an article or service not generally in short supply. This amendment does not make "refusal to supply" an offense in itself. However, a complaint concerning such practices can be brought to the Restrictive Trade Practices Commission. If the complaint is upheld, the Commission can recommend to the Minister of Finance that customs duties be modified so that the injured party can import supplies on competitive terms. Alternatively, it may order that one or more suppliers accept that customer on usual trade terms.[15]

Provincial pricing legislation

British Columbia, Alberta, and Manitoba have provincial legislation that prevents firms from selling below "landed" invoice cost plus a minimum markup, such as 5 percent. Such legislation outlaws predatory pricing. But the real intent appears to involve protecting limited-line retailers from "ruinous" competition were full-line stores to sell milk below cost as a loss leader. But although such legislation may be on the books, it has not been vigorously enforced.

More recently, newly enacted Provincial Trade Practices Legislation has focused on protecting consumers from misleading price advertising and the deceptive pricing practices of door-to-door salespeople. Particular attention has been paid to seeing that any comparison of a sale price with a so-called regular price is valid.

■ CONCLUSION

The Price variable offers an alert marketing manager many possibilities for varying marketing mixes. What pricing policies will be used depends on the pricing objectives. We looked at profit-oriented, sales-oriented, status quo-oriented, and product line pricing objectives.

A marketing manager must set policies about price flexibility, price levels over the product life cycle, who will pay the freight, and who will get discounts and allowances. While doing this, the manager should be aware of pricing legislation affecting these policies.

In most cases, a marketing manager must set prices—that is, administer prices. Starting with a list price, a variety of discounts and allowances may be offered to adjust for the "Something" being offered in the marketing mix.

Throughout this chapter, we have assumed that a list price has already been set. We have talked about what may be included (or excluded) in the "Something"—and what objectives a firm might set to guide its pricing policies. Price setting itself was not discussed. It will be covered in the next chapter—showing ways of carrying out the various pricing objectives and policies.

■ QUESTIONS AND PROBLEMS

1. Identify the strategic decisions a marketing manager must make in the Price area. Illustrate your answer for a local retailer.

2. How should the acceptance of a profit-oriented, a sales-oriented, or a status quo-oriented pricing objective affect the development of a company's marketing strategy? Illustrate for each.

3. Distinguish between one-price and flexible-price policies. Which is most appropriate for a supermarket? Why?

4. Cite two examples of continuously selling above the market price. Describe the situations.

5. Explain the types of competitive situations which might lead to a "meeting competition" pricing policy.

6. What pricing objective(s) is a skimming pricing policy most likely implementing? Is the same true for a penetration pricing policy? Which policy is probably most appropriate for each of the following products: (*a*) a new type of home lawn-sprinkling system, (*b*) a new low-cost meat substitute, (*c*) a new type of children's toy, (*d*) a faster computer?

7. Discuss unfair trade practices acts. To whom are they "unfair"?

8. How would our marketing structure change if manufacturers were required to specify fair trade prices on *all* products sold at retail and *all* retailers were required to use these prices? Would this place greater or lesser importance on the development of the manufacturer's marketing mix? What kind of an operation would retailing be in this situation? Would consumers receive more or less service?

9. Is price discrimination involved if a large oil company sells gasoline to taxicab associations for resale to individual taxicab operators for 2½ cents a gallon less than the price charged to retail service stations? What happens if the cab associations resell gasoline not only to taxicab operators, but to the general public as well?

10. Indicate what the final consumer really obtains when paying the list price for the following "products": (*a*) an automobile, (*b*) a portable radio, (*c*) a package of frozen peas, and (*d*) a lipstick in a jeweled case.

11. Are seasonal discounts appropriate in agricultural businesses (which are certainly seasonal)?

12. What are the "effective" annual interest rates for the following cash discount terms: (*a*) 1/10, net 60; (*b*) 1/5, net 10; (*c*) net 30?

13. Explain how a marketing manager might change his F.O.B. terms to make his otherwise competitive marketing mix more attractive.

14. What type of geographic pricing policy is most appropriate for the following products (specify any assumptions necessary to obtain a definite answer): (*a*) a chemical by-product, (*b*) nationally advertised candy bars, (*c*) rebuilt auto parts, (*d*) tricycles?

15. Explain how the prohibition of freight absorption (that is, requiring F.O.B factory pricing) might affect a producer with substantial economies of scale in production.

■ SUGGESTED CASES

4. Tot-Switch

23. Westco Machinery Company

■ NOTES

1. For more discussion of the behavior of satisfiers, see Herbert A. Simon, *Administrative Behavior,* 2d ed. (New York: Macmillan, 1961).

2. W. Warren Haynes, *Pricing Decisions in Small Business* (Lexington: University of Kentucky Press, 1962); and Alan Reynolds, "A Kind Word for 'Cream Skimming,'" *Harvard Business Review,* November-December 1974, pp. 113–20. See also Subhash C. Jain and Michael B. Laric, "A Framework for Strategic Industrial Pricing," *Industrial Marketing Management* 8 (1979), pp. 75–80.

3. Joseph W. McGuire, John S. Y. Chiu, and Alvar O. Elving, "Executive Incomes, Sales and Profits," *American Economic Review,* September 1962, pp. 753–61; "For the Chief, Sales Sets the Pay," *Business Week,* September 30, 1967, p. 174; and Alfred Rappaport, "Executive Incentives versus Corporate Growth," *Harvard Business Review,* July-August 1978, pp. 81–88.

4. "Squeeze on Product Lines," *Business Week,* January 5, 1974, p. 50 f; and "Pricing Strategy in an Inflation Economy," *Business Week,* April 6, 1974, pp. 43–49.

5. For an interesting discussion of the many variations from a one-price system in retailing, see Stanley C. Hollander, "The 'One-Price' System—Fact or Fiction?" *Journal of Marketing Research,* February 1972, pp. 35–40. See also Michael J. Houston, "Minimum Markup Laws: An Empirical Assessment," *Journal of Retailing* 57, no. 4 (Winter 1981), pp. 98–113.

6. For more discussion on price dealing, see Charles L. Hinkle, "The Strategy of Price Deals," *Harvard Business Review,* July-August 1965, pp. 75–85.

7. See, for example, "The Airline that Thrives on Discounting," *Business Week,* July 24, 1971, pp. 68–70. See also Zarrel V. Lambert, "Product Perception: An Important Variable in Pricing Strategy," *Journal of Marketing,* October 1970, pp. 68–76; and "Price and Choice Behavior," *Journal of Marketing Research,* February 1972, pp. 35–40.

8. "Grocery Coupons Are Seen Threatened by Growth of Fraudulent Redemptions," *The Wall Street Journal,* April 12, 1976, p. 26.

9. Jo Marney, "Cents-Off: Born 1898, Still Going Strong," *Marketing,* November 16, 1981. See also "Coupon Redemption Rates and Patterns," Vol. 6, 1979, and Vol. 7, 1982, published by the A. C. Nielsen Company of Canada; and "Couponing Marks Another Record Year with 3.6 Billion Used," *Marketing,* February 25, 1985, CP–I p. 3.

10. For discussion concerning European countries, see *Market Power and the Law* (Washington, D.C.: Organization for Economic Cooperation and Development Publication Center, 1970), 206 pp.

11. For a complete summary of all court cases through late 1973 under the Combines Investigation Act, see Appendixes A and B of *Proposals for a New Competition Policy for Canada—First Stage Bill C-227* (Ottawa: Department of Consumer and Corporate Affairs, November 1973).

12. Bruce Mallen, "The Combines Investigation Act: Canada's Major Marketing Statute," in *Cases and Readings in Marketing,* ed. W. H. Kirpalani and R. H. Rotenberg (Toronto: Holt, Rinehart & Winston of Canada, 1974), pp. 169–70. The same source was used in trying to assess the actual impact and the barriers to enforcement of other presently existing Combines Act Trade Practices Provisions.

13. D. N. Thompson, "Competition Policy and Marketing Regulation," in *Canadian Marketing: Problems and Prospects,* D. N. Thompson and David S. R. Leighton (Toronto: Wiley Publishers of Canada, 1973), pp. 14–15; also D. N. Thompson, "Resale Price Maintenance and Refusal to Sell: Aspects of a Problem in Competition of Policy," *University of Toronto Law Journal* 21 (1971) pp. 82–86.

14. This section draws heavily upon the corresponding discussion found in *Proposals for a New Competition Policy for Canada,* pp. 44–46 and 67–68.

15. Ibid.

Appendix E ■ Marketing arithmetic

When you finish this appendix, you should:

1. Understand the components of an operating statement (profit and loss statement).
2. Know how to compute the stockturn rate.
3. Understand how operating ratios can help analyze a business.
4. Understand how to calculate markups and markdowns.
5. Understand how to calculate return on investment (ROI) and return on assets (ROA).
6. Recognize the important new terms (shown in red).

Business students must become familiar with the essentials of the "language of business." Business people commonly use accounting language when discussing costs, prices, and profit. So you need to understand this terminology. Using accounting data is a practical tool in analyzing marketing problems.

The following discussion introduces the basic ideas underlying the operating statement, some commonly used ratios related to the operating statement, mark-ups, the markdown ratio, and ROI and ROA ratios. Other analytical techniques are discussed in various parts of the text—and are not treated separately here.

The Operating Statement

An operating statement for a wholesale or retail business—commonly referred to as a profit and loss statement—is presented in Figure E–1. A complete and detailed statement is shown so you will see the framework throughout the discussion—but the amount of detail on an operating statement is not standardized. Many companies use financial statements with much less detail than this one. Their emphasis is on clarity and readability—rather than detail. To understand an operating statement, however, you must know about its parts.

The **operating statement** is a simple summary of the financial results of the operations of a company over a specified period of time. Some beginning students may feel that the operating statement is complex—but as we shall see, this really isn't true. *The main purpose of the operating statement is determining the net profit figure—and presenting data to support that figure.*

Only three basic components

The basic components of an operating statement are *sales*—which come from the sale of goods or services; *costs*—which come from the making and selling process; and the balance—called *profit or loss*—which is just the difference between sales and costs. So there are only three basic components in the statement: *sales, costs,* and *profit (or loss).*

Time period covered may vary

There is no one time period which an operating statement covers. Rather, statements are prepared to satisfy the needs of a particular business. This may be at the end of each day—or at the end of each week. Usually, however, an operating statement summarizes results for one month, three months, six months, or a full year. Since the time period does vary, this information is included in the heading of the statement as follows:

XYZ Company
Operating Statement
For the (Period) Ended (Date)

Also, see Figure E–1.

Management uses of operating statements

Before going on to a more detailed discussion of the components of our operating statement, think about some of the uses for such a statement. A glance at

■ FIGURE E–1   An operating statement (profit and loss statement)

XYZ COMPANY
Operating Statement
For the Year Ended December 31, 198X

Gross sales			$54,000
Less: Returns and allowances			4,000
Net sales			$50,000
Cost of goods sold:			
Beginning inventory at cost		$ 8,000	
Purchases at billed cost	$31,000		
Less: Purchase discounts	4,000		
Purchases at net cost	27,000		
Plus freight-in	2,000		
Net cost of delivered purchases		29,000	
Cost of goods available for sale		37,000	
Less: Ending inventory at cost		7,000	
Cost of goods sold			30,000
Gross margin (gross profit)			20,000
Expenses:			
Selling expenses:			
Sales salaries	6,000		
Advertising expense	2,000		
Delivery expense	2,000		
Total selling expense		10,000	
Administrative expense:			
Office salaries	3,000		
Office supplies	1,000		
Miscellaneous administrative expense	500		
Total administrative expense		4,500	
General expense:			
Rent expense	1,000		
Miscellaneous general expenses	500		
Total general expense		1,500	
Total expenses			16,000
Net profit from operation			$ 4,000

Figure E–1 shows that a wealth of information is presented in a clear and concise manner. With this information, management can easily find the relation of its net sales to the cost of goods sold, the gross margin, expenses, and net profit. Opening and closing inventory figures are available—as is the amount spent during the period for the purchase of goods for resale. The total expenses are listed to make it easier to compare them with previous statements—and to help control these expenses.

All of this information is important to the management of a company. Assume that a particular company prepared monthly operating statements. It should be obvious that a series of these statements would be a valuable tool for the direction and control of the business. By comparing results from one month to the next, management can uncover unfavorable trends in the sales, expense, or profit areas of the business—and take the needed action.

A skeleton statement gets down to essential details

Let's refer to Figure E–1 and begin to analyze this seemingly detailed statement. The intention at this point is to get first-hand knowledge of the components of the operating statement.

As a first step, suppose we take all the items that have dollar amounts extended to the third, or right-hand, column. Using these items only, the operating statement looks like this:

Gross sales.	$54,000
Less: Returns and allowances	4,000
Net sales.	$50,000
Less: Cost of goods sold.	30,000
Gross margin	$20,000
Less: Total expenses	16,000
Net profit (loss)	$ 4,000

Is this a complete operating statement? The answer is yes. This skeleton statement differs from Figure E–1 only in supporting detail. All the basic components are included. In fact, the only items we *must* list to have a *complete* operating statement are:

Net sales.	$50,000
Less: Costs.	46,000
Net profit (loss)	$ 4,000

These three items are the *essence* of an operating statement. All other subdivisions or details are just useful additions.

Meaning of "sales"

Now let's define and explore the meaning of the terms that are used in the skeleton statement.

The first item is "sales." What do we mean by sales? The term **gross sales** is the total amount charged to all customers during some time period. It is certain, however, that there will be some customer dissatisfaction—or just plain errors in ordering and shipping goods. This results in returns and allowances—which reduce gross sales.

A **return** occurs when a customer sends back purchased products. The company either refunds the purchase price or allows the customer dollar credit on other purchases.

An **allowance** occurs when a customer is not satisfied with a purchase for some reason. The company gives a price reduction on the original invoice (bill), but the customer keeps the goods or services.

These refunds and price reductions must be considered when the net sales figure for the period is computed. Really, we are only interested in the revenue which the company manages to keep. This is **net sales**—the actual sales dollars the company will receive. Therefore, all reductions, refunds, cancellations, and so forth—made because of returns and allowances—are deducted from the original total (gross sales) to get net sales. This is shown below:

Gross sales.	$54,000
Less: Returns and allowances	4,000
Net sales.	$50,000

Meaning of "cost of goods sold"

The next item in the operating statement—**cost of goods sold**—is the total value (at cost) of all the goods sold during the period. We will discuss this computation later. Meanwhile, merely note that after the cost of goods sold figure is obtained, it is subtracted from the net sales figure to get the gross margin.

Meaning of "gross margin" and "expenses"

Gross margin (gross profit) is the money left to cover the cost of selling the products and managing the business. The hope is that a profit will be left after subtracting these expenses.

Selling expense commonly is the major expense below the gross margin. Note that in Figure E–1, all **expenses** are subtracted from the gross margin to get the net profit. The expenses in this case are the selling, administrative, and general expenses. (Note that the cost of purchases and cost of goods sold are not included in this total expense figure—they were subtracted from net sales earlier to get the gross margin.)

Net profit—at the bottom of the statement—is what the company has earned from its operations during a particular period. It is the amount left after the cost of goods sold and the expenses have been subtracted from net sales. Note: net sales and net profit are not the same—as many naive people believe. Many firms have large sales and no profits—or even losses!

Detailed Analysis of Sections of the Operating Statement

Cost of goods sold for a wholesale or retail company

The cost of goods sold section includes details which are used to find the "cost of goods sold" ($30,000 in our example).

In Figure E–1, it is obvious that beginning and ending inventory, purchases, purchase discounts, and freight-in are all necessary in calculating costs of goods sold. If we pull the cost of goods sold section from the operating statement, it looks like this:

Cost of goods sold		
Beginning inventory at cost		$ 8,000
Purchases at billed cost	$31,000	
Less: Purchase discounts	4,000	
Purchases at net cost	$27,000	
Plus: Freight-in	2,000	
Net cost of delivered purchases		29,000
Cost of goods available for sale		$37,000
Less: Ending inventory at cost		7,000
Cost of goods sold		$30,000

"Cost of goods sold" is the cost value of goods *sold*—that is, actually removed from the company's control—and not the cost value of goods on hand at any given time.

The inventory figures merely show the cost of merchandise on hand at the beginning and end of the period the statement covers. These figures may be obtained by a physical count of the merchandise on hand on these dates—or they may be estimated through a system of perpetual inventory bookkeeping which would show the inventory balance at any given time. The methods used in determining the inventory should be as accurate as possible—since these figures affect the cost of goods sold during the period, and net profit.

The net cost of delivered purchases must include freight charges and purchase discounts received—since these items affect the money actually spent to buy goods and bring them to the place of business. A **purchase discount** is a reduction of the original invoice amount for some business reason. For example, a cash discount may be given for prompt payment of the amount due. The total of such discounts is subtracted from the original invoice cost of purchases to get the *net* cost of purchases. To this figure we add the freight charges for bringing the goods to the place of business. This gives the net cost of *delivered* purchases. When the net cost of delivered purchases is added to the beginning inventory at cost, we have the total cost of goods available for sale during the period. If we now subtract the ending inventory at cost from the cost of the goods available for sale, we finally get the cost of goods sold.

One important point should be noted about cost of goods sold. The way the value of inventory is calculated varies from one company to another—and different methods can cause big differences on the operating statement. See any basic accounting textbook for how the various inventory valuation methods work.

Cost of goods sold for a manufacturing company

Figure E–1 shows the way the manager of a wholesale or retail business arrives at his cost of goods sold. Such a business *purchases* finished goods and resells them. In a manufacturing company, the "purchases" section of this operating statement is replaced by a section called "cost of goods manufactured." This section includes purchases of raw materials and parts, direct and indirect labor costs, and factory overhead charges (such as heat, light, and power)—which are necessary to produce finished goods. The cost of goods manufactured is added to the beginning finished-goods inventory to arrive at the cost of goods available for sale. Often, a separate cost of goods manufactured statement is prepared—and only the total cost of production is shown in the operating statement. See Figure E–2 for an illustration of the cost of goods sold section of an operating statement for a manufacturing company.

Expenses

"Expenses" go below the gross margin. They usually include the costs of selling, and the costs of administering the business. They do not include the cost of goods—either purchased or produced.

There is no "right" method for classifying the expense accounts or arranging them on the operating statement. They can just as easily be arranged alphabetically—or according to amount, with the largest placed at the top and so on down the line. In a business of any size, though, it is desirable to group the expenses in some way—and to use subtotals by groups for analysis and control purposes. This was done in Figure E–1.

Summary on operating statements

The statement presented in Figure E–1 contains all the major categories in an operating statement—together with a normal amount of supporting detail. Further detail can be added to the statement under any of the major categories—

■ **FIGURE E–2**   Cost of goods sold section of an operating statement for a manufacturing firm

Cost of goods sold:			
Finished goods inventory (beginning)...............		$ 20,000	
Cost of goods manufactured (Schedule 1)...........		100,000	
Total cost of finished goods available for sale		120,000	
Less: Finished goods inventory (ending)		30,000	
Cost of goods sold			$ 90,000

Schedule 1, Schedule of cost of goods manufactured

Beginning work in process inventory..................			15,000
Raw materials			
Beginning raw materials inventory		10,000	
Net cost of delivered purchases....................		80,000	
Total cost of materials available for use..............		90,000	
Less: Ending raw materials inventory..............		15,000	
Cost of materials placed in production		75,000	
Direct labor.......................................		20,000	
Manufacturing expenses			
Indirect labor	$4,000		
Maintenance and repairs	3,000		
Factory supplies	1,000		
Heat, light, and power............................	2,000		
Total manufacturing expenses		10,000	
Total manufacturing costs			105,000
Total work in process during period...................			120,000
Less: Ending work in process inventory			20,000
Cost of goods manufactured....................			$100,000

Note: The last item, cost of goods manufactured, is used in the operating statement to determine the cost of goods sold, as above.

without changing the nature of the statement. The amount of detail normally is determined by how the statement will be used. A stockholder may be given a sketchy operating statement—while the one prepared for internal company use may have a great amount of detail.

We have already seen that eliminating some of the detail in Figure E–1 did not affect the essential elements of the statement—net sales, costs, and net profit (or loss). Whatever further detail is added to the statement, its purpose is to help the reader see how those three figures were determined. A very detailed statement can easily run to several single-spaced pages—yet the nature of the operating statement is the same.

Computing the Stockturn Rate

A detailed operating statement can provide the data needed to compute the **stockturn rate**—a measure of the number of times the average inventory is sold during a year. Note that the stockturn rate is related to the *turnover during a year*—not the length of time covered by a particular operating statement.

The stockturn rate is a very important measure—because it shows how rapidly the firm's inventory is moving. Some businesses typically have slower turnover than others—but a drop in the rate of turnover in a particular business can be very alarming. For one thing, it may mean that the firm's assortment of products is no longer as attractive as it was. Also, it may mean that more working capital will be needed to handle the same volume of sales. Most businesses pay a lot of attention to the stockturn rate—trying to get faster turnover.

Three methods—all basically similar—can be used to compute the stockturn rate. Which method is used depends on the data available. These three methods are shown below—and usually give approximately the same results.*

$$\frac{\text{Cost of goods sold}}{\text{Average inventory at cost}} \qquad (1)$$

$$\frac{\text{Net sales}}{\text{Average inventory at selling price}} \qquad (2)$$

$$\frac{\text{Sales in units}}{\text{Average inventory in units}} \qquad (3)$$

Computing the stockturn rate will be illustrated only for Formula 1—since all are similar. The only difference is that the cost figures used in Formula 1 are changed to a selling price or numerical count basis in Formulas 2 and 3. Note: it is necessary—regardless of the method used—to have both the numerator and denominator of the formula in the same terms.

Using Formula 1, the average inventory at cost is computed by adding the beginning and ending inventories at cost—and dividing by 2. This average inventory figure is then divided *into* the cost of goods sold (in cost terms) to get the stockturn rate.

For example, suppose that the cost of goods sold for one year was $100,000. Beginning inventory was $25,000 and ending inventory, $15,000. Adding the two inventory figures and dividing by 2, we get an average inventory of $20,000. We next divide the cost of goods sold by the average inventory ($100,000 divided by $20,000) and get a stockturn rate of 5.

Further discussion of the use of the stockturn rate is found in Chapter 20.

Operating Ratios Help Analyze the Business

Many business people use the operating statement to calculate **operating ratios**—the ratio of items on the operating statement to net sales—and compare these ratios from one time period to another. They can also compare their own operating ratios with those of competitors. Such competitive data is often available through trade associations. Each firm may report its results to the trade

---

*Differences will occur because of varied markups and non-homogeneous product assortments. In an assortment of tires, for example, those with high markups might have sold much better than those with small markups—but with Formula 3, all tires would be treated equally.

association—and then summary results are distributed to the members. These ratios help management to control their operations. If some expense ratios are rising, for example, those particular costs are singled out for special attention.

Operating ratios are computed by dividing net sales into the various operating statement items which appear below the net sales level in the operating statement. Net sales is used as the denominator in the operating ratio—because it is this figure with which the business manager is most concerned—that is, the revenue actually received by the business.

We can see the relation of operating ratios to the operating statement if we think of there being an additional column to the right of the dollar figures in an operating statement. This additional column contains percentage figures—using net sales as 100 percent. This can be seen below:

Gross sales	$540.00	
Less: Returns and allowances	40.00	
Net sales	$500.00	100%
Cost of goods sold	350.00	70
Gross margin	150.00	30
Expenses	100.00	20
Net profit	$ 50.00	10%

The 30 percent ratio of gross margin to net sales in the above illustration shows that 30 percent of the net sales dollar is available to cover sales expenses and the administration of the business—and provide a profit. Note that the ratio of expenses to sales added to the ratio of profit to sales equals the 30 percent gross margin ratio. The net profit ratio of 10 percent shows that 10 percent of the net sales dollar is left for profit.

The usefulness of percentage ratios should be obvious. The percentages are easily figured—and much easier to work with than large dollar figures. With net sales as the base figure, they provide a useful means of comparison and control.

Note that because of the interrelationship of these various categories, only a few pieces of information are necessary to figure the others. In this case, for example, knowing the gross margin percent and net profit percent makes it possible to figure the expense and cost of goods sold percentages. Further, knowing just one dollar amount lets you figure all the other dollar amounts.

Markups

A **markup** is the dollar amount added to the cost of goods to get the selling price. The markup is similar to the gross margin. Gross margin and the idea of markups are related because the amount added onto the unit cost of a product by a retailer or wholesaler is expected to cover the selling and administrative expenses—and to provide a profit.

The markup approach to pricing is discussed in Chapter 20—so it will not be discussed at length here. A simple example will illustrate the idea, however. If a retailer buys an article which cost $1 when delivered to his store, then obviously he must sell it for more than this cost if he hopes to make a profit. So he might add 50 cents onto the cost of the article in order to cover his selling and other costs and, hopefully, to provide a profit. The 50 cents would be the markup.

It would also be the gross margin or gross profit on that item *if* it is sold—but note that it is *not* the net profit. His selling expenses may amount to 35 cents, 45 cents, or even 55 cents. In other words, there is no assurance that the markup will cover his costs. Further, there is no assurance that the customers will buy at the marked-up price. This may require markdowns—which are discussed later in this appendix.

Markup conversions

Sometimes it is convenient to talk in terms of markups on cost, while at other times markups on selling price are useful. To have some agreement, *markup* (without any explanation) will mean percentage of selling price. By this definition, the 50 cents markup on the $1.50 selling price is a markup of 33⅓ percent.

Some retailers and wholesalers have developed markup conversion tables—so they can easily convert from cost to selling price—depending on the markup on selling price they want. To see the interrelation, look at the two formulas below. They can be used to convert either type of markup to the other.

$$\text{Percentage markup on selling price} = \frac{\text{Percent markup on cost}}{100\% + \text{Percentage markup on cost}} \tag{4}$$

$$\text{Percentage markup on cost} = \frac{\text{Percent markup on selling cost}}{100\% - \text{Percentage markup on selling price}} \tag{5}$$

In the previous example, we had a cost of $1, a markup of 50 cents, and a selling price of $1.50. We saw that the markup on selling price was 33⅓ per-cent—and on cost, it was 50 percent. Let's substitute these percentage figures—in Formulas 4 and 5—to see how to convert from one basis to the other. Assume first of all that we only know the markup on selling price—and want to convert to markup on cost. Using Formula 5, we obtain:

$$\text{Percentage markup on cost} = \frac{33\tfrac{1}{3}\%}{100\% - 33\tfrac{1}{3}\%} = \frac{33\tfrac{1}{3}\%}{66\tfrac{2}{3}\%} = 50\%$$

If we know, on the other hand, only the percentage markup on cost, we can convert to markup on selling price as follows:

$$\text{Percentage markup on selling price} = \frac{50\%}{100\% + 50\%} = \frac{50\%}{150\%} = 33\tfrac{1}{3}\%$$

These results can be proved and summarized as follows:

$$
\begin{array}{l}
\text{Markup } \$0.50 = 50\% \text{ of cost, or } 33\tfrac{1}{3}\% \text{ of selling price} \\
\underline{+ \text{ Cost } \$1.00 = 100\% \text{ of cost, or } 66\tfrac{2}{3}\% \text{ of selling price}} \\
\text{Selling price } \$1.50 = 150\% \text{ of cost, or } 100\% \text{ of selling price}
\end{array}
$$

It is important to see that only the percentage figures change—while the money amounts of cost, markup, and selling price stay the same. Note, too, that when selling price is the base for the calculation (100 percent), then the cost percentage plus the markup percentage equal 100 percent. But when the cost of the product is used as the base figure (100 percent), it is obvious that the selling price percentage must be greater than 100 percent—by the markup on cost.

Markdown Ratios Help Control Retail Operations

The ratios we discussed above were concerned with figures on the operating statement. Another important ratio, the **markdown ratio**—is a tool used by many retailers to measure the efficiency of various departments and their whole business. But note—it is *not directly related to the operating statement.* It requires special calculations.

A **markdown** is a retail price reduction which is required because the customers will not buy some item at the originally marked-up price. This refusal to buy may be due to a variety of reasons—soiling, style changes, fading, damage caused by handling, or an original markup which was too high. To get rid of these products, the retailer offers them at a lower price.

Markdowns are generally considered to be due to "business errors"—perhaps because of poor buying, too high original markups, and other reasons. Regardless of the cause, however, markdowns are reductions in the original price—and are important to managers who want to measure the effectiveness of their operations.

Markdowns are similar to allowances—because price reductions are made. Thus, in computing a markdown ratio, markdowns and allowances are usually added together and then divided by net sales. The markdown ratio is computed as follows:

$$\text{Markdown \%} = \frac{\$ \text{ Markdowns} + \$ \text{ Allowances}}{\$ \text{ Net sales}} \times 100$$

The 100 is multiplied by the fraction to get rid of decimal points.

Returns are *not* included when figuring the markdown ratio. Returns are treated as "consumer errors"—not business errors—and therefore are *not* included in this measure of business efficiency.

Retailers who use markdown ratios keep a record of the amount of markdowns and allowances in each department—and then divide the total by the net sales in each department. Over a period of time, these ratios give management a measure of the efficiency of the buyers and salespeople in the various departments.

It should be stressed again that the markdown ratio is not calculated directly from data on the operating statement—since the markdowns take place before the products are sold. In fact, some products may be marked down and still not sold. Even if the marked-down items are not sold, the markdowns—that is, the reevaluations of their value—are included in the calculations in the time period when they are taken.

The markdown ratio is calculated for a whole department (or profit center)— *not* individual items. What we are seeking is a measure of the effectiveness of a whole department—not how well the department did on individual items.

Return on Investment (ROI) Reflects Asset Use

Another "off the operating statement" ratio is **return on investment (ROI)**—the ratio of net profit (after taxes) to the investment used to make the net profit—multiplied by 100 to get rid of decimals. "Investment" is not shown on the operating statement—but it is on the **balance sheet** (statement of financial condition)—another accounting statement—which shows the assets, liabilities, and net worth of a company. It may take some "digging" or special analysis, however, to find the right investment number.

"Investment" means the dollar resources the firm has "invested" in a project or business. For example, a new product may require $400,000 in new money—for inventory, accounts receivable, promotion, and so on—and its attractiveness may be judged by its likely ROI. If the net profit (after taxes) for this new product is expected to be $100,000 in the first year, then the ROI is 25 percent—that is, ($100,000 ÷ $400,000) × 100.

There are two ways to figure ROI. The *direct* way is:

$$\text{ROI (in \%)} = \frac{\text{Net profit (after taxes)}}{\text{Investment}} \times 100$$

The *indirect* way is:

$$\text{ROI (in \%)} = \frac{\text{Net profit (after taxes)}}{\text{Sales}} \times \frac{\text{Sales}}{\text{Investment}} \times 100$$

This way is concerned with net profit margin and turnover—that is:

$$\text{ROI (in \%)} = \text{Net profit margin} \times \text{Turnover} \times 100$$

This indirect way makes it clearer how to *increase* ROI. There are three ways:

1. Increase profit margin.
2. Increase sales.
3. Decrease investment.

Effective marketing strategy planning and implementation are ways of increasing profit margin and/or sales. And careful asset management can decrease investment.

ROI is a revealing measure of managerial effectiveness. Most companies have alternative uses for their funds. If the returns in the business aren't at least as high as outside uses, then the money probably should be shifted to the more profitable uses. Further, many companies must borrow to finance some of their operation. So the ROI should be higher than the cost of money—or the company should cut back until it can operate more profitably.

Some firms borrow more than others to make "investments." In other words, they invest less of their own money to acquire assets—what we have called "investments." If ROI calculations use only the firm's own "investment," this gives higher ROI figures to those who borrow a lot—which is called leveraging. To adjust for different borrowing proportions—to make comparisons among projects, departments, divisions, and companies easier—another ratio (ROA) has come into use. **Return on assets (ROA)** is the ratio of net profit (after taxes) to the assets used to make the net profit—times 100.

Both ROI and ROA measures are trying to get at the same thing—how effectively the company is using resources. These measures have become increasingly popular as profit rates have dropped and it becomes more obvious that increasing sales volume does not necessarily lead to higher profits—or ROI—or ROA. Further, inflation and higher costs for borrowed funds force more concern for ROI and ROA. Marketers must include these measures in their thinking—or top managers are likely to ignore their plans—and requests for financial resources.

■ QUESTIONS AND PROBLEMS

---

1. Distinguish between the following pairs of items which appear on operating statements: (a) gross sales and net sales, (b) purchases at billed cost and purchases at net cost, and (c) cost of goods available for sale and cost of goods sold.

2. How does gross margin differ from gross profit? From net profit?

3. Explain the similarity between markups and gross margin. What connection do markdowns have with the operating statement?

4. Compute the net profit for a company with the following data:

Beginning inventory (cost)	$ 15,000
Purchases at billed cost	33,000
Sales returns and allowances	25,000
Rent	6,000
Salaries	40,000
Heat and light	18,000
Ending inventory (cost)	25,000
Freight cost (inbound)	9,000
Gross sales	130,000

5. Construct an operating statement from the following data:

Returns and allowances	$ 15,000
Expenses	20%
Closing inventory at cost	60,000
Markdowns	2%
Inward transportation	3,000
Purchases	100,000
Net profit (5%)	30,000

6. Data given:

Markdowns	$ 10,000
Gross sales	100,000
Returns	8,000
Allowances	12,000

Compute net sales and percent of markdowns.

7. (a) What percentage markups on cost are equivalent to the following percentage markups on selling price: 20, 37½, 50, and 66⅔? (b) What percentage markups on selling price are equivalent to the following percentage markups on cost: 33⅓, 20, 40, and 50?

8. What net sales volume is required to secure a stockturn rate of 20 times a year on an average inventory at cost of $100,000, with a gross margin of 30 percent?

9. Explain how the general manager of a department store might use the markdown ratios computed for his various departments? Is this a fair measure? Of what?

10. Compare and contrast return on investment (ROI) and return on assets (ROA) measures. Which would be best for a retailer with no bank borrowing or other outside sources of funds; i.e., the retailer has put up all the money that is needed in the business?

Chapter 20 ■ Price setting in the real world

When you finish this chapter, you should:

1. Understand how most wholesalers and retailers set their prices—using markups.

2. Understand why turnover is so important in pricing.

3. Understand the advantages and disadvantages of average cost pricing.

4. Know how to use break-even analysis to evaluate possible prices.

5. Know how to find the most profitable price and quantity—using marginal analysis, and total revenue and total cost.

6. Know the many ways that price setters use demand estimates in their pricing.

7. Recognize the important new terms (shown in red).

"How should I price this product?" is a common problem facing marketing managers.

In the last chapter, we accepted the idea of a list price and went on to discuss variations from list. Now, we will see how the basic list price might be set in the first place.

For example, think about how a paint and wallpaper store might price a new item—a paint sprayer that costs the store $80. The store may arrive at a list price by adding the same dollar amount it adds to paint that costs $80. Or, the store may simply use a list price suggested by the sprayer's manufacturer. Or, the manager may price the sprayer based on estimates of demand . . . considering how many sprayers might be sold at different price levels.

As this example suggests, there are many ways to set list prices. But—for simplicity—these can be reduced to two basic approaches: *cost-oriented* and *demand-oriented* price setting. We will discuss cost-oriented approaches first. They are most common. Also, understanding the problems of relying only on a cost-oriented approach helps to show why demand must be considered to make good price decisions. Let's begin by looking at how most retailers and wholesalers set cost-oriented prices.

Pricing by Wholesalers and Retailers

Markups guide pricing by middlemen

Most retailers and wholesalers set prices by using a **markup**—a dollar amount added to the cost of goods to get the selling price. For example, suppose that a drug store buys a bottle of shampoo for $1. To make a profit, the drug

639

store obviously must sell this article for more than $1. If 50 cents is added to cover operating expenses and provide a profit, we say that the store is marking up the item 50 cents.

Markups, however, usually are stated as percentages—rather than dollar amounts. And this is where confusion sometimes arises. Is a markup of 50 cents on a cost of $1 a markup of 50 percent? Or should the markup be figured as a percentage of the selling price—$1.50—and therefore be 33⅓ percent? A clear definition is necessary.

Markup percent is based on selling price—a convenient rule

Unless otherwise stated, **markup (percent)** means percentage of selling price which is added to the cost to get the selling price. So the 50-cent markup on the $1.50 selling price is a markup of 33⅓ percent. Markups are related to selling price for convenience.

There is nothing wrong, however, with the idea of markup on cost. The important thing is to state clearly which markup percent we are using—to avoid confusion.

Managers often need to change a markup on cost to one based on selling price—or vice versa.[1] The calculations to do this are simple (see the section on markup conversion in Appendix E on marketing arithmetic).

Many use a "standard" markup percent

It's very common for a middleman to set prices on all of his products by applying the same markup percent. This makes pricing easier! When you think of the large number of items the average retailer and wholesaler carry—and the small sales volume of any one item—this approach makes sense. Spending the time to find the "best" price to charge on every item in stock (day-to-day or week-to-week) probably wouldn't pay.

Moreover, the same markup percent is often used by different companies in the same line of business. There is a reason for this. A standard markup will work only if it is large enough to cover the firm's operating expenses—and provide a reasonable profit. Firms in the same line of business often use the same markup because their operating expenses are usually similar. This also explains why the "customary" markup may vary across different types of business—where operating expenses are different.

Markups are related to gross margins

How do managers decide on a standard markup in the first place? It is usually based on information about the firm's *gross margin*. Managers regularly see gross margins on their profit and loss statements. (See Appendix E on marketing arithmetic—it follows Chapter 19—if you are unfamiliar with these ideas.) They know that unless there is a large enough gross margin, there won't be any profit. For this reason, they accept a markup percent that is close to their usual gross margin (percent).

Smart manufacturers pay attention to the gross margins and standard markups of middlemen in their channel. They usually allow trade (functional) discounts that are very similar to the standard markups expected by these middlemen.

Markup chain may be used in channel pricing	The markup used by different firms in a channel often varies. A **markup chain**—the sequence of markups used by firms at different levels in a channel—determines the price structure in the whole channel. For example, the markup chain in the channel for an electric drill may be 10 percent for the manufacturer, 20 percent for the power tool wholesaler, and 40 percent for the retail hardware store that sells it to consumers. The markup is figured on the *selling price* at each level of the channel.

The producer's selling price becomes the wholesaler's cost—the wholesaler's selling price becomes the retailer's cost—and this cost plus a retail markup becomes the retail selling price. Each markup should cover the costs of selling and running the business—and leave a profit. The markup chain can set the price structure in the whole channel. If some markup in the chain is "too high," the final price on a product may be more than customers are willing to pay!

Figure 20–1 illustrates the markup chain for the electric drill at each level of the channel system. The production (factory) cost of the drill is $21.60. In this case, the producer is taking a 10 percent markup and sells the goods for $24. The markup is 10 percent of $24 or $2.40. The producer's selling price now becomes the wholesaler's cost—$24. If the wholesaler is used to taking a 20 percent markup on selling price, the markup is $6—and the wholesaler's selling price becomes $30. $30 now becomes the cost for the hardware retailer. And if the retailer is used to a 40 percent markup, $20 is added, and the retail selling price becomes $50.

High markups don't always mean big profits	Some people—including many retailers—think high markups mean high profits. But this is often not true. A high markup may result in a price that's too high—a price at which few customers will buy. The key is the quantity sold at a particular margin. You can't earn much if you don't sell much—no matter how high your markup. But many retailers and wholesalers seem more concerned with the size of their markup on a single item than with their total profit.

Lower markups can speed turnover—and the stockturn rate	Some retailers and wholesalers, however, try to speed turnover to increase profit—even if this means reducing the markup. They realize that the business is running up costs over time. If they can sell a much greater amount in the same

■ FIGURE 20–1   Example of a markup chain and channel pricing

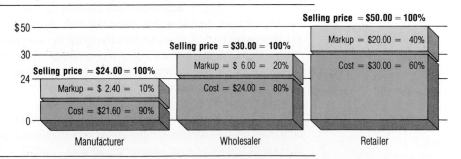

Items with a high stock-turn rate may have a lower markup.

time period, they may be able to take a lower markup—and still have a higher profit at the end of the period.

An important idea here is the **stockturn rate**—the number of times the average inventory is sold in a year. Various methods of figuring stockturn rates can be used (see the section "Computing the Stockturn Rate" in Appendix E). If the stockturn rate is low, this may be bad for profits.

At the very least, a low stockturn will increase inventory carrying cost and tie up working capital. If a firm with a stockturn of 1 (once per year) sells goods which cost it $100,000, that much is tied up in inventory all the time. But a stockturn of 5 requires only $20,000 worth of inventory ($100,000 cost divided by 5 turnovers a year).

Whether a stockturn rate is high or low depends on the industry and product involved. An annual rate of 1 may be expected by an auto parts wholesaler—while a grocery retailer would expect 10 to 12 stockturns for soap and detergents and 40 to 50 stockturns for fresh fruits and vegetables.

Supermarkets and mass-merchandisers run in fast company

We have noted that many middlemen use the same "customary" markup percent on different products for convenience. But some businesses—like supermarkets and mass-merchandisers—know the importance of fast turnover. They put low markups on fast-selling items—and higher markups on items which sell less frequently. For example, a mass-merchandiser may put a small margin (like 20 percent) on fast-selling health and beauty aids (toothpaste or shampoo) but put higher margins on appliances and clothing. Similarly, supermarket operators put low markups on fast-selling items like milk, eggs, and detergents. The markup on these items may be less than half the average markup for all grocery items, but this doesn't mean they are unprofitable. The small profit per unit is earned more often. Fast-moving goods are usually less expensive to sell, too. They take up valuable space for shorter periods, are damaged less, and tie up less working capital.

Food discounters carry the fast turnover idea even further. By pricing products even lower—attracting more customers from wider areas—they are able to operate profitably on even smaller margins.

Pricing by Producers

It's up to the producer to set the list price

Some markups eventually become customary in a trade. Most of the channel members tend to follow a similar process—adding a certain percentage to the previous price. Who sets price in the first place?

The basic list price usually is decided by the producer and/or brander of the product—a large retailer, a large wholesaler, or most often, the producer. Now we'll look at the pricing approaches of such firms. For convenience, we will call them "producers."

Customary formulas are common

Producers commonly use a cost-oriented approach. They may start with a dollar-cost-per-unit figure and add a markup—perhaps a customary percentage—to obtain the selling price. Or they may use some rule-of-thumb formula such as: *Production cost* × 3 = *Selling price.*

Each producer usually develops rules and markups related to its own costs and objectives. Yet even the first step—selecting the appropriate cost per unit to build on—isn't easy. Let's discuss several approaches to see how cost-oriented price setting really works.

Average-Cost Pricing Is Common and Dangerous

Average-cost pricing is adding a "reasonable" markup to the average cost of a product. The average cost per unit is usually found by studying past records. The total cost for the last year may be divided by all the units produced and sold in that period to get the "expected" average cost per unit for the next year. If the total cost was $5,000 for labor and materials and $5,000 for fixed overhead expenses—such as selling expenses, rent, and manager salaries—then "expected" total cost is $10,000. If the company produced 10,000 items in that time period, the "expected" average cost is $1 per unit. To get the price, the producer decides how much profit per unit seems "reasonable." This is added to the average cost per unit. If 10 cents is considered a reasonable profit for each unit, then the new price is set at $1.10. See Figure 20–2.

It does not make allowances for cost variations as output changes

This approach is simple. But it can also be dangerous. It's easy to lose money with average-cost pricing. To see why, let's follow this example further.

First, remember that the average cost of $1 per unit was based on output of 10,000 units. But, if in the next year only 5,000 units are produced and sold, the firm may be in trouble. Five thousand units sold at $1.10 each ($1.00 cost plus $.10 for "profit") yields a total revenue of only $5,500. The overhead is still fixed at $5,000, and the variable material and labor cost drops in half to $2,500—for a total cost of $7,500. This means a loss of $2,000, or 40 cents a unit. The method that was supposed to allow a profit of 10 cents a unit actually causes a loss of 40 cents a unit! See Figure 20–2.

■ FIGURE 20–2   Results of average-cost pricing

Calculation of planned profit if 10,000 items are sold	Calculation of actual profit if only 5,000 items are sold
Calculation of costs:	Calculation of costs:
Fixed overhead expenses .... $ 5,000	Fixed overhead expenses $5,000
Labor and materials................. 5,000	Labor and materials................. 2,500
Total costs 10,000	Total costs $7,500
"Reasonable" profit 1,000	
Total costs and planned profit $11,000	

Calculation of "reasonable" price for both possibilities:

$$\frac{\text{Total costs and planned profit}}{\text{Planned number of items to be sold}} = \frac{\$11,000}{10,000} = \$1.10 = \text{"Reasonable" price}$$

Calculation of profit or (loss):	Calculation of profit or (loss):
Actual unit sales (10,000) times price	Actual unit sales (5,000) times price
($1.10) = ... $11,000	($1.10) =....................... $5,500
Minus: Total costs................... 10,000	Minus: Total costs................. 7,500
Profit (loss) .... $ 1,000	Profit (loss) .... ($2,000)
Therefore: Planned ("reasonable") profit of $1,000 is earned if 10,000 items are sold at $1.10 each.	Therefore: Planned ("reasonable") profit of $1,000 is not earned. Instead, $2,000 loss results if 5,000 items are sold at $1.10 each.

The basic problem is that this method does not allow for cost variations at different levels of output. In a typical situation, economies of scale set in, and the average cost per unit continually drops as the quantity produced increases. (See Figure 20–3 for the typical shape of the average cost curve.) This is why mass production and mass distribution often make sense. This behavior of costs must be considered when setting prices.

■ FIGURE 20–3   Typical shape of average cost curve

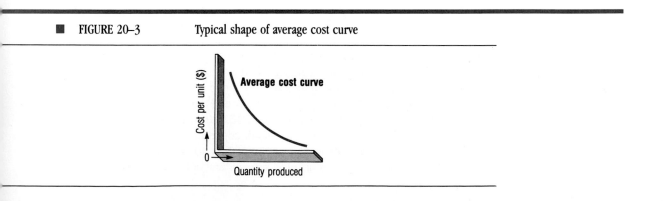

Marketing Manager Must Consider Various Kinds of Costs

Average-cost pricing may fail because total cost includes a variety of costs. And each of these costs changes in a *different* way as output changes. Any pricing method that uses cost must consider these changes. To understand why, however, we need to define *six types of costs*. Differences among these costs help explain why many companies have problems with pricing.

There are three kinds of total cost

1. **Total fixed cost** is the sum of those costs that are fixed in total—no matter how much is produced. Among these fixed costs are rent, depreciation, managers' salaries, property taxes, and insurance. Such costs stay the same even if production stops temporarily.

2. **Total variable cost**, on the other hand, is the sum of those changing expenses that are closely related to output—expenses for parts, wages, packaging, materials, outgoing freight, and sales commissions.

At zero output, total variable cost is zero. As output increases, so do variable costs. If a dress manufacturer doubles its output of dresses in a year, the total cost of cloth also (roughly) doubles.

3. **Total cost** is the sum of total fixed and total variable costs. Changes in total cost depend upon variations in total variable cost—since total fixed cost stays the same.

There are three kinds of average cost

The pricing manager usually is more interested in cost per unit than total cost—because prices are usually quoted per unit.

1. **Average cost** (per unit) is obtained by dividing total cost by the related quantity (that is, the total quantity which causes the total cost). See Table 20–1.

2. **Average fixed cost** (per unit) is obtained by dividing total fixed cost by the related quantity. See Table 20–1.

Fixed costs must be covered even if little is being produced.

■   TABLE 20–1   Cost structure of a firm

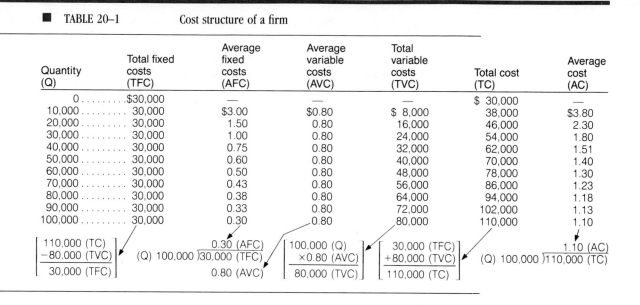

Quantity (Q)	Total fixed costs (TFC)	Average fixed costs (AFC)	Average variable costs (AVC)	Total variable costs (TVC)	Total cost (TC)	Average cost (AC)
0	$30,000	—	—	—	$ 30,000	—
10,000	30,000	$3.00	$0.80	$ 8,000	38,000	$3.80
20,000	30,000	1.50	0.80	16,000	46,000	2.30
30,000	30,000	1.00	0.80	24,000	54,000	1.80
40,000	30,000	0.75	0.80	32,000	62,000	1.51
50,000	30,000	0.60	0.80	40,000	70,000	1.40
60,000	30,000	0.50	0.80	48,000	78,000	1.30
70,000	30,000	0.43	0.80	56,000	86,000	1.23
80,000	30,000	0.38	0.80	64,000	94,000	1.18
90,000	30,000	0.33	0.80	72,000	102,000	1.13
100,000	30,000	0.30	0.80	80,000	110,000	1.10

$$\begin{bmatrix} 110,000 \text{ (TC)} \\ -80,000 \text{ (TVC)} \\ \hline 30,000 \text{ (TFC)} \end{bmatrix}$$ (Q) 100,000 $\overline{)30,000}$ $\dfrac{0.30 \text{ (AFC)}}{\text{(TFC)}}$ $\begin{bmatrix} 100,000 \text{ (Q)} \\ \times 0.80 \text{ (AVC)} \\ \hline 80,000 \text{ (TVC)} \end{bmatrix}$ $\begin{bmatrix} 30,000 \text{ (TFC)} \\ +80,000 \text{ (TVC)} \\ \hline 110,000 \text{ (TC)} \end{bmatrix}$ (Q) 100,000 $\overline{)110,000}$ $\dfrac{1.10 \text{ (AC)}}{\text{(TC)}}$

0.80 (AVC)

3. **Average variable cost** (per unit) is obtained by dividing total variable cost by the related quantity. See Table 20–1.

An example illustrates cost relations

Table 20–1 shows typical cost data for one firm. Here we assume that average variable cost is the same for each unit. Notice how average fixed cost goes down steadily as the quantity increases. Notice also how total variable cost increases when quantity increases, although the average variable cost remains the same. Average cost decreases continually, too. This is because average variable cost is the same and average fixed cost is decreasing. Figure 20–4 shows the three "average" curves.

Ignoring demand is the major weakness of average-cost pricing

Average-cost pricing works well if the firm actually sells the quantity which was used in setting the average cost price. Losses may result, however, if actual sales are *much lower* than expected. On the other hand, if sales are much higher than expected, then profits may be very good. But this will only happen by accident—that is, because the firm's demand is much larger than expected.

To use average-cost pricing, a marketing manager must make *some* estimate of the quantity to be sold in the coming period. But unless this quantity is related to price—that is, unless the firm's demand curve is considered—the marketing manager may set a price that doesn't even cover a firm's total cost! This can be seen in a simple example for a firm with the cost curves shown in Figure 20–4. This firm's demand curve is shown in Figure 20–5. It is important to see that customers' demands (and their demand curve) are still important—whether management takes time to analyze the demand curve or not.

In this example, whether management sets the price at a high $3 or a low $1.25, it will have a loss. At $3, only 10,000 units will be sold for a total revenue

■ FIGURE 20–4   Typical shape of cost (per unit) curves when AVC is assumed constant per unit

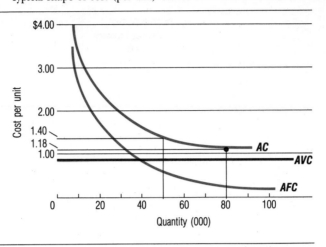

of $30,000. But total cost will be $38,000—for a loss of $8,000. At the $1.25 price, 50,000 units will be sold—for a loss of $7,500. If management tries to estimate the demand curve—however roughly—the price probably will be set in the middle of the range—say at $2—where a profit of $6,000 will be earned. See Figure 20–5.

In short, average-cost pricing is simple in theory—but often fails in practice. In stable situations, prices set by this method may yield profits—but not necessarily maximum profits. And note that such cost-based prices might be higher than a price that would be more profitable for the firm—as shown in Figure 20–5. When demand conditions are changing, average-cost pricing may be even more risky.

Figure 20–6 provides a simple overview of the relationships discussed above. Cost-oriented pricing suggests that the total number of units to be sold determines the *average* fixed cost per unit and thus the average total cost. Then, some amount of profit per unit is added to average total cost to get the cost-

■ FIGURE 20–5   Evaluation of various prices along a firm's demand curve

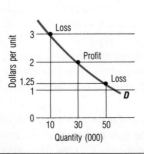

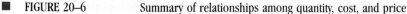

■   FIGURE 20–6   Summary of relationships among quantity, cost, and price

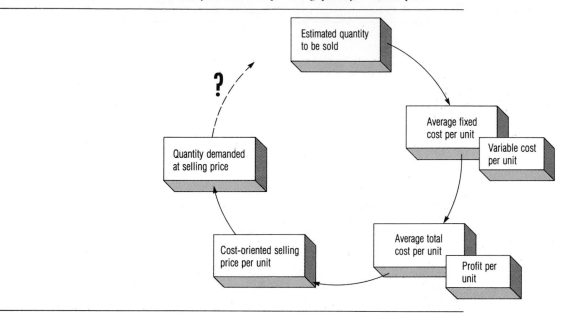

oriented selling price. But we are back where we started—when demand is considered—because the number of units sold will depend on the selling price—and the quantity sold (times price) determines total revenue (and total profit or loss). This figure emphasizes that a decision made in one area affects each of the others—directly or indirectly.[2] A manager who forgets this can make bad pricing decisions.

Experience curve pricing is even riskier

In recent years, some aggressive marketers—including Texas Instruments—have used a variation of average-cost pricing—called experience curve pricing. **Experience curve pricing** is average-cost pricing using an estimate of *future* average costs. This approach is based on the observation that over time—as an industry gains experience in certain kinds of production—managers learn new ways to reduce costs. The effect of such "learning" on costs varies in different businesses. Studies suggest that costs are reduced by about 15 to 20 percent each time total cumulative production experience doubles—at least in some industries. Some aggressive marketers expect that average costs will be lower in the future. So they set average-cost prices where they expect costs to be when products are sold in the future—not where they actually are when the strategy is set. This approach is seen more often when the market is growing rapidly (as in the electronics business) because cumulative production volume (experience) grows more *rapidly*.

If costs drop as expected, this approach can work fairly well—but it has the same risks as regular average-cost pricing—unless demand is included in the price setting. At the least, this means that the price setter has to estimate what quantity will be sold—to be able to read off the "right" experience curve price from the average cost curve. Further, remember that costs don't drop "automatically"—but only if managers continually find ways to be more efficient.[3]

Some Firms Add a Target Return to Cost

Target return pricing scores . . . sometimes

Target return pricing—adding a "target return" to the cost of a product—has become popular in recent years. With this approach, the price setter seeks to earn (1) a percentage return (say 10 percent per year) on the investment or (2) a specific total dollar return.

The method is a variation of the average-cost method—since the desired target return is added into total cost. As a simple example, if a small company had $10,000 invested and wished to make a 10 percent return on investment, it would add $1,000 to its annual total costs in setting prices.

This approach has the same weakness as other average-cost pricing methods. If the quantity that actually is sold is less than the quantity used in setting the price, then the target return is not earned—even though it seems to be part of the price structure. In fact, we already illustrated this problem. Look at Figure 20–2 again, and you will remember that we added $1,000 as an expected "reasonable profit"—or target return. But the return was much lower when the expected quantity was not sold. (It could be higher, too—but only if the quantity sold is much larger than expected.) Target return pricing clearly does not guarantee that the target will be hit.

Hitting the target in the long run

Managers in some larger firms—wanting to achieve a long-run target return objective—use another cost-oriented pricing approach—**long-run target return pricing**—adding a "long-run average target return" to the cost of a product. Instead of estimating the quantity they expect to produce in any one year, they assume that during several years' time their plants will produce at, say, 80 percent of capacity. They use this quantity when setting their prices.

No reference is made to current demand when setting current prices. Rather, demand and cost factors are estimated when the plant is built. In fact, it is the decision to build a plant of a certain size and capacity that determines later long-run target return prices.

Companies taking this longer-run view assume that there will be recession years when sales drop below 80 percent of capacity. For example, Owens Corning Fiberglas sells insulation. In years when there is little construction, output is low, and the target return is not earned. But they also have good years when more insulation is sold and the target return is exceeded. Over the long run, they expect that the target return will be achieved.

This long-run approach to target return pricing sounds simple. But like all pricing methods, it cannot be used mechanically. For example, "capacity" is a rather flexible concept—perhaps referring to a five-day, single-shift operation or to a seven-day, three-shift operation. So, long-run target return pricing need not lead to a unique price or a stable price. But companies using long-run target return pricing typically have stable prices and may be easy targets for more flexible competitors.

Break-Even Analysis Can Evaluate Possible Prices

Some price setters use break-even analysis to include expected revenue (and perhaps demand) in their pricing. They already know their costs fairly well. Now they want to know what price to set. Perhaps they are trying to decide among several prices which are somewhere close to their competition.

Break-even analysis evaluates whether the firm will be able to break even—that is, cover all its costs—with a particular price. This is important, because a firm must cover all costs in the long run—or there is not much point in being in business. This method focuses on the **break-even point (BEP)**—the quantity where the firm's total cost will just equal its total revenue.

Break-even charts help find the BEP

To help understand how break-even analysis works, look at Figure 20–7—an example of the typical break-even chart. Notice that the chart has lines which show total costs (total variable plus total fixed costs) and total revenues at different levels of production. The break-even point on the chart is at 75,000 units—

■ FIGURE 20–7   Break-even chart for a particular situation

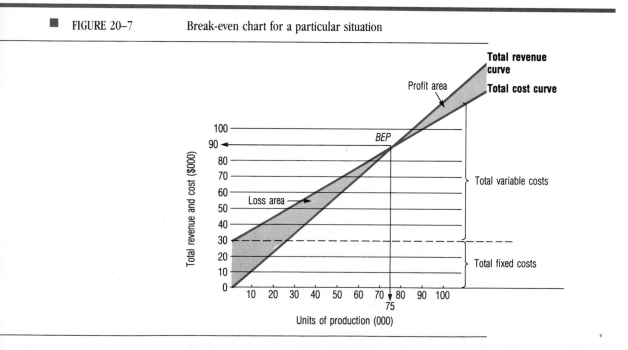

where the total cost and total revenue lines intersect. At that production level, total cost and total revenue are the same—$90,000.

This chart also shows some key assumptions that are made to simplify break-even analysis. Note that the total revenue curve is a straight line. This means that each extra unit sold adds the same amount to total revenue. Stated differently, this assumes that *any quantity may be sold at the same price.* For this chart, we are assuming a selling price of $1.20 a unit. You can see that the break-even quantity of 75,000 units sold at $1.20 each produces total revenue of $90,000.

In addition, the total cost curve in the chart is a straight line. This assumes that average variable cost (AVC) is the same at different levels of output. For Figure 20–7, the AVC is $.80 per unit.

The chart shows that below the break-even point, total cost is higher than total revenue—and a loss results. A profit would be made above the break-even point. The difference between the total revenue and total cost at a given quantity is the profit—or loss!

Break-even analysis can be very helpful—if used properly—so let's look at this approach more closely.

How to compute a break-even point

A break-even chart provides a useful summary, but it is convenient to be able to compute the break-even point.

In units, the BEP can be found by dividing total fixed costs (TFC) by the **fixed-cost (FC) contribution per unit**—the assumed selling price per unit minus the variable cost per unit. This may be stated as a simple formula:

$$\text{BEP (in units)} = \text{TC} \div \text{FC contribution per unit}$$

This formula makes sense when we think about it. If we are to break even, then total fixed costs must be covered. Therefore, we must figure the contribution which each unit will make to covering the total fixed costs (after paying for the variable costs to produce the item). When we divide this per-unit contribution into the total fixed costs which must be covered, we have the BEP (in units).

To illustrate the formula, let's use the same cost and price information as in Figure 20–7. The price per unit is $1.20. The average variable cost per unit is $.80. So the FC contribution per unit is $.40 ($1.20 − $.80). The fixed cost is $30,000 (see Figure 20–7). Substituting in the formula:

$$\text{BEP} = \$30,000 \div \$.40 = 75,000 \text{ units}$$

From this you can see that if this firm sells 75,000 units, it will exactly cover all its fixed and variable costs. If even one more unit is sold, then it will begin to show a profit—in this case, 40 cents per unit. Note that once the fixed costs are covered, the part of revenue formerly going to cover fixed costs is now all profit.

BEP can be stated in dollars, too

The BEP can also be figured in dollars. Here, the easiest method to remember is to compute the BEP in units and then multiply by the assumed per-unit price. If you multiply the selling price ($1.20) by the BEP in units (75,000) you get $90,000—the BEP in dollars.

Each possible price has its own break-even point	Often it is useful to compute the break-even point for each of several possible prices. Then, the marketing manager can consider the BEP for each price relative to what demand might be at that price. For example, you can quickly reject some possibilities when the expected quantity demanded at a given price is way below the break-even point for that price.
Target profit point can be figured, too	So far in our discussion of BEP we have focused on the quantity at which total revenue equals total cost—where profit is zero. We can also use a variation on the same approach to see what quantity is required to earn a certain level of profit. The analysis is the same as described above for the break-even point in units, but the amount of "target" profit is added to the total fixed cost figure—just as we discussed in the section on target returns. Then, when the fixed cost plus profit figure is divided by the contribution from each unit, the resulting quantity is the one that will earn the "target" profit.
Break-even analysis is helpful—but not a pricing solution	Break-even analysis is a useful approach. It is also very popular—because of the ease with which it can be applied by cost-oriented managers. But it is too often misunderstood. The graph—with its straight-line total revenue curve—makes it seem that any quantity can be sold at the assumed price. But this usually is not true. *It is the same as assuming a perfectly horizontal demand curve at that price.* In fact, most managers face down-sloping demand situations. And their total revenue curves *do not* keep going up. So, to really zero in on the most profitable price, marketers are better off to estimate the demand curve itself—and then use "marginal analysis," which is discussed next.

Traditional Demand and Supply Analysis Shows How to Maximize Profits

Most demand curves are down-sloping—and most supply curves are up-sloping. The intersection of these demand and supply curves seems to determine price—and, therefore, to take care of demand-oriented pricing. Unfortunately, reality is not quite that simple. Although such analysis may be suitable for whole industries, some refinements are necessary when applying it to an individual firm seeking to maximize profits.

We are seeking the biggest profit	In the following pages, we will discuss these refinements—concentrating on price setting in the many situations in which demand curves are down-sloping—that is, in monopolistic competition situations.[4] In these situations, the firm has carved out a little market for itself—and does have a pricing decision to make. By contrast, in pure or nearly pure competition, marketing managers have little difficulty with the pricing decision. They simply use the market price. (The special case of oligopoly will be treated later in the chapter.)

We will focus on how to *maximize* profits—not just on how to seek *some* profits. This has been the traditional approach of economic analysis. And it makes sense. If you know how to make the biggest profit, you can always adjust to pursue other objectives—while knowing how much profit you are giving up!

**Marginal analysis—
helps find the one
best price**

In monopolistic competition, a marketing manager faces a down-sloping demand curve. He must pick a price on that curve—and generally must offer that price to all potential buyers (to avoid price discrimination) for the life of the plan. If a lower price is chosen, additional units will be sold. But all customers—even those who might have paid more—pay this lower price. Therefore, a manager should consider the effect of alternative prices on total profit.

Marginal analysis can help make the best pricing decision. **Marginal analysis** focuses on the change in total revenue and total cost from selling one more unit—to find the most profitable price and quantity. This is a very useful—but technical—idea. It is treated more fully in the next several pages. Be sure to study the tables and figures.

**Marginal revenue
helps decide—can be
negative**

Marginal revenue is the change in total revenue which results from the sale of one more unit of a product. Since the firm's demand curve is down-sloping, this extra unit can be sold only by reducing the price of *all* items.

Table 20–2 shows the relationship between price, quantity, total revenue, and marginal revenue in a situation with a straight-line down-sloping demand curve.

If four units can be sold for a total revenue of $420 and five units for $460, then marginal revenue for the fifth unit is $40. Considering only revenue, it would be desirable to sell this extra unit. But will this continue if more units are sold at lower prices? No! Table 20–2 shows that negative marginal revenues occur at lower price levels. Obviously, this is not good for the firm! (Note: the *total* revenue that will be obtained if price is cut may still be positive, but the *marginal* revenue—the *extra* revenue gained—*may be positive* or *negative*.)

■ TABLE 20–2   Marginal revenue and price

(1) Quantity q	(2) Price p	(3) Total revenue (1) × (2) = TR	(4) Marginal revenue MR
0	$150	$ 0	
1	140	140	$140
2	130	260	120
3	117	351	91
4	105	420	69
5	92	460	40
6	79	474	14
7	66	462	−12
8	53	424	−38
9	42	378	−46
10	31	310	−68

Marketing managers know that the price which is set will affect the quantities that will be sold.

Marginal revenue curve and demand curve are different

The marginal revenue curve is always below a down-sloping demand curve, because the price of each "last unit" must be lower to sell more. This can be seen in Figure 20–8—where the data in Table 20–2 is plotted. The fact that the demand curve and the marginal revenue curves are different in monopolistic competition is very important. We will use both of them when finding the best price and quantity.

Marginal cost is needed, too

As we have already seen, various kinds of costs behave differently. Further, there is an important kind of cost which is similar to marginal revenue: marginal cost. This cost is vital to marginal analysis.

■ FIGURE 20–8   A plotting of the demand and marginal revenue data in Table 20-2

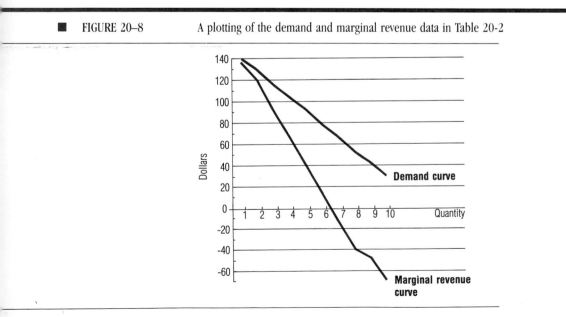

■ TABLE 20–3   Cost structure for individual firm

(1) Quantity Q	(2) Total fixed cost TFC	(3) Average fixed cost AFC	(4) Total variable cost TVC	(5) Average variable cost AVC	(6) Total cost (TFC + TVC = TC) TC	(7) Average cost (AC = TC ÷ Q) AC	(8) Marginal cost (per unit) MC
0..........	$200	$ 0	$ 0	$ 0	$200	Infinity	
1..........	200	200	96	96	296	$296	$ 96
2..........	200	200	116	58	316		20
3..........	200				331	110.33	
4..........	200	50			344		
5..........	200	40	155	31		71	11
6..........	200		168			61.33	13
7..........			183				15
8..........			223				
9..........			307		507	56.33	
10..........		20	510	51	710	71	203

Marginal cost is the change in total cost that results from producing one more unit. If it costs $275 to produce 9 units of a product and $280 to produce 10 units, then marginal cost is $5 for the 10th unit. In other words, marginal cost contrasted to average cost per unit is the additional cost of producing one more *specific unit,* while average cost is the average for *all units.*

Cost structure example

Table 20–3 shows how these costs can vary for a typical firm. *You should fill in the missing numbers on this table.* Notice that variable cost no longer is assumed constant per unit in Table 20–3. Here, we use the more realistic assumption that variable costs will go down for a while and then rise.

In Table 20–3, several important points should be noted. *First,* total fixed costs do not change over the entire range of output—but total variable costs increase continually as more and more units are produced. It is obvious, then, that total costs—the sum of total fixed costs and total variable costs—will increase as total quantity increases.

Second, average costs will decrease—for awhile—as quantity produced increases—since average costs are the sum of average fixed costs and average variable costs, and total fixed costs are divided by more and more units as output increases. For example—given a total fixed cost of $200—at a production level of four units, the average fixed cost is $50. At a production level of five units, the average fixed cost is $40.

Third, average costs in this table start rising for the last two units—because average variable costs have been increasing faster than average fixed costs have been decreasing. The firm may have been forced to use less efficient facilities and workers, to go into overtime work, or to pay higher prices for the materials it needed. This turn-up of the average cost curve is common—after the economies of scale "run out."

■   FIGURE 20–9   Per-unit cost curves (for data in Table 20-3)

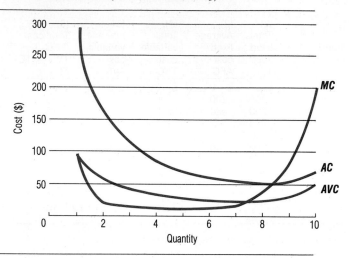

The marginal cost of just one more is important

The *marginal cost* column in Table 20–3 is the most important column for our purposes. It shows what each extra unit costs—and suggests the *minimum* extra revenue we should get for each additional unit. Like average cost, marginal cost drops, but it begins to rise again at a lower *level of output* than average cost does.

Although average cost per unit is going down over most of the quantity range, marginal cost *starts up earlier*—at five units. Figure 20–9 shows the behavior of the *average cost, average variable cost,* and *marginal cost* curves. Note that the marginal cost curve intersects the average variable cost and average cost curves from below *at their low points,* and then rises rapidly. This is how this curve typically behaves.

How to find the most profitable price and the quantity to produce

Since a manager must choose only *one* price level (for a time period), the problem is which one to choose. This price will determine the quantity that will be sold. To maximize profit, you should now see that a manager should be willing to supply more units if he can obtain a marginal revenue at least equal to the marginal cost of extra units. From this we get the following **rule for maximizing profit**: *the firm should produce that output where marginal cost is just less than or equal to marginal revenue.**

The selling price for this optimum quantity is found by referring to the demand curve—which shows what price customers are willing to pay for the optimum quantity. Note: *the optimum price is not found on the marginal revenue curve.*

This method of finding the most profitable price and quantity is a useful tool for a marketing manager. To make sure you understand it, study the following

---

*This rule applies in the typical situations where the curves are shaped similarly to those discussed here. Technically, however, we should add the following to the rule for maximizing profit: *the marginal cost must be increasing, or decreasing at a lesser rate than marginal revenue.*

example carefully. To make doubly sure that this approach is fully explained, we will calculate the most profitable price and quantity using total revenue and total cost curves first, and then show that the same answer is obtained with marginal curves. This will give you a check of the method—as well as help you see how the marginal revenue–marginal cost method works.

Profit maximization with total revenue and total cost curves

Table 20–4 provides data on total revenue, total cost, and total profit for a firm. Figure 20–10 graphs the total revenue, total cost, and total profit relationships. It is clear from the graph of the total profit curve that the most profitable quantity is six—this is the quantity where we find the greatest vertical distance between the TR curve and the TC curve. Table 20–4 shows that the most profitable price is $79 and a quantity of six will be sold.

You can see that beyond a quantity of six, the total profit curve declines. A profit-oriented marketing manager should not be interested in selling more than this number.

Profit maximization using marginal curves

Now we can apply the rule for maximizing profit using marginal curves. The same best quantity and price—six at $79—are obtained. See Figure 20–11—which is based on the data for marginal revenue and marginal cost in Table 20–4.

In Figure 20–11, the intersection of the marginal cost and marginal revenue curves occurs at a quantity of six. This is the most profitable quantity. But the best price must be obtained by going up to the demand curve and then over to the vertical axis—*not* by going from the intersection of MR and MC over to the vertical axis. Again, the best price is $79.

The graphic interpretation is supported by the data in Table 20–4. At a quantity of six, marginal revenue equals $14, and marginal cost is $13. There is a profit margin of $1—and this suggests that it might be profitable to offer seven

■ TABLE 20–4   Revenue, cost, and profit for an individual firm

(1) Quantity q	(2) Price p	(3) Total revenue TR	(4) Total cost TC	(5) Profit (TR − TC)	(6) Marginal revenue MR	(7) Marginal cost MC	(8) Marginal profit (MR − MC)
0	$150	$ 0	$200	$ −200			
1	140	140	296	−156	$140	$ 96	$+ 44
2	130	260	316	− 56	120	20	+100
3	117	351	331	+ 20	91	15	+ 76
4	105	420	344	+ 76	69	13	+ 56
5	92	460	355	+105	40	11	+ 29
6	79	474	368	+106	14	13	+ 1
7	66	462	383	+ 79	−12	15	− 27
8	53	424	423	+ 1	−38	40	− 78
9	42	378	507	−129	−46	84	−130
10	31	310	710	−400	−68	203	−271

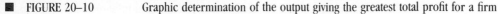

■ FIGURE 20–10   Graphic determination of the output giving the greatest total profit for a firm

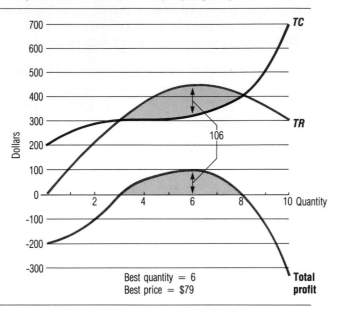

rather than six units. This is not the case, however. The marginal cost of the seventh unit is $15, while its marginal revenue is actually negative. Offering to sell seven units (instead of only six) will reduce total profit by $27.

It is important to realize that *total* profit is *not* near zero when MR equals MC. **Marginal profit**—the extra profit on the last unit—is near zero. But that is exactly why the quantity obtained at the MR–MC intersection is the most profitable. Marginal analysis shows that when the firm is finding the best price to charge, it should be willing to increase the quantity it will sell as long as the last unit it considers offering will yield *extra* profits.

Again, the marketing manager finally will choose only *one* price. Marginal analysis is useful in helping to set the best price to charge for all that will be sold. It might help to think of the demand curve as an "iffy" curve—*if* a price is selected, *then* its related quantity will be sold. Before the actual price is set, all these *if-then* combinations can be evaluated for profitability. But once a particular price is set, the results will follow—i.e., the related quantity will be sold.

A profit range is reassuring

We have been trying to find the most profitable price and quantity. But in a changing world, this is difficult. Fortunately, this optimum point is surrounded by a profitable range.

Note that in Figure 20–10, there are *two* break-even points rather than a single point—which was the case when we were discussing break-even analysis. The second break-even point falls farther to the right—because total costs turn up and total revenue turns down.

■   FIGURE 20–11   Alternate determination of the most profitable output and price for a firm

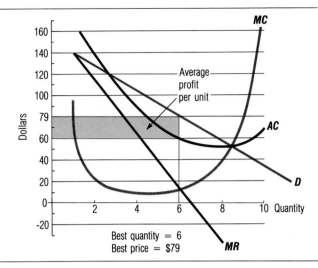

Best quantity = 6
Best price = $79

These two break-even points are important to note—they show the range of profitable operations. Although we are seeking the point of maximum profit, we know that this point is an ideal rather than a realistic possibility. So it is essential that the marketing manager knows there is a range of profit around the optimum—it is not just a single point. This means that pursuing the most profitable price is a wise policy.

How to lose less, if you must

The marginal approach to finding the most profitable output also will find the output which will be least unprofitable—when market conditions are so poor that the firm must operate at a loss.

If sales are slow, the marketing manager may even have to consider stopping production. When making this decision, fixed costs should be ignored—since these will continue regardless. Some fixed costs may even involve items that are so "sunk" in the business that they cannot be sold for anything near the cost shown on the company's records. The special-purpose buildings and machines of an unsuccessful company may be worthless to anyone else.

Marginal costs are another matter. If the firm cannot recover the marginal cost of the last unit (or, more generally, the variable cost of the units being considered), it should stop operations temporarily or go out of business. The only exceptions involve social or humanitarian considerations—or the fact that the marginal costs of closing temporarily are high and stronger demand is expected *soon.* But if marginal costs can be covered in the short run—even though all fixed costs cannot—the firm should stay in operation.

Marginal analysis helps get the most in pure competition

Marketing managers caught in pure competition also can apply marginal methods. They do not have a price decision to make—since the demand curve is flat. This means that the marginal revenue curve is flat at the same level. But

■ FIGURE 20–12   Finding the most profitable (or least unprofitable) price and quantity in pure
                        competition (in the short run)

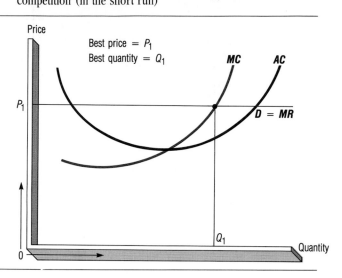

they do have output decisions. They can use the marginal revenue curve, therefore, with their own unique marginal cost curve to determine the most profitable
(or least unprofitable) output level. See Figure 20–12. Not incidentally, this approach leads to a different (and more profitable) output than the lowest average-
cost decision favored by some "commonsense" managers. Note—in Figure
20–12—that the quantity associated with the lowest average cost is *not* the most
profitable quantity.

Marginal Analysis Applies in Oligopoly, Too

Marginal analysis can be used whenever a firm can estimate its demand and
cost curves. The special kinked nature of the oligopoly demand curve is no
problem.

When demand kinks, marginal revenue drops fast

As we saw in Chapter 4, each competitor in an oligopoly faces a kinked demand curve. We said then that the tendency in such situations is to avoid the
use of Price—to avoid price cutting. Marginal analysis now helps us understand
this situation better.

The dashed part of the marginal revenue line in Figure 20–13 shows that
marginal revenue drops sharply at the kinked point. This is a technical but important matter. It helps explain why prices are relatively sticky at the kinked point.

■ FIGURE 20–13   Marginal revenue drops fast in an oligopoly

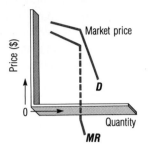

Even if costs change—and, therefore, if each firm's supply curve moves up or down—the MC curve still may cross the MR curve someplace along this drop. In this case, even though costs are changing—and there may seem to be a reason for changing the price—each firm should hold its price at the kinked price level—to maximize its profits!

A price leader usually sets the price

Most of the firms in an oligopoly are aware of the economics of their situation—at least intuitively. Usually, a **price leader** sets a price for all to follow—perhaps to maximize profits or to get a certain target return on investment—and (without any collusion) other members of the industry follow. This price may be maintained for a long time—or at least as long as all members of the industry continue to make a reasonable profit.

The price leader must take this responsibility seriously. If the followers are not able to make a reasonable profit at the market price, then they may try secret price cuts to expand sales. If very much of this happens, the price leader will lose business. And the situation may turn into a violent price war. Or there may be a temptation to collude—which is done, although it is illegal. Lacking an effective leader, the market may be unstable. And severe price cutting may be a continual threat.

A price leader may try to lead others to higher price levels if industry conditions seem to justify it—say, if labor costs have increased. Or the leader may try to get the industry price back up to former levels after a long period of price cutting. But this must be done carefully. The competitors may not "follow the leader." And the leader may lose heavily before being forced to retreat. The National Gypsum Company, for example, once tried to return industry prices to list price levels and was "chopped up" during its two-month effort. As a result, the firm vowed not to try to lead the industry in price actions again. Its managers said that in the future, "we are going to be absolutely convinced in the marketplace by the actions of our competitors before doing anything." Further, "if they demonstrate statesmanship, our participation will go with them. But if we see them being cute, we will react differently."[5]

Price leader should know costs and demand

A price leader should have a good understanding of its own and its competitors' cost structures—as well as an estimate of the industry demand curve. Setting too high a price may look attractive in the short run, but it may attract more competitors to the market and lead to trouble later—when capacity has expanded. Setting too low a price, on the other hand, can lead to action from antitrust officials who become concerned about small competitors. An optimal price may be one which is just high enough to support the marginal firm—the least efficient company whose production is needed to meet peak long-run demands.[6]

If the price leader chooses a price that others can accept, they may follow without any need for agreement. This "conscious parallel action" is deplored by those trying to preserve business competition, but it still has not been declared illegal. Indeed, it is hard to see how it can be. Each firm *must* administer its prices, and meeting competition is certainly legal. In fact, basically the same behavior is found in pure competition. So—as long as conspiracy is avoided—meeting competition in any market situation probably will continue to be acceptable.

Some Price Setters Do Estimate Demand

Cost-oriented pricing is relatively simple and practical. But it is also clear that most cost-oriented approaches require some estimate of the likely demand. And, as we have seen, estimating the demand curve may help avoid mistakes in pricing.

Actual use of demand curves is not very common in the real world. This is probably because many managers think the exact shape of the demand curve must be known to gain the benefits of this approach. They forget that the profitable "range" around the best price and quantity allows some lack of precision in demand estimates.

Yet, we do find marketers pricing as though they believe demand curves are present. The following sections discuss examples of these demand-related approaches.

Value in use pricing— how much will the customer save?

Industrial and commercial buyers think about costs when they make purchases. Many marketers who aim at industrial markets keep this in mind in setting prices. They use **value in use pricing**—which is setting prices that will capture some of what customers will save by substituting the firm's product for the one currently being used. For example, a manufacturer of an electronic word processor knows that his machine doesn't just replace a standard office typewriter, but also reduces secretarial costs. He can estimate the labor cost that will be saved and set a price for the word processor that will lead to less costly clerical output.

This approach to pricing is an extension of the marketing concept. It considers the customer's costs and objectives, not just those of the seller. It helps the manager to estimate what quantity will be demanded—especially for new products—by focusing on how much business may be taken away from existing products.[7]

Leader pricing—make it low to attract customers

Leader pricing is setting some very low prices—real bargains—to get customers into retail stores. The idea is not to sell large quantities of the leader items, but to get customers into the store to buy other products.[8] Certain products are picked for their promotion value and priced low—but above cost. In food stores, the leader prices are the "specials" that are advertised regularly—to give an image of low prices. Leader items usually are well-known, widely used items which customers don't stock heavily—milk, butter, eggs, or coffee—but on which they will recognize a real price cut.

Leader pricing may try to appeal to customers who normally shop elsewhere. But it can backfire—if they buy only the low-price leaders. To avoid hurting profits, managers often select leader items that aren't directly competitive with major lines—as when bargain-priced recording tape is the leader for a stereo equipment store.

Bait pricing—offer a "steal," but sell under protest

Bait pricing is setting some very low prices to attract customers—but trying to sell more expensive models or brands once the customer is in the store. For example, a furniture store may advertise a color TV for $199. But once bargain hunters come to buy it, sales clerks point out the disadvantages of the low-price TV and try to convince them to "trade-up" to a better (and more expensive) set. It's something like leader pricing. But here the seller *doesn't* plan to sell much at the low price. Some stores even make it very difficult to buy the "bait" item.

If bait pricing is successful, the demand for higher-quality products expands. But extremely aggressive and sometimes dishonest bait-pricing advertising has given this method a bad reputation. In fact, all throughout Canada bait-pricing is illegal, either specifically or indirectly.

Psychological pricing—some prices just seem right

Psychological pricing is setting prices which have special appeal to target customers. Some people feel there are whole ranges of prices which potential customers see as the same. So price cuts in these ranges do not increase the quantity sold. But just below this range, customers may buy more. Then, at even lower prices, the quantity demanded stays the same again. And so on. The kind of demand curve that leads to psychological pricing is in Figure 20–14. Vertical drops mark the price ranges which customers see as the same. Pricing research shows that there are such demand curves.[9]

Odd-even pricing is setting prices which end in certain numbers. For example, products selling below $50 often end in the number 5 or the number 9—such as $.49 or $24.95. For higher-priced products, prices are often $1 or $2 below the next even dollar figure—such as $99 rather than $100.

Some marketers use odd-even pricing because they feel that consumers react better to these prices—perhaps seeing them as "substantially" lower than the next highest even price. Marketers using these prices seem to assume that they have a rather jagged demand curve—that slightly higher prices will substantially reduce the quantity demanded. Odd-even prices were used long ago by

■ FIGURE 20–14   Demand curve when psychological pricing is appropriate

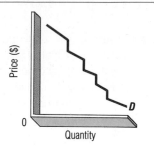

some retailers to force their clerks to make change. Then they had to record the sale and could not pocket the money. Today, however, it is not always clear why these prices are used—or whether they really work. Perhaps it is done simply because "everyone else does it."[10]

Prestige pricing: Make it high—but not cheap

Prestige pricing is setting a rather high price to suggest high quality or high status. Some target customers want the "best." So, they will buy at a high price. But if the price seems "cheap," they worry about quality and don't buy.[11]

Prestige pricing is most common for luxury products—such as furs and jewelry. It is also common in service industries—where the customer can't see the product in advance and relies on price to judge the quality that will be supplied. Target customers who respond to prestige pricing give the marketing manager an unusual demand curve. Instead of a normal down-sloping curve, the curve goes down for a while and then bends back to the left again. See Figure 20–15.

Price lining—a few prices cover the field

Price lining is setting a few price levels for a product class and then marking all items at these prices. This approach assumes that customers have a certain price in mind that they expect to pay for a product. For example, most neckties

■ FIGURE 20–15   Demand curve showing a prestige price situation

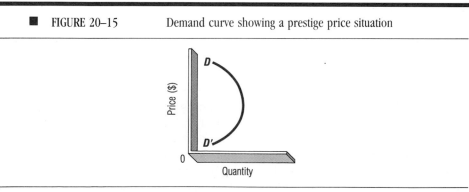

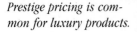

are priced between $5 and $15. In price lining, there will not be many prices in this range. There will be only a few. Ties will not be priced at $5, $5.50, $6, and so on. They might be priced at four levels—$5, $7.50, $10, and $15.

Price lining has advantages other than just matching the price of a product to what consumers expect to pay. The main advantage is simplicity—for both clerks and customers. It is less confusing than having many prices. Some customers may consider items in only one price class. Their big decision, then, is which item(s) to choose at that price. Price is no longer a question—unless the products at that price are not satisfactory. Then, the customer can be "traded-up" to the next price level.

For retailers, price lining has several advantages. Sales may increase because (1) they can offer a bigger variety in each price line and (2) it is easier to get customers to make decisions within one price line. Stock planning is simpler—because demand is larger at the relatively few prices. Price lining also can reduce costs because inventory needs are lower—even though large stocks are carried in each line. In summary, price lining results in faster turnover, fewer markdowns, quicker sales, and simplified buying.

Demand-backward pricing aids price lining

Demand-backward pricing is setting an acceptable final consumer price and working backward to what a producer can charge. It is commonly used by producers of final consumer products—especially shopping goods, such as women's and children's clothing and shoes. It is also used for toys or gifts for which customers will spend a specific amount—because they are seeking a "five-dollar" or a "ten-dollar" gift. Here, a reverse cost-plus pricing process is used. This method has been called "market-minus" pricing.

The producer starts with the retail price for a particular item and then works backward—subtracting the typical margins which channel members expect. This gives the approximate price that the producer can charge. Then, the average or planned marketing expenses can be subtracted from this price to find how much can be spent producing the item.

Demand estimates are needed if demand-backward pricing is to be successful. The quantity which will be demanded affects production costs—that is, where the firm will be on its average cost curve. Also, since competitors can be expected to make the best product possible, it is important to know customer needs—to set the best amount to be spent on manufacturing costs. By increasing costs a little, the product may be so improved in consumers' eyes that the firm will sell many more units. But if consumers only want novelty, additional quality may not increase the quantity demanded—and shouldn't be offered.

Demand-backward pricing is often used with "gift" items.

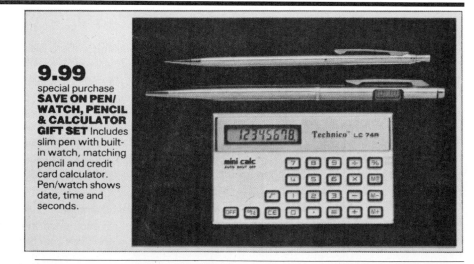

Pricing a Full Line

Our emphasis has been—and will continue to be—on the problem of pricing a single item—mainly because this makes our discussion clearer. But most marketing managers are responsible for more than one product. In fact, their "product" may be the whole company line! So we will discuss this matter briefly.

Full-line pricing—market- or firm-oriented?

Full-line pricing is setting prices for a whole line of products. How to do this depends on which of two basic strategies a firm is using.

In one case, all products in the company's line are aimed at the same general target market—which makes it important for all prices to be related to one another. For example, a TV manufacturer could offer several price and quality levels—to give its target customers some choice. (If it sells only high-priced models, many customers will be forced to buy other brands.) But the different prices should appear "reasonable" when the target customers are evaluating them.

In the other case, the different products in the line are aimed at entirely different target markets—and so there doesn't have to be any relation between the various prices. A chemical manufacturer of a wide variety of products with several target markets, for example, probably should price each product separately.

Usually, the marketing manager attempts to price products in a full line so that the prices will appear logically related and make sense to potential customers.[12] Most customers—especially industrial customers—feel that prices should be related to cost. And this must be considered in setting prices. Customers usually realize that small production runs or handling small quantities is likely to cost more—so they may be willing to pay higher prices for items which they know have a small market.

Cost is not much help in full-line pricing

The marketing manager must try to recover all costs on the whole line—perhaps by pricing quite low on competitive items and much higher on less competitive items. But estimating costs is difficult when there is a full line to price. The biggest problem is that there is no single "right" way to assign a company's fixed costs to each of the products. And if any method is carried through without considering demand, it may lead to very unrealistic prices. The marketing manager should judge demand for the whole line—as well as demand for each individual product in each target market—to avoid mistakes.

As an aid to full-line pricing, the marketing manager can assemble directly variable costs on the many items in the line—for calculating a floor under which prices will not be lowered. To this can be added a "reasonable" markup based on the quality of the product, the strength of the demand for the product, and the degree of competition. But finally, the image projected by the full line must be evaluated.

Complementary product pricing

Complementary product pricing is setting prices on several products as a group. This may lead to one product being priced very low so that the profits from another product will increase—and increase the product group's total profits. A new razor, for example, may be priced low to sell the blades—which continue to get dull. Or, Atari might set a "low" price for its video game consoles. Once customers buy the console, they will buy Atari's games to go with it—at a nice profit for Atari!

Complementary product pricing differs from full-line pricing because quite different production facilities may be involved—so there's no cost allocation problem. Instead, the problem is really understanding the target market and the demand curves for each of the complementary products. Then, various combinations of prices can be tried to see what set will be best for reaching the company's pricing objectives.

Bid Pricing Depends Heavily on Costs

A new price for every job

Bid pricing is offering a specific price for each possible job—rather than setting a price that applies for all potential customers. Building contractors, for example, must bid on possible projects. And many companies selling services (like cleaning or data processing) must submit bids for jobs they would like to have.

The big problem in bid pricing is estimating all the costs that will apply to each job. This may sound easy, but thousands of cost components may have to go into a complicated bid. Further, management must include an overhead charge and a charge for profit.

Demand must be considered, too

Competition must be considered when adding in overhead and profit. Usually, the customer will get several bids and accept the lowest one. So unthinking addition of overhead and profit should be avoided. Some bidders use the same overhead and profit rates on all jobs—regardless of competition—and then are surprised when they don't get some jobs.

Bidding can be expensive. So a marketing manager may want to be selective about which jobs to bid on—and select those where he feels he has the greatest chance of success. Thousands or even millions of dollars have been spent just developing bids for large industrial or government orders.[13]

Sometimes bids are bargained

Some buying situations (including much government buying) require the use of bids—and the purchasing agent must take the lowest bid. In other cases, however, bids may be called for and then the company submitting the *most attractive* bid—not necessarily the lowest—will be singled out for further bargaining. This may include price adjustments—but it also may be concerned with how additions to the job will be priced, what guarantees will be provided, and the quality of labor and supervisors who will do the job. Some projects—such as construction projects—are hard to define exactly. So it is important that the buyer be satisfied about the whole marketing mix—not just the price. Obviously, effective personal selling can be important here.

■ CONCLUSION

In this chapter, we discussed various approaches to price setting. Generally, retailers and wholesalers use traditional markups. Some use the same markups for all their items. Others have found that varying the markups may increase turnover and profit. In other words, demand is considered!

Cost-oriented pricing seems to make sense for middlemen—because they handle small quantities of many items. Producers must take price setting more seriously. They are the ones that set the "list price" to which others apply markups.

Producers commonly use average cost curves to help set their prices. But this approach sometimes ignores demand completely. A more realistic approach to average cost pricing requires a sales forecast. This may just mean assuming that sales in the next period will be roughly the same as in the last period. This *will* enable the marketing manager to set a price—but this price *may or may not* cover all costs and earn the desired profit.

Break-even analysis can be useful for evaluating possible prices. But management judgment must be used to evaluate the chance of reaching these possible break-even points. It does provide a rough and ready tool for eliminating obviously unworkable prices.

Traditional demand and supply analysis can be a useful tool for finding the most profitable price—and the quantity to produce. The most profitable *quantity* is found at the intersection of the marginal revenue and marginal cost curves. To determine the *most profitable price,* the manager takes the most profitable quantity to the firm's demand curve—to find what price target customers will be willing to pay for this quantity.

The major difficulty with demand-oriented pricing is estimating the demand curve. But experienced managers—aided perhaps by marketing research—can make estimates of the nature of demand for their products. Such estimates—even if they aren't exact—are useful. They get your thinking in the right "ballpark." Sometimes, when all that is needed is a decision about raising or lowering price, even "rough" demand estimates can be very revealing. Further, it is important to recognize that a firm's demand curve does not cease to exist simply because it is ignored. Some information is better than none at all. And it appears that some marketers do consider demand in their pricing. We saw this with leader pricing, bait pricing, odd-even pricing, psychological pricing, full-line pricing, and even bid pricing.

We have stressed throughout the book that the customer must be considered before anything is done. This certainly applies to pricing. It means that when managers are setting a price, they have to consider what customers will be willing to pay. This isn't always easy, but it is nice to know that there is a profit range around the "best" price. Therefore, even "guesstimates" about what potential customers will buy at various prices will probably lead to a better price than mechanical use of traditional markups or cost-oriented formulas.[14]

■ QUESTIONS AND PROBLEMS

1. Why do department stores seek a markup of about 40 percent when some discount houses operate on a 20 percent markup?

2. A manufacturer of household appliances distributed its products through wholesalers and retailers. The retail selling price was $250, and the manufacturing cost to the company was $100. The retail markup was 40 percent and the wholesale markup 25 percent. (*a*) What was the cost to the wholesaler? To the retailer? (*b*) What percentage markup did the manufacturer take?

3. Relate the concept of stock turnover to the rise of discounters. Use a simple example in your answer.

4. If total fixed costs are $100,000 and total variable costs are $200,000 at the output of 10,000 units, what are the probable total fixed costs and total variable costs at an output of 20,000 units? What are the average fixed costs, average variable costs, and average costs at these two output levels? Determine the price which should be charged. (Make any simplifying assumptions necessary to obtain a definite answer.)

5. Explain how target return pricing differs from average-cost pricing.

6. Construct an example showing that mechanical use of very large or very small markup might still lead to unprofitable operation while some intermediate price would be profitable. Draw a graph and show the break-even point(s).

7. The Smith Company's fixed costs for the year are estimated at $100,000. The variable costs are usually about 70 percent of sales. Sales for the coming year are expected to reach $380,000. What is the break-even point? Expected profit? If sales are forecast at only $200,000, should the Smith Company shut down operations? Why?

8. Distinguish among marginal revenue, average revenue, and price.

9. Draw a graph showing a demand and supply situation where marginal analysis correctly indicates that the firm should continue producing even though the profit and loss statement shows a loss.

10. Discuss the idea of drawing separate demand curves for different market segments. It seems logical because each target market should

have its own marketing mix. But won't this lead to a considerable number of demand curves and possible prices? And what will this mean with respect to functional discounts and varying prices in the marketplace? Will this be legal? Will it be practical?

11. Brown Bean Company has been enjoying a profitable year. Their product sells to wholesalers for 20 cents a can. After careful study, it has been decided that a 60 percent gross margin should be maintained. Their manufacturing costs are divided in this manner: material, 50 percent of cost; labor, 40 percent of cost; and 10 percent of cost for overhead. Both material and labor costs experienced a 10 percent increase. Determine the new price per can based on their present pricing methods. Is it wise to hold fast to a 60 percent margin, if a *price increase* would mean lost customers? Answer, using graphs and MC–MR analysis. Show a situation where it would be most profitable to (a) raise price, (b) leave price alone, (c) reduce price.

12. How does a prestige pricing policy fit into a marketing mix? Would exclusive distribution be necessary?

13. Cite a local example of the use of odd-even pricing and then evaluate whether you feel it makes sense.

14. Cite a local example of the use of psychological pricing and then evaluate whether you feel it makes sense.

15. Distinguish between leader pricing and bait pricing. What do they have in common? How can their use affect a marketing mix?

16. Is a full-line pricing policy available only to producers? Cite local examples of full-line pricing. Why is full-line pricing important?

■ SUGGESTED CASES

■ NOTES

1. Marvin A. Jolson, "A Diagrammatic Model for Merchandising Calculations," *Journal of Retailing,* Summer 1975, pp. 3–9.

2. Mary L. Hatten, "Don't Get Caught with Your Prices Down: Pricing in Inflationary Times," *Business Horizons,* March 1982, pp. 23–28; "Why Detroit Can't Cut Prices," *Business Week,* March 1, 1982, p. 110; and Douglas G. Brooks, "Cost Oriented Pricing: A Realistic Solution to a Complicated Problem," *Journal of Marketing,* April 1975, pp. 72–74.

3. "Selling Business a Theory of Economics," *Business Week,* September 8, 1973, pp. 85–90; Robert J. Dolan and Abel P. Jeuland, "Experience Curves and Dynamic Demand Models: Implications for Optimal Pricing Strategies," *Journal of Marketing,* Winter 1982, pp. 52–62; and Alan R. Beckenstein and H. Landis Gabel, "Experience Curve Pricing Strategy: The Next Target of Antitrust?" *Business Horizons* 25, no. 5 (September/October 1982), pp. 71–77.

4. Approaches for estimating price-quantity relationships are reviewed in Kent B. Monroe, *Pricing: Making Profitable Decisions* (New York: McGraw-Hill, 1979). For a specific example see Frank D. Jones, "A Survey Technique to Measure Demand under Various Pricing Strategies," *Journal of Marketing,* July 1975, pp. 75–77.

5. "National Gypsum Vows Not to Lead Industry Again in Price Action," *The Wall Street Journal,* July 17, 1970, p. 11; and "Gypsum Makers Move to Stop Sharp Discounts," *The Wall Street Journal,* December 3, 1969, p. 6. See also (re cigarette industry) Marvin A. Jolson and Noel B. Zabriskie, "Nonprice Parallelism in Oligopolistic Industries," *MSU Business Topics,* Autumn 1971, pp. 33–41.

6. See J. Howard Westing and Jon G. Udell, "Pricing and the Antitrust Laws," *Michigan Business Review,* November 1962, pp. 6–11.

7. Benson P. Shapiro and Barbara P. Jackson, "Industrial Pricing to Meet Customer Needs," *Harvard Business Review,* November-December, 1978, pp. 119–27; and "The Race to the $10 Light Bulb," *Business Week,* May 19, 1980, p. 124.

8. For an example applied to a high-price item, see "Sale of Mink Coats Strays a Fur Piece from the Expected," *The Wall Street Journal,* March 21, 1980, p. 30.

9. E. R. Hawkins, "Price Policies and Theory," *Journal of Marketing,* January 1954, p. 236. See also B. P. Shapiro, "The Psychology of Pricing," *Harvard Business Review,* July-August 1968, pp. 14–24; and C. Davis Fogg and Kent H. Kohnken, "Price-Cost Planning," *Journal of Marketing,* April 1978, pp. 97–106.

10. Dik W. Twedt, "Does the 9 Fixation in Retailing Really Promote Sales?" *Journal of Marketing,* October 1965, pp. 54–55; H. J. Rudolph, "Pricing and Today's Market," *Printers' Ink,* May 29, 1954, pp. 22–24; and "Strategic Mix of Odd, Even Prices Can Lead to Increased Retail Profits," *Marketing News,* March 7, 1980, p. 24.

11. Peter C. Riesz, "Price versus Quality in the Marketplace," *Journal of Retailing,* (Winter 1978), pp. 15–28; John J. Wheatly and John S. Y. Chiu, "The Effects of Price, Store Image, and Product and Respondent Characteristics on Perceptions of Quality," *Journal of Marketing Research,* May 1977, pp. 181–86; Arthur G. Bedeian, "Consumer Perception of Price as an Indicator of Product Quality," *MSU Business Topics,* Summer 1971, pp. 59–65; David M. Gardner, "An Experimental Investigation of the Price/Quality Relationship," *Journal of Retailing,* Fall 1970, pp. 25–41; N. D. French, J. J. Williams, and W. A. Chance, "A Shopping Experiment on Price-Quality Relationships," *Journal of Retailing,* Fall 1972, pp. 3–16; Michael R. Hagerty, "Model Testing Techniques and Price-Quality Relationships," *Journal of Consumer Research,* December 1978, pp. 194–205; J. Douglas McConnell, "Comment on 'A Major Price-Perceived Quality Study Reexamined,'" *Journal of Marketing Research,* May 1980, pp. 263–64; and K. M. Monroe and S. Petroshius, "Buyers' Subjective Perceptions of Price: An Update of the Evidence," in *Perspectives in Consumer Behavior,* ed. T. Robertson and H. Kassarjian (Glenview, Ill.: Scott Foresman 1981), pp. 43–55.

12. Alfred Oxenfeldt, "Product Line Pricing," *Harvard Business Review,* July-August, 1966, pp. 135–43.

13. Stephen Paranka, "Competitive Bidding Strategy," *Business Horizons,* June 1971, pp. 39–43; Wayne J. Morse, "Probabilistic Bidding Models; A Synthesis," *Business Horizons,* April 1975, pp. 67–74; and Kenneth Simmonds and Stuart Slatter, "The Number of Estimators: A Critical Decision for Marketing under Competitive Bidding," *Journal of Marketing Research,* May 1978, pp. 203–13.

14. For references to additional readings in the pricing area, see Kent B. Monroe, D. Lund, and P. Choudhury, *Pricing Policies and Strategies: An Annotated Bibliography* (Chicago: American Marketing Association, 1983).

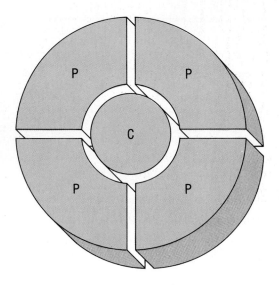

Product

Place

Promotion

Price

Customer

This part is concerned with tying together and extending the material we have been discussing throughout the book. Chapter 21 reemphasizes the need for focusing on target markets when planning marketing mixes—and shows how knowing about target markets as well as the goods classes can help you develop effective—and perhaps even breakthrough—strategies. Ways of developing and selecting such marketing plans are discussed—starting with "typical" marketing mixes and then adjusting them to the needs and preferences of target markets— in the light of competitors' actions and the company's own resources and objectives.

Controlling marketing plans and programs is the subject of Chapter 22. The interrelation of controlling and planning is emphasized—because the marketing management process is continuous—involving planning, implementing, and control—which leads to feedback to make better plans for the future.

Chapter 23 applies the material you have studied to international marketing. We will discuss the need to deal with even more uncontrollable and less familiar environments. This should not discourage an aggressive marketer because the potential rewards are great—and working in international markets can be very exciting and challenging.

Chapter 21 ■ Planning and implementing marketing programs

When you finish this chapter, you should:

1. Know that strategy planning is much more than assembling the four Ps.
2. Know how response functions can help plan marketing strategies.
3. Understand why typical mixes are a good starting point for planning.
4. Understand how marketing mixes are related to goods classes.
5. Know the content and differences among strategies, marketing plans, and a marketing program.
6. Know about allocating budgets for marketing plans.
7. Know about some graphical aids for implementing a marketing program.
8. Recognize the important new terms (shown in red).

"More than strategies must be planned."

In this chapter, we will finish our discussion of marketing strategy planning. We will emphasize *why* an individual firm should see each of its internal activities as part of a whole—and why a marketing manager must plan whole marketing mixes to satisfy target markets, rather than looking at only one or another of the four Ps.

Bob Miller manages an ice skating rink. He continually analyzes how satisfied his present customers are and keeps track of how many new ones are attracted by his advertising and free "school tours" sales promotions—to help him decide if and how much he can raise prices. Clearly, marketing mixes can't be planned just one P at a time.

Marketing Planning Is More than Assembling the Four Ps

They must be blended together

Marketing planning involves much more than assembling the four parts of a marketing mix. The four Ps must be *blended* together in a creative way—so that the "best" mix is developed for the firm's target market. This may mean that ideas of some specialists—the product manager, sales manager, physical distribution manager, and so on—may have to be adjusted to improve the whole mix.

Throughout the text, we have given the job of integrating the four Ps to the marketing manager. Now you should see the need for this integrating role. It is easy for specialists to focus on their own areas—and expect the rest of the company to work for or around them. This is especially true in larger firms—where specialists are needed—just because the size of the whole marketing job is too much for one person.

Need plans and program

Marketing managers must plan strategies, marketing plans, and, finally, a whole marketing program. As explained in Chapter 2, a marketing strategy is a "big picture" of what a firm will do in some target market—while a marketing plan includes the time-related details for that strategy—and a marketing program is a combination of the firm's marketing plans.

By now, it should be clear that each strategy which gets implemented must be carried out over a period of time. Some time schedule is implicit in any strategy. A marketing plan simply spells out this time period and the time-related details. Usually, we think in terms of some reasonable length of time, such as six months, a year, or a few years. But it might be only a month or two in some cases—especially when style and fashion are important factors. Or, a strategy might be implemented over several years—perhaps the length of a product life cycle or at least the early stages of the life of the product.

You can see that marketing strategy planning is a creative process—but it also is a logical process. It requires blending many of the ideas which we have discussed already in this book. So this chapter might be thought of as a review. Figure 21–1 shows the strategic decision areas which we have been talking about throughout the book. Now these must be integrated into logical marketing mixes, marketing strategies, marketing plans, and a marketing program.

■ FIGURE 21–1   Strategic decision areas

Product	Place	Promotion	Price
Features	Objectives	Objectives	Objectives
Accessories	Channels	Promotion blend	Flexibility
Installation	Market exposure	Salespeople	Level
Instructions	Kinds of middlemen	Kind	Changes over product
Service	Kinds and location	Number	life cycle
Warranty	of stores	Selection	Geographic terms
Product lines	Who handles	Training	Discounts
Packaging	transporting	Motivation	Allowances
Branding	and storing	Advertising	
	Service levels	Targets	
		Kinds of ads	
		Media type	
		Copy thrust	
		Prepared by whom	
		Sales promotion	
		Publicity	

Blending the Four Ps Takes Understanding of a Target Market

The marketing concept emphasizes that all of a firm's activities should be focused on its target markets. It logically follows, therefore, that if one fully understands the needs and attitudes of a target market, then combining the four Ps should be "easy." There are three gaps in this line of reasoning, however: (1) we don't always know as much as we would like to about the needs and attitudes of our target markets; (2) competitors are also trying to satisfy these or similar needs—and their efforts may force shifts of a firm's marketing mix; and (3) the other uncontrollable variables may be changing—and require more changes in marketing mixes.

Understanding leads to profitable mixes maybe

A clear understanding of the needs and attitudes of the firm's target market can make the development of a marketing mix "relatively" easy—even in the face of competition. Kodak, for example, has had continued success in the "consumer film market" by stressing good quality and convenience. It has prospered by following George Eastman's original philosophy: "You press the button, we do the rest." As segmenters, Kodak offered good film, made it conveniently available, and arranged for high-quality, rapid processing all over the world.

Kodak's successful marketing mix did not satisfy everyone, however—particularly those who wanted their pictures *immediately*. Polaroid came along to satisfy this market segment with a different marketing mix—including "instant pictures." They may not be as good as the pictures a production-oriented chemical engineer would like to deliver. But they are delivered fast (providing time utility)—and the speed makes up for the lower quality and higher price, at least for some customers. Polaroid's strategy was extremely profitable. To compete in this market, Kodak came out with its own "fast delivery" system in 1976—30 years after Kodak had rejected the Polaroid approach as "frivolous."

Kodak's move into the "instant picture" market may put it in the role of "me-too" imitator. On the other hand, market research showed that Polaroid was not satisfying everyone in the "instant picture" market. Even people who already owned a Polaroid said they might be interested in buying another kind of instant camera—if conditions were right. Desired features were: no need for timing, better color, no peeling, no waste paper, and no use of chemicals. As Kodak saw it, some customers wanted greater convenience in use—and better quality in their instant pictures. And Kodak has been able to capture a good share of the "instant picture" market.

Superior mixes may be breakthrough opportunities

When marketing managers fully understand their target markets, they may be able to develop marketing mixes which are obviously superior to "competitive mixes." Such understanding may provide breakthrough opportunities—until their competitors reach the same understanding of the market and decide to meet them "head-on." Taking advantage of these kinds of opportunities can lead to large sales—and profitable growth. This is why we have continually stressed the

Polaroid developed a marketing mix to do a very good job of satisfying the segment that wants "instant pictures."

importance of looking for breakthrough opportunities—rather than merely trying to patch up or improve present mixes.

Inferior mixes are easy to reject

Just as some mixes are clearly superior, some mixes are obviously inferior or unsuitable. For example, a national TV advertising campaign might make sense for a large company—but be completely out of the question for a small manufacturer offering a new product only in Quebec.

In-between mixes are harder to develop

Where competitors are hitting each other "head-on," it is even more important to understand the target market—and how it is likely to respond to alternative marketing mixes. Here, we have more need for estimating response functions.

Response Functions May Help Plan Better Strategies

A **response function** shows (mathematically and/or graphically) how the firm's target market is expected to react to changes in marketing variables. So, trying to estimate relevant response functions can be a real aid in developing better marketing mixes.

Response functions usually are plotted as curves showing how sales and profit will vary at different levels of marketing expenditures—but other relationships may be helpful, too. Possibilities include how sales and profits will vary if (1) prices are changed or (2) different promotion blends are used.

To deepen your understanding of response functions—and to show how they might be useful—we will first focus on response functions for each of the four Ps. See Figure 21–2, where possible response functions are graphed for each of the four Ps. The response function for the whole marketing mix will be discussed a little later.

These are just examples of the general shape of the curves which *might* be found in the real world. A particular company aiming at a particular target mar-

■   FIGURE 21–2   Four "illustrative only" response functions

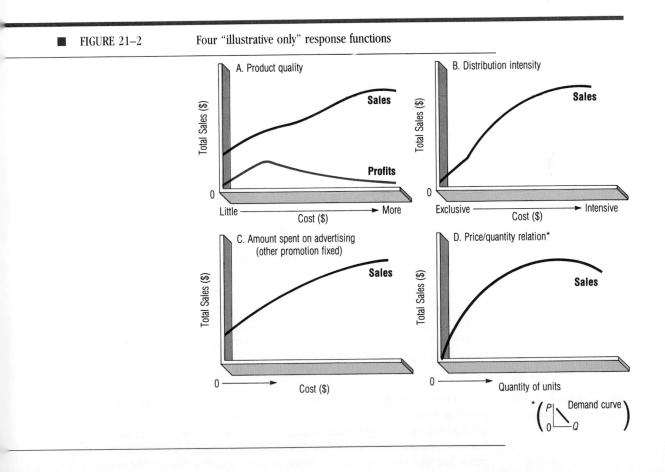

ket—and facing a particular group of competitors—might have quite different response functions. And these functions might lead a marketing manager to select very different mixes than competitors'—or than similar companies operating in the other markets. Again, the response functions illustrated here should be seen as examples only—*not* as typical responses.

The shape of such response functions is obviously critical to the selection of the "best" blend for each particular P—and for a whole marketing mix. Yet we do not know much about the precise shapes of the functions. Worse, there is no published source of empirically verified response functions for varying situations. The manager usually must develop his own response functions—using past experience and judgment, perhaps aided by marketing research. As difficult as such estimating may be, it is still necessary if a careful evaluation of alternatives is desired. Response functions do not "go away" if they are ignored—and decisions made without them may be just crude guesses.

Product quality response function

A response function for product quality may show that adding more quality (and features) will increase sales (perhaps even continuously up to a point)—but it may also increase costs and, therefore, result in a profit response function which reaches a high point and then declines. This "maximum point" is the "best" level for product quality (depending upon the firm's objectives, of course!). See Figure 21–2A.

Place-distribution intensity response function

A Place-related response function which focuses on the degree of market exposure desired (ranging from exclusive to intensive) might look like the response function shown in Figure 21–2B. The reason sales level off near the extreme of intensive distribution is that when most outlets already carry the product, little increase in sales can be expected from the last few, perhaps marginal, outlets.

Promotion—advertising response function

Figure 21–2C shows a possible response function for advertising. This figure suggests that even with no advertising, personal selling (and other promotion efforts) will get some sales results. But sales will be higher with some advertising. On the extreme right of the response function, the curve starts to level off—showing declining results from extra advertising. (Although picking the best level is beyond the scope of this text, it is important to note that the best point may not be at the highest sales level. Marginal analysis can be used here to show that as the response function begins to flatten out, the marginal return of sales to advertising dollar begins to decline.)

Price-demand curve response function

The Price-oriented response function shown in Figure 21–2D illustrates the impact of price level variations on sales and quantity sold. This figure is simply another way of showing the down-sloping demand curve which we have discussed in various parts of the text. Note that a down-sloping demand curve does mean that total sales will start declining at some quantity. Recall that marginal

L'eggs paid to achieve intensive distribution—because they thought it would increase sales.

revenue can go negative—and this means that total revenue is declining. It is not possible to increase total dollar sales indefinitely with price cuts!

A manager must estimate his own response functions

Estimating response functions is not easy. They are probably changing all the time. Further, there will be different response functions for each target market. Nevertheless, each marketing manager should make some estimate about the likely response of customers to the various ingredients he controls. This is where past experience—and careful analysis of how the same or similar customers are responding to competitors' mixes—is useful. If one firm has already tried a 10 percent price cut to encourage retailers to sell more by cutting their own prices, for example, and the retailers simply absorb the extra margin, then the response function for this kind of price cutting is not attractive. But another competitor may have increased the number of calls made on each retailer—with great results. Some marketing research might help a manager decide whether he also has such a response function—and whether increasing sales effort would be equally successful for his firm.

Estimating general marketing effort response functions

Besides trying to estimate response functions for each of the four Ps, it is desirable to estimate the general response function for all marketing effort in one marketing mix. Then, different response functions for alternative mixes can be compared when seeking the "best" mix for any particular target market. Such a generalized marketing response function is presented in Figure 21–3—showing the relation between marketing effort (in dollars) and sales (or profits) for one marketing mix.

Threshold effort is needed to get any sales

The shape of this response function probably is typical of the alternatives facing marketing managers. This response function shows that a higher level of

■ **FIGURE 21–3**   A marketing effort response function for one marketing mix

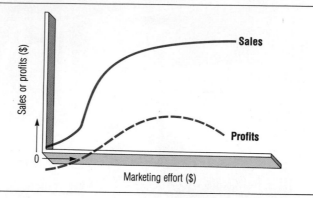

marketing expenditures *may* yield a higher level of sales (or profits). But just spending more and more money for marketing won't guarantee better profits. Further, there is not a straight-line relationship between marketing expenditures and sales (or profits). Instead, some expenditure may be necessary to get *any sales at all.* This is called the **threshold expenditure level**—the minimum expenditure level needed just to be in a market. After this level, small increases in expenditures may result in large increases in sales for awhile (as the curve rises rapidly)—after which, additional expenditures may lead to little or no increase in sales (where the sales curve flattens out) and a decline in profits.

The response function for a whole marketing mix is the result of the interaction of all the mix ingredients. There are techniques for estimating these functions—if we know the shape of all the mix ingredient functions. But this topic is beyond our scope.[1]

For our purposes, we'll have to be satisfied to know that it is possible to "roughly" estimate response functions for alternative mixes and that, therefore, it

■ **FIGURE 21–4**   Response functions for three different marketing mixes for next year

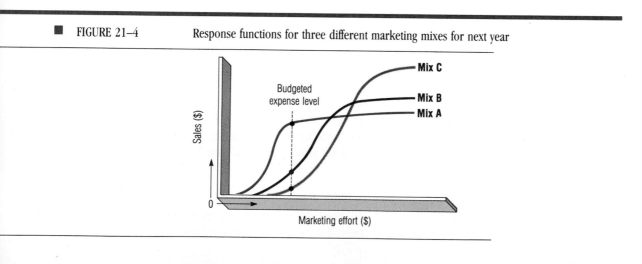

■ TABLE 21–1

Comparing the estimated sales, costs, and profits of four "reasonable" alternative marketing mixes*

Marketing mix	Price	Selling cost	Advertising cost	Total units	Sales	Total cost	Total profit
A	$15	$20,000	$ 5,000	5,000	$ 75,000	$ 70,000	$ 5,000
B	15	20,000	20,000	7,000	105,000	95,000	10,000
C	20	30,000	30,000	7,000	140,000	115,000	25,000
D	25	40,000	40,000	5,000	125,000	125,000	0

*For the same target market, assuming product costs per unit are $5 and fixed (overhead) costs are $20,000.

is possible to select the best one—given the firm's resources and objectives. Figure 21–4 shows three estimated response functions for three different mixes. If the marketing manager's budget were fixed at the level shown in Figure 21–4— and he wanted to maximize sales in the short run—then Mix A is clearly best.

If a manager didn't want to estimate whole functions, it would be useful to estimate the sales and costs of "reasonable" alternative marketing mixes and compare them for profitability. Table 21–1 illustrates such a comparison for a small appliance which is currently selling for $15—Line 1 in the example. Here, the marketing manager simply estimated the costs and likely results of four "reasonable" alternatives. And assuming profitability is the objective *and* there are adequate resources to consider each of the alternatives, then marketing Mix C is obviously the best alternative.

Typical mixes are a good starting point for marketing mix planning

Typical mixes are a good starting point for developing possible marketing mixes—and estimating their response functions. What others have done in similar situations must have satisfied someone—and can serve as a guide. And, if actual sales and cost data are available—or can be estimated—then at least a few points on response functions can be estimated. Beyond this, judgment or some marketing research will be needed. In this way, you can make use of past experience—while not relying on it blindly.

We will discuss typical marketing mixes in the next section. They will serve as a good starting point for developing unique marketing mixes—knowing the firm's own target market and its own objectives, resources, and competition.

During this discussion, try to develop a feel for which mix ingredients seem "most important." These will probably be the ones which have the most steeply rising response functions over reasonable cost levels—that's why they are typically used. For example, if personal selling is very important in a particular mix, this probably means that the personal selling response function is more attractive than the other marketing mix ingredients. Even so, a marketing manager will want to evaluate how good personal selling is (over a range of expenditures) before naively spending all his promotion money on personal selling or (maybe worse) all his marketing money on this one ingredient.

Typical Marketing Mixes Related to Goods Classes

Ideally, the ingredients of a good marketing mix will flow logically from all the relevant dimensions of a target market. Table 21–2 shows the kinds of market dimensions you might like to know—and their effect on the strategic decision areas. Usually, however, you do not or cannot know all that you would like to about a potential target market. You may know enough, however, to decide whether the product is a consumer good or an industrial good—and which goods class is most relevant.

The relevant goods classes have a direct bearing on marketing mix planning—because they are based on how potential customers view and buy the product—not on the characteristics of the products themselves. So, if you don't know as much as you would like about the potential customers' needs and attitudes, at least knowing how they would classify the company's product can give you a head start on developing a marketing mix. Further, it's reassuring to see that goods classes do summarize some of what you would like to know about target markets—as seen in Table 21–2.

A first step, then, is to put each product into the proper goods class. This will simplify the selection of Place and Promotion, especially—since goods classes suggest how and why various products are typically distributed and promoted.

Now let's tie together what we know about goods classes with a description of how and why various products typically are distributed and promoted. The major emphasis will be on how Place and Promotion are usually handled, although packaging and branding will be referred to when relevant.

Price will be more or less ignored in this discussion of typical behavior because, generally, Price is badly handled. Also, goods classes are not as relevant

■   TABLE 21–2   Relation of potential target market dimensions (including ones which are related to goods classes) to marketing mix decision areas

Potential target market dimensions	Effects on decision areas
1. Geographic location and other demographic characteristics of potential customers	Affects size of *Target Markets* (economic potential) and *Place* (where products should be made available) and *Promotion* (where and to whom to advertise)
2. Behavioral needs, attitudes, and how present and potential goods or services fit into customers' consumption patterns	Affects *Product* (design, packaging, length or width of product line) and *Promotion* (what potential customers need and want to know about the product offering, and what appeals should be used)
3. Urgency to get need satisfied and desire and willingness to compare and shop	Affects *Place* (how directly products are distributed from producer to consumer, how extensively they are made available, and the level of service needed) and *Price* (how much potential customers are willing to pay)

The ingredients of a good marketing mix typically flow logically from the relevant dimensions of a target market.

for pricing—except when they suggest inelasticity of demand, for example, as with impulse, emergency, specialty, and repair goods. After a manager has "roughed out" a mix based on goods classes, he probably should spend a good deal more time considering what would be the best price—in the light of the strength of the rest of the mix and the firm's objectives. We discussed this in Chapters 19 and 20.

"Typical" is not necessarily "right"

In the following paragraphs, we will describe the typical Place and Promotion methods used. Try to see the "why" of typical channels and typical promotion blends—rather than memorizing "right" answers. Although these are typical, they are not necessarily right for all situations. Some very profitable marketing mixes have departed from the typical—to satisfy some target markets better.

Typical Mixes for Consumer Goods

Convenience goods—get them where the customers are

Most convenience goods, especially staples, are relatively simple items—seldom requiring installation, service, or even much personal selling.

The scattered location of target customers and the typically small size of each purchase encourage the use of several middlemen—especially merchant wholesalers and retailers. It is impractical for manufacturers to set up their own retail outlets.

Staples

Since staples are often in the market maturity stage of the product life cycle—with large potential target markets—a manufacturer's promotion blend usually emphasizes mass selling. If a producer promotes a product effectively, the merchant wholesalers and retailers may not have to do much more than receive, break bulk, and store the appropriate assortment until needed.

Retailers usually do not voluntarily provide displays or special promotion aids—except for their own dealer brands. Therefore, producers and wholesalers' sales reps have to promote each product to wholesalers and retailers—and provide any store displays and point-of-purchase aids which are needed.

Impulse goods

With impulse goods, the need for intensive distribution and point-of-purchase display at the retail level is obvious. Basically, promotion of impulse goods is aimed at the channels—relying mainly on aggressive personal selling to the retailer. Although merchant wholesalers may stock the goods, the manufacturer usually has to go directly to retailers with his own salespeople to assure well-placed displays. This usually requires highly persuasive personal selling to the retailer. Consumer advertising may not be essential—unless several similar goods are competing in the channels. Then, a producer may have to promote his product to final consumers—to impress retailers and wholesalers that his product is the best impulse item available.

Emergency goods

Since emergency goods are regarded as necessities for special circumstances, they must have wide distribution—and must be available at times when regular outlets might not be open. A variety of retailers cater to emergency business—all-night gas stations, open-till-midnight food and beverage stores, and vending machines. Intensive distribution is needed to these outlets. And this can require intensive distribution to wholesalers to reach these outlets.

Little consumer promotion is needed—except what is necessary to remind buyers of the product's availability when an emergency occurs. Mass selling to consumers can be used if a producer wants to move a product from the emergency goods class—where brands are less important—to another class. Antifreeze manufacturers, for example, advertise to try to get motorists to install *their* brand all year long or early in the fall—to avoid the last-minute rush. But despite their efforts, many drivers still wait until the first freeze warning and then pour anything available into the radiator. At this point, having widespread distribution is all-important to the producer and wholesalers.

The main promotion job for these goods is in the channels—to get distribution. A very persuasive personal selling job may be needed if competitive products are available. As with impulse goods, mass selling can be used to impress channel members with the firm's offering.

Shopping goods—the direct route if necessary

Target customers for shopping goods—like the customers for convenience goods—are widely scattered. But shopping-goods customers are willing to make more of an effort to satisfy their needs. The producer needs fewer retail outlets—and direct-to-retail distribution is possible. Producer-to-consumer selling is unlikely, however, because consumers generally want to compare shopping goods. Retailers play a key role here.

Homogeneous shopping goods

Homogeneous shopping goods do not require attractive surroundings or knowledgeable sales personnel. For well-known manufacturers' brands of appliances, for instance, price is very important to some consumers. They are willing to go to back-alley discount houses, if necessary, to buy them. Unbranded soft goods—such as towels and children's clothing—may be dumped into bins, and customers will sort through them for the lowest-priced items.

A manufacturer of homogeneous shopping goods may decide that it is too difficult—or impossible—to upgrade the consumer image of the product—especially if it is in the later stages of the product life cycle. He may then drop selective distribution efforts and try to gain intensive distribution—with as many wholesale and retail outlets as possible.

Some retailers use personal selling to try to get potential customers to see that they offer more than just low price. Others—such as the mass-merchandisers—have gone to self-service and check-out counters for such products. They still advertise products, however—emphasizing low prices—to project a low-price image for *all* their products. Here, the objective is to "sell" the store—not just particular items.

Heterogeneous shopping goods

Heterogeneous shopping goods are compared by consumers on more than just price. For this reason, they require more retail display and often more personal selling—both to final consumers and to middlemen.

Producers frequently bypass wholesalers, because they *must* tell the sales story to retailers—sometimes including technical information that must be explained directly to the retail clerks. Since they must make the sales calls anyway, they feel they might as well take the orders and deliver the product themselves. Fairly direct channels are also encouraged by the willingness of retail buyers to make regular trips to central markets for home furnishings and clothing. Resident buyers also speed the direct movement of these goods—especially for style and fashion goods.

Mass selling may be used by manufacturers or retailers—to inform customers about the unique aspects of these heterogeneous goods. Copies of national advertisements may be sent to retailers—and displayed by the retailers to show customers that they offer nationally advertised products.

Generally, brand promotion is less important for these goods. Some manufacturers do little or no advertising for clothing and home furnishings—because consumers want to compare products in the store. Manufacturers may rely more on informed retail clerks. They may be paid promotion allowances—such as a $5 bonus for each new mattress sold. Personal contacts in the channels—stressing economic arguments and demonstrating effective selling techniques—are essential here.

Specialty goods—hold a favored position

Specialty goods are normally distributed through the same channels as those convenience or shopping goods they most nearly resemble. The favored status of these products makes it relatively easy to promote them to wholesalers and retailers—on the basis of profit potential.

Retailers advertising these products may use mass media—such as billboards and newspaper ads—just to remind customers where they are for sale.

However, specialty goods may require continued mass selling by the manufacturer. Consumers are fickle. If similar products are being promoted aggressively, the manufacturer does not want to risk losing brand familiarity. New customers are continually entering the market—and must be convinced that the product is a specialty good. This mass selling by producers also helps assure middlemen of continued customer acceptance.

Unsought goods— need some extra push

Unsought goods are in the introductory stage of their life cycle. All potential customers must be fully informed about them. Mass selling may be used by manufacturers to reach final consumers—but order getters may be needed to convince wholesalers and retailers of the profit potential of these products. If they aren't convinced, the products may not even reach the retail level.

A large, established firm just introducing an unsought good—one similar to the firm's other products—may be able to use the rest of its line and its reputation to get distribution for the new product. The producer may still have to pay for or supply all promotion, but it *is* able to get distribution.

A smaller producer—or a larger one going into a new market—may not be so lucky. It may have to resort to the use of less efficient middlemen, mail-order selling, or house-to-house selling.

Aggressive and persuasive personal selling is needed to put these products across—especially in the channels. But to impress the channel members, the products may have to be supported by mass selling—and even a pulling policy. Manufacturer's or wholesaler's salespeople may be needed to give demonstrations—and set up displays and point-of-purchase materials. Perhaps the producer will have to offer pricing deals. Personal salespeople may be needed to adapt a company's marketing mix to each individual situation.

Typical Mixes for Industrial Goods

For the industrial buyer, personal selling is important

Unlike final consumers, industrial buyers usually don't seek out the goods they need. By accepted practice, they wait for the seller to present products or ideas. If a technical story must be told, direct distribution may be desirable—or even necessary.

The promotion blends of both producers and middlemen tend to emphasize personal selling because most markets are relatively limited and concentrated—and the selling job is often technical. The specific marketing mix, however, varies by goods class.

Installations—president may become the sales rep

Some installations—specific buildings or pieces of property or custom-made machines—are unique and have special technical characteristics. Promotion must inform target customers about these products—and persuade them of the advantages. Usually, personal selling is the best method.

New installations are normally sold directly by the contractor's or manufacturer's own sales representative since (1) customers are relatively few and geographically concentrated, (2) the potential sales volume is large, and (3) there is need for design, technical assistance, and service of a kind that middlemen don't normally provide. Even smaller companies may sell directly. The president or executive officers often serve as the sales force.

Brokers often handle sales of used buildings and land rights—since buyers and sellers are not regularly in the market. These specialized middlemen know the market and can provide a useful service.

Accessory equipment—middlemen are often needed

With some accessory equipment, direct-to-user personal selling by the producer is common—and important (1) to convince users of the merits of buying a particular company's product and (2) to give technical assistance when necessary.

For other accessories, however, potential customers are spread out and still need frequent contact by experienced salespeople. For such products, large firms use manufacturers' agents or brokers in less populous areas—and smaller firms use them throughout the country. These agents provide continuous contact—and there is no cost to the producer until a sale is completed. The cost of the agents' regular sales calls is spread over a number of products—so the producer can get sales coverage without the high overhead sales costs of doing this job for himself for only one line.

If effective agents or brokers aren't available, then merchant wholesalers—such as mill supply houses or oil field supply houses—may be used. But relatively little sales effort can be expected from them. They may simply list the items in a catalog—and sell them if customers ask about them. Typically, their salespeople are not specialists—and can't be expected to provide a technical sales job or service.

Farm product raw materials—many small farmers

The large number of small farmers creates a real discrepancy of quantity—and perhaps of assortment. This creates many specialized middlemen. Assemblers gather farm products in rural areas—and commission merchants and merchant wholesalers handle these products in the terminal markets, as the products come closer to users.

Farm products usually require no promotion—except for the routine order taking which is needed to complete a sale. Usually, farm products are homogeneous commodities sold in almost pure competition—so channel systems have evolved to routinely bring buyers and sellers together.

Some farmers' cooperatives and trade associations try to differentiate their offerings—even to the extent of branding their products and spending fairly large sums on advertising. These mass selling efforts are not done by the individual producers, however.

Natural product raw materials—a few big producers

These products are produced by fewer and larger firms. There is little or no need for assemblers. There are few users—compared to final consumers. As a result, many of these producers handle distribution themselves—although smaller producers may use brokers or drop-shippers. The smaller firms need practically the same market coverage as the larger firms, but have less to sell and a smaller sales volume to cover selling costs.

Most of these products have reached the market maturity or even sales decline stages—and tend to be standardized. Prices—which usually are available in newspapers—are competitive. Promotion is not unimportant, however. Buyers still must decide from whom they will buy. So, opportunities exist for much persuasive personal selling by order getters. The personality of the particular salesperson—and the company image he conveys—can be the deciding factors.

Component parts and materials—personal contact may be vital

Most components producers are specialized—and cater to a relatively small, concentrated group of users. Since technical and design assistance may be needed, these producers normally deal directly with their target customers. If potential customers are numerous and widespread, however, agents may help locate and service new business. And they may be granted exclusive territories to encourage selling effort.

Promotion for these products must inform the prospective buyers about technical details—as well as price, quality, and delivery dependability.

Personal selling is the chief means of promoting component parts and materials. Some components are custom-made for specific applications—and sales reps are vital to assure that both buyers and sellers are aware of each other's needs and capabilities. Further, very persuasive salespeople are important because many competitors can offer the same technical service or even identical products. As with raw materials—given essentially homogeneous products and price—the competence and personality of the salesperson can be very important.

Supplies—middlemen rank high for maintenance items

Maintenance items are used widely—and are similar to convenience goods. Customers are widely spread—purchases of each item are relatively small—and little technical assistance or service is needed. Since this is an ideal situation for

Promotion for components informs buyers about technical details—as well as price, quality, and delivery dependability.

middlemen, merchant wholesalers are common in this field. Mill supply houses and office and stationery supply stores often serve as middlemen for maintenance items. They are contacted directly by larger producers in the major metro areas—and by manufacturers' agents in other areas. Smaller producers may use manufacturers' agents for all contacts with these merchant wholesalers.

For these goods, the producer's main promotion job is personal selling—in the channel—to get distribution. Some mass selling may be desirable to encourage wholesalers to stock the firm's products, but personal selling is vital—to actually get the wholesalers' business. The merchant wholesalers, then, provide an order-taking role.

Repair items

Repair items are used widely and—with some exceptions—may be distributed in the same way as maintenance items. Large customers may have complete repair facilities and prefer to buy repair parts directly. Smaller manufacturers and contractors usually prefer to have wholesalers carry the parts inventory—and perhaps handle the repair service, too.

Since most repair parts come directly from the original manufacturer, the main promotion job is to inform buyers of their availability. These products have a "captive market." Persuasion isn't necessary.

However, if the market is large enough to attract competitors—as with some automotive and electrical products—then persuasion must be used, too. The main promotion appeals are faster, more dependable service. Personal selling may have to be used to meet competition.

Operating supply items

Operating supply items—with few exceptions—are similar to maintenance items and are distributed in the same way. The exceptions are some bulky items—such as coal, lubricants, and fuel oil. Direct distribution of these supplies by the producer may be sensible because of variations in technical service needs (as for lubricants) or the large sales volumes (fuel oil). Drop-shippers commonly act as middlemen for the many small coal producers—to make the sales calls without handling the coal.

Services—usually are sold directly

Most "services" don't involve physical goods. There is nothing tangible to move through a distribution system. As a result, the producers typically sell directly to their customers. Where the potential customers are scattered, however, agents may enter to provide the initial contacts. Then the producer's own salespeople can follow up.

Since most service businesses have relatively undifferentiated products, their promotion objective is to persuade—they emphasize personal selling.

When a service is new, information about price, availability, and dependability is all that is needed. But competitors usually enter a profitable field quickly, and personal selling is then needed to persuade customers about the value of the service.

Special Factors May Affect the Typical Marketing Mix

A marketing manager may have to develop a mix which is not typical because of various market realities—including special characteristics of the product or target market, the competitive environment, and his own firm's special capabilities and limitations. It is useful to see how some of these market realities may affect marketing mix decisions.

Not all targets look the same

Size and geographic concentration affect sales contacts needed

If the sales potential of the target market is large enough, it may be possible to go directly to retailers, consumers, or users. This is especially true if the target customers are highly concentrated—as are the customers for many industrial goods. An obvious example is the clustering of auto manufacturers in Central Canada. For final consumer goods, however, potential customers usually are numerous and widely scattered—and buy in small quantities. Although the total market may be relatively large, it might be split up into small geographic segments—with too little demand in each market to support a direct approach.

Value of item and frequency and regularity of purchase

Even low-priced items such as groceries may be handled directly if they are purchased often and the total volume is large—as in the case of home-delivered milk and bread. But for products purchased infrequently—even though purchases are large—specialists such as commission merchants, agents, brokers, and other middlemen are useful. A critical factor is the cost of regularly providing the needed marketing functions—in relation to actual sales.

Customer preferences for personal contact

Customer preferences vary even within the same goods class. Some target customers—especially some industrial customers—don't like to deal with middlemen. Even though they may want only small quantities, they prefer to buy directly from manufacturers. The manufacturers may tolerate it because these customers sometimes buy larger quantities.

Other buyers, however, prefer the convenience of buying through a middleman—because they can telephone orders and get immediate action from a local source. Two quite different marketing mixes may be needed to fully satisfy both types of customers.

Not all products are the same

Some goods—because of their technical nature, perishability, or bulkiness—require *more direct* distribution than is implied by their goods class.

Technical products

Complicated products—such as conveyor systems and electronic data processing equipment—call for much technical selling ability, and expert installation and servicing. Wholesalers usually don't want—nor are they equipped—to provide all these required services.

Perishability

Perishable items—cut flowers, milk, and fresh seafood—may have to be handled directly. If many small producers are clustered together, specialists may develop to handle transportation, refrigeration, and storage. Complicated terminal markets—such as those dealing in fresh produce—may develop—along with many specialized commission merchants, brokers, merchant wholesalers, and truck wholesalers.

High-fashion items also are "perishable"—and call for more direct distribution to speed the flow to retailers. Sometimes retailers and final consumers even go directly to the producers—to see the latest fashion showings in New York or Paris.

Bulkiness

Transporting, handling, and storing costs rise when bulky products are moved—making it hard for middlemen to operate. If a producer can't make enough sales contacts when selling bulky items direct, brokers, manufacturers' agents, and especially drop-shippers may be used. They will make the sales contacts—and the producer will ship the goods directly to the customer.

Not all channel structures are the same

The marketing manager's "ideal" channel system may not be available or even possible—as we'll see next.

Availability of suitable and cooperative middlemen

The kinds of middlemen the marketing manager would like to use may not even be available—or willing to cooperate. This is more likely if the company enters a market late and competitors already have tied up the best middlemen—perhaps as part of a selective or exclusive distribution policy. *Aggressive market-oriented* middlemen usually aren't just waiting for someone to use them. They *may* be receptive to good proposals—but just another "me-too" mix won't interest them.

A toy manufacturer might like to have aggressive market-oriented middlemen in the channel—but they may not be interested.

The specific customers already being reached by each proposed middleman are very important. If these do not include the marketing manager's target markets, then that middleman doesn't have much to offer. A wholesaler specializing in groceries has a valuable customer list for the food business—but it is not of much value in distributing electronic machinery.

Uniformity of market coverage of available middlemen

The middlemen available in large urban areas may be very effective there—but may not cover outlying areas. Two channels may be needed to reach both areas. But it may also lead to a dual distribution problem. The middlemen who are suitable for outlying areas may also cover urban areas—but not as well. Everyone likes to work where sales are plentiful—and easy to make.

Nor does distribution through national or international companies guarantee uniform coverage. For example, Steinberg's has a much larger share of the retail grocery market in Quebec than in Ontario. And The Hudson's Bay Company has been stronger in Western Canada than in other regions. This simply means that, in practice, every channel must be custom-made for every target market.

Financing required in channel system

Adequate credit may be critical for smoothing the flow through a channel system. Some middlemen enter a channel mainly because they can give financial help to the members. This is the role of factors. But some merchant wholesalers also hold a secure position in a channel because of their strong financial condition—and willingness to meet the financial needs of other channel members. This is especially true in international markets.

Nature of the company itself—is it big, rich, and unprejudiced?

In deciding what kind of mix to offer and how to work within a channel system, each marketing manager—at every level in the system—must evaluate his company's capabilities, needs, and potential contributions to the channel. Realistically, it may be best to join a strong system—rather than try to be the channel captain.

Size of company and width of product line

A company's size affects its place in a channel system—because size affects discrepancies of quantity and assortment. A large producer already making a wide line of food or soap products, for example, may be in a good position to take on an additional product of the same type and handle it the same way—perhaps directly. In contrast, a smaller producer—or one with unrelated lines—may suffer from a discrepancy of quantity or discrepancy of assortment—or both—and would probably find middlemen more practical.

Financial strength

A company's financial strength is relevant if its customers need financial help. Firms unable to provide this financing may need specialized middlemen. Selling agents, factors, merchant wholesalers, or large retailers may be able to finance a producer or channel members—including users or final consumers. In fact, a captain's strength may depend heavily on financing ability.

Planning Must Use the Product Life Cycle

So far we have been emphasizing the development the "best" marketing strategy for some target market. This can be risky, however, if you forget that markets are continually changing. This means that you must plan strategies which can adjust to changing conditions. Although some environmental changes are completely uncontrollable—and even unpredictable—some other changes *are* more predictable. And these should be considered when developing a plan. In particular, the product life cycle should be given serious attention because, typically, marketing variables should change throughout a product's life cycle.[2]

Figure 21–5 shows some of the typical changes in marketing variables which might be needed over the course of a product life cycle. This figure is a good review. Notice that as the product life cycle moves on, the marketing manager should *expect* to find more products entering "his" market—and pushing the market closer to pure competition or oligopoly. This means that as the cycle moves along, he may want to shift from a selective to an intensive distribution policy *and* move from a skimming to a penetration pricing policy. The original marketing plan may even include these likely adjustments and the probable timing.

It is not necessary to make plans to last for the full length of a product life cycle. A firm can drop out of a market. But you must be aware that the cycle will move on—and you should make your own plans accordingly.

Nonprofit and Social Marketing

Defining terms   Nonprofit marketing is another activity whose importance has only recently been recognized. "Nonprofit marketing is conducted by organizations that oper-

■ FIGURE 21–5   Typical changes in marketing variables over the course of the product life cycle

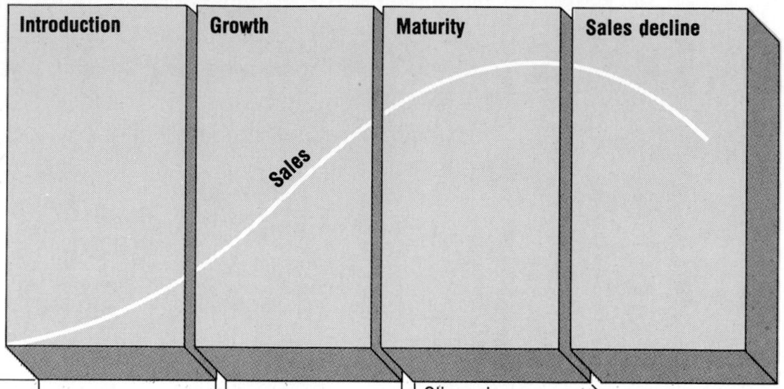

	Introduction	Growth	Maturity	Sales decline
		Sales		
Competitive situation	Monopoly	Monopolistic competition	Oligopoly or monopolistic competition heading toward pure competition	→
Product	One	Variety-try to find best product Build brand familiarity	All "same" Battle of brands	Some drop out
Place	Build channels Maybe selective distribution		→ Move toward more intensive distribution	→
Promotion	Pioneering-informing Build primary demand	Informing and persuading ————→ Persuading and Build selective demand ————————→ reminding Frantically competitive		
Price	Skimming or penetration	Meet competition (especially in oligopoly) ————→ or Price dealing and price cutting ————————————→		

ate in the public interest or to foster a cause and do not seek financial profits. It may involve organizations (religious groups, labor unions, trade associations), people (political candidates), places (resorts, convention centers, industrial sites), and ideas (stop smoking) as well as products and services."[3] Clearly, *nonprofit marketing* is a very broad term that covers many different types of marketing.

Social marketing is defined as "the design, implementation, and control of programs seeking to increase the acceptability of a social idea or practice in a target market."[4] Social marketing is usually, but not always, a form of nonprofit marketing. A liquor company that encourages responsible drinking or an automobile manufacturer that promotes safe driving are both examples of profit-making organizations engaged in social marketing.[5] Far more often, however, social marketing is carried out by nonprofit organizations.

The basic idea behind nonprofit marketing is easy to understand. The concept of marketing can be broadened to include much more than meeting consumer needs at a profit. Many organizations must face uncontrollable elements—and could effectively use the same marketing research techniques that business employs. There are nonprofit equivalents to the four Ps, (Product, Price, Promotion, or Place) though the exact form of each would be somewhat different. Target markets can be selected and appropriate marketing services put together by all kinds of nonprofit organizations.[6]

Differences and similarities with "for-profit" marketing

This call for broadening the concept of marketing was first published in 1969. Since then we have learned much more about the similarities and differences between for-profit and nonprofit marketing. We have learned that nonprofit organizations differ from profit-seeking ones in at least two important ways. (1) Lack of concrete objectives and a "bottom-line" profit target often keep nonprofit organizations from making the changes a marketing approach usually requires. Corporations, on the other hand, generally have to make such changes if they want to stay in business. (2) Churches, universities, hospitals, and libraries are labor-intensive. In such organizations, increased demand does not automatically make mass production, economies of scale, or other cost-saving innovations possible. In fact, marketing programs that increase demand may make things worse rather than better. So these organizations might use marketing to *reduce* the total demand for their services.

Figure 21–6 shows how social marketing is different in such areas as market analysis, market segmentation, organization, control, and the traditional mix areas of Product, Price, Promotion, and Place. These differences are important—and pose real problems for the social or nonprofit marketer. On the other hand, such differences do not mean that marketing has been broadened too far.

Marketing still has much to contribute to the nonprofit sector. A marketing attitude results in a more responsible social service organization willing to listen to the needs of its consumers. And that attitude should help such organizations realize that some products or services have outlived their usefulness and need to be replaced by new offerings.

The nonprofit organization which takes a marketing approach will think in terms of segmenting and of matching products with markets. Just as is done in the for-profit sector, marketing plans will be developed for each product-market segment that the nonprofit organization chooses to serve.

A marketing-minded nonprofit organization will also use marketing research and forecasting techniques—and appreciate such marketing concepts as the product life cycle, the innovation and diffusion process, and the theory of communication.

Companies Plan and Implement Marketing Programs

Several plans make a program

Most companies implement more than one strategic plan at the same time. A **marketing program** blends all of a firm's strategic plans into one "big" plan.

■   FIGURE 21–6   What's different about social marketing?

I.   Market analysis differences
      A.   Social marketers usually have:
            Less good secondary data available about their consumers.
      B.   Social marketers have more difficulty:
            Obtaining valid and reliable measures of key factors.
            Determining how important each such factor is in affecting consumer behavior.
            Getting consumer research studies funded, approved and completed.
II.   Market segmentation differences
      A.   Social marketers:
            Frequently do not have accurate behavior to use in identifying segments.
            Face pressure against segmentation that leads to the ignoring of certain groups.
            Often have target segments consisting of the most negatively disposed consumers.
III. Product strategy differences
      A.   Social marketers have:
            Less flexibility in shaping their products or offerings.
            More difficulty in formulating product concepts.
            More difficulty selecting and implementing long-term positioning strategies.
IV.   Pricing strategy differences
      A.   The development of a pricing strategy primarily involves trying to reduce the mone-
            tary, psychic, energy, and time costs of consumers.
      B.   Social marketers:
            Can encounter real difficulties in measuring their prices.
            Tend to have less control over consumer costs.
V.   Place strategy differences
      A.   Social marketers have more difficulty utilizing and controlling desired intermediaries.
VI.   Promotional strategy differences
      A.   Social marketers usually:
            Find paid advertising impossible to use.
            Must communicate relatively large amounts of complex information.
      B.   Social marketers often:
            Face pressure not to use certain types of appeals in their messages.
            Have difficulty conducting meaningful pretests of alternate appeals.
VII. Organizational design differences
      A.   Social marketers must function in organizations:
            Where marketing activities are poorly understood, weakly appreciated, and improp-
               erly located.
            Where plans (if any are developed) are treated as records rather than as action
               documents.
            That are especially poor in keeping organizational records.
VIII. Evaluation differences
      A.   Social marketers often find it difficult:
            Even to establish effectiveness measures.
            To estimate marketing contribution to the achievement of these objectives.

Source: Adapted from Paul N. Bloom and William D. Novelli, "Problems and Challenges in Social Marketing," *Journal of Marketing*, Spring 1981, pp. 79–88.

When the various plans in the company's program are quite different, there may be less concern with how well they fit together—except as they compete for the firm's usually limited resources.

When the plans are similar, however, the sales force may have to carry out several plans. Or, the firm's advertising department may have to develop the publicity and advertising for several plans. In such situations, product managers will try to get enough of the common resources, say, salespeople's time, for their own plan.

Forms for each strategy can make planning easier

Forms such as the one shown in Figure 21–7 improve the planning process—and help communicate its results to others, including top management who must review the plans. This form spells out everything that should be covered in a marketing plan.

■ FIGURE 21–7   A suggested format for a marketing plan

I. "Management summary": of the major dimensions of the marketing program suggested and the implications for the firm's financial resources and performance.
II. A review of the market situation
   A. Buyer
      1. Level of primary demand; trends, determinants
      2. Nature of selective demand; sensitivity to various marketing approaches
   B. Competition
      1. Identification, by type, of relevant competitors; trends
      2. Share of market and other competitive performance measures
      3. Competitive programs and anticipated changes in programs
   C. Channels
      1. Identification, by type, of channels that are important trends
      2. Nature of channel behavior; sensitivity to various marketing approaches
   D. Technology
      1. Changes affecting people, institutions, products, communication, etc.
   E. Government and the public interest
      1. Laws: trends, enforcement patterns
      2. Expectations; responsibilities; bargaining arena
III. A review of the firm/product/brand situation
   A. Performance
      1. Past goals; results to date on dimensions such as market share, awareness, trial, repeat purchase rates, and contribution
   B. Resources audit
      1. Financial strengths and weaknesses
      2. Skills: marketing, people, production, and R&D
   C. Organization
      1. Nature of organization and implications for incentives, authority, responsibility, and accountability for decisions and changes in decisions
   D. Existing program
      1. Product, price, channels, and communications strategies summarized for the past and current periods
   E. Critique of performance
      1. Firm/product/brand performance (versus past objectives) explained in terms of events and activities that affected it
IV. A review of problems and opportunities for the future
   A. Opportunities
      1. Factors that will enable the firm to realize equal or improved marketing performance during the next period
   B. Problems
      1. Factors that may jeopardize future improvements in marketing performance
   C. Objectives
      1. What specific goals for the next period (in particular) and future periods (in general)
      2. Priorities if goals contradictory (e.g., profit margin versus market share; penetration of existing markets versus market development effort)
V. Program
   A. Overview
      1. Outline of the basic strategy, stripped to its essentials in terms of positioning selection and critical activities to achieve marketing success; this is sometimes referred to as the "core strategy"

■ FIGURE 21–7 *(concluded)*

    B. Product strategy
       1. Branding, features, etc.
    C. Pricing strategy
       1. To channels, to buyers, margins, etc.
    D. Channels strategy
       1. Retailers/wholesalers to use, incentives and controls, etc.
    E. Communications strategy
       1. Mix of methods, messages, media, timing, and measurement
    F. Research strategy
       1. Information needs to improve decisions
       2. Cost versus value of such information
       3. Plans and procedures to gather information to improve marketing program decisions
  VI. Financial implications of the program
    A. Revenues
       1. Amount and timing
    B. Expenses
       1. Variable, fixed, discretionary distinctions
       2. May include: cost of goods, media and production, sampling, promotion, trade allowances, market research, sales force, physical distribution, and administration
    C. Investments
       1. Inventory, receivables, advertising, and sales training
    D. Statements
       1. Income (profit and loss) for past and future
       2. Budget (and/or cash flow statement)
       3. Balance sheet (sometimes not included)
 VII. Program implementation
    A. Determination of what will be done, by whom, when, where
    B. Manpower recruiting, training, controlling, directing, and compensating
    C. Coordination with other areas/departments of the company
VIII. Program performance
    A. Information system
       1. Who gets what information, for what purpose, when, about the performance of all or part of the program
    B. Additional research
       1. Tests, studies, etc. proposed to add to information usually gathered about program performance and reasons for that performance
  IX. Contingency plans
    A. Situation changes
       1. Probable versus possible development in market situation (e.g., change by competition) and in company situation (e.g., change in financial support); indicators to give earliest possible warning of these changes
    B. Importance of changes
       1. What changes mean for program performance either in total or in part
    C. Alternate plans
       1. What to do if the changes occur to maintain or improve marketing performance
   X. Appendixes
    A. Financial exhibits
    B. Research exhibits
    C. Sales call plans, media schedules, promotion cycles, and sales promotion schedules

Source: Kenneth G. Hardy, Michael R. Pearce, Thomas C. Kinnear, and Adrian B. Ryans, *Canadian Marketing, Cases and Concepts* (Toronto: Allyn & Bacon Canada, 1978), pp. 593–94.

Almost always, a company's resources are limited—so the marketing manager must make hard choices. He can't launch a plan to pursue every promising opportunity, Instead, limited resources force him to choose among alternative plans—while developing the program.

Find the best program by trial and error

How do you find the "best" program? There is no one best way of comparing various plans. Much reliance must be placed on management judgment. Yet some calculations are helpful, too. If a five-year planning horizon seems to be realistic for the firm's markets, then expected profits over the five-year period can be compared for each plan.

Assuming that the company has a profit-oriented objective, the more profitable plans could be looked at first—in terms of both potential profit and resources required. Also, the impact on the entire program should be evaluated. One profitable looking alternative might be a poor first choice because it will eat up all the company's resources—and sidetrack several plans which together would be more profitable.

Some juggling among the various plans—comparing profitability versus resources needed and available—moves the company toward the *most profitable* program.

A computer program can help if a large number of alternatives must be evaluated. Actually, however, the computer would merely do the same function—trying to match potential revenues and profits against available resources.[7]

Allocating Budgets for a Marketing Program

Once the overall marketing program and long-term plans have been set, shorter-term plans also must be worked out. Typically, companies use annual budgets—both to plan what they are going to do and to provide control over various functions. Each department may be allowed to spend its budgeted amount—perhaps by months. As long as departments stay within their budgets, they are allowed considerable (or complete) freedom.

Budgeting for marketing—50 percent, 30 percent, or 10 percent is better than nothing

The most common method of budgeting for marketing expenditures is to compute a percentage of sales—either past or forecasted sales. The virtue of this method is its simplicity. A similar percentage can be used automatically each year—eliminating the need to keep evaluating the kind and amount of marketing effort needed and its probable cost. It allows those executives who aren't too tuned into the marketing concept to "write off" a certain percentage or number of dollars—while controlling the amount spent. When a top company's managers have this attitude, they often get what they expect from their marketing activities—something less than the best results.

Find the task, budget for it

Mechanically budgeting a certain percentage of past or forecasted sales leads to expanding marketing expenditures when business is good and sales are rising, and cutting back when business is poor. It may be desirable to increase marketing expenditures when business is good—but when business is poor, the most sensible approach may be to be *more,* not less, aggressive!

Other methods of budgeting for marketing expenditures are:

1. Match expenditures with competitors.
2. Set the budget as a certain number of cents or dollars per sales unit (by case, by thousand, or by ton), using the past year or estimated year ahead as a base for computation.
3. Set aside all uncommitted revenue—perhaps including budgeted profits. Companies willing to sacrifice some or all of current profits for future sales may use this approach; that is, *invest* in marketing.
4. Base the budget on the number of new customers desired or the number required to reach some sales objective—as when entering new territories or increasing volume. This is called the **task method**—basing the budget on the job to be done.

Task method can lead to budgeting without agony

In the light of our continuing discussion about planning marketing strategies to reach objectives, the most sensible approach to budgeting marketing (and other functional) expenditures seems to be the *task method.*

The amount budgeted—using the task method—can be stated as a percentage of sales—but calculating the right amount is much more involved than picking up a past percentage. It requires a careful review of the strategic (and marketing) plans and the specific tasks to be accomplished this year—as part of each of these plans. The costs of these tasks, then, are totaled—to determine how much should be budgeted for marketing and the other business functions provided for in the plans. In other words, it should be possible to assemble the budgets directly from detailed strategic plans—rather than from historical patterns or ratios.

After the marketing department receives its budget for the coming year, it can, presumably, spend its money any way it sees fit. But if the previous planning-budgeting procedure has been followed, it makes sense to continue allocating expenditures within the marketing function according to the plans in the program.

Again, everyone in the marketing department—and in the business—should view the company as a total system and plan accordingly. If this is done, it is possible to eliminate some of the traditional planning-budgeting "fights"—which are often so agonizing because managers and departments are pitted against each other.

Program Implementation Must Be Planned

Up to now, we have been mainly concerned with planning strategies—that is, the "big picture." Plans and a program bring this down to earth—by adding the time-related details. Now we want to go a step further—illustrating graphical techniques which help marketing managers carry out their plans and program.

First, we will discuss techniques which are helpful for introducing new products or controlling special projects. Then we will consider aids for an ongoing program.

New products or projects can use PERT flowcharts

Some marketing managers find it helpful to draw flowcharts or diagrams of all the tasks that must be accomplished on schedule. In recent years, some firms have successfully applied such flowcharting techniques as CPM (critical path method) or PERT (program evaluation and review technique). These methods were originally developed as part of the U.S. space program (NASA) to ensure that the various contractors and subcontractors' efforts stayed on schedule—and reached their goals as planned.

Detailed flowcharts are used—to describe which marketing activities must be done in sequence—and which can be done concurrently. These charts also show the time needed for various activities. By totaling the time allotments along the various chart paths, the most critical (the longest) path—as well as the most desirable starting and ending dates for the various activities—can be shown.

Basically, a flowcharting effort follows a number of logical steps. First, a marketing strategy—or better, a marketing plan—is needed. Then the various elements of the strategy to be implemented over a period of time must be listed. Each of these elements, in turn, must be broken down into sub-elements or activities. A basic element such as sales promotion might include "Preparing a Sales Brochure." But this, in turn, would require detailed activities such as preparing performance charts and graphs, preparing rough copy, agency preparation of preliminary copy and layouts, and so on. These activities are then flowcharted to pinpoint the bottlenecks.

This flowcharting is *not* really complicated. Basically, what it requires is that all the activities—which have to be performed anyway—be identified ahead of time and their probable duration and sequence shown on one diagram. (Nothing more than addition and subtraction is used.) Working with such information should be part of the planning function anyway. Then the chart can be used for guiding implementation and control.

Regular plans call for monthly charts

Some marketing managers have found flowcharts helpful for keeping track of all the tasks in their ongoing plans. Each week or month in an ongoing 12-month plan, for example, can be graphed horizontally. How long each activity should take—and when it should be started and completed—can be seen. If it is clearly impossible to accomplish some of the jobs in the time allotted, this will become clear during the flowcharting process—and adjustments can be made. This might be necessary, for example, when several product managers have planned more work than the salespeople can do during one month.

Basically, this kind of flowcharting is like the scheduling done by production planners—where wall-size graphic aids are used. See Figure 21–8 for such a visual aid. Without such aids, it is easy to neglect some tasks—or to just naively assume that enough time will be available to do all of the necessary jobs. By planning ahead—aided by a visual approach—it's easier to avoid conflicts which can wreck the implementation of the company's plans and program.

■ FIGURE 21–8   Magnetic scheduling board

■ CONCLUSION

This chapter has shown the importance of developing whole marketing mixes—not just policies for the individual four Ps which hopefully will fit together into some logical whole. The marketing manager is responsible for developing a workable blend—integrating all of a firm's efforts into a coordinated whole which makes effective use of its resources and guides it toward its objectives. This requires thinking about response functions—how the four Ps affect sales and profit. Ultimately, however, managers must compare the market's responsiveness to possible marketing mixes. Ideally, they know the exact shape of the alternative response functions, but, in practice, they have to rely on past experience (to some extent), marketing research if they have the time, plus a lot of judgment.

They also can study typical marketing mixes—and their apparent effectiveness in the marketplace—for clues about what works and how well.

As a starting place for developing new marketing mixes, a marketing manager can use the goods classes which have served as a thread through this text. Even though he may not be able to fully describe the needs and attitudes of his target markets, he may be able to make reasonable judgments about the appropriate goods class for a particular product. This, in turn, will have direct relevance for selecting Place and Promotion policies.

Throughout the text, we have emphasized the importance of marketing strategy planning. In this chapter, we have gone on to show that the marketing manager must develop a marketing plan for carrying out each strategy and, then, merge a set of plans into a marketing program. If this planning has been effective, the budgeting should be relatively simple.

Finally, it is the marketing manager's job to co-ordinate the implementation of the whole marketing program. Two types of flowcharting techniques were discussed. Both may help in this most difficult job of coordinating the activities of the firm—to better satisfy its target customers.

■ QUESTIONS AND PROBLEMS

1. Discuss whether Kodak was an imitator or segmenter in the "instant picture" market.

2. Distinguish between competitive marketing mixes and "superior" mixes which might lead to breakthrough opportunities.

3. Distinguish between a general marketing effort response function and a response function for one of the four Ps.

4. Explain how the use of response functions—even if they must be crudely estimated—can be helpful in developing a marketing strategy.

5. Would a direct or some type of indirect channel of distribution be most appropriate for the following products? (Utilize the general factors discussed in this chapter and make any assumptions necessary to obtain a definite answer.) (*a*) Hedge clippers, (*b*) fly swatters, (*c*) earth-moving machinery, (*d*) fingernail clippers, (*e*) motor scooters, (*f*) grass seed, (*g*) picture frames, (*h*) trucks, (*i*) fresh apple cider.

6. For those products in the previous question where indirect distribution was the answer (in the light of the assumptions), indicate specifically the kinds of channels and the rest of the producer's marketing mix which might be appropriate.

7. Explain what marketing mix might be most appropriate for manufacturers of the following established products (assume average- to large-sized firms in each case and support your answer):

(*a*) a completely new home permanent wave concept packaged in a convenient kit, (*b*) a contracting service capable of bidding on projects up to large dams, (*c*) lumber, (*d*) production tools for finishing furniture, (*e*) glass for window repair.

8. Distinguish clearly between marketing plans and marketing programs.

9. Consider how the job of the marketing manager becomes more complex as he must develop and plan *several* strategies as part of a marketing program. Be sure to discuss how he might have to handle different strategies at different stages in the product life cycle. To make this more concrete, consider the job of a marketing manager for a sporting goods manufacturer.

10. Briefly explain the task method of budgeting.

11. Discuss how a marketing manager could go about choosing among several possible marketing plans, given that he must because of limited resources. Would the job be easier in the consumer goods or in the industrial goods area? Why?

12. Explain why the budgeting procedure is typically such an agonizing procedure, usually consisting of extending past budgets, perhaps with small modifications from current plans. How would the budgeting procedure be changed if the marketing program planning procedure discussed in the chapter were implemented?

■ **SUGGESTED CASES**

29. Visiting Nurses Association

31. Mayfair Detergent Company

■ **NOTES**

1. Albert J. Della Bitta, Kent B. Monroe, and John McGinnis, "Consumer Perceptions of Comparative Price Advertisements," *Journal of Marketing Research* 18 (November 1981), pp. 416–27; David A. Aaker, James M. Carman, and Robert Jacobson, "Modeling Advertising-Sales Relationships Involving Feedback: A Time Series Analysis of Six Cereal Brands," *Journal of Marketing Research* 19 (February 1982), pp. 116–25; J. B. Wilkinson, J. Barry Mason, and Christie H. Paksoy, "Assessing the Impact of Short-Term Variables," *Journal of Marketing Research* 19 (February 1982), pp. 72–86; Paul W. Farris and Mark S. Albion, "The Impact of Advertising on the Price of Consumer Products," *Journal of Marketing* 44, no. 3 (Summer 1980), pp. 17–35; and Leonard M. Lodish, "A User-Oriented Model for Sales Force Size, Product, and Market Allocations Decisions," *Journal of Marketing* 44, no. 3 (Summer 1980), pp. 70–78.

2. John E. Smallwood, "The Product Life Cycle: A Key to Strategic Marketing Planning," *MSU Business Topics,* Winter 1973, pp. 29–35; and Richard F. Savach and Laurence A. Thompson, "Resource Allocation within the Product Life Cycle," *MSU Business Topics,* Autumn 1978, pp. 35–44.

3. Joel A. Evans and Barry Berman, *Marketing* (New York: Macmillan, 1982), p. 624.

4. Philip Kotler, *Marketing for Nonprofit Organizations* (Englewood Cliffs, N.J.: Prentice-Hall, 1975), p. 283.

5. For a more detailed discussion of the scope and nature of social marketing, see Paul N. Bloom and William D. Novelli, "Problems and Challenges in Social Marketing," *Journal of Marketing,* Spring 1981, pp. 79–87.

6. Philip Kotler and Sidney J. Levy, "Broadening the Concept of Marketing," *Journal of Marketing,* January 1969, pp. 10–15.

7. For further discussion on evaluating and selecting alternative plans, see W. I. Little, "The Integrated Management Approach to Marketing," *Journal of Marketing,* April 1967, pp. 32–36; Leon Winer, "A Profit-Oriented Decision System," *Journal of Marketing,* April 1966, pp. 38–44 (this article discusses discounting of cash flows for different lengths of time); see also S. M. Lee and R. E. Nicely, "Goal Programming for Marketing Decisions: A Case Study," *Journal of Marketing,* January 1974, pp. 24–32; J. Fred Weston, "ROI Planning and Control," *Business Horizons,* August 1972, pp. 35–42; Richard T. Hise and Robert H. Strawser, "Application of Capital Budgeting Techniques to Marketing Operations," *MSU Business Topics,* Summer 1970, pp. 69–76; and Louis V. Gerstner, "Can Strategic Planning Pay Off?" *Business Horizons,* December 1972, pp. 5–16.

Appendix F ■ Why marketing management needs to be different for services*

---

*The area of services marketing is now receiving a great deal of attention after a long period of relative neglect. The article that appears as Appendix F was written by Professor Christopher H. Lovelock, who at the time was an Associate Professor of Business Administration at the Harvard Business School. It provides a most useful introduction to some of the similarities and differences between product and services marketing. The article is reprinted with permission of the American Marketing Association from *Marketing of Services*, ed. James H. Donnelly and William R. George (Chicago: American Marketing Association, 1980).

Services often compete with goods to offer similar core benefits to customers, but this does not mean that the marketing management tasks are the same. There are currently both generic and contextual differences between goods and services marketing. Although the latter are likely to narrow over time, the former will remain, requiring service marketers to play a number of roles not usually expected of their counterparts in manufacturing industries.

Let me start with an immediate concession to those who argue that the similarities between goods and services marketing outweigh the differences: I make no claim that the marketing of services is uniquely different from that of physical goods. If the two *were* uniquely different this would raise serious doubts as to the coherence of marketing as a functional area of management. My contention is simply that a different management approach is needed in services marketing.

Services, of course, often compete in the marketplace with goods that offer their users the same (or broadly similar) core benefits. For instance, buying a service may be an alternative to doing it yourself: examples range from lawncare and babysitting to janitorial services and industrial equipment maintenance. Too, using a rental service is frequently an alternative to owning a good. The Yellow Pages in any large city includes listings for a wide array of rental services, ranging from trucks to typewriters and from furniture to formal wear.

But just because a good and a service may be close competitors does not mean that the marketing management tasks for each are the same. A packaged foods marketer is likely to come to grief using similar strategies to market fast food restaurants; a successful automobile marketer will not necessarily find it easy to replicate that success in the rental car business; a marketing executive for a manufacturer of heavy electrical equipment will need to develop a new managerial style—as well as new strategies—if transferred to the same company's equipment servicing division.

It's my contention that marketing management tasks in the service sector can be differentiated from those in the manufacturing sector along two dimensions. The first relates to the generic differences between service products and physical goods products. The second concerns the management environment or context within which marketing tasks must be planned and executed. Let's look at each in turn.

Generic Differences between Goods and Services

Five generic differences can be identified that separate goods from services marketing. These involve the nature of the product itself, how that product is created, the marketer's ability (or inability) to stockpile the product, the nature of the distribution channels for the product, and the relative ease of determining costs for pricing purposes.

1. Nature of the product

"A good," writes Berry (1980), "is an object, a device, a thing; a service is a deed, a performance, an effort." Admittedly, goods are sometimes an integral part of a particular service, especially where rentals are concerned. But even in such an explicitly goods-oriented service as the car-rentals business, the relevant product attributes extend far beyond those normally associated with owning one's own car, including such elements as pick-up and drop-off locations (often in different cities), inclusive insurance, maintenance, free connecting airport shuttle buses, long-distance reservations, and speedy, courteous customer contact personnel.

From the customer's perspective, three distinctive characteristics of most service products are: their ephemeral, experiential nature; the emphasis on time as a unit of consumption; and the fact that people—both service employees and other customers—are often part and parcel of the service product. As we shall see, the relative importance of these characteristics varies according to whether the *target* of the service is the customer in person or the customer's possessions.

2. Different production methods

Producing a service typically involves assembling and delivering the output of a mix of physical facilities and mental or physical labor. Sometimes the customers' role is relatively passive, more often they are actually involved in helping create the service product. These factors make it hard for service organizations to control for quality and to offer customers a consistent product. As a former packaged goods marketer, turned hotel marketer, observed: "We can't control the quality of our product as well as a P&G control engineer on a production line can. . . . When you buy a box of Tide, you can reasonably be 99 and 44/100 percent sure that this stuff will work to get your clothes clean. When you buy a Holiday Inn room, you're sure at some lesser percentage that it will work to give you a good night's sleep without any hassle, or people banging on the walls, and all the bad things that can happen in a hotel." (Knisely, 1979a)

3. No inventories for services

Because a service is a deed or performance, rather than a tangible item, it cannot be inventoried. Of course the necessary equipment, facilities, and labor can be held in readiness to create the service, but these simply represent productive capacity, not the product itself. Unused capacity in a service organization is rather like a running tap in a sink with no plug: The flow is wasted unless customers (or possessions requiring servicing) are present to receive it. As a result, service marketers must work to smooth demand levels to match capacity.

4a. Lack of physical distribution channels for most services

The marketer's task in manufacturing firms includes developing distribution strategies for physically moving the product from the factory to the customer. Typically, this involves the use of one or more intermediaries. Because services delivered to the person of the customer are consumed as they are produced, the service factory, retail outlet, and consumption point are often one and the same. Hence distribution strategies in service organizations emphasize the *scheduling* of service delivery as much as the locations. And, unlike manufacturers, most service organizations have direct control over the service delivery outlet, either through outright ownership or tightly written franchise agreements.

However, physical distribution channels do exist for certain services performed on customers' goods. Examples include film processing, off-site equipment repair and maintenance, certain specialty cleaning services, and so forth. But these instances—involving drop-off at a convenient retail location and shipment to a plant where the necessary servicing is done—are the exception rather than the rule in the service sector.

4b. Availability of electronic distribution channels for some services

A rapidly growing approach to service distribution is through electronic distribution channels. Physical goods and people cannot yet be "teleported," as science fiction writers predict that some day they will. But services directed at the customer's mind—such as advice, education, entertainment, and information—can be telecommunicated through such channels as radio, television, the telephone, telecopying, or microwave relays. Moreover, the use of remote printers, video recorders, and telecopiers even makes it possible for such services to produce a hard copy at the receiving end—the closest we have yet come to "teleportation." Services directed at the customer's intangible assets—such as banking, insurance, and stockbroking—can also be distributed, faster than a speeding bullet, through telephone-based authorizations or automated electronic transmission systems.

Theaters, hotels, and transportation operators have long used travel and ticket agencies as intermediaries to handle inquiries, reservations, and ticket sales. Telecommunications now make it possible to deliver certain service products through independent retail intermediaries. One example is the availability in some cities of on-line banking services at supermarkets and department stores (Merliss and Lovelock, 1980). A second is the ability of libraries to sell on-line, computerized information services connected to data banks thousands of miles away. While marketing managers in such organizations face such traditional distribution problems as selecting outlets and determining commission structures (see, for instance, Davis and Star, 1977), they have some novel advantages over their manufacturing industry counterparts. Demand can be smoothed by use of variable, time-of-day pricing; supplies can be cut off instantly as an extreme form of sanction; and new products can be made available spontaneously at many different locations, since there are no lengthy "pipelines" to fill.

5. Determining costs for pricing purposes

Relative to manufacturing firms, it is much more difficult for service businesses to determine which fixed and operating costs are associated with which products—especially when several services are being produced concurrently by the same organization (Dearden, 1978). If a marketer does not know the average cost of producing a unit of service, it is hard to determine what the selling price should be.

The variable cost of selling one additional unit of service (e.g., an extra seat on an aircraft, an extra room in a hotel) is often minimal. Since demand may fluctuate widely by time of day (or week or season), this gives service marketers much greater flexibility than goods marketers to offer similar products at different prices to different market segments. The challenge is to ensure that the weighted average of all prices charged exceeds the average costs, thus looping the problem back to the tasks of cost determination and allocation.

Summary

Taken as a broad product class, services are distinguished from goods by several generic differences that have important implications for marketing management. Services are not homogeneous, of course; there are many different types (Lovelock, 1980). Yet although the generic differences described above may be more or less pronounced for a specific type of service, and although some goods may share certain features with some services, these generic differences will continue to require distinctions in marketing practice between the manufacturing and service sectors.

Contextual Differences between Goods and Services Marketing

Service marketers whose previous job was in the manufacturing sector—and particularly those who came from consumer packaged goods—often note sharp differences between their current and previous working environments. These differences presently include a narrow definition of marketing by other managers, limited appreciation for marketing skills, a different organizational structure, and a relative lack of competitive data. In addition, many service industries are experiencing a loosening of both government regulations and professional restrictions on management practices, with important strategic implications for marketing. Finally, there are special constraints and opportunities facing marketers in public and nonprofit organizations.

1. Narrow definition of marketing

Professional marketing management is still relatively new to the service sector. Many service industry executives, who tend to be operations oriented, still define marketing as simply advertising and public relations; others extend this definition only as far as sales and market research. Decisions in such areas as new product development, retail site location, pricing, and product line policy have traditionally been excluded from marketing's domain in the service sector. This situation is changing, but many service organizations still have a long way to go before they can be said to have adopted the marketing concept and implemented it across a broad range of managerial activities.

2. Lack of appreciation for marketing skills

The comedian, Rodney Dangerfield, whose perennial complaint is that "I don't get no respect," would probably feel very much at home as a marketing manager in most service firms. Knisely (1979b) records an interview with a Lever Bros. executive who had spent some time as a senior marketing manager in a large service organization; the latter observed: "You feel less loved and less needed. . . . In a service company which has perhaps been built on skills and disciplines that have not included large doses of marketing, you're selling—you're saying 'listen to me' as opposed to 'tell me, tell me.'"

Limited appreciation for marketing skills among other managers makes the service marketer's job just that much more difficult. Lack of clout limits his/her ability to win acceptance of new strategies—particularly if they require deviation from current practice; it may also constrain the amount of resources allocated to marketing.

3. Different organizational structures

As noted by Lovelock et al. (1981), service organizations frequently include a general management-type position at both corporate and field levels. Example of the latter would be a branch bank manager, a station manager for an airline or trucking company, or the general manager of a hotel.

These "field general managers," who usually report to operations, are engaged in marketing management tasks whether they recognize them as such or not. In particular, they are usually responsible for managing service personnel in regular contact with customers.

As noted earlier, service organizations generally control service outlets, the service equivalent of a retail store. But much of this benefit is lost if the "store" is not run in a way that balances marketing considerations against operational ones. This means that marketing managers at the corporate level must either develop an organizational structure, such as a matrix, that provides them with access to customer contact personnel, or they must ensure that "field general managers" possess marketing skills and are rewarded for good marketing practice. As noted by Czepiel (1980), most service businesses have some distance to travel before they achieve an organizational structure that integrates marketing and operations in ways calculated to deliver consistently high levels of service quality and customer satisfaction.

4. Lack of data on competitive performance

One of the differences felt most keenly by consumer goods marketers who have moved to the service sector is the lack of market data on their "brands." In many packaged goods businesses, historical data is available on brand performance extending back for many years; and detailed new Nielsen reports (or other retail audits) are published at regular intervals. However, in most service industries, as one bank marketing executive complained to Knisely (1979c), "there is an almost complete lack of historical competitive data. . . . Therefore, the product manager and his (advertising) agency are not able to monitor the results of their marketing efforts as tightly."

Because service organizations rarely use third parties to sell their products to customers, development of an independent retail audit similar to Nielsen would be difficult. (Ticket sales through travel agencies probably do not constitute a representative cross-section of the total sales base.) Many service businesses—from colleges to hotels—share sales information with similar institutions, but there is always the problem that some organizations may decline to participate or else supply deliberately biased information. And although some regulated industries are obliged to supply customer usage data to state or federal agencies, such data is usually highly aggregated for publication purposes.

5. Impact of government regulation and deregulation

Many service industries have traditionally been highly regulated in the United States. Regulatory agencies have mandated price levels, constrained distribution strategies by limiting transportation route structures and banking service areas, and, in some instances, prescribed product attributes. Additionally, self-imposed "professional ethics" have prohibited or restricted advertising in such fields as health care and the law.

Since the late 1970s there has been a trend toward complete or partial federal deregulation in several major service industries. Changes in the regulatory environment are taking place at the state level, too. Meantime, the Federal Trade Commission has achieved removal or relaxation of bans on advertising in certain professional service industries. These moves have frequently served to stimulate competition and to unfetter such key strategic elements as pricing, distribution, and advertising. As a result of deregulation, marketing will undoubtedly assume greater importance as a management activity in the industries in question.

6. Constraints and opportunities for non-business marketers

The past decade has seen greater application of marketing to public and non-profit services. But marketers need to be aware of the special context in which those services operate. In the public sector, priorities are often established externally by politicians, not management. Externally imposed constraints may include limiting the use of advertising, confining service delivery within established political boundaries, mandating service to "uneconomic" segments, establishing pricing policies, and even defining specific product attributes. Nonprofit marketers, meantime, may have to defer to the wishes of volunteer boards (Selby, 1978) and make compromises to retain the support of important donors.

On the other hand, many public and nonprofit services can be offered at prices well below the full costs of producing them; some are even offered free of charge. Free advertising time and space may be available in the form of public service announcements. And volunteers may offer their services free of charge for such marketing-relating tasks as personal selling and customer-contact at the point of service delivery.

Conclusion

The context within which many service marketers must work is often sharply different from that facing their counterparts in the manufacturing sector (especially in consumer packaged goods firms, where marketing expertise has achieved a high level of sophistication).

But as service businesses become more familiar with the contributions that marketing management can make, there will be greater acceptance of this function. This, in turn, will facilitate development of new organizational structures that give marketing a more equal status with operations in managing the business. Greater competition in service markets will spur efforts to develop more detailed, reliable market data. Finally, public and nonprofit service organizations, faced with greater financial stringency in the years ahead, are likely to develop more market-oriented operating strategies than they have historically, and to charge prices which cover a higher proportion of total costs.

Roles for Service Marketers

Reflecting the generic differences between goods and services, the life of a service marketer is, in my view, more varied than that of a goods marketer. To round out this paper, I'd like to look at some of the many roles played by service marketers—using the term *marketer* in its broadest sense to include all service managers with responsibilities that include managing customer relationships.

The service marketer as admissions director

With a few exceptions, usually confined to potentially dangerous products, the only qualification required of an adult wishing to buy a specific good is the ability to pay for it. By contrast, service marketers are much more likely to screen their customers against nonfinancial criteria before agreeing to sell their products. Since the customer is often part of the product and in close contact with service personnel, it may be very important for service businesses to ask: Which types of customers will we agree to serve?

In higher education, would-be college students must apply for admission to the college of their choice, and may be rejected if they fail to meet certain minimum aptitude standards laid down by the institution. Other types of services may or may not have a formal admissions process, yet they still employ screening procedures. The hospitality industry, for instance, recognizes that for any one customer, other guests are part of the product experience. Hence a service manager must ask: "How will the appearance and behavior of different types of customers affect the nature of the product experience? Should we set explicit (or implicit) standards and discourage patronage by those who fail to meet them?"

The proprietors of professional practices are often as concerned with the psychic satisfaction they obtain from their job as with the financial income they obtain. Once business exceeds a certain volume, they may start to become very selective about which jobs they accept, seeking to focus on those projects that will be challenging and satisfying; they may prefer more leisure time to obtaining additional income from a boring project.

The strategic questions here for service marketers are: How do we attract the customers we want, *when* we want them? And what procedures do we employ for evaluating prospective customers and tactfully screening out those whose business fails to meet our criteria?

In some instances, acceptance of a customer results in a long-term relationship, during the course of which numerous transactions take place. This results in an important role for . . .

The service marketer as club secretary

Many service businesses have much in common with clubs. You have to "join" them before you may use their services. Using almost any form of public utility requires a formal turning on of the supply and (usually) paying a predefined, monthly subscription. To use most bank services requires that you first open an account. Although credit-worthiness is frequently a necessary criterion for admission to "membership" in a service organization, other criteria may include possession of specific types or models of physical equipment, residence within defined political boundaries, evidence of intellectual aptitude, attainment of a certain age, and even personal chemistry between marketer and customer.

"Membership" can also be *de facto* rather than *de jure:* Regular users of a specific service outlet can often obtain preferential treatment over casual, one-time customers, reflecting personal recognition by the service provider.

The service manager's role as club secretary requires attention to such tasks as (1) setting monthly dues and supplementary fees, (2) admission procedures, (3) membership rights and privileges (these may have to be spelled out in contractual form in some instances), and (4) publication of the "club newsletter" (unlike many goods marketers, service marketers are much more likely to know their customers' names and addresses for billing and legal purposes; this greatly facilitates use of direct mail promotions, which can be included with the periodic financial statements sent to "members"). Finally, there must be established procedures for updating membership lists and handling resignations and terminations. This leads us to the role of . . .

The service marketer as police officer

Because customers are frequently involved in the service production process and often interact with other customers, service marketers may have to lay down formal rules for customer behavior. Sometimes such rules are required by law for safety purposes (consider how tightly our behavior is prescribed every time you take a commercial airline flight); at other times they are laid down by the service organization and relate to such behaviors as form of dress (e.g., restaurants, sailing schools), level of permitted noise (e.g., hotels), physical activity (e.g., health care), accurate completion of documents (e.g., banking), and avoidance of dangerous or inconsiderate activities (e.g., smoking in a nonsmoking area).

This raises the problem of how to get customers to conform to the desired standards, how to enforce behavior when exhortation fails, and how to discipline disobedient customers.

When violations are nonlegal in nature, a mixture of tact and firmness may be needed to achieve the desired effect without generating bad feelings and even an embarrassing "scene." If worst comes to worst, the disobedient customer can be escorted to the door. In practice, the marketer's role as police officer can be made much easier by effective implementation of the role of . . .

The service marketer as teacher

All but the simplest physical goods are accompanied by a set of instructions describing how to use the product. Dollar for dollar, services tend to be much more complex for first-time purchasers to buy and use than are goods. Compare using the bus system in a new city—perhaps a 50-cent purchase—with buying and using a new brand of soap (or soft drink). And compare buying a room and breakfast at a hotel—perhaps a $50 purchase—with buying and using a common household appliance of similar value. As a broad generalization, I think it's fair to say that the service purchase and usage process is considerably the more complex of the two. Typically it involves a sequence of steps, each of which must be successfully negotiated (usually in the presence of other people) before proceeding to the next.

Customers who fail to use a physical good correctly seldom cause problems for other users of the same product (car drivers are an exception). But, customers who misuse a service product may also interfere with the smooth running of the service operation, delay service personnel, and irritate other customers who are seeking service at the same time. This places a great premium on effective education of customers, through printed materials, retail signage, and assistance from customer contact personnel.

The information to be transmitted may include instructions on where and when to seek the service, what operating procedures to follow, how to identify and interact with customer service personnel, how to tender payment, how to dress, how to interact with other customers, and what to do (and what *not* to do) if problems arise.

Contributing to the need for effective education is the fact that the customer is frequently participating in a carefully stage-managed process, designed to achieve both operational efficiencies and creation of a desirable atmosphere. This, in turn, emphasizes the role of . . .

The service marketer as dramatist and choreographer

Among the tasks faced by many service organizations are designing the service setting and costuming the service personnel; employee uniforms may be necessary not only for practical purposes, but also to simplify customer recognition of relevant personnel. When customers arrive at the service outlet, they may be left to find their own way; alternatively their progress may be carefully stage managed. Service personnel often have a prepared script to deliver to customers, perhaps combining an introductory welcome with some information about how to use the service itself and some discreetly phrased guidelines concerning required or desired behavior.

The delivery of the core service is sometimes carefully choreographed, especially in more complex services that involve the presence of several specialist personnel, require cooperative behavior from customers, and employ a carefully sequenced delivery system. Examples range from good restaurants to airlines to dentists' offices.

Customer complaints tend to be more frequent and more emotional in service businesses, because quality control is harder to maintain and the customer is usually more immediately involved. Effective handling of such complaints is an important marketing task because, if done well, considerable good will may result, whereas, if done badly, the outcome may be permanent disaffection on the customer's part. Either outcome is likely to result in word-of-mouth advertising, the one positive and the other negative.

The final opportunity for theatrical action in the service transaction might be described as ringing down the curtain—closing out a specific customer contact in ways that leave good feelings on both sides and increase the likelihood of repeat usage.

The service marketer as demand engineer

Demand levels, as we have noted, often vary widely over time in a service business. Yet without warehouses to store the product, how can service managers bring supply and demand into balance?

Although supply cannot be inventoried, there may be opportunities for operations managers to adjust capacity levels and for marketing managers to smooth demand levels (Sasser, 1976). Successful demand management requires increasing demand in slack periods and decreasing demand on occasions when it would otherwise exceed capacity. It may entail such strategies as product enhancement in off-peak periods, selective pricing, and use of communications for both informational and persuasive purposes.

Another strategy is to inventory demand at times when it exceeds capacity. The service firm's ability to do this depends in part on the target of the service: It is difficult to keep people waiting in line for long unless a truly exceptional service is being offered. But if the target of the service is one of the customer's assets (such as an appliance to be repaired), then that item can be put in a holding area for days or even weeks. An alternative is to introduce a reservations system that establishes a mutually agreed time when the customer shall receive the service (or deliver a possession to be serviced). These may sound like operational procedures; the marketing task consists in designing and promoting them to be acceptable to customers.

The service marketer as manufacturer and product

Those who create the service product are often perceived by customers as part of the product. The higher their level of contact with customers, the more likely they are to be evaluated by customers as an attribute of the service. From an operational perspective, flight attendants are a much less important aspect of the airline product than flight crew and mechanics; but the marketing role played by the former is usually much more significant, since they are in much closer contact with customers.

The sales force and the production team are sometimes one and the same in service organizations—particularly in professional service firms such as consultants. Unfortunately, the fact that they are good service manufacturers does not necessarily make them convincing salespeople.

For some personal services, there is a veritable "service trinity," with a single individual running the service operation, seeking to market the service, and being equated by customers with the product. Few people have the skills to play all three roles successfully; marketing specialists can help such service professionals to understand the customer's viewpoint better and to develop an effective outreach strategy.

Summary and Conclusion

In this paper I've emphasized a management perspective in contrasting goods and services marketing.

It's my contention that the contextual differences between goods and services marketing are currently quite significant in many service businesses; but I believe they will become progressively less pronounced as service marketing evolves and moves up the learning curve.

On the other hand, I expect certain generic differences between services and goods marketing to remain. For many services, these differences will always require distinctive marketing strategies that cannot be transferred directly from goods marketing. As a result, service marketers will continue to play a wide variety of roles that, in certain respects, are richer and more interesting than those played by goods marketers.

I hope, in conclusion, that I have convinced you "why marketing management needs to be different for services."

■ REFERENCES

Berry, L. L. (1980) "Services Marketing Is Different." *Business,* May-June, pp. 24–29.

Czepiel, J. A. (1980) "Managing Customer Satisfaction in Consumer Service Business." Cambridge, Mass.: Marketing Science Institute.

Davis, N., and S. H. Star (1977) "The Information Bank." In S. H. Star et al., *Problems in Marketing.* New York: McGraw-Hill, pp. 551–80.

Dearden, J. (1978) "Cost Accounting Comes to Service Industries." *Harvard Business Review* 56 (September-October), pp. 132–40.

Knisely, G. (1979a) "Greater Marketing Emphasis by Holiday Inns Breaks Mold." *Advertising Age,* January 15.

_____ (1979b) "Listening to Consumer Is Key to Consumer or Service Marketing." *Advertising Age,* February 19.

_____ (1979c) "Financial Services Marketers Must Learn Packaged Goods Selling Tools." *Advertising Age,* March 19.

Lovelock, C. H. (1980) "Towards a Classification of Services." In C. W. Lamb and P. M. Dunne, *Theoretical Developments in Marketing.* Chicago: American Marketing Association, pp. 72–76.

Lovelock, C. H., E. Langeard, J. E. G. Bateson, and P. Eiglier (1981) "Some Organizational Problems Facing Marketing in the Service Sector."

In J. H. Donnelly and W. R. George, *Marketing of Services.* Chicago: American Marketing Association, pp. 168–71.

Merliss, P. P., and C. H. Lovelock (1980) "Buffalo Savings Bank," 9–581–065. Boston, Mass.: Intercollegiate Case Clearing House.

Sasser, W. E. (1976) "Match Demand and Supply in Service Industries." *Harvard Business Review* 54 (November-December), pp. 133–40.

Selby, C. C. (1978), "Better Performance from 'Nonprofits." *Harvard Business Review* 56 (September-October), pp. 92–98.

Chapter 22 ■ Controlling marketing plans and programs

When you finish this chapter, you should:

1. Understand how sales analysis can aid marketing strategy planning.

2. Understand the differences among sales analysis, performance analysis, and performance analysis using performance indices.

3. Understand the difference between natural accounts and functional accounts—and their relevance for marketing cost analysis.

4. Know how to do a marketing cost analysis for customers or products.

5. Understand the difference between the full-cost approach and the contribution margin approach.

6. Understand how planning and control can be combined to improve the marketing management process.

7. Understand what a marketing audit is—and when and where it should be used.

8. Recognize the important new terms (shown in red).

"Planning, implementing, and control—that's the basic management process."

Our primary emphasis so far has been on planning. Now, however, we must discuss **control**—the feedback process that helps the marketing manager learn (1) how ongoing plans are working and (2) how to plan for the future.

Keeping a firmer hand on the controls

A good manager wants to know: which products' sales are highest and why; whether the products are profitable; what is selling where; and how much the marketing process is costing. Knowing what's happening—in detail—is needed to improve the "bottom-line."

Unfortunately, the traditional accounting reports are usually of little help to the marketing manager—they are much too general. A particular company may be showing a profit, for example, while 80 percent of its business is coming from only 20 percent of its products—or customers. The other 80 percent may be unprofitable. But without special analyses, the managers won't know this. This 80/20 relationship is fairly common—and is often referred to as the 80/20 rule.

The Cello Packaging Company was a moderately successful firm. The new owners, however, wanted to increase profits. The managers were uncertain what to do. But after some detailed sales and cost analysis, some facts emerged. Many small customers were taking up too much sales time—while some larger, potentially profitable ones were being neglected. Further, considering all the technical service Cello provided, along with the very differentiated physical products, it was obvious that the prices for some large accounts were too low. The managers discovered that some of the value of the firm's "competitive advantage" was being given away. Only six months after its strategies were modified—for large as well as small customers—Cello's profits were above the objectives set by the new owners.

As this example shows, it is possible for the marketing manager to get detailed information about how his plans are progressing. This chapter discusses some of the kinds of information which can be available to the marketing manager—but only if he asks for and helps develop the necessary data.

This is an important chapter. And the techniques are not really complicated—basically requiring only arithmetic—and perhaps a computer if a large volume of adding and subtracting is required.[1]

Sales Analysis Shows What's Happening

Sales analysis—a detailed breakdown of a company's sales records—can be very informative—especially the first time it is done. Detailed data can quickly update marketing executives who are out of touch with what is happening in the market. In addition, routine sales analyses prepared each week, month, or year may show trends—and permit managers to check their hypotheses and assumptions.[2]

Some managers resist sales analysis—or any analysis for that matter—because they don't fully appreciate how valuable it can be to them. One top executive in a large consumer products firm made no attempt to analyze his company's sales—even by geographic area. When asked why, he replied: "Why should we? We're making money!"

But today's profit is no guarantee that you'll make money tomorrow. In fact, ignoring sales analysis can lead not only to poor sales forecasting but to poor decisions in general. One manufacturer did much national advertising on the assumption that the firm was selling all over the country. A simple sales analysis, however, showed that most present customers were within a 250-mile radius of the factory! In other words, the firm did not know who and where its customers were—and was wasting most of the money it spent on national advertising.

But a marketing manager must ask for it

Detailed sales analysis is only a possibility, however, unless the manager asks for the data. Valuable sales information is regularly buried in sales invoice files—after the usual accounting functions are completed. Manual analysis of such records is so burdensome that it is seldom done.

Today—with computers—effective sales analysis can be done easily and at relatively small cost—if marketing managers decide they want it done. In fact, the information desired can be obtained as a by-product of basic billing and accounts receivable procedures. The manager simply must be sure that identifying information on important dimensions such as territory, sales reps, and so forth is recorded in machine-processable form. Then, sales analysis and simple trend projections can easily be run.

With computers, effective sales analysis can be done easily and at relatively low cost.

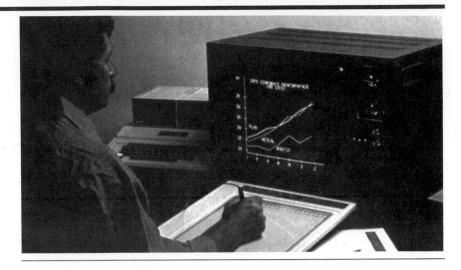

What to ask for varies

There is no one "best" way to analyze sales data. Several breakdowns may be useful—depending on the nature of the company and product—and what dimensions are relevant. Typical breakdowns include:

1. Geographic region—province, county, city, sales rep's territory.
2. Product, package size, grade, or color.
3. Customer size.
4. Customer type or class of trade.
5. Price or discount class.
6. Method of sale—mail, telephone, or direct sales.
7. Financial arrangement—cash or charge.
8. Size of order.
9. Commission class.

Too much data can drown a manager

While some sales analysis is better than none—or getting data too late for action—extremely detailed sales breakdowns can easily "drown" a manager in reports. Computers can print over 1,000 lines per minute—faster than any manager can read. So wise managers only ask for breakdowns which are likely to be useful. And to avoid having to cope with mountains of data—much of which may be irrelevant—most managers move on to *performance analysis.*

Performance Analysis Looks for Differences

Numbers are compared

Performance analysis looks for exceptions or variations from planned performance. In simple sales analysis, the figures are merely listed—without comparing them against standards. In performance analysis, comparisons are made.

One territory might be compared against another, against the same territory's performance last year, or against expected performance.

The purpose of performance analysis is to improve operations. The salesperson, territory, or other factors showing poor performance can be identified—and singled out for detailed analysis and corrective action. Or outstanding performances can be analyzed—to see if the successes can be explained and made the general rule.

Performance analysis doesn't have to be limited to sales. Other data can be analyzed, too. This data might include kilometers traveled, number of calls made, number of orders, or the cost of various tasks.

A performance analysis can be quite revealing—as shown in the following example.

Straight performance analysis—an illustration

A manufacturer of industrial products sold to wholesalers through five sales reps—each serving a separate territory. Total net sales for the year amounted to $2,386,000. Compensation and expenses of the sales force came to $198,000. This yielded a direct-selling expense ratio of 8.3 percent—that is, $198,000 ÷ $2,386,000 × 100.

This information—taken from a profit and loss statement—was interesting, but didn't explain what was happening from one territory to another. To get a clearer picture, the manager compared the sales results with other data *from each territory.* See Tables 22–1 and 22–2.

■ TABLE 22–1   Comparative performance of sales reps

Sales area	Total calls	Total orders	Order-call ratio	Sales by sales rep	Average sales rep order	Total customers
A	1,900	1,140	60.0%	$ 912,000	$800	195
B	1,500	1,000	66.7	720,000	720	160
C	1,400	700	50.0	560,000	800	140
D	1,030	279	27.1	132,000	478	60
E	820	165	20.1	62,000	374	50
Total	6,650	3,284	49.3%	$2,386,000	$634	605

■ TABLE 22–2   Comparative cost of sales reps

Sales area	Annual compensation	Expense payments	Total sales rep cost	Sales produced	Cost-sales ratio
A	$ 22,800	$11,200	$ 34,000	$ 912,000	3.7%
B	21,600	14,400	36,000	720,000	5.0
C	20,400	11,600	32,000	560,000	5.7
D	19,200	24,800	44,000	132,000	33.3
E	20,000	32,000	52,000	62,000	83.8
Total	$104,000	$94,000	$198,000	$2,386,000	8.3%

The sales reps in sales areas D and E obviously were not doing well. Sales were low—and marketing costs were high. Perhaps sales reps with more "push" could have done a better job—but the number of customers suggests that the potential might be low. Perhaps the whole plan needs revision.

The figures themselves, of course, don't provide the answers—but they do reveal the areas that need improvement. This is the main value of performance analysis. It is up to management to find the remedy—either by revising or changing the marketing plan.

Performance Indices Simplify Human Analysis

Comparing against "what ought to have happened"

With a straight performance analysis, the marketing manager can personally evaluate the variations among sales reps in an effort to explain the "why." This takes time, however—and sometimes the "poor" performances really aren't as bad as the bare sales figures seem to indicate. Some uncontrollable factors in a particular territory may automatically lower the sales potential. Or a territory just may not have good potential.

To get a better check on performance effectiveness, performance indices are used. With this approach, the marketing manager compares what did happen with "what ought to have happened."

A performance index is like a batting average

When standards have been set—that is, quantitative measures of what "ought to happen"—it is relatively simple to develop a **performance index**—a number—such as a baseball batting average—which shows the relation of one value to another.

Baseball batting averages are computed by dividing the actual number of hits by the number of times at bat (the possible number of times the batter could have had a hit) and then multiplying the result by 100 to get rid of decimal points. A sales performance index is computed the same way—by dividing actual sales by expected sales for the area (or sales rep, product, etc.) and then multiplying this figure by 100. If a sales rep is "batting" 82 percent, the index is 82.

A simple example shows where the problem is

Developing a performance index is shown in the following example—which assumes that population is an effective measure of sales potential.

In Table 22–3, the population of Canada is broken down by regions—as a percentage of the total population. The regions in this case are the Atlantic Provinces, Quebec, Ontario, the Prairies, British Columbia, the Yukon, and N.W.T.

The firm already has $1 million in sales—and now wants to evaluate performance in each region. The actual sales of $1 million—broken down in proportion to the population in the five regions—are shown in Column 2. This is what sales should have been if population were a good measure of future performance. Column 3 in Table 22–3 shows the actual sales for the year for each region. Column 4 shows measures of performance (performance indices)—Column 3 ÷ Column 2 × 100.

■ TABLE 22–3   Development of a measure of sales performances (by regions)

Regions	(1) Population as percent of Canada	(2) Expected distribution of sales based on population	(3) Actual sales	(4) Performance index
Atlantic	10	$ 100,000	$ 60,000	60
Quebec	28	280,000	300,000	107
Ontario	36	360,000	360,000	100
Prairies	16	160,000	180,000	113
British Columbia, Yukon and N.W.T.	10	100,000	100,000	100
Total	100	$1,000,000	$1,000,000	

The Atlantic region isn't doing as well as expected. Note that the population in the Atlantic region was 10 percent of the total population, and expected sales (based on population) were $100,000. Actual sales, however, were only $60,000. This means that the Atlantic region's performance index was only 60—actual sales were much lower than would be expected on the basis of population.

If population is a sound basis for measuring expected sales (an important if), the explanation for poor sales performance will have to be traced further. Perhaps salespeople in the Atlantic region are not doing as well as they should. Perhaps promotion there is not as effective as elsewhere. Or, competitive products may have entered the market in this region.

Whatever the cause, it should be clear that performance analysis does not solve problems. It points out potential problems—and it does this well.

A Series of Performance Analyses May Find the Real Problem

Performance analysis helps a marketing manager to see if the firm's marketing plans are working properly and, if not, to correct the problems. But this may require a series of performance analyses—as shown in the following example.

To get a feel for the passage of time, follow this example carefully—one table at a time. Try to anticipate the marketing manager's decision.

The case of Stereo, Inc.

Stereo's sales manager found that sales for the Ontario region were $130,000 below the quota of $14,500,000 (that is, actual sales were $14,370,000) for the January–June 1985 period. The quota was based on forecasted sales of the various types of stereo equipment which the company sells. Specifically, the quota was based on forecasts for each product type in each store in each sales rep's territory.

John Dexter—the sales manager—felt this difference was not too large (1.52 percent) and was inclined to forget the matter—especially since forecasts are

Big problems can go un-detected if managers do not analyze performance.

usually in error to some extent. He thought about sending a letter, however, to all sales reps and district supervisors in the region—a letter aimed at stimulating sales effort.

The overall story of what was happening to Stereo's sales in Ontario is shown in Table 22–4. What do you think the manager should do?

Hamilton district had the poorest performance—but it wasn't too bad. Before writing a "let's get with it" letter to Hamilton—and then relaxing—the sales manager decided to analyze the performance of the four sales reps in the Hamilton district. A breakdown of the Hamilton figures by sales reps is shown in Table 22–5. What conclusion or action is suggested now?

Since Ted Smith previously had been the top sales rep, the sales manager wondered if Smith were having trouble with some of his larger customers. Before making a drastic move, he obtained an analysis of Smith's sales to the five largest customers. See Table 22–6. What action could the sales manager take now? Should Smith be fired?

Smith's sales in all the large stores were down significantly—although his sales in many small stores were holding up well. It would seem that Smith's

■ TABLE 22–4   Sales performance—Ontario, January–June 1985 ($000)

District	Quota	Actual	Plus or minus	Performance to quota
Toronto	$ 4,675	$ 4,765	Plus $ 90	102%
Ottawa	3,625	3,675	Plus 50	101
Hamilton	3,000	2,800	Minus 200	93
London	3,200	3,130	Minus 70	98
Total	$14,500	$14,370	Minus $130	99%

■ TABLE 22–5   Sales performance—Hamilton district, January–June 1985 ($000)

Sales representative	Quota	Actual	Plus or minus		Performance to quota
Jane Johnson	$ 750	$ 780	Plus	$ 30	104%
Ted Smith	800	550	Minus	250	69
Bill Jones	790	840	Plus	50	106
Joe Carson	660	630	Minus	30	95
Total	$3,000	$2,800	Minus	$200	93%

■ TABLE 22–6   Sales performance—selected stores of Ted Smith in Hamilton district, January–June 1985 ($000)

Stores	Quota	Actual	Plus or minus		Performance to quota
1	$140	$ 65	Minus	$ 75	46%
2	110	70	Minus	40	69
3	105	60	Minus	45	57
4	130	65	Minus	65	50
5	205	150	Minus	55	73
Others	110	140	Plus	30	127
Total	$800	$550	Minus	$250	69%

■ TABLE 22–7   Sales performance—Ted Smith in Hamilton district, January–June 1985 ($000)

Product	Quota	Actual	Plus or minus		Performance to quota
Tape recorders	$ 70	$ 80	Plus	$ 10	114%
Portable radio-cassette players ..	430	160	Minus	270	37
Stereo receivers	150	150		0	100
Tape decks	100	110	Plus	10	110
Others	50	50		0	100
Total	$800	$550	Minus	$250	69%

problem was general. Perhaps he was just not working. Before calling him, the sales manager decided to look at Smith's sales of the four major products. Table 22–7 shows Smith's sales. What action is indicated now?

Smith was having real trouble with portable radio-cassette players. Was the problem Smith or the players?

Further analysis by products for the whole region showed that everyone in Ontario was having trouble with portable players—because a regional competitor was cutting prices. But higher sales on other products had hidden this fact. Since portable player sales had been doing all right nationally, the problem was only now showing up. You can see that this is *the* major problem.

Since overall company sales were going fairly well, many sales managers would not have bothered with this analysis. They might or might not have traced the problem to Smith. And without detailed sales records and performance analysis, the natural human reaction for Smith would be to blame business conditions—or aggressive competition—or some other handy excuse.

Stay home and use the computer

This case shows that total figures can be deceiving. Marketing managers should not jump on the first plane—or reach for the phone—until they have all the facts. Even worse than rushing to the scene would be a rash judgment based on incomplete information. Some students have wanted to fire Smith after they saw the store-by-store data (Table 22–6).

The home office should have the records and facilities to isolate problem areas—then rely on the field staff for explanations and assistance to locate the exact problem. Continuing detailed analysis usually gives better insights into problems, as this case shows. With computers, this can be done routinely and in great detail—*provided marketing managers ask for it.*

The "iceberg principle"—90 percent is below the surface

One of the most interesting conclusions to be drawn from the Stereo illustration is the **iceberg principle**—much good information is hidden in summary data.[3] Icebergs show only about 10 percent of their mass above water level—with the other 90 percent below water level—and not directly below, either. The submerged portion almost seems to be searching out ships that come too near.

The same is true of much business and marketing data. Since total sales may be large and company activities varied, problems in one area may be submerged below the surface. Everything looks calm and peaceful. But closer analysis may reveal jagged edges which can severely damage or even "sink" the business. The 90:10 ratio—or the 80/20 rule mentioned earlier—must not be ignored. Averaging and summarizing data can be helpful, but you should be sure that summaries don't hide more than they reveal.

Managers must look beyond summaries—to understand how their company is really doing.

Marketing Cost Analysis—Controlling Costs, Too

So far we have emphasized sales analysis. But sales come at a cost. And costs can and should be analyzed and controlled, too.

Detailed cost analysis has been very useful in the factory—but much less has been done with *marketing cost analysis.*[4] Accountants have shown little interest in the marketing process. Many think of salespeople as swingers who wine and dine customers, play golf all afternoon, and occasionally pick up orders. In this situation, they feel it is impossible to tie the costs of selling to particular products or customers. Many accountants feel, too, that advertising is almost a complete waste of money—that there is no way of relating it to particular sales. They wind up treating it as a general overhead cost—and then forget about it.

Marketing costs have a purpose

Careful analysis of most marketing costs, however, shows that the money is spent for a specific purpose—either to develop or promote a *particular product* or to serve *particular customers.* So it makes sense to allocate costs to specific market segments—or customers—or to specific products. In some situations, it is practical to allocate costs directly to the various geographical market segments being served. This may permit direct analysis of the profitability of the firm's target markets. In other cases, it may be desirable to allocate costs to specific customers—or specific products—and then add these costs for market segments—depending on how much of which products each customer bought.

In either case, marketing cost analysis usually requires a new way of classifying accounting data. Instead of using the natural accounts typically used for financial analysis, we have to use functional accounts.

Natural versus functional accounts—what is the purpose?

Natural accounts are the categories to which various costs are charged in the normal accounting cycle. These accounts include salaries, wages, social security, taxes, supplies, raw materials, auto, gas and oil expenses, advertising, and other such categories. These accounts are called "natural" because they have the names of their expense categories.

This is not the approach to cost analysis used in factories, however—and it is not the one we will use. In the factory, **functional accounts** show the *purpose* for which the expenditures are made. Factory functional accounts include shearing, milling, grinding, floor cleaning, maintenance, and so on. Factory cost accounting records are organized so that the cost of particular products or jobs can be calculated from them.

Marketing jobs are done for specific purposes, too. With some planning, the costs of marketing also can be assigned to specific categories—such as customers and products. Then their profitability can be calculated.

First, get costs into functional accounts

The first step in marketing cost analysis is to reclassify all the dollar cost entries in the natural accounts into functional cost accounts. For example, the many cost items in the natural *salary* account may be allocated to functional accounts with the following names: storing, inventory control, order assembly, packing and shipping, transporting, selling, advertising, order entry, billing, credit extension, and accounts receivable. The same is true for rent, depreciation, heat, light, power, and other natural accounts.

The way natural account amounts are shifted to functional accounts depends on the method of operation of the particular firm. It may require time studies, space measurements, actual counts, and managerial estimates.

Then reallocate to evaluate profitability of profit centers

The next step is to reallocate the functional costs to those items—or customers or market segments—for which the costs were spent. The most common reallocation of functional costs is to products and to customers. After these costs are allocated, the detailed totals can be combined in any way desired—for example, by product or customer class, region, and so on.

The costs allocated to the functional accounts equal in total those in the natural accounts. They are just organized in a different way. But instead of being used only to show total company profits, they can now be arranged to show the profitability of territories, products, customers, salespeople, price classes, order sizes, methods of distribution, methods of sales, or any other breakdown desired. Each unit can be treated as a profit center.

Cost analysis finds "No-profit Jones"— tracking down the loser

These ideas can be seen more clearly in the following example. In this case, the usual accounting approach—with natural accounts—shows that the company made a profit of $938 last month (Table 22–8). When a question is raised about the profitability of the company's three customers, the profit and loss statement can't help. The managers decide to use marketing cost analysis—because they want to know whether a change in the marketing mix will improve profit.

First, the costs in the five natural accounts are distributed to four functional accounts—sales, packaging, advertising, and billing and collection (see Table 22–9)—according to the functional reason for the expenses. Specifically, $1,000 of the total salary cost was for sales reps who seldom even come into the office—since their job is to call on customers; $900 of the salary cost was for packaging labor; and $600 was for office help. Assume that the office force split its time about evenly between addressing advertising material—and the billing and collection function. So the $600 is split evenly into these two functional accounts.

■ TABLE 22–8   Profit and loss statement

Sales		$17,000
Cost of goods sold		11,900
Gross margin		5,100
Expenses:		
Salaries	$2,500	
Rent	500	
Wrapping supplies	1,012	
Stationery and stamps	50	
Office equipment	100	
		4,162
Net profit		$ 938

■ TABLE 22–9   Spreading natural accounts to functional accounts

Natural accounts		Functional accounts			
		Sales	Packaging	Adver-tising	Billing and collection
Salaries	$2,500	$1,000	$ 900	$300	$300
Rent	500		400	50	50
Wrapping supplies	1,012		1,012		
Stationery and stamps	50			25	25
Office equipment	100			50	50
Total	$4,162	$1,000	$2,312	$425	$425

The $500 for rent was for the entire building—but 80 percent of the floor space was used for packaging and 20 percent for the office. Thus $400 is allocated to the packaging account. The remaining $100 is divided evenly between the advertising and billing accounts—because these functions used the office space about equally. Stationery, stamps, and office equipment charges are allocated equally to the latter two accounts for the same reason. Charges for wrapping supplies are allocated to the packaging account—because these supplies were used in packaging. In another situation, different allocations and even different accounts may be sensible—but these are workable here.

Calculating profitability of three customers

Now we can calculate the profitability of the company's three customers. But we need more information before we can allocate these functional accounts to customers or products. It is presented in Table 22–10.

Table 22–10 shows that the company's three products vary in cost, selling price, and sales volume. The products also have different "bulks"—and so the packaging costs aren't related to the selling price. For example, Product C is six times bulkier than A. When packaging costs are allocated to products, this must be considered. This is done by computing a new measure—a packaging unit—which is used to allocate the costs in the packaging account. Packaging units adjust for relative bulk—and the number of each type of product sold. While only 10 units of Product C are sold, it is bulky and requires 10 times 6—or 60 packaging units. This will cause more of the costs in the packaging account to be allocated to each unit of Product C.

Table 22–10 also shows that the three customers require different amounts of sales effort, place different numbers of orders, and buy different product combinations.

Jones seems to require more sales calls. Smith places many orders which must be processed in the office—with increased billing expense. Brown seems to be a great customer—since he placed only one order—and that order was for 70 percent of the sales of high-valued Product C.

The computations for allocating the functional amounts to the three customers are shown in Table 22–11. There were 100 sales calls in the period.

■ **TABLE 22–10**　　　　　Basic data for cost and profit analysis example

Products

Products	Cost/unit	Selling price/unit	Number of units sold in period	Sales volume in period	Relative "bulk" per unit	Packaging "units"
A	$ 7	$ 10	1,000	$10,000	1	1,000
B	35	50	100	5,000	3	300
C	140	200	10	2,000	6	60
			1,110	$17,000		1,360

Customers

Customers	Number of sales calls in period	Number of orders placed in period	Number of each product ordered in period A	B	C
Smith	30	30	900	30	0
Jones	40	3	90	30	3
Brown	30	1	10	40	7
Total	100	34	1,000	100	10

Assuming that all calls took the same amount of time, we can figure the average cost per call by dividing the $1,000 sales cost by 100 calls—giving an average cost of $10. Similar reasoning is used in breaking down the billing and packaging account totals. Advertising during this period was for the benefit of Product C only—so this cost is split among the units of C sold.

Calculating profit and loss for each customer

Now we can compute a profit and loss statement for each customer—combining his purchases and the cost of serving him. This is done in Table 22–12. A statement is prepared for each customer. And the sum of each of the four major components (sales, cost of goods sold, expenses, and profit) is the same as on the original statement (Table 22–8)—because all we've done is rearrange and rename the data.

The method is explained for customer Smith's statement in Table 22–12. Smith bought 900 units of A at $10 each and 300 units of B at $50 each—for the

■ **TABLE 22–11**　　　　　Functional cost account allocations

Sales calls	$1,000/100 calls	= $10/call
Billing	$425/34 orders	= $12.50/order
Packaging units costs	$2,312/1,360 packaging units	= $1.70/packaging unit or
		$1.70 for product A
		$5.10 for product B
		$10.20 for product C
Advertising	$425/10 units of C	= $42.50/unit of C

■ TABLE 22–12   Profit and loss statements for customers

	Smith	Jones	Brown	Whole company
Sales				
A	$9,000	$ 900	$ 100	
B	1,500	1,500	2,000	
C		600	1,400	
Total sales	$10,500	$ 3,000	$ 3,500	$17,000
Cost of goods sold				
A	6,300	630	70	
B	1,050	1,050	1,400	
C		420	980	
Total cost of goods sold	7,350	2,100	2,450	11,900
Gross margin	3,150	900	1,050	5,100
Expenses				
Sales calls ($10 each)	300	400.00	300.00	
Order costs ($12.50 each) ...	375	37.50	12.50	
Packaging costs				
A	1,530	153.00	17.00	
B	153	153.00	204.00	
C		30.60	71.40	
Advertising		127.50	297.50	
	2,358	901.60	902.40	4,162
Net profit (or loss)	$ 792	$ (1.60)	$147.60	$ 938

respective sales totals ($9,000 and $1,500) shown in Table 22–12. Cost of goods sold is computed in the same way. Thirty sales calls cost $300—30 times $10 each. He placed 30 orders (at an average cost of $12.50 each) for a total ordering cost of $375. Total packaging costs amounted to $1,530 for A (900 units purchased times $1.70 per unit) and $153 for B (30 units purchased times $5.10 per unit). There were no packaging costs for C—because Smith didn't buy any of Product C. Neither were any advertising costs charged to Smith—since all costs were spent promoting Product C—which he didn't buy.

Analyzing the results

We see now that Smith was the most profitable customer—yielding over 75 percent of the net profit.

This analysis shows that Brown was profitable, too—but not as profitable as Smith, because Smith bought three times as much. Jones was unprofitable— because he didn't buy very much and received one third more sales calls.

It is clear that the iceberg principle is operating again here. Although the company as a whole is profitable, customer Jones is not. Before dropping Jones, however, the marketing manager should study the figures and the marketing plan very carefully. Perhaps Jones should be called on less frequently—or maybe he will grow into a profitable account. Now he is at least covering some fixed costs.

Dropping him may only shift those fixed costs to the other two customers—making them look less attractive. (See the discussion on contribution margin later in this chapter.)

The marketing manager may also want to analyze the advertising costs against results—since this is a heavy advertising expense against each unit of Product C. Perhaps the whole marketing plan should be revised.

Cost analysis is not performance analysis

Such a cost analysis is not a performance analysis, of course. If the marketing manager had budgeted costs to various jobs, it would be possible to extend this analysis to a performance analysis. This would be logical—and perhaps even desirable—but few companies have moved this far.

As the cost of computer record keeping drops, we may see more companies doing marketing cost and performance analysis. They could then compute fairly realistic profit and loss statements for individual customers—just as some factory cost accounting systems develop cost estimates for products. Then these figures could be compared with "expected" figures—to evaluate and control the marketing plans.

Should All Costs Be Allocated?

We have discussed the general principles, but allocating costs is tricky. Some costs are likely to be fixed for the near future—regardless of what decision is made. And some costs are likely to be *common* to several products or customers—making allocation difficult.

Two basic approaches to handling this problem are possible—the full-cost approach and the contribution-margin approach.

Sometimes it is difficult to allocate functional costs to specific products, customers, or other categories.

Full-cost approach—everything costs something

In the **full-cost approach,** all functional costs are allocated to products, customers, or other categories. Even fixed costs are allocated in some way—as are common costs. Because all costs are allocated, it is possible to subtract costs from sales and find the profitability of various customers, and so on. This *is* of interest to some managers.

The full-cost approach requires that some difficult-to-allocate costs be split on some basis. The assumption here is that the services provided for those costs are equally beneficial to customers, to products, or to whatever group they are allocated. Sometimes this allocation is done mechanically. But often logical reasoning can support the allocation—if we accept the idea that marketing costs are incurred for a purpose. For example, advertising costs not directly related to specific customers or products *might* be allocated to *all* customers on the basis of their purchases—on the theory that advertising has helped bring in the sales.

Contribution margin—ignores some costs to get results

When we use the **contribution-margin approach,** all functional costs are not allocated in *all* situations. Why?

When various alternatives are being compared, it may be more useful to consider only the costs which are directly related to specific alternatives. Variable costs are particularly relevant here.

The contribution-margin approach focuses attention on variable costs—rather than on total costs. Total costs may include some fixed costs which do not change in the short run and can safely be ignored—or some common costs which are more difficult to allocate.[5]

The two approaches can lead to different decisions

The difference between the full-cost approach and the contribution-margin approach is important. Different decisions may be suggested by the two approaches—as we'll see in the following example.

Full-cost example

Table 22–13 shows a profit and loss statement—using the full-cost approach—for a department store with three operating departments. (These could be market segments or customers or products.)

■   TABLE 22–13   Profit and loss statement by department

	Totals	Department 1	Department 2	Department 3
Sales	$100,000	$50,000	$30,000	$20,000
Cost of goods sold	80,000	45,000	25,000	10,000
Gross margin	20,000	5,000	5,000	10,000
Other expenses				
Selling expenses	5,000	2,500	1,500	1,000
Administrative expenses	6,000	3,000	1,800	1,200
Total other expenses	11,000	5,500	3,300	2,200
Net profit or (loss)	9,000	(500)	1,700	7,800

The administrative expenses—which are the only fixed costs in this case—have been allocated to departments based on the sales volume of each department—a typical method of allocation. In this case, some managers argued that Department 1 was clearly unprofitable—and should be eliminated—because it showed a net loss of $500. Were they right?

To find out, see Table 22–14—which shows what would happen if Department 1 were eliminated.

Several facts become clear right away. The overall profit of the store would be reduced if Department 1 were dropped. Fixed costs of $3,000—now being charged to Department 1—would have to be allocated to the other departments. This would reduce net profit by $2,500—since Department 1 previously covered $2,500 of the $3,000 of fixed costs. This shifting of costs would then make Department 2 unprofitable!

Contribution-margin example

A contribution-margin income statement for the same department store is shown in Table 22–15. Note that each department has a positive contribution margin. Here the Department 1 contribution of $2,500 stands out better. This actually is the amount that would be lost if Department 1 were dropped. (This

■ TABLE 22–14   Profit and loss statement by department if Department 1 were eliminated

	Totals	Department 2	Department 3
Sales	$50,000	$30,000	$20,000
Cost of goods sold	35,000	25,000	10,000
Gross margin	15,000	5,000	10,000
Other expenses			
Selling expenses	2,500	1,500	1,000
Administrative expenses ...	6,000	3,600	2,400
Total other expenses ..	8,500	5,100	3,400
Net profit or (loss)	6,500	(100)	6,600

■ TABLE 22–15   Contribution-margin statement by departments

	Totals	Dept. 1	Dept. 2	Dept 3
Sales	$100,000	$50,000	$30,000	$20,000
Variable costs				
Cost of goods sold	80,000	45,000	25,000	10,000
Selling expenses	5,000	2,500	1,500	1,000
Total variable costs	85,000	47,500	26,500	11,000
Contribution margin	15,000	2,500	3,500	9,000
Fixed costs				
Administrative expenses	6,000			
Net profit	9,000			

example assumes that the fixed administrative expenses are *truly* fixed—that none of them would be eliminated if this department were dropped.)

A contribution-margin income statement shows the contribution of each department more clearly—including its contribution to both fixed costs and profit. As long as a department has some contribution-margin—and as long as there is no better use for the resources it uses—the department should be retained.

Contribution-margin versus full cost—choose your side

Using the full-cost approach often leads to arguments within a company. Any method of allocation can make some products or customers appear less profitable than if some other allocation method is used.

Assigning all common advertising costs to customers based on their purchases, for example, can be supported logically. But it also can be criticized on the grounds that it may make large-volume customers appear less profitable than they really are—especially if the marketing mix aimed at the larger customers emphasizes price more than advertising.

Those in the company who want the smaller customers to look more profitable will argue *for* this allocation method—on the grounds that general advertising helps "build" good customers because it affects the overall image of the company and its products.

Arguments over allocation methods can be deadly serious—because the method used may reflect on the performance of various company managers—and affect their salaries and bonuses. Product managers, for example, are vitally interested in how the various fixed and common costs are allocated to their products. Each, in turn, might like to have costs shifted to others' products.

Arbitrary allocation of costs also may have a direct impact on sales reps' morale. If they see their variable costs loaded with additional common or fixed costs over which they have no control, they may decide—What's the use?

To avoid these problems, the contribution-margin approach is often used. It is especially useful for evaluating alternatives—and for showing operating managers and salespeople how they're doing. The contribution-margin approach shows what they have actually contributed to covering general overhead and profit.

Top management, on the other hand, often finds full-cost analysis more useful. In the long run, some products, departments, or customers must pay for the fixed costs. Full-cost analysis has its place, too.

Planning and Control Combined

We have been treating sales and cost analyses separately up to this point. But management often will combine them to keep a running check on its activities—to be sure the plans are working—and to see when and where new strategies are needed.

Sales + Costs + Everybody helps = $8,150

Let's see how this works at the XYZ Hardware Company—a typical hardware retailer.

This firm netted $15,500 last year. Expecting no basic change in competition—and slightly better local business conditions—Jim Smith, the owner, set this year's profit objective at $16,300—an increase of about 5 percent.

Next he developed tentative plans to show how this higher profit could be made. He estimated the sales volumes, gross margins, and expenses—broken down by months and by departments in his store—that would be needed to net $16,300.

Table 22–16 is a planning and control chart which Jim developed to show the contribution each department should make each month. At the bottom of Table 22–16, the plan for the year is summarized. Notice that space is provided to insert the actual performance and a measure of variation—allowing both planning and control to be done with this chart.

Table 22–16 shows that Smith is focusing on the monthly contribution by each department. The purpose of monthly estimates is to get more frequent feedback—and allow faster adjustment of plans. Generally, the shorter the planning

■ TABLE 22–16 XYZ Hardware Company planning and control chart

| | Contribution to store | | | | | Store expense | Operating profit | Cumulative operating profit |
	Dept. A	Dept. B	Dept. C	Dept. D*	Total			
January								
Planned	2,700	900	400	−100	3,900	2,400	1,500	1,500
Actual								
Variation								
February								
Planned	2,000	650	250	−100	2,800	2,400	400	1,900
Actual								
Variation								
November								
Planned	3,200	750	250	0	4,200	2,400	1,800	10,650
Actual								
Variation								
December								
Planned	6,300	1,250	400	900	8,850	3,200	5,650	16,300
Actual								
Variation								
Total								
Planned	31,600	7,000	6,900	−400	45,300	28,800	16,300	16,300
Actual								
Variation								

*The objective of minus $400 for this department was established on the same basis as the objectives for the other departments, i.e., it represents the same percentage gain over last year, when Department D's loss was $420. Plans call for discontinuance of the department unless it shows marked improvement by the end of the year.

and control period, the easier it is to correct problems before they become emergencies.

In this example, a modified contribution-margin approach is being used—since some of the fixed costs can be allocated logically to particular departments. On this chart, the balance left after direct fixed and variable costs are charged to departments is called "Contribution to Store." The idea is that each department will contribute to covering *general* store expenses—such as top-management salaries and Christmas decorations—and to net profits.

In Table 22–16, we see that the whole operation is brought together when the monthly operating profit is computed. This contribution from each of the four departments is totaled—then general store expenses are subtracted to obtain the operating profit for each month.

Each department must plan and control, too

Table 22–17 shows a similar planning and control chart for a single XYZ department—Department B. In this table, actual results have been entered for the month of January. An unfavorable difference is revealed between planned and actual sales performance (−$1,400)—and gross profit (−$170).

Now the marketing manager must decide why actual sales were less than projected—and begin to make new plans. Possible hypotheses are: (1) prices were too high; (2) promotion was ineffective; (3) the product selection did not

■ TABLE 22–17   XYZ Hardware Company planning and control chart—Department B

	Sales	Gross profit	Direct expense Total	Direct expense Fixed	Direct expense Variable	Contribution to store	Cumulative-contribution to store
January							
Planned	6,000	1,800	900	600	300	900	900
Actual	4,600	1,630	830	600	115	800	800
Variation	−1,400	−170	70	0	70	−100	−100
February							
Planned	5,000	1,500	850	600	250	650	1,550
Actual							
Variation							
November							
Planned	7,000	2,100	1,350	1,000	350	750	5,750
Actual							
Variation							
December							
Planned	9,000	2,700	1,450	1,000	450	1,250	7,000
Actual							
Variation							
Total							
Planned	60,000	18,000	11,000	8,000	3,000	7,000	7,000
Actual							
Variation							

appeal to the target customers; and (4) errors might have been made in marking the prices or in totaling the sales figures.

Corrective action could take either of two courses: improving implementation efforts—or developing new, more realistic strategies.

The marketing manager must take charge

Computers are commonly used for data analysis in larger companies. Increasingly, smaller companies are buying computers, too.

But this kind of analysis is not possible unless the data is in machine-processable form—so it can be sorted and analyzed rapidly. Here, the creative marketing manager plays a crucial role—by insisting that the necessary data is collected. If the data he wishes to analyze is not captured as it comes in, information will be difficult—if not impossible—to get later. The only limitation on more effective and revealing data analysis is the imagination of the marketing manager—since machines can handle the drudgery.

The Marketing Audit

While crises pop, planning and control must go on

The analyses we have discussed so far are designed to help a firm plan and control its operations. They can help a marketing manager do a better job. Often, however, the control process tends to look at only a few critical elements—such as sales variations by product in different territories—and misses such things as the suitability of various marketing strategies—and the possible effectiveness of alternative mixes.

The marketing manager usually is responsible for day-to-day implementing as well as planning and control—and may not have the time to evaluate the effectiveness of the firm's efforts. Sometimes, crises are popping in several places at

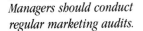
Managers should conduct regular marketing audits.

the same time. Attention must be focused on adjusting marketing mixes—or shifting strategies in the short run.

To make sure that the whole marketing program is evaluated *regularly*—not just in times of crisis—marketing specialists have developed a new concept—the marketing audit. It is similar to the accounting audit—or the personnel audit—both of which have been accepted by business for some time.

The **marketing audit** is a systematic, critical, and unbiased review and appraisal of the basic objectives and policies of the marketing function—and of the organization, methods, procedures, and people employed to implement the policies.[6] Table 22–18 shows what a working audit involves.

A marketing audit requires a detailed look at the company's current marketing plans—to see if they are still the "best" plans the firm can offer. Since customers' needs and attitudes change—and competitors are continually developing new and better plans—plans that are more than a year or two old may be getting out of date—or may even be obsolete. Sometimes, marketing managers are so close to the "trees that they can't see the forest." An outsider can help the firm see whether it really has focused on some unsatisfied needs—and is offering appropriate marketing mixes. Basically, the auditor uses our strategy planning framework—but instead of developing plans, he works backward—and evaluates the plans which are being implemented. He also evaluates the quality of the effort—looking at who is doing what and how well. This means interviewing customers, competitors, channel members, and employees. A marketing audit can be a big job—but if it helps assure that the company's strategies are on the right track and being implemented properly—it can be well worth the effort.

■ **TABLE 22–18** Guide to conducting the marketing audit

I. Mission
  A. Does the mission statement offer a clear guide to the product-markets of interest to the firm?
  B. Have objectives been established for the corporation as a whole and for marketing?
  C. Is information available for the review of corporate progress toward objectives, and are the reviews conducted on a regular (quarterly, monthly etc.) basis?
  D. Has corporate strategy been successful in meeting objectives?
  E. Are opportunities or problems pending that may require altering marketing strategy?
II. Marketing strategy
  A. Situation analysis
    1. Is marketing's role and responsibility in corporate strategy clearly specified?
    2. Are responsibility and authority for marketing strategy assigned to one executive?
    3. How well is the firm's marketing strategy working? Do problems exist?
    4. Are changes likely to occur in the marketing environment that may affect the firm's marketing strategy?
  B. Marketing plan and organization
    1. Are annual and longer-range marketing plans developed, and are they being used?

■ **TABLE 22–18**   *(continued)*

    2. Are the responsibilities of the various units in the marketing organization clearly specified?

    3. What are the strengths and limitations of the key members of the marketing orgainzation? What is being done to develop people?

    4. Is the organizational structure for marketing appropriate for implementing marketing plans?

  C. Target markets

    1. Has each target market been clearly defined and its importance to the firm established?

    2. Have demand, industry, and competition in each target market been analyzed and key trends, opportunities, and threats identified?

    3. Has the proper target market strategy (mass, grouping, or segmentation) been adopted?

    4. Should repositioning or exit from any product-market be considered?

  D. Objectives

    1. Have objectives been established for each target market, and are these consistent with corporate objectives and the available resources? Are the objectives realistic?

    2. Are sales, cost, and other information available for monitoring the progress of planned performance against actual results?

    3. Are regular appraisals made of marketing performance?

    4. Where do gaps exist between planned and actual results? What are the probable causes of the performance gaps?

  E. Marketing program

    1. Does the firm have an integrated marketing program made up of product, channel, price, advertising, and sales force strategies? Is the role selected for each mix element consistent with the overall program objectives, and does it properly complement other mix elements?

    2. Are adequate resources available to carry out the marketing program? Are resources committed to target markets according to the importance of each?

    3. Are allocations to the various marketing mix areas too low, too high, or about right in terms of what each is expected to accomplish?

    4. Is the effectiveness of the marketing program appraised on a regular basis?

III. Marketing program activities

  A. Product

    1. Is the product mix geared to the needs that the firm wants to meet in each product-market?

    2. Does the firm have a sound approach to product planning, and is marketing involved in product decisions?

    3. Are additions to, modifications of, or deletions from the product mix needed to make the firm more competitive in the marketplace?

    4. Is the performance of each product evaluated on a regular basis?

  B. Channels of distribution

    1. Has the firm selected the type and intensity of distribution appropriate for each of its product-markets?

    2. How well does each channel access its target market?

    3. Are channel intermediaries carrying out their assigned functions properly?

    4. Is the physical distribution function being managed as an integrated set of activities?

    5. Are desired customer service levels being reached, and are the costs of doing this acceptable?

  C. Pricing

    1. How responsive is each target market to price variations?

    2. What role and objectives does price have in the marketing mix?

    3. How do the firm's pricing strategy and tactics compare to those of competition?

    4. Is a systematic approach used to establish prices?

■ TABLE 22–18   *(concluded)*

5. Are there indications that changes may be needed in pricing strategy or tactics?
D. Advertising and sales promotion
    1. Have a role and objectives been established for advertising and sales promotion in the marketing mix?
    2. Is the budget adequate to carry out the objectives assigned to advertising and sales promotion?
    3. Do the media used represent the most cost-effective means of communicating with target markets?
    4. Do advertising copy and content effectively communicate the intended messages?
    5. How well does the advertising program measure up in meeting its objectives?
E. Sales force
    1. Are the role and objectives of personal selling in the marketing mix clearly specified and understood by the sales organization?
    2. Do the qualifications of salespeople correspond to their assigned role?
    3. Is the sales force of the proper size to carry out its function, and is it efficiently deployed?
    4. Are sales force results in line with management's expectations?
    5. Is each salesperson assigned performance targets, and are incentives offered to reward performance?
    6. Are compensation levels and ranges competitive?
IV. Implementation and control
    A. Have the causes of all performance gaps been identified?
    B. Is implementation of planned actions taking place as intended? Is implementation being hampered by other functional areas of the firm (e.g., manufacturing, finance)?
    C. Does the marketing plan require modification due to changing conditions, experience, or other factors?
    D. Has the audit revealed areas requiring additional study before action is taken?

Source: David W. Cravens, Gerald E. Hills, and Robert B. Woodruff, *Marketing Decision Making: Concepts and Strategy*, rev. ed. (Homewood, Ill.: Richard D. Irwin, 1980), pp. 480–81.

An audit shouldn't be necessary—but usually it is

A marketing audit takes a big view of the business—and evaluates the whole marketing program. It might be done by a separate department within the company—perhaps by a "marketing controller." Or, to avoid bias, it might be better to have it done by an outside organization—such as a management consulting firm.

Ideally, a marketing audit should not be necessary. A good manager does his very best in planning, implementing, and control—and should be continually evaluating the effectiveness of the operation.

In practice, however, managers often become identified with certain strategies—and pursue them blindly—when other strategies might be more effective. Since an outside view can give needed perspective, we may see greater use of marketing audits in the future.

■ CONCLUSION

In this chapter, we saw that sales and cost analysis can help a marketing manager control a marketing program—and that control procedures can be useful in planning. Controls lead to feedback that can aid planning.

Simple sales analysis just gives a picture of what has happened. But when sales forecasts or other data showing expected results are brought into the analysis, it is possible to evaluate performance—using performance indices.

Cost analysis also can be useful—if "natural" accounting costs are allocated to market segments, customers, products, or other categories—using functional cost breakdowns. There are two basic approaches to cost analysis—full-cost and contribution-margin. Using the full-cost approach, all costs are allocated in some way. Using the con-

tribution-margin approach, only the variable costs are allocated. Both methods have their advantages and special uses.

Ideally, the marketing manager should arrange for a constant flow of data that can be analyzed routinely—preferably by machine—to help control present plans and plan new strategies. A marketing audit may help this ongoing effort. Either a separate department within the company—or an outside organization—may conduct this audit.

It is clear that a marketing program must be controlled. Good control helps the marketing manager locate and correct weak spots—and at the same time find strengths which may be applied throughout the marketing program. Control works hand in hand with planning.

■ QUESTIONS AND PROBLEMS

1. Various breakdowns can be used for sales analysis, depending on the nature of the company and its products. Describe a situation (one for each) where each of the following breakdowns would yield useful information. Explain why.

a. By geographic region.
b. By product.
c. By customer.
d. By size of order.
e. By size of sales rep commission allowed (on each product or product group.)

2. Distinguish between a sales analysis and a performance analysis.

3. Explain carefully what the "iceberg principle" should mean to the marketing manager.

4. Explain the meaning of the comparative performance and comparative cost data in Tables

22–1 and 22–2. Why does it appear that eliminating sales areas D and E would be profitable?

5. Most sales forecasting is subject to some error (perhaps 5 to 10 percent). Is it proper to conclude then that variations in sales performance of 5 to 10 percent above or below quota are to be expected? If so, how should such variations be treated in evaluating performance?

6. Explain why there is controversy between the advocates of the net profit approach and the contribution-margin approach to cost analysis.

7. The profit and loss statement for June for the Browning Company is shown. If competitive conditions make price increases impossible—and management has cut costs as much as possible—should the Browning Company stop selling to hospitals and schools? Why?

Browning Company statement

	Retailers	Hospitals and schools	Total
Sales			
80,000 units at $0.70	$56,000		$56,000
20,000 units at $0.60		$12,000	12,000
Total......	56,000	12,000	68,000
Cost of goods sold.........	40,000	10,000	50,000
Gross margin....	16,000	2,000	18,000
Sales and administrative expenses:			
Variable.....	6,000	1,500	7,500
Fixed.......	5,600	900	6,500
Total......	11,600	2,400	14,000
Net profit (loss).........	$ 4,400	$ (400)	$ 4,000

8. Explain why it is so important for the marketing manager to be directly involved in the planning of control procedures.

9. Explain why a marketing audit might be desirable—even in a well-run company. Discuss who or what kind of an organization would be best to conduct a marketing audit. Would a marketing research firm be good? Would the present CA firms be most suitable?

■ **SUGGESTED CASES**

32. Weldwood of Canada, Ltd.
33. Diamond Jim's Pizza Company

34. Aluminum Products Limited

■ NOTES

1. Subhash Sharma and Dale D. Achabal, "STEMCOM: An Analytical Model for Marketing Control," *Journal of Marketing* 46, no. 2 (Spring 1982), pp. 104–13; James M. Hulbert and Norman E. Toy, "A Strategic Framework for Marketing Control," *Journal of Marketing,* April 1977, pp. 12–21; and Sam R. Goodman, *Techniques of Profitability Analysis* (New York: John Wiley & Sons, 1970), especially chap. 1.

2. Ed Weymes, "A Different Approach to Retail Sales Analysis," *Business Horizons* 25, no. 2 (March/April 1982), pp. 66–74; R. I. Haley and R. Gatty, "Monitor Your Markets Continuously," *Harvard Business Review,* May-June 1968, pp. 65–69; and D. H. Robertson, "Sales Force Feedback on Competitors' Activities," *Journal of Marketing,* April 1974, pp. 69–71.

3. Richard D. Crisp, *Marketing Research* (New York: McGraw-Hill, 1957), p. 144.

4. Patrick M. Dunne and Harry I. Wolk, "Marketing Cost Analysis: A Modularized Contribution Approach," *Journal of Marketing,* July 1977, pp. 83–94; Leland L. Beik and Stephen L. Buzby, "Profitability Analysis by Market Segments," *Journal of Marketing,* July 1973, pp. 48–53; D. R. Longman and M. Schiff, *Practical Distribution Cost Analysis* (Homewood, Ill.: Richard D. Irwin, 1955); Frank H. Mossman, Paul M. Fischer, and W. J. E. Crissy, "New Approaches to Analyzing Marketing Profitability," *Journal of Marketing,* April 1974, pp. 43–48; "Segmental Analysis: Key to Marketing Profitability," *MSU Business Topics,* Spring 1973, pp. 42–49; and V. H. Kirpalani and Stanley J. Shapiro, "Financial Dimensions of Marketing Management," *Journal of Marketing,* July 1973, pp. 40–47.

5. Technically, a distinction should be made between variable and direct costs, but we will use these terms interchangeably. Similarly, not all common costs are fixed costs, and vice versa, but the important point here is to recognize that some costs are fairly easy to allocate, and other costs are not.

6. A. R. Oxenfeldt, "The Marketing Audit as a Total Evaluation Program," in *Analyzing and Improving Marketing Performance: Marketing Audits in Theory and Practice* (New York: American Management Association, 1959), p. 26. See also John F. Grashof, "Conducting and Using a Marketing Audit," in *Readings and Cases in Basic Marketing,* 4th ed., ed. E. J. McCarthy, J. F. Grashof, and A. A. Brogowicz (Homewood, Ill.: Richard D. Irwin, 1984); Edward M. Mazze and John T. Thompson, Jr., "Organization Renewal: Case Study of a Marketing Department," *MSU Business Topics,* Summer 1973, pp. 39–44; and Alice M. Tybout and John R. Hauser, "A Marketing Audit Using a Conceptual Model of Consumer Behavior: Application and Evaluation," *Journal of Marketing* 45, no. 3 (Summer 1981), pp. 82–101.

Chapter 23 ■ Marketing strategy planning for international markets

When you finish this chapter, you should:

1. Understand the various ways that businesses can get into international marketing.

2. Understand what multinational corporations are.

3. Understand the kinds of opportunities in international markets.

4. Understand the market dimensions which may be useful in segmenting international markets.

5. Recognize the important new terms (shown in red).

"Did you know that more packaged spaghetti is eaten in Germany than in Italy?"

Planning strategies for international markets can be even harder than for domestic markets because cultural differences are more important. Also, the other uncontrollable variables may vary more. Each foreign market must be treated as a separate market—with its own sub-markets. Lumping together all people outside Canada as "foreigners"—or assuming they are just like Canadian customers—will almost guarantee failure.

Too much stereotyped thinking is applied to international marketing: "We wouldn't want to risk putting a plant over there and then having it nationalized," or "Fighting all that 'red tape' would be too much trouble," or "It sold here—it'll sell there" or "Just have the ad put into Spanish (or French, or German or—) and run it in all the papers."

This chapter tries to get rid of some of these misconceptions—and to suggest how marketing planning has to be adjusted when a firm goes into international marketing. We will see that a marketing manager must make several strategic decisions about international marketing: (1) whether the firm even wants to work in international markets at all and, if so, its degree of involvement, (2) in which markets, and (3) what organization arrangements should be made when it moves beyond its domestic activities. See Figure 23–1.

International markets are very important to Canada and many Canadian firms. Many opportunities exist outside this country. And as Table 23-1 shows, some Canadian firms are deeply involved—selling more abroad than in Canada. Coca-

■ TABLE 23–1   Top Canadian exporters, 1984

Rank by exports 1984	Total Canadian exports $000	Company	Rank in FP 500	Exports as percent of total sales	Percent change in exports versus 1983
1	10,614,462	General Motors of Canada Ltd.	1	65%	+17%
2	6,253,000	Ford Motor Co. of Canada	3	52	+62
3	4,412,350	Canadian Wheat Board	12	85	-5
4	3,823,000	Chrysler Canada Ltd.	8	61	+40
5	2,914,343	Canadian Pacific Ltd.	2	20	+28
6	1,876,165[1]	Alcan Aluminum Ltd.	7	27	+32
7	1,206,000	Alberta & Southern Gas Co.	66	81	-8
8	1,153,000	MacMillan Bloedel Ltd.	44	54	+9
9	1,028,000	Mitsui & Co. (Canada)	53	57	+5
10	1,000,000	Inco Ltd.	51	52	+54
11	959,073	Abitibi-Price Inc.	42	45	+26
12	943,411	Mitsubishi Canada Ltd.	71	74	+51
13	884,000	IBM Canada Ltd.	29	29	+46
14	874,532	Nova Corp.	22	23	-19
15	859,600	PetroCanada	14	18	+6
16	814,300	B.C. Resources Investment Co.	85	77	+14
17	781,000	Imperial Oil Ltd.	5	9	+24
18	741,000	Cargill Grain Co.	54	45	+138
19	727,100	TransCanada PipeLines Ltd.	17	17	+28
20	700,000	Shell Canada Ltd.	10	12	+73
21	649,963	Canadian Commercial Corp.	130	100	+28
22	588,511	Royal Canadian Mint	127	87	+42
23	566,908	Westcoast Transmission Co.	79	49	-9
24	550,900	Consolidated-Bathurst Inc.	56	34	+18
25	535,418	Pratt & Whitney Canada Inc.	132	83	+30
26	533,900	British Columbia Forest Products Ltd.	89	53	+10
27	522,000	Stelco Inc.	38	22	+25
28	499,712	Rio Algom Ltd.	80	44	+31
29	468,000	Canfor Corp.	86	45	+1
30	465,000	Agro Co. of Canada	154	90	-40
31	443,948	International Harvester Canada Ltd.	92	46	+95
32	429,158	Cansulex Ltd.	181	100	+77
33	427,000	Ontario Hydro	18	10	-4
34	419,000	Sumitomo Canada Ltd.	141	70	n.a.
35	406,891	Mobil Oil Canada Ltd.	60	26	+38
36	395,024	American Motors (Canada) Inc.	111	51	-4
37	388,000	Hydro-Quebec	21	9	+14
38	388,000	Canpotex Ltd.	194	100	+62
39	385,000	Boise Cascade Canada Ltd.	175	86	+24
40	374,400	Domtar Inc.	46	18	+11
41	364,118	Falconbridge Ltd.	119	50	+29
42	342,466	Crown Forest Industries Ltd.	118	46	+10
43	313,393	Canadair Ltd.	200	83	-9
44	310,542	Allied Canada Inc.	114	41	+44
45	306,500	Magna International Inc.	160	62	+41

■   TABLE 23–1   (*concluded*)

Rank by exports 1984	Total Canadian exports $000	Company	Rank in FP 500	Exports as percent of total sales	Percent change in exports versus 1983
46	304,000	Marubeni Canada Ltd.	112	39	n.a.
47	300,000	George Weston Ltd.	6	4	0
48	289,300	Suncor Inc.	59	18	−28
49	283,434	ProGas Ltd.	239	95	−2
50	279,700	Rockwell Int.'l of Canada	190	70	+67

n.a. = Not available.
[1]Converted from US$.

Source: "Who's Who in Selling to the World," *Financial Post 500*, Summer 1985, p. 113.

■   FIGURE 23–1   Strategic decisions about international marketing

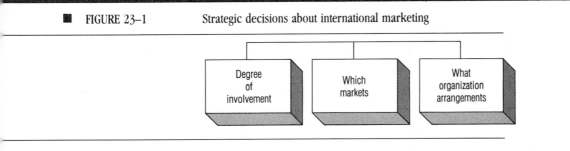

Cola, for example, recently moved past the halfway point—more than half of its profits come from international operations. Coca-Cola sees the day coming when as much as 75 percent of its earnings will be from abroad—because there will be more young people there than in aging North America.[1]

Let's look first at how important international marketing is, and then begin to consider the strategic decisions which a marketing manager must make when planning strategies for international markets.

Canada's Foreign Trade

Foreign trade accounts for about 20 percent of Canada's gross national product (GNP). This makes foreign trade as important a component of Canada's GNP as it is in Germany and the United Kingdom. The corresponding figure for the United States is about 10 percent.

United States the major trading partner

Table 23–2 reveals that Canada does most of its foreign trading with the United States. Although the proportions differ somewhat from year to year, Canada's trade with the United States is much more important than that with any other nation or trading group. Canada is also the major trading partner of the United States, but it accounts for only 20 to 22 percent of total U.S. foreign trade.

The United Kingdom became a member of the European Economic Community (EEC) on January 1, 1973. In a sense, Canada's second and third largest trading partners merged at that time. As Table 23–2 indicates, a significant volume of Canadian trade takes place with an expanded EEC and with Japan, now our third most important partner. However, total trade with Japan and the EEC combined is less that 20 percent of Canadian trade with the United States.

What Canada buys and sells

Canada has remained basically an exporter of natural resources and an importer of finished products. On the other hand, our large trading partners are big importers of primary products and large exporters of manufactured goods. Motor vehicles and parts now account for about two thirds of Canada's exports of manufactured end products. Other sales of end products have averaged between 10 percent and 12 percent of total exports. Why are motor vehicle exports so high? A duty-free market in automotive and related products was created by the Canada–U.S. Automotive Agreement of 1965. Many people are now interested in expanding Canada's free trading arrangements with the United States. However, political considerations, especially the different interests of states, provinces, and industries, will make negotiating such a free trade agreement very difficult.[2]

■ TABLE 23–2   Canadian import-export patterns

	What gets exported (percent)		What gets imported (percent)	
	1982	1984	1982	1984
Live animals	0.4%	0.5%	0.2%	0.1%
Food, feed, beverages, tobacco	11.7	9.1	7.2	6.3
Crude materials	17.6	15.6	13.0	8.7
Fabricated materials	32.9	31.6	17.7	18.2
End products	36.3	41.6	62.5	67.9
Special transactions	0.3	0.4	1.5	1.7

	Where it goes (percent)		Where it comes from (percent)	
	1982	1984	1982	1984
United States	67.9%	76.5%	70.5%	71.5%
United Kingdom	2.1	3.3	2.8	2.4
Other EEC	5.6	4.7	5.6	6.2
Japan	0.8	0.9	5.2	6.0
Other OECD	3.7	4.3	2.8	2.4
Other American	13.6	6.1	6.4	4.9
Other countries	6.3	4.2	6.7	6.6

Source: Adapted from *Statistics Canada*, Cat. 65-001, Summary of External Trade, December 1984.

Can Canadian manufacturers compete?

What kinds of products can Canadian manufacturers successfully produce? What items cannot be profitably manufactured because of foreign competition? Since these questions are so important, let's examine what one observer considers "significant Canadian conditions and circumstances" affecting new product development.

First, there is too often confusion between Canada's capability of producing (technically) a new product and its ability to market such a product profitably. A national fear of otherwise becoming "a technological colony" is by itself not a good enough reason for introducing costly new products. Also, the Canadian market is a relatively small one stretching for 3,500 miles. Often, large parts of that total market can be reached more cheaply by foreign manufacturers than they can by firms producing elsewhere in Canada. This nation has high labor costs and its productivity relative to other countries has steadily declined. Since Canada is not part of a large trading community such as one now finds in Europe, its problems as an exporter are increasing. Specifically, it does not have qualified access to markets large enough to allow Canadian plants to benefit from possible economies of scale. Finally, government policies often have the effect of discouraging product development in Canada.[3]

Finding a niche; the answer

A more recent investigation cited higher wages, diseconomies of small scale, difficulties in obtaining adequate financing, and the tax costs and administrative burdens of "big government" as problems confronting Canadian manufacturers. Despite these problems, the study showed that Canadian producers were capable of succeeding if their operations met one or more of the following conditions: (1) product superiority either in terms of technical product leadership or high quality; (2) process or manufacturing superiority, either technical process superiority or a unique combination of two or more processes within the same firm; (3) management philosophy and style, leading to the ability to compete economically in cost-sensitive markets, in spite of the Canadian disadvantages cited above; (4) customizing the product package, which generally involved a unique combination of product, process, and engineering skill, not necessarily technological superiority.[4]

Carefully engineered, well-designed Canadian products that meet the needs of specific customer segments are being successfully marketed both in Canada and abroad. Some examples include most of Northern Telecom's electronic equipment, tractors produced by Versatile Manufacturing Limited, hockey equipment from Cooper Canada, Ltd., and sailboats from Performance Sailcraft, Inc.[5]

The world product mandate

Many Canadian manufacturers are subsidiaries of foreign-owned corporations. Such organizations could compete successfully abroad if they were chosen by their parent company to market certain products internationally. In other words, the Canadian subsidiary might be given a "world product mandate" for certain items. The Canadian firm with such a mandate would design, engineer, and manufacture in Canada. A worldwide marketing effort would also be directed

■ FIGURE 23–2   How product mandates keep Black & Decker on top—A winner in world markets

It has not been easy, but the orbital sander made in Brockville, Ontario, by Black & Decker Canada, Inc., is holding its market position as the best value at the lowest price in Tokyo. The product, a leading competitor in price and quality in most world markets, including the United States, was the starting point for a textbook example of escape from industrial branch-plant status through world product mandating.

Since the Canadian company, wholly owned by Black & Decker Manufacturing Co. of Baltimore, sought the right to produce the sander exclusively for North America in 1968 and won the world mandate in 1972, it has become one of the strongest units in the Black & Decker organization. With 15 percent annual growth averages and 5 percent productivity improvements throughout the 1970s, Brockville outpaced the world organization. From that one successful power tool it has built an international business of eight mandated products. Three more are planned for next year. Between 40 percent and 50 percent of production is exported.

Though product mandating has long been a popular theory, few Canadian companies are involved. Black & Decker, one of the few, today counts its blessings in increased sales, net earnings and employment. But the real benefits, as in the case of Westinghouse Canada, Inc., and Canadian General Electric, Ltd., are to be found in that transformation from the branch plant attitude, feeding on protective tariffs, to a self-supporting operation taking on the world's best.

Now in its 60th year in Canada, Black & Decker took advantage of existing market conditions in 1968 when the Brockville plant asked the head office in Baltimore for a product mandate to help rationalize Canadian production. A U.S. surge in demand for consumer power tools had strained U.S. plant capacity, and the Canadians saw an opportunity to escape the limitations of strictly low-volume domestic production.

Part of the deal, of course, was that Brockville could handle a mandate as cheaply as any U.S. plant—something Canadians were confident of when calculating the economies of scale. The product agreed upon was the highly successful orbital sander, then produced in limited volumes in Canada.

The spin-offs were soon evident. Brockville's production capacity doubled the following year. The surge in U.S. exports and resulting lower costs served to rationalize production of items still made for Canadian markets alone. By 1972, the division had developed the lowest unit costs for the orbital sander of any Black & Decker plant in the world, and the parent company extended what had originally been a North American mandate into a world mandate.

The next project also proved to be a world-beater. It was the Workmate, a portable workbench-vise combination invented in Britain and produced in an earlier version with limited success by the U.K. division. Canada wanted to redesign the product into something stronger and more economical to produce and introduce it to what the company judged would be a more receptive North American market.

"We knew a small market couldn't justify the development costs," recalls president-designate Chelico. "But we also knew we had a winner. The United States started importing two years later, and our production went from 250,000 in 1974 to more than a million now."

With the substantial cash flow from two very high-volume products, the company now had the capital for more sophisticated R&D and investment in productivity improvement. The Workmate assembly line, resembling something out of the Henry Ford era, has had $10 million reinvested in it. This has resulted in production cost reductions to about half those of 1974.Three additional models have been developed, together with spin-off accessories for routers and power saws that extend the versatility of the original unit.

Source: Randall Litchfield, "How Product Mandates Keep Black & Decker on Top—A Winner in World Markets," *Financial Times of Canada,* June 4, 1982, p. 7.

from this country. Such mandates are, in fact, beginning to be assigned to Canadian subsidiaries.[6]

World product mandating is an exciting new development that may significantly increase Canada's exports of manufactured goods. It may mean that more Canadian subsidiaries will advance beyond the stage of branch manufacturing plant. Figure 23–2 shows the many benefits of world product mandating.

Government services available to exporters

Foreign trade and an acceptable balance-of-payments position is important—the Canadian government provides a number of services to would-be exporters. Most of this help comes from the Department of Regional Industrial Expansion. Its Fairs and Mission Branch arranges trade fair exhibits in foreign countries, trade missions to and from Canada, and visits by foreign buyers to Canadian sources of supply. The Market Development Group brings together Canadian manufacturers so they can collectively bid on foreign projects too large for any one firm. Canadian Trade Commissioners posted abroad act as export marketing consultants to interested sellers. They also serve as liaison officers between foreign buyers and Canadian exporters.[7]

Other federal agencies offer additional types of help. For example, the Export Development Corporation provides insurance to exporters, guarantees payment, and provides interim financing. The Canadian Commercial Corporation, also wholly owned by the Government of Canada, helps other governments and international agencies that want to purchase Canadian goods and services. The Canadian International Development Agency encourages exports by making foreign aid recipients "buy Canadian" whenever possible.

Many provinces have similar programs to encourage exports—and actively promote trade missions to various parts of the world. At both the provincial and federal level there has also been interest in establishing "official" or "state" trading companies. Such firms could cultivate foreign markets for many Canadian manufacturers unable to pursue export opportunities.

Degrees of Involvement in International Marketing

Attractive opportunities in foreign countries have led many companies into worldwide operations. The marketing concept is less understood in some foreign markets. So there are exciting opportunities for those who want to apply it abroad. There are varying degrees of involvement, however. A marketing manager can choose among six basic kinds of involvement—as shown in Figure 23–3—exporting, licensing, contract manufacturing, management contracting, joint venturing, and wholly-owned subsidiaries. Let's look at these possibilities now.

Exporting often comes first

Some companies get into international marketing by just exporting the products they are already producing. Sometimes this is just a way of "getting rid of" surplus output. For others, it comes from a real effort to look for new opportuni-

■   FIGURE 23–3   Kinds of involvement in international marketing that a marketing
                          manager can choose

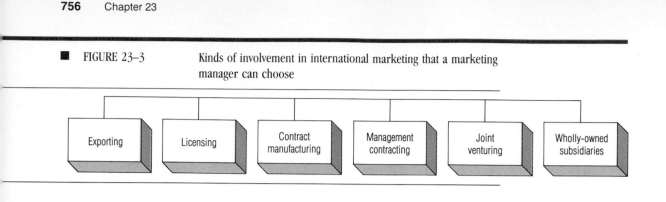

ties—i.e., the "market development" opportunities discussed in Chapter 3. Gerber (baby foods) entered international marketing by exporting.

Exporting is selling some of what the firm is producing to foreign markets.
Often this is tried without changing the product—or even the service or instruction manuals! As a result, some early efforts are not very satisfying—to buyers or
sellers.

Exporting gets a firm involved in a lot of government "red tape"—but handling
it can be mastered fairly quickly. Or it can be turned over to specialists—as many
large exporters do. Export agents can handle the paper work as the goods are
shipped outside the country. Then agents or merchant wholesalers can handle
the importing details. Even large manufacturers with many foreign operations
use international middlemen for some products or markets. They know how to
handle the sometimes confusing formalities and specialized functions. Even a
small mistake can tie goods up at national borders for days—or months.

Export departments within firms are often treated as "stepchildren" by the
regular departments. Increasingly, though, companies are aggressively pursuing
foreign market prospects as they find their foreign operations becoming more

*Exporting means selling
present products in for-
eign markets.*

profitable than domestic activities. Then, the export department's status rises—or exporting is integrated into the regular operation.

Some relationships get a firm more involved

Exporting doesn't have to involve permanent relationships. Of course, channel relationships take time to build and shouldn't be treated lightly. Sales reps' contacts in foreign countries are "investments," but it is relatively easy to cut back on these relationships—or even drop them.

Some firms, on the other hand, develop more formal and permanent relationships with nationals in foreign countries—including licensing, contract manufacturing, management contracting, and joint venturing.

Licensing is an easy way

Licensing is a relatively easy way to enter foreign markets. **Licensing** means selling the right to use some process, trademark, patent, or other right—for a fee or royalty. The licensee takes most of the risk—because it must invest some capital to use the right.

This can be an effective way of entering a market if good partners are available. (Gerber entered the Japanese baby food market in this way, but Gerber still exports to other countries.)

Contract manufacturing takes care of the production problems

Contract manufacturing means turning over production to others while retaining the marketing process. Sears used this approach as it opened stores in Latin America and Spain.

This approach can be especially good where labor relations are difficult—or there are problems obtaining supplies and "buying" government cooperation. Growing nationalistic feelings may make this approach more attractive in the future.

Management contracting sells know-how

Management contracting means the seller provides only management skills—the production facilities are owned by others. Some mines and oil refineries are operated this way—and Hilton operates hotels all over the world for local owners. This is a relatively low-risk approach to international marketing. No commitment is made to fixed facilities—which can be taken over or damaged in riots or wars. If conditions get too bad, the key management people can fly off on the next plane—and leave the nationals to manage the operation.

Joint venturing is more involved

Joint venturing means a domestic firm entering into a partnership with a foreign firm. As with any partnership, there can be honest disagreements over objectives—for example, about how much profit is desired and how fast it should be paid out—and operating policies. Where a close working relationship can be developed—perhaps based on a Canadian firm's technical and marketing know-how and the foreign partner's knowledge of the market and political connections—this approach can be very attractive to both parties. At its worst, it can be a nightmare and cause the Canadian firm to want to go into a wholly-owned operation. But the terms of the joint venture may block this for years.

More countries are requiring joint ventures—with nationals controlling at least 51 percent. Mexico and India have moved in this direction, for example.

Wholly-owned subsidiaries give more control

When a firm feels that a foreign market looks really promising, it may want to go the final step. A **wholly-owned subsidiary** is a separate firm—owned by a parent company. This gives complete control—and helps a foreign branch work more easily with the rest of the company.

Some multinational companies have gone this way. It gives them a great deal of freedom to move goods from one country to another. If a firm has too much capacity in a country with low production costs, for example, some production may be moved there from other plants—and then exported to countries with higher production costs. This is the same way that large firms in the United States ship goods from one area to another—depending on costs and local needs.

Multinational Corporations Evolve to Meet International Challenge

Multinational corporations have a direct investment in several countries and run their businesses depending on the choices available anywhere in the world. Well-known U.S.-based multinational firms include Coca-Cola, Eastman Kodak, Warner-Lambert, Pfizer, Anaconda, Goodyear, Ford, IBM, ITT, Corn Products, 3M, National Cash Register, H. J. Heinz, and Gillette. They regularly earn over a third of their total sales or profits abroad.[8]

Many multinational companies are American. But there are also many well-known foreign-based companies—such as Nestle, Shell (Royal Dutch Shell), Lever Brothers (Unilever), Sony, and Honda. They have well-accepted "foreign" brands—not only in the United States, but around the world. Such Canadian organizations as Alcan, Canron, CIL, Consolidated Bathurst, Massey-Ferguson, and Seagrams have a controlling or complete interest in U.S. firms.

Indeed, Canadian-owned firms are far more multinational than most of us realize. Some 22 Canadian-controlled firms appear in *Fortune* magazine's 1984

Gerber makes different marketing arrangements around the world.

list of "500 Largest Non-U.S. Industrial Corporations." (Another 8 Canadian-based but foreign-owned firms—the largest being General Motors of Canada—also appear on that list).

Multinational operations make sense to more firms

As a firm becomes more involved in international marketing, it may reach the point where it sees itself as a worldwide business. As a chief executive of Abbott Laboratories—a pharmaceutical company with plants in 22 countries—said, "We are no longer just a U.S. company with interests abroad. Abbott is a world-wide enterprise, and many major fundamental decisions must be made on a global basis."

Multinational companies have to view the world objectively to run their companies profitably.

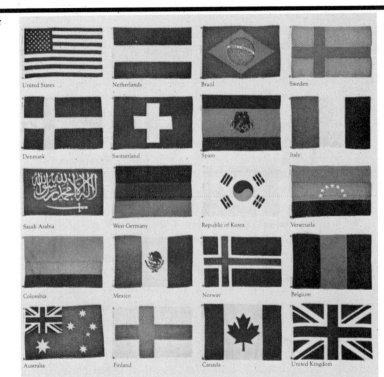

A Texas Instruments manager had a similar view: "When we consider new opportunities and one is abroad and the other domestic, we can't afford to look upon the alternative here as an inherently superior business opportunity simply because it is in the United States. We view an overseas market just as we do our market, say, in Arizona, as one more market in the world."

A General Motors manager sees this trend as "the emergence of the modern industrial corporation as an institution that is transcending national boundaries."[9]

Much of the multinational activity of the 1960s and early 1970s was U.S.-based firms expanding to other countries. As these opportunities became less attractive in the mid-1970s—due to the energy crisis, inflation, currency devaluations, labor unrest, and unstable governments—foreign multinational companies have been moving into the United States. The United States is, after all, one of the richest markets in the world.

Multinational companies overcome national boundaries

From an international view, multinational firms do—as the GM manager said—"transcend national boundaries." They see world market opportunities and locate their production and distribution facilities for greatest effectiveness. This has upset some nationalistic business managers and politicians. But these multinational operations may be hard to stop. They are no longer just exporting or importing. They hire local residents—and build local plants. They have business relationships with local business managers and politicians. These are powerful organizations which have learned to deal with nationalistic feelings and typical border barriers—treating them simply as uncontrollable variables.

We do not have "one world" politically as yet—but business is moving in that direction. We may have to develop new kinds of corporations and laws to govern multinational operations. The limitations of national boundaries on business and politics will make less and less sense in the future.

Identifying Different Kinds of International Opportunities

Firms usually start from where they are

A multinational firm which has accepted the marketing concept will look for opportunities in the same way that we have been discussing throughout the text, that is, looking for unsatisfied needs that it might be able to satisfy—given its resources and objectives.

The typical approach—and perhaps a very practical one, since we're talking about going into very unfamiliar markets—is to start with the firm's current products and the needs it knows how to satisfy, and then try to find new markets—wherever they may be—with the same or similar unsatisfied needs. This approach might lead to exporting—to "get our feet wet." Next, the firm might adapt the Promotion, and then the Product. Later, the firm might think about developing new products and new promotion policies. Some of these possibilities are shown in Figure 23–4. Here, the emphasis is on Product and Promotion—because Place would obviously have to be changed in new markets—and Price adjustments probably would be needed too.

■   FIGURE 23–4   International marketing opportunities as seen by a U.S. firm from the viewpoint of
its usual product-market in the United States

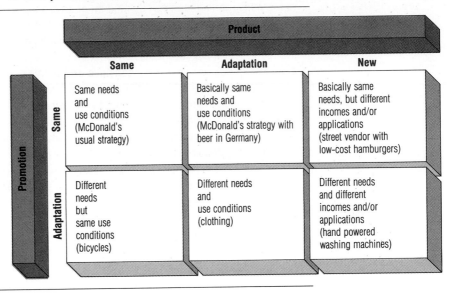

The "Same-Same" box in Figure 23–4 can be illustrated with McDonald's
(fast-food chain) entry into European markets. Its director of international marketing says, "Ronald McDonald speaks eight languages. Our target audience is
the same world-wide—young families with children—and our advertising is designed to appeal to them." The basic promotion messages must be translated, of
course, but the same strategy decisions which were made in the U.S. market
apply. McDonald's has adapted its Product in Germany, however, by adding beer
to appeal to adults who prefer beer to soft drinks. Its efforts have been extremely
successful so far.[10]

McDonald's and other firms expanding into international markets usually move
first into markets with good economic potential—such as Western Europe and
Japan. But if McDonald's or some other fast-food company wanted to move into
much lower-income areas, it might have to develop a whole new Product—perhaps a traveling street vendor with "hamburgers" made from soybean products.
This kind of opportunity is in the upper right-hand corner of Figure 23–4.

The lower left-hand box in this figure is illustrated by the different kind of
Promotion that is needed for just a simple bicycle. In some parts of the world, a
bicycle provides basic transportation—while in Canada, it is mainly a recreation
vehicle. So a different Promotion emphasis is needed in these different target
markets.

Both Product and Promotion changes will be needed as one moves to the
right along the bottom row of Figure 23–4. Such moves may increase the risk—
and obviously require more market knowledge.

The risk of opportunities varies by environmental sensitivity

International marketing means going into unfamiliar markets. This can increase risk. The farther you go from familiar territory, the greater the chance of making big mistakes. But not all products offer the same risk. It is useful to think of the risks running along a "continuum of environmental sensitivity." See Figure 23–5. Some products are relatively insensitive to the economic or cultural environment in which they are placed. These products may be accepted as is—or may require just a little adaptation to make them suitable for local use. Most industrial goods are near the insensitive end of this continuum.

At the other end of the continuum, we find highly sensitive products which may be difficult or impossible to adapt to all international situations. At this end, we find "faddy" or high-style consumer goods. It is sometimes difficult to understand why a particular product is well accepted in a home market—which makes it even more difficult to know how it might be received in a different environment.

This continuum helps explain why many of the early successes in international marketing were basic commodities such as gasoline, soap, transportation vehicles, mining equipment, and agricultural machinery. It also suggests that firms producing and/or selling highly sensitive products should carefully analyze how their products will be seen and used in new environments—and plan their strategies accordingly.[11] American-made blue jeans, for example, have been "status symbols" in Western Europe and Latin America—and producers have been able to sell them at premium prices through the "best" middlemen.

Evaluating opportunities in possible international markets

Judging opportunities in international markets uses the same principles we have been discussing throughout this text. Basically, each opportunity must be evaluated—considering the uncontrollable variables. But there may be more of these—and they may be more difficult to evaluate—in international markets. Estimating the risk involved in particular opportunities may be very difficult. Some countries are not politically stable. Their governments and constitutions come and go. An investment that was safe under one government might become the target for a take-over under another. Further, the possibility of foreign exchange controls—and tax rate changes—can reduce the chance of getting profits and capital back to the home country.

Because the risks are hard to judge, it may be wise to enter international marketing by exporting first—building know-how and confidence over time. Experience and judgment are even more important in unfamiliar areas. Allowing time to develop these skills among a firm's top management—as well as its inter-

◼ FIGURE 23–5   Continuum of environmental sensitivity

Insensitive		Sensitive
Industrial goods	Basic commodity-type consumer goods	Faddy or high-style consumer goods

national managers—makes sense. Then the firm will be in a better position to estimate the prospects and risks of going further into international marketing.

International Marketing Requires Even More Segmenting

Success in international marketing requires even more attention to segmenting. There are over 140 nations with their own unique differences! There can be big differences in language, customs, beliefs, religions, race, and even income distribution patterns from one country to another. This obviously complicates the segmenting process. But what makes it even worse is that there is less good data as one moves into international markets. While the number of variables increases, the quantity and quality of data go down. This is one reason why some multinational firms insist that local operations be handled by natives. They, at least, have a "feel" for their markets.

Most of the discussion in the rest of this chapter will emphasize final consumer differences, because they are likely to be greater than intermediate customer differences. Also, we will consider regional groupings and stages of economic development—which can aid your segmenting.

Regional Groupings May Mean More than National Boundaries

While national boundaries are a common and logical dimension for segmenting markets, sometimes it makes more sense to treat several nearby countries with similar cultures as one region—Central America or Latin America, for example. Or if several nations have banded together to have common economic boundaries, then these nations may be treated as a unit. The outstanding example is the European Economic Community (EEC). They have dared to abandon old ideas and nationalistic prejudices—in favor of cooperative efforts to reduce tariffs and other controls, which are commonly applied at national boundaries.

These cooperative arrangements are very important, because the taxes and restrictions at national borders can be annoying—but can also greatly reduce marketing opportunities. **Tariffs**—taxes on imported goods—vary, depending on whether the country is trying to raise revenue or limit trade. Restrictive tariffs often block all movement. But even revenue-producing tariffs cause red tape and discourage free movement of goods. Quotas act like restrictive tariffs. **Quotas** set the specific quantities of goods which can move in or out of a country. Great market opportunities may exist in a country, but import quotas (or export controls applied against a specific country) may discourage outsiders from entering. The Canadian government, for example, has worked to control Japan's export of cars to Canada. (Otherwise, we would have had even more Japanese cars entering the Canadian market!)

GATT works on tariff reduction

Until 1948, most countries in the world made bilateral (two-way) arrangements on trade. In 1948, most of the nations of the free world accepted the idea of multilateral negotiations—when they signed the *General Agreement on Tariffs and Trade* (GATT). They agreed to meet every two years and negotiate for reductions in tariffs among their countries. This organization is still going strong. Several major negotiation conferences have been very effective in lowering tariffs—and encouraging greater trade.

This multinational bargaining is especially important because most major trading nations use the **most-favored-nation clause**—which says that a significant tariff reduction offered to one nation immediately will be offered to all participating nations.

Coal and Steel Community surrendered some national sovereignty

The first supranational (above-national) economic organization developed in 1952—when Belgium, France, Germany, Italy, Luxembourg, and the Netherlands signed the *Coal and Steel Community Pact*. In this agreement, some national sovereignty was surrendered to the larger body—for the purpose of establishing a free market for iron ore, steel scrap, coal, and steel.

The objective of the Coal and Steel Community was development of a regional—rather than national—pattern for the production and distribution of these products. Since none of these countries was self-sufficient in steel production, the agreement made sense. It showed that economic integration—even without political integration—was possible when it was logical and benefited all the countries involved.

European Economic Community works toward full economic union

As a result of the smooth functioning of the Coal and Steel Community, these same six nations met in Rome in 1957 to sign a treaty establishing a *European Economic Community* (EEC) and a European Atomic Energy Community. They were, in effect, applying the concept behind the Coal and Steel Community to their entire economic life. These six nations formed the nucleus of the European Common Market.

By the middle 1960s, it was clear that this large free-trade market was breaking down old nationalistic and restrictionist attitudes, expanding employment and investment, reducing prices, and generally helping to raise the standard of living in these communities. So impressive were the advances made by the Common Market nations that Denmark, Ireland, and the United Kingdom joined in 1973. Over 20 other nations in Western Europe and Africa are associate members. And others have concluded free-trade agreements with the EEC—removing tariffs on industrial products.[12]

Long term, however, high energy costs may test the EEC concept. Most of the countries are dependent on foreign oil, but the impact is falling much more heavily on some of the less-developed members of the community. There is talk in the EEC—and elsewhere—of setting up cartels or agreements to control the marketing of goods. We may be in for a new round of protectionism.

Other groups are following the EEC

Organizations similar to the European Economic Community have formed in other parts of the world. But none of these groups has yet had the success of the

EEC—because of border and civil wars, revolutions, and strong nationalistic and protectionist tendencies. Nevertheless, strategy planning should include a serious consideration of such organizations.

Stages of Economic Development Help Define Markets

International markets vary widely—within and between countries. Some markets are more advanced and/or growing more rapidly than others. And some countries—or parts of a country—are at different stages of economic development. This means their demands—and even their marketing systems—will vary.

To get some idea of the many possible differences in potential markets—and how they affect strategy planning—let's discuss six stages of economic development. These stages are helpful—but must be qualified—because they greatly oversimplify the real world for a number of reasons. In the first place, different parts of the same country may be at different stages of development—so it isn't possible to identify a single country or region with only one stage. Secondly, the growing influence of multinational companies—and eager governments in some less-developed countries—has led to the skipping of one or two stages due to the infusion of outside or government capital. For example, the building of uneconomic steel mills to boost national pride—or the arrival of multinational corporations—might lead to a substantial jump in stages. This "stage-jumping" does not destroy the six-stage process. Rather, it merely explains why more rapid movements have taken place in some situations.

Stage 1—agricul-tural—self-supporting

In this stage, most people are subsistence farmers. There may be a simple marketing system—perhaps weekly markets—but most of the people are not even in a money economy. Some parts of Africa and New Guinea are in this stage. In a practical marketing sense, these people are not a market—they have no money to buy goods.

Stage 2—preindustrial or commercial

Some countries in Sub-Sahara Africa and the Middle East are in this second stage. During this stage, we see more market-oriented activity. Raw materials such as oil, tin, and copper are extracted and exported. Agricultural and forest crops such as sugar, rubber, and timber are grown and exported. Often this is done with the help of foreign technical skills and capital. A commercial economy may develop along with—but unrelated to—the subsistence economy. These activities may require the beginnings of a transportation system to tie the extracting or growing areas to shipping points. A money economy operates in this stage.

Industrial machinery and equipment are imported. And huge construction projects may import many special supplies. There is also the need for imports—including luxury goods—to meet the living standards of technical and supervisory people. These may be handled by company stores—rather than local retailers.

The relatively few large landowners—and those who benefit by this business activity—may develop expensive tastes. The few natives employed by these

Japan—like Canada and the United States—is at the stage of economic development where exporting manufactured products is important.

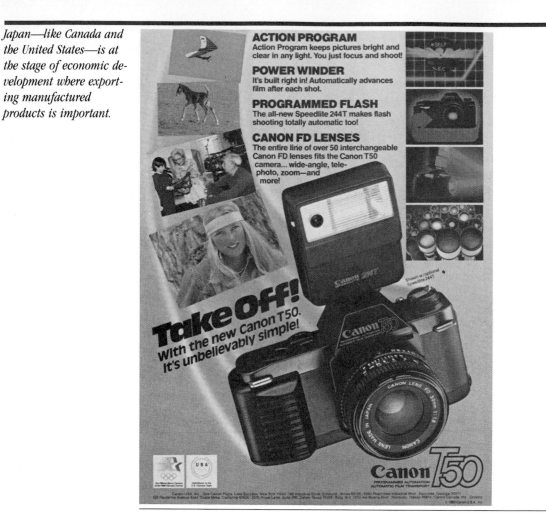

larger firms—and the small business managers who serve them—may form a small, middle-income class. But most of the population is still in the first stage—for practical purposes, they are not in the market. This total market may be so small that local importers can easily handle the demand. There is little reason for local manufacturers to try to supply it.

Stage 3—primary manufacturing

In this third stage, there is some processing of metal ores or the agricultural products that once were shipped out of the country in raw form. Sugar and rubber, for example, are both produced and processed in Indonesia. The same is true for oil on the Persian Gulf. Multinational companies may set up factories to take advantage of low-cost labor. They may export most of the output, but they do stimulate local development. More local labor becomes involved in this stage. A domestic market develops. Small local businesses are starting to handle some of the raw material processing.

Even though the local market expands in this third stage, a large part of the population is still at the subsistence level—almost entirely outside the money economy. But a large foreign population of professionals and technicians may still be needed to run the developing agricultural-industrial complex. The demands of this group and of the growing number of wealthy natives are still quite different from the needs of the lower class and the growing middle class. A domestic market among the local people begins to develop. But local manufacturers still may have trouble finding enough demand to keep them in business.

Stage 4—non-durable and semi-durable consumer goods manufacturing

At this stage, small local manufacturing begins—especially in those lines that need only a small investment to get started. Often, these industries grow out of small firms that developed to supply the processors dominating the last stage. For example, plants making sulfuric acid and explosives for extracting mineral resources might expand into soap manufacturing. And recently, multinational firms have speeded development of countries in this stage with investments in promising opportunities.

Paint, drug, food and beverage, and textile industries develop in this stage. The textile industry is usually one of the first to develop. Clothing is a necessity. This early emphasis on the textile industry in developing nations is one reason the world textile market is so competitive.

Some of the small manufacturers become members of the middle- or even upper-income class. They help to expand the demand for imported goods. As this market grows, local businesses begin to see enough volume to operate profitably. So the need for imports to supply non-durable and semi-durable goods is less. But consumer durables and capital goods are still imported.

Stage 5—capital goods and consumer durable goods manufacturing

In this stage, the production of capital goods and consumer durable goods begins. This includes automobiles, refrigerators, and machinery for local industries. Such manufacturing creates other demands—raw materials for the local factories, and food and fibers for clothing for the rural population entering the industrial labor force.

Industrialization has begun. But the economy still depends on exports of raw materials—either wholly unprocessed or slightly processed.

It still may be necessary to import special heavy machinery and equipment in this stage. Imports of consumer durable goods may still compete with local products. The foreign community and the status-conscious wealthy may prefer these imports.

Stage 6—exporting manufactured products

Countries that have not gone beyond the fifth stage are mainly exporters of raw materials. They import manufactured goods and equipment to build their industrial base. In the sixth stage, exporting manufactured goods becomes most important. The country specializes in certain types of manufactured goods—such as iron and steel, watches, cameras, electronic equipment, and processed food.

Many opportunities for importing and exporting exist at this stage. These countries have grown richer and have needs—and the purchasing power—for a wide variety of products. In fact, countries in this stage often carry on a great deal of trade with each other. Each trades those goods in which it has production advantages. In this stage, almost all consumers are in the money economy. And there may be a large middle-income class. Canada, the United States, most of the Western European countries, and Japan are at this last stage.[13]

It is important to see that it is not necessary to label a whole country or geographic region as being in one stage. Certainly, different parts of Canada have developed differently and might properly be placed in different stages. It may help to understand the full implications of the stages if you try to identify geographic areas within Canada which are in each of these stages. Then, by careful thinking about the kind of public and private facilities found in these areas, you can get a better understanding about the likely character of international markets.

How These Stages Can Be Useful in Finding Market Opportunities

A good starting point for estimating present and future market potentials in a country—or part of a country—is to estimate its present stage of economic development and how fast it is moving to another stage. Actually, the speed of movement, if any, and the possibility that stages may be skipped may suggest whether market opportunities are there—or are likely to open. But just naming the present stage can be very useful in deciding what to look at and whether there are prospects for the firm's products.

Fitting the firm to market needs

Manufacturers of automobiles, expensive cameras, or other consumer durable goods, for example, should not plan to set up a mass distribution system in an area that is in Stage 2 (the preindustrial) or even Stage 3 (the primary manufacturing stage). The market would be too limited.

But among the foreign population and the wealthy landowners, there may be a small but very attractive market for luxury items. A simple distribution system with one or a few middlemen may be quite adequate. Even the market for Canadian "necessities"—items such as canned foods or drug products—may not be large yet. Large-scale selling of these consumer items requires a large base of cash or credit customers—but as yet, too few are part of the money economy.

On the other hand, a market in the non-durable goods manufacturing stage (Stage 4) has more potential—especially for durable goods producers. Incomes and the number of potential customers are growing. There is no local competition yet.

Opportunities might still be good for durable goods imports in Stage 5—even though domestic producers are trying to get started. But more likely, the local government would raise some controls to aid local industry. Then the foreign producer might have to license local producers—or build a local plant.

Areas or countries in the final stage often are the biggest and most profitable markets. While there may be more competition, many more customers have

Coke has successfully used similar strategies around the world—but most companies need to adjust their marketing mixes for different countries.

higher incomes. We have already seen how income distribution shifted in Canada. This can be expected during the latter stages—when a "mass market" develops.

Other Market Dimensions May Suggest Opportunities, Too

Considering country or regional differences—including stages of economic development—can be useful as a first step in segmenting international markets. After finding some possible areas (and eliminating unattractive ones), we must look at more specific market characteristics.

We discussed potential dimensions in the Canadian market. It's impossible to cover all possible dimensions in all world markets. But some of the ideas discussed for Canada certainly apply in other countries. So, here, we will just outline some dimensions of international markets—and show some examples to emphasize that depending on half-truths about "foreigners" won't work in increasingly competitive international markets.

The number of people in our world is staggering

Although our cities may seem crowded with people, Canada's population of just over 25 million is only one half of 1 percent of the world's population—which is over 4 billion.

Numbers are important

Instead of a boring breakdown of population statistics, let's look at a map showing area in proportion to population. Figure 23–6 makes Canada look unimportant—because of our small population in relation to land area. In contrast, Western Europe is much larger, and the Far Eastern countries are even bigger.

But people are not spread out evenly

People everywhere are moving off the farm and into industrial and urban areas. Shifts in population—combined with already dense populations—have led to extreme crowding in some parts of the world.

Figure 23–7 shows a map of the world emphasizing density of population. The darkest shading shows areas with more than 250 persons per square mile.

Developing interurbias in Canada show up clearly as densely populated areas. Similar areas are found in Western Europe, along the Nile River Valley in Egypt, and in many parts of Asia. In contrast, many parts of the world (like our prairie provinces) have few people.

Population densities are likely to increase in the near future. Birth rates in most parts of the world are high—higher in Africa, Latin America, Asia, and Oceania than in Canada and the United States—and death rates are declining as modern medicine is more widely accepted. Generally, population growth is expected in most countries. But the big questions are: How rapidly?—and—Will

■ FIGURE 23–6   Map of the world showing area in proportion to population

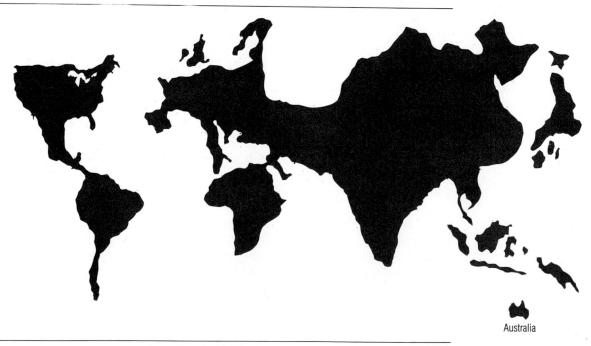

Australia

Source: Drawn by J. F. McCarthy.

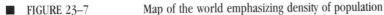

■ FIGURE 23–7   Map of the world emphasizing density of population

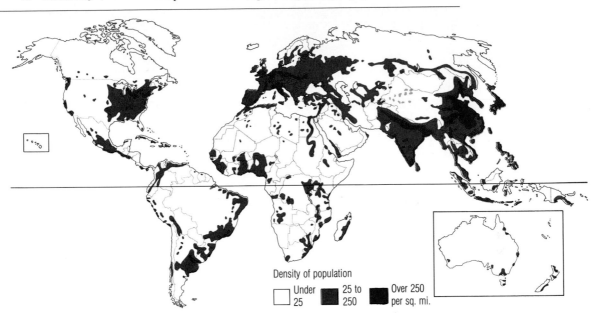

Density of population

☐ Under 25   ■ 25 to 250   ■ Over 250 per sq. mi.

Source: Adapted from Norton Ginsberg, *Atlas of Economic Development*, by permission of the University of Chicago Press. Copyright 1961 by the University of Chicago.

output increase faster than population? This is important to marketers—because it affects how rapidly these countries move to higher stages of development, and become new markets for different kinds of products.

You must sell where the income is

Profitable markets require income—as well as people. The best available measure of income in most countries is **gross national product (GNP)**—the total market value of goods and services produced in a year. Unfortunately, this may not give a true picture of consumer well-being in many countries—because the method commonly used for figuring GNP may not be accurate for very different cultures and economies. For instance, do-it-yourself activities, household services, and the growing of produce or meat by family members for their own use are not usually figured as part of GNP. Since the activities of self-sufficient family units are not included, GNP can give a false picture of economic well-being in less-developed countries.

Gross national product, though, is useful and sometimes the only available measure of market potential in many countries. Figure 23–8 shows the population and GNP of major regions of the world—except the USSR and mainland China. You can see that the more developed industrial regions have the biggest share of the world's GNP. This is why so much trade takes place between these countries—and why many companies see them as the more important markets.

■ FIGURE 23–8 Population (1982) and gross national product (1979) of major geographic regions of the world

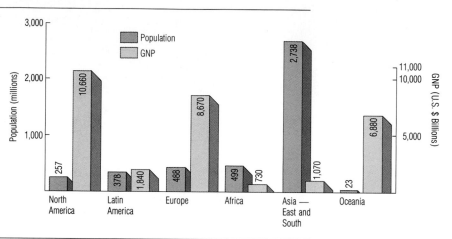

Source: *Statistical Abstract of the United States, 1982–1983*, p. 856, and *Yearbook of National Accounts Statistics, 1980*, vol. II (New York: United Nations, 1982), pp. 3–9.

Income per person can be more helpful

GNP per person is a commonly available figure—but it can be a misleading estimate of market potential. When GNP per person is used for comparison, we assume that the wealth of each country is distributed evenly among all consumers. This is seldom true. In a developing economy, 75 percent of the population may be on farms and receive 25 percent or less of the income. And there may be unequal distribution along class or racial lines.

To provide some examples, the GNP per person for several countries is shown in Figure 23–9. The range is wide, from $205 (in U.S. dollars) per person per year in India to $19,428 in the United Arab Emirates.

A business, and a human opportunity

You can see that much of the world's population lives in extreme poverty. Many of these countries are in the early stages of economic development. Most of their people work on farms—and live barely within the money economy.

These people, however, have needs. And many are eager to improve themselves. But they may not be able to raise their living standards without outside help. This presents a challenge and an opportunity to the developed nations—and to their business firms.

Some companies—including Canadian firms—are trying to help the people of less-developed countries. Corporations such as Pillsbury, Corn Products, Monsanto, and Coca-Cola have developed nutritious foods that can be sold cheaply—but still profitably—in poorer countries. One firm sells a milk-based drink (Samson)—with 10 grams of protein—to the Middle East and the Caribbean areas. Such a drink can make an important addition to diets. Poor people in less-developed lands usually get only 8 to 12 grams of protein per day in their normal diet (60 to 75 grams are considered necessary for an adult).[14]

■ FIGURE 23–9   Gross national product per capita for major regions of the world and selected countries (in 1979 U.S. dollars)

	GNP per capita for countries	GNP per capita for regions
North America		$10,660
United States	$10,777	
Canada	9,586	
Latin America		1,840
Brazil	1,809	
Mexico	1,749	
Venezuela	3,622	
Haiti	228	
Europe		8,670
United Kingdom	7,192	
France	10,720	
West Germany	12,419	
Italy	5,686	
Sweden	12,831	
Portugal (1978)	1,816	
Middle East		2,850
Israel	4,969	
United Arab Emirates	19,428	
Africa		730
Algeria	1,639	
Egypt	435	
Kenya	394	
Nigeria (1977)	717	
Rwanda	206	
South Africa	1,940	
East and South Asia		1,070
India	205	
Pakistan	291	
Japan	8,627	
Indonesia	331	
Oceania		6,880
Australia	8,836	
New Zealand	6,896	

Source: *Yearbook of National Accounts Statistics, 1980*, vol. II, (New York: United Nations, 1982) pp. 3–9.

Reading, writing, and marketing problems

The ability of a country's people to read and write has a direct influence on the development of the economy—and on marketing strategy planning. Certainly, the degree of literacy affects the way information is delivered—which in marketing means promotion. And, unfortunately, only about two thirds of the world's population can read and write.

Low literacy sometimes causes difficulties with product labels and instructions—for which we normally use words. In highly illiterate countries, some manufacturers found that placing a baby's picture on food packages is unwise. Illiterate natives believed that the product was just that—a ground-up baby! Singer Sewing Machine Company met this lack of literacy with an instruction book that used no words.

Even in Latin America—which has generally higher literacy rates than Africa or Asia—a large number of people cannot read and write. Marketers have to use symbols, colors, and other non-verbal means of communication if they want to reach the masses.

Careful Market Analysis Is Vital

The opportunities in international marketing are exciting ones—but diversity presents a real challenge to target marketers. Careful market analysis is especially important—since there often are differences that we would not pick up unless we were aggressively seeking out all the possibilities.

What are you drinking?

Tastes do differ across national boundaries. French Burgundy wine going to Belgium must have a higher sugar content than the Burgundy staying in France. Burgundy going to Sweden must have still higher sugar content to be sold successfully there.

Milk-drinking habits also differ greatly. Scandinavians consider milk a daily staple—while Latins feel that milk is only for children. A former French premier was able to get his picture on the front page of every Paris newspaper simply by drinking a glass of milk in public.

Organizing for International Marketing

Until a firm develops a truly worldwide view of its operations, it usually is desirable to have someone in charge of international matters. The basic concern should be to see that the firm transfers its domestic know-how into international operations.

Organization should transfer know-how

As the firm moves beyond just a few international locations, the managers might want to develop regional groupings—clustering similar kinds of countries into groups. This smooths the transfer of know-how among operations in similar environments. Regional groupings may also reduce the cost of supervision.

Regional groups, however, may be less useful than groups based on other relevant dimensions—such as the stage of economic development, or perhaps language. The important thing is to develop an organization which enables the local managers to control matters that require "local feel," while at the same time sharing their accumulating experience with colleagues who face similar problems.

Each national market should be thought of as a separate market. To the extent that they are really different from each other, top management will have to delegate a great deal of responsibility for strategy planning to these local managers. In extreme cases, it may not even be possible for the local managers to fully explain some parts of their plans. In such cases, they can be judged only by their results. Then, the organizational setup would be such that these managers are given a great deal of freedom—but are tightly controlled against their own plans. Top management need not have a deep understanding of its various markets. Instead, it can simply insist that the various managers stick to their budgets and meet the plans which they, themselves, create. When the firm reaches this stage, it is being managed like a well-organized domestic corporation—which insists that its managers (of divisions and territories) meet their own plans, so that the whole company's program works out as intended.[15]

■ CONCLUSION

The international market is large—and keeps growing in population and income. Many North American companies are becoming aware of the opportunities open to alert and aggressive businesses.

The great variations in stages of economic development, income, population, literacy, and other factors, however, mean that foreign markets must be treated as many separate target markets—and studied carefully. Lumping foreign nations together under the common and vague heading of "foreigners"—or, at the other extreme, assuming that they are just like Canadian customers—almost guarantees failure. So does treating them like common Hollywood stereotypes.

Involvement in international marketing usually begins with exporting. Then, a firm may become involved in joint ventures or wholly-owned subsidiaries in several countries. Companies that become this involved are called multinational corporations. Some of these corporations have a global outlook—and are willing to move across national boundaries as easily as national firms move across state boundaries.

Much of what we have said about marketing strategy planning throughout the text applies directly in international marketing. Sometimes Product adaptations or changes are needed. Promotion messages must be translated into the local languages. And, of course, new Place arrangements and Prices are needed. But blending the four Ps still requires a knowledge of the all-important customer.

The major "roadblock" to success in international marketing is an unwillingness to learn about and adjust to different peoples and cultures. To those who are willing to make these adjustments, the returns can be great.

■ QUESTIONS AND PROBLEMS

1. Discuss the "typical" evolution of corporate involvement in international marketing. What impact would a whole-hearted acceptance of the marketing concept have on the evolutionary process?

2. Distinguish between licensing and contract manufacturing in a foreign country.

3. Distinguish between joint ventures and wholly-owned subsidiaries.

4. Discuss the long-run prospects for (a) multinational marketing by Canadian firms producing in Canada only and (b) multinational firms willing to operate anywhere.

5. Discuss how a manufacturer interested in finding new international marketing opportunities might organize its search process. What kinds of opportunities would it look for first, second, and so on?

6. Discuss how the approaches to market segmenting (which were described in Chapter 9) might have to be modified when one moves into international markets.

7. Evaluate the growth of "common markets" in relation to the phases of economic development of the members. Is this basically a movement among the developing countries which are seeking to "catch up"?

8. Discuss the prospects for a Latin American entrepreneur who is considering building a factory to produce machines which would manufacture cans for the food industry. His country happens to be in Stage 4—the non-durable and semi-durable consumer goods manufacturing stage. The country's population is approximately 20 million, and there is some possibility of establishing sales contacts in a few nearby countries.

9. Discuss the value of gross national product per capita as a measure of market potential. Refer to specific data in your answer.

10. Discuss the possibility of a multinational marketer using essentially the same promotion campaign in Canada and in many international markets.

11. Discuss the kinds of products which you feel may become popular in Europe in the near future. Does the material on Canadian consumption behavior—discussed earlier in the text—have any relevance here?

12. Discuss the importance of careful target marketing within the European Common Market.

13. Discuss how a multinational firm might organize to develop an effective organization.

■ **SUGGESTED CASES**

26. Canadian Inland

27. Highland Manufacturing Company

■ NOTES

1. "How Coke Runs a Foreign Empire," *Business Week,* August 25, 1973, pp. 40–43.

2. B. W. Wilkinson, "Canadian-United States Free Trade: The Issue for Canada," *Cost and Management* 41 (November 1967), pp. 7–11. Reprinted in B. E. Mallen and E. A. Litvak, *Marketing Canada,* 2d ed. (Toronto: McGraw-Hill of Canada, 1968), pp. 328–35.

3. S. S. Grimley, "Canadian Factors in the Generation and Evaluation on New Product Ideas," *Business Quarterly* 39 (Summers 1974), pp. 32–39.

4. J. R. M. Gordon and Peter R. Richardson, "Why Manufacture in Canada," *Business Quarterly* 42 (Winter 1977), p. 43.

5. Margaret Wente, "Grand Designs," *Canadian Business,* May 1978, pp. 38–43.

6. For a more detailed discussion of world product mandating in a Canadian context, see *Working Group on Industrial Policies, Multinationals, and Industrial Strategy: The Role of World Product Mandates* (Ottawa: Science Council of Canada, September 1980).

7. C. S. Mayer and J. E. Flynn, "Canadian Small Business Abroad: Opportunities, Aids and Experiences," *Business Quarterly* 38 (Winter 1973), pp. 33–47.

8. Theodore Levitt, "The Globalization of Markets," *Harvard Business Review* 61, no. 3 (May-June 1983), pp. 92–102.

9. Thomas Hout, Michael E. Porter, and Eileen Rudden, "How Global Companies Win Out," *Harvard Business Review* 60, no. 5 (September-October 1982), pp. 98–108; "Multi-national Companies," *Business Week,* April 20, 1963, pp. 62–86; "Multi-national Firms Now Dominate Much of World's Production," *The Wall Street Journal,* April 18, 1973,

p. 1 f; "Japanese Multinationals Covering the World with Investment," *Business Week,* June 16, 1980, pp. 92–99; and David A. Heenan and Warren J. Keegan, "The Rise of Third World Multinationals," *Harvard Business Review,* January-February 1979, pp. 101–9.

10. "McDonald's Brings Hamburger (with Beer) to Hamburg," *Advertising Age,* May 30, 1977, p. 61.

11. Warren J. Keegan, "A Conceptual Framework for Multinational Marketing," *Columbia Journal of World Business,* November 1972, pp. 67–78.

12. Robert R. Jones, "Executive's Guide to Antitrust in Europe," *Harvard Business Review,* May-June 1976, pp. 106–18.

13. This discussion is based on William Copulsky's, "Forecasting Sales in Underdeveloped Countries," *Journal of Marketing,* July 1959, pp. 36–37. Another set of stages is interesting although less marketing oriented. See W. W. Rostow, *The Stages of Economic Growth—A Non-Communist Manifesto* (New York: Cambridge University Press, 1960).

14. *The Wall Street Journal,* August 8, 1968, p. 1.

15. Christopher A. Bartlett, "MNCs: Get off the Reorganization Merry-Go-Round," *Harvard Business Review* 61, no. 2 (March-April 1983), pp. 138–46; James M. Hulbert, William K. Brant, and Raimar Richers, "Marketing Planning in the Multinational Subsidiary: Practices and Problems," *Journal of Marketing* 44, no. 3 (Summer 1980), pp. 7–16; Pravin Banker, "You're the Best Judge of Foreign Risks," *Harvard Business Review* 61, no. 2 (March-April 1983), pp. 157–65; and Martin D. J. Buss, "Managing International Information Systems," *Harvard Business Review* 60, no. 5 (September-October 1982), pp. 153–62.

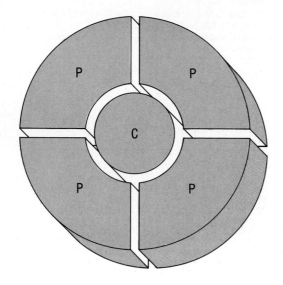

Product

Place

Promotion

Price

Customer

There is only one chapter in this part—but it is an important one. It discusses how good a job marketing is doing—and in particular whether "marketing costs too much." The authors' position is basically that marketing has been doing a pretty good job—but there is room for improvement. Marketing—and our whole economic system—face severe challenges. It will take some new thinking—and people with new ideas—to help our country and our business firms meet the challenges of the future. This chapter does not present answers. Rather, it tries to encourage your thinking about what you're going to do with your life—and what contribution you will make to our society.

Chapter 24 ■ Marketing in a consumer-oriented society: Appraisal and challenges

When you finish this chapter, you should:

1. Understand why marketing must be evaluated differently at the micro and macro levels.

2. Understand why the text argues that micro-marketing costs too much.

3. Understand why the text argues that macro-marketing does not cost too much.

4. Know some of the challenges facing marketers in the future.

"Does marketing cost too much?"

Does marketing cost too much? This is a fundamental question. Many people feel strongly that marketing does cost too much—that it is a waste of resources which would be better used elsewhere. In Chapter 1—and at various times throughout the text—we referred to criticisms of marketing and to the possible effects of business practices on consumer welfare. But we have *not* tried to answer the underlying question—whether marketing costs too much—believing that you needed more information before you could answer that question.

We have tried to provide the necessary background in this book. The focus has been mainly on the *micro* view of marketing—that is, marketing as seen through the eyes of the marketing manager. Now that you have a better understanding of what the marketing manager does—and how he contributes to the *macro*-marketing process—you should be able to consider whether marketing costs too much. That's what this chapter is about.

Your answer is very important. Your own business career and the economy in which you will live will be affected by your answer.

Do auto manufacturers, for example, produce as high quality cars as they could—or did in the "good old days"? Do producers of food and drug products spend too much advertising their own brands instead of offering more generics—at lower prices? Do we have too many retailers and wholesalers—all taking "too big" markups? Some critics of marketing would answer Yes! to *all* these important questions. Such critics probably want to change our political and legal environments—and the world in which you'll live and work. Do you agree with these critics? Or are you fairly satisfied with the way our system works? How will you "vote" on your consumer ballot?

Marketing Must Be Evaluated at Two Levels

As we saw in Chapter 1, it is useful to distinguish between two levels of marketing: the *micro* level (how individual firms run) and the *macro* level (how the whole system works). Some complaints against marketing are aimed at only one of these levels at a time. In other cases, the criticism *seems* to be directed to one level—but actually is aimed at the other. Some critics of specific ads, for example, probably would not be satisfied with *any* advertising. When evaluating marketing, we must treat each of these levels separately.

How Should Marketing Be Evaluated?

Different nations have different social and economic objectives. Dictatorships, for example, may be concerned mainly with satisfying the needs of society as seen by the political elite. In a socialist state, the objective might be to satisfy society's needs as defined by government planners. In still other economies, the objective might be to build up the country militarily—or economically.

Nations' objectives determine criteria

While different nations may have different objectives, each nation needs some kind of macro-marketing system to accomplish those objectives. How a macro-marketing system operates should depend on the objectives of a particular nation. Therefore, the effectiveness of any nation's macro-marketing system can only be evaluated in terms of that nation's objectives.

In Canada, the customer is assumed to be right—usually.

Consumer satisfaction is the objective in Canada

Historically, *the basic objective of our market-directed economic system has been to satisfy consumer needs as they—the consumers—see them.* This objective implies that political freedom and economic freedom go hand in hand—and that citizens in a free society have the right to live as they choose.

This is no place for a long discussion of the merits of this objective. Economists, philosophers, politicians, and business managers have long debated the trade-offs between consumer satisfaction and efficient use of resources. Perhaps the debate—along with changing social and economic conditions—will eventually lead to a change in our basic objective. However, this hasn't happened yet. And there is little evidence that the majority of Canadian consumers are willing to give up the freedom of choice they now enjoy.

Therefore, let's try to evaluate the operation of marketing in the Canadian economy—where the present objective is to satisfy consumer needs *as consumers see them.* This is the essence of our system. The business firm that ignores this fact does so at its own peril.

Can Consumer Satisfaction Be Measured?

Since consumer satisfaction is our objective, marketing effectiveness must be measured by *the extent of this satisfaction.* Unfortunately, consumer satisfaction is hard to define—and harder to measure.

Economic utility provides satisfaction, but . . .

Economists believe that consumer satisfaction is derived from the amount of economic utility—form, time, place, and possession utility—provided by goods and services. However, no satisfactory method of measuring economic utility has been developed. Further, some consumers may consider "psychic utility" more important than economic utility for some products.

Satisfaction depends on individual aspirations

Measuring consumer satisfaction is even more difficult because satisfaction depends on your level of aspiration or expectation.[1] Less prosperous consumers begin to expect more out of an economy as they see the higher living standards of others. Also, aspiration level tends to rise with repeated successes and fall with failures. Products considered satisfactory one day may not be satisfactory the next day, or vice versa. Most of us now expect cars to work—almost without maintenance! For early car owners (in the 1910s and 20s), breakdowns and flat tires were common. A "Sunday drive" often included fixing several flats—on a dusty road—with no helpful CAA on call! Thus, consumer satisfaction is a highly personal concept which does not provide a stable standard for evaluating marketing effectiveness.

A hierarchy of satisfaction exists

To complicate things further, consumers appear to have a hierarchy of needs—and different levels of satisfaction. Some consumer needs may be well satisfied, while others are not. For example, while a consumer may be very satisfied with products that meet lower-level needs—say for food—that consumer's higher-level needs may not be satisfied at all. In fact, a consumer may be dissatisfied with life in general—and for reasons which are quite unrelated to marketing.

Because of all these factors, it is extremely difficult to make exact quantitative estimates of consumer satisfaction.

Measuring macro-marketing must be subjective

Macro-marketing is concerned with *efficiency* (in terms of use of resources) and *fairness* (in terms of distribution of output to all parties involved)—while accomplishing the society's objectives.

If the objective is maximizing consumer satisfaction, then total satisfaction—of everyone—must be measured. But there is no quantitative way of measuring aggregate consumer satisfaction. So our evaluation of macro-marketing effectiveness will have to be subjective.

The consumer/citizens' votes can be your guide

The supreme test, probably, is whether the macro-marketing system satisfies enough individual consumer/citizens so that they vote—at the ballot box—to keep it running. So far, we have done so in Canada . But growing support for consumerism issues—and more government involvement in the market—suggests that satisfaction with our present system—as it is operating—is not complete. This should be of concern to supporters of our present system.

Measuring micro-marketing can be less subjective

Measuring micro-marketing effectiveness is also difficult. But it can be done. And individual business firms can and should try to measure how well their products satisfy their customers (or why their products fail). Methods which have been used include attitude research studies, unsolicited consumer responses (usually complaints), opinions of middlemen and salespeople, market test results, and profits.[2]

Satisfaction can be loosely measured by company profits

In our market-directed system, it is up to each customer to decide how effectively individual firms satisfy his or her needs. Usually, customers are willing to pay higher prices or buy more of those goods which satisfy them. Thus, efficient marketing plans can increase profits—and profits can be used as a rough measure of a firm's efficiency in satisfying customers.

Evaluating marketing effectiveness is difficult—but not impossible

Because it's hard to measure consumer satisfaction—and, therefore, the effectiveness of micro- and macro-marketing—it is easy to see why there might be different views on the subject. If the objective of the economy is clearly defined, however—and the argument is stripped of emotion—the big questions about marketing effectiveness probably can be answered.

In this chapter, we will argue that micro-marketing (how individual firms and channels operate) frequently *does* cost too much but that macro-marketing (how the whole marketing system operates) *does not* cost too much, *given the present objective of the Canadian economy—consumer satisfaction.* These positions should not be accepted as "gospel" but rather as points of view. In the end, you will have to make your own decision.[3]

Micro-Marketing Often *Does* Cost Too Much

Throughout the text, we have been exploring what marketing managers could or should do to help their firms do a better job of satisfying customers—while achieving company objectives. Many firms are implementing highly successful marketing programs. At the same time, however, many other firms are still too production-oriented and inefficient in their operations. For the customers of these latter firms, micro-marketing often *does* cost too much.

Many consumers are discontented

While North American consumers are not in a revolutionary mood, it is clear that many of them are not happy with the marketing efforts of some firms. "Helping consumers get a fair deal when shopping" ranks very high among public concerns. Only inflation, unemployment, government spending, welfare, and taxes rank higher. Consumers are also quite concerned about the high price and poor quality of many products—products whose performance didn't live up to advertised claims—and poor after-sale service and repairs.[4]

Many consumers are complaining

Despite the usual claim, "Satisfaction Guaranteed," there are many consumers who find reason to complain. Hundreds of complaints and inquiries are received daily by Better Business Bureaus across Canada, by federal, provincial, and local consumer protection agencies, by consumer spokesmen and consumer columnists for local newspapers, and, of course, by retailers and manufacturers.[5]

Consumers should be encouraged to complain

To further dramatize the problem, a recent study of consumer complaints found that as many as 50 percent of all serious complaints are never reported. Further, many of those that are reported never get fully resolved. The authors of the study concluded that "business should be alarmed at the amount of unresolved dissatisfaction that apparently exists in the marketplace." They advised firms to: (1) *encourage* customers to speak out when things go wrong, (2) make it more convenient for them to do so, and (3) develop careful, speedy procedures to handle complaints. Most important, company attitudes must be changed to ensure that complaining consumers are not viewed as "the enemy."[6]

The failure rate is high

Further evidence that most firms are too production-oriented and not nearly as efficient as they could be—is the fact that many new products fail. New and old businesses fail regularly, too. The main reason for such failure is poor management—or just plain managerial incompetence.

Incompetence and bad management lead to higher costs of operation—and reduce the effectiveness of the business system in general. Generally speaking, marketing inefficiencies are due to one or more of three reasons:

1. Lack of interest in—or understanding of—the sometimes fickle customer.
2. Improper blending of the four Ps—caused in part by an overemphasis on production and/or internal problems as contrasted with a customer orientation.
3. Lack of understanding of—or adjustment to—uncontrollable variables.

The company can get in the way of the customer	Serving the customer is plainly the role of business. Yet some producers seem to feel that customers eagerly await any product they turn out. So they worry about internal problems and ignore customer needs.

Middlemen, too, often get tied up in their own internal problems. Goods may be stocked where it is convenient for the retailer to handle them—rather than for consumers to find them. And fast-moving, hard-to-handle goods may not be stocked at all—"They are too much trouble," or "We're always running out."

Similarly, some accounting and financial managers try to cut costs by encouraging the production of standardized, "me-too" products—even though this may not serve customers well.

None of these managers understands a business as a "total system" responsible for satisfying consumer needs. |
| **The high cost of poor marketing mixes** | Perhaps lack of concern for the customer is most noticeable in the ways the four Ps are combined—or forced—into a marketing mix. This can happen in many ways—as the following discussion shows.

Product—"Forget the customer, full speed ahead!"

Some production-oriented managers develop a company's product—not to meet the needs of certain target customers but rather—to satisfy some pet idea held by themselves or their friends. They sometimes produce products too high or too low in quality—or too complicated for many target markets. Or they like long production runs of easy-to-make standardized products—to lower costs. Often they aren't worried about quality control. Until very recently, most Canadian manufacturers lacked any quality control procedures. Then, to compound these errors, the packaging people frequently put an ill-conceived product in a container that is easy to make and fill—but that doesn't really protect the product or appeal to the customer.

These poorly designed, poorly packaged products then are turned over to the sales department to unload on the market. Sometimes these products can be moved only with overly aggressive (or even dishonest) promotion. Middlemen may join in this aggressive selling if they are given high enough markups—or additional advertising or promotion allowances.

Place—"Don't rock the boat or sell to chains"

Sales managers don't make adjustments in channels as often as they should. This is partly because of personal relationships in their channels and partly because—being human—they prefer not to "rock the boat." Yet such inflexibility can be costly—especially in view of the "scrambling" we saw in the channels of distribution.

Some old-time salespeople are so tied to the idea of small independent wholesalers and retailers that they even refuse to sell chain stores or large firms. Their personal relationships with their old customers may make business more pleasant. But they don't necessarily contribute to efficiency and profits. The continued use of obsolete and overly expensive channels supports the charge of "too many" wholesalers and retailers. |

Price—"Pick a price, any high price"

Prices often are set on a cost-plus basis. This method of pricing may ignore customer demand—and lead to unnecessarily high (*and* less profitable) prices. Many business managers consider both margin and expected volume in pricing products. But margins are fairly definite, while volume is only predictable. So they choose high margins—which may lead to high prices and reduced volume.

Promotion—"Let our advertising geniuses and star sales reps do it"

If a product is poorly designed—or if inadequate channels are employed—or if cost-plus pricing is used—it's easy to see why promotion may be costly. Aggressive selling may be needed to try to overcome previous mistakes.

Even if a good job is done on the other three Ps, however, Promotion is sometimes inefficient and costly. As we saw, sales managers and advertising managers may not cooperate—each feeling that his own techniques are the most effective and need no support from the other.

Until recently, the value of market research was not taken very seriously in most firms. Some advertising executives still feel that all a promotion campaign needs is their creative genius.

Sales management also has its problems. There are many types of sales jobs. Recruiting the right person for each is difficult. Further, the very nature of the sales job makes it difficult to measure sales performance.

Careful analysis and management are necessary to build a productive sales force at a reasonable cost. Unfortunately, many sales managers—although former "star" sales reps—are not up to this tough management job.

Company objectives may force higher-cost operation

Top-management decisions on company objectives may increase the cost of marketing unnecessarily. Seeking growth for growth's sake, for example, might lead to excessive spending for promotion. Diversification for diversification's sake could require costly new arrangements for Place. Or if the established firms already have won a "competitive advantage"—a new firm may be forced to offer second-rate marketing mixes.

For these reasons, marketing managers should be alert to such dangers—and be involved in shaping the firm's objectives. Recognizing the importance of marketing, progressive firms have given marketing management a greater voice in determining company objectives. Unfortunately, though, in many more firms, marketing is still looked on as the department that "gets rid of" the product.

Micro-marketing does cost too much—but things are changing

It appears that marketing does cost too much in many firms. Despite much publicity, the marketing concept has not *really* been applied in many places. Sales managers may have been renamed "marketing managers"—and vice presidents of sales called "vice presidents of marketing"—but nothing else changed. Marketing mixes were still put together by production-oriented managers in the same old ways.

But not all business firms and marketers should be criticized. Increasing numbers *are* becoming customer-oriented. And many of these are paying more attention to market-oriented strategic planning—to more effectively carry out the marketing concept.

Further, some organizations have developed codes of ethics to guide members' behavior. Some of these developments are responses to the consumerism movement. But others reflect long-established company policies. Even more industry groups might be willing to get together to discuss how to do a better job (with good intentions), but they are held back by fear of possible antitrust action.[7]

Competition continues to encourage the elimination of unnecessary costs *and* institutions. Distribution channels are continually shifting as better ways are found for doing the marketing job. Limited-function wholesalers have developed in many lines. Discount houses and mass-merchandisers have pushed out many small, conventional retail stores—which did not recognize changing customer demands.

One encouraging sign is the end of the idea that anybody can run a business successfully. This never was true. Today, the growing complexity of business is drawing more and more professionals into the field. This includes not only professional business managers but psychologists, sociologists, statisticians, and economists.

Managers who adopt the marketing concept as a way of business life do a better job. As more of these managers rise in business, we can look forward to much lower micro-marketing costs.

Macro-Marketing Does *Not* Cost Too Much

Many criticisms of marketing take aim at the operation of the macro-marketing system. These criticisms suggest that (1) advertising and promotion in general are socially undesirable and (2) that the macro-marketing system causes an improper allocation of resources, restricts income and employment, and leads to an unfair distribution of income. Most of these complaints imply that some micro-marketing activities should not be permitted—and because they are, macro-marketing costs too much or yields poor results.

Much of this criticism comes from those who have their own version of the ideal way to run an economy. Some of the most severe critics of our marketing system are theoretical economists who use the pure-competition model as their ideal. They want consumers and producers to have free choice in the market—but they are critical of the way the present market operates. Meanwhile, other critics would scrap our market-directed system and substitute the decisions of government planners—thus reducing freedom of choice in the marketplace. These different views should be kept in mind when evaluating criticisms of marketing.

In the following discussion, the word *business* probably could be substituted for *marketing* in most places. Marketing is the most exposed arm of business, but it is nearly impossible to separate this arm from the rest of the body. A criticism of marketing at the macro level usually (1) implies a criticism of our entire market-directed economic system as it now exists and (2) suggests that some modification—or an entirely different system—would be more effective. Let's look at some of these positions to help you form your own opinion.

Is pure competition the welfare ideal?

A major criticism of our macro-marketing system is that it permits—or even encourages—the allocation of too many resources for marketing activities—thus reducing consumer "welfare." This argument is concerned with how the economy's resources (land, labor, and capital) are allocated for producing and distributing goods. These critics usually feel that scarce resources could be better spent on producing goods than on marketing them. This argument assumes that marketing activities are unnecessary and do not create value. Being technical, it assumes that pure competition is the ideal for maximizing consumer welfare.

In pure competition, economists assume that consumers are "economic men," that is, they are well informed about all available offerings and will choose rationally among the alternatives to maximize their own welfare. Therefore, these critics feel that emotional or persuasive advertising (1) discourages the economic comparison required for an ideal pure-competition economy and (2) is wasteful because society doesn't need it.

Theoretical economic analysis can show convincingly that pure competition will provide greater consumer welfare than monopolistic competition—*provided* all the conditions and assumptions of pure competition are met. But are they?

Different people want different things

Our present knowledge of consumer behavior and people's desire for different products pretty well demolishes the economists' "economic man" assumption—and therefore the pure-competition ideal.[8] A pioneer in monopolistic competition analysis—E. H. Chamberlin—also argues logically against the pure-competition ideal. He observes that people, in fact, are different and that they do have different demands. He translates these differences into demands for different products. Given this type of demand (down-sloping demand curves), monopoly elements naturally develop. He concludes that "monopoly is necessarily a part of the welfare ideal . . ."[9]

People are different, and as consumers they want different things.

Once we admit that not all consumers know everything—and that they have varied demands—the need for a variety of micro-marketing activities becomes clear.

Micro-efforts expand macro-output through innovation

Some critics feel that marketing helps create monopoly, or at least monopolistic competition. Further—they feel—this leads to higher prices, restriction of output, and reduction in the national income and employment.

It is true that firms in a market-directed economy try to carve out separate monopolistic markets for themselves. This may have the short-run effect of restricting output (depending on the shape of the demand and supply curves)—and raising prices on *that particular new product.*

Are customers taken advantage of, however? They don't *have* to buy the new product unless they feel it is a better value. The old products are still available. Ironically, the prices may even be lower on the old products to meet the new competition—yet their sales may decline because customers shift to the new product.

Over several years, the profits of the innovator may rise—but the rising profits also encourage further innovation by competitors. This leads to new investments—which contribute to economic growth and raise the level of national income and employment.

The increasing profits also attract competition. The profits then begin to drop as competitors enter—and begin producing somewhat similar products. (Recall the rise and fall of industry profit during the product life cycle.)

It is certainly true that the performance of micro-marketing activities in monopolistic competition can lead to a different allocation of resources than would be found in a pure-competition economy. But this allocation of resources probably results in greater consumer satisfaction. Let's look at advertising, for example.

Is advertising a waste of resources?

Advertising is the most criticized of all micro-marketing activities. Indeed, many ads *are* annoying, insulting, misleading, and downright ineffective. This is one reason why micro-marketing often does cost too much. However, advertising can also make both the micro- and macro-marketing processes work better.

Advertising can result in lower prices

Advertising is a relatively economical way of informing large numbers of potential customers about a firm's products. Provided that a product satisfies customer needs and wants, advertising can increase demand for the product—resulting in economies of scale in manufacturing, distribution, and sales. Because these economies may more than offset advertising costs, advertising can actually *lower* prices to the consumer.[10] In addition, advertising can reduce the time and effort consumers must spend searching for products.[11] It may also increase competition. In recent years, for example, U.S. regulatory bodies have encouraged advertising by doctors, lawyers, optometrists, and pharmacists—as a means of stimulating price competition.

Advertising stimulates economic growth

At the macro level, the increased demand brought about by advertising gives producers a faster return on their investment. This in turn stimulates further investment, encourages innovation, creates jobs, raises personal incomes, and generates economic growth.

Does marketing make people buy things they don't need?

From our discussion so far, it seems that the performance of micro-marketing activities aimed at satisfying consumer needs and wants does *not* lead to an improper allocation of resources. Giving individuals what they want, after all, is the purpose of our market-directed economic system. However, some critics feel that most firms—especially large corporations—do not really cater to the needs and wants of the consumer. Rather, they use powerful persuasive techniques—television advertising in particular—to manipulate consumers into buying whatever the firms wish to sell.

Advertising is criticized—but it can result in lower prices and stimulate economic growth.

Historian Arnold Toynbee, for example, felt that American consumers have been manipulated into buying products which are not necessary to satisfy "the minimum material requirements of life." Toynbee saw American firms as mainly trying to fulfill "unwanted demand"—demand created by advertising—rather than "genuine wants." He defined genuine wants as "wants that we become aware of spontaneously, without having to be told by Madison Avenue that we want something that we should never have thought of wanting if we had been left in peace to find out our wants for ourselves."[12]

What are the minimum requirements of life?

One flaw in this line of reasoning is the problem of determining "the minimum material requirements of life." Does this mean that people should go back to living in caves or log cabins? Which products consumed today are unnecessary—and therefore should be abandoned?

Obviously, some value judgments must be made to answer such questions—and few of us share the same values. One critic suggested, for example, that North Americans could and *should* do without items such as pets, newspaper comic strips, second family automobiles, motorcycles, snowmobiles, campers, recreational boats and planes, cigarettes, aerosol products, pop and beer cans, and hats.[13] You may agree with some of those. But who should determine "minimum material requirements of life"—consumers or critics?

Which wants are really "genuine"?

Another problem with Toynbee's argument is the notion that people should be "left in peace" to discover their own wants. Actually, while our basic needs may be innate, almost all our wants for specific need-satisfying goods and services are learned. Moreover, these wants are learned not only through advertising, but also through other sources—including our family, friends, teachers, reference groups, and so on.

For example, North American consumers did not stand up and shout for refrigerators, cars, and kidney dialysis machines before they were told that such products were available. Does this mean that these products don't satisfy genuine needs and wants?

Consumers are not puppets

The idea that firms can manipulate consumers to buy anything they choose to produce simply isn't true. A consumer who buys a can of soda pop that tastes terrible won't buy another can of that brand—regardless of how much it's advertised. In fact, many new products fail the test of the marketplace. Not even large corporations are assured of success every time they launch a new product. Consider, for example, the dismal fate of products such as Ford's Edsel, Du Pont's Corfam, Campbell's Red Kettle Soups, and RCA's computers.

Satisfying needs and wants is not a static process

Consumer needs and wants are constantly changing. Few of us would care to live the way our grandparents lived when they were our age—let alone like the pioneers who traveled west in covered wagons. The critics must realize that marketing's job is not just to satisfy consumer wants as they exist at any particular point in time. Rather, as Engledow has stated:

> One of marketing's most critical functions is the creative function—utilizing the capabilities of the firm *to produce a better solution to a want than any that might be envisioned by the consumer* with his limited perception of technological and marketing possibilities. [Emphasis added.][14]

Indeed, it is this continuous search for better solutions to consumer needs that makes our competitive market-directed system work so effectively.

Does marketing make people materialistic?

Along with charges of creating unwanted demand, many critics have accused marketing of distorting people's tastes—and making them too materialistic. There is no doubt that marketing relies heavily on materialistic values. And some over eager advertisers have perhaps been guilty of suggesting product-oriented solutions to all life's problems. However, there is much disagreement as to whether marketing creates materialistic values—or simply appeals to already existing values.

Anthropologists have discovered that, even in the most primitive societies, people want to adorn themselves with trinkets and accumulate possessions. In fact, in some tribal villages, a person's social status is measured by how many goats or sheep that person owns. Further, the tendency for ancient pharaohs and kings to surround themselves with wealth and treasures can hardly be attributed to the persuasive powers of the advertising agencies!

The idea that marketers create and serve "false tastes"—as defined by individual critics—has been rebutted by a well-known economist—George Stigler— who said:

> The marketplace responds to the tastes of consumers with the goods and services that are salable, whether the tastes are elevated or depraved. It is unfair to criticize the marketplace for fulfilling these desires, when clearly the defects lie in the popular tastes themselves. I consider it a cowardly concession to a false extension of the idea of democracy to make sub rosa attacks on public tastes by denouncing the people who serve them. It is like blaming waiters in restaurants for obesity.[15]

Marketing reflects our own values

Among the scholars who have studied materialism, the consensus appears to be that—in the short run—marketing reflects social values, while—in the long run—it enhances and reinforces them. And as Webster has pointed out:

> To the extent that materialism represents a consensus of opinion expressed by the public through its votes in the marketplace as well as the polling place, it is hard to criticize it without challenging the foundation of democracy and capitalism.[16]

Material goods do improve the quality of life

In the final analysis, the issue is not really materialism versus some other alternative. Rather, it is how much materialism is "necessary." More is not always better. The quality of life should not be measured strictly in terms of quantities of material goods. But when material goods are viewed as the means to an end—rather than the end itself—they *do* make it possible to satisfy higher-level needs. Modern household appliances, for example, have greatly reduced the amount of time and effort that must be spent on household duties—leaving homemakers free to pursue other interests. And more dependable cars have expanded people's geographic horizons—affecting where they can live and work and play. Not having "wheels" would drastically change many people's life styles—and even their self images.

Consumers ask for it, consumers pay for it

Certainly, we do not now have the economists' "ideal"—pure competition. But the monopolistic competition typical of our economy is the result of customer preferences—*not* manipulation of markets by business. Monopolistic competition may seem costly at times—when we look at micro-level situations—but it works fairly well at the macro level—in serving the welfare of consumers who have many varied demands.

All these demands add to the cost of satisfying consumers. The total cost is larger than it would be if spartan, undifferentiated products were offered at the factory door on a take-it-or-leave-it basis to long lines of buyers.

But if the role of the marketing system is to serve consumers, then the cost of whatever services they demand cannot be considered excessive. It is just the cost of serving consumers the way they want to be served.

Does macro-marketing cost enough?

The question, Does marketing cost too much? has been answered by one well-known financial expert with another question, Does distribution cost enough?[17] His analysis showed that marketing is an important part of our economic system. And he suggested that perhaps even more should be spent on marketing—since "distribution is the delivery of a standard of living"—that is, the satisfaction of consumers' basic needs and wants.

The role of marketing and business in our market-directed economy is to satisfy consumers. Production can't do this job alone—nor can marketing. It makes little sense to think of production and marketing separately. They are different sides of the same coin.

Marketing reflects people's values.

Mass production requires mass distribution—and our macro-marketing system helps make the whole market-directed economic system work well. In this sense, then, macro-marketing does *not* cost too much. Some of the activities of individual business firms may cost too much. And if these micro-level activities are improved, the performance of the macro system probably will improve. But regardless, our macro-marketing system performs a vital role in our economic system—and does *not* cost too much.

Challenges Facing Marketers

We have said that our macro-marketing system does *not* cost too much—given the present objective of our economy—while admitting that the performance of many business firms leaves a lot to be desired. This presents a challenge to serious-minded students and marketers. What needs to be done—if anything?

We need better performance at the micro level

Some business executives seem to feel that in a market-directed economy, they should be completely "free." They don't understand that ours is a market-directed system—and that the needs of consumer/citizens must be served. Instead, they focus on their own internal problems, and don't satisfy consumers very well.

We need better planning

Most firms are still production-oriented. Some hardly plan at all. Others simply extend this year's plans into next year. Progressive firms are beginning to realize that this doesn't work in our fast changing marketplaces. Market-oriented strategy planning is becoming more important in many companies. More attention is being given to the product life cycle—because marketing variables should change through the product's life cycle.

May need more social responsiveness

A good business manager would put himself in the consumer's position. A useful rule to follow might be: Do unto others as you would have others do unto you. In practice, this means developing satisfying marketing mixes for specific target markets. This may mean building in more quality or more safety. The consumers' long-run satisfaction should be considered, too. How will the product hold up in use? What about service guarantees?

Note, however, that this would not always mean producing the "highest quality" that could be produced or offered for sale. Low-quality, short-lived products might be acceptable in certain circumstances—as long as the target market understood what it was getting.

Production-oriented business managers often neglect this market-oriented rule. It often is difficult—or impossible—to determine what grade or quality is being offered at what prices. Labels, salespeople, and advertising may offer no help at all. Further, the producers may not even know—because no specific customer-related quality has been built into the product. They may *feel* it is better—

because higher-cost components have been installed. And these higher-cost components may result in higher prices, but they may not contribute to consumer satisfaction. In such cases, you can see why some promotion people—faced with production-oriented bosses—resort to aggressive, or even deceptive and fraudulent, promotion to "get rid of the goods."

It seems doubtful that production-oriented approaches will work in the future. Tougher competition—and more watchful government agencies—may force the typical production-oriented business managers to change their thinking—just to survive.

May need more environmental awareness

Besides focusing more on consumers' needs, marketers must be sensitive to environmental concerns. A lack of understanding of uncontrollable variables— and a failure to recognize new environmental trends—are major causes of marketing failure. Conditions around the world are changing rapidly—as social-economic-political systems grow more and more interdependent. Marketing managers cannot afford to conduct "business as usual."

Of special concern are environmentalists—who are trying to protect our scarce resources by limiting their use. This movement—coupled with high energy prices and slower population growth—will probably reduce economic growth and lead to more government control—and more restrictions on marketing managers.

The objective of increasing consumer satisfaction is often at odds with the environmentalists' objective of preserving the quality of our natural environment. Environmental costs have traditionally been ignored by the marketing system. Resources such as air and water have been seen as "free commodities." Now marketers must face the fact that they will have to give greater consideration to social costs in their decision making. They may have to ignore potentially profitable opportunities which are ecologically dangerous. They must give more thought to how products will be consumed over time and ultimately disposed of. Finally, marketers must contend with the higher prices that will be necessary to cover environmental costs—knowing that this will probably reduce both sales and profits.

Marketing managers must be aware of environmental concerns.

The Canadian focus on the environment

Canadian concerns with ecology and resource shortages have had a somewhat different focus than that in other countries.[18] There have been two major studies of the possibility of Canada becoming a "Conserver Society" rather than one that emphasizes continuous economic growth and ever increasing consumption.[19] Articles both "for" and "against" the conserver society concept appeared in a number of magazines after the two research teams published their findings. Numerous conferences, seminars, and workshops continue to be held on the subject. Indeed, interest in the conserver society was at one time so great that a new quarterly publication, *Conserver Society Notes—Canada's Leading Magazine on the War On Waste,* evolved out of a Science Council of Canada guide to conserver literature.

What would marketing be like in a conserver society? For the Science Council of Canada's answer to this question, look at Figure 24–1. Note the indictment of modern marketing techniques and the plea for a new approach to pricing that incorporates social costs. Many conserver society proponents consider Canada's adoption of conserver values as socially and morally desirable rather than as an unfortunate necessity. Others promote a conserver stance only because they believe it is ecologically necessary. However, all conserver society advocates take issue with the position that "more is always better." They do not believe per capita Canadian consumption can continue to rise in a world of overpopulation, scarce resources, and expensive energy.

We may need new laws

One of the advantages of a market-directed economic system is that its operation is relatively automatic—but in our version of this system, consumer/citizens provide certain constraints (laws). And these constraints can be modified at any time. So it is important for business managers to realize that their actions may cause new constraints—they do not have the right to do anything they want.

■ FIGURE 24–1   The conserver society: An operational definition

The concept of a conserver society arises from a deep concern for the future and the realization that decisions taken today in such areas as energy and nonrenewable resources, for example, may have an irreversible and possibly destructive impact in the medium to long term.

The necessity for a conserver society derives from our perception of the world as finite and of nonrenewable resources as limited, as well as from our recognition of increasing global interdependence.

A conserver society is, on principle, against waste. Therefore, it is society which

Promotes economy of design of all systems, i.e., "doing more with less."
Favors reuse or recycling, and wherever possible, reduction at the source.
Questions the ever-growing per capita demand for consumer goods artificially encouraged by modern marketing techniques.
Recognizes that a diversity of solutions in many systems, such as energy and transportation, might in effect increase their overall economy, stability, and resiliency.

In a conserver society, the pricing mechanism should not just reflect the private cost, but rather should reflect the total cost to society, including net energy used, ecological impact, and social considerations. This will permit the market system to allocate resources in a manner that more closely reflects societal needs, both immediate and long term.

Source: Science Council of Canada, *Conserver Society Notes,* May–June 1976, p. 2.

Need tougher enforcement of present laws

Before piling on too many new or different constraints, however, it probably would be wise to apply and vigorously enforce the ones we have. The antitrust laws, for example, have often been applied to protect competitors from each other when in fact they were intended to protect competition. Refocusing present constraints could make a big difference. Consumer and Corporate Affairs Canada seems to have a very definite consumer-oriented emphasis.[20] Provincial and local authorities also are taking stronger stands—for example, with respect to product safety, truth-in-lending, and deceptive advertising.

The results of strict enforcement of present laws could be far reaching if more price fixers, fraudulent or deceptive advertisers, and others who are obviously violating existing laws—and thereby affecting the performance of the macro-marketing system—were sent to jail or given heavy fines. A quick change in attitudes might occur if top managers—those who plan strategy—were prosecuted, rather than the salespeople or advertisers who are expected to "deliver" on weak or undifferentiated strategies.

In other words, if the government made it clear that it was serious about improving the performance of our economic system, much could be achieved within the present system—*without* adding new constraints or trying to "patch up" the present ones.

Need better-informed and politically active business leaders

Further, it probably would be desirable for business leaders to expand their understanding of—and efforts to improve—our macro system. More communication with legislators, government administrators, and consumer advocates could increase awareness of each others' problems, perceptions, and even use of terminology. Confusion or differences regarding the meaning of words such as: *competition, product, market, consumer needs, rationality,* and *information* can make a big difference.[21]

Need better-informed consumers

We also may need some changes to help potential customers choose among the confusing array of goods and services on the market. Legislation to ensure that consumers do have grounds for comparing products (for example, life expectancy of light bulbs and appliances) would be useful. Consumer education programs designed to teach people how to buy more effectively could also be a help.

But great care must be used here—so that the consumer's free choice *really* is preserved. If only easily measurable characteristics are used, consumers might be encouraged to use quantitative criteria, when qualitative characteristics (for example, style, taste, freshness, and fun in use) might be more important for many buyers.

Need socially responsible consumers

We have been stressing the responsibility of producers to act responsibly—but consumers have responsibilities, too. This is usually ignored by consumer advocates.[22] Some consumers abuse returned-goods policies, change price tags in self-service stores, and expect attractive surroundings and courteous, well-trained sales and service people—but want discount prices. Others are

People behave differently as consumers and citizens.

downright abusive to salespeople. Others think nothing of "ripping off" businesses—because "they're rich."

Canadians tend to perform their dual role of consumer/citizens with something of a split personality. We often behave one way as consumers—and then take the opposite position at the ballot box. For example, while our beaches and parks are covered with garbage and litter, we urge our political representatives to take stiff action to curb pollution. We protest sex and violence in the media—and then flock to see *Friday the 13th,* and other R- or X-rated movies. We complain about high energy costs—and then purchase low-efficiency appliances.

Let's face it. There is a wealth of information already available to aid consumer decision making. The consumerism movement has encouraged nutritional labeling, open dating, unit pricing, truth-in-lending, plain-language contracts and warranties, and so on. And government agencies publish many consumer buying guides—as do organizations such as The Consumers Association of Canada. Yet the majority of consumers continue to ignore most of this information.

We may need to modify our macro-marketing system

Our macro-marketing system is built on the assumption that we are trying to satisfy consumers. But with resource shortages and high energy costs, how far should the marketing concept be allowed to go?

Should marketing managers limit consumers' freedom of choice?

Achieving a "better" macro-marketing system is certainly a desirable objective. But an important question is what role should a marketer play in his role as a producer. As a consumer/citizen, there is no doubt that he has the right and obligation to contribute his view and vote to improve our system. But as a producer, what should he do?

This is extremely important, because some marketing managers—especially those in large corporations—can have an impact far larger than in their role as a consumer/citizen. Should they, for example, deliberately refuse to produce "energy-gobbling" appliances or cars—even though there is strong demand? Or should they be expected to install safety devices which inevitably will increase costs—and which are *not* desired by potential customers?

These are very difficult questions to answer. Some things which marketing managers can do are clearly in both the firm's and consumers' interests—in that they lower costs and/or improve the options available to consumers. Other choices, however, might actually reduce consumer choice and would seem to be at odds with a desire to improve the effectiveness of our macro-marketing system.

Consumer/citizens should vote on the changes

It seems fair to suggest, therefore, that marketing managers should be expected to improve and expand the range of goods and services they make available to consumers—always trying to better satisfy the needs and preferences of potential customers. This is the job we have assigned to business.

To the extent that pursuing this objective makes "excessive" demands on scarce resources—or causes an "intolerable" level of ecological damage—then consumer/citizens have every right and responsibility to vote for laws to restrict the many individual firms which are trying to satisfy consumers' needs. This is the role which we as consumers have assigned to the government—to ensure that the macro-marketing system works effectively.

It is important to recognize that some critics of marketing are really interested in basic changes in our macro-marketing system. And some basic changes *might* be accomplished by *seemingly minor* modifications in our present system. Allowing some government agency (for example, the Department of Consumer and Corporate Affairs) to prohibit the sale of products for seemingly good reasons may establish a precedent which would lead to major changes we never expected. (Bicycles, for example, are a very hazardous consumer product—should they continue to be sold?) Clearly, such government actions could seriously reduce consumers' present "right" to freedom of choice—including "bad" choices.[23]

Therefore, consumer/citizens should be careful to distinguish between proposed changes designed simply to modify our system and those designed to change it—perhaps drastically. In either case, the consumer/citizen should have the opportunity to make the decision (through elected representatives). This decision should not be left in the hands of a few well-placed managers or government planners.

Marketing people may be even more necessary in the future

Regardless of the changes which might be voted by consumer/citizens, some kind of a marketing system will be needed in the future. Further, if satisfying more subtle needs—such as for the "good life"—becomes our objective, it could be even more important to have market-oriented firms. It may be necessary, for example, not only to define individual's needs, but also society's needs—perhaps for a "better neighborhood" or "more enriching social experiences," and so on. As one goes beyond tangible physical goods into more sophisticated need-satisfying blends of goods and services, the trial-and-error approach of the typical production-oriented manager becomes even less acceptable.

■ CONCLUSION

Macro-marketing does *not* cost too much. Business has been assigned the role—by consumers—of satisfying their needs. Customers find it satisfactory—and even desirable—to permit businesses to cater to them and even to stimulate wants. As long as consumers are satisfied, macro-marketing will not cost too much—and business firms will be permitted to continue as profit-making entities.

It must always be remembered that business exists at the consumers' discretion. It is mainly by satisfying the consumer that a particular business firm—and our economic system—can justify its existence and hope to keep operating.

In carrying out this role granted by consumers, the activities of business firms are not always as effective as they might be. Many business managers do not understand the marketing concept—or the role that marketing plays in our way of life. They seem to feel that business has a God-given right to operate as it chooses. And they proceed in their typical production-oriented ways. Further, many managers have had little or no training in business management—and are not as competent as they should be. As a result, micro-marketing *does* cost too much. The situation is being improved, however, as training for business expands and as more competent people are attracted to

marketing and business generally. Clearly, *you* have a role to play in improving marketing activities in the future.

Marketing has new challenges to face in the future. *Our* consumers may have to settle for a lower standard of living. Resource shortages, high energy costs, and slowing population growth may all combine to reduce our income growth. This may force consumers to shift their consumption patterns—and politicians to change some of the rules governing business. Even our present market-directed system may be threatened.

To keep our system working effectively, individual business firms should work toward more efficient and socially responsible implementation of the marketing concept. At the same time, individual consumers have the responsibility to consume goods and services in an intelligent and socially responsible way. Further, they have the responsibility to vote and ensure that they get the kind of macro-marketing system they want. What kind do you want? What can and should you do to ensure that fellow consumer/citizens will vote for your system? Is your system likely to satisfy you, personally, as well as another macro-marketing system? You don't have to answer these questions right now—but your answers will affect the future you will live in and how satisfied you will be.

■ QUESTIONS AND PROBLEMS

1. Explain why marketing must be evaluated at two levels. Also, explain what criteria you feel should be used for evaluating each level of marketing, and defend your answer. Explain why your criteria are "better" than alternative criteria.

2. Discuss the merits of various economic system objectives. Is the objective of the Canadian economic system sensible? Do you feel more con-

sumer satisfaction might be achieved by permitting some sociologists—or some public officials—to determine how the needs of the lower-income or less-educated members of the society should be satisfied? If you approve of this latter suggestion, what education or income level should be required before an individual is granted free choice by the social planners?

3. Should the objective of our economy be maximum efficiency? If your answer is yes, efficiency in what? If not, what should the objective be?

4. Cite an example of a critic using his own value system when evaluating marketing.

5. Discuss the conflict of interests among production, finance, accounting, and marketing executives. How does this conflict contribute to the operation of an individual business? Of the economic system? Why does this conflict exist?

6. Why does the text indicate that the adoption of the marketing concept will encourage more efficient operation of an individual business? Be specific about the impact of the marketing concept on the various departments of a firm.

7. It appears that competition sometimes leads to inefficiency in the operation of the economic system in the short run. Many people argue for monopoly in order to eliminate this inefficiency. Discuss this solution to the problem of inefficiency.

8. How would officially granted monopolies affect the operation of our economic system? Specifically, consider the effect on allocation of resources, the level of income and employment, and the distribution of income. Is the effect any different than if a monopoly were obtained through winning out in a competitive market?

9. Is there any possibility of a pure-competition economy evolving naturally? Could legislation force a pure-competition economy?

10. Comment on the following statement: Ultimately, the high cost of marketing is due only to consumers.

11. Should the consumer be king or queen? How should we decide this issue?

12. Should marketing managers, or business managers in general, be expected to refrain from producing profitable products which some target customers want but which may not be in their long-run interest? Or, should firms be expected to produce "good" products which offer a lower rate of profitability than usual? What if only a break-even level is obtainable? What if the products are likely to be unprofitable, but the company is also producing other products which are profitable so that on balance it will still make some profit? What criteria are you using for each of your answers?

13. Should a marketing manager or a business refuse to produce an "energy-gobbling" appliance which some consumers are demanding? Similarly, should it install an expensive safety device which does not appear to be desired by potential customers and inevitably will increase costs? Are the same principles involved in both of these questions? Explain.

14. Discuss how much slower economic growth or even no economic growth would affect your college community—and in particular its marketing institutions.

■ **SUGGESTED CASES**

■ NOTES

1. This section is based on Jack L. Engledow, "Was Consumer Satisfaction a Pig in a Poke?" *MSU Business Topics,* April 1977, pp. 88–90.

2. James U. McNeal, "Consumer Satisfaction: The Measure of Marketing Effectiveness," *MSU Business Topics,* Summer 1969, p. 33.

3. For an extensive discussion of the problem and mechanics of measuring the efficiency of marketing, see Stanley C. Hollander, "Measuring the Cost and Value of Marketing," *Business Topics,* Summer 1961, pp. 17–26; and Reavis Cox, *Distribution in a High-Level Economy* (Englewood Cliffs, N.J.: Prentice-Hall, 1965).

4. Hiram C. Barksdale and William D. Perreault, Jr., "Can Consumers Be Satisfied?" *MSU Business Topics,* Spring 1980, pp. 19–30.

5. K. G. Hardy, M. R. Pearce, T. C. Kinnear, and A. B. Ryans, *Canadian Marketing, Cases and Concepts* (Toronto: Allyn & Bacon Canada, 1978), pp. 521–52.

6. Alan R. Andreasen and Arthur Best, "Consumers Complain—Does Business Respond?" *Harvard Business Review,* July-August 1977, pp. 100–1.

7. Gene Laczniak, "Frameworks for Analyzing Marketing Ethics," *Journal of Macromarketing* 3, no. 1 (Spring 1983), pp. 7–18.

8. F. M. Nicosia, *Consumer Decision Processes* (Englewood Cliffs, N.J.: Prentice-Hall, 1966), p. 39

9. E. H. Chamberlin, "Product Heterogeneity and Public Policy," *American Economic Review,* May 1950, p. 86.

10. For more on this point see Robert L. Steiner, "Does Advertising Lower Consumer Prices?" *Journal of Marketing,* October 1973, pp. 19–26; and Robert L. Steiner, "Marketing Productivity in Consumer Goods Industries—A Vertical Perspective," *Journal of Marketing,* January 1978, pp. 60–70.

11. George J. Stigler, "The Economics of Information," *Journal of Political Economy,* June 1961, p. 213.

12. Arnold J. Toynbee, *America and World Revolution* (New York: Oxford University Press, 1966), pp. 144–45. See also John Kenneth Galbraith, *Economics and the Public Purpose* (Boston: Houghton-Mifflin, 1973), pp. 144–45.

13. Russell J. Tomsen, "Take It Away," *Newsweek,* October 7, 1974, p. 21.

14. Engledow, "Was Consumer Satisfaction a Pig in a Poke," p. 92.

15. "Intellectuals Should Re-Examine the Marketplace; It Supports Them, Helps Keep Them Free; Prof. Stigler," *Advertis-*

ing Age, January 28, 1963. See also E. T. Grether, "Galbraith versus the Market: A Review Article," *Journal of Marketing,* January 1968, pp. 9–14; and E. T. Grether, "Marketing and Public Policy: A Contemporary View," *Journal of Marketing,* July 1974, pp. 2–7.

16. Frederick Webster, *Social Aspects of Marketing* (Englewood Cliffs, N.J.: Prentice-Hall, 1974), p. 32.

17. Paul M. Mazur, "Does Distribution Cost Enough?" *Fortune,* November 1947.

18. Stanley J Shapiro, "Marketing in a Conserver Society," *Business Horizons,* April 1978.

19. Kimon Valaskakis, Peter S Sindell, and J. Graham Smith, *The Selective Conserver Society* (Montreal: GAMMA,1976); Science Council of Canada Report No. 27, *Canada as a Conserver Society: Resource Uncertainties and the Need for New Technologies* (Ottawa: Minister of Supply and Services Canada, 1977).

20. Department of Consumer and Corporate Affairs, "Who We Are and What We Do," Cat.RG23-25/1975 (Ottawa: Information Canada, 1975).

21. R. Bauer and S. Greyser, "The Dialogue that Never Happens," *Harvard Business Review,* November-December 1967, pp. 2–12 and 186–90; and T. Levitt, "Why Business Always Loses," *Harvard Business Review,* March-April 1968, pp. 81–89.

22. James T. Roth and Lissa Benson, "Intelligent Consumption: An Attractive Alternative to the Marketing Concept," *MSU Business Topics,* Winter 1974, pp. 30–34; and Robert E. Wilkes, "Fraudulent Behavior by Consumers," *Journal of Marketing,* October 1978, pp. 67–75; and "How Shoplifting Is Draining the Economy," *Business Week,* October 15, 1979, pp. 119–23.

23. Dan R. Dalton and Richard A. Cosier, "The Four Faces of Social Responsibility," *Business Horizons* 25, no. 3 (May/June 1982), pp. 19–27; Y. Hugh Furuhashi and E. Jerome McCarthy, *Social Issues of Marketing in the American Economy* (Columbus, Ohio: Grid, 1971); James Owens, "Business Ethics; Age-Old Ideal, Now Real," *Business Horizons,* February 1978, pp. 26–30; Steven F. Goodman, "Quality of Life: The Role of Business," *Business Horizons,* June 1978, pp. 36–37; William F. Dwyer, "Smoking: Free Choice," *Business Horizons,* June 1978, pp. 52–56; Stanley J. Shapiro, "Marketing in a Conserver Society," *Business Horizons,* April 1978, pp. 3–13; and Johan Arndt, "How Broad Should the Marketing Concept Be?" *Journal of Marketing,* January 1978, pp. 101–3.

 **Cases**

Guide to the Use of These Cases

Cases can be used in many ways. And the same case can be analyzed several times for different purposes.

"Suggested cases" are listed at the end of most chapters, but these cases can also be used later in the text. The main criterion for the order of these cases is the amount of technical vocabulary—or text principles—which are needed to read the case meaningfully. The first cases are "easiest" in this regard. This is why an early case can easily be used two or three times—with different emphasis. Some early cases might require some consideration of Product and Price, for example, and might be used twice, perhaps in regard to place planning and later pricing. In contrast, later cases which focus more on Price might be treated more effectively *after* the Price chapters are covered.

■ 1. FOODCO, INC.

It is now 1983, and Mr. Robert Donald, newly elected president of Foodco, Inc., is faced with some serious problems. Foodco, Inc., is a 115-year-old Toronto-based food processor. Its multi-product lines are widely accepted under the "Foodco" brand. The company and subsidiaries prepare, can, package, and sell canned and frozen foods. Beginning with beef, the company expanded to include pineapple from Hawaii as well as other fruits, vegetables, pickles and condiments, British Columbian salmon, and can manufacturing. Operating more than 27 processing plants in Canada, Foodco became one of the largest Canadian food processors—with annual sales (in 1982) of $348,065,000.

Until 1980, Foodco was a subsidiary of a major midwestern meat-packing company, and many of the present managers came up through the meat-packing industry. Foodco's last president recently said: "Almeat's (the meat-packing firm) influence is still with us. Foodco has always been run like a meat-packer. As long as new products show a potential for an increase in the company's sales volume, they are produced. Traditionally, there has been little, if any, attention paid to margins. We are well aware that profits will come through good products."

Jim Warren, a 25-year Foodco employee and now production manager, is in full agreement with the multi-product–line policy. Mr. Warren said: "Volume comes from satisfying needs. We at Foodco will can, pack, or freeze any meat, vegetable, or fruit we think the consumer might want." He also admitted that much of the expansion in product lines was encouraged by economics. The typical plants in the industry are not fully used. By adding new products to use this excess capacity, costs are spread over greater volume. So the production department is always looking for new ways to make more effective use of its present facilities.

The wide expansion of product lines coupled with Foodco's line-forcing policy has resulted in 85 percent of the firm's sales coming from supermarket chain stores—such as Safeway, Kroger, and A&P. Smaller stores are generally not willing to accept the Foodco policy—which requires that any store wanting to carry its brand name must be willing to carry the whole line of 68 varieties of fruits, vegetables, and meats. Mr. Warren explains, "We know that only large stores can afford to invest the amount of money in inventory that it would take to adequately stock our products. But, the large stores are the volume! We give consumers the choice of any Foodco product they want, and the result is maximum sales." Many small retailers have complained about Foodco's policy, but they have been considered to be too small in potential sales volume per store to be of any significance.

In 1983, a stockholders' revolt over low profits (in 1982, they were only $10,101) resulted in Foodco's president and two of its five directors being removed. Robert Donald, a lawyer who had been a staff assistant to the chairman of the board, was elected president. One of the first things he decided to focus on was the variable and low levels of profits earned in the past several years. A comparison of Foodco's results with comparable operations of some large competitors supported Mr. Donald's concern. In the past 10 years, Foodco's closest competitors have had an average profit return on shareholder's investment of 6 to 11 percent, while Foodco averaged only 3.8 percent. Further, Foodco's sales volume, $348,065,000 in 1982, has not increased much from the 1956 level (after adjusting for inflation)—while operating costs have soared upward. Profits for the firm were about $8 million in 1956. The closest they have come since then is about $6 million—in 1964.

In his last report to the Foodco board of directors, the outgoing president blamed his failure on an inefficient marketing department. He wrote, "Our marketing department has deteriorated. I can't exactly put my finger on it, but the overall quality of marketing people has dropped, and morale is bad. The team just didn't perform." When Mr. Donald confronted Jack Kenny—the vice president of marketing—with this charge; his reply was, "It's not our fault. I think the company made a key mistake after Word War II. It expanded horizontally—by increasing its number of product offerings—while major competitors were expanding vertically, growing their own raw materials and making all of their packing materials. They can control quality and make profits in manufacturing which can be used in marketing. I lost some of my best people from frustration. We just aren't competitive enough to reach the market the way we should with a comparable product and price."

In further conversation with Kenny, Mr. Donald learned more about the nature of Foodco's market. Although all the firms in the food-processing industry advertise widely to the consumer market, there has been no real increase in the size of the market for processed foods. Further, consumers aren't very selective. If they can't find the brand of food they are looking for, they'll pick up another brand rather than go without a basic part of their diet. No company in the industry has much effect on the price at which its products are sold. Chain store buyers are used to paying about the same price per case for any competitor's product—and won't exceed it. They will, however, charge any price they wish on a given brand sold at retail (That is, a 48-can case of sweet peas might be purchased from any supplier for $17.28, no matter whose product it is. Generally, the shelf price for each is no more than a few pennies different, but chain stores occasionally attract customers by placing a well-known brand on "sale.")

At this point, Mr. Donald is wondering why Foodco isn't as profitable as it once was. Also, he is puzzled as to why the competition is putting products on the market with low potential sales volume. For example, one major competitor recently introduced a line of dietary fruits and vegetables.

Discuss Foodco's policies and what it might do to improve its situation.

■ 2. KASKAID COMMUNICATIONS*

After graduating with a degree in business administration, Glen Kask decided to combine a career in a large organization with some entrepreneurial activities. Craft shops and gift stores were selling large volumes of Northwest Coast Indian artifacts. Carvings, paintings, and prints were extremely popular items. The newly opened Museum of Man at the University of British Columbia, which featured a vast collection of Indian art, further stimulated interest. Kask had wanted for some time to develop a line of educational coloring books. He decided to integrate the growing interest in native art with his concept of an educational coloring book. The idea was to create a product that would be instructional and amusing for youngsters.

Kask saw the market as including local residents of the Greater Vancouver and Victoria areas, tourists looking for souvenirs, and teachers. He believed that most of the books would be bought by adults for children.

An artist friend of Kask's agreed to prepare 32 line drawings and a front and back cover for a royalty of five cents per book. He asked for a $450 advance payment, which represented royalties on the first 9,000 copies. Preliminary inquiries with a local printer indicated that 5,000 copies could be produced for $500. Kask estimated, based on some experience, that the cost of binding, trimming, and shipping would be seven cents per book. As he was going to operate from his home, Kask "guesstimated" that overhead expenses would be a modest three cents per book. Using these preliminary figures, Glen decided to go ahead with the project. He commissioned his friend to proceed with the drawings.

Some weeks later, as the artist was progressing quickly with the drawing, Kask arranged a meeting

---

*This case was written by Dr. Robert Wyckham, who at the time of its preparation was associated with Simon Fraser University. Ms. Ann Pobst assisted with the preparation of the case.

Original cost estimate	$ per book
Royalty for artist (9,000—$450)	.05
Printing (5,000—$500)	.10
Binding, trimming, shipping	.07
Overhead	.03
Total	$.25

with the printer. To his surprise, the printer refused to honor the price originally quoted by his assistant. He also said that the desired paper stock was not available in British Columbia, would have to be ordered from Ontario, and could only be obtained by the boxcar load. Discouraged and annoyed, Glen shopped around for a new printer. He finally found a printer who would produce the coloring book on a high-quality paper for $1,300 for 3,000 copies.

When the three thousand copies had been made, Kask found that his binding and trimming costs had worked out to be just under seven cents per book. However, shipping and overhead were much more expensive than originally estimated. The various delays and alternate arrangements resulted in costs of 19 cents per copy.

Final costs	$ per book
Royalty	.05
Printing ($1,300)	.43
Binding and trimming	.07
Overhead and shipping	.19
	$.74

Based on his final costs, Glen decided to offer the coloring books for $1.25 per copy to retailers, leaving him a gross profit of $.51 per book. He did not suggest a retail price to the outlets, as he was aware of various markup practices which would result in prices ranging from $1.98 to $2.49.

To obtain distribution for his product, Kask began making sales calls on gift shops, cruise shop offices, Indian residential schools, Chambers of Commerce, service clubs, British Columbia Ferries, school boards, and the Boy Scouts organization. He had hoped that the Boy Scouts and the Indian residential schools would buy the coloring books to use to sell in fund-raising projects. Glen

felt that Chambers of Commerce and service clubs would buy the books to give away to visitors and exchange students. He considered his product ideal for youngsters looking for an activity on the multitude of routes of the B.C. Ferries. School art teachers, he thought, would be interested in exposing their students to local art. Kask also looked into the idea of setting up a coloring contest. He envisaged a group of local merchants sponsoring a contest and providing prizes to youngsters who did an excellent job coloring the book. To encourage immediate use, Glen prepared packages with sets of felt pens attached to the coloring books.

After one year of operation, Kask found he had sold about half his inventory and made a modest profit. His most productive distribution channel turned out to be gift shops, especially those heavily frequented by visitors to British Columbia. Many of the retailers liked the idea of the feltpen/coloring book package, and they sold well. Some gift shops reordered, while others did not seem able to move the books.

Kask received no response from the operators of gift shops on cruise ships. He discovered that B.C. Ferries had a policy forbidding the sale of coloring books on board ship because of the potential damage from crayons and felt pens. The Boy Scouts showed no interest. While the Indian residential schools would not buy any of his coloring books, they produced one of their own. Kask did not feel that there would be much competition from this product. He was not able to organize a campaign to reach service clubs and the Chambers of Commerce.

Some schools purchased the coloring book in quantity. Others, Kask discovered, purchased single copies and photocopied sufficient numbers to supply their classes. Kask determined that, while he could take action to recover the retail value of the copied books through small claims court, the amount involved was too small to be worth the trouble.

Kask was somewhat discouraged by his experience. He had invested a great deal of time and effort in the project and had received a very small return. He realized that he had learned a good deal about manufacturing and marketing of a

Income.	$1,916.25
Cost of goods sold.	843.15
Gross margin	$1,073.10
Operating expenses	357.00
Profit before taxes	$ 716.10

printed product and that there were potentially good profits to be made from this knowledge. How would he get a return on his invested dollars and on his experience?

The first problem was the current inventory, Kask saw a number of alternatives:

1. Continue as at present and make calls on retailers. Do so until current stocks are used up and then drop the project.
2. Try to unload the current stock to a few retailers at cost (about $.75 per book) or try to sell the total stock to a novelty or book company.
3. Identify new potential retail outlets. For example: participate at craft fairs popular at some of the ferry terminals; establish a booth at the multitude of craft fairs during the Christmas season; make contact with street vendors in the Gastown area, which is very popular with tourists; set up a booth at the Pacific National Exhibition.

4. Try to place the book in stores specializing in educational materials, such as the Teachers' Store.
5. Approach the British Columbia Ministry of Tourism to see if it would purchase the books for distribution at tourist information offices.
6. Contact major travel agencies to see if they would be interested in including the coloring book in their welcome packages for tourists; contact airlines to see it they would buy the coloring book to hand out to children on their flights.
7. A final alternative would be to scrap the remainder of the copies and see the project as a worthwhile experience.

A second decision, which was related to the solution chosen for the first problem, was whether to create new companion products. Kask realized he now had sufficient development, production, and marketing know-how to better exploit the markets for similar new products. What he did not know was whether the financial returns would be worth his efforts.

What should Mr. Kask do about the current inventory? Should he create new companion products?

■ 3. APEX CHEMICAL COMPANY

Apex Chemical Company is a large manufacturer of basic chemicals and polymer resins located in Alberta. Tom Zang, a bright young engineer, has been working for Apex as a research engineer in the polymer resins laboratory. His job is to do research on established resins—to find new, more profitable applications for resin products.

During the last five years, Tom has been under heavy pressure from top management to come up with an idea that would open up new markets for the company's foamed polystyrene.

Two years ago, Tom developed the "spiral-dome concept," a method of using the foamed polystyrene to make dome-shaped roofs and other struc-

tures. He described the procedure for making domes as follows: The construction of a spiral dome involves the use of a specially designed machine which bends, places, and bonds pieces of plastic foam together into a predetermined dome shape. In forming a dome, the machine head is mounted on a boom, which swings around a pivot like the hands of a clock, laying and bonding layer upon layer of foam board in a rising spherical form.

According to Tom, polystyrene foamed boards have several advantages:

1. Foam board is stiff—but can be formed or bonded to itself by heat alone.

2. Foam board is extremely lightweight and easy to handle. It has good structural rigidity.
3. Foam board has excellent and permanent insulating characteristics. (In fact, the major use for foamed board is as an insulator.)
4. Foam board provides an excellent base on which to apply a variety of surface finishes.

Using his good selling abilities, Tom had little trouble convincing top management of the soundness of the idea.

According to a preliminary study by the marketing department, the following were areas of construction that could be served by the domes:

1. Bulk storage.
2. Cold storage.
3. Educational construction.
4. Industrial tanks (covers for).
5. Light commercial construction.
6. Planetariums.
7. Recreational construction (such as a golf-course starter house).

The study focused on uses for existing dome structures. Most of the existing domes are made of concrete or some cement base material. It was estimated that large savings would result from using foam boards—due to the reduction of construction time.

Because of the new technology involved, the company decided to do its own contracting (at least for the first four to five years after starting the sales program). It felt this was necessary to make sure that no mistakes were made by inexperienced contractor crews. (For example, if not applied properly, the plastic may burn.)

After building a few domes to demonstrate the concept, the company contacted some leading architects across the country. Reactions were as follows:

It is very interesting, but you know that the Fire Marshal of Toronto will never give his OK.

Your tests show that foamed domes can be protected against fires, but there are no *good* tests for unconventional building materials as far as I am concerned.

I like the idea, but foam board does not have the impact resistance of cement.

We design a lot of recreational facilities, and kids will find a way of poking holes in the foam.

Building codes around Vancouver are written for wood and cement structures. Maybe when the codes change.

After this unexpected reaction, management didn't know what to do. Tom still thinks the company should go ahead. He feels that a few reports of well-constructed domes in leading newspapers would go a long way toward selling the idea.

What should Apex do? Why did it get into the present situation?

■ 4. THE TOT-SWITCH*

Jim Halstrum, the inventor of the Tot-Switch, was confronted with an interesting and perplexing dilemma in the early summer of 1980. He was faced with the choice of leaving his product in the hands of Innovation Promotions Limited or using legal means to obtain control over Tot-Switch and finding another method of producing and marketing it.

The Tot-Switch was created by Halstrum to solve a problem he had observed in his own home. While recuperating from an illness in March 1977, he noticed how often his two children, aged two and three years, asked their mother to turn lights on. He also noticed that the lights were left on as the children moved from one area to another in the

*This case was written by Robert Wyckham, who at the time of its preparation was associated with Simon Fraser University.

house to play. Jim thought that if he could devise some method whereby the youngsters could turn the lights on and off he would save his wife innumerable steps and perhaps cut his hydro bill.

After tinkering with pulleys and switches, Halstrum was able to develop the prototype of the Tot-Switch. A string-and-pulley system allowed the children to operate the light switches. He put a number of these crude attachments on light switches throughout his house and immediately discovered an added bonus. The children were able to light their own way to the bathroom at night.

Halstrum received encouragement from friends who were impressed by the system. Some asked Jim to put together sets for their homes. During 1977 he made numerous changes in design and materials until the light switch system was durable, easy to install, and easy to use.

After 10 months of experimentation Halstrum took two major steps. First, he made arrangements to patent his invention. He took out patents on five different designs in Canada. He also applied for patents in the United States and Japan. The total cost of his patents was $4,050.[1] Second, he consulted with Dr. Roger Vergin, a professor of business administration at Simon Fraser University. Professor Vergin agreed to install the switch systems in two daycare centers with which he was associated in Bellingham, Washington.

Six months of use and abuse by the children in the two daycare centers indicated that the switch systems worked very well. They did not break down, and the youngsters found them easy to use. At this point Vergin recommended to Halstrum that he try to sell the concept to a manufacturer.

In the second week of July 1978, Jim Halstrum mailed 50 prototypes of his switch to manufacturers and distributors across Canada. Over the next month or so he received a varied response:

1. McDonald's restaurant chain expressed interest in the switch as a promotional item. They would be willing to purchase 2.5 million units if

Halstrum could sell the units for eight cents apiece.

2. A number of electric utility companies were favorably disposed toward the product. They were orienting their promotion toward conservation, and the switches fit this theme. However, because of federal regulations, none of the utilities was able to help develop and market the product.

3. A sizable number of small manufacturers and distributors felt the product had merit. They wrote asking for additional information.

At this point, a friend told Halstrum about a company called Innovation Promotions Limited. Innovation Promotions had been formed recently by a lawyer, John Pobst, and an engineer, Fred Jamison, for the purpose of new product development. In their separate professional practices Pobst and Jamison had observed the problems that inventors have in exploiting their new products. They decided that they could assist inventors and build a healthy business in new product development. At the time that Halstrum contacted Innovation Promotions, the company had one product under contract for development.

After a number of meetings with Pobst and Jamison, Halstrum agreed to a contract which would give Innovation Promotions Limited control over the product for five years. The contract, which was effective October 2, 1979, contained the following conditions:

1. Innovation Promotions would research the market, develop the product for mass production, promote, and handle sales of the product.

2. Halstrum was to receive a royalty of 25 cents on each unit sold.

3. Innovation Promotions must sell a minimum of 30,000 units in the first year and 450,000 units over the next four years.

4. If at any time Innovation Promotions failed to fulfill their agreement, Halstrum would regain control over the product.

During the late fall of 1979, Innovation Promotions contracted with a plastics manufacturer in Vancouver to produce the product. The switch was

---

[1] Canadian patent, $750; U.S. patent, $1,000; Japanese patent, $1,300; other patent costs, $1,000.

modified and engineered to allow mass production. A two-cavity mold was produced at a cost of $5,600. This resulted in a production cost of 27 cents per unit. An eight-cavity model, which would have cost $18,000, would have reduced production costs to 10 cents per unit.

A creative director from an advertising agency was hired to develop a name for the product and design the package. The name chosen was the Tot-Switch. It was selected because it described the product in use and was catchy. The package design was executed by a local packaging firm. Jamison decided to use an innovative skin-tight plastic-coated package, which, although expensive (35 cents per unit), was thought to be a selling feature to the trade.

It was decided that the Tot-Switch should retail for $4.99. Up to this point no market or consumer research had been done. Pobst and Jamison were of the opinion that the six-month test at the day-care centers was an adequate evaluation of the worth of the product.

Production began in January 1980; an initial run of 2,500 units was produced. The costs of production and markups for the first production run were as follows:

	Per unit
Retail selling price	$4.99
Retail margin	2.50
Wholesale selling price	$2.49
Production cost	.27
Packaging cost	.35
Royalty to Halstrum	.25
Taxes	.16
Royalty to Innovation Promotions*	
Shipping	
Advertising	1.46
	$2.49

*Innovation Promotions had invested about $23,000 in the Tot-Switch to this point.

As a first thrust into the marketplace, Innovation Promotions decided to use a mail-order marketing approach. An advertisement was prepared and placed in the Ontario, British Columbia, and Alberta regional editions of *TV Guide* for the first and third weeks in February. The advertisement included an encouragement for multiple purchases by offering a quantity discount. Prices, including mailing and handling costs, were as follows: one, $5.49; two, $4.75 per unit; three, $4.58 per unit; five or more, $3.75 per unit.

Halstrum was very disappointed with the performance of Innovation Promotions Limited. He felt that the $4.99 price was much too high. His original idea was to sell the product for about $1.99. Although he could understand the benefits of using mass advertising to make people aware of the Tot-Switch, he felt that the mail order idea was a waste of time. Halstrum pointed to the fact that only about 500 units had been sold on the basis of the *TV Guide* ads.

"They are never going to sell the required 30,000 units by September. Sales at the Thunderbird Electrical stores are not going well. I understand a California manufacturer has shown interest, but he wants national advertising support. Pobst and Jamison are negotiating with a local wholesaler on a deal for 300,000 units, but I can't see anything resulting from the discussions. They have also talked with the Paraplegic Society of British Columbia. Apparently the society wants to promote the product through their magazine and is asking for a fifty-cent fee for each unit sold. As far as I'm concerned they just haven't been able to put the thing together. They probably should have gone the traditional route through the department stores. McDonald's is still interested, and if I could get the production costs down and McDonald's price up I might be able to move a fantastic number of units in one quick sale."

On the basis of what was known at the time, did the decision to go with Innovations Promotions Limited make sense? What should Mr. Halstrum do now?

■ 5.   INDIAN STEEL COMPANY

Indian Steel Company is one of the two major producers of wide-flange beams in the Montreal area. The other major producer in the area is the Quebec Steel, Ltd. (QSL)—which is several times larger than Indian as far as production capacity on this particular product is concerned.

Wide-flange beams are one of the principal steel products used in construction. They are the modern version of what are commonly known as "I-beams." QSL rolls a full range of wide flanges from 6 to 36 inches. Indian entered the field about 25 years ago—when it converted an existing mill to produce this product. This mill is limited to flanges up to 24 inches, however. At the time of the conversion, it was estimated that customer usage of sizes over 24 inches was likely to be small. In the past few years, however, there has been a definite trend toward the larger and heavier sections.

The beams produced by the various competitors are almost identical—since customers buy according to standard dimensional and physical-property specifications. In the smaller size range, there are a number of competitors, but above 14 inches, only QSL and Indian compete in the Montreal area. Above 24 inches, QSL has had no competition.

All the steel companies sell these beams through their own sales forces. The customer for these beams is called a "structural fabricator." This fabricator typically buys unshaped beams and other steel products from the mills and shapes them according to the specifications of each customer. The fabricator sells to the contractor or owner of a building or structure being built.

The structural fabricator usually sells on a competitive-bid basis. The bidding is done on the plans and specifications prepared by an architectural or structural engineering firm—and forwarded to him by the contractor wanting the bid. Although several hundred structural fabricators compete in the region, relatively few account for the majority of wide-flange tonnage. Since the price is the same from all producers, they typically buy beams on the basis of availability (i.e., availability to meet pro-duction schedules) and performance (reliability in meeting the promised delivery schedule).

Several years ago, Indian production schedulers saw that they were going to have an excess of hot-rolled plate capacity in the near future. At the same time, a new production technique was developed which would enable a steel company to weld three plates together into a section with the same dimensional and physical properties and almost the same cross-section as a rolled wide-flange beam. This technical development appeared to offer two advantages to Indian: (1) it would enable Indian to use some of the excess plate capacity, and (2) larger sizes of wide-flange beams could be offered. Cost analysts showed that by using a fully depreciated plate mill and the new welding process it would be possible to produce and sell larger wide-flange beams at competitive prices, i.e., at the same price charged by QSL.

Indian's managers were excited about the possibilities—because customers usually appreciate having a second source of supply. Also, the new approach would allow the production of up to a 60-inch depth of section and an almost 30-inch width of flange. With a little imagination, these larger sizes could offer a significant breakthrough for the construction industry.

Indian decided to go ahead with the new project. As the production capacity was being converted, the salespeople were kept well informed of the progress. They, in turn, promoted this new capability—emphasizing that soon they would be able to offer a full range of beam products. Several general information letters were sent to the trade, but no advertising was used. Moreover, the market development section of the sales department was very busy explaining the new possibilities of the process—particularly to fabricators at engineering trade associations and shows.

When the new production line was finally ready to go, the market reaction was disappointing. In general, the customers were wary of the new product. The structural fabricators felt they could not use it without the approval of their customers—because It would Involve deviating from the speclfled rolled sections. And as long as they could still get the rolled section, why make the extra effort for something unfamiliar—especially with no price advantage. The salespeople were also bothered with a very common question: How can you take plate which you sell for about $450 per ton and make a product which you can sell for $460? This questlon came up frequently and tended to divert the whole discussion to the cost of production—rather than to the way the new product might be used.

Evaluate Indian's situation. How could it gain greater acceptance for its new product?

■ 6. WEST CITY'S COMMITTEE ON FITNESS*

The members of the Mayor's Committee on Fitness listened attentively to Professor Henry Morgan, chairman of its research subcommittee. The committee had been formed 12 months earlier when the mayor of West City had invited each of a number of clubs and organizations concerned with fitness and health—the YMCA, the medical association, the parks and recreation commission, sports clubs, and so forth—to appoint a representative to the committee. In his invitation, the mayor suggested the following objectives for the Committee on Fitness to consider:

1. To indicate to the people of West City the opportunities existing within the community for living more fully through personal involvement.
2. To suggest ways in which every member of the community can be encouraged to take part in his or her own way in fun-associated activity on a regular basis.
3. To involve the citizens of West City in physical activity—particularly of a vigorous nature, over an extended period of time.

Committee representatives subsequently discussed the reason for the formation of the committee. They generally agreed that there was a genuine need to develop programs designed to meet the objectives given in the mayor's invitation. The sedentary life styles of the people, developed over the last century as industrialization and urbanization increased, had led to some serious problems. A large proportion of the community's health costs, existing inefficiencies in labor productivity, and even low enjoyment or satisfaction with life itself could be attributed to inappropriate lifestyles. Lack of physical activity and fitness, poor eating habits, and excessive use of alcohol, tobacco, and drugs could all be viewed as contributing factors. The level of physical fitness was considered especially important since it was known that people with high physical activity levels also ate better and made far less use of alcohol, tobacco, and drugs.

The members of the committee agreed that the objectives for the committee should go well beyond the first and second points mentioned by the mayor. It would not be enough "to indicate" or "to suggest." Rather, the committee should strive to bring about increased participation of the citizens of West City in physical activities of a "vigorous nature" over an "extended period of time." Since there was no well-known method of creating the major shift in life styles and behavior that achievement of the objectives would require, the committee decided to seek the cooperation of several experts in physiology, human kinetics, recreation, and applied behavioral science on the staff of the local university. Accordingly, a research subcommittee was formed with the assistance of various faculty members. Professor Henry Morgan was chosen as the subcommittee's chairman.

After meeting several times, the research com-

---

*This case was prepared by Dr. John Liefeld, who at the time of its preparation was associated with the Department of Consumer Studies at the University of Guelph.

EXHIBIT 1:   Attitude responses—physical activity

Statement	Disagree	Disagree somewhat	Agree somewhat	Agree
1. In our modern society there is no need for strenuous physical activity	69.4%	11.6%	9.3%	9.6%
2. I would participate more in physical activities if my doctor advised me to be more active	15.3	4.3	18.8	61.6
3. My athletic skills and capabilities are below average	34.7	21.9	22.2	21.3
4. I don't know enough about the role of exercise in health and fitness	43.3	16.5	21.1	19.1
5. I enjoy being a spectator of sports and physical activities more than being a participant	33.6	15.4	21.7	29.3
6. The companionship and socializing I get when participating in physical activities are more important to me than the health benefits of physical activities	35.0	23.9	27.1	14.0
7. I would participate more in physical activities and sports but I am embarrassed about my lack of physical skills	55.1	17.3	14.8	12.8
8. The health benefits of physical activities and sports are more important to me than the companionship and socializing I get from such activities	14.0	22.3	25.5	38.1
9. Medical science can keep us healthy and fit; exercise is not necessary	84.4	6.8	5.1	3.7
10. I prefer active recreations such as skating, swimming, or other physical activities to passive recreations such as reading, watching TV, or doing crafts	14.8	22.5	19.7	43.0
11. I would participate more in physical activities but my job is too tiring	43.6	14.0	23.5	18.9
12. I like my body the way it is	34.8	27.9	16.8	20.5
13. I want to know more about exercise, health, and fitness	11.4	11.4	31.1	46.0
14. In the summer it is too hot for me to participate in physical activities	66.0	16.7	9.6	7.6
15. I am personally commited to participation in active physical activities	45.5	13.9	15.9	24.7
16. I would participate more in physical activities and sports but there are not enough facilities in West City (i.e., fields, gyms, pools, courts, etc.)	57.9	16.6	13.8	11.7
17. In our modern society there is a real need for strenuous physical activity	15.1	14.2	21.7	49.0
18. It is important to me to be physically fit in order to manage my daily life and make my work and leisure more meaningful	5.9	10.5	20.4	63.2
19. I am too busy to participate in physical activities	45.0	17.6	27.8	9.6
20. I would participate in more physical activities if more of my friends would also participate	37.6	13.1	29.3	19.0
21. When I start some form of physical activity I always continue it	28.2	26.7	21.3	23.9
22. In the past year, I would have participated more in physical activities and sports but the programs cost too much money	54.7	12.9	18.6	13.8
23. A nutritious diet by itself will guarantee health and fitness	63.7	19.0	12.5	4.8
24. I would participate more in physical activities and sports but I don't have the time	34.0	14.7	32.9	18.4
25. Other people think I am fit	21.5	21.8	33.5	23.2

mittee approved the following statement of its objectives:

> To describe the current physical activities, fitness capabilities, and predispositions toward physical activities of West City residents in a manner which will: (a) provide measures for use in future evaluations of the impact and effectiveness of programs implemented by the mayor's committee, (b) help to identify target markets and objectives suitable for program development, and (c) provide information which is useful in designing and implementing programs.

Given these objectives, the research committee then designed a research project to measure three main classes of variables: (1) attitudes related to fitness, (2) rates of participation in physical activities, and (3) attitudes toward fitness and health. Using volunteer university and high school students as interviewers, 354 interviews were conducted in West City homes. A significant response bias was experienced in this interviewing as students reported that people who were overweight or negative in their attitudes toward physical activities were less likely to agree to be interviewed.

Striking findings were revealed when two activity indices were calculated. In the week prior to the study, 55 percent of the sample had an activity index number of 2.3 or less. To achieve an index number of 2.3, the individual need only move his or her body for 14 hours out of the 168-hour week. In other words, two hours or less per day of movement was the norm for 55 percent of the sample. Even given a sample that was biased toward those who are more fit—very little physical activity took place in the week prior to the study!

In terms of the index for the previous year's activity, similar results were reported. Seventy-one percent of the sample had an index score of 200 or less. To achieve this index number, the individual need only move his or her body for one and a quarter hours a day every day of the year. This means that they spent less than 5.2 percent of the year in any kind of movement. That a very large majority of the residents of West City are extremely sedentary was an inevitable conclusion.

The responses of the subjects to the survey's

EXHIBIT 2: Physical activities during the past year

	Number of respondents		Number of respondents
Walking to, or at, work	236	Gardening	213
Walking for recreation	180	Snow shovelling	186
Jogging	64	Social dancing	129
Competitive running	7	Dancing classes	11
Calisthenic exercises	79	Yoga	22
Recreational bicycling	97	Horseback riding	9
Bicycling to work	32	Boxing, judo, karate	7
Bicycle racing	3	Tennis	41
Recreational swimming	171	Table tennis	30
Competitive swimming	3	Badminton	27
Platform diving	5	Handball or squash	8
Skin diving	4	Volleyball	21
Scuba diving	1	Curling	20
Recreational sailing	15	Bowling	50
Sailboat racing	3	Golfing	44
Recreational skating	45	Touch football	17
Figure skating	2	Soccer	9
Competitive skating	2	Hardball	7
Downhill skiing	23	Softball	20
Cross-country skiing	29	Ice hockey	16
Snow shoeing	6	Floor hockey	10
Repairs around the house	209	Basketball	20

probing as to attitudes are summarized in Exhibit 1. The physical activities of respondents during the previous year are presented in Exhibit 2, and the reasons given for so participating are shown in Exhibit 3.

EXHIBIT 3: Reasons for participating in physical activity (multiple responses possible)

	Percent of subjects
1. It makes me feel good	85.6
2. To maintain health and fitness	80.7
3. To help control weight	63.7
4. For social contacts	56.9
5. For excitement	42.4
6. Advised to do so by doctor	16.1
7. To get recognition and admiration from friends	12.5

After Professor Morgan's presentation, the committee discussed the implication of the research findings for the programs the mayor's committee might introduce. Some members of the committee advocated programs that would increase the number of organized fitness-related activities people could select. Others argued for an educational program to make people more knowledgeable about the relationship between fitness and health. A third group maintained that fitness motivation was the central problem. They insisted that programs designed either to educate or to offer more activities were doomed to failure until people could be motivated to change their way of life.

Given the data presented, what are the problems confronting the committee? What, if anything, can marketing contribute to their solution?

■ 7. **WOODWARDS' DEPARTMENT STORES: HOLIDAY TRAVEL***

During the summer of 1977, executives of Woodwards, a multi-unit western Canadian department store chain with headquarters in Vancouver, had to decide about their involvement in the travel agency business. The decision boiled down to a choice between accepting an offer from Maple Leaf Travel, Ltd., to operate agencies within Woodwards' stores as a licensee or developing agencies owned and operated by the department store.

Woodwards had been founded in Vancouver in 1892 by Mr. C. W. Woodward. By 1977 the company had sales of over $653 million and profits of $8.3 million from 21 stores in British Columbia and Alberta. Woodwards served a wide cross-section of the consumer population and, although there was variation from store to store, tended to be most attractive to the middle socio-economic market.

Holiday Carousels, Ltd., which had operated travel agencies in eight Woodwards Stores, went

out of business in the early summer of 1977. The Holiday Carousels organization had created a unique physical unit to house their agencies. Called carousels, they were semicircular in design, attractively decorated, and occupied about 300 square feet of floor space.

Woodwards' management considered the sales growth of Holiday Carousels promising, with average sales of approximately $700,000 to $800,000 per unit per month in the spring of 1977. Each unit employed the equivalent of four full-time agents. (Industry rules of thumb suggest that an experienced agent should sell about $300,000 of travel per month.)

Woodwards' executives determined to continue to offer travel agency service to their customers for the following reasons:

1. The results of the Holiday Carousel experience were promising.
2. Increasing disposable incomes, smaller families, and larger numbers of senior citizens suggested a growing travel market.
3. Travel was seen as a natural complement to a

---

*This case was written by Dr. Robert G. Wyckham, who at the time of its preparation was associated with the Faculty of Business Administration at Simon Fraser University.

full-line department store image and to the existing level of customer traffic.

4. That level of customer traffic, plus customer confidence and loyalty to Woodwards, provided an excellent opportunity for travel sales.

5. There was a high potential profit per square foot of space occupied.

6. A travel agency service was necessary in order to remain competitive with other department store chains who were in the travel business.

After receiving proposals from a number of travel agencies, Woodwards' management decided to compare the Maple Leaf offer with the alternative of setting up their own travel agencies.

Maple Leaf Travel, Ltd., was a Vancouver-based travel agency with all national and international accreditations. It was owned, in part, by the credit unions of the province, which had more than 600,000 members. Total revenue of the travel agency in 1976 exceeded $2 million, the bulk of which was developed by direct mail to credit union members.

The Maple Leaf proposal was based on immediate reopening of the Park Royal, West Vancouver, travel office. Other offices would be opened when, by mutual agreement, a sufficiently smooth operating system had been achieved. Additional openings would occur first on the Lower Mainland of British Columbia and later Alberta.

Maple Leaf required about 300 square feet of space for an initial staff of two. Hours would be 9:30 A.M. to 5:30 P.M., Monday to Friday. Experiments with evening and Saturday openings were also to be carried out. Location of the travel office within each store was to be based on a trade-off between the need for traffic flow and visibility, the consumers' need for privacy, and the travel agents' need for relative quiet.

The lease agreement requested by Maple Leaf was as follows:

1. Five years with a five-year renewal clause.
2. 300 square feet of space initially; option to increase to 600 square feet as business warrants.

3. Rent formula:
   1.0% of net sales of less than $250,000.
   1.5% of net sales of $250,000 to $499,999.
   2.0% of net sales of $500,000 to $999,999.
   1.5% of net sales of $1,000,000 to $1,500,000.
   1.0% of net sales of more than $1,500,000.

Assuming an average commission rate of 9 percent, Maple Leaf Travel estimated a break-even point of sales of $411,000 in the first year. Pro forma contribution for the first year was estimated conservatively at $4,000 and optimistically at $16,000.

Three markets were identified for potential development: credit union members in the Woodwards' trading areas, current Woodwards' customers, and the general public. Cooperative direct-mail and newspaper advertising were suggested as the most productive forms of promotion.

In analyzing the alternative possibility, the creation of wholly owned and operated units, Woodwards' executives outlined some financial and other advantages:

1. The contribution to overhead and profit of travel outlets owned by Woodwards was estimated to be 2.6 percent on annual sales of $1 million compared to 1.625 percent from Maple Leaf Travel.

2. Because of the fixed nature of many expenses, it was thought that the contribution rate from owned agencies would increase as sales grew.

3. Advantageous advertising rates and in-house advertising expertise could be extended to a travel business operated directly by Woodwards.

4. Having control over an important service to Woodwards' customers was felt to be an advantage. Ownership was also seen as leading to greater flexibility in promotion, rate of growth, and operating characteristics.

5. Through various merchandising and promotional activities Woodward already was generating customer traffic; owned travel agencies would result in greater benefits to Woodwards from this traffic.

6. Woodwards had a "built-in" market, the corporate travel of executives, and direct access to a large number of employees.

7. Individuals expert in the travel business were available, and accounting services with travel agency experience could be retained.

A number of disadvantages of ownership were pointed out. In any new business the first weeks and months are difficult. A large amount of executive time would likely have to be allocated to the travel business, a business in which Woodward executives lacked any great degree of prior experience. There would also likely be some fairly substantial losses in the initial period before accreditations were received and business was built up.

A number of advantages would also be forgone if the Maple Leaf proposal was not accepted. The major potential loss was the opportunity to have more direct exposure to hundreds of thousands of credit union members. Also, Woodwards rather than Maple Leaf Travel would have to absorb any losses incurred in the start-up period. Any lease arrangements with Maple Leaf, in contrast, would be based on that firm's sales. There would, therefore, always be a positive contribution to Woodwards even if the travel agencies did not make a profit. Finally, Maple Leaf had marketing and operating systems already in place. Hence the amount of time Woodwards' executives would have to apply to the travel business would be greatly reduced.

Which of these two alternatives should Woodwards select? How would you support the recommendation?

■ 8. LAST MOUNTAIN SKI RESORT, LTD.*

Last Mountain, a popular, family oriented, "local" ski resort,[1] is located in the Okanagan Valley of central British Columbia. In the early summer of 1978, the 10th anniversary of Last Mountain, John Barlee and Frank Jobes decided that they should conduct a study of their skier-customers to obtain information to assist them in planning for the future.

The Last Mountain resort is situated 12 miles south and west of Kelowna, a city of about 55,000. Kelowna is a fast-growing community (67 percent growth in 1968–77), with personal disposable income per capita slightly below the national average. To the east and south of Last Mountain lie the towns of Westbank, Peachland, and Summerland and the city of Penticton (population 23,000).

Jobes and Barlee had purchased Last Mountain from the original owner and developer in the fall of 1974. During their ownership no major changes or expansions had been carried out. Although sales and profits varied from year to year depending on snow and weather conditions, the company was in good financial shape. Barlee, who was the managing partner, was on the mountain every day and so was aware of some of the skiers' concerns. Most frequent comments concerned the need for more lifts and problems in grooming the slopes. The road and the parking lot were also sources of some discontent. Skiers had also made suggestions about the cafeteria in the day lodge, the rental shop, and the ski school. Management was interested in the skiers' perceptions of the appropriateness of the days and hours of operation of the mountain and whether there was general satisfaction among skiers.

Last Mountain has two ski lifts. The major facility is a 3,000-foot Muehler double chair which has a vertical rise of just over 600 feet. A second lift is

---

*This case was written by Dr. Robert Wyckham, who at the time of its preparation was associated with Simon Fraser University.

[1]Last Mountain is considered a "local" ski resort because, for the most part, it serves the local market. Ski resorts that attract customers from long distances are known as "destination" resorts.

a Dopplemaier T-bar which is situated on a hill with a 250-foot vertical rise. The resort has under lease from the provincial government ample land and slopes to accommodate additional lifts. There are two or three areas to which skiers currently hike in order to find fresh snow and new challenges.

As at all ski resorts, the length of the lift lines is always a concern for customers and management. At Last Mountain, according to Barlee, lift lines are long only during the Christmas holidays and on weekend days when conditions are ideal. Barlee's experience was that lift lines at the other central Okanagan resorts, Big White, Apex Alpine, and Silver Star, were longer than those at Last Mountain.

To make new facilities economic, either the current customer group would have to ski more often, new skiers would have to be attracted, or prices would have to be raised. It was estimated that a new T-bar extending from the top of the current T-bar to cover about 300 vertical feet would cost $150,000 to $200,000.

The ski terrain at Last Mountain is ideally suited for skiers in the beginner to intermediate categories. Trails from all areas come together in one location making it possible for families and groups to stay in contact with each other. Families, ladies' groups and youngsters (including school groups) make up the majority of Last's daytime customers. At night the mountain is popular with teenagers and working people who cannot ski during the day.

The composition of the customers attracted by Last Mountain means that it is important that the slopes be well groomed. Moguls must not be allowed to build up, and, whenever possible, icy areas must be dealt with.[2] Slope grooming was a particular concern for night skiing under the lights when sudden drops in temperature created icy conditions. Well-groomed slopes of smooth soft snow were felt to be ideal by Last's skiers.

In Barlee's opinion, better snow grooming equipment would result in better slope conditions. During the 1977–78 season the grooming machinery had suffered a number of breakdowns. As well, Barlee was considering an attachment called a powder-maker, which would do a better job of dealing with icy slopes.

The road to Last Mountain from the highway is approximately seven miles long; the last four miles are gravel. Although the road is fairly wide and has only two relatively steep areas, skiers complain at times about how the road is being maintained by the Department of Highways. John Barlee feels that only the commitment of a great deal of management time backed up by solid consumer complaints would move the Highways Department to improve and pave the road.

Parking is only a problem at Last over the Christmas period and on sunny weekends after falls of new snow. There is space that could be bulldozed and new parking provided. Another way of dealing with the situation would be to hire staff to guide cars so as to park more cars in the existing lots.

From time to time various comments and recommendations had been made to staff members by customers about the cafeteria, the ski rental shop, and the ski school. According to Barlee, there was no consistency to these comments, and he would like to know whether there are concerns that should be addressed.

In designing the study the first problem that had to be dealt with was the population to be sampled. Jobes favored sampling a number of season pass holders, while Barlee wanted to get information from both season pass skiers and those who paid cash. No problems would be encountered in sampling season pass holders as a complete list of names and addresses was available. However, there was no easy way to get to the skier who paid cash. Jobes and Barlee debated whether to put the study off to the next year and interview the casual skier on the mountain during the ski season. They also considered some sort of telephone survey which would identify respondents as: skiers or non-skiers; regular Last Mountain skiers, occasional Last Mountain skiers. or non-Last Mountain skiers; Last Mountain season pass holders or Last Mountain cash customers.

Finally, after much argument, they decided that because research done previously had indicated that season pass holders made up almost half of

---

[2]Moguls are bumps which build up on a ski hill as a result of the turning actions of skiers.

the "skier days" on the mountain, and because many pass holders were repeat customers from year to year, only season pass skiers would be surveyed. This decision made the study considerably less expensive than the telephone alternative.

Each season pass holder was mailed a questionnaire on June 1, 1978. A letter from John Barlee was attached. The letter encouraged response by indicating that Last Mountain was considering changes and wanted ideas from skiers. A total of 973 questionnaires were mailed. By June 30, 1978, the cut-off date, a total of 236 completed questionnaires were returned.

Two thirds of the sample classified themselves as intermediate skiers; almost 1 in 5 said they felt they were novices; fewer than 1 in 10 reported that they were either experts or first-year skiers. Sixty-five percent of the respondents were 25 or younger. More than half of the sample members indicated that they had held Last Mountain passes for two years or more.

TABLE 1

Sample characteristics

	Percent
Skiing capability:	
Expert	7%
Intermediate	67
Novice	18
First year	8
	100
Age:	
16 or less	38
17–25	27
25 or older	35
	100
Years as Last pass holder	
1	45
2	32
3-4	14
5 or more	9
	100

On the positive side 68 percent said the road was satisfactory; 71 percent found the parking satisfactory; 62 percent felt the service in the ski rental shop was good; 79 percent said that the rental equipment was of good quality; 95 percent reported that the lift operators were friendly and helpful; 62 percent said the lift lines were okay; 83 percent indicated that the chair runs were well groomed; 58 percent said they felt that the correct number of moguls were left on the chair runs; 86 percent felt that the T-bar slopes were well groomed; 66 percent said the right number of moguls were left on the T-bar runs; 73 percent said the food, drinks, and service in the cafeteria were good; 90 percent gave a positive response to the quality of ski lessons.

In terms of the time of operation, 60 percent wanted the Mountain open on Mondays (currently Last was closed on Mondays during the day and open on Monday evenings for special groups only); 56 percent suggested that Last should be open later into the spring (traditionally Last closed before the Easter break); 93 percent said they like the present hours of operation (day skiing was from 10 A.M. to 4 P.M., and evening skiing was from 5 P.M. to 11 P.M.). Overall, 94 percent said they were pleased with the 1977-78 season at Last Mountain, and 88 percent thought they might buy a pass for the next year.

On the negative side, 67 percent said there was insufficient ski rental equipment. Almost 40 percent said that lift lines were too long and that service in the rental shop was poor. About 30 percent were dissatisfied with the road, the parking, the quantity of moguls on the chair runs (too many), the quantity of moguls on the T-bar (too few), and prices in the cafeteria.

Although about one third of the total sample said road conditions were unsatisfactory, dissatisfaction tended to be lower among older respondents. In general the comments from skiers were related to two different types of road conditions: when the road was covered with new snow and when the snow was removed by plows or melted by warm weather. Earlier and more frequent grading to remove washboard areas, better culverts, and paving were suggested for the latter condition.

More than 7 of 10 respondents indicated that they were happy with the parking situation. Older sample members tended to be less pleased with the parking. The comments suggested quite a diversity of opinion. Some felt that there was always plenty of parking space; others were adamant that a larger parking lot was required; still others indicated that the space was adequate but that better organization was needed to improve utilization. There were suggestions that more and better plowing of the parking lot was needed.

Only about 14 percent of the sample replied to the questions about ski rentals. Almost 7 of 10 of those respondents said there was not enough rental equipment available. Older customers tended to be much more dissatisfied with all aspects of the ski rental operation. More and better qualified personnel were suggested.

Almost all sample members gave positive responses to the questions about the lift operators. However, almost 4 in 10 said lift lines were too long. From the comments it was clear that long lift lines were a problem during peak periods only. The largest number of suggestions were for the building of additional lifts.

The comments and suggestions from respondents indicated a diversity of opinion about the nature of the skiing conditions desired. Some wanted more grooming, more packing of new snow, and fewer moguls. Others asked that the moguls be left so that they would become bigger and suggested leaving the fresh powder unpacked.

There were a number of negative comments about the bumps on the T-bar track. Older respondents said there were too many moguls; younger respondents said there were too few.

Although most sample members indicated that the food service was good, the older people were more likely to feel that the food value was satisfactory while the younger people were more impressed by the service. The most frequent complaints were that the cafeteria area was often overcrowded; that bag lunches could not be eaten in the cafeteria (an area on the main floor of the lodge was set aside for bag lunches); and that liquor was sold in the cafeteria, which many felt was inappropriate in a "family area."

Very few comments were made about the operation of the ski school. There were suggestions related to the organization of the ski classes to make sure the same students were always with the same instructor. Smaller classes were also recommended.

Sixty percent of respondents wanted the mountain open on Mondays. Some suggested that because of the shortness of the ski season Last should open seven days a week; others recommended opening Monday evenings only; still others felt it was necessary to be closed one day a week for repairs and maintenance.

Fifty-six percent wanted a longer season. Only two sample members made specific suggestions about having Last stay open longer into the spring.

Although more than 9 in 10 respondents said they like the present hours of operation, some suggestions were made: keep night skiing open until midnight, especially on weekends; do not close lifts between day and night skiing periods; extend day skiing to 5 P.M. and start night skiing at 6 P.M.

Only 6 percent of the sample said they were not pleased with the operation of the mountain. A number of people indicated that the new owners had done a good job. There were negative comments about the general appearance of the lodge and area. More and better housekeeping, litter clean-up, and washroom maintenance were recommended. Quite a number of concerns were raised about the problems associated with having a bar at a family recreation facility.

Eighty-eight percent of the respondents said they may renew their season pass; more than half said they definitely plan to renew.

Was the research project well designed and well executed. On the basis of what you learned, what course of action would you follow if you were in charge of Last Mountain?

■ 9. WEST COAST INTERNATIONAL RESOURCES*

The president (Carl McKay) of a large integrated forest products company in Vancouver had been approached regarding the purchase of a "sash and door" manufacturing plant. The company, Firply Framing, would provide an ideal complementary operation to West Coast International because wooden sash, window, and door frames must be manufactured from high-grade export quality lumber—the very product category McKay was currently having trouble in selling to his overseas (especially European and Japanese) markets.

*This case was written by Dr. Lindsay Meredith, who at the time of its preparation was associated with Simon Fraser University.

McKay's decision had to be made soon since it was quickly established that two other large multinational producers were considering the purchase of Firply. The West Coast market analyst, on the basis of short notice, was only able to provide the documentation in Exhibits 1, 2, 3, and 4. McKay knew that further information would simply not be forthcoming in time for his decision.

A brief check on Firply reaffirmed McKay's previous knowledge of the company:

1. It was a well-run organization with no discernible problems in quality control.

2. Firply tended toward a "going rate" pricing policy. Rarely were the Firply management initia-

EXHIBIT 1:   Estimated Canadian market for wooden windows units ($000)

	Value of all industry shipments								
	1962	1963	1964	1965	1966	1967	1968	1969	1970
Domestic shipments:									
Wooden sash, window, or window units	40,548	42,252	36,369	38,885	38,692	40,527	40,548	42,252	40,980
Wooden window and door frames	9,267	6,656	8,291	8,104	8,248	7,785	8,786	8,009	5,816
Total domestic shipments	49,815	48,908	44,660	46,989	46,940	48,312	49,334	50,261	46,796
Imports:									
Window, door, and window frames	N/A	1,229	1,816	1,972	1,844	1,955	1,950	1,904	1,439
Domestic consumption	N/A	50,137	46,476	48,961	48,784	50,267	51,284	52,165	48,235

EXHIBIT 2:   Estimated Canadian market for metal windows ($000)

	Value of all industry shipments								
	1962	1963	1964	1965	1966	1967	1968	1969	1970
Domestic shipments:									
Aluminum	31,265	37,416	43,759	44,446	43,232	49,025	53,556	59,526	67,730
Steel	4,519	3,802	3,159	4,121	3,844	3,256	4,029	4,109	4,752
Hermetically sealed	12,506	14,108	16,629	15,980	17,707	14,345	15,605	16,130	17,776
Total domestic shipments	48,290	55,326	63,547	64,547	64,783	66,626	73,190	79,765	90,258
Imports:									
Metal windows and shutters	N/A	N/A	932	1,154	1,884	1,667	550	404	486
Insulating multi-pane window units	N/A	N/A	294	126	89	290	412	569	631
Total value of imports	N/A	N/A	1,226	1,280	1,973	1,957	962	973	1,117
Domestic consumption	N/A	N/A	64,773	65,827	66,756	68,583	74,152	80,738	91,375

EXHIBIT 3: Sash, door, and other millwork plants, all industry shipments of goods of own manufacture for major product categories only*

Wooden Window Units	1963	1964	1965	1966	1967	1968	1969
Wooden window units, covered with metals, (all kinds)	4,870	6,492	5,127	5,098	3,531	3,998	3,970
Wooden window units, sashless, panoramic, double hung, etc.	18,334	17,471	19,836	22,247	26,167	27,734	28,403
Wooden window sash, storm, screen, etc. (Excluding units)	13,279	9,771	10,452	10,137	8,713	7,032	10,301
Wooden window or door frames, knock down or other	8,027	7,699	6,750	7,506	7,079	6,159	5,231

*Note categories in Exhibit 3 do not add to summaries in Exhibit 1.

EXHIBIT 4: Canadian housing starts, all areas

Year	Total Canadian dwelling completions
1962	126,682
1963	128,191
1964	150,963
1965	153,037
1966	162,192
1967	149,242
1968	170,993
1969	195,286
1970	175,827

tors of a price increase or decrease, and, as characteristic of most firms in the forest products business, they appeared to be acutely aware of the need to respond to import competitors' prices.

3. Firply maintained a relatively constant share of the Canadian market—seldom moving from its position as one of the larger Canadian suppliers with sales in the range of $6 to $8 million.

4. The product line of the company appeared attractive to McKay. Firply was active in the four major product categories indicated in Exhibit 3. Furthermore, the nature of production oper-

ations allowed the company to concentrate output in any one or more of the categories. McKay felt this to be an advantage in that, if the company was purchased, he could "fine tune" output to the growth sectors of the window, sash, and door market.

5. Finally, McKay knew that, with the homogeneous products and standardized production technology which characterized the wooden window, sash, and door market, the performance of the individual companies would be affected more by total industry activity than by competitive advantage.

McKay was very aware of one last piece of information. He had limited data on which to base a decision that must be made immediately.

Should West Coast International Resources execute their option to purchase Firply Framing? Justify your answer. Given that West Coast International did complete the purchase (and given the profile of market demand from Exhibit 3), what recommendations, if any, would you, as market analyst, make to Carl McKay concerning changes in the four product lines currently produced by Firply Framing?

■ 10. COMP-U-CARD CANADA, INC.*

Comp-u-Card (CUC) was an electronic shopping service which provided consumers with the opportunity to purchase brand-name products at savings of as much as 40 percent. CUC Canada, Inc., was a Canadian-owned licensee of a U.S. company that had operated since May 1983.

The arrival of CUC had been a huge success, to the dismay of local merchants. Manufacturers and retailers had to respond to the deepening penetration by CUC into their various markets.

Comp-u-Card of America was launched in the summer of 1972 as a discount buying service for consumer durables. The service soon evolved into an electronic shopping service, providing access to a database of 60,000 brand names in a wide variety of product areas including major appliances, photographic equipment, china, sports goods, and watches. Once consumers had a fairly specific idea of what they wanted, they called a toll-free number with the product information. "Shopping consultants" fed the information to the computer which then tracked the products and accessed the CUC price. Prices quoted included tax and delivery charges. If a consumer decided to buy, the computer placed the order with the nearest vendor (wholesaler or retailer) and took care of the accounting and payment service. Payment was made through VISA, MasterCard, or by personal cheque. CUC arranged to have the item delivered to the customer and estimated the date of arrival. In addition to its telephone shopping service, CUC offered an interactive home computer service which was more flexible. Users could "call up" products by selecting product features or price rather than having a specific model in mind.

In the spring of 1984, 100 wholesalers/distributors across Canada were listed with CUC. They agreed to sell at a lower price to members of CUC because it created a "ready" market to which they would not have had access otherwise. The in-

creased sales allowed them to take advantage of the volume discounts offered by manufacturers. While the vendors were authorized dealers, they did not accept the responsibility for servicing merchandise sold through CUC, although the items came with the manufacturer's full warranty.

CUC used credit card listings to identify those people with credit limits toward the high end of the scale who also had good credit ratings. These people were "invited" by CUC to become members. By January 1984, there were 40,000 members in Canada and 2.5 million in the United States. Membership fees were $25 (U.S.) and $35 (Canadian). The potential market in the United States alone was 75 million adult credit cardholders.

The promotional literature sent to potential members emphasized saving time, effort, and money on name-brand products. CUC aimed its appeal at consumers who not only put a premium on their time, but who also appreciated the value of their dollar. There were no traffic or parking hassles, and time was not wasted looking for the store with the right model or size, once the consumer had decided to buy a particular product. Personal disposable income had been increasing steadily while the time available to spend it had not.

Comparison shopping had become a way of life for middle- to upper-income consumers, and membership in CUC afforded substantial savings of up to 40 percent of the list price.

CUC also offered its members a means by which they could negotiate with local merchants for a lower price. Equipped with the knowledge of a product's price obtained through CUC, members approached their local retailers to bargain for a reduction. Transactions made with a merchant in their own town allowed CUC members all the previous advantages of buying from a known source together with the added attraction of a better price.

CUC reduced waiting time in stores, but the convenience lay primarily in the savings it offered since it was still necessary to compare items and

---

*This case was prepared by Shelagh M. Deeley under the direction of Professors Carl A. Lawrence and Ken Wong, who at the time of its preparation were associated with Queen's University.

prices. Consequently, the legwork was not really eliminated. Carol Street, a Toronto lawyer and CUC member, said "It's kind of difficult to buy something over the phone if you haven't seen it and compared it with others, so you do usually have to shop around. But the savings are definitely worth it. The dishwasher I bought sells in most stores for around $1,150. I got it for $860."

Some items did not lend themselves to this type of shopping. CUC offered no provision for returns: merchandise was not sent on approval so consumers had to be certain of their selection. If goods were received in damaged condition, the responsibility lay with the consumer to contact the manufacturer directly. Customers had to be prepared to wait for delivery, rather than being able to take the merchandise home with them. Consumers buying major appliances, such as dishwashers, not only had to make their own "hook-up" arrangements following delivery but also arrange for the service of their purchases.

An additional consideration for would-be members was whether or not their total savings on purchases made through CUC over the year would warrant the annual membership fee.

The bulk of CUC's revenues came from the annual membership fees. Membership had been increased substantially through the introduction of a joint VISA/CUC card. The association with the familiar VISA card gave CUC the higher profile it needed in order to gain wider acceptance for its revolutionary concept. The contribution to revenues made by merchandise service fees had increased as a result of growing membership. This fee was charged by CUC for handling the sale of the product and was included in the price quoted to members. CUC's interactive home computer service was responsible for the access fees' contribution to funds. The membership in this system had increased by 50 percent over the 1983/84 financial year. Finally, CUC obtained revenues from licensing its operations in Canada and the United Kingdom. A comparison of income statements for the financial years 1982, 1983, and 1984 appears in Exhibit 1.

While CUC was determined to expand its membership in the electronic shopping system, it also had other irons in the fire and was experimenting with variations on the theme.

A video extension of the home computer service called "shopping channel" had been introduced into several areas in the United States during 1983 via cable television. Viewers of shopping channel, having paid the CUC annual fee, were entitled to order the televised merchandise, which carried the normal CUC discount. The management of CUC was interested in expanding this service into other markets.

EXHIBIT 1: Comp-U-Card Canada, Inc., consolidated income statement for the year ended January 31

Year ended January 31	1984	1983	1982
Revenues:			
Membership fees	$5,088,000	$1,663,000	$1,097,000
Merchandise service fees	1,433,000	917,000	535,000
Licensing fees	1,740,000	966,000	
Access fees	549,000	366,000	109,000
Interest income	459,000	204,000	21,000
Other	219,000	40,000	17,000
Total revenues	9,488,000	4,156,000	1,779,000
Expenses:			
Operating	3,603,000	2,762,000	1,953,000
Marketing	2,576,000	1,413,000	1,506,000
General and administrative	3,009,000	2,198,000	1,901,000
Research and development	70,000	50,000	625,000
Interest	199,000	252,000	378,000
Total expenses	9,457,000	6,675,000	6,363,000
Net income (loss)	31,000	(2,519,000)	(4,584,000)

Another field of investigation in May 1983 was Comp-U-Store. This concept involved a kiosk, containing an interactive video terminal, located in a department store. The original test terminal displayed items from J. P. Stevens, a manufacturer of bed and bath fashions, in three stores in the United States. Shoppers browsed through an extensive selection of sheets, towels, etc.—more than the store could ever carry in inventory—and placed their order directly with the manufacturer. CUC owned the mainframe and leased time to the manufacturer. The department store received a percentage of the profit from the manufacturer for making the space available on the shop floor for the kiosk.

In Canada, CUC had introduced its Comp-U-Claim service for insurance companies. Insurers telephoned the service either to obtain a replacement price quote on cash claims or to place an order for the item to be replaced through Comp-U-Claim. CUC charged a fixed amount for each quote and stipulated a minimum number of quotes each month in return for the service.

How successful do you think Comp-U-Card Canada will become? How will local retailers and wholesalers be affected? What can these local intermediaries do to protect themselves?

■ 11. MASON SPORTS SHOP

Bob and Mary Mason graduated from a state university in Alberta in 1981. With some family help, they were planning to open a small ski equipment shop in Banff, Alberta. They were sure that by offering friendly, personal service they would have something unique and be able to compete with the many other ski shops in town. They were well aware that there are already many competitors because many "ski bums" choose the Banff area as a place to live—and then try to find a way to earn a living there. By keeping the shop small, however, the Masons hoped to be able to manage most of the activities themselves—keeping costs down and also being sure of good service for their customers.

Now they are trying to decide which line—or lines—of skis they should carry. Almost all the major manufacturers' skis are offered in the competing shops, so Bob and Mary are seriously considering specializing in the King brand—which is not now carried by any local stores. In fact, the King sales rep has assured them that if they are willing to carry the line exclusively, then King will not sell its skis to any other retailers in Banff. This appeals to Bob and Mary because it would given them something unique—a new kind of American-made skis which is just being introduced into the Canadian market with supporting full-page ads in skiing magazines. The skis have an injected foam core that is anchored to boron and fiberglass layers above and below by a patented process which causes the fiberglass to penetrate the foam. The process is the result of several years of experimenting by a retired space capsule designer—Kurt King. He felt that it should be possible to apply "space technology" to building lighter and more responsive skis. Now his small company—King Manufacturing Company—is ready to sell the new design as "recreational skis" for the large "beginner" and "intermediate" markets. Jim Vane, the King sales rep, is excited about the possibilities and compares the King ski development to the Head ski (first metal ski), and Prince tennis racket (first "outsize" racket) developments which were big successes. Both of these successes were built on the pioneering work of one man—Mr. Head—who Jim feels is very much like Mr. King—a "hard-working genius."

The Masons are interested because they would have a unique story to tell about skis which could satisfy almost every skier's needs. Further, the suggested retail prices and markups were similar to those of other manufacturers, so the Mason Ski Shop could emphasize the unique features of the King skis while keeping their prices competitive.

The only thing that worries the Masons about committing so completely to the King line is that there are many other manufacturers—both domestic and foreign—which claim to offer unique features. In fact, most ski manufacturers regularly come out with new models and features, and the Masons realize that most consumers are confused about the relative merits of all of the offerings. In the past, Bob himself has been reluctant to buy "off-brand" skis—preferring instead to stay with major names such as Hart, Head, K2, and Rossignol. So he wonders if a complete commitment to the King line is wise. On the other hand, the Masons do want to offer something unique. They don't want to run just another ski shop carrying lines which are available "everywhere." The King line isn't their only possibility, of course. There are other "off-brands" which are not yet carried in Banff. But the Masons like the idea that King is planning to give national promotion support to the skis during the introductory campaign. They feel

that this might make a big difference in how rapidly the new skis are accepted. And if they provide friendly sales assistance and quick binding-mounting service, perhaps their chances for success will be even greater. Another reason for committing to the King line is that they like the sales rep, Jim Vane, and are sure he would be a big help in their initial stocking and set-up efforts. They talked briefly with some other firms' salespeople at the major trade shows, but had not gotten along nearly so well with any of them. In fact, most of the sales reps didn't seem too interested in helping a newcomer—preferring instead to talk with and entertain buyers from established stores. The major ski shows are over, so any more contacts with manufacturers will mean the Masons must take the initiative. But from their past experience, this doesn't sound too appealing. Therefore, they seem to be drifting fast toward specializing in the King line.

Evaluate the Masons' and Jim Vane's thinking. What should the Masons do?

■ 12. MILLER SHOES LIMITED*

John Daniels gazed out the window that overlooked the busy streets of the city. It was noon and people poured from the buildings into the summer sunshine. He mused to himself, "I wonder how many of those career women would buy high-fashion shoes at bargain prices?"

Mr. Daniels was the operations manager for Miller Shoes, a company that sold primarily high-fashion shoes through 15 outlets in a major Canadian city. The company was a successful merchandiser of shoes to fashion-conscious men and women. Miller shoes started at $30 and ran to $80 per pair. The majority of the shoes were im-

_____

*This case was written by Professor Ken Hardy, who at the time of its preparation was associated with the University of Western Ontario.

ported from Spain, Italy, and England. Some shoes were private-branded for Miller, some were unbranded, and some were well-known imported brands. At least three quarters of the shoes were sold to women.

Mr. Daniels said, "Our success has been due to a keen sense of fashion on the part of our major buyer. Through his constant contact with Montreal and New York, he has been able to outguess the market almost every year. Our styles tend to be about one year ahead of the rest of the city. This puts us just a few months behind Montreal and other fashion centers. However, I have been struck by the general inefficiency in the shoe retailing business. Here in the city we have hundreds of tiny shoe retail shops, each of them carrying inventory and only selling a few dozen pairs of shoes a day.

Because of the high margins, most of the shops manage to break even.

"In most cases the markup on shoes is 50 percent of the retail price and the clerks are poorly trained. Furthermore, the clerks sometimes knowingly sell poorly fitting shoes to people because of the commission structure on which they are paid.

"Now, in our existing operation we have high-fashion merchandise in our downtown stores, and if lines do not move within a few months, we move them out to the suburban stores. It occurred to me that some of these slower-moving shoes have wide appeal and could be mass retailed. With an efficient outlet turning a high volume, we could lower the price by as much as 25 percent.

"For instance, a pair of imported women's shoes now retailing for $80 could be sold for as little as $59. What I visualize is a 6,000-square-foot store with a large glass front, broadloomed, at a location on one of the main streets. There is such a location available to us right now, and it has a parking lot beside it. Rather than have the shoes tucked away at the back, we would put our inventory on shelves all around the store, and salaried clerks would be available to conduct fittings. However, they would allow a consumer a chance to browse among the many styles. We would advertise 25 percent savings on the store front and perhaps use direct mail to reach the surrounding apartment dwellers and career women in the various offices nearby. Obviously, we would not want to use the Miller name on the discount center as it might rub off on our high-fashion shoe stores. We would create a name for the new store that would have connotations both of fashion and saving.

"What bothers me is the basic concept of selling high-fashion shoes at a substantial discount. It occurs to me that women have to be able to judge the quality of the shoes in order to realize that there would be a substantial saving offered to them. Some women can judge shoe quality, and some of them seem to do a considerable amount of shopping around. When they spot our shoes, would they recognize the savings? I hope word-of-mouth advertising would carry us after the initial store opening period.

"I still have some nagging doubts. It's such an obvious void in the market that I can't understand why, so far as I know, no one has attempted this retail strategy in Canada."

If you were Daniels, would you open this type of shoe store? Defend your position.

■ 13. McINTOSH FILING SYSTEM*

Herb Simpson had just finished a telephone conversation with the president of his largest customer, Office Supplies Limited, and he was angry. He had spoken to Jake Berry about a written request that Berry had sent him for a private-label version of McIntosh's 10 largest selling sizes of general and specialized "Target" brand file folders.

Office Supplies Limited (OSL) had managed to secure private-label names for more than 40 big sellers in its nationwide operations from pens and pencils to staplers, tape, and standard office forms. Now Jake was demanding that a line equivalent in quality to "Target" brand file folders, which held almost 60 percent of the market, be manufactured under the OSL label. Herb's consternation at OSL's request was in part caused by the fact that this was the third time OSL had made such a demand.

On both previous occasions Herb had turned down the request, and OSL had continued to buy and actively support all of McIntosh's lines with excellent growth results. OSL accounted for almost 23 percent of the total business of Herb's division, and Target brand file folders represented about 43 percent of this volume.

Herb had spent his whole working life with McIntosh, and he took personal affront at Jake's

---

*This case was written by Professor Ken Hardy, who at the time of its preparation was associated with the University of Western Ontario.

request because some 20 years earlier Herb had recommended Jake to OSL when Jake had graduated from university.

McIntosh Filing Systems was a division of STL. STL had acquired a regional manufacturer of business forms on the verge of bankruptcy—McIntosh Paper and Office Forms. STL made this business a success by moving it into the production of general and specialized file folders, labels, and markers for the office.

Herb knew the McIntosh policies on private-label business because its position in the matter had been well publicized. A former international chairman, Harry Winston Prince, had allowed several plants to become dependent on sales of private-label products for selected large paper companies. In the mid-50s a competitor had underbid on two of the three contracts, which resulted in numerous layoffs and the temporary closing of two McIntosh plants. From that time until his death in 1960, Prince had vigorously opposed any suggestions of private-label manufacturing.

STL was a multinational multiproduct company headquartered in the United States. In Canada, McIntosh Filing was one of five strategic business units within the company. STL sales revenue in 1984 was $180 million, and McIntosh sales were $20 million. McIntosh's business had grown rapidly, paralleling the growth in white-collar employment. It had been fed by a steady flow of file folders, 1,000 types of file markers and labels, and a variety of indexing systems. Available in every size, color, and type, no competitor could match McIntosh's scope in that end of the business. About 30 percent of McIntosh's file folder business was in specialized lines such as: oversized blueprint and engineer drawings; adhesive-bearing files for storage of telexes and messages; rapid read "see through" files for medical markets; washable, greaseproof, and waterproof files for marine, oil field, and other hazardous environmental markets; and spring-loaded files for carry-on transport markets such as couriers and short-haul truckers.

Competitors to McIntosh were mostly small regional paper converters, but excess capacity in the industry was substantial, and these converters were always hungry for orders. To complicate matters, Herb faced the fact that some of these converters bought base stocks for custom folders and labels from McIntosh, a situation that Herb believed had not hurt McIntosh. In fact selling to converters had made a significant contribution to plant overhead.

Herb's distribution consisted of 10 regional stationery suppliers, OSL, and more than 35 local stationers who had wholesale and retail operations. On average, the 10 regional stationers each had about six branches, while the local stationers each had one wholesale outlet and three or four retail locations. The regional suppliers sold directly to large corporations and to some retailers. By contrast, OSL's main volume was essentially retail to small businesses and walk-in trade with very few wholesale-type sales to large accounts.

Herb had real concern about the local stationers, who were seriously discussing the formation of buying groups. This would be done in order to obtain discounts on volume from vendors and thus compete more effectively with OSL's 60 retail stores and the big four regionals. None of Herb's other accounts was nearly as sharp at marketing or retailing as OSL, which had carved a real name for itself in every major city in the country. OSL's profits were the highest in the industry, its brands almost as well known as those of some key vendors, and its expansion plans aggressive. OSL was known to have attempted to buy a regional converter, but according to industry gossip, negotiations had broken down on price.

Herb was confident that McIntosh's brand names were well entrenched within the market, despite the fact that cash flow from McIntosh's operations had been put into new product work rather than into major advertising to users. Herb was very concerned that if OSL acquired a private label they would sell at a discount and possibly bring down all market prices. Across all lines of file folders, Herb averaged a 35 percent margin, but the high-volume sellers sought by OSL averaged only a 20 percent margin.

It was unclear to Herb whether OSL would continue to sell his branded Target line alongside OSL's private-label folders if OSL successfully concluded a private-label contract. OSL's history had been to sell branded and OSL private label side by side in most cases, especially if the branded product such as writing pens had a high quality, high recognition name in the market.

Herb had always been intrigued by the idea of custom merchandising and pricing McIntosh's total line to certain specific target market segments. For example, Herb believed some large specific markets such as insurance companies might welcome a merchandise assortment of file folders, labels, and markers priced and packaged to meet their particular needs. He thought that this same type of idea was "theoretically" feasible for an many as 10 different commercial market segments representing probably 40 percent of McIntosh's total sales. There were at least 100,000 end customers who bought in total $10 million in file folders. According to the Office Products Association, 80 percent of the volume was purchased by the largest 20 percent of the end customers.

Herb knew that Jack McIntosh, the president of McIntosh, continued to look to him for outstanding performance. In fact, in the elevator that morning Jack had said, "Say, I just saw John Moxie's lab report on his Magnof file project, and I'm really excited. It looks like that could give a real boost to your profits, Herb." STL had also just received patent approval on a new electronic security system for locking paper files. Herb had to get back to OSL's president by Friday of that week under threat that OSL would go private label with someone else if it wasn't McIntosh.

What position should Simpson take with Office Supplies Limited?

■ 14. COOPER LUMBER COMPANY

Bill Cooper—now 55 years old—has been a salesman for over 30 years. He started selling in a department store, but gave it up after 10 years to work in a lumberyard because the future looked much better in the building materials industry. After drifting from one job to another, he finally settled down and worked his way up to manager of a large wholesale building materials distribution warehouse in Hamilton, Ontario. In 1962, he decided to go into business for himself, selling carload lots of lumber to large retail yards in the Niagara Peninsula area.

He made arrangements to work with several large lumber mills in British Columbia. They would notify him when a carload of lumber was available to be shipped, specifying the grade, condition, and number of each size board in the shipment. Bill wasn't the only person selling for these mills, but he was the only one in his area. He was not obligated to take any particular number of carloads per month—but once he told the mill he wanted a particular shipment, title passed to him and he had to sell it to someone. Bill's main function was to buy the lumber from the mill as it was being shipped, find a buyer, and have the railroad divert the car to the buyer.

Bill has been in this business for 20 years, so he knows all of the lumberyard buyers in his area very well—and is on good working terms with them. Most of his business is done over the telephone from his small office, but he tries to see each of the buyers about once a month. He has been marking up the lumber between 4 and 6 percent—the standard markup, depending on the grades and mix in each car—and has been able to make a good living for himself and his family. The "going prices" are widely publicized in trade publications, so the buyers can easily check to be sure Bill's prices are competitive.

In the last few years, however, interest rates have been high for home loans, and the building boom slowed down. Bill's profits did too, but he decided to stick it out—figuring that people still needed housing and that business would pick up again.

Six months ago, an aggressive salesman—

much younger than Bill—set up in the same business covering about the same area but representing different lumber mills. This new salesman charges about the same prices as Bill, but undersells him once or twice a week in order to get the sale. Many lumber buyers—knowing that they were dealing with a homogeneous product—seem to be willing to buy from the lowest-cost source. This has hurt Bill financially and personally—because even some of his "old friends" are willing to buy from the new man if the price is lower. The near-term outlook seems dark, since Bill doubts if there is enough business to support two firms like his, especially if the markup gets shaved any closer. Now, they seem to be splitting the business about equally—as the newcomer keeps shaving his markup. The main reason Bill is getting some orders is because the lumber mills make up different kinds of carloads (varying the number of different sized products), and specific lumberyards want his cars rather than his competitor's cars.

A week ago, Bill was contacted by Mr. Pope, representing the Pope and White particleboard manufacturing plant. Mr. Pope knew that Bill was well acquainted with the local building supply dealers and wanted to know if he would like to be the sole distributor for Pope and White in that area—selling carload lots, just as he did lumber. Mr. Pope gave Bill several brochures on particleboard, a product introduced about 20 years ago, describing how it can be used as a cheaper and better subflooring than the standard lumber usually used. The particleboard is also made with a wood veneer so that it can be used as paneling in homes and offices. He told Bill that the lumberyards could specify the types and grades of particleboard they needed—unlike lumber where they choose from carloads that are already made up. Bill knew that a carload of particleboard cost about 30 percent more than a carload of lumber—and that sales would be less frequent. In fact, he knew that this product had not been as well accepted in his area as many others because no one had done much promotion in his area. But the 20 percent average markup looked very tempting—and the particleboard market was expanding.

Bill has three choices:

1. Take Mr. Pope's offer and sell both products.
2. Take the offer and drop lumber sales.
3. Stay strictly with lumber and forget the offer.

Mr. Pope is expecting an answer within another week, so Bill has to decide soon.

Evaluate what Bill Cooper has been doing. What should he do now? Why?

■ 15.   PARTITIONS CANADA LIMITED*

Colin Dennis, the president of Partitions Canada, called Bruce Laine, the firm's controller, into his office. "Most of our branch centers may appear to be making a good profit, but the overall profit picture of the company is pretty poor. All of our unit costs seem reasonable, and our selling prices are in line with our competitors. Your idea of decentralizing everything by making each branch an individual profit center and each department in the plant accountable for its expenses may have been a good one but it hasn't improved anything. We still can't tell why we're not making much profit.

"A friend at the club was telling me that he increased his overall profits by 6 percent by centralizing the management of his distribution. He not only reduced his distribution costs by 20 percent but improved the level of service being provided to customers. He also thinks sales have gone up 7 or 8 percent because of better service. Distribution may be where our problem lies. I think that we've got distribution costs that are spread across both the sales and production departments. Nobody's

*This case was written by Mr. Gerry Byers, who at the time of its preparation was associated with the Business Division at Humber College.

really keeping track of these expenses, and nobody's coordinating our distribution activities. I'm thinking of hiring a manager of physical distribution to make recommendations and carry out the necessary changes."

Partitions Canada, Ltd., is a branch of a U.S. firm, with manufacturing facilities in Cambridge, Ontario. The firm was established in Canada in 1961. It has enjoyed rapid growth, at least partly due to the continuing surge in the construction of large buildings. The growth was also due to an aggressive sales program which included a massive distribution network stimulated by an environment of competition within the firm itself.

The company manufactures semi-permanent but movable partitions and portable dividers used in office buildings, hospitals, schools, small shopping centers, and other institutions. Distribution is through branch centers in 18 Canadian cities. Sales are made to building owners and large tenants both directly and through architects, interior designers, consulting engineers, and contractors. Smaller office installations are sold through large stationery retailers, stationery wholesalers, and office furniture and equipment suppliers.

The branch centers are located in Victoria, Vancouver, Calgary, Edmonton, Regina, Winnipeg, Thunder Bay, Sudbury, Windsor, London, Hamilton, Toronto, Kingston, Cornwall, Ottawa, Montreal Quebec City, and St. John, N.B. Each branch consists of a small office, warehouse, and light manufacturing area where panels can be cut and painted or coated to customers' requirements. A small staff is maintained for this purpose as well as for installation if required.

This distribution structure was originally regarded as being an ideal arrangement in a market that stretched across Canada for 5,000 miles in a belt that was scarcely 200 miles wide. Transportation over the two national railroads could be very economical, although somewhat slow, if carload lots were shipped. Although communications might be expensive, autonomous management and the fact that each branch was a profit center meant that most decisions could be made without clearing with Head Office. Actually, individual managers often competed against each other for contracts in adjacent territories. The sales volume and profit performance of successful branch managers was flaunted monthly in the faces of the others to stimulate aggressive selling and cost cutting.

The company's policy provided for freight to distribution centers, warehousing, and packing costs to be averaged and incorporated into a uniform base price charged to the local distribution centers. They could also compete fairly and uniformly with each other regardless of where in Canada they were located. These centers could then compete effectively against smaller local manufacturers who would otherwise have underbid the company due to transportation differentials.

Rather than maintain large inventories, the managers were inclined to place specific orders with the warehouse at Cambridge for whatever was required for each job. They also usually requested that each order be packed completely in a separate unit and that it be shipped directly to the job site. Such practices meant that branches were saved the costs associated with maintaining a large inventory, "picking" an individual order, custom cutting and finishing panels, packing and loading, and providing local transportation to the job site.

Orders, in all their detail, were phoned in to Cambridge collect—in order to speed up delivery. The back-up paperwork followed by mail. Invariably, orders were accompanied by special instructions requesting shipments to be sent out by the following day. Although the actual installation at the job site might not be required for another month, the managers had experienced erratic deliveries by rail and therefore wanted to allow lots of time so as to protect their reputation with customers.

The effects of these practices and policies were felt by the Production Department at Head Office. Transportation, warehousing, custom cutting, and packing came under the jurisdiction of the production manager, Bill Prouse. He was constantly harassed by Dennis to fulfill every request by the branch managers. Errors in order filling and delayed shipments were continually brought to his attention.

Mike Alberts, the warehouse and shipping manager, who was also responsible for the finished-goods inventory, found it very difficult to maintain adequate stocks of all sizes in all finishes. He constantly had to order up special runs from the manufacturing department. Robbie Dixon, who was in charge of manufacturing, complained that he could never get a large enough production run to effect any economies of scale. He often had to pay overtime in order to meet the demands of the sales department.

Although the railroads had created special incentive-rate tariffs for large shipments, Sergio Cericola, the traffic manager, found that he could rarely ship even a carload at a time. Individually packed job orders were so irregular in shape that there was generally a lot of wasted volume in the railway cars. When Cericola tried to hold back orders to consolidate shipments, he got complaints from the field about these delays.

Branch managers would often order shipments on flat cars instead of box cars so that unloading at scattered job sites could be done more easily with forklift trucks where no receiving dock was available. However, flat cars cost more to ship on than box cars; requests for such flat cars were also filled more slowly by the railroads. Flat car shipments also had to have extra protection so that merchandise would arrive in usable condition.

Dennis eventually hired a physical distribution manager to review the situation and to recommend whatever changes were necessary to deal with existing problems.

What changes should that physical distribution manager be recommending? What special studies, if any, might he have to conduct?

■ 16. NEW START FURNITURE*

Sam Jones was dissatisfied with his current job with the Department of Transport at the Calgary Airport. He wanted a position or career with more challenge and personal responsibility. One of the alternatives he was considering was opening a store in the town of Cochrane, Alberta.

Sam had joined the Canadian Airforce after his graduation from high school. He performed various duties including aircrew member on submarine spotters during his 10 years in the Airforce. Upon leaving the Airforce he earned an economics degree from the University of Victoria. After graduating, Sam went to work for the Canadian Department of Transport. His first assignment was to develop plans for leasing the retail space in the new $136 million airport then under construction in Calgary.

Both Sam and his wife liked the idea of living in a small town. Upon getting the assignment in Cal-

gary, they had explored the small towns surrounding the city. Eventually, they decided to locate in Cochrane, a small but fast-growing town situated in the valley of the Bow River, some 20 kilometers northwest of Calgary. The population of the town had increased from some 500 people in 1970 to 2,000 in 1978. A major developer had plans to build an additional 400 to 500 new homes in Cochrane over the next three years.

The area surrounding Cochrane was changing rapidly from farming and ranching to small hobby farms and acreages. Most of the people living on the acreages worked in Calgary. Their homes varied, but most were large and expensive. As a result of increased building in the area, the district's school population had grown from 300 students in the mid-1960s to over 1,750 students in 1978.

Industrial employment in the Cochrane district had also increased in the last few years. In 1977 Canron opened a plant to produce reinforced concrete pipe; the plant employed between 50 and 75 people. Spray Lake Saw Mills and Domtar Construction Products had plants in Cochrane em-

*This case was written by Dr. James B. Graham, who at the time of its preparation was associated with the Faculty of Management at the University of Calgary.

ploying a total of 150 people. Three natural gas processing plants, each with approximately 50 employees, were also operating in the area. With the exception of the Domtar plant, all these industries had located in the Cochrane district within the last 10 years. Over half the people working in these plants commuted from Calgary.

Prior to the period of industrial expansion and subdivision of the surrounding land, Cochrane's merchants had served the large ranches and farms located in the area. A good variety of services had been available in Cochrane including a hotel, a lumberyard, a hardware store, four garages offering repair services, three bulk gasoline distribution centers, a dry goods store, a drug store, a bank, a barber shop, two restaurants, a supermarket, a medical clinic, and a veterinary clinic.

The services offered had expanded in the last five years. A number of small construction and oil well servicing firms located in Cochrane. In 1977 two new shopping centers had opened. These centers were small but greatly expanded the retail space available in the town. A new supermarket, several arts and crafts shops, a bakery, a delicatessen, a pool room, a sporting goods shop, a jewelry store, a laundromat, a dentist office, a second lumberyard, and other service establishments such as a bookkeeping agency and real estate firms had quickly rented the space. A new provincial building containing a liquor store, new medical clinic, and a Fish and Wildlife office had also opened in the last year. Mr. Jones was not sure how well these new stores were doing. He had heard rumors that several were not achieving the sales volume they had expected.

Mr. Jones observed that most of the older businesses had a well established clientele. The store owners were relaxed, friendly, and had good relationships with their customers. They always seemed to have time to discuss the weather, town politics, or family happenings with those customers. Casual conversation revealed that the reaction of the newer residents of Cochrane to the local merchants' way of doing business varied. Some people enjoyed the relaxed, unhurried atmosphere of the small town. Others were extremely impatient with the "poor service and high prices." These people tended to shop in the nearby Calgary stores where prices were slightly lower and variety somewhat greater.

Mr. Jones believed that Cochrane's growth might make it possible for him to operate a furniture store in that community. He felt that he could offer a friendly, reassuring environment that would attract customers. He hoped to be able to sell good quality, stylish, attractive furniture to people living or moving into the area.

Sam realized that people often bought new furniture when their life situation changed. They bought new furniture as their families expanded or became smaller. Also, people liked to buy new furniture when they moved. The newer, large warehouse-type furniture stores located in the southern section of Calgary were farther away from the rapidly expanding northwestern part of that city than was Sam's proposed Cochrane location. He wondered, therefore, if he could attract not only local residents but also people moving into northwestern Calgary to his local store.

He was particularly intrigued by the success of MacKay's Ice Cream Parlour in attracting Calgarians. Each evening and Sunday afternoon in the spring, summer, and fall, large numbers of Calgarians drove to Cochrane for "homemade" ice cream. At times the line of people waiting to be served stretched for half a block down Main Street. Obviously, people would travel for some kinds of products so why not for an important purchase like furniture?

Mr. Jones realized the marketing mix offered by his store would be critical to its success or failure. He wondered about the size of store, the price range, the furniture to carry, the advertising strategy, the level and type of salesperson to hire. And, of course, he could not be certain that a furniture store would be successful.

How should Mr Jones decide whether or not to go ahead with his plans? If he does, what marketing mix would be appropriate?

■ 17. BLACK & DECKER COMPANY*

In April 1984, the management of Black and Decker (B&D) were poised on the brink of an extremely challenging time. The $300 million (U.S.) acquisition of General Electric's small appliance division had just been completed, representing B&D's attempt to dramatically expand its product line. Black & Decker, Canada, Inc., and Canadian General Electric were included in the deal. According to the agreement, B&D had three years to make the transition from GE's brand name.

B&D faced the question of rebuilding its image to include household products. Laurence Farley, chief executive officer for B&D, told a group of GE retailers at a meeting in February 1984, "Changing the G.E. brand name will not be easy, nor will it happen overnight. But we're convinced that it can be done successfully."

The Black & Decker Manufacturing Company of Towson, Maryland, was founded in 1910. In 1984, B&D was the world's leader in producing and selling both industrial and consumer power tools. However, the company faced saturation in its core business (consumer power tools) with limited growth potential. B&D also faced competition from the Japanese, who were experts in low-cost production. One Japanese firm, Makita, was already milking profits from B&D's cash cow, industrial power tools, matching B&D's market share of 20 percent within a three-year period.

One of B&D's divisions had over-expanded during the 1970s. Sales for this division had then plummeted, causing it to be largely responsible for the $77 million loss suffered by B&D in 1982.

Farley began housecleaning to streamline operations worldwide and capitalize on B&D's strengths. Unprofitable divisions were sold, three plants were closed, and a layer of corporate management was eliminated. These moves strengthened the company's financial position by increasing liquidity and reducing leverage. In 1983

the company had a profit of $44 million. The first quarter of 1984 was encouraging. Unit sales were up by 20 percent, and profits increased by 85 percent to a record of $26.7 million.

In 1983 the company had experienced major restructuring and was revamping its entire strategy under the new president, Laurence Farley. In the past, B&D had allowed each subsidiary to have complete control over all operations in the belief that the individual companies knew their own markets best. This autonomy included the design of component parts and decisions regarding which products were offered. Several of B&D's products had been available in some markets and not in others. The DUSTBUSTER (a cordless vacuum), for example, was marketed in only three countries—France, the United Kingdom, and the United States.

The new president believed that the old policy was incompatible with his concept of "globalization"—the marketing of a standard product suitable for sale worldwide, rather than a custom product intended for a specific market only. The GE acquisition provided the opportunity to expand sales dramatically since small appliances were thought to lend themselves to standardization. It was also a field were the Japanese were not yet a major factor.

B&D had launched several household items via their expertise in cordless appliance technology. These products bore their own brand name and were designed to capture market niches that were previously unidentified. They accounted for 13 percent of B&D's total sales in 1983. Items such as the DUSTBUSTER, which were marketed under their trade name rather than the B&D logo, were runaway successes and paved the way into the household appliance market.

Prior to the acquisition, GE was number one in the small appliance business holding a 50 percent market share in items such as toaster ovens, portable mixers, and irons. Sales for 1983 topped $470 million, but after-tax profits were only 3 percent of sales due to GE's high manufacturing costs. B&D

---

*This case was prepared by Ms. Shelagh M. Deely under the direction of Professors Carl Lawrence and Ken Wong, who at the time of its preparation were associated with Queen's University.

could provide lower costs with its more efficient factories. GE top management decided that it could use its own technology and financial resources more effectively in markets for major appliances and high technology. The management and 125-person sales force of the GE small appliance operations were retained and transferred to B&D after the acquisition.

Black & Decker was determined to triple its size and become a $5 billion company by 1989. Farley believed that the small appliance business could be made more profitable by increasing sales volume. He wanted to try to push the brand image harder and thereby command higher prices. He reasoned that when products are similar, price becomes the deciding factor for the consumer and profits suffer as a result. The SPACEMAKER series, developed and introduced by GE, was a perfect test case. The SPACEMAKER series was designed to hang beneath kitchen cabinets, thereby saving counter space, and consisted of a toaster oven, electric knife, can opener, and coffee maker. The series would be sold as a high-priced, color-coordinated group that could be bought separately, with the intention that when consumers returned for a particular item, they would choose one that matched what they already had.

Several crucial questions faced the top management of B&D after the acquisition. Among these were the following:

1. A powerful brand name has character and helps a high-quality product to be perceived as such. Establishing an enduring brand name would not be an easy task:

a. Appliance sales historically followed the rate of growth of the population, and, as that rate slowed, increased competition for market share was likely to ensue.
b. The quality of products from different manufacturers had become increasingly similar since major marketers had access to the same technology. Thus, marketing expenses were growing, as manufacturers responded to the ever-higher cost of reaching the consumer.
c. The influence of the retailer and retailers' own

store brands was growing in many parts of the world.

The "recognition level"[1] and reputation of GE needed to be transferred to B&D. Management was aware that a well-conceived and smooth transition was vital for success. How was the switch of brand name to be accomplished over the next few years?

2. Contribution towards retailers' profits from housewares products had always been low, and the retailers wanted reassurance that these skimpy margins would be improved under the B&D name. The SPACEMAKER line of products had proved to be successful beyond all expectations, and retailers were continually disappointed that demands were always in excess of deliveries. They had to be reassured that B&D would live up to their promise that five times the number of SPACEMAKER items would be produced in 1984 in order to meet this demand and alleviate the back order problem. Some retail purchasing agents had already been stocking up on competitors brands to guard against the possibility of losing sales owing to inadequate inventories.
3. Decisions had to be made concerning whether or not B&D should continue GE's "stock balancing policy," under which retailers could return unsold merchandise to GE at year-end in exchange for new models. Retailers were clearly concerned about being left with old stock under the B&D current policy of "you bought it, it's yours."
4. Traditional hardware stores, home centers, catalog showrooms, and discount department stores were the distribution outlets for power tools that were familiar to B&D. These were somewhat different from the retail and discount departments that carried housewares. B&D had to face the frenzy that accompanied the competition with other housewares manufacturers for retail shelf space. This would be a new experience for the B&D marketing staff,

---

[1]"Recognition level" refers to the extent to which the general public is familiar with the name brand in question.

and management was concerned with how this task should be handled.

5. Black & Decker made its name through the power tool industry and now faced a completely different target market. Research had shown that women were more familiar with Black & Decker than first thought, mainly because they bought drills, etc., as gifts for their husbands or friends. Retailers were not quite so sure, though, how easy it would be to "sell a lady on a Black & Decker toaster."

Did the GE purchase make sense for Black & Decker? Would you bet on the company doing well in the small appliance business?

■ 18.   YORK FURNITURE COMPANY

Mrs. Carol King has been operating the York Furniture Company for 10 years and has slowly built the sales to $900,000 a year. Her store is located in the downtown shopping area of a city of 150,000 population. This is basically a factory town, and she has deliberately selected "blue-collar" workers as her target market. She carries some higher-priced furniture lines but puts great emphasis on budget combinations and easy credit terms.

Mrs. King is most concerned because she feels she may have reached the limit of her sales growth—sales have not been increasing during the last two years. Her newspaper advertising seems to attract her target customers, but many of these people come in, shop around, and then leave. Some of them come back, but most do not. She feels her product selections are very suitable for her target market and is concerned that her salespeople do not close more sales with potential customers. She has discussed this matter several times with her salespeople. They say they feel they ought to treat all customers alike—the way they personally want to be treated. They feel their role is just to answer questions when asked—not to make suggestions or help customers arrive at their selections. They feel this would be too much of a "hard sell."

Mrs. King argues that this behavior is interpreted as indifference by the customers who are attracted to the store by her advertising. She feels that customers must be treated on an individual basis—and that some customers need more encouragement and suggestion than others. Moreover, she feels that some customers will actually appreciate more help and suggestions than the salespeople themselves might. To support her views, she showed her salespeople the data from a study about furniture store customers (Tables 1 and 2). She tried to explain to them about the differences in demographic groups and pointed out that her store was definitely trying to aim at specific groups. She argued that they (the salespeople) should cater to the needs and attitudes of their customers—and think less about how they would like to be treated themselves. Further, she suggested that she may have to consider changing the sales compensation plan if they don't "do a better job." Now they are paid a salary of $13,000 to $20,000 per year (depending on years of service) plus a 1 percent commission on sales.

Evaluate Mrs. King's thinking. What would you advise her to do?

TABLE 1

In shopping for furniture I found (find) that	Demographic groups				Marital status	
	Group A	Group B	Group C	Group D	Newly-weds	Married 3–10 yrs.
I looked at furniture in many stores before I made a purchase..........................	78%	57%	52%	50%	66%	71%
I went (am going) to only one store and bought (buy) what I found (find) there...............	2	9	10	11	9	12
To make my purchase I went (am going) back to one of the stores I shopped in previously.....	48	45	39	34	51	49
I looked (am looking) at furniture in no more than three stores and made (will make) my purchase in one of these..................	20	25	24	45	37	30
No answer.................................	10	18	27	27	6	4

TABLE 2   The sample design

Demographic status

Upper class (group A); 13% of sample
   This group consisted of managers, proprietors, or executives of large businesses. Professionals, including doctors, lawyers, engineers, college professors and school administrators, research personnel. Sales personnel, including managers, executives, and upper-income salespeople above level of clerks.
   Family income over $30,000.

Middle class (group B); 37% of sample
   Group B consists of white-collar workers including clerical, secretarial, sales clerks, bookkeepers, etc.
   It also includes school teachers, social workers, semiprofessionals, proprietors or managers of small businesses; industrial foremen and other supervisory personnel.
   Family income between $20,000 and $40,000.

Lower middle class (group C); 36% of sample
   Skilled workers and semiskilled technicians were in this category along with custodians, elevator operators, telephone linemen, factory operatives, construction workers, and some domestic and personal service employees.
   Family income between $10,000 and $40,000.
   No one in this group had above a high school education.

Lower class (group D); 14% of sample
   Nonskilled employees, day laborers. It also includes some factory operatives, domestic and service people.
   Family income under $15,000.
   None had completed high school; some had only grade school education.

■ 19. NEWMAN DANCE STUDIO

Anne Newman has been operating the Newman Dance Studio for five years—in a suburban community of about 50,000. Slowly, she has built a clientele—mostly young girls whose mothers want them to have some ballet experience.

The studio is conveniently located downtown—within walking distance of two grade schools (grades one to five) and one middle school (grades six to eight). Some of Anne's customers come from these schools, but even more come from more remote schools. Most are driven and picked up by their mothers.

A few competitors are offering classes in their homes to neighborhood children, but none of them has facilities or quality of instruction comparable to Anne's. The school district offers some classes at lower prices on Saturday and during the summer, but Anne has not considered them to be real competition.

Most of Anne's students come only one hour a week, and slowly make enough progress so that Anne can hold spring recitals to show off the girls' accomplishments to their parents and friends. Even first-year students are able to make a reasonable showing—and "success" in the spring recital tends to encourage mothers to re-enroll their daughters in the fall classes. Anne has not had much luck developing an interest in summer classes—and last year she stopped trying. She decided that her students associated ballet with the nine-month school year. So Anne took off for a three-month summer vacation. Fortunately, there had been enough business in the previous nine months so she could afford to do this.

Now it is February 1983, and Anne is very much concerned about her financial prospects for the future. Declining school enrollments (which cut state educational support payments) and rising costs (including rising heating gas costs) have forced the school board to take some drastic measures. One of these was changing the school schedule to start later so the students are getting up later and going to school later—thereby saving energy during the dark morning hours. There is some doubt whether this really did accomplish its purpose, but the school system has decided that the new schedule will be continued indefinitely.

The schools now open at 8:40 A.M. and close at 3:40 P.M. instead of 3 P.M. This has drastically cut into Anne's after-school business.

At first Anne did not see the implications when the change was announced for January 1983. But it quickly became clear that her 3:30–4:20 class was at the wrong time when no one signed up for the class during the first week of January. Not only did she lose many of the girls who were formerly enrolled in her 3:30 class, but enrollment in the later classes dropped almost in half. Some of the 3:30 girls did move to the 4:30 and 5:30 classes, but probably only about 20 percent of them. It is hard to get exact figures on enrollment because there's usually at least a 20 percent turnover from fall to winter to spring terms. Anne has become

used to a continual flow of new girls. Few girls stay more than a couple of years—because the program is not designed to build serious ballet students, but rather to cater to the "recreational" ballet student. But, it is quite clear to Anne that the change in school schedule has drastically cut her business—and she is trying to decide what to do for the spring term and beyond. In fact, the school schedule change just precipitously compounds the problem of fewer young girls coming along—as a result of parents having fewer children. This has been worrying Anne for some time, but now she must face an immediate problem as well as the longer-term trend.

Given that most parents seem to need about a half hour to get their children from school to the studio, she could move the starting time of the first class to about 4:15 (from 4:30) to try to use a little more after-school time. But this would still mean that she could only offer two "prime-time" classes after school (instead of the three which she offered before) because classes starting after 6 P.M. seem to be viewed as "too late." Alternately, she could forget about trying to change the after-school schedule and try to fill later times with older, more serious students. Anne has the credentials and training to offer more advanced courses, but so far there hasn't been much demand for them. The local school district does offer some adult education classes at lower prices—and this may take care of the older market.

Another possibility that Anne is considering is to persuade the local school system to allow "early release" of interested students—with a view to filling the 3:40–4:20 or a 3:10–4:00 slot. Anne knows that some children are now being released an hour early for advanced training in ice skating. But few students are involved, and she fears that such an arrangement for ballet is not likely because her students aren't "advanced."

Now that the total amount of time available between the end of school and dinner is almost an hour shorter, some parents may feel that there just isn't enough time for extra recreation activities. This may help account for the substantial drop in business after school. Anne's Saturday business has not been affected by the change in school schedule, but very few of the weekday students have moved to Saturday, either. This concerns her for the long run because total revenue has dropped about one quarter—bringing her studio below the break-even point. Clearly, the studio needs more students to break even because it cannot cut costs very easily. Rent, light, taxes, insurance, and other fixed costs can't be changed. Further, her two part-time assistants are paid a fixed amount for the five after-school periods and Saturday.

Saturday classes could use some more students—enrollments have declined slightly over the last few years as the "baby boom" has ended. Similarly, the after-school market has dropped some in the last few years. But the immediate problem is the new after-school market. Something must be done after school if the business is to survive. Before and after the school schedule change, the following numbers of students were enrolled in the various classes at approximately $3.50 per class:

Class	Jan. 1984	Jan. 1985
3:30–4:20	20	0
4:30–5:20	20	9
5:30–6:20	18	9
6:30–7:20	10	6

What has happened to the Newman Dance Studio? What would you recommend Anne Newman do?

■ 20. THE NIAGARA PENINSULA REHABILITATION CENTRE*

The Niagara Peninsula Rehabilitation Centre, founded in 1970, is located in St. Catharines, Ontario. The center is a community resource which acts as an outpatient service fully equipped to provide rehabilitative care. There is normally no cost to patients since their expenses are covered by the Ontario Health Insurance Programme. The center is financed in part by the Ontario Ministry of Health as well as from community funds.

In the past five years, the center has treated more than 4,000 patients from across the Niagara Peninsula. These patients suffer from such disabilities as stroke, arthritic and cardiac disorders, respiratory ailments, industrial and home accidents, and hearing or speech disorders. A medical referral is needed for treatment at the center. The center has a staff of approximately 40, two thirds of whom are directly involved in the treatment process.

The objective of the center is to provide each patient with a controlled treatment program that deals with the patient's disability and facilitates a return to home or occupational environment. On the initial visit to the center, both patient and family are seen by the medical doctor and the social worker. The emphasis is on assessment of the emotional, social, and family situations as they relate to the physical disability. If required, a number of services, including counseling and referral to community resources, are provided. The center is divided into four departments—physiotherapy, occupational therapy, speech pathology/audiology, and advisory services (social work).

Although the center is located at the southern boundary of the city of St. Catharines (with a total population in 1976 of approximately 125,000), it has a mandate to serve the entire Niagara Peninsula (total population approximately 300,000). Its assigned territory includes the communities of Dunnville, Fort Erie, Grimsby, Niagara Falls, Niagara-on-the-Lake, Port Colborne, Welland, and of course the city of St. Catharines. Patients who, because of their disability or the inadequacy of public transportation, would otherwise be unable to be present for treatment may use the center's own transport system. Those conveyed who are able to

---

*This case was written by Dr. Ronald Rotenberg, who at the time of its preparation was associated with the School of Administrative Studies at Brock University.

pay for all or some of their transportation costs are expected to do so.

Physiotherapy and occupational therapy are generally available in some regional hospitals when a patient is hospitalized. The Niagara Rehabilitation Centre is able to treat such patients once they are discharged from hospital but still need rehabilitation care. In addition, the center is unique in providing speech therapy and audiology services. It is the only institution in the Peninsula that brings all these services together under one roof. The center has been successful in its mission. It has grown steadily to the point where it was operating at almost full utilization of capacity in 1978, having dealt with over 1,500 cases in the 1977 calendar year.

In January of 1978, Dr. Allen Kroll, Director of Speech Pathology and Audiology at the Niagara Peninsula Rehabilitation Centre, casually asked Dr. Ronald Rotenberg of the Brock University business program whether marketing might be applicable to a situation which had developed at the rehabilitation center. While he wasn't sure any problem existed, Dr. Knoll indicated that the director of the center, Evelyn Tipson, had expressed some concern over the fact that a relatively high proportion of the patients treated at the center came from the city of St. Catharines. The number of patients from areas other than St. Catharines were not fully represented at the center. Dr. Kroll wondered whether "marketing" could aid in the analysis and perhaps solution of the situation. On the other hand, he expressed some doubts as to the applicability and appropriateness of advertising. Furthermore, he felt that Miss Tipson probably had even stronger feelings about the appropriateness of utilizing commercial promotion to advance the goals of a rehabilitation center. Nevertheless, it was decided that a meeting between Miss Tipson, Dr. Kroll, and Dr. Rotenberg could prove to be of some benefit to the center.

Such a meeting took place the following week. It began with Miss Tipson expressing concern over the fact that patients from the communities outside of St. Catharines were underrepresented at the center. There was *no immediate urgency* to resolve the situation, since the center was already operating at near capacity. However, she felt it would be better in the long run if the patient mix at the center more closely reflected the actual population distribution of the Niagara Peninsula at large. (Exhibit 1 compares the geographic mix of patients treated at the center for 1974 to 1977 inclusive with the actual geographic distribution of population in 1976 of the Niagara Peninsula.)

A number of other issues and concerns were reviewed at the same meeting. First, the possibility existed of some kind of rivalry between the medical facilities (hospitals and doctors) in Niagara Falls and those in St. Catharines. Perhaps doctors in the Falls would not normally refer their patients to a St. Catharines-based rehabilitation center even if that center were the only one of its kind in the Peninsula. It was also felt that doctors in the communities of Dunnville and Grimsby were more likely to refer their patients to the Chedoke Hospital in Hamilton because that institution was closer. There had been no formal studies of former patients to determine their degree of satisfaction with the center. While patients could only come to the center on a doctor's referral, it was not really known whether patients generally asked a physician for a referral, or whether the doctor, or possibly a nurse, initiated most referrals. Although Miss Tipson believed that most of the 300 doctors in a position to refer patients knew of the center's existence, she felt some of them might not be aware of the full range of its available facilities and services. In addition, there was no information as to physicians' images of, and attitudes toward, the center. Finally, nothing was known either of the general public's degree of awareness of the rehabilitation center or of the center's image among those who knew of its existence.

After some discussion, Miss Tipson reiterated that there was no urgency in dealing with the situation. Nevertheless, she felt it would be desirable to have a more proportionate representation of area residents as patients at the center. While acknowledging "marketing" could be applicable in helping to analyze and correct the situation, she felt advertising of any kind would not be appropriate. Such advertising could give the impression that the rehabilitation center is in desperate need

EXHIBIT 1   Breakdown of patients by geographic locations in Niagara region

Geographic distribution of patients	Percent of total region population	1977		1976		1975		1974	
		Number	Percent	Number	Percent	Number	Percent	Number	Percent
Dunnville............	3.1%	1	.1%	2	.2%	2	.2%	6	.7%
Fort Erie	6.3	34	2.2	23	1.9	26	2.8	28	3.4
Grimsby	4.3	10	.6	4	.3	12	1.3	16	1.9
Lincoln..............	3.9	55	3.5	30	2.4	23	2.4	28	3.4
Niagara Falls	18.3	98	6.3	115	9.3	104	11.1	69	8.2
Niagara-on-the-Lake...	3.4	43	2.8	22	1.8	22	2.4	26	3.1
Pelham	2.7	33	2.1	46	3.7	32	3.4	35	4.2
Port Colborne........	5.6	49	3.2	21	1.8	23	2.4	16	1.9
St. Catharines	32.1	994	64.0	732	59.5	525	56.0	425	50.7
Thorold	4.0	81	5.2	68	5.5	45	4.8	33	3.9
Wainfleet............	1.6	4	.3	2	.2	1	.1	5	.6
Welland.............	12.5	140	9.0	154	12.5	117	12.5	146	17.4
West Lincoln.........	2.5	4	.3	9	.7	5	.5	3	.4
Other...............		6	.4	2	.2	1	.1	2	.2
Total referred ...		1,522	100.0	1,230	100.0	938	100.0	838	100.0

of patients. It could also contravene an unwritten code of ethics or practice which states that hospitals (or other such public institutions) "don't advertise." In the past, the rehabilitation center had used audio visual tapes/displays for the public and letters to doctors. Although she considered displays an acceptable method of communication, there had never been any formal evaluation of their effectiveness. Miss Tipson wondered whether the use of tapes and displays should be continued or even expanded through the utilization of (temporary) displays in shopping malls throughout the Niagara region.

Regardless of the additional or intensified method of communication (if any) ultimately chosen, Miss Tipson felt that there had to be some reasonable justification. The center's operating grant did not provide for any extensive promotional program. In order to implement any such program, the center would have to apply for additional funding either to the Ministry of Health or some other granting agency. Miss Tipson did, however, mention that volunteers from the community might be able to aid in gathering the data required before any decision regarding promotion was made.

What marketing problem, if any, does the rehabilitation center face? If you believe a marketing problem exists, what information is needed before any marketing decisions can be taken or any marketing plan prepared? What marketing action could be taken with a limited budget of $2,000–$3,000 a year?

■ **21.   PENNFIELD PHARMACEUTICAL LABORATORIES***

Until 1983, Pennfield Pharmaceutical Laboratories had been marketing tranquilizers under cross licensing arrangements with U.S. firms who hold international patents. At the same time, Pennfield Laboratories in Vancouver had worked with a number of pharmacology professors from a well-known Canadian university to develop a distinctively better tranquilizer with a minimum number of side effects.

The laboratory, after extensive testing and submission of its findings to the Food and Drug

*This case was written by professor Peter Banting, who at the time of its preparation was associated with McMaster University.

Directorate, received approval to market its product—Penntab—in Canada. In addition to obtaining Canadian patent protection of its formulation, Pennfield Laboratories had patents pending in the United States and was in the process of securing patent protection in other countries.

The pharmaceutical industry is one of extremely high risk. New products continually displace existing products, frequently before they have reached a profitable stage of market development. High risk in the industry is accentuated by the randomness of discovery in research and development. Thus, product obsolescence forces pharmaceutical firms to innovate or perish. It therefore becomes essential to obtain widespread distribution and acceptance of a new product as quickly as possible. This necessitates heavy promotional expenditures in the introductory phase of the product's life cycle, including medical journal advertising, direct mail, personal selling by detail salespeople, and free samples to the physicians.

Drugs are quite unlike most consumer products. They are not sought when the customer is healthy; rather, they are desperately needed when the individual is ill. In short, demand is uncertain, hinging on the vagaries of illness. Furthermore, the individual is seldom able to compare prices and effectiveness. Price elasticity is not a determining factor for sales volume. The physician's decision to prescribe any particular drug is the overriding factor.

Prices for tranquilizers range from $3.75 per hundred to $33 per hundred (including prescription fee), with most clustered about the $6 per hundred price at the retail level. Most new drugs are high priced.

Pennfield management, enthusiastic about the performance of Penntab, considered it to be foremost in the tranquilizer field. Nevertheless, management lines divided in sharp conflict when the issue was raised: At what price shall we sell Penntab? The controller of the company suggested that since the ultimate customer was primarily concerned with relief, lower price would have no effect on increasing sales volume. He suggested that to recoup the company's heavy investment in developing Penntab, plus the high costs of introducing it to the market, it was imperative that Penntab be priced at the $33 per hundred retail price level. On the other hand, the production manager pointed out that at the anticipated sales volume, he could produce Penntabs for 95 cents a hundred. He then went on to argue that doctors invariably consider the earning power of their patients before prescribing a drug. By pricing high, he contended, Pennfield would never be able to penetrate the mass market and sell the volume of Penntabs he was expected to manufacture. Moreover, he questioned the physician's willingness to differentiate Penntab as being superior when there is a proliferation of competing tranquilizers, all vying for the same customers.

At this point, Pennfield's president invited the vice president of marketing development to offer his views on how best to price Penntab.

At what price should Penntab be retailed? Would generic substitution affect Penntab's price? If so, how?

■ 22. CANADIAN HYDROGARDENS LIMITED*

Hydroponics is the science of growing plants without earth. The word means, literally, "water-working." It involves growing plants in an inert me-

dium, such as gravel, which will give them support, and feeding them by means of aqueous nutrient solutions. The gravel is put in a water-tight bed, and seedlings are planted in it. A nutrient solution is periodically and automatically pumped through the bed each day and is allowed to drain back into a tank at the foot of the bed, where it collects and

---

*This case was written by Professor Peter Banting, who at the time of its preparation was associated with McMaster University.

is eventually re-pumped through the culture. The level of nutrients in the tank is measured at various time intervals, and nutrients are added as they are consumed by the growing plants. The nutrient solution is primarily made of nitrogen, phosphorus, and potassium.

The whole operation takes place within the greenhouses, where humidity, air circulation, and carbon dioxide levels can be precisely monitored and controlled. In this way, the plants are protected from adverse weather conditions, from pests, and from soil-borne diseases, and they can be grown year round. Because of the controlled conditions, the plant receives the best treatment it possibly could: it grows in an almost "perfect" environment. A wide variety of vegetables, fruits, and flowers have been grown successfully using hydroponic techniques.

Experiments in cultivating plants in water containing dissolved inorganic ingredients, rather than soil, were conducted in England as early as 1699. But it was not until 1929 that Dr. W. F. Gericke of the University of California gave the technique the name "hydroponics" and succeeded in growing 25-foot tall tomato plants hydroponically. Pan American Airlines was the first commercial user, growing fresh vegetables hydroponically on Wake Island to supply its aircraft crew and passengers. During the Second World War, the British grew produce hydroponically in Iraq, and military production in 1952 was reported at 8 million pounds. Most recently, NASA has experimented with hydroponic food propagation aboard earth-orbiting satellites.

Canadian Hydrogardens, Ltd., began on a small scale in St. Catharines, Ontario, when the original three founders of the company constructed a small quonset-style greenhouse covered with a translucent fiberglass skin. They built it on rented land and outfitted it with hydroponic equipment. This greenhouse would be used experimentally to study and gain experience in the technical aspects of hydroponic culture and to test the economic and marketing feasibility of a hydroponic tomato-growing operation.

The company's primary objectives were stated in its "Articles of Incorporation" on July 10, 1982,

as follows: "to plant, grow, nurture, sell, and otherwise deal in vegetables, fruits, and foods of all kinds by hydroponic-related process or processes, or by any other process.

During its first 10 months of operation, the company grew two crops of tomatoes, leaf lettuce, and seedless cucumbers. Other experimental crops grown by Canadian Hydrogardens included zucchini, celery, bell peppers, hot peppers, and endive.

The numerous technical problems that developed during this time period were basically due to lack of experience and insufficient knowledge of the chemistry of the required nutrient solutions. However, the project did produce enough returns to warrant the group's optimism in proceeding with their venture.

In June 1983 the operations were moved to newly purchased land in Ancaster, Ontario, and 20,000 square feet of hydroponic growing space were subsequently added. The expansion program was partly financed by bringing in new partners who contributed $45,000. The balance of the company's financial needs were raised through the sale of a debenture issue. By January 1986 the physical plant alone was valued at $150,000 by management.

Six principals own Canadian Hydrogardens. They are a youthful and well-educated management group. All are within the 26–32 age range. Four of the group have MBAs or an undergraduate business degree so they are familiar with modern management concepts. In addition, two are engineers, one is a lawyer, and one has a masters degree in chemistry. Only the marketing vice president, John Stevens, is employed full-time with the company. The remainder of the management team hold responsible full-time jobs in the Hamilton-Toronto area and contribute to the hydroponic operation on a part-time basis.

Of all the vegetables that might be grown, tomatoes were found to benefit the most from hydroponic growing conditions. Consequently, Canadian Hydrogardens, Ltd., decided to emphasize commercial tomato production. While construction of the Ancaster complex was underway, John Stevens began "missionary selling" in the Hamilton area, visiting supermarket chains, independent grocers, and wholesalers to interest them in his product. He managed to attract a considerable amount of interest in his sample batch of hydro-ponically-grown tomatoes, but not one of the prospects he approached would give him a firm commitment to buy. They all said: "Come back to see us when you have grown your crop and have a ready supply available." John also encountered resistance from large chain purchasers, such as Loblaws, who demonstrated strong loyalty to existing suppliers of Ontario-grown hothouse tomatoes. In sum, there was no way John could estimate demand for his product until he had actually grown at least one full crop.

Because the hydroponic greenhouse environment is as near perfect as possible with optimum feeding, root support, temperature, and air circulation, Canadian Hydrogardens is able to produce tomatoes that offer many advantages over field-grown and soil-grown hothouse tomatoes.

These advantages include:

1. *Better appearance*—the tomatoes are larger and more uniform in size and shape. They have a deeper red color, and the company picks them so that the greenery of the petal (calyx) is still attached (a feature not found in competing products).
2. *Superior flavor*—the tomatoes are meatier in texture and taste better.
3. *Longer shelf life*—hydroponically grown tomatoes have a lasting quality which allows them three to four times the shelf life of normal tomatoes.
4. *Faster maturity*—optimal conditions ensure faster growth and maturity.
5. *Reduced water requirement*—because the nutrient solution is recycled many times, water is conserved.
6. *Reduced labor requirement*—automatic watering, feeding, and aeration reduce manpower needs compared to soil culture.
7. *Elimination of plant hazards*—under controlled conditions the potential dangers of wind, drought, snow, hail, excessive cold and heat, or nutrient deficiencies are eliminated.

8. *Disease and pest reduction*—since no soil is used, soil-borne diseases and pests are eliminated, and no toxic herbicides or pesticides are required.
9. *Cleanliness*—operating conditions and procedures are cleaner.
10. *Year-round production*—crops can be grown all year.

Unfortunately, these attributes are not without their costs. One reason for high cost is the initial capital intensity of the hydroponic operation. In addition, heating costs for the greenhouses are rising at an astonishing rate. Heating is done by natural gas and currently runs at about 25 percent of operating expenses. Consumers' Gas officials estimate the price of their product will double in the next two years. Consequently, the greatest disadvantage of hydroponically grown tomatoes is that they must command a premium price due to their higher cost structure.

Canadian Hydrogardens had identified their tomatoes with the brand name "Ripe & Ready." They are priced at 10 to 20 cents per pound (retail) above imported tomatoes and 5 to 10 cents per pound above Ontario soil-grown hothouse tomatoes.

For most of the year, imports of low quality come to the Ontario market from Mexico, California, and Florida. Although their coloring, size, and flavor are poor and they don't have the attractive green calyx attached, the prices of these tomatoes are reasonable. Competing against them are Ontario soil-grown hothouse tomatoes. They have become established as the premium tomato with many large grocery chains. In August, the flood of locally grown field tomatoes decreases prices significantly, creating an even greater price differential between Ripe & Ready and other tomatoes.

After the seedlings of their first commercial crop had been planted, a Canadian Hydrogarden management meeting was called to discuss marketing plans for Ripe & Ready tomatoes. Many crucial questions remained unanswered. As the principals of the company talked, the following questions were articulated:

"Will the consumer be willing to change his or

her buying habits and purchase a tomato that is grown hydroponically?"

"Should we even tell the consumer that Ripe & Ready tomatoes are grown hydroponically? If we do identify our product as hydroponic, what is the best way to communicate this idea?"

"Will the consumer be willing to pay the price differential for the difference in quality?"

"What are the possible way of getting Ripe & Ready tomatoes to the consumer?"

How would you answer the questions raised at the pre-launch meeting?

■ 23. THE WESTCO MACHINERY COMPANY

The Westco Machinery Company is a leading manufacturer in the wire machinery industry. It has patents covering over 200 machine variations, but it is rare for Westco's customers to buy more than 30 different types in a year. The machines are sold to wire and small-tubing manufacturers—when they are increasing production capacity or replacing outdated equipment.

Established in 1895, the company has enjoyed a steady growth to its present position with annual sales of $35 million.

Some six firms compete in the wire machinery market. Each is about the same size and manufactures basically similar machinery. Each of the competitors has tended to specialize in its own geographic area. Four of the competitors are in Eastern Canada, and two—including Westco—are on the West Coast. All of the competitors offer similar prices and sell FOB their factories. Demand has been fairly strong in recent years. As a result, all of the competitors have been satisfied to sell in their geographic areas and avoid price cutting. In fact, price cutting is not a popular idea because about 20 years ago one firm tried to win additional business and found that others immediately met the price cut but industry sales (in units) did not increase at all. Within a few years, prices returned to their earlier level, and since then competition has tended to focus on promotion.

Westco's promotion has depended largely on six company sales reps who cover British Columbia and the Prairies. They usually are supported by sales engineers when the company is close to making a sale. Some advertising is done in trade journals. And direct mailings are used occasionally, but the main promotion emphasis is on personal selling. Personal contact outside Western Canada, however, is through manufacturers' agents.

James Tang, president of Westco is not satisfied with the present situation. Industry sales have leveled off and so have Westco's sales—although the firm has continued to hold its share of the market. Tang would like to find a way to compete more effectively in the other regions because he sees that there is great potential outside of Western Canada—if he can only find a better way of reaching it.

Competitors and buyers agree that Westco is the top-quality producer in the industry. Its machines have generally been somewhat superior to others in terms of reliability, durability, and productive capacity. The difference, however, usually has not been great enough to justify a higher price—because the others are able to do the necessary job—unless Westco's sales rep convinces the buyer (and other influencers) that the extra quality will help improve the buyer's product and lead to fewer production line breakdowns. The sales rep can also try to "sell" the company's better sales engineers and technical service people. But if a buyer is only interested in comparing delivered prices for basic machines, the Westco's price must be at least competitive to get the sale. In short, if such a buyer had a choice between Westco's and another machine *at the same price,* Westco would probably get the business. But it's clear that Westco's price would have to be at least competitive in such cases.

The average wire machine sells for about $125,000 FOB shipping point. Shipping costs within any of the three major regions averages about $1,500—but another $1,000 to $2,000 must be added on shipments from Western Canada to Ontario and Quebec (or vice versa).

Mr. Tang is thinking about expanding his market by being willing to absorb the extra $1,000 to $2,000 in freight costs which would be incurred if a customer in Eastern Canada were to buy from his Western Canada location. By so doing, he would not be cutting price in those markets but rather reducing his net return. He feels that his competitors would not see this as price competition—and therefore would not resort to cutting prices themselves. Further, he thinks such a move would be legal—because all the customers in each major region would be offered the same price.

The sales manager, Robert Dixon, feels that the proposed freight absorption plan might actually stimulate price competition in the eastern markets—and perhaps in Western Canada as well. He proposes instead that Westco hire some sales reps to work the Eastern markets—selling "quality"—rather than relying on the manufacturers' agents. He feels that two additional sales reps in each of these regions would not increase costs too much—and could greatly increase the sales from these markets over that brought in by the agents. With this plan, there would be no need to absorb the freight and risk disrupting the status quo. This is especially important, he argues, because competition in the East is somewhat "hotter" than in the West—due to the number of competitors in those regions. Much expensive entertaining, for example, seems to be required just to be considered as a potential supplier. In contrast, the situation has been rather quiet in the West—because only two firms are sharing this market. The "eastern" competitors don't send any sales reps to western Canada—and if they have any manufacturers' agents they haven't gotten any business in recent years.

Mr. Tang agrees that Mr. Dixon has a point, but since industry sales are leveling off, he feels that the competitive situation might change drastically in the near future anyway and he would rather be a leader in anything that is likely to happen rather than a follower. He is impressed with Mr. Dixon's comments about the greater competitiveness in the other markets, however, and therefore is unsure about what should be done.

Evaluate Westco's strategy planning in the light of its market situation, and explain what it should do now.

■ 24. PERRY MANUFACTURING COMPANY

Perry Manufacturing Company, is a manufacturer of industrial cutting tools. These tools include such items as lathe blades, drill press bits, and various other cutting edges used in the operation of large metal cutting, boring, or stamping machines. The president of the company, Chuck Perry, takes great pride in the fact that his company—whose $2,759,000 sales in 1982 is small by industry standards—is recognized as a producer of the highest-quality line of cutting tools to be found.

Competition in the cutting-tool industry is intense. Perry Manufacturing Company competes not only with the original manufacturers of the machines, but also with many other larger manufacturers offering cutting tools as one of their many different product lines. This has had the effect, over the years, of standardizing the price, specifications, and in turn, the quality of the competing products of all manufacturers.

About a year ago, Mr. Perry was tiring of the financial pressure of competing with companies enjoying economies of scale. At the same time, he noted that more and more potential cutting-tool customers were turning to small, custom, tool-and-die shops because of specialized needs that could not be met by the mass production firms. Mr. Perry felt that perhaps he should consider some basic strategy changes. Although he was unwilling to become strictly a custom producer, Mr. Perry felt that the recent trend toward buying customized cutting edges suggested the development of new markets which might be too small for the large, multiproduct–line companies to serve profitably. But, he thought, the new markets might be large enough to earn a good profit for a flexible company of Perry's size.

An outside company, Mothison Research Associates, was hired to study the feasibility of serving these potential new markets. The initial results were encouraging. It was estimated that Perry might increase sales by 50 percent and double profits by servicing the emerging market.

Next, Mr. Perry had the sales manager develop a team of three technical specialists to maintain continuous contact with potential cutting-tool customers. They were supposed to identify any present or future needs that might exist in enough cases to make it possible to profitably produce a specialized product. The technical specialists were not to take orders or "sell" Perry to the potential customers. Mr. Perry felt that only through this policy could these representatives easily gain access to the right persons.

The initial feedback from the technical specialists was most encouraging. Many firms (large and small) had special needs—although it often was necessary to talk to the shop foreman or individual machine operators to find these needs. Most operators were "making do" with the tools available. Either they didn't know customizing was possible or doubted that their supervisors would do anything about it if it were suggested that a more specialized tool would increase productivity. But these operators were encouraging because some felt that it would be easier to get specialized tools ordered if they were already produced and in stock than if they had to be custom-made. The company, therefore, decided to continually add high-quality products to meet the ever-changing, specialized needs of users of cutting tools and edges.

The potential customers of Perry's specialized tools were widely scattered. The average sale per customer is not expected to exceed $300 at a time, but the sale will be repeated several times within a year. Because of the widely dispersed market and low sales volume per customer, Mr. Perry doesn't feel that selling the products direct—as is done by small custom shops—is practical. At the present time, the Perry Manufacturing Company distributes 90 percent of its regular output through a large industrial wholesaler—which serves the Manitoba-Ontario border. This wholesaler, although very large and well known, is having trouble moving cutting tools. It is losing sales of cutting tools in some cities to newer wholesalers specializing in the cutting-tool industry. The new wholesalers are able to give more technical help to potential customers and therefore better service. Borman Supply's chief executive is convinced that the newer, less-experienced concerns will either realize that a substantial profit margin can't be maintained along with their aggressive strategies or they will eventually go broke trying to "overspecialize."

From Mr. Perry's standpoint, the present wholesaler has an established reputation and has served Perry Manufacturing well in the past. The traditional wholesaler has been of great help to Perry in holding down the firm's inventory costs—by increasing the amount of inventory maintained in the 34 branch wholesale locations operated by Borman Supply. Although Mr. Perry has received several complaints about the lack of technical assistance given by the wholesaler's sales reps—as well as their lack of knowledge about the new products available from their company—he feels that the present wholesaler is providing the best service it can. All its sales reps have been told about the new products at a special training session, and a new page has been added to the catalog they carry with them. So Mr. Perry classifies the complaints as "the usual things you hear when you're in business."

Mr. Perry feels that there are more urgent problems than a few complaints—profits are declining. Sales of the new cutting tools are not nearly as high as forecast—even though all indications are that the company's new products should serve the intended markets perfectly. The high costs involved in producing small quantities of special products and the technical specialist team—together with lower-than-expected sales—have significantly reduced the firm's profits. Mr. Perry is wondering whether it is wise to continue to try to cater to the needs of specific target markets when the results are this discouraging. He also is considering increasing advertising expenditures in the hope that customers will "pull" the new products through the channel.

Evaluate Perry Manufacturing Company's strategy. What should Mr. Perry do now?

■ **25. LAFONTAINE POTTERIES LIMITED***

Founded in 1908, Lafontaine Potteries Limited is Quebec's leading manufacturer of glazed and unglazed giftware. In addition, it had contracted with a local firm to manufacture wrought iron ware which it assembles with a pottery line. There are approximately a hundred product items in each of the company's two product lines. Some of these items are:

1. *Glazed and unglazed giftware:* cups and saucers, tea and coffee pots, mugs and steins, ash trays, planters, tidbit servers, barbecue sets of plates and mugs, fancy flower pots, casseroles, wall plaques, rustic TV dinnerware sets, vases, and "Habitant" dinnerware sets.
2. *Wrought iron ware:* wrought iron is matched up with the company's pottery items to make smokers, planters, casseroles, and coffee warmers, cocktail and barbecue sets, and umbrella stands.

Of the company's $8 million sales volume, approximately 65 percent is realized in pottery items. The major portion of Lafontaine's line of products is low-priced and is merchandised primarily in variety stores, department stores, and independent retail gift shops. Thirty percent of the firm's sales are made through large retail chains.

The head office and main show room of Lafontaine are located on St. Hubert Street in Montreal. While all of the firm's total product line is displayed in the showroom, not all items are in stock. The company maintains inventories only of those product items which have proved sales success and show excellent future market potential. A branch sales office is located in Toronto.

Lafontaine is family owned and operated. Guy Lafontaine is not only president of the company, but also senior sales executive. Andre Lafontaine, Guy's younger brother, is vice president in charge of finance and office management. The third and youngest brother, Roland, who is vice president of operations, handles all the firm's manufacturing activities. The sales manager for the province of Ontario is Guy Lafontaine's son-in-law, Sam Stone. Mr. Stone lives in an apartment adjacent to the firm's Toronto showroom and is responsible for it. He is the firm's only salesperson in Ontario and covers the entire province. Roland's son-in-law, Charles Denis, covers the Maritime provinces four times a year assisted by a French-Canadian salesperson who lives in New Brunswick. Both work out of the Montreal office. The western provinces, including British Columbia, are handle by Thomas Jones, who lives in Vancouver, and Jack Shore, a Winnipeg resident. Both salespeople operate out of the Montreal office, visiting Montreal at least a half dozen times a year. The province of Quebec is supervised by Guy and accounts for 40 percent of the company's total sales. Six salespeople in Quebec report directly to the president.

Ontario provides 30 percent of the company's total sales volume. Most of these sales are made directly by the Montreal home office to the head buyers of such large companies as T. Eaton Co.,

*This case was written by Professor Peter Banting, who at the time of its preparation was associated with McMaster University.

Simpsons-Sears, Woolworth, Zellers, Kresge, and so on. Sam Stone's responsibility is to ensure that these house accounts are satisfactorily serviced. Because Mr. Stone is the only salesperson in Ontario, few sales are made to independent retail stores.

For the past two years, sales expenses have increased dramatically—so much so that Guy has repeatedly expressed concern over Lafontaine's shrinking profit margin. Guy has consistently argued that the problem is twofold: (1) expenses are too high and (2) the company is not maximizing the potential market that could be developed in Ontario by employing more salespeople.

Unlike his brother, Roland does not feel that the solution lies in hiring more salespeople to cover the province of Ontario. He contends such action would involve building or leasing a warehouse in addition to the Toronto showroom to adequately service retailers. The result would be even higher expenses for the company.

On the other hand, Sam Stone argues that the solution would be to employ the services of a regional wholesaler in Toronto who would sell directly to independent Ontario retailers. This wholesaler, with whom Sam is familiar, is a small family owned organization that has been importing and distributing a few Japanese-made pottery goods but is primarily a jobber for Canadian manufacturers and has a ready-made clientele of small independent stores. Mr. Stone believes that Lafontaine should retain its large house accounts but let this wholesaler handle all other sales in Ontario.

Guy's reaction to this suggestion is mixed. He thinks the idea should be carefully considered, yet such a radical change in policy might have implica-

tions for the company's total operations. For example, might it not be a good idea to employ small wholesalers in all the other provinces too? In this way, costs could be cut down significantly for the simple reason that the salespeople currently serving these areas would no longer be needed. In addition, the company would gain increased market coverage.

Andre feels that this idea is a good one, but he wonders whether Lafontaine would in fact obtain maximum coverage. How could Lafontaine expect a wholesaler of similar product lines to push Lafontaine's products more than their present line?

Guy's response is that wholesalers not currently in this product line would be the type to approach. However, this raises the question of whether they would have either the appropriate captive market of retailers or the product knowledge to effectively realize Lafontaine's objectives.

According to Andre: "It is all very fine and dandy to concern oneself with getting maximum market potential. But in return for the assistance of regional wholesalers, what does Lafontaine have to offer in the form of monetary compensation? Do we have the necessary margin to make it attractive for these people not only to handle our products but also to push them? Aren't we putting the cart before the horse? After all, we operate as a wholesaler. How can we expect other wholesalers to operate within our margin, particularly at this moment when it isn't a very profitable one?"

Should Lafontaine sell through a wholesaler in Ontario? Should Lafontaine consider employing middlemen for the entire Canadian market?

■ 26. CANADIAN INLAND*

Inland Manufacturing Corporation, a medium-sized U.S. manufacturer of aluminum products, entered Canada in 1957 by acquiring the assets of two Canadian extrusion[1] companies. These two companies were then merged into a single Canadian extrusion enterprise with plants in Toronto and Hamilton.

Canadian Inland has two main divisions—industrial and consumer. The industrial division produces semi-fabricated extrusions which are supplied to manufacturers. The consumer division produces finished aluminum products, such as garden furniture, aluminum ladders, umbrella-type clothes lines, scaffolding, moldings, cabinet edgings, etc. In addition, Inland owns several aluminum door and window firms. Canadian Inland's sales reached $20 million in 1980.

The parent company's international division looks after all foreign operations. These include plants in France, Germany, Belgium, Spain, Italy, England and Canada. All subsidiaries operate with a reasonably high degree of autonomy. Of the foreign subsidiaries, however, the Canadian firm is the only one with a consumer products division. It alone has experience, know-how, and marketing knowledge in the consumer area.

Having successfully cultivated the home market, with the prior approval of the parent company the Canadian firm decided to probe foreign markets. The objective was to stimulate demand for Inland's products in the foreign markets and make Inland's other subsidiaries recognize the potential for consumer sales in their respective markets. Sales volume developed by the Canadian company, when sufficiently large, would be turned over for the local subsidiary to expand and ultimately result in the establishment of domestic manufacturing by the sister subsidiary.

On this basis, the Canadian consumer division went "international" in January of 1979. The sales manager, John Foreman, believed that the growing affluence of the European worker, his developing taste for leisure, and his life-style preferences would permit the company's consumer products to quickly gain market acceptance.

John's first step was to investigate foreign markets. The Ontario Ministry of Industry and Tourism in March 1980 was organizing a trade mission to Europe. After some consultations with members of the department, John accepted their invitation to join this trade mission, which toured Italy, Germany, Holland, France, and England. During the course of the trip, John was officially introduced to leading buyers for department store chains, import-houses, wholesalers, and buying groups. The two-week trip convinced John Foreman that there was ample buying power in some of the countries to make the exportation of Canadian-made aluminum consumer products a profitable undertaking.

On his return trip to Canada, John's next step was to obtain credit references for the firms he considered as potential distributors. To those judged acceptable, he sent letters expressing interest and including samples, prices, and other relevant information.

The first orders received were from a German wholesaler who imported on his own account. Sales in this market totaled $60 thousand in 1980. Similar success was achieved in France and England. Italy, on the other hand, did not produce sales. This was attributed to the semi-luxury nature of the company's products. John Foreman concluded that due to the lower level of incomes in Italy, Italians had developed a predisposition toward "making do" with serviceable items, rather than looking for goods and services that would make life easier.

In Canada, Inland distributes through merchant hardware distributors and buying groups, such as co-operatives and hardware chains. In foreign markets, however, there is no recognizable pattern, and channel systems vary from country to country.

---

*This case was written by Professor Peter Banting, who at the time of its preparation was associated with McMaster University.

[1]Extrusion is the process of forcing aluminum billets under great heat and pressure through dies to form predetermined shapes.

In one country, sales are made to an individual who stocks goods on his own account. In another, an agent, a buying group, or a hardware wholesaler is engaged. To avoid mixing channels of distribution, Inland has only one account in each country. The chosen distributor enjoys exclusive representation.

In Germany Inland distributes through a wholesaler based in the Southern Ruhr, which is the central distribution area for Western Germany. This wholesaler has a force of five salespeople: one covering the Bavarian area, one the Ruhr Valley, one on the northern area around Bremen and Hanover, one in West Berlin, and one in the Heidelberg-Manheim territory. The firm specializes in small housewares and has contacts with leading buying groups, wholesalers, and department stores. John Foreman was impressed with the firm's aggressiveness and knowledge of merchandising techniques. He noted that they had won an award from a large American vacuum cleaner firm as their best single foreign representative in 1978, which he considered a good indication of sales ability.

In France the company sells to a Paris-based buying group of a chain of hardware wholesalers with representation throughout the country. It was felt that this group would provide excellent coverage of the market because of their extensive distributive network.

In Denmark the Canadian company's line is sold to a buying group representing a chain of hardware retailers. This group recently expanded to include their counterparts in Sweden, Finland, and Norway. Together, they purchase goods for about 500 hardware retailers. The buying power of the Scandinavians is quite high, and it is expected that Inland's products will prove very successful in this market.

In The United Kingdom an importer-distributor, who both buys on his own account and acts as a sales agent, handles the company's line. This firm sells to department stores and hardware wholesalers. The distribution chain in England is quite cumbersome, and the company had found it difficult to attain acceptance in the British market. John Foreman, however, is convinced that this

market has the highest potential of all the foreign countries. To date, the do-it-yourself market in Great Britain had brought in a lot of business in aluminum moldings.

The Australian market was established indirectly and successfully. A number of letters were received from Australian merchants who had heard of Inland through the Department of Industry, Trade and Commerce. The supply of garden furniture in Australia was small and prices were high. Prices were quoted and samples sent to the businessmen recommended by the Canadian trade commissioner. The distributor selected is an Australian importer who operates a chain of discount houses and retails on his own account. This firm discovered it could land aluminum furniture in Melbourne at prices competitive with American and Japanese imports.

The Venezuelan market was developed by an American who came to Canada from Venezuela in search of new lines. Inland attributes success in Venezuela to the efforts of this aggressive and capable agent. He has built a sizable trade in aluminum ladders.

In Trinidad and Jamaica, Inland's consumer products are handled by traders who carry such diversified lines as insurance, apples, plums, fish, and so on. They have been successful in selling aluminum ladders.

The sales manager's export strategy is as follows:

1. Product—no product modifications will be made in selling to foreign customers. This might be considered later, after a substantial sales volume has developed.
2. Price—the company will not concern itself with retail prices and will not publish suggested list prices. Distributors add their own markups to their landed cost. Supply prices will be kept as low as possible. This is accomplished by:
a. Removing advertising expenses and other strictly domestic overhead charges from price calculations.
b. Finding the most economical packages for shipment (smallest volume per unit).
c. Bargaining with carriers to obtain the lowest shipping rates possible.

3. Promotion—removal of advertising expenses from price calculations is accomplished because the firm does no advertising in foreign markets. Brochures and sales literature already being used in Canada are supplied to foreign distributors. Inland will continue to promote its consumer products by participating in overseas trade shows. These are manned by the consumer sales manager. All exhibition inquiries are forwarded to the firm's distributor in that country.

4. Distribution—new distributors will be contacted through foreign trade shows. John Foreman considers large distributors desirable. He feels, however, that they are not as receptive as smaller distributors to a new unestablished product line. Consequently, he prefers to appoint small distributors. Larger distributors may by appointed after the company has gained a strong consumer franchise.

5. Financing—Inland sees no need to provide financial help to distributors. The company views its major contribution as providing operational products at the lowest possible price.

6. Marketing and planning assistance—John Foreman contends that foreign distributors know their own markets best. Consequently, they are best equipped to plan for themselves.

7. Selection of foreign markets—the evaluation of foreign market opportunities for the company's consumer products is based primarily upon disposable income and life-style patterns. For example, John fails to see any market in North Africa for his products, which he categorizes as a semi-luxurious line. It is his opinion that cheaper products such as wooden ladders (often home-made) are preferred to pre-fabricated aluminum ladders in regions such as North Africa, Italy, and Spain. Venezuela, on the other hand, he contends is a more highly industrialized market with luxury tastes. Thus, John sees Inland's consumer products as being essentially tailored for a highly industrialized and affluent society.

What do you think of John Foreman's approach to probing foreign markets and to selecting distribution channels? What overseas distribution strategy would you design for Inland?

■ 27. HIGHLAND MANUFACTURING CO., LTD.*

Serious swimmers in most parts of the world today wear swimming goggles to protect their eyes. With the increasing availability of swimming facilities in many countries and exposure to water sports in the Olympic Games, more and more people of all ages are taking up swimming as a sport, thus creating a demand for goggles. This demand for goggles in international markets has been taken advantage of by a Canadian firm, Highland Manufacturing Co., Ltd., located in Burnaby, a suburb of Vancouver, British Columbia.

With the aid of a team of highly skilled in-house technicians, Highland produces over 20 different sizes and models of goggles, the most popular brand being "Arena." Each goggle is packed in an attractive package for visual appeal, but no further modifications are made for the export market.

The target market for Arena goggles is the serious adult swimmer, particularly the athlete, who is conscious of high product quality and safety and does not mind paying a higher price for the quality assurance provided by a well-known brand name. By producing only high-quality goggles with optimum features, Highland prices its products at the higher end of the spectrum and does not attempt to compete in the "low end" market. The officials of the 1984 Los Angeles Olympic Games were so impressed with Highland's product as compared to other competitive products that they prescribed Arena as the official swim goggle for the games.

---

*This case was written by Mr. George Jacob, who at the time of its preparation was associated with the British Columbia Institute of Technology.

Highland started producing swim goggles in 1970. Initial sales were sporadic and confined to local markets only. From time to time goggles were custom-made for various dealers in Canada and the United States, such as Jantzen, ABC Sports, AMF Voit, etc. However, the market for goggles in other parts of the world, particularly Europe, was not looked into until 1979 when research showed that a large potential existed for exports to that area.

To enter the European market Highland concentrated on a strategy of engaging a well-known distributor who had distribution facilities worldwide. Finding such a distributor was no easy task as many different types of middlemen with widely varying degrees of capabilities operate in international markets. The company participated in two well-known trade fairs, the International Sports Equipment fair in Munich and the International Trade Fair of Sporting Goods, Camping Equipment, and Garden Furniture, Cologne, also in West Germany. These promotional efforts paid off as Highland succeeded in engaging the world-famous firm Adidas Fabrique de Chaussures de Sport (SARL) as their primary distributor with exclusive rights to distribute swim goggles under the brand name of Arena. Adidas is a French firm located in Lindersheim, France, engaged in the manufacture and sales of sports footwear, leather balls, swimwear, and other sporting accessories. They have well-established markets in Europe, North America, Australia, and South Africa. In all these markets Arena goggles are sold through specialty retail outlets.

A major problem facing Highland is the duplication of its product in various markets abroad. No sooner is a feature introduced than it is copied by some competing manufacturer. Although Arena is a registered trademark in several countries, pirating of Highland's product features is common but prosecution of the violators is time-consuming and costly. Hence, rather than take the violators to court, Highland finds it more profitable to concentrate its energies on improving the design and features of its product.

While export sales are steadily expanding in North America and Europe for Arena goggles, the Pacific Rim markets offer a real challenge. A variety of swim goggles, some equal in quality to Highland's products, are produced in the Pacific Rim countries, notably Japan and Taiwan, and are offered at comparatively cheaper prices to prospective consumers.

Research statistics on water sports, such as those shown in Exhibits 1 and 2 on industrialized countries, are not available for several of the Pacific Rim countries. However, market visits show that there is keen demand for swim goggles.

Should Highland enter the Pacific Rim markets? If so, how?

EXHIBIT 1:   Number of registered swimmers

Country	Number of swimmers
West Germany	510,708
Great Britain	300,000
Netherlands	210,000
France	94,000
Austria	60,000

Source: Swimming Association of each country. Figures are for 1983.

EXHIBIT 2:   Registered swimmers by age, West Germany

Year	Children	Young people	Adults	Total
1978	287,747	75,775	195,735	559,257
1979	276,030	75,812	197,397	549,239
1980	276,111	78,183	198,326	543,620
1981	254,718	80,336	197,013	532,067
1982	243,127	82,480	194,575	520,182
1983	231,505	79,666	199,537	510,708

Source: Schimm-Verband e.V. Mitglied Der Federation Internationale de Natation.

■   28.   MULTI FOODS LIMITED*

Burt Mann has been the marketing director of Multi Foods Limited for the last four years—since he arrived from international headquarters in New York. Multi Foods—headquartered in Toronto—is a subsidiary of a large U.S.-based consumer packaged-food company with world-wide sales of more than $2 billion in 1982. Its Canadian sales were just under $250 million—with the Quebec and Ontario markets accounting for 65 percent of the company's Canadian sales.

The company's product line includes such items as cake mixes, puddings, pie fillings, pancakes, and prepared foods. The company has successfully introduced at least six new products every year for the last five years. Its most recent new product was a line of frozen dinners successfully launched last year. Products from Multi Foods are known for their high quality and enjoy much brand preference throughout Canada—including the Province of Quebec.

Sales of the company's products have risen every year since Mr. Mann has taken over as marketing director. In fact, the company's market share has increased steadily in each of the product categories in which it competes. The Quebec market has closely followed the national trend except that, in the past two years, total sales growth in that market began to lag.

According to Burt Mann, a big advantage of Multi Foods over its competitors is the ability to coordinate all phases of the food business from Toronto. For this reason, Mr. Mann meets at least once a month with his product managers—to discuss developments in local markets that might affect marketing plans. While each manager is free to make suggestions—and even to suggest major departures from current marketing practices—Mr. Mann has the final say.

One of the product managers, Jac Seine, expressed great concern at the last monthly meeting about the weak performance of some of the com-

pany's products in the Quebec market. While a broad range of possible reasons—ranging from inflation to politics—were reviewed to try to explain the situation, Mr. Seine maintained it was due to a basic lack of understanding of that market. Not enough managerial time and money has been spent studying the Quebec market. As a result, Seine felt that the current marketing approach to that market needed to be reevaluated. An inappropriate marketing plan may well be responsible for the sales slowdown. After all, "80 percent of the market is French-speaking. It's in the best interest of the company to treat that market as being separate and distinct from the rest of Canada."

Mr. Seine supported his position by showing that per capita consumption in Quebec of many product categories (in which the firm competes) is above the national average (Table 1). Research projects conducted by Multi Foods also support the "separate and distinct" argument. The firm has found—over the years—many French-English differences in brand attitudes, life styles, usage rates, and so on.

Mr. Seine argued that the company should develop a unique Quebec marketing plan for some or all of its brands. He specifically suggested that the French-language advertising plan for a particular brand be developed independently of the plan for English Canada. Currently, the agency assigned to the brand just translates its English-language ads for the French market. Mr. Mann pointed out that the existing advertising approach assured Multi Foods of a uniform brand image across Canada. However, the discussion that followed suggested that a different brand image might be needed in

---

TABLE 1   Per capita consumption index, Province of Quebec (Canada = 100)

Cake mixes...	103	Pie fillings..........	115
Pancakes	91	Frozen dinners......	84
Puddings	111	Prepared packaged	
Salad dressings	87	foods	89
Molasses.....	129	Cookies............	119
Soft drinks....	122		

---

*This case was adapted from one written by Professor Robert Tamilia, University of Quebec at Montreal.

the French market if the company wanted to stop the brand's decline in sales.

The executives also discussed the food distribution system in Quebec. The major supermarket chains have their lowest market share in that province. Independents are strongest there—the "mom-and-pop" food stores fast disappearing outside Quebec remain alive and well in the province. Traditionally, these stores have stocked a higher proportion (than supermarkets) of their shelf space with national brands—a point of some interest to Multi Foods.

Finally, various issues related to discount policies, pricing structure, sales promotion, and cooperative advertising were discussed. All of this suggested that things were different in Quebec—and that future marketing plans should reflect these differences to a greater extent than they do now.

After the meeting, Burt Mann stayed in his office to think about what had been said. Although he agreed with the basic idea that the Quebec market was in many ways different, he wasn't sure how far his company should go in recognizing this fact. He knew that regional differences in food tastes and brand purchases existed not only in Quebec, but in other parts of Canada as well. People were people, on the other hand, with far more similarities than differences.

Mr. Mann was afraid that giving special status to one region might conflict with top management's objective of achieving standardization whenever possible. He was also worried about the long-term effect of such a policy change on costs, organizational structure, and brand image. Still, enough product managers had expressed their concern over the years about the Quebec market to make him wonder if he shouldn't modify the current approach. Perhaps they could experiment with a few brands—and just in Quebec. He could cite the "language difference" as the reason for trying Quebec rather than any of the other provinces. But Mr. Mann realizes that any change of policy could be seen as the beginning of more change, and what would New York think? Could he explain it successfully there?

Evaluate this situation. What would you tell Burt Mann? What are the future implications of your recommendations?

■ 29. VISITING NURSES ASSOCIATION (VNA)

The Visiting Nurses Association (VNA) is a nonprofit organization which has been operating—with varying degrees of success—for 20 years. Some of its funding comes from the local United Way—to provide emergency nursing services for those who can't afford to pay. The balance of the revenues—about 90 percent of the $1.2 million annual budget—comes from charges made directly to the client or to third-party payers—including insurance companies and the federal government—for Medicare or Medicaid services.

Janet Brown has been executive director of the VNA for two years now—and has developed a well-functioning organization—able to meet the requests for service which come to it from some local doctors and from the discharge officers at local hospitals. Some business also comes to the association by self-referral—the client finding the name of the association in the Yellow Pages of the local telephone directory.

The last two years have been a rebuilding time—because the previous director had had personnel problems. This led to a weakening of the association's image with the local referring agencies. Now, the image is more positive. But Janet is not completely satisfied with the situation. By definition, the Visiting Nurses Association is a nonprofit organization—but it still has to cover all its costs in order to meet the payroll, rent payments, telephone expenses, and so on—including her own salary. She can see that while the association is growing slightly and now breaking even, it doesn't have much of a cushion to fall back on if (1) people stop needing as many nursing services, (2) the government changes its rules about paying for the association's kind of nursing services—either cutting back on what would be paid for or reducing the amount that would be paid for specific services—or (3) if new competitors enter the market. In fact, the latter possibility is of great concern to Janet. Some hospitals—squeezed for revenue—are expanding into home health care. And "for-profit" organizations (e.g., Kelly Home Care Services) are expanding around the country—to provide home health care services—including nursing services of the kind offered by VNA. These for-profit organizations appear to be efficiently run—offering good service at competitive—and sometimes even lower—prices than some non-profit organizations. And they seem to be doing this at a profit—which suggests that it would be possible for them to lower their prices if the non-profit organizations tried to compete on price.

Janet is trying to decide whether she should ask her board of directors to let her move into the whole home health care market—i.e., move beyond just nursing.

Now, the VNA is primarily concerned with providing professional nursing care in the home. But her nurses are much too expensive for routine health-care activities—such as helping fix meals, bathing and dressing patients, and so on. The "full cost" of a nurse is about $50 per hour. Besides, a registered nurse is not needed for these jobs. All that is required is an ability to get along with all kinds of people—and a willingness to do this kind of work. Generally, any mature person can be fairly quickly trained to do the job—following the instructions and under the general supervision of a physician, a nurse, or family members. The "full costs" of aides are $5 to $10 per hour for short visits—and as low as $50 per 24 hours for a live-in aide who has room and board supplied by the client.

There seems to be a growing demand for home health care services as more women have joined the work force and can't take over home health care when the need arises—either due to emergencies or long-term disabilities. And with older people living longer, there are more single-survivor

family situations where there is no one nearby to take care of their needs. Often, however, there are family members—or third-party payers such as the government or insurers—who would be willing to pay for such services. Now, Janet sometimes assigns nurses to this work—because the VNA is not in a position to send home health-care aides. Sometimes she recommends other agencies, or suggests one or another of three people who have been doing this work on their own—part-time. But with growing demand—she is wondering if the VNA should get into this business—hiring aides as needed.

Janet is concerned that a new, competitive, full-service home health care organization—which would provide both nursing services *and* less-skilled home health care services—might be more appealing to the local hospitals and other referrers. She can see the possibility of losing nursing service business if the VNA does not begin to offer a more complete service. This would cause real problems for the VNA—because overhead costs are more or less fixed. A loss in revenue of as little as 10 to 20 percent could require laying off some nurses—or perhaps laying off some secretaries, giving up part of the office, and so on.

Another reason for expanding beyond nursing services—using para-professionals and relatively unskilled personnel—is to offer a better service to present customers *and* make more effective use of the organization structure which has been developed over the last two years. Janet estimates that the administrative and office capabilities could handle 50 to 100 percent more clients without straining the system. It would be necessary to add some clerical help—if the expansion were quite large—as well as expanding the hours when the switchboard was open. But these increases in overhead would be minor compared to the present proportion of total revenue which goes to covering overhead. In other words, additional clients could increase revenue and assure the survival of the association—providing a cushion to cover the normal fluctuations in demand—and providing some security for the administrative personnel.

Further, Janet feels that if the VNA were successful in expanding its services—and therefore could generate some surplus—it would be in a position to extend services to those who aren't now able to pay. One of the worst parts of her job is refusing service to clients whose third-party benefits have run out—or for whatever reason can no longer afford to pay the association. Janet is uncomfortable about having to cut off service, but must schedule her nurses to provide revenue-producing services if she's going to be able to meet the payroll every two weeks. By expanding to provide more services, she might be able to keep serving more of these non-paying clients. This possibility excites her because her nurse's training has instilled a deep desire to serve people—whether they can pay or not. This continual need to cut off service—because people can't pay—has been at the root of many disagreements—and even arguments—between the nurses serving the clients and Janet, as director and representative of the board of directors.

Expanding into home health care services won't be easy. It may require convincing the nurses' union that the nurses should be available on a 24-hour schedule—rather than the eight-to-five schedule six days a week, which is typical now. It would also require some decisions about relative pay levels for nurses, para-professionals, and home health care aides. It would also require setting prices for these different services and telling the present customers and referral agencies about the expanding service.

These problems aren't bothering Janet too much, however, because she thinks she could handle them. She is sure that home health care services are in demand and could be supplied at competitive prices.

Her primary concern is whether this is the right thing for a nurses' association to do. The name of her group is the Visiting Nurses Association, and its whole history has been oriented to supplying *nurses' services*. Nurses are dedicated professionals who bring high standards to any job they undertake. The question is whether the VNA should offer "less professional" services. Inevitably, some of the home health care aides will not be as dedicated as the nurses might like them to be. And this might reflect unfavorably on the nurse image. At the same time, however, Janet is concerned about the future of the Visiting Nurses Association—and her own future.

What should Janet Brown do? Why?

■ 30.   BRAMALEA REALTY, LTD.*

Bramalea Realty, Ltd., is a small independent real estate firm located in Lethbridge, Alberta. Because of its success the company has recently decided to expand operations from residential real estate to office development. The decision to move into this area was felt by management to be sound because of the buoyant economy Alberta was experiencing in the 70s and the fact that all projections for business, population, and construction were very positive for the next decade. Although most of this activity was centered in Calgary, Edmonton, and points north, it was felt that considerable spillover was affecting Lethbridge, which is located in the southwest corner of the province and has a population of 50,000.

Bramalea's accountant had indicated that he noticed some figures in the *Financial Post Survey of Markets* indicating that Lethbridge's growth rate per decade was 35 percent—significantly higher than the Canadian average of 10 percent and even 1 percent higher than the Alberta average. In the same publication he found Lethbridge to have a market rating of 86 percent above the national average and also higher than Edmonton and Calgary. This, he surmised, was a result of high retail expenditures per capita and a large retail drawing

*This case was written by Professor D. W. Balderson, who at the time of its preparation was associated with the University of Lethbridge.

from the smaller communities surrounding Lethbridge. Although Bramalea's management was a bit hesitant to move so quickly, they were aware that the demand for office space increased in proportion to population, income, and retail expenditures and these variables were all rapidly increasing. The accountant pointed to the fact that construction in Lethbridge was going ahead strongly and that it would be an ideal time for Bramalea to enter this area of office development.

As a result, Bramalea purchased a site one block from the central business district—with plans to construct an office building. Although the site contained an old building, it would be replaced with a four-story office building of about 40,000 square feet.

Before going ahead with construction Bramalea decided to do some research on the type of facilities which prospective tenants would prefer (e.g., underground parking, recreation facilities, restaurant, etc.). They felt that acting on the results of this research would increase their chances for a high early occupancy rate of at least 90 percent, which they were going to require to make the project financially feasible. Results of their investigation revealed the following in addition to revealing tenant preferences regarding amenities desired.

1. Confirmation that the population of Lethbridge was growing at a rate of 35 percent per decade (*FP Survey of Markets*), whereas the Canadian average is 10 percent.

2. Confirmation that the market rating index of Lethbridge was 86 percent above the national average in 1979 (*FP Survey of Markets*).

3. Per capita retail sales for Lethbridge in 1979 was $5,924—considerably above the Canadian average of $3,190.

4. Population projections for Lethbridge:

1979	50,000
1984	58,000
1989	66,000

5. Present supply of office space in Lethbridge (1979) was estimated at 425,000 square feet with a vacancy rate of 20 percent.

6. Averages for other cities in Canada show an average of about 6.5 to 7 square feet per capita in space at 90 percent occupancy.

7. There did not appear to be a great demand for restaurant or recreation facilities because the major preference was to be close to downtown.

In view of this information Bramalea is still planning to proceed with construction of the building, but they are now a bit worried.

Should Bramalea be concerned about the results of their most recent research? How should Bramalea have gone about assessing the market potential for their new office building? What additional information, if any, is required at this point? What would you advise Bramalea to do at this time?

■ 31.   **MAYFAIR DETERGENT COMPANY***

Mike Powell is product manager for Protect Deodorant Soap. He was just transferred to the Canadian company from World Headquarters in New York and is anxious to make a good impression. He is working on developing and securing management approval of next year's marketing plan for Protect. His first step involves submitting a draft marketing plan to Gerry Holden who has recently been appointed group product manager.

Mike's marketing plan is the single most important document he will produce on his brand assignment. Written annually, the marketing plan does three main things:

1. It reviews the brand's performance in the past year, assesses the competitive situation, and highlights problems and opportunities for the brand.

*This case was prepared by Mr. Daniel Aronchick, who at the time of its preparation was Marketing Manager at Thomas J. Lipton, Limited.

2. It spells out marketing, advertising, and sales promotion strategies and plans for the coming year.

3. Finally, and most importantly, the marketing plan sets out the brand's sales objectives and advertising/promotion budget requirements.

In preparing this marketing plan, Mike gathered the information in Table 1.

Mike was aware of the regional disparities in the bar soap market and recognized the significant regional skews.

1. The underdevelopment of the deodorant bar segment in Quebec with a corresponding overdevelopment of the beauty bar segment. Research showed this was due to cultural factors. An identical pattern is evident in most European countries where the adoption of deodorant soaps has been slower than in North America. For similar reasons, the development of perfumed soaps is highest in Quebec.

2. The overdevelopment of synthetic bars in the Prairies. These bars, primarily in the deodorant segment, lather better in the hard water of the Prairies. Non-synthetic bars lather very poorly in hard-water areas and leave a soap film.

3. The overdevelopment of the "all-other" segment in Quebec. This segment, consisting of smaller brands, fares better in Quebec, where 40 percent of the grocery trade is done by independent stores. Conversely, large chain grocery stores predominate in Ontario and the Prairies.

Mike's brand, Protect, is a highly perfumed deodorant bar. His business is relatively weak in the key Ontario market. To confirm this share data, Mike calculated consumption of Protect per thousand people in each region (see Table 2).

These differences are especially interesting since per capita sales of total bar soap products are roughly equal in all provinces.

A consumer attitude and usage research study had been conducted approximately a year ago. This study revealed that consumer top-of-mind awareness of the Protect brand differed greatly across Canada. This was true despite the even expenditure of advertising funds in past years. Also, trial of Protect was low in the Maritimes, Ontario, and British Columbia. (Table 3).

The attitude portion of the research revealed that consumers who had heard of Protect were aware of its main attribute of deodorant protection via a high fragrance level. This was the main sell-

TABLE 1 Past 12-month share of soap market (percent)

	Maritimes	Quebec	Ontario	Manitoba/ Saskatchewan	Alberta	British Columbia
Deodorant segment:						
Zest	21.3%	14.2%	24.5%	31.2%	30.4%	25.5%
Dial	10.4	5.1	12.8	16.1	17.2	14.3
Lifebuoy	4.2	3.1	1.2	6.4	5.8	4.2
Protect	2.1	5.6	1.0	4.2	4.2	2.1
Beauty bar segment:						
Camay	6.2	12.3	7.0	4.1	4.0	5.1
Lux	6.1	11.2	7.7	5.0	6.9	5.0
Dove	5.5	8.0	6.6	6.3	6.2	4.2
Lower-priced bars:						
Ivory	11.2	6.5	12.4	5.3	5.2	9.0
Sunlight	6.1	3.2	8.2	4.2	4.1	8.0
All others: (including stores' own brands)	26.9	30.8	18.6	17.2	16.0	22.6
Total soap market	100.0	100.0	100.0	100.0	100.0	100.0

TABLE 2   Standard cases of three-ounce bars consumed per 1,000 people in 12 months

	Maritimes	Quebec	Ontario	Manitoba/ Saskatchewan	Alberta	British Columbia
Protect...............	4.1	10.9	1.9	8.1	4.1	6.2
Sales index.............	66	175	31	131	131	100

TABLE 3   Usage results (in percent)

	Maritimes	Quebec	Ontario	Manitoba/ Saskatchewan	Alberta	British Columbia
Respondents aware of Protect...............	20%	58%	28%	30%	32%	16%
Respondents ever trying Protect...............	3	18	2	8	6	4

ing point in the copy strategy, and it was well communicated through Protect's advertising. The other important finding was that consumers who had tried Protect were satisfied with the product. Some 72 percent of those trying Protect had repurchased the product at least twice.

One last pressing issue for Protect was the pending delisting of the brand by two key Ontario chains. These chains, which controlled about half the grocery volume in Ontario, were dissatisfied with the level at which Protect was moving off the shelves.

With this information before him, Mike now had to resolve the key aspect of the brand's marketing plan for the following year: how to allocate the advertising and sales promotion budget by region.

Protect's total advertising/sales promotion budget was 22 percent of sales. With forecast sales of $3.2 million, this budget amounted to a $700,000 marketing expenditure. Traditionally such funds had been allocated in proportion to population (Table 4).

Mike's inclination is to skew spending even more heavily into Ontario where the grocery chain delisting problem exists. In the previous year, 36 percent of Protect's budget was allocated to Ontario, which accounted for only 12 percent of Protect's sales. Mike wants to increase Ontario spending to 45 percent of the total budget by taking funds evenly from all other areas. Mike expects this will increase business in the key Ontario market, which has over a third of Canada's population.

Mike then presented this plan to Gerry, his newly appointed group product manager. Gerry strongly disagreed. He had also been reviewing Protect's business and felt that advertising and rally promotion funds had historically been misallocated. It was his firm belief that, to use his words: "A brand should spend where its business is." Gerry believed that the first priority in allocating funds regionally was to support the areas of strength. He went on to suggest to Mike that there was more business to be had in the brand's strong areas, Quebec and the Prairies, than in chasing

TABLE 4   Allocation of marketing budget, by population

	Maritimes	Quebec	Ontario	Manitoba/ Saskatchewan	Alberta	British Columbia	Canada
Percent of population	10%	27%	36%	8%	8%	11%	100%
Possible allocation of budget based on population......	$70M	$190M	$253M	$55M	$55M	$77M	$700M
Percent of Protect business at present.......	7%	51%	12%	11%	11%	8%	100%

sales in Ontario. Therefore, Gerry suggested that spending for Protect in the coming year be proportional to the brand's sales by region rather than to regional population.

Mike felt this was wrong, particularly in light of the Ontario situation. He asked Gerry how the Ontario market should be handled. Gerry suggested the conservative way to build business in Ontario was to consider investing incremental marketing funds. However, before these incremental funds are invested, a test of this Ontario investment proposition should be conducted. Gerry recommended that in a small area or town in Ontario an investment-spending test market be conducted for 12 months to see if the incremental spending resulted in higher sales and profits—profits large enough to justify the higher spending. In other words, an investment payout would have to be assured before spending any extra money in Ontario.

Mike felt this approach would be a waste of time and unduly cautious, given the importance of the Ontario market.

Should Protect's advertising and promotion funds be allocated by region in proportion to past sales, by regional population, or in some other fashion? Why?

■ 32. WELDWOOD OF CANADA, LTD.*

Weldwood of Canada is a large forest products company based in Vancouver, British Columbia. Major product divisions include plywood, paneling, pulp, and lumber. The company is fully integrated. Operations include everything from logging camps and manufacturing plants to approximately 25 retail branches located coast-to-coast in Canada.

Susan McKay, Central Division Manager for Weldwood, had to make training and remuneration decisions regarding her sales reps (see Exhibit 1). The decisions were complicated by a number of factors:

1. Head Office had indicated that due to the downturn in 1981, a maximum of four reps could be recommended for maximum salary increments based on performance.
2. Two of the branches in her division were showing signs of atypical performance. Windsor's sales and gross profits were down substantially due to that district's reliance on the automobile industry, which suffered badly in 1981.

---

*This case was prepared by Professor Lindsay Meredith, who at the time of its preparation was associated with Simon Fraser University.

EXHIBIT 1

TO: S. McKay, Central Division Manager

FROM: L. Meredith, Sales Analyst II

DATE: February 1, 1982

Attached [Exhibit 2] is the sales and gross profit analysis for our representatives in the Central Division. I hope this will be of some use in your efforts to determine:

(a) Which of the employees from Central Division you wish to send to the annual training program in order to improve sales performance.
(b) Those employees you wish to recommend for maximum salary increments due to outstanding performance in the previous year.

The representatives have been ranked according to sales achievement for 1981.

On the other hand, Ottawa, a new branch, was experiencing rapid growth. One of the Central Division objectives for 1982 and 1983 was to penetrate this market as rapidly as possible in an attempt to capture a large share of the residential construction contractors' business.

3. McKay knew that sales volume figures for reps could be misleading to the extent that much of Weldwood's product mix (approximately 85 lines) generated substantially different gross profits. Just because a representative produced a substantial sales volume did not automatically imply an associated large gross profit. Furthermore, the price a representative might obtain for the company's products was, within limits, a function of how well he or she could negotiate terms with the customer.

The Ottawa sales force was doing well for relative "newcomers" to the company (see "Basis Month Average" column). Their gross profit/sales ratios were above average (Brumec, 10.3; Kyle, 13.2; and Blackman, 14.8). Consideration of their sales volumes (which fell in the middle to lower end of the distribution) had to be tempered by the fact that Ottawa was a new branch and these salespeople were still developing new accounts. Andrews, Davis, Gordon, and McDonald all had gross profit/sales ratios below average (6.8, 6.6, 6.5, and 6.5, respectively). They all had at least one year's experience with Weldwood. They all came from branches where their colleagues were able to substantially "outperform" them. Finally, these people all fell in the middle to lower range of the sales volume ranking.

McKay, after careful consideration of the data, recommended that:

1. Richards, McCain, and Pederson receive maximum salary increments.
2. Andrews, Davis, Gordon, and McDonald receive further training in order to upgrade their sales skills.

Given the wide range of possible recommendations, why did Susan McKay select these people? Give your justification for her decision.

EXHIBIT 2   Analysis of sales staff ranked according to average sales dollars per month and average gross profit per month as at December 31

Basis month average	Name	Location	Sales rank	Average sales per month	G.P. rank	Average G.P. per month	Other duties
12	S. Richards	Toronto	1	312,510	2	34,915	
12	R. McCain	Toronto	2	301,950	3	34,134	
7	N. Walker	Hamilton	3	299,420	6	28,560	
10	G. Pedersen	Kingston	4	295,650	1	35,478	
12	L. Nielson	Hamilton	5	287,777	4	29,842	
12	J. Morrison	Thunder Bay	6	284,920	9	25,643	
8	B. Brumec	Ottawa	7	280,000	5	28,840	
12	G. Andrews	Thunder Bay	8	273,255	11	18,581	
12	E. Davis	Kingston	9	268,125	10	17,696	
12	F. Gordon	Hamilton	10	230,122	12	14,958	
12	F. Scott	Thunder Bay	11	228,500	13	14,853	SSR*
6	J. Kyle	Ottawa	12	214,752	8	28,400	
12	M. Fisk	Kingston	13	204,912	14	13,319	SSR
4	R. Blackman	Ottawa	14	193,155	7	28,520	ASR†
12	A. Hobson	Windsor	15	181,122	16	9,056	
12	A. McDonald	Toronto	16	150,110	15	9,757	
12	P. Greenway	Windsor	17	115,055	17	5,753	
12	E. Fleischer	Windsor	18	92,110	18	4,606	

*SSR—staff sales representatives; i.e., sales personnel who take an active part in running the branch office in addition to their limited duties as traveling sales representatives.
†ASR—advisory sales representative; i.e., technical specialists who act as resource people to other sales staff and customers in addition to maintaining some of their own sales accounts.

■ 33. DIAMOND JIM'S PIZZA COMPANY

Diamond Jim's Pizza Company (DJ's) is a small owner-managed pizza take-out and delivery business with three stores located in Ontario. DJ's stores obtain their business by telephone or walk-in orders. They prepare their pizzas at each store location. In addition to pizzas, DJ's also sells and delivers a limited selection of soft drinks.

DJ's first store has been very successful. Much of the store's success is attributed to being close to The York University campus—which enrolls more than 15,000 students. Most of these students live within five miles of this DJ's store.

The Scarborough store has been moderately successful. It serves mostly residential customers in the Scarborough area. Recently, the store had advertised—using direct-mail flyers—to several office buildings within three miles of the store. The flyers describe DJ's willingness and ability to cater large orders for office parties, business luncheons, etc. This promotion has been quite successful. With this new program and DJ's solid residential base of customers in Scarborough, improved profitability at the Scarborough location seems assured.

DJ's Peterborough location has experienced mixed results during the past three years. The Peterborough store receives only about 50 percent of its customer orders from residential delivery requests. That store's new manager, Bill Hendricks, believes the problem with residential pizza delivery in Peterborough is due to distribution of residential neighborhoods in the area. Peterborough has several large industrial plants (mostly auto industry related) that are located throughout the city. Small, mostly factory-worker neighborhoods are distributed in between the various plant sites. As a result, DJ's store location can service only two or three of these small neighborhoods on one delivery run.

Most of the Peterborough store's potential seems to be in serving the large industrial plants. Many of these plants work two or three work shifts—five days a week. During each work shift, workers are allowed one half-hour "lunch" break—which usually occurs at 11 A.M., 8 P.M., or 2:30 A.M. (depending on the shift).

Generally, a customer will call from a plant about 30 minutes before a scheduled lunch break and order several (5 to 10) pizzas for a work group. DJ's may receive many orders of this size from the same plant (i.e., from different groups of workers). The plant business is very profitable for several reasons. First, a large number of pizzas can be delivered at the same time to the same location, saving transportation costs. Second, plant orders usually involve many different toppings (double cheese, pepperoni, mushrooms, hamburger) on each pizza. This results in $10 to $15 revenue per pizza. The delivery drivers also like delivering plant orders because the tips are usually $1 or $2 per pizza.

Despite the profitability of the plant orders, there are several factors which make it difficult to serve the plant market. DJ's store is located 5 to 8 minutes from most of the plant sites, so DJ's must prepare the orders within 20 to 25 minutes after the telephone order is received. Often, bottlenecks in oven capacity preclude getting all the orders heated at the same time. Further, the current preparation crew often cannot handle peak order loads in the time available.

Generally, plant workers will wait as long as 10 minutes past the start of their lunch break before ordering from various vending trucks which arrive at the plant sites during lunch breaks. (Currently, no other pizza delivery stores can adequately service plant locations.) But, there have been a few instances when workers refused to pay for pizzas that were only five minutes late! Worse yet, if the same work group gets a couple of late orders, they are lost as future customers. Bill Hendricks believes that the inconsistent profitability of the Peterborough store is a result of lost plant customers.

In an effort to rebuild the plant delivery business, Bill is considering various methods to assure prompt customer delivery service. Bill feels that the potential demand during lunch breaks is significantly above DJ's present capacity. Bill also knows that if he tries to satisfy all phone orders on some peak days, he will be unable to provide prompt customer service and may lose additional plant customers.

Bill has outlined three alternatives that may be used to reestablish the Peterborough store's plant business. He has developed these alternatives to discuss with DJ's owner. Each alternative is briefly described below.

Alternative 1: Determine practical capacities during peak volume periods using existing equipment and personnel. Accept orders only up to that capacity and decline orders beyond. This approach will assure prompt customer service and product quality and also minimize or eliminate losses presently incurred resulting from customers' rejection of late deliveries. Financial analysis of this alternative—shown in Table 1—indicates that a potential daily profit of $1,230 could result from the successful implementation of this alternative.

Alternative 2: Add additional equipment (one oven and one delivery car) and hire additional staff

to handle peak loads. This approach would assure timely customer delivery and product quality as well as provide additional capacity to service unmet demand. A conservative estimate of potential daily demand for plant orders compared to current capacity and proposed increased capacity appears in Table 2. The cost of acquiring the additional equipment and relevant information related to depreciation and fixed costs appears in Table 3.

Using this alternative, the following additional pizza preparation and delivery personnel costs would be required:

	Hours required	Cost per hour	Total additional daily cost
Delivery personnel	6	5	$30.00
Preparation personnel	8	5	40.00
			$70.00

The addition of even more equipment and the personnel that would be needed to service all unmet demand was not considered in this alternative

---

TABLE 1 Practical capacities and sales potential of current equipment and personnel

	11 A.M. break	8 P.M. break	2:30 A.M. break	Daily totals
Current capacity (pizzas)	48	48	48	144
Average selling price per unit.......................	12.50	12.50	12.50	12.50
Sales potential............	$600	$600	$600	$1,800
Variable cost (approximately 40 percent of selling price)*	240	240	240	720
Contribution margin of pizzas	360	360	360	1,080
Beverage sales (2 medium-sized beverages per pizza ordered at 75¢ apiece)†................	72	72	72	216
Cost of beverages (30¢ per beverage).............	22	22	22	66
Contribution margin of beverages	50	50	50	150
Total contribution margin of pizza and beverages	$410	$410	$410	$1,230

*The variable cost estimate of 40 percent of sales includes variable costs of delivery to plant locations.
†Amounts shown are not physical capacities (there is almost unlimited physical capacity), but potential sales volume is constrained by number of pizzas that can be sold.

TABLE 2   Capacity and demand for plant customer market

	Estimated daily demand	Current daily capacity	Proposed daily capacity
Pizza units (1 pizza)	280	144	192

TABLE 3   Cost of required additional assets

	Cost	Estimated useful life	Salvage value	Annual depreciation*	Daily depreciation†
Delivery car (equipped with pizza warmer)	$ 8,000	5 years	$1,000	$1,400	$4.00
Pizza oven	$20,000	8 years	$2,000	$2,250	$6.43

* Annual depreciation is calculated on a straight-line basis.
† Daily depreciation asumes a 350-day (plant production) year. All variable expenses related to each piece of equipment (e.g., utilities, gas, oil) are included in the variable cost of a pizza.

because the current store is not large enough for more ovens and related personnel.

Alternative 3: Add additional equipment and personnel as described in alternative 2, but move to a new location that would reduce delivery lead times to two to five minutes. This move would probably allow DJ's to service all unmet demand. This is possible because the reduction in delivery time will provide for additional "oven" time. In fact, DJ's might have excess capacity using this approach.

A suitable store space is available which is located adjacent to approximately the same number of residential customers (including many of the store's current residential customer neighborhoods). The available site is slightly larger than needed, and the rent is higher. Relevant cost information on the proposed site appears below:

Additional rental expense of
 proposed site over current site ....$ 1,200 per year
Cost of moving to new
 site (one-time cost) $10,000

Bill Hendricks presented each of the three alternatives to DJ's owner—Bob Major. Bob was pleased that Bill had "done his homework" in putting together these alternatives. He concluded

that Bill should make the final decision on what to do (being sure that profits increase) and offered the following comments and concerns:

1. He agreed that the plant market was extremely sensitive to delivery timing. Product quality and pricing, although important, were of secondary importance to delivery.
2. He agreed that plant demand estimates were conservative. "In fact they may be 10 to 20 percent low."
3. He was concerned that under alternative 2, and especially under alternative 3, much of the store's capacity would go unused over 80 percent of the day.
4. He was concerned that DJ's had a bad reputation with plant customers because the prior store manager was not sensitive to timely plant delivery.

He suggested that Bill devise a promotion plan to reestablish DJ's reputation with the plants.

Evaluate DJ's present strategies for the Peterborough store. What should Bill do? Why? Suggest possible promotion plans if alternative 3 is chosen.

■ 34. ALUMINUM PRODUCTS LIMITED*

Fred Barrie is the owner-manager of Aluminum Products Limited, a small fabricator of aluminum garden furniture located in the town of Pickering, Ontario. Fred started his business in 1950, at first making aluminum extrusions for door and window frames. However, the business became so competitive that Fred decided to make aluminum garden chairs, chaise lounges, and garden tables. He found this market much more stable in total annual sales. Furthermore, he liked it better because there was much less chance of losing a big sale because of a slightly higher price.

Aluminum Products Limited's sales of garden furniture were made at the consumer level through independent hardware and variety stores. These stores were supplied by distributors, who were the immediate customers of Aluminum Products Limited. Fred employed one salesperson to call on a total of 23 distributors. The distributors are broken down in the following fashion: one in Charlottetown, Prince Edward Island, one in St. John's, Newfoundland, one in Yarmouth, Nova Scotia, and one in Halifax; one in Moncton, New Brunswick, and one in Fredericton; two in Montreal, one in Quebec City, and one in Hull, Quebec; three in Toronto, one in Hamilton, one in London, and one in Sudbury, Ontario; one in Winnipeg, one in Regina, one in Edmonton, one in Calgary, and three in Vancouver.

In addition to receiving regular calls from Aluminum Products Limited's salespeople, the distributors were also given promotional assistance by Aluminum Products Limited. In 1982 the company had spent $9,600 in advertising and sales promotion funds to assist the 23 distributors in selling Aluminum Products Limited products. Although this amounted to a relatively small amount on a per distributor basis, Fred felt his company received a lot of mileage from point-of-purchase displays which accounted for $6,000 of the total promotional budget. These displays consisted of self-supporting cardboard easels painted in phosphorescent colors which the retailer could display beside a pile of folded Aluminum Products Limited garden products. One of these cardboard displays would be shipped to the distributor with every 25 items purchased from Aluminum Products Limited. The rest of the promotional budget was spent on cooperative advertising. If one of the distributor's customers advertised Aluminum Products Limited products, and the distributor had shared the cost of the ad with the retailer, he need only send proof of this expense and Aluminum Products Limited would reimburse the distributor with a dollar amount equivalent to as much as 3 percent of the distributor's purchases of Aluminum Products Limited products. During 1982, distributors had claimed $3,600 from Aluminum Products Limited in cooperative advertising expenditures. The total of Aluminum Products Limited advertising and sales promotion expenditures had typically averaged around 4 percent of total sales during the past five years.

By mid-January of 1983, Fred, after pouring over his annual statement, began to plan his marketing program for the coming summer. In particular, he began to think about the possibility of intensifying his distribution by selling through large chain and discount store operations such as Home Hardware, Kresge, Woodwards, The Bay, Eaton's, Simpsons, etc. If he were to do this, he would have to hire a new salesperson since his present salesperson was already overworked calling on the 23 distributors. The more he thought about this approach, the more Fred liked the idea. Thus he began to figure out a budget that would include selling through the large chains, hiring an additional salesperson, and increasing advertising and sales promotion expenditures.

In working out his budget, he first considered what the new sales possibly would be. He felt that by doubling his sales force he would probably double his sales, but he decided to estimate a more conservative increase of 60 percent for the first year. The new salesperson would cost an addi-

---

*This case was written by Professor Peter Banting, who at the time of its preparation was associated with McMaster University.

tional $12,000 in salary, and normal expenses would run another $13,000, based on Fred's experience with the present salesperson. The new salesperson also would be offered the 4 percent commission on net sales which Fred currently allowed his salesperson. Advertising and promotion would be increased by 2 percent, from 4.1 percent to 6.1 percent of sales, to allow for the increased amount of promotion which Fred felt would be necessary to sell Aluminum Products Limited products through the chain and department stores. On this basis, Fred developed a objected operating statement for 1983 which indicated that a net profit of $9,710 would result from the new distribution strategy.

In January of 1984, when Fred reviewed the actual results of the year's operations under the new distribution strategy, he was disappointed to see that although sales had increased, they had not met the level he had projected and the firm had incurred a net loss of almost $20,000.

What do you think of Fred Barrie's planning methods? What might have led to the firm not achieving its projected 1983 profits? What methods might he use in developing a more accurate plan for 1984?

Illustration credits

■ Author index

A

Aaker, David A., 394 n, 706 n
Abell, Derek F., 61 n, 104 n
Achabal, Dale D., 742 n
Achenbaum, Alvin A., 239 n
Achral, Ravi Singh, 61 n
Ackerman, Kenneth B., 504 n
Adams, Kendall A., 477 n
Albion, Mark S., 706 n
Alderson, Wroe, 21 n, 24 n, 30 n, 420 n
Allen, M. G., 102 n, 107 n
Alpert, M. I., 241 n
Anderson, Paul F., 107 n, 362 n
Andreasen, Alan R., 61 n, 803 n
Andrus, Roman, 536 n
Ansoff, H. Igor, 107 n
Apple, David L., 61 n, 452 n
Applebaum, William, 477 n
Arbeit, S., 317 n
Armstrong, Gary M., 565 n
Armstrong, Muriel, 133 n
Arndt, Johan, 803 n
Aronchick, Daniel, 860 n
Assael, Henry, 317 n
Ayal, Igal, 393 n

B

Babcock, A. W., 394 n
Bacon, Frank R., Jr., 85 n, 107 n,
    378 n, 385 n, 394 n
Bagnall, James, 565 n
Balderson, D. W., 859 n
Banker, Pravin, 777 n
Banting, Peter M., 133 n, 477 n, 843 n,
    844 n, 850 n, 852 n, 868 n
Barksdale, Hiram C., 61 n, 803 n
Barlee, John, 819–21
Barnes, J. G., 165 n
Barnhill, J. Allison, 133 n
Barrie, Fred, 868–69
Bartlett, Christopher A., 777 n
Bass, Stephen J., 452 n

Bates, Albert D., 452 n
Bateson, John E. G., 282 n, 719 n
Bauer, R., 803 n
Beard, A. D., 240 n
Bearden, William O., 240 n
Beckenstein, Alan R., 671 n
Beckman, M. Dale, 112 n, 252 n
Beckman, T. N., 477 n
Bedeian, Arthur G., 671 n
Behrman, Douglas N., 565 n
Beik, Leland L., 747 n
Bell, James E., Jr., 201 n
Bellenger, Danny N., 165 n, 317 n,
    362 n, 565 n
Bellizzi, J. A., 363 n
Bennear, Mark, Jr., 504 n
Bennett, P. D., 565 n
Bennett, Roger C., 61 n
Bennigson, A. I., 394 n
Bennigson, L. A., 394 n
Benson, Lissa, 803 n
Berkman, Harold W., 252 n
Berman, Barry, 706 n
Bernhardt, K. L., 133 n
Berry, L. L., 710, 719 n
Best, Arthur, 803 n
Beswick, Charles A., 565 n
Bettman, James R., 239 n, 240 n
Bird, M. Murphy, 504 n
Blackwell, R. D., 240 n
Blair, Patricia, 133 n
Blanding, Warren, 504 n
Bliss, Perry, 362 n
Bloom, Paul N., 30 n, 698 n, 706 n
Boisvert, J. M., 252 n
Bonoma, Thomas V., 30 n, 282 n,
    299 n, 536 n
Borchert, G. T., 311 n, 312 n, 317 n
Bouchard, Jacques, 252 n
Bowersox, Donald J., 416 n, 504 n
Boychuk, Ron, 252 n
Boyd, Harper W., Jr., 165 n

Brant, William K., 777 n
Brechin, Marion, 133 n
Brewer, John, 61 n
Brien, Richard H., 165 n
Britt, S. H., 209 n, 394 n
Brogowicz, A. A., 26 n, 747 n
Brooks, Douglas G., 671 n
Brown, Barbara E., 169
Brown, James R., 420 n
Brown, Janet, 857–59
Brown, M. P., 477 n
Brown, S. W., 362 n
Buck, Wayne, 463
Bucklin, Louis P., 362 n, 416 n, 420 n,
    427 n
Buell, Victor P., 394 n
Burnett, John J., 30 n
Burnett, Stephen C., 394 n
Burns, Alvin C., 240 n
Burns, Robert, 355
Busch, Paul, 565 n
Buss, Martin, D. J., 165 n, 777 n
Butler, Marion, 169
Butler, Thomas W., Jr., 85 n, 107 n,
    378 n, 385 n, 394 n
Buzby, Stephen L., 747 n
Buzzell, Robert D., 452 n, 477 n
Byers, Gerald, 504 n, 832 n

C

Calantone, Roger J., 317 n
Calder, Bobby J., 165 n
Campbell, Donald, 165 n
Capon, Noel, 565 n
Cardozo, Richard N., 107 n
Carman, James A., 240 n
Carman, James M., 420 n, 706 n
Carson, Rachel, 114
Cash, Harold C., 565 n
Catry, Bernard, 394 n
Chamberlin, E. H., 789, 803 n
Chambers, T. E., 39 n

■ Subject index

*This book has been set Linotron 202 in 9 point Helvetica
leaded 3 points. Part and chapter numbers and titles are
20 point Garamond Bold condensed. The text sets 27 picas
with a maximum type area of 35 picas 9 points by 49 picas.*